Re

BENSON and HEDGES Golfer's Handbook 1989

Eighty-sixth year of publication

Editor Laurence Viney
Associate Editor Bernard Gallacher

MACMILLAN

This edition published 1989 by
MACMILLAN PRESS LIMITED
Stockton House, 1 Melbourne Place, London WC2B 4LF

British Library Cataloguing in Publication Data
A CIP catalogue record for this book is available from the British Library.

ISBN 0–333–47405–8
ISBN 0–333–47406–6 Pbk

Note
Whilst every care has been taken in compiling the information contained in this book, the Publishers, Editors and Sponsors accept no responsibility for any errors or omissions.

Correspondence
Letters on editorial matters should be addressed to:
The Editor, Benson & Hedges Golfer's Handbook
Macmillan Press Limited
Stockton House
1 Melbourne Place
London WC2B 4LF

Enquiries about despatch, invoicing and commercial matters should be addressed to:
Customer Services Department
Macmillan Press Limited
Houndmills
Basingstoke
Hampshire RG21 2XS

Advertising
Enquiries about advertising space in this book should be addressed to:
Communications Management International
Chiltern House
120 Eskdale Avenue
Chesham
Buckinghamshire HP5 3BD

Illustrations for Centenary Clubs reproduced by kind permission of the Clubs.

Consultant Editor Klaus Boehm

Maps by Pete Ferris (colour), Chartwell (black and white)

Typeset by Matrix, 21 Russell St, London WC2.

Printed and bound in Great Britain by Richard Clay Ltd, Bungay, Suffolk.

Contents

Part IV: Tournament Results

Part V: The Government of the Game

Part VI: Golf History

Part VII: Interesting Facts and Record Scoring

Foreword

1988 saw the continued growth of golf in Europe and widespread success for European professionals. While the focus of publicity is always aimed at the professional tournaments in the five continents, the Amateur game flourishes even with years of waiting for membership of a Club and with public courses full all day. Encouragingly however, plans for new courses are announced nearly every week. The last great expansion was nearly 100 years ago and limited to Great Britain. That in the USA came about 30 years later and in Europe only now is the game taking hold of the populace. This is especially so in France, Germany, Sweden and Spain where more new courses are coming into use than elsewhere. In the USA, with its vast resources and unlimited land available, new facilities continue to appear. In Great Britain too more courses are being planned than for many years past.

Two reasons for the resurgence of interest are the television coverage of championships and professional tournaments, with aspiring young amateurs hoping one day to emulate their heroes they watch on the screen, and enterprising companies and a few municipalities which are prepared to put up the substantial capital sums necessary to acquire the many acres on which to design and build a course. If the game continues to attract new adherents for years to come, investment in golf's future will be fully justified.

How is it that so many people have such confidence in golf's future? Part of the answer is in the nature of the game itself and its advantages compared with other sports:

1 It can be played at almost any age by both sexes and, through the universal handicapping system, the poor player can compete with the best.

2 Every course presents a different challenge to the player.

3 It is a simple game to understand but difficult to master.

4 In this country and many others the weather and climate seldom make play impossible, however unpleasant the conditions.

5 The Rules and Etiquette produce a standard of behaviour which is the envy of many other sports and games.

6 Through the Royal and Ancient and USGA working in harness and harmony, the standards of the game are identical throughout the world.

7 Lastly, and perhaps most importantly, for every player there is always the opportunity to improve his performance.

This last incentive is the key. Testing a new theory, which produces a round several strokes better than normal, spurs the individual with enthusiasm even though the spell may only last a week or two. For him the elusive secret of the game, which he has at last triumphantly found, fades away, but there is always another theory to try the following week.

Mention of the Royal and Ancient, the joint custodian of golf with the USGA, prompts comment on the leadership and financial support the Club gives to the game in the UK and, with the USGA, throughout the world. With a comparatively small staff, the Club works in close association with representative bodies, especially the Home Unions, Overseas Associations, Council of National Golf Unions and many others. The substantial funds available from the impressive annual staging of the Open are reinvested in the game through many organisations and through the Golf Foundation, which has proved a major force in discovering talent through its coaching in schools. The Foundation's contribution to the game needs the support of all golfers and the pitifully small number of clubs who regularly send donations to it is depressing.

Protestation of insufficient finance should fall on deaf ears. Is it that some Club Committees with latent attitudes of male chauvinism, apply their principles equally to avoiding support of youth as well? 50p per member from all clubs in GB would produce over £400,000.

Until recently golf in Great Britain involved much less financial outlay than most other countries. Club membership fees are much lower than those in, say, USA, Japan and continental Europe. In many British Clubs the subscription covers the day-to-day running expenses, but little or no allowance is made for future capital expenditure to improve the course, clubhouse or other facilities. Minor reconstruction of a course, such as extending a hole by moving the green on by 50 yards, can involve an outlay of several thousand pounds and clubs should be encouraged to create the reserves necessary for such improvements. Good husbandry of a course needs professional advice of which Amateur Green Committees should not hesitate to avail themselves. There are signs however that the attitudes of Club Committees that subscriptions should be kept low is slowly changing, although few Club members yet accept the need to pay higher rates to ensure a Club's future prosperity.

1989 is both a Ryder Cup and Walker Cup year. It would be a major reversal of the form in recent matches if the Amateurs were to emulate their Curtis and Ryder Cup colleagues and win for the first time in the USA, but the side will have every support in their attempt to do so. Preparations for the Ryder Cup at the Belfry in September are at an advanced stage and the PGA must be right to make it an all-ticket match as the large crowds expected could become too great both for comfort and the road system around the Club.

Limitation of tickets may also keep away that tiny element among spectators whose behaviour at some recent events was so alien to the game. Those who come to cheer an opponent's shot which strays into the rough or a bunker, must somehow be kept away so as not to mar the occasion for players and other spectators alike. The match promises to be an occasion to be remembered, particularly if Tony Jacklin and his side can pull off a third consecutive win.

Laurence Viney
Berkhamsted, December 1988

SF 199B

Televised Tournaments 1989

The thirteen Tournaments listed below will be shown on BBC Television, except Carrolls Irish Open on June 22–25 which will be on Irish Television only. Pictorial plans, designed to benefit the viewer, of the holes of nine of the courses to be televised are shown in this section.

In the plans, holes have been treated individually to give as clear a pictorial representation as possible: this means, however, that each hole is not necessarily to scale with its neighbours. Rather than following the actual north-south layout of the courses, most holes are represented as they will appear to the viewer – in other words, as if seen from high-up behind the tee.

Users should also note that at Woburn the holes on the course have been re-numbered as shown.

Date	**Tournament**	**Course**
6–9 April	US Masters	Augusta, Georgia
4–7 May	Epson Grand Prix of Europe	St Pierre, Chepstow
26–29 May	Volvo PGA Championship	Wentworth, Surrey
1–4 June	Dunhill British Masters	Woburn, Bedfordshire
22–25 June	Carrolls Irish Open	Portmarnock, Co. Dublin
12–15 July	Bell's Scottish Open	Gleneagles, Perthshire
20–23 July	118th Open Championship	Royal Troon, Ayrshire
10–13 August	Benson and Hedges International	Fulford, York
7–10 Sept	Panasonic European Open	Walton Heath, Surrey
22–24 Sept	Johnnie Walker Ryder Cup	The Belfry, Warwickshire
28 Sept–1 Oct	Dunhill Cup	St Andrews, Fife
12–15 Oct	Suntory World Match Play	Wentworth, Surrey
26–29 Oct	Volvo Masters	Valderrama, Spain

St Pierre Course

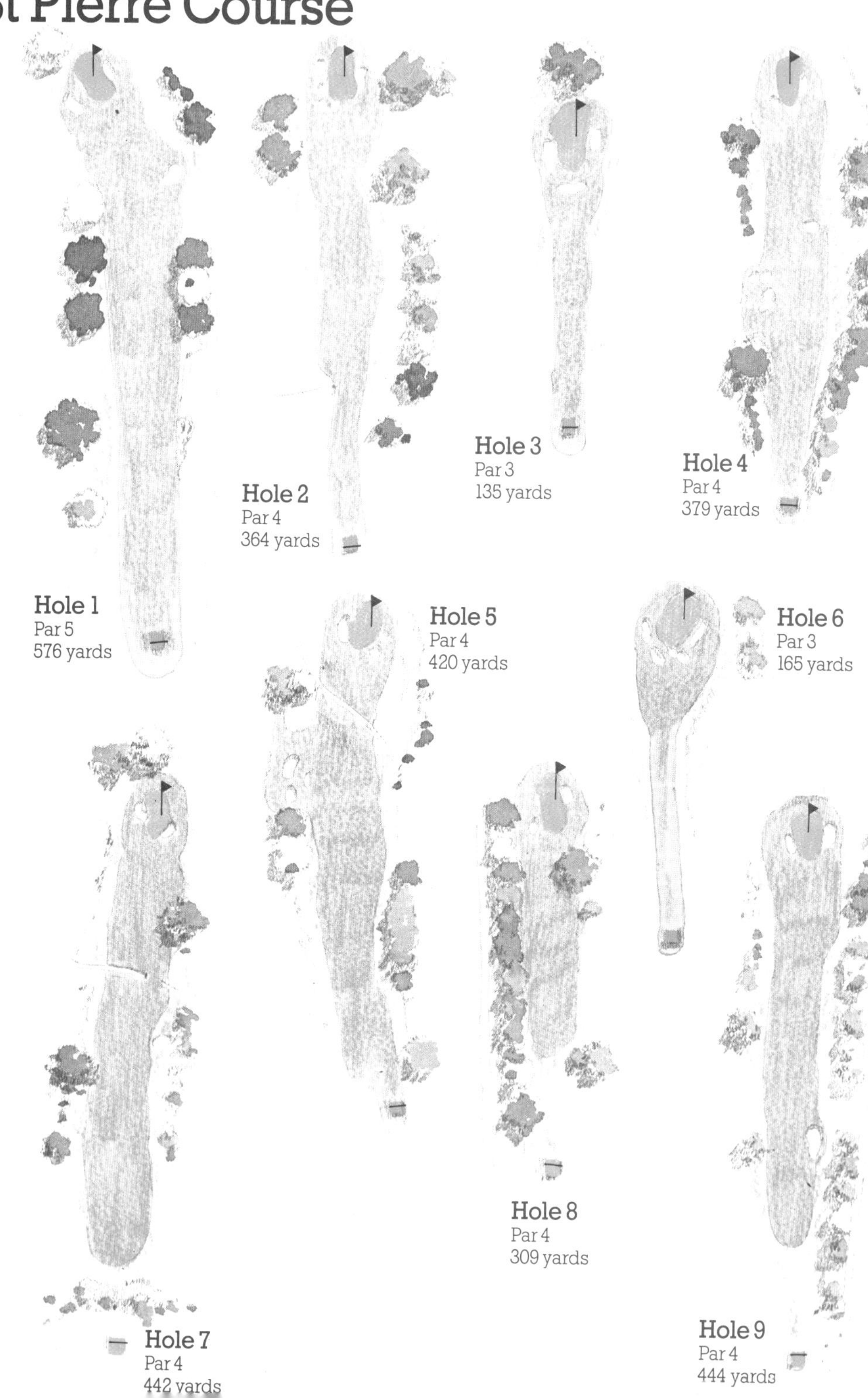
Hole 1
Par 5
576 yards
Hole 2
Par 4
364 yards
Hole 3
Par 3
135 yards
Hole 4
Par 4
379 yards
Hole 5
Par 4
420 yards
Hole 6
Par 3
165 yards
Hole 7
Par 4
442 yards
Hole 8
Par 4
309 yards
Hole 9
Par 4
444 yards

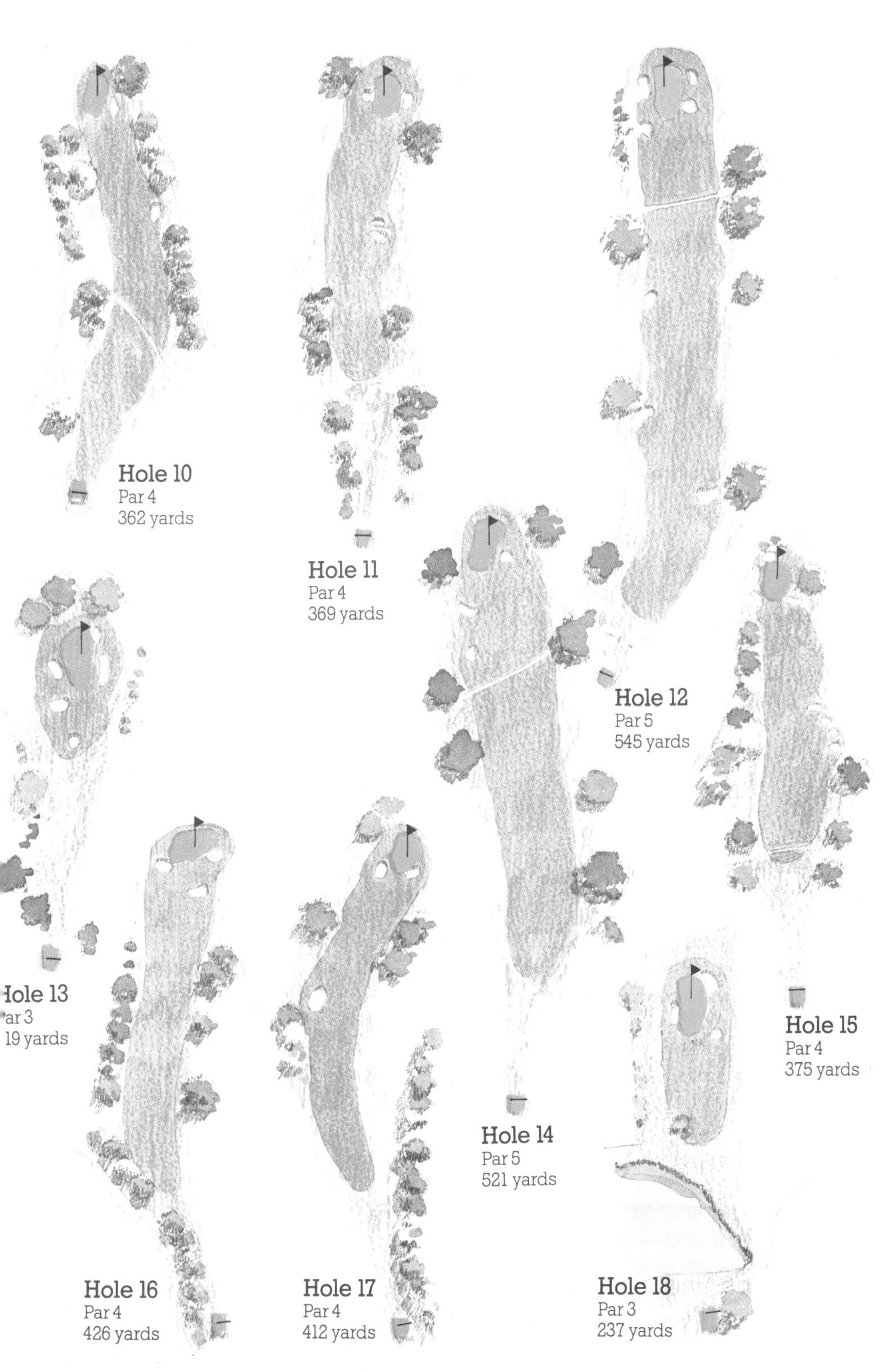
Hole 10
Par 4
362 yards
Hole 11
Par 4
369 yards
Hole 12
Par 5
545 yards
Hole 13
Par 3
19 yards
Hole 14
Par 5
521 yards
Hole 15
Par 4
375 yards
Hole 16
Par 4
426 yards
Hole 17
Par 4
412 yards
Hole 18
Par 3
237 yards

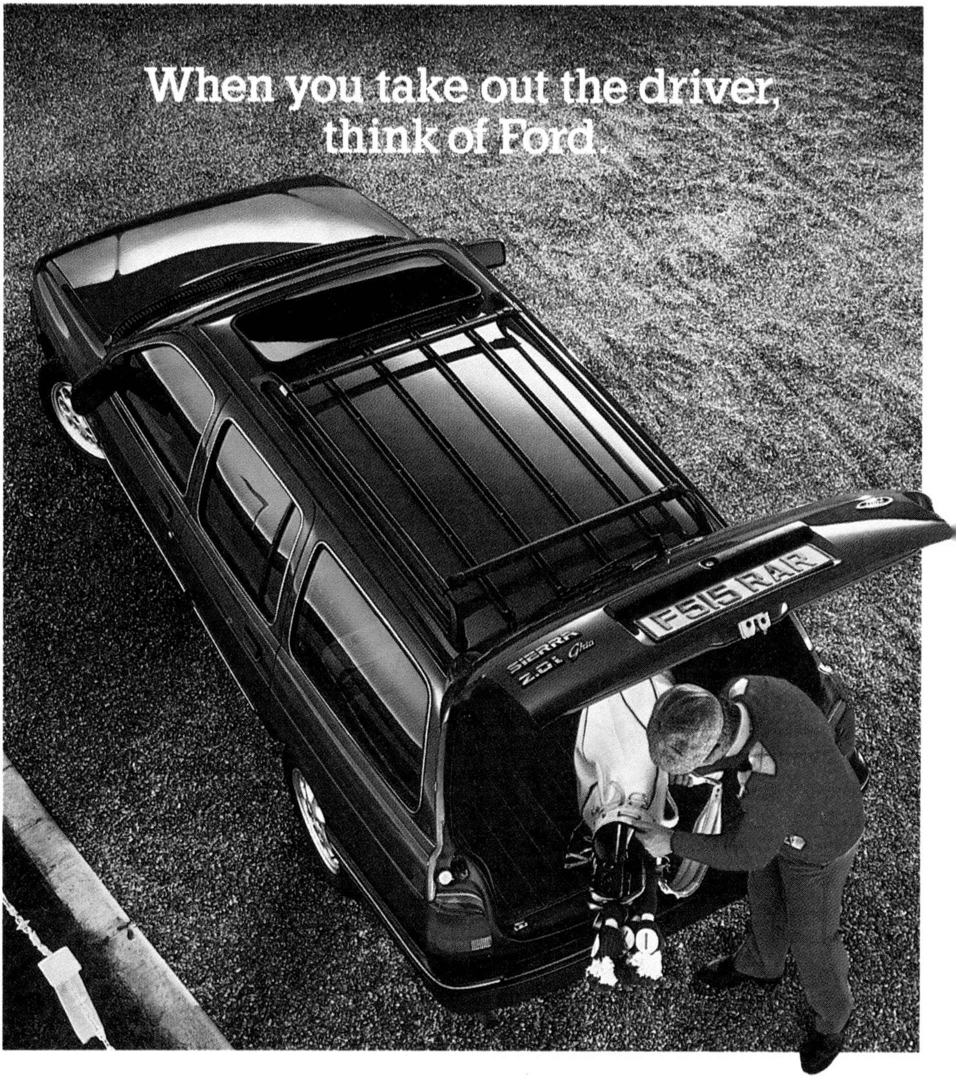

Ford in Golf 1989

Ford Motor Company's involvement with golf spans the whole spectrum of the game, through the Ford in Golf programme.

The Ford Ladies Golf Classic, the first event in the UK on the 1989 Ladies Professional circuit, is to be held once again at the Woburn Golf and Country Club, 26–29 April. This year, the increased prize fund of £50,000 should certainly produce exciting and competitive play, when Laura Davies will surely be hoping to repeat her 1988 success.

At the 118th Open Championship at Royal Troon, 20–23 July, the Ford Courtesy Car Fleet will again be in operation. As official suppliers to the Royal and Ancient, twenty-six Ford cars will transport the world's top players to and from the course. In addition, a static display of the model range will feature in the tented village area.

The Ford Amateur Golf Tournament is now the oldest event of its kind, and remains one of the most popular on the club amateur golf calendar. From an initial entry of over 150,000 competitors at club level, sponsored by the Ford Dealer organisation, top scorers progress to the National Trials for each of the home nations, and compete for a place in one of the four 12-man national teams.

The Ford Home Internationals Final, undoubtedly the highlight of the tournament, will be staged at The Belfry. Only three weeks prior to the Ryder Cup, the Ford finalists will compete over three days for the prestigious trophy in Ryder Cup format, under the guidance of four professional captains.

The Ford Amateur Tournament continues to support the Golf Foundation through prize draws held at all participating clubs and Ford dealers. This year's top prize will be a superb new Fiesta car. Almost £150,000 has been raised to date, permitting the Golf Foundation to maintain its valuable contribution to the development of junior golf.

Ford has been a manufacturer in Britain for 77 years and as the company goes from strength to strength, its commitment to golf at all levels continues to grow.

Tommy Horton and his English team, 1988

Wentworth Golf Club West Course

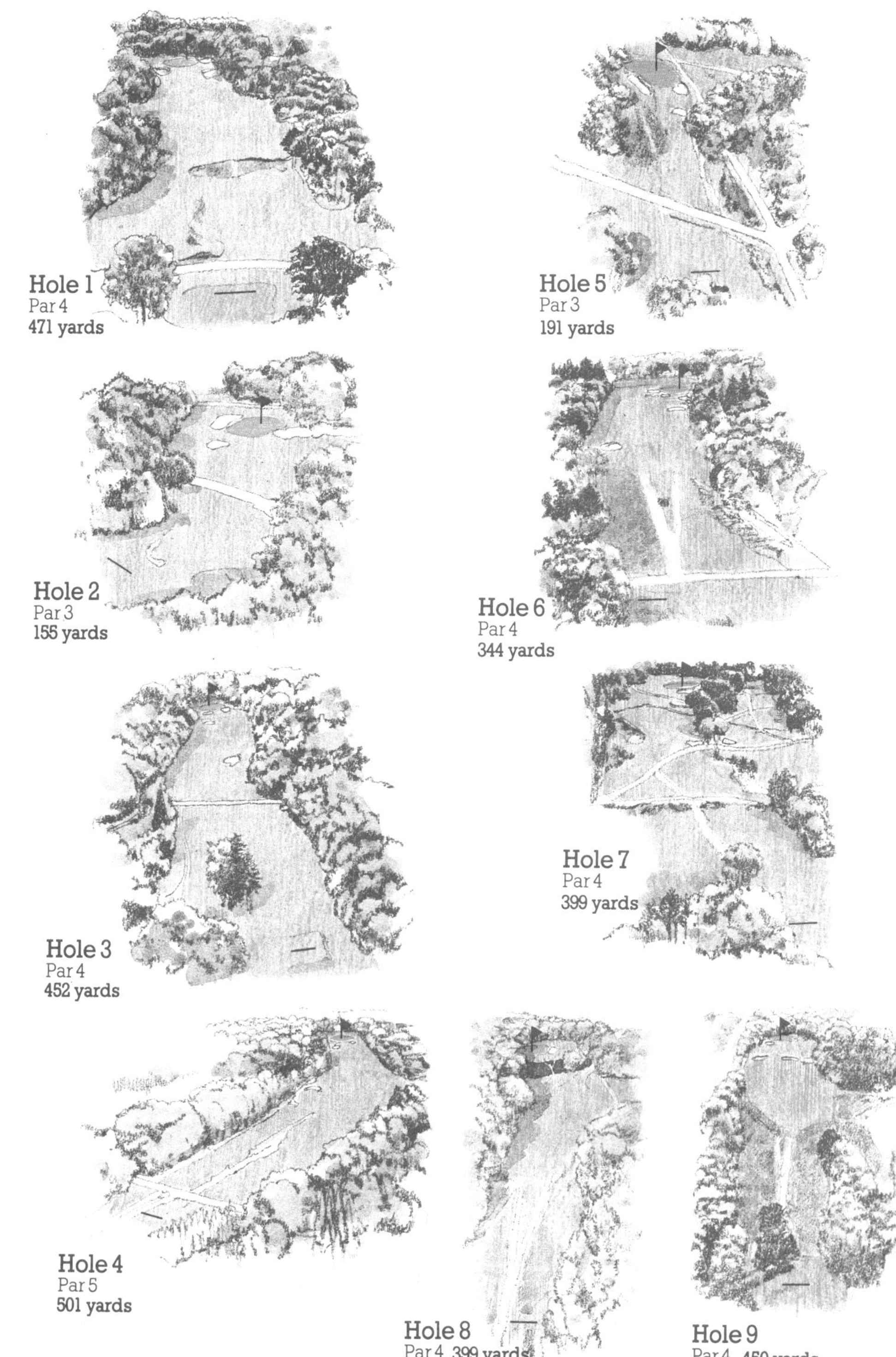

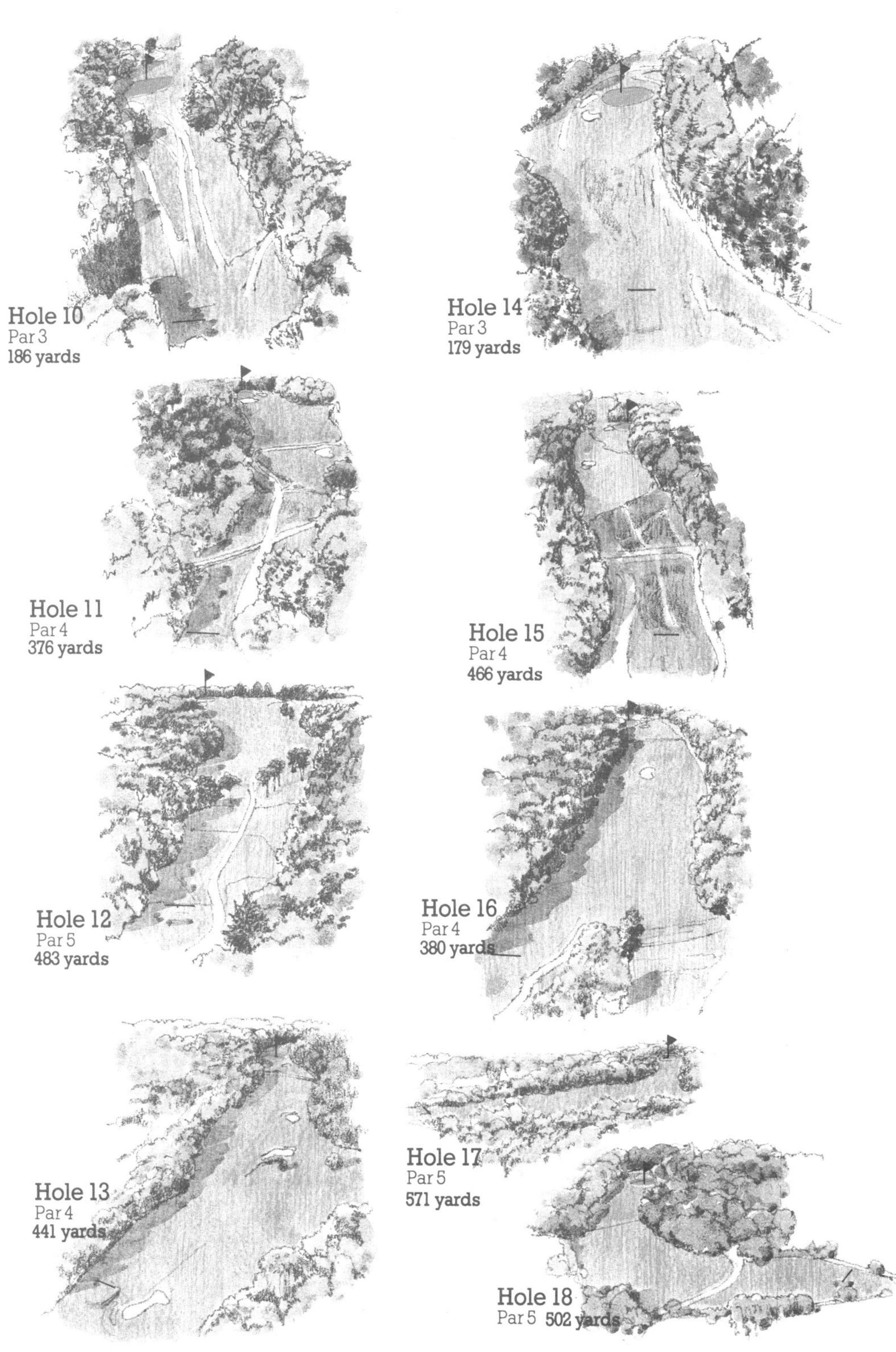
Hole 10
Par 3
186 yards
Hole 14
Par 3
179 yards
Hole 11
Par 4
376 yards
Hole 15
Par 4
466 yards
Hole 12
Par 5
483 yards
Hole 16
Par 4
380 yards
Hole 13
Par 4
441 yards
Hole 17
Par 5
571 yards
Hole 18
Par 5 502 yards

Wild Flowers on British Golf Courses

Clarissa Titcomb

In a time when more and more of our countryside is being destroyed for development or for agriculture, it is a comforting thought that at least small areas of that beauty will be saved on our golf courses. We not only protect the wild flowers and animals; we also enrich our own lives. Natural wild flower swards, purple heather, prickly gorse and skylarks singing over-head are very much a part of the attraction of golf. It would not be the same to most golfers if played on plastic turf in a sterile environment.

Many nationally threatened habitats such as heathland, chalk downland, wetland and ancient woodland are found on golf courses, which, in Great Britain, cover an area of land just less than the area of Bedfordshire. These courses are, in effect, a chain of unofficial nature reserves. Not only do they constitute important refuges for many of our common plants, but there are some species in the British flora which owe their very survival to golf courses. The game of golf is here to stay. As a consequence the land contained within the boundaries of the courses will be protected for generations.

Plants can be visualised as the important fuelling power near the bottom of a complex web linking all living things. Woodlands tend to have a less diverse array of wild flowers in their cool dark centres than at their boundaries. Golf courses therefore serve to break up densely wooded areas to allow in more light. A great floral diversity of both open country and forest species is found on the edge of woodland and in the areas where tracks have been made through the trees. Insects, especially butterflies, are also abundant here, finding the right combination of light and food plants. These insect populations serve, in turn, as food for birds and animals higher up in the food chain.

Bluebells, primroses, wood anemones, dog's mercury and yellow archangel are generally regarded as indicators of ancient woodland. All of these flower early in the year before the leaf canopy develops to shade out the light. White Webbs golf course, situated just one mile from the M25 in Middlesex, harbours all these species as well as the garlic-smelling ramson, greater stitchwort and common dog violet. The early purple orchid is another woodland species found amongst the carpet of bluebells.

Garlic-smelling ramsons carpet the ground in stretches of damp woodland.

Meadows and permanent pastures were once a familiar and beautiful part of the British countryside with their wealth of colourful flowers such as oxeye daisies, buttercups and orchids and home to many insects. Today though, modern agriculture with its emphasis on arable crops and dependence on herbicides and fertilisers, has made these flower-rich grasslands a rarity. Some ancient and unimproved grasslands are, however, represented on golf courses. High Post in Wiltshire is renowned for its rich chalk downland wildlife, whilst the West Kent course contains important herb-rich areas. Fragrant herbs such as wild marjoram are found alongside the springy clumps of purple thyme. The bee orchid, so named because the lip of its flower resembles a bee, also grows interspersed with wild parsnip, man orchid, and the beautiful quaking grass. Such a diversity is reflected in the considerable range of invertebrates, many of which have specific plant needs. The small blue butterfly which feeds on kidney vetch and the marbled white feeding on scabious and knapweeds, are both found at West Kent.

North Foreland golf course resembles a green island in a sea of urban development and contains one of the few areas of chalk grassland left on the Isle of Thanet. The rough areas of the course are home to many flowers which themselves attract 22 species of butterfly and numerous other insects.

Heathlands are one of Britain's most threatened habitats. Each year vast tracts are destroyed to make way for roads and housing. In Hertfordshire, where heathland has all but disappeared due to agricultural improvement or lack of traditional management, relict stands of heather can still be found on parts of Chorleywood and Berkhamsted golf courses. A significant proportion of all heathland south of London is found on golf courses. Examples include Royal Ashdown, Worplesdon, St Georges Hill, Piltdown and West Hill.

Ophrys apifera: *it is not hard to guess how the bee orchid got its name.*

The most abundant and conspicuous shrubby species on heathlands are common heather, bell heather, cross-leaved heather and gorse. Lichens and mosses are frequently found covering the areas between the heather. West Sussex golf course contains an area of quaking bog in which are found the carnivorous round-leaved sundew, the bog asphodel, cranberry and the wispy white flowers of the cottongrass.

One of the most significant contributions made by golf courses is to the conservation of coastal habitats such as cliff-top grasslands, sand dunes and saltmarshes. Many areas of the fragile duneland habitat have been saved from competing coastal developments, such as holiday resorts, by the presence of these relatively undisturbed golfing areas. Great variations of terrain occur on links land; from the towering sandhills at Royal Birkdale to the treeless flat turf at Deal and the dark impenetrable sea-woods at Formby. The rough, too, has its varieties, though on all courses the harsh dune grass is found. The plants which thrive in the sand dunes often have extensive root systems and adaptations to minimise water loss.

Saunton golf course in Devon has a particularly colourful, annual showing of the three species of evening primrose and also the blue vipers bugloss. There are 13 species of orchid found amongst the damp lower-lying areas between the dunes. Other plants worthy of note on this golf course are the bog pimpernel, pink centaury, yellow bartsia, burnet rose, seaside pansy and the carline thistle. The name, 'Carlina', commemorates Charlemagne who, according to legend, used this plant 1200 years ago to cure his soldiers of the plague.

Burnham and Berrow, also on the west coast of England, is well known for its mass of marsh and pyramidal orchids and especially for the marsh helleborine and the rare bee orchid. Small white clumps of the rapidly vanishing species, star-of-Bethlehem, grace some of the hollows in the dunes. Perhaps the most interesting plant found in this course is the tall, brown-flowered clustered-club-rush recorded in only three other places in the world. This rush is peculiar because it flowers on the tip of the spike and not halfway down the stem as in other rushes.

Prickly sea buckthorn with its silvery foliage and brilliant orange berries has started to overrun many dunes on the British links courses. Although it stabilises the dunes, it tends to shade out the smaller plants. As it coexists with bacteria, the nitrogen content of the soil is increased, which by no means suits other, more desirable plants.

In the rich farmlands of north-east Fife, where modern agricultural methods and afforestation have squeezed out so much of our native flora and fauna, golf links have become havens for wildlife. On the St Andrews golf courses, extensive areas of rough are left largely untouched and support a variety of wild flowers. The tall, spiky leaves of marram grass and sea-lyme grass

Woburn Golf and Country Club

Duke's Course

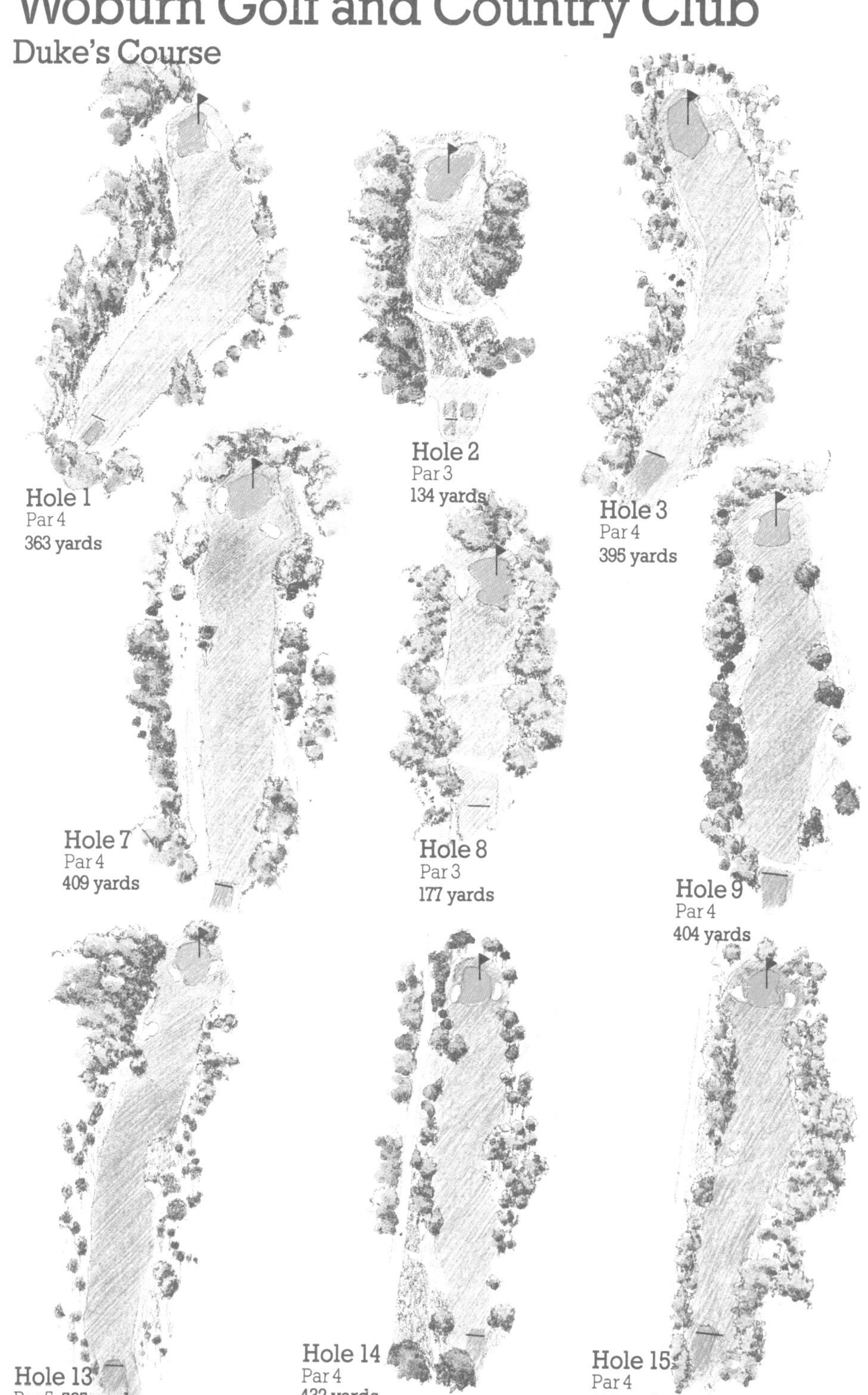

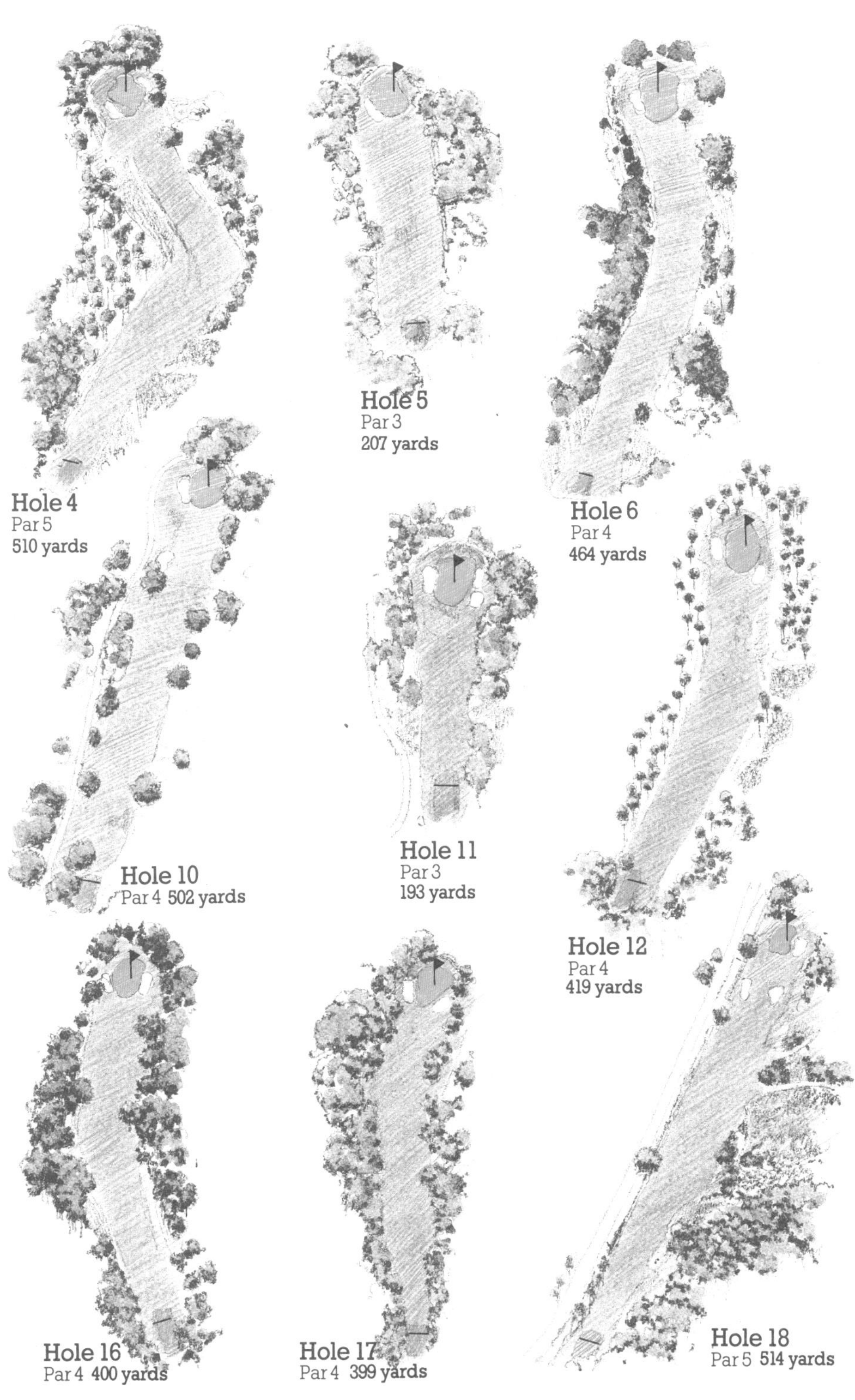
Hole 4
Par 5
510 yards
Hole 5
Par 3
207 yards
Hole 6
Par 4
464 yards
Hole 10
Par 4 502 yards
Hole 11
Par 3
193 yards
Hole 12
Par 4
419 yards
Hole 16
Par 4 400 yards
Hole 17
Par 4 399 yards
Hole 18
Par 5 514 yards

can be seen in many areas. As new dunes build up, those behind become sheltered from the salt and sand-laden winds, allowing a variety of plants including mosses and lichens to colonise the stable grassland – birdsfoot trefoil with its yellow and red 'pea' flowers, haresfoot clover, aptly named for its fluffy seedheads and the rare blue fleabane.

Dense thickets of golden-flowered gorse are a common springtime sight on heaths and cliff-tops.

The sand dune system of Kent's Sandwich Bay golf courses has an exceedingly rich flora and is of interest for both its plant communities and its individual species. Because of its close proximity to Europe, several of the plants are continental species at the north-western limit of their range. On the links at Princes, those areas containing the best colonies of the nationally rare bedstraw broomrape are left unmown, whilst on the adjacent Royal St Georges course, a seasonal warden has been engaged over recent summers specifically to guard the larger stands of the spectacular lizard orchid. The botanical name for the lizard orchid is somewhat multi-lingual. *Himantoglossum* is Greek for 'strap-tongue' and *hircinum* is Latin for 'goat-like' and refers to the smell of the plant. Three feet high, purplish green, festooned like a maypole, it often appears unexpectedly and alone, staying for a year before vanishing for good. At Royal St Georges, however, there is a large, stable population which is carefully managed and protected throughout the year. Other scarce species found in large numbers at Sandwich include the green-winged and man orchids, marsh helleborine, fenugreek and sharp rush.

Saltmarshes are mineral-rich areas which tend to attract both industrialists and farmers who may want to reclaim the fertile land for agriculture. Golf courses such as Burnham and Berrow and Royal West Norfolk, which contain parts of a saltmarsh, are thereby acting as a buffer zone preventing any destructive human intervention. Regular flooding is a common feature of saltmarshes and plants must therefore be able to tolerate salt water. The flowers of the common sea lavender often turn the marshes blue in summer, whilst the pink of the thrift and the mauve sea asters provide other splashes of colour.

Many courses contain damp areas, which have not been ploughed, improved with fertilisers, or drained. The rare fritillary favours these damp meadows and can be found on White Webbs and Brickendon Grange golf courses. The darker petals of these attractive purple flowers are marked with a chequered pattern which resembles the one used by the Romans on their diceboxes, for which their word was *fritillarus*. The buds are long, flat, narrow and pointed at the end and the markings evidently suggested to someone those of a reptile skin – hence the alternative vernacular name for the plant, 'snakes head'.

The distinctive snakes head fritillary grows only in undisturbed damp meadowland often preserved on golf courses.

Water features, natural or artificial are often incorporated into golf courses, serving as a golfing hazard, as well as providing an aesthetic function. These areas are relatively undisturbed, free from fishermen, sailors and other recreational users. Reedbeds can flourish and floating aquatics have the chance to become established. Enville and Edgbaston golf courses both have beautiful water features containing a vast array of aquatic plants including water lilies, yellow flag and reedmace.

Water hazards may not be beloved of golfers but they provide an ideal habitat for marsh plants such as water mint.

Damp alder woodlands occur on many courses, with their continued existence due to sympathetic management by the golf clubs. Meadowsweet which used to be used against malaria, is found in these damp areas on Canterbury golf course, along with honeysuckle, ragged robin, wood horsetail and marsh violet. In the wettest section of the Sene Valley golf course, also in Kent, the woodland grades into a fen-carr community, dominated by grey willow and young white willow. In the open ground between the trees, there is a species-rich, tall herb sward including water mint, marsh thistle, rushes, reeds and great willowherb.

Most golf courses mentioned are well-known and often busy, especially during the flowering season. They are known to support abundant and diverse floral communities, but the smaller, less acclaimed courses harbour as wide, or an even wider range of plants, especially those which have fewer golfing members and therefore suffer less damage from trampling.

Golfers are becoming increasingly aware of the role they play in preserving and protecting much of the British flora and fauna. Many greenkeepers actively encourage animals to take up residence on their courses and do their utmost to protect the established plants. With a little guidance, most of the natural areas of wildlife importance could be expanded to provide new protected habitats for a wide range of species including birds, butterflies and flowers. This improvement of the wildlife value of golf courses is one of the aims of the Golf Course Wildlife Trust (GCWT), which offers a specialist technical advisory service to golf clubs.

How lucky we are, as golfers, to be able to combine a sport we love with a walk in some of the most beautiful, unspoilt countryside. How sad it is that soon golf courses may be one of the only places in which to see so many of the plants that we, so often, take for granted. It falls to those of us who play golf and to those who are responsible for the management of golf courses to look after these valuable areas, both for the community and for the survival of our British wildlife.

The photographs are taken from Field Guide to British Wildflowers *by F Perring, M Walters and A Gagg, published by Macmillan Press, May 1989. Reproduced by kind permission of Andrew N. Gagg, Photoflora.*

Gleneagles Kings Course

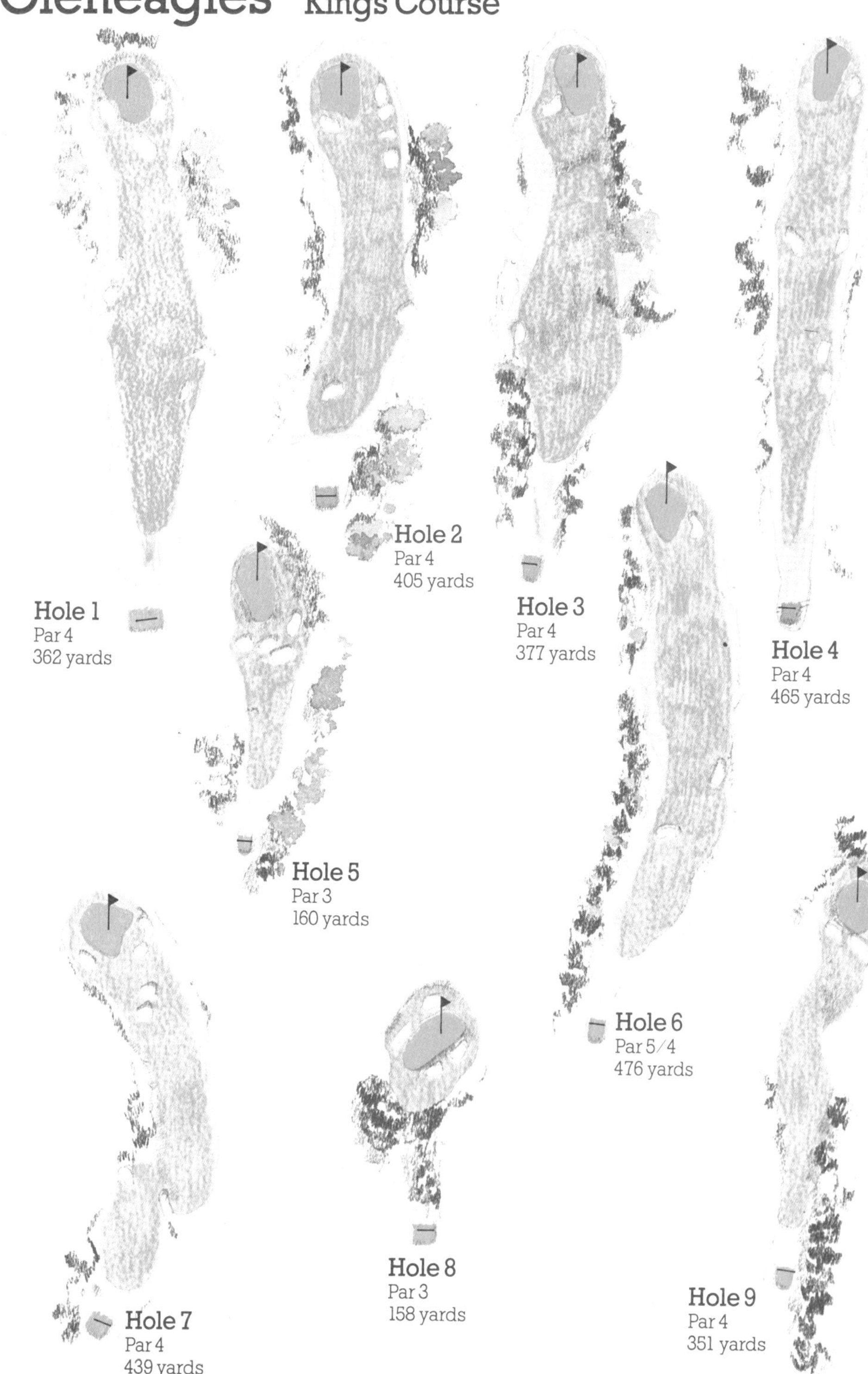

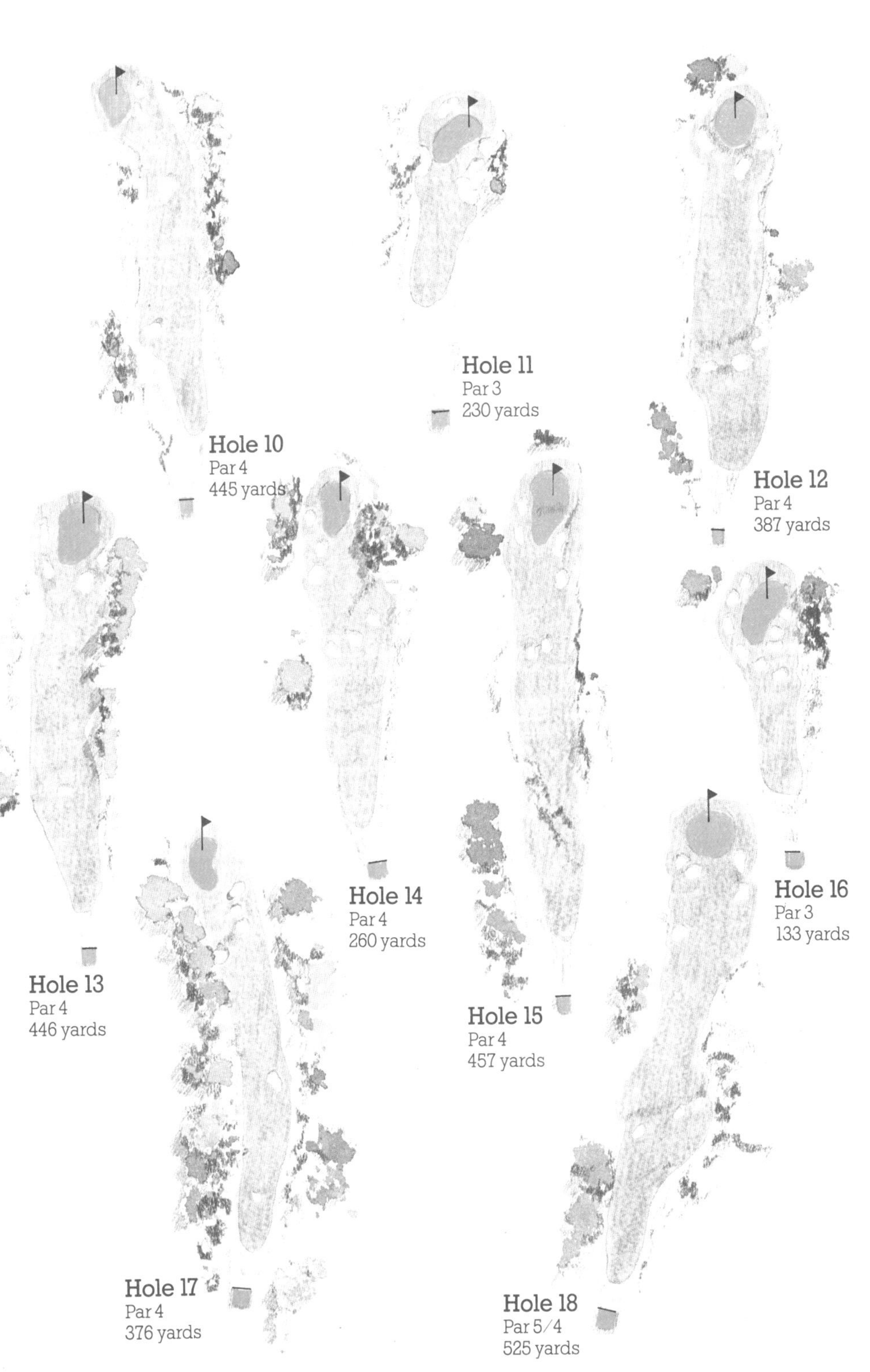
Hole 10
Par 4
445 yards
Hole 11
Par 3
230 yards
Hole 12
Par 4
387 yards
Hole 13
Par 4
446 yards
Hole 14
Par 4
260 yards
Hole 15
Par 4
457 yards
Hole 16
Par 3
133 yards
Hole 17
Par 4
376 yards
Hole 18
Par 5/4
525 yards

British Clubs Celebrating their Centenaries in 1989

England

Beverley & East Riding

The Beverley & East Riding Golf Club course is laid out on Westwood, a pleasant area of common land to the west of the town of Beverley. The land is owned by the local council but its management is under the jurisdiction of 12 Pasture Masters elected annually under an Act passed in 1836. The Club pays a rent to the Pasture Masters based on the number of 'gaits' which, if the Club did not cut the grass on the course, could otherwise be let to farmers for the grazing of their cattle and sheep!

The Club started with 50 members and a 9-hole course on which play was permitted only in the winter months and on weekdays. The annual subscription was one guinea. The course was extended to 18 holes in 1895 and the layout much altered during the next few years, mainly to accommodate the transfer of the Clubhouse from Black Mill to its present location at Anti Mill. Only four of the original nine holes still exist.

Summer play was not permitted by the Pasture Masters until 1907 and then only over 9 holes. Permission was given for summer play over the full course in 1919 but it was not until 1933 that golf could be played on Sundays.

Initially, ladies formed a separate club with their own 9 holes. They amalgamated with the men's Club in 1912. An artisans' section, the 'Beavers', which had been instituted in 1908, was also amalgamated with the Club in 1963.

Captain 1989: David Hannam
Secretary: Bernard Hiles
Professional: Ian Mackie

Bungay and Waveney Valley

The Waveney Valley Golf Club was founded in Bungay on 8th January, 1889. A 9-hole course was marked out on Outney Common by Willie Fernie, Professional at Great Yarmouth, and came into use four weeks later. By June 1889 the Club had 57 members. Two of these were Henry Rider Haggard and his wife, who had a long association with the Club. In 1894 a Clubhouse was built and was enlarged in 1904. In 1901 James Braid advised on the layout of an 18-hole course. In 1907, with membership at 160, Bungay was added to the title 'to assist strangers to locate the Club'. In 1916 a military camp on the common caused the temporary discontinuance of the Club, but in 1919 it was revived. An Artisans' Golf Club used the course from 1906.

Financial difficulties during the Second World War were alleviated by the green fees of US Servicemen stationed locally. Problems

Royal Troon CHAMPIONSHIP COURSE

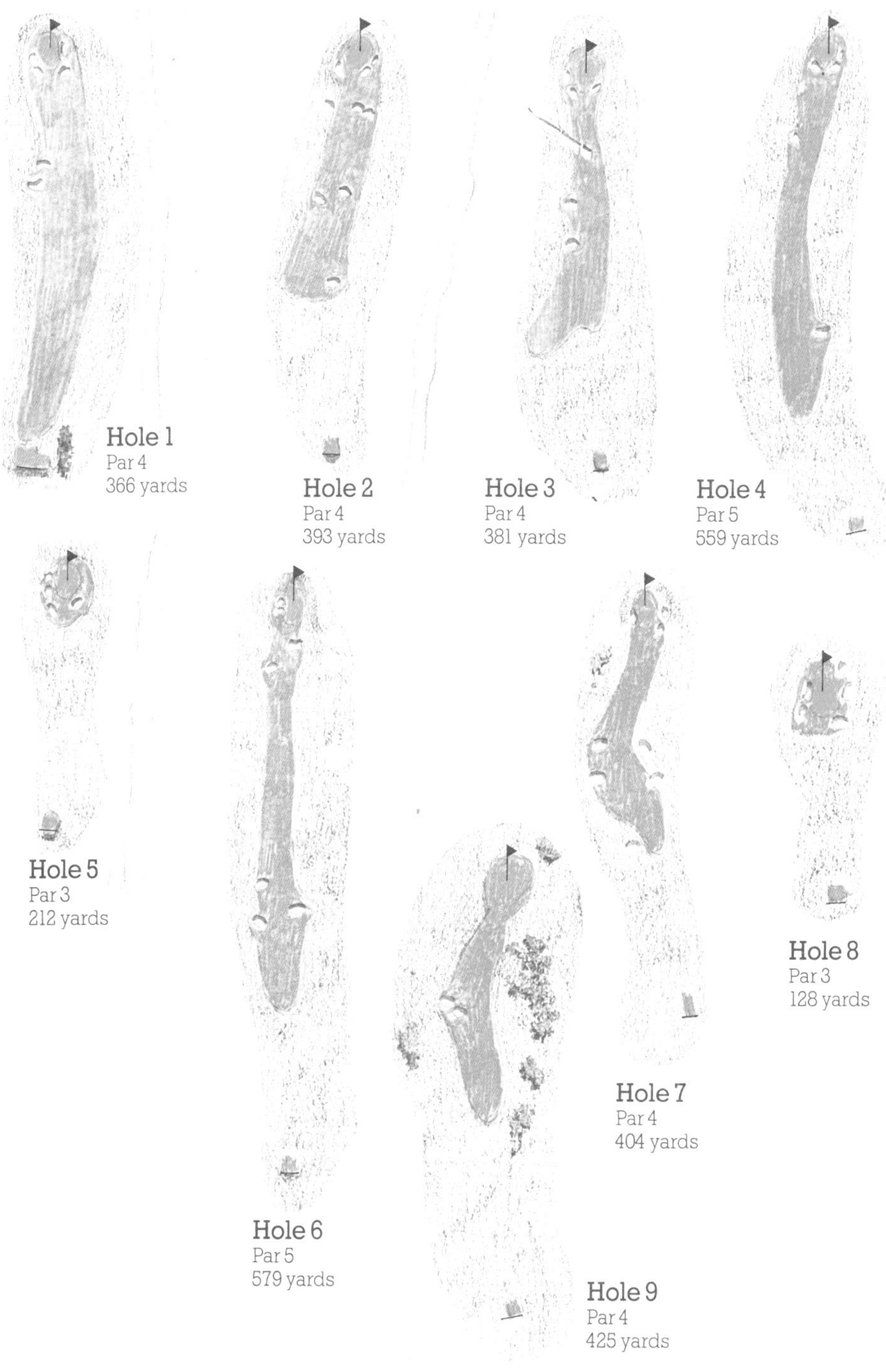

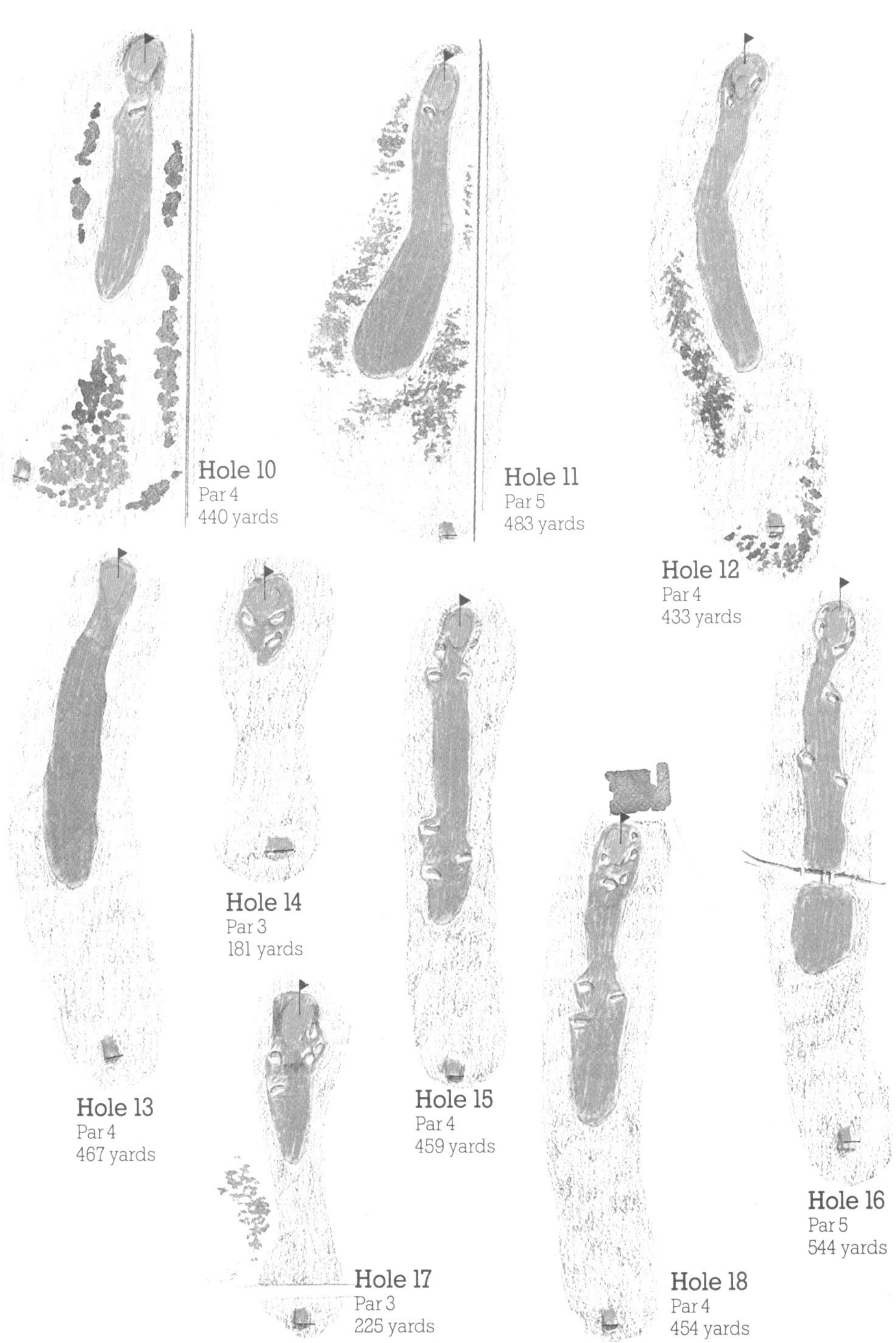

Hole 10
Par 4
440 yards
Hole 11
Par 5
483 yards
Hole 12
Par 4
433 yards
Hole 13
Par 4
467 yards
Hole 14
Par 3
181 yards
Hole 15
Par 4
459 yards
Hole 16
Par 5
544 yards
Hole 17
Par 3
225 yards
Hole 18
Par 4
454 yards

returned after the war and membership fell to 70 in 1957. A regime of severe economies promoted by an energetic secretary earned the Club a newspaper headline 'The Do It Yourself Club'. Today, after two decades of rapid progress, the Club has a membership of over 600, an attractive course lying in the loop of the River Waveney, the boundary between Norfolk and Suffolk, and a fine new Clubhouse opened in 1985.

Captain 1989: G Nichols
Secretary: WJ Mann
Professional: N Whyte

Disley

In 1889 three gentlemen met with a view to forming a golf club in Disley. They were Dr Hodgkinson (a throat specialist in Manchester) and two Disley men, Mr W Bell and Mr JA Hutton. Without the foresight of these gentlemen there would have been no golf course in Disley and countless thousands of people would have been the poorer for that.

Disley is in the north-east corner of Cheshire, with the Derbyshire boundary about a mile away. The terrain is more like the Peak District country than the lush pastures of Cheshire, but for all that, the members are tremendously proud of belonging to the Cheshire Union. The Club first had three holes, quickly made up to six and by 1891, a 9-hole course was in being. Around the middle of the 1890s a full 18-hole course was made and about 80 male members played on it until 1925 when the layout of the 18 holes was revised.

Dr Hodgkinson was the first Captain of the Club and presented a beautiful Gold Medal which is played for annually over two rounds. The Club President from 1889 to 1939 was Lord Newton, who resided part of each year in nearby Lyme Hall.

A Clubhouse was built in 1905 off the course but in 1979 a large functional Clubhouse was built on the course itself. The illustration shows Smyley Hall, a treasured possession of the Club. The barn on the left is the original Club room.

The two men famous in Disley golf are Israel Sidebottom, who had a domestic handicap of plus 7 and who played regularly for Cheshire and in several English Amateur Championships, and Neville Parker, who was Hon Secretary from 1927 until his death in 1978, giving 51 years of service to the Club.

Captain 1988: K Bleakley
Secretary: JA Lomas
Professional: AG Esplin

Epsom

A form of golf had been played on Epsom Downs close to the famous racecourse from about 1880. Two well-known pioneers of the game, W Laidlaw Purves and TW Lang had 'knocked about on the heath', but it was not until 1888 that some Epsom College masters cut holes in the turf near the LSWR station. The Club was formed in 1889, the Lord of the Manor, JS Strange, being invited to be President, perhaps an early example of the tact for which the Club is well-known. The Earl of Rosebery, yet to lead in his Derby winners, had to be content as a Vice-President.

The course was an amalgamation of the holes played by the Epsom masters and the ideas of TW Lang and was ready for play with remarkable speed by 6th April. Willie Mcwatt of Musselburgh was appointed Professional in 1891 and remained with the Club until 1922. The first Clubhouse was opened on 29th October 1892 and the Rosebery Medal and Brooks Cup competitions date from that day.

Many famous professionals, including Harry Vardon, JH Taylor, James Braid, Jack White and later Arthur Havers, all Open Champions, played exhibition matches at Epsom. The course cannot have been easy with Vardon winning one day with 81 and 76, which was a new professional record.

The present course is 18 holes, 5725 yards, with a par of 68. Being only 15 miles from central London, it has a membership of over 600 and is well-known for its welcome and hospitality.

Secretary: KH Watson
Professional: R Wynn

Fakenham

When instituted in February 1889, its name was Fakenham and Hempton Golf Club. The first annual subscription was £1.1.0 and there were 41 members. Club prizes were the Hammond Cup and Hastings Cup (Medal), played for twice yearly. The Club continued under this name until 1935, when it was changed to the Flag Moor Golf Club until 1942: the course was on land used jointly with the racecourse. Its length was 5438 yards, bogey 74.

The course was ploughed up in 1942 to assist the war effort and the Club found a temporary home at the local Sculthorpe air base during 1946–47.

In 1967 informal talks with the local council and the Fakenham Racecourse Company resulted in the present 9-hole course being designed by Cotton, Pennink, Lawrie & Partners, the well-known golf architects. It formed part of a sports complex comprising golf, bowls and squash clubs under the control of the North Norfolk District Council, until the Golf Club purchased the Centre in 1981.

Thereafter, the course was improved by the construction of alternate tees, increasing the length to 5992 yards with a Standard Scratch of 69. It is predominantly a parkland course and crosses the racecourse track at two points, resulting in the closure of the golf course six times in the year on race meeting days. The illustration is a view of the 1st green and 2nd fairway.

Visitors are made very welcome by the resident Club Professional and in the Centre itself, where the attractive lounge bar caters for all needs.

Captain 1989: Barry Anderson
Secretary: Graham Cocker
Professional: J Westwood

Kenilworth

1989 sees the Club celebrating its centenary. The initial course was laid out at Castle Farm but in 1937 facilities were transferred to Crew Lane where now exists one of the most popular courses in Warwickshire. Continual investment into the course along with its proximity to Midland motorway networks makes it sought after by visitors who are made most welcome.

Major plans for centenary celebrations include a Festival of Golf Week in August and also a top pro-am on Monday 18th September which coincides with the Ryder Cup week at The Belfry.

The present Clubhouse was opened by Henry Cooper in 1972 and complements a pretty course which has beautiful views over the Warwickshire countryside. At 6400 yards, it offers a good test of golfing ability whilst its medium terrain is by no means arduous.

Club Captains 1988: Ken Bullock, Ron Saywell
Secretary: Berwyn Edwards
Professional: Sidney Mouland

Limpsfield Chart

Limpsfield Chart is one of the oldest Clubs in Surrey, only Guildford, Reigate, Redhill and Epsom are older. The Manorial Land at Limpsfield offered splendid opportunities for golf and several gentlemen of the neighbourhood saw the possibility and established a committee for the purpose of 'framing a golf course'. The Lord of the Manor, Granville William Gresham Leveson-Gower, was approached and gave his permission to have a course laid out.

James Paxton, professional at Royal Eastbourne, was employed to lay out 9 holes. The course was heather-and tree-lined as it is today, suiting those who hit the ball straight. It became a favourite course for Londoners, one of whom wrote to *The Times* describing it as 'a tough course set malignantly in a forest of gorse where the wise set forth with a pocket-full of repaints and a bottle of iodine'.

Several of the early members were local clergy. Later members included Prince and Princess Arthur of Connaught, Mrs (later Lady) Winston Churchill, the Hon B Bowes-Lyon who was great uncle to the renowned Surrey and England cricketer, HDG Leveson-Gower, and more recently Colin Cowdrey.

Fulford Golf Club, York

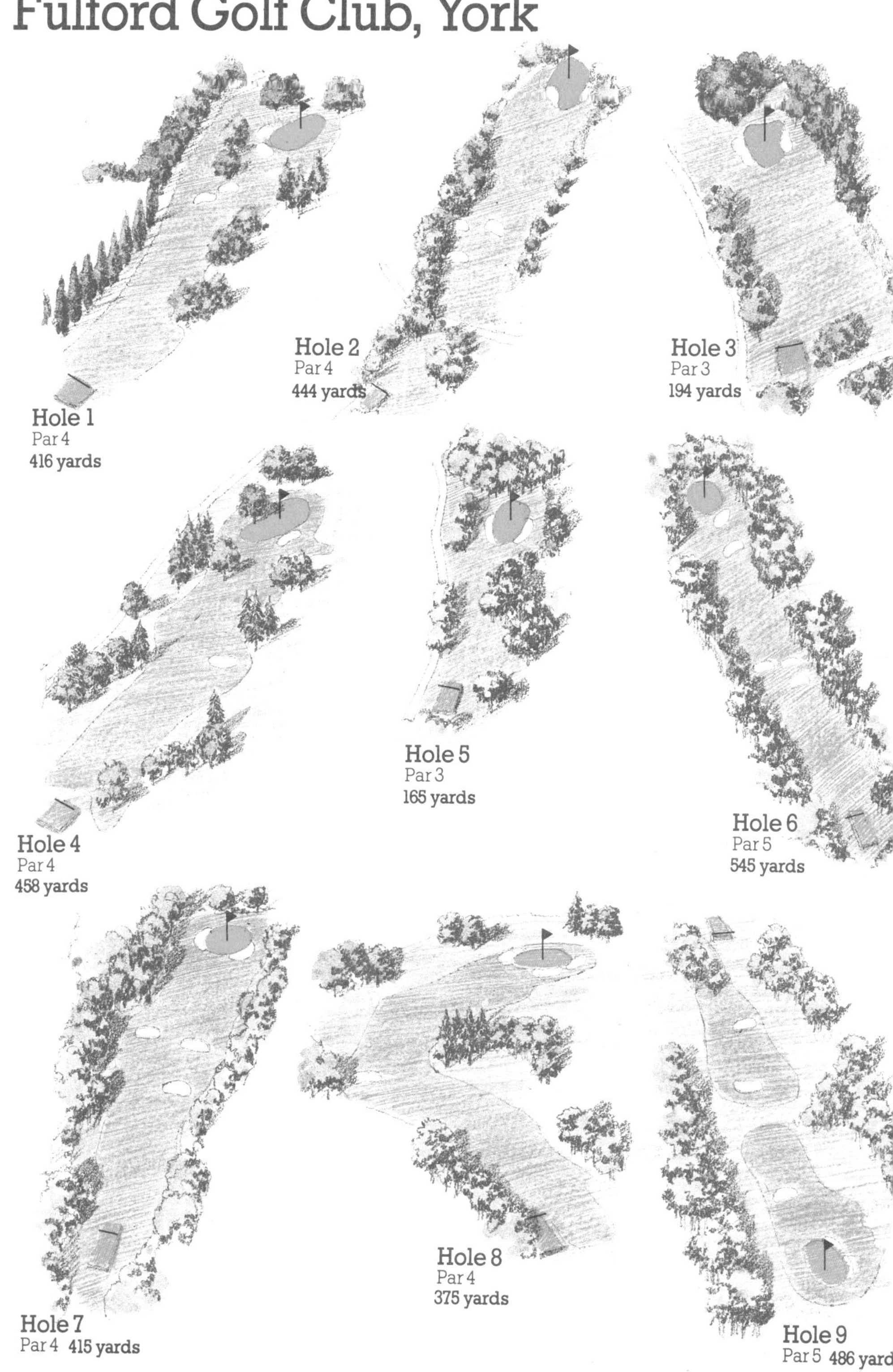

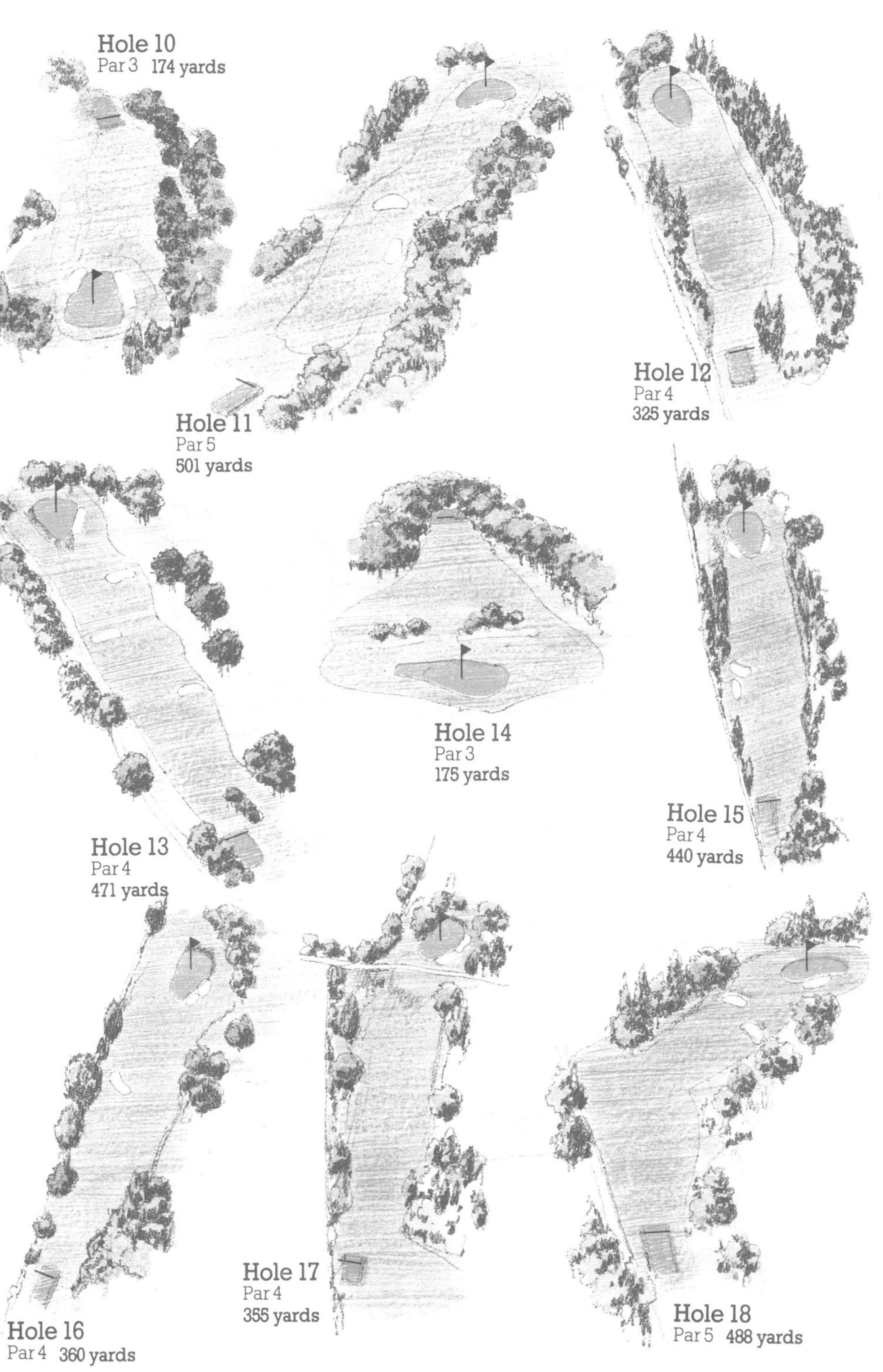
Hole 10
Par 3 174 yards
Hole 11
Par 5
501 yards
Hole 12
Par 4
325 yards
Hole 13
Par 4
471 yards
Hole 14
Par 3
175 yards
Hole 15
Par 4
440 yards
Hole 16
Par 4 360 yards
Hole 17
Par 4
355 yards
Hole 18
Par 5 488 yards

The Club emblem is a grasshopper, originating from the Gresham family, early ancestors of the Leveson-Gowers, and is also the emblem of the Royal Exchange, Martin's Bank and Gresham College. The Club has a strong artisan section, also known as 'The Gresham'.

In 1971 the then Lord of the Manor, Major Richard Leveson-Gower, offered some 350 acres of the Common, including the Golf Course, to the National Trust, which granted a lease to the Club 'at 1/- per annum if called for'.

The course, while perhaps now less malignant, retains it original natural beauty, as will be seen from the view from the 10th hole, typical of the whole course.

Captain 1988: Brian Barnett
Secretary: J Braidson

Littlehampton

Littlehampton Club still plays its golf on the same stretch of links land just across the River Arun, near its estuary, on the west side of the town. For many years the quickest way to the Clubhouse and course was by ferry-boat across the river which was preferable to the detour over the footbridge. As with some other Clubs, Littlehampton suffered a disastrous fire in 1985 when all its records were destroyed, but by careful research in the local library and other sources a few dedicated members have uncovered much of its early history.

Being near to Arundel, the Club has had close connections with the Dukes of Norfolk, one member of the family having always been President of the Club. The Patron is Lavinia, Duchess of Norfolk, widow of the 16th Duke, who took a keen interest and did so much for the Club. He rescued it in 1957 when the finances were in a poor state and handed it back to the members as a going concern in 1974. As sitting tenants of a low-rent leasehold property the members were able to purchase the freehold eight years later.

After the fire the Clubhouse was rebuilt. The first floor containing the new communal rooms has a splendid view over the course. While the direction and layout of most of the holes has been altered over the years, the ground has not and several features from the first plan of holes remain, including the ruined fort built as part of the coast defences in the last century. The course was redesigned by JH Taylor and Fred Hawtree in 1923–24 when several of the less interesting holes were eliminated.

Many Sussex Championships have been played at Littlehampton. The Club has a strong membership of both sexes and is proud of its reputation for welcoming visitors.

Captain 1988: Peter Gimson
Secretary: Keith Palmer
Professional: Clive Burgess

Ludlow

Shropshire's oldest Golf Club plays and, since its inception in 1889, has always played, on a tract of heathland, in the parish of Bromfield some 2 miles to the north-west of the ancient town of Ludlow, just off the A49 Shrewsbury Road. Play has only been interrupted by two World Wars, when the course was used for the accommodation of troops and military hardware. The original course consisted of 9 holes only, but was extended in 1922 to its existing 18 holes under the advice and direction of James Braid.

Although situated in the middle of rich agricultural country, the course enjoys the benefit of a gravel subsoil, growing fine textured fairway grass and draining quickly in the wettest of weather. Like Royal Ascot and other courses, the layout lies within the periphery of the local (Ludlow) racecourse and provides a fine test of golf, abounding in natural hazards in the shape of a profuse growth of gorse and broom bounding some of the narrow fairways, and with a quarry which comes into play on two holes. Although the course itself is level, there are fine views of the rolling south Shropshire hills, with Ludlow Castle and the church tower conspicuous on the skyline.

The Clubhouse was extended and modernised in 1983 to meet expanding membership, which now stands at about 550. The course is 6266 yards long with a par and SSS of 70.

Captain 1989: ER Wilks
Administrator: AR Wilcox
Professional: Graham Farr

Macclesfield

Fifteen 'Gentlemen interested in the formation of a Golf Club' met at the Bull's Head Hotel, Macclesfield, on 30th October, 1889. The idea was Mr WHL Cameron's and those attending included two bank managers, a solicitor, two parsons and a doctor, a quite normal spread of professions for the time. The Club was founded there and then, officers elected and arrangements made to play on land owned by a Mr Warren of Upton Hill Farm. The ground, consisting of fields, was 'mowed, rolled prepared for play'. Such rapid improvisation was helped a month later by the advice of Mr Lowe. Professional and Greenkeeper at St Anne's-on-Sea, who considered the layout of all but two holes satisfactory.

Little is known of the subsequent history of the Club due to a fire in 1912 which destroyed the Clubhouse and all early records. However it is clear that the move from the Upton course to Hollins occurred in 1901, largely due to the complaints of the farmer. Another fire in 1964, while again destroying records, provided the opportunity to rebuild the Clubhouse and, with the great increase of interest in the game, two further extensions in 1977 and 1985 have given it the reputation of being one of the finest Clubhouses in Cheshire. The course has been altered over the years, but not since 1968 when a public footpath had to be re-routed and the 8th hole extended to 510 yards.

The Club is celebrating its centenary by providing china tankards and wall plates showing the illustration of the Clubhouse seen here, reproduced from a painting by the 1988–89 Captain, Mr D Collier.

Captain 1988: D Collier
Secretary: W Eastwood
Professional: T Taylor

Minchinhampton

The following is a Minute dated 14th March 1889. 'It was unanimously resolved that a Golf Club be formed to be called "The Minchinhampton Common Golf Club", that the Headquarters of the Club be at the Old Lodge Inn and that a Professional be engaged by the Club for three months from 1st April'. Thus the oldest club in Gloucestershire came into being.

An 18-hole course was laid out by Robert Wilson, the Club's first Professional and a 9-hole Ladies' Course was also made. Although not all the holes remain the same, the Minchinhampton Old Course today is similar to that played in 1889.

After 80 years of continuous play on Minchinhampton Common, it was decided that conditions had become so difficult, due to the influx of people and cars, that a new and enclosed site, within the neighbourhood, had to be found.

Walton Heath Championship Course

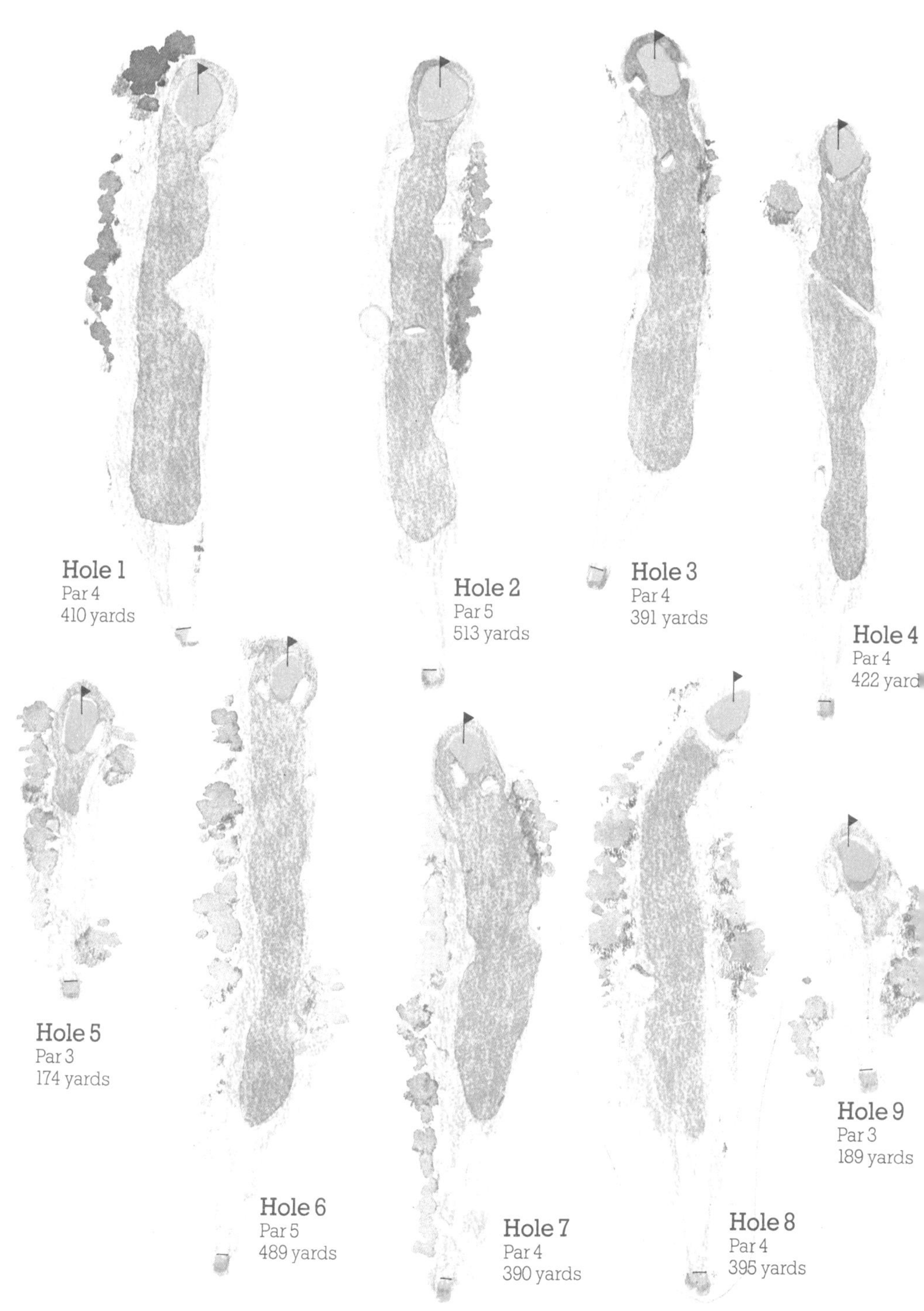

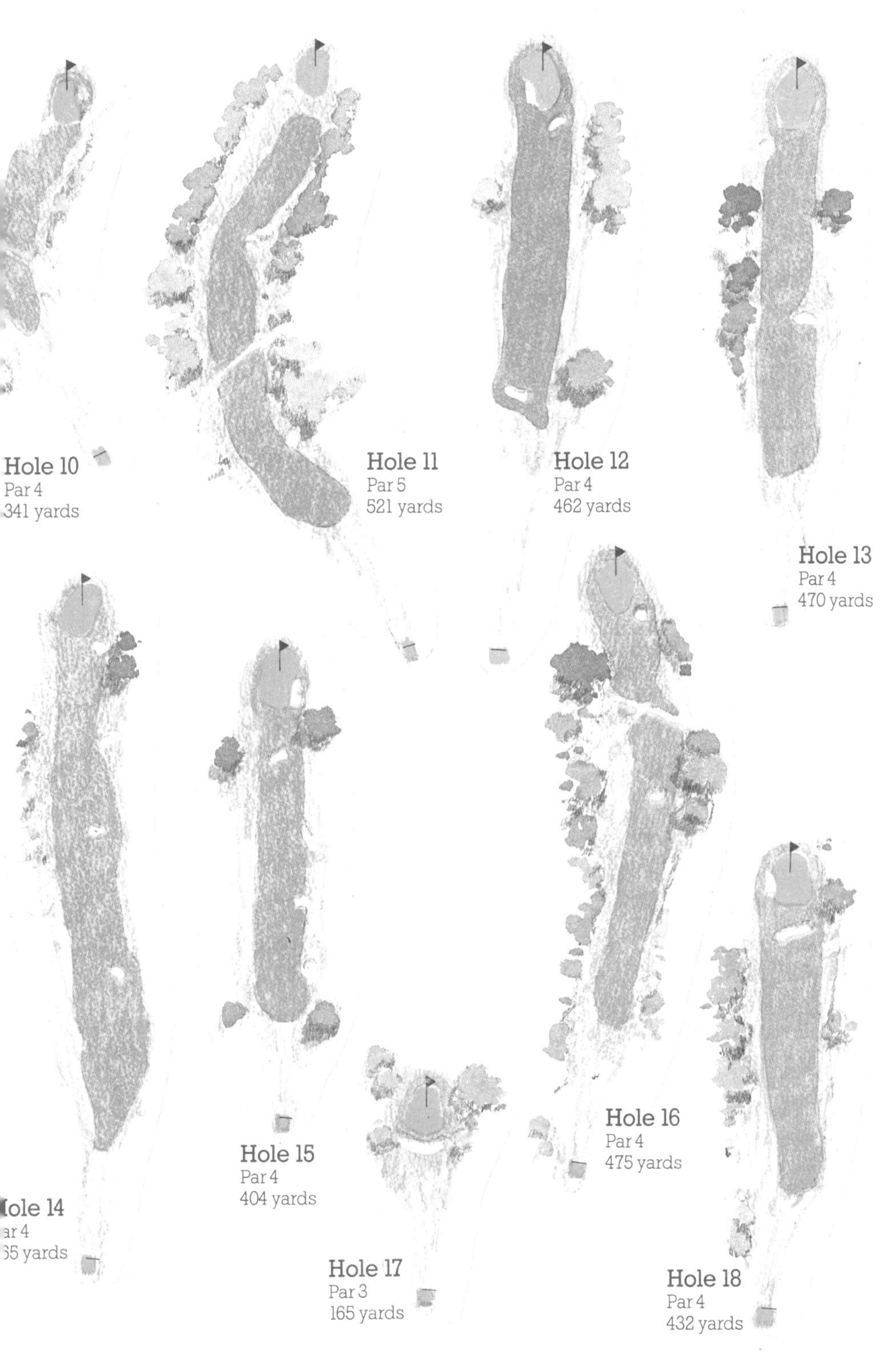

Hole 10
Par 4
341 yards
Hole 11
Par 5
521 yards
Hole 12
Par 4
462 yards
Hole 13
Par 4
470 yards
ole 14
ar 4
yards
Hole 15
Par 4
404 yards
Hole 16
Par 4
475 yards
Hole 17
Par 3
165 yards
Hole 18
Par 4
432 yards

In 1972, 134 acres of farmland were purchased between Minchinhampton and Avening, about three miles from the Old Course. Mr FW Hawtree, the well-known golf architect, designed the course and the result is evidence of his ability to produce a first class course, without affecting the natural beauty of the surroundings, nor involving excessive reconstruction.

The course is characterised by its long tees, giving both a par 71 and 72 course, as well as a County Green for the Ladies. There are two starting points, each nine holes boasting two par 3s and two par 5s and offers a fair test for all golfers. The illustration shows the New Course and Clubhouse.

Captain: DG Martin
Secretary: DR Vickers
Professional: C Steele

Royal Birkdale

This famous Club which celebrates its centenary in 1989, is rated as one of the great golf courses in the world.

It has staged many major events, including six Open Championships, two Ryder Cup matches, The British Amateur, The Walker Cup, The Ladies British Open and The Curtis Cup.

The decision to form a golf club at Birkdale was made on the 30th July 1889 by eight golf enthusiasts. They leased a piece of land near the Portland Hotel and converted it into a 9-hole golf course. This sufficed until March 1897, when the land was required for building development, and an area of 190 acres of sandhills was leased, on which the present course stands.

The expression 'A natural golf course' is particularly apt when applied to the Birkdale Links, as the fairways run in valleys between high sandhills stretching along the Lancashire coast, an area once described by Bernard Darwin as the most heavenly golfing country in the world.

The course was re-modelled by Messrs Hawtree and Taylor in 1933, and is arranged in two loops of 9 holes, each hole being separated from its neighbour, and having its own individual character. It provides a very fair test of golf and can be equally enjoyed by tiger and rabbit alike.

In the same year, a magnificent Clubhouse was built, and this has been improved and modernised to provide three lounges and dining accommodation to seat 140 with panoramic views of the course and the Welsh hills.

Captain 1989: AN Stephenson
Secretary: N Crewe
Professional: RN Bradbeer

Sidmouth

Situated in a sheltered and scenically beautiful part of the south-east Devon coastland, Sidmouth has developed into a very popular and enthusiastically organised Club. In 1889, the original membership consisted of 30 golfers who paid an annual subscription of one guinea for the privilege of playing on the 6-hole course available at that time. By 1891 the course had been enlarged to 9 holes and in 1905, with the help of JH Taylor, an 18-hole course was designed approximating, with the exception of the 9th green and the 10th tee, to the present course although many improvements to tees and greens have been made over the years.

The present Clubhouse was built in 1905 and, although a pleasant building, it is now being developed and improved.

The course is rather short at 5109 yards, but due to its sloping and undulating character and wooded nature, and with the 9th green 325 feet higher than the Clubhouse, it presents players with a testing variety of challenges. The par is 66 and club golfers are pleased to play to their handicaps at Sidmouth. The uninterrupted views across Lyme Bay to Portland and the backcloth of thick forest to the west make playing the course an enjoyable experience. During the holiday season many visitors to the resort play the course.

The 1985 English Amateur Champion, Roger Winchester, is a member of the Club and, in the years between the wars, Sidney Easterbrook, an assistant Professional with the Club until 1930, played in Ryder Cup matches and was Irish Open Champion.

Captain 1989: David Govier
Secretary: David Matthews
Professional: Mervyn Kemp

Stinchcombe Hill

Stinchcombe Hill Golf Club was constituted on 13th October 1889 and the first few holes were opened for play at the end of November in the same year. The founding Committee was helped by the Worcestershire Golf Club who not only provided opposition on the field of play but also the first Greenkeeper, William Lewis, and the founder Secretary, Herbert Goldingham, who continued in the post for 21 years. The Club soon had 100 members with 52 gentlemen paying a guinea each subscription while 48 Ladies paid half that sum. The rough scrub through which the course ran produced record scores in the high 80s, but the course matured and improved when in the twenties and thirties it had the reputation of one of the finest courses in the South-West.

In 1929 Sir Stanley Tubbs, a former Captain and President of the Club, acquired the Stinchcombe Hill thus solving ownership problems, and gave it for public use, subject to a 99 year lease, to the Club and the Dursley Artisans Club, which also plays over the Hill. Stinchcombe Hill also has close links with Australian clubs.

In 1944 the Clubhouse was destroyed by fire. It was initially replaced progressively by a number of wooden buildings and not until the early eighties was a staged rebuilding completed.

The present course, which now has an automatic watering system, is of modest length at under 6000 yards, but any player who returns a nett 68 should be well pleased. Seven hundred feet high, with magnificent views, including across the Severn estuary, the course is relatively flat and can boast of challenging holes, avoiding fairways adjacent or parallel to each other. There can be few better places to spend some time than on Stinchcombe Hill, especially with a golf club in hand.

Captain 1989: Geoffrey Beetham
Secretary: Geoffrey Beetham
Professional: BE Valentine

Sutton Coldfield

Golf had been played on the town side of Sutton Park for many years. Steps to regularise the activity were taken by several local gentlemen in October 1889 with the creation of Sutton Coldfield Golf Club. Play continued at the Town Gate for a while but the difficulties associated with this venue led to a move across the Park to the present Streetly site in 1891. The antiquity of this part of the Park is emphasised by the presence of the Roman road, Icknield Street, which forms a prominent feature of several holes on the course. In 1893 work began to extend the course to 18 holes and many modifications were subsequently made over the years. However shortly after the Great War, Dr Alister Mackenzie, who a decade later began work with Bobby Jones and Clifford Roberts on what became the Augusta National Golf Club in Georgia, was engaged to suggest improvements to the layout. While the present course is by no means solely Mackenzie's work, much of his legacy remains.

Today the Club has a fine natural heathland course where a premium is placed on accurate driving. Excellent drainage means that the course is playable in all but the very worst of weather conditions.

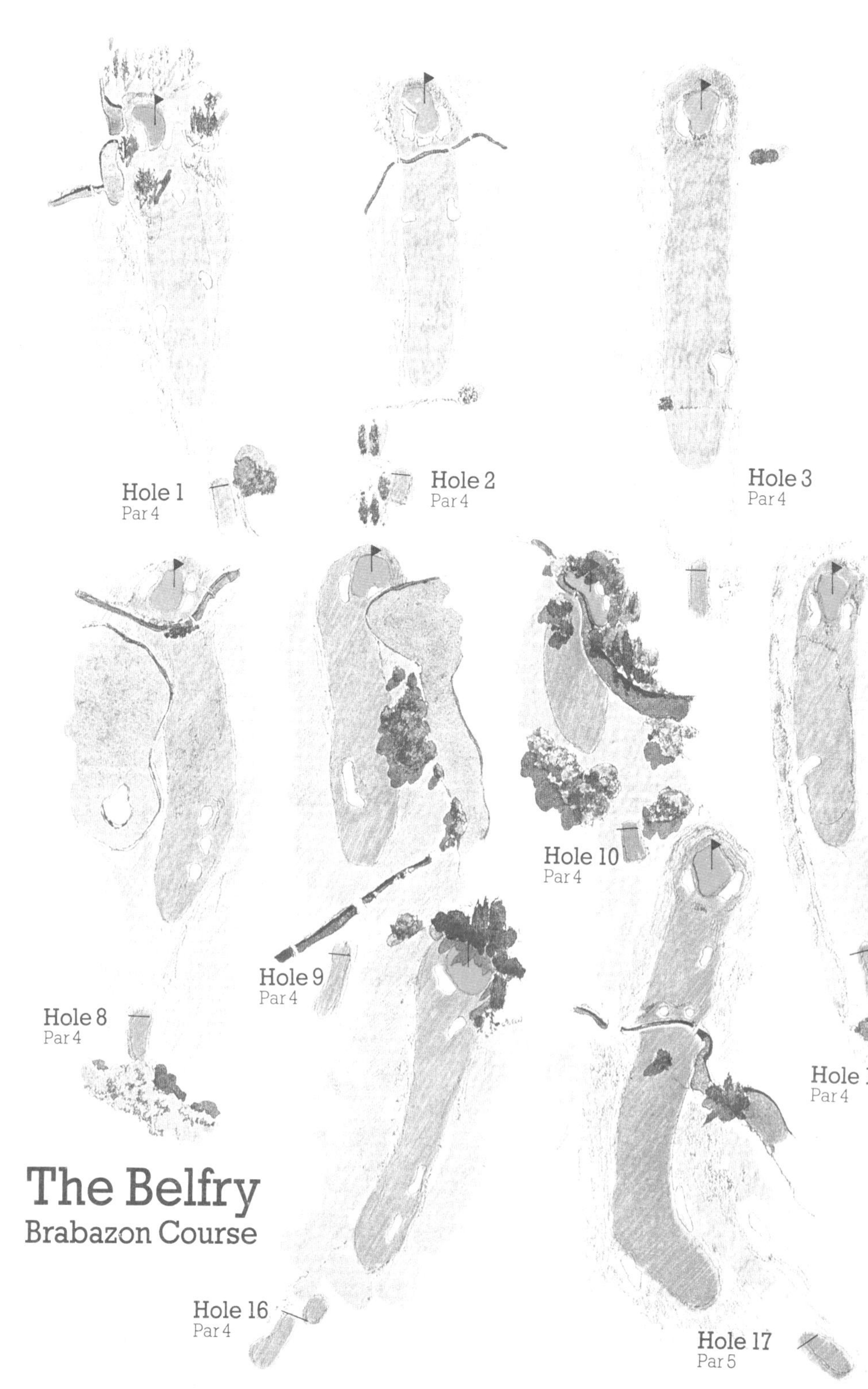

Hole 1
Par 4
Hole 2
Par 4
Hole 3
Par 4
Hole 10
Par 4
Hole 9
Par 4
Hole 8
Par 4
Hole
Par 4
The Belfry
Brabazon Course
Hole 16
Par 4
Hole 17
Par 5

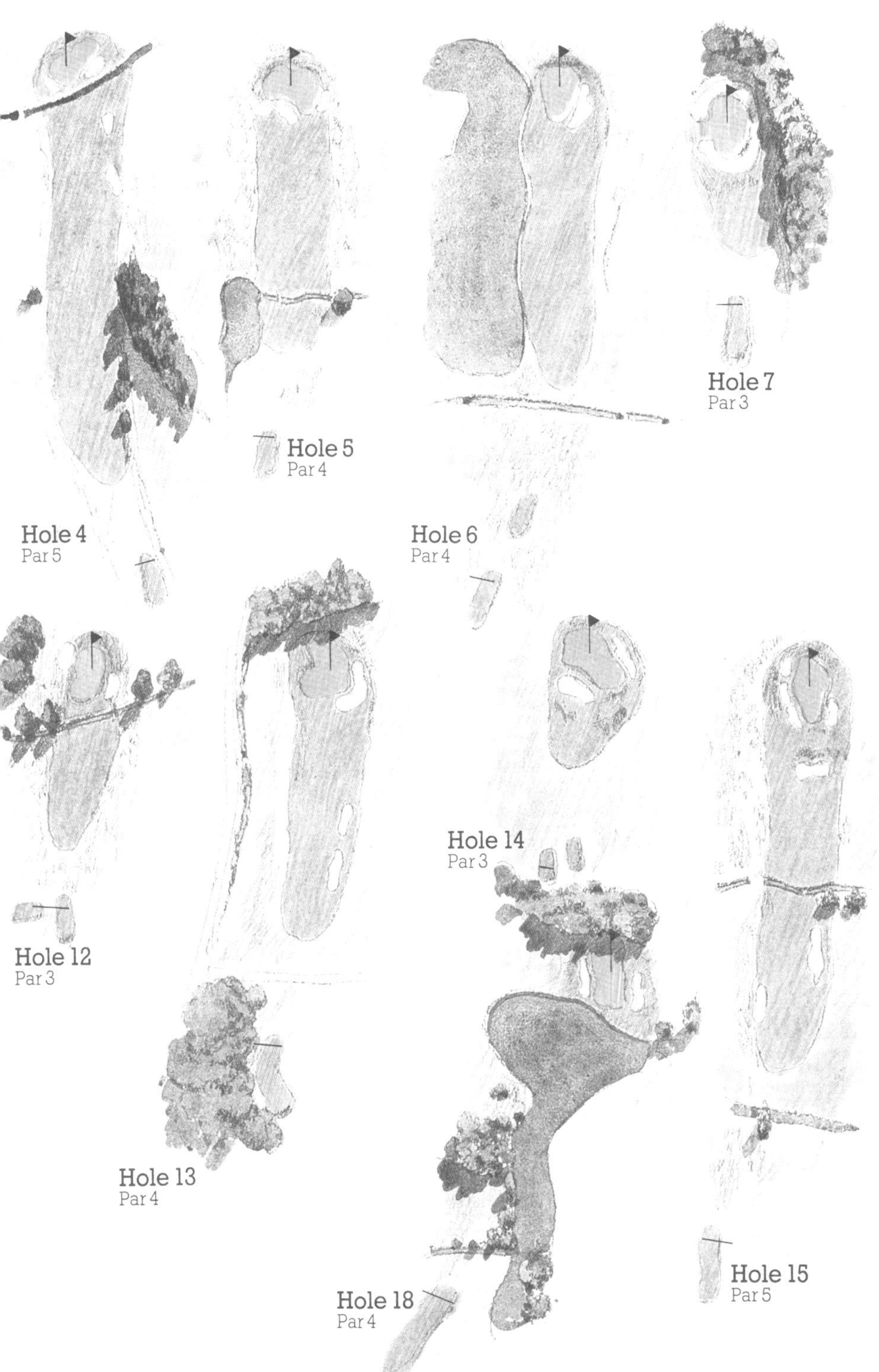
Hole 4
Par 5
Hole 5
Par 4
Hole 6
Par 4
Hole 7
Par 3
Hole 12
Par 3
Hole 13
Par 4
Hole 14
Par 3
Hole 18
Par 4
Hole 15
Par 5

Until local government reorganisation, successive Mayors of the Royal Borough served as Presidents of the Club. In this centenary year there are over 500 members of various categories and a thriving Ladies' Club, which was founded in 1893. The history of the Club has been published and copies are available from the Secretary.

Captain 1989: AG Imlah
Secretary: AJ Bishop
Professional: JK Hayes

Tunbridge Wells

Tunbridge Wells Golf Club was founded and built by Mr W Bruce Dick, the proprietor of the Spa Hotel in Tunbridge Wells. Mr Dick, a player of international standard, was a true lover of the game and constructed the golf course in the grounds of the hotel at first for his own amusement. As the game grew in popularity so the Club grew in membership and soon had established itself as a course in its own right. The Spa Hotel retained ownership of the course until 1975 when it was purchased by the members from the then owner of the hotel and President of the Golf Club, Mr JA McNab.

The course, at only 4500 yards, nevertheless represents a true test of the short game and can be said to be one of the most picturesque 9-hole courses in Kent.

A major part of the Club's history has been its friendliness and loyalty of members, combined with the fact that between the years 1920–1979 the Club had only two Professionals, Sam and John Humphrey, who were father and son, an unusual record much to be admired. A par of 65 with a standard scratch of 62 means the course is rarely bettered and, despite the ravages of the October 1987 hurricane, retains many of its finest woodland features.

Captain 1989: Gordon King
Secretary: Eric Goulden
Professional: Richard Mudge

West Cornwall

West Cornwall Golf Club at Lelant, near St Ives, was formed in December 1889 and is the oldest golf club in Cornwall. Nine holes were laid out on the 'Links Land' on the southern shores of St Ives Bay and the estuary of the River Hayle. The original glebe land together with an earlier village of Lelant had been covered with sand by the seventeenth century. A Ladies 9-hole course came into being in 1892 and the original 9-hole course was extended to 18 holes certainly by 1896. The present 18 holes follow this 18-hole course except for three holes. The Clubhouse, built in 1900, has been changed, but the Ladies Pavilion, built in 1913, has been little altered.

The land was originally leased from Mr Tyringham, the local squire, but in 1920 the 'towans' (Cornish for sandhill or dune) was purchased by members for £4000.

The Learmonth family, served the Club from 1911 to 1978. Father Jim was Greenkeeper from 1911 and later also Professional until 1946. Son Jock served as Professional until 1978, giving up greenkeeping in 1962.

Jim Barnes, winner of the Open in 1925, the US Open in 1921, the USPGA in 1916 and 1919 was a regular caddy at West Cornwall until he emigrated to America in 1906 at the age of 19.

Captain 1989: BL Portman
Secretary: WS Richards
Professional: Paul Atherton

Wilmslow

Most people's idea of the ideal inland golf course is that it should be set against a rural backcloth away from the pressure of industry, it should be demanding but not monstrously long, it should have good quality greens throughout the year, a limited membership and good off-course facilities. This, in essence, is what The Wilmslow Golf Club is. It lies on the edge of the northern stockbroker belt, tucked away in a delightful rural setting which the modern age has not seriously disturbed and yet it is only 18 miles away from the centre of Manchester, with good access to the motorway network and the Manchester International Airport.

On Monday, 21st October 1889, four gentlemen – three of whom were members of the then Lytham and St Anne's Golf Club – met and decided to form The Wilmslow Golf Club, rights having been negotiated to play over farmland lying between Alderley Edge and Wilmslow. G Lowe, the Professional at Lytham, laid out 9 holes on this farmland and on 30th November 1889 the first medal competition was played. By the end of the first year the Club had 30 members and a year later 59 members, by which time the course had been extended to 18 holes.

In the spring of 1903, the Club moved some two miles westwards to its present site near Great Warford. It is not known who was responsible for the original layout of the course on this site but since then it has been significantly altered on four occasions – in 1910 by Sandy Herd, in 1929 by James Braid, in 1936 by Hawtree and Taylor and the last alteration, by Donald Steel, will be brought into play in 1989.

In addition to some National and many County Amateur events, the Club has hosted seven Greater Manchester Open Tournaments (1975–81) and The Martini International Golf Tournament (1983).

Captain 1989: Lord Carlisle of Bucklow
Secretary: CA Skelton
Professional: J Nowicki

Scotland

Blairgowrie

'I think this is the most beautiful inland green I have ever seen' commented old Tom Morris of St Andrews when visiting Blairgowrie on 6th June, 1889 to suggest improvements and to play over the 9 holes already roughly laid out. Old Tom's expense account appears in the annual accounts: 'Paid Tom Morris fee for advice regarding golfing green and other expenses coming to Blairgowrie – £1.14s1d.' He grasped the opportunity to arrange a local agency for the sale of his clubs.

The 9-hole course was formally opened on 9th June 1889. Membership was so encouraging that later in the year, a fund was launched to erect a wooden pavilion with 20 golf boxes therein.

By spring 1891, all nine greens had been returfed. That autumn, the country gentlemen members overcame the transport problem by providing a stable which was taken over by the Club on the understanding that any member stabling a horse there should subscribe £1 for life use or 2/6d for annual use. On 27th June, 1892, the first five young lady members were admitted. There are now some 250 lady members out of a total membership of 1200. Perhaps the most famous exhibition match played over the Blairgowrie course was on 11th July 1901 between James Braid, the reigning British Open Champion, and equally famous Harry Vardon.

The long-awaited extension of the course to 18 holes was completed in 1927. Additional land was acquired and professional advice taken from the famous golfer and course designer James Braid, mentioned above. The re-designed Rosemount course was opened in June 1934. (6592 yards). A substantial new Clubhouse was opened in 1939 – the Club's Jubilee Year.

Then, to meet demand, a second 18-hole course called Lansdowne (6865 yards) was opened in June 1974, giving the Club two top quality 18-hole courses as well as a most interesting and attractive 9-holer.

In 1985, the Clubhouse was extended and refurbished to provide excellent facilities for members and visitors alike. So, it was hardly surprising to hear a recent visitor, one of some 13,000 annually , echo old Tom Morris's remarks

St Andrews Old Course

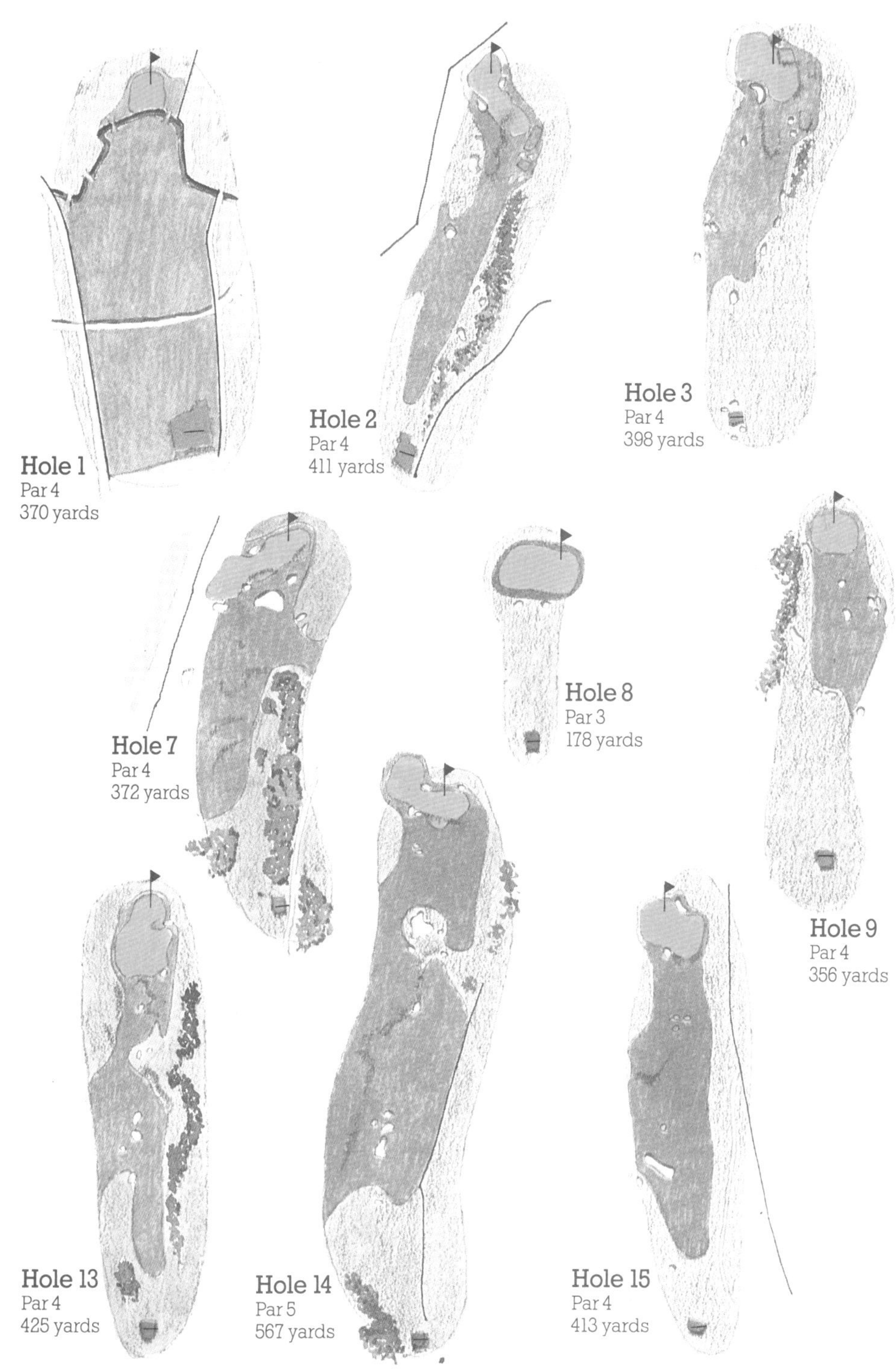

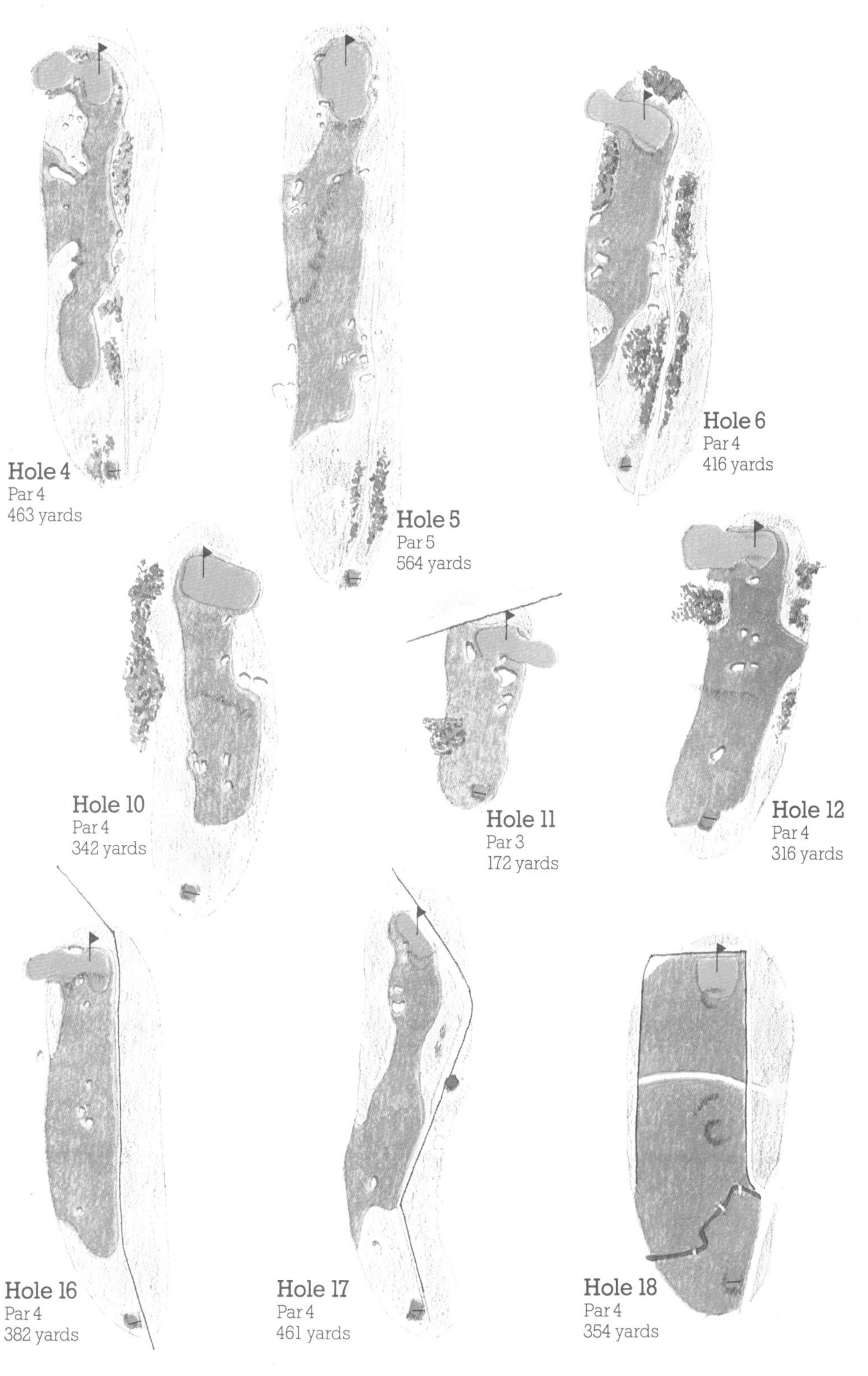
Hole 4
Par 4
463 yards
Hole 5
Par 5
564 yards
Hole 6
Par 4
416 yards
Hole 10
Par 4
342 yards
Hole 11
Par 3
172 yards
Hole 12
Par 4
316 yards
Hole 16
Par 4
382 yards
Hole 17
Par 4
461 yards
Hole 18
Par 4
354 yards

not only about the beauty of the courses but also about their challenge, the variety of wild life, deer, red squirrels and birds galore he had seen and on the quality of the Club facilities.
Captain 1989: Bill Christie
Secretary: Denis Kirkland
Professional: Gordon Kinnoch

Dunaverty

Dunaverty Golf Club is situated at the southernmost tip of the beautiful Mull of Kintyre peninsula. The breathtaking views of the Antrim hills in the west and eastwards to the Ayrshire coast down to the Mull of Galloway have to be seen to be fully appreciated. The 18 holes measure 4597 yards for a par of 64, but it's a tough test for the handicap golfer when the wind blows from the sea. Under the shadow of Dunaverty rock, where once stood McDonald castle, alas! now gone, the area is rich in history and with the sandy beaches there is plenty for non-golfers in the family to occupy themselves on holiday. Looking west towards the Irish coast, the illustration shows the 10th green and par 4 11th.

The Club welcomes visitors throughout the year with the fee for a round only £3.00 or £5.00 for a day ticket. Weekly and fortnightly green fees are also available with no prior bookings required.

The new Clubhouse, built in the mid-1970s, replaced two corrugated tin buildings which had become a well-known landmark. A welcome change was the start of Sunday play, which has proved popular and rewarding for all. The small membership of 220 showed great enterprise in raising the funds to purchase the land of 12 holes, which became available six years ago.

The Club's best-known member, Belle Robertson, British Ladies Champion in 1981, Scottish Champion on seven occasions and nine times a Curtis Cup International, has carried the name of Dunaverty all over the globe. She started her career at Dunaverty and has never forgotten her home club and has been appointed Honorary Captain for the Club's centenary year.

Captain 1989: Robert Millar
Match Secretary: Hamish Paterson
Treasurer: Archie Cameron

Forres

Forres Golf Club was formed on 26th April, 1889, after a meeting in the Courthouse of 23 local gentlemen interested in having a course on a suitable site at Kinloss. Present at the meeting and Founder Officials were Mr RB Finlay QC, MP, elected President, Mr John Burn, Provost of Forres, elected Captain and the Secretary, Mr John Leask, a solicitor. A 9-hole course was laid out, supervised by Alex Brown, Professional at Nairn. In 1890 the course was extended to 18 holes with the expert assistance of Andrew Kirkaldy of St Andrews. The land was rent free, membership 120 and annual subscription 10/6d.

In March 1904, due to problems of land ownership and recurring tidal encroachment from Findhorn Bay, it was decided that the course at Kinloss would have to be abandoned. The Cluny Hill Hydropathic Company, owners of a 9-hole course at Muiryshade, was approached and agreement reached for Forres GC members to join at 18/6d annual subscription. The sale of the Clubhouse and equipment at Kinloss realised £3 4s 6d. The Muiryshade course, laid out by Nairn Professional J Dalgeish, was opened on 5th September 1904 with an exhibition match featuring Harry Vardon, Jack White, James Braid and J Dalgeish. In 1912 the course was extended to 18 holes. The illustration shows today's Clubhouse and 18th green with Cluny Hill behind.

When in 1944 Sir Robert M'Vitie Grant bought the land, he gifted it to the people of Forres and it was administered jointly by the Golf Club and Town Council. Since 1975 the Management Committee has comprised representatives of the Club and Moray Council.

Hugh B Stuart of Eisenhower Trophy and Walker Cup fame, was brought up on Muiryshade and is a past Captain and Honorary Member of the Club.

Captain 1989: George Barrie
Secretary: George Reaper
Professional: Sandy Aird

Golspie

Golspie Golf Club was founded by members of the Sutherland Golfing Society in the spring of 1889. Previously, the society had organised competitions over the links at Golspie, as well as at other venues in the area.

Originally, a 9-hole course was laid out and a small hut sufficed as a Clubhouse. By 1905, however, the Club extended the course to 18 holes and in 1907 a new Clubhouse was constructed. The 18-hole layout was subsequently altered following reports by Archie Simpson of Royal Aberdeen in 1907 and James Braid in 1925. This gave the Club the course which largely exists today.

The order of holes has altered with two changes in Clubhouse location. First, in 1952 and in response to the threat of coastal erosion, the 1907 Clubhouse was removed away from the shore and extended. In 1967, a new Clubhouse was constructed to a very modern design about $^1/_4$ of a mile from the village. This is the existing Clubhouse and was substantially enlarged in 1985.

The course measures some 5800 yards in length and has, in recent years received more of the recognition which generations of visitors to the area have felt to be its due. In 1985, it was one of the courses which hosted the qualifying rounds of the Amateur Championship which was played at nearby Royal Dornoch. The Northern Counties Cup visited Golspie for the first time in 1987.

Captain 1989: H Bruce Field
Secretary: IG Smith

Lenzie

The Club is one of the oldest in Dunbartonshire. Golf started in Lenzie in April 1889, on a 9-hole course but a few months later moved to another 9-hole course on the present site. The first captain was James Stewart and his Stewart Medal is still played for annually.

The course was extended to 18 holes in 1907 and now measures 5982 yards, SSS 69. Its most famous hole is called Alma, the 5th, a par 4 without a bunker but with the second shot played up a hill which is one of the steepest in Scotland. Once you reach the green there are magnificent views over the Gadloch to the Campsie Hills.

Interestingly, Lenzie's two most famous players are ladies. Moira Paterson was a Scottish internationalist and Curtis Cup player and she won the British Ladies Championship in 1952. Janette Robertson was also a Scottish international and Curtis Cup player; she won the British Girl's Championship in 1950 and the Scottish Ladies on four occasions.

Captain 1989: John A Chisholm
Secretary: Alan W Jones
Professional: Malcolm Campbell

Lockerbie
(formerly Annandale Golf Club)

'A meeting of gentlemen favourable to the formation of a Golf Club was held on 10 July 1889' . . . so the first Minute relates, and led to golf being played on the Lambhill Course for the first time in September 1889. With the exception of seven years at the turn of the century when the Club was in dispute with the Landlord over £1 per annum rent, golf has been played continuously on the course during the last hundred years.

It is situated on the hill overlooking Lockerbie and provides many beautiful views for the golfer as he plays the short but testing course of 5418 yards. To the south there are the Cumbrian

Fells, the Hills of Dumfriesshire in the west and the Moffat Hills in the north. Situated close to the A74 it is an ideal venue for a golfing holiday with six other courses within a 13 mile radius.

The original 9-hole course was planned by Bob Ferguson of Musselburgh, re-designed by James Braid in 1927 with the extension to 18 holes in 1986 being designed by two local Professionals, Gordon Gray of Dumfries and County Golf Club and Lee Johnson formerly of Powfoot Golf Club.

Following the opening of the new extension on 21st June 1986 by the former Minister of Sport, Sir Hector Monro MP, visitors increased dramatically, returning often to play on the enviable greens and fairways.

Still a small Club with only 310 members, Lockerbie is proud to have as an Honorary Member, Ken Brown, a member of the Ryder Cup Team on five occasions, and whose family have very close ties with the area.

It is now the Club's intention to extend the existing Clubhouse to offer better facilities for visitors.

Captain 1989: Dr K McQueen
Secretary: James Carruthers

Moray

The first Moray Golf Club at Lossiemouth was formed in 1875 but lapsed after some years and the present Club was founded by gentlemen from the nearby town of Elgin in 1889. The fine testing 18-hole course proved quite inadequate to cope with the large numbers anxious to play golf in such a beautiful place and a 9-hole relief course was built in 1905 and later extended to 18 holes. Andrew Kirkaldy, Old Tom Morris and Harry Colt were all involved in laying out the Old Course, and Charles Neaves, Archie Simpson and, much later, Sir Henry Cotton with the design of the New Course.

Herbert Asquith, when Prime Minister, and Ramsay MacDonald were both members. The first was attacked by suffragettes on the 17th green and the second was expelled from the Club in 1916 for his political views. An attempt to reinstate him in 1924 when he was Prime Minister failed to gain the necessary support. The 6643 yard Old Course is the home of one of the oldest amateur tournaments in the world, first played in 1894, and it is adjudged to be one of the finest tests on the Scottish Tartan Tour circuit. The New Course, with its aptly named Bermuda Triangle, is also a fine test of golf. The climate is one of the mildest and driest in Scotland and golf can be played all the year round. The SSS of the Old Course is 72 and of the New Course 69. The current membership is 1056.

Captain 1989: W Farquhar Thomson
Secretary: James Hamilton
Professional: Alistair Thomson

Ranfurly Castle

One of the finest inland courses in the West of Scotland, Ranfurly Castle is noted for the excellent condition in which the course is always maintained.

The Club came into being, along with many at the time, with the growth of the railways in the late nineteenth century. It became popular for golfers to come by train from Glasgow, about half an hour's journey, to stay in the splendid Ranfurly Hotel, alas no more, for a golfing weekend in Bridge of Weir.

The course was designed by Wm Campbell of Prestwick originally as 9 holes, and extended to 18 in 1895 by Willie Park of Musselburgh on rented land, but a disagreement arose on the renewal of the lease. The reason for this has been difficult to establish, but may have had something to do with the Club's wish to continue with Sunday golf – a touchy subject in Scotland at the turn of the century.

As a result the present site was purchased, then rough farm and moorland and a new course, layed out after consultation with Andra' Kirkaldy, and Clubhouse, designed by JA Campbell, were opened in 1905.

Many well-known figures have been associated with the Club over the years. In the period from 1889 to 1905, various matches and competitions were held and the best known professionals of the day took part, including JH Taylor, Sandy Herd, Andra' Kirkaldy and Willie Fernie. In later years many notable personalities were among the members. These include Leslie Taylor, runner-up in the 1956 British Amateur, Jim McBeath, runner-up in the 1964 Scottish Amateur, Walker Cup player Roy McGregor, the McLeod brothers and the late Wilbur Muirhead, a past Captain of the R and A.

Captain 1989/90: CC Reedie
Secretary: Mrs TJ Gemmell
Professional: Kevin Stables

Ireland

Dooks

Dooks Golf Club, founded in 1889, is a testing 18-hole links situated in one of the most picturesque corners of the Ring of Kerry. A breathtaking panoramic view of Dingle Bay and the majestic McGillycuddy Reeks in the background, make Dooks an idyllic golfing holiday location.

Opened as a 9-hole links for the landed gentry of the last century, Dooks has always been the friendliest of Clubs where visitors are welcome. In fact, the Great Southern and Western Railway Company opened a special flag stop at Caragh Bridge to cater for the visiting golfers of the late 1800s.

Dooks, an Irish word meaning rabbit warren, is on 100 acres of sandy terrain which was part of the Beresford-McGregor Estate. When the lease ran out in 1965, the Club, after a nationwide campaign, was allowed to purchase the property. Through a unique voluntary labour scheme, nine new holes were built by the members and the 18-hole course, (Par 70, SSS 68) was opened by Mr Cecil Ewing, President of the GUI in 1970.

Dooks has since gone from strength to strength. A watering scheme to the greens was installed in 1972 and the Clubhouse was renovated and enlarged in 1977-78.

Care has been given to the greens in recent years, and, as a result, the popularity of Dooks as a true test of golf has grown. Societies now regard Dooks as an ideal venue; green fees have always been reasonable, resulting in a large increase in the number of visitors who savour its challenging links and friendly atmosphere.

Credit for the high esteem in which Dooks is held today must rest with the tremendous dedication of the members who have worked diligently to improve the links and Club through their unselfish efforts and this is indeed aptly expressed in the Club motto 'Per Ardua Ad Astra'.

Captain 1989: Joseph O'Dwyer
Secretary: Michael Shanahan

Killymoon

Killymoon demesne, part of the historic Stewart Castle (designed by Nash) and estate, lies a short distance to the south-east of Cookstown, a market town in the middle of Ulster. There, largely due to the influence of one Hugh Adair, an 18-hole course was laid out in the year 1889. Within a few years, however, the original 18 holes had shrunk to nine due to maintenance costs and the scarcity of aficionados. This same terrain forms part of the present layout and play on it has continued without interruption until today.

The prosperous Adair family was largely instrumental in keeping the game alive in the region. Hugh's son, John, a keen golfer, helped purchase the land of the course and Clubhouse and, as owner and President, exercised for many years autocratic control over both. His daughter, Rhona, who was naturally a member of the Club, won the British Ladies Open Championship in 1900 and 1904, besides being runner-up in 1901. Earlier in 1890 Killymoon, with eight other equally youthful clubs, helped to found the Golfing Union of Ireland, the first of the National Unions.

Despite sporadic slumps, the growth of the Club continued over the years, thanks to the popularity of the game, reflected in the unusual arrangement by which passing trains stopped on request at the course. The land was acquired in 1943 allowing further development, including the planting of thousands of trees. The Clubhouse, destroyed by fire in 1963, was speedily replaced. A further 60 acres of land was purchased which enabled play to return in 1974 to the original concept of 18 holes. In preparation for the centenary year a new Clubhouse is well on the way to completion.

Captain 1989: Stan Heron
Secretary: Dr John McBride
Professional: Paul Leonard

Royal County Down, Newcastle

Usually known as Newcastle Co Down, it is one of the great Irish courses, renowned all over the world. Playing the course is an essential part of any Irish golfing pilgrimage and it has been said that no golfer can claim to have played all the best courses unless he has tested his skill at Newcastle. In a majestic setting by the sea 30 miles south of Belfast, beneath the Mountains of Mourne, the course remains one of enchanting beauty. Soon after the Club's formation in March 1889 Tom Morris came to advise on the layout of holes for the princely fee of £4; it is not stated whether this included his travelling expenses from St Andrews. His suggestions made great use of the many sandhills, gorse and springy turf. Harry Vardon, playing in a Professional Tournament in 1896, said the course 'held its own against all others' and Horace Hutchinson, that great observer of the Victorian golfing scene, said it was 'second to none in the kingdom'.

In 1908 Ben Sayers advised on a new layout, which involved increasing the length with new tees and greens and other changes, but the course remains basically as Tom Morris's first design. 1908 was also the year the Club was granted Royal status.

Many Irish Amateur and Professional Championships have been played at Newcastle. The Club has also hosted the Curtis Cup in 1968, the Home Internationals twice, the Amateur in 1970, when Michael Bonallack won for the fifth time, and seven British Ladies' Championships. The first, in 1899 was won by the 17-year-old May Hezlet of Royal Portrush. She was successful too in 1907 when it was again played at Newcastle. On this occasion she defeated her sister, Florence, in the final. It is curious that three out of the five subsequent Ladies' Championships have been won by French Ladies, Mlle Thion de la Chaume (later Mme René Lacoste and mother of Catherine Lacoste, the 1969 champion) in 1927, Vicomtesse de Saint Sauveur (Lally Vagliano) 1950 and Mlle Brigid Varangot 1963.

Captain 1987/88: Ian WL Webb
Secretary: RH Cotton
Professional: ET Jones

Golfing Hotel Compendium

This year the Golfing Hotel Compendium *has almost doubled in size and is now a prime source of information for golfers wishing to find the most comfortable place to stay at or close to some of the finest golf courses in the country. This section has been compiled from the premier hotels of the British Isles which include golf among their many attractions.*

If readers wish to especially recommend an establishment which is not listed in this edition of the Benson & Hedges Golfer's Handbook *the editors will be happy to be advised.*

England: South West

Bel Alp House Country Hotel

Haytor, Near Bovey Tracey, South Devon
Tel (03646) 2177
Small elegant country house in a most spectacular setting providing a remarkable standard of food, comfort and hospitality. Close to many excellent South Devon golf courses plus perfect peace and quiet.

Boskerris Hotel

Carbis Bay, St Ives, Cornwall TR26 2NQ
Tel (0736) 795295
Boskerris Hotel does not have its own golf course, but by a unique arrangement with 12 of Cornwall's clubs is able to offer free golf within the price of accomodation. (See advertisement page 46 for further details.)

Budock Vean Golf and Country House Hotel

Mawnan Smith, Falmouth, Cornwall TR11 5LG
Tel (0326) 250288
Challenging 9-hole (18 tee) private golf course set in sub-tropical grounds, free to guests. Excellent amenities, luxurious surroundings, top quality service and cuisine. (See advertisement page 61 for further details.)

Culloden House Hotel

Westward Ho!, Devon
Tel (02372) 79421
The Golfer's hotel – run by golfers for golfers. All-in package includes green fees (choice of eight courses). Full English breakfast, home cooking for your dinner (four courses of course).

Greyholme Hotel

St Albans Road, Torquay, Devon
Tel (0803) 38229
Situated beside Torquay Golf Club, golf arranged at Teignmouth, Churston and other nearby courses. En suite rooms, super food, bar never closes. Societies catered for. Prices from £28.00 per day including green fees.

Highfield House Hotel

123 Bay View Road, Buckleigh, Westward Ho!, Devon
Tel (02372) 73970
Superb inclusive golfing holidays. 5 challenging courses including 2 championship courses, Royal North Devon and Saunton Golf Club. Comfortable en suite rooms. Excellent cuisine. Fully licensed bar. Terms on application.

Hotel Riviera

estcliff Gardens, Bournemouth, Dorset BH2 5HL
Tel (0202) 22845
Finest position overlooking the sea. Ideal for golfing holidays with a variety of superb golf courses within a radius of 15 miles. 35 bedrooms en suite, colour TV, tea making facilities, lift, night porter and attractive golfers bar.

Hotel Collingwood
11 Priory Road, Bournemouth BH2 5DF
Tel **(0202) 27575**
Situated in central Bournemouth, with 9 golf courses within 6 miles. Tee times arranged, parking, licensed, indoor pool, leisure centre, snooker, nightly entertainment. Early breakfast, late evening meal available from £25.00 DBB.

Langstone Cliff Hotel
Dawlish, Devon EX7 0NA
Tel **(0626) 865155**
64 bedroom hotel overlooking the sea. Set in 19 acre grounds. Indoor and outdoor heated swimming pool, snooker, table tennis, hard court tennis. Six 18-hole golf courses within 12 miles.

Lee Bay Hotel
Lee, North Devon EX34 8LP
Tel **(0271) 63503**
One of the west country's leading hotels where all the sportsman's needs, as well as wives and families, are professionally catered for. (See advertisement page 55 for further details.)

Manor Crest Hotel
Hendford, Yeovil, Somerset BA20 1TG
Tel **(0935) 23116**
Tx **46580** ***Fax*** **706607**
Only two miles from Yeovil golf course. This beautifully furnished mansion, dating from 1735, stands in the town centre providing traditional hospitality in a location that is an ideal base for touring Somerset and Dorset.

Preston House Hotel
Saunton, Braunton, North Devon EX33 1LG
Tel **(0271) 890472**
Beautiful Victorian privately owned residence overlooking the sea. Spectacular coastal views. All rooms en suite – sauna, solarium, spa bath, excellent cuisine. Golfing at three centres nearby. Reduced green fees at Saunton. (See advertisement page 53 for further details.)

St Enodoc Hotel
Rock, Nr Wadebridge, Cornwall PL27 6LA
Tel **(0208 86) 3394**
Comfortable hotel adjoining St Enodoc Golf Club with its renowned championship links and second 18-hole course. Hotel Club provides squash, snooker, sauna, jacuzzi, solarium, gymnasium. Sailing, water sports, windsurfing close by.

St Mellion Hotel
St Mellion Golf & Country Club, St Mellion, Saltash, Cornwall PL12 6SD
Tel **(0579) 50101**
Modern hotel situated next to the St Mellion complex. 24 rooms. AA and RAC ***. Two golf courses (the Nicklaus and the Old), indoor pool, tennis, squash and badminton courts.

The Crown Hotel
West Street, Blandford, Dorset DT11 7AJ
Tel **(0285) 56626**
A superb Georgian building ideally situated for the many fine golf courses in the area.

The Dormy Hotel and Leisure Club
New Road, Ferndown, Dorset BH22 8ES
Tel **(0202) 872121**
De Vere 4-star hotel adjacent to Ferndown Golf Course, offering sporting and leisure activities combined with a high standard of accomodation and cuisine. (See advertisement page 53 for further details.)

The Hartnoll Country House Hotel
Bolham, Tiverton, Devon EX16 7RA
Tel **(0884) 252777**
We are a small country house hotel set back in its own grounds. We specialise in sporting breaks and have a high proportion of very regular trade from this source.

The York Hotel
The Avenue, Minehead, Somerset TA24 5AN
Tel **(0643) 5151**
Fully licensed hotel with good food and comfortable rooms only 3 minutes drive from Minehead and West Somerset Golf Club. A private members club with full facilities – set between Exmoor and the sea.

Tredragon Hotel
Mawgan Porth, Near Newquay, Cornwall TR8 4DQ
Tel **(0637) 860213**
Family run hotel, rurally set between Newquay and Padstow, grounds with direct access to Sandy Cove. Indoor pool complex. Special all inclusive golf packages. AA Hospitality award. An Inter hotel.

Treglos Hotel

Constantine Bay, Near Padstow, Cornwall PL28 8JH
Tel (0841) 520727

Country hotel in its own grounds, overlooking the sea and golf course. 45 luxury bedrooms, heated indoor pool, large car park. Owner managed and renowned for hospitality and good food, with central heating and log fires.

Trevose Golf and Country Club

Constantine Bay, Padstow, Cornwall PL28 8JB
Tel (0841) 520208
Fax (0841) 521057

Located on the North coast of Cornwall, Trevose offers an idyllic golfing paradise. 18 and 9-hole courses, 3 tennis courts, swimming pool. Self catering accommodation and restaurant. Brochure on request.

Ullswater Hotel

Westcliff Gardens, Bournemouth, Dorset BH2 5HW
Tel (0202) 25181

Central location on Westcliff of Bournemouth, 5 minutes from the town centre and close to all amenities, with free parking, licensed bar, and snooker room. All bedrooms have colour T.V., telephone and tea-making facilities. Special weekend and midweek breaks.

Whitsand Bay Hotel Golf & Country Club

Portwrinkle, Crafthole, By Torpoint, Cornwall
Tel (0503) 30276

Spectacularly sited 18-hole uncrowded golf course, overlooking the ocean in Cornish fishing hamlet, with first tee 100 yards from front door. Leisure complex, heated indoor swimming pools, sauna, solarium, massage/beauty salons.

England: South East

Abbotsley Golf & Squash Club

Eynesbury Hardwicke, St Neots, Cambridgeshire
Tel (0480) 215153

Cosy moated country house amidst picturesque golf course. Beamed dining room with delightful inglenook fireplace. All bedrooms en suite. Internationally renowned golf schools with Vivien Saunders. Squash and golf range. (See advertisement page 63 for further details.)

Abingdon Lodge Hotel

Marcham Road, Abingdon, Oxon OX14 1TZ
Tel (0235) 553456

Modern hotel with restaurants and bar five miles from Oxford at the junction of the A34/A415. Nearest golf course situated 4 miles away at Frilford Heath.

Berystede Hotel

Bagshot Road, Ascot, Berks SL5 9JH
Tel (0334) 23311

Victorian country house hotel set in 6 acres with own putting green and croquet lawn. Superb restaurant and comfortable bedrooms. Close to Sunningdale, Wentworth, The Berkshire, Swinley Forest and Royal Ascot Golf Courses. Special weekend and group rates.

Burlington Hotel

The Esplanade, Sheringham, Norfolk NR26 8LJ
Tel (0263) 822224

The hotel that really overlooks the sea. Sheringham golf course 4 minutes away, Cromer golf club 4 miles away. Our friendly staff and our elegant surroundings will help you to relax during your stay with us. For the more discerning real ales are served in our bar.

Cooden Resort Hotel

Cooden Beach, Bexhill-on-Sea, East Sussex TN39 4TT
Tel (0424) 32281

Situated on the beach just 200 yards from mainline station and adjacent to Golf club. Indoor Health club, Sovereign Bar, candlelit dinners in Grill Room. All rooms with bath/shower, TV, direct dial telephone. Ideal for conferences.

Gatton Manor Hotel and Golf Club

Ockley, Nr Dorking, Surrey RH5 5PQ
Tel (0306) 79555/6

Attached to 18-hole golf course set in 200 acres. Situated between London and the South Coast, 15 miles from Gatwick airport. Twin/double bedded rooms, some overlooking the first tee.

Goodwood Park Hotel

Goodwood, Chichester, West Sussex PO18 0QB
Tel (0243) 775537
Tx 869173 GPK HTL

Standing on the 12,000 acre Goodwood Estate, with 89 well equipped bedrooms, conference rooms and fine restaurant. In association with Country Club Hotels, Spring 1989 sees the unveiling of a superb leisure club and in August a magnificent 18-hole golf course created in the beautiful Goodwood Parkland.

Holiday Inn, Slough/Windsor

Ditton Road, Langley, Slough SL3 8PT
Tel (0753) 44244
Located close to Junction 5 of the M4 Motorway. Easy access to Stoke Poges, Wentworth, Sunningdale and Moor Park. Excellent leisure facilities. Special Weekend rates. Courtesy coach to Heathrow airport.

Hotel Mildenhall AA **

Blackfriars Street, Kings Lynn, Norfolk
Tel (0553) 775146
A modernised coaching inn in an old market town. 50 en suite bedrooms, lovely restaurant with a good traditional menu. Two bars and real ale. 5 minutes from Kings Lynn Golf Club. Four more clubs within easy reach. (See advertisement page 61 for further details.)

Ifield Court Hotel

Ifield Avenue, Crawley, West Sussex RH11 0JH
Tel (0293) 34807
2 weeks free parking for Gatwick. All rooms have private bathrooms. Family run a la carte restaurant.

Lansdowne Hotel

King Edward's Parade, Eastbourne, East Sussex BN21 4EE
Tel (0323) 25174
Play 36 holes a day on choice of 6 courses; we book your tee-off time. Two nights with green fees, light lunch at club and use of our drying room: 15 January to 31 March £86.00; 1 April to 31 May £89.00; 1 June to 31 August £95.00; 1 October to 30 November £95.00. Extra days pro rata. (See advertisement page 53 for further details.)

Le Strange Arms Hotel

Golf Course Road, Old Hunstanton, Norfolk PE36 6JJ
Tel (04853) 34411
Three-star country house hotel with lawns sweeping down to the beach. 30 bedrooms with private facilities. An ideal base for Hunstanton, Royal West Norfolk and Kings Lynn Golf Courses.

Morston Hall

Morston, Holt, Norfolk NR25 7AA
Tel (0263) 741041
Large Country House circa 1690 with luxury en suite bedrooms, informal atmosphere and secluded gardens. Individual 4-star cuisine. Local courses: Brancaster, Hunstanton, Sheringham and Cromer.

Newtown House Hotel

Manor Road, Hayling Island, Hampshire
Tel (0705) 466131
Delighfully set in own grounds with tennis, heated swimming pool. 28 bedrooms all en suite, with TV, teasmaking, hair driers. Fully licensed, excellent cuisine. Half a mile from Hotel-Hayling Golf Links, playable in any weather.

Old Thorns golf course, Hotel and Restaurants

Old Thorns, Longmoor Road, Liphook, Hampshire GU30 7PE
Tel (0428) 724555
Old Thorns is a rare combination of an 18-hole championship golf course, European and Japanese restaurants, hotel and leisure centre set in 400 acres of magnificent Hampshire countryside.

Quinns Hotel

48 Sheen Road, Richmond, Surrey TW9 1AW
Tel 01 940 5445
Very quiet and centrally located hotel close to many sporting venues. Basic and en suite rooms available all with radio, intercom, colour television. Car parking in own grounds. Unbeatable rates available.

Selsdon Park Hotel

Addington Road, Sanderstead, Croydon, Surrey CR2 8YA
Tel 01 657 8811
Traditional country house set in 200 acres of parkland with an 18-hole championship course and residents' exclusive tropical leisure complex. (See advertisement page 72 for further details.)

The Compleat Angler

Marlow Bridge, Marlow, Bucks SL7 1RG
Tel (06284) 4444
Standing on the banks of the river Thames, ideal for top management conferences, private dinners/lunches, a perfect setting for wedding receptions, 42 bedrooms/4 luxury suites. Restaurant offering French/English cuisine, terrace bar.

The Imperial Hotel

North Drive, Great Yarmouth, Norfolk NR30 1EQ
Tel (0493) 851113
A privately run four crown hotel. All rooms have en suite facilities, and our rambouillet restaurant has an excellent local reputation. Golf inclusive holidays are available playing at the Yarmouth course.

The Rose & Crown Hotel
Harnham Road, Harnham, Salisbury, Wilts SP2 8JQ
Tel **(0722) 27908**
Tx **47224**
A 13th century Inn set in a beautiful rose garden on the banks of the river Avon, under the shadow of the spire of Salisbury Cathedral. One and a half miles from South Wiltshire Golf Club.

Thorpeness Golf Club Hotel
Thorpeness, Near Leiston, Suffolk IP16 4NH
Tel **(0728 85) 2176**
Modern luxury hotel adjoining the clubhouse on one of East Anglia's finest 18-hole courses. Situated on the lovely, unspoiled Suffolk coast. Ideal, too for non-golfers. (See advertisement page 63 for further details.)

White Horse Hotel
Station Road, Leiston, Suffolk IP16 4HD
Tel **(0728) 830694**
Close to 3 excellent courses, in the heart of Suffolk heritage coast. Friendly bars, excellent food, 12 rooms (6 en suite) all with TV and telephone. Bargain weekend breaks all year.

England: Midlands

Broomhill Hotel
Holdenby Road, Spratton, Northampton NN6 8LD
Tel **(0604) 845959**
A privately owned 3-star country house hotel offering high standard cuisine and 13 superb en suite bedrooms. Five miles from Northampton, 3 miles from Northamptonshire County Golf Course. Fully licensed.

Peterborough Moat House
Thorpe Wood, Peterborough PE3 6SG
Tel **(0733) 260000**
3-star hotel adjacent to golf course. Special weekend breaks including dinner/dance on Saturday evening. Full leisure complex with pool. For details write or telephone Brenda Ross, Sales Manager.

Poolway House
Gloucester Road, Coleford, Gloucester GL16 8BN
Tel **(0594) 33937**
A 16th century family hotel with licensed restaurant. This is a listed building two minutes away from Coleford Golf Course and thirty minutes from St Pierre and Rolls of Monmouth. All rooms are en suite with television and central heating. ETB 4 crowns.

Sutton Court Hotel
60–66 Lichfield Road, Sutton Coldfield, West Midlands B74 2NA
Tel **021 355 6071**
Privately owned 3-star hotel, 64 individually designed bedrooms and Courtyard Restaurant enjoying a fine reputation for international cuisine. 8 golf courses within 15 minutes' drive, including Belfry Ryder Cup course.

Telford Hotel Golf and Country Club
Great Hay, Sutton Hill, Telford, Shropshire TF7 4DT
Tel **(0952) 585642**
Overlooking the Ironbridge Gorge and encompassed by its own 9 and 18-hole golf courses, this hotel offers comfort and style in addition to extensive leisure facilities featuring swimming, snooker and squash. (See advertisement page 61 for further details.)

Terrick Hall Country Hotel
Hill Valley, Whitchurch, Shropshire SY13 4JZ
Tel **(0948) 3031/3020**
Surrounded by the Hill Valley golf courses. Prime tee times each day for residents. First class accomodation, all 15 rooms en suite, excellent restaurant and bar. Tennis, snooker and squash.

Tewkesbury Park Hotel Golf and Country Club
Lincoln Green Lane, Tewkesbury, Gloucester GL20 7DN
Tel **(0684) 295405**
This 82 bedroom hotel with modern facilities surrounded by its own 18-hole course, combined with heated indoor pool, sauna, whirpool, steam room, multi-gym, snooker, squash and all weather tenniscourts.

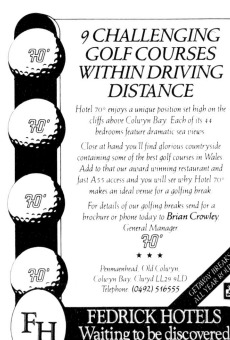

The Belfry

Wishaw, North Warwickshire B76 9PR
Tel **(0675) 70301**
Set in 370 acres of parkland, the championship Brabazon course, venue of the 1985 and 1989 Ryder Cup, par 73 and easier Derby course, par 70. Green fees Derby Weekday £9.00 and Weekend £11.00. Brabazon Weekday £20.00 and Weekend £22.00. 4-star hotel on site.

The Cedars Hotel

Cedar Road, Loughborough, Leicestershire LE11 2AB
Tel **(0509) 214459**
37 bedrooms with en suite facilities. Colour television, radio, telephones. Outdoor heated swimming pool, sauna, and solarium. 6 golf courses within easy reach. RAC and AA 3-star.

The Golf Hotel

The Broadway, Woodhall Spa, Lincolnshire LN10 6SG
Tel **(0526) 53535**
51 bedrooms with private facilities set in 7 acres of lawns and woodland adjacent to the Woodhall Spa Golf Club. Special rates available to golfing parties. (See advertisement page 57 for further details.)

The Grange and Links Hotel

Sea Lane, Sandilands, Sutton-on-Sea, Lincolnshire
Tel **(0521) 41334**
Grade A hotel with own 18-hole links course. Two tennis courts, snooker room, ballroom. Renowned for good food, friendliness, comfort and service. Within easy reach are Seacroft golf club and Woodhall Spa.

The Greenway

Shurdington, Cheltenham, Gloucestershire GL51 5UG
Tel **(0242) 862352**
Tx **437216** *Fax* **0242 862780**
16th century country house hotel set in formal gardens and surrounded by hundreds of acres of parkland. Convenient for Lilley Brook, Cotswold hills, Cirencester and Broadway golf clubs.

The Olde School and Manor Hotel

Church Street, Bloxham, Nr Banbury, Oxon OX15 4ET
Tel **(0295) 720369**
Old style country hotel near museum, thatched cottages, open countryside. 30 bedrooms with facilities, ironing boards, hairdryers. Six conference rooms, games room, squash, art studio for art weekends, open fires.

Welcombe Hotel and Golf Course

Warwick Road, Stratford-upon-Avon, Warwickshire CV37 0NR
Tel **(0789) 295252**
A 4-star Jacobean style mansion set within its own 6,202 yards golf course and 150 acres of parkland. Special packages available on request.

England: North

Alma Lodge

149 Buxton Road, Stockport, Greater Manchester
Tel **(061) 483 4431**
Located on the Southern edge of Stockport, within easy access to M63, M56, M6 and M62. 58 bedrooms with 1 suite, all rooms have radio, colour TV, direct dial telephone, hairdryer, tea and coffee making facilities, etc. Extensive car park. 7 miles from Manchester Airport.

Dean Court Hotel

Duncombe Place York YO1 2EF
Tel **(0904) 625082**
Situated in the heart of York, adjacent to York Minster and within walking distance of shops and tourist attractions. Handy for three local golf courses. A warm welcome awaits you.

Downe Arms

Wykeham, Scarborough, North Yorkshire YO13 9QB
Tel **(0723) 862471**
Situated on A170, 6 miles from Ganton and Scarborough. Rooms en suite, colour TV, and tea making facilities. Bars and restaurant. Ring Philip Mort for reservations.

Golden Lion

Market Square, Ley Burn, North Yorkshire DL8 5AS
Tel **(0969) 22161**
Set in the heart of Yorkshire Dales, we offer dinner, bed and breakfast and green fees. Play at any of our 6 local golf courses from £30.00 a day.

Harewood Arms Hotel

Harrogate Road, Harewood, nr Leeds, West Yorkshire LS17 9LH
Tel (0532) 886556
Ideally located for businessmen and tourists. Seven miles from the commercial centre of Leeds and seven miles from the Spa town of Harrogate. The Hotel is conveniently situated for discovering the Yorkshire Dales, its charms and abundance of things to see and do. (See advertisement page 71 for further details.)

Leasowe Castle Hotel

Moreton, Wirral
Tel (051) 606 9191
All bedrooms have bath/shower, colour television, trouser press, hairdryer. There are 12 golf courses in the area. Special golf break tariff. Sea fishing. (See advertisement page 55 for further details.)

Metropole Hotel

3 Portland Street, Southport, Merseyside PR8 1LL
Tel (0704) 36836
Situated within 5 minutes of Royal Birkdale. Fully licensed, private facilities, special golf terms. Golfing proprietors can assist with golf bookings. Colour brochure on request.

Motel Leeming

Bedale, North Yorkshire DL9 1DT
Tel (0677) 23611
Modern·family run hotel in the middle of North Yorkshire. Four courses within 20 minutes. Special packages at sensible prices. Clean rooms, good cooking, laundry service.

Shaw Hill Hotel Golf and Country Club

Preston Road, Whittle-Le-Woods, Chorley, Lancashire PR6 7PP
Tel (02572) 69221
RAC and AA 3-star hotel golf and country club. A la carte restaurant. 22 bedrooms, all en suite, overlooking an 18-hole championship course. Special mini breaks rates available. (See advertisement page 59 for further details.)

The Bold Hotel

Lord Street, Southport PR9 0BE
Tel (0704) 32578/38497
Situated centrally on one of the most beautiful boulevards in Britain. Surrounded by some of the best golfing courses in Britain. There are also superb shops, parks and historical monuments.

The Dormy House

Royal Lytham & St Anne's Golf Club, Links Gate, Lytham St Anne's, Lancashire FY8 3LQ
Tel (0253) 724206
Ideal for small parties wishing to play the championship course. Accomodation for men only. Apply to the secretary. (See advertisement page 63 for further details.)

The George Washington Hotel

Stone Cellar Road, Washington, Tyne and Wear NE37 1PH
Tel (091) 417 2626
Everything for the golfer, championship course, floodlit driving range and professional. Accomodation offers every comfort. Facilities include snooker, squash and leisure club.

The Wensleydale Heifer

West Witton, Wensleydale, North Yorkshire DL8 4LS
Tel (0969) 22322
A 17th century dales Inn, with 20 en suite bedrooms, restaurant and bistro. Ideally placed for Catterick and Bedale Courses. Golfing breaks a speciality. A Consort Hotel. AA/RAC 2-star.

Viking Hotel

North Street, York YO1 1JF
Tel (0904) 659822
Tx 57937 *Fax* (0904) 641793
Situated only a few miles from the famous York Fulford Golf Course, the Viking hotel is a 4-star hotel complex with 188 bedrooms, 2 restaurants plus a health & leisure club and is situated in the heart of historic York. (See advertisement page 59 for further details.)

Isle of Man

Castletown Golf Links Hotel

Derbyhaven, Castletown, Isle of Man
Tel (0624) 822201
Situated on our own peninsula, our championship golf course of 6,700 yards, with all holes having sea views, is a real test of links golf. The hotel facilities are of a luxurious three star standard.

The Heronston Hotel
Bridgend Mid-Glamorgan

Luxury Hotel with 76 Superb Suites
Situated 4 miles off the M4

Three Golf Championship Courses within 3 miles of hotel

Indoor and Outdoor Heated Swimming Pool with Sauna, Steam Room, Solarium and Jacuzzi

Transportation can be arranged to various activities

Special Terms for Weekend Breaks

The Hotel with the Personal Touch

The HERONSTON HOTEL
Ewenny, Bridgend, Mid-Glamorgan.
Tel 0656 68811 Telex 498232 Fax 0656 767391

LUXURY CORNISH GOLFING HOTEL

Set in 65 acres of sub-tropical grounds, with beautifully laid out private golf course, championship all-weather tennis courts and fabulous indoor pool – this hotel offers superb facilities free to all guests.

Idyllically situated on the banks of the romantic Helford River,with private foreshore for boating, both the hotel and golf course enjoy delightful views.

All guest rooms offer style and comfort, and excellent standards of service combined with top class cuisine prepared and presented with care and originality make us confident of satisfying the most discerning guest.

We invite you to visit the hotel and enjoy the luxury of a peaceful, healthy holiday, in elegant surroundings.

BUDOCK VEAN
GOLF AND COUNTRY HOUSE HOTEL

MAWNAN SMITH FALMOUTH CORNWALL TR11 5LG TEL (0326) 250288

TELFORD HOUSE

Overlooking the Ironbridge Gorge and encompassed by its own 18-hole championship and 9-hole par 9 golf courses. This hotel offers comfort and style in addition to extensive leisure facilities featuring swimming, snooker and squash.

Hotel Mildenhall & Motel

Kings Lynn, Norfolk PE30 1NN
Tel: Kings Lynn (0553) 775146

AA★★. When you visit Kings Lynn to play Golf, to see Royal Sandringham or just to relax, why not stay with us in one of our beautifully appointed bedrooms. Enjoy your lunch or dinner in our restaurant, choosing from either the Hotel menu or very wide A la Carte menu. Have a glass of Real Ale in our Copper Bar or join our Saturday night Dinner Dance. Traditional Sunday Roast Beef is our speciality. We know you love to play Golf, but there are lots of places to explore in Norfolk, so **make us your stepping off point.** Resident Managers: Barry & Helen Anderson.

Wales: North

Hotel 70°

Penmaenhead, Old Colwyn, Colwyn Bay, Clwyd
Tel (0492) 516555
Luxury modern hotel situated on the cliff tops with breathtaking views. Each of the 44 bedrooms has every modern facility. Superb award winning restaurant. (See advertisement page 57 for further details.)

Wales: Central

Oxford Arms Hotel

Duke Street, Kington, Herefordshire
Tel (0544) 230322
16th Century coaching inn located 1 mile from Kington Golf Course – highest course in England and Wales. Challenging 18-hole course. Ten other courses within a half hour drive.

St Davids Hotel

Harlech, Gwynedd LL46 2PT
Tel (0766) 780366
A large comfortable hotel overlooking Royal St Davids golf course, Cardigan Bay and Snowdonia, the ideal base for golfing in North West Wales. Fully inclusive golf packages on several courses. Societies welcome.

The Royal Oak Hotel

The Cross, Welshpool, Powys SY21 7DG
Tel (0938) 2217
A privately owned hotel dating back to the 17th century, to the time of the Jacobites. The restaurant enjoys a good reputation for fine food, and a warm and friendly atmosphere. Welshpool Golf Course is 2 miles from the hotel. All inclusive weekend breaks available.

Trefeddian Hotel

Aberdovey, Gwynedd, Wales LL35 0SB
Tel (065 472) 213
3-star hotel with 46 rooms, all with bath or shower en suite, central heating, telephone and colour T.V. Indoor pool, putting green, tennis court, games room. Overlooks the golf links and sea. Golfers' tariff and brochure sent on request.

Wales: South

Fairways Hotel

Seafront, Porthcawl CF36 3LS
Tel (065 671) 2085
A recently renovated, privately owned hotel, overlooking the Bristol Channel. Situated five minutes from the M4. 28 bedrooms, many with bathroom and shower en suite. Three 18-hole golf courses, the Royal Portcawl, Pyle & Kenfig and Southerndown all within a few minutes drive. Table d'hote and full a la carte menu. (See advertisement page 67 for further details.)

Heronston Hotel

Ewenny, Bridgend, Mid-Glamorgan CF35 5AW
Tel (0656) 68811
4 miles off M4. Three championship courses within 3 miles of Hotel. Indoor and outdoor heated swimming pools with sauna, steam room, solarium and jacuzzi. Transport can be arranged to various activities. Special terms for weekend breaks. (See advertisement page 61 for further details.)

Hotel Mariners

Mariners Square, Harverfordwest, Pembrokeshire SA61 2DU
Tel (0437) 3353
Situated in quiet town centre, 28 rooms with colour television, the majority with en suite bathroom. Fully licensed with bar lunches and dinner. Special weekend rates.

St Pierre Hotel, Golf & Country Club

Chepstow, Gwent NP6 6YA
Tel (02912) 5261
14th century mansion house, comprising 108 bedrooms, en suite facilities and leisure club including swimming pool, squash, badminton, tennis, snooker, spa bath, sauna, steamroom, gymnasium, health and beauty salon, and brown and green bowling with restaurants and bars.

The Mill at Glynhir

Llandybie, Near Ammanford, Dyfed SA18 2TE
Tel (0269) 850672
FREE golf to residents. Overlooking Glynhir golf course. Indoor swimming pool. Special bargain breaks all the year round. All rooms en suite, television and radio etc. Excellent food. (See advertisement page 67 for further details.)

Scotland: West

Ardmory House Hotel

Ardmory Road, Ardbeg, Rothesay, Isle of Bute PA20 0PG
Tel **(0700) 2346**
Ideally situated for Bute's three panoramic golf courses – each offering unbelievable value for money – the hotel boasts personal attention, breathtaking views, superb cuisine. All rooms en-suite, special 3-day rates.

Beechwood Country House Hotel

Harthope Place, Moffat, Dumfriesshire DG10 9RS
Tel **(0683) 20210**
Situated in a delightful garden overlooking Moffat and the Upper Annan Valley which is renowned for fishing and walking. Golf, tennis and riding available nearby. Excellent restaurant and wine list.

Clonyard House Hotel

Colvend, Dalbeattie, Kirkshire DG5 4QW
Tel **(0556) 663372**
Family run country hotel in quiet grounds. Excellent restaurant, also informal meals in our lively bar. Ground floor rooms with facilities including direct dial telephones. Four golf courses within a 10 mile radius.

Grandtully Hotel

Strathtay, Nr Pitlochry, Perthshire PH9 0PL
Tel **(08874) 207**
Small family hotel in the heart of Perthshire Highlands. Four 18-hole courses within 10 miles and 9-hole course 5 minutes walk from the hotel. Also salmon fishing on the River Tay.

Kinloch Hotel

Blackwaterfoot, Isle of Arran
Tel **(077086) 444**
Beside the world's only 12-hole golf course. Breathtaking test of links skill. Six other courses nearby. Swimming pool, tennis, sauna, squash court, solarium. Full en suite facilities. Special golfers' rates.

Kirkton Jean's Hotel

47 Main Street, Kirkoswald, Ayrshire
Tel **(06556) 220**
Play golf at the famous Turnberry Golf Course, or any of 20 superb golf courses including Royal Troon, Prestwick and five Open qualifying courses all within 35 minutes. Or visit Culzean Castle and National Park which is nearby. This 18th century coaching inn situated in the heart of the Burns country, offers 9 twin rooms with en suite showers, colour TV and tea and coffee making facilities.

Kirroughtree Hotel

Newton Stewart, Wigtownshire DG8 6AN
Tel **(0671) 2141**
Unlimited free golf at 2 courses including a championship course. Luxurious country house hotel with finest French cuisine provided by our top continental trained chefs. Please send for details. AA 4-star RAC (See advertisement page 71 for further details.)

North West Castle Hotel

Seafront, Stranraer, South West Scotland DG9 8EH
Tel **(0776) 4413**
This RAC 4-star hotel offers free golf midweek at Stranraer Golf Club. Facilities include indoor swimming pool, curling rink (October to April) and well equipped games room. Weekly terms from £210.00 DBB.

Stirling Arms Hotel

Stirling Road, Dunblane, Perthshire FK15 9EP
Tel **(0786) 822156**
17th Century coaching inn on the banks of the Allam Water, conveniently situated for main road/rail access, perfect location for businessmen, tourists, golfers (Gleneagles 10 minutes) and anglers. Excellent restaurant.

Sun Court Hotel

19 Crosbie Road, Troon, Ayrshire KA10 6HF
Tel **(0292) 312727**
Overlooking Royal Troon and the sea. Excellent restaurant, four squash courts, lawn tennis and real tennis. Special rates for golf groups.

The Fernhill Golf Hotel

Heugh Road, Portpatrick, Nr Stranraer DG9 8TD
Tel **(077 681) 220**
Golf package holidays available throughout the year in this three-star AA and RAC hotel. Golf at the scenic Portpatrick club and championship Stranraer. Send for illustrated coloured brochure.

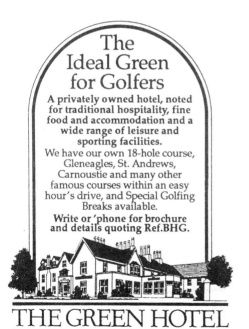

The Marine Highland Hotel
Troon, Ayrshire KA10 6HE
Tel **(0292) 314444**
Magnificent 4-star hotel, overlooking 18th Fairway of Royal Troon Championship Course. It comprises 72 bedrooms and suites; leisure and sports club; conference and banqueting centre; 2 restaurants and 3 bars.

Turnberry Hotel and Golf Courses
Turnberry, Ayrshire KA26 9LT
Tel **(0655) 31000**
Tx **777779** ***Fax*** **0655 31706**
Situated overlooking Scotland's South West Ayrshire coast. Within its 360 acres are a luxury hotel, golf and leisure resort with few equals in the world.

Scotland: East

Alton Burn Hotel
Alton Burn Road, Nairn
Tel **(0667) 52051/53325**
Family hotel with superb views of Moray Firth. Overlooking Nairn West Championship Golf Course. 26 rooms with bathrooms. Practice golf area, putting green, tennis courts, outdoor heated swimming pool.

Alvey House Hotel
Golf Course Road, Newtonmore, Inverness-shire PH20 1AT
Tel **(05403) 260**
STB 3 Crowns hotel situated 50 yards from the 1st tee of the lovely Newtonmore Golf Course. Ideal holiday course, set in the beautiful Spey Valley, with three other 18-hole courses within easy reach.

Angus Thistle Hotel
101 Marketgait, Dundee DD1 1QU
Tel **(0382) 26874**
The Angus Thistle is a modern four star hotel in the centre of Dundee and is particularly handy for the superb golf courses at Carnoustie and St Andrews. It has 58 bedrooms including three luxury suites with Jacuzzi. All rooms have colour TV, trouser press, hairdryer, tea and coffee making facilities, etc.

Balcraig House Hotel
By Scone, Perth PH2 7PG
Tel **(0738) 51123** ***Fax*** **0738 33449**
Country house hotel with luxury accommodation, in parkland setting. We are in close proximity to all major courses in the area, including Gleneagles, Carnoustie, St Andrews, Blairgowrie and others. Special group rates on request. Assistance with itinerary. Contact Derek MacKintosh.

Ballathie House Hotel
Kinclaven by Stanley, Perthshire PH1 4QN
Tel **(025083) 268** ***Tx*** **76216**
A superior country house hotel overlooking the River Tay. Budget and deluxe accommodation. Totally restored. 15 minutes from Perth and Blairgowrie, Rosemount (10 minutes), Gleneagles (40 minutes), Carnoustie and St Andrews (55 minutes).

Bayswell
Bayswell Park, Dunbar, East Lothian EH42 1AE
Tel **(0368) 62225**
Golfers have a choice of 14 splendid courses and the Bayswell overlooks the Firth of Forth. The hotel is centrally heated. All rooms en suite, with colour TV, and tea/coffee making facilities.

Bridgend Hotel
257 High Street, Kinross, Tayside KY13 7EN
Tel **(0577) 63413**
Ideally situated just one mile from Junction 6 on the M90. 40 minutes drive from St Andrews, Gleneagles, Carnoustie. 14 bedrooms – undergoing refurbishment early 1989. 120 seater restaurant – lunch/evening meal. Function facilities for 250. (See advertisement page 65 for further details.)

Burghfield House Hotel
Dornoch, Sutherland IV25 3HN
Tel **(0862) 810212**
42 bedroom country house hotel a few minutes from the golf course. Superb restaurant. Golf packages on Royal Dornoch and nearby courses.

Clayton Caravan Park
Nr St Andrews, Fife KY16 9YA
Tel **(0334) 870242**
(5 miles West of St Andrews on A91)
Facilities include touring pitches with electrical hook-ups. Full toilet facilities. Restaurant, bar, games room. We can arrange course bookings if required. Please ring or write for details.

Columba House

Manse Road, Kingussie, Inverness PH21 1JF
Tel **(05402) 402**
Come and enjoy a round at any of six beautiful courses amidst the magnificent Highland scenery of the lovely Spey Valley. Small parties. Group rates. For further details contact Ian Shearer. (See advertisement page 69 for further details.)

Cullen Bay Hotel

Cullen, Banffshire AB5 2XA
Tel **(0542) 40432**
Magnificent views overlooking Cullen Bay and Golf Course. Within easy reach of 12 courses, we provide good food, a friendly atmosphere and have two bars, a restaurant, lounge and garden.

Dalmore Hotel

Rosemount, Blairgowrie
Tel **(0250) 2150**
All day seven days a week fully licensed hotel adjacent to Rosemount Golf Course. Meals all day. 18-hole mini golf course. Bed and breakfast and evening meal.

Dornoch Castle

Dornoch, Sutherland IV25 3SD
Tel **(0862) 810216**
Formerly a Bishop's palace, the hotel has 20 bedrooms. The panelled cocktail bar, elegant lounge and Bishop's Room restaurant overlooking historic Dornoch Cathedral. An INTER hotel AA RAC STB Commended 3 crowns. (See advertisement page 67 for further details.)

Glencoe Hotel

8 Links Parade, Carnoustie, Angus DD7 7JF
Tel **(0241) 53273**
Directly opposite the 1st tee of the Championship Course. 11 bedrooms, the majority with private bathrooms. All with colour television and direct dial telephone. 2-star AA and RAC.

Gleneagles Hotel

Auchterarder, Perthshire PH3 1NF
Tel **(07646) 2231**
In additon to championship golf courses, Gleneagles boasts an indoor sports and leisure complex, tennis courts, the Gleneagles Jackie Stewart Shooting School and of course the luxury of Scotland's first and foremost 5-star hotel. (See advertisement page 24 for further details.)

Golf Hotel

34 Dirleton Avenue, North Berwick, East Lothian EH39 4BH
Tel **(0620) 2202**
Family run hotel ideal for golfers wishing to play any of East Lothian's 16 courses. Starting times arranged. Lounge bar, TV lounge, rooms with private bathroom and colour TV.

Greenlawns

13 Seafield Street, Nairn IV12 4HG
Tel **(0667) 52738**
Greenlawns is situated close to golf courses, beaches, bowling greens, tennis/squash courts, swimming pool, riding stables and fishing. Within easy reach of Loch Ness, Cawdor and Brodie Castles, Culloden Battlefield. An ideal centre for touring northern Scotland.

Highlander Hotel

Newtonmore, Inverness-shire
Tel **(054 03) 341**
Tx **75577** ***Fax*** **054 03 708**
We are a modern family run hotel with 67 bedrooms. Recent extensions include a conference room and 60ft lounge. There are several good golf courses nearby. 'Highland Night' entertainment is on most evenings. Parties and individuals catered for.

Letham Grange

Colliston, by Arbroath DD11 4RL
Tel **(0241) 89373** ***Fax*** **0241 89414**
20 bedroom Victorian Mansion, with 18-hole championship standard golf course, first class facilities, set in the heartland of golf. Company/Society golf breaks welcome. (See advertisement page 67 for further details.)

Lockerbie House Hotel

Boreland Road, Lockerbie, Dumfries and Galloway DG11 2RG
Tel **(05762) 2610**
Free golf on two courses at Lockerbie and Moffat. Lockerbie House is an 1814 Georgian Mansion, built by the Queensbury family predominantly in Adam style, with 30 en suite rooms, set in 80 acres of parkland. (See advertisement page 69 for further details.)

Lomond Hills Hotel

Freuchie, Nr Falkland, Fife KY7 7EY
Tel **(0337) 57329/57498**
25 bedrooms, all with facilities. Close to many golf courses including St Andrews. Two day golf breaks including dinner from £61.00. Candlelit restaurant, sauna. Large car park. STB 3 crowns AA, RAC.

Lockerbie Country House Hotel

Lockerbie House was originally a family mansion and still retains, in some measure, the charm and elegance of a private residence.

Situated in 78 acres of tranquil park and woodland which contains roe deer, red squirrels and other wildlife. The trees around the house and in the parkland add the finishing touch, some dating back 150 years.

Free golf on two courses at Lockerbie and Moffat Lockerbie House.

Tel: (05762) 2610

The Bein Inn Glenfarg

RAC** **Perthshire PH2 9PY** AA**
Telephone: 057-73 216
"A TRUE GOLFERS PARADISE"

With Carnoustie, Gleneagles, St. Andrews, Rosemount, Downfield, Ladybank and many more wonderful courses all within 30 minutes drive from THE BEIN INN. Traditional and comfortably appointed THE BEIN INN is situated in beautiful Glen Farg, just off the M90 – 8 miles from Perth, 30 miles from Edinburgh. All bedrooms with private bath, T.V. and telephone, are spacious, bright and modern. Superb a la carte meals together with a comprehensive wine list are served in a character dining room all at reasonable prices.

An ideal venue for your golfing holiday. A family run hotel with great atmosphere.

SPECIAL BARGAIN BREAKS AVAILABLE
A la Carte Dinner, Bed and Breakfast—£67 per person for 2 days, reduced rate for longer stays—7 days £212.50 per person, (sharing twin or double rooms)

Please send for brochure and terms or telephone Glenfarg (057 73) 216
"YOU'LL BE ASSURED OF A WARM WELCOME"

MURRAY PARK HOTEL

Crieff Perthshire PH7 3DJ

Tel (0764) 3731

A charming pink stoned Victorian house, set in its own grounds, it has been tastefully altered over the years to keep in touch with today's standards. Murray Park is an important golf hotel which specialises in good food and good cheer. We even like golfers!!

Special golf packages arranged, please contact Ann or Noel Scott tel: (0764) 3731

4 crowns commended, AA two stars and Taste of Scotland.

Manse Road, Kingussie, Inverness-shire PH21 1JF
Tel. Kingussie 402

AA* RAC*
STB 3 CROWNS

A welcoming family run small country house hotel offering you the best in Highland hospitality. Traditional home cooking & baking. Licensed Rooms with colour TV, mini bar, telephone, tea making. En suite available. Tennis, putting, croquet. **Luxury Holiday Cottages** also available. Phone now for our colour brochure.

Proprietors – Ian and Myra Shearer

Marine Hotel
Cromwell Road, North Berwick, East Lothian EH39 4LZ
Tel **(0620) 2406**
Golfers in North Berwick have a choice of 14 splendid courses and the superb Marine Hotel overlooks the famous West Links. (See advertisement page 65 for further details.)

Murray Park Hotel
Crieff, Perthshire PH7 3DJ
Tel **(0764) 3731**
A charming pink stoned Victorian house, set in its own grounds, it has been tastefully altered over the years to keep in touch with today's standards. Murray Park is an important golf hotel which specialises in good food and good cheer. Special golf packages arranged. 4 crowns commended, AA two stars and Taste of Scotland. (See advertisement page 69 for further details.)

Parkway Hotel
Abbotshall Road, Kirkcaldy, Fife KY2 5PQ
Tel **(0592) 262143**
3-star hotel geared to golfers' needs within 30 minutes drive of 35 courses including Gleneagles and St Andrews. Superb restaurant serving many specialities and well stocked bar. 2 night breaks from £55.00 p.p. DBB.

Rosemount Golf Hotel
Golf Course Road, Blairgowrie, Perthshire PH10 6LJ
Tel **(0250) 2604**
Rosemount close by, Gleneagles, St Andrews, Carnoustie, etc within easy reach. Twelve en suite rooms plus self-catering chalets in lovely grounds. Or try shooting, fishing, walking or skiing nearby.

Seafield Lodge Hotel
Woodside Avenue, Grantown-on-Spey PH26 3JN
Tel **(0479) 2152**
A 2-star hotel run by the resident proprietors, Nancy and Peter Austen. Too small for coaches, yet large enough to provide a good restaurant and comfortable lounge bar, where a cosmopolitan group of sportsmen congregate. The subject of a major refurbishment, all rooms now boast private bathrooms, colour T.V., tea making equipment and direct dial telephones. New this year, we have 2 luxury suites.

Skean Dhu Hotel
Farburn Terrace, Dyce, Aberdeen AB2 0DW
Tel **(0224) 723101**
Approximately 5 miles from Aberdeen with 219 bedrooms containing full private facilities. Restaurant, coffee shop, catering/conference for 300 and own leisure complex. Nearby are several high standard golf courses.

Spey Valley Hotel
Seafield Avenue, Grantown-on-Spey PH26 3EJ
Tel **(0479) 2942**
A privately owned, family run, fully licensed country hotel with 18 bedrooms in beautiful Spey Valley. Six courses within a 20 mile radius and championship courses also available.

St Andrews Golf Hotel
St Andrews, Fife KY16 9AS
Tel **(0334) 72611**
Most comfortable, traditional Scottish hotel (all bedrooms en suite). Fine restaurant. Extensive cellar. On the seafront 200 yards from the 'Old Course'. Let us arrange your golf in Scotland.

Stakis Earl Grey Hotel
Earl Grey Place, Dundee DD1 4DE
Tel **(0382) 29271**
Luxury 4-star Hotel located within 45 minutes of 50 major golf courses with St Andrews and Carnoustie on the doorstep. Car park and leisure facilities available. Special golfing holidays available.

The Bein Inn Hotel
Glenfard, Perthshire PH2 9PY
Tel **(057 73) 216**
Excellent facilities in beautiful surroundings. 8 miles from Perth and within 30 minutes of Carnoustie, Gleneagles, St Andrews, Downfield and Ladybank. (See advertisement page 69 for further details.)

The Green Hotel
2 The Muirs, Kinross, Tayside KY13 7AS
Tel **(0577) 63467**
Superb hotel and leisure complex with own 18-hole golf course within an easy hour's drive of Gleneagles, St Andrews, Carnoustie, Rosemount and over a score of other well respected courses. Golf breaks available.

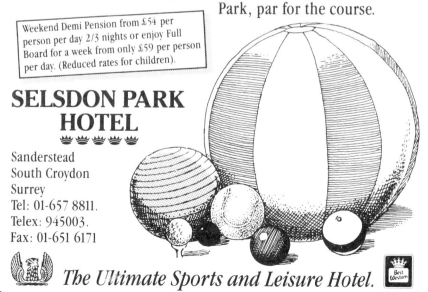

The Highland Haven Hotel and Leisure Centre

Shore Street, Macduff, Banffshire AB4 1UB
Tel **(0261) 32408**
Well appointed family run hotel overlooking the Deveron Bay and Moray Firth Golf. Golf courses nearby are Duff House Royal Golf Club, Royal Tarlair Golf Club, and Turriff Golf Club. Special weekend breaks available. An Inter hotel. STB 4 crowns. AA and RAC.

The Kings of Kinloch Hotel

Meigle, Perthshire PH12 8QX
Tel **(08284) 273**
Country house hotel situated within easy reach of thirty golf courses. We have eight en suite bedrooms and six self-catering chalets. Special weekend breaks available. Phone Meigle 273.

The Lundin Links Hotel

Leven Road, Lundin Links, Fife KY8 6AP
Tel **(0333) 320207**
Fax **0333 320930**
Surrounded by top class golf courses (35 within 25 mile radius, including St Andrews), and close to fine beaches, we offer good value golfing holidays and super Winter Bargains! (See advertisement page 59 for further details).

The Moulin Inn

11–13 Kirchmichael Road, Pitlorchy, Tayside PH16 5EH
Tel **(0796) 2196/2221**
Originally a 17th century coaching inn, surrounded by lovely walking country. 1 mile from Pitlochry golf course for which we can offer a 5 day ticket Monday to Friday for £15.00. Please ring for tariff.

The Old Manor Hotel

Leven Road, Lundin Links, Fife KY8 6AJ
Tel **(0333) 320368**
Live in comfort and enjoy good food (Egon Ronay etc) while looking onto Lundin Links golf course (an 'Open' qualifier) and the sea. All rooms have television, telephone and teamakers. AA ***; STB 4-crown commended. (See advertisement page 63 for further details.)

The Park Hotel

John Street, Montrose, Angus DD10 8RJ
Tel **(0674) 73415** ***Tx*** **76367**
A short distance from Montrose Medal course. Privately owned hotel, 59 bedrooms all with colour TV and most with private bathrooms. (See advertisement page 57 for further details.)

The Royal Marine Hotel

Golf Road, Brora, Sutherland KW9 6WS
Tel **(0408) 21252** ***Tx*** **76165**
The North's Favourite Golfing and Fishing Hotel. Country house hotel with its own heated indoor swimming pool, snooker table, and 4 lane curling rink. Chef's cuisine, comfortable rooms with all facilities.

PGA European Tour	WPG European Tour	UK & Ireland Men's Amateur	UK & Ireland Women's Amateur	USPGA Tour	Date	Event
					January	
				•	5-8	Mony Tournament of Champions, LaCosta, California
				•	12-15	Bob Hope Chrysler Classic, La Quinta, California
				•	19-22	Phoenix Open, Scotsdale, Arizona
				•	26-29	AT&T Pebble Beach National Pro-Am, Pebble Beach, California
					February	
				•	2-5	Los Angeles Nissan Open, Nissan Riviera, California
				•	9-12	Hawaiian Open, Honolulu
				•	16-19	Shearson Lehman Hutton Andy Williams Open, Torrey Pines CC, California
				•	23-26	Doral Ryder Open, Doral CC, Miami, Florida
•					23-26	Tenerife Open, Golf del Sur
					March	
•					1-4	Dubai Open, Emirates GC
				•	2-5	Honda Classic, Coral Springs, Florida
•					9-12	Open de Baleares, Santa Ponsa, Majorca
				•	9-12	The Nestlé Invitational, Bay Hill, Florida
•					16-19	IMG Catalan Open, Pals, Gerona
				•	16-19	The Players Championship, Sawgrass, Ponte Vedra Florida
				•	23-26	USF&G Classic, New Orleans, Louisiana
•					24-27	AGF Open, La Grande Motte
				•	30-2 Apr	Independent Insurance Agent Open, Houston, Texas
•					30-2 Apr	Volvo Open, Is Molas, Sardinia
					April	
				★	6-9	**The Masters, Augusta, Florida**
				•	6-9	Deposit Guaranty Classic, Hattiesburg, Massachusetts
•					6-9	Jersey Open, La Moye
		•			7-9	Central England Men's Foursomes, Woodhall Spa

PGA European Tour	WPG European Tour	UK & Ireland Men's Amateur	UK & Ireland Women's Amateur	USPGA Tour	Date	Event
					April cont'd	
•					13-16	Cannes Open, Cannes Mougins
	•				13-16	Rome Classic, Ogliata, Rome
				•	13-16	MCI Heritage Classic, Hilton Head Island, S Carolina
		•			19-20	Peter McEvoy Trophy, Copt Heath
•					20-23	Cepsa Madrid Open, Puerta de Hierro
	•				20-23	TBA
				•	20-23	K Mart Greater Greensboro Open, N Carolina
		•			22-23	West of England Open Amateur Stroke-Play Championship, Saunton
	•				26-29	Ford Ladies Classic, Woburn
•					27-30	Peugeot Spanish Open, El Saler, Valencia
				•	27-30	Las Vegas Invitational, Nevada
					May	
•					4-7	Epson Grand Prix, St Pierre, Chepstow
	•				4-7	Ladies Portuguese Open, Parque de Floresta, Lagos
				•	4-7	GTE Byron Nelson Classic, Las Colinas, Texas
		•			6-7	Berkshire Trophy, The Berkshire Ascot
•					11-14	Volvo Belgian Open, Royal Waterloo
	•				11-14	Guia Ladies Masters, Quinta de Marinha, Estoril
				•	11-14	Memorial Tournament, Muirfield Village, Ohio
		•			12-14	Tillman Trophy, Hunstanton
		•			13-14	England v Spain, El Prat, Barcelona
			•		14-17	Welsh Ladies Team, Caernarvonshire
			•		15-20	Scottish Ladies Close, Moray
			•		17-20	Irish Ladies Close, Westport
			•		18-20	Welsh Ladies Close, Caernarvonshire
•					18-21	Lancia Italia Open, Monticello
	•				18-21	Players Championship, TBA
				•	18-21	Colonial National Invitational, Colonial, Texas
		•			19-21	Brabazon Trophy, Royal Liverpool
			•		23-27	English Ladies Close, Burnham & Berrow
	•				25-28	Hennessy Ladies Cup, St Germain, Paris
	•				25-28	Irish Open, Lahinch
				•	25-28	BellSouth Atlanta Classic, Atlanta, Georgia
•					26-29	Volvo PGA Championship, Wentworth
		•			31-1 Jun	Lagonda Trophy, Camberley Heath
		•			31-2 Jun	England Open Seniors' Championship, West Sussex and Ham Manor

PGA European Tour	WPG European Tour	UK & Ireland Men's Amateur	UK & Ireland Women's Amateur	USPGA Tour		
					June	
•					1-4	Dunhill British Masters, Woburn
	•				1-4	BMW Ladies Classic, Hubbelrath, Dusseldorf
				•	1-4	Kemper Open, Irving, Texas
		•			5-10	Amateur Championship, Royal Birkdale and Hillside
•					8-11	Wang Four Stars Pro-Am, Moor Park
	•				8-11	Ladies Scottish Open, Haggs Castle
				•	8-11	Manufacturers Hanover Westchester Classic, New York
			•		13-17	Ladies British Open Amateur, Hoylake
•					15-18	NM English Open, The Belfry
	•				15-18	Third Open de France Féminin, Fourqueux
				★	15-18	**US Open, Oak Hill, Rochester, New York**
•					22-25	Carrolls Irish Open, Portmarnock
	•				22-25	Ladies Dutch Open, Haagsche, Wassenaar
				•	22-25	Canadian Open, Glen Abbey, Ontario
		•			23-24	Lytham Trophy, Royal Lytham & St Annes
			•		24-25	Welsh Open Amateur Stroke Play, Newport
			•		24-25	Irish Ladies Senior Club Cup, Longford
		•			28-2 Jul	European Mens Team Championship, Royal Porthcawl
•					29-2 Jul	Peugeot French Open, Chantilly
	•				29-2 Jul	St Moritz Ladies Classic, Engadine
				•	29-2 Jul	Beatrice Western Open, Butler National, Oak Brook, Illinois
		•			30-1 Jul	Midland Open Amateur Championship, Sutton Coldfield and Little Aston
					July	
•					5-8	Torras Monte Carlo Open, Mont Angel
	•				6-9	Ladies Spanish Open, TBA
				•	6-9	Canon Greater Hartford Open, Cromwell, Connecticut
•					12-15	Bell's Scottish Open, Gleneagles
		•			12-16	European Boys Team Championship, Lyckoma (Sweden)
	•				13-16	Bloor Homes Eastleigh Classic, Fleming Park
				•	13-16	Anheuser-Busch Classic, Kingsmill, Williamsburg, Virginia
			•		17-20	Irish Girls Close, Athlone
		•			20	Midland Boys Championship, Longcliffe
★		★			20-23	**Open Championship, Royal Troon**
				•	20-23	Hardee's Golf Classic, Oakwood, Illinois

PGA European Tour	WPG European Tour	UK & Ireland Men's Amateur	UK & Ireland Women's Amateur	USPGA Tour	Date	Event
					July cont'd	
			•		23-27	Welsh Girls Close, Carmarthen
•					27-30	KLM Dutch Open, Kennemer, Zandvoort
•					27-30	Volvo British Seniors Open, Turnberry
	•				27-30	Lufthansa Ladies German Open, Worthsee, Munich
				•	27-30	Buick Open, Warwick Hills, Michigan
			•		29-30	Irish Ladies Close Stroke Play Foursomes, Kilkenny
		•			31-5 Aug	English Amateur Championship, Royal St George's
					August	
			•		1-4	English Girls, Edgbaston and Moseley
•					3-6	Scandinavian Enterprises Open, Drottingholm
	•				3-6	Weetabix Ladies British Open, Ferndown
				•	3-6	Federal Express St Jude Classic
			•		8-10	English Ladies Stroke Play, Nottingham Ladies
		•			9-11	British Seniors Championship, Moortown and Alwoodley
		•			10-11	Boys International, Nairn
•					10-13	Benson & Hedges International, Fulford
	•				10-13	First Icelandair Ladies Open, Akureyri
				★	10-13	**PGA Championship, Kemper Lakes, Illinois**
		•			12	Boys GB & Ireland v Continent of Europe, Nairn
			•		14-15	Girls Home Internationals, Carlisle
		•			14-18	Boys Championship, Nairn
		•			16-17	Walker Cup, Peachtree (USA)
			•		16-18	English Ladies Intermediate, Warrington
			•		16-19	Girls British Open Championship, Carlisle
•					17-20	PLM Open, Bokskogon
	•				17-20	Ladies Danish Open, Rungsted
				•	17-20	The International
		•			22	Youths International England v Scotland, Ashburnham
			•		22-26	Ladies British Open Amateur Stroke Play, Southerness
		•			23	Youths GB & Ireland v Continent of Europe, Ashburnham
		•			24-26	Youths Championship, Ashburnham
•					24-27	German Open, Frankfurt
	•				24-27	Gislaved Ladies Open, Isaberg
				•	24-27	NEC World Series of Golf
		•			25-27	Midlands Amateur Championship, Moortown
•					31-3 Sep	Ebel Euro Masters Swiss Open, Crans-sur-Sierre
	•				31-3 Sep	Variety Club Celebrity Classic, Calcot Park
				•	31-3 Sep	Greater Milwaukee Open

PGA European Tour	WPG European Tour	UK & Ireland Men's Amateur	UK & Ireland Women's Amateur	USPGA Tour	Date	Event
					September	
			•		6-8	Home Internationals, Westport
•					7-10	Panasonic European Open, Walton Heath
	•				7-10	Godiva European Masters, Golf du Bercuit, Brussels
				•	7-10	BC Open, En-Joie, Endicott, New York
		•			8-9	English Champion Club Tournament, Southport and Ainsdale
		•			13-15	Home Internationals, Ganton
•					14-17	Lancôme Trophy, St Nom la Breteche, Paris
	•				14-17	Ladies European Open, Kingswood
				•	14-17	Bank of Boston Classic, Pleasant Valley, Massachusetts
•	•				21-24	HCS Mixed Open, Eindhoven
				•	21-24	Southern Open
			•		22-23	Vagliano Trophy, Venice
•					22-24	Johnnie Walker Ryder Cup, The Belfry
		•			24	English County Champion Tournament, Woodbridge
•					25-26	Equity & Law Challenge, Royal Mid-Surrey
•					28-1 Oct	Dunhill Cup, St Andrews
•					28-1 Oct	UAP under 25 European Open, TBA
	•				28-1 Oct	Third Ladies Italian Open, Carimate
				•	28-1 Oct	Centel Classic, Tallahassee, Florida
		•			29-1 Oct	English County Finals, St Enodoc
					October	
			•		4-5	Senior British Open Amateur, Wrexham
•					5-8	German Masters, Stuttgart
	•				5-8	TBA
		•			5-8	Central England Open Mixed Foursomes, Woodhall Spa
				•	5-8	Nabisco Texas Open, Oak Hill, San Antonio, Texas
•					12-15	Suntory World Matchplay, Wentworth
	•				12-15	Laing Charity Ladies Classic, Stoke Poges
				•	12-15	Pensacola Open, Tiger Point, Gulf Breeze, Florida
•					19-22	Portuguese Open, Quinta do Lago
	•				19-22	Woolmark Ladies Matchplay Championship, Barcelona
				•	19-22	Walt Disney World/Oldsmobile Classic, Lake Buena Vista, Florida
•					26-29	Volvo Masters, Valderrama
	•				26-29	AGF, Biarritz Ladies Open, Biarritz
				•	26-29	Nabisco Golf Championships, Pebble Beach, California

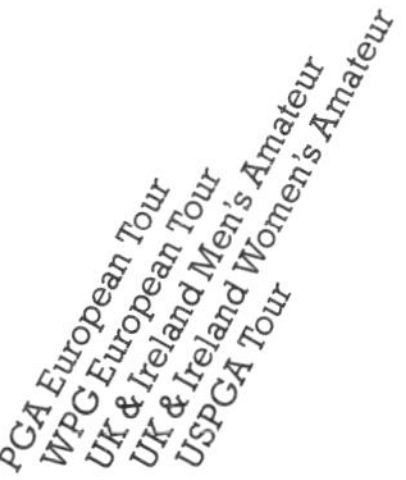

PGA European Tour	WPG European Tour	UK & Ireland Men's Amateur	UK & Ireland Women's Amateur	USPGA Tour	Date	Event
					November	
•				•	2-5	Kirin Cup, Yomiuri, Tokyo
	•				2-5	Qualitair La Manga Classic, La Manga
•	•				9-12	Benson & Hedges Trophy (Mixed Team), Aloha, Marbella
				•	9-12	Isuzu Kapalua International
	•				14-17	TBA
•					16-19	Philip Morris World Cup, Las Brisas
•					23-26	TBA
				•	23-26	Skins Game
				•	30-3 Dec	J C Penney Classic
					December	
•					2-7	PGA European Tour qualifying school, La Manga
				•	7-10	Chrysler Team Championship

Buyer's Guide to Good Golfing and Golf Course Maintenance

This compact but informative guide to manufacturers and organisations offering services to Golf Clubs and individual golfers has once again been expanded to include a greater number of categories. The editors do not necessarily endorse the information supplied.

Club Management and Training Courses

Club Management Services

50 Town Street, Duffield, Derby DE6 4GG
Tel (0332) 84007

Provision of training courses in Golf Club Management. Existing correspondence courses for Secretary/Managers and Stewards. Management consultancy and staff recruitment for Golf Clubs in Great Britain and in Europe.

Event Organisers

3D Golf Promotion Plc

62 Carcluie Crescent, Ayrshire KA7 4SZ
Tel **(0292) 42206/43989** ***Tx*** **776483** ***Fax*** **0292 4261**

UK'S NOS 1 GOLF SPECIALIST PGA approved organisers of overseas Pro-Am series. golf tuition week and golf school series with the UK's top teachers, home and abroad. FULL COLOUR BROCHURE AVAILABLE.

Golf Accessory Suppliers

Avant Leisure Ltd

1 Grange Road, Kingston-upon-Thames, Surrey KT1 2QU ***Tel*** **01 546 0366**

Designers and manufacturers of golf accessories. Flipofax pocket guide; Greenpal utility tool; Visiview score and plan holder; club cleaning and care kit; Gripsure grip conditioner; pick-up ball retriever; rainwear suits; sports bag; accessory bags and kits. (See advertisement page 85 for further details.)

Dunlop Golf Division

PO Box 8, Normanton, West Yorkshire WF6 1YX
Tel **(0924) 89686**

Manufacturers of golf balls (Maxfli DDH 500, Tour Ltd MD, Dunlop 65i) and golf clubs under Dunlop and Maxfli brands. A wide range of bags, gloves, holdalls, umbrellas and accessories are also available.

J B Halley & Co Ltd

Granville Works, Conduit Lane, Hoddesdon, Herts ***Tel*** **(0992) 468386**

Manufacturers of golf clubs and accessories for over 100 years. Over 90% of our equipment is British made and we supply 76 countries.

Pro-line Sports (UK) Ltd

256 Holtye Road, East Grinstead, West Sussex RH19 3EY ***Tel*** **(0342) 323851**
Tx **957139** ***Fax*** **0342 326855**

Suppliers of golfing accessories to both the pro shop and the retail trade. Pro-line's range is competitively priced and includes golf bags, umbrellas, gloves, club covers, sports bags, leather and waterproof golf shoes.

Slazenger Golf Division

PO Box 8, Normanton, West Yorkshire WF6 1YX
Tel **(0924) 896868**

Slazenger manufacture a range of stylish equipment. Balls include 480 Interlock balata, surlyn and two piece. Clubs include Silver Panther, Seve XTC Graphite. Stylish bags, luggage and accesories to complement the range.

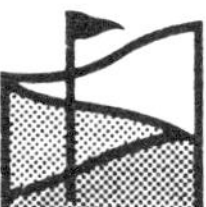

Tran Am Sports & Leisure Ltd

William House, Gore Road, New Milton, Hampshire BH25 6RJ ***Tel*** **(0425) 620580**
Tran Am sports and leisure international distributors for Stirling golf clubs, Baleno waterproof clothing, Rukka windproof sweaters, ASL socks and Starke golf bags. The international company that specialises in service.

Golf Ball Manufacturers

Dunlop Golf Division

PO Box 8, Normanton, West Yorkshire WF6 1YX ***Tel*** **(0924) 896868**
Manufacturers of golf balls (Maxfli DDH 500, Tour Ltd MD, Dunlop 65i) and golf clubs under Dunlop and Maxfli brands. A wide range of bags, gloves, holdalls, umbrellas and accessories are also available.

Kestrel Products Ltd

Unit 34, Cwmdu Estate, Skewen, Neath, West Glamorgan SA10 6RP
Tel **(0792) 817884** ***Fax*** **0792 812913**
Manufacturers of rubber tees for ranges and golf mats and one piece golf balls. Includes low bounce for crazy golf, mid-compression for ranges and practice and high compression for golfers and up-market ranges.

Slazenger Golf Division

PO Box 8, Normanton, West Yorkshire WF6 1YX
Tel **(0924) 896868**
Slazenger manufacture a range of stylish equipment. Balls include 480 Interlock balata, surlyn and two piece. Clubs include Silver Panther, Seve XTC Graphite. Stylish bags, luggage and accesories to complement the range.

Golf Cars/Trolleys and Buggies

Aero Golf Equipment

Winsport House, Leicester Road, Lutterworth, Leicestershire LE17 4PL
Tel **(04555) 56073** ***Fax*** **0455 209298**
AERO DYNAMICS A new company utilising Aerospace technology to produce the ultimate in game improvement clubs. Also a unique golf bag and combined golf trolley offering ease of use combined with lightness.

KingKaddy Ltd

Ninelands Lane, Garforth, Leeds LS25 1NT
Tel **(0532) 320151** ***Fax*** **0532 860739**
KingKaddy powered golf caddies have been tested by professionals over the most arduous courses. The KingKaddy Mark 2 and the KingKaddy Pacer are designed for reliable service at realistic price. Available from your Pro-Shop. Details from the above address.

Mitsui Machinery Sales (UK) Ltd

Oakcroft Road, Chesssington, Surrey KT9 1SA
Tel **01 397 5111**
Suppliers of top selling Yamaha golf car. Available through a national network of distributors. Various schemes include lease purchase or seasonal hire contracts to Clubs.

Moderncross Ltd

162 Rugeley Road, Chase Terrace, Walsall WS7 8NT ***Tel*** **(05436) 4215**
Sales-Hire-Service. Petrol driven golf cars for golf days, and all sporting, leisure, social and business events.

Pleasure Products Ltd

Redhouse Industrial Estate, Middlemore Lane West, Aldridge, Walsall, West Midlands WS9 8EL ***Tel*** **(0922) 743737**
Manufacturers of the 'SUPATROL' power driven golf trolley. Strong, reliable and quiet in operation. Competitively priced with 12 months' guarantee and full after sales service. Available from pro-shop.

Powakaddy International Ltd

Sittingbourne Industrial Park, Sittingbourne, Kent ME10 3JH ***Tel*** **(0795) 73555**
Manufacturers and distributors worldwide of electronic self-propelled golf trolleys. Both the Powkaddy Classic and Rio models are maintenance free. Enjoyed by more than 100,000 golfers worldwide.

Golf Club Manufacturers

Browning Sports Ltd

37d Milton Trading Estate, Milton, Abingdon, Oxon OX14 4RT ***Tel*** **(0235) 833939**
Browning are established manufacturers of quality clubs, bags and accessories. Club ranges to match all standards of play, mens and ladies models, including Ceramic Plus, Tour Class, Mirage, Lady Mirage and Premier.

Slazenger Golf Division

PO Box 8, Normanton, West Yorkshire WF6 1YX
Tel **(0924) 896868**
Slazenger manufacture a range of stylish equipment. Balls include 480 Interlock balata, surlyn and two piece. Clubs include Silver Panther, Seve XTC Graphite. Stylish bags, luggage and accessories to complement the range.

Slotline Golf Europe Ltd

Largo Road, St Andrews, Fife
Tel **(0334) 77017 Call Free 0800 83 33 77**
Manufacturers of INERTIAL PUTTERS, E-MAX IRONS and WOODS and the new LADY RAMPANT COPPER/GRAPHITE IRONS and WOODS. Free advice and customisation service always available from professional staff.

Taylor Made (Great Britain) Ltd

Annecy House, Gastons Wood, Reading Road, Basingstoke, Hants RG24 0TW
Tel **(0256) 479797**
Taylor made metalwoods are the number one choice of tour professionals. The comprehensive range of metalwoods now are also fitted with a choice of graphite and titanium shafts. TPF irons, and TDA putters complete the range of products.

Tran Am Sports & Leisure Ltd

William House, Gore Road, New Milton, Hampshire BH25 6RJ ***Tel*** **(0425) 620580**
Tran Am sports and leisure international distributors for Stirling golf clubs, Baleno waterproof clothing, Rukka windproof sweaters, ASL socks and Starke golf bags. The international company that specialises in service.

Golf Club Grips

Avon Industrial Polymers Ltd

Bath Road, Melksham, Wiltshire SN12 8AA
Tel **(0225) 707666** ***Tx*** **44142**
Avon's range of pioneering golf grip designs includes the Chamois, Charger Procushion and Pro-select grips, suitable for all skill levels from the high handicap player to the professional. (See advertisement page 80 for further details).

Golf Club Repairers

B G Golf Factors

Golf House, Ivinghoe, Nr Leighton Buzzard, Beds ***Tel*** **(0296) 668696**
Manufacturing the Cypress Point range of clubs, bags and other accesories for supply to the golf profession.

David Watkinson Golf Co

Unit 6, Moat Lodge Industrial Estate, Stock Chase, Maldon, Essex CM9 7AA
Tel **(0621) 58510**
Manufacturers of hand crafted Persimmon woods and complete repair facility from refinishing woods to rechroming irons.

Golf Course Architects

British Association of Golf Course Architects

Hon Secretary, 5 Oxford Street, Woodstock, Oxford OX7 1TQ ***Tel*** **(0993) 811976**
Professional Association of qualified golf course architects officially recognised by the R & A and English Golf Union.

Golf Development International NV (Joan F Dudok Van Heel)

4 Beukenlaan, 1640 St Genesius-Rode, Belgium
Tel **(02) 358 3387**
Architecture, design and construction – supervision of golf courses. Consultancy on golf course and club management. Feasibility studies – promoting and developing the game of golf.

Hamilton Stutt & Co

12 Bingham Avenue, Poole, Dorset BH14 8NE
Tel **(0202) 708406**
Founder member of the British Association of Golf Course Architects. One of Europe's most experienced golf architects. Personal attention to each new project – only a limited number accepted each year.

Hawtree & Son

5 Oxford Street, Woodstock, Oxford OX7 1TQ
Tel **(0993) 811976**
Hawtree & Son celebrates 77 years of golf architectural service throughout the world. (See advertisement page 82 for further details.)

I R H (Development Services) Ltd

5 Cortes Crescent, Edinburgh EH3 7AL
Tel **031-220 1707**
Fax **031 220 1626**
Co-ordination and management of all project elements including concept, planning approvals, golf course design and construction, related infrastructure and landscaping. Projects range from course alterations to substantial integrated developments as at Collingtree Park, Northampton. (See advertisement page 88 for further details.)

John Jacobs Golf Associates Ltd

68A High Street, Walkern, Stevenage, Herts SG2 7PG
Tel **(0438) 86 438** ***Fax*** **0438 86 788**
Golf architects/consultants offering a complete service, through feasibility, design and contract management. Leaders in the golf centre design and development field. Architects of the new South Course at Wentworth. (See advertisement page 82 for further details.)

Golf Course Maintenance

Claymore Grass Machinery (UK)

Waterloo Road, Waterloo Industrial Estate, Bidford-on-Avon, Warwickshire BS0 4JH
Tel **(0789) 490177**
High quality grass cutting machinery for all types of terrain is available from Claymore. Distributors for Greens, Roberine and Bolens mowers with sales and service centres throughout the UK. From superfine golf green pedestrian cylinder and ride-on diesel hydrostatic cylinder mowers to lawn tractors and trailed gang mowers. The accent is on comfort, ease and efficiency. (See advertisement page 88 for further details.)

Watermation Ltd

Monument Way E, Woking, Surrey GU21 5LY ***Tel*** **(04862) 70303**
Manufacturers and installers of top quality golf course irrigation equipment, including computer controllers (TW1 and TW2) and pop-up sprinklers (GN range) made from brass and bronze with rubber covers.

Golf Financial Services

Golf Plus – Golf Financial Services Ltd

308–314 Kings Road, Reading, Berkshire RG1 4PA
Tel **(0734) 61022** ***Tx*** **848511** ***Fax*** **0734 662237**
Golf Plus, the credit card designed exclusively for golfers. Approved by the PGA, Golf Plus offers members a comprehensive range of golfing services and benefits through the Golf Plus Club.

Golf Holidays

Meridian Holidays

12–16 Dering Street, London W1R 9AE
Tel **01 493 2777**
Choose Meridian for over 10 years experience in arranging golf holiday packages in Europe. Self-catering or hotel holidays in France, Spain or Portugal with value and style. ABTA/IATA/ATOL.

Golf Practice Equipment

Golf Aids of Reading

470 Reading Road, Winnersh, Wokingham, Berkshire RG11 5ET ***Tel*** **(0836) 240509**
Manufacturers of probably the finest range of golf practice nets in Europe. Exclusive green polyethylene netting also sold by the roll for multi-purpose uses.

Irrigation Equipment and Installation

Grundfos Pumps Ltd

Grovebury Road, Leighton Buzzard, Bedfordshire LU7 8TL
Tel **(0525) 850000** ***Tx*** **825544**
Manufacturers of Electro submersible pumps for water supply, booster pumps for sports turf irrigation, water boosting, circulation/transfer and a wide range of heating and hot water service circulation pumps.

Sportsground Irrigation Co

6 Stuart Road, Market Harborough LE16 9PQ
Tel **(0858) 63153**
Fax **0858 410085**
Irrigation engineers, specialising in golf course equipment and installations. Annual service contracts offered on any system.
(See advertisement page 80 for further details.)

Watermation Ltd

Monument Way E, Woking, Surrey GU21 5LY
Tel **(04862) 70303**
Manufacturers and installers of top quality golf course irrigation equipment, including computer controllers (TW1 and TW2) and pop-up sprinklers (GN range) made from brass and bronze with rubber covers.

Personalised Golf Merchandise

Club Sports

Solent Business Centre, Unit 018, Millbrook Road, West Millbrook, Southampton SO1 0HW
Tel **(0703) 702654**
Club Sports promoting YOUR NAME on our range of PACKAGED ACCESSORIES. We offer a complete range, from Airflow balls to packets of tees, from shoe laces to bag towels.

Professional Bodies

British Association of Golf Course Architects

Hon Secretary, 5 Oxford Street, Woodstock, Oxford OX7 1TQ
Tel **(0993) 811976**
Professional Association of qualified golf course architects officially recognised by the R & A and English Golf Union.

Institute of Groundmanship
19–23 Church Street, The Agora, Wolverton, Milton Keynes, Bucks MK12 5LG
Tel **(0908) 312511**
Educational and training programmes; turf advisory service; annual conference; monthly journal; I0G sports and leisure world trade exhibitions; Groundsman of the Year awards. The professional body for groundsmen and greenkeepers.

Publishers and Book Sellers

Superbbooks Ltd
18 Wellington Road, Hastings, East Sussex TN34 3RN
Tel **(0424) 720313** ***Fax*** **0424 720565**
Publishers of diaries, handbooks and score cards for golf clubs on an entirely free of charge basis. (See advertisement page 85 for further details.)

Menswear

Burberrys of London
29/53 Chatham Place, London E9 6LP
Tel **01 985 3344**
A comprehensive range of golf bags and holdalls, in five colour ways and matching golf umbrellas, head covers, shoes, etc. Also available, a comprehensive collection of golf clothing for men and women. (See advertisement page 4 for further details.)

Womenswear

Burberrys of London
29/53 Chatham Place, London E9 6LP
Tel **01 985 3344**
A comprehensive range of golf bags and holdalls, in five colour ways and matching golf umbrellas, head covers, shoes, etc. Also available, a comprehensive collection of golf clothing for men and women. (See advertisement page 4 for further details.)

S R Leisure
26 Stirling Close, Pattison South Industrial Estate, District 8, Washington, Tyne & Wear NE38 8QD
Tel **(091) 415 3344**
That – specialist ladies outer clothing, jackets, gillets, skirts, trousers, plus 2's, cullottes; in polycottons, Trevira and corduroy. Also showerproof oversuits in the comfortable fabric Climaguard, 100% waterproof with the Aquatex membrane, Tactel.

Rainwear

Burberrys of London
29/53 Chatham Place, London E9 6LP
Tel **01 985 3344**
A comprehensive range of golf bags and holdalls, in five colour ways and matching golf umbrellas, head covers, shoes, etc. Also available, a comprehensive collection of golf clothing for men and women. (See advertisement page 4 for further details.)

S R Leisure
26 Stirling Close, Pattison South Industrial Estate, District 8, Washington, Tyne & Wear NE38 8QD ***Tel*** **(091) 415 3344**
That – specialist ladies outer clothing, jackets, gillets, skirts, trousers, plus 2's, cullottes; in polycottons, Trevira and corduroy. Also showerproof oversuits in the comfortable fabric Climaguard, 100% waterproof with the Aquatex membrane, Tactel.

Sunderland Sportswear Ltd
PO Box 14, Glasgow G2 1ER
Tel **041–552 3261** ***Fax*** **041 552 8518**
Sunderland Sportswear manufacture high-quality golf rainwear and umbrellas in Scotland, all rainsuits are tour tested and guaranteed waterproof, a variety of fabrics including Gore-tex, Aquatex and Bretex being used.

Tran Am Sports & Leisure Ltd
William House, Gore Road, New Milton, Hampshire BH25 6RJ ***Tel*** **(0425) 620580**
Tran Am sports and leisure international distributors for Stirling golf clubs, Baleno waterproof clothing, Rukka windproof sweaters, ASL socks and Starke golf bags. The international company that specialises in service.

W L Gore & Associates (UK) Ltd
Kirkton Campus, Livingston, West Lothian
Tel **(0506) 412525**
Gore-tex fabric golf suits are the ultimate in waterproof and breathable rain suits. The unique gore-tex membrane allows perspiration to escape yet is guaranteed waterproof.

Suppliers of Golf Prizes

Derek Burridge Trophies
5–11 Hanbury Road, Acton, London W3 8RF
Tel **01 992 5948/7313**
The country's leading suppliers of golf prizes. We offer a vast range of silverplate, crystal, china, clocks, leather goods and sporting trophies, all at trade prices. Glass and silver plate in house engraving service. (See advertisement page 46 for further details.)

CLAYMORE

CLAYMORE
GRASS MACHINERY
BIDFORD & ARBROATH

Roberine

Bolens

Part I
1988 Season

The Open 1988

The return of the Open to Royal Lytham and St Annes after a break of nine years was a Championship Committee decision which raised questions with some. It is the only course on the Open rota which is entirely surrounded by residential housing. Could it cope with the greater crowds expected than those in 1979? Was there sufficient space for the many more exhibition, entertainment and trade marquees now necessary? Would available car parking areas be near enough and sufficient? In the event, the Club and area survived the test to the satisfaction of the vast majority. Indeed the crowd on the Sunday was the largest recorded for any day of an Open, a record 41,332.

© Peter Dazeley Photography

Ballesteros wins the Cup for the third time. His 65 was the best-ever last round score of any winner.

There was never any doubt that the course, immaculately prepared, would fail to present problems to the greatest players. The roll-call of earlier Open Champions at Lytham, Bobby Jones, Bobby Locke, Peter Thomson, Gary Player, Bob Charles, Tony Jacklin and Seve Ballesteros proved its quality. No United States professional had won there. Would the spell be broken? It was not to be. But for a disastrous first round, the US Open Champion, Curtis Strange, would have been contesting the finish. His three subsequent rounds of 68, 69 and 68 were only equalled by the winner. Strange's was a major case of 'if only'.

Faldo's Open record is remarkable. He was 7th in 1978; except for 1985 when he was among the also-rans on the last day, he has in ten years never been lower than 19th, in 1979, and has averaged 7th. Few of the great Champions in their heyday, when there were far fewer competitors, equalled such a record. That he was in full contention to retain his title until the 63rd hole was a magnificent achievement.

The drama of the Saturday when the storms caused cancellation of play for the day and a later start on Sunday was the first such postponement since 1970 at St Andrews. There were also breaks for an hour or so at Sandwich in 1985 and Turnberry in 1986. For the Championship Committee, men who serve golf so faithfully, postponement of a round is a difficult decision. Once the condition of the course makes play impossible, usually through greens being under water, they hope stopping play will only be for an hour or so. If postponed and then restarted, players already on the course can return to the spot where they stopped. Cancellation of a round usually means an extra day and all the consequent alterations to schedules of players, officials and attendants. Once the Committee had decided that two rounds on Sunday was not an option, Saturday's round was cancelled, with the last round to be played on Monday.

To return to the first day, one recent champion, Greg Norman, had not recovered from hitting a hidden rock when playing an iron shot in the US Open at Brookline and had withdrawn. Nearly all the other major figures were there. After two rounds Nick Price of Zimbabwe led on 137, a shot ahead of Ballesteros, with Stadler, Faldo, Bean, Couples, Lyle and Tway still decidedly in the hunt. Casualties failing to better 148, the cut-off score, included Trevino, Baker-Finch, Mize, Floyd, Sutton, Canizares,

Green, Calcavecchia and, strangely, all seven Swedes who had qualified.

© Peter Dazeley Photography

Nick Price, who was still level with Ballesteros at the 16th hole in the last round.

The 3rd round was stopped soon after midday when nearly two inches of rain had fallen in 24 hours, leaving the greens and some fairways unplayable. At first it was hoped that two rounds could be completed on the Sunday, but soon it was clear that the course was unlikely to be ready in time for an early start, even if the rain ceased. Thus the Championship had to be extended to an extra day on the Monday. Not many had started their 3rd round well in the conditions, but Hubert Green was disappointed having completed eight holes in five under par.

© Matthew Harris

Nick Faldo, who finished third, studies a putt – if only a few more had dropped!

By midnight on Saturday four holes were completely under water. The green staff, working through the night, and with the rain clearing, managed to transform the course, making a start possible next morning a little later than usual. No praise can be too high for their efforts to make play possible so soon after the downpour.

On Sunday morning the Championship really came alive. David J Russell, as he had at Birkdale in 1983, went out in 29 but again slipped badly to 39 back. By the evening Price led at 7 under, followed by Faldo and Ballesteros 5 under and Lyle 4 under. Larry Nelson was the leading American one stroke further back. There was sympathy for Price as the three players snapping at his heels had each been Open Champion in the previous four years.

© Matthew Harris

Seve Ballesteros delighted at laying his chip dead from the semi-rough at the 72nd hole to clinch the title.

After nine holes Ballesteros had drawn level and he took the lead at the 11th. Price had one back with a birdie 3 at the 12th to Seve's 4 and was still only one behind on the 16th tee. There Price saw his rival hole a putt for another birdie 3. The 17th was halved and Price was on the 18th green in two, with Ballesteros over to the left beyond the hole in an uncomfortable lie in the short rough. He then played a marvellous chip which lipped the hole and left him stone-dead for his 4 and a win by two strokes.

Faldo never looked the winner after the first nine holes in 34 and in the end he finished six shots behind. It was a disappointment for him, especially after his fine effort on the US Open play-off against Strange. The headline 'Faldo fails' was unnecessary. In the last 25 years only Trevino and Watson have won the Open two years in succession and few holders have finished third in their attempt to retain the title.

While no US player threatened in the last round, their strength in depth is evident. In the first 40 players there were 19 Americans and 10 Europeans.

The US Majors

The Masters

© Matthew Harris

Sandy Lyle, the first British winner of the Masters.

Sandy Lyle became the first British golfer to win the Masters. Previously the only non-Americans who had worn the famous Green Jacket were Player who won on three occasions, Ballesteros twice and Langer once. That the three favourites before the start should be Greg Norman, Ballesteros and Lyle, who had already won two US Tour tournaments in January and March, showed the strength of the overseas challenge to United States hegemony.

Until the last round Norman was not in contention. Eleven strokes behind, he then produced a 64, the best round of the week gaining seven shots on Lyle to finish 5th equal. Otherwise no one did better scores than 66, by Zoeller in the 2nd round and Price in the 4th. Ballesteros never played with inspiration and while Langer was only four strokes off at the start of the last day, he did not threaten.

Lyle has such a phlegmatic approach to the game that his destructive shots never seem to worry him. This had been apparent in his 1985 victory in the Open at Sandwich when he fluffed a clip from the rough near the 72nd green then calmly played another from long grass at the fringe close enough to hole the putt comfortably.

He had played at Augusta on six occasions since 1980; he did not receive an invitation in 1982 and 1984. The invitation to play is one way the Masters maintains its unique reputation. Another is the awesome quality of the course with which no liberties can be taken and an inaccurate stroke nearly always means an extra shot. The greens too with their alarming slopes, tricky borrows and lightening speed strike fear in the best of players. The winner's award of the Green Jacket is the thrill of his life for the first-time winner.

Lyle's lack of outward emotion, whatever may be the thoughts in that fair head above the tall frame, is a worry to rivals. His expression seldom alters whether its a birdie or three putts for a two over par six. When in the lead such an attitude can be disconcerting to his partner in the final round.

He played with confidence from the start, beginning with a steady 71 to share the lead with Mark Calcavecchia, followed by a 67 on the Friday, which no one bettered all week except Zoeller in the second, and Norman and Price in the last round. On Saturday evening Lyle led Calcavecchia by two shots. Out in 34 on Sunday he gained two more on him. After the 10th was halved in 4, Calcavecchia produced a brilliant spell of 3,3,4 against par of 4,3,5 and Lyle's three over par 5,5,5, gaining five shots and snatching the lead. Calcavecchia was playing a hole ahead of Lyle, but Lyle reacted with aplomb, matching his rival's score at the next two holes and gaining a stroke at the 16th with a well-judged 12 foot putt for a 2, which needed a substantial borrow. This effort brought him back to level again.

Lyle equalled Calcavecchia's conventional

par 4 at the 17th. With the honour at the 18th he chose a 1-iron for his tee shot to avoid the fairway bunkers and promptly drove into one of them 250 yards ahead. By then he knew Calcavecchia had had a 4 and a birdie was required if he was to win. There followed as remarkable a shot as he will ever play in such circumstances. A 7-iron of 150 yards from the bunker sailed over the flag-stick, pitching 12 feet beyond and rolling back four feet with the slope. He had been putting well and, carefully assessing the borrow, gently stroked his ball into the hole from eight feet for a 3.

Seldom have so many supporting Britons watching in person or on TV had greater excitement in golf.

In the last round only Stadler had threatened at one point to catch the leaders, but his chance disappeared a few holes back.

The US Open

© Matthew Harris

Curtis Strange, US Open Champion, wins his long-expected first Major, but only after a play-off with Faldo.

Curtis Strange won the US Open at The Country Club, Brookline, near Boston, Massachusetts, in a play-off with Nick Faldo, who so nearly emulated Tony Jacklin's feat of 20 years earlier in holding the Open and US Open titles at the same time. The last man to achieve it was Tom Watson in 1982. Faldo played as well as anyone from tee to green, but once again the putts would not drop. He did not putt badly in any of his five rounds. In carrying the European flag when each of the other contenders faded, he played consistent par golf or a little better. Ballesteros, after a first round 68 once again failed to produce his attacking play in a US Championship and fell away to 288 and 30th place. Lyle, who also started well, finished a stroke ahead of Seve. Of the other Europeans both Langer and Brown failed to make the cut.

Scott Simpson, the holder, who had done little of note since his win at Olympic, San Francisco, finished equal 6th with Azinger, who, one feels, will win a major soon. Pate, O'Meara and DA Weibring finished equal 3rd, but never really threatened the two leaders in the later stages.

Strange, striving for his first major, was favourite from the start. The battle for the lead developed into a two-man race between him and Faldo from round 3; on the Sunday, Faldo started one behind Strange and was still one more on the 17th tee, but Strange surprisingly took three putts there from no distance. Faldo played the 18th well and, with Strange bunkered near the green, he looked the winner, but a fine recovery shot gave Strange a half and the 18-hole play-off.

Faldo was not at his best next day, missing several greens early on but recovering well, failing to make par only at the 3rd in the first six holes. Strange had gone one up at the 5th with a birdie and the next five holes were halved in par or better. Faldo fell two behind at the 11th. It was cut and thrust through the 12th to 15th, each player winning holes alternately. The 16th was halved in a par 3. Faldo finally gave way, playing each of the last two holes in one over par and losing them both.

The Country Club, traditionally the only Club in the United States with the capital 'T', again proved a real test. At both previous Opens there, those of 1913 and 1963, a play-off had been necessary, the young amateur Francis Ouimet beating Harry Vardon and Ted Ray is one of the biggest upsets in Championship history and 50 years later, Julian Boros winning from Jack Cupitt and Arnold Palmer. (It is an interesting statistic that since 1920 there have been 19 play-offs in the US Open and only seven in the Open.) The Country Club was one of the four founding Clubs of the USGA and has maintained its reputation having also been host to five US Amateur Championships and two Walker Cups.

USPGA

The USPGA, played at Oak Tree, Edmond, Oklahoma, produced another surprise winner in Jeff Sluman, one of the smallest men on the Tour, who scored 272 with a final round of 65.

His only previous entry into the headlines was his tie with Sandy Lyle in the 1986 Tournament Player Championship, when he lost the sudden-death play-off. This time he won convincingly by three strokes from Paul Azinger, with Tommy Nakajima three more and Nick Faldo equal with Tom Kite one stroke further back at 279.

Since 1980, when Jack Nicklaus won the USPGA for the fifth time, all winners have been US Open Champions or were to be subsequently, except Sutton in 1983 and Bob Tway in 1986. Tway holed a memorable pitch shot at the 18th to edge out Greg Norman. It was Sluman's holing of an approach of 110 yards at the 590-yard 5th hole for an eagle 3, which set him on his way to victory, giving him a two stroke lead on Nick Faldo, his playing partner, who had just recovered to within two strokes of the lead. Sluman became the first man since Jerry Pate in the 1970 US Open to win a major as his first Tour success.

Having come within two strokes at the 4th and managed a birdie 4 to Sluman's eagle at the 5th, Faldo dropped a shot at the 7th to go four behind. By then it was all but over. Sluman made a few errors on the back 9 holes but pitched well and made telling putts to finish in 65.

It was yet another disappointment for Faldo, whose record in the 1988 majors was outstanding: 30th at Augusta in the Masters, losing a play-off after finishing 1st equal in the US Open, 3rd at Lytham in the Open and now 4th equal in the USPGA, a record which has seldom been bettered, but yet with no outright victory.

Apart from Faldo the European Tour contingent failed disappointingly. Ballesteros, Langer and Brown all missed the cut and Woosnam would also have failed to reach round 3 for he had already retired after 27 holes with a fierce headache, due to the 95°F-plus shade temperature; such was the heat that ice packs encased in plastic for wearing round the neck, lasting about 90 minutes, were provided.

The old order changeth. A few years back it would have been a sensation if Nicklaus, Palmer, Trevino and Zoeller had all missed the cut, as each did at Oak Tree; nor was Watson in contention. With so many first-time winners of Tour events since January 1988, one speculates who will emerge to win several events this year. Azinger, Sluman, Tway, Calcavecchia, Price, O'Meara and DA Weibring must be candidates. Is a burning desire to win losing its flame among the thousands upon thousands of dollars to be won for finishing in the top 50 of the merit order? One sincerely hopes not. Will there evver again be a great triumvirate like Palmer, Player and Nicklaus with Trevino in support? Personalities who can win consistently are surely needed to maintain spectator enthusiasm.

US Major Championships 1988

The US Masters
at Augusta National GC, Augusta, Georgia

Name	Score	Prize $
S Lyle	71-67-72-71–281	183800
M Calcavecchia	71-69-72-70–282	110200
C Stadler	76-69-70-68–283	69400
B Crenshaw	72-73-67-72–284	48900
D Pooley	71-72-72-70–285	36500
G Norman	77-73-71-64–285	36500
F Couples	75-68-71-71–285	36500
D Frost	73-74-71-68–286	31000
T Watson	72-71-73-71–287	28000
B Langer	71-72-71-73–287	28000
L Wadkins	74-75-69-70–288	23000
S Ballesteros	73-72-70-73–288	23000
R Floyd	80-69-68-71–288	23000
D Tewell	75-73-68-74–289	18500
N Price	75-76-72-66–289	18500
D Pohl	78-70-69-73–290	16000
F Zoeller	76-66-72-76–290	16000
M McNulty	74-71-73-72–290	16000
TC Chen	76-73-72-70–291	13500
H Green	74-70-75-72–291	13500
C Strange	76-70-72-74–292	11200
J Nicklaus	75-73-72-72–292	11200
C Beck	73-70-76-73–292	11200
M McCumber	79-71-72-71–293	9600
R Wrenn	69-75-76-74–294	7975
P Stewart	75-76-71-72–294	7975
I Aoki	74-74-73-73–294	7975
G Koch	72-73-74-75–294	7975
R Davis	77-72-71-75–295	7100
M O'Grady	74-73-76-73–296	6500
N Faldo	75-74-75-72–296	6500
S Jones	74-74-75-73–296	6500
B Tway	74-73-74-76–297	5667
T Nakajima	74-72-77-74–297	5667
L Nelson	69-78-75-75–297	5667

US Open Championship
at The Country Club, Brookline, Massachusetts

Name	Score	Prize $
C Strange	70-67-69-72–278	180000
N Faldo	72-67-68-71–278	90000
(Strange won play-off)		
DA Weibring	71-69-68-72–280	41370
S Pate	72-69-72-67–280	41370

M O'Meara	71-72-66-71–280	41370
S Simpson	69-66-72-74–281	24414
P Azinger	69-70-76-66–281	24414
F Zoeller	73-72-71-66–282	20903
B Gilder	68-69-70-75–282	20903
P Stewart	73-73-70-67–283	17870
F Couples	72-67-71-73–283	17870
L Wadkins	70-71-70-73–284	14781
D Pohl	74-72-69-69–284	14781
L Mize	69-67-72-76–284	14781
A Bean	71-71-72-70–284	14781
B Crenshaw	71-72-74-67–284	14781
J Sindelar	76-68-70-71–285	11981
M McNulty	73-72-72-68–285	11981
H Irwin	71-71-72-71–285	11981
R Floyd	72-73-72-67–285	11981
S Hoch	71-72-71-72–286	10344
P Jacobsen	76-70-76-64–286	10344
B Eastwood	74-72-69-71–286	10344
C Beck	73-72-71-70–286	10344
J Haas	73-67-74-73–287	8855
D Barr	73-72-72-70–287	8855
C Stadler	70-73-71-73–287	8855
B Tway	77-68-73-69–287	8855
M Wiebe	75-70-73-69–287	8855
S Lyle	68-71-75-73–287	8855
*B Mayfair	71-72-71-73–287	–
T Nakajima	74-72-69-73–288	7726
M McCumber	72-72-71-73–288	7726
K Green	72-70-70-76–288	7726
S Ballesteros	69-74-72-73–288	7726
T Watson	74-71-69-75–289	7002
D Ishii	73-73-75-68–289	7002
M Lye	75-71-71-72–289	7002
T Kite	72-69-73-75–289	7002

(* Denotes Amateur)

USPGA Championship

at Edmond Country Club, Oklahoma

Name	Score	Prize $
J Sluman	69-70-68-65–272	160000
P Azinger	67-66-71-71–275	100000
T Nakajima	69-68-74-67–278	70000
T Kite	72-69-71-67–279	45800
N Faldo	67-71-70-71–279	45800
D Rummels	73-64-68-75–280	32500
B Gilder	66-75-71-68–280	32500
D Pohl	69-71-70-71–281	28000
M O'Meara	70-71-70-71–282	21500
G Norman	68-71-72-71–282	21500
P Stewart	70-69-70-73–282	21500
R Floyd	68-68-74-72–282	21500
K Knox	72-69-68-73–282	21500
S Jones	69-68-72-73–282	21500
C Stadler	68-73-75-67–283	16500
J Mahaffey	71-71-70-71–283	16500
R Zokol	70-70-74-70–284	11500
N Price	74-70-67-73–284	11500
J Overton	68-66-76-74–284	11500
O Pavin	71-70-75-68–284	11500
M McNulty	73-70-67-74–284	11500
D Graham	70-67-73-74–284	11500
M Calcavecchia	73-69-70-72–284	11500
B Crenshaw	70-71-69-74–284	11500

Volvo European Tour 1988

Colin Callander

On the face of things European golf seems to have changed little during the last decade. A glance at the records reveals that in 1978 it was a young Spaniard who won the Harry Vardon Trophy for the third successive season. Ten years later it was the same Severiano Ballesteros who headed the Order of Merit for the fifth time in his career. But such statistics can be greatly misleading. The Spaniard might have been the dominant force in European professional golf for much of the last decade but around about him there has been an incredible transformation in the European game. In 1978 Ballesteros captured four Tour titles, the Martini International, the Dutch Open, the Scandinavian Open and the Swiss Open, with his official earnings amounting to £54,348 from a total purse for the season of just £1.2 million. In 1988 the Tour, now under the umbrella sponsorship of Volvo, offered a total prize fund in excess of £10 million. Ballesteros ended the season with rather more than £501,000 which included a £50,000 bonus from the major sponsors for heading the Order of Merit.

But it is not just in terms of the prize money available that there has been a boom in European professional golf over the last decade. Indeed such riches would not have been possible had the leading European professionals themselves not found a new role on the worldwide golfing stage. Ten years ago no Briton or European had won one of golf's four Majors for nine years. Success outside the confines of the European Tour was rare. How, a mere ten years on, the Europeans have assumed a role which once seemed to belong to the Americans almost by right. It is the Europeans who are now the dominant force in world golf. Sitting at the tail end of 1988 we can see that the top Europeans have won seven Majors in the space of the last six years. Europe has won the biennial Ryder Cup match on two successive occasions and hardly a week seems to go by without one member of the Tour winning in some far flung land. It is against this background that we must view the domestic scene in Europe in 1988.

© Peter Dazeley Photography

Seve Ballesteros with four Tour wins in addition to the Open.

© Peter Dazeley Photography

Sandy Lyle, winner of the Dunhill Masters in June and the World Match-Play at Wentworth in October, with his defeated opponent, Faldo. It was Sandy's fifth final, but first victory.

It is a measure of Europe's new-found success that it would be fair to argue that Sandy Lyle, with victories in The Masters, the Greater

Greensboro Open and the Phoenix Open in the States as well as in the Dunhill British Masters and the Suntory World Match Play Championship, was the finest golfer in the world in 1988. But in terms of the Volvo Tour itself the Scot has to be placed behind Ballesteros when the honours are handed out. The statistics themselves reveal that in 1988 Ballesteros had no peer within the confines of Europe.

- He won five times – the Open de Baleares, The Open, the Scandinavian Enterprise Open, the German Open and the Lancôme Trophy – to finish the season with a record haul of £501,559.
- In just 14 tournament appearances he had 11 top-ten finishes and missed the cut just once.
- In the same 14 appearances he averaged £32,254 per tournament or almost £10,000 more than his nearest rival.
- And in 54 tournament rounds during the season he was a total of 130 under par.

All this would have been impressive enough but he also produced the highlight of the season in winning The Open at Royal Lytham and St Annes.

For the first time in many years Ballesteros chose to enter the first official event of the season. It might just have been because one of this companies was promoting the tournament, but it was a fruitful decision nonetheless because the Spaniard left the Open de Baleares in Mallorca with the £33,330 first-place cheque firmly in his grasp. Ballesteros had four-putted the final green during the first round but eventually pulled away to win by six strokes from his compatriot, José-Maria Olazabal, and win his first big title for almost a year. Ballesteros' uncharacteristically fast start to the season meant that he had no qualms about missing the next two events in Barcelona and Biarritz which left the way clear for some of the lesser lights to shine.

One of the most noticeable features of the 1988 season on the Volvo Tour was the number of times – eight in all – that tournaments were won by competitors who had never previously won in Europe. This trend began when David Whelan won the Barcelona Open and continued when David Llewellyn captured the ensuing AGF Open in Biarritz. Llewellyn's triumph in Biarritz, during which he scored a 60 in the penultimate round, which might have been a 59 had he not three-putted the final green, was hardly a major surprise. He had produced a string of high finishes over a number of years and had been touted in several quarters to win a European title to add to the three which he had already won on the Safari Circuit. But Whelan was a different case altogether. This 26 year-old Englishman had just emerged from his sixth visit to the European Tour Qualifying School at La Manga and had no previous form whatsoever. Nevertheless he produced a 12 under par aggregate of 276 at El Prat and then despatched Mark Mouland, Barry Lane and Nick Faldo in a four hole sudden-death play-off. Not surprisingly, the £33,330 winner's cheque was the biggest the penniless Whelan had ever received and proved ample compensation for the endless hours he had spent over the winter months changing his swing under the tutelage of David Leadbetter.

© Peter Dazeley Photography

Bernhard Langer had a disappointing season, winning only the Epson Match-Play at St Pierre. His putting was suspect. Note left hand below right grip of the putter.

After Whelan and Llewellyn had produced the goods, the Tour then returned to some semblance of normality when Zimbabwe's Mark McNulty captured his seventh Tour title in the Cannes Open at Mougins before there were two more tournaments in which the new boys triumphed. Such a phrase could be termed as rather misleading in connection with England's Derrick Cooper because he had been a member of the European Tour for almost ten years before he came from nowhere to capture the Cepsa Madrid Open at Puerta de Hierro. But in the case of Mike Harwood, who won the subsequent Portuguese Open at Quinta do Lago, the label is much more apt. Harwood, an Australian, first appeared in Europe in 1986 a matter of months after he had won his country's PGA title, but in the subsequent two seasons he seldom hit the headlines finishing, respectively, 93rd and 92nd on the Order of Merit. Such progress as this was, it did little to suggest to the British and

Continental golfing public that in 1988 the 29 year-old from Melbourne would win once and produce another five top-20 finishes to end the year in 29th place on the Order of Merit table with prize money totalling £68,843.

Looked at in a generous light, this plethora of early first-time winners suggested that the Volvo Tour now had considerably more strength in depth, than had been the case a number of seasons before. That is undoubtedly true to a point but there then followed a sequence of nine tournaments, all of which were won by golf's equivalent of the 'A-Team'. In order this group comprised Bernhard Langer (the Epson Grand Prix of Europe Match-Play Championship), Mark James (Peugeot Spanish Open), Greg Norman (Lancia Italian Open), Ian Woosnam (Volvo PGA Championship), Sandy Lyle (Dunhill British Masters), Rodger Davis (Wang Four Stars Pro-Celebrity), José-Maria Olazabal (Volvo Belgian Masters), Nick Faldo (Peugeot French Open) and José Rivero (Monte Carlo Open) who amongst them had won 79 European Tour titles leading into 1988. With the benefit of hindsight, a number of pointers emerge from these results, the most important of which was that in 1988 it was still the Old Guard who dominated the bigger tournaments. With due respect to Peter Baker (Benson & Hedges International) and Barry Lane (Bell's Scottish Open), it can be seen that in the tournaments which attracted the strongest fields it was invariably one of the seasoned campaigners who won. One needs to look no further than the feats of the ubiquitous Seve Ballesteros to be reminded of that fact.

© Peter Dazeley Photography

Two of the several first-time 1988 winners, Peter Baker in the Benson & Hedges at Fulford and Barry Lane in Bell's Scottish Open at Gleneagles

Entering the half-way mark of the 1988 Volvo tour, which in its entirety stretched across seven months and visited nine countries, Ballesteros had fallen to fourth place behind Mark McNulty, Nick Faldo and José-Maria Olazabal on the Order of Merit table. But in the space of his next five tournament appearances he was to end any speculation that the Vardon Trophy might end up in someone else's grasp. He did not enter the Bell's Scottish Open, won by Barry Lane, the KLM Open, which went to Mark Mouland, the Benson & Hedges International, captured by Peter Baker (the 1987 Rookie of the Year) or the Carrolls Irish Open and the Panasonic European Open, both won by Ian Woosnam, but he triumphed in The Open at Royal Lytham and St Annes, the Scandinavian Enterprise Open at Drottningholm, the German Open at the Frankfurter Club and the Lancôme Trophy at St Nom la Breteche as well as finishing tied for second alongside Woosnam but behind Chris Moody in the Ebel European Masters at Crans-sur-Sierre. The form of Woosnam also tends to lend support to the argument that, while a number of new figures did emerge, it was not at the expense of those the Americans might describe as 'major leaguers'. The Welshman had been a revelation during 1987, heading the Order of Merit in Europe, winning eight titles worldwide, and winning in excess of £1,000,000 during the season. That being the case, it might have been expected that he would suffer some reaction the following year, in the end it did not materialise. It is true that he had a miserable start to the season, made worse by his decision to change allegiance to a new club manufacturer. He was also out of action for more than a month during June and July after sustaining a wrist injury falling off a motorcycle, but over the season as a whole he still won three times in Europe to finish a creditable fourth in the Order of Merit table.

Another leading figure who must also count his 1988 campaign as something of a success was Spain's José-Maria Olazabal whose earlier triumph in the Volvo Belgian Open was repeated in the German Masters in Stuttgart where he finished two strokes ahead of Sweden's Anders Forsbrand and Ireland's Des Smyth. Olazabal might be termed as the 'sleeper' of the season. Always in the shadow of his more illustrious compatriot from Santander and seldom the focus of huge media attention, he nevertheless recorded six top-five finishes in addition to his two victories to end the season with £285,964 in official earnings. Olazabal's second victory of the year came just before the week of the inaugural English Open at Royal Birkdale which, despite its attractive title, turned out to be arguably the low point of the season. Despite arduous efforts on the part of the Tour authorities, a sponsor could not be found; thus the tournament went ahead with just £180,000 in total prize money and only a handful of Europe's top-20 in the field. Under the circumstances it will not go down as one of the highlights of Howard Clark's career, although his win did mark this first victory for more than a year and his first on English soil since the PGA Championship in 1984. After an event bereft of incident, not to mention a sizable crowd to watch, it was something of a relief that the next tournament on the calendar, namely the Suntory World Match Play Championship, turned out to be one of the finest of the year. The weather might have been foul but it did little to dampen the enthusiasm for a Championship which is sometimes slated as a mere vehicle to raise money for the stars on the International Management Group's books but which has, despite this taint, grown in stature in leaps and bounds since its inception in 1964.

© Matthew Harris

José-María Olazabal, the engaging Spaniard, had a consistent record, finishing third in Merit Order, with wins in the Belgian Open and German Masters.

After his incredible start to the season, during which he won three times in the States and twice in Europe, Sandy Lyle had been noticeably less successful during July and August giving rise to some suggestions that he had tired himself out with his hectic early schedule. With this in mind it is perhaps no coincidence that he had a full fortnight off prior to winning his first Match Play title at Wentworth. Certainly there was no sign of leaden limbs as he despatched Nick Price in his opening match, demolished Seve Ballesteros 7 and 6 in the semi-finals and then pipped Nick Faldo 2 and 1 in one of the most enthralling final battles seen for years. For Lyle this triumph at Wentworth laid a ghost to rest. Four times before he had reached the final but had succumbed on each occasion. This time round he made amends in front of a massive crowd which had willingly returned for an extra day after torrential rain on the Saturday night had caused a 24-hour postponement of play. Returning to our original theme, the Suntory will be remembered, not just for Lyle's welcome win, but also because it served as another timely reminder that the European Tour now seems to have the edge over its counterpart in the States. In a non-Ryder Cup year such a statement might be difficult to argue, albeit during the second round of the Suntory some definite proof did emerge. Billed almost as a match between the Tours, the Wentworth crowd lapped it up as all four representatives from the European Tour defeated their rivals from across the Atlantic. First Ian Woosnam crushed the USPGA champion Jeff Sluman 7 and 6 and then Lyle polished off Price by 3 and 2. Faldo made it 3-0 for the homesters, beating Joey Sindelar 5 and 4 before Seve Ballesteros finished the job by putting out Mark McCumber, the US Players' champion, on the 37th hole.

© Matthew Harris

Ian Woosnam, less successful than in 1987, still won three important tournaments: the Volvo PGA, Carroll's Irish Open and the Panasonic.

European success was also a feature which carried over into the ensuing Dunhill Cup at St Andrews although on this occasion it was not the same four men who did the damage, but rather an unheralded team of Irishmen which comprised Eamonn Darcy, Des Smyth and Ronan Rafferty. Their triumph might have been one of the most unexpected of the season, but it was also one of the most richly deserved. Having ousted Canada in the first round, the Irish trio then proceeded to beat the top seeds from USA and the defending champions from England before ending Australia's hopes of a third success in the final. The subsequent celebrations matched anything seen before at Landsdowne Road and lasted long enough to see Rafferty win the Equity and Law Challenge at Royal Mid-Surrey and Smyth add the Jersey Open title to his name. Such has been the growth in interest centred around the European Tour in recent times that smaller events like the Jersey Open – shuffled around the calendar to fill the inevitable gaps. Though one of the most popular tournaments as far as the pros themselves are concerned, the Jersey tournament has found itself clashing with both the US Masters and the USPGA. In 1988 it fell on the penultimate week of the season when the top names wanted nothing more than to prepare for the inaugural Volvo Masters.

The Volvo Masters, staged at Valderrama in Southern Spain, was a new concept brought about as a result of the Swedish car giant's association with the Tour. Seen as the grand finale to the European season, just as the Nabisco World Championship of Golf is on the USPGA Tour, it offered £350,000 in prize money plus a further inducement to enter in that a bonus pool of £200,000 was also available to the leading 15 competitors on the Order of Merit who agreed to tee up in Spain. Not surprisingly the event produced one of the strongest fields of the season. It could not affect Seve Ballesteros' unassailable lead at the top of the money list, but it did result in a win for the man who was, at one and the same time, both the most consistent and the most unfortunate competitor of the year. Earlier in 1988 Nick Faldo had been bridesmaid more often than Elizabeth Taylor has been a bride. Though this victory was his second of the season after the Peugeot French Open, most of us will remember instead the ones which got away. Altogether the former Open champion finished runner-up seven times during the course of the Volvo tour – in the Barcelona Open, the Spanish Open, the Dunhill British Masters, the Benson & Hedges, the Irish Open, the European Open and the Suntory – but he suffered his most galling moment when he lost out in an 18-hole play-off to Curtis Strange in the US Open. With this spate of second place finishes in mind it was entirely appropriate that Faldo's win in Spain should elevate him to second on the Order of Merit table behind Ballesteros. It was a place he had occupied for much of the European season.

European Tour Results 1988

Open De Baleares
at Santa Ponsa Mallorca

Name	Score	Prize £
S Ballesteros	70-68-67-67—272	33330
J-M Olazabal	68-73-64-73—278	22200
G Brand Jr	76-68-70-66—280	12520
R Rafferty	73-70-70-70—283	8490
B Lane	71-73-67-72—283	8490
M Poxon	72-72-69-70—283	8490
J Jacobs	71-73-68-72—284	6000
D Smyth	73-71-72-69—285	5000
M James	73-70-71-72—286	3646
M Pinero	72-71-74-69—286	3646
P Jones	72-72-71-71—286	3646
P Baker	71-73-70-72—286	3646
J Slaughter	68-72-73-73—286	3646
C McClellan	71-73-73-69—286	3646

Barcelona Open
at Real Club de Golf El Prat Barcelona

Name	Score	Prize £
D Whelan	68-65-74-69—276	33330
M Mouland	71-68-69-68—276	14906
N Faldo	66-68-71-71—276	14906
B Lane	71-69-67-69—276	14906
(D Whelan won play-off)		
J Rystrom	70-69-68-71—278	8470
S Torrance	75-68-68-68—279	7000
D Gilford	68-73-68-71—280	4433
M Mackenzie	72-68-68-72—280	4433
P Harrison	71-68-73-68—280	4433
C O'Connor Jr	72-69-71-68—280	4433
P Teravainen	68-71-69-72—280	4433
P Baker	75-69-70-66—280	4433

AGF Biarritz Open

at Biarritz GC

Name	Score	Prize £
D Llewellyn	64-69-60-65—258	23691
C O'Connor Jr	66-66-65-68—265	15787
B Lane	71-65-63-67—266	8002
J Rivero	67-63-69-67—266	8002
M James	67-69-65-66—267	4705
G Brand Jr	64-69-68-66—267	4705
M Allen	67-66-69-65—267	4705
P Walton	65-66-67-69—267	4705
S Bishop	64-70-68-66—268	2771
N Hansen	68-66-66-68—268	2771
J Rutledge	66-67-66-69—268	2771
E Darcy	63-71-67-67—268	2771

Cannes Open

at Cannes Mougins

Name	Score	Prize £
M McNulty	72-71-70-66—279	31588
R Commans	70-68-72-72—282	16453
J Sindelar	69-74-69-70—282	16453
D Durnian	72-69-74-70—285	9477
T Charnley	71-75-74-66—286	7330
J Rutledge	72-75-71-68—286	7330
H Clark	70-72-73-72—287	5686
P Walton	71-73-68-76—288	4065
J-M Olazabal	74-69-72-73—288	4065
O Sellberg	71-77-70-70—288	4065
J Anglada	72-74-71-71—288	4065
W Riley	68-75-75-71—289	3156
M Allen	71-73-76-69—289	3156

Cepsa Madrid Open

at Real Club de Puerta de Hierro

Name	Score	Prize £
D Cooper	70-68-69-68—275	33330
M Pinero	69-69-67-71—276	17360
M Martin	69-69-68-70—276	17360
S Ballesteros	69-68-69-72—278	10000
H Clark	69-76-71-64—280	6190
M McNulty	71-67-71-71—280	6190
J Morgan	68-72-68-72—280	6190
M James	71-70-69-70—280	6190
B Gallacher	69-71-70-70—280	6190
I Gervas	65-69-73-74—281	3840
D Ray	72-73-69-67—281	3840

Lancia Italian Open

at Monticello Milan

Name	Score	Prize £
G Norman	69-68-63-70—270	35319
C Parry	65-68-67-71—271	23531
R Rafferty	66-70-67-69—272	13271
D Durnian	67-70-68-68—273	9794
R Chapman	66-68-69-70—273	9794
G Brand Jr	67-68-70-69—274	6889
I Woosnam	68-68-69-69—274	6889
P Parkin	65-72-68-70—275	5024
P Senior	70-69-67-69—275	5024
D Whelan	63-71-70-72—276	4070
B Shearer	67-70-71-68—276	4070
B Lane	67-69-71-70—277	3354
C Montgomerie	68-71-68-70—277	3354
R Davis	65-74-69-69—277	3354
J Rivero	66-68-71-72—277	3354

Epson Grand Prix of Europe Match-Play Championship

at St Pierre Chepstow Gwent

First Round:

K Brown (Scot) beat M Persson (Swe) 2 and 1
D Smyth (Ire) beat J Hawkes (SA) 5 and 4
C O'Connor Jr (Ire) beat M Mouland (Wal) 3 and 2
R Davis (Aus) beat P Way (Eng) 1 hole
D Durnian (Eng) beat N Ratcliffe (Aus) 5 and 3
G Ralph (Eng) beat B Lane (Eng) 1 hole
B Longmuir (Scot) beat O Sellberg (Swe) at 19th
B Marchbank (Scot) beat P Hartmann (USA) 4 and 2
T Johnstone (Zim) beat J Rivero (Sp) 1 hole
A Forsbrand (Swe) beat P Malley (USA) 3 and 1
J Morgan (Eng) beat T Charnley (Eng) 3 and 2
GJ Brand (Eng) beat D Llewellyn (Wal) 3 and 1
A Garrido (Sp) beat M James (Eng) at 19th
C Mason (Eng) beat J O'Leary (Ire) 4 and 2
R Lee (Eng) beat E Darcy (Ire) 5 and 3
H Clark (Eng) beat J-M Olazabal (Sp) 2 holes
M Roe (Eng) beat G Levenson (SA) 3 and 1
M Martin (Sp) beat H Baiocchi (SA) 3 and 1
P Walton (Ire) beat J Bland (SA) at 19th
P Fowler (Aus) beat J-M Canizares (Sp) 2 and 1
I Mosey (Eng) beat S Torrance (Scot) 3 and 2
DA Russell (Eng) beat R Rafferty (N Ire) 1 hole
DJ Russell (Eng) beat D Feherty (N Ire) at 20th
R Chapman (Eng) beat M Pinero (Sp) 1 hole
(All first round losers received £1715)

Second Round:

I Woosnam (Wal) beat K Brown (Scot) 2 and 1
D Smyth (Ire) beat C O'Connor Jr (Ire) at 21st
R Davis (Aus) beat D Durnian (Eng) 1 hole
G Ralph (Eng) beat M Lanner (Swe) 1 hole
B Langer (W Ger) beat B Longmuir (Scot) at 19th
T Johnstone (Zim) beat B Marchbank (Scot) at 19th

Second Round cont'd:

J Morgan (Eng) beat A Forsbrand (Swe) 5 and 3
GJ Brand (Eng) beat G Brand Jr (Scot) 2 and 1
A Garrido (Sp) beat N Faldo (Eng) 2 and 1
C Mason (Eng) beat R Lee (Eng) 2 and 1
H Clark (Eng) beat M Roe (Eng) 2 and 1
M Martin (Sp) beat P Senior (Aus) 3 and 2
M Kuramoto (Jap) beat P Walton (Ire) 1 hole
I Mosey (Eng) beat P Fowler (Aus) 1 hole
DJ Russell (Eng) beat DA Russell (Eng) 1 hole
M McNulty (Zim) beat R Chapman (Eng) 3 and 2
(All second round losers received £3000)

Third Round:

D Smyth (Ire) beat I Woosnam (Wal) 2 and 1
R Davis (Aus) beat G Ralph (Eng) 4 and 3
B Langer (W Ger) beat T Johnstone (Zim) 2 and 1
J Morgan (Eng) beat GJ Brand (Eng) at 19th
C Mason (Eng) beat A Garrido (Sp) at 20th
H Clark (Eng) beat M Martin (Sp) 4 and 2
M Kuramoto (Jap) beat I Mosey (Eng) at 20th
M McNulty (Zim) beat DJ Russell (Eng) 5 and 4
(All third round losers received £4750)

Quarter Finals:

R Davis (Aus) beat D Smyth (Ire) 3 and 1
B Langer (W Ger) beat J Morgan (Eng) 1 hole
H Clark (Eng) beat C Mason (Eng) 5 and 4
M McNulty (Zim) beat M Kuramoto (Jap) 3 and 2
(Quarter final losers received £9,100)

Semi-Finals:

M McNulty (Zim) beat H Clark (Eng) 3 and 2
B Langer (W Ger) beat R Davis (Aus) 1 hole

Play-off for 3rd and 4th place:

R Davis (Aus) beat H Clark (Eng) 3 and 2
(Davis won £17190 and Clark won £13750)

Final:

B Langer (W Ger) beat M McNulty (Zim) 4 and 3
(Langer won £50000 and McNulty won £30500)

Peugeot French Open

at Chantilly Paris

Name	Score	Prize £
N Faldo	71-67-68-68—274	47236
D Durnian	65-68-69-74—276	24600
W Riley	72-67-67-70—276	24600
C Moore	71-69-69-69—278	13084
D Feherty	72-70-66-70—278	13084
P Senior	70-69-68-72—279	9919
R Rafferty	73-69-74-64—280	7794
D Williams	73-67-69-71—280	7794
M MacKenzie	72-70-68-72—282	5526
S Torrance	69-73-70-70—282	5526
M Martin	75-68-65-74—282	5526
A Forsband	72-72-67-71—282	5526
C Strange	70-73-70-70—283	4563

Wang Four Stars National Pro-Celebrity

at Moor Park GC Herts

Name	Score	Prize £
R Davis	69-63-71-72—275	30000
J-M Canizares	69-67-69-71—276	16350
E Darcy	67-68-69-72—276	16350
D Ray	67-69-69-74—279	9300
M Harwood	69-70-70-72—281	7300
B Lane	71-69-69-72—281	7300
G Brand Jr	69-70-71-72—282	4284
E Dussart	70-74-67-71—282	4284
M Roe	72-71-66-73—282	4284
J Slaughter	68-73-71-70—282	4284
D Smyth	71-71-71-69—282	4284

Volvo PGA Championship

at Wentworth

Name	Score	Prize £
I Woosnam	67-70-70-67—274	50000
S Ballesteros	67-68-71-70—276	26040
M James	68-72-68-68—276	26040
R Chapman	70-71-71-66—278	13850
M McNulty	67-71-69-71—278	13850
J Hawkes	67-70-70-72—279	10500
J Bland	72-70-69-69—280	7740
B Langer	67-66-74-73—280	7740
S Lyle	70-76-68-66—280	7740
N Faldo	71-70-71-69—281	6000
J-M Canizares	69-68-70-75—282	5340
J-M Olazabal	68-66-78-70—282	5340

Jersey Open

at La Moye Jersey

Name	Score	Prize £
D Smyth	69-68-69-67—273	20330
R Chapman	68-68-68-69—273	13540
(D Smyth won play-off)		
C Mason	66-68-69-71—274	5795
P Way	71-69-65-69—274	5795
R McFarlane	67-70-65-72—274	5795
N Hansen	68-69-69-68—274	5795
D Whelan	71-68-68-68—275	3660
C O'Connor Jr	66-71-69-70—276	2887
C Moody	64-71-69-72—276	2887
S Bottomley	68-70-70-69—277	2265
S Tinning	68-69-71-69—277	2265
D Gilford	71-70-68-68—277	2265

Dunhill Masters'

at Woburn G & CC Milton Keynes

Name	Score	Prize £
S Lyle	66-68-68-71—273	41660
N Faldo	72-67-67-69—275	21705
M McNulty	69-69-72-65—275	21705
J-M Olazabal	69-68-71-68—276	12500
R Rafferty	72-67-71-69—279	10600
M James	68-75-71-67—281	8125
P Walton	73-68-71-69—281	8125
J-M Canizares	74-71-69-68—282	6250
K Brown	74-67-74-68—283	4875
R Davis	70-71-70-72—283	4875
B Shearer	70-71-71-71—283	4875
L Trevino	69-75-70-69—283	4875

Volvo Belgian Open

at Bercuit Brussels

Name	Score	Prize £
J-M Olazabal	67-69-64-69—269	33330
M Smith	67-73-63-70—273	22200
GJ Brand	69-70-67-71—277	11260
O Sellberg	68-71-70-68—277	11260
P Baker	68-73-67-70—278	8470
E Romero	72-69-71-67—279	5620
T Johnstone	69-68-71-71—279	5620
R Rafferty	68-70-69-72—279	5620
S Bennett	71-72-69-67—279	5620
M Lanner	73-69-68-70—280	3840
C Mason	69-68-73-70—280	3840
G Brand Jr	71-66-74-70—281	3240
W Riley	68-69-71-73—281	3240
T Armour III	68-72-71-70—281	3240

PLM Open

at Flomen Falsterbo Sweden

Name	Score	Prize £
F Nobilo	63-68-71-68—270	33126
H Clark	68-69-68-66—271	22064
P Fowler	65-69-72-70—276	10267
A Forsbrand	67-66-72-71—276	10267
C Montgomerie	66-67-74-69—276	10267
O Sellberg	69-68-72-69—278	6957
A Sorensen	69-68-71-71—279	5963
C Parry	67-67-76-70—280	4094
T Charnley	66-66-76-72—280	4094
M Persson	68-71-72-69—280	4094
S Bennett	72-69-67-72—280	4094
M Mouland	68-74-69-69—280	4094
S Tinning	72-68-74-67—281	3200

Johnnie Walker Monte Carlo Open

at Mont Angel

Name	Score	Prize £
J Rivero	65-64-67-65—261	35013
M McNulty	66-62-68-67—263	23342
S Ballesteros	65-66-67-68—266	13151
L Stephen	72-68-62-66—268	10504
H Baiocchi	67-68-67-68—270	8887
N Faldo	71-65-69-67—272	7352
J Hawkes	66-70-71-66—273	5777
BE Smith	71-67-68-67—273	5777
G Levenson	67-66-70-71—274	4445
P Senior	70-68-67-69—274	4445
M Allen	69-71-70-65—275	3209
A Garrido	68-68-68-71—275	3209
B Shearer	73-67-65-70—275	3209
C Parry	68-65-68-74—275	3209
M Calero	69-67-71-68—275	3209
A Sherborne	65-69-72-69—275	3209
P Teravainen	72-64-68-71—275	3209
M Persson	68-69-65-73—275	3209

Bell's Scottish Open

at Gleneagles Perthshire

Name	Score	Prize £
B Lane	70-67-66-68—271	41660
J Rivero	64-70-72-68—274	21705
S Lyle	68-69-69-68—274	21705
R Chapman	68-68-67-72—275	12500
P Fowler	71-63-69-73—276	10600
J-M Olazabal	71-70-67-69—277	8125
M Lanner	71-71-72-63—277	8125
D Gilford	69-70-70-69—278	5362
R Davis	74-66-68-70—278	5362
R Weir	66-72-67-73—278	5362
D Graham	71-69-70-68—278	5362
M O'Meara	70-69-67-73—279	4046
M Harwood	68-65-75-71—279	4046
I Woosnam	68-71-71-69—279	4046

Scandinavian Enterprise Open

at Ullna GC Stockholm

Name	Score	Prize £
S Ballesteros	67-70-66-67—270	41660
G Taylor	67-68-71-69—275	27760
G Marsh	66-66-77-67—276	14075
P Senior	66-68-72-70—276	14076
KH Han	68-69-69-71—277	9675

Name	Score	Prize £
G Brand Jr	65-71-68-73—277	9675
C Stadler	68-69-69-72—278	6450
C Parry	64-69-73-72—278	6450
R Boxall	72-66-68-72—278	6450
B Ogle	73-67-69-70—279	4480
P McWhinney	66-68-78-67—279	4480
R Rafferty	70-68-72-69—279	4480
DJ Russell	68-68-66-77—279	4480

English Open
at Royal Birkdale Lancs

Name	Score	Prize £
H Clark	72-71-67-69—279	30000
P Baker	73-70-69-70—282	20000
D Smyth	74-65-70-74—283	10150
P McWhinney	75-67-74-67—283	10150
S McAllister	73-69-73-69—284	7000
M Martin	74-71-72-67—284	7000
DJ Russell	74-70-70-71—285	5400
T Charnley	74-73-69-70—286	4130
B Longmuir	74-70-72-70—286	4130
R Boxall	74-71-76-66—287	3300
M Mouland	75-73-70-69—287	3300
M James	74-68-75-70—287	3300
M Poxon	76-70-72-70—288	2575
B Gallacher	72-73-72-71—288	2575
M Pendaries	74-74-72-68—288	2575
A Murray	79-70-70-69—288	2575
D Cooper	74-73-71-70—288	2575
C Moody	72-68-72-76—288	2575
P Walton	77-69-71-71—288	2575
A Sherborne	72-74-69-73—288	2575

KLM Dutch Open
at Hilversum

Name	Score	Prize £
M Mouland	72-68-69-65—274	41660
D Smyth	71-67-67-70—275	27760
C Mason	69-69-72-66—276	14075
T Johnstone	68-66-68-74—276	14075
M Martin	71-72-68-66—277	10600
J-M Olazabal	69-67-71-71—278	8125
C Parry	70-70-67-71—278	8125
A Murray	65-76-67-71—279	5616
D Williams	68-71-68-72—279	5616
M McNulty	70-69-67-73—279	5616
L Carbonetti	70-72-69-69—280	4185
M Roe	69-66-73-72—280	4185
M Persson	70-69-69-72—280	4185
D Graham	73-70-69-68—280	4185

Carrolls Irish Open

at Port Marnock Co Dublin Eire

Name	Score	Prize £
I Woosnam	68-70-70-70—278	38689
J-M Olazabal	66-70-74-75—285	15443
D Smyth	68-73-71-73—285	15443
M Pinero	69-68-75-73—285	15443
N Faldo	71-68-73-73—285	15443
E Darcy	69-68-75-74—286	6102
P Walton	69-68-75-74—286	6102
B Shearer	69-70-77-70—286	6102
M Sludds	70-72-71-73—286	6102
R Chapman	73-71-69-73—286	6102
P Mitchell	70-70-74-73—287	4004
M Roe	71-70-75-71—287	4004
M James	75-69-71-72—287	4004

Benson & Hedges International Open

at Fulford York

Name	Score	Prize £
P Baker	68-68-66-69—271	41660
N Faldo	68-68-66-69—271	27760
(P Baker won play-off)		
J-M Olazabal	70-71-66-65—272	14075
C Parry	68-68-69-67—272	14075
M James	72-69-68-65—274	10600
S Lyle	70-67-69-69—275	8750
C O'Connor Jr	70-65-71-70—276	7500
H Clark	72-70-68-67—277	5362
E Dussart	68-71-69-69—277	5362
D Smyth	70-70-65-72—277	5362
M McNulty	68-68-68-73—277	5362
D Durnian	75-69-70-64—278	3866
H Baiocchi	71-69-71-67—278	3866
J Anderson	72-69-70-67—278	3866
P Walton	71-70-68-69—278	3866
G Marsh	71-68-69-70—278	3866

Lufthansa German Open

at Frankfurt

Name	Score	Prize £
S Ballesteros	68-68-65-62—263	47244
G Brand Jr	67-69-62-70—268	31464
M Clayton	68-68-68-65—269	15959
B Longmuir	71-67-67-64—269	15959
M James	71-69-65-65—270	12000
R Boxall	68-69-62-72—271	7965
D Smyth	66-69-69-67—271	7965
C Mason	67-71-66-67—271	7965
BE Smith	67-67-69-68—271	7965
P Senior	67-69-66-70—272	5253

Name	Score	Prize £
F Nobilo	67-68-69-68—272	5253
M Smith	71-66-67-68—272	5253
C Parry	67-71-67-68—273	4266
J Hawkes	68-70-71-64—273	4266
D Durnian	67-70-65-71—273	4266
P Norton	70-65-71-67—273	4266

Ebel European Masters Swiss Open

at Crans-sur-Sierre Switzerland

Name	Score	Prize £
C Moody	68-68-67-65—268	65543
I Woosnam	68-66-66-69—269	29312
S Ballesteros	65-68-68-68—269	29312
A Forsbrand	67-71-67-64—269	29312
P Senior	70-68-64-68—270	16651
R Rafferty	70-66-69-67—272	13764
G Brand Jr	70-68-67-68—273	9107
D Frost	70-68-72-63—273	9107
J-M Olazabal	73-69-65-66—273	9107
B Ogle	73-68-65-67—273	9107
N Faldo	67-67-71-68—273	9107
M Mouland	68-70-72-64—274	6221
P Walton	71-69-66-68—274	6221
I Baker-Finch	71-71-68-64—274	6221
F Nobilo	67-72-67-68—274	6221

Panasonic European Open

at Walton Heath Surrey

Name	Score	Prize £
I Woosnam	65-66-64-65—260	50000
N Faldo	66-65-66-66—263	33300
J-M Olazabal	65-70-64-67—266	15493
S Lyle	69-65-67-65—266	15493
M James	66-70-63-67—266	15493
G Brand Jr	65-70-67-65—267	10500
C Parry	68-70-67-63—268	9000
J Rivero	68-65-66-70—269	7500
B Ogle	71-68-66-65—270	6360
P Baker	67-68-66-69—270	6360
D Durnian	64-67-69-71—271	5170
M McNulty	67-66-70-68—271	5170
M Lanner	68-63-69-71—271	5170
R Rafferty	67-74-64-67—272	4410
M Harwood	66-67-70-69—272	4410
D Williams	68-68-64-72—272	4410

German Masters

at Stuttgart

Name	Score	Prize £
J-M Olazabal	69-72-70-68—279	47770
A Forsbrand	75-68-70-68—281	24878
D Smyth	71-68-71-71—281	24878
T Purtzer	68-72-72-70—282	13232
M McNulty	69-72-71-70—282	13232
R Rafferty	75-69-72-68—284	9315
S Ballesteros	72-70-68-74—284	9315
J Hawkes	78-70-69-68—285	6793
J Rivero	71-71-72-71—285	6793
P Walton	70-71-75-70—286	5503
M Lanner	69-70-71-76—286	5503
E Darcy	66-76-71-74—287	4772
N Faldo	73-71-72-71—287	4772
S Lyle	69-75-72-72—288	4213
D Feherty	73-69-70-76—288	4213
I Mosey	70-72-72-74—288	4213

Suntory World Match-Play Championship

at Wentworth

First Round:

J Sluman beat N Serizawa 6 and 5
J Sindelar beat B Lane 5 and 4
N Price beat R Davis 2 and 1
M McCumber beat M McNulty 1 hole
(Each loser received £10000)

Second Round:

I Woosnam beat J Sluman 7 and 6
N Faldo beat J Sindelar 5 and 4
S Lyle beat N Price 3 and 2
S Ballesteros beat M McCumber at 37th
(Each loser received £15000)

Semi-Finals:

S Lyle beat S Ballesteros 7 and 6
N Faldo beat I Woosnam 1 hole

3rd and 4th place play-off

As play was abandoned on October 9th, the play-off was cancelled and the players shared the prize money.
(Ballesteros and Woosnam received £25000)

Final:

S Lyle beat N Faldo 2 and 1
(Lyle won £75000 and Faldo £40000)

Lancôme Trophy
at St Nom la Breteche Paris

Name	Score	Prize £
S Ballesteros	64-66-68-71—269	66660
J-M Olazabal	69-66-69-69—273	44400
G Norman	71-72-68-67—278	22520
S Lyle	75-63-68-72—278	22520
R Rafferty	71-70-75-63—279	16940
R Davis	71-73-71-65—280	14000
J Rivero	71-68-69-70—281	8220
P Baker	70-67-74-70—281	8220
C Moody	71-68-72-70—281	8220
J Bland	71-69-69-72—281	8220
C O'Connor Jr	72-72-70-67—281	8220
T Johnstone	74-71-67-69—281	8220
R Boxall	70-77-69-65—281	8220
J Hawkes	75-68-67-71—281	8220

Dunhill Nations Cup
at Old Course St Andrews

Preliminary Round:

ZIMBABWE 2; ARGENTINA 1
M Shumba beat E Romero 73 75
A Edwards beat M Fernandez 73-75
T Price lost to V Fernandez 75-72

SWEDEN 3; SINGAPORE 0
M Persson beat M Murugiah 74-77
A Forsbrand beat B Fung 76-80
O Sellberg beat SW Lim 71-78
(Each loser received £1720)

First Round:

USA 3; PHILIPPINES 0
C Strange beat E Bagtas 70-75
C Beck beat R Lambares 68-81
M McCumber beat F Minoza 72-75

IRELAND 2; CANADA 1
R Rafferty lost to D Barr 69-67
E Darcy beat D Halldorson 69-72
D Smyth beat R Zokol 69-76

SPAIN 3; ZIMBABWE 0
S Ballesteros beat T Price 72-74
J Rivero beat A Edwards 68-72
J-M Olazabal beat M Shumba 74-78

AUSTRALIA 3; BRAZIL 0
R Davis beat R Navarro 69-73
D Graham beat C Dluosh 68-79
G Norman beat P Diniz 71-73

ENGLAND 3; FRANCE 0
M James beat F Regard 66-75
B Lane beat M Tapia 70-75
N Faldo beat E Dussart 65-70

First Round cont'd:

SCOTLAND 3; THAILAND 0
G Brand Jr beat B Ruangkit 74-76
C Montgomerie beat S Meesawad 72-80
S Lyle beat S Springsangar 70-73

JAPAN 3; DENMARK 0
N Ozaki beat J Rasmuaawn 69-77
T Ozaki beat S Tinning 68-69
H Meshiai beat A Sorensen 72-75

WALES 3; SWEDEN 0
D Llewellyn beat M Persson 72-75
M Mouland beat O Sellberg 70-71
I Woosnam beat A Forsbrand 69-75
(Each loser received £4300)

Quarter-Finals:

AUSTRALIA 2; WALES 1
D Graham beat M Mouland 67-76
R Davis beat D Llewellyn 69-70
G Norman lost to I Woosnam 73-71

IRELAND 2; USA 0
R Rafferty beat M McCumber 71-72
D Smyth finished level with C Beck 71-71
E Darcy beat C Strange 66-68

SPAIN 3; JAPAN 0
S Ballesteros beat N Ozaki 72-74
J Rivero beat H Meshiai 65-68
J-M Olazabal beat T Ozaki 68-69

ENGLAND 2; SCOTLAND 1
B Lane lost to G Brand Jr 73-71
M James beat C Montgomerie 69-71
N Faldo beat S Lyle 67-68
(Each loser received £8600)

Semi-Finals:

AUSTRALIA 2; SPAIN 1
G Norman beat S Ballesteros 67-69
R Davis beat J Rivero 71-72
D Graham lost to J-M Olazabal 73-69

IRELAND 2; ENGLAND 1
R Rafferty lost to B Lane 68-65
D Smyth beat N Faldo 69-70
E Darcy beat M James 68-72

Play-off for 3rd and 4th place:

SPAIN 2; ENGLAND 1
J-M Olazabal lost to N Faldo 67-66
S Ballesteros beat B Lane 71-72
J Rivero beat M James 69-70
(England won £15290 each and Spain won £21024 each)

Final:

IRELAND 2; AUSTRALIA 1
D Smyth beat R Davis 71-73
R Rafferty beat D Graham 69-74
E Darcy lost to G Norman 71-63
(Australia won £28669 each and Ireland won £57,339 each)

Equity & Law Challenge

at Royal Mid-Surrey

Name	Points	Pars	Prize £
R Rafferty	21	31	20000
B Lane	20	31	10000
D Cooper	20	25	6500
M Roe	19	34	4000
E Romero	19	31	3000
D Durnian	19	29	2000
C Mason	18	32	1400
R Drummond	18	30	1000
J-M Olazabal	16	33	930
S Bennett	16	33	930
P Walton	16	32	880
M Allen	16	27	850
T Charnley	15	33	820
A Sherborne	15	33	820

(Competitors scored 1 point for a birdie, 2 points for an eagle and 3 points for an albatross. The position for players with equal points was decided by a countback of pars.)

Peugeot Spanish Open

at Real de Pedrena Santander

Name	Score	Prize £
M James	63-68-63-68—262	27703
N Faldo	68-67-62-68—265	18456
R Boxall	63-64-70-69—266	10406
GJ Brand	70-66-64-68—268	7677
C O'Connor Jr	67-66-69-66—268	7677
E Darcy	71-68-67-64—270	4986
J-M Olazabal	71-66-65-68—270	4986
M Martin	70-67-65-68—270	4986
G Brand Jr	69-68-68-66—271	3241
D Cooper	69-71-63-68—271	3241
D Williams	67-66-69-69—271	3241
C Montgomerie	69-64-70-68—271	3241

Portuguese Open

at Quinta do Lago

Name	Score	Prize £
M Harwood	73-70-68-69—280	33330
E Darcy	69-70-72-70—281	22200
P Baker	74-68-67-73—282	11260
D Smyth	70-74-68-70—282	11260
P Fowler	71-68-73-71—283	8470
I Gervas	74-70-69-71—284	7000
P Harrison	69-73-73-70—285	5500
J Rivero	73-72-71-69—285	5500
R Boxall	74-71-69-72—286	3646
GJ Brand	73-73-73-67—286	3646
T Johnstone	72-71-71-72—286	3646
M Mackenzie	74-70-70-72—286	3646
R Rafferty	71-71-70-74—286	3646
W Westner	74-70-73-69—286	3646

Volvo Masters

at Valderrama Spain

Name	Score	Prize £
N Faldo	74-71-71-68—284	58330
S Ballesteros	68-72-74-72—286	38860
S Lyle	68-71-75-74—288	21910
I Woosnam	75-74-70-70—289	17500
R Chapman	71-77-70-75—293	13540
E Darcy	74-71-74-74—293	13540
M Lanner	77-70-74-73—294	8522
A Sorensen	76-67-76-75—294	8522
P Fowler	77-71-71-75—294	8522
C O'Connor Jr	78-73-70-73—294	8522
J-M Canizares	76-76-67-76—295	6230
N Hansen	77-72-75-71—295	6230
H Clark	73-73-74-76—296	5490
M Pinero	74-71-81-70—296	5490
N Coles	78-76-72-71—297	5140

Europcar Cup

at Biarritz France

Pos		Score
1	Sweden (M Lanner, J Rystrom, J Parnevik, M Persson)	810
2	Spain (A Garrido, I Gervas, J Anglada, M Martin)	817
3	England (D Cooper, G Ralph, A Charnley, D Williams)	820
	Ireland (D Jones, J Heggarty, M Sludds, P Walton)	820
5	France	828
6	Wales (P Thomas, M Litton, G Davies, H Davies-Thomas)	830
7	Italy	832
8	West Germany	838
9	Scotland (W Longmuir, R Drummond, W McColl, M Miller)	840

(4 Rounds of Stroke-play, the best 3 scores to count towards team total)

Benson & Hedges Trophy

at Moraleja Golf Club Madrid Spain

Pos		Score
1	M McNulty (Zimbabwe) and M-L de Lorenzi Taya (France)	276
2	J M Cancares (Spain) and T Abitbol (Spain)	277
3	W Longmuir (Scotland) and F Descampe (Belgium)	278
	A Stubbs (England) and S Strudwick (England)	278
5	D Cooper (England) and P Conley (USA)	280
	A Sherborne (England) and K Douglas (England)	280
7	M Pinero (Spain) and M Figueras-Dotti (Spain)	282
	J Rivero (Spain) and X Wunsch-Ruiz (Spain)	282
	M Lanner (Sweden) and M Wennersten From (Sweden)	282
10	S Bishop (England) and D Dowling (England)	284

Kirin World Championship of Golf

at Kapalua Maui Hawaii

Day 1	European Tour beat Japan	9—3
	USA beat Australia/New Zealand	10-2
Day 2	Japan beat Australia/New Zealand	7-5
	USA beat European Tour	10-2
Day 3	Australia/New Zealand beat European Tour	7-5
	USA beat Japan	9-3

(Points: USA 29, European Tour 16, Australia/New Zealand 14, Japan 12)

Final	USA beat European Tour	8-4
3rd place play-off	Australia/New Zealand beat Japan	8-4

Team Prize Money

USA	$360000
European Tour	$210000
Australia/New Zealand	$180000
Japan	$150000

World Cup

at Royal Melbourne Victoria Australia

Pos		Score
1	United States	
	(B Crenshaw 275, M McCumber 285)	560
2	Japan	
	(T Ozaki 276, M Ozaki 285)	561
3	Australia	
	(P Senior 278, R Mackay 284)	562
4	Canada	
	(D Barr 277, B Franklin 292)	569
5	Scotland	
	(G Brand Jr 279, C Montgomerie 291)	570
6	New Zealand	
	(F Noble 284, G Turner 287)	571
Individual		
	B Crenshaw (USA)	275
	T Ozaki (Japan)	276
	D Barr (Canada)	277
	P Senior (Australia)	278

Safari Tour 1988

Nigerian Open
at Ikoyi Club Lagos

Name	Score	Prize £
V Singh	72-70-68-71—281	8829
M Miller	65-72-73-71—281	5886
(V Singh won play-off)		
M Gregson	73-71-69-71—284	2982
P Akakasiaka	72-70-70-72—284	2982
P Kent	70-70-68-77—285	2050
J Lebbie	70-73-71-71—285	2050
J Morgan	70-78-68-71—287	1366
A Stevens	69-69-76-73—287	1366
D Wood	70-74-73-70—287	1366

Ivory Coast Open
at President GC Yamoussoukro

Name	Score	Prize £
GJ Brand	68-71-67-69—275	12819
R Fish	69-73-67-68—277	8538
J Annable	69-67-71-72—279	4330
T Stevens	70-69-72-68—279	4330
J Higgins	71-70-67-72—280	2752
J McHenry	74-74-66-66—280	2752
V Singh	72-70-69-69—280	2752
J Morgan	70-72-70-69—281	1923
E Dussart	74-68-71-69—282	1723
W Grant	70-76-70-67—283	1425
M Miller	71-70-70-72—283	1425
D Blakeman	76-69-69-69—283	1425

555 Kenya Open
at Muthaiga GC Nairobi

Name	Score	Prize £
C Platts	66-65-72-68—271	11442
M Mouland	71-67-70-64—272	7751
V Singh	71-68-67-69—275	4328
P Harrison	69-71-70-66—276	3406
P Kent	72-69-68-69—278	2885

Name	Score	Prize £
D James	72-64-72-71—279	1850
C Laurence	73-70-66-70—279	1850
C Mason	69-72-67-71—279	1850
R McFarlane	68-76-67-68—279	1850
A Stubbs	71-68-71-69—279	1850

Zimbabwe Open

at Chapman GC Harare

Name	Score	Prize £
R Chapman	63-70-71-71—275	7356
V Singh	64-68-72-72—276	4901
C Mason	65-70-71-71—277	2280
C Montgomerie	66-72-66-73—277	2280
D William	66-70-67-74—277	2280
J Higgins	64-72-71-71—278	1324
M Mouland	64-74-68-72—278	1324
M Roe	64-69-74-71—278	1324

Zambia Open

at Lusaka GC Zambia

Name	Score	Prize £
D Llewellyn	72-70-68-70—280	12500
R Fish	71-72-70-68—281	8320
G Ralph	72-73-71-71—287	4690
J Pinsent	72-73-74-70—289	3460
J Higgins	67-79-70-73—289	3460
J McHenry	77-71-76-66—290	2435
C Platts	72-74-71-73—290	2435
S Cipa	73-70-73-75—291	1875
J Morgan	76-71-75-70—292	1680
G Turner	73-76-74-70—293	1440
V Singh	76-74-72-71—293	1440
M Krantz	75-72-73-74—294	1250
J Vingoe	73-73-75-73—294	1250
M Miller	73-73-75-74—295	1125
E Murray	79-69-75-72—295	1125
J Spence	77-75-71-73—296	1013
P Harrison	75-73-73-75—296	1013
J Gervas	75-74-72-75—296	1013

Safari Tour Money List 1988

Pos	Name	Total Prize Money £
1	V Singh (Fii)	22252
2	R Fish (Eng)	18134
3	C Platts (Eng)	15328
4	D Llewellyn (Wal)	14143
5	GJ Brand (Eng)	13139
6	M Mouland (Wal)	9076
7	M Miller (Scot)	8913
8	J Higgins (Eng)	8911
9	R Chapman (Eng)	8521
10	T Stevens (Eng)	8066
11	J McHenry (Ire)	6959
12	P Kent (Eng)	6736
13	J Pinsent (Eng)	5972
14	J Morgan (Eng)	5509
15	G Ralph (Eng)	5509
16	J Annable (Eng)	5505
17	P Harrison (Eng)	4938
18	C Montgomerie (Scot)	4877
19	M Gregson (Eng)	4635
20	C Manson (Eng)	4131
21	C Laurence (Eng)	4128
22	P Akakasiaka (Nig)	3824
23	D Wood (Eng)	3818
24	D Jagger (Eng)	3571
25	D Blakeman (Eng)	3515
26	D Williams (Eng)	3506
27	A Stubbs (Eng)	3428
28	F Regard (Fr)	3400
29	W Grant (Eng)	3351
30	S Cipa (Eng)	3055
31	E Dussart (Fr)	3019
32	D James (Scot)	3010
33	G Harvey (Scot)	2968
34	P Cowen (Eng)	2956

PGA European Tour Final Statistics

PGA European Tour Prize Money, 1988

	Official Money	No of OM Events	Average OM Prize Fund	'Approved' Money	Total
	£		£	£	£
1979	1,102,220 (76.43%)	23	48,439	340,000 (23,57%)	1,442,220
1980	1,304,830 (76.22%)	22	59,310	407,100 (23.78%)	1,711,930
1981	1,442,555 (74.85%)	22	65,570	363,925 (20.15%)	1,806,480
1982	1,885,975 (82.07%)	26	72,537	412,060 (17.93%)	2,298,035
1983	2,410,931 (85.72%)	27	89,293	401,405 (14.28%)	2,812,336
1984	2,908,879 (85.49%)	26	111,880	493,886 (14.51%)	3,402,765
1985	3,460,726 (72.71%)	26	133,109	1,298,864 (27.29%)	4,759,590
1986	4,333,178 (76.55%)	26	166,661	1,327,300 (23.45%)	5,660,478
1987	5,755,137 (72.90%)	27	213,153	2,139,155 (27.10%)	7.894,292
1988	7,913,251 (78.77%)	30	263,775	2,132,317 (21.23%)	10,045,568

Details of 1988 Prize Money

	£		£
Official Prize Money in 30 Volvo Order of Merit Tournaments	7,682,124		
Extra Prize Money beyond 65th place	31,127		
Volvo Bonus Pool	200,000		7,913,251
Other 'Approved' Prize Money not in Volvo Order of Merit			
	£	£	
Special Events:			
Volvo Seniors British Open	149,790		
Dunhill Cup: Finals	583,716		
European Pre-qualifying	54,255		
Equity & Law Challenge	84,000		
Europcar Cup	74,160		
Benson & Hedges Trophy (PGA European Tour Members)	60,000		
Suntory World Match-play Championship	265,000		
Kirin Cup (PGA European Tour Members)	196,883		
World Cup (PGA European Tour Members)	196,883	1,589,179	
Pro-Ams: with Tournaments	149,180		
One-day Official	170,201	319,381	
Satellite Tournaments: Rolex Trophy	29,026		
Bolton Old Links Tournament	15,000		
Belstaff Young Masters	15,000		
Broadstone Tournament	15,000		
Motorola Southern PGA Championship	69,000		
UAP Under 25s Championship	70,006		
Pre-qualifying for Open Championship: Regionals	4,725		
Finals	6,000	223,757	2,132,317
			10,045,568
Safari Tour			
Prize Money from 5 Tournaments		319,646	

PGA Final Statistics, 1988

(Provided by Phillips Radio Communication Systems)

Driving Distance

		Yards
1	S Ballesteros	272
2	W Riley	269
3	I Woosnam	267
4	J De Forest	266
	S Lyle	266
	J Rutledge	266
7	D Cooper	265
	P Walton	265
	I Young	265
10	S Torrance	264
11	B Longmuir	263
12	B Lane	262
13	G Brand Jr	260
	R Chapman	260
	R Davis	260
	J Rivero	260
17	M Allen	259
	P Fowler	259
	M Lanner	259
	M Mackenzie	259
	E Romero	259
22	H Clark	258

Fairways Hit

		%
1	E Dussart	75
2	N Faldo	74
3	A Garrido	73
4	M Clayton	71
5	M McNulty	70
6	DA Russell	69
7	H Baiocchi	68
	D Gilford	68
	D Llewellyn	68
	C Mason	68
	J Morgan	68
12	J-M Canizares	67
	D Durnian	67
	M James	67
	C Parry	67
	R Rafferty	67
	A Sorenson	67

Fairways Hit cont'd

		%
18	T Charnley	66
	A Murray	66
	J Rivero	66
21	GJ Brand	65
	M Martin	65
	P Mitchell	65
	C O'Connor Jr	65
	M Pinero	65

Greens in Regulation

		%
1	M James	75.2
2	N Faldo	75
	I Woosnam	75
4	S Torrance	74
5	J-M Olazabal	73
6	P Fowler	72
	S Lyle	72
	P Mitchell	72
	C Parry	72
10	A Garrido	71
	R Rafferty	71
12	H Baiocchi	70
	T Charnley	70
	H Clark	70
	E Darcy	70
	R Davis	70
	B Lane	70
	J Rivero	70
19	R Chapman	69
	M McNulty	69
	C Mason	69
	O Moore	69
	J Morgan	69
	A Murray	69
	F Nobilo	69
	D Williams	69
	S Ballesteros	69
	GJ Brand	69
	D Durnian	69

Putts Per Round

		Avg
1	S Ballesteros	28.25
2	P Baker	29.00
3	C O'Connor Jr	29.19
4	M Martin	29.20
5	M Pinero	29.25
6	J Heggarty	29.36
7	R Boxall	29.42
8	G Ralph	29.64

Putts Per Round cont'd

		%
9	J Jacobs	29.67
10	M McNulty	29.69
11	J Haas	29.75
12	J Morgan	29.82
13	R Rafferty	29.90
14	P Curry	30.00
	N Faldo	30.00
	S Lyle	30.00
	DA Russell	30.00
18	C Montgomerie	30.07
	A Sorensen	30.07
20	J Calero	30.11
21	D Llewellyn	30.13
22	G Brand Jr	30.14
	N Hansen	30.14
24	S Bennett	30.15
	A Sherborne	30.15

Sand-Saves

		%
1	I Woosnam	76
2	J Rystrom	67
3	M Pinero	60
4	D Durnian	59
	N Faldo	59
6	M James	58
7	S Lyle	57
8	F Allem	56
	R Chapman	56
	M Jonsson	56
11	S Ballesteros	55
	P Fowler	55
	J Jacobs	55
	P Mitchell	55
	J Slaughter	55
16	J Morgan	54
17	M Clayton	53
	J Rivero	53
19	H Clark	52
	G Ralph	52
21	B Lane	51
	W Riley	51

The 1988 Volvo Order of Merit

1988 Official Money List

Pos	Name	Country	Official Prize Money £
1	Severiano Ballesteros	Sp	451,559.59
2	Nick Faldo	Eng	347,971.47
3	José-Maria Olazabal	Sp	285,964.33
4	Ian Woosnam	Wal	234,990.64
5	Sandy Lyle	Scot	186,017.98
6	Mark McNulty	Zim	180,991.55
7	Des Smyth	Ire	171,951.02
8	Mark James	Eng	152,900.37
9	Ronan Rafferty	N Ire	132,394.66
10	José Rivero	Sp	131,079.42
11	Gordon Brand Jr	Scot	129,296.79
12	Peter Baker	Eng	125,182.08
13	Howard Clark	Eng	124,373.64
14	Barry Lane	Eng	119,209.83
15	Eamonn Darcy	Ire	112,335.22
16	Peter Senior	Aus	103,101.47
17	Roger Chapman	Eng	99,758.15
18	Mark Mouland	Wal	95,580.95
19	Chris Moody	Eng	95,567.27
20	Denis Durnian	Eng	94,909.32
21	Rodger Davis	Aus	93,203.49
22	Anders Forsbrand	Swe	89,880.90
23	Christy O'Connor Jr	Ire	84,456.52
24	Craig Parry	Aus	81,782.54
25	Miguel Martin	Sp	76,184.19
26	Carl Mason	Eng	75,887.22
27	Richard Boxall	Eng	72,392.80
28	Gordon J Brand	Eng	69,908.20
29	Mike Harwood	Aus	68,843.27
30	Bernhard Langer	W Ger	66,368.38
31	Philip Walton	Ire	66,155.98
32	Derrick Cooper	Eng	65,101.68
33	Frank Nobilo	NZ	64,706.19
34	Wayne Riley	Aus	63,782.92
35	Manuel Pinero	Sp	63,006.12
36	Peter Fowler	Aus	59,521.61
37	José-Maria Canizares	Sp	54,474.75
38	Tony Johnstone	Zim	53,792.85
39	Tony Charnley	Eng	51,604.31
40	David Whelan	Eng	51,450.83
41	Jeff Hawkes	SA	51,034.93
42	David J Russell	Eng	50,782.40
43	David Williams	Eng	48,580.03
44	Mats Lanner	Swe	43,533.75
45	David Feherty	N Ire	43,346.29
46	Mark Roe	Eng	42,835.37
47	Mike Smith	USA	42,828.55
48	Eduardo Romero	Arg	42,752.93
49	David Llewellyn	Wal	42,680.30

Pos	Name	Country	Official Prize Money £
50	Andrew Murray	Eng	42,252.11
51	Sam Torrance	Scot	42,251.69
52	Colin Montgomerie	Scot	39,201.42
53	Mike Clayton	Aus	39,041.01
54	Michael Allen	USA	37,351.07
55	Stephen Bennett	Eng	37,162.23
56	John Morgan	Eng	36,262.84
57	Ove Sellberg	Swe	35,964.76
58	Jim Rutledge	Can	34,507.49
59	Malcolm Mackenzie	Eng	34,313.20
60	Bill Longmuir	Scot	34,029.34
61	John Bland	SA	33,888.63
62	Ian Mosey	Eng	33,576.75
63	Andrew Sherborne	Eng	33,288.29
64	Jerry Anderson	Can	33,195.36
65	Gerry Taylor	Aus	31,542.50
66	Magnus Persson	Swe	30,957.60
67	David Gilford	Eng	30,626.07
68	Hugh Baiocchi	SA	29,781.23
69	Ossie Moore	Aus	29,208.23
70	Philip Harrison	Eng	29,088.00
71	Brett Ogle	Aus	28,936.93
72	Neil Hansen	Eng	28,716.96
73	Ron Commans	USA	27,995.81
74	Manuel Calero	Sp	27,665.99
75	Martin Poxon	Eng	26,852.58
76	Peter Mitchell	Eng	26,623.93
77	Brian Marchbank	Scot	26,174.21
78	Anders Sorensen	Den	26,016.22
79	Johan Rystrom	Swe	25,605.20
80	Bob Shearer	Aus	25,331.01
81	John Slaughter	USA	25,181.43
82	David A Russell	Eng	25,165.56
83	Juan Anglada	Sp	25,161.83
84	Antonio Garrido	Sp	24,374.85
85	Paul Curry	Eng	24,243.14
86	David Ray	Eng	23,238.15
87	Glenn Ralph	Eng	22,721.78
88	Emmanuel Dussart	Fr	20,987.16
89	Vicente Fernandez	Arg	20,653.08
90	Peter McWhinney	Aus	20,579.56
91	John Jacobs	USA	20,438.26
92	Jimmy Heggarty	N Ire	20,266.23
93	Ignacio Gervas	Sp	19,812.13
94	Paul Way	Eng	19,736.56
95	Ross McFarlane	Eng	19,715.90
96	Simon Bishop	Eng	19,656.92
97	Bob E Smith	USA	18,560.17
98	Ken Brown	Scot	18,112.46
99	Bernard Gallacher	Scot	18,017.63
100	Peter Teravainen	USA	17,774.74
101	Lyndsay Stephen	Aus	17,388.80
102	Andrew Oldcorn	Eng	16,704.39
103	Jerry Haas	USA	16,242.01
104	Bill Malley	USA	15,820.53
105	Paul Kent	Eng	15,522.62
106	Emilio Rodriguez	Sp	14,936.14
107	Stephen McAllister	Scot	14,714.16
108	Keith Waters	Eng	14,650.48
109	Ian Young	Scot	14,152.35
110	Armando Saavedra	Arg	14,055.11
111	Gavin Levenson	SA	13,942.22
112	Ross Drummond	Scot	13,871.54
113	Mats Hallberg	Swe	13,867.08
114	Michael King	Eng	13,673.64
115	Grant Turner	Eng	13,488.95

European Tour 1989

All exempt categories

1 Winners of the PGA Championship, the Open Championship and Order of Merit in the last 10 years.

2 Winners of the Tournament Players' Championship in the last 5 years.

3 Winners of the European Open in the last 5 years.

4 Winners of the European Masters Tournaments for 6 years commencing 1984.

5 **Tournament Winners:** Winners of the PGA European Tour events for three years. 1986 winners exempt for 1989; 1987 winners exempt for 1989 and 1990; 1988 winners exempt for 1989, 1990 and 1991.

6 Members of the last named European Ryder Cup Team.

7 The top 40 from the 1988 Career Money List.

8 10 Sponsors' Invitations

9 National/Regional Orders of Merit

Information not available at time of going to press.

10 Past winners of the tournament in question.

11 The top 120 from the 1988 Volvo Order of Merit.

12 **Qualifying School:** The top 50 from the 1988 PGA European Tour Qualifying School.

13 Players finishing between 121 and 151 (inclusive) on the 1988 Volvo Order of Merit

14 Players finishing between 51st and 107th place in the 1988 PGA European Tour Qualifying School.

15 **Past Champions**

(a) European-born former winners of PGA European Tour events not otherwise eligible for membership ranked according to the number of individual past successes.

(b) European-born former members of Ryder Cup, World Cup, Hennessy Cup and Double Diamond Teams are eligible for membership.

General: Regular Fields
For regular full-field PGA European Tour competitions, starting fields will be 144.

1988 All Exempt European Tour

Category 1

Winners PGA	*Eligible*	*Expires*	
	1st Jan	31 Dec	
Ian Woosnam *(Wal)*	1989	1998	
Bernhard Langer *(W Ger)*	1988	1997	
Rodger Davis *(Aus)*	1987	1996	
Paul Way *(Eng)*	1986	1995	
Howard Clark *(Eng)*	1985	1994	
Tony Jacklin *(Eng)*	1983	1992	
Vicente Fernandez *(Arg)*	1980	1989	

Winners Open

Severiano Ballesteros *(Sp)*	1989	1998	
Nick Faldo *(Eng)*	1988	1997	
Greg Norman *(Aus)*	1987	1996	
Sandy Lyle *(Scot)*	1986	1995	
Tom Watson *(USA)*	1984	1993	
Bill Rogers *(USA)*	1982	1991	No in Category 13

Category 2

Winners TPC

Jaime Gonzalez *(Bra)*	1985	1989	No in Category 1

Category 3

Winners European Open

Gordon Brand Jr *(Scot)*	1985	1989	No in Category 1

Category 4

Winners European Masters

Chris Moody *(Eng)*	1989	1993	
Anders Forsbrand *(Swe)*	1988	1992	
José-Maria Olazabal *(Sp)*	1987	1991	
Craig Stadler *(USA)*	1986	1990	
Jerry Anderson*(Can)*	1985	1989	No in Category 5

Category 5

Tournament Winners

David Whelan *(Eng)*	1989	1991
David Llewellyn *(Wal)*	1989	1991
Mark McNulty *(SA)*	1989	1991
Derrick Cooper *(Eng)*	1989	1991
Mike Harwood *(Aus)*	1989	1991
Mark James *(Eng)*	1989	1991
José Rivero *(Sp)*	1989	1991
Barry Lane *(Eng)*	1989	1991
Mark Mouland *(Wal)*	1989	1991
Peter Baker *(Eng)*	1989	1991

Winners PGA	*Eligible*	*Expires*	
Frank Nobilo *(NZ)*	1989	1991	
Des Smyth (Ire)	1989	1991	
Sam Torrance *(Scot)*	1988	1990	
Mats Lanner *(Swe)*	1988	1990	
Eamonn Darcy *(Ire)*	1988	1990	
Peter Senior *(Aus)*	1988	1990	
Noel Ratcliffe *(Aus)*	1988	1990	
Mark O'Meara *(USA)*	1988	1990	
Robert Lee *(Eng)*	1988	1990	
John Bland *(SA)*	1987	1989	
David Feherty *(N Ire)*	1987	1989	
Ove Sellberg *(Swe)*	1987	1989	
Antonio Garrido *(Sp)*	1987	1989	
John Morgan *(Eng)*	1987	1989	
Greg J Turner *(NZ)*	1987	1989	No in Category 25

Category 6

European Ryder Cup Team

Ken Brown *(Scot)*	1987	1989	No in Category 1

Category 7

Top 40 Career Money List

José-Maria Canizares *(Sp)*	1989	1989	
Manuel Pinero *(Sp)*	1989	1989	
Hugh Baiocchi *(SA)*	1989	1989	
Ronan Rafferty *(N Ire)*	1989	1989	
Gordon J Brand *(Eng)*	1989	1989	
Bernard Gallacher *(Scot)*	1989	1989	
Christy O'Connor Jr *(Ire)*	1989	1989	
Graham Marsh *(Aus)*	1989	1989	
Neil Coles *(Eng)*	1989	1989	
Carl Mason *(Eng)*	1989	1989	
Brian Barnes *(Scot)*	1989	1989	
Brian Waites *(Eng)*	1989	1989	
Roger Chapman *(Eng)*	1989	1989	
John O'Leary *(Ire)*	1989	1989	
Bob Charles *(NZ)*	1989	1989	No in Category 15

Category 8

Sponsor's Invitations

No in Category 10

Category 9

National/Regional Orders of Merit

Information not available at time of going to press.

Category 10

Past winners of the tournament in question

Category 11

Top 120 Members from the 1988 Volvo Order of Merit

	Eligible	*Expires*	*Ranking in Category*
	1st Jan	31st Dec	
Denis Durnian *(Eng)*	1989	1989	20
Craig Parry *(Aus)*	1989	1989	24
Miguel Angel Martin *(Sp)*	1989	1989	25
Richard Boxall *(Eng)*	1989	1989	27
Philip Walton *(Ire)*	1989	1989	31
Wayne Riley *(Aus)*	1989	1989	34
Peter Fowler *(Aus)*	1989	1989	36
Tony Johnstone *(Zim)*	1989	1989	38
Tony Charnley *(Eng)*	1989	1989	39
Jeff Hawkes *(SA)*	1989	1989	41
David J Russell *(Eng)*	1989	1989	42
David Williams *(Eng)*	1989	1989	43
Mark Roe *(Eng)*	1989	1989	46
Mike Smith *(USA)*	1989	1989	47
Eduardo Romero *(Arg)*	1989	1989	48
Andrew Murray *(Eng)*	1989	1989	50
Colin Montgomerie *(Scot)*	1989	1989	52
Mike Clayton *(Aus)*	1989	1989	53
Michael Allen *(USA)*	1989	1989	54
Stephen Bennett *(Eng)*	1989	1989	55
Jim Rutledge *(Can)*	1989	1989	58
Malcolm Mackenzie *(Eng)*	1989	1989	59
Bill Longmuir *(Scot)*	1989	1989	60
Ian Mosey *(Eng)*	1989	1989	62
Andrew Sherborne *(Eng)*	1989	1989	63
Gerry Taylor *(USA)*	1989	1989	65
Magnus Persson *(Eng)*	1989	1989	66
David Gilford *(Eng)*	1989	1989	67
Ossie Moore *(Aus)*	1989	1989	69
Philip Harrison *(Eng)*	1989	1989	70
Brett Ogle *(Aus)*	1989	1989	71
Neil Hansen *(Eng)*	1989	1989	72
Ron Commans *(USA)*	1989	1989	73
Manuel Calero *(Sp)*	1989	1989	74
Martin Poxon *(Eng)*	1989	1989	75
Peter Mitchell *(Eng)*	1989	1989	76
Brian Marchbank *(Scot)*	1989	1989	77
Anders Sorenson *(Den)*	1989	1989	78
Johan Rystrom *(Swe)*	1989	1989	79
Bob Shearer *(Aus)*	1989	1989	80
John Slaughter *(USA)*	1989	1989	81
David A Russell *(Eng)*	1989	1989	82
Juan Anglada *(Sp)*	1989	1989	83
Paul Curry *(Eng)*	1989	1989	85
David Ray *(Eng)*	1989	1989	86
Glenn Ralph *(Eng)*	1989	1989	87
Emmanuel Dussart *(Fr)*	1989	1989	88
Peter McWhinney *(Aus)*	1989	1989	90
John Jacobs *(USA)*	1989	1989	91
Jimmy Heggarty *(N Ire)*	1989	1989	92
Ignacio Gervas *(Sp)*	1989	1989	93
Ross McFarlane *(Eng)*	1989	1989	95
Simon Bishop *(Eng)*	1989	1989	96
Bob E Smith *(USA)*	1989	1989	97
Peter Teravainen *(USA)*	1989	1989	100
Lyndsay Stephen *(Aus)*	1989	1989	101
Andrew Oldcorn *(Eng)*	1989	1989	102
Jerry Haas *(USA)*	1989	1989	103
Bill Malley *(USA)*	1989	1989	104
Paul Kent *(Eng)*	1989	1989	105
Emilio Rodriguez *(Sp)*	1989	1989	106
Stephen McAllister *(Scot)*	1989	1989	107
Keith Waters *(Eng)*	1989	1989	108
Ian Young *(Scot)*	1989	1989	109
Armando Saavedra *(Arg)*	1989	1989	110

	Eligible	*Expires*	*Ranking in Category*
Gavin Levenson *(SA)*	1989	1989	111
Ross Drummond (Scot)	1989	1989	112
Mats Hallberg *(Swe)*	1989	1989	113
Michael King (Eng)	1989	1989	114
Grant Turner *(Eng)*	1989	1989	115
Philip Parkin *(Wal)*	1989	1989	116
Bryan Norton *(USA)*	1989	1989	118
Marc Pendaries *(Fr)*	1989	1989	119
Steen Tinning *(Den)*	1989	1989	120

No in Category 74

Category 12

Top 50 from 1988 Qualifying School

	1st Jan	31st Dec	
Jesper Parnevik *(Swe)*	1989	1989	1
Vijay Singh *(Fij)*	1989	1989	2
Paul Mayo *(Wal)*	1989	1989	3
Ulf Nilsson *(Swe)*	1989	1989	4
Lief Hederstroem *(Swe)*	1989	1989	5
Miguel Angel Jimenez *(Sp)*	1989	1989	6
Johan Tumba *(Swe)*	1989	1989	7
Alberto Binaghi *(It)*	1989	1989	8
David Jones *(N Ire)*	1989	1989	9
David James *(Scot)*	1989	1989	10
Sandy Stephen *(Scot)*	1989	1989	11
Joe Higgins *(Eng)*	1989	1989	12
Andrew Stubbs *(Eng)*	1989	1989	13
Steven Thompson *(Scot)*	1989	1989	14
Mikael Krantz *(Swe)*	1989	1989	15
Paul Carrigill *(Eng)*	1989	1989	16
Manuel Moreno *(Sp)*	1989	1989	17
Paul Broadhurst *(Eng)*	1989	1989	18
Wayne Stephens *(Eng)*	1989	1989	19
Mark Davis *(Eng)*	1989	1989	20
Rick Hartmann *(USA)*	1989	1989	21
Jamie Howell *(USA)*	1989	1989	22
Luis Carbonetti *(Arg)*	1989	1989	23
Paul Hoad *(Eng)*	1989	1989	24
Brian Evans *(Eng)*	1989	1989	25
Magnus Jonsson *(Swe)*	1989	1989	26
Jean-Ignace Mouhica *(Fr)*	1989	1989	27
Jean Van de Velde *(Fr)*	1989	1989	28
Marc Farry *(Fr)*	1989	1989	29
Chris Van Der Velde *(Hol)*	1989	1989	30
Steven Bottomley *(Eng)*	1989	1989	31
Don Klenk *(USA)*	1989	1989	32
Carlos Franco *(Par)*	1989	1989	33
Juan Rosa *(Sp)*	1989	1989	34
Kris Moe *(USA)*	1989	1989	35
José Davila *(Sp)*	1989	1989	36
José Cantero *(Arg)*	1989	1989	37
Juan Quiros *(Sp)*	1989	1989	38
Lee Jones *(Eng)*	1989	1989	39
Michael Miller *(Scot)*	1989	1989	40
Stephen Hamill *(N Ire)*	1989	1989	41
Eugene Elliott *(USA)*	1989	1989	42
Richard Fish *(Eng)*	1989	1989	43
Kevin Dickens *(Eng)*	1989	1989	44
John McHenry (Ire)	1989	1989	45
Peter Cowen *(Eng)*	1989	1989	46
Christopher Gray *(Eng)*	1989	1989	47
Daniel Lozano *(Sp)*	1989	1989	48
Francis Quinn *(USA)*	1989	1989	49
Mariano Aparicio *(Sp)*	1989	1989	50

No in Category 50

Category 13

121–151 1988 Volvo Order of Merit

	Eligible	*Expires*	*Ranking in Category*
	1st Jan	31st Dec	
Magnus Sunesson *(Swe)*	1989	1989	122
Andrew Chandler *(Eng)*	1989	1989	123
Kyi Hla Han *(Bur)*	1989	1989	124
John De Forest *(USA)*	1989	1989	125
Frederic Regard *(Fr)*	1989	1989	127
Mitch Adcock *(USA)*	1989	1989	129
Teddy Webber *(Zim)*	1989	1989	130
Santiago Luna *(Sp)*	1989	1989	132
Wayne Smith *(Aus)*	1989	1989	133
Vaughan Somers *(Aus)*	1989	1989	134
Bill McColl *(Scot)*	1989	1989	135
Craig McClellan *(USA)*	1989	1989	136
Peter Jones *(Aus)*	1989	1989	137
Paul Thomas *(Wal)*	1989	1989	139
Russell Weir *(Scot)*	1989	1989	141
Neal Briggs *(Eng)*	1989	1989	143
Ronald Stelten *(USA)*	1989	1989	144
Martin Sludds *(Ire)*	1989	1989	148
Emanuele Bolognesi *(It)*	1989	1989	149
Jeremy Bennett *(Eng)*	1989	1989	151
			No in Category 20

Category 14

51–107 from the 1988 Qualifying School

	1st Jan	31st Dec	
Andrea Canessa *(It)*	1989	1989	52
Christopher Platts *(Eng)*	1989	1989	53
Thomas Levet *(Fr)*	1989	1989	54
Silvio Grappasonni *(It)*	1989	1989	55
Paolo Quirici *(Swi)*	1989	1989	56
Carl Magnus Stroemberg *(Swe)*	1989	1989	57
Tim Planchin *(Fr)*	1989	1989	58
Robin Mann *(Eng)*	1989	1989	60
Griffin Rudolph *(USA)*	1989	1989	61
Daniel Westermark *(Swe)*	1989	1989	62
Ruud Bos *(Hol)*	1989	1989	63
Martin Schiene *(USA)*	1989	1989	64
Daniel Silva *(Port)*	1989	1989	66
Marco Durante *(It)*	1989	1989	67
Wayne Henry *(Eng)*	1989	1989	68
Alessandro Rogato *(It)*	1989	1989	70
Paul Hunstone *(Eng)*	1989	1989	72
Clive Tucker *(Eng)*	1989	1989	73
Brendan McDaid *(Ire)*	1989	1989	74
Oliver Eckstein *(W Ger)*	1989	1989	75
Willie Milne *(Scot)*	1989	1989	77
Johnny Young *(Ire)*	1989	1989	78
David Curry *(Eng)*	1989	1989	79
Jonas Saxton *(USA)*	1989	1989	80
Colin Brooks *(Scot)*	1989	1989	81
Jacob Rasmussen (Den)	1989	1989	82
José Cabo *(Sp)*	1989	1989	83
José Rozadilla *(Sp)*	1989	1989	84
Kyle Kelsall *(Eng)*	1989	1989	85
Nicholas Godin *(Eng)*	1989	1989	86
José Carriles *(Sp)*	1989	1989	87
James Spence *(Eng)*	1989	1989	88
Steven Bowman *(USA)*	1989	1989	89
John Hawksworth *(Eng)*	1989	1989	90
Michel Tapia *(Fr)*	1989	1989	91
Anthony Gilligan *(Aus)*	1989	1989	92

	Eligible	*Expires*	*Ranking in Category*
Barry Conser *(USA)*	1989	1989	93
Laurent Lassalle *(Fr)*	1989	1989	94
Magnus Granqvist *(Swe)*	1989	1989	95
Tony Ashton *(Eng)*	1989	1989	96
Peter Harrison *(Eng)*	1989	1989	97
Alfonso Pinero *(Sp)*	1989	1989	98
Jonathan Nichols *(USA)*	1989	198	99
José Buendia *(Sp)*	1989	1989	100
Michael McLean *(Eng)*	1989	1989	101
Thomas Nilsson *(Swe)*	1989	1989	102
Frederic Martin *(Fr)*	1989	1989	103
Paul Carman *(Eng)*	1989	1989	104
James Annable *(Eng)*	1989	1989	105
Per-Arne Brostedt *(Swe)*	1989	1989	106
Paul Girvan *(Scot)*	1989	1989	107

No in Category 51

Category 15

Past Champions/Ryder Cup/Double Diamond/Hennessy-Cognac/World Cup Players

Francisco Abreu *(Sp)*
Peter Alliss *(Eng)*
Alfonso Angelini *(It)*
Laurie Ayton *(Eng)*
Manuel Ballesteros *(Sp)*
Brian Bamford *(Eng)*
Harry Bannerman *(Scot)*
Valentin Barrios *(Sp)*
Maurice Bembridge *(Eng)*
Jamie Benito *(Sp)*
Roberto Bernardini *(It)*
Fred Boobyer *(Eng)*
Ken Bousfield *(Eng)*
Hugh Boyle *(Ire)*
Harry Bradshaw *(Ire)*
Andrew Brooks *(Scot)*
Peter Butler *(Eng)*
Manuel Cabrera *(Sp)*
Renato Campagnoli *(It)*
Aldo Casera *(It)*
Alex Caygill *(Eng)*
David Chillas *(Scot)*
Clive Clark *(Eng)*
John Cockin *(Swe)*
Tony Coop *(Eng)*
Patrick Cotton *(Fr)*
Simon Cox *(Wal)*
Gordon Cunningham *(Scot)*
Kim Dabson *(Eng)*
Fred Daly *(Ire)*
Baldovino Dassu *(It)*
Peter Dawson *(Eng)*
Craig Defoy *(Wal)*
Flory Van Donck *(Bel)*
Jan Dorrestein *(Hol)*
Norman Drew *(N Ire)*
Richard Emery *(Eng)*
Max Faulkner *(Eng)*
Martin Foster *(Eng)*
Angel Gallardo *(Sp)*
Jamie Gallardo *(Sp)*
Jean Garaialde *(Fr)*
Manuel Garcia *(Sp)*
John Garner *(Eng)*
German Garrido *(Sp)*
Torsten Giedeon *(W Ger)*
Peter Gill *(Eng)*
Karl-Heinz Goegele *(W Ger)*
U Grappasonni *(It)*
Malcolm Gregson *(Eng)*
Tony Grubb *(Eng)*
Jack Hargreaves *(Eng)*
Liam Higgins *(Ire)*
Jimmy Hitchcock *(Eng)*
Vince Hood *(Eng)*
Tommy Horton *(Eng)*
Brian Huggett *(Wal)*
David Huish *(Scot)*
Warren Humphreys *(Eng)*
Bernard Hunt *(Eng)*
Geoffrey Hunt *(Eng)*
Guy Hunt *(Eng)*
David Ingram *(Scot)*
Hugh Jackson *(Ire)*
John Jacobs *(USA)*
David Jagger *(Eng)*
Nick Job *(Eng)*
Ernie Jones *(N Ire)*
Frank Jowle *(Eng)*
Manfred Kessler *(W Ger)*
Krister Kinell *(Swe)*
Sam King *(Eng)*
Jimmy Kinsella *(Ire)*
Bill Large *(Eng)*
Arthur Lees *(Eng)*
Eric Lester *(Eng)*
Massimo Mannelli *(It)*
Manuel Mantes *(Sp)*
Jimmy Martin *(Ire)*
Steve Martin *(Scot)*
Doug McClelland *(Eng)*
Paddy McGuirk *(Ire)*
Angel Miguel *(Sp)*
Sebastian Miguel *(Sp)*
Ralph Moffitt *(Eng)*
Hedley Muscroft *(Eng)*
Christy O'Connor *(Ire)*
Peter Oosterhuis *(Eng)*
John Panton MBE *(Scot)*
Bernard Pascassio *(Fr)*
Andrew Phillips *(Wal)*
Lionel Platts *(Eng)*
Eddie Pollend *(Ire)*
Manuel Ramos *(Sp)*
Frank Rennie *(Scot)*
Manuel Sanchez *(Sp)*
Doug Sewell *(Eng)*
Paddy Skerritt *(Ire)*
David Snell *(Eng)*
Ramon Sota *(Sp)*
Arnold Stickley *(Eng)*
Norman Sutton *(Eng)*
David Talbot *(Eng)*
David Thomas *(Wal)*
Phillippe Toussaint *(Bel)*
Peter Townsend *(Eng)*
David Vaughan *(Wal)*
Charlie Ward *(Eng)*
Gery Watine *(Fr)*
Ross Whitehead *(Eng)*
Peter Wilcock *(Eng)*
George Will *(Scot)*
Norman Wood *(Scot)*

No in Category 113

Breakdown of nationalities of those eligible for membership in 1989

Category	England	USA	Spain	Scotland	Australia	Sweden	France	Ireland	Italy	Wales	Argentina	N Ireland	South Africa	Denmark	New Zealand	Zimbabwe	Canada	Holland	W Germany	Brazil	Burma	Fiji	Paraguay	Portugal	Switzerland	
1	4	2	1	1	2					1	1								1							13
2																				1						1
3				1																						1
4	1	1	1			1											1									5
5	7	1	2	1	3	2		2		2		1	1		2	1										25
6				1																						1
7	5		2	2	1			2				1	1		1											15
11	27	10	5	6	10	3	2	1		1	2	1	2	2		1	1									74
12	14	6	7	4		6	3	1	1	1	2	2						1				1	1			50
13	3	4	1	2	3	1	1	1	1	1						1					1					20
14	15	6	5	3	1	5	5	2	4					1				1	1					1	1	51
Totals	76	30	24	21	20	18	11	9	6	6	5	5	4	3	3	3	2	2	2	1	1	1	1	1	1	256

Summary

Argentina	5
Australia	20
Brazil	1
Burma	1
Canada	2
Denmark	3
England	76
Fiji	1
France	11
Holland	2
Ireland	9
Italy	6
New Zealand	3
Northern Ireland	5
Paraguay	1
Portugal	1
Scotland	21
Spain	24
South Africa	4
Sweden	18
Switzerland	1
USA	30
Wales	6
West Germany	2
Zimbabwe	3

Sony Ranking

The World Ranking System for Professional Golf

In the spring of 1986 the Sony Corporation announced the launch of a world ranking system for professional golf. The Sony Ranking, which is sanctioned by the Royal and Ancient Golf Club of St Andrews, is a specially developed computerised ranking which provides an authoritative reference source to the relative performance of the world's top players.

The official events from all the geographical circuits are graded according to their status and the quality and strength of the players participating. Points are then awarded to each player dependent upon his finish and the tournament's grade, with additional bonus points taking into account the strength of the field.

The Sony Ranking is based on a three year 'rolling' period weighted in favour of the more recent results and is issued each Monday at the completion of the week's tournaments from around the world.

Gradings

Grade 1	The Masters	(USA)
	US Open Championship	(USA)
	The Open Championship	(Eur)
	PGA Championship	(USA)
Grade 1a	The Players Championship	(USA)
Grade 2	The Nestlé Invitational	(USA)
	Memorial Tournament	(USA)
	Volvo PGA Championship	(Eur)
	NEC World Series	(USA)
	Panasonic European Open	(Eur)
	Trophée Lancôme	(Eur)
	Japan Open	(Jpn)
	Dunlop Pheonix	(Jpn)
	Australian Open	(ANZ)
Grade 3	Leading Tournaments and Championships. (Majority of USPGA Tour events and leading events on European, Japanese and Australia/New Zealand Tours)	
Grade 4	Intermediate Tournaments. (Majority of remaining events on US, European and Japanese Tours and leading events on Australia/New Zealand, South African and Asian Tours)	
Grade 5	Other Tournaments (Safari Tour, other events on US, European and Japanese Tours and remaining events on the Australia/New Zealand, South African and Asian Tours)	
Grade 6	Minor and Regional Events (Canadian and South American events and regional events on Japanese Tour)	

Points

50 points are awarded to the winner in a Grade 1 event with 30 points for second place, 20 for third, 15 for fourth, 12 for fifth down to a single point for 50th place. In Grade 1a 40 points go to the winner down to one point for 40th place. There is a reduced scale of points through Grades 2 to 6 where 'Bonus Points' are awarded dependent on the number of Top 50 ranked players that are participating in the event.

'Rolling' Three Year period

The Sony Ranking is based on a 'rolling' three year period weighted in favour of the more recent years as follows:

Current 52 wk period	Points multiplied by 4
Previous 52 wk period	Points multiplied by 2
52 wk period, 2 years ago	Points multiplied by 1

Sony Ranking

at 31December 1988

					Year Totals			Weeks 1–49		
Pos	**Name** (1985/87)	**Circuit**		**Points**	**1985 ×1**	**1986 ×2**	**1987 ×4**	**1985/7 Total**	**1985/7 Minus**	**1988 Plus**
1	**Seve Ballesteros** (2)	Eur	1	1458	181	336	652	1169	−675	964
2	**Greg Norman** (1)	ANZ	1	1365	85	582	564	1231	−658	797
3	**Sandy Lyle** (4)	Eur	2	1297	125	126	628	879	−502	920
4	**Nick Faldo** (14)	Eur	3	1103	25	82	516	623	−324	804
5	**Curtis Strange** (5)	USA	1	1092	137	144	592	873	−505	724
6	**Ben Crenshaw** (10)	USA	2	070	0	128	540	668	−334	584
7	**Ian Woosnam** (6)	Eur	4	854	58	120	652	830	−444	468
8	**David Frost** (22)	Afr	1	843	30	122	404	556	−293	580
9	**Paul Azinger** (11)	USA	3	825	7	86	556	649	−328	504
10	**Mark Calcavecchia** (31)	USA	4	819	0	46	408	454	−227	592
11	**Masashi Ozaki** (18)	Jpn	1	781	29	202	360	591	−310	500
12	**Chip Beck** (36)	USA	5	770	10	116	280	406	−208	572
13	**Tom Kite** (21)	USA	6	726	71	168	324	563	−317	480
14	**Lanny Wadkins** (8)	USA	7	721	127	130	440	697	−412	436
15	**Bernhard Langer** (3)	Eur	5	696	184	316	612	1112	−648	232
16	**Payne Stewart** (7)	USA	8	672	85	212	420	717	−401	356
17	**Ken Green** (57)	USA	9	661	30	90	144	264	−147	544
18	**Mark McNulty** (9)	Afr	2	645	31	206	436	673	−352	324
19	**Fred Couples** (46)	USA	10	638	37	20	280	337	−187	488
20	**J-M Olazabal** (49)	Eur	6	629	1	162	144	307	−154	476
21	**Joey Sindelar** (67)	USA	11	599	67	90	76	233	−150	516
22	**Rodger Davis** (13)	ANZ	2	589	48	226	352	626	−337	300
23	**Larry Nelson** (23)	USA	12	576	31	56	464	551	−291	316
24	**David Ishii** (25)	USA	13	532	27	112	376	515	−271	288
25	**Mark O'Meara** (26)	USA	14	518	123	128	252	503	−318	328
26T	**Mark McCumber** (54T)	USA	15T	516	48	24	200	272	−160	404
	Steve Pate (73)	USA	15T	516	20	28	164	212	−116	420
28	**Larry Mize** (12)	USA	17	511	47	110	488	645	−346	212
29	**Tom Watson** (16)	USA	18	505	62	126	428	616	−339	228
30T	**Jeff Sluman**(75)	USA	19	503	18	22	168	208	−113	408
	Isao Aoki (19)	Jpn	2	503	70	214	296	580	−325	248
32	**Tsun'ki Nakajima** (15)	Jpn	3	494	125	288	204	617	−371	248
33	**Scott Simpson** (17)	USA	20	493	38	50	504	592	−315	216
34	**Bob Tway** (30)	USA	21	486	31	308	144	483	−257	260
35	**Mike Reid** (51)	USA	22	485	29	34	224	287	−158	356
36	**Dan Pohl** (29)	USA	23	473	41	154	296	491	−266	248
37	**Craig Stadler** (27T)	USA	24	461	99	98	296	493	−296	264
38	**Ian Baker-Finch** (40)	ANZ	3	454	49	132	184	365	−207	296
39	**Scott Hoch** (27T)	USA	25	452	45	104	344	493	−269	228
40	**Don Pooley** (32)	USA	26	445	22	106	304	432	−227	240
41	**Nick Price** (47)	Afr	3	438	44	72	220	336	−190	292
42	**Peter Senior** (38)	ANZ	4	429	10	54	316	380	−195	244
43	**Jay Haas** (56)	USA	27	405	23	66	176	265	−144	284
44	**Ronan Rafferty** (58T)	Eur	7	395	24	58	180	262	−143	276
45	**Gordon Brand Jr** (33)	Eur	8	387	70	320	425	230	−230	192
46	**Masah'o Kuramoto** (45)	Jpn	4	364	67	108	172	347	−207	224
47	**Corey Pavin** (24)	USA	28	361	118	114	296	528	−323	156
48	**Bruce Lietzke** (105T)	USA	29	360	28	56	64	148	− 88	300
49	**Des Smyth** (130T)	Eur	9	343	18	54	40	112	− 65	296
50	**Mark James** (108)	Eur	10	336	34	48	64	146	− 90	280

The Curtis Cup

Lewine Mair

© Matthew Harris

The Great Britain and the Ireland team with the non-playing Captain, Diane Bailey, and Vice-Captain, Elizabeth Boatman holding the Cup.

It was during the practice days for the Curtis Cup at Royal St George's that Sue Shapcott, at 18 the youngest member of the Great Britain and Ireland side, made a typically pertinent observation concerning the different attire of the two teams. Where the home side were swinging away in their shirt sleeves, the Americans were not only wrapped in woollies but, said Sue, for she had seen them changing in the locker-rooms, they had on thermal underwear! 'It could help,' she suggested, mischievously, 'if it were to get really cold. . . '

There was a similarly prophetic remark from Ireland's Claire Hourihane who, in what was one of the less happy talking points of an otherwise great week, was never given a game over the two days. Looking across at the limp flag on the 18th green, Miss Hourihane spoke of how Great Britain and Ireland were lucky in that they had had opportunities in earlier practice sessions to see Royal St George's in wind. 'If it blows this week,' she said, 'the Americans will be looking at a course they've never seen before.'

It got colder and windier and, as Judy Bell, the gamest of American captains was to say, such conditions certainly contributed to the American defeat.

In truth, our girls felt the cold, too, on the second day. However, as was noted at the time, they never looked as chilled and shivery as the Americans – partly, one suspects, because Diane Bailey, the British captain, was forever dinning into her troops how important it was that they should look confident and in control at all times.

This insistence that they were to hold their heads high undoubtedly enabled Shirley Lawson, Scotland's only representative, to win an opening single on a day when the 'chipping twitch' bedevilling her game was at its most treacherous. She duffed almost all of her little chips but, far from letting the problem eat into her confidence, she elsewhere unleashed some positively regal shots, with her drives arguably the best on either side. Dr Pat Cornett, her opponent, may know a thing or two about psychology, but the Scot's playing pattern had her stumped. Small wonder that, at the end of her one hole defeat, she could not hold back the tears.

Those who, incidentally, wonder what has become of Miss Lawson since Royal St George's might like to know that, when she returned from overseas to play in the Home Internationals at Barassie later in the year, her 'chipping twitch' was very definitely on the mend. Her solution one of having her trolley-puller standing in close and talking her through the shot. 'Straight back, straight through, keep your head down,' was the gist of the instruction.

Good luck messages had poured in from everywhere on the days leading up to the Curtis Cup, with Jill Thornhill the recipient of a bouquet of flowers so long in the stem as to have someone suggest she had best arrange them in her golf bag!

As was the case when Great Britain and Ireland won at Prairie Dunes, Mrs Bailey had been impressing on her players the importance of getting away to a good start. The 7 which Linda Bayman and Julie Wade amassed at the 1st hole in the opening match was hardly what she had in mind but, to their credit, this most positive of pairings went on to defeat Tracy Kerdyk and Kathleen Scriver by two and one.

The second foursome, that in which Sue Shapcott and Karen Davies defeated Cindy Scholefield and Carol Thompson by five and four, was one which gave untold pleasure to that former triple British Champion and *Daily Telegraph* golf correspondent, Enid Wilson. Miss Wilson, who played in the original match against the Americans in 1932, said that she never thought she would live to see the day when our girls would outplay the Americans on and around the greens. 'They putted like angels' she declared. What is more, Miss Scholefield and Mrs Thompson were no ordinary Americans, for Cindy Scholefield is the coach at UCLA, while Carol Thompson went on to share individual honours with Italy's Stefania Croce in the World Cup in September.

As for the third foursome, that was a shared affair between Jill Thornhill and Vicki Thomas and Lesley Shannon and Caroline Keggi.

This lunchtime lead was increased to 6–3 at the end of afternoon singles in which, apart from the aforementioned Miss Lawson, both Jill Thornhill and Julie Wade were on the winning side.

© Peter Dazeley Photography

Jill Thornhill, who belied her veteran status and continued her succession of wins in her third successive appearance in the match.

But it was Mrs Bayman's halved match with Tracy Kerdyk which, of all the first day activities, will linger longest in the memory. One down mounting the 18th tee and in imminent danger of losing a point, the local heroine holed from off the green for the most dramatic of eagles.

'There's still a long way to go,' said a rightly tentative Mrs Bailey when asked to address the press at the half-way stage. Her players echoed what she had to say but where, a few years ago, their thoughts might have been focussing more on whether or not they would manage to stay ahead, they were on this occasion radiating confidence. Interestingly, none among them had felt particularly nervous, even on the first day. Indeed, it was only when Julie Wade teed up in the World Amateur team championships in Sweden that she said she recognised what 1st tee nerves were all about. 'In the Curtis Cup, all I ever wanted was to get started . . .'

The Americans hit back at the start of the

second day at Royal St George's, with Tracy Kerdyk, possibly the strongest of the Americans, and Kathleen Schrivner defeating Linda Bayman and Julie Wade. But Karen Davies and Sue Shapcott won again, while Jill Thornhill and Vicki Thomas had a resounding win – the most decisive of any – when they defeated Cindy Scholefield and Carol Thompson by six and five.

© Matthew Harris

Diane Bailey congratulates Linda Bayman on her win in the singles on the second day.

With Great Britain and Ireland's lead now 8–4, the three points picked up on an ever more windswept final afternoon by Sue Shapcott, Vicki Thomas and Linda Bayman were all that were needed for a final scoreline of 11–7. Of that trio, Sue Shapcott emerged from the contest with more points than anyone on either side – namely, three. As for Mrs Bayman, she bagged two and a half – no bad effort for one playing amid all the additional pressures of having the match in her own backyard.

Mrs Thornhill may have been disappointed to have lost her final single to Carol Thompson in what she insists is her last Curtis Cup. However, the fact is that in the three Curtis Cups she has played since 1984, she has lost only twice while collecting an extraordinary haul of eight and a half points.

That the Americans were devastated to lose the Curtis Cups twice in a row was no understatement. Judy Bell could not have been more sporting in the way in which she congratulated Mrs Bailey and her players and also in the way in which she handled so diplomatically the question of the wintry weather Royal St George's had provided as a backcloth to this mid-summer fixture. 'We have known days like the first day at home, but today's conditions, I have to say, belong, exclusively, to you . . .' When the conversation turned to the American players, though, this charming official was too overcome to say any more: 'I'm afraid I'm a bit emotional on the subject of my team,' she said, softly.

Fittingly, the highlights of the match, which had been watched by ten thousand spectators and more, were recorded for posterity by the BBC. When it was shown, a few days later, Mrs Bayman was otherwise engaged but made arrangements to video the programme. Later, when she sat back to enjoy what was, indisputably, the highlight of her golfing career, she found the video churning out half an hour on pig farming!

Results

First Day – Foursomes

Great Britain & Ireland		United States	
L Bayman and J Wade (2 and 1)	1	T Kerdyk and K Scrivner	0
S Shapcott and K Davies (5 and 4)	1	C Scholefield and C Thompson	0
J Thornhill and V Thomas	1/2	L Shannon and C Keggi	1/2
	2 1/2		1/2

Singles

Great Britain & Ireland		United States	
L Bayman	1 1/2	T Kerdyk	1/2
J Wade (2 holes)	1	C Scholefield	0
S Shapcott	0	C Thompson (1 hole)	1
K Davies	0	P Sinn (4 and 3)	1
S Lawson (1 hole)	1	P Cornett	0
J Thornhill (3 and 2)	1	L Shannon	0
	3 1/2		2 1/2

Second Day – Foursomes

Great Britain & Ireland		United States	
L Bayman and J Wade	0	T Kerdyk and K Scrivner (1 hole)	1
S Shapcott and K Davies (2 holes)	1	L Shannon and C Keggi	0
J Thornhill and V Thomas (6 and 5)	1	C Scholefield and C Thompson	0
	2		1

Singles

Great Britain & Ireland		United States	
J Wade	0	T Kerdyk (2 and 1)	1
S Shapcott (3 and 2)	1	C Keggi	0
S Lawson	0	K Scrivner (4 and 3)	1
V Thomas (5 and 3)	1	P Cornett	0
L Bayman (1 hole)	1	P Sinn	0
J Thornhill	0	C Thompson (3 and 2)	1
	3		3

Aggregate: Great Britain & Ireland, 11: United States, 7

The Amateurs

Raymond Jacobs

It goes without saying that the finest accomplishments in the amateur year of 1988 were by the Great Britain and Ireland women's team, who at Royal St George's – by a nice irony, an all-male bastion of a Club – successfully defended the Curtis Cup against the United States and by the corresponding men's side, who at Stockholm won the Eisenhower Trophy for the third time after a second interval of 12 years. These sterling exploits are, however, dealt with in detail elsewhere. For the purposes of this contribution pride of place for achievement must rest at a source a good deal less obvious – the Championship Committee of the Royal and Ancient Club.

Of course, it was a complete coincidence that the Committee took a decision which had been argued for both by Bruce Critchley and myself in last year's edition of *The Golfer's Handbook*. From 1991 onwards the Walker Cup match, when played in these islands, will be moved from its traditional date in May to September, as will the Amateur Championship, which will be held at the end of August or in early September, the exact date depending on whether or not it is a Walker Cup year. Thus in two years' time the match against the United States at Portmarnock will be on 5th and 6th September (instead of 29th and 30th May, as originally planned) and the Amateur Championship will follow from 10th to 15th September at Ganton.

The Committee explained its decision, whose implications and importance will surely be felt and recognised sooner rather than later, under four main headings. Firstly, the match and the championship, along with the home Internationals and, every other year, the Eisenhower Trophy, will have more impact as fitting climaxes to the amateur season. Secondly, instead of having to announce a team in December to play the following May, the selectors will be able to take into account form that is much more up to date, not least in the four national championships, always decided at the end of July and the beginning of August. Thirdly, the new placings in the calendar will not affect the normal date of the US Amateur Championship.

But fourthly, and perhaps most importantly of all, the condition of the courses in the British Isles used for leading events is invariably better in the autumn, when whatever has passed for summer has still brought a growth and maturity unattainable in spring. Equally, the condition of the games of the leading players is healthier in method and sharper from competition than it can ever be from having only recently emerged from under the dead hand of winter. It should help players and selectors too, that the British Youths' Championship, now in an August limbo, will be brought forward to June, when it will have greater stature and significance.

Whether these changes in the programme succeed in making a closer contest of the Walker Cup remains to be seen. It detracts nothing from the victories of the last two Curtis and Ryder Cup sides to say that their causes were not exactly compromised by the selection procedures adopted by the United States. In distinction from what has proved to be the more than resistible blend of the quixotic, the eccentric, and the perverse, American Walker Cup teams have invariably been chosen from strength, not as a reward for consistency or for not being a college golfer. On that basis, the selection of Walker Cup teams from the British Isles continues to be at one perpetual disadvantage – the haemorrhaging of talent to the professional ranks for which there are less strong compensating transfusions than are available to the United States.

Maybe the time is not faraway when, as for the Ryder Cup matches, the side for the Walker Cup will be expanded by recruitment from the continent of Europe. There was much wringing of hands in chagrin when, in 1979 at The Greenbrier, the score in national anthems at the flag-raising ceremony before the match was 3-1 to Europe. Two years later the majority was 4-1, but defeat was even more humbling. But after the close result in 1983 came two triumphs and there has been enough evidence to suggest that inclusion of continentals into the Walker Cup team would stiffen resistance and concentrate equally the minds of the Americans and the British and Irish candidates.

Mind you, few would envy the task of the

Royal and Ancient Club's Selection Committee, who are currently responsible for nominating all British and Irish teams, if their net had to be cast more widely. Presumably it would be necessary to include knowledgeable and experienced judges from the continent and that would not make the selection process any easier than the complex series of decisions that have always been necessary. Some form of points system might be introduced; an unofficial table for the British season has been compiled, but if any semblance of the amateur tradition is to be even faintly maintained, that attendance at tournaments must never be made compulsory, then a system comparable with that applying to the Ryder Cup side cannot be acceptable.

After all that, the principal achievements of 1988 were: the first victory by a Swedish golfer in the Amateur Championship; the first success for a French golfer in the Youths' Championship; and another plume in the French *chapeau* with their victory in the European Boys' team championship. In fact, a British player did not reach the British final at Royal Porthcawl, in which Christian Hardin beat a South African, Ben Fouchee, to become the third continental winner all in this decade, after Philippe Ploujoux and José-Maria Olazabal. In the Youths' at Royal Aberdeen Christian Cevaer defeated Craig Cassells in a play-off, and again on Scottish territory, at Renfrew, France overcame the host country for the junior title. The balance was somewhat restored, however, when Britain and Ireland gained victories over the Continent of Europe in the matches at both senior and youths level.

© Matthew Harris

Christian Hardin, British Amateur Champion at Royal Porthcawl, the first Swede ever to win.

As a warning against complacency the fledgling European amateur title went overseas, to the 1986 Australian champion, David Ecob, but the four home countries were able to produce the customary crop of exceptional performances – in England by Russell Claydon, Peter Broadhurst, and Peter McEvoy, in Scotland by Jim Milligan and Craig Everett, in Ireland by Garth McGimpsey, and in Wales by Keith Jones and Simon Pardoe. If these players took the pre-eminent roles, honourable walk-on parts were adopted by, among others, Bobby Eggo and Stephen Easingwood, respective winners of the English and Scottish open stroke play titles, for Ireland by Paul McGinlay, who became the first to win both the Irish and Scottish Youths' championships and for Wales by Neil Roderick, who won his country's stroke play for the second time and nearly achieved a title double.

© Matthew Harris

Russell Claydon, who won the English Amateur at Royal Birkdale and several other events during the year.

As well as beating David Curry at the 40th hole in the final of the English championship at Royal Birkdale, Claydon won two 72-hole tournaments, the Berkshire and Lagonda Trophies and nearly embarrassed the best of Europe's young professionals by finishing a close second in the UAP Open at Le Prieuré, near Paris. Broadhurst preceded his transfer to professionalism by winning the Lytham Trophy and returning to the Lancashire course to take the amateur medal in the Open Championship. McEvoy, in advance of his indispensable part in the Eisenhower Trophy victory, won the inaugural English Mid-Amateur championship by no fewer than 20 strokes, strongly suggesting that unless the age limit was sharply reduced from 35, say by ten years, the award might as well be inscribed The Peter McEvoy Perpetual Trophy. No such certainties could be hinted at for the future outcome of events elsewhere. The headlong compulsion to turn professional would see to that.

Paradoxically, Milligan, who achieved the difficult distinction of winning the Scottish championship over his home course at Barassie, beating a teenager, Andrew Coltart, at the 36th hole in the final, intends to remain an amateur. Everett, who won the West and East of Scotland titles and the old-established Leven Gold Medal (all over 72 holes) seemed a likelier professional candidate. McGimpsey, meanwhile, responded smartly to his omission from the last Walker Cup side, becoming only the second player to win in the same season the East, West and Close championships of Ireland. Ireland, the European team champions, emerged as winners of their quadrangular contest against France, Germany, and Sweden only to suffer severe disappointment in the home International matches at Muirfield.

Ireland seemed certain to retain the Raymond Trophy when, having drawn with Wales and beaten Scotland, they stood 4-1 up after the foursomes games against England. To retrieve a desperate situation England had to take the singles 7-3 and this they did to achieve an improbable clean sweep. Wales, for years accustomed to living on scraps, but since the beginning of this decade increasingly a force in both team and individual events, combined these advances in the person of Jones. Aged 19 and the son of the Worplesdon Club's secretary, Jones won his national title by beating Roderick at the 40th hole in the final at Harlech and had the best record of anyone in the home Internationals by taking $5^1/_2$ points from a possible six. As encouraging for the future of Welsh (and British) golf, however, was the achievement of Pardoe, from Goring and Streatley but born in Wrexham, who beat David Haines by 3 and 2 in the final of the British Boys' Championship at Formby – an unprecedented second successive victory in that event by a golfer from The Principality. The old order, happily, is nothing like as predictable as it used to be, and golf in the British Isles is all the better for that.

Eisenhower Trophy 1988

The Great Britain & Ireland winning Eisenhower Trophy team with Geoffrey Marks, the non-playing Captain.

Played every two years, the Eisenhower Trophy is for teams of four Amateurs from each country competing at Stroke Play, with the three best scores in each round to count. It was first held in 1958 when Australia won at St Andrews. Bobby Jones, confined to a wheel-chair through a crippling disease of the spine, captained the United States team on his last visit here. It was the occasion when he received the Freedom of St Andrews in an emotional ceremony, the first US citizen to be so honoured since Benjamin Franklin. Last year was the 16th time the Trophy was held, with Sweden the 15th country in which it had been played.

On nearly every occasion the USA team has dominated the contest, winning nine times and being second in four. Australia and Great Britain and Ireland had two wins each and Japan and Canada, the holders, one. The US dominance can be partly explained in that their winning teams over the years have included Nicklaus, Kite, Wadkins, Crenshaw, Koch, Pate, Hoch and Tway before each turned professional.

On this occasion at the Ullna course, Akersberga, near Stockholm, the Great Britain and Ireland team was led by Peter McEvoy, with Garth McGimpsey, Jim Milligan and Eoghan O'Connell in support. Previously Great Britain and Ireland had won in 1964 at Ogliato, Italy and, after a 12-year gap, in 1976 at Penina, Portugal. After a further 12 years, the prospects of another win were propitious.

If ever a leader played his full part, McEvoy did with rounds of 72, 71, 70 and 71. He won the individual prize comfortably by six shots at 284 from Ecob of Australia. Only Ronnie Shade in 1966 in Mexico City had previously achieved a British outright victory in the individual contest, although Michael Bonallack tied with Vinny Giles at Melbourne in 1968.

© Larry Petrillo/Matthew Harris

Peter McEvoy, who won the individual title by six strokes and inspired the team with his consummate play.

Leading from the front as he did, McEvoy would be the first to agree that it was a full team effort with the other three members contributing their part. Each of them had only one round which did not count and, while McEvoy alone featured in the first six individual scores, the others all played steadily after the team had established an early lead. Six strokes ahead going into the last day, McEvoy was playing in the penultimate pair and showed great character in completing a round of 71 which, but for three putts on the 16th and 18th greens would have been 69. Every shot was a test of his determination and stamina and he played his part without apparent stress as manfully as any man ever has.

Under the captaincy of Geoffrey Marks, the team developed an excellent spirit and it is significant that two of the side, McEvoy and McGimpsey, who were controversially dropped from the 1987 Walker Cup team, now played a prominent part in the team's great win.

Results

at Ullva, Sweden

(Figures in brackets are discarded scores)

1 **Great Britain and Ireland**		882
P McEvoy	72-71-70-71	
G McGimpsey	(76)-72-74-78	
J Milligan	75-(80)-(74)-79	
E O'Connell	73-75-72-(80)	
2 **United States**		887
K Johnson	(77)-73-76-(78)	
E Meeks	76-73-73-77	
J Sigel	71-(78)-(78)-77	
D Yates	72-76-70-73	
3 **Australia**		895
D Ecob	70-71-75-74	
B Hughes	80-80-(78)-(77)	
L Peterson	(85)-(84)-69-76	
S Robinson	76-80-72-72	
4 **Sweden**		897
5 **France**		899
6 **Denmark**		906
7 **Spain**		914
8 **Canada**		915
9 **New Zealand**		916

Individual

P McEvoy (GB)	72-71-70-71—284
D Ecob (Australia)	70-71-75-74—290
D Yates (USA)	72-76-70-73—291
J Lindberg (Sweden)	73-75-74-75—297
J Arruti (Spain)	73-72-79-73—297
P Barques (France)	77-73-72-76—298

WPGET Professional Review of the Year

Lewine Mair

Marie-Laure de Lorenzi Taya had a magnificent season, winning seven events of the tour and nearly £100,00 in prize money.

Though it was Laura Davies who first brought our women professionals to the fore when she went over to the States and won the US Women's Open, Marie-Laure de Lorenzi Taya kept things simmering nicely in a 1988 season in which she won seven titles, or eight if you count the Benson and Hedges Mixed Team Trophy at the end of the year. Fittingly for a golfer who was brought up in Biarritz and who nowadays lives in Barcelona, Marie-Laure won the French Open by way of her first title and the Spanish Open as a finale. That she so dominated the circuit was something which worried the tour's Executive Director, Joe Flanagan, for he feared that she might be looking for fresh pastures to conquer in 1989. To his relief, Marie-Laure assured him that she had no such plans. As the mother of a four-year-old daughter, Laura, nothing matters more to this great golfer that that she should be able to spend her weeks off – she took five of them over the last season – in Barcelona. Were she to play in America, she explained, she would have to go over there for 12 weeks at a time in order to give herself a fair chance, and for her to spend such a long spell over there would be counter-productive in that she would always be worrying about what was going on at home. What she will do, though, is to take up those American invitations which go with the winning of the European Order of Merit, namely the Dinah Shore and the US Open.

It is not too difficult to explain why, of all tournaments, there was none more exciting than the Biarritz Classic. In the first place it was being played over the course where Marie-Laure grew up. Secondly, it was the only tournament of the year in which Marie-Laure and Laura Davies were to be locked together in the closing stages. At the beginning of the tournament, the locals' applause was reserved exclusively for Marie-Laure. But it did not take long for the people to warm to her big hitting rival and, by the weekend, they were revelling in the fact that their tournament should have developed into a battle between the two finest women golfers in Europe. After a record-breaking three-round tally of 200, Laura was one shot ahead going into the last round, a lead she increased to three after opening with an eagle to Marie-Laure's somewhat hesitant six. It was at the 16th that the French player finally succeeded, with a birdie, in hauling herself alongside Laura but, having taken that all-important step, she promptly fell behind again by spilling three putts at the short 17th. Laura did what she had to do in terms of keeping her tee shot straight down the tree-lined 18th and went on to sew up a title which, in terms of satisfaction, must have ranked alongside that win in the Jamie Farr Toledo Classic where she had gone down the stretch with none other than her great heroine, Nancy Lopez. Quite apart from the fact that she had beaten Marie-Laure, Laura was more than a little elated at securing a top-ten finish on the European Order of Merit. In so doing, she had fulfilled one half of her stated ambition for 1988, to finish in the top-ten of both of US and European money lists.

Liselotte Neumann, Swedish winner of the US Women's Open, another great European win following Laura Davies in 1987.

From Biarritz she headed for the LPGA circuit with a view of going to work on the thirteenth place she occupied there at that time. She knew it would take nothing less than a third win (aside from having won in Toledo she had won in Tucson) but, at the end of a season in which she had probably asked just too much of herself, that win never materialised. Nor, as it turned out, did she win America's Rookie of the Year award, that honour going to Lotta Neumann who, having followed Laura as the US Open champion, finished second in the Mazda tournament in Japan to pull up in 12th place on the LPGA money list to Laura's 15th. However, for Laura to have pocketed $160,440 from her 20 tournaments in American and £41,871 from her ten tournaments at home, not to mention the countless yen she won at the end of the season in Japan, all added up to a thoroughly satisfying year for a player who could have been forgiven had she suffered some kind of reaction to the winning of the US Open the year before. There were plenty of girls on the European circuit who felt exhausted at the mere mention of the kind of hectic schedule Laura was following. Having envied Marie-Laure the way in which she would come back fresh to the circuit each time she took a week off, they were all wondering if they would do better were they to pace themselves more sensibly.

Alison Nicholas found herself in a position towards the end of last year when she had no option but to carry on and on and on . . . After playing quite beautifully to win her third title of the year in Guernsey, Alison had a very real chance of catching Marie-Laure on the money list. She made the gamest of efforts but, in the wake of that Guernsey win, was just too tired to pick herself up, mentally, for the following week's Laing Classic at Stoke Poges. Crucially, she finished 37th in the Laing to Marie-Laure's first, albeit things were not finally decided until the week of the Woolmark Match play championship where Marie-Laure defeated her in the 36-hole final. While Marie-Laure was winning alongside McNulty in Spain to push her prize money for the season close to the £100,000 mark, Alison was playing for a first time in Japan. Interestingly, the little Yorkshire golfer has been 'big' in Japan – Alison Nicholas towels and umbrellas are apparently all the rage out there – ever since she won the 1987 British Women's Open using a set of Japanese clubs.

Alison Nicholas who kept pace with Marie-Laure until near the season's end.

Mention must be made of Corinne Dibnah, the Australian who played such glorious golf to follow Alison as the British Open champion. However, in looking a little further down the money list, one cannot but pick out Marie Wennersten From for her achievement in winding up in 12th place at a time when she was almost six months pregnant. At five and a half months pregnant, the Swede had caused great excitement when she went into the third and final round of the Spanish Open at La Manga with a one shot lead over Marie-Laure. She then went to two ahead at the second. But, as one who had played herself, although not competitively, when eight months pregnant, Marie-Laure was not as in awe of her playing partner as might otherwise have been the case. The French player moved into top gear and swept past the Swede, ultimately finishing first with her promising compatriot, Corinne Soules, second.

Though individual success stories were many, nothing perhaps, was more important in 1988, than the success of the tour as a whole after the break from the PGA Everything depended on whether or not the women professionals got the right man at the helm and, to their relief, Joe Flanagan, who became their Executive Director at the start of the season, was soon into the swing of things. 'He was never a stranger,' said Dale Reid, who had been more than a little worried at the girls' decision to go it alone. 'He's been great with the players, great with the sponsors. What more could we ask?'

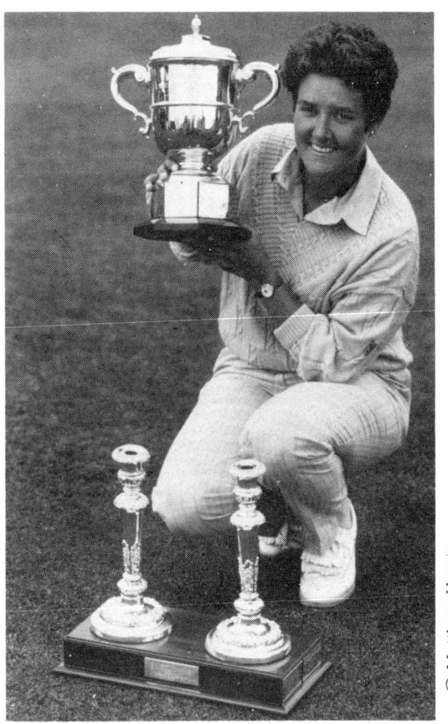

Corrine Dibnah from Australia won the Ladies British Open at Lindrick.

WPGET Tour 1988

Ford Ladies' Classic

at Woburn G & CC Milton Keynes Buckinghamshire

Name	Score	Prize £
L Davies	72-76-69-75—292	6000
C Dibnah	74-72-73-74—293	4100
M Walker	69-75-74-76—294	3000
C Panton	74-73-74-74—295	2440
T Abitbol	71-78-69-78—296	1960
M Wennersten From	75-78-71-73—297	1433
B Helbig	73-79-70-75—297	1433
M-L de Lorenzi Taya	73-69-77-78—297	1433
A Sheard	76-72-71-79—298	1060

Marbella Ladies' Open

at Marbella Spain

Name	Score	Prize £
L Maritz	70-68-76-69—283	9000
C Dibnah	72-71-73-70—286	5265
D Reid	71-69-72-74—286	5265
C Panton	70-71-74-72—287	3600
K Lunn	70-76-72-70—288	2655
K Epinasse	68-73-70-77—288	2655
S Strudwick	72-73-73-72—290	1920
P Gonzalez	70-71-72-77—290	1920
M Garner	73-75-69-74—291	1530
D Heinicke	72-71-77-72—292	1200
P Grice-Whittaker	71-76-71-74—292	1200
A Nicholas	77-71-69-75—292	1200
G Stewart	70-75-70-77—292	1200
B Huke	73-77-72-71—293	1011
S Gronberg	77-72-72-72—293	1011

Hennessy Cognac Ladies' Cup

at St Germain Paris

Name	Score	Prize £
M-L de Lorenzi Taya	75-72-66-71—284	11250
M Jones	74-70-69-72—285	6580
A Nicholas	72-72-71-70—285	6580

Name	Score	Prize £
G Stewart	73-70-70-73—286	4500
K Cockerill	76-72-69-72—289	3600
J Connachan	73-74-75-70—292	2815
B New	75-72-70-75—292	2815
A Jones	76-80-69-68—293	2210
C Baker	71-75-73-75—294	1583
C Dibnah	75-75-69-75—294	1583
R Lautens	74-76-74-70—294	1583
S Strudwick	80-70-75-69—294	1583
M Wennersten From	75-79-69-71—294	1583
D Barnard	74-71-75-75—295	1265
L Maritz	73-71-78-73—295	1265

British Olivetti Tournament

at Moor Hall GC Sutton Coldfield

Name	Score	Prize £
A Nicholas	71-72-69-71—283	4500
J Connachan	72-71-69-72—284	3075
M Garner	73-72-69-71—285	2250
D Clum	71-68-73-74—286	1830
K Douglas	69-74-73-71—287	1470
A Munt	74-72-73-69—288	1245
S Strudwick	72-72-72-73—289	1065

Portuguese Ladies' Open

at Vilamoura

Name	Score	Prize £
P Conley	69-76-72-74—291	6000
C Dibnah	75-74-70-73—292	4100
C Panton	74-77-73-70—294	3000
B New	75-75-70-75—295	2440
D Reid	73-79-75-71—298	1565
D Dowling	74-72-79-73—298	1565
G Stewart	75-72-74-77—298	1565
J Hill	73-74-74-77—298	1565
J Furst	77-76-75-71—299	1000
P Gonzalez	77-72-75-75—299	1000

Broadway Wirral Classic

at Caldy GC Wirral Cheshire

Name	Score	Prize £
B New	68-71-75-69—283	4500
C Panton	70-72-72-72—286	3075
A Jones	74-72-72-69—287	2250
L Maritz	75-71-74-69—289	1650
J Arnold	71-70-74-74—289	1650
L Mullard	75-70-74-72—291	1155
J Forrest	74-73-69-75—291	1155

Bowring Ladies' Scottish Open

at Cawder Glasgow

Name	Score	Prize £
C Panton	71-71-76-75—293	6000
D Dowling	73-75-71-75—294	3180
M Garner	74-72-76-72—294	3180
A Nicholas	72-74-76-72—294	3180
L Behan	75-71-76-74—296	1464
P Conley	75-71-76-74—296	1464
J Connachan	72-73-79-72—296	1464
K Lunn	75-71-81-69—296	1464
S Van Wyk	74-68-79-75—296	1464

St Moritz Classic

at St Moritz Switzerland

Name	Score	Prize £
J Arnold	72-70-74-69—285	9000
C Panton	73-74-70-69—286	6090
M-L de Lorenzi Taya	71-72-74-70—287	4020
A Nicholas	72-72-72-71—287	4020
S Strudwick	71-77-72-68—288	2655
B Helbig	71-73-74-70—288	2655
L Maritz	72-76-68-73—289	2070
C Baker	75-71-74-70—290	1470
C Soules	74-74-72-70—290	1470
K Lunn	75-71-73-71—290	1470
C Dibnah	74-73-72-71—290	1470

Bloor Homes Eastleigh Classic

at Fleming Park GC Eastleigh Hampshire

Name	Score	Prize £
C Dibnah	62-62-69-63—256	6000
D Hutton	64-64-62-67—257	3550
D Lofland	62-68-65-62—257	3550
C Baker	66-65-63-65—259	2440
A Jones	65-62-68-65—260	1960
K Lunn	67-66-66-62—261	1540
D Petrizzi	62-66-67-66—261	1540
K Douglas	64-65-69-64—262	1220
D Dowling	65-67-67-64—263	1060

Godiva Ladies' European Masters

at Royal Antwerp Belgium

Name	Score	Prize £
K Lunn	70-68-67-71—276	15000
M-L de Lorenzi Taya	69-65-69-75—278	10000
R Lautens	70-73-66-70—279	7400
L Davies	69-74-70-68—281	6000
P Conley	72-67-72-72—283	3812
S Gronberg	68-71-75-69—283	3812
L Mullard	69-69-71-74—283	3812
S Strudwick	70-73-71-69—283	3812
J Connachan	73-68-71-72—284	2550
D Dowling	72-68-68-77—285	2150
F Descampe	72-74-68-71—285	2150

Letting French Open

at Fourqueux St Germain Paris

Name	Score	Prize £
M-L de Lorenzi Taya	71-72-75-72—290	10500
C Bourtayre (*)	69-76-71-74—290	
(de Lorenzi Taya won play-off)		
A Nicholas	74-73-73-72—292	6142
L Planos	74-68-74-76—292	6142
D Dowling	72-75-72-74—293	3780
B New	73-72-72-76—293	3780
C Panton	72-76-79-67—294	2835
J Connachan	74-75-73-73—295	2415
A Jones	74-74-76-72—296	1638
L Percival	76-75-73-72—296	1638
G Stewart	75-71-77-73—296	1638
J Greco	75-73-72-76—296	1638
D Reid	70-77-71-78—296	1638

(* denotes amateur)

James Capel Guernsey Open

at Royal Guernsey CI

Name	Score	Prize £
A Nicholas	68-72-67-67—274	6000
A Sheard	74-67-68-67—276	4100
K Douglas	65-74-72-67—278	3000
A Jones	73-71-67-68—279	2440
J Arnold	69-73-68-70—280	1960
C Dibnah	76-68-65-73—282	1540
T Hammond	68-74-69-71—282	1540
P Conley	67-72-73-71—283	1140
K Lunn	76-69-67-71—283	1140

Guia Ladies' Masters

at Quinta da Marinha Portugal

Name	Score	Prize £
L Maritz	72-74-67—213	7500
A Nicholas	74-74-68—216	3543
M Wennersten From	74-71-71—216	3543
T Abitbol	72-72-72—216	3543
K Lunn	71-70-75—216	3543
C Dibnah	70-72-75—217	2025
S Moon	76-71-71—218	1600
C Panton	71-71-76—218	1600
M Garner	75-70-75—220	1275
S Strudwick	76-73-72—221	1033
D Petrizzi	71-78-72—221	1033
G Stewart	71-74-76—221	1033

Volmac Dutch Ladies' Open

at Rosendaelsche Arnhem

Name	Score	Prize £
M-L de Lorenzi Taya	75-74-72-74—295	9000
K Douglas	71-74-75-76—296	6090
K Espinasse	76-71-74-76—297	4440
S Strudwick	79-73-73-73—298	2745
P Gonzalez	75-74-76-73—298	2745
P Conley	77-74-73-74—298	2745
M Wennersten From	78-72-71-77—298	2745
J Greco	78-75-73-74—300	1650
A Nicholas	74-73-75-78—300	1650
P Smillie	76-77-76-72—301	1137
S Sronberg	77-79-73-72—301	1137
G Stewart	79-74-75-73—301	1137
A Munt	74-77-76-74—301	1137
S de Kraat	76-73-76-76—301	1137
D Reid	74-73-77-77—301	1137

BMW Ladies' German Open

at Hubbelrath Düsseldorf

Name	Score	Prize £
L Neumann	74-71-74-71—290	9000
M-L de Lorenzi Taya	71-74-69-77—291	6090
D Reid	78-74-73-69—294	4020
G Stewart	71-73-73-77—294	4020
J Arnold	75-73-69-78—295	2880
K Douglas	77-76-72-71—296	2430
D Dowling	78-75-73-71—297	1920
M Wennersten From	75-76-70-76—297	1920
A Nicholas	74-73-74-77—298	1440
C Panton	74-70-76-78—298	1440
J Connachan	74-76-76-73—299	1150
B Lunsford	76-73-76-74—299	1150
B New	75-76-73-75—299	1150

Burleigh Ladies' European Open

at Kingswood Surrey

Name	Score	Prize £
D Reid	68-72-71-72—283	9000
A Nicholas	71-69-67-77—284	6090
M Scobling	72-65-73-75—285	4440
C Dibnah	72-76-67-71—286	3600
L Mullard	72-68-70-77—287	2880
L Maritz	71-70-74-75—290	2430
A Jones	70-74-73-74—291	1790
K Scrivner	69-76-72-74—291	1790
D Hutton	71-72-73-75—291	1790
K Clark	72-71-75-74—292	1240
B New	74-74-70-74—292	1240
M Wennersten From	71-73-68-80—292	1240
S Moon	74-76-70-73—293	1015
K Espinasse	72-73-74-74—293	1015
P Nilsson	69-74-75-75—293	1015
P Gonzalez	70-76-70-77—293	1015

Laing Ladies' Classic

at Stoke Poges Berks

Name	Score	Prize £
M-L de Lorenzi Taya	67-67-69—203	6000
C Griffiths	71-75-64—210	4100
P Conley	67-72-72—211	2720
C Dibnah	73-70-68—211	2720
J Brown	72-68-74—214	1810
D Reid	71-72-71—214	1810
C Panton	72-71-72—215	1420
L Davies	72-75-69—216	1140
T Hammond	70-73-73—216	1140

Weetabix Ladies' British Open

at Lindrick Yorks

Name	Score	Prize £
C Dibnah	73-73-74-75—295	15000
S Little	73-77-69-76—295	10280
(C Dibnah won play-off)		
A Nicholas	76-73-75-72—296	7400
K Lunn	72-79-75-73—299	6000
J Soulsby	75-77-75-73—300	4800
K Douglas	76-70-78-77—301	4050
K Imrie*	76-72-77-76—301	
L Davies	72-78-79-73—302	3200
M Wennersten From	72-82-72-76—302	3200

Name	Score	Prize $
D Dowling	76-80-75-73—304	2110
D Heinicke	75-79-70-80—304	2110
L Maritz	77-76-77-74—304	2110
D Reid	78-76-74-76—304	2110
G Stewart	73-77-77-77—304	2110
N Way*	78-79-70-77—304	
M-L de Lorenzi Taya	73-79-74-79—305	1720
T Yarwood*	79-76-77-73—305	

(* denotes amateur)

Swedish Ladies' Open
at Delsjö

Name	Score	Prize £
M-L de Lorenzi Taya	70-70-69-66—275	9000
P Conley	69-68-71-70—278	6090
A Nicholas	70-71-72-67—280	4440
K Douglas	65-72-73-72—282	3600
C Dibnah	70-69-73-71—283	2655
D Dowling	71-70-71-71—283	2655
L Neumann	73-70-74-67—284	1920
S Strudwick	69-72-72-71—284	1920
D Hutton	71-71-72-71—285	1312
C Panton	73-70-68-74—285	1312
D Reid	74-72-71-68—285	1312
X Wunsch-Ruiz	74-66-74-71—285	1312

Danish Ladies' Open
at Rungsted GC

Name	Score	Prize £
F Descampe	70-73-76-66—285	9000
P Conley	72-73-74-70—289	4710
L Davies	72-74-73-70—289	4710
L Neumann	74-71-76-68—289	4710
R Comstock	71-77-71-71—290	2880
K Lunn	75-70-73-73—291	2090
D Reid	71-70-78-72—291	2090
M Wennersten From	69-71-76-75—291	2090
C Duffy	72-74-72-74—292	1370
D Heinicke	73-77-71-71—292	1370
A Nicholas	70-74-76-72—292	1370
M-L de Lorenzi Taya	68-71-78-76—293	1110
B New	70-69-77-77—293	1110

Variety Club Celebrity Classic

at Calcot Park Berks

Name	Score	Prize £
A Nicholas	68-67-69—204	6500
D Reid	70-68-70—208	4400
M Burton	75-70-66—211	3400
J Forrest	76-67-69—212	2700
D Dowling	71-71-71—213	2100
P Conley	75-71-68—214	1525
T Hammond	71-73-70—214	1525
D Hutton	70-71-74—215	1100

Biarritz Ladies' Open

at Biarritz France

Name	Score	Prize £
L Davies	65-67-68-67—267	7500
M-L de Lorenzi Taya	67-65-69-67—268	5075
C Dibnah	71-68-65-69—273	3700
K Lunn	71-68-67-69—275	3000
J Arnold	72-72-67-67—278	2212
P Conley	73-72-68-65—278	2212
D Barnard	69-71-68-71—279	1600
F Dassu	69-70-70-70—279	1600
D Reid	71-68-69-72—280	1200
S Strudwick	70-73-68-69—280	1200

Toshiba Players' Championship

at Old Thorns Hants

Name	Score	Prize £
D Reid	70-76-75-73—294	7500
P Conley	72-79-68-75—294	5075
(D Reid won play-off)		
J Brown	76-76-71-72—295	2781
C Dibnah	70-72-75-78—295	2781
D Dowling	78-75-69-73—295	2781
M Thomson	73-78-72-72—295	2781
L Davies	69-78-77-72—296	1600
K Douglas	75-74-74-73—296	1600
K Lunn	74-83-69-73—299	1275
J Connachan	77-79-73-71—300	1033
A Nicholas	76-75-76-73—300	1033
A Jones	77-76-77-70—300	1033

Italian Open

at Ca Della Nave Venice

Name	Score	Prize £
L Davies	65-67-69-68—269	10500
M-L de Lorenzi Taya	67-76-67-68—278	5495
K Douglas	72-66-65-75—278	5495
D Reid	68-67-70-73—278	5495
P Gonzalez	70-66-73-70—279	3360
C Panton	71-70-71-70—282	2835
J Connachan	70-74-69-70—283	2240
C Dibnah	70-69-71-73—283	2240
K Lunn	72-73-67-72—284	1785
P Conley	71-74-65-75—285	1400
F Dassu	69-73-69-74—285	1400
R Lautens	71-71-70-73—285	1400
J Ralls	72-69-74-70—285	1400
B New	72-73-70-71—286	1159
M Thomson	71-70-70-75—286	1159
X Wunsch-Ruiz	70-71-71-74—286	1159

Qualitair Spanish Open

at La Manga

Name	Score	Prize £
M-L de Lorenzi Taya	71-68-68—207	6000
C Soules	67-74-70—211	4100
D Reid	70-75-67—212	2720
F Descampe	72-73-67—212	2720
P Conley	70-72-71—213	
M Wennersten From	69-69-75—213	
A Nicholas	75-68-71—214	
A Jones	71-71-72—214	
F Dassu	75-69-71—215	
E Glass	71-70-74—215	
X Wunsch-Ruiz	70-74-71—215	
C Dibnah	74-73-69—216	
B New	72-70-74—216	
M Lunn	74-70-72—216	

Woolmark Ladies' Matchplay Championship

at Vallromanos Barcelona Spain

Semi-Finals:

M-L de Lorenzi Taya beat C Griffiths 1 hole
A Nicholas beat M Thomson 2 and 1

Play-off for 3rd and 4th place:

M Thomson beat C Griffiths 1 hole
(M Thomson won £3300 and C Griffiths £2500)

Final:

M-L de Lorenzi Taya beat A Nicholas 4 and 2
(M-L de Lorenzi Taya won £10000 and A Nicholas won £4400)

WPGET Woolmark Order of Merit 1988

1988 WPGET Money List

Pos		Name	Official Money £	No of Events
1	(6)	**M-L de Lorenzi Taya** (France)	99360.16	20
2	(4)	**Alison Nicholas**	76409.88	24
3	(3)	**Corinne Dibnah** (Australia)	66906.57	25
4	(1)	**Dale Reid**	56905.21	24
5	(26)	**Peggy Conley** (USA)	47867.58	24
6	(20)	**Karen Lunn** (Australia)	47455.25	25
7	(11)	**Catherine Panton**	45463.33	25
8	(2)	**Laura Davies**	41871.00	10
9	(7)	**Kitrina Douglas**	37879.80	23
10	(10)	**Debbie Dowling**	30731.25	23
11	(—)	**Laurette Maritz** (South Africa)	28362.66	13
12	(35)	**Marie Wennersten From** (Sweden)	27793.88	18
13	(19)	**Suzanne Strudwick**	27594.83	23
14	(18)	**Beverley New**	26344.07	23
15	(31)	**Anne Jones** (Australia)	24312.94	25
16	(9)	**Jane Connachan**	23916.89	21
17	(—)	**Janice Arnold** (New Zealand)	23064.16	17
18	(16)	**Gillian Stewart**	21114.90	14
19	(—)	**Regine Lautens** (Switzerland)	18478.33	18
20	(13)	**Maureen Garner**	17774.16	22
21	(32)	**Muriel Thomson**	17414.41	21
22	(27)	**Karine Espinasse** (France)	17308.10	19
23	(8)	**Liselotte Neumann** (Sweden)	16400.00	4
24	(46)	**Louise Mullard** (Australia)	16274.82	25
25	(39)	**Dennise Hutton** (Australia)	16267.90	13
26	(94)	**Caroline Griffiths**	16051.83	25
27	(—)	**Florence Descampe** (Belgium)	15928.85	8
28	(42)	**Patricia Gonzalez** (Colombia)	15324.21	21
29	(14)	**Alison Sheard**	14542.71	19
30	(15)	**Federica Dassu** (Italy)	14133.66	22
31	(28)	**Janet Soulsby**	13651.50	23
32	(—)	**Marjorie Jones** (USA)	12599.00	12
33	(—)	**Sofia Gronberg** (Sweden)	12403.00	17
34	(33)	**Corinne Soules** (France)	12166.83	16
35	(12)	**Susan Moon** (USA)	11929.60	21
36	(23)	**Brenda Lunsford** (USA)	11894.33	24
37	(—)	**Tania Abitbol** (Spain)	11409.51	18
38	(54)	**Julie Brown**	11174.08	20
39	(34)	**Barbara Helbig** (W Germany)	10850.57	20
40	(—)	**Lori Planos** (Spain)	10721.78	10
41	(37)	**Elizabeth Glass**	10350.91	21
42	(—)	**Xoniz Wunsch-Ruiz** (Spain)	10283.81	19
43	(30)	**Diana Heinicke** (USA)	10080.00	19
44	(40)	**Maxine Burton**	9666.20	25
45	(41)	**Rica Comstock** (USA)	9567.99	22
46	(—)	**Tracy Hammond**	9216.75	21
47	(—)	**Alison Munt** (Australia)	9182.66	17
48	(—)	**Linda Percival**	9027.65	22
49	(29)	**Beverley Huke**	8952.66	23

Pos		Name	Official Money £	No of Events
50	(84)	**Michele Scobling**	8462.28	13
51	(43)	**Diane Barnard**	8423.50	23
52	(36)	**Rae Hast**	7843.21	23
53	(49)	**Pia Nilsson** (Sweden)	7255.50	9
54	(51)	**Connie Baker** (Canada)	7104.00	7
55	(—)	**Debbie Petrizzi** (USA)	6966.86	22
56	(60)	**Julia Hill**	6880.75	18
57	(—)	**Helen Hopkins** (Australia)	6720.62	21
58	(38)	**Sonja Van Wyk** (South Africa)	6675.75	18
59	(57)	**Jo Rumsey**	6623.86	24
60	(85)	**Jane Forrest**	6172.00	11

Position in 1987 in brackets
Nationality is British unless otherwise stated

Women's Amateur Golf 1988

Lewine Mair

Home county rivalry

1988 was a year in which England's professional approach to the amateur game showed signs of having rubbed off on the other home countries, with Scotland preparing as never before for the Home Internationals they won at Barassie in September. Though Wales were no doubt happy enough at contributing two players, Karen Davies and Vicki Thomas, to the Curtis Cup side which was to win at Royal St George's in June, it clearly hurt the Scots and the Irish that they had but a player apiece to England's four. What is more, all three of Wales, Scotland and Ireland were given food for thought when, in mid-season, the British teams chosen, simultaneously, for the World Team championships were exclusively English affairs. It was not a case of England having got lucky. Rather was it a matter of English players receiving their just rewards for, as had happened in 1987, they were dominating the British championships. Where, in 1987, Janet Collingham had defeated Sue Shapcott in the final of the British Match Play championship so, in 1988, the final was another all-English concern in which Joanne Furby of Yorkshire defeated Julie Wade. Alison Macdonald, an English schoolgirl, albeit one with Scottish connections, followed Lincolnshire's Helen Dobson as British Girl champion while, when it came to the British Women's Stroke Play, Karen Mitchell took over as champion from Linda Bayman. The British Seniors', too, fell into English hands, with Catherine Bailey, who had performed so well for Surrey over 1988, winning at Littlestone.

National championships

With the Curtis Cup side having been announced at the end of the Avia Foursomes won by Karen Mitchell and Paul Way's sister, Nicola, it goes without saying that much interest attached to whether the Curtis Cup girls would clean up in the national championships. Julie Wade, of England's four Curtis Cup runners, won the English at Little Aston when she defeated Sue Shapcott in a match wherein the standard augured well for our chances in the Curtis Cup. In Scotland, Shirley Lawson defeated Fiona Anderson to bag what was her first senior Scottish title. It was an achievement which spoke volumes for Miss Lawson's temperament for, as a Curtis Cup recruit who did not have quite the same weighty credentials as the other seven members of the side, she felt that this was one championship she simply had to win. As a subsidiary pressure, she had the worry of having to contain the beginnings of that chipping twitch which was to terrorise her all summer. With Karen Davies still at university in the States and Vicki Thomas not at her considerable best, the Welsh title went to that wonderfully dogged little left-hander, Sharon Roberts. As for the Irish championship, Claire Hourihane, Ireland's lone member of the Curtis Cup team, went out early on to pave the way for a win by Laura Bolton.

Ladies British Open

For Miss Hourihane, that early loss was one which maybe contributed to the fact that she alone, of the Curtis Cup girls, was not given a game as the Great Britain and Ireland side triumphed in such style at Royal St George's. Typically, this enviably organised little Irish golfer hit back the following week to reach the semi-finals of the British Match-Play, a championship whose winner, Joanne Furby, had not only missed out on playing in the Curtis Cup but had failed even to feature on that team's short list. That the Great Britain and Ireland side had given all they had to their 11 – 7 defeat of the Americans should not be allowed to take away from Miss Furby's win the week after. The beaten Americans were decidedly dangerous, while there were plenty of other useful players from overseas. Miss Furby, the most phlegmatic of souls, played and putted magnificently over the five days. Her straightness off the tee was uncanny while, even if there were those who commented on how her backswing was not according to the textbook, most appreciated what her coach, Nigel Sumner, had to say about the way in which her swing will look better and better as she gets stronger. Not the most obviously athletic of girls, she has been dutifully following all the exercises handed out by Sumner. Running features on the list, as do wrist strengthening routines.

In the wake of that win, Miss Furby had every reason to suppose that her fortunes on the team front might take a turn for the better. Though she had won the 1987 English championship, she had been a humble reserve when at the start of 1988, England chose junior sides for the Vilmorin Trophy and the European Team championships which they were to win in Belgium. Nor, of course, had she featured in the thoughts of the Curtis Cup selectors. Though she was not given a place in the World Cup side - the three slots there went to MissWade, Miss Shapcott and Linda Bayman who were to finish a creditable third in Sweden - she was named as one of two players to go to New Zealand, the other being the promising Lora Fairclough. At last she had something to look forward to but, in the meantime, she had the kind of experience in the Home Internationals which must have had her thinking that she was fated in the amateur arena.

Scotland's triumph at Baracassie

In Home Internationals there are foursomes each morning, singles each afternoon, with each player having a possible six games over the three days. With Miss Furby the reigning British champion, the expectation was that England would use her all or most of the time, especially bearing in mind that the World Cup players had returned to these shores from Sweden only on the eve of the event and were patently the worse for wear. As it transpired, she played only twice. On the first afternoon she holed a glorious putt across the home green to collect half a point from her match with Scotland's Kathryn Imrie, arguably the most successful player of the series. Then, after having played not at all over the second day and the third morning, she was sent out at the top of the England side in their singles series against Ireland. The English captain, Judy Baymire, had thought, reasonably enough, that Miss Furby would be playing Laura Bolton, a clever girl who, with a job in the realm of engineering, spends more of her time concerned with the launching of spacecraft than golf balls. However, Ireland had slipped the Irish champion down the list and Miss Furby, who had so little golf under her belt, found herself up against an in-form Mary McKenna and was duly beaten out in the country. Though it has to be said that Scotland were decidedly lucky to play the English on a first day when they were the reverse of settled after the World Cup contingent had hurried north only at the last moment, the host nation deserved success. To their credit, they made the most of the fact that they were so well placed to practise and play together at Barassie, while they had also taken the unprecedented step of paying for Shirley Lawson, their champion, and Kathryn Imrie, who had been the leading amateur in the British Open championship, to return for the week from the States. Miss Lawson and Miss Imrie each played a key role in Scotland's success, while no one will forget the part played by Scotland's Lindsey Anderson who was never on the losing side.

Viewing the season as a whole, there is no escaping the fact that the top amateurs, like their professional counterparts, were in danger of playing too much for their own good. Nowadays, when so much store is set by proper preparation for a championship, it seems oddly contradictory that the top women in these islands are expected to play in their major championship, the British Match Play, hard on top of a Curtis Cup. Again, for a golfing nation so well organised as the British to have no decent interval between the World Cup in Sweden and the Home Internationals, similarly goes against the grain.

Too much competition?

For all of this, none among the more 'overworked' players seemed to suffer irreparable damage in terms of confidence. Sue Shapcott, who was involved in internationals at youth and senior level besides playing in all the major individual championships, rounded off her season by reaching the final of the Australian Amateur championship. No bad result to set alongside her runner-up berth in the English and her wins in each of the French Girls' championship and the Welsh Open Stroke Play. As for Julie Wade whose name is linked with Miss Shapcott's when players from abroad talk in terms of the British players they fear the most, she was tired enough to be glad of a break, but not too tired to be talking, excitedly, of the new season ahead.

USPGA Tour Results 1988

Bob Hope Chrysler Classic
at La Quinta California

Name	Score	Prize $
J Haas	63-68-69-68-70—338	180000
D Edwards	66-71-71-65-67—340	108000
B Tway	69-66-67-67-72—341	68000
P Stewart	72-71-67-67-65—342	44000
M O'Meara	71-66-68-68-69—342	44000
S Hoch	69-66-72-68-68—343	36000
G Morgan	71-67-71-67-68—344	31166
C Beck	72-67-69-66-70—344	31166
L Thompson	68-66-76-70-64—344	31166
G Sauers	69-67-69-70-70—345	26000
P Azinger	67-68-65-70-75—345	26000
C Strange	74-68-66-72-66—346	21000
A Magee	65-70-68-73-70—346	21000
F Couples	68-72-69-70-67—346	21000

Phoenix Open
at TAC Scottsdale Arizona

Name	Score	Prize $
S Lyle	68-68-68-65—269	117000
F Couples	67-65-67-70—269	70200
(S Lyle won play-off)		
D Frost	67-66-70-68—271	44200
D Love III	63-68-66-76—273	31200
B Lohr	68-70-70-66—274	22831
G Morgan	68-66-71-69—274	22831
K Green	70-68-67-69—274	22831
K Brown	66-71-70-67—274	22831
C Beck	66-63-75-71—275	17550
J Carter	71-68-66-70—275	17550
TC Chen	68-68-70-69—275	17550
M McCumber	69-71-66-70—276	14300
K Knox	72-68-68-68—276	14300
T Purtzer	68-70-68-71—277	11050
L Mize	69-72-68-68—277	11050
P Jacobsen	70-70-66-71—277	11050
J Mudd	69-68-70-70—277	11050
D Barr	67-71-67-72—277	11050

Nissan Los Angeles Open

at Riviera CC California

Name	Score	Prize $
C Beck	65-69-65-68—267	135000
B Sander	70-69-66-66—271	66000
M O'Grady	69-68-66-68—271	66000
M Reid	67-69-67-69—272	33000
E Fiori	66-68-68-70—272	33000
T Purtzer	69-68-67-69—273	26062
J Haas	65-68-69-71—273	26062
S Elkington	69-67-66-72—274	22500
D Hammond	66-68-73-67—274	22500
H Sutton	70-68-68-69—275	20250

Hawaiian Open

at Waialae CC Honolulu

Name	Score	Prize $
L Wadkins	68-71-66-66—271	108000
R Zokol	66-71-65-70—272	64800
J Huston	72-67-69-66—274	40800
G Sauers	71-68-67-69—275	28800
F Allem	69-69-68-70—276	24000
T Watson	69-70-66-72—277	19425
L Roberts	68-66-70-73—277	19425
B Eastwood	69-69-73-66—277	19425
J Carter	69-68-71-69—277	19425
JC Snead	70-67-73-68—278	15000
D Ishii	70-68-69-71—278	15000
D Eichelberger	75-66-69-68—278	15000

AT & T Pebble Beach National Pro-Am

at Pebble Beach Cypress Point and Spyglass Hill California

Name	Score	Prize $
S Jones	72-64-70-74—280	126000
B Tway	72-73-67-68—280	75600
(S Jones won play-off)		
G Norman	68-75-72-66—281	47600
T Sieckmann	69-68-75-70—282	27562
C Stadler	68-70-71-73—282	27562
B Langer	72-67-70-73—282	27562
J Carter	70-71-70-71—282	27562
M Calcavecchia	67-69-75-72—283	21700
T Watson	68-72-72-72—284	18900
M O'Meara	69-73-71-71—284	18900
D Canipe	70-76-68-70—284	18900

Shearson Lehman Brothers-Andy Williams San Diego Open

at Torrey Pines GC La Jolla California

Name	Score	Prize $
S Pate	68-66-67-68—269	117000
J Haas	69-67-68-66—270	70200
G Morgan	74-62-67-68—271	37700
J Sindelar	68-67-68-68—271	37700
W Wood	66-68-68-70—272	22035
T Kite	68-65-69-70—272	22035
R Maltbie	67-68-68-69—272	22035
B Foxon	69-65-66-72—272	22035
M Calcavecchia	66-68-70-68—272	22035
D Pooley	67-65-71-70—273	15600
G Koch	66-68-69-70—273	15600
JD Blake	69-71-67-66—273	15600
F Couples	63-71-68-71—273	15600

Doral Ryder Open

at Doral CC Miami Florida

Name	Score	Prize $
B Crenshaw	70-69-69-66—274	180000
M McCumber	71-68-68-68—275	88000
C Beck	68-68-70-69—275	88000
R Floyd	69-71-68-68—276	48000
L Nelson	68-71-70-68—277	36500
J Sindelar	71-69-69-68—277	36500
J Mahaffey	69-72-69-67—277	36500
S Hoch	72-70-68-68—278	29000
G Morgan	69-69-73-67—278	29000
B Lietzke	69-71-68-70—278	29000
R Wrenn	70-68-72-69—279	22000
C Stadler	71-73-67-68—279	22000
E Fiori	69-71-69-70—279	22000
T Kite	68-70-73-68—279	22000

Honda Classic

at Eagle Trace Fort Lauderdale Florida

Name	Score	Prize £
J Sindelar	68-70-68-70—276	126000
P Stewart	73-71-67-67—278	52266
E Fiori	70-67-71-70—278	52266
S Lyle	74-64-70-70—278	52266
J Mudd	70-67-72-70—279	24587
B Lohr	73-73-66-67—279	24587
W Grady	72-69-70-68—279	24587
T Byrum	70-68-71-70—279	24587
F Couples	73-70-69-68—280	18900
K Green	70-70-73-67—280	18900
R Floyd	71-69-68-72—280	18900

Hertz Bay Hill Classic

at Bay Hill Orlando Florida

Name	Score	Prize $
P Azinger	66-66-73-66—271	135000
T Kite	69-68-69-70—276	81000
A Magee	66-70-73-71—280	43500
D Frost	70-66-75-69—280	43500
D Pooley	68-74-73-66—281	30000
P Stewart	68-72-70-72—282	23475
J Sindelar	68-73-73-68—282	23475
C Stadler	73-68-70-71—282	23475
B Lietzke	69-72-71-70—282	23475
D Eichelberger	72-65-71-74—282	23475
G Rudolph	70-69-73-71—283	16500
G Norman	73-70-73-67—283	16500
D Barr	70-70-74-69—283	16500
B Crenshaw	70-71-74-68—283	16500

USF&G Classic

at Lakewood CC New Orleans Louisiana

Name	Score	Prize $
C Beck	69-64-65-64—262	135000
L Wadkins	67-65-69-68—269	81000
D Forsman	68-68-70-65—271	51000
C Peete	69-70-67-66—272	36000
L Mize	68-68-70-67—273	30000
G Ladehoff	68-68-68-70—274	27000
J Cook	70-70-67-68—275	24187
P Fabel	70-67-68-70—275	24187
T Watson	68-69-71-68—276	18000
P Wrenn	68-71-68-69—276	18000
M Lye	71-70-68-67—276	18000
D Hammond	68-71-70-67—276	18000
L Clements	69-68-68-71—276	18000
R Cochran	71-69-66-70—276	18000

Panasonic-Las Vegas Invitational

at Las Vegas Desert Inn and Spanish Trail Nevada

Name	Score	Prize $
G Koch	68-73-66-67—274	250000
M O'Meara	65-75-69-66—275	122222
P Jacobsen	71-66-68-70—275	122222
J Sindelar	70-72-68-66—276	52361
G Sauers	69-71-68-68—276	52361
R Fehr	67-74-67-68—276	52361
C Byrum	65-72-67-72—276	52361
D Canipe	71-69-68-68—276	52361
P Stewart	70-72-66-69—277	38889
D Hammond	68-75-66-68—277	38889

Tournament Players' Championship

at Tournament Players' Club Sawgrass Florida

Name	Score	Prize $
M McCumber	65-72-67-69—273	225000
M Reid	68-69-73-67—277	135000
D Frost	67-71-68-72—278	65000
F Allem	73-72-65-68—278	65000
C Byrum	66-73-69-70—278	65000
L Wadkins	70-72-67-70—279	43437
G Morgan	69-70-71-69—279	43437
P Stewart	71-65-71-73—280	36250
D Pohl	69-69-70-72—280	36250
W Levi	70-71-71-68—280	36250
G Norman	66-74-68-73—281	26500
M Wiebe	71-70-71-69—281	26500
T Kite	67-73-69-72—281	26500
C Beck	73-67-69-72—281	26500
B Crenshaw	69-71-69-72—281	26500
B Langer	71-72-67-72—282	17535
P Jacobsen	69-75-69-69—282	17535
M Hulbert	74-69-69-70—282	17535
G Sauers	70-71-70-71—282	17535
J Sindelar	69-72-67-74—282	17535
C Peete	70-69-71-72—282	17535
G Kock	70-72-69-71—282	17535

Greater Greensboro Open

at Forest Oaks CC Greensboro North Carolina

Name	Score	Prize $
S Lyle	68-63-68-72—271	180000
K Green	68-67-69-67—271	108000
(S Lyle won play-off)		
J Sluman	64-65-73-71—273	68000
S Hoch	67-67-69-72—275	48000
G Morgan	68-68-71-72—279	40000
T Purtzer	74-66-72-69—281	
K Parry	71-70-70-70—281	
C Beck	70-70-72-69—281	
D Hammond	67-67-73-74—281	
TC Chen	66-71-75-70—282	
J Sindelar	70-72-72-68—282	
K Clearwater	69-73-71-69—282	
R Campbell	74-70-67-71—282	

MCI Heritage Classic

at Harbour Town GC Hilton Head Is South Carolina

Name	Score	Prize $
G Norman	65-69-71-66—271	126000
G Morgan	71-64-69-68—272	61600
D Frost	69-64-69-70—272	61600
F Couples	68-65-68-73—274	33600
D Ogrin	67-69-71-69—276	26600
P Azinger	65-70-73-68—276	26600
D Tewell	72-69-69-67—277	21816
C Strange	70-70-71-66—277	21816
DA Weibring	68-71-68-70—277	21816
S Pate	71-69-70-68—278	17500
M McCumber	72-67-69-70—278	17500
R Cochran	73-68-69-68—278	17500

Independent Insurance Agent Houston Open

at The Woodlands Houston Texas

Name	Score	Prize $
C Strange	69-68-66-67—270	126000
G Norman	65-70-68-67—270	75600
(C Strange won play-off)		
T Kite	69-69-66-68—272	47600
B Tennyson	68-68-70-69—275	30800
J Carter	71-69-68-67—275	30800
T Simpson	68-70-69-69—276	25200
M Donald	67-69-72-70—278	22575
B Lietzke	73-68-69-68—278	22575
D Rummells	72-68-70-69—279	18900
J Renner	70-70-68-71—279	18900
B Clampett	73-68-70-68—279	18900
C Peete	69-70-69-72—280	14700
H Sutton	66-70-73-71—280	14700
B Crenshaw	73-65-71-71—280	14700

Mony Tournament of Champions

at La Costa CC Carlsbad California

Name	Score	Prize $
S Pate	66-66-70—202	90000
L Nelson	68-67-68—203	54000
D Barr	67-66-73—206	29000
N Faldo	70-65-71—206	29000
K Clearwater	69-67-73—209	19000
JC Snead	69-69-71—209	19000
P Azinger	68-73-69—210	15062
M McCumber	72-68-70—210	15062
D Tewell	69-71-70—210	15062
P Stewart	68-71-71—210	15062

GTE Byron Nelson Golf Classic

at TPC Las Colinas Irving Texas

Name	Score	Prize $
B Lietzke	66-69-66-70—271	135000
C Rose	66-69-67-69—271	81000
(B Lietzke won play-off)		
D Graham	68-69-67-68—272	43500
B Crenshaw	66-65-70-71—272	43500
J Cook	70-64-69-70—273	27375
P Azinger	73-68-63-69—273	27375
M Calcavecchia	70-66-68-69—273	27375
C Stadler	68-66-68-72—274	22500
N Price	71-68-66-69—274	22500
T Watson	67-73-71-64—275	18750
F Couples	70-71-65-69—275	18750
D Frost	66-70-70-69—275	18750

Colonial National Invitation

at Colonial CC Fort Worth Texas

Name	Score	Prize $
L Wadkins	67-68-70-65—270	135000
J Sindelar	71-65-67-68—271	56000
M Calcavecchia	68-69-68-66—271	56000
B Crenshaw	69-67-68-67—271	56000
C Rose	67-68-65-74—274	30000
M Wiebe	72-67-69-67—275	25125
S Hoch	67-68-71-69—275	25125
D Graham	71-66-70-68—275	25125
C Beck	71-70-69-67—277	21000
D Frost	74-66-69-68—277	21000

Memorial Tournament

at Muirfield Village GC Dublin Ohio

Name	Score	Prize $
C Strange	73-70-64-67—274	160000
D Frost	69-70-68-69—276	78220
H Irwin	70-68-68-70—276	78220
A Magee	70-70-68-74—282	39115
J Huston	69-70-72-71—282	39115
L Wadkins	79-66-71-67—283	26880
J Haas	72-75-69-67—283	26880
P Stewart	72-69-67-75—283	26880
G Norman	71-74-67-71—283	26880
P Jacobsen	68-74-72-69—283	26880
S Hoch	74-73-64-72—283	26880
N Price	74-67-71-72—284	18970
P Azinger	72-69-71-72—284	18970
C Beck	72-76-69-67—284	18970

Kemper Open

at TPC Avenel Potomac Maryland

Name	Score	Prize $
M Hatalsky	68-66-68-72—274	144000
T Kite	67-67-71-69—274	86400
(M Hatalsky won play-off)		
C Stadler	70-70-64-72—276	46400
M Reid	69-68-67-72—276	46400
B Gilder	72-65-71-69—277	30400
J Hallet	68-65-72-72—277	30400
C Peete	68-70-70-70—278	24100
J Mahaffey	68-68-68-74—278	24100
D Mast	72-68-68-70—278	24100
L Mize	69-70-69-70—278	24100

Manufacturers Hanover Westchester Classic

at Westchester CC Rye New York

Name	Score	Prize $
S Ballesteros	72-68-69-67—276	126000
G Norman	73-69-70-64—276	52266
D Frost	71-68-69-68—276	52266
K Green	71-68-67-70—276	52266
(S Ballesteros won play-off)		
S Elkington	68-70-69-71—278	28000
L Roberts	66-71-73-70—280	22662
D Mast	71-68-68-73—280	22662
B Eastwood	69-72-72-67—280	22662
B Chamblee	70-68-73-69—280	22662
J Sluman	74-70-68-69—281	18200
T Armour	73-69-71-68—281	18200
S Simpson	71-69-71-71—282	13300
JC Snead	68-73-70-71—282	13300
B Kratzert	73-71-66-72—282	13300
T Nakajima	73-71-71-67—282	13300
J Hallet	70-71-69-72—282	13300
JD Blake	71-72-72-67—282	13300

Provident Classic

at Valleybrook Hixon Tennessee

Name	Score	Prize $
P Blackmar	66-64-69-65—264	81000
P Stewart	65-67-67-65—264	48600
(P Blackmar won play-off)		
M Hayes	70-69-63-67—269	23400
BR Brown	69-69-65-66—269	23400
J Dent	66-66-67-70—269	23400
L Thompson	66-67-69-68—270	13612
B Glasson	68-69-68-65—270	13612
J Hallet	67-65-69-69—270	13612
B Bergin	69-67-65-69—270	13612
B Britton	63-70-66-71—270	13612
R Cochran	66-69-67-68—270	13612

Georgia-Pacific Atlanta Classic

at Atlanta CC Marietta Georgia

Name	Score	Prize $
L Nelson	63-66-66-73—268	126000
C Beck	67-66-70-66—269	75600
P Azinger	66-67-66-71—270	47600
L Wadkins	69-68-70-65—272	28933
B Wadkins	64-69-68-71—272	28933
D Rummells	67-69-67-69—272	28933
N Price	68-71-68-66—273	22575
C Rose	68-71-66-68—273	22575
S Hoch	70-65-68-71—274	20300
W Levi	68-69-68-70—275	18200
M Calcavecchia	67-71-67-70—275	18200

St Jude Federal Express Classic

at Colonial CC Cordova Tennessee

Name	Score	Prize $
J Mudd	68-68-67-70—273	171692
N Price	73-64-71-66—274	83938
P Jacobsen	68-68-72-66—274	83938
D Rummells	70-69-66-71—276	39425
L Mize	70-68-70-68—276	39425
T Simpson	68-68-68-72—276	39425
C Strange	69-71-67-70—277	30761
T Kite	71-69-67-70—277	30761

Canadian Open

at Glen Abbey GC Oakville Ontario

Name	Score	Prize $
K Green	70-65-68-72—275	135000
S Verplank	69-70-67-70—276	66000
B Glasson	70-71-68-67—276	66000
M Sullivan	71-70-69-67—277	33000
D Barr	72-68-71-66—277	33000
M Wiebe	72-69-70-67—278	27000
G Smith	71-71-70-67—279	22593
L Rinker	77-65-65-72—279	22593
W Grady	69-72-68-70—279	22593
J Delsing	70-67-68-74—279	22593
B Tway	71-69-66-74—280	17250
J Huston	70-73-64-73—280	17250
L Mize	66-71-71-72—280	17250

Anheuser-Busch Golf Classic

at Kingsmill GC Williamsburg Virginia

Name	Score	Prize $
T Sieckmann	69-66-66-69—270	117000
M Wiebe	68-70-64-68—270	70200
(T Sieckmann won play-off)		
G Sauers	68-71-67-66—272	37700
K Knox	67-69-65-71—272	37700
J Sluman	70-67-72-64—273	24700
M McCumber	68-69-69-67—273	24700
F Zoeller	67-68-69-70—274	19581
T Simpson	69-71-69-65—274	19581
P Jacobsen	67-65-69-73—274	19581
J Coston	75-67-65-67—274	19581
J Sindelar	70-70-69-66—275	14950
C Kite	67-73-65-70—275	14950
T Byrum	65-73-70-67—275	14950

Hardee's Golf Classic

at Oakwood CC Coal Valley Illinois

Name	Score	Prize $
B McCallister	68-62-63-68—261	108000
D Forsman	64-66-67-67—264	64800
S Randolph	64-67-69-66—266	40800
B Fabel	67-66-67-67—267	24800
S Jones	67-69-67-64—267	24800
S Hoch	69-65-67-66—267	24800
B Lohr	68-68-66-66—268	19350
R Cochran	66-64-69-69—268	19350
T Sieckmann	67-67-69-66—269	15600
J Dent	66-68-68-67—269	15600
D Barr	69-67-67-66—269	15600
R Barr Jr	66-67-70-66—269	15600
D Ogrin	67-68-69-66—270	12600
G Sauers	62-73-70-66—271	11100
J Huston	68-69-65-69—271	11100

Canon Sammy Davis Jr-Greater Hartford Open

at TPC of Connecticut Cromwell Connecticut

Name	Score	Prize $
M Brooks	66-65-69-69—269	126000
J Sindelar	65-72-67-65—269	61600
D Barr	69-67-70-63—269	61600
(M Brooks won play-off)		
R Black	66-69-65-70—270	30800
M Calcavecchia	67-66-67-70—270	30800
B Upper	67-66-69-69—271	24325
R Maltbie	64-68-72-67—271	24325

Name	Score	Prize $
B McCallister	68-66-69-69—272	19600
B Faxon	65-69-69-69—272	19600
L Clements	68-70-68-66—272	19600
G Archer	70-66-67-69—272	19600
K Perry	67-68-68-70—273	15400
M Hayes	67-69-69-68—273	15400

Beatrice Western Open

at Butler National GC Oak Brook Illinois

Name	Score	Prize $
J Benepe	71-68-69-70—278	162000
P Jacobsen	70-65-69-75—279	97200
B Faxon	71-69-71-69—280	52200
I Aoki	71-73-67-69—280	52200
DA Weibring	70-71-69-71—281	34200
D Forsman	68-69-71-73—281	34200
H Irwin	73-69-69-71—282	27112
B Glasson	69-73-71-69—282	27112
M Hatalsky	66-79-68-69—282	27112
M Calcavecchia	71-71-67-73—282	27112

The International

at Castle Pines GC Castle Rock Colorado

Name	Points	Prize $
J Sindelar	+17	180000
D Pohl	+13	88000
S Pate	+13	88000
M Wiebe	+12	48000
C Beck	+11	40000
D Love III	+9	36000
B Crenshaw	+8	33500
B Lietzke	+6	31000

Modified Stableford with points awarded as follows: double eagle +8; eagle +5; birdie +2; par 0; bogey −1; double bogey or worse −3.

Buick Open

at Warwick Hills G & CC Grand Blanc Michigan

Name	Score	Prize $
S Verplank	66-66-70-66—268	126000
D Tewell	68-70-68-64—270	75600
F Couples	66-69-71-65—271	47600
T Norris	69-66-71-66—272	33600
B Crenshaw	70-71-66-67—274	26600
J Hallet	67-69-69-69—274	26600
G Sauers	68-71-68-68—275	20370
J Renner	68-72-68-67—275	20370
D Rummells	68-71-66-70—275	20370
K Knox	69-68-69-69—275	20370
S Hoch	66-72-68-69—275	20370

NEC World Series of Golf

at Firestone CC Akron Ohio

Name	Score	Prize $
M Reid	70-65-71-69—275	162000
T Watson	74-69-64-68—275	97200
(M Reid won play-off)		
I Baker-Finch	68-67-71-71—277	52200
L Nelson	70-70-66-71—277	52200
S Lyle	69-67-71-71—278	36000
C Beck	71-69-69-70—279	31350
S Pate	74-67-74-64—279	31350
B Crenshaw	73-67-68-72—280	28100
J Haas	69-73-69-70—281	25300
B Lietzke	70-69-72-70—281	25300
J Sluman	71-73-71-67—282	22600
G Norman	72-71-69-71—283	20800
M McCumber	70-71-66-77—284	19100

BC Open

at Endicott New York

Name	Score	Prize $
B Glasson	66-68-65-69—268	90000
B Lietzke	68-71-67-64—270	44000
W Levi	66-71-66-67—270	44000
J Sluman	68-70-68-65—271	22000
D Pooley	67-66-70-68—271	22000
K Green	66-70-72-65—273	16750
B Bryant	68-68-67-70—273	16750
F Couples	70-67-69-67—273	16750
J Sindelar	67-65-70-72—274	12500
LT Broeck	66-69-68-71—274	12500
K Perry	69-70-66-69—274	12500
K Knox	68-70-68-68—274	12500
I Baker-Finch	69-68-67-70—274	12500

Bank of Boston Classic

at Pleasant Valley CC Sutton Massachusetts

Name	Score	Prize $
M Calcavecchia	71-67-70-66—274	108000
D Pooley	75-68-69-73—275	64800
F Zoeller	68-69-69-70—276	31200
D Rummells	70-69-70-67—276	31200
J Mahaffey	70-69-70-67—276	31200
S Pate	68-68-69-72—277	20100
W Levi	71-67-69-70—277	20100
W Grady	71-68-69-69—277	20100
D Waldorf	71-70-69-68—278	14400
DA Weibring	68-68-69-73—278	14400
C Rose	71-70-71-66—278	14400
R Maltbie	71-71-66-70—278	14400
D Hammond	67-73-71-67—278	14400
B McCallister	73-69-70-66—278	14400

Greater Milwaukee Open

at Tuckaway CC Franklin Wisconsin

Name	Score	Prize $
K Green	70-69-61-68—268	126000
D Pohl	70-72-66-66—274	46200
D Hammond	68-69-68-69—274	46200
J Gallacher Jr	67-67-72-68—274	46200
M Calcavecchia	71-68-69-66—274	46200
N Price	70-71-67-67—275	25200
C Pavin	66-72-70-68—276	21816
T Simpson	70-70-70-66—276	21816
D Ogrin	70-66-70-70—276	21816
D Barr	66-68-68-75—277	18000

Nabisco Texas Open

at Oak Hills CC San Antonio Texas

Name	Score	Prize $
C Pavin	64-63-66-66—259	108000
R Wrenn	69-68-68-62—267	64800
P McGowan	68-68-67-65—268	40800
T Kite	67-64-69-69—269	28800
B Wadkins	64-71-69-66—270	20340
M Sullivan	63-67-77-63—270	20340
P Stewart	69-65-68-68—270	20340
T Pernice Jr	65-66-67-72—270	20340
R Maltbie	68-67-68-67—270	20340
D Pooley	67-69-69-66—271	14400
J Mudd	68-66-70-67—271	14400
B Crenshaw	67-65-69-70—271	14400
J Haas	66-65-73-67—271	14400

Nabisco Championships of Golf

at Pebble Beach California

Name	Score	Prize $
C Strange	64-71-70-74—279	360000
T Kite	72-65-70-72—279	216000
(C Strange won play-off)		
K Green	67-70-69-74—280	104666
P Stewart	73-70-64-73—280	104666
M Calcavecchia	70-71-65-74—280	104666
P Jacobsen	71-70-67-73—281	72000
F Couples	75-67-67-73—282	68000
M Reid	72-72-68-73—285	55800
S Verplank	69-70-72-74—285	55800
G Koch	71-72-68-74—285	55800
B Tway	69-70-71-75—285	55800
J Mudd	70-71-68-76—285	55800
B Lietzke	69-68-70-78—285	55800

Gatlin Brothers Southwest Classic

at Fairway Oaks G & RC Abilene Texas

Name	Score	Prize $
T Purtzer	64-72-69-64—269	72000
M Brooks	64-68-70-67—269	43200
(T Purtzer won play-off)		
B Gardner	69-68-69-65—271	27200
D Pohl	70-69-66-67—272	17600
B Bryant	66-68-68-70—272	17600
M O'Meara	71-70-68-64—273	12950
T Armour	71-70-64-68—273	12950
P Azinger	66-70-69-68—273	12950
D Barr	69-67-68-69—273	12950
H Twitty	68-68-70-68—274	10400
D Love III	73-65-70-66—274	10400

Southern Open

at Green Island CC Columbus Georgia

Name	Score	Prize $
D Frost	70-68-65-67—270	72000
B Tway	71-66-66-67—270	43200
(D Frost won play-off)		
D Forsman	67-66-69-69—271	20800
G Archer	70-66-70-65—271	20800
D Barr	72-68-61-70—271	20800
M Hulbert	67-66-69-70—272	14400
LT Broeck	68-65-69-71—273	12050
J Sluman	63-67-74-69—273	12050
C Pavin	69-70-66-68—273	12050
M Donald	67-70-71-65—273	12050

Walt Disney World Golf Classic

at Lake Buena Vista and Magnolia Palm

Name	Score	Prize $
B Lohr	62-67-66-68—263	126000
C Beck	66-68-63-66—263	75600
(B Lohr won play-off)		
F Zoeller	64-69-66-70—269	40600
B Lietzke	69-67-65-68—269	40600
D Pohl	68-68-68-66—270	25550
P Azinger	67-68-62-73—270	25550
M Donald	68-67-70-65—270	25550
R Wrenn	66-68-71-66—271	19600
G Sauers	69-67-67-68—271	19600
M Wiebe	69-67-68-67—271	19600
L Nelson	72-63-67-69—271	19600
T Kite	68-68-66-72—272	15400
K Green	70-64-68-70—272	15400

Centel Classic

at Killearn G & CC Tallahassee Florida

Name	Score	Prize $
B Glasson	67-69-68-68—272	90000
T Armour	70-71-65-68—274	54000
B Lohr	69-67-68-71—275	29000
C Perry	67-71-66-71—275	29000
K Perry	69-66-69-72—276	18250
M Donald	70-66-70-70—276	18250
B Gardner	68-69-70-69—276	18250
J Overton	68-70-73-66—277	14500
B Langer	66-70-71-70—277	14500
G Archer	68-69-70-70—277	14500
K Knox	67-71-69-71—278	12500

Deposit Guaranty Classic

at Hattiesburg Massachusetts

Name	Score	Prize $
F Conner	65-70-69-63—267	36000
B Mogg	68-67-70-67—272	21600
D Ogrin	68-69-68-68—273	13600
R Thompson	72-64-69-69—274	7875
K Young	68-70-66-70—274	7875
J Hart	70-68-70-66—274	7875
J Adams	69-71-66-68—274	7875

Pensacola Open

at Tiger Point Florida

Name	Score	Prize $
A Magee	70-68-67-66—271	72000
K Green	68-68-69-67—272	29866
T Byrum	72-64-65-71—272	29866
B Leitzke	71-67-67-67—272	29866
D Pohl	66-71-70-67—274	16000

USLPGA Tour Results 1988

Mazda Classic
at Stonebridge G & CC Deerfield Beach Florida

Name	Score	Prize $
N Lopez	69-68-71-75—283	30000
M Figueras-Dotti	70-70-72-73—285	18500
J Inkster	74-71-75-68—288	8434
H Farr	70-74-73-71—288	8434
J Stephenson	72-71-71-74—288	8433
P Sheehan	71-72-71-74—288	8433
A Benz	69-72-73-74—288	8433
M Foyer	71-70-72-75—288	8433
L Peterson	72-75-71-71—289	4054
K Postlewait	70-73-73-73—289	4054
A Alcott	70-73-72-74—289	4053
P Rizzo	67-72-76-74—289	4053

Orient Leasing Hawaiian Ladies Open
at Turtle Bay CC Oahu

Name	Score	Prize $
A Okamoto	69-72-72—213	45000
D Richard	73-73-68—214	24000
J Carner	70-71-73—214	24000
B Daniel	70-73-72—215	13000
K Postlewait	70-73-72—215	13000
J Stephenson	68-75-72—215	13000
M Bozarth	73-72-71—216	7500
P Sheehan	73-72-71—216	7500
C Gerring	71-72-73—216	7500
J Delk	71-69-76—216	7500
L Young	77-73-67—217	4981
L Rittenhouse	75-72-70—217	4980
T Ohsako	74-71-72—217	4980
J Inkster	72-73-72—217	4980
P Bradley	75-69-73—217	4980

Sarasota Classic

at Bent Tree G & RC Sarasota Florida

Name	Score	Prize $
P Sheehan	71-72-72-67—282	33750
J Carner	70-74-73-68—285	18000
J Rosenthal	71-70-74-70—285	17999
S Turner	69-74-73-70—286	10687
B Daniel	68-73-72-73—286	10687
C Morse	73-74-72-68—287	7256
J Inkster	72-75-72-68—287	7256
P Hammel	70-78-70-71—289	5850
J Stephenson	68-78-73-71—290	5006
C Walker	72-73-71-74—290	5006

Circle K Tucson Open

at Randolph Park GC Tucson Arizona

Name	Score	Prize $
L Davies	63-74-69-72—278	45000
R Walton	69-64-76-70—279	27750
P Sheehan	68-68-72-72—280	20250
J Stephenson	73-69-68-71—281	15750
M Bozarth	73-70-69-70—282	12750
R Jones	70-70-72-71—283	10500
S Turner	72-66-73-73—284	8850
C Walker	75-70-73-67—285	6421
N Lopez	71-73-71-70—285	6420
O-H Ku	72-69-71-73—285	6420
H Farr	71-70-71-73—285	6420
J Coles	72-66-74-73—285	6420

Standard Register/Samaritan Turquoise Classic

at Moon Valley Phoenix Arizona

Name	Score	Prize $
O-H Ku	71-68-70-72—281	52500
D Mochrie	70-72-71-69—282	28000
A Okamoto	71-71-70-70—282	28000
A Alcott	65-73-73-73—284	16625
C Walker	67-71-73-73—284	16625
C Johnson	70-76-70-69—285	10559
H Farr	74-69-71-71—285	10558
J Inkster	72-71-70-72—285	10558
N Brown	74-69-75-69—287	6840
S Turner	75-73-68-71—287	6840
J Geddes	73-74-68-72—287	6840
D Ammaccapane	70-72-71-74—287	6840
R Jones	70-71-70-76—287	6840

Santa Barbara Open

at La Purisima and Sandpiper Santa Barbara California

Name	Score	Prize $
R Jones	70-70-72—212	45000
M McGeorge	68-72-75—215	27750
M Blackwelder	72-72-73—217	18000
K Postlewait	71-73-73—217	18000
S Turner	66-76-76—218	12750
C Hill	71-76-72—219	7701
C Walker	74-72-73—219	7701
S Furlong	71-74-74—219	7701
A Okamoto	71-74-74—219	7701
S Palmer	71-73-75—219	7701
C Morse	70-73-76—219	7700

Kemper Women's Open

at Princeville Makai Kauai Hawaii

Name	Score	Prize $
B King	73-72-66-69—280	45000
B Daniel	72-66-70-73—281	27750
T Green	70-71-73-68—282	20250
A Okamoto	71-71-69-72—283	15750
A Alcott	70-71-70-73—284	12750
A Ritzman	73-68-73-72—286	9675
C Walker	70-71-72-73—286	9675
M-C Cheng	73-74-71-69—287	6421
H Farr	73-74-70-70—287	6420
J Carner	70-71-74-72—287	6420
R Jones	70-73-70-74—287	6420
M Bozarth	68-71-72-76—287	6420

AI Star/Centinela Hospital Classic

at Rancho Park GC Los Angeles California

Name	Score	Prize $
N Lopez	71-72-67—210	60000
M Figueras-Dotti	70-70-70—210	37000
(N Lopez won play-off)		
C Walker	73-71-67—211	27000
K Shipman	73-70-69—212	19000
A Alcott	69-70-73—212	19000
M Nause	73-75-65—213	11400
A Benz	73-72-68—213	11400
S Turner	72-68-73—213	11400
J Inkster	70-70-73—213	11400
P Hammel	74-71-69—214	7160
H Stacy	71-73-70—214	7160
R Hood	73-70-71—214	7160
N Ledbetter	72-71-71—214	7160
S Quinlan	73-68-73—214	7160

Nabisco Dinah Shore Invitational

at Mission Hills CC Rancho Mirage California

Name	Score	Prize $
A Alcott	71-66-66-71—274	80000
C Walker	73-65-69-69—276	42000
R Jones	73-67-68-71—279	26000
C Keggi*	75-71-66-69—281	—
N Lopez	74-69-70-69—282	18000
M Figueras-Dotti	70-69-70-73—282	18000
D Mochrie	76-71-70-67—284	14431
J Geddes	75-73-66-70—284	14431
D Coe	77-67-70-70—284	14430
D Massey	72-68-73-72—285	10643
J Stephenson	69-72-70-74—285	10643

(* denotes amateur)

San Diego Inamori Classic

at Stoneridge CC San Diego California

Name	Score	Prize $
A Okamoto	69-71-63-69—272	33750
C Walker	68-67-69-69—273	20812
J Dickinson	68-71-68-67—274	15187
N Lopez	70-68-72-68—278	11812
M Nause	71-71-69-68—279	8719
O-H Ku	68-70-69-72—279	8719
M Moore	71-70-71-69—281	5625
A Alcott	72-70-67-72—281	5625
D Germain	69-72-68-72—281	5625
P Sheehan	67-71-69-74—281	5624

USX Classic

at Pasadena Yacht & CC St Petersburg Florida

Name	Score	Prize $
R Jones	67-69-69-70—275	33750
K Postlewait	68-69-69-69—275	20812
(R Jones won play-off)		
B Bunkowsky	71-70-67-69—277	15187
C Chillemi	70-70-71-67—278	10687
D White	68-68-71-71—278	10687
L Connelly	70-75-70-65—280	6413
V Fergon	68-70-74-68—280	6412
C Hill	71-68-70-71—280	6412
T Johnson	71-69-68-72—280	6412

Crestar

at Sleepy Hole CC Portsmouth Virginia

Name	Score	Prize $
J Inkster	70-70-69—209	45000
R Jones	73-66-70—209	21250
N Lopez	71-68-70—209	21250
B King	69-68-72—209	21250
(J Inkster won play-off)		
A Alcott	71-70-69—210	10700
M Berteotti	68-69-73—210	10700
S Turner	68-68-74—210	10700
H Farr	72-68-71—211	7800
A Finney	72-71-69—212	6352
C Walker	69-73-70—212	6352
L Adams	70-71-71—212	6351
J Coles	73-71-69—213	4805

Chrysler-Plymouth Classic

at Navesink CC Chatham New Jersey

Name	Score	Prize $
N Lopez	68-70-66—204	37500
J Stephenson	77-71-64—212	23125
M Ward	71-74-68—213	15000
A Ritzman	68-71-74—213	15000
M Figueras-Dotti	70-70-74—214	10625
O-H Ku	71-75-69—215	7542
S Turner	73-72-70—215	7542
M Bozarth	73-70-72—215	7541

Corning Classic

at Corning CC Corning New York

Name	Score	Prize $
S Turner	71-63-69-70—273	48750
J Carner	74-70-65-66—275	26000
O-H Ku	69-64-71-71—275	25999
P Sheehan	67-70-73-69—279	17062
J Britz	70-71-69-70—280	13812
M Foyer	72-70-70-70—282	11375
S Quinlan	71-73-70-69—283	8558
K Young	73-66-74-70—283	8558
M-C Cheng	73-69-71-70—283	8558
L Kean	70-73-69-72—284	6035
D Massey	77-68-67-72—284	6035
D Mochrie	74-70-68-72—284	6035
B King	69-69-70-76—284	6034

Mazda LPGA Championship

at Jack Nicklaus Centre Kings Island Ohio

Name	Score	Prize $
S Turner	70-71-73-67—281	52500
A Alcott	68-71-69-74—282	32375
M Figueras-Dotti	74-70-71-69—284	15890
K Postlewait	74-69-69-72—284	15890
S Little	72-71-69-72—284	15890
A Okamoto	71-71-69-73—284	15890
A Benz	70-71-69-74—284	15890
M Berteotti	74-70-68-73—285	9100
S Quinlan	69-68-79-70—286	7415
J Geddes	73-70-70-73—286	7414
J Dickinson	74-69-69-74—286	7414
L Adams	73-71-73-70—287	5793
M Bozarth	72-70-73-72—287	5793
D Germain	72-69-71-75—287	5793

McDonald's Championship

at Du Pont CC Wilmington Delaware

Name	Score	Prize $
K Postlewait	69-68-69-70—276	75000
P Sheehan	68-66-69-74—277	46250
J Stephenson	71-70-68-69—278	27084
N Lopez	71-66-72-69—278	27083
D Mochrie	70-67-68-73—278	27083
J Rosenthal	70-72-70-68—280	15084
C Walker	71-70-69-70—280	15083
J Dickinson	70-69-71-70—280	15083
T Green	75-71-67-68—281	10126
A Alcott	70-71-71-69—281	10125
V Fergon	73-68-69-71—281	10125
L Garbacz	69-72-69-71—281	10125

Rochester International

at Locust Hill CC Pittsford New York

Name	Score	Prize $
M-C Cheng	71-77-66-73—287	45000
P Sheehan	73-71-69-74—287	24000
N Lopez	72-69-71-75—287	24000
(M-C Cheng won play-off)		
N Brown	73-72-72-71—288	15750
C Rarick	73-70-72-74—289	11625
D Ammaccapane	68-72-75-74—289	11625
D Mochrie	77-69-74-70—290	8325
J Dickinson	73-74-71-72—290	8325
L Peterson	72-75-65-79—291	7050

Mayflower Classic

at The CC of Indianapolis Indiana

Name	Score	Prize $
T-J Myers	68-69-68-71—276	60000
A Alcott	71-65-71-70—277	32000
A Okamoto	70-68-67-72—277	32000
J Dickinson	71-69-70-70—280	19000
S Turner	70-67-71-72—280	19000
M McGeorge	73-66-72-70—281	14000
V Skinner	72-69-73-68—282	10533
A Benz	70-73-69-70—282	10533
T Green	68-71-73-70—282	10533
J Inkster	65-72-74-72—283	7667
D Ammaccapane	71-69-70-73—283	7666
D White	68-67-74-74—283	7666
M Figueras-Dotti	75-74-72-71—292	6001
C Morse	73-73-71-75—292	6000

Lady Keystone Open

at Hershey CC Hershey Pennsylvania

Name	Score	Prize $
S Furlong	68-72-65—205	45000
S Turner	73-65-67—205	27750
(S Furlong won play-off)		
V Skinner	71-69-67—207	20250
S Steinhauer	69-70-69—208	13000
S Palmer	69-69-70—208	13000
C Walker	68-69-71—208	13000
B King	68-71-70—209	7900
M Bozarth	68-70-71—209	7900
A Okamoto	67-70-72—209	7900
J Inkster	67-73-70—210	6001
P Jordan	69-70-71—210	6000
P Sheehan	72-71-68—211	5100
L Adams	71-68-72—211	5100

Sara Lee Classic

at Hermitage Nashville Tennessee

Name	Score	Prize $
P Rizzo	70-70-67—207	50250
T Green	70-71-66—207	23729
S Turner	71-69-67—207	23729
K Williams	69-71-67—207	23728
(P Rizzo won play-off)		
N Brown	72-69-67—208	11139
J Dickinson	70-68-70—208	11139
R Jones	69-68-71—208	11138
D Richard	71-66-71—208	11138

Jamie Farr Toledo Tournament

at Glengarry CC Toledo Ohio

Name	Score	Prize $
L Davies	69-70-69-69—277	41250
N Lopez	68-70-69-73—280	25437
J Stephenson	70-72-70-71—283	16500
B King	72-69-68-74—283	16499
M Blackwelder	74-71-70-71—286	11687
N Taylor	71-69-73-74—287	9625
T Green	73-74-72-69—288	8112
L Adams	74-72-75-69—290	6806
S LeVeque	75-76-67-72—290	6806
H Farr	75-71-75-71—292	5513
A Read	73-74-72-72—292	5513

US Women's Open Championship

at Baltimore CC Maryland

Name	Score	Prize $
L Neumann	67-72-69-69—277	70000
P Sheehan	70-72-68-70—280	35000
D Mochrie	70-69-76-68—283	21679
C Walker	70-74-68-71—283	21679
J Stephenson	72-72-71-69—284	14393
M Berteotti	75-71-68-71—285	11826
A Benz	70-72-71-72—285	11826
K Albers	73-70-72-71—286	9726
J Inkster	71-68-75-72—286	9726
V Fergon	70-71-75-71—287	8315
B Daniel	77-71-66-73—287	8315
B King	76-74-71-67—288	7038
A Okamoto	75-73-71-69—288	7038
K Hanson	73-72-73-70—288	7038
N Lopez	72-74-71-71—288	7038
J Carner	69-73-76-71—289	5954
N Brown	71-73-72-73—289	5954
K Cockerhill	73-70-72-74—289	5954
M-C Cheng	74-76-70-70—290	5070
C Johnson	73-74-73-70—290	5070
R Jones	74-70-74-72—290	5070
M Figueras-Dotti	77-71-69-73—290	5070
T Green	71-70-71-78—290	5070
R Hood	77-72-71-71—291	4310
D Lasker	73-71-74-73—291	4310
J Dickinson	71-76-71-73—291	4310
S Quinlan	69-75-74-73—291	4310
D White	72-70-73-76—291	4310
C Semple*	79-71-70-72—292	—
K Guadagnino	72-72-75-73—292	3820
S Turner	73-72-73-74—292	3820
J Rosenthal	74-73-71-74—292	3820

(* denotes amateur)

Boston Five Classic

at Sheraton Tara CC Danvers Massachusetts

Name	Score	Prize $
C Walker	66-69-70-69—274	45000
K Young	71-69-75-67—282	19125
P Sheehan	77-68-67-70—282	19125
J Geddes	71-71-69-71—282	19125
J Stephenson	71-69-69-73—282	19125
B King	71-69-70-73—283	10500
D Eggeling	74-71-73-66—284	7500
S Quinlan	69-73-72-70—284	7500
C Marino	70-70-72-72—284	7500
C Rarick	70-70-72-72—284	7500
D Lasker	74-71-71-69—285	5300
L Neumann	72-72-70-71—285	5300
B Daniel	71-71-72-71—285	5300

Du Maurier Classic

at Vancouver GC Coquitlam Canada

Name	Score	Prize $
S Little	74-65-69-71—279	75000
L Davies	69-71-70-70—280	46250
S Turner	68-72-70-72—282	33750
N Brown	72-74-71-68—285	19938
D Richard	72-72-71-70—285	19938
J Stephenson	70-72-73-70—285	19937
A Alcott	72-70-71-72—285	19937
R Jones	72-71-71-72—286	13000
O-H Ku	74-72-71-70—287	10148
C Walker	73-68-73-73—287	10148
P Rizzo	73-70-70-74—287	10147
D Massey	72-68-73-74—287	10147

Atlantic City Classic

at Sands CC Somers Point New Jersey

Name	Score	Prize $
J Inkster	72-69-65—206	33750
B Daniel	66-68-72—206	20812
(J Inkster won play-off)		
R Jones	74-66-70—210	11109
B King	70-69-71—210	11109
D Massey	69-69-72—210	11109
M Nause	67-70-73—210	11109
S Quinlan	71-69-71—211	6637
C Marino	72-73-67—212	5569
S Palmer	69-70-73—212	5568
S Turner	74-69-70—213	4313
K Shipman	72-70-71—213	4313
C Walker	68-73-72—213	4313

Planters Pat Bradley International

at Willow Creek GC High Point North Carolina

Name	Points	Prize $
M Nause	14	62500
D Massey	13	35000
J Dickinson	13	35000
A Okamoto	12	20000
N Lopez	11	10500
J Britz	10	8500
D Germain	10	8500
A Alcott	9	6750
J Anderson	9	6750
J Rosenthal	9	6750
J Inkster	7	5250

Nestlé World Championship of Women's Golf

at Pine Isle Resort Burford Georgia

Name	Score	Prize $
R Jones	70-69-66-74—279	81500
L Neumann	70-73-71-66—280	43000
P Sheehan	70-73-68-70—281	21167
S Turner	71-70-70-70—281	21167
N Lopez	67-72-71-71—281	21166
A Okamoto	67-71-73-73—284	10500
A Alcott	68-74-75-68—285	7625
C Walker	71-73-70-71—285	7625

Greater Washington Open

at Bethesda CC Bethesda Maryland

Name	Score	Prize $
A Okamoto	69-70-67—206	33750
B Daniel	68-69-70—207	18000
C Chillemi	72-64-71—207	17999
S Sanders	68-73-67—208	11812
D Massey	73-70-66—209	8719
J Dickinson	67-74-68—209	8718
A Benz	71-72-67—210	4927
A Alcott	70-71-69—210	4927
D Coe	70-70-70—210	4927
J Inkster	71-69-70—210	4927

Ocean State Open

at Alpine CC Cranston Rhode Island

Name	Score	Prize $
P Jordan	73-68-70—211	22500
M Edge	72-72-69—213	7988
L Adams	74-69-70—213	7988
M Ward	72-70-71—213	7988
J Briles	70-71-72—213	7987
S Palmer	71-69-73—213	7987
J Pitcock	75-63-75—213	7987
S Redman	71-71-72—214	3525
K Young	69-73-72—214	3525
M Nause	73-67-74—214	3525
V Fergon	77-70-68—215	2427
J Britz	69-75-71—215	2427
P Hammel	72-71-72—215	2427

Rail Charity Classic

at Rail GC Springfield Illinois

Name	Score	Prize $
B King	68-68-71—207	37500
M Ward	70-68-71—209	23125
D White	66-75-70—211	15000
S Palmer	69-70-72—211	15000
D Eggeling	71-74-69—214	7825
C Marino	70-73-71—214	7825
V Fergon	68-74-72—214	7825
D Ammaccapane	71-69-74—214	7825
N Brown	68-70-76—214	7825
S Haynie	71-72-72—215	5001

Cellular One Ping Championship

at Riverside CC Portland Oregon

Name	Score	Prize $
B King	71-70-72—213	37500
C Walker	68-77-69—214	23125
S Sanders	68-76-71—215	15000
M Blackwelder	72-71-72—215	15000
J Rosenthal	70-77-69—216	8917
S Turner	73-72-71—216	8917
P Hammel	70-72-74—216	8916
C Rarick	76-70-71—217	5875
D McHaffie	73-72-72—217	5875
B Daniel	71-72-74—217	5875
D White	73-74-71—218	4422
J Geddes	75-72-71—218	4422
S Haynie	71-71-76—218	4421

Safeco Classic

at Meridian Valley CC Seattle Washington

Name	Score	Prize $
J Inkster	76-70-65-67—278	33750
O-H Ku	71-70-71-69—281	20812
J Stephenson	71-72-67-72—282	15187
S Turner	73-75-67-68—283	11812
D Ammaccapane	73-70-68-73—284	9562
J Carner	70-71-70-74—285	7256
B Daniel	71-69-71-74—285	7256
J Geddes	74-73-72-67—286	5288
N Lopez	72-75-70-69—286	5287
R Jones	72-71-74-69—286	5287

Konica San José Classic

at Almaden G & CC San José California

Name	Score	Prize $
K Guadagnino	69-71-67—207	45000
C Marino	70-70-68—208	27750
R Jones	73-69-68—210	18000
M McGeorge	69-69-72—210	18000
B Daniel	73-70-68—211	12750
M Berteotti	68-71-73—212	10500
K Young	69-75-69—213	7500
L Adams	71-71-71—213	7500
K Postlewait	69-73-71—213	7500
J Inkster	69-69-75—213	7500
J Carner	71-74-69—214	4852
P Rizzo	72-73-69—214	4852
K Monaghan	72-71-71—214	4852
B King	73-69-72—214	4852
M Blackwelder	71-69-74—214	4852
J Stephenson	71-69-74—214	4852

Mazda Japan Classic

at Musashigaoka GC Saitama

Name	Score	Prize $
P Sheehan	72-67-67—206	67500
L Neumann	70-66-70—206	41625
(P Sheehan won play-off)		
J Rosenthal	70-73-67—210	27000
Y Moriguchi	67-72-71—210	27000
R Walton	69-74-68—211	16050
A Okamoto	73-68-70—211	16050
S Little	70-70-71—211	16050

USLPGA Money Winners

Place	Name	Official Money $
1	S Turner	347255
2	N Lopez	322154
3	R Jones	318973
4	C Walker	311784
5	A Alcott	291722
6	A Okamoto	284156
7	P Sheehan	258671
8	B King	248876
9	J Inkster	233513
10	J Stephenson	228659
11	K Postlewait	199089
12	O-H Ku	165063
13	J Dickenson	160440
14	L Davies	154950
15	M Figueras-Dotti	152468
16	L Neumann	147104
17	B Daniel	137039
18	DP Mochrie	131861
19	M Nause	130409
20	S Little	123731
21	J Carner	121218
22	T Green	109134
23	D Massey	109094
24	A Benz	108978
25	M-C Cheng	108489

Top 100 US Money Winners, 1988

Place	Name	Official Money $
1	C Strange	$1147644
2	C Beck	916818
3	J Sindelar	813732
4	K Green	779181
5	T Kite	760405
6	M Calcavecchia	751912
7	S Lyle (GB)	726934
8	B Crenshaw	696895
9	D Frost	691500
10	L Wadkins	616596
11	P Azinger	594850
12	S Pate	582473
13	M McCumber	559111
14	P Stewart	553571
15	M Reid	533343
16	P Jacobsen	526765
17	G Norman (Aus)	514854
18	J Sluman	503321
19	B Lietzke	500815
20	J Haas	490409
21	F Couples	489822
22	M O'Meara	438311
23	J Mudd	422022
24	G Koch	414694
25	L Nelson	411284
26	S Hoch	397599
27	D Pohl	396400
28	M Wiebe	392166
29	B Tway	381966
30	B Glasson	380651
31	S Verplank	366045
32	B Lohr	315536
33	D Barr (Can)	291244
34	G Morgan	288002
35	G Sauers	280719
36	M Brooks	280636
37	C Stadler	278313
38	D Rummells	274800
39	T Watson	273216
40	D Forsman	269440
41	J Mahaffey	266416
42	N Price (SA)	266300
43	A Magee	261954

44	D Hammond	256010
45	S Jones	241877
46	D Pooley	239534
47	M Hatalsky	239019
48	C Rose	228976
49	B McCallister	225660
50	C Pavin	216768
51	F Zoeller	209564
52	R Wrenn	209404
53	D Tewell	209196
54	T Sieckmann	209151
55	C Byrum	208853
56	T Simpson	200748
57	T Purtzer	197740
58	E Fiori	193765
59	B Wadkins	193022
60	J Carter	191489
61	W Levi	109073
62	L Mize	187823
63	DA Weibring	186677
64	N Faldo (GB)	179120
65	J Benepe	176055
66	T Armour	175461
67	T Byrum	174378
68	J Hallet	170993
69	R Floyd	169549
70	K Knox	168099
71	S Ballesteros (Sp)	165202
72	H Irwin	164996
73	F Allem (SA)	163911
74	B Faxon	162656
75	D Love III	156068
76	D Edwards	151513
77	R Maltbie	150602
78	J Huston	150301
79	S Elkington	149972
80	R Cochran	148960
81	T Nakajima (Jap)	148304
82	B Gilder	144523
83	R Zokol	142153
84	J Cook	139916
85	K Perry	139421
86	D Ogrin	138807
87	C Peete	138310
88	H Sutton	137296
89	L Roberts	136890
90	JD Blake	131937
91	B Gardner	130859
92	R Mediate	129829
93	D Mast	128568
94	M Hulbert	127752
95	L Rinker	125471
96	M Donald	118509
97	S Randolph	117132
98	M O'Grady	116153
99	M Sullivan	115994
100	D Canipe	114180

USPGA Tour Official Statistics

Stroke Averages

1	G Norman	69.38
2	C Beck	69.46
3T	T Kite	69.53
	S Lyle	69.53
5	P Stewart	69.54
6T	B Crenshaw	69.58
	D Frost	69.58
8	T Watson	69.74
9	F Couples	69.76
10	P Azinger	69.77

Greens in Regulation

1	J Adams	.739
2	D Barr	.736
3	B Lietzke	.718
4	T Norris	.715
5	G Sauers	.714
6	C Peete	.712
7	D Pohl	.711
8	J Mahaffey	.710
9	C Beck	.706
10	R Mediate	.703

Putting Leaders

1	D Pooley	1.729
2T	M Hatalsky	1.731
	S Lyle	1.731
4	P Azinger	1.736
5T	D Forsman	1.740
	K Green	1.740
7T	N Price	1.741
	W Wood	1.741
9	B Crenshaw	1.742
10	P Stewart	1.743

Eagle Leaders

1	K Green	21
2	M Calcavecchia	17
3	J Sindelar	14
4	G Sauers	13
5T	D Waldorf	12
	J Hallet	12
7	Five tied with	11

Drive Distance

1	S Thomas	284.6
2	C Stadler	279.5
3	G Norman	279.4
4	B Glasson	278.4
5	D Pohl	277.9
6	D Love III	276.4
7	J Adams	276.1
8T	D Waldorf	275.6
	K Perry	275.6
10	M Calcavecchia	275.5

Driving Accuracy

1	C Peete	.825
2	M Reid	.777
3	C Stange	.767
4	T Kite	.757
5	D Edwards	.755
6	F Allem	.753
7	B Lietzke	.750
8	J Renner	.746
9T	L Nelson	.740
	L Mize	.740

Par Breakers

1	K Green	.236
2	F Couples	.234
3T	P Stewart	.228
	P Azinger	.228
5	G Norman	.227
6T	C Beck	.225
	M Calcavecchia	.225
8T	D Rummells	.218
	D Forsman	.218
10	S Lyle	.217

Birdie Leaders

1	D Forsman	465
2	M Calcavecchia	461
3	M Wiebe	434
4	D Rummells	432
5	J Sluman	417
6	F Couples	416
7	J Sindelar	413
8	P Stewart	412
9	S Hoch	411
10	T Byrum	408

Sand-Saves

1	Greg Powers	.635
2	J Sluman	.610
3	DA Weibring	.596
4	D Frost	.593
5	L Rinker	.589
6	J Inman	.587
7	M Hatalsky	.575
8	B Britton	.565
9	T Kite	.563
10	R Zokol	.562

Awards

Golf Writers' Association Trophy

Awarded to the man or woman who, in the opinion of Golf Writers, has done most for golf during the year

1951 Max Faulkner
1952 Miss Elizabeth Price
1953 JB Carr
1954 Mrs Roy Smith (Miss Frances Stephens)
1955 Ladies' Golf Union's Touring Team
1956 JC Beharrell
1957 DJ Rees
1958 Harry Bradshaw
1959 Eric Brown
1960 Sir Stuart Goodwin (sponsor of international golf)
1961 Commdr RCT Roe (ex-hon secretary, PGA)
1962 Mrs Marley Spearman, British Ladies' Champion 1961-1962
1963 MSR Lunt, Amateur Champion, 1963
1964 Great Britain and Ireland Team, winners of Eisenhower Trophy – JB Carr (non-playing Captain), MF Bonallack, MSR Lunt, RDBM Shade, R Foster
1965 Gerald Micklem, golf administrator, President, English Golf Union
1966 RDBM Shade, Scottish Amateur Champion for fourth successive year; Eisenhower Trophy Best individual score, 1966; runner-up Amateur Championship, 1966
1967 John Panton
1968 Michael Bonallack
1969 Tony Jacklin
1970 Tony Jacklin
1971 British Walker Cup Team – MF Bonallack, R Carr, R Foster, CW Green, W Humphreys, JS Macdonald, G McGregor, GC Marks, DM Marsh, HB Stuart
1972 Miss Michelle Walker
1973 PA Oosterhuis
1974 PA Oosterhuis
1975 Golf Foundation
1976 Great Britain and Ireland Team, winners of Eisenhower Trophy – Sandy Saddler (non-playing captain), John Davies, Ian Hutcheon, Mike Kelley, Steve Martin
1977 C O'Connor
1978 Peter McEvoy
1979 S Ballesteros
1980 Sandy Lyle
1981 B Langer
1982 G Brand Jr
1983 N Faldo
1984 S Ballesteros
1985 European Ryder Cup Team
1986 Great Britain and Ireland Curtis Cup Team
1987 European Ryder Cup Team
1988 S Lyle

Harry Vardon Trophy

Currently awarded to the PGA member heading the Order of Merit at the end of the season

1937	CA Whitcombe	1966	P Alliss
1938	TH Cotton	1967	ME Gregson
1939	RA Whitcombe	1968	BGC Huggett
1940–45	*In abeyance*	1969	B Gallacher
1946	AD Locke	1970	NC Coles
1947	NG Von Nida	1971	PA Oosterhuis
1948	CH Ward	1972	PA Oosterhuis
1949	CH Ward	1973	PA Oosterhuis
1950	AD Locke	1974	PA Oosterhuis
1951	J Panton	1975	Dale Hayes
1952	H Weetman	1976	S Ballesteros
1953	F van Donck	1977	S Ballesteros
1954	AD Locke	1978	S Ballesteros
1955	DJ Rees	1979	AWB Lyle
1956	H Weetman	1980	AWB Lyle
1957	EC Brown	1981	B Langer
1958	BJ Hunt	1982	G Norman
1959	DJ Rees	1983	N Faldo
1960	BJ Hunt	1984	B Langer
1961	C O'Connor	1985	AWB Lyle
1962	C O'Connor	1986	S Ballesteros
1963	NC Coles	1987	I Woosnam
1964	P Alliss	1988	S Ballesteros
1965	BJ Hunt		

Rookie of the Year

1960	T Goodwin	1974	C Mason
1961	A Caygill	1975	No Award
1962	No Award	1976	M James
1963	A Jacklin	1978	AWB Lyle
1964	No Award	1979	MJ Miller
1966	R Liddle	1980	P Hoad
1967	No Award	1981	J Bennett
1968	B Gallacher	1982	G Brand Jr
1969	P Oosterhuis	1983	G Turner
1970	S Brown	1984	AP Parkin
1971	D Llewellyn	1985	P Thomas
1972	S Torrance	1986	J-M Olazabal
1973	P Elson	1987	P Baker
		1988	C Montgomerie

Avia Watches' Woman Golfer of the Year

1982	Jane Connachan
1983	Jill Thornhill
1984	Gillian Stewart
	Claire Waite
1985	Belle Robertson
1986	Great Britain and Ireland Curtis Cup Team
1987	Linda Bayman
1988	Great Britain and Ireland Curtis Cup Team

Benson and Hedges Golfer's Handbook Golfer of the Year

1983	Tom Watson
1984	Lee Trevino
1985	Sandy Lyle
1986	Greg Norman
1987	Ian Woosnam

Byron Nelson Award

Awarded for most victories on USPGA Tour

1955	Cary Middlecoff	1978	Tom Watson
1956	Ted Kroll	1979	Tom Watson
1957	Arnold Palmer	1980	Tom Watson
1958	Ken Venturi	1981	Bruce Lietzke
1959	Gene Littler		Ray Floyd
1960	Arnold Palmer		B Rogers
1961	Arnold Palmer	1982	Calvin Peete
1962	Arnold Palmer		Craig Stadler
1963	Arnold Palmer	1983	Seve Ballesteros
1964	Jack Nicklaus		Hal Sutton
1965	Jack Nicklaus		Fuzzy Zoeller
1966	Billy Casper		Lanny Wadkins
1967	Jack Nicklaus		Calvin Peete
1968	Billy Casper		Gil Morgan
1969	Dave Hill		Mark McCumber
1970	Billy Casper		Jim Colbert
1971	Lee Trevino	1984	Denis Watson
1972	Jack Nicklaus		Tom Watson
1973	Jack Nicklaus	1985	Curtis Strange
1974	Johnny Miller		Lanny Wadkins
1975	Jack Nicklaus	1986	Bob Tway
1976	Ben Crenshaw	1987	Curtis Strange
1977	Tom Watson	1988	

The US Vardon Trophy

The award is made to the member of the USPGA who completes 80 rounds or more, with the lowest scoring average over the calendar year.

1948	Ben Hogan	1968	Billy Casper
1949	Sam Snead	1969	Dave Hill
1950	Sam Snead	1970	Lee Trevino
1951	Lloyd Mangrum	1971	Lee Trevino
1952	Jack Burke	1972	Lee Trevino
1953	Lloyd Mangrum	1973	Bruce Crampton
1954	Ed Harrison	1974	Lee Tevino
1955	Sam Snead	1975	Bruce Crampton
1956	Cary Middlecoff	1976	Don January
1957	Dow Finsterwald	1977	Tom Watson
1958	Bob Rosburg	1978	Tom Watson
1959	Art Wall	1979	Tom Watson
1960	Billy Casper	1980	Lee Trevino
1961	Arnold Palmer	1981	Tom Kite
1962	Arnold Palmer	1982	Tom Kite
1963	Billy Casper	1983	Ray Floyd
1964	Arnold Palmer	1984	Calvin Peete
1965	Billy Casper	1985	Don Pooley
1966	Billy Casper	1986	Scott Hoch
1967	Arnold Palmer	1987	Dan Pohl
		1988	Chip Beck

US Rookie of the Year

Awarded by Golf Digest

1957	Ken Venturi	1973	Tom Kite
1958	Bob Goalby	1974	Ben Crenshaw
1959	Joe Campbell	1975	Roger Moore Maltbie
1960	Mason Rudolph	1976	J Pate
1961	Jacky Cupit	1977	G Marsh
1962	Jack Nicklaus	1978	Pat McGowan
1963	Ray Floyd	1979	John Fought
1964	RH Sikes	1980	Gary Hallberg
1965	Homero Blancas	1981	M O'Meara
1966	John Schlee	1982	Hal Sutton
1967	Lee Trevino	1983	Nick Price
1968	Bob Murphy	1984	Corey Pavin
1969	Grier Jones	1985	Phil Blackmar
1970	Ted Hayes	1986	Brian Claar
1971	Hubert Green	1987	Keith Clearwater
1972	Lanny Wadkins	1988	Jim Benepe

Bobby Jones Award

Awarded by USGA for distinguished sportsmanship in golf

1955	Francis Ouimet	1972	Michael Bonallack
1956	Bill Campbell	1973	Gene Littler
1957	Babe Zaharias	1974	Byron Nelson
1958	Margaret Curtis	1975	Jack Nicklaus
1959	Findlay Douglas	1976	Ben Hogan
1960	Charles Evans Jr	1977	Joseph C Dey
1961	Joe Carr	1978	Bob Hope and Bing Crosby
1962	Horton-Smith	1979	Tom Kite
1963	Patty Berg	1980	Charles Yates
1964	Charles Coe	1981	Mrs JoAnne Carner
1965	Mrs Edwin Vare	1982	WJ Patton
1966	Gary Player	1983	Mrs Maureen Garrett
1967	Richard Tufts	1984	J Sigel
1968	Robert Dickson	1985	Fuzzy Zoeller
1969	Gerald Micklem	1986	Jess W Sweetser
1970	Roberto De Vicenzo	1987	Tom Watson
1971	Arnold Palmer	1988	Isaac B Grainger
		1989	Chi-Chi Rodriguez

Arnold Palmer

Awarded to the USPGA leading money-winner

1981	Tom Kite
1982	Craig Stadler
1983	Hal Sutton
1984	Tom Watson
1985	Curtis Strange
1986	Greg Norman
1987	Paul Azinger
1988	Curtis Strange

USPGA Player of the Year Award

The award is made on the basis of points gained by winning the major events (30 points), the TPC and World Series (20), tour events (10), and additional points for final Top 10 positions in the Money List and Scoring Averages.

1948	Ben Hogan	1968	*Not awarded*
1949	Sam Snead	1969	Orville Moody
1950	Ben Hogan	1970	Billy Casper
1951	Ben Hogan	1971	Lee Trevino
1952	Julius Boros	1972	Jack Nicklaus
1953	Ben Hogan	1973	Jack Nicklaus
1954	Ed Furgol	1974	Johnny Miller
1955	Doug Ford	1975	Jack Nicklaus
1956	Jack Burke	1976	Jack Nicklaus
1957	Dick Mayer	1977	Tom Watson
1958	Dow Finsterwald	1978	Tom Watson
1959	Art Wall	1979	Tom Watson
1960	Arnold Palmer	1980	Tom Watson
1961	Jerry Barner	1981	Bill Rogers
1962	Arnold Palmer	1982	Tom Watson
1963	Julius Boros	1983	Hal Sutton
1964	Ken Venturi	1984	Tom Watson
1965	Dave Marr	1985	Lanny Wadkins
1966	Billy Casper	1986	Bob Tway
1967	Jack Nicklaus	1987	Paul Azinger
		1988	Curtis Strange

Golf Foundation Review of the Year

Chris Plumridge

© Peter Dazeley Photography

Bill Campbell, Captain of the Royal and Ancient, St Andrews, presents the R and A Trophy to the winner, Sweden. The Klippaus Gymnasieskola Team: Peter Elustrom, Peter Olsson and Daniel Lang.

Following in the wake of further international success, most notably that of the Curtis Cup and Eisenhower Trophy teams, 1988 brought a further increase in the number of young people wishing to involve themselves in the activities of the Golf Foundation.

It is paradoxical however, that in this time of great prosperity within the game these international successes have placed a strain on the Foundation's funds. The Foundation's policy is not to refuse a new school or junior group into the Coaching Scheme for Schools and Junior Groups which is the main sphere of its work. Thus, the more groups that join the Scheme, the greater the strain on resources.

Traditionally, the Foundation has received the bulk of its income from the ordinary club golfer who has contributed to the Annual Appeal or has entered the various draws and competitions whose proceeds are donated to the Foundation. The companies which back these types of promotions are to be applauded. The R and A and the golf industry also contribute greatly to the Foundation's funds but, quite simply, the supply of money is not keeping pace with the demand to play.

It is still an unwelcome statistic that of the 2000 plus clubs there are in the four home countries, only just over 300 contribute anything to the Annual Appeal. Solving this perennial problem is one of the Foundation's chief objectives. In terms of communicating with clubs, the Foundation mails information and details regularly throughout the year to all club secretaries. Yet the response to appeals for contributions remains stubbornly slow. The Foundation recognises that secretaries are beleaguered with paperwork and administrative duties and that giving time to the Foundation's cause may not always be possible. The suggestion therefore, that one of the members, either male or female, becomes the Golf Foundation's representative within the club is one which has a great deal of merit. The post would be officially recognised by the Foundation and the representative would receive regular information on all the Foundation's activities to act upon where necessary. It is the sort of position that would appeal to an older member with a great interest in junior golf who has retired. Apart from helping the Foundation in its fund-raising, the representative would also be helping to secure the future membership of that particular club. Interested parties please apply!

In the area of competitive golf, the number of entries reflected the growing demand. The Golf Foundation Team Championship for Schools attracted entries from over 1000 schools. Each school enters a team of three players and, following regional qualifying rounds, the winners go forward to the National Finals in the four home countries. The National Champion Schools then qualify for the International Final which, in 1988 was held over the Old Course at Sunningdale. Eleven teams qualified for the International Final with New Zealand, represented by the Hamilton Boys' School, appearing for the first time.

Bill Campbell, Captain of the Royal and Ancient, St Andrews, presents the PGA European Tour Trophy to Steven Alker, Hamilton High School, New Zealand.

Defending champions were the Klippans Gymnasieskola from Sweden who won at Foxhills in 1987 and they again proved too strong for the other teams, finally recording a nine stroke victory over New Zealand. There was some consolation for New Zealand in the outstanding performance of Steven Alker whose rounds of 71 and 68 won the PGA European Tour Trophy for the lowest individual score. His aggregate of 139 was the lowest in the 17-year history of the Championship and represented marvellous golf. Bill Campbell, Captain of the R and A, presented the R and A Trophy to the winning Swedish team. The second year of the Golf Foundation/NatWest Bank Age Group also attracted an increased entry. Over 1700 junior golfers, both boys and girls, entered and, following regional qualifying rounds, 52 boys and 27 girls won through to the finals at Patshull Park.

Once again, the scoring was quite remarkable in these Championships which are played off scratch with no account of handicaps. Lee Westwood from Worksop and Mhairi McKay from Turnberry became the first double winners of the Championships. Westwood, winner of the Under-15 title last year took the Under-16s this time with a 36-hole aggregate of 151 while Mhairi McKay, winner of the Under-13s in 1987, triumphed in the Under-14s with a 79. The best round of the finals came from Under-15 winner Ben Collier from Callander with a 73 while Under-14 winner Sam Pigott from West Malling produced a 74. It is clear from the enthusiasm of all the entrants that these Championships are achieving their aims of providing meaningful competition to youngsters in categories relevant to their age and physical development.

In every area of activity the Golf Foundation experienced its busiest year in 1988. The Coaching Scheme for Schools and Junior Groups now looks after the tuitional needs of some 40,000 children; the Merit Award Scheme has seen over 3000 awards made in the four categories available; the Golf Foundation Eclectic Competition attracted over 2500 entries during the school holidays.

The administration of all these activities is an enormous exercise. It is all handled most efficiently by the staff at headquarters, led by the Executive Director, Lesley Attwood. In order that their work on behalf of the future of British golf does not flounder, it is up to every golfer in the country to do what he or she can to help. Companies also have a responsibility to ensure that tomorrow's golfers are not held back by today's economic restrictions.

Golf Foundation Tournament Winners

Age-group Winners, 1988

at Patshull Park Shropshire

Boys

Under 16

Lee Westwood (Worksop)	74-77—151
David Cooper (Drumpellier)	76-76—152
James Grundy (Radyr)	74-78—152
Stuart Davis (Breadsall Priory)	77-77—154

Under 15

Ben Collier (Callander)	73-79—152
Chris Sheppard (Southerndown)	77-77—154
Phillip Kenyon (Hillside)	77-77—154
Matthew Pearson (Abbeydale)	85-76—161

Under 14

Sam Pigott (West Malling)	74
David Rose (North Shore)	76
Christopher Sands (Heswell)	77
Stuart Wilson (Whitby)	78

Under 13

Peter Drew (Worthing)	77
Iain Ferrie (Bedlingtonshire)	79
Robert McCrea (Worcestershire)	80
Jamie Little (Hartsbourne)	80

Girls

Under 16

Valerie Melville (Clydesdale and District)	79-84—163
Chloe Pout (Chestfield Whitstable)	83-82—165
Elaine Ratcliffe (Sandiway)	83-82—165
Nicola Brixton (Wakefield)	85-84—169
Geraldine Doran (Royal County Down)	83-86—169

Under 15

Jane Williamson (Hadley Wood)	88-80—168
Andrea Murray (Heysham)	87-84—171
Victoria Smith (Burton-on-Trent)	85-87—172
Sarah Phillips (Lakey Hill)	84-98—182

Under 14

Mhairi McKay (Turnberry)	79
Samantha Atkinson (Sundridge Park)	87
Charlotte Afford (Drayton Park)	88
Nicola Gorman (Balmoral, Belfast)	91

Team Championship for Schools, 1988

International Final at Foxhills Surrey

Klippans Gymnasieskola, Sweden

Daniel Lang	144
Peter Olsson	144
Peter Elvstrom	148
	436

Lycée Bellevue, France

Pascal Edmond	151
Christophe Muniesa	151
Frederic Cupillard	153
	455

Bury Grammar School, England

Richard Booth	150
Garry Winstanley	154
Christopher Hinton	163
	467

Verslunarskoli, Iceland

Gunnar Sigurdsson	154
Gunnar Hansson	161
Hordur F Hardarson	170
	485

Glan-y-Mor Comprehensive, Wales

Richard Lee Evans	154
Gary Hire	157
David Owen Westcott	180
	491

Hamilton Boys High School, New Zealand

Steven Alker	139
David Smail	152
Maurice Campbell	154
	445

The Modern School, India

Daniel Samir Chopra	149
Vivek Bhandari	153
Utpal Kumar Das	162
	464

Peterhead Academy, Scotland

Stephen Docherty	153
Hamish Love	155
Roy Livingstone	172
	480

Summerhill College, Ireland

Gerard Sproule	159
James Sproule	165
Ivan McLoughlin	166
	490

Golf Foundation/Aer Lingus Schools'Team Championship

Year	Winning Team	Country	Venue
1972	Buckhaven High School	Scotland	Ballybunion
1973	Acklam High School	England	Ballybunion
1974	Millfield School	England	Portmarnock
1975	Perth Academy	Scotland	Ballybunion
1976	Brockenhurst College	England	Portmarnock
1977	Millfield School	England	Foxhills
1978	Sundsgardens Folkhogskola	Sweden	Connemara
1979	St Fachtna's	Ireland	Baltray
1980	Hugh Christie School	England	Portmarnock
1981	Tangvallaskolan	Sweden	Portmarnock
1982	Porthcawl Comprehensive	Wales	Carlow
1983	Ysgol John Bright	Wales	Ballybunion
1984	Marr College	Scotland	Lahinch
1985	Marr College	Scotland	Waterville

Golf Foundation Team Championship for Schools

for the R & A Trophy

1986	Tonbridge School	England	Sunningdale
1987	Klippans Gymnasieskola	Sweden	Foxhills
1988	Klippans Gymnasieskola	Sweden	Sunningdale

Part II
Courses and Clubs in the UK and Europe

Golf Clubs and Courses in the UK and Europe

1. Geographical Divisions

In England, Ireland and Wales clubs are listed in alphabetical order within counties, which are themselves arranged alphabetically. All English clubs are now listed under their geographical county and not the county of affiliation. In Scotland, clubs are listed in alphabetical order within the regions recognised by the Scottish Golf Union. In Europe, the clubs are listed in alphabetical order within each country, based on the nearest town or city. All clubs and courses are listed in the index at the back of the book.

2. Explanation of details given

a After the name of the club is the date when founded (where available) and a note saying whether the **course** on which the club plays is publicly or privately owned.

b The address is the postal address of each club or course. If the postal county is different from the one under which the club or course is listed, it will be shown in the address.

c The membership figure denotes the total number of members,. The number of lady members (**L**), the number of juniors (**J**) and of five day members (**5**) are sometimes shown separately.

d Telephone numbers for secretaries and professionals are shown if different from the club telephone number.

e **V'trs:** this shows what restrictions (if any) are in force for visitors.
(i) **WD** Weekdays; **WE** Weekends: **BH** Bank Holidays.
If no days stated, the particular restrictions apply at all times.
(ii) **U** Unrestricted, ie casual visitors may play on the days stated unrestricted.
M With a Member, ie casual visitors are not allowed. Only visitors playing with a member are permitted on the days stated.
H Handicap certificate required.
I Introduction, ie visitors are permitted on the days stated if they have a letter of introduction from their own club, their own club's membership card, or a handicap certificate.
XL No ladies allowed on the days stated.
NA No visitors allowed.
SOC Recognised Golfing Societies welcome if previous arrangements made with secretary.

f **Fees:** green fees are only quoted for visitors if they are permitted to play unaccompanied by a member. The basic cost per round is shown first, then, in brackets, the cost of a weekend and/or Bank Holiday round where this is available to unaccompanied visitors. Green fees for visitors playing with a Member are not given. Weekly (W), monthly (M) and fortnightly (F) terms are shown where available.

Index

England: South-East

Kent

1 Aquarius
2 Ashford
3 Barnehurst
4 Bearsted
5 Beckenham Place Park
6 Bexley Heath
7 Broome Park
8 Canterbury
9 Cherry Lodge
10 Chestfield (Whitstable)
11 Chislehurst
12 Cobtree Manor Park
13 Corinthian
14 Cranbrook
15 Cray Valley
16 Darenth Valley
17 Dartford
18 Deangate Ridge
19 Edenbridge G&CC
20 Eltham Warren
21 Faversham
22 Gillingham
23 Hawkhurst
24 Herne Bay
25 High Elms
26 Holtye
27 Hythe Imperial
28 Knole Park
29 Lamberhurst
30 Langley Park
31 Leeds Castle
32 Littlestone
33 Lullingstone Park
34 Magpie Hall Lane
35 Mid Kent
36 Nevill
37 North Foreland
38 Poult Wood
39 Prince's
40 Rochester & Cobham Park
41 Royal Blackheath
42 Royal Cinque Ports
43 Royal St George's
44 Ruxley
45 St Augustines
46 Sene Valley Folkestone & Hythe
47 Sheerness
48 Shooter's Hill
49 Shortlands
50 Sidcup
51 Sittingbourne & Milton Regis
52 Sundridge Park
53 Tenterden
54 Tunbridge Wells
55 Walmer & Kingsdown
56 West Kent
57 West Malling
58 Westgate & Birchington
59 Whitstable & Seasalter
60 Wildernesse
61 Woodlands Manor
62 Wrotham Heath

Middlesex

1 Airlinks
2 Ashford Manor
3 Brent Valley
4 Bush Hill Park
5 Crews Hill
6 Ealing
7 Enfield
8 Finchley
9 Fulwell
10 Grim's Dyke
11 Hampstead
12 Harefield Place
13 Harrow School
14 Haste Hill
15 Hendon
16 Highgate
17 Hillingdon
18 Holiday Inn
19 Horsenden Hill
20 Hounslow Heath
21 Lime Trees Park
22 Mill Hill
23 Muswell Hill
24 North Middlesex
25 Northwood
26 Perivale Park
27 Picketts Lock
28 Pinner Hill
29 Ruislip
30 Stanmore
31 Strawberry Hill
32 Sudbury
33 Trent Park
34 Twickenham
35 West Middlesex
36 Whitewebbs
37 Wyke Green

Surrey

1 The Addington
2 Addington Court
3 Addington Palace
4 Banstead Downs
5 Barrow Hills
6 Betchworth Park
7 Bramley
8 Burhill
9 Camberley Heath
10 Chessington Golf Centre
11 Chipstead
12 Coombe Hill
13 Coombe Wood
14 Coulsdon Court
15 Croham Hurst
16 Crondall
17 Cuddington
18 Dorking
19 Drift
20 Dulwich & Sydenham Hill
21 Effingham
22 Epsom
23 Farnham
24 Farnham Park
25 Fernfell G&CC
26 Foxhills
27 Gatton Manor Hotel
28 Goal Farm
29 Guildford
30 Hankley Common
31 Hindhead
32 Hoebridge Golf Centre
33 Home Park
34 Kingswood
35 Laleham
36 Leatherhead
37 Limpsfield Chart
38 Malden
39 Mitcham
40 Moore Place
41 New Zealand
42 North Downs
43 Oaks Sports Centre
44 Purley Downs
45 Puttenham
46 RAC Country Club
47 Redhill & Reigate
48 Reigate Heath
49 Richmond
50 Richmond Park
51 Roehampton
52 Royal Mid-Surrey
53 Royal Wimbledon
54 St George's Hill
55 Sandown Park
56 Selsdon Park Hotel
57 Shillinglee Park
58 Shirley Park
59 Silvermere
60 Surbiton
61 Tandridge
62 Thames Ditton & Esher
63 Tyrrells Wood
64 Walton Heath
65 Wentworth
66 West Byfleet
67 West Hill
68 West Surrey
69 Wimbledon Common
70 Wimbledon Park
71 Windlemere
72 Woking
73 Woodcote Park
74 Worplesdon

Sussex (East)

1 Bognor Regis
2 Copthorne
3 Cottesmore
4 Cowdray Park
5 Effingham Park
6 Gatwick Manor
7 Goodwood
8 Ham Manor
9 Haywards Heath
10 Hill Barn
11 Ifield
12 Littlehampton
13 Mannings Heath
14 Pyecombe
15 Selsey
16 Tilgate
17 West Chiltington
18 West Sussex
19 Worthing

Sussex (West)

1 Ashdown Forest Hotel
2 Brighton & Hove
3 Cooden Beach
4 Crowborough Beacon
5 Dale Hill
6 The Dyke
7 East Brighton
8 Eastbourne Downs
9 Hastings
10 Highwoods (Bexhill)
11 Hollingbury Park (Brighton)
12 Horam Park
13 Lewes
14 Peacehaven
15 Piltdown
16 Royal Ashdown Forest
17 Royal Eastbourne
18 Rye
19 Seaford
20 Seaford Head
21 Waterhall
22 West Hove
23 Willingdon

Public courses are set in italic

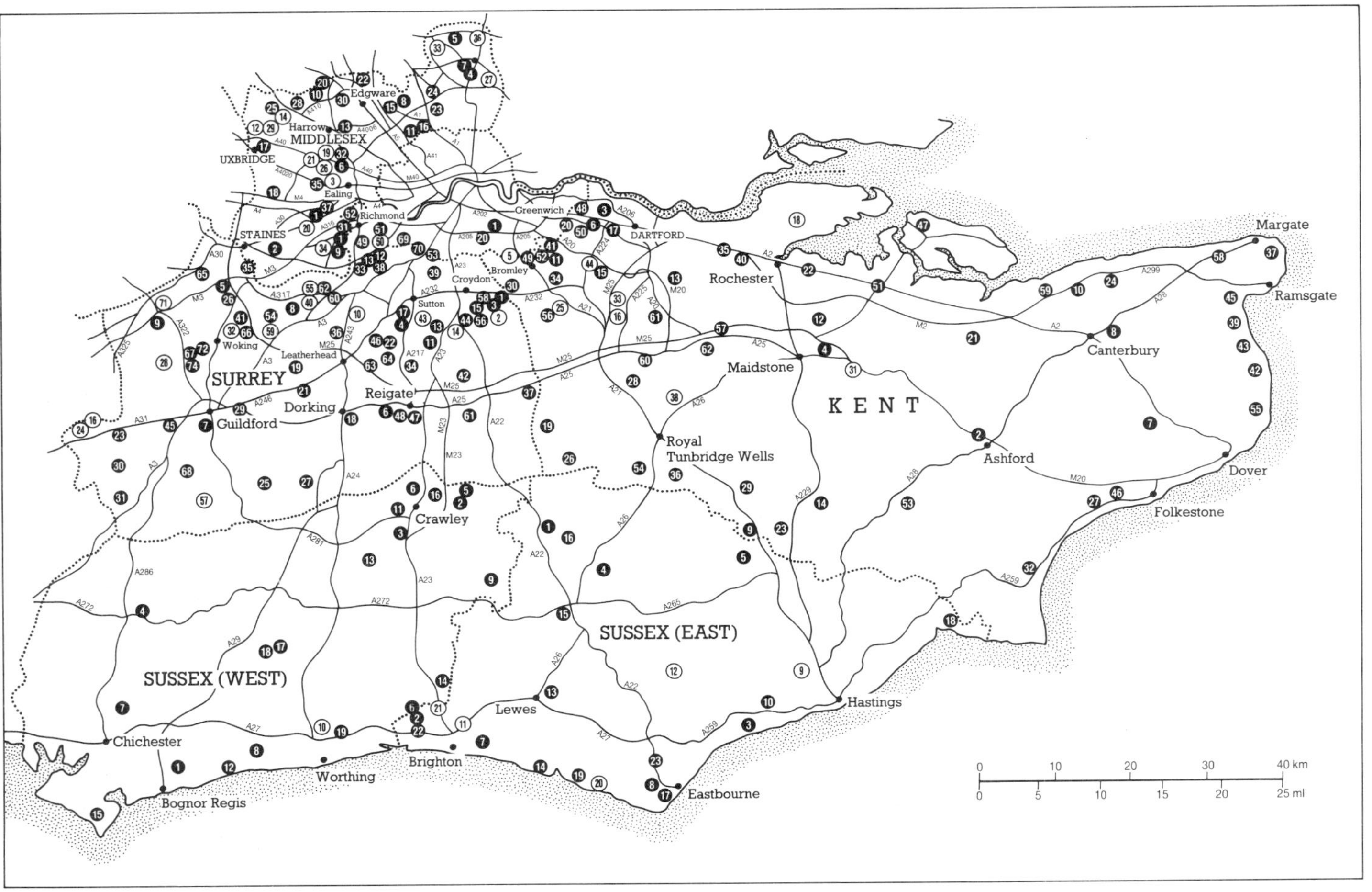
Edgware
Harrow
MIDDLESEX
UXBRIDGE
Ealing
Richmond
STAINES
Greenwich
DARTFORD
Bromley
Croydon
Sutton
Woking
Leatherhead
SURREY
Reigate
Dorking
Guildford
Crawley
Rochester
Maidstone
Royal Tunbridge Wells
K E N T
Canterbury
Margate
Ramsgate
Ashford
Dover
Folkestone
SUSSEX (EAST)
Hastings
Lewes
SUSSEX (WEST)
Chichester
Bognor Regis
Worthing
Brighton
Eastbourne
0 10 20 30 40 km
0 5 10 15 20 25 ml

England: South

Berkshire
1 Bearwood
2 Berkshire
3 Calcot Park
4 Datchet
5 Downshire
6 East Berkshire
7 Eton College
8 Goring & Streatley
9 Hawthorn Hill
10 Hurst
11 Lavender Park Golf Centre
12 Maidenhead
13 Newbury & Crookham
14 Reading
15 Royal Ascot
16 The Royal Household
17 Sonning
18 Sunningdale
19 Sunningdale Ladies
20 Swinley Forest
21 Temple
22 West Berkshire
23 Winter Hill

Buckinghamshire
1 Abbey Hill
2 Beaconsfield
3 Buckingham
4 Burnham Beeches
5 Chesham & Ley Hill
6 Chiltern Forest
7 Denham
8 Ellesborough
9 Farnham Park
10 Flackwell Heath
11 Gerrards Cross
12 Harewood Downs
13 Hazlemere G&CC
14 Iver
15 Ivinghoe
16 Little Chalfont
17 Stoke Poges
18 Stowe
19 Weston Turville
20 Wexham Park
21 Whiteleaf
22 Windmill Hill
23 Woburn

Hampshire
1 Alresford
2 Alton
3 Ampfield Par Three
4 Andover
5 Army Golf Club
6 Barton-on-Sea
7 Basingstoke
8 Basingstoke Hospitals
9 Bishopswood
10 Blackmoor
11 Bramshaw
12 Brokenhurst Manor
13 Burley
14 Corhampton
15 Dibden
16 Dunwood Manor
17 Fleetlands
18 Fleming Park
19 Gosport & Stokes Bay
20 Great Salterns
21 Hartley Wintney
22 Hayling
23 Hockley
24 Leckford & Longstock
25 Lee-on-the-Solent
26 Liphook
27 Meon Valley Hotel
28 New Forest
29 North Hants
30 Old Thorns Hotel CC
31 Ordnance Survey
32 Petersfield
33 Portsmouth
34 Romsey
35 Rowlands Castle
36 Royal Winchester
37 Southampton
38 Southwick Park
39 Southwood
40 Stoneham
41 Tidworth Garrison
42 Tylney Park
43 Waterlooville

Isle of Wight
1 Cowes
2 Freshwater
3 Newport IW
4 Osborne
5 Ryde
6 Shanklin & Sandown
7 Ventnor

Oxfordshire
1 Badgemore Park
2 Burford
3 Cherwell Edge
4 Chesterton
5 Chipping Norton
6 Frilford Heath
7 Henley
8 Huntercombe
9 North Oxford
10 RAF Benson
11 Southfield
12 Tadmarton Heath

Public courses are set in italic

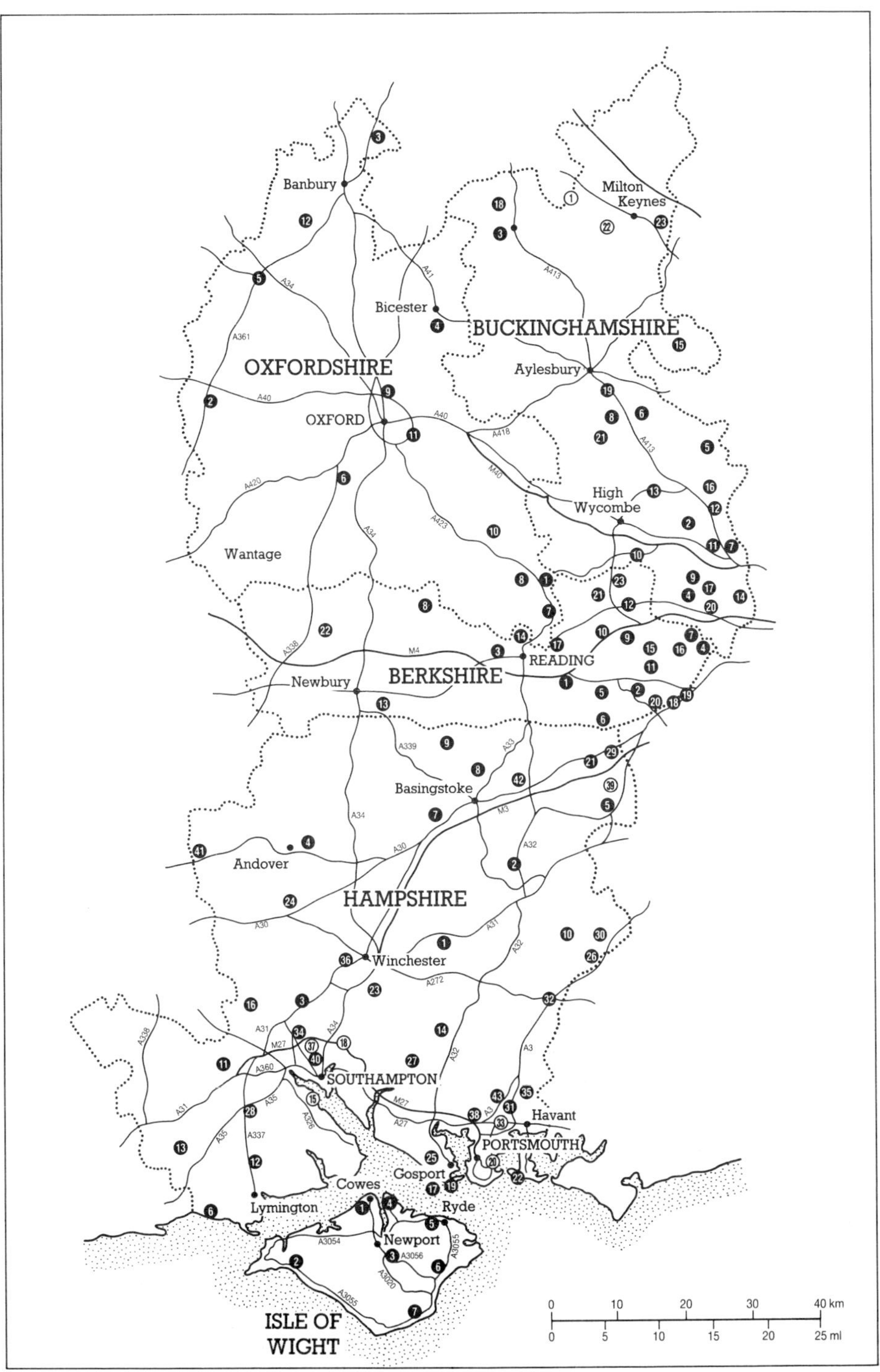

Banbury
Milton Keynes
Bicester
BUCKINGHAMSHIRE
OXFORDSHIRE
Aylesbury
OXFORD
High Wycombe
Wantage
READING
BERKSHIRE
Newbury
Basingstoke
Andover
HAMPSHIRE
Winchester
SOUTHAMPTON
Havant
PORTSMOUTH
Gosport
Cowes
Lymington
Ryde
Newport
ISLE OF WIGHT
A34
A361
A41
A413
A40
A418
M40
A420
A423
A338
M4
A339
A33
M3
A30
A32
A31
A272
A3
M27
A360
A35
A337
A326
A27
A3054
A3056
A3055
A3020
0
10
20
30
40 km
0
5
10
15
20
25 ml

England: South-West

Avon
1 Bath
2 Bristol & Clifton
3 Chipping Sodbury
4 Clevedon
5 Entry Hill
6 Filton
7 Fosseway CC
8 Henbury
9 Knowle
10 Lansdown
11 Long Ashton
12 Mangotsfield
13 Saltford
14 Shirehampton Park
15 Tracy Park
16 Weston-super-Mare
17 Worlebury

Cornwall
1 Bude & North Cornwall
2 Budock Vean Hotel
3 Carlyon Bay
4 Culdrose
5 Falmouth
6 Isles of Scilly
7 Launceston
8 Looe Bindown G&CC
9 Mullion
10 Newquay
11 Perranporth
12 Praa Sands
13 St Austell
14 St Enodoc
15 St Mellion
16 Tehidy Park
17 Tregenna Castle Hotel
18 Trevose
19 Truro
20 West Cornwall
21 Whitsand Bay Hotel

Devon
1 Axe Cliff
2 Bigbury
3 Chulmleigh
4 Churston
5 Downes Crediton
6 East Devon
7 Elfordleigh Hotel C&GC
8 Exeter G&CC
9 Holsworthy
10 Honiton
11 Ilfracombe
12 Manor House Hotel
13 Newton Abbot (Stover)
14 Okehampton
15 Royal North Devon
16 Saunton
17 Sidmouth
18 Staddon Heights
19 Tavistock
20 Teignmouth
21 Thurlestone
22 Tiverton
23 Torquay
24 Torrington
25 Warren
26 Wrangaton (South Devon)
27 Yelverton

Dorset
1 Ashley Wood
2 Bridport & West Dorset
3 Broadstone
4 Came Down
5 Christchurch
6 Ferndown
7 Highcliffe Castle
8 Isle of Purbeck
9 Knighton Heath
10 Lakey Hill
11 Lyme Regis
12 Meyrick Park
13 Parkstone
14 Queen's Park
15 Sherborne
16 Wareham
17 Weymouth

Gloucestershire
1 Broadway
2 Cirencester
3 Cleeve Cloud
4 Cleeve Hill
5 Cotswold Edge
6 Cotswold Hills
7 Forest of Dean
8 Gloucestershire Hotel
9 Lilley Brook
10 Lydney
11 Minchinhampton
12 Painswick
13 Stinchcombe Hill
14 Tewkesbury Park Hotel
15 Westonbirt

Somerset
1 Brean
2 Burnham & Berrow
3 Enmore Park
4 Kingweston
5 Mendip
6 Minehead & West Somerset
7 Taunton & Pickeridge
8 Vivary Park
9 Wells
10 Windwhistle G&CC
11 Yeovil

Wiltshire
1 Bremhill Park
2 Brinkworth
3 Broome Manor
4 Chippenham
5 High Post
6 Kingsdown
7 Marlborough
8 North Wilts
9 RAF Upavon
10 RMCS Shrivenham
11 Salisbury & South Wilts
12 Swindon
13 West Wilts

Public courses are set in italic

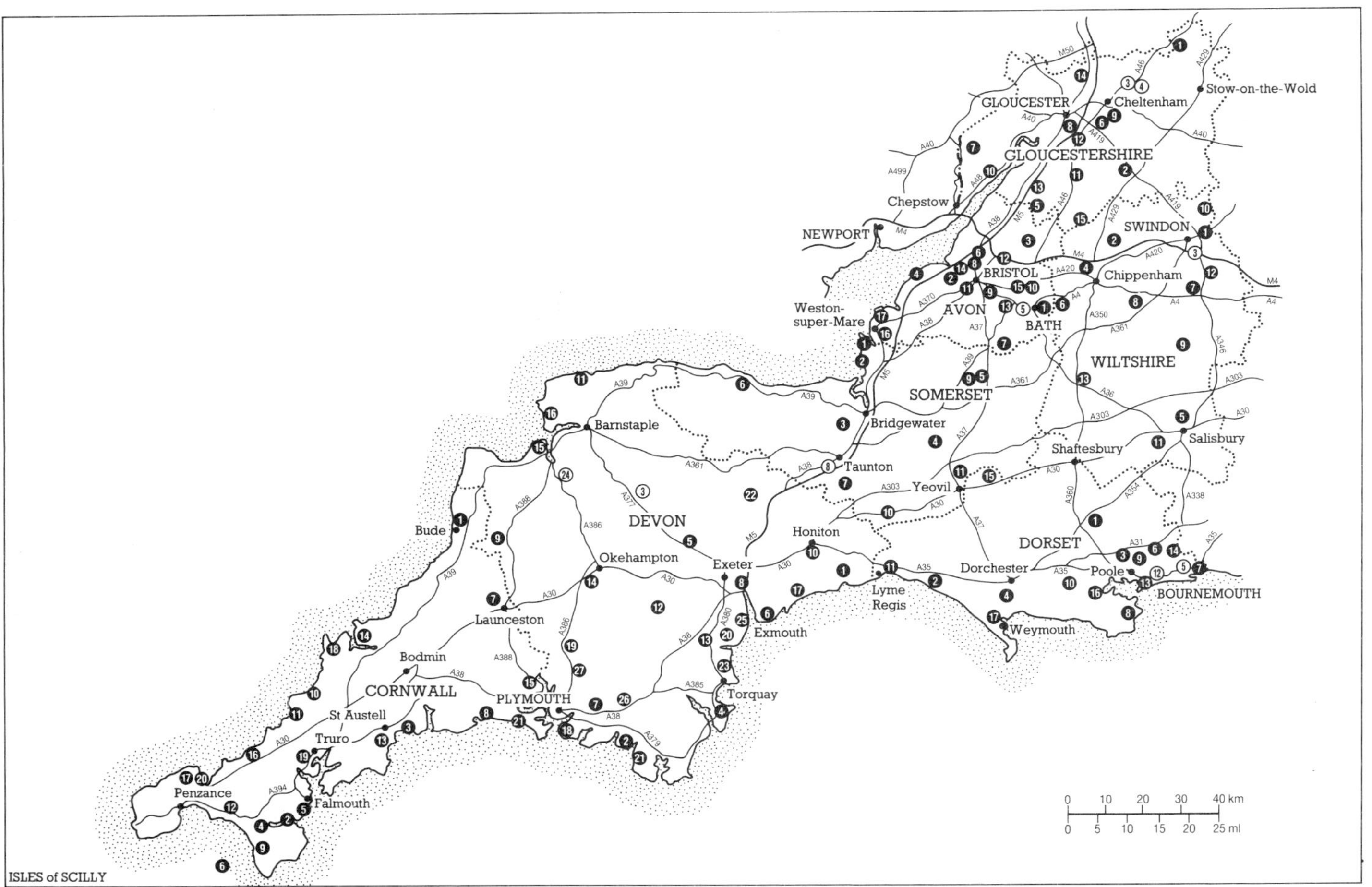
GLOUCESTER
Cheltenham
Stow-on-the-Wold
GLOUCESTERSHIRE
Chepstow
NEWPORT
SWINDON
BRISTOL
Chippenham
Weston-super-Mare
AVON
BATH
WILTSHIRE
SOMERSET
Barnstaple
Bridgewater
Salisbury
Shaftesbury
Taunton
Yeovil
Bude
DEVON
Honiton
DORSET
Okehampton
Exeter
Dorchester
Poole
BOURNEMOUTH
Lyme Regis
Launceston
Exmouth
Weymouth
Bodmin
CORNWALL
PLYMOUTH
Torquay
St Austell
Truro
Penzance
Falmouth
ISLES of SCILLY
0 10 20 30 40 km
0 5 10 15 20 25 ml

England: East Anglia

Bedfordshire
1 Aspley Guise & Woburn Sands
2 Beadlow Manor Hotel G&CC
3 Bedford & County
4 Bedfordshire
5 Colworth
6 Dunstable Downs
7 Griffin
8 John O'Gaunt
9 Leighton Buzzard
10 Millbrook
11 Mowsbury
12 South Beds
13 Stockwood Park
14 Tilsworth
15 Wyboston Lakes

Cambridgeshire
1 Abbotsley
2 Cambridgeshire Moat House Hotel
3 Ely City
4 Girton
5 Gog Magog
6 March
7 Orton Meadows
8 Peterborough Milton
9 Ramsey
10 St Ives (Hunts)
11 St Neot's
12 Thorpe Wood

Essex
1 Abridge G&CC
2 Ballards Gore
3 Basildon
4 Belfairs
5 Belhus Park Municipal
6 Bentley G&CC
7 Birch Grove
8 Boyce Hill
9 Braintree
10 Bunsay Downs
11 Burnham-on-Crouch
12 Canons Brook
13 Channels
14 Chelmsford
15 Chigwell
16 Chingford
17 Clacton
18 Colchester
19 Fairlop Waters
20 Forrester Park
21 Frinton
22 Hainault Forest
23 Hartswood
24 Harwich & Dovercourt
25 Havering
26 Ilford
27 Maldon
28 Maylands
29 Orsett
30 Pipps Hill CC
31 Quietwaters
32 Rochford Hundred
33 Romford
34 Royal Epping Forest
35 Saffron Walden
36 Skips
37 Southend-on-Sea
38 Stoke by Nayland
39 Theydon Bois
40 Thorndon Park
41 Thorpe Hall
42 Three Rivers
43 Towerlands
44 Upminster
45 Wanstead
46 Warley Park
47 Warren
48 West Essex
49 Woodford

Hertfordshire
1 Aldenham G&CC
2 Arkley
3 Ashridge
4 Batchwood Hall
5 Berkhamsted
6 Bishops Stortford
7 Boxmoor
8 Brickendon Grange
9 Brookmans Park
10 Bushey G&CC
11 Bushey Hall
12 Chadwell Springs
13 Cheshunt Park
14 Chorleywood
15 Dyrham Park CC
16 East Herts
17 Elstree
18 Hadley Wood
19 Harpenden
20 Harpenden Common
21 Hartsbourne CC
22 Hatfield London
23 Knebworth
24 Letchworth
25 Little Hay
26 Mid Herts
27 Moor Park
28 Old Fold Manor
29 Panshanger
30 Porters Park
31 Potters Bar
32 Redbourn
33 Rickmansworth
34 Royston
35 Sandy Lodge
36 South Herts
37 Stevenage
38 Verulam
39 Welwyn Garden City
40 West Herts
41 Whipsnade Park

Norfolk
1 Barnham Broom Hotel
2 Bawburgh
3 Costessey Park
4 Dereham
5 Eaton
6 Fakenham
7 Feltwell
8 Gorleston
9 Great Yarmouth & Caister
10 Hunstanton
11 King's Lynn
12 Links Country Park Hotel
13 Mundesley
14 RAF Marham
15 Royal Cromer
16 Royal Norwich
17 Royal West Norfolk
18 Ryston Park
19 Sheringham
20 Sprowston Park
21 Swaffham
22 Thetford

Suffolk
1 Aldeburgh
2 Beccles
3 Bungay & Waveney Valley
4 Bury St Edmunds
5 Cretingham
6 Diss
7 Felixstowe Ferry
8 Flempton
9 Fornham Park
10 Haverhill
11 Ipswich (Purdis Heath)
12 Links (Newmarket)
13 Newton Green
14 Rookery Park
15 Royal Worlington & Newmarket
16 Rushmere
17 Southwold
18 Stowmarket
19 Thorpeness Hotel
20 Waldringfield Heath
21 Warren Heath
22 Woodbridge

Public courses are set in italic

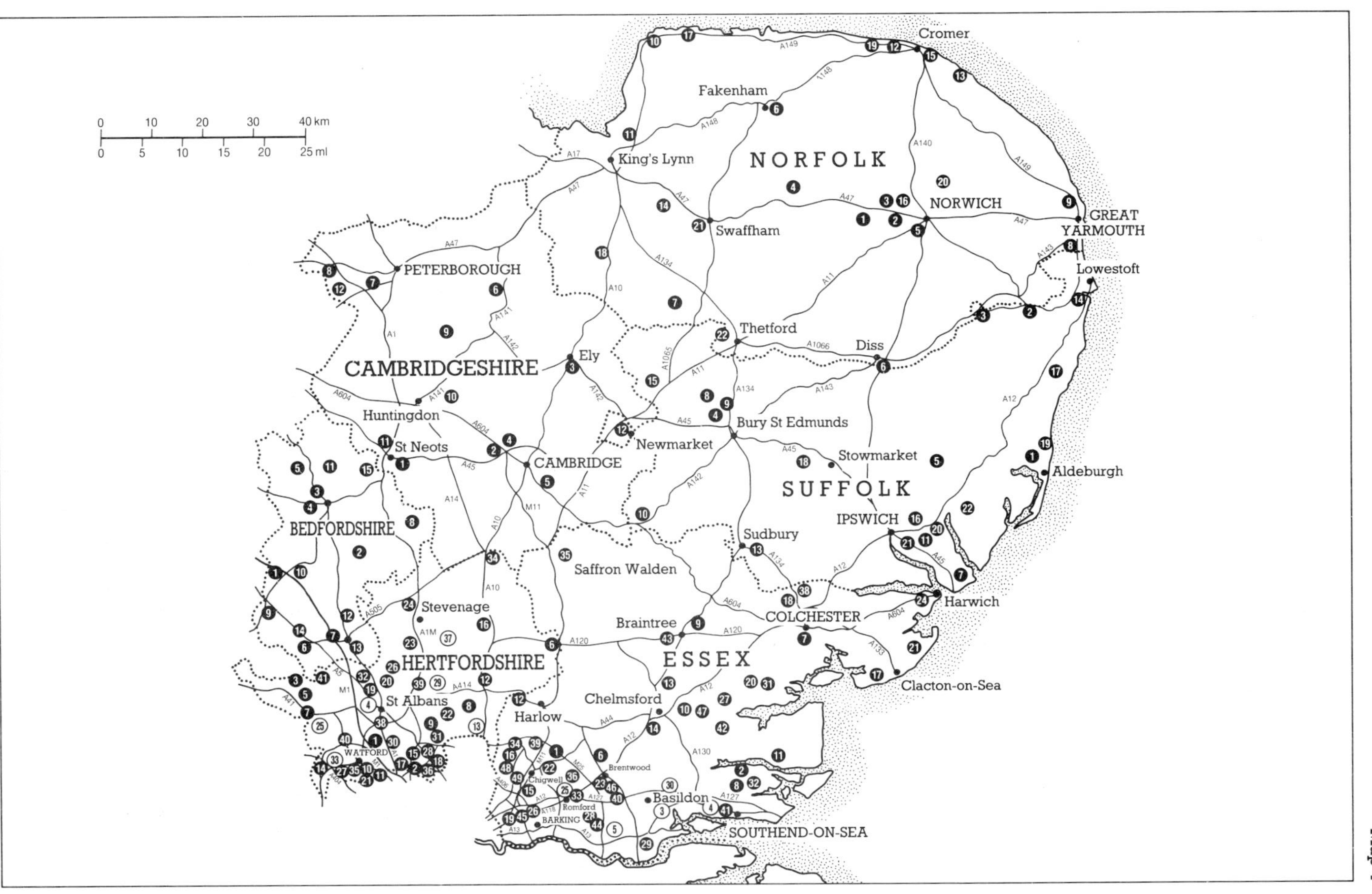
0 10 20 30 40 km
0 5 10 15 20 25 ml
Cromer
Fakenham
King's Lynn
NORFOLK
NORWICH
Swaffham
GREAT YARMOUTH
Lowestoft
PETERBOROUGH
Thetford
Diss
CAMBRIDGESHIRE
Ely
Huntingdon
Bury St Edmunds
St Neots
Newmarket
CAMBRIDGE
Stowmarket
Aldeburgh
SUFFOLK
BEDFORDSHIRE
IPSWICH
Sudbury
Saffron Walden
Harwich
Stevenage
COLCHESTER
Braintree
HERTFORDSHIRE
ESSEX
Clacton-on-Sea
St Albans
Chelmsford
Harlow
WATFORD
Brentwood
Chigwell
Basildon
Romford
BARKING
SOUTHEND-ON-SEA

England: East Midlands

Leicestershire

1 Birstall
2 Charnwood Forest
3 Cosby
4 Enderby
5 Glen Gorse
6 Hinckley
7 Humberstone Heights
8 Kibworth
9 Kirby Muxloe
10 Leicestershire
11 Lingdale
12 Longcliffe
13 Luffenham Heath
14 Lutterworth
15 Market Harborough
16 Melton Mowbray
17 Oadby
18 RAF North Luffenham
19 Rothley Park
20 Scraptoft
21 Ullesthorpe Court
22 Western Park
23 Whetstone
24 Willesley Park

Lincolnshire

1 Belton Park
2 Blankney
3 Boston
4 Burghley Park
5 Canwick Park
6 Carholme
7 Elsham
8 Gainsborough
9 Lincoln
10 Louth
11 Market Rasen & District
12 Millfield
13 North Shore
14 RAF Waddington
15 Sandilands
16 Seacroft
17 Sleaford
18 Spalding
19 Stoke Rochford
20 Sutton Bridge
21 Woodhall Spa

Northamptonshire

1 Cold Ashby
2 Daventry & District
3 Delapre
4 Kettering
5 Kingsthorpe
6 Northampton
7 Northamptonshire County
8 Oundle
9 Priors Hall
10 Rushden
11 Staverton Park
12 Wellingborough
13 Woodlands Vale

Nottinghamshire

1 Beeston Fields
2 Bulwell Forest
3 Chilwell Manor
4 Coxmoor
5 Edwalton
6 Kilton Forest
7 Mapperley
8 Newark
9 Nottingham City
10 Notts
11 Oxton
12 Radcliffe on Trent
13 Retford
14 Ruddington Grange
15 Rushcliffe
16 Serlby Park
17 Sherwood Forest
18 Stanton-on-the-Wolds
19 Wollaton Park
20 Woodhouse
21 Worksop

Public courses are set in italic

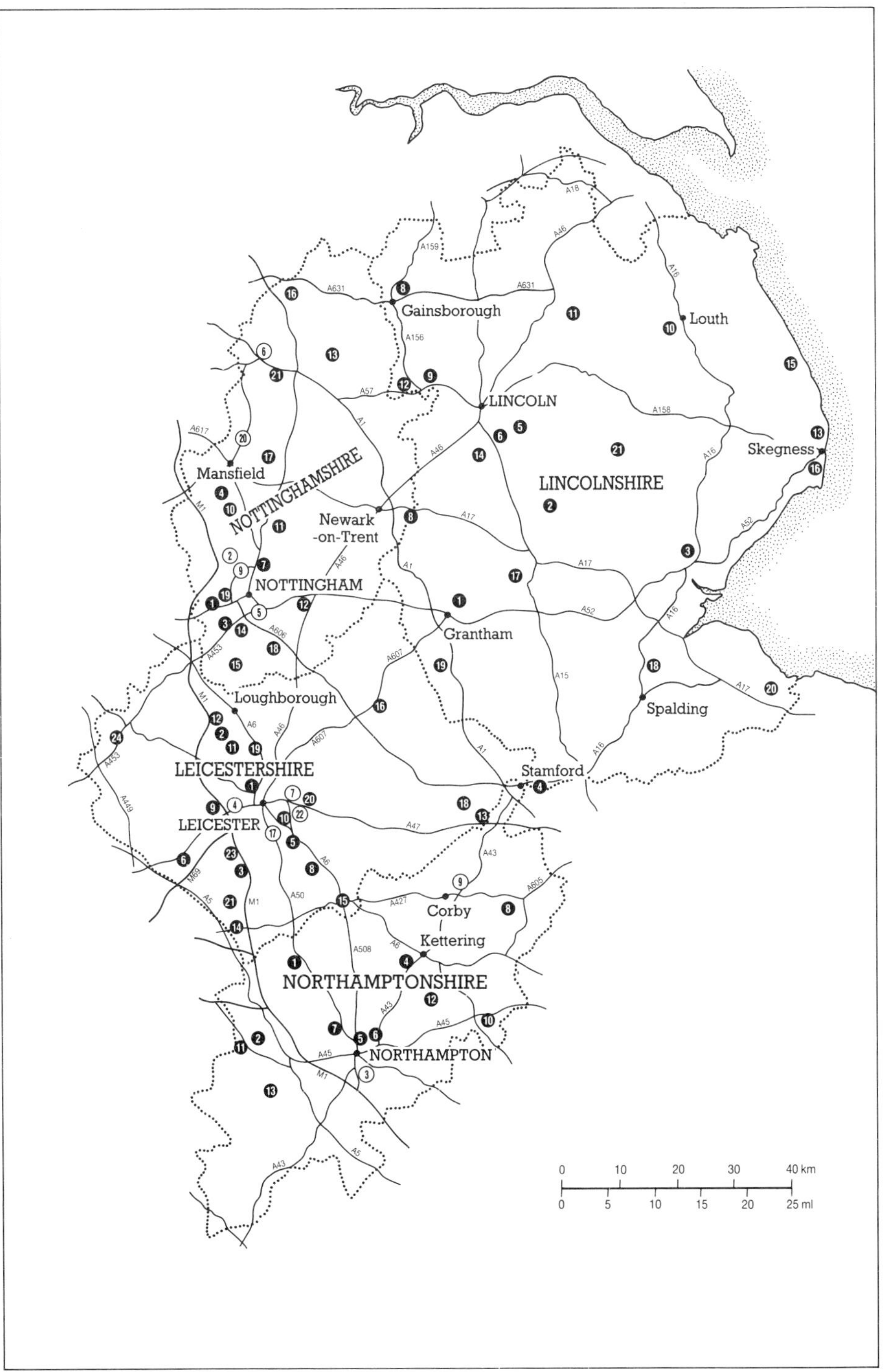

Gainsborough
Louth
LINCOLN
Skegness
LINCOLNSHIRE
Mansfield
NOTTINGHAMSHIRE
Newark
-on-Trent
NOTTINGHAM
Grantham
Loughborough
Spalding
LEICESTERSHIRE
Stamford
LEICESTER
Corby
Kettering
NORTHAMPTONSHIRE
NORTHAMPTON
0 10 20 30 40 km
0 5 10 15 20 25 ml

England: West Midlands

Derbyshire
1 Alfreton
2 Allestree Park
3 Ashbourne
4 Bakewell
5 Blue Circle
6 Breadsall Priory
7 Buxton & High Peak
8 Cavendish
9 Chapel-en-le-Frith
10 Chesterfield
11 Chesterfield Municipal
12 Chevin
13 Derby
14 Erewash Valley
15 Glossop & District
16 Hallowes
17 Ilkeston
18 Kedleston Park
19 Matlock
20 Mickleover
21 Ormonde Fields
22 Pastures
23 Shirland
24 Sickleholme
25 Stanedge

Hereford & Worcester
1 Belmont House
2 Blackwell
3 Churchill and Blakedown
4 Droitwich
5 Evesham
6 Habberley
7 Herefordshire
8 Kidderminster
9 King's Norton
10 Kington
11 Leominster
12 Little Lakes
13 Pitcheroak
14 Redditch
15 Ross-on-Wye
16 Tolladine
17 Worcester G&CC
18 Worcestershire

Shropshire
1 Bridgnorth
2 Church Stretton
3 Hawkstone Park
4 Hill Valley G&CC
5 Lilleshall Hall
6 Llanymynech
7 Ludlow
8 Market Drayton
9 Meole Brace
10 Oswestry
11 Shifnal
12 Shrewsbury
13 Telford Hotel G&CC
14 Wrekin

Staffordshire
1 Alsager G&CC
2 Barlaston
3 Beau Desert
4 Branston
5 Brocton Hall
6 Burslem
7 Burton-on-Trent
8 Craythorne Golf Centre
9 Drayton Park
10 Goldenhill
11 Greenway Hall
12 Ingestre Park
13 Lakeside (Rugeley)
14 Leek
15 Newcastle Municipal
16 Newcastle-under-Lyme
17 Onneley
18 Stafford Castle
19 Stone
20 Tamworth
21 Trentham
22 Trentham Park
23 Uttoxeter
24 Westwood
25 Whittington Barracks
26 Wolstanton

Warwickshire
1 Atherstone
2 City of Coventry (Brandon Wood)
3 Kenilworth
4 Ladbrook Park
5 Leamington & County
6 Maxstoke Park
7 Newbold Comyn
8 Nuneaton
9 Purley Chase
10 Rugby
11 Stratford-on-Avon
12 Warwick
13 Welcombe Hotel

West Midlands
1 The Belfry
2 Bloxwich
3 Boldmere
4 Brand Hall
5 Calderfields
6 Cocks Moor Woods
7 Copt Heath
8 Coventry
9 Coventry Hearsall
10 Dartmouth
11 Druids Heath
12 Dudley
13 Edgbaston
14 Enville
15 Forest of Arden G&CC
16 Fulford Heath
17 Gay Hill
18 Grange
19 Great Barr
20 Hagley
21 Halesowen
22 Handsworth
23 Harborne
24 Harborne Church Farm
25 Hatchford Brook
26 Hilltop
27 Himley Hall
28 Lickey Hills
29 Little Aston
30 Moor Hall
31 Moseley
32 North Warwickshire
33 North Worcestershire
34 Olton
35 Oxley Park
36 Patshull Park
37 Penn
38 Pype Hayes
39 Robin Hood
40 Sandwell Park
41 Shirley
42 South Staffordshire
43 Sphinx
44 Stourbridge
45 Sutton Coldfield
46 Swindon
47 Walmley (Wylde Green)
48 Walsall
49 Warley

Public courses are set in italic

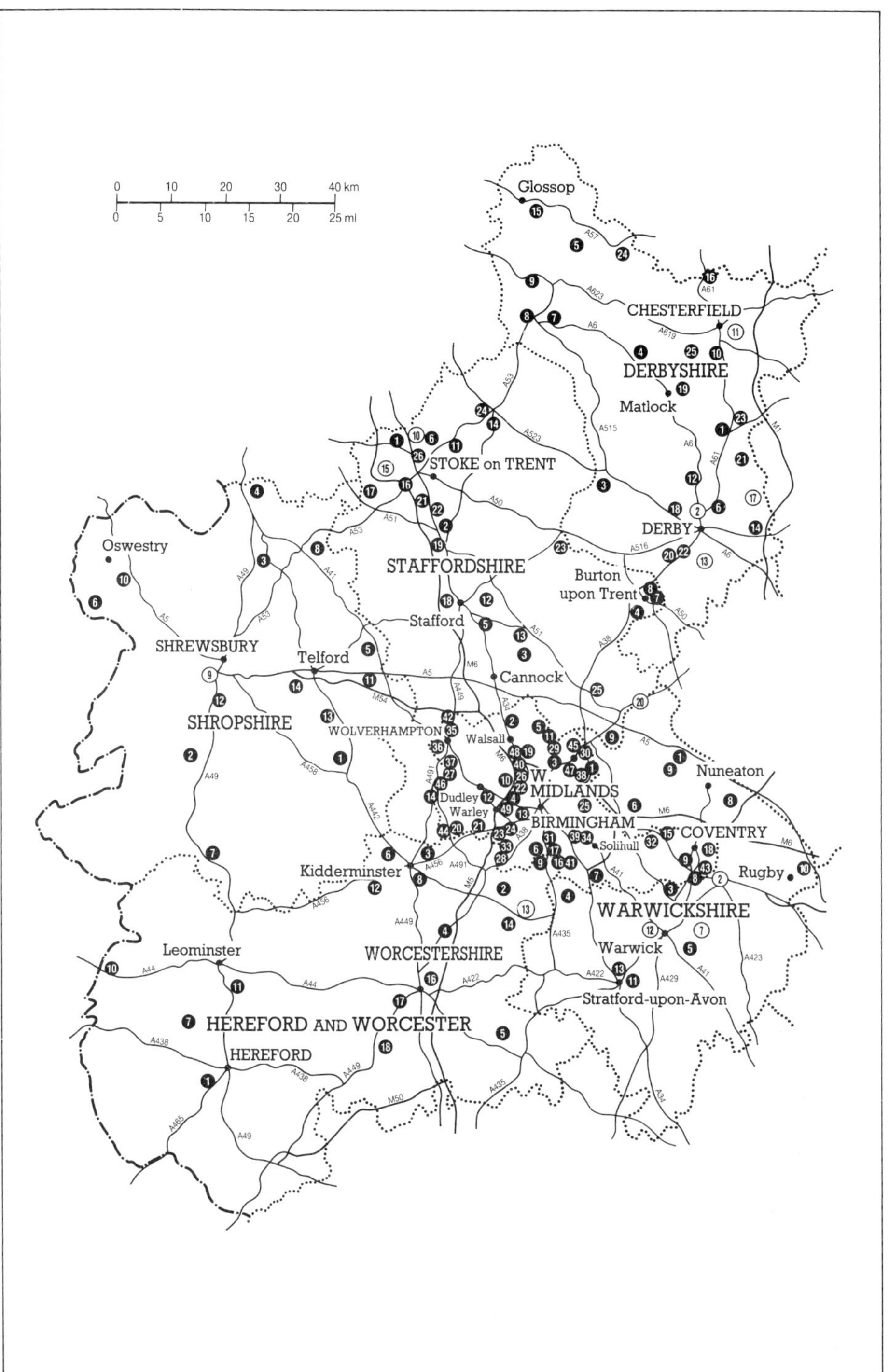

0 10 20 30 40 km
0 5 10 15 20 25 ml
Glossop
CHESTERFIELD
DERBYSHIRE
Matlock
STOKE on TRENT
DERBY
Oswestry
STAFFORDSHIRE
Burton upon Trent
Stafford
SHREWSBURY
Telford
Cannock
SHROPSHIRE
WOLVERHAMPTON
Walsall
W. MIDLANDS
Nuneaton
Dudley
Warley
BIRMINGHAM
COVENTRY
Solihull
Rugby
Kidderminster
WARWICKSHIRE
Leominster
WORCESTERSHIRE
Warwick
Stratford-upon-Avon
HEREFORD AND WORCESTER
HEREFORD

England: Yorkshire & Humberside

Humberside

1 Beverley & East Riding
2 Boothferry (Spaldington)
3 Bridlington
4 Brough
5 Cleethorpes
6 Driffield
7 Flamborough Head
8 Ganstead Park
9 Grimsby
10 Hainsworth Park
11 Hessle
12 Holme Hall
13 Hornsea
14 Hull
15 Immingham
16 Kingsway
17 Normanby Hall
18 Scunthorpe
19 Springhead Park
20 Sutton Park
21 Withernsea

Yorkshire (North)

1 Aldwark Manor
2 Ampleforth College
3 Bedale
4 Bentham
5 Catterick Garrison
6 Crimple Valley
7 Easingwold
8 Filey
9 Fulford (York)
10 Ganton
11 Ghyll
12 Harrogate
13 Heworth
14 Kirkbymoorside
15 Knaresborough
16 Malton & Norton
17 Masham
18 Oakdale
19 Pannal
20 Pike Hills
21 Richmond
22 Ripon City
23 Scarborough North Cliff
24 Scarborough South Cliff
25 Selby
26 Settle
27 Skipton
28 Thirsk & Northallerton
29 Whitby
30 York

Yorkshire (South)

1 Abbeydale
2 Austerfield Park
3 Barnsley
4 Beauchief Municipal
5 Birley Wood
6 Concord Park
7 Crookhill Park
8 Doncaster
9 Doncaster Town Moor
10 Dore & Totley
11 Grange Park
12 Hallamshire
13 Hickleton
14 Hillsborough
15 Lees Hall
16 Lindrick
17 Phoenix
18 Renishaw Park
19 Rotherham
20 Roundwood
21 Sheffield Transport Dept
22 Silkstone
23 Sitwell Park
24 Stocksbridge & District
25 Tankersley Park
26 Thorne
27 Tinsley Park
28 Wath-upon-Dearne
29 Wheatley

Yorkshire (West)

1 Alwoodley
2 Baildon
3 Ben Rhydding
4 Bingley (St Ives)
5 Bradford
6 Bradford Moor
7 Bradley Park
8 Branshaw
9 Calverley
10 Castle Fields
11 City of Wakefield
12 Clayton
13 Cleckheaton & District
14 Crosland Heath
15 Dewsbury District
16 East Bierley
17 Elland
18 Ferrybridge 'C'
19 Fulneck
20 Garforth
21 Gotts Park
22 Halifax
23 Halifax Bradley Hall
24 Halifax West End
25 Hanging Heaton
26 Headingley
27 Headley
28 Horsforth
29 Howley Hall
30 Huddersfield
31 Ilkley
32 Keighley
33 Leeds
34 Lightcliffe
35 Longley Park
36 Low Laithes
37 Marsden
38 Meltham
39 Middleton Park
40 Moor Allerton
41 Moortown
42 Mount Skip
43 Normanton
44 Northcliffe
45 Otley
46 Outlane
47 Painthorpe House
48 Phoenix Park
49 Pontefract & District
50 Pontefract Park
51 Queensbury
52 Rawdon
53 Riddlesden
54 Roundhay
55 Ryburn
56 Sand Moor
57 Scarcroft
58 Shipley
59 Silsden
60 South Bradford
61 South Leeds
62 Temple Newsam
63 Todmorden
64 Wakefield
65 West Bowling
66 West Bradford
67 Wetherby
68 Whitwood
69 Woodhall Hills
70 Woodsome Hall
71 Wortley

Public courses are set in italic

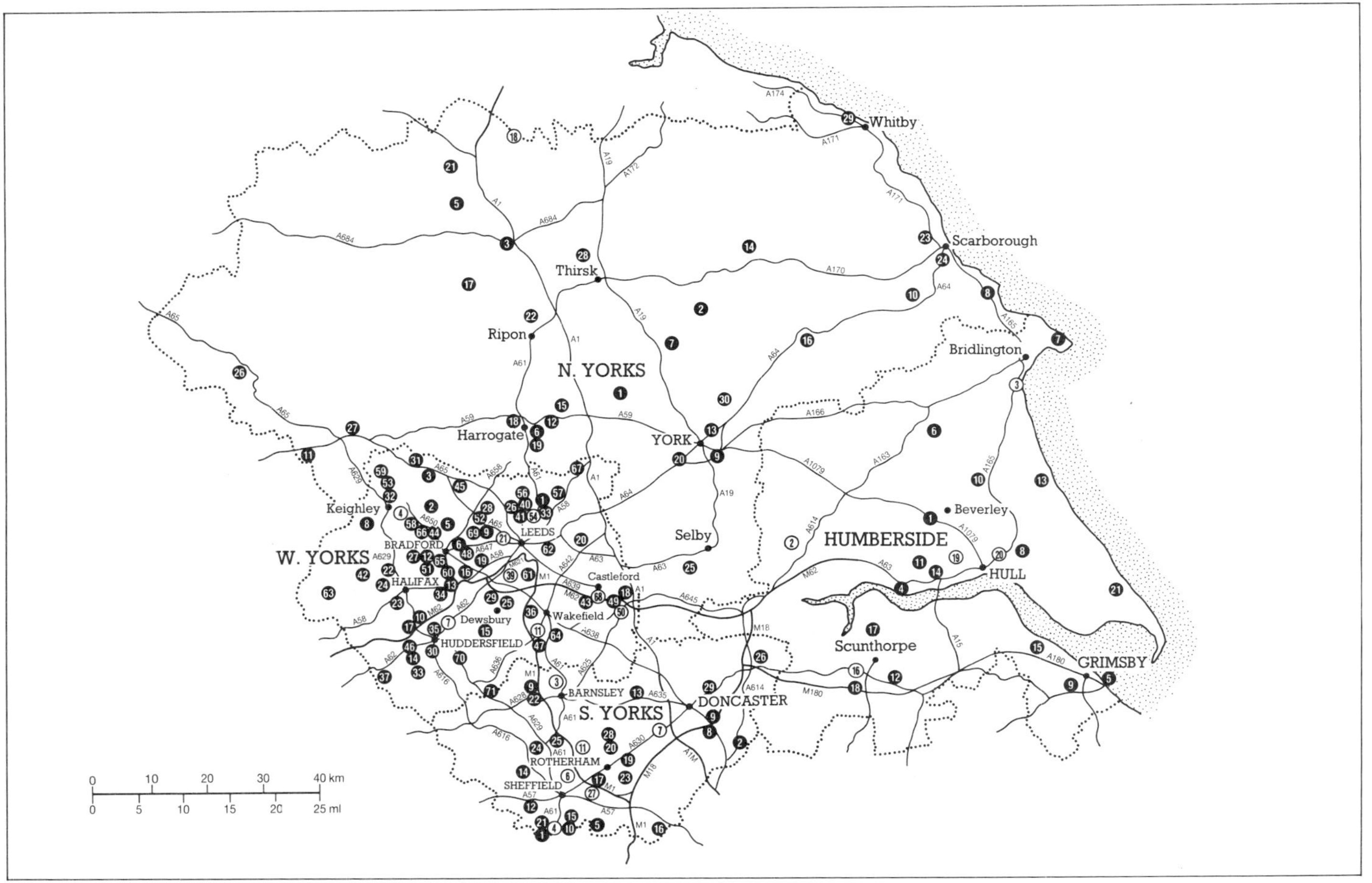
N. YORKS
W. YORKS
S. YORKS
HUMBERSIDE
Whitby
Scarborough
Bridlington
Beverley
HULL
GRIMSBY
Scunthorpe
DONCASTER
YORK
Selby
Thirsk
Ripon
Harrogate
LEEDS
Castleford
Wakefield
Dewsbury
BRADFORD
HALIFAX
HUDDERSFIELD
Keighley
BARNSLEY
ROTHERHAM
SHEFFIELD
0 10 20 30 40 km
0 5 10 15 20 25 ml

England: North West

Cheshire

1 Alderley Edge
2 Astbury
3 Avro
4 Birchwood
5 Bramhall
6 Chester
7 Congleton
8 Crewe
9 Delamere Forest
10 Eaton
11 Ellesmere Port
12 Helsby
13 Knights Grange
14 Knutsford
15 Lymm
16 Macclesfield
17 Malkins Bank
18 Mere G&CC
19 New Mills
20 Poulton Park
21 Prestbury
22 Queen's Park
23 Romiley
24 Runcorn
25 St Michael Jubilee
26 Sandbach
27 Sandiway
28 Stockport
29 The Tytherington
30 Upton-by-Chester
31 Vicars Cross
32 Walton Hall
33 Warrington
34 Widnes
35 Widnes Municipal
36 Wilmslow

Isle of Man

1 Castletown
2 Douglas Municipal
3 Howstrake
4 Peel
5 Port St Mary
6 Ramsey
7 Rowany

Lancashire

1 Accrington & District
2 Alt
3 Ashton & Lea
4 Bacup
5 Baxenden & District
6 Blackburn
7 Blackpool North Shore
8 Blackpool Park
9 Burnley
10 Chorley
11 Clitheroe
12 Colne
13 Darwen
14 Dean Wood
15 Duxbury Park
16 Fairhaven
17 Fishwick Hall
18 Fleetwood
19 Great Harwood
20 Green Haworth
21 Heysham
22 Hindley Hall
23 Ingol Golf & Squash Club
24 Knott End
25 Lancaster G&CC
26 Lansil
27 Leyland
28 Lobden
29 Longridge
30 Lytham (Green Drive)
31 Marsden Park
32 Morecambe
33 Nelson
34 Ormskirk
35 Penwortham
36 Pleasington
37 Poulton-le-Fylde
38 Preston
39 Rishton
40 Rossendale
41 Royal Lytham & St Annes
42 St Annes Old Links
43 Shaw Hill G&CC
44 Silverdale
45 Towneley
46 Turton
47 Whalley
48 Wilpshire

Manchester (Greater)

1 Altrincham Municipal
2 Ashton-on-Mersey
3 Ashton-under-Lyne
4 Beacon Park
5 Blackley
6 Bolton
7 Bolton Municipal
8 Bolton Old Links
9 Brackley Municipal
10 Bramall Park
11 Breightmet
12 Brookdale
13 Bury
14 Castle Hawk
15 Cheadle
16 Chorlton-cum-Hardy
17 Crompton & Royton
18 Davenport
19 Davyhulme Park
20 Deane
21 Denton
22 Didsbury
23 Disley
24 Dukinfield
25 Dunham Forest G&CC
26 Dunscar
27 Ellesmere
28 Fairfield Golf & Sailing Club
29 Flixton
30 Gathurst
31 Gatley
32 Great Lever & Farnworth
33 Greenmount
34 Haigh Hall
35 Hale
36 Harwood
37 Hazel Grove
38 Heaton Moor
39 Heaton Park
40 Horwich
41 Houldsworth (Levenshulme)
42 Leigh
43 Lowes Park
44 Manchester GC Ltd
45 Marple
46 Mellor & Townscliffe
47 North Manchester
48 Northenden
49 Oldham
50 Pike Fold
51 Prestwich
52 Reddish Vale
53 Ringway
54 Rochdale
55 Saddleworth
56 Sale
57 Springfield Park
58 Stamford
59 Stand
60 Swinton Park
61 Tunshill
62 Walmersley
63 Werneth
64 Werneth Low
65 Westhoughton
66 Whitefield
67 Whittaker
68 Wigan
69 William Wroe
70 Withington
71 Worsley

Merseyside

1 Allerton Park
2 Arrowe Park
3 Ashton-in-Makerfield
4 Bidston
5 Bootle
6 Bowring
7 Bromborough
8 Caldy
9 Childwall
10 Eastham Lodge
11 Formby
12 Formby Ladies'
13 Grange Park
14 Haydock Park
15 Hesketh
16 Heswall
17 Hillside
18 Hoylake Municipal
19 Huyton & Prescot
20 Leasowe
21 Lee Park
22 Liverpool Municipal
23 Prenton
24 Royal Birkdale
25 Royal Liverpool
26 St Helens
27 Southport & Ainsdale
28 Southport Municipal
29 Southport Old Links
30 Wallasey
31 Warren
32 West Derby
33 West Hoyle
34 West Lancashire
35 Wirral Ladies
36 Woolton

Public courses are set in italic

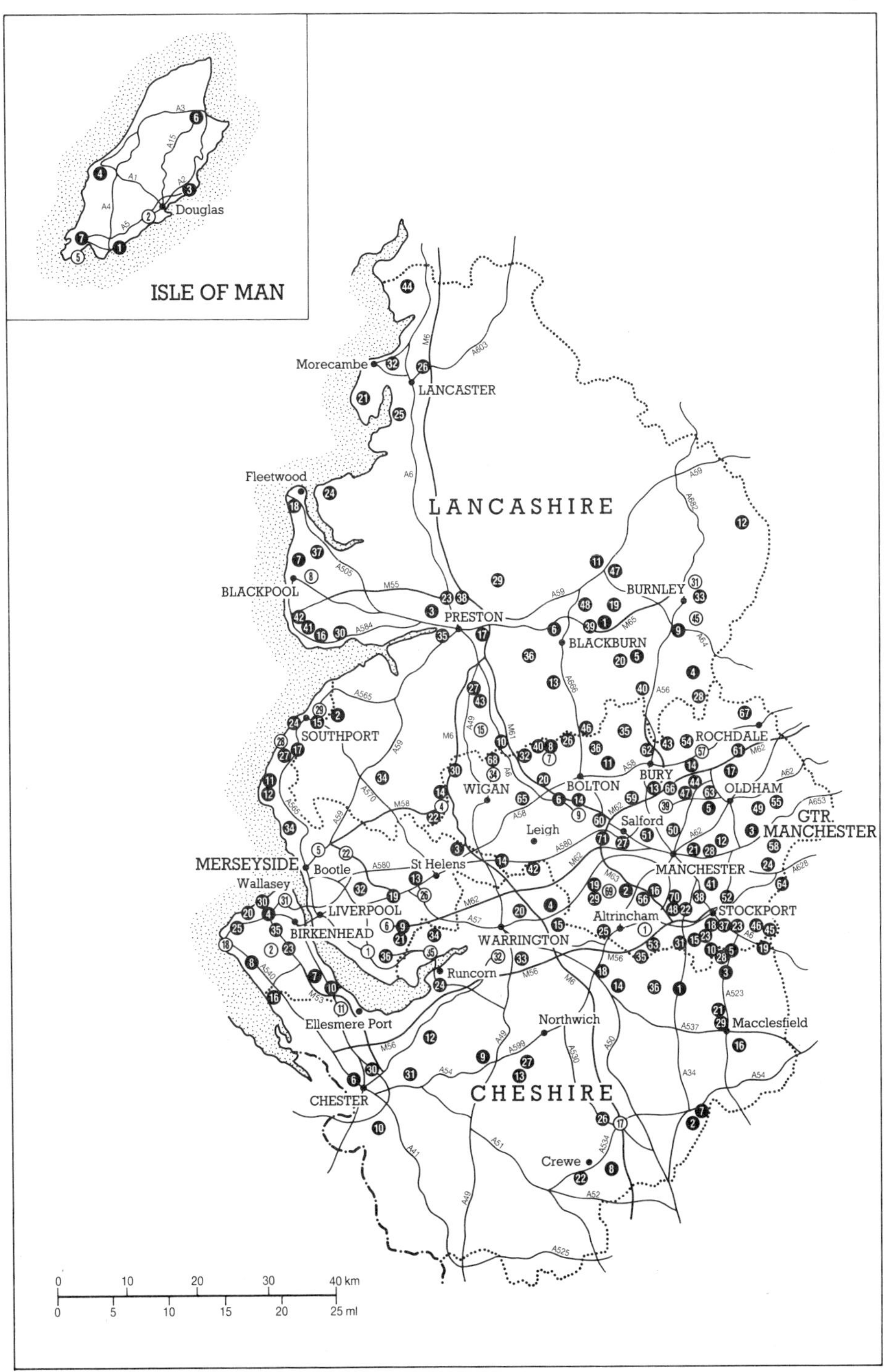
ISLE OF MAN
Douglas
LANCASHIRE
Morecambe
LANCASTER
Fleetwood
BLACKPOOL
PRESTON
BURNLEY
BLACKBURN
ROCHDALE
SOUTHPORT
WIGAN
BOLTON
BURY
OLDHAM
GTR. MANCHESTER
Leigh
Salford
MERSEYSIDE
Bootle
St Helens
MANCHESTER
Wallasey
LIVERPOOL
BIRKENHEAD
WARRINGTON
Altrincham
STOCKPORT
Runcorn
Ellesmere Port
Northwich
Macclesfield
CHESHIRE
CHESTER
Crewe
0 10 20 30 40 km
0 5 10 15 20 25 ml

England: North

Cleveland
1 Billingham
2 Castle Eden & Peterlee
3 Cleveland
4 Eaglescliffe
5 Hartlepool
6 Middlesbrough
7 Middlesbrough Municipal
8 Saltburn
9 Seaton Carew
10 Tees-side
11 Wilton

Cumbria
1 Alston Moor
2 Appleby
3 Barrow
4 Brampton (Talkin Tarn)
5 Carlisle
6 Cockermouth
7 The Dunnerholme
8 Furness
9 Grange Fell
10 Grange-over-Sands
11 Kendal
12 Keswick
13 Kirkby Lonsdale
14 Maryport
15 Penrith
16 St Bees
17 Seascale
18 Sedbergh
19 Silecroft
20 Silloth-on-Solway
21 Stoneyholme
22 Ulverston
23 Windermere
24 Workington

Durham
1 Aycliffe
2 Barnard Castle
3 Beamish Park
4 Bishop Auckland
5 Blackwell Grange
6 Brancepeth Castle
7 Chester-Le-Street
8 Consett & District
9 Crook
10 Darlington
11 Dinsdale Spa
12 Durham City
13 Hobson Municipal
14 Mount Oswald
15 Roseberry Grange
16 Seaham
17 South Moor
18 Stressholme
19 Woodham G&CC

Northumberland
1 Allendale
2 Alnmouth
3 Alnmouth Village
4 Alnwick
5 Arcot Hall
6 Bamburgh Castle
7 Bedlingtonshire
8 Bellingham
9 Berwick-upon-Tweed
10 Blyth
11 Dunstanburgh Castle
12 Hexham
13 Magdalene Fields
14 Morpeth
15 Newbiggin-by-the-Sea
16 Ponteland
17 Prudhoe
18 Rothbury
19 Seahouses
20 Stocksfield
21 Tynedale
22 Warkworth
23 Wooler

Tyne & Wear
1 Backworth
2 Birtley (Portobello)
3 Boldon
4 City of Newcastle
5 Close House
6 Garesfield
7 George Washington Hotel
8 Gosforth
9 Gosforth Park
10 Heworth
11 Houghton-le-Spring
12 Newcastle United
13 Northumberland
14 Ravensworth
15 Ryton
16 South Shields
17 Tynemouth
18 Tyneside
19 Wallsend
20 Washington
21 Wearside
22 Westerhope
23 Whickham
24 Whitburn
25 Whitley Bay

Public courses are set in italic.

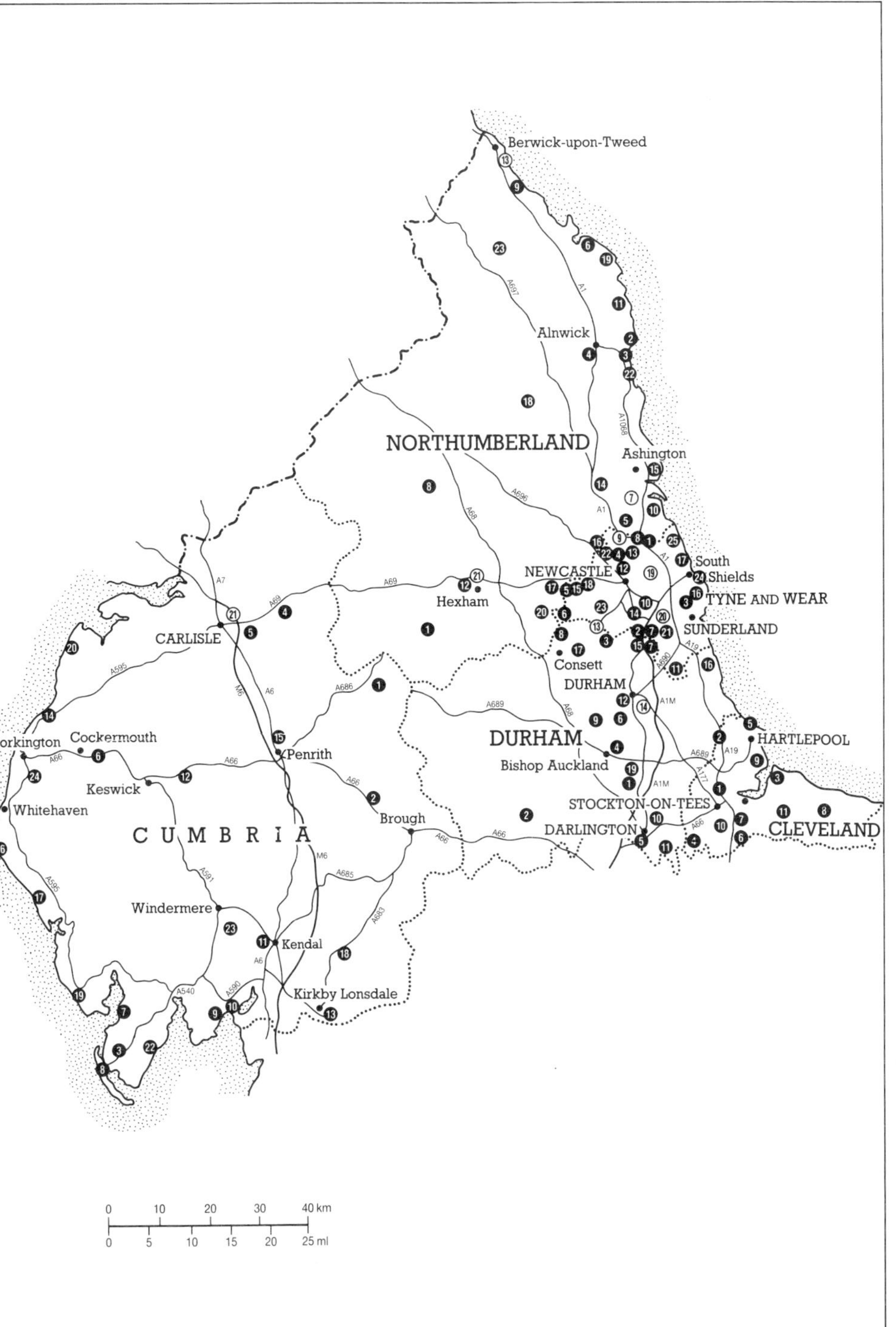
Berwick-upon-Tweed
Alnwick
NORTHUMBERLAND
Ashington
NEWCASTLE
South Shields
TYNE AND WEAR
SUNDERLAND
Hexham
CARLISLE
Consett
DURHAM
DURHAM
HARTLEPOOL
Bishop Auckland
STOCKTON-ON-TEES
DARLINGTON
CLEVELAND
Cockermouth
Workington
Penrith
Keswick
Whitehaven
CUMBRIA
Brough
Windermere
Kendal
Kirkby Lonsdale
0 10 20 30 40 km
0 5 10 15 20 25 ml

Ireland

Connacht

Co Galway
1 Athenry
2 Ballinasloe
3 Connemara
4 Galway
5 Gort
6 Loughrea
7 Mount Bellew
8 Oughterard
9 Portumna
10 Tuam

Co Leitrim
11 Ballinamore
12 Carrick-on-Shannon

Co Mayo
13 Achill Island
14 Ballina
15 Ballinrobe
16 Ballyhaunis
17 Belmullet
18 Castlebar
19 Castlemorris
20 Mulrany
21 Swinford
22 Westport

Co Roscommon
23 Athlone
24 Ballaghaderreen
25 Boyle
26 Castlerea
27 Roscommon

Co Sligo
28 Ballymote
29 County Sligo
30 Enniscrone
31 Strandhill

Leinster

Co Carlow
1 Borris
2 Carlow

Co Dublin
3 Balbriggan
4 Ballinascorney
5 Beaverstown
6 Beech Park
7 Corballis
8 Deer Park
9 Donabate
10 Dun Laoghaire
11 Forrest Little
12 Hermitage
13 The Island
14 Killiney
15 Kilternan Hotel
16 Lucan
17 Malahide
18 Newlands
19 Portmarnock
20 Rush
21 Skerries
22 Slade Valley
23 Woodbrook

Dublin City
24 Carrickmines
25 Castle
26 Clontarf
27 Edmondstown
28 Elm Park G&SC
29 Foxrock
30 Grange
31 Howth
32 Milltown
33 Rathfarnham
34 Royal Dublin
35 St Anne's
36 Stackstown
37 Sutton

Co Kildare
38 Athy
39 Bodenstown
40 Cill Dara
41 Clongowes
42 Curragh
43 Knockanally
44 Naas

Co Kilkenny
45 Callan
46 Castlecomer
47 Kilkenny

Co Laois
48 Abbey Leix
49 Heath (Portlaoise)
50 Mountrath
51 Portarlington
52 Rathdowney

Co Longford
53 Co Longford

Co Louth
54 Ardee
55 County Lough
56 Dundalk
57 Greenore

Co Meath
58 Gormanston College
59 Headfort
60 Laytown and Bettystown
61 Royal Tara
62 Trim

Co Offaly
63 Birr
64 Edenderry
65 Tullamore

Co Wexford
66 Courtown
67 Enniscorthy
68 New Ross
69 Rosslare
70 Wexford

Co Westmeath
71 Moate
72 Mullingar

Co Wicklow
73 Arklow
74 Baltinglass
75 Blainroe
76 Bray
77 Coollattin
78 Delgany
79 Greystones
80 Wicklow
81 Woodenbridge

Munster

Co Clare
1 Drumoland Castle
2 Ennis
3 Kilkee
4 Kilrush
5 Lahinch
6 Shannon
7 Spanish Point

Co Cork
8 Bandon
9 Bantry
10 Charleville
11 Cobh
12 Cork
13 Doneraile
14 Douglas
15 Dunmore
16 East Cork
17 Fermoy
18 Glengarriff
19 Kanturk
20 Kinsale
21 Macroom
22 Mallow
23 Mitchelstown
24 Monkstown
25 Muskerry
26 Skibbereen
27 Youghal

Co Kerry
28 Ballybunion
29 Ceann Sibeal
30 Dooks
31 Kenmare
32 Killarney
33 Parknasilla
34 Tralee
35 Waterville

Co Limerick
36 Adare Manor
37 Castletroy
38 Limerick
39 Newcastle West

Co Tipperary
40 Cahir Park
41 Carrick on Suir
42 Clonmel
43 Nenagh
44 Rockwell College
45 Roscrea
46 Templemore
47 Thurles
48 Tipperary

Co Waterford
49 Dungarvan
50 Lismore
51 Tramore
52 Waterford

Ulster

Co Antrim
1 Ballycastle
2 Ballyclare
3 Ballymena
4 Bushfoot
5 Cairndhu
6 Carrickfergus
7 Cushendall
8 Dunmurry
9 Greenisland
10 Larne
11 Lisburn
12 Massereene
13 Royal Portrush
14 Whitehead

Co Armagh
15 County Armagh
16 Craigavon
17 Lurgan
18 Portadown
19 Tandragee

Belfast
20 Ballyearl Golf Centre
21 Balmoral
22 Belvoir Park
23 Cliftonville
24 Fortwilliam
25 Gilnahirk
26 The Knock
27 Knockbracken
28 Malone
29 Ormeau
30 Shandon Park

Co Cavan
31 Belturbet
32 Blacklion
33 Cabra Castle
34 County Cavan
35 Virginia

Co Donegal
36 Ballbofey & Stranorlar
37 Ballyliffin
38 Buncrana
39 Bundoran

List continued on p.224

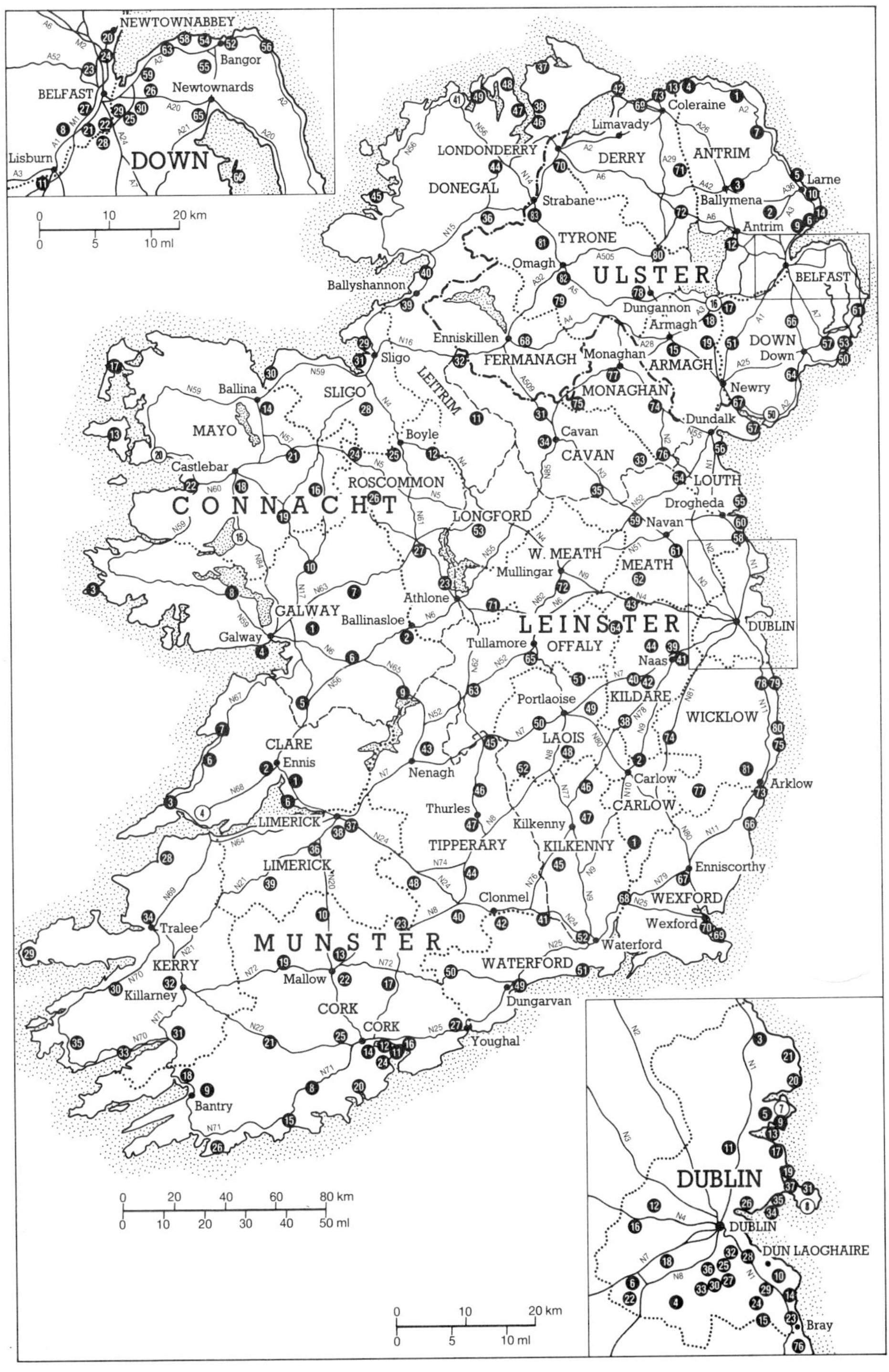
ULSTER
CONNACHT
LEINSTER
MUNSTER
DONEGAL
LONDONDERRY
DERRY
ANTRIM
TYRONE
FERMANAGH
ARMAGH
DOWN
MONAGHAN
CAVAN
SLIGO
LEITRIM
MAYO
ROSCOMMON
LONGFORD
GALWAY
W. MEATH
MEATH
LOUTH
OFFALY
KILDARE
DUBLIN
WICKLOW
LAOIS
CARLOW
KILKENNY
WEXFORD
CLARE
LIMERICK
TIPPERARY
WATERFORD
KERRY
CORK
Coleraine
Limavady
Larne
Ballymena
Antrim
Strabane
Omagh
BELFAST
Dungannon
Armagh
Enniskillen
Monaghan
Newry
Down
Dundalk
Ballyshannon
Sligo
Ballina
Castlebar
Boyle
Cavan
Drogheda
Navan
Mullingar
Athlone
Ballinasloe
Galway
Tullamore
Naas
Portlaoise
Carlow
Arklow
Ennis
Nenagh
Thurles
Kilkenny
LIMERICK
Enniscorthy
Clonmel
Wexford
Waterford
Tralee
Mallow
Killarney
Dungarvan
CORK
Youghal
Bantry
NEWTOWNABBEY
Bangor
Newtownards
Lisburn
DOWN
DUN LAOGHAIRE
Bray
0 10 20 km
0 5 10 ml
0 20 40 60 80 km
0 10 20 30 40 50 ml

Ireland (contd)

40 Donegal
41 Dunfanaghy
42 Greencastle
43 Gweedore
44 Letterkenny
45 Narin & Portnoo
46 North West
47 Otway
48 Portsalon
49 Rosapenna

Co Down
50 Ardglass
51 Banbridge
52 Bangor
53 Bright Castle
54 Carnalea
55 Clandeboye
56 Donaghadee
57 Downpatrick
58 Helen's Bay
59 Holywood
60 Kilkeel
61 Kirkistown Castle
62 Mahee Island
63 Royal Belfast
64 Royal County Down
65 Scrabo
66 The Spa
67 Warrenpoint

Co Fermanagh
68 Enniskillen

Co Londonderry
69 Castlerock
70 City of Derry
71 Kilrea
72 Moyola Park
73 Portstewart

Co Monaghan
74 Castleblayney
75 Clones
76 Nuremore
77 Rossmore

Co Tyrone
78 Dungannon
79 Fintona
80 Killymoon
81 Newtownstewart
82 Omagh
83 Strabane

Public courses are set in italic

Scotland: North

Angus
1 Arbroath
2 Brechin Golf & Squash Club
3 Buddon Links
4 Burnside
5 Caird Park
6 Caird Park
7 Camperdown
8 Carnoustie Championship
9 Downfield
10 Edzell
11 Forfar
12 Kirriemuir
13 Letham Grange
14 Monifieth Golf Links
15 Montrose
16 Panmure

Argyll & Bute
1 Blairmore & Strone
2 Bute
3 Carradale
4 Colonsay
5 Cowal
6 Craignure
7 Dunaverty
8 Glencruitten
9 Innellan
10 Islay
11 Kyles of Bute
12 Lochgilphead
13 Machrihanish
14 Millport
15 Port Bannatyne
16 Rothesay
17 Tarbert
18 Tobermory
19 Vaul

North
Caithness, Inverness, Nairn, Orkney, Shetland, Sutherland & Western Isles
1 Abernethy
2 Alness
3 Askernish
4 Boat-of-Garten
5 Bonar-Bridge & Ardgay
6 Brora
7 Carrbridge
8 Elgin
9 Forres
10 Fort Augustus
11 Fort William
12 Fortrose & Rosemarkie
13 Gairloch
14 Garmouth & Kingston
15 Golspie
16 Grantown
17 Helmsdale
18 Hopeman
19 Invergordon
20 Inverness
21 Kingussie
22 Lochcarron
23 Lybster
24 Moray
25 Muir of Ord
26 Nairn
27 Nairn Dunbar
28 Newtonmore
29 Orkney
30 Reay
31 Royal Dornoch
32 Sconser
33 Shetland
34 Skeabost
35 Stornaway
36 Strathpeffer Spa
37 Stromness
38 Tain
39 Tarbat
40 Thurso
41 Torvean
42 Traigh
43 Westray
44 Wick

North-East (Aberdeen, Banff & Kincardineshire)
1 Aboyne
2 Auchenblae
3 Auchmill
4 Ballater
5 Balnagask
6 Banchory
7 Braemar
8 Buckpool
9 Cruden Bay
10 Cullen
11 Deeside
12 Duff House Royal
13 Dufftown
14 Dunecht House
15 Fraserburgh
16 Hazlehead
17 Huntly
18 Insch
19 Inverallochy
20 Inverurie
21 Keith
22 Kemnay
23 King's Links
24 Kintore
25 McDonald
26 Murcar
27 Newburgh-on-Ythan
28 Oldmeldrum
29 Peterhead
30 Royal Aberdeen
31 Royal Tarlair
32 Spey Bay
33 Stonehaven
34 Strathlene
35 Tarland
36 Torphins
37 Turriff
38 Westhill

Perthshire & Kinross
1 Aberfeldy
2 Alyth
3 Auchterarder
4 Bishopshire
5 Blair Atholl
6 Blairgowrie
7 Comrie
8 Craigie Hill
9 Crieff
10 Dalmunzie
11 Dunkeld & Birnam
12 Dunning
13 Glenalmond
14 Gleneagles Hotel
15 Green Hotel
16 Killin
17 King James VI
18 Milnathort
19 Muckhart
20 Murrayshall
21 Muthill
22 North Inch
23 Pitlochry
24 Royal Perth Golfing Society
25 St Fillans
26 Strathtay
27 Taymouth Castle

Public courses are set in italic

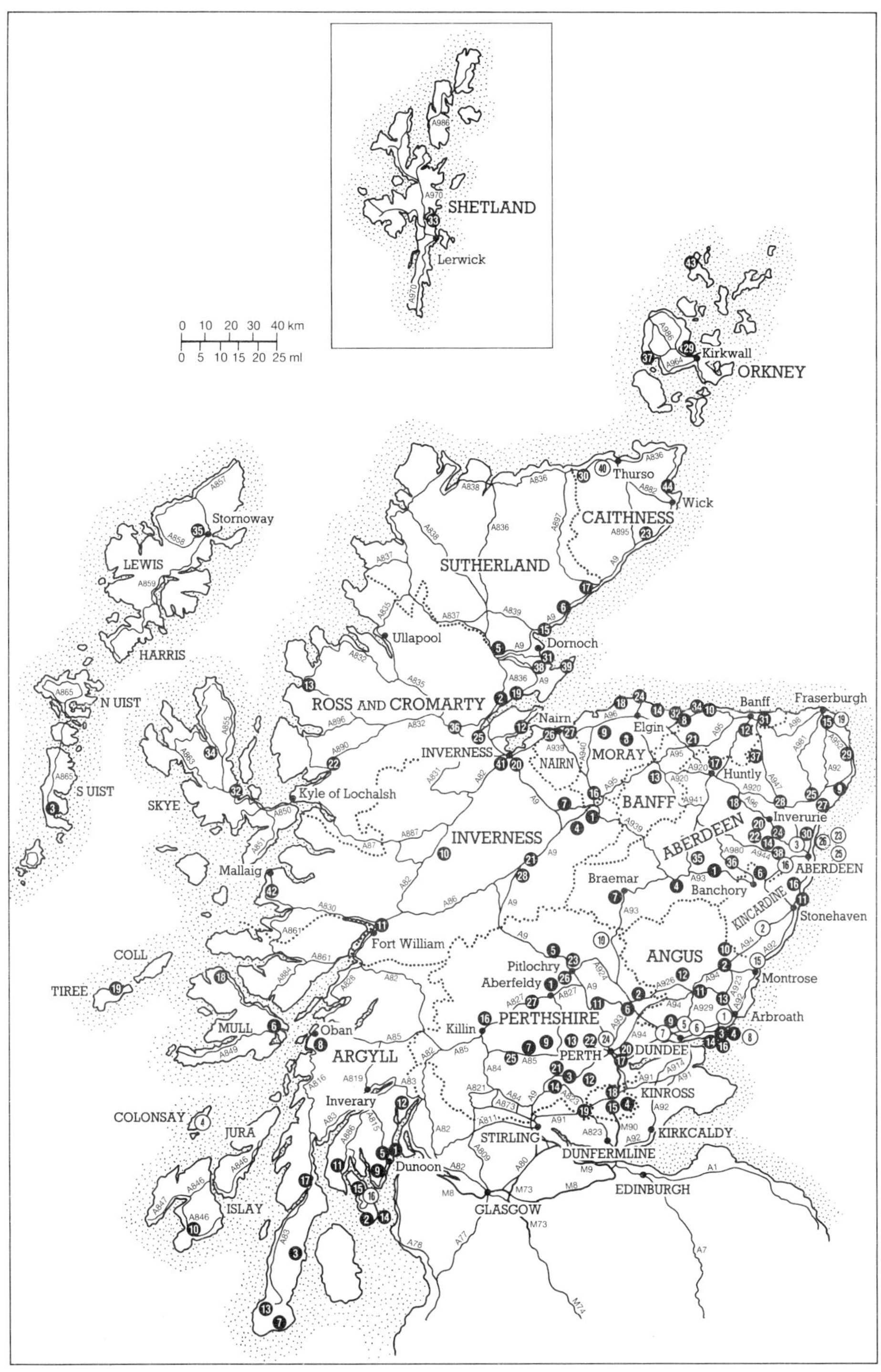

SHETLAND
Lerwick
ORKNEY
Kirkwall
Thurso
Wick
CAITHNESS
SUTHERLAND
Stornoway
LEWIS
HARRIS
N UIST
S UIST
SKYE
Ullapool
Dornoch
ROSS AND CROMARTY
INVERNESS
Kyle of Lochalsh
Nairn
NAIRN
MORAY
Elgin
BANFF
Banff
Fraserburgh
Huntly
Inverurie
ABERDEEN
Braemar
Banchory
KINCARDINE
Stonehaven
Mallaig
Fort William
COLL
TIREE
MULL
Oban
ARGYLL
Inverary
Killin
PERTHSHIRE
Pitlochry
Aberfeldy
ANGUS
Montrose
Arbroath
PERTH
DUNDEE
KINROSS
KIRKCALDY
STIRLING
DUNFERMLINE
EDINBURGH
GLASGOW
Dunoon
COLONSAY
JURA
ISLAY
0 10 20 30 40 km
0 5 10 15 20 25 ml

Scotland: South

Ayrshire
1 Annanhill
2 Ardeer
3 Auchenharvie
4 Ballochmyle
5 Beith
6 Belleisle
7 Brodick
8 Caprington
9 Corrie
10 Dalmilling
11 Girvan
12 Glasgow Gailes
13 Irvine
14 Irvine Ravenspark
15 Kilbirnie Place
16 Kilmarnock (Barassie)
17 Lamlash
18 Largs
19 Lochranza
20 Loudoun Gowf Club
21 Machrie Bay
22 Maybole
23 New Cumnock
24 Prestwick
25 Prestwick St Cuthbert
26 Prestwick St Nicholas
27 Routenburn
28 Royal Troon
29 Seafield
30 Shiskine
31 Skelmorlie
32 Troon Municipal
33 Turnberry Hotel
34 West Kilbride
35 Western Gailes
36 Whiting Bay

Borders (Berwickshire, Peeblesshire, Roxburghshire & Selkirkshire)
1 Duns
2 Eyemouth
3 Galashiels
4 Hawick
5 The Hirsel
6 Innerleithen
7 Jedburgh
8 Kelso
9 Langholm
10 Lauder
11 Melrose
12 Minto
13 Peebles
14 St Boswells
15 Selkirk
16 Torwoodlee

Clackmannanshire
1 Alloa
2 Alva
3 Braehead
4 Dollar
5 Tillicoultry
6 Tulliallan

Dunbartonshire
1 Balmore
2 Bearsden
3 Cardross
4 Clober
5 Clydebank Municipal
6 Clydebank and District
7 Cumbernauld
8 Dougalston
9 Douglas Park
10 Dullatur
11 Dumbarton
12 Hayston
13 Helensburgh
14 Hilton Park
15 Kirkintilloch
16 Lenzie
17 Milngavie
18 Vale of Leven
19 Windyhill

Fife
1 Aberdour
2 Anstruther
3 Auchterderran
4 Balbirnie Park
5 Ballingry
6 Burntisland Golf House Club
7 Canmore
8 Crail Golfing Society
9 Cupar
10 Dunfermline
11 Dunnikier Park
12 Falkland
13 Glenrothes
14 Golf House Club
15 Kinghorn
16 Kirkcaldy
17 Ladybank
18 Leslie (Fife)
19 Leven Links
20 Leven Municipal Course
21 Lochgelly
22 Lundin
23 Lundin Ladies
24 Pitreavie
25 St Andrews
26 St Michael's
27 Saline
28 Scotscraig
29 Thornton

Glasgow
1 Alexandra Park
2 Bishopsbriggs
3 Cathcart Castle
4 Cathkin Braes
5 Cawder
6 Cowglen
7 Deaconsbank
8 Glasgow
9 Haggs Castle
10 King's Park
11 Knightswood
12 Lethamhill
13 Linn Park
14 Littlehill
15 Pollok
16 Ralston
17 Ruchill
18 Sandyhills
19 Williamwood

Lanarkshire
1 Airdrie
2 Bellshill
3 Biggar
4 Blairbeth
5 Bothwell Castle
6 Calderbraes
7 Cambuslang
8 Carluke
9 Carnwath
10 Coatbridge
11 Colville Park
12 Crow Wood
13 Douglas Water
14 Drumpellier
15 East Kilbride
16 Easter Moffat
17 Hamilton
18 Hollandbush
19 Kirkhill
20 Lanark
21 Larkhall
22 Leadhills
23 Mount Ellen
24 Shotts
25 Strathaven
26 Strathclyde Park
27 Torrance House
28 Wishaw

The Lothians
1 Baberton
2 Bathgate
3 Braidhills No 1
4 Braidhills No 2
5 Broomieknowe
6 Bruntsfield Links Golfing Society
7 Burgh Links
8 Carrick Knowe
9 Craigentinny
10 Craigmillar Park
11 Dalmahoy
12 Deer Park CC
13 Duddingston
14 Dunbar
15 Dundas Park
16 Gifford
17 Glencorse
18 Greenburn
19 Gullane
20 Haddington
21 Harburn
22 Kilspindie
23 Kingsknowe
24 Liberton
25 Linlithgow
26 Longniddry
27 Lothianburn
28 Luffness New
29 Merchants of Edinburgh
30 Mortonhall
31 Murrayfield
32 Musselburgh
33 Musselburgh Old Course
34 Newbattle
35 Niddry Castle
36 North Berwick
37 Polkemmet
38 Portobello
39 Prestonfield
40 Pumpherston
41 Ratho Park
42 Ravelston
43 Royal Burgess Golfing Society of Edinburgh
44 Royal Musselburgh
45 Silverknowes
46 Swanston
47 The Honourable Company of Edinburgh Golfers
48 Torphin Hill
49 Turnhouse
50 Uphall
51 West Linton
52 West Lothian
53 Winterfield

Renfrewshire
1 Barshaw
2 Bonnyton
3 Caldwell
4 Cochrane Castle
5 East Renfrewshire
6 Eastwood
7 Elderslie
8 Erskine
9 Fereneze
10 Gleddoch
11 Gourock
12 Greenock
13 Kilmacolm
14 Lochwinnoch
15 Old Ranfurly
16 Paisley
17 Port Glasgow
18 Ranfurly Castle
19 Renfrew
20 Whinhill
21 Whitecraigs

List continued on p.228

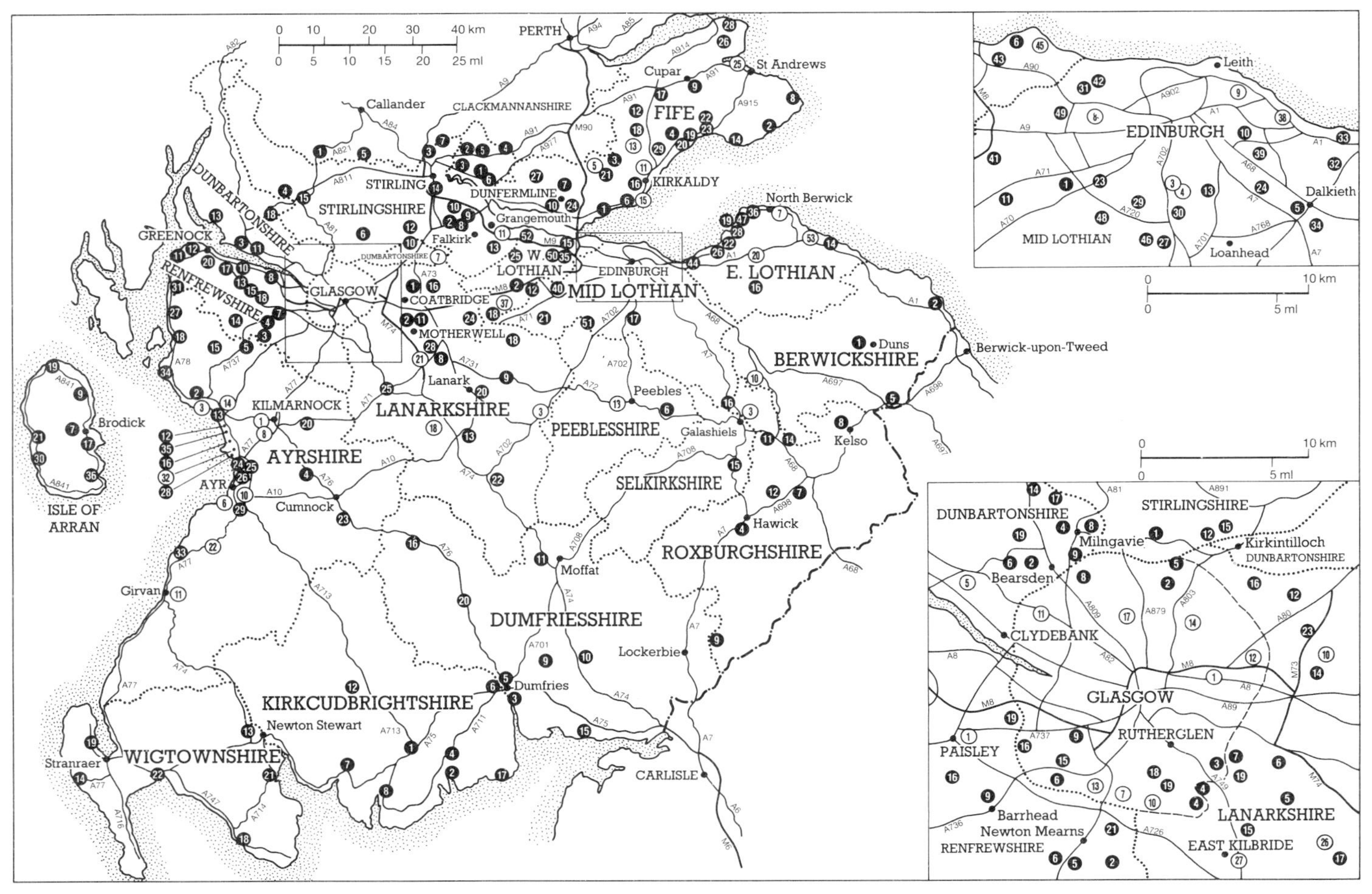
PERTH
Callander
CLACKMANNANSHIRE
STIRLING
STIRLINGSHIRE
DUNFERMLINE
Grangemouth
Falkirk
FIFE
Cupar
St Andrews
KIRKALDY
North Berwick
E. LOTHIAN
W. LOTHIAN
MID LOTHIAN
EDINBURGH
BERWICKSHIRE
Duns
Berwick-upon-Tweed
Kelso
ROXBURGHSHIRE
Hawick
Galashiels
SELKIRKSHIRE
Peebles
PEEBLESSHIRE
Moffat
DUMFRIESSHIRE
Lockerbie
CARLISLE
Dumfries
KIRKCUDBRIGHTSHIRE
Newton Stewart
WIGTOWNSHIRE
Stranraer
Girvan
AYR
AYRSHIRE
Cumnock
KILMARNOCK
LANARKSHIRE
Lanark
MOTHERWELL
COATBRIDGE
GLASGOW
DUNBARTONSHIRE
GREENOCK
RENFREWSHIRE
Brodick
ISLE OF ARRAN
40 km
25 ml
Leith
Dalkieth
Loanhead
10 km
5 ml
STIRLINGSHIRE
Kirkintilloch
Milngavie
Bearsden
CLYDEBANK
RUTHERGLEN
LANARKSHIRE
EAST KILBRIDE
PAISLEY
Barrhead
Newton Mearns
RENFREWSHIRE

Scotland: South (contd)

South (Dumfriesshire, Kirkudbrightshire & Wigtownshire)
1 Castle Douglas
2 Colvend
3 Crichton Royal
4 Dalbeattie
5 Dumfries & County
6 Dumfries & Galloway
7 Gatehouse
8 Kirkcudbright
9 Lochmaben
10 Lockerbie
11 Moffat
12 New Galloway
13 Newton Stewart
14 Portpatrick Dunskey
15 Powfoot
16 Sanquhar
17 Southerness
18 St Medan
19 Stranraer
20 Thornhill
21 Wigtown & Bladnoch
22 Wigtownshire County

Stirlingshire
1 Aberfoyle
2 Bonnybridge
3 Bridge of Allan
4 Buchanan Castle
5 Callander
6 Campsie
7 Dunblane New
8 Falkirk
9 Falkirk Tryst
10 Glenbervie
11 Grangemouth
12 Kilsyth Lennox
13 Polmont
14 Stirling
15 Strathendrick

Public courses are set in italic

Wales

Clwyd
1 Abergele & Pensarn
2 Bryn Morfydd
3 Denbigh
4 Flint
5 Hawarden
6 Holywell
7 Mold
8 Old Colwyn
9 Old Padeswood
10 Padeswood & Buckley
11 Prestatyn
12 Rhuddlan
13 Rhyl
14 Ruthin-Pwllglas
15 St Melyd
16 Vale of Llangollen
17 Wrexham

Dyfed
1 Aberystwyth
2 Ashburnham
3 Borth & Ynyslas
4 Cardigan
5 Carmarthen
6 Cilgwyn
7 Glynhir
8 Haverfordwest
9 Milford Haven
10 Newport (Pembs)
11 St Davids City
12 South Pembrokeshire
13 Tenby

Gwent
1 Blackwood
2 Caerleon
3 Greenmeadow
4 Llanwern
5 Monmouth
6 Monmouthshire
7 Newport
8 Pontnewydd
9 Pontypool
10 Rolls of Monmouth
11 St Mellons
12 St Pierre
13 Tredegar & Rhymney
14 Tredegar Park
15 West Monmouthshire

Gwynedd
1 Aberdovey
2 Abersoch
3 Bala
4 Betws-y-Coed
5 Caernarfon
6 Conwy (Caernarvonshire)
7 Criccieth
8 Dolgellau
9 Ffestiniog
10 Llandudno (Maesdu)
11 Llandudno (North Wales)
12 Llanfairfechan
13 Nefyn & District
14 Penmaenmawr
15 Portmadoc
16 Pwllheli
17 Rhos-on-Sea Residential
18 Royal St David's
19 St Deiniol

Isle of Anglesey
1 Anglesey
2 Baron Hill
3 Bull Bay
4 Holyhead
5 Llangefni

Mid Glamorgan
1 Aberdare
2 Bargoed
3 Bryn Meadows G&CC
4 Caerphilly
5 Castell Heights
6 Creigiau
7 Llantrisant & Pontyclun
8 Maesteg
9 Merthyr Tydfil
10 Morlais Castle
11 Mountain Ash
12 Mountain Lakes
13 Pontypridd
14 Pyle & Kenfig
15 Rhondda
16 Royal Porthcawl
17 Southerndown
18 Whitehall

Powys
1 Brecon
2 Builth Wells
3 Cradoc
4 Knighton
5 Llandrindod
6 Machynlleth
7 Old Rectory Country Club
8 St Giles GC Newtown
9 St Idloes
10 Welshpool

South Glamorgan
1 Brynhill
2 Cardiff
3 Dinas Powis
4 Glamorganshire
5 Llanishen
6 Radyr
7 RAF St Athan
8 Wenvoe Castle
9 Whitchurch (Cardiff)

West Glamorgan
1 Clyne
2 Fairwood Park
3 Glynneath
4 Inco
5 Langland Bay
6 Morriston
7 Neath
8 Palleg
9 Pennard
10 Pontardawe
11 Swansea Bay

Public courses are set in italic

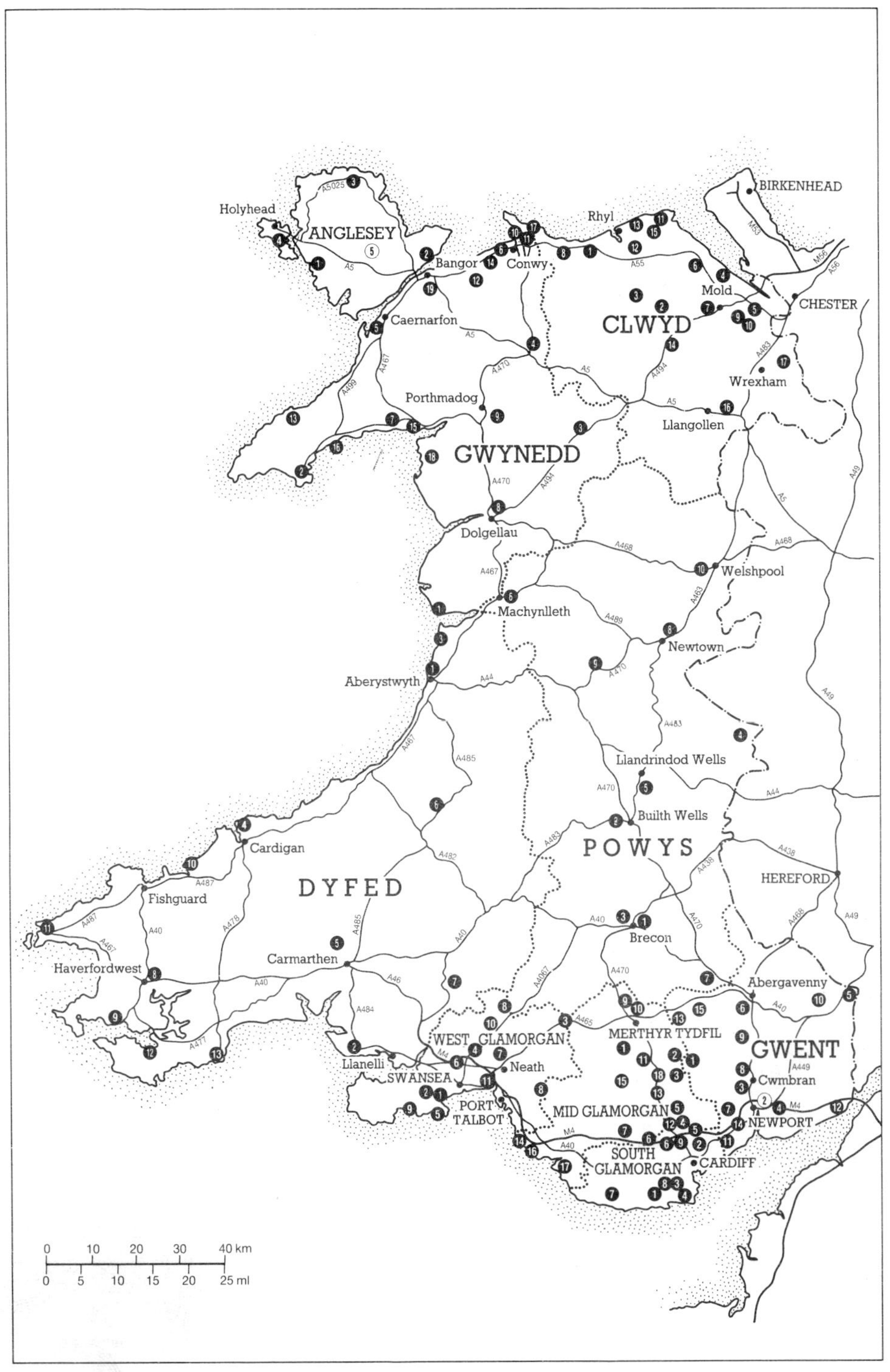

ANGLESEY
Holyhead
Bangor
Caernarfon
Conwy
Rhyl
BIRKENHEAD
Mold
CHESTER
CLWYD
Wrexham
Llangollen
Porthmadog
GWYNEDD
Dolgellau
Welshpool
Machynlleth
Newtown
Aberystwyth
Llandrindod Wells
Builth Wells
POWYS
Cardigan
DYFED
Fishguard
HEREFORD
Brecon
Haverfordwest
Carmarthen
Abergavenny
MERTHYR TYDFIL
GWENT
WEST GLAMORGAN
Neath
Llanelli
SWANSEA
Cwmbran
PORT TALBOT
MID GLAMORGAN
NEWPORT
SOUTH GLAMORGAN
CARDIFF
0 10 20 30 40 km
0 5 10 15 20 25 ml

Northern France

Key to Map

1 Ajoncs d'Or (Saint-Brieuc)
2 Amiens
3 Andaines (La Fertéˆ Maécˆ)
4 Benodet-Quimper (Quimper)
5 Boisgelin (Paimpol)
6 Bondues (Lille)
7 Bréˆhal
8 Brest-Iroise (Landerneau)
9 Brigode (Lille)
10 Cabourg-Le Home (Cabourg)
11 Cherbourg
12 Clair-Vallon (Cabourg)
13 Coutainville
14 Deauville
15 Dieppe
16 Dinard
17 Dunkerque
18 Étretat
19 Flandres (Lille)
20 Fontenay (Montebourg)
21 Granville (Bréˆhal)
22 Hardelot
23 Le Havre
24 Nampont Saint-Martin (Montreuil)
25 Omaha Beach (Bayeux)
26 Pen Guen (Saint Cast)
27 Quimper Cournouaille (Quimper)
28 Rennes
29 Rouen
30 Sables-d'Or (Sables-d'Or-les-Pins)
31 Saint-Gatien (Deauville)
32 Saint Malo-Le Tronchet (Saint-Malo)
33 Saint-Samson (Lannion)
34 Sart (Lille)
35 Le Touquet
36 Le Vaudreuil (Rouen)
37 Wimereux

Public courses are set in italic

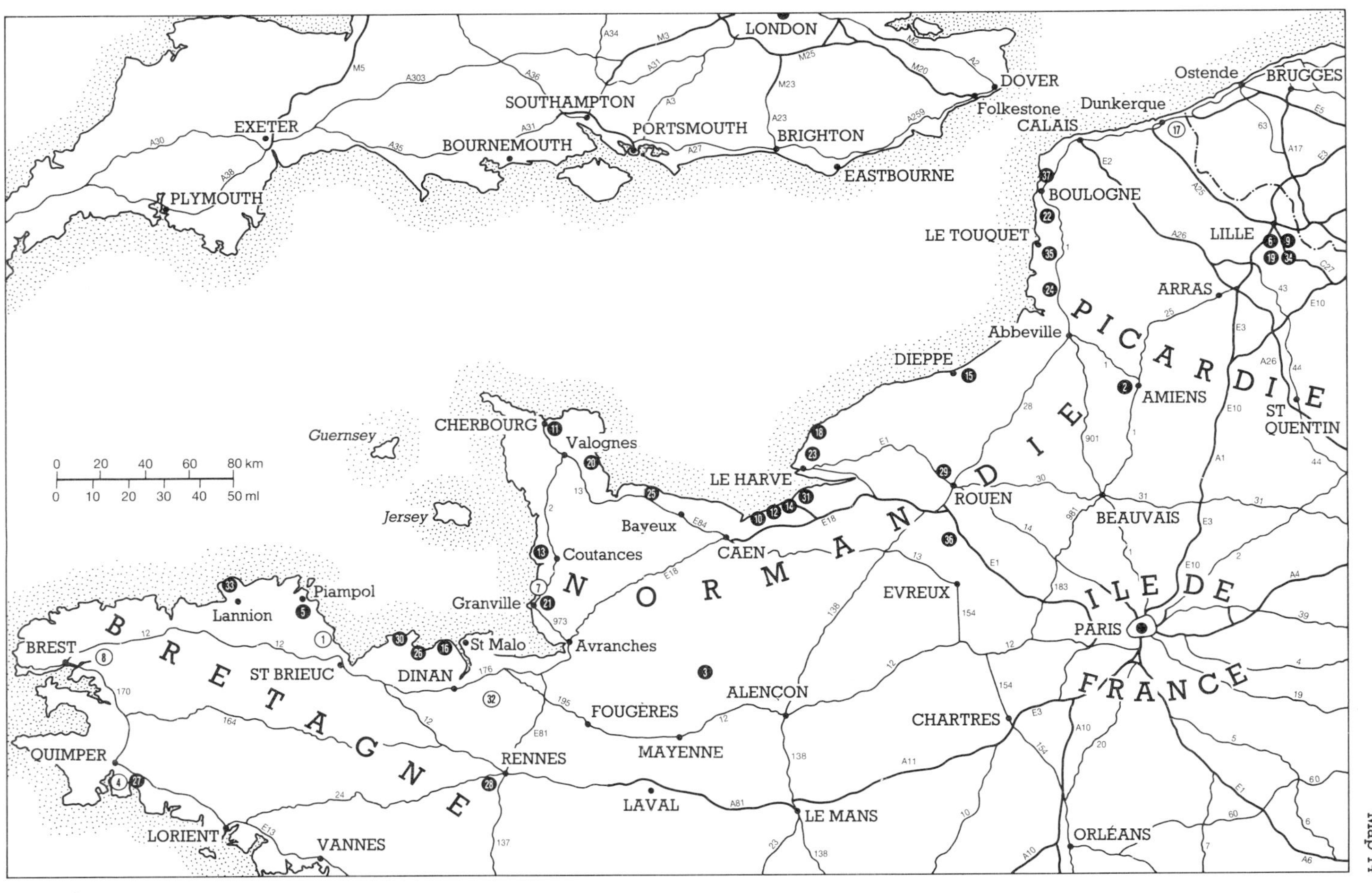

LONDON
DOVER
Folkestone
BRIGHTON
EASTBOURNE
PORTSMOUTH
SOUTHAMPTON
BOURNEMOUTH
EXETER
PLYMOUTH
Ostende
BRUGGES
Dunkerque
CALAIS
BOULOGNE
LE TOUQUET
LILLE
ARRAS
AMIENS
ST QUENTIN
Abbeville
DIEPPE
ROUEN
BEAUVAIS
PARIS
EVREUX
CHARTRES
ORLÉANS
LE HARVE
CAEN
Bayeux
Valognes
CHERBOURG
Coutances
Granville
Avranches
St Malo
DINAN
ALENÇON
LE MANS
MAYENNE
FOUGÈRES
LAVAL
RENNES
Guernsey
Jersey
Piampol
Lannion
ST BRIEUC
BREST
QUIMPER
LORIENT
VANNES
PICARDIE
ILE DE FRANCE
NORMANDIE
BRETAGNE
0 20 40 60 80 km
0 10 20 30 40 50 ml

Spain: Costa del Sol

Key to Map
1 Almerimar (Almería)
2 Aloha (Marbella)
3 Atalaya Park G&CC (Marbella)
4 Las Brisas (Marbella)
5 Club de Campo de Málaga (Málaga)
6 El Candado (Málaga)
7 La Duquesa G&CC (Algeciras)
8 Guadalmina (Marbella)
9 Mijas (Málaga)
10 Los Moriscos (Motril)
11 Los Naranjos (Marbella)
12 Nerja G&CC (Málaga)
13 El Paraiso (Marbella)
14 Playa Serena (Almería)
15 Río Real (Marbella)
16 Sotogrande (Algeciras)
17 Torrequebrada (Málaga)
18 Valderrama (Algeciras)

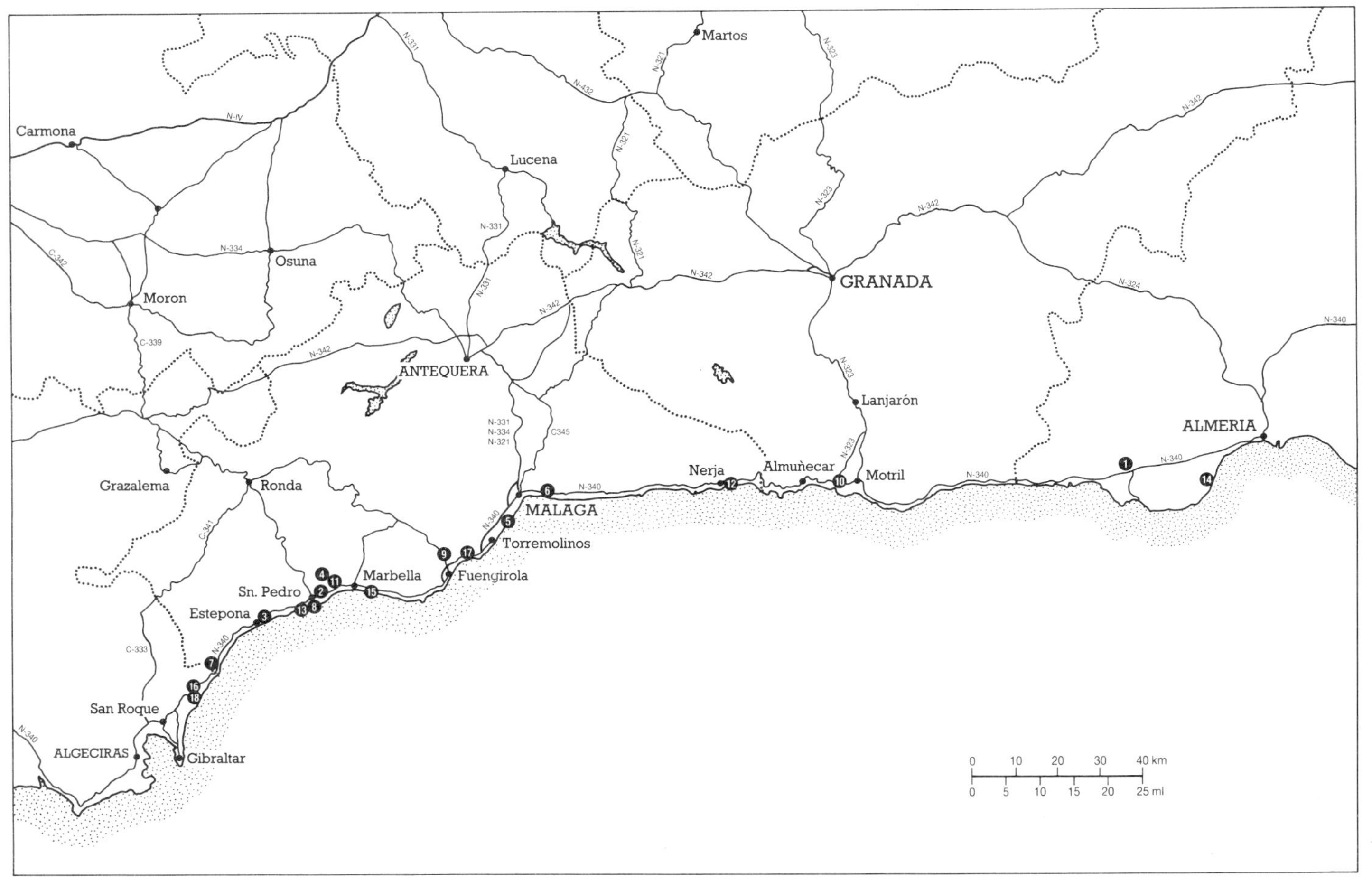
Martos
Carmona
Lucena
Osuna
Moron
GRANADA
ANTEQUERA
Lanjarón
ALMERIA
Nerja
Almuñecar
Motril
Grazalema
Ronda
MALAGA
Torremolinos
Marbella
Fuengirola
Sn. Pedro
Estepona
San Roque
ALGECIRAS
Gibraltar
N-331
N-432
N-IV
N-321
N-323
N-342
N-334
C-342
N-324
N-340
C-339
N-331 N-334 N-321
C345
C-341
C-333
0 10 20 30 40 km
0 5 10 15 20 25 ml

Golf Courses of the UK and Europe

England

Avon

Bath (1880)

Private
Sham Castle, Bath BA2 6JG
Tel **(0225) 25182**
Mem 650
Sec PB Edwards
Pro P Hancox (0225) 66953
Holes 18 L 6369 yds SSS 70
Recs Am–67 M Bloxham
Pro–68 G Brand
V'trs H SOC
Fees £10 (£12) 1988 prices
Loc $1\frac{1}{2}$ miles SE of Bath off A36

Bristol & Clifton (1891)

Private
Beggar Bush Lane, Failand, nr Clifton, Bristol BS8 3TH
Tel **(0272) 393117**
Mem 800
Sec Cdr PA Woollings RN (0272) 393474
Pro P Mawson (0272) 393031
Holes 18 L 6294 yds SSS 70
Recs Am–65 P Godsland
Pro–64 P Oosterhuis
V'trs WD–UH WE/BH–MH
Fees On request
Loc 2 miles W of suspension bridge. 4 miles S of M5 Junction 19

Chipping Sodbury (1954)

Private
Chipping Sodbury, nr Bristol BS17 6PU
Tel **(0454) 312024 (Members)**
Mem 740
Sec KG Starr (0454) 319042
Pro S Harris (0454) 314087
Holes New 18 L 6912 yds SSS 73
Old 9 L 6194 yds SSS 69
Recs New: Am–66 D Wood (1988)
Pro–68 J Nicholas (1988)
V'trs WD–U SOC WE–Sun pm only
H Sat/Sun am–XL
Fees New £9 (£11) Old £2.50
Loc M4 Junc 18 5 miles. M5 Junc 14 9 miles. 12 miles NE of Bristol
Mis (Steward) (0454) 315822

Clevedon (1908)

Private
Castle Road, Clevedon BS21 7AA
Tel **(0272) 873140**
Mem 700
Sec Capt (Retd) M Sullivan (0272) 874057
Pro C Langford (0272) 874704
Holes 18 L 5887 yds SSS 69
Recs Am–69 G Say (1987)
Pro–67 G Ryall (1987)
V'trs WD–U H NA Wed am
WE/BH–H I NA before 11am SOC–Mon only
Fees £12 (£15)
Loc Holly Lane, Walton, Clevedon, M5 Junction 19 or 20

Entry Hill (1985)

Public
Entry Hill, Bath BA2 5NA
Tel **(0225) 834248**
Mem 347
Sec J Sercombe (0272) 868972
Pro T Tapley
Holes 9 L 4206 yds SSS 61
Recs Am–66 N Jorephani
V'trs WD–U WE–booking only
Fees 18 holes–£4 9 holes–£2.50
Loc 1 mile S of Bath off A367
Mis Entry Hill GC plays here

Filton (1909)

Private
Golf Course Lane, Bristol BS12 7QS
Tel **(0272) 692021**
Mem 600
Sec DF O'Leary (0272) 694169
Pro JCN Lumb (0272) 694158
Holes 18 L 6277 yds SSS 70
Recs Am–66 S Hurley
V'trs WD–U WE/BH–M
Fees £10
Loc 4 miles N of Bristol

Fosseway CC (1970)

Private
Charlton Lane, Midsomer Norton, Bath BA3 4BD
Tel **(0761) 412214**
Mem 280
Sec RF Jones (Mgr)
Holes 9 L 4148 yds SSS 61
V'trs U exc Wed–M after 5pm
Sun–NA before 1.30pm
Fees £4.75 (£5.75)
Loc 10 miles SW of Bath on A367

Henbury (1891)

Private
Westbury-on-Trym, Bristol BS10 7QB
Tel **(0272) 500660**
Mem 435 117(L) 68(J) 140(5)
Sec JW Estill (0272) 500044
Pro P Stow (0272) 502121
Holes 18 L 6039 yds SSS 70
Recs Am–63 R Tugwell
Pro–67 B Sandry
V'trs WD–H WE–M SOC–Tues & Fri
Fees £12.50
Loc N Bristol (centre 3 miles)

Knowle (1905)

Private
Fairway, Brislington, Bristol BS4 5DF
Tel **(0272) 776341**
Mem 700
Sec Mrs JD King (0272) 770660
Pro GM Brand (0272) 779193
Holes 18 L 6016 yds SSS 69
Recs Am–64 SD Hurley, D Hares
Pro–64 S Brown
V'trs WD–H or I exc Thurs
WE/BH–H or I SOC–Thurs
Fees £10 (£12)
Loc 3 miles S of Bristol, Brislington Hill off A4

Lansdown (1894)

Private
Lansdown, Bath BA1 9BT
Tel **(0225) 25007**
Mem 725
Sec (0225) 22138
Pro T Mercer (0225) 20242
Holes 18 L 6267 yds SSS 70
Recs Am–65 C Edwards, A Lyddon (1984)
Pro–66 D Ray (1987)
V'trs WD–U WE–H SOC
Fees £10 (£12)
Loc By Bath racecourse. 2 miles NW of town. M4 Junction 18 6 miles

For map index see page 203.

Long Ashton (1893)

Private
The Clubhouse, Long Ashton, Bristol BS18 9DW
Tel **(0272) 392229**
Mem 700
Sec RE Burniston (0272) 392316
Pro DP Scanlan (0272) 392265
Holes 18 L 6051 yds SSS 70
Recs Am–65 A Rogers
Pro–65 D Snell
V'trs WD–U H WE/BH–I H
SOC–Wed
Fees £15 (£18)
Loc 3 miles S of Bristol on B3128

Mangotsfield (1975)

Private
Carsons Road, Mangotsfield, Bristol BS17 3LW
Tel **(0272) 565501**
Mem 450
Sec I Chapman
Pro M Watts
Holes 18 L 5297 yds SSS 66
V'trs U
Fees £3.50 (£5)
Loc City centre 3 miles

Saltford (1904)

Private
Golf Club Lane, Saltford
Tel **(0225) 873220**
Mem 650
Sec V Radnedge (02217) 3513
Pro D Millensted (0225) 872043
Recs Am–68 S Godfrey
V'trs U
Fees £12 (£15)
Loc Bath 6 miles. Bristol 7 miles

Shirehampton Park (1907)

Private
Park Hill, Shirehampton, Bristol BS11 0UL
Tel **(0272) 823059**
Mem 600
Sec (0272) 822083
Pro K Spurgeon (0272) 822488
Holes 18 L 5486 yds SSS 67
Recs Am–64 MJ Bessell
Pro–63 M Steadman
V'trs WD–U WE–M
Fees £11
Loc M5 Junction 18 $1^1/_2$ miles

Tracy Park (1976)

Private
Tracy Park, Bath Road, Wick, nr Bristol BS15 5RN
Tel **(027 582) 2251**
Mem 700
Sec Capt J Seymour–Williams
Pro G Aitken (027 582) 3521
Holes 27 holes Avon L 6834 yds SSS 73; Bristol L 6861 yds SSS 73; Cotswold L 6203 yds SSS 70
Recs Am–70 G Ryall
Pro–72 M Kedworth
V'trs WD/WE(phone first)
SOC–WD/WE by arrangement
Fees £8 (£10)
Loc 8 miles E of Bristol off A420 Bristol–Chippenham road. 5 miles N of Bath, M4 Junction 18

Weston-super-Mare (1892)

Private
Uphill Road, Weston-super-Mare
Tel **(0934) 21360**
Mem 630
Sec RH White (0934) 26968
Pro T Murray (0934) 33360
Holes 18 L 6279 yds SSS 70
Recs Am–67 GD Robert
Pro–69 A Lees, WJ Branch
V'trs U SOC
Fees £9 (£12) W–£35
Loc Weston–super–Mare

Worlebury (1908)

Private
Monks Hill, Weston-super-Mare BS22 9SX
Tel **(0934) 623214**
Mem 640
Sec RT Bagg (0934) 625789
Pro G Marks (0934) 418473
Holes 18 L 5967 yds SSS 69
Recs Am–65 N Roseff
Pro–68 S Hall
V'trs U SOC–WD
Fees £9 (£13.50)
Loc 2 miles NE of town centre

Bedfordshire

Aspley Guise & Woburn Sands (1914)

Private
West Hill, Aspley Guise, Milton Keynes MK16 8DX
Tel **(0908) 582264**
Mem 530
Sec TE Simpson (0908) 583596
Pro G McCarthy (0908) 582974
Holes 18 L 6248 yds SSS 70
Recs Am–67 D Williams, N Abrahams
Pro–68 P Webster
V'trs WD–UH WE/BH–MH
SOC–Wed & Fri
Fees £11 D–£14
Loc 2 miles W of M1 Junction 13

Beadlow Manor Hotel G & CC

Private
Beadlow, Shefford SG17 5PH
Tel **(0525) 60800**
Mem 700
Sec LN Kershaw
Pro KF Robson (0525) 60800/61292
Holes 18 L 6238 yds SSS 71
9 L 6042 yds SSS 70
Recs Am–71 C Skinner
Pro–68 KF Robson
V'trs U H SOC
Fees £10 (£12) D–£15
Loc 2 miles W of Shefford on A507
Mis Hotel, restaurants and Health and Fitness Centre

Bedford & County (1912)

Private
Green Lane, Clapham, Bedford MK41 6ET
Tel **(0234) 52617**
Mem 600
Sec E Bullock (0234) 52617
Pro E Bullock (0234) 59189
Holes 18 L 6347 yds SSS 70
Recs Am–66 C Allen (1980)
Pro–66 M King (1978)
V'trs WD–U WE–M SOC
Fees £10.50 D–£12.50
Loc 2 miles NW of Bedford on A6

Bedfordshire (1891)

Private
Bromham Rd, Biddenham, Bedford MK40 4AF
Tel **(0234) 53241**
Mem 600
Sec TA Nutt (0234) 61669
Pro G Buckle (0234) 53653
Holes 18 L 6185 yds SSS 69
Recs Am–64 CM Beard
Pro–65 K Warren
V'trs WD–U (phone first) WE–M before noon SOC–WD
Fees £10 D–£12
Loc $1^1/_2$ miles NW city boundary A428

Colworth (1985)

Private
Unilever Research, Sharnbrook, Bedford MK44 1LQ
Tel **(0234) 222502**
Mem 350
Sec SG Pound (0234) 222238
Holes 9 L 2500 yds
Recs Am–57 J Barrett (1988)
V'trs NA
Loc 10 miles N of Bedford off A6

Dunstable Downs (1907)

Private
Whipsnade Road, Dunstable LU6 2NB
Tel **(0582) 604472**
Mem 550
Sec PJ Nightingale
Pro M Weldon (0582) 662806
Holes 18 L 6184 yds SSS 70
Recs Am–65 RA Durrant
Pro–67 J Macdonald, SL King
V'trs WD–H WE–M
SOC–Tues/Thurs/Fri
Fees On application
Loc M1 Junction 11. Dunstable 2 miles

Griffin (1985)

Private
c/o 3 Hillcrest Avenue, Luton LU2 7AB
Tel **(0582) 415573**
Mem 350
Sec Mrs L Weedon (0582) 579511
Holes 9 L 5354 yds SSS 66
Recs Am–73 A Halliday (1987)
V'trs WD–U WE/BH–M (exc Sun am–NA) SOC
Fees £3 (£5)
Loc M1 Junction 11. 3 miles W of Luton on A505 between Dunstable and Caddington
Mis Catering by arrangement

John O'Gaunt (1948)

Private
Sutton Park, Sandy, Biggleswade SG19 2LY
Tel **(0767) 260360**
Mem 1100
Sec DJ Wallace
Pro R Round (0767) 260694
Holes John O'Gaunt 18 L 6513 yds SSS 71; Carthagena 18 L 5869 yds SSS 68
Recs Am–64 N Wharton
Pro–67 SC Evans
V'trs WD–U WE–H
Fees £18 (£30)
Loc 3 miles NE Biggleswade on B1040
Mis Advisable phone before visit

Leighton Buzzard (1925)

Private
Plantation Road, Leighton Buzzard
Tel **(0525) 373812**
Mem 600
Sec FJ Clements (0525) 373525
Pro LJ Muncey (0525) 372143
Holes 18 L 5366 yds SSS 68
Recs Am–65 D Horne
V'trs WD exc Tues–U WE/BH–MH
Fees £12 D–£15
Loc 1 mile N of L Buzzard

Millbrook

Private
Millbrook, Ampthill
Tel **(0525) 404683**
Mem 250
Sec CF Grimwood (0525) 712001
Pro T Devine (0525) 402269
Holes 18 L 6473 yds SSS 72
V'trs WD–U exc Thurs WE–before 9.30am
Fees £10 (£15)
Loc Millbrook Village

Mowsbury (1975)

Private
Kimbolton Road, Bedford
Tel **(0234) 771042**
Mem 425
Sec MW Gray
Pro P Ashwell
Holes 18 L 6514 yds SSS 71
Recs Pro–66
V'trs U
Fees £3.80 (£5.70)
Loc 3 miles N of Bedford
Mis Driving range

South Beds (1894)

Private
Warden Hills, Luton
Tel **(0582) 55201**
Mem 750
Sec JJ Hackett (0582) 591500
Pro E Cogle (0582) 591209
Holes 18 L 6342 yds SSS 70
9 L 4954 yds SSS 64
V'trs WE/BH–H SOC
Ladies Day–Tues
Fees 18 hole course: £10 D–£15 (£14 D–£20)
9 hole course: £5.50 (£8.50)
Loc 3 miles N of Luton on E side of A6

Stockwood Park (1973)

Public
London Rd, Luton
Tel **(0582) 413704**
Mem 550
Sec DW Thompson
Pro D Hunt
Holes 18 L 5567 yds SSS 69
Recs Am–73 RM Harris
Pro–66 T Minshall
V'trs U
Fees £3.25 (£4.60)
Loc 1 mile S of centre on A6

Tilsworth

Public
Dunstable Rd, Tilsworth, Dunstable
Tel **(0525) 210721/210722**
Mem 160
Pro N Webb
Holes 9 L 2773 yds SSS 35
V'trs U
Fees £3 (£4) 18 holes
Loc 2 miles N of Dunstable on A5

Wyboston Lakes (1978)

Public
Wyboston Lakes, Wyboston MK44 3AL
Tel **(0480) 219200**
Mem 250
Sec B Chinn (Mgr)
Pro P Ashwell (0480) 212501
Holes 18 L 5711 yds SSS 69
V'trs U SOC
Fees £6 (£8)
Loc S of St Neots off A1 and St Neots by-pass

Berkshire

Bearwood (1986)

Private
Mole Road, Sindlesham RG11 5DB
Tel **(0734) 760060**
Mem 570
Sec C Dyer OBE
Pro B Tustin
Holes 9 L 2814 yds Par 35
V'trs WD–H before 4pm–M after 4pm WE/BH–M
Fees 9 holes £5
Loc B3030 1½ miles N of Arborfield Cross. M4 Junction 10
Mis 9 hole pitch and putt

Berkshire (1928)

Private
Swinley Road, Ascot SL5 8AY
Tel **(0990) 21495**
Mem 935
Sec Maj. PD Clarke (0990) 21496
Pro KA Macdonald (0990) 22351
Holes Red Course 18 L 6356 yds SSS 70; Blue Course 18 L 6258 yds SSS 70
V'trs WD–I WE/BH–M
Loc 3 miles from Ascot on A332

Calcot Park (1930)

Private
Calcot, nr Reading
Tel **(0734) 427124**
Mem 700
Sec SD Chisholm
Pro A Mackenzie (0734) 427797
Holes 18 L 6283 yds SSS 70
Recs Am–66 SA Scott
Pro–63 C Defoy
V'trs WD–U WE/BH–M
Fees £15
Loc 3 miles W of Reading on A4

Datchet (1890)

Private
Buccleuch Road, Datchet
Tel **(0753) 43887**
Mem 200 50(L) 25(J) 110(5)
Sec Sqd Ldr WJ Brooks
Pro P Stanwick (0753) 42755
Holes 9 L 5978 yds SSS 69
Recs Am–66 R Blyfield
Pro–63 N Wood
V'trs WD–U before 3pm M–after 3pm WE–M
Fees £7 D–£10
Loc Slough, Windsor 2 miles

Downshire (1973)

Public
Easthampstead Park, Wokingham
Tel **(0344) 424066**
Sec G Legouix
Pro G Legouix
Holes 18 L 6382 yds SSS 70

For map index see page 203.

Recs Am–67 T Smith
Pro–66 M King
V'trs U SOC
Fees Summer £5 Winter £3.35
Loc Off 9 Mile Ride
Mis Easthampstead GC and Downshire GC play here

East Berkshire (1904)

Private
Ravenswood Ave, Crowthorne
Tel (0344) 772041
Mem 700
Sec WH Short
Pro A Roe (0344) 774112
Holes 18 L 6315 yds SSS 70
Recs Am–65 J Davies
Pro–65 N Coles
V'trs I WE/BH–M SOC
Fees £20
Loc Nr Crowthorne Station

Easthampstead (1973)

Public
Easthampstead Park, Wokingham
Tel (0344) 424066
Sec G Legouix
Holes Play over Downshire Course

Eton College (1973)

Private
Eton College, Windsor
Tel (0753) 66461
Mem 500
Sec PTC Croker (0753) 55299
Holes 9 L 3560 yds SSS 58
Recs Am–55 DL Morkill
V'trs NA

Goring & Streatley (1893)

Private
Rectory Road, Streatley-on-Thames RG8 9QA
Tel (0491) 872688
Mem 740 110(L) 80(J) 120(5)
Sec J Menzies (0491) 873229
Pro R Mason (0491) 873715
Holes 18 L 6266 yds SSS 70
Recs Am–65 DG Lane
Pro–65 C DeFoy
V'trs WD–U WE/BH–M SOC–WD
Fees £14
Loc 10 miles NW of Reading on A417

Hawthorn Hill (1985)

Public
Drift Road, Hawthorn Hill, Maidenhead SL6 3ST
Tel (0628) 771030/75588
Sec CD Smith
Pro G Edmonds
Holes 18 L 6212 yds SSS 70
V'trs U
Fees £6 (£7.50)
Loc 4 miles S of Maidenhead on A330
Mis Floodlit driving range

Hurst (1979)

Public
Sandford Lane, Hurst, Wokingham
Tel (0734) 345143
Pro G Legouix
Holes 9 L 3015 yds
V'trs U
Fees Summer £2.50 Winter £1.65
Loc Reading 5 miles. Wokingham 3 miles

Lavender Park Golf Centre

Public
Swinley Road, Ascot
Tel (0344) 884074
Pro B Cutt
Holes 9 L 1104 yds SSS 27
V'trs U
Fees £1.20 (£1.40)
Mis Driving range

Maidenhead (1898)

Private
Shoppenhangers Road, Maidenhead SL6 2PZ
Tel (0628) 20545
Mem 450
Sec To be appointed
Pro R Newman (0628) 24067
Holes 18 L 6360 yds SSS 70
Recs Am–66 M Briggs (1985), L Hawkins (1986)
Pro–64 AN Walker, G Wolstenholme
V'trs WD–before 4.30pm by request; M after 4.30pm WE–M
Fees £15 R/D
Loc Maidenhead Station 1/2 mile

Newbury & Crookham (1873)

Private
Bury's Bank Road, Greenham Common, Newbury RG15 8BZ
Tel (0635) 40035
Mem 626
Sec RF Church (0635) 40035
Pro DW Harris (0635) 31201
Holes 18 L 5880 yds SSS 68
Recs Am–63 D Rosier (1984)
Pro–61 M Howell (1986)
V'trs WD–U WE–M (recognised club members) H
Fees £12
Loc 2 miles SE of Newbury

Reading (1910)

Private
Kidmore End Road, Emmer Green, Reading RG4 8SG
Tel (0734) 472169
Mem 700
Sec ANH Weekes (0734) 472909
Pro TP Morrison (0734) 476115
Holes 18 L 6204 yds SSS 70
Recs Am–65 MG King
Pro–64 AP Morley
V'trs Mon–Thurs–U Fri/WE/BH–M
Fees £16
Loc 2 miles N of city off Peppard Road (B481)

Royal Ascot (1887)

Private
Winkfield Road, Ascot SL5 7LJ
Tel (0990) 25175
Mem 600
Sec J Young
Pro C Dell (0990) 24656
Holes 18 L 5709 yds SSS 68
Recs Am–66 K Rixon
V'trs WD–U before 5pm M after 5pm SOC
Fees £11
Loc Bracknell 3 miles. Windsor 4 miles
Mis Within boundaries of racecourse

The Royal Household

Private
Buckingham Palace, London SW1
Tel (01) 930 4832
Mem 200
Sec A Jarred
Holes 9 L 4560 yds SSS 62
V'trs Strictly by invitation with a member
Loc The Home Park Private Windsor Castle

Sonning (1914)

Private
Sonning-on-Thames
Tel (0734) 693332
Mem 500
Sec PF Williams
Pro RT McDougall (0734) 692910
Holes 18 L 6345 yds SSS 70
Recs Am–66 MT Rapley
Pro–65 B Lane
V'trs WD–U WE–M
Fees On application
Loc South side of A4 nr Sonning

Sunningdale (1901)

Private
Sunningdale SL5 9RW
Tel (0990) 21681
Mem 800
Sec K Almond
Pro K Maxwell (0990) 20128
Holes Old 18 L 6586 yds SSS 71
New 18 L 6676 yds SSS 71
Recs Old: Am–66 MC Hughesdon
Pro–62 N Faldo
New Am–65 M Lunt
Pro–64 GJ Player
V'trs WD–I WE–M
Fees £39
Loc Sunningdale Station 1/4 mile on A30

Sunningdale Ladies (1902)

Private
Cross Road, Sunningdale
Tel (0990) 20507
Mem 400
Sec BWJ Ford
Holes 18 L 3622 yds SSS 60
V'trs WD/WE–by appointment. No 3 or 4 balls before 11am
Fees D–Ladies £9 (£11) Men £12 (£14)
Loc Sunningdale Station ¼ mile

Swinley Forest (1909)

Private
Coronation Road, Ascot SL9 5LE
Tel (0990) 20197
Mem 335
Sec IL Pearce
Pro RC Parker
Holes 18 L 6001 yds
Recs Am–64 EF Storey, ER Sermon Pro–64 P Alliss
V'trs M
Loc S of Ascot

Temple (1909)

Private
Henley Road, Hurley, Maidenhead SL6 5LH
Tel (062 882) 4248
Mem 500
Sec Capt RM Brounger (062 882) 4795
Pro Alan Dobbins (062 882) 4254
Holes 18 L 6206 yds SSS 70
Recs Am–66 AR Millar
V'trs WD–I WE/BH–M SOC
Fees £20
Loc Between Maidenhead and Henley on A423. M4 Junction 8/9. M40 Junction 3

West Berkshire (1975)

Private
Chaddleworth, Newbury RG16 0HS
Tel (04882) 574
Mem 350
Sec Norman Edwards
Pro FS Boobyer
Holes 18 L 7053 yds SSS 74
Recs Am–74 J Pocock, D Murphy, B Claringbold Pro–69 M Howell, B Laing
V'trs U SOC
Fees £6 (£10)
Loc M4 Junction 14 on A338 to Wantage

Winter Hill (1976)

Private
Grange Lane, Cookham SL6 9RP
Tel (062 85) 27613
Mem 600
Sec GB Charters-Rowe
Pro P Hedges (062 85) 27610
Holes 18 L 6408 yds SSS 71
Recs Am–70
V'trs WD–U WE–M SOC
Fees £13 (£16)
Loc Maidenhead Centre 3 miles

Buckinghamshire

Abbey Hill (1975)

Public
Monks Way, Two Ash, Milton Keynes MK8 8AA
Tel (0908) 562408
Mem 350
Sec A Hennessy (0908) 563386
Pro S Harlock (0908) 563845
Holes 18 L 6193 yds SSS 69
Recs Am–67 T Mernagh Pro–67 H Stott
V'trs U
Fees On application
Loc 2 miles S of Stony Stratford

Beaconsfield (1914)

Private
Beaconsfield HP9 2UR
Tel (0494) 676545
Mem 862
Sec PI Anderson
Pro M Brothers (0494) 676616
Holes 18 L 6469 yds SSS 71
Recs Am–66 D Haines Pro–63 E Murray
V'trs WD–H WE–N/A
Fees £15
Loc 8 miles N of Slough. 2 miles E of Beaconsfield

Buckingham (1914)

Private
Tingewick Road, Buckingham MK18 4AE
Tel (0280) 813282
Mem 600
Sec D Rolph (0280) 815566
Pro T Gates (0280) 815210
Holes 18 L 6082 yds SSS 69
Recs Am–71 RJ Gillam
V'trs WD–U WE–M SOC
Fees £14
Loc 1½ miles on Oxford Road

Burnham Beeches (1891)

Private
Burnham, Slough SL1 8EG
Tel (062 86) 61150
Mem 670
Sec AJ Buckner (Mgr) (062 86) 61448
Pro T Buckner (062 86) 61661
Holes 18 L 6415 yds SSS 71
Recs Am–67 M Orris Pro–64 H Flatman
V'trs WD–I WE/BH–M
Fees £15 D–£18.50
Loc 4 miles W of Slough

Chesham & Ley Hill (1919)

Private
The Club House, Ley Hill, Chesham HP5 1UZ
Tel (0494) 784541
Mem 380
Sec RJ Carter
Holes 9 L 5158 yds SSS 65
Recs Am–67 GL Keen Pro–69 TE Lebroge
V'trs Mon/Wed/Thurs–U Fri–U before 1pm; –M after 1pm; Tues–M after 3pm WE–M; SOC–Wed & Thurs
Fees £4.50
Loc Chesham 2 miles
Mis Course closed Sun after 2pm from 1st Apr–30th Sept

Chiltern Forest (1921)

Private
Aston Hill, Halton, Aylesbury HP22 5NQ
Tel (0296) 630899
Mem 500
Sec LEA Clark (0296) 631267
Pro C Skeet
Holes 9 L 6038 yds SSS 70
Recs Am–69 K Symonds
V'trs WD–U WE–M SOC
Fees £9
Loc 5 miles SE of Aylesbury

Denham (1910)

Private
Tilehouse Lane, Denham UB9 5DE
Tel (0895) 832022
Mem 550
Sec Wing Commander D Graham
Pro J Sheridan (0895) 832801
Holes 18 L 6439 yds SSS 71
Recs Am–66 DMA Steel Pro–68 J Sheridan
V'trs WD (Mon–Thurs) I H WE(Fri–Sun)/BH–M
Fees £14 D–£23
Loc 3 miles NW of Uxbridge

Ellesborough (1906)

Private
Butlers Cross, nr Aylesbury HP17 0TZ
Tel (0296) 622375
Mem 780
Sec KM Flint (0296) 622114
Pro S Watkins (0296) 623126
Holes 18 L 6310 yds SSS 70
Recs Am–66 N Lucas, NM Allen, P Stevens Pro–68 G Will
V'trs WE/BH–M WD–I or H SOC–Wed & Thurs only
Fees On application
Loc 1 mile W of Wendover

Farnham Park (1974)

Public
Park Road, Stoke Poges, Slough
Tel (028 14) 3332
Mem 500
Sec Mrs M Brooker (0753) 42537
Pro S Cannon
Holes 18 L 5847 yds SSS 68
Recs Am–69 N Harrison, D Ivall
Pro–68 T Bowers
V'trs U
Fees £3.60 (£5)
Loc 2 miles N of Slough

Flackwell Heath (1920)

Private
High Wycombe HP10 9PE
Tel (062 85) 20027
Mem 750
Sec JJR Barton (062 85) 20929
Pro B Plucknett (062 85) 23017
Holes 18 L 6150 yds SSS 69
Recs Am–65 P Dougan
Pro–65 J Hoskison
V'trs WD–H WE–M SOC–Wed–Fri
Fees £16
Loc Between High Wycombe & Beaconsfield off the A40. M40 Junction 3 from London

Gerrards Cross (1934)

Private
Chalfont Park, Gerrards Cross SL9 0QA
Tel (0753) 883263
Mem 780
Sec PH Fisher
Pro AP Barr (0753) 885300
Holes 18 L 6295 yds SSS 70
Recs Am–65 JB Berney
Pro–63 AP Barr
V'trs WD–H WE/BH–M
Fees £16, £11 after 3pm
Loc 1 mile from station off A413

Harewood Downs (1908)

Private
Cokes Lane, Chalfont St Giles HP8 4TA
Tel (024 04) 2308
Mem 350
Sec RM Lennard (024 04) 2184
Pro GC Morris (024 04) 4102
Holes 18 L 5958 yds SSS 69
Recs Am–65 AL Parsons
Pro–65 JM Hume
V'trs WD–H WE/BH–M SOC
Loc A413 to Amersham

Hazlemere G & CC (1982)

Private
Penn Road, Hazlemere, High Wycombe HP15 7LR
Tel (0494) 714722
Mem 560
Sec DE Hudson
Pro SR Morvell (0494) 718298
Holes 18 L 6039 yds SSS 69
Recs Pro–65 J Bennett, R Green (1987)
V'trs WD–U WE–booking req SOC–WD
Fees £14 (£18)
Loc 3 miles NE of High Wycombe on B474
Mis Buggies available for hire

Iver (1983)

Private
Hollow Hill Lane, Iver SL0 0JJ
Tel (0753) 655615
Mem 350
Sec T Notley
Pro T Notley
Holes 9 L 3107 yds
V'trs U SOC
Fees 18 holes £4 (£5.30)
9 holes £2.60 (£3.30)
Loc 1 mile to Langley station, off Langley Park Road

Ivinghoe (1967)

Private
Wellcroft, Ivinghoe, nr Leighton Buzzard LU7 9EF
Tel (0296) 668696
Mem 200
Sec Mrs SE Garrad (0296) 662478
Pro PW Garrad
Holes 9 L 4508 yds SSS 62
Recs Am–61 J Dillon
Pro–60 R Garrad
V'trs U
Fees 18 holes £4.50 (£5)
36 holes £5.50 (£6)
Loc Tring 3 miles. Dunstable 2 miles

Little Chalfont (1981)

Private
Lodge Lane, Little Chalfont, nr Amersham
Tel (024 04) 4877
Mem 450
Sec JM Dunne
Pro P Gibbins (024 04) 2942
Holes 9 L 5852 yds SSS 68
Recs Am–76 D Brown
Pro–66 P Gibbins (1987)
V'trs WD–U WE–M
Fees £5 (£7)
Loc Station $1^1/_2$ miles

Stoke Poges (1908)

Private
Park Road, Stoke Poges SL2 4PG
Tel (0753) 26385
Mem 700
Sec RC Pickering
Pro K Thomas (0753) 23609
Holes 18 L 6654 yds SSS 71
Recs Am–65 BA Price
Pro–65 J Hudson
V'trs WD–I or H WE/BH–M
Fees £8 (£14)
Loc 2 miles N of Slough

Stowe (1974)

Private
Stowe, Buckingham MK18 5EH
Tel (0280) 813650
Mem 300
Sec Mrs SA Cross (0280) 813684
Holes 9 L 4573 yds SSS 63
V'trs WD/WE dawn–1pm & after 7pm–U; School holidays–M SOC
Loc M1 Junction 16–A5–A43–A413. 4 miles from Buckingham on A413 to Brickley.

Weston Turville (1974)

Private
New Road, Weston-Turville, nr Aylesbury HP22 5QT
Tel (0296) 24084
Mem 410
Sec AK Holden
Pro G George (0296) 25949
Holes 13 L 6782 yds SSS 72
Recs Am–73 B Duff
V'trs U (exc Sun before noon)
Fees £6.50 (£8.50)
Loc $2^1/_2$ miles SE of Aylesbury

Wexham Park (1979)

Private
Wexham Street, Wexham, nr Slough SL3 6NB
Tel (028 16) 3271
Mem 650
Sec JWE Mulley (0753) 24615
Pro D Morgan (028 16) 3425
Holes Wexham 18 L 5836 yds SSS 68; Old Grange 9 L 2383 yds SSS 32
V'trs U SOC–WD
Fees 18 hole course £4 (£5.50)
9 hole course £2.60 (£3.30)
Loc 2 miles N of Slough
Mis Private club on public land

Whiteleaf (1904)

Private
Whiteleaf, Aylesbury
Tel (084 44) 3097
Mem 250
Sec LS Edwards
Pro KS Ward (084 44) 5472
Holes 9 L 2756 yds SSS 66
Recs Am–64 M Copping
Pro–63 MM Caines
V'trs WD–U WE–M
Fees 18 holes £10; 36 holes £15
Loc Princes Risborough 2 miles

Windmill Hill (1972)

Public
Tattenhoe Lane, Bletchley, Milton Keynes MK3 7RB
Tel (0908) 78623
Sec J Drage
Pro C Clingan (0908) 78623
Holes 18 L 6773 yds SSS 72
Recs Am–69 RJ Long
Pro–66 C Defoy

For explanation of abbreviations see page 202.

V'trs U SOC
Fees £3.50 (£4.80)
Loc 4 miles M1 Junction 14 on A421
Mis Floodlit driving range

Woburn (1976)

Private
Bow Brickhill, Milton Keynes
Tel (0908) 70756
Pro A Hay (0908) 647987
Holes Duke's 18 L 6913 yds SSS 74; Duchess 18 L 6641 yds SSS 72
Recs Duke's Am–68
Pro–65 R Lee, M James, MA McNulty, W Westner
V'trs WD–H (by arrangement) WE–M
Fees By arrangement
Loc 4 miles W of M1 Junc 13

Cambridgeshire

Abbotsley (1986)

Private
Eynesbury Hardwicke, St Neots PE19 4XN
Tel (0480) 215153
Mem 700
Sec J Wisson (0480) 74000
Pro V Saunders
Holes 18 L 6150 yds SSS 71
Recs Am–72 J Morrow (1987)
Pro–69 S Whymark (1984)
V'trs WD–U SOC WE–M before 10am –U after 10am BH–U
Fees £8 (£13)
Loc 2 miles SE St Neots (B1046). 12 miles W of Cambridge. M11 Junction 13 on to A45
Mis Floodlit driving range. Hotel accommodation on site

Cambridgeshire Moat House Hotel (1974)

Private
Bar Hill, Cambridge CB3 8EU
Tel (0954) 80555
Mem 350
Sec GW Huggett
Pro GW Huggett (0954) 80098
Holes 18 L 6734 yds SSS 72
Recs Am–68 P Way
Pro–68 P Townsend
V'trs I
Fees £14 (£22.50)
Loc 5 miles NW of Cambridge on A604
Mis Buggies for hire

Ely City (1961)

Private
Cambridge Road, Ely CB7 4HX
Tel (0353) 2751
Mem 750
Sec GA Briggs
Pro F Rowden (0353) 3317 (Touring Pro H Baiocchi)
Holes 18 L 6686 yds SSS 72
Recs Am–68 N Evans
Pro–66 L Trevino
V'trs WD–U WE–H SOC–Tues–Fri
Fees £14 (£20)
Loc 12 miles N of Cambridge

Girton (1936)

Private
Dodford Lane, Cambridge
Tel (0223) 276169
Mem 650
Sec Mrs MA Cornwell
Pro J Sharkey
Holes 18 L 6000 yds SSS 69
Recs Am–66 J Clough
V'trs WD–U WE/BH–M SOC
Fees WD–£12
Loc 3 miles N of Cambridge

Gog Magog (1901)

Private
Shelford Bottom, Cambridge CB2 4AB
Tel (0223) 247626
Mem 1050
Sec T Murphy
Pro I Bamborough (0223) 246058
Holes Old 18 L 6386 yds SSS 70
New 9 L 5833 yds SSS 68
Recs Am–64 RW Guy, MT Seaton, DWG Woods, R Claydon
Pro–64 G Wolstenholme, PJ Butler
V'trs WD–I WE/BH–M SOC–Tues & Thurs
Fees Old £17 New £10
Loc 2 miles S of Cambridge on A1307
Mis Buggies not allowed

March (1922)

Private
Frogs Abbey, Grange Rd, Knights End, March
Tel (0354) 52364
Mem 300
Sec RA Philpott (0354) 54604
Pro F Kiddie
Holes 9 L 6278 yds SSS 70
Recs Am–68 JW Kisby
V'trs H WE–M
Fees £7
Loc 18 miles E of Peterborough

Orton Meadows (1987)

Public
Ham Lane, Peterborough PE2 0UU
Mem 270
Sec K Boyer (0733) 238508
Pro N Grant (0733) 237478
Holes 18 L 5800 yds SSS 68
Recs Am–75 T Graves (1988)
Pro–67 R Mann (1987)
V'trs U (always phone Pro)
Fees £3.70 (£5.50)
Loc 2 miles SW of Peterborough on A605
Mis 12 hole pitch and putt

Peterborough Milton (1937)

Private
Milton Ferry, Peterborough PE6 7AG
Tel (0733) 380204
Mem 700
Sec PJ Bishop (0733) 380489
Pro NS Bundy (0733) 380793
Holes 18 L 6431 yds SSS 71
Recs Am–67 J Mitchell (1988)
Pro–69 B Barnes, G Will
V'trs WD–U WE–M SOC
Fees £15
Loc 4 miles W of Peterborough on A47

Ramsey (1964)

Private
4 Abbey Terrace, Ramsey, Huntingdon PE17 1DD
Tel (0487) 813573
Mem 750
Sec R Muirhead (0487) 812600
Pro BJ Puttick (0487) 813022
Holes 18 L 6136 yds SSS 70
Recs Am–66 DP Smith (1987)
Pro–69 S Turner (1985)
V'trs WD–U WE–Restricted until 10.30am
Fees £12 (£18)
Loc 12 miles SE of Peterborough

St Ives (Hunts) (1923)

Private
St Ives, Huntingdon PE17 4RS
Tel (0480) 64459
Mem 320
Sec R Hill IPFA (0480) 68392
Pro A Headley (0480) 66067
Holes 9 L 6052 yds SSS 69
Recs Am–67 Fl–Lt CJB Murdoch
Pro–61 P Alliss
V'trs WD–U WE–after 11am
Fees £8 (£12)
Loc 5 miles E of Huntingdon

St Neot's (1890)

Private
Crosshall Road, St Neot's PE19 4AE
Tel (0480) 74311
Mem 600
Sec RJ Marsden (0480) 72363
Pro G Bithrey (0480) 76513
Holes 18 L 6027 yds SSS 69
Recs Am–67 JR Gray
Pro–65 M Gallagher, H Flatman
V'trs H
Fees £9 D–£12 (£13 D–£18)
Loc 1 mile W of St Neot's on A45
Mis Buggy £9 D–£15

Thorpe Wood (1975)

Public
Nene Parkway, Peterborough PE3 6SE
Tel (0733) 267701
Mem 850
Sec R Palmer (0733) 63758

For map index see page 203.

Pro D Fitton, R Fitton
Holes 18 L 7086 yds SSS 74
Recs Am–74 N Brownlie, JN Dodd, J Brady
Pro–71 R Fitton
V'trs U
Fees £3.70 (£5.50)
Loc 3 miles W of town on A47

Channel Islands

Alderney (1969)

Private
Route des Carrieres, Alderney
Tel **(048 182) 2835**
Mem 520
Sec A Eggleston
Holes 9 L 2528 yds SSS 33
Recs Am–29 M Hugman
Pro–28 PL Cunningham
V'trs U
Fees £8 (£10)
Loc 1 mile E of St Anne

L'Ancresse

Private
L'Ancresse, Guernsey
Tel **(0481) 47408**
Mem 312
Sec BD Tullier (0481) 56275
Holes Share L'Ancresse course with Royal Guernsey

La Moye (1902)

Private
La Moye, St Brelade
Tel **(0534) 42701**
Mem 1250
Sec D Lowton (0534) 43401
Pro D Melville (0534) 43130
Holes 18 L 6741 yds SSS 72
Recs Am–69 BJ McCarthy (1987)
Pro–62 Gordon Brand Jr
V'trs IH SOC–after 9.30am
Fees £18 (£20) W–£80
Loc 6 miles W of St Helier

Royal Guernsey (1890)

Private
L'Ancresse, Guernsey
Tel **(0481) 47022**
Mem 880
Sec GJ Nicolle (0481) 46523
Pro N Wood (0481) 45070
Holes 18 L 6206 yds SSS 70
Recs Am–64 R Eggo (1986)
Pro–64 P Cunningham
V'trs WD–U WE–NA H SOC
Fees £9 D–£11 W–£35 F–£52
Loc 5 miles N of St Peter Port

Royal Jersey (1878)

Private
Grouville, Jersey
Tel **(0534) 54416**
Mem 1300
Sec RC Leader
Pro T Horton (0534) 52234
Holes 18 L 6023 yds SSS 69
Recs Am–68 TA Gray (1988)
Pro–64 P Le Chevalier (1988)
V'trs WD–H after 10am WE/BH–H after 2.30pm (Winter 12.30pm)
Fees £18 (£25) W–£80 F–£150
Loc 4 miles E of St Helier

St Clements (1925)

Private
St Clements, Jersey
Tel **(0534) 21938**
Mem 90
Sec D Leybourne (0534) 54823
Pro R Marks
Holes 9 L 3972 yds SSS 61
Recs Am–61 T Gray, B McCarthy
V'trs U Sun am–NA
Fees £6
Loc 1 mile E of St Helier
Mis Book by telephone

Western Golf Range

Public
The Mount, Val de la Mare, St Quens, Jersey
Tel **(0534) 81947/82787**
Sec J Le Brun (Mgr) (0534) 82629
Pro C Wackeb (0534) 82787
Holes 12 holes Par 3 SSS 36
V'trs U
Fees 12 holes £3 (£3.25)
Loc Five Mile Road, St Quens Bay
Mis Driving range

Cheshire

Alderley Edge (1907)

Private
Brook Lane, Alderley Edge SK9 7RU
Tel **(0625) 585583**
Mem 212 80(L) 40(J) 40(5)
Sec AJ Hayes (0625) 523213
Pro M Stewart (0625) 584493
Holes 9 L 5836 yds SSS 68
Recs Am–65 FA Hardy, DJ Austin
Pro–65 R Boughey
V'trs M or H
Fees £9 (£11)
Loc 12 miles S of Manchester

Astbury (1922)

Private
Peel Lane, Astbury, nr Congleton CW12 4RE
Tel **(0260) 272772**
Mem 600
Sec T Williams
Pro SR Bassil
Holes 18 L 6269 yds SSS 70
Recs Am–65 AJA Hurst (1983)
Pro–69 I Mosey (1979)
V'trs WD–H or M WE–M SOC–Thurs only
Fees £12
Loc 1 mile S of Congleton off A34 via Astbury village
Mis Play before 4pm

Avro (1980)

Private
British Aerospace, Woodford
Tel **(061) 439 5050**
Mem 400
Sec AP Johnson (0625) 874402
Holes 9 L 5735 yds SSS 68
Recs Am–73 R Wheeler (1988)
V'trs M
Fees £4 (£6)

Birchwood (1979)

Private
Kelvin Close, Birchwood, Warrington
Tel **(0925) 818819**
Mem 1009
Sec A Jackson
Pro D Cooper (0925) 812876
Holes 18 L 6760 yds SSS 73
Recs Am–65 MJ Conroy
Pro–69 P Hunstone
V'trs U SOC Mon & Thurs
Fees £10 (£14)
Loc M62 Junction 11 2 miles

Bramhall (1905)

Private
Ladythorn Road, Bramhall, Stockport SK7 2EY
Tel **(061) 439 4057**
Mem 290 160(L) 85(J) 100(5)
Sec F Chadfield (061) 439 4393
Pro B Nield (061) 439 1171
Holes 18 L 6300 yds SSS 70
Recs Am–64 AE Hill (1987)
Pro–66 I Higby (1987)
V'trs U (exc Thurs) SOC
Fees £12 (£14)
Loc Stockport

Chester (1900)

Private
Curzon Park, Chester CH4 8AR
Tel **(0244) 675130**
Mem 750
Sec PM Pritchard (0244) 677760
Pro G Parton (0244) 671185
Holes 18 L 6487 yds SSS 71
Recs Am–68 M Weetman
Pro–66 D Screeton
V'trs WD–U WE–U H SOC
Fees £10 (£12)
Loc Chester 1 mile

Congleton (1897)

Private
Biddulph Road, Congleton CW12 3LZ
Tel **(0260) 273540**
Mem 380
Sec FT Pegg

For explanation of abbreviations see page 202.

Pro JA Colclough (0260) 271083
Holes 9 L 5704 yds SSS 65
Recs Am–65 IR Hollinshead
Pro–59 N Coles
V'trs U
Fees On application
Loc $1^1/_2$ miles from town on A527

Crewe (1911)

Private
Fields Road, Haslington, Crewe CW1 1TB
Tel **(0270) 584099 (Sec)**
(0270) 584227 (Steward)
Mem 601
Sec DG Elias B.Sc
Pro R Rimmer (0270) 585032
Holes 18 L 6181 yds SSS 69
Recs Am–66 VG McCandless
Pro–68 A Thompson
V'trs WD–U WE/BH–M SOC
Fees £12 (1988)
Loc 2 miles NE of Crewe Station. 5 miles W of M6 Junction 16

Delamere Forest (1910)

Private
Station Road, Delamere, Northwich CW8 2JE
Tel **(0606) 882807**
Mem 400
Sec L Parkin
Pro D Comboy (0606) 883307
Holes 18 L 6305 yds SSS 70
Recs Am–66 B Stockdale
Pro–63 M Bembridge
V'trs U (WE–2 balls only)
Fees £13 (£16)
Loc 10 miles E of Chester

Eaton (1965)

Private
Eaton Park, Eccleston, Chester CH4 9JF
Tel **(0244) 671420**
Sec RT Robinson (0244) 680474
Pro A Mitchell (0244) 680170
Holes 18 L 6446 yds SSS 71
V'trs I SOC–WD
Loc 3 miles S of Chester

Ellesmere Port (1971)

Public
Chester Road, Hooton, South Wirral L66 1QH
Tel **(051) 339 7502**
Mem 350
Sec B Turley (051) 355 8800
Holes 18 L 6432 yds Par 71
SSS 71
Recs Am–69 A Waterhouse
Pro–67 B Evans, A Caygill
V'trs SOC–WD WE–Arrange with Pro
Fees £2.60 (£3.20)
Loc 9 miles N of Chester on A41

Helsby (1902)

Private
Tower's Lane, Helsby, Warrington WA6 0JB
Tel **(09282) 2021**
Mem 600
Sec N Littler
Pro I Wright (09282) 5457
Holes 18 L 6260 yds SSS 70
Recs Am–69 F Wood, JJ Spruce
Pro–68 I Wright
V'trs WE–NA SOC
Fees £10
Loc Off A56 into Primrose Lane, first right Towers Lane

Knights Grange (1983)

Public
Grange Lane, Winsford
Tel **(06065) 52780**
Mem 132
Sec A Peters (06065) 3521
Pro S McCarthy
Holes 9 L 6240 yds SSS 70
V'trs U SOC
Fees 18 holes £1.85 (£2.35)
9 holes £1.45 (£1.60)
Loc Signposted from centre to Knights Grange Sports Complex

Knutsford (1891)

Private
Mereheath Lane, Knutsford
Tel **(0565) 3355**
Mem 135
Sec D Francis (0565) 4001 (H)
Pro A Wilson
Holes 9 L 6288 yds SSS 70
Recs Am–65 B Stockdale
Pro–65 D Cooper
V'trs I Wed pm–NA SOC
Fees £10 (£12)
Loc Town $^1/_2$ mile

Lymm (1907)

Private
Whitbarrow Road, Lymm WA13 9AN
Tel **(092 575) 2177**
Mem 400 100(L) 75(J) 50(5)
Sec JM Pearson (092 575) 5020
Pro GJ Williams (092 575) 5054
Holes 18 L 6304 yds SSS 70
Recs Am–68 CN Brown (1987)
Pro–69 S Lyle (1987)
V'trs U
Fees £11 (£13)
Loc 5 miles SE of Warrington

Macclesfield (1889)

Private
The Hollins, Macclesfield
Tel **(0625) 23227**
Mem 400
Sec W Eastwood (0625) 615845
Pro T Taylor (0625) 616952
Holes 12 L 6184 yds SSS 69
Recs Am–69 RA Johnson, B Hodkinson
Pro–67 M Gregson
V'trs WD/BH–I WE–M
Fees £7
Loc 1 mile SE town centre

Malkins Bank

Public
Sandbach
Tel **(0270) 765931**
Pro D Wheeler
Holes 18 L 6178 yds SSS 69
Fees £3 (£3.65)
Loc M6 Junction 17

Mere G & CC (1934)

Private
Mere, Knutsford WA16 6LJ
Tel **(0565) 830155**
Mem 350 150(L) 100(J)
Sec AB Turner
Pro EP Goodwin (0565) 830219
Holes 18 L 6849 yds SSS 73
Recs Am–68 CR Smethurst
Pro–69 N Faldo
V'trs WE/BH–NA Wed & Fri–NA Mon/Tues/Thurs–H SOC
Fees £25
Loc 1 mile E M6 Junction 19
Mis Driving range. Buggies

New Mills (1907)

Private
Shaw Marsh, New Mills
Tel **(0663) 43485**
Mem 250
Sec W Hyde (0663) 43816
Pro I Scott (0663) 46161
Holes 9 L 5924 yds SSS 68
Recs Am–72 R Palmer, S Hewson
Pro–67 A Ellis, A Murray
V'trs WD–U WE–M SOC
Fees D–£6

Poulton Park (1980)

Private
Dig Lane, Cinnamon Brow
Tel **(0925) 812034**
Mem 360
Sec B Carr
Pro A Baguley (0925) 825220
Holes 9 L 4918 metres SSS 66
Recs Am–70 S Bennett
V'trs WD–NA 5–6pm
WE–NA noon to 2pm
Fees £6.50 (£8)
Loc Off Crab Lane, Fearnhead

Prestbury (1920)

Private
Macclesfield Road, Prestbury, Macclesfield SK10 4BJ
Tel **(0625) 829388**
Mem 725
Sec JL Carter (0625) 828241
Pro TW Rastall (0625) 828242

For map index see page 203.

Holes 18 L 6359 yds SSS 71
Recs Am–66 R Foster, JE Allen
Pro–68 M Faulkener
V'trs WD–I WE–M
Fees £15 (1988 prices)
Loc $2^1/_2$ miles NW of Macclesfield

Queen's Park (1985)

Public
Queen's Park Gardens, Crewe
Tel **(0270) 666724**
Mem 280
Sec JG Jones (0270) 583478
Pro M Williams
Holes 9 L 5370 yds Par 68
V'trs WD–U WE–U after 8.30am SOC
Fees £2.20 (£2.70)
Loc $1^1/_4$ miles from Crewe centre off Victoria Avenue

Romiley (1897)

Private
Goosehouse Green, Romiley, Stockport SK6 4LJ
Tel **(061) 430 2392**
Mem 750
Sec GM Beresford (061) 430 7257
Pro GS Ogden (061) 430 7122
Holes 18 L 6335 yds SSS 70
Recs Am–64 N Ryan
Pro–67 D Roberts
V'trs U SOC
Fees £10 (£15)
Loc Station $^3/_4$ mile

Runcorn (1909)

Private
Clifton Road, Runcorn
Tel **(092 85) 72093 (members)**
(092 85) 74214 (secretary)
Mem 375 90(L) 100(J)
Sec GE Povey OBE JP
Holes 18 L 6035 yds SSS 69
Recs Am–67 I Rockliffe
V'trs WD–U exc comp days H SOC
Fees £8 (£9.50)

St Michael Jubilee

Public
Dundalk Road, Widnes
Tel **(051) 424 0989**
Mem 300
Sec W Hughes
Holes Play over Widnes Municipal

Sandbach (1923)

Private
Middlewich Road, Sandbach CW11 9EA
Tel **(0270) 762117**
Mem 215 100(L) 50(J)
Sec AF Pearson
Holes 9 L 5533 yds SSS 67
Recs Am–64 K Brooks
V'trs WD–U WE/BH–M
Fees £9
Loc Sandbach 1 mile
Mis No catering Mon & Thu

Sandiway (1921)

Private
Sandiway CW8 2DJ
Tel **(0606) 882606**
Mem 650
Sec VFC Wood (0606) 883247
Pro J Law (0606) 883180
Holes 18 L 6435 yds SSS 72
Recs Am–67 AE Hill
Pro–65 D Huish
V'trs I H
Fees £15 (£20)
Loc Chester 15 miles on A556

Stockport (1906)

Private
Offerton Road, Offerton, Stockport SK2 5HL
Tel **(061) 427 2001**
Mem 495
Sec HE Bagshaw (061) 427 4425
Pro R Tattersall (061) 427 2421
Holes 18 L 6319 yds SSS 71
Recs Am–65 KR Gorton
Pro–66 E Lester
V'trs U
Fees £12 (£15)
Loc 1 mile along A626 from Hazel Grove to Marple

The Tytherington (1986)

Private
Macclesfield SK10 2JP
Tel **(0625) 617622**
Mem 200
Sec S Wilson
Pro S Wilson
Holes 18 L 6717 yds SSS 72
V'trs U
Fees £14 D–£20 (£20 D–£30)
Loc Nr Macclesfield on Manchester Road

Upton-by-Chester (1934)

Private
Upton Lane, Chester CH2 1EE
Tel **(0244) 381183**
Mem 750
Sec JB Durban
Pro PA Gardner
Holes 18 L 5875 yds SSS 68
Recs Am–63 JD Norbury
Pro–66 A Perry
V'trs U SOC–WD
Fees £10 (£12)
Loc Off Liverpool Road, near 'Frog' PH

Vicars Cross (1939)

Private
Vicars Cross, Chester
Tel **(0244) 335174**
Mem 650
Sec DC Chilton
Pro FA Nickells
Holes 18 L 5857 yds SSS 68
Recs Am–63 MK Jones
V'trs U
Fees £10 (£12.50)
Loc 2 miles E of Chester

Walton Hall

Public
Warrington Road, Higher Walton, Warrington WA4 5LU
Tel **(0925) 66775**
Mem 245 38(L) 37(J)
Sec D Judson (0925) 571028
Pro MJ Slater (0925) 63061
Holes 18 L 6843 yds SSS 73
Recs Am–70 R Davies (1988)
V'trs U
Fees £3.65 (£4.50)
Loc 2 miles S of Warrington

Warrington (1903)

Private
Hill Warren, Appleton
Tel **(0925) 61620**
Mem 875
Sec RO Francis (0925) 61775
Pro AW Fryer (0925) 65431
Holes 18 L 6305 yds SSS 70
Recs Am–66 JR Bennett
Pro–65 EG Lester
V'trs U SOC–Wed & Thurs
Fees £9.50 (£14)
Loc 3 miles S of Warrington

Widnes (1924)

Private
Highfield Road, Widnes WA8 7DT
Tel **(051) 424 2440**
Mem 800
Sec M Cresswell
(051) 424 2995
Pro F Robinson (051) 424 2995
Holes 18 L 5719 yds SSS 68
Recs Am–65 F Whitfield (1985), WK George (1986)
Pro–64 A Murray
V'trs WD–U WE–NA on comp days SOC–WD
Fees £8 (£10)
Loc Station $^1/_2$ mile

Widnes Municipal (1977)

Public
Dundalk Road, Widnes
Tel **(051) 424 6230**
Mem 200
Sec R Doran
Pro R Bilton (0295) 65241
Holes 18 L 5612 yds SSS 67
Recs Am–73
V'trs U
Mis St Michael Jubilee Club plays here

Wilmslow (1889)

Private
Great Warford, Mobberley, Knutsford WA16 7AY
Tel **(056 587) 2579**
Mem 670
Sec CA Skelton (056 587) 2148
(0625) 861429 (home)

For explanation of abbreviations see page 202.

Pro J Nowicki (056 587) 3620
Holes 18 L 6500 yds SSS 71
Recs Am–68 A O'Connor, TB Taylor
Pro–64 J O'Leary
V'trs U Wed–NA before 2pm
Fees On application
Loc $3^{1}/_{2}$ miles W of Alderley Edge

Cleveland

Billingham (1967)

Private
Sandy Lane, Billingham
TS22 5NA
Tel **(0642) 554494/533816**
Mem 800
Sec AG Shirley (0642) 533816
Pro P Bradley (0642) 557060
Holes 18 L 6430 yds SSS 71
Recs AM–66 M Ure (1988)
Pro–65 P Harrison (1988)
V'trs WD–after 9am H WE/BH–M SOC
Fees D–£11 (NA)
Loc W boundary of Billingham adjacent to A19 E of bypass
Mis No catering Mon

Castle Eden & Peterlee (1927)

Private
Castle Eden, Hartlepool
Tel **(0429) 836220**
Mem 650
Sec P Robinson
Pro T Jenkins (0429) 836689
Holes 18 L 6297 yds SSS 70
Recs Am–66 G Border (1987)
V'trs U
Fees £7 (£8)
Loc 2 miles S of Peterlee

Cleveland (1887)

Private
Queen Street, Redcar TS10 1BT
Tel **(0642) 483693**
Mem 674
Sec LR Manley (0642) 471798
Pro D Masey (0642) 483462
Holes 18 L 6707 yds SSS 72
Recs Am–68 M Watson, NBJ Fick
Pro–70 B Hardcastle
V'trs WD–after 9.30am Sun/BH–no parties SOC
Fees £8 (£12.50)
Loc S bank of River Tees

Eaglescliffe (1914)

Private
Yarm Road, Eaglescliffe, Stockton-on-Tees
Tel **(0642) 780098**
Mem 470
Sec JG Liddle (0642) 780238
Pro J Munro (0642) 780588
Holes 18 L 6275 yds SSS 70
Recs Am–67 B Skipper
Pro–67 J Munro
V'trs H
Fees £10 (£12.50)
Loc 3 miles S of Stockton-on-Tees

Hartlepool (1906)

Private
Hart Warren, Hartlepool
Tel **(0429) 274398**
Mem 600
Sec WE Storrow (0429) 870282
Pro ME Cole (0429) 267473
Holes 18 L 6255 yds SSS 70
Recs Am–67 G Bell (1987)
Pro–66 G Brown (1987)
V'trs WD–U SOC
Fees £9 (£12) W–£40
Loc N boundary of Hartlepool

Middlesbrough (1908)

Private
Brass Castle Lane, Middlesbrough TS8 9EE
Tel **(0642) 316430**
Mem 900
Sec JM Jackson (0642) 311515
Pro DJ Jones (0642) 311766
Holes 18 L 5582 metres SSS 69
Recs Am–61 R Boxall
Pro–66 D Jagger
V'trs U
Fees £11 D–£12.50
Loc 3 miles S of town centre

Middlesbrough Municipal (1977)

Public
Ladgate Lane, Middlesbrough TS5 7YZ
Tel **(0642) 315533**
Mem 510
Sec J Dilworth (0642) 468893
Pro M Nutter (0642) 315361
Holes 18 L 6314 yds SSS 70
Recs Am–69 NBJ Fick
Pro–67 B Gallagher
V'trs U
Fees £3.75 (£5)
Loc 3 miles S of centre on A174
Mis Floodlit driving range

Saltburn (1894)

Private
Hob Hill, Saltburn-by-the-Sea
Tel **(0287) 22812**
Mem 800
Sec I Mackay (0287) 32768
Pro R Broadbent (0287) 24653
Holes 18 L 5846 yds SSS 68
V'trs U
Fees £8 (£10)

Seaton Carew (1874)

Private
Tees Road, Hartlepool TS25 1DE
Tel **(0429) 266249**
Mem 650
Sec T Waite (0429) 267645
Pro W Hector
Holes Old Course 6604 yds SSS 72
Brabazon 6802 yds SSS 73
Recs Am–66 M Kelley
Pro–67 JW Johnson
V'trs U SOC
Fees £10 (£12)
Loc Hartlepool 2 miles

Tees-side (1901)

Private
Acklam Road, Thornaby TS17 7JS
Tel **(0642) 676249**
Mem 600
Sec W Allen (0642) 616516
Pro K Hall (0642) 673822
Holes 18 L 6472 yds SSS 71
V'trs WD–before 4.30pm WE–after 11am BH–M before 11am SOC
Fees £8 (£12)
Loc 2 miles S of Stockton on A1130. $^{1}/_{2}$ mile from A19 on A1130

Wilton (1949)

Private
Wilton, Redcar TS10 4QY
Tel **(0642) 465265**
Mem 700
Sec DW Lewis (0642) 477570
Pro AL Maskell
Holes 18 L 6043 yds SSS 69
Recs Am–64 N Crapper
Pro–68 S Hunt
V'trs WD–U Sat–NA Sun/BH–U SOC
Fees £9 (£9)
Loc 3 miles W of Redcar on A174

Cornwall

Bude & North Cornwall (1891)

Private
Burn View, Bude EX23 8DA
Tel **(0288) 2006**
Mem 320 135(L) 60(J)
Sec BWA Watson
Pro P Sanders (0288) 3635
Holes 18 L 6202 yds SSS 70
Recs Am–67 D Cann
Pro–70 C Pennington
V'trs U SOC
Fees £9 W–£30 F–£45
Loc Bude Town Centre

Budock Vean Hotel (1922)

Private
Falmouth
Tel **(0326) 250288**
Mem 250
Sec FG Benney (0326) 250060
Holes 9 L 3100 yds SSS 66
Recs Am–61 RJ Sadler
Pro–64 D Short
V'trs H
Fees £7 (£9)
Loc Falmouth 5 miles

For map index see page 203.

Carlyon Bay (1926)

Private
Carlyon Bay, St Austell
Tel **(072 681) 4250**
Mem 600
Sec CH Farmer
Pro NJ Sears (072 681) 4228
Holes 18 L 6510 yds SSS 71
Recs Am–69 M Boggia
Pro–65 N Coles
V'trs U
Fees £8.50 (£10) W–£40
Loc 2 miles E of town
Mis Buggies for hire

Culdrose

Private
Royal Naval Air Station, Culdrose
Tel **(0326) 4121 (Ext 7113)**
Mem 100
Sec D Ashman (0326) 4121 (Ext 7149)
Holes 9 L 6412 yds SSS 71
V'trs M

Falmouth (1928)

Private
Swanpool Road, Falmouth
Tel **(0326) 311262**
Mem 600
Sec DJ de C Sizer (0326) 40525
Pro D Short (0326) 316229
Holes 18 L 5581 yds SSS 67
Recs Am–65 JL Gresson
Pro–65 G Brand Jr
V'trs U SOC
Fees £8 (£8) W–£40
Loc 1/2 mile W of Swanpool Beach

Isles of Scilly (1904)

Private
St Mary's, Isles of Scilly TR21 0NF
Tel **(0720) 22692**
Mem 380
Holes 9 LL 5974 yds SSS 69
Recs Am–69 M Twynham
V'trs U Sun–M
Fees £7 W–£15.50
Loc Hughtown 1 1/2 miles

Launceston (1928)

Private
St Stephen, Launceston
Tel **(0566) 3442**
Mem 750
Sec BJ Grant (0566) 3442
Pro J Tozer
Holes 18 L 6374 yds SSS 70
Recs Am–67 H Reid
Pro–67 G Smith
V'trs U SOC
Fees £10 (£12)
Loc 1 mile N of Launceston off Bude Road

Looe Bindown G & CC (1933)

Private
Bin Down, nr Looe PL13 1PX
Tel **(05034) 247**
Mem 350
Sec K Wood
Holes 18 L 5940 yds SSS 68
V'trs U SOC
Fees £8.50 (£10) W–£36
Loc 3 miles E of Looe

Mullion (1895)

Private
Cury Helston TR12 7BP
Tel **(0326) 240276**
Mem 800
Sec D Watts (0326) 240685
Pro M Singleton (0326) 241176
Holes 18 L 5610 yds SSS 67
Recs Am–66 PA Gilbert
Pro–68 BJ Hunt, P Alliss
V'trs H (restricted comp days and open days) SOC–WD
Fees £9 W–£30 F–£45
Loc 6 miles S of Helston
Mis No dogs on course or in clubhouse

Newquay (1890)

Private
Tower Road, Newquay TR7 1LT
Tel **(0637) 872091**
Mem 500
Sec G Binney (0637) 874354
Pro P Muscroft (0637) 874830
Holes 18 L 6140 yds SSS 69
Recs Am–65 I Veale
Pro–69 PJ Yeo
V'trs WD/Sat–H Sun–M
Fees £10 W–£40
Loc Centre 1/2 mile

Perranporth (1927)

Private
Budnick Hill, Perranporth TR6 0AB
Tel **(0872) 572454**
Mem 550
Sec VG Hill (0872) 573701/ 572206 (day)
Pro DC Mitchell (0872) 572317
Holes 18 L 6208 yds SSS 70
Recs Am–65
Pro–68
V'trs H SOC
Loc 1/2 mile NW of town centre

Praa Sands (1971)

Private
Praa Sands, Germoe Cross Roads, Penzance TR20 9TQ
Tel **(0736) 763445**
Mem 350
Sec D & K Phillips (Props)
Pro RA Hamilton
Holes 9 L 4036 yds SSS 60
Recs Am–59 P Lorys
V'trs U exc Sunday am
Fees £6 W–£28
Loc 7 miles from Penzance on A394 Penzance–Helston road, at Praa Sands

St Austell (1912)

Private
Tregongeeves, St Austell
Tel **(0726) 74756**
Mem 780
Sec SH Davey
Pro M Rowe (0726) 68621
Holes 18 L 5981 yds SSS 69
Recs Am–67 AC Nash
V'trs SOC exc comp days
Fees £9 (£12)
Loc 1 1/2 miles W of St Austell

St Enodoc (1890)

Private
Rock, Wadebridge PL27 6LB
Tel **(020 886) 3216**
Mem 1050
Sec Col L Guy OBE
Pro NJ Williams (020 886) 2402
Holes Church 18 L 6207 yds SSS 70; Holywell 18 L 4165 yds SSS 61
Recs Am–66 G Brand
Pro–67 Dai Rees
V'trs Main course–H
Short course–U; (max h'cap 24, ladies 36) SOC
Fees Church £13 W–£46
Holywell £8 W–£32
Loc Wadebridge 6 miles

St Mellion (1976)

Private
St Mellion, nr Saltash PL12 6SD
Tel **(0579) 50101**
Mem 700
Sec D Webb (Mgr)
Pro T Moore (0579) 50724
Holes Resort Course 18 L 5927 yds SSS 68; Jack Nicklaus Course 18 L 6626 yds SSS 72
V'trs H SOC
Loc Tamar Bridge
Mis Buggies. Driving range

Tehidy Park (1922)

Private
Camborne TR14 0HH
Tel **(0209) 842208**
Mem 1000
Sec PM Green
Pro J Dumbreck (0209) 842914
Holes 18 L 6222 yds SSS 70
Recs Am–65 S Hurley
Pro–67 J Sharkey
V'trs H
Fees £10 (£15)
Loc 3 miles N of Camborne

Tregenna Castle Hotel (1982)

Private
St Ives TR26 2DE
Tel **(0736) 795254**
Mem 127
Sec D Houghton
Pro L Knapp
Holes 18 L 3645 yds SSS 57
V'trs U SOC
Fees D–£6
Loc Town centre 1 mile

Trevose (1924)

Private
Constantine Bay, Padstow
Tel **(0841) 520208**
Mem 625
Sec P Gammon, I Savage
Pro G Alliss (0841) 520261
Holes 18 L 6608 yds SSS 72
9 L 1367 yds SSS 29
Recs Am–67 C Phillips
Pro–66 N Burch
V'trs H SOC
Fees On application
Loc 4 miles W of Padstow
Mis 3 & 4 ball starting times restricted all year–phone Club

Truro (1937)

Private
Treliske, Truro TR1 3LG
Tel **(0872) 72640**
Mem 800
Sec BE Heggie (0872) 78684
Pro NK Bicknell (0872) 76595
Holes 18 L 5347 yds SSS 66
Recs Am–61 AJ Ring
Pro–63 M Hoyle
V'trs U SOC
Fees £10 (£13) W–£40 M–£80
Loc 2 miles W of Truro on A390

West Cornwall (1889)

Private
Lelant, St Ives TR26 3DZ
Tel **(0736) 753319**
Mem 825
Sec WS Richards (0736) 753401
Pro P Atherton (0736) 753177
Holes 18 L 5854 yds SSS 68
Recs Am–65 MC Edmunds
V'trs H
Fees £7 (£8) W–£30
Loc 2 miles E of St Ives

Whitsand Bay Hotel (1909)

Private
Portwrinkle, Torpoint
Tel **(0503) 30470 or 30276 (hotel)**
Mem 370
Sec GG Dyer (0503) 30418
Pro S Poole (0503) 30778
Holes 18 L 5512 yds SSS 67
Recs Am–62 GG Dyer
Pro–63 M Faulkner
V'trs H SOC
Fees £8 (£9)
Loc Plymouth 6 miles

Cumbria

Alston Moor (1906)

Private
The Hermitage, Alston
CA9 3DB
Tel **(0498) 81675**
Mem 250
Sec AR Frater (0498) 81953
Holes 9 L 5380 yds SSS 66
Recs Am–67 A Rutherford
V'trs U SOC
Fees £4 (£4.50)
Loc Alston 2 miles on B6277

Appleby (1903)

Private
Appleby
Tel **(076 83) 51432**
Mem 600
Sec B Waites
Holes 18 L 5914 yds SSS 68
Recs Am–63 K Bush
Pro–69 SS Scott
V'trs U
Fees £4.50 (£6)
Loc 2 miles S of Appleby

Barrow (1921)

Private
Rakesmoor Lane, Hawcoat,
Barrow-in-Furness
Tel **(0229) 25444**
Mem 400 128(L) 80(J)
Sec FG Leigh (0229) 24174
Pro M Booth (0229) 23121
Holes 18 L 6209 yds SSS 70
Recs Am–66 NL Brooks
V'trs U
Fees £8 (£8) W–£25
Loc Hawcoat

Brampton (Talkin Tarn) (1907)

Private
Brampton
Tel **(069 77) 2255**
Mem 750
Sec IJ Meldrum (0228) 23155
Pro S Harrison (069 77) 2000
Holes 18 L 6420 yds SSS 71
Recs Am–70 N Johnstone (1988)
V'trs U
Fees £7 (£9) W–£24
Loc On B6413, 1 mile SE of Brampton

Carlisle (1908)

Private
Aglionby, Carlisle
Tel **(0228) 513303**
Mem 870
Sec C Baker, JA Griffiths
Pro JS More (0228) 513241
Holes 18 L 6278 yds SSS 70
Recs Am–66 PL Jack
Pro–65 D Pearce (1988)
V'trs WD–after 9.30am & 1.30pm WE–after 10am & 2.30pm NA–Tues pm and comp days SOC–Wed and Fri
Fees £12 (£15)
Loc 2 miles E of Carlisle

Cockermouth (1896)

Private
Embleton, Cockermouth
Tel **(059 681) 223**
Mem 430
Sec RD Pollard (0900) 822650
Holes 18 L 5496 yds SSS 67
Recs Am–65 S Gabb
V'trs WD–U before 5pm exc Wed WE–Sun NA before 11am and 2–2.30pm SOC
Fees £6 (£6)
Loc 4 miles E of town

The Dunnerholme (1905)

Private
Askam-in-Furness
Tel **(0229) 62675**
Mem 300
Sec JH Mutton (0229) 62979
Holes 10 L 6101 yds SSS 69
Recs Am–68 H Bayliff
Pro–70 JB Ball
V'trs U
Fees £5 (£6)
Loc 6 miles N of Barrow on A595 Whitehaven–Workington road

Furness (1872)

Private
Walney Island, Barrow-in-Furness
Tel **(0229) 41232**
Mem 700
Sec D Clamp
Pro K Bosward
Holes 18 L 6418 yds SSS 71
Recs Am–67 A Miles (1986)
Pro–65 A Chandler, GJ Brand (1984)
V'trs U
Fees £6 (£8)
Loc Walney Island

Grange Fell (1952)

Private
Cartmel Road, Grange-over-Sands
LA11 6HB
Tel **(044 84) 2536**
Mem 260
Sec JB Asplin (044 84) 2021
Holes 9 L 4826 metres SSS 66
Recs Am–68 GB Wolstenholme AI Bremner, N Bremner, D Airey, G Park
Pro–66 F Robinson
V'trs U
Fees £5 (£7)

For map index see page 203.

Grange-over-Sands (1919)

Private
Meathop Road, Grange-over-Sands LA11 6QX
Tel (044 84) 3180
Mem 255 95(L) 25(J)
Sec JR Green (044 84) 2717
Holes 18 L 5660 yds SSS 68
Recs Am–64 S McMillan
Pro–67 G Cuthbert
V'trs U
Fees £7 (£10)
Loc Grange station ½ mile

Kendal (1891)

Private
The Heights, Kendal
Tel (0539) 24079
Mem 460
Sec EF Millar (0539) 20840
Pro J Brennand (0539) 23499
Holes 18 L 5550 yds SSS 67
Recs Am–63 J Brennand
Pro–63 P Tupling, GC Norton
V'trs U H SOC
Fees £6.50 (£9)

Keswick (1978)

Private
Threlkeld Hall, nr Keswick CA12 4HH
Tel (07687) 83324
Mem 410
Sec DS Cowan (07687) 72147
Holes 18 L 6175 yds SSS 72
Recs Am–71 BD Airey (1987)
Pro–69 I Clark (1984)
V'trs U SOC
Fees £8
Loc 4 miles E of Keswick A66

Kirkby Lonsdale

Private
Casterton Road, Kirkby Lonsdale
Mem 130 30(L) 20(J)
Sec P Jackson (0468) 72085
Holes 9 L 4058 yds SSS 60
V'trs U
Fees £3
Loc 1 mile on Sedbergh Road

Maryport (1905)

Private
Bankend, Maryport CA15 6PA
Tel (0900) 812605
Mem 260
Sec NH Cook (0900) 815652 (home)
(0900) 815661 (office)
Holes 18 L 6272 yds SSS 71
Recs Am–70 JA Scott
V'trs U
Fees £6 (£7) W–£20
Loc 1 mile N of Maryport off B5300

Penrith (1890)

Private
Salkeld Road, Penrith CA11 8SG
Tel (0768) 62217/65429
Mem 850
Sec Sqn Ldr I Troughton RAF (Retd) (0768) 62217
Pro CB Thomson (0768) 62217
Holes 18 L 6026 yds SSS 69
Recs Am–64 JM Nutter
Pro–65 K Bousefield
V'trs H WE/BH–10.06–11.30am & after 3pm
Fees £10 (£12)
Loc ½ mile E of Penrith
Mis No dogs on course or in clubhouse

St Bees (1931)

Private
Rhoda Grove, Rheda, Frizington CA26 3TE
Tel (0946) 82295
Mem 300
Sec JB Campbell (0946) 812105
Holes 9 L 5082 yds SSS 65
Recs Am–66 E Gulliksen
V'trs U
Fees £4 (£5)
Loc 4 miles S of Whitehaven

Seascale (1893)

Private
The Banks, Seascale CA20 1QL
Tel (094 67) 28202/28800
Mem 550
Sec C Taylor (094 67) 28662
Holes 18 L 6416 yds SSS 71
Recs Am–67 D Weston, ID Stavert, G Shuttleworth (1987)
Pro–68 EC Anderson
V'trs U SOC
Fees £10 (£12)
Loc 15 miles S of Whitehaven

Sedbergh (1896)

Private
The Riggs, Sedbergh
Mem 70
Sec AD Lord (0587) 20993
Holes 9 L 2067 yds SSS 61
Recs Am–64 S Gardner
V'trs U
Fees £2
Loc 1 mile S of Sedbergh at Millthorp

Silecroft (1903)

Private
Silecroft, Millom LA18 4AG
Tel (0657) 4250
Mem 370
Sec M O'N Wilson JP
(0657) 4160
Holes 9 L 5712 yds SSS 68
Recs Am–67 B Graham
V'trs WD–U WE–often restricted until 5pm BH–until 5.30pm
Fees £5 R/D
Loc 3 miles N of Millom through village towards shore

Silloth-on-Solway (1906)

Private
Silloth, nr Carlisle CA5 4AD
Tel (0965) 31179
Mem 600
Sec J Todd
Pro D Forsythe
Holes 18 L 6343 yds SSS 70
Recs Am–66 C Wallace
V'trs U H SOC
Fees D–£8 (D–£12) 5D–£30
Loc 22 miles W of Carlisle. Adjacent Silloth centre

Stoneyholme (1974)

Public
Carlisle
Tel (0228) 34856
Mem 290
Sec DJ Scott (0228) 38098
Pro S Fox
Holes 18
Recs Am–69
V'trs U
Fees £2.20
Loc 1 mile E of Carlisle

Ulverston (1894)

Private
Bardsea Park, Ulverston
Tel (0229) 52824
Mem 700
Sec DB Sharpe (0229) 53523
Pro MR Smith (0229) 52806
Holes 18 L 6092 yds SSS 69
Recs Am–67 D Weston
Pro–71 JA Raisbeck
V'trs U
Fees £10 (£12) 3D–£30

Windermere (1892)

Private
Cleabarrow, Windermere LA23 3NB
Tel (096 62) 3123
Mem 760
Sec KR Moffat
Pro WSM Rooke (096 62) 3550
Holes 18 L 5006 yds SSS 65
Recs Am–58 P Chapman (1988)
Pro–60 P Carman
V'trs U
Fees £12 (£14)
Loc 1½ miles E of Bowness

Workington (1922)

Private
Branthwaite Road, Workington
Tel (0900) 3460
Mem 475 125(L) 100(J)
Sec JK Walker (0900) 5420
Pro J Forsythe
Holes 18 L 6252 yds SSS 70
Recs Am–65 A Drabble
V'trs H SOC
Fees £8 (£10)
Loc 2 miles E of town

Derbyshire

Alfreton (1893)

Private
Oakerthorpe, Alfreton
Tel **(0773) 832070**
Mem 260
Sec D Tomlinson (0246) 862661
Pro JR Turnbull (0773) 832070
Holes 9 L 5074 yds SSS 65
Recs Am–64 N Cluskey
Pro–65 J Smith
V'trs WD exc Mon–U before 4.30pm–M after 4.30pm WE/Mon–M SOC
Fees £6.50 (£8)
Loc Alfreton

Allestree Park (1949)

Public
Allestree Hall, Allestree, Derby
Tel **(0332) 550616**
Mem 250
Sec PWJ Bye (0332) 512099
Pro RG Brown
Holes 18 L 5749 yds SSS 68
Recs Am–66 J McCann
V'trs U WE–booking req SOC
Fees £3 (£3.50)
Loc 2 miles N of Derby on A6

Ashbourne (1910)

Private
Clifton, Ashbourne
Tel **(0335) 42078**
Mem 350
Sec NPA James (0335) 42077
Holes 9 L 5388 yds SSS 66
V'trs U SOC
Fees £6 (£8)
Loc 2 miles W of Ashbourne on A515 Litchfield Road

Bakewell (1899)

Private
Station Road, Bakewell DE4 1GB
Tel **(062) 981 2307**
Mem 205 67(L) 40(J) 21(5)
Sec PS Newell
Pro TE Jones
Holes 9 L 5240 yds SSS 66
Recs Am–64 MH Piggott
V'trs U SOC
Fees £6 (£10)
Loc 1/2 mile NE of town centre and A6

Blue Circle (1985)

Private
Cement Works, Hope S30 2RP
Tel **(0433) 20317**
Mem 116
Sec DS Smith
Holes 9 L 5252 yds SSS 66
Recs Am–69 B Harper
V'trs NA
Loc Hope Valley

Breadsall Priory (1976)

Private
Moor Road, Morley, Derby DE7 6DL
Tel **(0332) 832235**
Mem 450
Sec A Busman (Gen Mgr)
Pro A Smith (0332) 834425
Holes 18 L 6402 yds SSS 71
Recs Am–70 A Thomas
Pro–66 M Glynn
V'trs WD–H WE–NA SOC
Fees D–£12
Loc A61 Breadsall, left into Croft Lane, left into Rectory Lane, right on to Moor Road
Mis Driving range

Buxton & High Peak (1887)

Private
Townend, Buxton
Tel **(0298) 3453**
Mem 600
Sec D Poole (0298) 6923
Pro RM Head (0298) 3112
Holes 18 L 5954 yds SSS 69
Recs Am–66 MP Higgins, D Moss
Pro–65 AJH Ellis
V'trs U
Fees £8 (£10)
Loc NE boundary of town on A6

Cavendish (1925)

Private
Gadley Lane, Buxton SK17 6XD
Tel **(0298) 3494**
Mem 650
Sec DN Doyle–Davidson (0298) 3256
Pro J Nolan (0298) 5052
Holes 18 L 5833 yds SSS 68
Recs Am–65 J Slack
Pro–63 I Buckley (1988)
V'trs U SOC–by prior arrangement with Pro
Fees £9 (£12)
Loc 3/4 mile W of Buxton Station

Chapel-en-le-Frith (1905)

Private
The Cockyard, Manchester Road, Chapel-en-le-Frith, Stockport SK12 6UH
Tel **(0298) 812118**
Mem 535
Sec JW Dranfield (0298) 813943
Pro DJ Cullen
Holes 18 L 6089 yds SSS 69
Recs Am–70 F Fletcher
Pro–66 H Hunt
V'trs U
Fees £8 (£12)
Loc Stockport 13 miles on A6 (B5470)

Chesterfield (1897)

Private
Walton, Chesterfield S42 7LA
Tel **(0246) 279256**
Mem 551
Sec CD Yates (0246) 566032
Pro M McLean (0246) 276297
Holes 18 L 6326 yds SSS 70
Recs Am–65 I Wyatt
Pro–66 K Nagle, B Hutchison
V'trs WD–U WE–M SOC
Fees £10
Loc 2 miles SW of Chesterfield

Chesterfield Municipal (1934)

Public
Murray House, Crow Lane, Chesterfield S41 0EQ
Tel **(0246) 73887**
Pro J Delany
Holes 18 L 6044 yds SSS 69
V'trs U
Fees £1.70 (£2.20)
Loc Chesterfield
Mis Tapton Park play here

Chevin (1894)

Private
Duffield, Derby
Tel **(0332) 841864**
Mem 500 66(L) 61(J) 8(5)
Sec F McCabe
Pro W Bird (0332) 841112
Holes 18 L 6057 yds SSS 69
Recs Am–65 C Radford (1987)
Pro–65 DJ Russell (1985)
V'trs WD–U WE–M SOC exc Sat
Fees £8 (£12)
Loc 5 miles N of Derby on A6

Derby (1923)

Public
Shakespeare Street, Sinfin, Derby DE2 9HD
Tel **(0332) 766323**
Mem 400
Sec P Davidson (0332) 764265
Pro RG Brown (0332) 766462
Holes 18 L 6183 yds SSS 69
Recs Am–65
V'trs U
Fees £1.80 (£2.80)

Erewash Valley (1905)

Private
Stanton-by-Dale, nr Ilkeston
Tel **(0602) 323258**
Mem 400
Sec D Knowles (0602) 322984
Pro MJ Ronan (0602) 324667
Holes 18 L 6487 yds SSS 71
Recs Am–69 DL Clarke
Pro–68 MJ Ronan
V'trs WE BH–NA before noon SOC–WD

Fees £12 (£14)
Loc Midway Nottingham and Derby. M1 Junction 25

Glossop & District (1894)

Private
Sheffield Road, Glossop
Tel **(045 74) 3117**
Mem 250
Sec J Dickson (045 74) 62713
Pro C Wadsworth
Holes 11 L 5716 yds SSS 68
Recs Am–66 DM Pike
Pro–68 S Sewgolum
V'trs U SOC
Fees £6 (£7)
Loc 1 mile E of town off A57

Hallowes (1892)

Private
Dronfield, Sheffield S18 6UA
Tel **(0246) 413149**
Mem 600
Sec EE Vessey (0246) 413734
Pro P Seal (0246) 411196
Holes 18 L 6342 yds SSS 71
Recs Am–67 JW Benson
Pro–67 R Ellis
V'trs WD–U WE/BH–M (phone first)
Fees £7 D–£10
Loc 6 miles S of Sheffield on A61 (not by-pass)

Ilkeston (1929)

Public
Peewit West End Drive, Ilkeston
Mem 90
Sec SJ Rossington (0602) 320304
Holes 9 L 4116 yds SSS 60
V'trs U
Fees On application
Loc Town centre $^1/_2$ mile

Kedleston Park (1947)

Private
Kedleston, Derby DE6 4JD
Tel **(0332) 840035**
Mem 900
Sec K Wilson
Pro J Hetherington (0332) 841685
Holes 18 L 6643 yds SSS 72
Recs Am–67 AF Simms
Pro–68 R Meek
V'trs U
Fees £12 (£15)
Loc 4 miles N of Derby

Matlock (1907)

Private
Chesterfield Road, Matlock DE4 5LF
Tel **(0629) 582191**
Mem 375 45(L) 50(J) 45(5)
Sec AJ Box
Pro M Deeley (0629) 584934
Holes 18 L 5989 yds SSS 69
V'trs WD–U WE–M SOC–WD
Fees £12.50 W–£50 M–£100
Loc $1^1/_2$ miles NE Matlock on A632

Mickleover (1923)

Private
Uttoxeter Road, Mickleover
Tel **(0332) 513339 (clubhouse)**
Mem 600
Sec D Rodgers (0332) 512092 (home)
Pro S Hadfield (0332) 518662
Holes 18 L 5708 yds SSS 68
Recs Am–64 CRJ Ibbotson
Pro–63 A Skingle
V'trs U SOC–Tues & Thurs
Fees £10 (£13)
Loc 3 miles W of Derby on A516/B5020

Ormonde Fields

Private
Nottingham Road, Codnor, Ripley
Tel **(0773) 42987**
Mem 460
Sec RN Walters (0773) 47301
Pro S Illingworth
Holes 18 L 5812 yds SSS 68
Recs Am–67 S Clarke, S Butt
Pro–67 C Jepson
V'trs U SOC
Fees £5 (£7)
Loc A610 Ripley to Nottingham Road. M1 Junction 26 5 miles

Pastures (1969)

Private
Pastures Hospital, Mickleover
Tel **(0332) 513921 (ext 348)**
Mem 320
Sec S McWilliams
Holes 9 L 5005 yds SSS 64
Recs Am–64 I Smith (1983), C Whyatt (1987)
V'trs M SOC–WD
Loc 4 miles W of Derby

Shirland (1977)

Private
Lower Delves, Shirland DE5 6AU
Tel **(0773) 832515**
Mem 360
Sec RT Yorke (0773) 604764
Pro NB Hallam (0773) 834935
Holes 18 L 5948 yds SSS 69
V'trs U SOC
Fees £5 (£6.50)
Loc 1 mile N of Alfreton, off A61 by Shirland Church

Sickleholme (1898)

Private
Bramford, Sheffield S30 2BH
Tel **(0433) 51306**
Mem 250 100(L) 72(J) 80(5)
Sec WT Scott
Pro PH Taylor
Holes 18 L 6064 yds SSS 69
Recs Am–63 IL Fletcher
Pro–65 AP Highfield
V'trs U exc Wed am
Fees £12.50 (£15)
Loc Between Hathersage and Hope (A625)

Stanedge (1934)

Private
Walton Hay Farm, nr Chesterfield
Tel **(0246) 566156**
Mem 260
Sec J Hine (0246) 234392
Holes 9 L 4867 yds SSS 64
Recs Am–64
Pro–65
V'trs WD–U before 2pm–M after 2pm Sat–M Sun–NA before 4pm–M after 4pm
Fees £7
Loc 5 miles SW of Chesterfield off B5057

Tapton Park (1934)

Public
Murray House, Crow Lane, Chesterfield S41 0EQ
Mem 450
Sec D Griffiths (0246) 475260
Holes Play over Chesterfield Municipal

Devon

Axe Cliff (1896)

Private
Squires Lane, Axmouth, Seaton EX12 2BJ
Tel **(0297) 20499**
Mem 380
Sec J Hankins (0297) 20219
Holes 18 L 5111 yds SSS 65
Recs Am–65 P Cricard
V'trs U H SOC
Fees £9
Loc Town centre $^3/_4$ mile nr Yacht Club

Bigbury (1923)

Private
Bigbury, Kingsbridge TQ7 4BB
Tel **(0548) 810207**
Mem 850
Sec BJ Perry (0548) 810557
Pro S Lloyd (0548) 810412
Holes 18 L 6076 yds SSS 69
Recs Am–65 CS Yeoman
Pro–67 S Lloyd
V'trs I H SOC
Fees £12
Loc Plymouth 15 miles

Chulmleigh (1976)

Private
Leigh Road, Chulmleigh EX18 7BL
Tel **(0769) 80519**
Mem 150
Sec PN Callow
Holes 18 L 1440 yds Par 3
Recs Am–53 S Hooper
Pro–54 D Sheppard
V'trs U
Fees £3 D–£4.50
Loc 1 mile N of A377 Exeter–Barnstaple road

Churston (1890)

Private

Churston, Brixham

Tel **(0803) 842218**

Mem 640

Sec DR Griffin (0803) 842751

Pro R Penfold (0803) 842894

Holes 18 L 6201 yds SSS 70

Recs Am–64 MWL Hampton
Pro–67 JM Green

V'trs U (recognised club members)
NA–Tues am

Fees On application

Loc Torquay $5^1/_4$ miles

Downes Crediton (1976)

Private

Hookway, Crediton EX17 3PE

Tel **(036 32) 3991**

Mem 650

Sec RE Langhorne (036 32) 3025

Pro H Finch (036 32) 4464

Holes 18 L 5858 yds SSS 68

V'trs U

Fees £10 (£12)

Loc Off A377 at entrance
to Crediton

East Devon (1902)

Private

**North View Road, Budleigh Salterton
EX9 6DQ**

Tel **(039 54) 2018**

Mem 850

Sec RSB Luckman (039 54) 3370

Pro T Underwood
(039 54) 5195

Holes 18 L 6214 yds SSS 70

Recs Am–68 P Newcombe
Pro–69 B Huggett

V'trs H SOC

Fees £12

Loc 12 miles SE of Exeter

Elfordleigh Hotel C & GC (1932)

Private

Elfordleigh, Plympton, Plymouth

Tel **(0752) 336428**

Mem 309

Sec A Dunstan (0752) 703824

Pro I Marshall (0752) 336428

Holes 9 L 5609 yds SSS 67

Recs Am–65 M Tunnicliff (1987)
Pro–66 M Ellis

V'trs WD–U WE–phone first

Fees £7 (£8)

Loc 4 miles E of Plymouth

Exeter G & CC (1895)

Private

Countess Wear, Exeter EX2 7AE

Tel **(039 287) 4139**

Mem 896

Sec C Greetham

Pro M Rowett (039 287) 5028

Holes 18 L 6061 yds SSS 69

Recs Am–63 G Milne (1988)
Pro–64 G Laing

V'trs WD–U WE–I SOC–Thurs only

Fees £12

Holsworthy (1937)

Private

Kilatree, Holsworthy

Tel **(0409) 253177**

Mem 350

Sec B Megson (0409) 253701
(home)

Holes 18 L 5935 yds SSS 68

Recs Am–66 A Ramsey
Pro–67 G Ryall, R Troake

V'trs WD–U Sun–after 12 noon

Fees £7 W–£28

Loc 1 mile W of town

Honiton (1896)

Private

Middlehills, Honiton EX14 8TR

Tel **(0404) 3633**

Mem 820

Sec KT Melton (0404) 44422

Pro J Mackie (0404) 2943

Holes 18 L 5931 yds SSS 68

Recs Am–70 R Bumpstead
Pro–65 I Read

V'trs U (recognised club member)
BH–NA SOC

Fees £11 (£14)

Loc 1 mile S of Honiton.
M5 Junction 25

Ilfracombe (1892)

Private

Hele Bay, Ilfracombe EX34 9RT

Tel **(0271) 62176**

Mem 510

Sec MC Duffin

Pro D Hoare (0271) 63328

Holes 18 L 5857 yds SSS 68

Recs Am–67 RC Beer

V'trs H SOC WD–NA 12–2pm
WE/BH–after 10am–NA
12–2pm

Fees £10 5D–£35

Loc Between Ilfracombe and
Combe Martin

Manor House Hotel (1929)

Private

Moretonhampstead

Tel **(0647) 40355**

Mem 250

Sec R Lewis

Pro R Lewis

Holes 18 L 6016 yds SSS 69
Pro–65 R Emerson

V'trs U SOC

Fees £12 (£15)

Loc 15 miles SW of Exeter

Newton Abbot (Stover) (1930)

Private

Newton Abbot TQ12 6QQ

Tel **(0626) 52460**

Mem 861

Sec R Smith

Pro M Craig (0626) 62078

Holes 18 L 5834 yds SSS 68

Recs Am–65 RH Knott,
JP Langmead
Pro–67 Brian Barnes

V'trs H SOC–Thurs

Fees £13 R/D 1988 prices

Loc 3 miles N of Newton Abbot
on A382

Okehampton (1913)

Private

Okehampton EX20 1EF

Tel **(0837) 2113**

Mem 400

Sec To be appointed

Pro P Blundell (0837) 3541

Holes 18 L 5300 yds SSS 67

Recs Am–67 MS Moore
Pro–H Finch

V'trs U SOC

Fees On application

Loc S boundary of Okehampton,
signposted from traffic lights

Royal North Devon (1864)

Private

**Golf Links Road, Westward Ho!
EX39 1HD**

Tel **(023 72) 73824**

Mem 900

Sec EJ Davies (023 72) 73817

Pro G Johnston (023 72) 77598

Holes 18 L 6644 yds SSS 72

Recs Am–66 D Boughey
Pro–66 P Dawson,
KDG Nagle, MF Foster

V'trs On request

Fees £10 D–£12

Loc Bideford 2 miles

Saunton (1897)

Private

Saunton, nr Braunton

Tel **(0271) 812436**

Mem 1030

Sec WE Geddes

Pro JA McGhee (0271) 812013

Holes East 18 L 6703 yds SSS 73
West 18 L 6322 yds SSS 71

Recs East Am–69 J Langmead
Pro–70 D Talbot
West Am–67 ME Jewell
Pro–69 P Berry

V'trs U H

Fees £13 (£15) W–£65

Loc 7 miles W of Barnstaple

Sidmouth (1889)

Private

**Cotmaton Road, Sidmouth
EX10 8SX**

Tel **(0395) 513023**

Mem 700

Sec DE Matthews (0395) 513451

Pro M Kemp (0395) 516407

Holes 18 L 5188 yds SSS 65

Recs Am–59 N Winchester
Pro–64 E Murray

V'trs U SOC

Fees D–£10 (£12) W–£40

Loc $^1/_2$ mile W of town centre.
12 miles SE of M5 Junction 30

For map index see page 203.

Staddon Heights (1895)

Private
Plymstock, Plymouth PL9 9SP
Tel (0752) 402475
Mem 620
Sec MG Holliday
Pro M Grieve (0752) 492630
Holes 18 L 5861 yds SSS 68
Recs Am–64 R Clark, D Roberts
Pro–62 GC Smale
V'trs WE–H SOC–WD
Fees £8 D–£10 (£10 D–£12)
5D–£30 Summer £25 Winter
Loc SE Plymouth

Tavistock (1891)

Private
Down Road, Tavistock PL19 9AQ
Tel (0822) 612049
Mem 650
Sec BG Steer (0822) 612344
Pro R Hall (0822) 612316
Holes 18 L 6250 yds SSS 70
Recs Am–66 MG Symons
Pro–69 S Chadwick,
N Bicknell
V'trs U SOC–WD
Fees £8 (£10)
Loc Whitchurch Down

Teignmouth (1924)

Private
Teignmouth TQ14 9NY
Tel (062 67) 3614
Mem 900
Sec D Holloway (062 67) 4194
Pro P Ward (062 67) 2894
Holes 18 L 6142 yds SSS 69
Recs Am–65 JH Laidler (1980)
Pro–66 P Millhouse (1987)
V'trs H (recognised club member)
SOC–WD WE–M before 4pm
Fees £12 (£15)
Loc 2 miles N of Teignmouth on
B3192

Thurlestone (1897)

Private
Thurlestone, nr Kingsbridge
Tel (0548) 560405/560221
Mem 700
Sec R Marston (0548) 560405
Pro N Whitley (0548) 560715
Holes 18 L 6337 yds SSS 70
Recs Am–66 RP Knott
Pro–67 PJ Yeo
V'trs I or H
Fees £12 W–£53 1988 prices
Loc Kingsbridge 5 miles

Tiverton (1932)

Private
Post Hill, Tiverton EX16 4NE
Tel (0884) 252114 (Clubhouse)
Mem 475 130(L) 55(J) 250(5)
Sec Maj DLJ Hicks (0884) 252187
Pro RE Freeman (0884) 254836
Holes 18 L 6263 yds SSS 71
Recs Am–65 SC Waddington
Pro–70 A Moore
V'trs I H
Fees On application
Loc 5 miles W of M5 Junction 27.
1½ miles E of Tiverton on
B3391

Torquay (1910)

Private
Petitor Road, St Marychurch, Torquay
TQ1 4QF
Tel (0803) 314591
Mem 800
Sec BG Long
Pro M Ruth (0803) 39113
Holes 18 L 6192 yds SSS 69
Recs Am–62 AR Copping
Pro–66 D Short
V'trs H SOC
Fees £12 (£15)
Loc Torquay

Torrington (1932)

Public
Weare Trees, Torrington
EX38 7EZ
Tel (023 72) 22229
Mem 423
Sec GSC Green ((023 72) 72792
Holes 9 L 4418 yds SSS 62
Recs Am–65 P Wheeler
V'trs U Sun am–NA
Fees £6 5D(Mon–Fri)–£20
Loc Torrington 1 mile on
Weare Gifford Road

Warren (1892)

Private
Dawlish
Tel (0626) 862255
Mem 550
Sec TE Allen
Pro G Wicks (0626) 864002
Holes 18 L 5968 yds SSS 69
Recs Am–65 J Langmead (1987)
V'trs U
Fees £10 (£12) W–£45
Loc 1½ miles E of Dawlish

Wrangaton (South Devon) (1895)

Private
Wrangaton, South Brent TQ10 9HJ
Tel (036 47) 3229
Mem 350
Sec RR Hine
Holes 9 L 5790 yds SSS 68
Recs Am–66 SR Bryant
Pro–67 FG Robins
V'trs U exc Wed pm and Sun
(Mar–Oct)
Fees £8
Loc Dartmoor, 10 miles SW of
Ashburton

Yelverton (1904)

Private
Golf Links Road, Yelverton
PL20 6BN
Tel (0822) 853618
Mem 700
Sec Maj (Retd) DR Bettany
(0822) 852824
Pro A MacDonald (0822) 853593
Holes 18 L 6288 yds SSS 70
Recs Am–67 P Newcombe (1987)
V'trs H SOC
Fees £10 (£12) W–£25
Loc 6 miles N of Plymouth on
A386

Dorset

Ashley Wood (1983)

Private
Tarrant Rawston, Blandford Forum
DT11 9HN
Tel (0258) 52253
Mem 500
Sec E Butterworth (0258) 53267
Pro S Taylor
Holes 9 L 6227 yds SSS 70
Recs Am–68 D Thorn, S Ricketts
Pro–67 S Taylor (1988)
V'trs WD–U WE–phone first
Fees £7.50 (£12)
Loc 1½ miles SW of Blandford

Boscombe (1938)

Public
Queen's Park, Bournemouth
Mem 337
Sec TI Williams (0202) 874843
Holes Play over Queen's Park
course

Boscombe Ladies (1953)

Private
Queen's Park Pavilion, Queen's
Park,
West Drive, Bournemouth
Tel (0202) 36198
Mem 90
Sec Mrs DM Read (0202) 34170
Holes Play over Queen's Park
course

Bournemouth & Meyrick Park (1890)

Private
Meyrick Park, Bournemouth
BH2 6LH
Tel (0202) 20307
Mem 590
Sec R Easton
Holes Play over Meyrick Park
course

Bridport & West Dorset (1891)

Private
East Cliff, West Bay, Bridport DT6 4EP
Tel **(0308) 22597**
Mem 600
Sec PJ Ridler
Pro JE Parish (0308) 421095
Holes 18 L 5246 yds SSS 66
Recs Am–63 M Rees
Pro–66 Bishop R Crockford
V'trs U
Fees £10 (£12)
Loc 1½ miles S of Bridport

Broadstone (1898)

Private
Wentworth Drive, Station Approach, Broadstone BH18 8DQ
Tel **(0202) 693363**
Mem 750
Sec JM Cowan (0202) 692595
Pro N Tokely (0202) 692835
Holes 18 L 6129 yds SSS 70
Recs Am–65 JH Nash (1988)
Pro–64 S Hamill (1988)
V'trs WD–H after 9.30am
WE/BH–after 10am(Summer)
NA(Winter) SOC–WD
Fees £16 D–£19 (£18 D–£22)
Loc 4 miles N of Poole

Came Down (1905)

Private
Came Down, Dorchester DT2 8NR
Tel **(030 581) 2531**
Mem 700
Sec D Stuckes (Mgr) (030 581) 3494
Pro R Preston (030 581) 2670
Holes 18 L 6224 yds SSS 71
Recs Am–69
V'trs H Sun am–NA SOC
Fees £11 (£14) W–£38
Loc 2 miles S of Dorchester

Christchurch (1977)

Public
Iford Bridge, Barrack Road, Christchurch
Tel **(0202) 473817**
Mem 350
Sec BG Dodd (0202) 872818
Pro P Troth
Holes 9 L 4824 yds SSS 64
Recs Am–65 D Pearcey
V'trs U
Fees £3.20 (£3.70)
Loc Boundary of Bournemouth on Christchurch Road
Mis Golf range £1.15 (50 balls)

Ferndown (1923)

Private
119 Golf Links Road, Ferndown BH22 8BU
Tel **(0202) 872022**
Mem 700
Sec MR Lovett (0202) 874602
Pro DN Sewell (0202) 873825
Holes 18 L 6442 yds SSS 71
9 L 5604 yds SSS 68
Recs Old Am–66 JHA Leggett
Pro–68 DN Sewell
New Am–67 G Howell
Pro–68 DN Sewell
V'trs WD/WE–I H (after 9.30am)
SOC–WD
Fees Old £20 (£25) New £10 (£15)
Loc 6 miles N of Bournemouth

Highcliffe Castle (1913)

Private
107 Lymington Road, Christchurch BH23 4LA
Tel **(042 52) 72953**
Mem 350 100(L) 50(J)
Sec DW Blakeman (042 52) 72210
Pro R Crockford (042 52) 6640
Holes 18 L 4655 yds SSS 63
Recs Am–58 S Jenkins
Pro–60 D Sewell
V'trs I
Fees £8.50 (£10.50)
Loc Bournemouth 8 miles

Isle of Purbeck (1892)

Private
Studland BH19 3AB
Tel **(092 944) 361**
(Members) (092 944) 210
Mem 600
Sec J Robinson
Pro P Sowerby (092 944) 354
Holes 18 L 6283 yds SSS 71
9 L 2022 yds SSS 30
Recs Am–67 N Holman
Pro–72 K Sparkes
V'trs U H SOC
Fees Purbeck £16 (£18)
Dene £8
Loc Swanage 2 miles

Knighton Heath (1976)

Private
Francis Avenue, West Howe, Bournemouth BH11 8NX
Tel **(0202) 572633**
Mem 700
Sec R Bestwick
Pro M Torrens (0202) 578275
Holes 18 L 6206 yds SSS 70
Recs Am–65 P Holbert (1988)
Pro–65 M Thomas (1988)
V'trs WD–H after 9.30am
WE–H after 10.30am
Fees On request
Loc 3 miles N of Poole nr junction of A348/A3049

Lakey Hill (1978)

Private
Hyde, nr Wareham BH20 7NT
Tel **(0929) 471776/471941**
Mem 750
Sec JI Mullins
Pro G Packer (0929) 471574
Holes 18 L 6146 yds SSS 69
V'trs WD–U WE–M SOC–WD
Fees £9 (£12)
Loc Worgret Heath, Wareham

Lyme Regis (1894)

Private
Timber Hill, Lyme Regis
Tel **(029 74) 2963**
(029 74) 2043 (steward)
Mem 650
Sec RG Fry
Pro A Black (029 74) 3822
Holes 18 L 6262 yds SSS 70
Recs Am–64 L Thompson (1988)
Pro–66 MD Dack (1987)
V'trs H WD–U after 9.15am (1pm Thurs) Sun–U after 12 noon SOC
Fees £15 (£16)
Loc Between Lyme Regis and Charmouth off A3502/A35

Meyrick Park (1894)

Public
Bournemouth BH2 6LH
Tel **(0202) 290871**
Mem 335
Sec K Holmes (0202) 577375
Pro N Jordan (0202) 290862
Holes 18 L 5878 yds SSS 69
Recs Am–66 GG Burton
V'trs U
Fees £6
Mis Bournemouth Club plays here. Closed Sun pm

Parkstone (1910)

Private
Links Road, Parkstone, Poole BH14 9JU
Tel **(0202) 708025**
Mem 500 160(L) 50(J)
Sec DFC Thomas (0202) 707138
Pro N Blenkarne (0202) 708092
Holes 18 L 6250 yds SSS 70
Recs Am–65 RA Latham
Pro–63 P Alliss
V'trs H WD–NA before 9.30am and 12.30–2.10pm WE–NA before 9.45am and 12.30–2.30pm
Fees £16 D–£18 (£20 D–£21)
Loc 3 miles W of Bournemouth off A35

Queen's Park (1905)

Public
Queen's Park, South Drive, Bournemouth
Tel **(0202) 36198**
Mem 900
Sec JG Sharkey (0202) 36817
Holes 18 L 6505 yds SSS 72
Recs Am–69 M Butcher
Pro–66 A Caygill, H Boyle
V'trs U SOC
Fees Oct–Apr £6 May–Sept £7
Loc 2 miles NE Bournemouth
Mis Closed Sun pm. Boscombe club plays here

Sherborne (1895)

Private
Clatcombe, Sherborne DT9 4RN
Tel **(0935) 812475**
Sec A Mouncer (0935) 814431
Pro A Pakes (0935) 812274
Holes 18 L 5949 yds SSS 68
Recs Am–66 S Edgeley (1987)
Pro–63 M Thomas
V'trs H
Fees £12 (£15)
Loc 1 mile N of town

Wareham (1922)

Private
Sandford Road, Wareham BH20 4DH
Tel **(092 95) 54147**
Mem 300
Sec T Kelly
Pro A Frampton
Holes 12 L 5294 yds SSS 66
Recs Am–64 CA Whitcombe
V'trs WD–U WE–M SOC
Fees £8
Loc On A351

Weymouth (1909)

Private
Weymouth DT4 0PF
Tel **(0305) 784994**
Mem 650
Sec E Dickinson (0305) 773981
Pro D Lochrie (0305) 773997
Holes 18 L 5980 metres SSS 69
Recs Am–68 L Peters
Pro–65 D Bennett
V'trs WD/WE–H SOC
Fees £10 (£13)
Loc A354–last exit on Manor roundabout

Durham

Aycliffe (1977)

Public
School Lane, Newton Aycliffe
Tel **(0325) 314334**
Mem 65
Sec WJ Findley (0325) 318390
Pro R Lister (0325) 310820
Holes 9 L 6054 yds SSS 69
V'trs U
Fees £2 (£3.50)
Loc Sports complex on A6072 from A68. Station and town $1^{1}/_{2}$ miles
Mis Floodlit driving range

Barnard Castle (1898)

Private
Harmire Road, Barnard Castle
Tel **(0833) 37237**
Mem 600
Sec AW Lavender (0833) 38355
Pro J Harrison (0833) 31980
Holes 18 L 5838 yds SSS 68
Recs Am–65 M Porter (1984)
Pro–64 C Hamilton (1983)
V'trs U SOC
Fees £7 (£10) 5D–£20
Loc N boundary of Barnard Castle

Beamish Park (1950)

Private
Beamish, Stanley DH9 0RH
Tel **(091) 370 1133**
Mem 520
Sec A Curtis (091) 370 1382
Pro C Cole (091) 370 1984
Holes 18 L 6205 yds SSS 70
Recs Am–67 A Stewart
V'trs WD/Sat–U before 4pm
Sun–NA SOC
Fees £7 (£9)
Loc Beamish, nr Stanley

Bishop Auckland (1893)

Private
High Plains, Bishop Auckland
Tel **(0388) 602198**
Mem 680
Sec H Taylorson (0388) 663648
Pro W Laird (0388) 661618
Holes 18 L 6420 yds SSS 71
Recs Am–67 RL Aisbitt
Pro–65 BL Hunt
V'trs H (closed Good Friday and Christmas Day)
Fees £8 (£10)
Loc $^{1}/_{2}$ mile NE of Bishop Auckland

Blackwell Grange (1930)

Private
Briar Close, Blackwell, Darlington DL3 8QX
Tel **(0325) 464464**
Mem 650
Sec F Hewitson (Hon)
(0325) 465265
Pro R Givens (0325) 462088
Holes 18 L 5609 yds SSS 67
Recs Am–64 HP Jolly, S Santon, MW Rogers
Pro–63 M Gregson
V'trs U exc Wed 11am–2.30pm–NA Sat–booking only Sun–comps in progress SOC
Fees £9 (£11)
Loc 1 mile S of Darlington on A66

Brancepeth Castle (1924)

Private
Brancepeth Village, Durham DH7 8EA
Tel **(091) 378 0075**
Mem 760 108(L) 81(J) 105(5)
Sec DC Carver
Pro D Howdon (091) 378 0183
Holes 18 L 6415 yds SSS 71
Recs Am–67 D Curry, P Page
V'trs WD–U WE–NA SOC
Fees £12 (£16)
Loc $4^{1}/_{2}$ miles W of Durham City on A690

Chester-Le-Street (1909)

Private
Lumley Park, Chester-Le-Street DH3 4NS
Tel **(091) 388 3218**
Mem 400 130(L) 90(J)
Sec WB Dodds
Pro MA Strong (091) 389 0157
Holes 18 L 6054 yds SSS 69
Recs Am–68 SJ Watson
V'trs WD–U WE–NA before 10.30am or 12–2pm or by arrangement
Fees £8 (£10)
Loc $^{1}/_{4}$ mile E of Chester-Le-Street

Consett & District (1911)

Private
Elmfield Road, Consett DH8 5NN
Tel **(0207) 502186**
Mem 650
Sec JJ Horrill (0207) 562261
Pro T Jenkins (0207) 580210
Holes 18 L 6001 yds SSS 69
Recs Am–65 H Ashby
V'trs WD–U SOC–exc Sat
Fees £7 (£10)
Loc 12 miles NW of Durham on A691. Gateshead 12 miles on A692

Crook (1919)

Private
Low Job's Hill, Crook
Tel **(0388) 762429**
Mem 450
Sec R King (0388) 746400 (home)
Holes 18 L 6075 yds SSS 69
Recs Am–66 N Tweddle
V'trs U SOC
Fees £6 (£7)
Loc $^{1}/_{2}$ mile E of Crook (A690)

Darlington (1908)

Private
Haughton Grange, Darlington DL1 3JD
Tel **(0325) 463936**
Mem 410 87(L) 110(J) 70(5)
Sec J Welsh (0325) 355324
Pro I Todd (0325) 462955
Holes 18 L 6272 yds SSS 70
Recs Am–64 H Teschner
Pro–67 M Gallacher
V'trs U 9.30–12 & 1.30–5pm SOC
Fees £10 (£12)
Loc Off Salters Lane, NE of Darlington

Dinsdale Spa (1910)

Private
Middleton St George, Darlington DL2 1DW
Tel **(0325) 332222**
Mem 826
Sec N Sharp (0325) 332297
Pro D Dodds (0325) 332515
Holes 18 L 6078 yds SSS 69
Recs Am–64 PF Ward (1984)
Pro–69 DM Edwards (1980)

V'trs WD–U WE–M BH–M SOC
Fees £8 D–£9.50
Loc 5 miles SE of Darlington

Durham City (1887)

Private
Littleburn, Langley Moor DH7 8HL
Tel **(091) 378 0069**
Mem 750
Sec JT Ross
Pro S Corbally (091) 378 0029
Holes 18 L 6211 yds SSS 69
Recs Am–66 A Ramshaw, K Cheseldine
V'trs WD–U NA–WE SOC
Fees £8 (£12)
Loc 1½ miles W of Durham

Hobson Municipal (1978)

Public
Hobson, nr Burnopfield, Newcastle-upon-Tyne
Tel **(0207) 70941**
Mem 500
Sec G Allan (0207) 236980
Pro J Ord (0207) 71605
Holes 18 L 6502 yds SSS 71
Recs Am–69 D Dunn (1987)
V'trs U SOC
Fees D–£4.25 (D–£5.50)
Loc Between Gateshead and Consett on A692

Mount Oswald

Private
South Road, Durham City DH1 3TQ
Tel **(0385) 67527**
Mem 106
Sec G Clark
Holes 18 L 6009 yds SSS 69
Recs Am–64 J Mee (1986)
Pro–66 J Mathews (1984)
V'trs U SOC
Fees £5 D–£7 (£6 D–£9)
Loc SW of Durham on South Road (A1050)

Roseberry Grange

Public
Grange Villa, Chester-Le-Street DH2 3NF
Tel **(091) 370 0670**
Mem 350
Sec R Handy (0207) 233022
Pro A Hartley (091) 370 0660
Holes 18 L 5628 yds SSS 68
Recs Am–67 M Ridley (1988)
Pro–65 B Rumney (1988)
V'trs U SOC
Fees £4 (£5)
Loc 3 miles W of Chester-Le-Street on A693

Seaham (1911)

Private
Dawdon, Seaham SR7 7RD
Tel **(091) 581 2354**
Mem 550
Sec GE Gustord (091) 526 4044
Holes 18 L 5972 yds SSS 69
Recs Am–64 J Sanderson Jr (1984)
V'trs U SOC
Fees £8 (£12)
Loc Dawdon

South Moor (1925)

Private
The Middles, Craghead, Stanley DH9 6AG
Tel **(0207) 232848**
Mem 518
Sec R Harrison (091) 370 0515
Holes 18 L 6445 yds SSS 71
Recs Am–67 JE Handy
Pro–65 A Webster
V'trs U
Fees On application
Loc 8 miles NW of Durham

Stressholme (1976)

Public
Snipe Lane, Darlington
Tel **(0325) 53073**
Mem 550
Sec DP Fawcett (0325) 483383
Pro FC Thorpe (0325) 461002
Holes 18 L 6511 yds SSS 71
Recs Am–69 S Aitken
Pro–64 N Coles
V'trs U
Fees £5 (£6)
Loc 2 miles S of Darlington on A167

Woodham G & CC (1983)

Private
Burnhill Way, Newton Aycliffe DH5 4PM
Tel **(0325) 320574**
Mem 250
Sec GE Golightly
Pro J Graham
Holes 18 L 6727 yds SSS 72
Recs Am–74 S Raby
V'trs U SOC
Fees £6 (£7)
Loc 1 mile N of Newton Aycliffe
Mis Starting times WE/BH

Essex

Abridge G & CC (1964)

Private
Epping Lane, Stapleford Tawney RM4 1ST
Tel **(04028) 388**
Mem 560
Sec PG Pelling (04028) 396/7
Pro Bernard Cooke (04028) 333
Holes 18 L 6703 yds SSS 72
Recs Am–68 NK Burch
Pro–68 David Feherty
V'trs WD–H WE/BH–NA
Fees £17
Loc Theydon Bois or Epping Station 3 miles
Mis No catering Fri

Ballards Gore (1980)

Private
Gore Road, Canewdon, Rochford
Tel **(037 06) 8917**
Mem 500+
Sec NG Patient
Pro M Pierce (037 06) 8924
Holes 18 L 7062 yds SSS 74
V'trs WD–U WE–M after 12.30pm (summer) 11.30am (winter) SOC
Fees WD–£12
Loc 1½ miles NE of Rochford

Basildon (1967)

Public
Kingswood, Basildon
Tel **(0268) 3297**
Mem 200 30(L) 20(J)
Sec AM Burch (0268) 3849
Pro W Paterson (0268) 3532
Holes 18 L 6120 yds SSS 69
Recs Am–67 R Reeve
Pro–63 W Longmuir
V'trs U SOC
Fees £5.25 (£10)
Loc 1 mile S of Basildon off Kingswood roundabout

Belfairs (1926)

Public
Eastwood Road North, Leigh-on-Sea SS9 4LR
Tel **(0702) 526911**
Mem 300
Sec BJ Orr
Pro R Foreman (0702) 520202
Holes 18 L 5871 yds SSS 68
V'trs WD–U exc Thurs am WE/BH–booking req
Fees £6 (£9)
Mis Southend GC and Belfairs GC play here

Belhus Park Municipal (1972)

Public
Belhus Park, South Ockendon RM15 4QR
Tel **(0708) 854260**
Sec L Bourne (Mgr) (0708) 852248
Pro S Wimbleton
Holes 18 L 5450 yds SSS 66
Recs Am–67 M Jennings, J Bearman
Pro–63 R Joyce
V'trs U
Fees £3.95 (£6)
Loc 1 mile N of A13/M25 Dartford Tunnel
Mis Floodlit driving range. Thurrock Belhus Park GC plays here

Bentley G & CC (1972)

Private
Ongar Road, Brentwood CM15 9SS
Tel **(0277) 73179**
Mem 525
Sec JA Vivers
Pro K Bridges (0277) 72933

Holes 18 L 6709 yds SSS 72
Recs Am–71 J Moody (1987), L Balkwell (1988) Pro–69 S Cipa (1988), B Smith (1988)
V'trs WD–U WE–M after noon BH–after 11am SOC–WD
Fees £10 D–£14
Loc 18 miles E of London. M25 Junction 28 3 miles

Birch Grove (1970)

Private
Layer Road, Colchester, Essex CO2 0HS
Tel (0206) 34276
Mem 250
Sec Mrs M Marston
Holes 9 L 4150 yds SSS 62
Recs Am–63 A Green (1988) Pro–56
V'trs WD/BH–U WE–Sun after 1pm SOC
Fees £6 (£7)
Loc 3 miles S of Colchester on B1026

Boyce Hill (1921)

Private
Vicarage Hill, Benfleet SS7 1PD
Tel (0268) 793625
Mem 600
Sec JE Atkins
Pro G Burroughs (0268) 752565
Holes 18 L 5882 yds SSS 68
Recs Am–65 RCD Gilbert Pro–61 G Burroughs
V'trs WD–UH WE/BH–MH SOC–Thurs only
Fees £15 R/D
Loc 4 miles N of Southend

Braintree (1891)

Private
Kings Lane, Stisted, Braintree CM7 8DA
Tel (0376) 24117
Mem 600
Sec HW Hardy (0376) 46079
Pro T Parcell (0376) 43465
Holes 18 L 6026 yds SSS 69
Recs Am–65 M Hawes, M Davis
V'trs WD–U WE/BH–H SOC
Fees £12 (£15)
Loc 1 mile W of Braintree off A120 towards Stisted

Bunsay Downs (1982)

Public
Little Baddow Road, Woodham Walter, nr Maldon CM9 6RW
Tel (024 541) 2648/2369
Sec RP Gorham (Mgr) (024 541) 2648
Holes 9 L 2913 yds SSS 68
V'trs WD–U WE/BH teeing–off times may be pre–booked up to 7 days in advance
Fees 18 holes £5 (£5.50) 9 holes £4 (£4.50)
Loc 7 miles E of Chelmsford off A414
Mis Indoor driving range

Burnham-on-Crouch (1923)

Private
Creeksea, Burnham-on-Crouch
Tel (0621) 782282
Mem 450
Sec DG Morrison
Holes 9 L 5866 yds SSS 68
Recs Am–66 D Clarke Pro–64 FJ Winser
V'trs WD–U WE–NA before noon
Fees £7 (£10)
Loc 1½ miles W of town

Canons Brook (1962)

Private
Elizabeth Way, Harlow CM19 5BE
Tel (0279) 21482
Mem 650
Sec GE Chambers
Pro R Yates (0279) 418357
Holes 18 L 6745 yds SSS 73
Recs Am–68 H Cornick Pro–65 G Burroughs
V'trs WD–U WE/BH–NA
Fees £13 R/D
Loc 25 miles N of London

Channels (1983)

Private
Belsteads Farm Lane, Little Waltham, Chelmsford
Tel (0245) 440005
Mem 650
Sec SM Everitt
Pro IB Sinclair (0245) 441056
Holes 18 L 6033 yds SSS 69
V'trs WD SOC–WD
Fees £8.75
Loc 3 miles N of Chelmsford
Mis Pitch and putt course

Chelmsford (1893)

Private
Widford, Chelmsford
Tel (0245) 250555
Mem 650
Sec Wg Cdr BA Templeman–Rooke (0245) 256483
Pro GD Bailey (0245) 257079
Holes 18 L 5912 yds SSS 68
Recs Am–67 G Turner Pro–65 C Platts
V'trs WD–I WE/BH–M
Fees On application
Loc Off A12 at Widford roundabout

Chigwell (1925)

Private
High Road, Chigwell IG7 5BH
Tel (01) 500 2059
Mem 650
Sec G Kitson
Pro C Baker (01) 500 2384
Holes 18 L 6279 yds SSS 70
Recs Am–66 AM Ronald Pro–66 H Flatman
V'trs WD–I WE/BH–M
Fees £12 D–£16
Loc 13½ miles NE of London (A113)

Chingford (1923)

Public
158 Station Road, Chingford, London E4
Tel (01) 529 2107
Mem 350
Sec F Singleton (01) 527 6548
Pro LH and R Gowers (01) 529 5708
Holes 18 L 6136 yds SS 70
Recs Am–65 P Barnes Pro–65 R Gowers
V'trs U
Mis Red coats must be worn

Clacton (1892)

Private
West Road, Clacton-on-Sea CO15 1AJ
Tel (0255) 424331
Mem 475
Sec IM Simpson (0255) 421919
Pro SJ Levermore (0255) 426304
Holes 18 L 6243 yds SSS 70
Recs Am–67 A Hull Pro–65 S Bryan
V'trs WE/BH–1st tee not before 11am, 10th tee not before 12.30pm SOC
Fees £10 (£15)
Loc In town boundary on sea front

Colchester (1909)

Private
Braiswick, Colchester CO4 5AU
Tel (0206) 852946
Mem 330 90(L) 70(J) 160(5)
Sec PB Stokes (0206) 853396
Pro P Hodgson (0206) 853920
Holes 18 L 6319 yds SS 70
Recs Am–63 B Booth Pro–68 A Parcell
V'trs WD–H WE/BH–NA SOC
Fees £10 D–£16
Loc ¾ mile NW of Colchester North Station on road to West Bergholt

Fairlop Waters (1987)

Public
Forest Road, Barkingside, Ilford IG6 3JA
Tel (01) 500 9911
Mem 800
Sec J Topping
Pro A Bowers (01) 501 1881
Holes 18 L 6288 yds SSS 72
V'trs U
Fees £3.50 (£5.50)
Loc 2 miles from S end of M11, by Fairlop underground station
Mis Driving range. 9 hole Par 3

Forrester Park (1975)

Private
Beckingham Road, Great Totham, Maldon
Tel **(0621) 891406**
Mem 400
Sec T Forrester-Muir
Holes 9 L 2675 yds SSS 66
V'trs WD-U WE-NA before noon SOC-WD
Fees £6 (£8)
Loc Maldon 3 miles on Tiptree Road

Frinton (1896)

Private
1 The Esplanade, Frinton-on-Sea CO13 9EP
Tel **(0255) 671618**
Mem 700
Sec ATH Turtill
Pro P Taggart (0255) 674618
Holes 18 L 6259 yds SSS 70
9 L 2508 yds SSS 33
Recs Am-67 IA Quick
Pro-66 CS Denny
V'trs H WE/BH-NA before 11.30am SOC
Fees £12 D-£15 9 holes-£5
Loc 18 miles E of Colchester

Hainault Forest (1912)

Public
Chigwell Row, Hainault Forest
Tel **(01) 500 2097**
Mem 500 60(L) 50(J)
Sec E Bayley (01) 590 0804
Pro AE Frost (01) 500 2131
Holes No 1 18 L 5754 yds SSS 67
No 2 18 L 6445 yds SSS 71
Recs No 1 Am-65 TG Patmore
Pro-65 A Frost
No 2 Am-66 K Saunders
Pro-68 AE Frost Jr
V'trs U
Fees £3.50 (£5)
Loc Hog Hill, Redbridge

Hartswood (1967)

Public
King George's Playing Fields, Brentwood
Tel **(0277) 218714**
Sec J Thompson (0227) 218850
Pro J Stanion
Holes 18 L 6238 yds SSS 70
Recs Am-70 A Cornell
Pro-70 W Longmuir
V'trs U SOC
Fees £3.40 (£5)
Loc Brentwood
Mis Hartswood Club plays here

Harwich & Dovercourt (1906)

Private
Parkeston Road, Harwich
Tel **(0255) 3616**
Mem 350
Sec BQ Dunham
Holes 9 L 2931 yds SSS 68
V'trs WD-U SOC
Fees On application
Loc A120 to roundabout to Parkeston Quay, course entrance 20 yds on left

Havering

Public
Risebridge Chase, Lower Bedfords Road, Romford
Tel **(0708) 22942**
Sec P Jennings (0708) 41429
Pro P Jennings (0708) 41429
Holes 18 L 6252 yds SSS 70;
9 hole Par 3
V'trs WD-U WE-at certain times
Fees £2.95 (£4.50)
Loc 2 miles from Brentwood Junction of M25, off A12
Mis Risebridge Club plays here

Ilford (1907)

Private
Wanstead Park Road, Ilford
Tel **(01) 554 5174**
Mem 579
Sec DGJ Hoare (01) 554 2930
Pro K Ashdown (01) 554 0094
Holes 18 L 5710 yds SSS 68
Recs Am-63 M Pinner
Pro-64 B Huggett, A Campbell
V'trs U
Fees £6 (£9)

Maldon (1891)

Private
Beeleigh Langford, Maldon CM9 7SS
Tel **(0621) 53212**
Mem 460
Sec JC Rigby
Holes 9 L 6197 yds SSS 69
Recs Am-71 R Byford
Pro-67 S Levermore
V'trs WD-U WE-M SOC
Fees £7 D-£9 (£8 D-£10)
Loc 3 miles NW of Maldon on B1019

Maylands (1936)

Private
Harold Park, Romford
Tel **(040 23) 42055**
Mem 600
Sec (040 23) 73080
Pro JS Hopkin (040 23) 46466
Holes 18 L 6351 yds SSS 70
Recs Am-68 M Stokes
Pro-67 RA Knight
V'trs WD-I WE/BH-M
Fees £13 (£20)
Loc 2 miles E of Romford. 1 mile from M25 Junction 28
Mis Buggies available for hire

Orsett (1898)

Private
Brentwood Road, Orsett RM16 3DS
Tel **(0375) 891352**
Mem 900
Sec RA Bond
Pro R Newberry (0375) 891797
Holes 18 L 6575 yds SSS 72
Recs Am-68 A Pollock, I Quick
Pro-69 H Flatman, G Burroughs
V'trs WD-H SOC-Mon-Wed only
Fees £17
Loc 4 miles NE of Grays on A128. M25 Junction 30/31

Pipps Hill CC

Private
Aquatels Recreation Centre, Cranes Farm Road, Basildon
Tel **(0268) 23456**
Holes 9 L 2829 yds SSS 67
V'trs U SOC
Fees On application
Loc Adjacent A127 London-Southend road

Quietwaters (1974)

Private
Colchester Road, Tolleshunt D'Arcy, nr Maldon CM9 8HX
Tel **(0621) 860410**
Mem 640
Sec PD Keeble (Mgr)
Pro D Pugh (0621) 860576
Holes 18 L 6450 yds SSS 71
Recs Am-71 M Keeble (1988)
Pro-68 K Ashdown (1988)
V'trs WD-U WE-M BH-U after 2pm SOC
Fees On application
Loc 8 miles S of Colchester off B1026

Risebridge (1973)

Public
Risebridge Chase, Lower Bedford Road, Havering
Tel **(0708) 27376**
Sec B Wyles (0708) 44581
Holes Play over Havering course

Rochford Hundred (1893)

Private
Rochford
Tel **(0702) 544302**
Mem 300 150(L) 60(J) 210(5)
Sec D Gardner
Pro GN Shipley
Holes 18 L 6256 yds SSS 70

For map index see page 203.

Recs Am–65 DK Wood
Pro–65 C Tucker
V'trs WD–U WE–M
Fees On application
Loc 4 miles N of Southend-on-Sea

Romford (1894)

Private
Heath Drive, Gidea Park, Romford RM2 5QB
Tel (0708) 40007 (Members)
Mem 690
Sec BE Fox (0708) 40986
Pro H Flatman (0708) 49393
Holes 18 L 6377 yds SSS 70
Recs Am–68 D Girdlestone
V'trs WD–I WE–NA SOC
Fees £12 D–£18
Loc 1 mile E of Romford. 3 miles W of M25 Junction 29

Royal Epping Forest (1888)

Public
Forest Approach, Station Road, Chingford, London E4 7AZ
Tel (01) 529 6407
Mem 278 43(L) 25(J)
Sec CD Loomes (01) 529 2195
Pro R Gowers (01) 529 2708
Holes 18 L 6620 yds SSS 70
Recs Am–68 A Johns
Pro–65 R Gowers
V'trs WE–booked times
Fees £3.70 (£5.50)
Loc Bury Road, London E4. 250 yds E of Chingford Stn
Mis Red coats or trousers compulsory

Saffron Walden (1919)

Private
Windmill Hill, Saffron Walden CB10 1BX
Tel (0799) 22689 (Members)
Mem 900
Sec (Manager) KW Reddall (0799) 22786
Pro P Davis (0799) 27728
Holes 18 L 6608 yds SSS 72
Recs Am–67 AD Emery (1988)
Pro–68 S Jackson (1983)
V'trs WD–UH WE/BH–M SOC
Fees £17
Loc On B184 at entry to town.

Skips (1973)

Private
Horsemanside, Tysea Hill, Stapleford Abbots RM4 1JU
Tel (040 23) 48234
Sec D Brautigan
Holes 18 L 6146 yds SSS 71
V'trs NA Season ticket holders only
Loc Romford 3 miles off B175

Southend-on-Sea (1953)

Public
Belfairs Park, Southend-on-Sea
Tel (0702) 524836
Mem 80
Sec RL Steedon (0702) 352925
Holes Play over Belfairs Municipal

Stoke by Nayland (1972)

Private
Keepers Lane, Leavenheath, Colchester CO6 4PZ
Tel (0206) 262836
Mem 1250
Sec J Loshak
Pro K Lovelock (0206) 262769
Holes Gainsborough 18 L 6471 yds SSS 71; Constable 18 L 6498 yds SSS 71
Recs Gainsborough Am–66 RW Mann
Pro–69 PL Cowan
V'trs WE/BH–H after 10am
WD–U SOC
Fees £10 D–£13 (£13 D–£16)
Loc Off A134 Colchester–Sudbury road on to B1036

Theydon Bois (1897)

Private
Theydon Bois, Epping CM16 4EH
Tel (037 881) 2279
Mem 600
Sec JD Edgar (037 881) 3054
Pro JD Edgar (037 881) 2460
Holes 18 L 5472 yds SSS 68
Recs Am–67 SJ Alen
V'trs Thurs am–restricted WE–M
Fees £10 (£15)
Loc 1 mile S of Epping

Thorndon Park (1920)

Private
Ingrave, Brentwood CM13 3RH
Tel (0277) 811666
Mem 300 140(L) 60(J) 130(5)
Sec JE Leggitt (0277) 810345
Pro BV White (0277) 810736
Holes 18 L 6455 yds SSS 71
Recs Am–66 MES Davis
Pro–65 BJ Hunt, B Waites
V'trs WD–I WE/BH–M
Fees £13.50 D–£20
Loc 2 miles SE of Brentwood on A128

Thorpe Hall (1907)

Private
Thorpe Hall Avenue, Thorpe Bay SS1 3AT
Tel (0702) 582205
Mem 750
Sec RCP Hunter
Pro R Smith (0702) 588195
Holes 18 L 6259 yds SSS 71
Recs Am–68 B Hillsden
Pro–67 L Platts
V'trs WD–H WE/BH after 12 noon–H
Fees On application
Loc E of Southend-on-Sea

Three Rivers (1973)

Private
Stow Road, Purleigh, nr Chelmsford CM3 6RR
Tel (0621) 828631
Mem 600
Sec AR Peck
Pro L Platts
Holes 18 L 6609 yds SSS 72
9 L 1071 yds Par 3 course
V'trs WD–U WE/BH–M
SOC Tues/Thurs mainly
Fees £12 R/D WE–NA
Loc 5 miles S of Maldon

Towerlands (1985)

Private
Panfield Road, Braintree CM7 5BJ
Tel (0376) 26802
Mem 290
Sec DJ Collar (0376) 26802
Holes 9 L 2703 yds SSS 66
V'trs WD–U WE–after 2pm
SOC–WD
Fees 18 holes £5.50 (£7.50)
9 holes £3.50
Loc 1 mile NW of Braintree
Mis Driving range

Upminster (1928)

Private
114 Hall Lane, Upminster
Tel (040 22) 20249
Mem 900
Sec Mrs J Wylie (040 22) 22788
Pro N Carr (040 22) 20000
Holes 18 L 5951 yds SSS 68
Recs Am–64 AT Bird
V'trs WD–U WE/BH–NA
Fees £10
Loc Station 3/4 mile

Wanstead (1893)

Private
London E11
Tel (01) 989 0604
Mem 650
Sec BJ Preston (01) 989 3938
Pro D Pugh (01) 989 9876
Holes 18 L 6262 yds SSS 69
Recs Am–64 BJ Hilsdon
Pro–64 N Coles, P Brown
V'trs WD–I WE/BH–M
Fees £15
Loc Epping Forest boundary

Warley Park (1975)

Private
Magpie Lane, Little Warley, Brentwood
Tel (0277) 224891
Mem 600
Sec SP Greene

Pro P O'Conner (0277) 212552
Holes 18 L 6261 yds SSS 70
9 L 3166 yds SSS 35
Recs Am–69 B Preston
V'trs WD–U WE–M
Fees £12
Loc 2 miles S of Brentwood

Warren (1932)

Private
Woodham Walter, Maldon CM9 6RW
Tel **(024 541) 3258/3198**
Mem 380 55(L) 70(J) 125(5)
Pro M Walker (024 541) 4662
Holes 18 L 6211 yds SSS 69
Recs Am–66 C Laurence
Pro–66 H Flatman
V'trs WD–I WE–M
Fees £10 D–£12
Loc 7 miles E of Chelmsford off A414

West Essex (1900)

Private
Stewardstonebury, Chingford, London E4 7QL
Tel **(01) 529 0928**
Mem 645
Sec PH Galley MBE (01) 529 7558
Pro C Cox (01) 529 4367
Holes 18 L 6317 yds SSS 70
Recs Am–66 KG Budd
Pro–EE Whitcombe
V'trs WD–UH WE/BH–MH SOC–Mon/Wed/Fri
Fees £15 D–£18
Loc Bury Road, 3/4 mile N of Chingford Station. M25 Junction 26

Woodford (1889)

Private
Sunset Avenue, Woodford Green
Tel **(01) 504 0553/4254**
Mem 400 64(L) 52(J) 80(5)
Sec IG Fowler (01) 504 3330
Pro A Johns (01) 504 4254
Holes 9 L 5743 yds SSS 68
Recs Am–65 LW Burgess
V'trs WD–U WE–M
Fees £4.50
Loc 11 miles NE of London

Gloucestershire

Broadway (1896)

Private
Willersey Hill, Broadway, Worcs WR12 7LG
Tel **(0386) 858997**
Mem 400 120(L) 70(J) 140(5)
Sec KS Lawrance (0386) 853683
Pro J Freeman (0386) 853275
Holes 18 L 6211 yds SSS 70
Recs Am–66 DM Fletcher
Pro–66 D Steele, R Adams
V'trs H
Fees £12 (£14)
Loc 1 1/2 miles E of Broadway (A44)

Cirencester (1893)

Private
Cheltenham Road, Cirencester GL7 7BH
Tel **(0285) 653939**
Mem 650
Sec ND Jones (0285) 652465
Pro M Thomas (0285) 656124
Holes 18 L 6021 yds SSS 69
Recs Am–64 D Rollo
Pro–67 DJ Rees
V'trs BH–H SOC–WD
Fees £12 (£14)
Loc 1 1/2 miles N of Cirencester on A435

Cleeve Cloud (1976)

Public
Cleeve Hill, nr Cheltenham
Mem 290
Sec MJ Lee (024 267) 2025
(024 267) 3733 (Home)
Pro D Finch (024 267) 2592
Holes 18 L 6444 yds SSS 71
V'trs U (exc Sun am) SOC
Fees £3.50 (£4.50)

Cleeve Hill (1976)

Public
Cleeve Hill, nr Prestbury, Cheltenham
Tel **(024 267) 2025**
Pro M Steadman (024 267) 2592
Holes 18 L 6169 yds SSS 70
V'trs U
Fees £3 (£3.80)
Loc 3 miles N of Cheltenham

Cotswold Edge (1980)

Private
Rushmire, Wotton-under-Edge GL12 7PT
Tel **(0453) 844167**
Mem 650
Sec NJ Newman
Pro I Watts (0453) 844398
Holes 18 L 6170 yds SSS 69
V'trs WD–U WE/BH–NA before 11am SOC
Fees £7 (£10)
Loc 2 miles NE of Wotton-under-Edge on B4058 Tetbury road

Cotswold Hills (1902)

Private
Ullenwood, nr Cheltenham GL3 9QT
Tel **(0242) 522421**
Mem 700
Sec Lt Col PG Roberson
(0242) 515264
Pro N Boland (0242) 515263
Holes 18 L 6716 yds SSS 72
Recs Am–68 R Day
Pro–68 SD Brown (1987)
V'trs I (recognised club members)
Fees £9 (£12)
Loc 3 miles S of Cheltenham

Forest of Dean (1974)

Private
Lords Hill, Coleford GL16 8BD
Tel **(0594) 32583**
Mem 450
Sec J Hamilton (Mgr)
Pro J Nicol (0594) 33689
Holes 18 L 5519 yds SSS 67
V'trs U SOC
Fees £8 D–£10 (£9 D–£11)
Loc Town 1/2 mile on Parkend Road
Mis Hotel in centre of course

Gloucestershire Hotel (1976)

Private
Matson Lane, Gloucester
Tel **(0452) 25653**
Mem 500
Sec R Jewell
Pro R Jewell, P Darnell
(0452) 411331
Holes 18 L 6127 yds SSS 69
9 L 1980 yds SSS 27
Recs Am–69 J Northam
Pro–65 P Darnell
V'trs U
Fees £8 (£10)
Loc 2 miles S of Gloucester off Painswick Road

Lilley Brook (1922)

Private
Cirencester Road, Charlton Kings, Cheltenham GL53 8EG
Tel **(0242) 526785**
Mem 700
Sec K Skeen
Pro F Hadden (0242) 525201
Holes 18 L 6226 yds SSS 70
Recs Am–64 B Mitten (1987)
Pro–67 M Steadman (1982), G Ryall (1987) N Blenkarne (1987)
V'trs H or I (recognised club members) SOC–WD
Fees £14 D–£18 (£20)
Loc 3 miles SE of Cheltenham on A435

Lydney (1909)

Private
Lydney
Tel **(0594) 42614**
Mem 300
Sec DA Barnard (0594) 43940
Holes 9 L 5382 yds SSS 66
Recs Am–63 MA Barnard (1988)
Pro–68 F Goulding
V'trs WD–U WE–M SOC
Fees £6 W–£18
Loc Off Lakeside Avenue

Minchinhampton (1889)

Private
Minchinhampton, Stroud (New course) GL6 8BE
Tel **(045 383) 2642 (Old course)**
(045 383) 3866 (New course)
Mem 1600
Sec DR Vickers (045 383) 3866
Pro C Steele (045 383) 3860
Holes Old 18 L 6295 yds SSS 70
New 18 L 6675 yds SSS 72
Recs Old Am–67 PH Fisher, AL Scott
Pro–67 RA Brown
New Am–68 RD Broad (1988)
Pro–67 GH Marks, G Ryall
V'trs U subject to availability of starting times SOC
Fees Old course £7 (£8)
New course £12 (£15)
Loc Old–3 miles E of Stroud.
New–5 miles E of Stroud

Painswick (1891)

Private
Painswick, nr Stroud
Tel **(0452) 812180**
Mem 230
Sec RJ May
Holes 18 L 4780 yds SSS 64
Recs Am–61 J Woolley
V'trs WD/Sat–U Sun–M SOC
Fees £5 (£7)
Loc Painswick
Mis Apr–Oct course closes at 2pm Sun

Stinchcombe Hill (1889)

Private
Dursley GL11 6AQ
Tel **(0453) 2015**
Mem 500
Sec GH Beetham
Pro A Valentine (0453) 3878
Holes 18 L 5710 yds SSS 68
Recs Am–64 PC French (1979)
Pro–64 I Bolt (1984)
V'trs WD–U WE/BH–NA before 10.30am SOC
Fees £10 (£12) W–£30 F–£50 M–£80
Loc Dursley town centre 1 mile

Tewkesbury Park Hotel (1976)

Private
Lincoln Green Lane, Tewkesbury GL20 7DN
Mem (0684) 295405
Sec Maj. JD McCarthy
Pro P Cane (0684) 294892
Holes 18 L 6533 yds SSS 72
Recs Am–68 RN Roper
Pro–68 N Job
V'trs WD–U H SOC–WD
WE–residential SOC only
Fees £14 (£16)
Loc ½ mile S of town on A38. 2 miles M5 Junction 9
Mis 6 hole Par 3 £2

Westonbirt (1971)

Private
Westonbirt, Tetbury GL8 8QG
Tel **(066 88) 242**
Mem 200
Sec Bursar, Westonbirt School
Pro C Steele (045 383) 3860
Holes 9 L 4504 yds SSS 61
Recs Am–62 S Dunlop
V'trs U SOC–WD
Fees D–£3.20 (£3.20)
Loc 3 miles S of Tetbury off A433

Hampshire

Alresford (1890)

Private
Cheriton Road, Alresford SO24 0PN
Mem 470
Sec P Kingston (0962) 733746
Pro M Scott (0962) 733998
Holes 11 L 5986 yds SSS 69
Pro–67 J Hay
V'trs U H WE–after 12 noon SOC
Fees £8.50 D–£12 (£15)
Loc 1 mile S of town centre

Alton (1908)

Private
Old Odiham Road, Alton GU34 4BU
Tel **(0420) 82042**
Mem 340
Sec JHJ Powers (0252) 613061
Pro M Smith (0420) 86518
Holes 9 L 5744 yds SSS 68
Recs Am–65 I McInally (1987)
Pro–65 A Stevens (1988)
V'trs U (exc comp days) SOC–WD
Fees £7 (£10)
Loc 2 miles N of Alton. 6 miles S of Odiham off A32

Ampfield Par Three (1963)

Private
Winchester Road, Ampfield, nr Romsey SO51 9BQ
Tel **(0794) 68480**
Mem 500
Sec Mrs S Baker
Pro R Benfield (0794) 68750
Holes 18 L 2478 yds SSS 53
Recs Am–49 R Bailey
Pro–49 A Timms
V'trs WD–U WE/BH–H (phone first) SOC
Fees £5 (£8.50)
Loc On A31 Winchester to Romsey

Andover (1907)

Private
51 Winchester Road, Andover SP10 2EF
Tel **(0264) 23980**
Mem 415 60(L) 40(J)
Sec Maj BF Gerhard MBE (0264) 58040
Pro A Timms (0264) 24151
Holes 9 L 5933 yds SSS 68
Recs Am–69 D Critcher
Pro–67 A Timms
V'trs WD–U WE/BH–NA before noon SOC
Fees £8 (£10)
Loc 1 mile S of town centre

Army Golf Club (1883)

Private
Laffan's Road, Aldershot GU11 2HF
Tel **(0252) 541104**
Mem 800
Sec RT Crabb(Sec/Mgr) (0252) 540638
Pro P Thompson (0252) 547232
Holes 18 L 6579 yds SSS 71
Recs Am–69 G Young
Pro–69 I Young
V'trs WD–I WE–M
Fees £15 (special rates for Forces)
Loc Between Aldershot and Farnborough

Barton-on-Sea (1897)

Private
Marine Drive, Barton-on-Sea BH25 7DY
Tel **(0425) 615308**
Mem 392 117(L) 30(J)
Sec CJ Wingfield
Pro P Coombs (0425) 611210
Holes 18 L 5565 yds SSS 67
Recs Am–63 RM Tuddenham
Pro–66 P Alliss
V'trs H WD–U WE/BH–NA before 11.15am SOC–Mon/Wed/Fri
Fees £15 (£18) R/D
Loc New Milton, 1½ miles M27 Junction 1

Basingstoke (1928)

Private
Kempshott Park, Basingstoke RG23 7LL
Tel **(0256) 465990**
Mem 725
Sec PA Gill
Pro Ian Hayes (0256) 51332
Holes 18 L 6309 yds SSS 70
Recs Am–68 M Gatrall (1988)
Pro–66 K Bowden (1988)
V'trs WD–H WE–M SOC–Wed & Thurs
Fees £12
Loc 3 miles W of Basingstoke on A30. M3 Junction 7
Mis Buggy hire £10 per round

Basingstoke Hospitals

Private
Aldermaston Road, Basingstoke
Tel **(0256) 20347**
Mem 275
Sec EEL Rowlands, R Fowler (Mgr)
Holes 9 L 5480 yds SSS 67
V'trs WD–U before 4.30pm–M after 4.30pm WE–contact Mgr SOC
Fees £6 (£8)
Loc $1^1/_2$ miles N of town centre

Bishopswood (1978)

Private
Bishopswood Lane, Tadley, Basingstoke RG26 6AT
Tel **(073 56) 5213**
Mem 400
Sec MW Phillips
Pro K Pickett
Holes 9 L 6474 yds SSS 71
Recs Am–69 C Wilkins (1987) Pro–68 R Boxall (1983)
V'trs U SOC
Fees £5 (£6.50) 18 holes
Loc 6 miles N of Basingstoke off A340
Mis Floodlit driving range

Blackmoor (1913)

Private
Whitehill Bordon GU35 9EH
Tel **(04203) 2775**
Mem 630 85(L) 60(J)
Sec Maj HRG Spiller
Pro A Hall (04203) 2345
Holes 18 L 6213 yds SSS 70
V'trs H
Fees £11 D–£17.50 WE–NA
Loc $^1/_2$ mile W of Whitehill on A325

Bohunt Manor (1923)

Private
Liphook
Mem 60
Sec IR Baker, 29 Headley Road, Liphook
Holes Play over Liphook

Bramshaw (1880)

Private
Brook, Lyndhurst SO43 7HE
Tel **(0703) 813433**
Mem 900 116(L) 39(J) 195(5)
Sec FS Prince
Pro W Wiltshire (0703) 813434
Holes Forest 18 L 5753 yds SSS 68
Manor 18 L 6257 yds SSS 70
Recs Forest Am–67 G Hill Pro–66 W Wiltshire
Manor Am–67 G Lovelady Pro–67 D Allen
V'trs WD–U WE–M
Fees On application
Loc Southampton 10 miles

Brokenhurst Manor (1919)

Private
Sway Road, Brokenhurst
Tel **(0590) 23332**
Mem 800
Sec CF Mackintosh
Pro C Bonner (0590) 23092
Holes 18 L 6216 yds SSS 70
Recs Am–64 K Weeks Pro–66 D Haslam
V'trs WD–after 9.30am H SOC NA Tues–Ladies' Day
Fees £20 (£30)
Loc Brokenhurst 1 mile on B3055

Burley (1905)

Private
Burley, Ringwood BH24 4BB
Tel **(042 53) 2431**
Mem 470
Sec GR Kendall
Holes 9 L 3126 yds SSS 69
Recs Am–70 N Carpenter, W Medd
V'trs U
Fees £10 (£10) W–£40
Loc 4 miles SE of Ringwood

Corhampton (1885)

Private
Sheeps Pond Lane, Droxford, Southampton SO3 1QZ
Tel **(0489) 877279**
Mem 600
Sec P Taylor
Pro J Harris (0489) 877638
Holes 18 L 6088 yds SSS 69
Recs Am–66 R Edwards (1988) Pro–65 P Dawson (1987)
V'trs WD–UH WE/BH–M SOC–Mons & Thurs
Fees £11 D–£16.50
Loc 9 miles S of Winchester
Mis Buggies for hire £10 per round

Dibden (1974)

Public
Main Road, Dibden, Southampton SO4 5TB
Tel **(0703) 845596**
Mem 300
Sec WW Brown
Pro A Bridge
Holes 18 L 6206 yds SSS 70 Pro–63 I Young (1988)
V'trs U
Fees £3.60 (£5.30)
Loc 10 miles W of Southampton. $^1/_2$ mile from Dibden roundabout on A326 Fawley road

Dunwood Manor (1969)

Private
Shootash Hill, Romsey SO5 10GF
Tel **(0794) 40549**
Mem 700
Sec Mrs H Johnson, K Heathcote (Gen Mgr)
Pro G Stubbington (0794) 40663
Holes 18 L 6004 yds SSS 69
Recs Am–71 A Devlin Pro–61 G Stubbington
V'trs WE/BH–restricted SOC–WD
Fees £9 D–£13
Loc Romsey 4 miles on A27

Fleetlands (1961)

Private
Fareham Road, Gosport
Tel **(0705) 822351**
Mem 120
Sec L Watling
Holes 9 L 4775 yds SSS 63
Recs Am–66 I Carter
V'trs M at all times

Fleming Park (1973)

Public
Fleming Park, Eastleigh
Tel **(0703) 612797**
Mem 250
Sec C House
Pro D Miller
Holes 18 L 4436 yds SSS 62
Recs Am–J Butcher Pro–D Miller
V'trs U
Fees £2.80 (£4)
Loc 6 miles N of Southampton

Gosport & Stokes Bay (1885)

Private
Military Road, Haslar, Gosport PO12 2AT
Tel **(0705) 581625**
Mem 170
Sec T Jopling (0705) 527941
Holes 9 L 5668 yds SSS 69
Recs Am–69 M Stubley (1986) Pro–65 P Dawson (1985)
V'trs U Sun–after noon
Fees D–£8 (May–Oct) D–£6 (Nov–Apr)
Loc S Boundary of Gosport

Great Salterns (1914)

Public
Portsmouth Golf Centre, Eastern Road, Portsmouth PO3 6QB
Tel **(0705) 664549**
Pro T Healey
Holes 18 L 5970 yds SSS 68
V'trs U
Fees £5
Loc 1 mile off M27 on A2030
Mis Southsea Club plays here. Driving range

For map index see page 203.

Hartley Wintney (1891)

Private
London Road, Hartley Wintney, nr Basingstoke
Tel **(025 126) 2214**
Mem 410
Sec BD Powell (025 126) 4211
Pro T Barter (025 126) 3779
Holes 9 L 6096 yds SSS 69
Recs Am–70 M Wild
Pro–63 R Lewington
V'trs WE/BH restricted
Wed–Ladies' Day SOC–Tues & Thurs
Fees £8 (£15)
Loc A30 London Road, Hartley Wintney between Camberley and Basingstoke

Hayling (1883)

Private
Ferry Road, Hayling Island PO11 0BX
Tel **(0705) 463712/463777**
Mem 900
Sec RCW Stokes (0705) 464446
Pro Ray Gadd (0705) 464491
Holes 18 L 6489 yds SSS 71
Recs Pro–66 F Gilbride
Am–66 D Harrison, K Weeks
V'trs H WE/BH–after 10.30am SOC
Loc 5 miles S of Havant on A3023

Hockley (1915)

Private
Twyford, nr Winchester SO21 1PL
Tel **(0962) 713461**
Mem 750
Pro T Lane (0962) 713678
Holes 18 L 6260 yds SSS 70
Recs Am–67 PE Anthony, CJ Hyde, GP Cole
Pro–66 P Dawson
V'trs WD–U WE/BH–M
Fees £13
Loc Winchester Station 2 miles on A333

Leckford & Longstock (1929)

Private
Leckford, Stockbridge SO20 65G
Tel **(0264) 810710**
Mem 200
Sec LG Lucas
Pro LG Lucas
Holes 9 L 3251 yds SSS 71
V'trs M
Loc 5 miles W of Andover

Lee-on-the-Solent (1905)

Private
Brune Lane, Lee-on-the-Solent
Tel **(0705) 550207**
Mem 700
Sec (0705) 551170
Pro John Richardson (0705) 551181
Holes 18 L 5991 yds SSS 69
Recs Am–65 S Richardson
Pro–66 M Faulkner
V'trs WD–UH WE–MH SOC–Thurs
Fees D–£14
Loc 3 miles S of Fareham

Liphook (1922)

Private
Liphook GU30 7EH
Tel **(0428) 723271**
Mem 800
Pro I Large
Holes 18 L 6207 yds SSS 70
Recs Am–70 R Tuddenham, M Wiggett
Pro–66 TR Pinner
V'trs IH (max 24) WE–NA before 1pm Sun
Fees £12 D–£18 (£20 D–£25)
Loc 18 miles SW of Guildford on A3
Mis Bohunt Manor Club plays here

Meon Valley Hotel (1977)

Private
Sandy Lane, Shedfield, Southampton SO3 2HQ
Tel **(0329) 833455**
Mem 500
Sec CM Terry
Pro J Stirling
Holes 18 L 6519 yds SSS 71
Recs Am–69 CW A'Court (1986)
Pro–67 J Garner (1987)
V'trs H SOC
Fees £13 (£16)
Loc 2 miles NW of Wickham. N off A334

New Forest (1888)

Private
Southampton Road, Lyndhurst SO43 7BU
Tel **(042 128) 2450/2752**
Mem 700
Sec M Swann
Pro K Gilhespy
Holes 18 L 5748 yds SS 68
Recs Am–65 C White
Pro–67 S Clay, R Brown
V'trs U (exc Sun am)
Fees £5 (£5)
Loc On A35 Bournemouth to Southampton road

North Hants (1904)

Private
Minley Road, Fleet GU13 8RE
Tel **(0252) 616443**
Mem 700
Sec IR Goodliffe
Pro S Porter (0252) 616655
Holes 18 L 6257 yds SSS 70
Recs Am–66 MC Hughesdon (1976)
JS Cheetham (1988)
Pro–67 B Hunt
V'trs WD–UH WE–MH
Fees £15
Loc 3 miles W of Farnborough on B3013. M3 Junction 4

Old Thorns Hotel CC (1982)

Private
London Kosaido Company Ltd, Longmoor Road, Liphook GU30 7PE
Tel **(0428) 724555**
Sec GM Jones
Pro Philip Loxley
Holes 18 L 6447 yds SSS 71
Pro–69 I Aoki (1982)
V'trs U SOC
Fees £16 (£22) SOC D–£38
Loc 1 mile off A3 from Liphook, on Longmoor Road
Mis 34 buggies for hire

Ordnance Survey (1934)

Private
Southampton Municipal, Bassett, Southampton
Tel **(0703) 768407**
Mem 90
Sec MB Swan, 68A Wolsley Road, Freemantle, Southampton (0703) 788393
Holes Play over Southampton Municipal

Petersfield (1881)

Private
Heath Road, Petersfield GU31 4EJ
Tel **(0730) 63725**
Mem 314(M) 87(L) 85(J)
Sec RDJ Maxwell (0730) 62386
Pro S Clay (0730) 67732
Holes 18 L 5751 yds SSS 68
Recs Am–70 P Tupper
Pro–69 S Clay
V'trs U WE–NA before 10.30am
Fees £7 (£10.50) D–£10 (£14) 1987 prices
Loc 1/2 mile E of centre

Portsmouth (1926)

Public
Crookhorn Lane, Widley, Portsmouth PO7 5QL
Tel **(0705) 372210**
Mem 450
Sec D Houlihan (0705) 381640
Pro R Brown
Holes 18 L 6259 yds SSS 70
V'trs U SOC (arrange with Pro)
Fees £5.10
Loc 1 mile N of city on B2177

Romsey (1925)

Private
Nursling, Southampton SO1 9XW
Tel **(0703) 732218**
Mem 500
Sec FG Biles (0703) 734637
Pro SS Howard (0703) 736673
Holes 18 L 5752 yds SSS 68
Recs Am–66 NP Woodward
Pro–64 J Slade
V'trs WD–U WE/BH–M

For explanation of abbreviations see page 202.

Fees £6
Loc $4^1/_2$ miles NW of Southampton (A3057)

Rowlands Castle (1902)

Private
Links Lane, Rowlands Castle PO9 6AE
Tel (0705) 412216
Mem 500 150(L) 60(J)
Sec Capt. AW Aird (0705) 412784
Pro P Klepacz (0705) 412785
Holes 18 L 6627 yds SSS 72
Recs Am–70 N Cole, C Anderson
Pro–66 M Gregson
V'trs H WD–U WE–phone first
SOC–Tues/Thurs/Fri
Fees £14 R/D (£18) 1988 prices
Loc 3 miles N of Havant.
9 miles S of Petersfield

Royal Winchester (1888)

Private
Sarum Road, Winchester SO22 5QE
Tel (0962) 52462
(0962) 65048 (Members)
Mem 600
Sec RD Tingey
Pro DP Williams (0962) 62473
Holes 18 L 6218 yds SSS 70
Recs Am–67 R Elliot, J Curren
Pro–67 B Lane, D Feherty
V'trs WD–UH WE/BH–M SOC–WD
Fees £15
Loc W of Winchester off A31

Southampton (1935)

Public
Golf Course Road, Bassett, Southampton
Tel (0703) 768407
Mem 400
Sec KG Kennard (0703) 582659
Pro J Cave
Holes 18 L 6218 yds SSS 70
9 L 2391 yds SSS 33
Recs Am–64 P Dedman
Pro–62 SW Murray
V'trs U
Fees 18 holes £3.40 (£5.20)
9 holes £1.70 (£2.60)
Loc 2 miles N of city centre

Southsea (1972)

Private
The Mansion, Eastern Road, Portsmouth
Tel (0705) 664549
Mem 500
Sec KP Parker (0705) 812435
Holes Play over Great Salterns

Southwick Park (1977)

Private
Pinsley Drive, Southwick PO17 6EL
Tel (0705) 380131
Mem 600 60(L)
Sec NW Price
Pro J Green (0705) 380442
Holes 18 L 5970 yds SSS 68
Recs Am–67 R Edwards
Pro–64 G Hughes
V'trs WD–U before 11am only
SOC–Tues
Fees On application. Servicemen reduced rate
Loc Southwick Village $^1/_2$ mile

Southwood (1977)

Public
Ively Road, Farnborough GU14 0LJ
Tel (0252) 548700
Mem 570
Sec R Hammond
Pro R Hammond
Holes 18 L 5553 yds SSS 67
Recs Am–69 (1988)
Pro–65 (1988)
V'trs U
Fees £5
Loc 1 mile W of Farnborough off A325

Stoneham (1908)

Private
Bassett, Southampton SO2 3NE
Tel (0703) 768151
Mem 750
Sec Mrs AM Wilkinson
(0703) 769272
Pro I Young (0703) 768397
Holes 18 L 6310 yds SSS 70
Recs Am–65 R Park
Pro–63 J Martin
V'trs WD–U WE–NA
SOC–Mon/Thurs/Fri
Fees £12 (£15)
Loc 2 miles N of city

Tidworth Garrison (1908)

Private
Tidworth
Tel (0980) 42321
Mem 600
Sec Lt Col DFT Tucker
(0980) 42301
Pro T Godsen (0980) 42393
Holes 18 L 5990 yds SSS 69
Recs Am–65 JN Flemming
V'trs U SOC–Tues/Thurs/Fri
Fees £10 (£12) 1988 prices
Loc Tidworth 1 mile on Bulford Road

Tylney Park (1973)

Private
Rotherwick, Basingstoke
Tel (025 672) 2079
Mem 700
Sec JC York
Pro C de Bruin
Holes 18 L 6108 yds SSS 69
Recs Am–70 D Curd
Pro–65 C de Bruin
V'trs WD–U WE–M or H
Fees £9.50 (£12)
Loc Hook 1 mile on A30

Waterlooville (1907)

Private
Cherry Tree Ave, Cowplain, Portsmouth
PO8 8AP
Tel (0705) 252661
Mem 800
Sec Mrs B Southwell
(0705) 263388
Pro J Hay (0705) 256911
Holes 18 L 6647 yds SSS 72
Recs Am–66 D Hickman (1987)
Pro–66 H Stott (1988)
V'trs WD/WE–MH (Sun am–XL)
SOC
Fees £12 D–£15
Loc 10 miles N of Portsmouth on A3

Hereford & Worcester

Belmont House (1983)

Private
Belmont, Hereford HR2 9SA
Tel (0432) 277445
Mem 370
Sec MJ Francis
Pro M Welsh
Holes 18 L 6448 yds SSS 71
V'trs U SOC
Fees On application
Loc $1^1/_2$ miles S of Hereford on A465

Blackwell (1893)

Private
Blackwell, nr Bromsgrove B60 1PY
Tel (021) 445 1781
Mem 300 100(L) 30(J)
Sec S Allen (021) 445 1994
Pro H MacDonald (021) 445 3113
Holes 18 L 6202 yds SSS 71
Recs Am–68 AJ Thomson
Pro–64 M Bembridge
V'trs WD–U WE/BH–M
Fees £18
Loc 3 miles E of Bromsgrove

Churchill and Blakedown (1926)

Private
Churchill Lane, Blakedown, nr Kidderminster
Tel (0562) 700200
Mem 350
Sec JH Lidstone (0384) 73161
Holes 9 L 5399 yds SSS 67
Recs Am–64 CMM Lea
Pro–61 R Livingston
V'trs WD–U WE–M
Fees D–£7.50
Loc 3 miles N of Kidderminster on A453

Droitwich (1897)

Private
Ford Lane, Droitwich WR9 0BQ
Tel **(0905) 770129**
Mem 728
Sec MJ Taylor (0905) 774344
Pro CS Thompson (0905) 770207
Holes 18 L 6040 yds SSS 69
Recs Am–63 J Bickerton
V'trs WD–U WE/BH–M SOC–Wed & Fri
Fees £12
Loc 1 mile N of town off A38. M5 Junction 5

Evesham (1894)

Private
Craycombe, Fladbury, Pershore, Worcs WR10 2QS
Tel **(0386) 860395**
Mem 300
Sec FG Vincent (0386) 552373
Pro R Gray
Holes 9 L 6418 yds SSS 71
V'trs WD–M H NA on comp/match days SOC
Fees £8
Loc 4 miles W of Evesham (B4084) adjacent to Fladbury Village

Habberley (1924)

Private
Trimpley Road, Kidderminster DY11 5RG
Tel **(0562) 745756**
Mem 400
Sec DB Lloyd (0562) 823509
Holes 9 L 5440 yds SSS 67
Recs Am–62 D Kwei
V'trs WD–U WE–M SOC
Fees £7
Loc 3 miles NW of town

Herefordshire (1909)

Private
Raven's Causeway, Wormsley, nr Hereford HR4 8LY
Tel **(0432) 71219**
Mem 600 75(L) 85(J) 55(5)
Sec C Jones (0432) 760662
Pro D Hemming
Holes 18 L 6069 yds SSS 69
Recs Am–66 J Wilson
Pro–61 B Barnes
V'trs U
Fees £8 (£10) W–£35
Loc 6 miles NW of Hereford
Mis Buggy for hire

Kidderminster (1909)

Private
Russell Road, Kidderminster
Tel **(0562) 822303**
Mem 800
Sec J Sanders
Pro NP Underwood (0562) 740090
Holes 18 L 6223 yds SSS 70
V'trs WD only
Fees £11.50
Loc Kidderminster Station 1 mile

King's Norton (1892)

Private
Brockhill Lane, Weatheroak
Tel **(0564) 826789**
Mem 950
Sec LNW Prince (Sec/Mgr)
Pro C Haycock (0564) 822822
Holes 18 L 6754 yds SSS 72
9 L 3290 yds SSS 36
Recs Am–69 PR Swinburne
Pro–66 M Gregson, P Oosterhuis
V'trs WD–U WE–NA SOC
Fees £10 D–£12
Loc 8 miles S of Birmingham. M42 Junction 3, 2 miles

Kington (1926)

Private
Bradnor Hill, Kington
Mem 420
Sec FH Bradley (054 48) 355
Pro WCL Griffiths
Holes 18 L 5786 yds SSS 68
Recs Am–68 A Marshmann, AW Lyle
V'trs U
Fees £5 (£7)
Loc 1 mile N of Kington

Leominster (1967)

Private
Ford Bridge, Leominster, Herefordshire HR6 0LE
Tel **(0568) 2863**
Mem 360
Sec JA Ashcroft (043 272) 493
Pro R Price
Holes 9 L 2657 yds SSS 66
Recs Am–67 G Price
Pro–66
V'trs I or H
Fees £6 (£8.50)
Loc 3 miles S of Leominster on A49

Little Lakes (1975)

Private
Lye Head, Bewdley DY12 2UZ
Tel **(0299) 266385**
Mem 340 50 (L)
Sec T Norris
Pro M Laing
Holes 9 L 6247 yds SSS 72
Pro–70 R Lane (1986)
V'trs WD–U WE–U
Fees £4.50 (£5.50)
Loc 2½ miles W of Bewdley off A456

Pitcheroak (1973)

Public
Plymouth Road, Redditch
Tel **(0527) 41054**
Mem 120
Sec A Sharp (0527) 24594
Pro D Stewart
Holes 9 L 4584 yds SSS 63
V'trs U
Fees £2.50 (£3.50)
Loc Plymouth Road, Redditch

Redditch (1913)

Private
Lower Grinsty, Green Lane, Callow Hill, Redditch B97 5PJ
Tel **(0527) 43309**
Mem 756
Sec C Holman
Pro F Powell (0527) 46372
Holes 18 L 6671 yds SSS 72
V'trs WD–U SOC
Fees £12
Loc 3 miles SW of town centre. Heathfield Road off A441

Ross-on-Wye (1903)

Private
Two Park, Gorsley, Ross-on-Wye HR9 7UT
Tel **(098 982) 267**
Mem 720
Sec GH Cason (098 987) 650 (Home)
Pro A Clifford (098 982) 439
Holes 18 L 6500 yds SSS 73 Par 72
Recs Am–69 J Stordy
Pro–71 G Brand Jr
V'trs U SOC Wed–Fri (2 per week for 16+ players)
Fees £15 (£18)
Loc By M50 Junction 3 (Newent). 5 miles N of Ross-on-Wye

Tolladine (1895)

Private
The Fairway, Tolladine Road, Worcester WR4 9BA
Tel **(0905) 21074**
Mem 300
Sec AJ Wardle (0905) 54841
Holes 9 L 5174 yds SSS 67
V'trs WD–U before 5pm WE/BH–M
Fees £5 (£8)
Loc M5 Junction 6 Warndon 1 mile

Worcester G & CC (1898)

Private
Boughton Park, Worcester
Tel **(0905) 422555**
Mem 1100
Sec JM Kennedy
Pro C Colenso (0905) 422044
Holes 18 L 5919 yds SSS 68
Recs Am–67 M Jeffs
Pro–66 BJ Hunt
V'trs WD–U WE–M
Fees £12 (£15)
Loc 1¼ miles W of city

Worcestershire (1879)

Private
Wood Farm, Malvern Wells WR14 4PP
Tel **(068 45) 3905**
Mem 770
Sec GR Scott (068 45) 5992
Pro GM Harris (068 45) 64428

Holes 18 L 6449 yds SSS 71
Recs Am–67 PM Guest
Pro–67 R Larratt
V'trs WD–H WE–H after 10am
Fees £12 (£15) W–£45 1988 prices
Loc 2 miles S of Gt Malvern off A449/B4209

Hertfordshire

Aldenham G & CC (1975)

Private
Radlett Road, Aldenham, nr Watford
Tel (0923) 85 3929
Mem 475
Sec DW Phillips
Pro A McKay (0923) 85 7889
Holes 18 L 6500 yds SSS 71
V'trs U
Fees £8 D–£12 (£15)
Loc Ladbroke Hotel 1/4 mile on A41. M1 Junction 5 1/2 miles

Arkley (1909)

Private
Rowley Green Road, Barnet EN5 3HL
Tel (01) 449 0394
Mem 350
Sec JG Duncan
Pro M Squire (01) 440 8473
Holes 9 L 6045 yds SSS 69
Recs Am–67 SN McWilliams
Pro–63 LV Baker
V'trs WD–U WE–M SOC–Wed & Thurs
Fees £9 D–£12
Loc Barnet Station 2 miles

Ashridge (1932)

Private
Little Gaddesden, Berkhamsted HP4 1LY
Tel (044 284) 2244
Mem 650
Sec Mrs MA West
Pro G Pook (Golf Mgr) (044 284) 2307
Holes 18 L 6508 yds SSS 71
Recs Am–66 Sqd Ldr CI Skellern
Pro–66 JRM Jacobs
V'trs Ring Sec for bookings
Fees On application
Loc 5 miles NW of Berkhamsted on B4506

Batchwood Hall (1935)

Public
Batchwood Hall, St Albans
Tel (0727) 3349
Mem 300
Sec M Waldron
Pro J Thomson
Holes 18 L 6465 yds SSS 71
Recs Am–67 M Cassidy
Pro–62 PP Wynne
V'trs U
Loc NW corner of town

Berkhamsted (1890)

Private
Berkhamsted HP4 2QB
Tel (0442) 863730
Mem 280 113(L) 119(J) 150(5)
Sec JF Robinson (0442) 865832
Pro BJ Proudfoot (0442) 865851
Holes 18 L 6568 yds SSS 72
Recs Am–64 N Leconte (1986)
Pro–69 S Proudfoot (1987)
V'trs U H WE–M before 11.30am SOC–Wed & Fri
Fees On application
Loc 1 1/2 miles E of town centre

Bishop's Stortford (1910)

Private
Dunmow Road, Bishop's Stortford CM23 5HP
Tel (0279) 54027
Mem 700
Sec G Ditchfield (0279) 54715
Pro V Duncan (0279) 51324
Holes 18 L 6440 yds SSS 71
Recs Am–69 M Whitlock
Pro–66 J Bennett
V'trs WD–U WE–M SOC
Fees £10 D–£12 W–on application
Loc 26 miles S of Cambridge
Mis Buggies for hire

Boxmoor (1890)

Private
18 Box Lane, Hemel Hempstead
Tel (0442) 42434
Mem 225
Sec E Duell (0442) 62427
Holes 9 L 4854 yds SSS 64
Recs Am–57 D Boyd, A Reeves
V'trs U Sun–NA
Fees £5 (Sat £6)
Loc 1 mile W on A41

Brickendon Grange (1964)

Private
Brickendon, nr Hertford
Tel (099 286) 228
Mem 600
Sec N Martin (099 286) 258
Pro J Hamilton (099 286) 218
Holes 18 L 6325 yds SSS 70
Recs Am–70 J Paterson, M Passingham
Pro–67 S James, K Robson
V'trs WD–U WE/BH–M SOC
Fees On application
Loc 3 miles S of Hertford

Brookmans Park (1930)

Private
Brookmans Park, Hatfield AL9 7AT
Tel (0707) 52487
Pro MMR Plumbridge (0707) 52468
Holes 18 L 6454 yds SSS 71
Recs Am–67 N Jarman
Pro–66 GR Burroughs
V'trs WD–UH WE/BH–M SOC
Fees D–£13
Loc 3 miles S of Hatfield

Bushey G & CC (1980)

Private
High Street, Bushey WD2 1BJ
Tel (01) 950 2283
Mem 600
Sec Mr and Mrs Paterson
Pro G Atkinson (01) 950 2215
Holes 9 L 3000 yds SSS 69
V'trs WD–before 6pm WE/BH–after 2pm Wed–closed
Fees 18 holes £9 (£12)
9 holes £5 (£7)
Loc 2 miles S of Watford M1/M25

Bushey Hall (1896)

Private
Bushey Hall Drive, Bushey WD2 2EP
Tel (0923) 225802
Mem 500
Sec CA Brown
Pro D Fitzsimmons (0923) 222253
Holes 18 L 6087 yds SSS 69
Recs Am–65 G Kemble
V'trs U Sun/BH–M
Fees On application
Loc 1 mile SE of Watford

Chadwell Springs (1974)

Private
Hertford Road, Ware SG12 9LE
Tel (0920) 3647
Mem 350
Sec (0920) 61447
Pro AN Shearn
Holes 9 L 3021 yds SSS 69
V'trs WD–U WE–M or I
Fees £4 (£6)
Loc Midway between Ware and Hertford on A119

Cheshunt Park (1976)

Public
The Club House, Park Lane, Cheshunt EN7 6QD
Tel (0992) 24009
Mem 350
Sec JG Duncan
Pro C Newton (0992) 24009
Holes 18 L 6608 yds SSS 71
V'trs U
Fees £4 (£5.50)
Loc A10 London–Cambridge; turn off at College Road junction. Proceed along Churchgate
Mis Cheshunt Club plays here

Chorleywood (1890)

Private
Common Road, Chorleywood WD3 5LN
Tel (092 78) 2009
Mem 180 55(L) 40(J)
Sec LW Turner
Holes 9 L 2838 yds SSS 67

For map index see page 203.

Recs Am–65 SM McCready
Pro–64 H Bradshaw
V'trs WD–U exc Tues & Thurs am
WE–Sat pm only
Fees £6 (£7.50)
Loc 3 miles W of Rickmansworth
off A404

Dyrham Park CC (1963)

Private
Galley Lane, Barnet
Tel (01) 440 3361
Mem 300
Sec DU Prentice
Pro W Large (01) 440 3904
Holes 18 L 6369 yds SSS 70
V'trs M–welcome WD SOC–Wed
Loc London 10 miles on A1
Mis Guests must be accompanied
by a member

East Herts (1898)

Private
Hamels Park, Buntingford SG9 9NA
Tel (0920) 821923
Mem 500
Sec JA Harper (0920) 821978
Pro James Hamilton
(0920) 821922
Holes 18 L 6449 yds SSS 71
Recs Am–68 JA Watts
Pro–R Joyce
V'trs WD–H WE–M
Fees On application
Loc 1/4 mile N of Puckeridge
on A10

Elstree (1984)

Private
Watling Street, Elstree WD6 3AA
Tel (01) 953 6115
Mem 550
Sec G Stoneman
Pro G Stoneman (01) 207 5680
Holes 18 L 6100 yds SSS 69
Recs Am–68 C Woodcock (1987)
V'trs U SOC
Fees On application
Loc A5183, 1 mile N of Elstree.
8 miles N of London.
M1 Junction 4, 2 miles
Mis Pay and play course; 40 bay
floodlit driving range

Hadley Wood (1922)

Private
Beech Hill, Hadley Wood, Barnet
EN4 0JJ
Tel (01) 449 4486
Mem 600
Sec JE Linaker (Sec/Mgr)
(01) 449 4328
Pro A McGinn (01) 449 3285
Holes 18 L 6473 yds SSS 71
Recs Am–67 CC Holton
Pro–67 PP Elson
V'trs WD–H or I WE/BH–M
Fees On application
Loc 10 miles N London off A111
between Potters Bar and
Cockfosters. 2 miles S of
M25 Junction 24

Harpenden (1894)

Private
Hammonds End, Harpenden
Tel (058 27) 2580
Mem 800
Sec H Pitcock
Pro DH Smith (058 27) 67124
Holes 18 L 6363 yds SSS 70
Recs Am–67 B Bulmer (1987)
V'trs WD–U WE/BH–M SOC exc
Thurs, Ladies Day
Fees £11 D–£18
Loc 6 miles N of St Albans

Harpenden Common (1931)

Private
East Common, Harpenden AL5 1BL
Tel (058 27) 2856
Mem 700
Sec HN Hobbs (058 27) 5959
Pro N Lawrence (0582) 460655
Holes 18 L 5651 yds SSS 67
Pro–65 R Mitchell (1988)
V'trs WD–U WE–M SOC
Fees £8.50
Loc 4 miles N of St Albans

Hartsbourne CC (1946)

Private
Hartsbourne Avenue, Bushey Heath
WD2 1JW
Tel (01) 950 1113
Mem 400
Sec RJH Jourdan
Pro Geof Hunt (01) 950 2836
Holes 18 L 6305 yds SSS 70
9 L 5432 yds SSS 70
Recs Am–67 E Silver
Pro–62 P Oosterhuis
V'trs NA
Loc 5 miles SE of Watford

Hatfield London (1976)

Private
Bedwell Park, Essendon, Hatfield
AL9 6JA
Tel (0707) 42624
Mem 100
Sec T Takizawa
Holes 18 L 6878 yds SSS 73
V'trs U
Fees £7 (£18)
Loc B158

Knebworth (1908)

Private
Deards End Lane, Knebworth SG3 6NL
Tel (0438) 812752
Mem 900
Sec JC Wright
Pro MW Blainey (0438) 812757
Holes 18 L 6428 yds SSS 71
Recs Am–64 PR Robinson
Pro–66 J Hudson, P Mitchell
V'trs WD–U H WE–M SOC–WD (Fri
max 24)
Fees On application
Loc 1 mile S of Stevenage

Letchworth (1905)

Private
Letchworth SG6 3NQ
Tel (0462) 683203
Mem 900
Sec BM Barber
Pro SJ Mutimer (0462) 682713
Holes 18 L 6057 yds SSS 69
Recs Am–67 RF Croft
Pro–66 NC Coles
V'trs WD–U WE–M SOC–Wed–Fri
Fees £13
Loc Letchworth off A505

Little Hay (1977)

Public
Box Lane, Bovingdon,
Hemel Hempstead
Tel (0442) 833798
Pro D Johnson
Holes 18 L 6610 yds SSS 72
Recs Pro–69
V'trs U
Fees £3.60 (£5)
Loc Off A41 at Box Lane

Mid Herts (1893)

Private
Gustard Wood, Wheathampstead
AL4 8RS
Tel (058 283) 3385
Mem 500(M) 125(L)
Sec CJ Bowen (058 283) 2242
Pro NG Brown (058 283) 2788
Holes 18 L 6060 yds SSS 69
Recs Am–68 P Mayles (1987)
Pro–66 H Baiocchi, R Morris,
J Pinsent (1987)
V'trs WD–U exc Tues WE/BH–M
SOC
Fees On application
Loc 6 miles N of St Albans

Moor Park (1923)

Private
Rickmansworth
Tel (0923) 773146
Mem 1950
Sec JA Davies
Pro ER Whitehead
Holes High 18 L 6903 yds SSS 73
West 18 L 5823 yds SSS 68
Recs High Am–69 RY Mitchell
Pro–67 M King
West Am– 63 AJ Eisner
Pro–63 AD Locke, A Lees,
EE Whitcombe
V'trs WD–I WE/BH–M
Fees On request
Loc Moor Park Station 3/4 mile.
Rickmansworth Station 1 mile.
M25 Junction 18, 1 mile

Old Fold Manor (1910)

Private
Hadley Green, Barnet EN5 4QN
Tel **(01) 449 1650**
Mem 500
Sec DV Dalingwater (01) 440 9185
Pro P Jones (01) 440 7488
Holes 18 L 6473 yds SSS 71
Recs Am–66 A Clark
Pro–68 SL King
V'trs WD–I/H WE–M
Fees £15
Loc 1 mile N of Barnet on A1000

Panshanger (1976)

Public
Old Herns Lane, Welwyn Garden City
Tel **(0707) 332837**
Mem 352
Sec JJ Travers (07072) 68979
Pro A Hall
Holes 18 L 6626 metres SSS 72
Recs Am–71 S Walton (1987)
Pro–70 R Green
V'trs U
Fees £4.50 (£5)
Loc 2 miles off A1, B1000 to Hertford

Porters Park (1899)

Private
Shenley Hill, Radlett WD7 7AZ
Tel **(092 76) 6262**
Mem 550
Sec MC Stamford (092 76) 4127
Pro D Gleeson (092 76) 4366
Holes 18 L 6313 yds SSS 70
Recs Am–65 J Putt
Pro–64 P Townsend
V'trs WD–H (phone first) WE/BH–M SOC–Wed&Thurs
Fees £18–£25
Loc Radlett Station 1/2 mile

Potters Bar (1923)

Private
Darkes Lane, Potters Bar EN6 1DE
Tel **(0707) 52020**
Mem 550
Sec F Ireland
Pro R Watkins (0707) 52987
Holes 18 L 6273 yds SSS 70
Recs Am–66 RR Davis
Pro–65 D McClelland
V'trs WD–H WE–M SOC–Mon/Tues/Fri
Loc Potters Bar Station 1/2 mile

Redbourn (1970)

Private
Kinsbourne Green Lane, Redbourn, nr St Albans
Tel **(058 285) 3493**
Sec WM Dunn (058 285) 2150
Pro S Baldwin
Holes 18 L 6407 yds SSS 71
9 L 1361 yds SSS 27
V'trs WD–U exc 4.30–6.15 pm WE/BH–NA before 3pm SOC
Fees 18 holes £7 (£8)
9 holes £2.50–£4
Loc 4 miles N of St Albans. 4 miles S of Luton. 1 mile S of M1 Junction 9

Rickmansworth (1937)

Public
Moor Lane, Rickmansworth WO3 1QL
Tel **(0923) 773163**
Mem 240
Sec LJ Miller (01) 958 3028
Pro I Duncan (0923) 775278
Holes 18 L 4412 yds SSS 62
Recs Am–62 L Silver
V'trs U
Fees £3.50 (£5)
Loc SE of town. M25 Rickmansworth exit. A4145 towards Watford

Royston (1893)

Private
Baldock Road, Royston
Tel **(0763) 42177 (Members)**
Mem 700
Sec Mrs S Morris (0763) 42696
Pro M Hatcher (0763) 43476
Holes 18 L 6032 yds SSS 69
Recs Am–65 T Moss
Pro–63 B Waites
V'trs WD–U WE/BH–M SOC
Fees £9
Loc Royston

Sandy Lodge (1910)

Private
Northwood, Middx
Tel **(092 74) 25429**
Mem 500
Sec JN Blair
Pro A Fox (092 74) 25321
Holes 18 L 6340 yds SSS 70
Recs Am–67 JM Brew, IC Goode
Pro–64 A Jacklin
V'trs WD/WE/BH–M
Fees £15
Loc Adjacent Moor Park Station, Rickmansworth

South Herts (1899)

Private
Totteridge, London N20 8QU
Tel **(01) 445 0117**
Mem 800
Sec AA Dogan (01) 445 2035
Pro RS Livingston (01) 445 4633
Holes 18 L 6470 yds SSS 71
9 L 1581 yds
Recs Am–67 R Neil (1964)
Pro–66 D Thomas (1966)
V'trs WD–IH WE/BH–M
Fees D–£18
Loc 10 miles N of London

Stevenage (1980)

Public
Aston Lane, Stevenage SG2 7EL
Tel **(043 888) 424**
Mem 475
Sec ET Messent (043 888) 322
Pro DW Astill
Holes 18 L 6451 yds SSS 71 Par 3
Recs Pro–71 R Mitchell, R Whitehead
V'trs U
Fees £3 (£4.35)
Loc Off A602 to Hertford
Mis Driving Range. 9 hole Par 3

Verulam (1905)

Private
London Road, St Albans AL1 1JG
Tel **(0727) 53327**
Mem 600
Sec RJ McMillan
Pro P Anderson (0727) 61401
Holes 18 L 6432 yds SSS 71
Recs Am–70
Pro–65 R Mitchell
V'trs WD–U WE/BH–NA
Fees £10 (reduced Mon–£6)
Loc 1 miles S of town on A1081

Welwyn Garden City (1922)

Private
Mannicotts, High Oaks Road, Welwyn Garden City AL8 7BP
Tel **(0707) 322722**
Mem 700
Sec JL Carragher (0707) 325243
Pro H Arnott (0707) 325525
Holes 18 L 6200 yds SSS 69
Recs Am–65 I Fordyce (1985)
Pro–63 N Faldo (1988)
V'trs U–Sun–M after noon
Fees £12.50 (£20)
Loc 3/4 mile N of Hatfield. From A1 take B197 to Valley Road

West Herts (1890)

Private
Cassiobury Park, Watford WD1 7SL
Tel **(0923) 224264**
Mem 600
Sec RAS Gordon (0923) 36484
Pro CS Gough (0923) 220352
Holes 18 L 6488 yds SSS 71
Recs Am–68 SA Masson
Pro–67 R Whitehead
V'trs WD–I WE/BH–M SOC–Wed & Fri
Fees £10.50
Loc Between Watford and Rickmansworth off the A412

For map index see page 203.

Whipsnade Park (1974)

Private
Studham Lane, Dagnall HP4 1RH
Tel **(044284) 2330**
Mem 400
Sec D Whalley
Pro M Lewendon
Holes 18 L 6812 yds SSS 72
Recs Am–71 A Calder
V'trs WD–U WE–M SOC–WD
Fees £11 D–£15
Loc S of Whipsnade Zoo between Dagnall and Studham

Humberside

Beverley & East Riding (1889)

Private
The Westwood, Beverley HU17 8RG
Tel **(0482) 867190**
Mem 460
Sec BJ Hiles (0482) 868757
Pro I Mackie (0482) 869519
Holes 18 L 5937 yds SSS 69
Recs Am–64 I Woodhead, D Hannam
Pro–69 NS Bundy
V'trs U SOC–WD
Fees £5.50 (£8)
Loc Beverley–Walkington Road

Boothferry (Spaldington) (1981)

Public
Spaldington Lane, Spaldington, Howden, Goole
Tel **(0430) 430364**
Mem 650
Sec A Atkin (0405) 5141
Pro S Wilkinson
Holes 18 L 6593 yds SSS 72
Recs Am–70 R Giles (1988)
Pro–70 M Ingham (1984)
S Rolley (1987)
Fees £3 (£6.40)
Loc 3 miles N of Howden on B1288. M62 Junction 37

Bridlington (1905)

Private
Belvedere Road, Bridlington YO15 3NA
Tel **(0262) 672092**
Mem 663
Sec C Wilson (0262) 674679
Pro D Rands (0262) 674721
Holes 18 L 6330 yds SSS 70
V'trs U Sun–after 11.15am
Fees £7 D–£9 (£11 D–£13)
Loc Bridlington Station $1^1/_2$ miles

Brough (1891)

Private
Brough HU15 1HB
Tel **(0482) 667374**
Mem 650
Sec HJ Oldroyd (0482) 667291
Pro G Townhill (0482) 667483
Holes 18 L 6189 yds SSS 69
Recs Am–64 PWJ Greenhough, MJ Kelley
Pro–63 A Thompson
V'trs WD–U Wed after 2pm
Fees £12
Loc 10 miles W of Hull on A63

Cleethorpes (1896)

Private
Kings Road, Cleethorpes DN35 0PN
Tel **(0472) 814060**
Mem 750
Sec GB Standaloft
Pro E Sharp (0472) 812059
Holes 18 L 6015 yds SSS 69
Recs Am–67 DB Short
Pro–64 D Ramsey
V'trs Wed pm–NA Sat pm/Sun am–XL
Fees £7 (£10)
Loc Cleethorpes 1 mile

Driffield (1938)

Private
Sunderlandwick, Driffield
Tel **(0377) 43116**
Mem 384
Sec K Pickles (0377) 44069
Holes 9 L 6227 yds SSS 70
V'trs U
Fees £6 (£10)
Loc 10 miles S of Bridlington

Flamborough Head (1932)

Private
Lighthouse Road, Flamborough, Bridlington YO15 1AR
Tel **(0262) 850333**
Mem 400
Sec WR Scarle (0262) 676494
Holes 18 L 5438 yds SSS 66
Recs Am–63 GR Allen
Pro–63 P Dawson
V'trs U
Fees £7 (£9) W–£28
Loc 5 miles NE of Bridlington

Ganstead Park (1976)

Private
Longdales Lane, Coniston, Hull HU11 4LB
Tel **(0482) 811280**
Mem 350
Sec RB Barker
Pro M Smee (0482) 811121
Holes 18 L 6534 yds SSS
Recs Am–67 M Smee (1987)
Pro–67 H Clark
V'trs U H WE–NA before noon SOC
Fees £6 (£9)
Loc 2 miles E of Hull boundary on A165

Grimsby (1923)

Private
Little Coates Road, Grimsby DN34 4LU
Tel **(0472) 42823**
Mem 550 150(L) 70(J)
Sec AD Houlihan (0472) 42630
Pro S Houltby (0472) 356981
Holes 18 L 6068 yds SSS 69
Recs Am–66 M James
Pro–66 BJ Hunt
V'trs WD–U Sat pm/Sun am–XL
Fees £8.50 (£11) W–£30
Loc 1 mile W of centre

Hainsworth Park (1983)

Private
Brandesburton, Driffield YO25
Tel **(0964) 542362**
Mem 300
Sec BW Atkin (Prop)
Holes 9 L 5360 yds SSS 66
V'trs WD–U WE–U after 4pm SOC–WD
Fees £4.50 (£6)
Loc 8 miles N of Beverley (A165). Bridlington 15 miles

Hessle (1906)

Private
Westfield Road, Cottingham
Tel **(0482) 650171**
Mem 600
Sec RL Dorsey
Pro G Fieldsend (0482) 650190
Holes 18 L 6638 yds SSS 72
Recs Am–68 A Wright (1984)
Pro–69 B Thompson (1980)
V'trs WD–U exc Tues 9.15am–1pm WE–M
Fees £10 (£15)
Loc 3 miles SW of Cottingham

Holme Hall (1908)

Private
Holme Lane, Bottesford, Scunthorpe DN16 3RF
Tel **(0724) 849185 (Steward)**
Mem 490 110(L) 75(J) 3(5)
Sec AHF Holtby (0724) 862078
Pro M Haines (0724) 851816
Holes 18 L 6475 yds SSS 71
Recs Am–67 S Steele, A Thain, K Blow, FW Wood
Pro–66 B Thompson
V'trs WD–U WE–M H SOC–WD
Fees £8 D–£12
Loc 4 miles SE of Scunthorpe. M180 Junction 4

Hornsea (1908)

Private
Rolston Road, Hornsea HU18 1XG
Tel **(0964) 532020**
Mem 550
Sec BW Kirton
Pro B Thompson (0964) 534989
Holes 18 L 6461 yds SSS 71
Recs Am–65 P Binnington (1986)
Pro–67 B Thompson (1985)
V'trs WD–U WE–Restricted SOC
Fees £10 (£15)
Mis No catering Mon

Hull (1921)

Private
The Hall, 27 Packman Lane,
Kirk Ella, Hull HU10 7JT
Tel **(0482) 653026**
Mem 756
Sec R Toothill (0482) 658919
Pro D Jagger (0482) 653074
Holes 18 L 6242 yds SSS 70
Recs Am–64 JD Dockar, R Roper
Pro–66 D Dunk, N Hunt,
S Smith, D Jagger
V'trs U WE–NA
Fees £12 R/D
Loc 5 miles W of Hull

Immingham (1975)

Private
Church Lane, Immingham, Grimsby
Tel **(0469) 75298**
Mem 350 60(L) 50(J)
Pro J Moffat (0469) 75493
Holes 18 L 5809 yds SSS 68
Recs Am–67 J Lea, C Robinson
V'trs Sun–NA before noon
Fees £5
Loc Civic Centre, $^1/_2$ mile behind
St Andrew's Church

Kingsway

Public
Kingsway, Scunthorpe DN15 7ER
Tel **(0724) 840945**
Sec RD Highfield
Pro C Mann
Holes 9 L 1915 yds SSS 59
V'trs U
Fees £1.10 (£1.40)
Loc Berkeley Circle 300 yds

Normanby Hall (1978)

Public
Normanby Park, Scunthorpe
Tel **(0724) 720226**
Mem 566
Sec ID Reekie (0724) 280444
(ext 850)
Pro C Mann
Holes 18 L 6548 yds SSS 71
Recs AM–
V'trs U SOC–WD
Fees £4 (£5.50)
Loc Normanby Park, 5 miles
N of Scunthorpe

Scunthorpe (1936)

Private
Ashby Decoy, Burringham Road,
Scunthorpe DN17 2AB
Tel **(0724) 842913/866561**
Mem 450 105(L) 50(J)
Sec EA Willsmore
Pro J Corden (0724) 868972
Holes 18 L 6281 yds SSS 71
Recs Am–69 R Mortimer
V'trs U SOC–WD
Fees £12 (Sat–£12 Sun NA)

Springhead Park (1903)

Public
Willerby Road, Hull
Tel **(0482) 656309**
Mem 449
Sec F Coggrave (0482) 656776
Pro B Herrington
Holes 18 L 6439 yds SSS 71
Recs Am–69 AD Hill, A Wright
Pro–65 S Rolley
V'trs U
Fees £2.70 (£3.50)

Sutton Park (1935)

Public
Salthouse Road, Hull
Tel **(0482) 74242**
Mem 650
Sec CD Smith (0482) 781039
Pro P Rushworth (0482) 711450
Holes 18 L 6251 yds SSS 70
Recs Am–67 A Wright
Pro–64 L Herrington
V'trs U
Fees £2.70 (£3.50)
Loc 3 miles E of city centre

Withernsea (1909)

Private
Chestnut Ave, Withernsea HU19 2PG
Tel **(0964) 612258**
Mem 296 47(L) 42(J) 207(5)
Sec F Buckley (0964) 612214
Holes 9 L 5112 yds SSS 64
Recs Am–62 SH Kellet
Pro–63 Gordon Townhill
V'trs WD–U WE–NA Sun am SOC
Fees £5 (£5) W–£20
Loc 17 miles E of Hull.
S side of Withernsea

Isle of Man

Castletown (1892)

Private
104 Ballycriy Park, Colby
Tel **(0624) 834422**
Mem 300
Sec TH Dore
Pro MC Crowe (0624) 822125
Holes 18 L 6716 yds SSS 72
Recs Am–68 WR Ennett
V'trs U SOC (arrange with Pro)
Fees £7 (£8)
Loc $1^1/_4$ miles E of Castletown

Douglas (1937)

Private
Pulrose Road, Douglas
Mem 450
Sec WR Moore (0624) 25760
Holes Play over Douglas Municipal

Douglas Municipal (1927)

Public
Pulrose Park, Douglas
Tel **(0624) 75952**
Sec NR Devereau
Holes 18 L 6080 yds SSS 69
Recs Am–63
V'trs U
Fees £4 D–£6 W–£20
Loc Douglas Pier 1 mile

Howstrake (1914)

Private
Groudle Road, Onchan
Tel **(0624) 20430**
Mem 400
Sec JC Davies
Holes 18 L 5367 yds SSS 66
Recs Am–62 TP Kniveton
Pro–69
V'trs U SOC
Fees £5 (£7)
Loc 1 mile N of Douglas

Peel (1896)

Private
Rheast Lane, Peel
Tel **(062 484) 2227**
Mem 500
Sec DR Forth (062 484) 3456
(mornings)
Holes 18 L 5914 yds SSS 68
Recs Am–64 J Sutton
V'trs WD–U WE/BH–not before
10.30am
Fees £6 (£8)
Loc 10 miles W of Douglas

Port St Mary

Public
Port St Mary
Sec JM Keggen (0624) 833133
Holes 9 L 2711 yds SSS 66
V'trs U
Fees £1 W–£4
Loc Callow Road

Ramsey

Private
Tel **(0624) 813365/812244**
Mem 870
Sec SA Lockwood (0624) 812397
Holes 18 L 6019 yds SSS 69
Recs Am–65 S Boyd
Pro–65 S Lyle
V'trs U H for comps SOC
Fees £7 (£8)
Loc W boundary of Ramsey.
N of Douglas

Rowany (1895)

Private
Port Erin
Tel (0624) 834108
Mem 500
Sec RJS Mawson (Mgr) (0624) 834988
Holes 18 L 5840 yds SSS 69
Recs Am–68 A Cain
V'trs U H–Open comps SOC
Fees £6.50 (£7.50)
Loc South of island

Isle of Wight

Cowes (1908)

Private
Crossfield Avenue, Cowes PO31 8HN
Tel (0983) 292303
Mem 250
Sec RE Wootton (0983) 295802
Holes 9 L 5880 yds SSS 68
Recs Am–69 I Graham
V'trs I H Thurs–NA before 4pm (Ladies Day) Fri–NA after 5pm Sun am–NA
Fees £8 W–£40
Loc Entry on Crossfield Avenue (private road); nr Cowes High School

Freshwater Bay

Private
Afton Down, Freshwater
Tel (0983) 752955
Mem 450
Sec HGV Gordon
Holes 18 L 5628 yds SSS 68
Recs Am–68 K Garrett (1984)
Pro–66 T Underwood (1981)
V'trs U SOC
Fees £10 (£12) W–£50 2W–£70
Loc 400 yds off Military Road

Newport IW (1896)

Private
St George's Down, nr Shide, Newport PO30 3BA
Tel (0983) 525076
Mem 300
Sec J Ambrose
Holes 9 L 5704 yds SSS 68
Recs Am–65 J Burton (1987)
V'trs WD–U WE–NA before noon
Fees £8.50
Loc 1 mile SE of Newport

Osborne (1903)

Private
Club House, East Cowes
Tel (0983) 295421
Mem 260 90(L)
Sec Mrs M Butler
Pro I Taylor (0983) 295649
Holes 9 L 6286 yds SSS 70
V'trs U exc Ladies' Day 11am–2.30pm–NA Sun–NA after 11.30am SOC
Fees £10 (£12) 5D–£30
Loc S of East Cowes in grounds of Osborne House

Ryde (1921)

Private
Ryde House Park, Ryde
Tel (0983) 614809
Mem 450
Sec F Cockayne (0983) 64388
Pro Steve Ward (0983) 62088
Holes 9 L 5220 yds SSS 66
Recs Am–65 B Marshall, D Chalon
Pro–64 T Underwood, D Allen
V'trs U
Fees £6 (£7.50)
Loc On main Ryde/Newport road

Shanklin & Sandown (1900)

Private
Fairway Lake, Sandown PO36 9PR
Tel (0983) 403217
Mem 700
Sec GA Wormald
Pro P Warner (0983) 404424
Holes 18 L 6000 yds SSS 69
Recs Am–66 D McToldridge
Pro–65 R Wynn
V'trs U SOC–WD
Fees £14 (£16) 5D–£55 W–£70 F–£120
Loc Sandown

Ventnor (1892)

Private
Steephill Down Road, Ventnor
Tel (0983) 853326
Mem 180
Sec R Hose (0983) 853198
Holes 9 L 5772 yds SSS 68
Recs Am–73 IH Guy
V'trs U
Fees £6 (£7)
Loc NW boundary of Ventnor

Kent

Aquarius (1913)

Private
Marmora Rd, Honor Oak, London SE22
Tel (01) 693 1626
Mem 350
Sec PA Mutton
Pro F Private
Holes 9 L 5034 yds SSS 65
Recs Am–62 R Hare
Pro–63 F Private
V'trs M
Loc SE London

Ashford (1904)

Private
Sandyhurst Lane, Ashford TN25 4NT
Tel (0233) 20180
Mem 650
Sec AH Story (0233) 622655
Pro H Sherman (0233) 629644
Holes 18 L 6246 yds SSS 70
Recs Am–66 L Donovan, KC Elvin
Pro–63 RS Fidler
V'trs WD–UH WE/BH–H SOC
Fees D–£13 (D–£16)
Loc Ashford 1½ miles (A20)

Barnehurst (1903)

Private
Mayplace Road, East Barnehurst DA7 6JU
Tel (0322) 523746
Mem 250
Sec GE Audsley (0322) 54612
Pro S Barr (0322) 51205
Holes 9 L 5320 yds SSS 66
Recs Am–64
Pro–64
V'trs Mon/Wed/Fri–U Other days restricted
Fees £3.60 (£5.70)
Loc Between Crayford and Bexley Heath

Bearsted (1898)

Private
Ware Street, Bearsted, nr Maidstone
Tel (0622) 38389
Mem 648
Sec (0622) 38198
Pro T Simpson (0622) 38024
Holes 18 L 6253 yds SSS 70
Recs Am–68 D Jenner (1987)
Pro–69 G Norton (1982)
V'trs WD–I H WE–H M Recognised GC members only SOC
Fees £12 D–£18
Loc Maidstone 2½ miles

Beckenham Place Park (1907)

Public
Beckenham Hill Road, Beckenham SE6
Tel (01) 650 2292
Mem Approx 180
Sec L Snashfold (01) 659 8086
Pro B Woodman (01) 658 5374
Holes 18 L 5722 yds SSS 68
Recs Am–62 S Champion
Pro–65 T Cotton
V'trs U
Fees £4.90 (£7)
Loc 2 miles S of Catford SE6
Mis Course shared with Braeside GC

Bexley Heath (1907)

Private
Mount Road, Bexley Heath
Tel (01) 303 6951
Mem 350
Sec RJ Cawston
Holes 9 L 5239 yds SSS 66
Recs Am–65 D Fillary
V'trs WD–H before 4pm
Fees £7
Loc Station 1 mile

For explanation of abbreviations see page 202.

Braeside (1947)

Public

The Mansion, Beckenham Place Park, Beckenham

Tel **(01) 650 2292**
Mem 150
Sec R Oliver
Holes Play over Beckenham Place Park

Bromley (1948)

Public

Magpie Hall Lane, Bromley, Kent

Tel **(01) 462 8001**
Mem 100
Sec BJ Pratt (01) 310 5434
Pro Alan Hodgeson (01) 462 7014
Holes Play over Magpie Hall Lane Course

Broome Park (1981)

Private

Barham, nr Canterbury CT4 6QX

Tel **(0227) 831701**
Sec D Lees (Hon)
Pro T Britz (0227) 831701 Ext 264
Holes 18 L 6610 yds SSS 72
Recs Am–66 M Smedley (1988)
Pro–66 B Impett (1984)
V'trs H WE–NA before noon SOC
Fees £12 (£15)
Loc M2/A2–A260 Folkestone road, $1^1/_2$ miles on RH side

Canterbury (1927)

Private

Scotland Hills, Canterbury CT1 1TW

Tel **(0227) 463586**
Mem 720
Sec G Good (0227) 453532
Pro P Everard (0227) 462865
Holes 18 L 6245 yds SSS 70
Recs Am–66 RJ Davies
Pro–64 K Redford
V'trs UH Sun am–NA
SOC–Tues & Thurs
Fees £13 D–£17.50 Sat–£16 Sun–£20
Loc 1 mile E of town centre on A257

Cherry Lodge (1969)

Private

Jail Lane, Biggin Hill, nr Westerham

Tel **(0959) 72250**
Mem 840
Sec D Downard (Mgr)
Pro N Child (0959) 72989
Holes 18 L 6908 yds SSS 74
Short course 6031 yds SSS 69
Recs Am–70 N Lancaster (1984)
Pro–69 B Cameron (1986)
V'trs WD–U WE–M
Fees £14
Loc 15 miles SW of London
Mis Buggies available

Chestfield (Whitstable) (1925)

Private

103 Chestfield Road, Whitstable CT5 3LU

Tel **(022 779) 2243**
Mem 630
Sec DA Kemp (Mgr) (022 779) 2365
Pro J Brotherton (022 779) 3563
Holes 18 L 6126 yds SSS 69
Recs Am–67 RA Howard, S Reid, M Wilson
Pro–64 B Cameron
V'trs WD–H WE–Sat after 11am Sun after 3pm
Fees On application
Loc 1 mile S of A229 and Chestfield Station

Chislehurst (1894)

Private

Camden Place, Chislehurst BR7 5HJ

Tel **(01) 467 3055**
Mem 740
Sec NE Pearson (01) 467 2782
Pro AS Costorphine (01) 467 6798
Holes 18 L 5128 yds SSS 65
Recs Am–62 DC Theobald (1987)
Pro–61 J Bennett
V'trs WD–H WE–M
Fees D–£20
Loc Charing Cross 20 mins

Cobtree Manor Park

Public

Chatham Road, Boxley, Maidstone

Tel **(0622) 53276**
Mem 500
Sec AD Pearce (0622) 671847
Pro M Drew
Holes 18 L 5716 yds SSS 68
V'trs WD–U WE/BH–(book 1 wk in advance) SOC–WD
Fees £4.50 (£6.50)
Loc Town centre 3 miles on A229 road to Chatham

Corinthian (1987)

Private

Gay Dawn Farm, Fawkham, nr Dartford, DA3 8LZ

Tel **(04747) 7559**
Mem 300
Sec SJ Billings
Holes 9 L 3118 yds SSS 36
V'trs WD–UH WE/BH–M SOC
Fees £5
Loc 4 miles S of Dartford Tunnel. 1 mile E of Brands Hatch along Fawkham Valley road
Mis Artificial greens

Cranbrook (1969)

Private

Benenden Road, Cranbrook TN17 4AL

Tel **(0580) 712833/712934**
Mem 700
Sec HM Borissow (0580) 712833
Pro G Potter (0580) 712934
Holes 18 L 6128 yds SSS 70
Recs Am–67 S Coulter
Pro–70 S Barr
V'trs WD–U WE/BH–U exc comp days SOC
Fees £8 (£11)
Loc 15 miles S of Maidstone. Sissinghurst $1^1/_4$ miles
Mis Buggies for hire Apr–Oct

Cray Valley (1972)

Private

Sandy Lane, St Paul's Cray, Orpington

Tel **(0689) 31927**
Mem 700
Sec R Hill (0689) 39677
Pro T Morgan (0689) 37909
Holes 18 L 5624 yds SSS 67
9 L 2100 yds SSS 60
V'trs WD–U WE–H SOC
Fees £6 (£8)
Loc 15 miles SW of London

Darenth Valley (1973)

Public

Station Road, Shoreham, nr Sevenoaks TN14 7SA

Tel **(09592) 2944 (Steward)**
Pro P Edwards (09592) 2922
Holes 18 L 6356 yds SSS 71
Recs Pro–68 B Owens P Edwards
V'trs WD–U SOC
Fees £6 (£8.75)
Loc 3 miles N of Sevenoaks off A225

Dartford (1897)

Private

Dartford Heath, Dartford

Tel **(0322) 23616**
Mem 600
Sec MJF Meason (0322) 26455
Pro A Blackburn (0322) 26409
Holes 18 L 5914 yds SSS 68
Recs Am–66 G Wright
Pro–66 C Tucker
V'trs WD–I WE–M H
Fees £11 (£5)
Loc Town centre 2 miles

Deangate Ridge (1972)

Public

Hoo, Rochester ME3 8RZ

Tel **(0634) 251180**
Mem 800
Sec JA Penfold (0474) 52495
Pro B Aram (0634) 251180
Holes 18 L 6300 yds SSS 70
Recs Am–67 AJ Rossiter (1985)
Pro–64 AJ Russell (1986)
V'trs U
Fees £2.95 (£4.20)
Loc Nr Isle of Grain

For map index see page 203.

Edenbridge G & CC (1973)

Private
Crouch House Road, Edenbridge TN8 5LQ
Tel (0732) 865097
Mem 800
Sec Mrs S Mitchell
Pro (0732) 865202
Holes 18 L 6604 yds SSS 72
Recs Am–72 I Martyr
V'trs WE/BH–U after 11am SOC–WD
Fees £7 (£10 After 12.30pm–£8)
Loc M25 Junction 6. Gatwick Airport 20 mins
Mis 16-bay floodlit driving range. 9-hole beginners' course

Eltham Warren (1890)

Private
Clubhouse, Bexley Road, Eltham, London SE9 2PE
Tel (01) 850 1166
Mem 400
Sec P Standish (01) 850 4477
Pro IA Coleman
Holes 9 L 5840 yds SSS 68
Recs Am–66 G Janes
V'trs WD–I WE/BH–M SOC
Fees £12
Loc Eltham

Faversham (1910)

Private
Belmont Park, Faversham
Tel (079 589) 251
Mem 700
Sec DB Christie (079 589) 561
Pro GG Nixon (079 589) 275
Holes 18 L 6021 yds SSS 69
Recs Am–65 R Chapman
Pro–67 D Place
V'trs WD–I or H WE–M SOC
Fees £12
Loc Town and M2, 2 miles

Foxgrove

Private
Westgate Road, Beckenham
Tel (01) 650 1707
Sec FG Wyatt
Holes Play over Beckenham Place Park

Gillingham (1908)

Private
Woodlands Road, Gillingham
Tel (0634) 50999
Mem 450 100(L) 50(J) 120(5)
Sec LP O'Grady (0634) 53017
Pro S Barrow (0634) 55862
Holes 18 L 5911 yds SSS 68
Recs Am–65 T Williamson
Pro–64 P Clark
V'trs WD–I H WE/BH–M
Fees £8 D–£11
Loc A2/M2, 2 miles

Hawkhurst (1968)

Private
High Street, Hawkhurst TN18 4JS
Tel (058 05) 2396
Mem 300
Sec AW Shipley
Pro T Collins (058 05) 3600
Holes 9 L 5769 yds SSS 68
Recs Am–70 B Betts
Pro–68 R Cameron
V'trs WD–U
Fees £8 (£10)
Loc 14 miles S of Tunbridge Wells on A268

Herne Bay (1889)

Private
Eddington, Herne Bay CT6 7PG
Tel (0227) 4097
Mem 400
Sec B Warren 0227) 373964
Pro D Lambert (0227) 374727
Holes 18 L 5466 yds SSS 67
Recs Am–65 SJ Wood
Pro–65 C Clark
V'trs WD–U WE/BH–H after 11am SOC–WD
Fees £10 D–£15 (£15)
Loc Herne Bay/Canterbury road

High Elms (1969)

Public
High Elms Road, Downe, Orpington
Tel (0689) 58175
Mem 270
Sec P Argent (01) 462 2940
Pro A Hodgson
Holes 18 L 6210 yds SSS 70
Recs Am–68 I Farman
Pro–A Hodgson
V'trs U
Fees £4.50 (£6.50)
Loc Off A21 via Shire Lane

Holtye (1893)

Private
Holtye, Cowden TN8 7ED
Tel (034 286) 635
Mem 480
Sec JP Holmes (034 286) 576
Pro M Scarles
Holes 9 L 5259 yds SSS 66
Recs Am–65 PD Scarles, JA Couling
Pro–64 S Frost
V'trs WD–U WE–NA before noon SOC–Tues only
Fees On application
Loc 4 miles E of E Grinstead on A264. 6 miles W of Tunbridge Wells

Hythe Imperial (1950)

Private
Prince's Parade, Hythe CT21 5RN
Tel (0303) 67441
Mem 300
Sec GE May (0303) 67554
Pro G Ritchie
Holes 9 L 5511 yds SSS 67
Recs Am–63 PI Kaye
Pro–64 SH Sherman
V'trs U H SOC
Fees £8 (£10) W–£30
Loc On the coast 4 miles W of Folkestone

Knole Park (1924)

Private
Seal Hollow Road, Sevenoaks TN15 0HJ
Tel (0732) 452709
Mem 600
Sec DJL Hoppe (0732) 452150
Pro PE Gill (0732) 451740
Holes 18 L 6249 yds SSS 70
Recs Am–64 RW Seamer
V'trs WD–Restricted WE/BH–M H SOC
Fees £14 D–£22
Loc Seal Hollow Road

Lamberhurst (1890)

Private
Church Road, Lamberhurst TN3 8DT
Tel (0892) 890241
Mem 700
Sec A Steward-Brooks (0892) 890591
Pro M Travers (0892) 890552
Holes 18 L 6249 yds SSS 70
Recs Am–71 MJ Collett
Pro–69 N Stott
V'trs WD–UH WE–M
Fees £15 (£15)
Loc 5 miles SE of Tunbridge Wells

Langley Park (1910)

Private
Barnfield Wood Road, Beckenham BR3 2SZ
Tel (01) 650 2090
Mem 650
Sec JL Smart (01) 658 6849
Pro GT Ritchie (01) 650 1663
Holes 18 L 6488 yds SSS 71
Recs Am–66 T Trodd
Pro–65 P Mitchell (1987)
V'trs WD–I WE–M SOC–WD
Fees £16
Loc Bromley South Station 1 mile

Leeds Castle (1928)

Public
Leeds Castle, nr Maidstone ME17 1PL
Tel (062 780) 467
Pro C Miller
Holes 9 L 6017 yds SSS 69
Recs Pro–66
V'trs U

For explanation of abbreviations see page 202.

Fees £5.95 (9 holes)
Loc A20, 1 mile from M20 at Park Gate Inn entrance
Mis Booking system for 9 holes

Littlestone (1888)

Private
Littlestone, New Romney TB28 8RB
Tel (0679) 62310
Mem 450
Sec JD Lewis (0679) 63355
Pro Glynne Williams (0679) 62231
Holes 18 L 6417 yds SSS 71
9 hole course 3996 yds Par 64
Recs Am–67 G Godmon (1984), S Wood (1988)
Pro–67 T Gale (1985)
V'trs WD–H WE–by arrangement
Fees On application
Loc 15 miles S of Ashford

Lullingstone Park (1967)

Public
Park Gate, Chelsfield, nr Orpington
Tel (0959) 34542
Mem 400
Sec GS Childs
Pro G Lloyd
Holes 18 and 9 holes
Loc Off Orpington by-pass A224

Magpie Hall Lane (1948)

Public
Magpie Hall Lane, Bromley
Tel (01) 462 7014
Pro A Hodgson
Holes 9 L 5538 yds SSS 66
Recs Am–66 HE Harding, KW Miles
V'trs U
Loc Off Bromley Common (A21)
Mis Bromley Club plays here

Mid Kent (1909)

Private
Singlewell Road, Gravesend
Tel (0474) 52387
Mem 1050
Sec AF Reid (0474) 568035
Pro R Lee (0474) 332810
Holes 18 L 6206 yds SSS 70
V'trs WD–H WE–M
Fees On application
Loc 25 miles SE of London

Nevill (1914)

Private
Benhall Mill Road, Tunbridge Wells TN2 5JW
Tel (0892) 27820
Mem 400 200(L) 120(J) 150(5)
Sec RA White (0892) 25818
Pro P Huggett (0892) 32941
Holes 18 L 6336 yds SSS 70
Recs Am–66 A Sykes (1975)
Pro–66 M Warner (1988)
V'trs WD–H WE/BH–M
Fees WD–£14
Loc Tunbridge Wells 1 mile

North Foreland (1903)

Private
Kingsgate, Broadstairs, Thanet
Tel (0843) 62140
Mem 800
Sec LCR Hemmings
Pro M Lee (0843) 69628
Holes 18 L 6374 yds SSS 70
Recs Am–66 P Walton
Pro–66 G Will
V'trs WD–H WE–NA am –H pm
Fees Summer £11 (£14) Winter £9 (£14) Approach & Putt £3 (£4)
Loc Broadstairs Station 1½ miles
Mis 18 holes Approach and Putt

Poult Wood (1974)

Public
Poult Wood, Higham Lane, Tonbridge
Tel (0732) 364039
Mem 500
Sec A Hope (0732) 366180
Pro K Adwick
Holes 18 L 5569 yds SSS 67
V'trs U SOC–WD
Fees £4.25 (£6)
Loc 2 miles N of Tonbridge off A227

Prince's (1904)

Private
Sandwich Bay, Sandwich
Tel (0304) 611118
Mem 550
Sec G Rowlands (0304) 612000
Pro P Sparks (0304) 613797
Holes 27 hole Championship course 3×9 holes: Dunes/Himalayas/Shore. Combined courses 6238–6947 yds. Par 71–72. SSS 70–73.
Recs Himalayas/Shore Am–67 M Goodin
Pro–69 M Mannelli
Dunes/Himalayas Am–69 S Wood
V'trs U SOC–WD/WE (book with G Ramm)
Fees £16 D–£18 (£18 D–£21)
Loc Sandwich Bay

Rochester & Cobham Park (1891)

Private
Park Pale, by Rochester ME2 3UL
Tel (047 482) 3411
Mem 720
Sec Maj JW Irvine (Mgr)
Pro M Henderson (047 482) 3658
Holes 18 L 6467 yds SSS 71
Recs Am–67 JW Baldwin
Pro–67 M Henderson
V'trs WD–UH WE–M before 5pm SOC–Tues & Thurs
Fees £16
Loc 3 miles E of Gravesend turn on A2

Royal Blackheath (1608)

Private
Court Road, Eltham, London SE9 5AF
Tel (01) 850 1795
Mem 600
Sec K Angus
Pro I McGregor (01) 850 1763
Holes 18 L 6216 yds SSS 70
Recs Am–66 DM Woolmer
Pro–66 WC Thomas
V'trs U SOC
Fees £25
Loc Charing Cross–Mottingham 20 mins

Royal Cinque Ports (1892)

Private
Golf Road, Deal
Tel (0304) 374328
Mem 1015
Sec NS Phillips (0304) 374007
Pro A Reynolds (0304) 374170
Holes 18 L 6744 yds SSS 72
Recs Am–65 MF Bonallack
Pro–63 GD Manson
V'trs I
Fees On application
Loc Deal

Royal St George's (1887)

Private
Sandwich CT13 9PB
Tel (0304) 617308
Mem 700
Sec Capt. RJ Hitchen RN (0304) 613090
Pro N Cameron (0304) 617380
Holes 18 L 6534 yds SSS 72
Recs Am–67 H Berwick
Pro–64 C O'Connor Jr
V'trs WD–IH SOC–WD WE–M
Fees £21 D–£28
Loc Sandwich 1 mile

Ruxley (1975)

Public
Sandy Lane, St Paul's Cray, Orpington
Tel (0689) 71490
Mem 250
Sec D Simpson
Pro R Cornwell
Holes 18 L 5017 yds SSS 65
Recs Am–63 D Curtis
Pro–63 L Turner
V'trs WD–U WE/BH–before 11.30am
Fees £6 (£7.50)
Loc Off Ruxley roundabout on A20 at Sidcup

Sene Valley Folkestone & Hythe (1888)

Private
Sene, Folkestone CT18 8BL
Mem 650
Sec GL Hills (0303) 68513
Pro T Dungate (0303) 68514
Holes 18 L 6287 yds SSS 70

For map index see page 203.

Recs Am–65 J Hamilton
Pro–69 G Will
V'trs WD–H or I SOC
Fees £12 (£15)
Loc 2 miles N of Hythe on B2065

Sevenoaks Town (1927)

Private
Knole Park, Seal Hollow Road, Sevenoaks
Mem 45
Holes Play over Knole Park course

Sheerness (1906)

Private
Power Station Road, Sheerness
Tel **(0795) 662585**
Mem 450
Sec JW Gavins
Holes 18 L 6500 yds SSS 71
Recs Am–68 JD Simmance
V'trs WD–U WE/BH–arrange with Sec
Fees £8 (£12)
Loc Sittingbourne 9 miles. M20, M2 or A2 to A249

Shooter's Hill (1903)

Private
Lowood, Eaglesfield Road, London SE18 3DA
Tel **(01) 854 1216**
Mem 310 60(L) 31(J) 265(5)
Sec BR Adams (01) 854 6368
Pro M Ridge (01) 854 0073
Holes 18 L 5736 yds SSS 68
Recs Am–63 M Holland
Pro–64 N Coles, G Will, S Scott
V'trs WD–I WE/BH–M SOC–Tues & Thurs only
Fees £16 WD only
Loc Blackheath 4 miles

Shortlands (1897)

Private
Meadow Road, Shortlands, Bromley BR2 0PB
Tel **(01) 460 2471**
Mem 525
Sec Mrs L Burrows
Pro J Bates
Holes 9 L 5261 yds SSS 66
Recs Am–64 B Kent
Pro–61 D Pratt
V'trs M
Loc Bromley, Kent

Sidcup (1891)

Private
Hurst Road, Sidcup DA15 9AE
Tel **(01) 300 2864**
Mem 350
Sec C Baker
Pro R Taylor
Holes 9 L 5692 yds SSS 67
Recs Am–65 R Harris
Pro–64 D Webb

V'trs WD–H WE/BH–M
Fees £10
Loc On A222. A2/A20, 2 miles

Sittingbourne & Milton Regis (1929)

Private
Wormdale, Newington, Sittingbourne ME9 7PX
Tel **(0795) 842261**
Mem 325 100(L) 72(J) 175(5)
Sec HDG Wylie
Pro JR Hearn (0795) 842775
Holes 18 L 6121 yds SSS 69
Recs Am–67
Pro–62
V'trs WD–H Sat–NA Sun–M SOC–Tues & Thurs
Fees £11
Loc 1 mile N of M2 Junction 5 on A249

St Augustines (1907)

Private
Cottington Road, Cliffsend, Ramsgate
Tel **(0843) 590333**
Mem 300 80(L) 55(J) 120(5)
Sec R James
Pro DB Scott (0843) 590222
Holes 18 L 5138 yds SS 65
Recs Am–59 Dr S Hutton
Pro–61 P Mitchell
V'trs H SOC–WE
Fees £14 (£16) W–£44 M–£104.50
Loc 2 miles S of Ramsgate. Follow signs to St Augustines Cross

Sundridge Park (1902)

Private
Garden Lane, Bromley BR1 3NE
Tel **(01) 460 1822**
Mem 1167 99(L) 51(J) 189(5)
Sec BC Moor (Sec/Mgr) (01) 460 0278
Pro B Cameron (01) 460 5540
Holes East 18 L 6410 yds SSS 71
West 18 L 6027 yds SSS 69
Recs East Am–65 W Hodkin (1988)
Pro–64 R Cameron
West Am–67 P Lyons (1987)
Pro–65 R Fidler
V'trs H SOC–WD
Fees £20 D–£25
Loc 1 mile N of Bromley off Plaistow Lane opposite Sundridge Park Station. M25 Junction 3 Southbound. M25 Junction 4 Northbound

Tenterden (1905)

Private
Woodchurch Road, Tenterden
Tel **(058 06) 3987**
Mem 350
Sec WG Dobbs (058 06) 3128
Pro H Sherman
Holes 9 L 5119 yds SSS 65
V'trs U Sun–NA before noon
Fees On application
Loc Tenterden 1 mile

Tunbridge Wells (1889)

Private
Langton Road, Tunbridge Wells TN4 8XH
Tel **(0892) 23034**
Mem 245 64(L) 44(J)
Sec EM Goulden (0892) 36918
Pro RC Mudge (0892) 41386
Holes 9 L 4684 yds SSS 62
Recs Am–59 EC Chapman
Pro–59 J Humphrey
V'trs WD–U WE/BH–M
Fees 18 holes D–£12
Loc Tunbridge Wells, by Spa Hotel and Marchant's Garage

Walmer & Kingsdown (1909)

Private
The Leas, Kingsdown, Deal CT14 8EP
Tel **(0304) 373256**
Mem 550
Sec BW Cockerill
Pro T Hunt (0304) 363017
Holes 18 L 6451 yds SSS 71
Recs Am–69 A Randall
Pro–70 M Lee
V'trs WD–U WE–after 11.30am SOC
Fees D–£11 (£13) W–£50 F–£77
Loc $2^1/_2$ miles S of Deal

West Kent (1916)

Private
Downe
Tel **(0689) 53737**
Mem 355 150(L) 120(5)
Sec AM Watt (0689) 51323
Pro RS Fidler (0689) 56863
Holes 18 L 6369 yds SSS 70
Recs Am–62 DC Smith
Pro–65 H Baiocchi
V'trs WD–HI WE/BH–M
Fees £16
Loc Orpington 5 miles

West Malling (1974)

Private
Addington, nr Maidstone
Tel **(0732) 844785**
Mem 550
Sec MR Ellis
Pro P Foston
Holes Spitfire 18 L 6142 yds Par 70
Hurricane 18 L 6240 yds Par 70
Recs Am–70 R Parkhouse
Pro–71 P Way
V'trs WD–U WE–UH after 11.30am
Fees £12 (£14)
Loc A20 London Road

Westgate & Birchington (1893)

Private
Domneva Road, Westgate-on-Sea
Tel **(0843) 31115**
Mem 325
Sec AJ Read
Pro R Game

Holes 18 L 4926 yds SSS 65
Recs Am–60 Miss W Morgan
Pro–60 J Hickman
V'trs WD–U WE/BH–NA before 10.30am H or I
Fees £6 (£7)
Loc Westgate Station 1/4 mile

Whitstable & Seasalter (1910)

Private
Collingwood Road, Whitstable CT5 1EB
Tel (0227) 272020
Mem 250
Sec D Spratt (0227) 273589
Holes 9 L 5284 yds SSS 63
V'trs WD–U WE–M
Fees £10
Loc Whitstable Station 1 mile

Wildernesse (1890)

Private
Seal, Sevenoaks
Tel (0732) 61526
Mem 800
Sec Brigadier TG Williams (0732) 61199
Pro W Dawson (0732) 61527
Holes 18 L 6478 yds SSS 72
Recs Am–66 P Benka, M Pinner
Pro–65 I Grant
V'trs WD–I WE/BH–M
Fees £16
Loc 2 miles E of Sevenoaks A25

Woodlands Manor (1928)

Private
Woodlands, Sevenoaks TN15 6AB
Tel (095 92) 3805
Mem 650
Sec EF Newman, J Mills (095 92) 3806
Pro N Allen (095 92) 4161
Holes 18 L 5858 yds SSS 68
Pro–65 N Coles
V'trs WD–U WE–H NA before noon SOC–WD
Fees £9 (£15)
Loc 4 miles S of M25 Junction 3. Off A20 between W Kingsdown and Otford

Wrotham Heath (1906)

Private
Seven Mile Lane Comp, Sevenoaks TN15 8QZ
Tel (0732) 884800
Mem 200 70(L) 55(J) 50(5)
Sec JD Majendie (0732) 883099
Pro H Dearden (0732) 883854
Holes 9 L 5823 yds SSS 68
Recs Am–66 R Sloman (1983)
V'trs WD–H WE/BH–M SOC–Fri only
Fees £12 D–£15
Loc 8 miles W of Maidstone on B2106. Juntion of M26/A20 1 mile

Lancashire

Accrington & District (1893)

Private
West End, Oswaldtwistle, Accrington
Tel (0254) 32734
Mem 350
Sec JE Pilkington (0254) 35070
Pro W Harling (0254) 31091
Holes 18 L 5954 yds SSS 69
Recs Am–64 J Rothwell
V'trs WD/WE–U SOC
Fees £5 (£6)

Alt (1975)

Public
Park Road, West Southport
Tel (0704) 30435
Mem 68
Sec SD Ireland (051) 526 6914
Pro W Fletcher (0704) 35268
Holes 18 L 5939 yds SSS 69
V'trs U (Phone to book)
Fees £2.40 (£3)
Loc N of Marine Lake

Ashton & Lea (1913)

Private
Tudor Ave, off Blackpool Rd, Lea, nr Preston PR4 0XA
Tel (0772) 7246480
Mem 900
Sec MG Gibbs (0772) 735282
Pro P Laugher (0772) 720374
Holes 18 L 6286 yds SSS 70
Recs Am–67 E Walsh (1979)
Pro–66 J Hawkesworth (1988)
V'trs U SOC
Fees £9.50 (£11)
Loc 3 miles W of Preston off A583

Bacup (1912)

Private
Maden Road, Bacup OL13 8HY
Tel (0706) 873170
Mem 395
Sec J Garvey (0706) 874485
Holes 9 L 5656 yds SSS 67
Recs Am–65 M Butcher
Pro–67 H Higgins
V'trs U
Fees £6 (£7)
Loc Bankside Lane

Baxenden & District (1913)

Private
Top o' th'Meadow, Baxenden, nr Accrington
Tel (0254) 34555
Mem 250
Sec L Howard (0706) 213394
Holes 9 L 5740 yds SSS 68
Recs Am–67 JJ Walsh
Pro–66 C Tobin
V'trs U
Fees £4 (£5)
Loc 2 miles SE of Accrington

Blackburn (1894)

Private
Beardwood Brow, Blackburn BB2 7AX
Tel (0254) 51122
Mem 440 110(L) 120(J)
Sec M Pattison
Pro (0254) 55942
Holes 18 L 6100 yds SSS 70
Recs Am–64 GH Readett
Pro–66 M Foster
V'trs U SOC–WD
Fees £8.50 (£11)
Loc In town

Blackpool North Shore (1904)

Private
Devonshire Road, Blackpool FY2 0RD
Tel (0253) 51017
Mem 820
Sec DS Walker (0253) 52054
Pro B Ward (0253) 54640
Holes 18 L 6443 yds SSS 71
Recs Am–67 T Foster (1988)
Pro–63 C O'Connor
V'trs U SOC (restricted WE)
Fees £12 (£13)
Loc 1/2 mile behind North prom

Blackpool Park (1925)

Public
North Park Drive, Blackpool FY3 8LS
Tel (0253) 33960
Mem 700
Pro B Purdie (0253) 31004
Holes 18 L 6192 yds SSS 69
Recs Am–65 AV Moss
Pro–68 D Lewis
V'trs U
Fees £4 (£5)
Loc 1 1/2 miles E of centre, adjacent to Stanley Park

Burnley (1905)

Private
Glen View, Burnley
Tel (0282) 21045
Mem 600
Sec G Dean (0282) 24328
Pro RM Cade (0282) 55266
Holes 18 L 5891 yds SSS 69
Recs Am–65 ID Gradwell, L Samuels, DA Brown
Pro–66 JS Steer
V'trs U SOC
Fees £8 (£10)
Loc From centre via Manchester Road to Glenview Road

Chorley (1898)

Private
Hall o' th' Hill Heath, Charnock, nr Chorley PR6 9HX
Tel **(0257) 480263**
Mem 380
Sec GA Birtill (025 72) 63024
Pro P Wesselingh (0257) 481245
Holes 18 L 6277 yds SSS 70
Recs Am–65 WG Bromilow
Pro–66 M Hughes
V'trs WD–I WE–by arrangement SOC
Fees On application
Loc 1 mile S of town

Clitheroe (1891)

Private
Whalley Road, Clitheroe BB7 1PP
Tel **(0200) 22618**
Mem 750 122(L) 68(J)
Sec JB Kay (0200) 22292
Pro P Geddes (0200) 24242
Holes 18 L 6045 yds SSS 71
Recs Am–68 S Holden
V'trs U
Fees £13 (£15)
Loc 2 miles S of town

Colne (1901)

Private
Law Farm, Skipton Old Road, Colne
Tel **(0282) 863391**
Mem 280
Sec RG Knowles (0282) 67158
Holes 9 L 5961 yds SSS 69
Recs Am–68 DP Murphy
V'trs U exc comp days SOC
Fees £7 (£9)
Loc $1^1/_2$ miles N of town

Darwen (1893)

Private
Winter Hill, Darwen
Tel **(0254) 71287**
Mem 360 70(L) 100(J) 40(5)
Sec J Kenyon (0254) 581983
Pro W Lennon (0254) 776370
Holes 18 L 5752 yds SSS 68
Recs Am–66
Pro–65
V'trs U
Fees £7 (£9)
Loc Town centre $1^1/_2$ miles

Dean Wood (1922)

Private
Laford Lane, Up Holland, Skelmersdale WN8 0QZ
Tel **(0695) 622980**
Mem 850
Sec J Walls (0695) 622219
Pro AB Coop
Holes 18 L 6097 yds SSS 70
Recs Am–66 D Dawber, JB Dickinson, D Parkin
Pro–66 RA Morris
V'trs WD–U WE/BH–M SOC
Fees £12 (£15)
Loc 4 miles W of Wigan (A577)

Duxbury Park (1975)

Public
Duxbury Hall Road, Duxbury Park, Chorley PR7 4AS
Tel **(025 72) 77049**
Mem 200
Sec E Mayor (Hon) (0257) 792681
Pro D Clark (025 72) 65380
Holes 18 L 6270 yds SSS 70
Recs Am–74 A Jones
Pro–66 J Anglada
V'trs U
Fees £3 (£4)
Loc $1^1/_2$ miles S of Chorley off Wigan Lane

Fairhaven (1895)

Private
Lytham Hall Park, Ansdell, Lytham St Annes FY8 4JU
Tel **(0253) 794531**
Mem 845
Sec B Hartley (0253) 736741
Pro (0253) 736976
Holes 18 L 6883 yds SSS 73
Recs Am–65 SG Birtwell
Pro–65 R Commans
V'trs U SOC–WD
Fees £13 (£17)
Loc Lytham 2 miles. St Annes 2 miles. M55 Junction 4

Fishwick Hall (1912)

Private
Glenluce Drive, Farringdon Park, Preston
Tel **(0772) 798300**
Mem 450
Sec RR Gearing (0772) 796866
Pro H Smith (0772) 795870
Holes 18 L 6028 yds SSS 69
V'trs Apply to Sec SOC
Fees £9 (£12)
Loc 1 mile E of town centre nr junction of A59 and M6 Junction 31

Fleetwood (1932)

Private
Golf House, Princes Way, Fleetwood FY7 8AF
Tel **(039 17) 3114**
Mem 548
Sec K Volter (039 17) 3661
Pro CT Burgess (039 17) 3661
Holes L 18 L 6723 yds SSS 72
S 18 L 6437 yds SSS 71
Recs L Am–69 JC Roberts
S Am–64 JC Roberts
Pro–70 S Bennett
V'trs U SOC
Fees £8 (£10)
Loc 1 mile W of town centre

Great Harwood (1895)

Private
Harwood Bar, Great Harwood
Tel **(0254) 884391**
Mem 162 60(L) 30(J)
Sec A Garraway (0254) 886802
Pro K Caven (0254) 886728
Holes 9 L 6413 yds SSS 71
Recs Am–68 J Aspinall
Pro–64 AH Padgham
V'trs U
Fees £7 (£8)
Loc Nr Blackburn

Green Haworth (1914)

Private
Green Haworth, Accrington BB5 3SL
Tel **(0254) 37580**
Mem 200
Sec K Lynch
Holes 9 L 5470 yds SSS 67
Recs Am–66 R Peters
V'trs WD–U WE/BH–M SOC
Ladies only after 5pm Wed
Fees £5 (£6)
Loc Willows Lane

Heysham (1910)

Private
Trumacar Park, Middleton Road, Heysham, Morecambe LA3 3JH
Tel **(0524) 51011**
Mem 400
Sec A Hesketh
Pro R Williamson (0524) 52000
Holes 18 L 6224 yds SSS 70
Recs Am–66 PW Coyle, B Bielby, S Swinton
Pro–64 H Clark
V'trs U
Fees £8 D–£11 (Sat £9 D–£12 Sun £15)
Loc Morecambe 2 miles

Hindley Hall (1905)

Private
Hall Lane, Hindley, Wigan WN2 2SQ
Tel **(0942) 55131**
Mem 430
Sec R Bell (0942) 58356
Pro P Shepherd (0942) 55991
Holes 18 L 5840 yds SSS 68
Recs Am–63 JB Dickinson
Pro–65
V'trs I SOC
Fees £7 (£9)
Loc $2^1/_2$ miles S of Wigan. M61 Junction 6

Ingol Golf & Squash Club (1983)

Private
Tanterton Hall Road, Ingol, Preston PR2 7BY
Tel **(0772) 734556**
Mem 500
Sec H Parker

Holes 18 L 6345 SSS 70
V'trs U SOC
Fees £8 (£10)
Loc A6 $1^1/_2$ miles NW of Preston. M6 Junction 32

Knott End (1911)

Private
Wyreside, Knott End on Sea, Blackpool FY6 0AA
Tel **(0253) 810254**
Mem 660
Sec C Desmond (0253) 810576
Pro K Short (0253) 811365
Holes 18 L 5351 metres SSS 68
Recs Am–66 DJ Martel
V'trs WD–U WE/BH–by arrangement SOC–WD
Fees £9 (£12) Special rate for 10+
Loc Over Wyre, Knott End on Sea, nr Blackpool

Lancaster G & CC (1932)

Private
Ashton Hall, Ashton-with-Stodday, nr Lancaster LA2 0AJ
Tel **(0524) 752090**
Mem 539 175(L) 141(J) 16(5)
Sec Mrs JM Ireland (0524) 751247
Pro R Head (0524) 751802
Holes 18 L 6422 yds SSS 71
Recs Am–67 R Whiteside, D Armistead
V'trs H (arrange with Sec or Pro)
Fees £13
Loc $2^1/_2$ miles S of Lancaster on A588

Lansil (1947)

Private
Caton Road, Lancaster LA1 3PD
Tel **(0524) 39269**
Mem 310
Sec FM Parker (0524) 67143
Holes 9 L 5608 yds SSS 67
Recs Am–68 DC Whiteway
V'trs WD–U WE–U after 1pm
Fees £4 (£6)
Loc A683, 2 miles E of centre

Leyland (1924)

Private
Wigan Road, Leyland
Tel **(0772) 421359**
Mem 400
Sec RE Wilkinson (0772) 436457
Pro C Burgess (0772) 23425
Holes 18 L 6105 yds SSS 69
Recs Am–66 G Norris
Pro–66 D Screeton
V'trs WD–U WE–M
Fees £8
Loc $^3/_4$ mile off M6 Junction 28

Lobden (1888)

Private
Whitworth, nr Rochdale
Tel **(0706) 343228**
Mem 220
Sec A Taylor (0706) 49000
Holes 9 L 5770 yds SSS 68
Recs Am–67 C Turner
V'trs U
Fees £5 (£6.50)
Loc 4 miles N of Rochdale

Longridge (1877)

Private
Fell Barn, Jeffrey Hill, Longridge, nr Preston
Tel **(077 478) 3291**
Mem 400
Sec J Greenwood (077 478) 2765
Pro NS James (077 478) 3291
Holes 18 L 5678 yds SSS 68
Recs Am–68 RP Wood
V'trs U
Fees £7 (£9)
Loc 8 miles NE of Preston off B6243

Lytham (Green Drive) (1922)

Private
Ballam Road, Lytham FY8 4LE
Tel **(0253) 734782**
Mem 700
Sec R Kershaw (0253) 737390
Pro I Howieson (0253) 737379
Holes 18 L 6038 yds SSS 69
Recs Am–64 C Rymer (1988)
Pro–64 E Romero (11988)
V'trs U H WE–NA SOC–WD
Fees £15 (£18)
Loc Lytham St Annes

Marsden Park (1969)

Public
Townhouse Road, Nelson
Tel **(0282) 67525**
Mem 140
Sec D Manley (0282) 63750
Pro N Brown
Holes 18 L 5806 yds SSS 68
Recs Am–66 MN Davies
Pro–74 T Gillett
V'trs U
Fees D–£3.50 (D–£4.50)
Loc Signposted Walton Lane, Nelson

Morecambe (1904)

Private
Clubhouse, Bare, Morecambe LA4 6AJ
Tel **(0524) 418050**
Mem 1100
Sec Maj. BC Hodgson (0524) 412841
Pro D Helmn (0524) 415596
Holes 18 L 5766 yds SSS 68
Recs Am–64 J Swallow, DP Carney
Pro–63 B Gallacher, P Oosterhuis
V'trs U H SOC
Fees £7.50 (£10)
Loc On sea front

Nelson (1902)

Private
Kings Causeway, Brierfield, Nelson
Tel **(0282) 64583**
Mem 500
Sec RW Baldwin
Pro R Geddes (0282) 67000
Holes 18 L 5961 yds SSS 69
Recs Am–65 S Duerden (1987)
Pro–68 H Shoesmith
V'trs WD–U exc Thurs pm
WE–U exc Sat before 4pm
Fees £8 (£10)
Loc 2 miles N of Burnley

Ormskirk (1899)

Private
Cranes Lane, Lathom, Ormskirk L40 5UJ
Tel **(0695) 72112**
Mem 300
Sec PD Dromgoole (0695) 72227
Pro J Hammond (0695) 72074
Holes 18 L 6350 yds SSS 70
Recs Am–63 DJ Eccleston
Pro–67 MJ Slater
V'trs I Sat–NA SOC
Fees £16 (£19) Wed–£19
Loc 2 miles E of Ormskirk

Penwortham (1908)

Private
Blundell Lane, Penwortham, Preston PR1 0AX
Tel **(0772) 743207**
Mem 700
Sec J Parkinson (0772) 744630
Pro J Wright (0772) 742345
Holes 18 L 5915 yds SSS 68
Recs Am–62 A Gillespie
Pro–66 W Fletcher
V'trs WD–U WE–no parties
Fees £10.50 (£12.60)
Loc $1^1/_2$ miles W of Preston

Pleasington (1890)

Private
Nr Blackburn BB2 5JF
Tel **(0254) 21028**
Mem 442
Sec L Ingham (0254) 22177
Pro GJ Furey (0254) 21630
Holes 18 L 6445 yds SSS 71
Recs Am–64 SG Birtwell (1983)
Pro–66 S Holden (1988)
V'trs H
Fees £12 (£15)
Loc 3 miles W of Blackburn

Poulton-le-Fylde (1982)

Private
Myrtle Farm, Breck Road, Poulton, nr Blackpool
Tel **(0253) 892444**
Mem 250
Sec K Slapp (0253) 893150

Pro C Mawdsley
Holes 9 L 2979 yds SSS 69
Recs Am–74 D Barker (1986)
Pro–70 J Wraith (1985)
V'trs U
Fees £2.10 (£4.20)
Loc 3 miles E of Blackpool

Preston (1892)

Private
Fulwood Hall Lane, Fulwood, Preston PR2 4DD
Tel **(0772) 794234 (Clubhouse)**
(0772) 700436 (Steward)
Mem 800
Sec JB Dickinson (0772) 700011
Pro PA Wells (0772) 700022
Holes 18 L 6249 yds SSS 70
Recs Am–65 MA Holmes, J Wright
Pro–66 JM Hulme
V'trs U H SOC–WD
Fees £11 (£13)
Loc $1^1/_2$ miles W of M6 Junction 32

Rishton (1925)

Private
Eachill Links, Hawthorn Drive, Rishton BB1 4HG
Tel **(0254) 884442**
Mem 250
Sec G Haworth (0254) 60226 (after 6pm)
Holes 9 L 6199 yds SSS 69
Recs Am–71 J Catlow
Pro–71 G Furey (1983)
V'trs WD–U WE–M
Fees £6
Loc 3 miles E of Blackburn

Rossendale (1903)

Private
Ewood Lane, Head Haslingden, Rossendale BB4 6LH
Tel **(0706) 213056**
Mem 600
Sec WP Whittaker (0706) 216234
Pro S Nicholls (0706) 213616
Holes 18 L 6262 yds SSS 70
Recs Am–67 A Siddle
V'trs WD/Sun–U Sat–M SOC
Fees £8 (£10)
Loc 7 miles N of Bury near end of M66 (Haslingden exit)

Royal Lytham & St Annes (1886)

Private
Links Gate, Lytham St Annes FY8 3LQ
Tel **(0253) 724206**
Mem 600
Sec Maj AS Craven (Retd)
Pro E Birchenough (0253) 720094
Holes 18 L 6697 yds SSS 73
Recs Am–66 R Foster, T Craddock
Pro–65 C O'Connor, BGC Huggett, W Longmuir, S Ballesteros
V'trs WD–I H
Fees £25
Loc Town centre 1 mile

Shaw Hill G & CC

Private
Whittle–le–Woods, Chorley
Tel **(025 72) 69221**
Mem 500
Sec RM Hodson
Pro I Evans (025 72) 79222
Holes 18 L 6467 yds Par 72 SSS 71
Recs Am–68 A Squires
Pro–69 I Evans
V'trs U
Fees £10 R/D
Loc A6, $1^1/_2$ miles N of Chorley. M61 Junction 8. M6 Junction 28

Silverdale (1906)

Private
Red Bridge Lane, Silverdale, Carnforth LA5 0SP
Tel **(0524) 701300**
Mem 513
Sec EF Wright (04482) 3782
Holes 9 L 5288 yds SSS 67
Recs Am–66
V'trs U exc Sun (Summer)–M
Fees £6 (£10)
Loc 3 miles NW of Carnforth, adjacent to Silverdale station

St Annes Old Links (1901)

Private
Highbury Road, Lytham St Annes FY8 2LD
Tel **(0253) 723597**
Mem 975
Sec DJM Hemsted (0253) 723597
Pro GG Hardiman (0253) 722432
Holes 18 L 6647 yds SSS 72
Recs Am–66 RD Squire, AC Nash
Pro–66 AD Sowa, T Webber, GL Parslow
V'trs WD–NA before 9.15am and 12–2pm WE/BH–by arrangement with Sec SOC
Fees £15 (£20)
Loc Midway between St Annes and Blackpool off A584

Towneley (1932)

Public
Towneley Park, Todmorden Road, Burnley
Tel **(0282) 51636**
Mem 250
Sec B Walsh (0282) 26459
Pro D Whittaker (0282) 38473
Holes 18 L 5840 yds SSS 68
9 hole course
V'trs U
Fees £2.95 (£3.40)
Loc $1^1/_2$ miles E of town
Mis New 9 hole course open

Turton (1907)

Private
Woodend Farm, Bromley Cross, nr Bolton
Tel **(0204) 852235**
Mem 200 47(L) 31(J) 25(5)
Sec D Jackson (0204) 594171
Holes 9 L 5805 yds SSS 68
Recs Am–67 TD Bullough
V'trs U Comp days–NA Sun–M before 10am
Fees £6
Loc $3^1/_2$ miles N of Bolton

Whalley (1912)

Private
Long Leese Barn, Clerkhill, Whalley, nr Blackburn
Tel **(025 482) 2236**
Mem 475
Sec PC Burt (025 482) 2367
Pro K Caven
Holes 9 L 5953 yds SSS 69
Recs Am–67 G Richards
V'trs WD/BH–U WE–U exc Sat Apr–Oct SOC
Fees £5 (£8)
Loc 7 miles E of Blackburn

Wilpshire (1889)

Private
72 Whalley Road, Wilpshire, Blackburn BB1 9LF
Tel **(0254) 48260/49691**
Mem 650
Pro W Slaven (0254) 49558
Holes 18 L 5911 yds SSS 68
Recs Am–64 H Green, MJ Savage
Pro–64 D Whelan
V'trs WD–U WE/BH–on request
Fees £10 (£13)
Loc 3 miles NE of Blackburn off A666

Leicestershire

Birstall (1901)

Private
Station Road, Birstall, Leicester
Tel **(0533) 674450**
Mem 350 86(L) 57(J)
Sec Ms S Wells (0533) 674322
Pro R Ball (0533) 675245
Holes 18 L 6203 yds SSS 70
Recs Am–68 K Wells, NH Abel, D Hunter Walker
Pro–67 L Platts
V'trs Mon/Wed/Fri–I Other days–M
Fees £12
Loc 3 miles N of town

Charnwood Forest (1890)

Private
Breakback Road, Woodhouse Eaves, Loughborough LE12 8TA
Tel **(0509) 890259**
Mem 250
Sec F Hand MC (0509) 231389
Holes 9 L 6202 yds SSS 70

Recs Am–65 G Wolstenholme (1987)
V'trs H SOC
Fees £9 (£12)
Loc M1 Junction 23, 3 miles

Cosby (1895)

Private
Chapel Lane, Cosby, nr Leicester
Tel (0533) 864759
Mem 625
Sec JD Horsburgh (0533) 866197
Pro D Bowring (0533) 848275
Holes 18 L 6277 yds SSS 70
V'trs WD–U before 4pm WE–M SOC–WD–H
Fees £10
Loc 7 miles S of Leicester

Enderby (1986)

Public
Mill Lane, Enderby, Leicester
Tel (0533) 849388
Mem 50
Sec LJ Speake (0533) 841133
Pro C D'Araujo
Holes 9 L 4356 yds SSS 61
V'trs U
Fees £2.25 (£2.75) 18 holes
Loc Enderby 2 miles. M2 Junction 21/M69 Junction 1

Glen Gorse (1933)

Private
Glen Road, Oadby, Leicester LE2 4RF
Tel (0533) 712226/714159
Mem 358 96(L) 65(J)
Sec K McKay (0533) 714159
Pro R Larratt (0533) 713748
Holes 18 L 6641 yds SSS 72
Recs Am–68 IR Middleton, P Toon
Pro–66 DT Steele
V'trs WD–U WE/BH–M SOC–WD
Fees £14
Loc 3 miles S of Leicester on A6

Hinckley (1983)

Private
Leicester Road, Hinckley LE10 3DR
Tel (0455) 615124
Mem 500
Sec J Toon
Pro R Jones (0455) 615014
Holes 18 L 6462 yds SSS 71
Championship course: 18 L 6592 yds SSS 71
Recs Pro–67 K Dickens (1987)
V'trs WD–U WE–NA Sun after noon SOC
Fees £12 (£14)
Loc NE Boundary of Hinckley on A47

Humberstone Heights (1978)

Public
Gipsy Lane, Leicester
Tel (0533) 761905
Mem 320
Sec S Day (0533) 674835
Pro P Highfield (0533) 764674
Holes 18 L 6444 yds SSS 71
Recs Am–64 D Butler (1987)
Pro–67 R Adams (1985)
V'trs U
Fees £3 (£4)
Loc 3 miles E of city centre off A47

Kibworth (1905)

Private
Weir Road, Kibworth Beachamp, Leicester LE8 0LP
Tel (053 753) 2301
Mem 550
Sec Mrs W Potter
Pro A Strange (053 753) 2283
Holes 18 L 6282 yds SSS 70
Recs Am–67 EE Feasey
Pro–67 J Briars
V'trs WD–U WE–M SOC
Fees £11
Loc 9 miles SE of Leicester on A6

Kirby Muxloe (1910)

Private
Station Road, Kirby Muxloe, nr Leicester LE9 9EN
Tel (0533) 393107
Mem 425
Sec SF Aldwinckle (0533) 393457
Pro RT Stephenson (0533) 392813
Holes 18 L 6303 yds SSS 70
Recs Am–69 M Reay
Pro–65 Peter Thomson
V'trs WD–U before 3.45pm SOC H M–no restrictions
Fees £10 (£12.50 with Captain's permission only)
Loc 3 miles W of Leicester

Leicestershire (1890)

Private
Evington Lane, Leicester LE5 6DJ
Tel (0533) 736035
Mem 750
Sec JL Adams (0533) 738825
Pro K Dixon Pickup (0533) 736730
Holes 18 L 6330 yds SSS 70
Recs Am–65 A Martinez, G Wolstenholme
Pro–63 H Henning, I Mosey, S Sherratt
V'trs U H SOC
Fees £14 (£17)
Loc 2 miles E of Leicester

Lingdale (1967)

Private
Joe Moores Lane, Woodhouse Eaves, Loughborough
Tel (0509) 890035
Mem 450
Sec D Wardle
Pro P Highfield (0509) 890684
Holes 9 L 6114 yds SSS 72
Recs Am–71 DS Cameron
V'trs U SOC
Fees D–£6 (£8)
Loc Loughborough 6 miles. 4 miles from M1 Junction 23

Longcliffe (1905)

Private
Nanpantan, Loughborough
Tel (0509) 216321
Mem 550
Sec G Harle (0509) 239129
Pro I Bailey (0509) 231450
Holes 18 L 6551 yds SSS 71
Recs Am–70 D Dunkerley, D Mee
Pro–68 M Reay
V'trs WD–U WE–M
Fees £13
Loc Loughborough 2½ miles. M1 Junction 23

Luffenham Heath (1911)

Private
Ketton, Stamford, Lincs PE9 3UU
Tel (0780) 720205
Mem 555
Sec IF Davenport
Pro JA Lawrence (0780) 720298
Holes 18 L 6254 yds SSS 70
Recs Am–66 RD Christian, E Lloyd
Pro–67 PJ Butler, RL Moffitt
V'trs U SOC–WD
Fees On application
Loc 5 miles W of Stamford on A6121

Lutterworth (1904)

Private
Lutterworth, Leicester
Tel (045 55) 2532
Mem 350
Sec H Cooke
Pro N Melvin
Holes 18 L 5570 yds SSS 67
Recs Am–67 M Moore
Pro–71 M Faulkner
V'trs WD–U WE–M SOC
Fees £10
Loc ¼ mile M1. 4 miles M6

Market Harborough (1898)

Private
Oxendon Road, Market Harborough
Tel (0858) 63684
Mem 360
Sec JNT Lord (0536) 771771
Pro N Gilks

For map index see page 203.

Holes 9 L 6080 yds SSS 69
Recs Am–68 RC Gadd, W Sneath
Pro–69 P Highfield, R Adams
V'trs WD–U SOC
Fees £6
Loc 1 mile S of M Harborough

Melton Mowbray (1925)

Private
Waltham Rd, Thorpe Arnold, Melton Mowbray
Tel **(0664) 62118**
Mem 380
Sec Mrs TD Hudson (0664) 78312
Holes 9 L 6200 yds SSS 70
Recs Am–65 N Street (1985)
Pro–66 W Hill
V'trs U before 3pm–M after 3pm
Fees £8 (£10)
Loc 2 miles NE of Melton Mowbray

Oadby (1974)

Public
Leicester Road Racecourse, Oadby, Leicester LE2 4AB
Tel **(0533) 700326/700215**
Mem 361 27(L) 43(J)
Sec C Chamberlain (0533) 889862
Pro S Ward (0533) 709052
Holes 18 L 6228 yds SSS 69
Recs Am–65 S Davis (1988)
Pro–73 C O'Connor Jr
V'trs U SOC–WD
Fees £3 (£3.50)
Loc 2 miles S of Leicester

RAF North Luffenham (1975)

Private
RAF North Luffenham, Oakham LE15 8RL
Tel **(0780) 720041 (Ext 295/240)**
Mem 215 53(L) 11(J)
Sec CJ Sheffield (Ext 295)
Holes 9 L 5997 yds SSS 69
Recs Am–72 KP Hickman
V'trs M
Fees £3
Loc RAF N Luffenham, 1/2 mile from S shore of Rutland Water

Rothley Park (1911)

Private
Westfield Lane, Rothley, Leicester LE7 7LH
Tel **(0533) 302019**
Sec BS Durham (0533) 302809
Pro PJ Dolan (0533) 303023
Holes 18 L 6487 yds SSS 71
Recs Am–67 EE Feasey
Pro–68 PJ Dolan
V'trs U
Fees £14 (£17)
Loc 6 miles N of Leicester, W of A6

Scraptoft (1928)

Private
Beeby Road, Scraptoft, Leicester LE7 9SJ
Tel **(0533) 419000**
Mem 450
Sec GER Papworth (0533) 418863
Pro S Sherratt (0533) 419138
Holes 18 L 6166 yds SSS 69
Recs Am–66 D Gibson, CM Harries
Pro–A Bownes
V'trs WD–U WE–M SOC–WD
Fees £10 (£14)
Loc 3 miles E of Leicester

Ullesthorpe Court (1976)

Private
Frolesworth Road, Ullesthorpe, Lutterworth
Tel **(0455) 209023**
Mem 600
Sec PE Woolley
Pro M Henney (0455) 209150
Holes 18 L 6206 yds SSS
Recs Am–70
Pro–68
V'trs U SOC–WD
Fees £9.50
Loc 3 miles NW of Lutterworth

Western Park (1920)

Public
Scudamore Road, Leicester LE3 1UQ
Tel **(0533) 872339/876158**
Mem 470 36(L) 31(J)
Sec T Elliot (0533) 874749
Pro BN Whipham (0533) 872339
Holes 18 L 6532 yds SSS 71
V'trs U
Fees £3.50 (£4.50)
Loc 4 miles W of Leicester

Whetstone (1965)

Private
Cambridge Road, Whetstone, Leicester
Tel **(0533) 862399**
Mem 50
Sec H Mitchell
Pro EL Callaway
Holes 9 L 3005 yds SSS 69
V'trs U
Loc S boundary of Leicester

Willesley Park (1921)

Private
Tamworth Road, Ashby-de-la-Zouch LE6 5PF
Tel **(0530) 411532**
Mem 600 99(L) 38(J)
Sec TR Hodgetts (0530) 414596
Pro C Hancock (0530) 414820
Holes 18 L 6310 yds SSS 70
Recs Am–64 PM Baxter
Pro–66 R Swain
V'trs WD–H WE/BH–H after 9.30am SOC
Fees £15 (£18)
Loc 2 miles S of Ashby on A453. M1 Junctions 22/23/24. A42(M) Junction 10

Lincolnshire

Belton Park (1890)

Private
Belton Lane, Londonthorpe Road, Grantham NG31 9SH
Tel **(0476) 63355**
Mem 950
Sec JH Roberts (0476) 67399
Pro B McKee (0476) 63911
Holes 27 Brownlow L 6412 yds SSS 71; Ancaster L 6109 yds SSS 69; Belmont L 5857 yds SSS 68
Recs Am–69 DF Price
Pro–65 S Bennett
V'trs U SOC–WD 9.30am–12.30pm and 2–5pm
Fees 18 holes £12 (£14)
27/36 holes £16 (£18)
Loc Grantham 2 miles

Blankney (1903)

Private
Blankney, Lincoln
Tel **(0526) 20263**
Mem 400 100(L) 60(J) 100(5)
Sec BH Clipsham
Pro G Bradley (0526) 20202
Holes 18 L 6402 yds SSS 71
V'trs WD–U WE–M SOC
Fees £8 D–£11 (£15)
Loc 10 miles SE of Lincoln on B1188

Boston (1962)

Private
Cowbridge, Horncastle Road, Boston PE22 7EL
Tel **(0205) 62306**
Mem 650 110(L) 41(J)
Sec DE Smith (0205) 50589
Pro TR Squires
Holes 18 L 5825 yds SSS 68
Recs Am–67 SG Wood
Pro–64 G Cullen
V'trs U
Fees £9 (£11)
Loc 2 miles N of Boston on B1183

Burghley Park (1890)

Private
St Martin's, Stamford PE9 3JX
Tel **(0780) 53789**
Mem 500 80(L) 80(J) 120(5)
Sec PH Mulligan
Pro G Davies (0780) 62100
Holes 18 L 6133 yds SSS 69
Recs Am–65 PG Barker
Pro–70 B Thomson
V'trs WD–U WE/BH–NA SOC
Fees £12
Loc 1 mile S of town. Turn off A1 at roundabout

Canwick Park (1893)

Private
Canwick Park, Washingborough Road, Lincoln
Tel (0522) 22166
Mem 500
Sec PJ Richardson
(0522) 694851
Pro S Williamson
Holes 18 L 6300 yds SSS 70
Recs Am–68 R Britt Robinson
V'trs WD–U WE–M
Fees £7 (£10)
Loc 2 miles S of Lincoln

Carholme (1906)

Private
Lincoln
Tel (0522) 36811
Mem 550
Sec BW Robinson (0522) 751580
Pro G Leslie (0522) 33263
Holes 18 L 6086 yds SSS 69
Recs Am–69 R Taylor
V'trs U (exc Sun)
Fees On application
Loc Town centre 1 mile

Elsham (1900)

Private
Barton Road, Elsham, nr Brigg DN20 0LS
Tel (0652) 688382
Mem 600
Sec HG Markham (0652) 680291
Pro R McKiernan (0652) 680 432
(home) (0652) 680 235
Holes 18 L 6411 yds SSS 71
Recs Am–72 A Shepherd
Pro–69 MT Hoyle
V'trs WE–M SOC–WD
Fees £10
Loc Off M180 nr Brigg

Gainsborough (1900)

Private
Thonock, Gainsborough DN21 1PZ
Tel (0427) 3088
Mem 470
Sec DJ Garrison
Pro G Stafford (0427) 2278
Holes 18 L 6504 yds SSS 71
Recs Am–67
V'trs U H WE/BH–M SOC–WD
Fees £8 D–£10
Loc Gainsborough
Mis Floodlit driving range

Lincoln (1891)

Private
Lincoln
Tel (042 771) 210
Mem 600
Sec D Boag (042 771) 721
Pro A Carter (042 771) 273
Holes 18 L 6400 yds SSS 70
Recs Am–66 A Thain, P Taylor
Pro–65 M James
V'trs H WE–by appointment
Fees £10 D–£14 (£10 D–£15)
Loc 12 miles W of Lincoln

Louth (1965)

Private
Crowtree Lane, Louth LN11 9LJ
Tel (0507) 602554
Mem 820
Sec Maj E Coombes (0507) 603681
Pro AJ Blundell (0507) 604648
Holes 18 L 6477 yds SSS 71
Recs Am–70 A Murray
Pro–A Caygill
V'trs U SOC–WD
Fees £8 D–£10 (£10 D–£12)
Loc Town centre 1/2 mile

Market Rasen & District (1922)

Private
Legsby Road, Market Rasen LN8 3DZ
Tel (0673) 842416
Mem 485
Pro AM Chester
Holes 18 L 6043 yds SSS 69
Recs Am–66 C Osbourne
V'trs WD–I WE–M
Fees £9
Loc 1 mile E of town

Millfield (1985)

Private
Laughterton, Lincoln
Tel (042 771) 255
Sec A Hunter
Pro P Lester
Holes 18 L 5583 yds SSS 67
Fees £3 R/D
Loc 12 miles W of Lincoln
Mis Inland links course

North Shore (1910)

Private
North Shore Road, Skegness PE25 1DN
Tel (0754) 3298
Mem 595
Sec RC Sykes (0754) 67280
Pro J Cornelius (0754) 4822
Holes 18 L 6134 yds SSS 69
Recs Am–72 R Peacock (1988)
V'trs H SOC–WD
Fees £10 (£12)
Loc 1 mile N of town centre

RAF Waddington

Private
Waddington, Lincoln LN5 9NB
Tel (0522) 720271
Mem 45
Sec Cpl JDT Richardson (Ext 244)
Holes 18 L 5223 yds SSS 66
Recs Am–68 T Graham (1987)
V'trs By prior arrangement
Fees £2
Loc A607 Lincoln–Grantham

Sandilands (1900)

Private
Sandilands, Sutton-on-Sea LN12 2RJ
Tel (0521) 41432
Mem 500
Sec D Mumby (0521) 41617
Pro D Vernon (0521) 41600
Holes 18 L 5995 yds SSS 69
Recs Am–66 JR Payne
Pro–63 FG Allott
V'trs U SOC
Fees £7 D–£10 (£10 D–£12)
Loc 1 mile S of Sutton-on-Sea off A52

Seacroft (1895)

Private
Seacroft, Skegness PE25 3AU
Tel (0754) 3020
Mem 340 190(L) 90(J)
Sec HK Brader (0754) 3741
Pro R Lawie (0754) 69624
Holes 18 L 6478 yds SSS 71
Recs Am–64 TH Bowman
Pro–67 J Heib (1988)
V'trs U WE–XL before 11am
Fees £9 (£11)
Loc S boundary of Skegness

Sleaford (1905)

Private
South Rauceby, Sleaford NG34 8PL
Tel (052 98) 273
Mem 650
Sec DBR Harris
(0529) 303535
Pro T Hutton (052 98) 644
Holes 18 L 6443 yds SSS 71
Recs Am–66 A Hare (1987)
V'trs U SOC–WD
Fees £9.50 (£14)
Loc 1 mile W of Sleaford on A153

Spalding (1922)

Private
Surfleet, Spalding PE11 4DG
Tel (077 585) 234
Sec WE Codling (077 585) 386
Pro J Spencer (077 585) 474
Holes 18 L 5847 yds SSS 68
Recs Am–65 G Palmer
Pro–65 J Spencer
V'trs U H SOC–Thurs
Fees On application
Loc 4 miles N of Spalding off A16

Stoke Rochford (1924)

Private
Great North Rd, nr Grantham
Tel **(047 683) 275**
Mem 515
Sec JM Butler
Pro A Dow (047 683) 218
Holes 18 L 6204 yds SSS 70
Recs Am–66 A Hare
Pro–65 A Dow
V'trs WE–U after 10.30am
Fees On application
Loc 6 miles S of Grantham, at service station on A1

Sutton Bridge (1914)

Private
New Road, Sutton Bridge
Tel **(0406) 350323**
Mem 330
Sec KC Buckle (0945) 870455
Pro M Cunningham
Holes 9 L 5804 yds SSS 68
Pro–62 CJ Norton
V'trs WD–U WE–NA
Fees £8
Loc Wisbech 8 miles

Woodhall Spa (1905)

Private
Woodhall Spa LN10 6PU
Tel **(0526) 52511**
Mem 450
Sec SR Sharp
Pro P Fixter
Holes 18 L 6866 yds SSS 73
Recs Am–68 FW Wood
Pro–68 EB Williamson
V'trs U–booking essential SOC
Fees £12 (£14.50)
Loc 19 miles SE of Lincoln

Manchester (Greater)

Acre Gate (1974)

Private
Pennybridge Lane, Flixton, Urmston, Manchester
Tel **(061) 748 1226**
Mem 200
Sec J Stenstrom (061) 748 7721
Holes Play over William Wroe Municipal

Altrincham Municipal

Public
Stockport Road, Timperley, Altrincham
Tel **(061) 928 0761**
Mem 285
Sec WD Wilson (061) 928 5659
Pro R West
Holes 18 L 6204 yds SSS 69
Recs Am–67
Pro–67
V'trs U
Fees £2.50 (£3.75)
Loc 9 miles SW of Manchester

Ashton-on-Mersey (1898)

Private
Church Lane, Sale, Cheshire M33 5QQ
Tel **(061) 973 3220**
Mem 180 70(L) 40(J) 60(5)
Sec AH Marsland
Pro MJ Williams (061) 962 3727
Holes 9 L 3073 yds SSS 69
Recs Am–68 B Armitage, M Gleave
Pro–67 R Williamson, D Cooper
V'trs WD–U (exc Tues after 5pm & Wed before 5pm) WE–M
Fees £8
Loc 5 miles W of Manchester

Ashton-under-Lyne (1913)

Private
Gorsey Way, Hurst, Ashton-under-Lyne
Tel **(061) 330 1537**
Mem 450
Sec G Musgrave (061) 339 8655
Pro C Boyle (061) 308 2095
Holes 18 L 6209 yds SSS 70
V'trs WD–U WE/BH–M SOC
Fees £11
Loc 8 miles E of Manchester

Beacon Park (1982)

Public
Beacon Lane, Dalton, Up Holland, Wigan WN8 7RU
Tel **(0695) 622700**
Mem 245
Sec JC McIlroy (0704) 892930
Pro R Peters
Holes 18 L 5927 yds SSS 69
Recs Am–68 D Parkin, I Donaldson
V'trs U
Fees £1.90 (£2.30)
Loc Signposted from Up Holland and Parbold. Close to Ashurst Beacon and M58/M6
Mis Private club playing over public course

Blackley (1907)

Private
Victoria Avenue, East Manchester M9 2HW
Tel **(061) 643 2980**
Mem 500
Sec CB Leggott (061) 643 4116
Pro M Barton (061) 643 3912
Holes 18 L 6235 yds SSS 70
Recs Am–65 D Royle
Pro–66 J Nixon
V'trs WD–U WE–M
Fees £8
Loc N Manchester area

Bolton (1912)

Private
Lostock Park, Bolton BL6 4AJ
Tel **(0204) 43278**
Mem 600
Sec H Cook (0204) 43067
Pro R Longworth (0204) 43073
Holes 18 L 6215 yds SSS 70
Recs Am–66 JB Hope, DE Roocroft
Pro–67 WSM Rooke
V'trs U SOC
Fees Mon/Tues & Thurs/Fri–£10
Wed/WE/BH–£12
Loc 3½ miles W of town. M61 exit Horwich 1½ miles

Bolton Municipal (1931)

Public
Links Road, Chorley New Road, Bolton, Lancs BL2 9XX
Tel **(0204) 42336**
Pro AK Holland
Holes 18 L 6012 yds SSS 69
Recs Am–67 PK Abbott
Pro–68 L Alamby
V'trs U SOC–WD
Fees £3.50 (£3.80)
Loc A673, 3 miles W of Bolton. M61 Junction 6
Mis Regent Park Club plays here

Bolton Old Links (1898)

Private
Chorley Old Road, Montserrat, Bolton, Lancs BL1 5SU
Tel **(0204) 40050**
Mem 650
Sec E Monaghan (0204) 42307
Pro P Horridge (0204) 43089
Holes 18 L 6406 yds SSS 72
Recs Am–66 L Mooney (1981)
Pro–66 M Adamson (1988)
V'trs U exc comp Sats
Fees £10 (£15)
Loc 3 miles NW of Bolton on B6226

Brackley Municipal (1977)

Public
Bullows Road, Little Hulton
Tel **(061) 790 6076**
Mem 90
Sec RG Steel (061) 790 5072
Pro K Bates
Holes 9 L 3003 yds SSS 69
V'trs U
Fees £1.40 (£1.65)
Loc Walkden 2 miles off A6

Bramall Park (1894)

Private
20 Manor Road, Bramhall, Stockport, Cheshire SK7 6NW
Tel **(061) 485 3119**
Mem 715
Sec JH Spedding
Pro RL Johnson (061) 485 2205
Holes 18 L 6214 yds SSS 70
Recs Am–68 B Steele
V'trs I

Fees £12 (£15)
Loc 8 miles S of Manchester. A6 to Bramhall Lane A5102. Turn right at Carrwood Road

Breightmet (1911)

Private
Red Bridge, Ainsworth, nr Bolton
Tel **(0204) 27381**
Mem 200
Sec R Weir
Holes 9 L 6448 yds SSS 71 Pro–68 P Alliss
V'trs WE–NA SOC–WD
Fees £8 (£10)
Loc 3 miles on Bury side

Brookdale (1905)

Private
Woodhouses, Failsworth
Tel **(061) 681 4534**
Mem 650
Sec G Glass (061) 681 8996
Pro P Devalle (061) 681 2655
Holes 18 L 6040 yds SSS 68
Recs Am–65 G Lever
V'trs U SOC–WD
Fees £6.75 (£7.75)
Loc 5 miles N of Manchester

Bury (1890)

Private
Unsworth Hall, Blackford Bridge, Bury BL9 9TJ
Tel **(061) 766 2213**
Mem 410
Sec JP Meikle
Pro M Peel
Holes 18 L 5961 yds SSS 69
Recs Am–67 MN Seddon Pro–PWT Evans
V'trs U SOC
Fees £8 (£10)
Loc A56, 5 miles N of Manchester. 3 miles N of M62 Junction 17

Castle Hawk (1975)

Private
Heywood Road, Castleton, Rochdale
Tel **(0706) 40841**
Mem 200
Sec A Kershaw
Pro K Caven
Holes 27 L 3160 yds SSS 55
Recs Am–57 R Baker Pro–56 G Bond
V'trs U SOC
Fees £3 (£4)
Loc Castleton Station 1 mile

Cheadle (1885)

Private
Shiers Drive, Cheadle, Cheshire SK8 1HW
Tel **(061) 428 2160**
Mem 350
Sec PP Webster (061) 485 4540
Pro GH Butler (061) 428 9878
Holes 9 L 5006 yds SSS 65
Recs Am–62 RP Bullock, PR Shortt Pro–63 F Memmott
V'trs H I M NA–Tues & Sat SOC
Fees D–£8 (£10))
Loc 1 mile S of Cheadle Village

Chorlton–cum–Hardy (1903)

Private
Barlow Hall, Manchester M21 2JJ
Tel **(061) 881 3139**
Mem 350
Sec FE Collis (061) 881 5830
Pro D Screeton (061) 881 9911
Holes 18 L 6003 metres SSS 69
Recs Am–63 JR Berry Pro–65 FS Boobyer
V'trs U SOC
Fees £10 (£13)
Loc 4 miles S of Manchester A5103/A5145

Crompton & Royton (1913)

Private
High Barn, Royton, Oldham OL2 6RW
Tel **(061) 624 2154**
Mem 620
Sec T Donovan (061) 624 0986
Pro DA Melling
Holes 18 L 6212 yds SSS 70
Recs Am–65 JA Osbaldeston Pro–65 D Durnian
V'trs U SOC–WD
Fees £7 (£9)
Loc Oldham 3 miles

Davenport (1913)

Private
Middlewood Road, Poynton, Stockport
Tel **(0625) 877321**
Mem 600
Sec TD Swindells (0625) 876951
Pro W Harris (0625) 877319
Holes 18 L 6006 yds SSS 69
Recs Am–65 I Muir Pro–67 B Evans
V'trs U (exc Sat–NA)
Fees £8 (Sun–£10)
Loc 5 miles S of Stockport

Davyhulme Park (1910)

Private
Gleneagles Road, Davyhulme, Manchester M31 2SA
Tel **(061) 748 2856**
Mem 600
Sec EW Travis (061) 748 2260
Pro H Lewis (061) 748 3931
Holes 18 L 6237 yds SSS 70
Recs Am–67 TF Sharp Pro–68 KG Geddes, D Rees
V'trs U Comp days–M after 3pm SOC
Fees £9.50 (£11.50)
Loc 7 miles SW of Manchester

Deane (1906)

Private
Off Junction Road, Deane, Bolton
Tel **(0204) 61944**
Mem 300
Sec J Bolton (0204) 651808
Pro D Martindale
Holes 18 L 5511 yds SSS 67
Recs Am–62 N Hazzleton
V'trs WD–U WE–Restricted
Fees £10
Loc 4 miles W of Bolton

Denton (1909)

Private
Manchester Road, Denton M34 2NU
Tel **(061) 336 3218**
Mem 520
Sec R Wickham
Pro R Vere (061) 336 2070
Holes 18 L 6290 yds SSS 70 Pro–68 D Cooper, S Scanlon, D Durnian
V'trs WD–U WE/BH–M SOC
Fees £7
Loc 5 miles SE of Manchester

Didsbury (1891)

Private
Ford Lane, Northenden, Manchester M22 4NQ
Tel **(061) 998 9278**
Mem 752
Sec B Hughes (Sec/Mgr)
Pro P Barber (061) 998 2811
Holes 18 L 6273 yds SSS 70
Recs Am–65 RI Walker
V'trs WD–UH WE–M after 11am SOC
Fees £10 (£12)
Loc 6 miles S of Manchester

Disley (1889)

Private
Stanley Hall Lane, Disley,nr Stockport, Cheshire
Tel **(0663) 63266**
Mem 600
Sec JA Lomas (Hon Sec)
Pro AG Esplin (0663) 62884
Holes 18 L 6015 yds SSS 69
Recs Am–68 A Peck Pro–63 B Charles
V'trs U
Fees £8 (£10)
Loc 6 miles S of Stockport

Dukinfield (1913)

Private
Yew Tree Lane, Dukinfield, Cheshire
Tel **(061) 338 2340**
Mem 199 46(L) 27(J)
Sec KP Parker (061) 338 2669
Holes 16 L 5544 yds SSS 67
Recs Am–69 S Woolley
V'trs WD–U (exc Wed) WE–M
Fees £6
Loc 6 miles E of Manchester

Dunham Forest G & CC (1961)

Private
Oldfield Lane, Altrincham, Cheshire WA14 4TY
Tel **(061) 928 2605**
Mem 600
Sec Mrs S Klaus
Pro I Wrigley (061) 928 2727
Holes 18 L 6636 yds SSS 72
V'trs WD–U WE/BH–M SOC exc 12.45–1.45pm
Fees £14 (£17.50)
Loc 1 mile SW of Altrincham

Dunscar (1908)

Private
Longworth Lane, Bromley Cross, Bolton BL7 9QY
Tel **(0204) 53321**
Mem 420
Sec TM Yates (0204) 51090
Pro G Treadgold (0204) 592992
Holes 18 L 5968 yds SSS 69
Recs Am–64 JW Smethurst
Pro–66 W Slater
V'trs U WE–Restricted
Fees £8 (£10)
Loc 3 miles N of Bolton off A666

Ellesmere (1913)

Private
Old Clough Lane, Worsley, nr Manchester M28 5HZ
Tel **(061) 790 2122**
Mem 330 80(L) 75(J) 50(5)
Sec AC Kay (061) 790 7108
Pro J Pennington (061) 790 8591
Holes 18 L 5957 yds SSS 69
Recs Am–67 JA Pugh
Pro–66 G Weir
V'trs U exc comp days (recognised club members, check first with Pro) SOC–WD
Fees £7.50 (£8.50)
Loc 6 miles W of Manchester at junction of M62/A580

Fairfield Golf & Sailing Club (1892)

Private
Booth Road, Audenshaw, Manchester M34 5GA
Tel **(061) 370 1641**
Mem 550
Sec J Humphries
Pro DM Butler (061) 370 2292
Holes 18 L 5664 yds SSS 68
Recs Am–65 PW Wrigley, ARS Pownell
V'trs U SOC–WD
Fees £8 (£10)
Loc East boundary A635

Flixton (1893)

Private
Church Road, Flixton, Manchester
Tel **(061) 748 2116**
Mem 250
Sec JG Frankland (061) 747 0296
Pro P Reeves
Holes 9 L 6441 yds SSS 71
Recs Am–69 P O'Brien
Pro–65 P Reeves
V'trs U
Fees £4 (£6)
Loc 6 miles SW of Manchester

Gathurst (1913)

Private
Miles Lane, Shevington, nr Wigan WN6 8EW
Tel **(025 75) 2861**
Mem 300
Sec J Clarke (025 75) 2432
Pro D Clarke (025 75) 4909
Holes 9 L 6308 yds SSS 70
Recs Am–67 S Ainscough
Pro–66 D Clarke
V'trs WD–U before 5pm WE/BH/ Wed–M SOC–WD
Fees £6.90
Loc 4 miles W of Wigan. 1 mile S of M6 Junction 27

Gatley (1911)

Private
Waterfall Farm, Styal Road, Heald Green, Cheadle, Cheshire SK8 3TW
Tel **(061) 437 2091**
Mem 400
Sec WW Tibbitts (061) 485 2943
Pro M Proffitt (061) 436 2830
Holes 9 L 5934 yds SSS 68
Recs Am–64 N Pattinson
Pro–63 C Timperley
V'trs WE/Tues–NA Other days–by prior arrangement with Sec
Fees £8
Loc 7 miles S of Manchester. Manchester Airport 2 miles

Great Lever & Farnworth

Private
Lever Edge Lane, Bolton
Tel **(0204) 62582**
Mem 470
Sec PJ Holt (0204) 72550
Holes 18 L 5859 yds SSS 69
Recs Am–68 J Dickinson
Pro–65 SC Evans
V'trs U
Fees £4.50 (£6.50)
Loc Town centre $1\frac{1}{2}$ miles

Greenmount (1920)

Private
Greenmount, nr Bury
Tel **(020 488) 3712**
Mem 180
Sec HJ Billingham (020 488) 3401
Holes 9 L 4920 yds SSS 64
Recs Am–62 G Dalziel
V'trs WD–U exc Tues WE–M
Fees £5
Loc 3 miles N of Bury

Haigh Hall (1972)

Public
Haigh Hall Country Park, Haigh, Wigan WN2 1PE
Tel **(0942) 831107**
Mem 150
Sec J McAllister (0942) 833337
Pro I Lee
Holes 18 L 6423 yds SSS 71
Recs Am–67 J Silcock (1987)
Pro–66 K Waters (1988)
V'trs U
Fees £2.50 (£3.25)
Loc 3 miles NW of town

Hale (1903)

Private
Rappax Road, Hale, Cheshire
Tel **(061) 980 4225**
Mem 305
Sec RV Nichols
Holes 9 L 5780 yds SSS 68
Recs Am–66 JR Barlow
Pro–65 D Durnian
V'trs WD–U exc Thurs–NA before 5pm WE/BH–M SOC
Fees £10
Loc 2 miles S of Altrincham

Harwood (1926)

Private
"Springfield", Roading Brook Road, Bolton BL2 5HT
Tel **(0204) 22878**
Mem 374
Sec D Bamber (0204) 22878
Pro MW Evans (0204) 398472
Holes 9 L 5960 yds SSS 69
Recs Am–67 PM Lay, N Stirling
V'trs WD–U WE–M SOC
Fees £8
Loc Harwood, 4 miles NE of Bolton

Hazel Grove (1912)

Private
Club House, Hazel Grove, nr Stockport SK7 6LU
Tel **(061) 483 3217**
Mem 550
Sec HAG Carlisle (061) 483 3978
Pro ME Hill (061) 483 7272
Holes 18 L 6300 yds SSS 70
Recs Am–67 A Hill
Pro–67 M Slater
V'trs U
Fees £11 (£15)
Loc 3 miles S of Stockport

Heaton Moor (1892)

Private
Heaton Mersey, Stockport
Tel **(061) 432 2134**
Mem 350
Sec AA Gibbon (061) 432 6458
Pro CR Loydall (061) 432 0846
Holes 18 L 5876 yds SSS 68

Recs Am–67 RM Short
Pro–66 D Cooper
V'trs U
Fees £7.50 (£9)
Loc Greater Manchester

Heaton Park (1912)

Public
Heaton Park, Prestwich, Manchester
Tel **(061) 798 0295**
Mem 150
Sec AF Roberts (061) 681 1476
Pro J Pennington (061) 798 0295
Holes 18 L 5849 yds SSS 68
Recs Am–66 J Griffiths (1986), S Pilling (1988)
Pro–65 AP Thomson, B Evans, I Collins, M Gray
V'trs U
Fees £3.50 (£5)
Loc N Manchester

Horwich (1895)

Private
Victoria Road, Horwich BL6 5PH
Tel **(0204) 696980**
Mem 180
Sec GR Sharp (0204) 696298
Holes 9 L 5404 yds SSS 67
Recs Am–65 M Derbyshire
V'trs M SOC–WD
Loc 5 miles W of Bolton

Houldsworth (Levenshulme) (1910)

Private
Wingate House, Higher Levenshulme, Manchester M19 3JW
Tel **(061) 224 5055**
Mem 300
Sec JB Hogg (061) 336 5044
Pro David Naylor (061) 224 4571
Holes 18 L 6078 yds SSS 69
Recs Am–67 R Arnold
Pro–63 D Vaughan
V'trs U SOC
Fees £6.00 (£8)
Loc 4 miles S of Manchester

Leigh (1906)

Private
Kenyon Hall, Culcheth, Warrington WA3 4BG
Tel **(092 576) 3130**
Mem 700
Sec GD Riley (092 576) 2943
Holes 18 L 5853 yds SSS 68
Recs Am–64 J Critchely
Pro–67 D Coles
V'trs U H SOC
Fees £9 (£12)
Loc At Culcheth

Lowes Park (1914)

Private
Hill Top, Walmersley, Bury BL9 6SU
Tel **(061) 764 1231**
Mem 250
Sec E Brierley (0706) 67331
Holes 9 L 6043 yds SSS 69
Recs Am–69 MJ Bailey (1984)
V'trs WD–U exc Wed–NA Sat comp days–NA Sun–by appointment only
Fees WD–£6 Sun–£7
Loc 2 miles NE of town boundary off A56

Manchester GC Ltd (1882)

Private
Hopwood Cottage, Rochdale Road, Middleton, Manchester M24 2QP
Tel **(061) 643 2718**
Mem 600
Sec RE Tattersall (061) 643 3202
Pro B Conner (061) 643 2638
Holes 18 L 6450 yds SSS 72
Recs Am–66 RE Tattersall, M Russell
Pro–65 I Mosey, D Cooper
V'trs WD–U WE–NA
Fees £12
Loc 7 miles N of city. M62 Junction 20

Marple (1892)

Private
Hawk Green, Marple, Stockport, Cheshire
Tel **(061) 427 2311**
Mem 300 70(L) 60(J) 30(5)
Sec M Gilbert (061) 427 6364
Pro N Wood (061) 449 0690
Holes 18 L 5506 yds SSS 67
V'trs WD–U exc Thurs–NA WE/BH–M SOC
Fees £6.50
Loc 2 miles from High Lane North off A6

Mellor & Townscliffe (1894)

Private
Tarden Mellor, nr Stockport, Cheshire SK6 5NA
Tel **(061) 427 2208**
Mem 470
Sec K Bounds
Holes 18 L 5939 yds SSS 69
Recs Am–67 CW Axon, MG Senior, GD Williams
Pro–64 MJ Slater
V'trs U
Fees £8 (£10)
Loc 7 miles SE of Stockport

North Manchester (1894)

Private
Rhodes House, Manchester Old Road, Middleton, Manchester M24 4PE
Tel **(061) 643 2941**
Mem 300 60(L) 38(J) 80(5)
Sec J Fallon (061) 643 9033
Pro M Vipond (061) 643 7094
Holes 18 L 6542 yds SSS 72
Recs Am–66 J Cheetham
Pro–69 M Vipond
V'trs U
Fees £10 (£14)
Loc 5 miles N of Manchester. M62 Junction 18

Northenden (1913)

Private
Palatine Road, Manchester M22 4FR
Tel **(061) 998 4738**
Mem 600
Sec JM Fleet (Mgr) RH Newall (Hon Sec)
Pro A Malcolm (061) 945 3386
Holes 18 L 6435 yds SSS 71
Recs Am–67 JEB Waddell
Pro–64 D Durnian
V'trs U SOC
Fees £12 (£15)
Loc 5 miles S of Manchester

Old Manchester (1818)

Private
Tel **(061) 766 4157**
Mem 60
Sec PT Goodall
Holes Club without a course

Oldham (1892)

Private
Lees New Road, Oldham
Tel **(061) 624 4986**
Mem 300 45(L) 35(J)
Sec BC Heginbotham (04577) 6326
Pro A Laverty (061) 626 8346
Holes 18 L 5045 yds SSS 65
Recs Am–66 D Maloney (1987)
Pro–65 E Smith
V'trs U SOC–WD
Fees £8 (£10)
Loc 200 yds off Oldham–Stalybridge road

Pike Fold (1909)

Private
Cooper Lane, Victoria Avenue, Blackley, Manchester M9 2QQ
Tel **(061) 740 1136**
Mem 200
Sec GVW Kendell (061) 766 6788
Holes 9 L 5789 yds SSS 68
Recs Am–68 M Hazelden, T Salmon, C Neill
Pro–66 JE Wiggett
V'trs WD–U WE/BH–M SOC
Fees £5 R/D (£3)
Loc 5 miles N of city

Prestwich (1908)

Private
Hilton Lane, Prestwich
Tel **(061) 773 2544**
Mem 447
Sec MT Thornton (061) 736 3084
Pro GP Coope
Holes 18 L 4522 yds SSS 63

For map index see page 203.

Recs Am–61 M Garrod
V'trs WD–U WE–NA before 3pm SOC
Fees £7 (£9)
Loc 3 miles N of Manchester

Reddish Vale (1912)

Private
Southcliffe, Reddish, Stockport, Cheshire SK5 7EE
Tel **(061) 480 2359**
Mem 450
Sec JL Blakey (061) 432 6544
Pro RA Brown (061) 480 3824
Holes 18 L 6086 yds SSS 69
Recs Am–64 KR Gorton
Pro–67 R Williamson
V'trs WD–U WE–M SOC
Fees £8.50
Loc 1 mile NNE of Stockport

Regent Park (1932)

Private
Links Road, Chorley New Road, Bolton, Lancs BL2 9XX
Tel **(0204) 44170**
Mem 130
Sec A Cunliffe
Holes Play over Bolton Municipal

Ringway (1909)

Private
Hale Mount, Hale Barns, Altrincham, Cheshire WA15 8SW
Tel **(061) 980 4468**
Mem 352 165(L) 41(J) 25(5)
Sec D Wright (061) 980 2630
Pro N Ryan (061) 980 8432
Holes 18 L 6494 yds SSS 71
Recs Am–67 RE Preston
V'trs Fri/Tues before 2pm & Sun before 11am–M
Fees £16 (£18)
Loc 8 miles S of Manchester off M56 Junction 6 (A538)

Rochdale (1888)

Private
Edenfield Road, Bagslate, Rochdale OL11 5YR
Tel **(0706) 46024 (Clubhouse)**
Mem 625
Sec (0706) 43818
Pro FW Accleton (0706) 522104
Holes 18 L 5981 yds SSS 69
Recs Am–66 J Hawkard, R Kershaw
Pro–66 P Butler, P Cowan
V'trs U
Fees £10 (£12)
Loc M62 Junction 20, 3 miles on A680

Saddleworth (1904)

Private
Uppermill, nr Oldham, Lancs
Tel **(04577) 3653**
Mem 620
Sec IG Bennett
Pro ET Shard
Holes 18 L 5976 yds SSS 69
Recs Am–67 P Smethurst
Pro–69 M Melling, A Gillies
V'trs U
Fees £8 (£10.50)
Loc 5 miles E of Oldham
Mis Buggy for hire

Sale (1913)

Private
Sale Lodge, Golf Road, Sale, Cheshire M33 2LU
Tel **(061) 973 3404**
Mem 580
Sec E Tootill (061) 973 1638
Pro M Lake (061) 973 1730
Holes 18 L 6351 yds SSS 70
Recs Am–67 JR Barlow
V'trs U SOC–WD
Fees £9 (£15)
Loc North boundary of Sale

Springfield Park (1928)

Public
Marland, Rochdale
Tel **(0706) 49801**
Mem 200
Sec B Wynn (0706) 526064
Pro D Wills
Holes 18 L 5209 yds SSS 66
Recs Am–68 B Walsh
Pro–67 ME Hill
V'trs U
Fees £2.75 (£2.75) 1987 prices
Loc West boundary of Rochdale

Stamford (1900)

Private
Oakfield House, Huddersfield Road, Stalybridge, Cheshire SK15 3PY
Tel **(04575) 2126**
Mem 500
Sec RH Makin
Pro B Badger (04575) 4829
Holes 18 L 5524 yds SSS 67
Recs Am–66 H Fletcher
V'trs WD–U WE comp days–after 2.30pm SOC–WD (min 12 members)
Fees £8 (£12.50)
Loc NE boundary of Stalybridge on B6175

Stand (1904)

Private
The Dales, Ashbourne Grove, Whitefield, Manchester M25 7NL
Tel **(061) 766 2388**
Mem 700
Sec TE Thacker (061) 766 3197
Pro M Dance (061) 766 2214
Holes 18 L 6411 yds SSS 71
Recs Am–68 JE Cooke
Pro–69 N Hunt
V'trs U SOC–WD
Fees £8 (£10)
Loc 5 miles N of Manchester

Swinton Park (1926)

Private
East Lancashire Road, Swinton, Manchester M27 1LX
Tel **(061) 794 1785**
Mem 425 92(L) 50(J)
Sec F Slater (061) 794 0861
Pro J Wilson (061) 793 8077
Holes 18 L 6675 yds SSS 72
Recs Am–66 J Thornley (1984)
V'trs WD–U WE–M SOC–Tues
Fees £10
Loc On A580 5 miles NW of Manchester

Tunshill (1901)

Private
Club House, Kiln Lane, Milnrow, nr Rochdale
Tel **(0706) 342095**
Mem 180
Sec D Kennedy
Pro P Lunt (0706) 861982
Holes 9 L 5812 yds SSS 68
Recs Am–66 D Williams
V'trs WD–U WE–NA Mar–Oct SOC
Fees £5 (£5.50) 1988 prices
Loc 2 miles E of Rochdale. M62 Junction 21

Walmersley (1906)

Private
Garrett's Close, Walmersley, Bury
Tel **(061) 764 1429**
Mem 350
Sec HH Coles (061) 764 0018
Holes 9 L 5588 yds SSS 70
Recs Am–67 I Bamborough
V'trs U exc Tues–(Ladies Day) Sat–(Mens Comp day) Sun–M SOC–Wed–Fri
Fees £5
Loc 2 miles N of Bury (A56)

Werneth (1909)

Private
Green Lane Garden Suburb, Oldham OL8 3AZ
Tel **(061) 624 1190**
Mem 350
Sec JH Barlow
Pro T Morley
Holes 18 L 5296 yds SSS 66
Recs Am–62 LA Lawton
V'trs WD–U WE–M SOC
Fees WD–£8
Loc 2 miles S of town centre

Werneth Low (1912)

Private
Gee Cross, Hyde, Tameside
Tel **(061) 368 2503**
Mem 245 50(L) 60(J)
Sec R Watson (061) 368 7388
Pro A Bacchus (061) 336 6908
Holes 9 L 5734 yds SSS 68
Recs Am–67 ST Madden
Pro–57 D Cooper
V'trs U Sun–NA BH–M

Fees £8.50 (Sat £13.50)
Loc On Werneth Low–2 miles from centre

Westhoughton (1929)

Private
Long Island, Westhoughton, Bolton BL5 2BR
Tel **(0942) 811085**
Mem 225 50(L) 30(J)
Sec F Atkinson
Pro B Sharrock
Holes 9 L 5834 yds SSS 68
Recs Am–64 T Woodward
V'trs WD–U WE/BH–M
Fees £4
Loc 4 miles SW of Bolton

Whitefield (1932)

Private
Higher Lane, Whitefield, Manchester M25 7EZ
Tel **(061) 766 2728**
Mem 500
Sec Mrs RL Vidler (061) 766 2904
Pro P Reeves (061) 766 3096
Holes 18 L 6041 yds SSS 69
18 L 5714 yds SSS 68
V'trs U SOC–WD
Fees £8.50 (£12.80)
Loc 4 miles N of Manchester. M62 Junction 17

Whittaker (1906)

Private
Littleborough, Lancs OL15 0LH
Tel **(0706) 78310**
Mem 120
Sec GA Smith (0484) 28546
Holes 9 L 5576 yds SSS 67
Recs Am–65 P Davies
Pro–65 MT Hoyle
V'trs Tues pm/Sun–NA SOC
Fees £4.50 (£5.50)
Loc $1^1/_2$ miles N of Littleborough off A58

Wigan (1898)

Private
Arley Hall, Haigh, Wigan WN1 2UH
Tel **(0257) 421360**
Mem 250
Sec J Crompton (0257) 41051
Holes 9 L 6058 yds SSS 69
Recs Am–68 RM Hodson
V'trs WD–U
Fees £8 (£10)
Loc 4 miles N of Wigan off A5106/B5239. M6 Junction 27

William Wroe (1973)

Public
Pennybridge Lane, Flixton, Manchester
Tel **(061) 748 8680**
Pro R West
Holes 18 L 4395 yds SSS 60
Recs Am–45 FJ Barrow
Pro–48 GR Johnston
V'trs U booking req
Fees £2.50 (£3.75)
Loc 6 miles SW of Manchester close to M63
Mis Acre Gate Club plays here

Withington (1892)

Private
243 Palatine Road, West Didsbury, Manchester M20 8UD
Tel **(061) 445 3912**
Mem 340 97(L) 38(J) 30(5)
Sec A Larsen (061) 445 9544
Pro RJ Ling (061) 445 4861
Holes 18 L 6410 yds SSS 71
Recs Am–70 C Webb
V'trs U H
Fees £10 (£12)
Loc 6 miles S of Manchester

Worsley (1894)

Private
Stableford Avenue, Monton Green, Eccles, Manchester
Tel **(061) 789 4202**
Mem 625
Sec B Dean
Pro C Cousins
Holes 18 L 6217 yds SSS 70
Recs Am–66 B Dean
Pro–68 FS Boobyer
V'trs I NA–9–9.45am and 12.15–1.30pm
Fees £10
Loc 5 miles W of Manchester

Merseyside

Allerton Park (1934)

Public
Liverpool
Tel **(051) 428 1046**
Mem 300
Sec HG Drew (051) 427 4057
Pro J Large
Holes 18 L 5084 yds SSS 64
Recs Am–63 N McCormick
V'trs U
Fees £1
Loc 5 miles S of city centre

Arrowe Park (1931)

Public
Arrowe Park, Woodchurch, Birkenhead, Wirral
Tel **(051) 677 1527**
Mem 200
Sec K Finlay (051) 645 7602
Pro C Scanlon (051) 677 1527
Holes 18 L 6377 yds SSS 70
V'trs U
Fees £3
Loc 3 miles from centre on A552. M53 Junction 3, 1 mile

Ashton-in-Makerfield (1902)

Private
Garswood Park, Liverpool Road, Ashton-in-Makerfield
Tel **(0942) 727267**
Mem 500
Sec H Howard Elce
(0942) 727745
Pro P Allan (0942) 724229
Holes 18 L 6120 yds SSS 69
Recs Am–67 GS Lacy
V'trs WD–restricted Wed WE/BH–M SOC
Fees £7
Loc Town centre 1 mile

Bidston (1913)

Private
Scoresby Road, Leasowe, Moreton L46 1QQ
Tel **(051) 638 3412**
Mem 500
Sec LA Kendrick (051) 638 8685
Pro JR Law (051) 630 6650
Holes 18 L 6207 yds SSS 70
Recs Am–67 P Whitehouse
Pro–68 JM Hume
V'trs WD–U WE–M SOC
Fees £5.50 (£9.36)

Bootle (1934)

Public
Dunnings Bridge Road, Litherland L30 2PP
Tel **(051) 928 6196**
Mem 300
Sec J Morgan (051) 922 4792
Pro J Payn (051) 928 1371
Holes 18 L 6362 yds SSS 70
Recs Am–64 S Ashcroft
Pro–69 R Boobyer
V'trs U SOC
Fees £2.30 (£3.40)
Loc 5 miles N of Liverpool
Mis Book by phone

Bowring (1913)

Public
Bowring Park, Roby Road, Huyton, Lancs
Tel **(051) 489 1901**
Mem 80
Sec J Cahill (051) 489 5985
Pro D Weston
Holes 9 L 5592 yds SSS 66
Recs Am–67 G Spurrier
V'trs U
Fees £2.20
Loc M62 motorway

Bromborough (1904)

Private
Raby Hall Road, Bromborough
Tel **(051) 334 2155**
Mem 600
Sec LB Silvester (051) 334 2978
Pro P Andrew (051) 334 4499

For map index see page 203.

Holes 18 L 6650 yds SSS 73
Recs Am–68 DP Jones
V'trs U (Arrange with Pro in advance)
Fees £12 (£15)
Loc Mid Wirral, M53 Junction 4

Caldy (1908)

Private
Links Hey Road, Caldy, Wirral L48 1NB
Tel **(051) 625 5660**
Mem 800
Sec JK Mayberry
Pro K Jones (051) 625 1818
Holes 18 L 6665 yds SSS 73
Recs Am–66 PT Bailey, J Greenough
Pro–68 G Harvey, B McColl, P Hoad
V'trs WD–9.00–9.30am–M 9.30am–1pm–U 1–2pm–M After 2pm–U WE/BH–M Advance booking req.
Fees D–£13 After 2pm–£10
Loc $1^1/_2$ miles S of West Kirby
Mis Buggies for hire

Childwall (1913)

Private
Naylor's Road, Gateacre, Liverpool L27 2YB
Tel **(051) 487 0654**
Mem 650
Sec L Upton
Pro N Parr (051) 487 9871
Holes 18 L 6425 yds SSS 71
Recs Am–66 M Gamble
V'trs WE/BH/Tues–restricted
Fees £8.50 (£13)
Loc 2 miles from M62. 7 miles E of Liverpool city centre

Eastham Lodge (1973)

Private
Ferry Road, Eastham, Wirral L62 0AP
Tel **(051) 327 1483**
Mem 520
Sec A Robertson (051) 327 3003
Pro I Jones (051) 327 3008
Holes 15 L 5826 yds SSS 68
Recs Am–64 EI Bradshaw
Pro–66 I Jones
V'trs WD–U WE/BH–M SOC–Tues
Fees £8.50
Loc 6 miles S of Birkenhead on A41. M53 Junction 5

Formby (1884)

Private
Golf Road, Formby, Liverpool L37 1LQ
Tel **(070 48) 74273**
Mem 600
Sec A Thirlwell (070 84) 72164
Pro C Harrison (070 48) 73090
Holes 18 L 6871 yds SSS 74
Recs Am–67 DJ Eccleston
Pro–65 NC Coles
V'trs I
Fees £22 (£25)
Loc Adjacent to Freshfield Station

Formby Ladies' (1896)

Private
Formby, Liverpool L37 1LQ
Tel **(070 48) 74127**
Sec Mrs V Bailey (070 48) 73493
Pro C Harrison (070 48) 73090
Holes 18 L 5426 yds SSS 71
Recs Am–60 CD Lee
V'trs U
Fees £12 (£15)
Loc Near Southport

Grange Park (1891)

Private
Toll Bar, Prescot Road, St Helens WA10 3AD
Tel **(0744) 22980 (members)**
Mem 700
Sec JE Jarman (0744) 26318
Pro PG Evans (0744) 28785
Holes 18 L 6480 yds SSS 71
Recs Am–68 GS Lacy (1988)
Pro–66 R Ellis (1986)
V'trs I
Fees £11 (£15)
Loc $1^1/_2$ miles W of St Helens centre on A58

Haydock Park (1877)

Private
Golborne Park, Rob Lane, Newton-le-Willows WA12 0HX
Tel **(092 52) 4389**
Mem 380 130(L)
Sec G Tait (092 52) 28525
Pro PE Kenwright (092 52) 6944
Holes 18 L 6014 yds SSS 69
Recs Am–65 D Pilkington, P Boydell, K Sargent
V'trs M SOC–WD exc Tues
Fees £13
Loc M6 Junction 23

Hesketh (1885)

Private
Cockle Dick's Lane, Cambridge Road, Southport PR9 9QQ
Tel **(0704) 30226**
Mem 580
Sec PB Seal (0704) 36897
Pro J Donoghue (0704) 30050
Holes 18 L 6478 yds SSS 72
Recs Am–68 G Brand
Pro–64 D Hayes
V'trs WD–U WE/BH–limited SOC
Fees £12 D–£15 (£14 D–£18)
Loc 1 mile N of town centre

Heswall (1901)

Private
Cottage Lane, Gayton Heswall, Wirral L60 8PB
Tel **(051) 342 2193**
Mem 902
Sec CPR Calvert (051) 342 1237
Pro AE Thompson (051) 342 7431
Holes 18 L 6472 yds SSS 72
Recs Am–67 J Butterworth
Pro–64 K Jones
V'trs U BH–NA SOC–Wed & Fri
Fees D–£12 (D–£17) SOC–£12 (Min 24)
Loc 8 miles NW of Chester

Hillside (1911)

Private
Hastings Road, Southport
Tel **(0704) 69902**
Mem 800
Sec PW Ray (0704) 67169
Pro B Seddon (0704) 68360
Holes 18 L 6850 yds SSS 74
Recs Am–67 P Way
Pro–66 M O'Grady, R Craig
V'trs By arrangement with Sec
Fees D–£20 (£25)
Loc Southport

Hoylake Municipal

Public
Carr Lane, Hoylake, Wirral
Tel **(051) 632 2956/4883**
Mem 250
Sec A Peacock (051) 653 3164
Pro R Boobyer (051) 632 2956
Holes 18 L 6330 yds SSS 70
Recs Am–67 S Roberts (1983)
Pro–64 T Bennett (1982)
V'trs U WE–phone 1 week in advance–block booking times in operation SOC
Fees £3
Loc Liverpool 10 miles

Huyton & Prescot (1905)

Private
Hurst Park, Huyton
Tel **(051) 489 1138**
Mem 700
Sec Mrs E Holmes (051) 489 3948
Pro R Pottage (051) 489 2022
Holes 18 L 5738 yds SSS 68
Recs Am–67
V'trs WD–U WE–M
Fees £12 (£15)
Loc 7 miles E of Liverpool

Leasowe (1891)

Private
Leasowe Road, Moreton, Wirral L46 3RD
Tel **(051) 677 5852**
Mem 450
Sec R Kerr
Pro I Higby (051) 678 5460
Holes 18 L 6204 yds SSS 70
Recs Am–63 J Maddocks
V'trs U Sun–M
Fees £10 (£12)

Lee Park (1954)

Private
Childwall Valley Road, Gateacre, Liverpool L27 3YA
Tel **(051) 487 9861 (Clubhouse)**
Mem 450
Sec Mrs D Barr (051) 487 3882
Holes 18 L 6024 yds SSS 69
Recs Am–69 RA Knight
Pro–67 I Bramall
V'trs U
Fees On application
Loc Liverpool centre 7 miles

Liverpool Municipal (1967)

Public
Ingoe Lane, Kirkby, nr Liverpool L32 4SS
Tel **(051) 546 5435**
Mem 250
Pro D Weston
Holes 18 L 6571 yds SSS 71
Recs Am–70 J Paton (1986)
Pro–70
V'trs U WE–booking required
Fees £2.20 (£2.20)
Loc M57 exit to B5192
Mis Kirkby Club plays here

Park (1915)

Private
Park Road, Southport
Tel **(0704) 30133**
Mem 250
Sec W Halsall
Holes Play over Southport Municipal Links

Prenton (1905)

Private
Golf Links Road, Prenton, Birkenhead
Tel **(051) 608 1461/1053**
Mem 360 110(L) 38(J) 50(5)
Sec PE Manley (051) 608 1053
Pro R Thompson (051) 608 1636
Holes 18 L 6411 yds SSS 71
Recs Am–68 CJ Farey, AJ Rainford, WJ Beattie
V'trs U SOC–Mon/Wed/Fri
Fees £12 (£16) W–£40
Loc Outskirts of Birkenhead. M53 Junction 3

RLGC Village Play (1895)

Private
Hoylake, Wirral
Mem 40
Sec J Chapman (051) 625 7013
Holes Play over Royal Liverpool

Royal Birkdale (1889)

Private
Waterloo Road, Southport PR8 2LX
Tel **(0704) 69903/69928**
Sec NT Crewe (0704) 67920
Pro R Bradbeer (0704) 68857
Holes 18 L 6703 yds SSS 73
Pro–64 M O'Meara
V'trs I
Loc 1½ miles S of Southport

Royal Liverpool (1869)

Private
Meols Drive, Hoylake L47 4AL
Tel **(051) 632 3101/2**
Mem 650
Sec JR Davidson
Pro J Heggarty (051) 632 5868
Holes 18 L 6804 yds SSS 74
Recs Am–69 R Hayes
Pro–64 B Waites
V'trs I SOC
Fees £24 (£29)
Loc 10 miles W of Liverpool

St Helens (1985)

Public
St Helens, Lancs
Tel **(0744) 813149**
Mem 150
Sec MH Devenish (0744) 31955
Pro PR Parkinson
Holes 18 L 5941 yds SSS 69
Recs Am–74 D Tierney, M Venney
V'trs U
Fees £2.10
Loc Sherdley Park, 2 miles E of town on A570
Mis Sherdley Park Club plays here

Southport & Ainsdale (1907)

Private
Bradshaws Lane, Ainsdale, Southport PR8 3LG
Tel **(0704) 78092**
Mem 340 100(L) 60(J) 130(5)
Sec DA Wood (0704) 78000
Pro M Houghton (0704) 77316
Holes 18 L 6612 yds SSS 73
Recs Am–67 JB Dickinson (1982), JL Plaxton (1983)
Pro–67 DJ Russell, DI Vaughan (1983)
Pro (L)–69 B New, M Walker, K Ehrnlund (1984)
V'trs WD–I before 4pm–M after 4pm WE/BH–M SOC
Fees £17 (NA)
Loc 3 miles S of Southport on A565

Southport Municipal

Public
Park Road, Southport
Tel **(0704) 35286**
Pro W Fletcher
Holes 18 L 6253 yds SSS 69
Pro–67 W Fletcher (1986)
V'trs U
Fees £2.50 (£3.50)
Loc N end of Southport promenade
Mis Park Club plays here

Southport Old Links (1926)

Private
Moss Lane, Southport
Tel **(0704) 24294/28207**
Mem 370
Sec WAD Sims
Holes 9 L 6486 yds SSS 71
Recs Am–68 J Robinson
V'trs U exc WE comp days BH–NA SOC–WD
Fees £7.50 (£10) SOC–£7 each
Loc Churchtown District

Wallasey (1891)

Private
Bayswater Road, Wallasey L45 8LA
Tel **(051) 639 3630**
Mem 350 90(L) 55(J) 45(5)
Sec DF Haslehurst (051) 691 1024
Pro M Adams (051) 638 3888
Holes 18 L 6607 yds SSS 73
Recs Am–68 P Morgan
Pro–66 P Barber
V'trs U
Fees £16 (£20)
Loc Wallasey Grove Road Station

Warren (1911)

Public
Grove Road, Wallasey
Tel **(051) 639 5730**
Mem 100
Sec LRJ Lyon (051) 630 1907
Pro K Lamb
Holes 9 L 5914 yds SSS 68
Recs Am–66 J Hayes
Pro–66 JA MacLachlan
V'trs U
Fees £2.40
Loc Wallasey, Wirral

West Derby (1896)

Private
Yew Tree Lane, Liverpool L12 9HQ
Tel **(051) 228 1540**
Mem 575
Sec S Young (051) 254 1034
Pro N Brace (051) 220 5478
Holes 18 L 6322 yds SSS 70
Recs Am–66 M Gamble
Pro–67 AC Coop
V'trs U
Fees £10 (£14)
Loc East Liverpool

West Hoyle

Private
Carr Lane, Hoylake, Wirral
Mem 170
Sec RG Jones (051) 632 2475
Holes Play over Hoylake Municipal

For map index see page 203.

West Lancashire (1873)

Private
Blundellsands, Crosby, Liverpool L23 8SZ
Tel **(051) 924 4115**
Mem 700
Sec DE Bell (051) 924 1076
Pro D Lloyd (051) 924 5662
Holes 18 L 6756 yds SSS 73
Recs Am–69 G Boardman
Pro–66 C Mason
V'trs U SOC
Fees £14 (£17) £8 after 4pm
Loc Midway between Liverpool and Southport off A565
Mis Traditional links

Wirral Ladies (1894)

Private
93 Bidston Road, Birkenhead
Tel **(051) 652 5797**
Mem 550
Sec Mrs DP Cranston-Miller (051) 652 1255
Pro M Jones (051) 652 2468
Holes 18 L 4966 yds SSS 70 (Ladies)
18 L 5170 yds SSS 66 (Men)
Recs Am–71 Miss H Lyall
V'trs U
Fees £10
Loc Birkenhead 1/2 mile. M53 2 miles

Woolton (1901)

Private
Doe Park, Speke Road, Woolton, Liverpool L25 7TZ
Tel **(051) 486 1601**
Mem 600
Sec KG Jennions (051) 486 2298
Holes 18 L 5706 yds SSS 68
Recs Am–64 AP Powell
Pro–66 DJ Rees
V'trs U exc comp days
Fees £9 (£15)
Loc South Liverpool
Mis Buggy and power trolley hire

Middlesex

Airlinks

Private
Southall Lane, Hounslow TW5 9PE
Tel **(01) 561 1418**
Sec J Shortland
Holes 18 L 5883 yds SSS 68

Ashford Manor (1898)

Private
Fordbridge Road, Ashford TW15 3RT
Tel **(0784) 252049**
Mem 800
Sec BJ Duffy (0784) 257687
Pro M Finney (0784) 255940
Holes 18 L 6372 yds SSS 70
Recs Am–66 NM Curtis, GA Homewood
Pro–64 David Talbot
V'trs I
Fees £16 (£20)
Loc Ashford, off A308

Brent Valley (1938)

Public
Church Road, Hanwell, London W7
Tel **(01) 567 1287 (bookings)**
Mem 350
Sec P Bryant
Pro P Bryant
Holes 18 L 5426 yds SSS 66
Recs Am–65 S Harper (1985)
Pro–61 R Green (1988)
V'trs U SOC
Fees £4 D–£6 (£5.50)
Loc Off Greenford Avenue, Hanwell

Bush Hill Park (1895)

Private
Bush Hill, Winchmore Hill, London N21 2BU
Tel **(01) 360 5738**
Mem 696
Sec DJ Clark
Pro GW Low (01) 360 4103
Holes 18 L 5809 yds SSS 68
Recs Am–65 T Sheaff
Pro–68 ST Murray
V'trs WD–U WE–M SOC
Fees £12
Loc 9 miles N of city centre

Crews Hill (1920)

Private
Cattlegate Road, Crews Hill, Enfield EN2 8AZ
Tel **(01) 363 0787**
Mem 600
Sec EJ Hunt (01) 363 6674
Pro J Reynolds (01) 366 7422
Holes 18 L 6208 yds SSS 70
Recs Am–68 S Bishop
Pro–66 P Hunt
V'trs WD–U H WE/BH–M SOC
Fees On application
Loc 2 1/2 miles N of Enfield. M25 Junction 24

Ealing (1923)

Private
Perivale Lane, Greenford UB5 8SS
Tel **(01) 997 2595**
Mem 600
Sec CFS Ryder (01) 997 0937
Pro A Stickley (01) 997 3959
Holes 18 L 6216 yds SSS 70
Recs Am–65 A Rogers
Pro–64 R Verwey
V'trs WD–U WE–M
Fees On application
Loc Marble Arch 6 miles on A40

Enfield (1893)

Private
Old Park Road South, Enfield EN2 7DA
Tel **(01) 363 0083/3921**
Mem 610
Sec AJ Hollis (01) 363 3970
Pro Ian Martin (01) 366 4492
Holes 18 L 6137 yds SSS 70
Recs Am–66 A Rogers
Pro–66 L Fickling
V'trs WD–I WE/BH–M SOC–WD
Fees £12 D–£15
Loc 1 mile NE of Enfield

Finchley (1929)

Private
Nether Court, Frith Lane, London NW7 1PU
Tel **(01) 346 2436**
Mem 450
Sec JR Pearce
Pro D Brown (01) 346 5086
Holes 18 L 6411 yds SSS 71
Recs Am–65 D Chatterton
Pro–67 T Moore
V'trs WD–U WE–pm only SOC
Fees £15 (£21)
Loc 8 miles NW of Charing Cross

Fulwell (1904)

Private
Hampton Hill TW12 1JY
Tel **(01) 977 3188**
Mem 600
Sec MCN Reding (01) 977 2733
Pro D Haslam (01) 977 3844
Holes 18 L 6490 yds SSS 71
Recs Am–68 KD Corcoran, SR Warin
Pro–63 P Buchan
V'trs WD–I WE–M
Fees £15 (£20)
Loc Opposite Fulwell Station

Grim's Dyke (1910)

Private
Oxhey Lane, Hatch End, Pinner HA5 4AL
Tel **(01) 428 4093**
Mem 575
Sec PH Payne (01) 428 4539
Pro N Macdonald (01) 428 7484
Holes 18 L 5600 yds SSS 67
Recs Am–65 J Thornton (1988)
Pro–64 BJ Hunt (1978)
V'trs U Sun–M H SOC
Fees D–£17 (D–£19)
Loc 2 miles W of Harrow (A4008)

Hampstead (1894)

Private
Winnington Road, London N2 0TU
Tel **(01) 455 0203**
Mem 533
Sec JH Dyson
Pro PJ Brown (01) 455 7089
Holes 9 L 5812 yds SSS 68
Recs Am–66 RDA Smith
Pro–62 GT Adams

V'trs WD–U WE–NA
Fees £12.50 D–£15 (£18)
Loc N of Hampstead Heath off Hampstead Lane

Harefield Place (1947)

Public
The Drive, Harefield Place, Uxbridge UB10 8PA
Tel (0895) 31169
Mem 490
Sec BL Russell (01) 561 6619
Pro P Howard (0895) 37287
Holes 18 L 5711 yds SSS 68
Recs Am–65 S Mylward
Pro–64 A Barr G Cullen
V'trs U
Fees £4.30
Loc 2 miles N of Uxbridge

Harrow School (1978)

Private
Harrow-on-the-Hill
Mem 190 80(L) 30(J)
Sec DA Fothergill (01) 422 5237
Holes 9 L 1775 yds SSS 30
V'trs M
Loc Harrow School

Haste Hill (1933)

Public
The Drive, Northwood
Tel (092 74) 22877
Mem 250
Sec ETA Rishton (Hon) (01) 866 3175
Pro T Le Brocq (Mgr)
Holes 18 L 5794 yds SSS 68
Recs Am–68 J Joyce
V'trs U
Fees £3.50 (£5.50)
Loc Northwood

Hendon (1900)

Private
off Sanders Lane, Devonshire Road, London NW7 1DG
Tel (01) 346 6023
Mem 500
Sec DE Cooper
Pro S Murray (01) 346 8990
Holes 18 L 6241 yds SSS 70
Recs Am–68 AL MacLeod
Pro–66 SWT Murray
V'trs WD–U WE/BH–bookings SOC
Fees £13 D–£16 (£21)
Loc 10 miles N of London. M1 Junction 2

Highgate (1904)

Private
Denewood Road, Highgate, London N6 4AH
Tel (01) 340 1906
Mem 593
Sec J Zuill (01) 340 3745
Pro R Turner (01) 340 5467
Holes 18 L 5964 yds SSS 69
Recs Am–66 D Kingsman, P Bax
Pro–66 I Martin (1987)
V'trs WD–U exc Wed am–M WE/BH–M SOC
Fees £16
Loc London 5 miles off A1

Hillingdon (1892)

Private
18 Dorset Way, Hillingdon, Uxbridge UB10 0JR
Tel (0895) 39810
Mem 375
Sec LAN Holland (0895) 33956
Pro DJ McFadden (0895) 51980
Holes 9 L 5459 yds SSS 67
Recs Am–67 M Weir
Pro–69 P Cheyney
V'trs WD–U (exc Thurs 12–4pm–lady members only) WE pm–M H SOC–Mon/Tues/Fri
Fees 18 holes D–£9
Loc 1 mile E of Uxbridge, by RAF Station, Uxbridge

Holiday Inn (1975)

Private
Stockley Road, West Drayton
Mem 80
Sec J O'Loughlin (0895) 444232
Pro NC Coles
Holes 9 L 3800 yds SSS 32
V'trs U SOC
Fees 18 holes–£2 (£3)
Loc In grounds of Holiday Inn

Horsenden Hill (1935)

Public
Woodland Rise, Greenford
Tel (01) 902 4555
Mem 130
Sec V Le Picq (01) 903 3143
Pro T Martin
Holes 9 L 3264 yds SSS 56
V'trs U
Fees £2.20 (£3.30)
Loc Greenford

Hounslow Heath (1979)

Public
Staines Road, Hounslow TW4 5DS
Tel (01) 570 5271
Mem 310
Sec E Rogan
Pro P Cheyney
Holes 18 L 5820 yds Par 69 SSS 68
V'trs U Tee off times–WE booking essential
Fees £3.75 (£4.75)
Loc Opposite Green Lane, Staines Road, Hounslow

Lime Trees Park (1984)

Public
Ruislip Road, Northolt UB5 6QZ
Tel (01) 845 3180
Mem 490
Sec AJ Besgrove
Pro B Mylward
Holes 9 L 5789 yds SSS 69
V'trs U SOC
Fees 18 holes £3.20 (£4.20)
9 holes £2.10 (£2.40)
Loc Turn off Western Avenue (A40) at Polish war memorial towards Yeading

Mill Hill (1925)

Private
100 Barnet Way, Mill Hill, London NW7 3AL
Tel (01) 959 2282
Mem 450
Sec FH Scott (01) 959 2339
Pro A Daniel (01) 959 7261
Holes 18 L 6309 yds SSS 70
Recs Am–65 H Aarons
Pro–67 J Hudson
V'trs WD–UH WE/BH–UH after 11.30am
Fees £12 (£20)
Loc Burnt Oak and Edgeware Stations

Muswell Hill (1893)

Private
Rhodes Avenue, Wood Green, London N22 4UT
Tel (01) 888 2044
Mem 500
Sec JAB Connors (01) 888 1764
Pro IB Roberts (01) 888 8046
Holes 18 L 6474 yds SSS 71
Recs Am–67 PJ Montague
Pro–65 H Weetman
V'trs U SOC
Fees £20 (£25–book with Pro)
Loc Bounds Green station 1 mile

North Middlesex (1928)

Private
The Manor House, Friern Barnet Lane, London N20 0NL
Tel (01) 445 1732
Mem 560
Sec D Dalingwater (01) 445 1604
Pro ASR Roberts (01) 445 3060
Holes 18 L 5611 yds SSS 67
Recs Am–65 M Cohen
Pro–64 S Levermore
V'trs WD–I WE/BH–restricted at certain times
Fees £10 (£17)
Loc Charing Cross 10 miles

Northwood (1891)

Private
Rickmansworth Road, Northwood HA6 2QW
Tel (092 74) 25329
Mem 420 240 (L)50(J) 111(5)
Sec CW Pipe (092 74) 21384
Pro CJ Holdsworth (092 74) 20112
Holes 18 L 6493 yds SSS 71
Recs Am–68 BE Marsden(1987)
Pro–67 J Bland (1977)
V'trs WD–H WE/BH–NA SOC
Fees £14
Loc 3 miles E of Rickmansworth

For map index see page 203.

Perivale Park (1932)

Public
Ruislip Road, East Greenford
Tel (01) 578 1693
Mem 200
Sec C Jonas
Pro P Bryant
Holes 9 L 5296 yds SSS 65
Recs Am–64
V'trs U
Fees £3.60 (£4.40)
Loc 1 mile E of Greenford

Picketts Lock (1973)

Public
Picketts Lock Lane, Edmonton, London N9 0AS
Tel (01) 803 3611
Sec JS Davie (01) 803 4756
Pro RG Gerken
Holes 9 L 2496 yds SSS 64
Recs Am–31 M Yates
Pro–30 JTB Rayner
V'trs U
Fees £1.20 (£1.45)
Loc Edmonton, North London

Pinner Hill (1929)

Private
Pinner Hill HA5 3YA
Tel (01) 866 0963
Mem 640
Sec M Crouch
Pro J Rule (01) 866 2109
Holes 18 L 6293 yds SSS 70
Recs Am–63 SR Warrin
Pro–67 TH Cotton, G Player, T Wilkes, G Low, J Warren
V'trs WD–U Sun/BH–M
Fees On request
Loc West Pinner Green 1 mile

Ruislip (1936)

Public
Ickenham Road, Ruislip
Tel (0895) 632004/638081
Mem 500
Sec SMD Dunlop
Pro D Nash (0895) 638835
Holes 18 L 5235 yds SSS 67
Recs Am–66 T Burchell
Pro–59 P Glozier
V'trs U
Fees £3.60 (£5)
Loc W Ruislip BR/LTE Station

Stanmore (1893)

Private
Gordon Avenue, Stanmore HA7 2RL
Tel (01) 954 4661
Mem 500
Sec PF Wise (01) 954 2599
Pro VR Law (01) 954 2646
Holes 18 L 5881 yds SSS 68
Recs Am–66 H Preston
Pro–66 G Low
V'trs WD–H WE/BH–M SOC
Fees WD–£12 (£5 public days)
Loc E boundary of Harrow

Strawberry Hill (1900)

Private
Wellesley Road, Twickenham
Tel (01) 894 1246
Mem 350
Sec RC Meer (01) 894 0165
Pro P Buchan (01) 892 2082
Holes 9 L 2381 yds SSS 62
Recs Am–61 RE Heryet
Pro–59 H Fullicks, K Bousfield, R Gerken
V'trs WD–U WE–M(XL)
Fees £8
Loc Strawberry Hill Station
Mis Course designed by JH Taylor 1910

Sudbury (1920)

Private
Bridgewater Road, Wembley HA0 1AL
Tel (01) 902 0218
Mem 640
Sec JA Smith (01) 902 3713
Pro R Beard (01) 902 7910
Holes 18 L 6282 yds SSS 70
Recs Am–63 T Greenwood
Pro–65 J Gill
V'trs WD–H Sun–M
Fees £15 (£19)
Loc Junction of A4005/A4090

Trent Park (1973)

Public
Bramley Road, Southgate, London N14
Tel (01) 366 7432
Mem 500
Sec C Nolan
Pro C Easton
Holes 18 L 6008 yds SSS 69
Recs Am–66 P Craig
Pro–64 V Law
V'trs U SOC
Fees £3.60 (£4.85)
Loc Opp Oakwood Tube

Twickenham (1977)

Public
Staines Road, Twickenham
Tel (01) 979 6946
Mem 232
Sec E Eldridge (01) 892 5579
Pro PA Tickle (01) 979 0032
Holes 9 L 6014 yds SSS 69
V'trs U
Fees £2.40 (£4.20)
Loc 2 miles NW of Hampton Court

West Middlesex (1891)

Private
Greenford Road, Southall
Tel (01) 574 3450
Mem 700
Sec PJ Furness
Pro L Farmer (01) 574 1800
Holes 18 L 6242 yds SSS 70
Recs Am–65 J Walsh
Pro–64 L Farmer
V'trs WD–U WE–after 3pm
Fees Tues/Thurs/Fri–£9.50 (£16)
Mon & Wed–£5.85
Loc Junction of Uxbridge Road and Greenford Road

Whitewebbs (1932)

Public
Beggars Hollow, Clay Hill, Enfield EN2 9JN
Tel (01) 363 2951
Mem 475
Sec SC Barnard (01) 804 8465
Pro D Lewis (01) 363 4454
Holes 18 L 5755 yds SSS 68
Recs Am–65 I Morley
Pro–68 D Lewis
V'trs U
Fees £3.60 (£4.85)
Loc 1 mile N of Enfield Town

Wyke Green (1928)

Private
Syon Lane, Isleworth
Tel (01) 560 8777
Mem 618
Sec Maj. WE Lyndon Moore TD
Pro A Fisher (01) 847 0685
Holes 18 L 6242 yds SSS 70
Recs Am–65 MR Johnson
Pro–64 C DeFoy
V'trs U
Fees £12 (£17)
Loc Gillettes Corner (A4) ½ mile

Norfolk

Barnham Broom Hotel (1977)

Private
Barnham Broom, Norwich NR9 4DD
Tel (060 545) 393
Mem 520
Sec A Long (Man Dir)
P Ballingall (Golf Dir)
Pro S Beckham
Holes 18 L 6603 yds SSS 72
Recs Am–70 G Parkhill (1981)
Pro–66 G Davies (1986), S Bennett (1987)
V'trs I or H WE/BH–NA (exc hotel residents) SOC
Fees £14 (NA) £12–residents
Loc 8 miles SW of Norwich off A47. 4 miles NW of Wymondham off A11

Bawburgh

Private
Long Lane, Bawburgh
Tel (0603) 746390
Mem 300
Sec RJ Mapes
Pro R Waugh

For explanation of abbreviations see page 202.

Holes 9 L 5278 yds SSS 66
Recs Am–69 S Manser
Pro–69 R Waugh
V'trs Sun–Restricted before 11am
SOC–WD by arrangement
Fees 18 holes £6 (£12.50)
9 holes £4
Loc S of A47, 1 mile from Norwich ring road. Turn left at Round Well PH. Rear of Royal Norfolk Showground

Costessey Park (1983)

Private
Costessey Park, Costessey, Norwich NR8 5AL
Tel (0603) 746333
Mem 500
Sec BA Howson
Pro R Foster (0603) 747085
Holes 18 L 5853 yds SSS 68
V'trs U SOC–WD
Fees £9 (£10)
Loc 3 miles W of Norwich, turn off A47 at Round Well PH

Dereham (1934)

Private
Quebec Road, Dereham NR19 2DS
Tel (0362) 693122
Mem 560
Sec N Dodds (0362) 695900
Pro S Fox (0362) 695631
Holes 9 L 6225 yds SSS 70
Recs Am–63 L Varney
Pro–65 M Elsworthy
V'trs H WE–M
Fees £8.50 (£10)
Loc Town centre 1/2 mile

Eaton (1910)

Private
Newmarket Road, Norwich NR4 6SF
Tel (0603) 52881
Mem 425 130(L) 70(J) 205(5)
Sec J Drinkwater (0603) 51686
Pro F Hill (0603) 52478
Holes 18 L 6125 yds SSS 69
Recs Am–65 SW Abel (1987)
Pro–65 M Spooner (1988)
V'trs I WE–NA before noon
Fees £14 (£18)
Loc S Norwich

Fakenham (1973)

Private
Fakenham
Tel (0328) 2867
Mem 450
Sec G Cocker (0328) 55665
Pro J Westwood (0328) 3534
Holes 9
Recs Am–70 D Hood
Pro–70 M Leeder
V'trs WD–U WE–starting times alternate Sun am SOC
Fees £8 (£11)
Loc Racecourse

Feltwell (1976)

Private
Wilton Road, Feltwell
Mem 290
Sec Fl Lt KW Wright MBE DFM RAF (Retd) (0842) 828795
Holes 9 L 6260 yds SSS 70
V'trs U
Fees £5 (£7)
Loc 1 mile S of Feltwell Village on B1112
Mis Course laid out on former Feltwell aerodrome.

Gorleston (1906)

Private
Warren Road, Gorleston, Gt Yarmouth NR31 6JT
Tel (0493) 661802
Mem 750
Sec PG Rudd (0493) 661911
Pro RL Moffit (0493) 662103
Holes 18 L 6400 yds SSS 70
Recs Am–68 J Maddock (1981)
V'trs U H SOC
Fees £10 (£12) W–£30
Loc S of Gorleston off A12

Great Yarmouth & Caister (1882)

Private
Beach House, Caister-on-Sea, Gt Yarmouth
Tel (0493) 720421
Mem 700
Sec AA Hunton (0493) 728699
Pro N Catchpole
Holes 18 L 6284 yds SSS 70
Recs Am–67 M Sperrin
Pro–66 E Murray
V'trs WE–NA before noon SOC
Fees £8 (£10)
Loc Caister–on–Sea

Hunstanton (1891)

Private
Hunstanton
Tel (048 53) 2811
Mem 650 250(L) 60(J)
Sec Wg Cdr AC Reed
Pro J Carter (048 53) 2751
Holes 18 L 6670 yds SSS 72
Recs Am–66 RDBM Shade (1966)
Pro–65 ME Gregson (1967)
V'trs WD–U after 9.30am WE/BH–U after 10.30am SOC
Fees £16 (£21) W–£75
Loc 1/2 mile NE of Hunstanton

King's Lynn (1923)

Private
Castle Rising, King's Lynn PE31 6BD
Tel (055 387) 656
Mem 980
Sec GJ Higgins (055 387) 654
Pro C Hanlon (055 387) 655
Holes 18 L 6646 yds SSS 72
Recs Am–74 S Webster (1988)
Pro–68 M Davis (1988)
V'trs WD–UH WE/BH–NA SOC
Fees £14 (£20)
Loc 4 miles NE of King's Lynn

Links Country Park Hotel (1979)

Private
West Runton, Cromer
Tel (026 375) 691
Mem 220
Sec G Harvey
Pro G Harvey
Holes 9 L 4814 yds Par 66
SSS 64
Recs Am–68 R Rouse
Pro–65 R Mann
V'trs U
Fees £5 (£6)
Loc 2 miles E of Sheringham

Mundesley (1903)

Private
Links Road, Mundesley NR11 8ES
Tel (0263) 720279
Mem 400
Sec BD Baxter (0263) 720095
Pro TG Symmons
Holes 9 L 5410 yds SSS 66
V'trs U exc Wed 12–3pm Sun–NA before 11.30am
Fees £8 (£12)
Loc 7 miles S of Cromer

RAF Marham (1974)

Private
RAF Marham, Kings Lynn PE33 9NP
Mem 160
Sec BW Sutherland (0760) 337261 (Ext 208)
Holes 9 L 5280 yds SSS 66
V'trs By prior arrangement–course situated on MOD land; WD–U WE–U exc Sun am
Fees £5
Loc Near Narborough, 11 miles SE of Kings Lynn
Mis Course may be closed without prior notice

Royal Cromer (1888)

Private
Overstrand Road, Cromer NR27 0JH
Tel (0263) 512884
Mem 655
Sec Fl Lt E Robertson
Pro RJ Page (0263) 512267
Holes 18 L 6508 yds SSS 71
Recs Am–69 C Lamb (1988)
Pro–71 M Few (1988)
V'trs H SOC–WD
Fees £15 (£20)
Loc 1 mile E of Cromer

Royal Norwich (1893)

Private
Drayton High Road, Hellesdon, Norwich
Tel **(0603) 45712**
Mem 780
Sec DF Cottier (0603) 429928
Pro B Lockwood (0603) 408459
Holes 18 L 6603 yds SSS 72
Recs Am–67 A Barker
Pro–66 HJ Boyle
V'trs WE/BH–Restricted SOC
Fees £15 R/D
Loc 1/2 mile W of ring road on Fakenham Road

Royal West Norfolk (1892)

Private
Brancaster, King's Lynn PE31 8AX
Tel **(0485) 210223**
Mem 660
Sec Maj. N Carrington Smith
Pro RE Kimber (0485) 210616
Holes 18 L 6428 yds SSS 71
Recs Am–67 AH Perowne
Pro–66 M Elsworthy
V'trs U WE–M (Jul–Sept)
Fees £14 (£20)
Loc 7 miles E of Hunstanton on A419

Ryston Park (1932)

Private
Ely Road, Denver, Downham Market PE38 0HH
Tel **(0366) 382133**
Mem 320
Sec AJ Wilson (0366) 383834
Holes 9 L 6292 yds SSS 70
Recs Am–66 JP Alflatt (1975)
V'trs WE–M
Fees £10
Loc 1 mile S of Downham Market on A10

Sheringham (1891)

Private
Sheringham
Tel **(0263) 822038**
Mem 750
Sec MJ Garrett (0263) 823488
Pro MT Leeder (0263) 822980
Holes 18 L 6464 yds SSS 71
Recs Am–70 PR Little
Pro–69 M Few
V'trs U H SOC
Fees £16 (£21)
Loc 1/2 mile W of town centre

Sprowston Park (1980)

Private
Wroxham Road, Sprowston, Norwich NR7 8RP
Tel **(0603) 410657**
Mem 650
Sec TA Mower
Pro C Potter (0603) 415557
Holes 18 L 5985 yds SSS 69
Recs Am–69 S Terrington
Pro–65 N Catchpole
V'trs H WE–U before 5pm
Fees No green fees WE
Loc 2 miles NE of city centre
Mis Floodlit driving range

Swaffham (1922)

Private
Cley Road, Swaffham
Tel **(0760) 721611**
Mem 450
Sec R Joslin (0760) 22487
Pro CJ Norton (036 621) 284
Holes 9 L 6252 yds SSS 70
Recs Am–68 G Head
Pro–64 CJ Norton
V'trs WD–U WE–M Sun am–NA
Fees £10
Loc Swaffham 1 1/2 miles

Thetford (1912)

Private
Brandon Road, Thetford IP24 3NE
Tel **(0842) 2258**
Mem 650
Sec RJ Ferguson (0842) 2169
Pro N Arthur (0842) 2662
Holes 18 L 6504 yds SSS 71
Recs Am–69 RE Clarke
Pro–69 B White
V'trs H SOC–WE (by arrangement)
Fees £14 (£16)
Loc Brandon Road (B1107) off A11

Northamptonshire

Cold Ashby (1974)

Private
Cold Ashby, nr Northampton NN6 7EP
Tel **(0604) 740548**
Mem 500 40(L) 40(J)
Sec D Croxton
Pro K Dickens, A Pauly (0604) 740099
Holes 18 L 5957 yds SSS 69
Recs Am–68 D France (1986)
Pro–61 D Dunk (1985)
V'trs WD–U WE–U after 10.30am (if booked) SOC
Fees £8 (£9.50)
Loc 5 miles E of M1 Junction 18, between Leicester and Northampton

Daventry & District (1922)

Private
Norton Road, Daventry
Tel **(0327) 702829**
Mem 300
Sec F Higham (0327) 703204
Pro M Higgins
Holes 9 L 2871 yds SSS 67
V'trs WD–U Sun–NA before 11am SOC
Fees £4.50 (£5.50)
Loc Norton Road

Delapre (1976)

Public
Eagle Drive, Nene Valley Way, Northampton
Tel **(0604) 64036/63957**
Mem 500
Sec JS Corby (0604) 63957
Pro J Corby (0604) 64036
Holes 18 L 6293 yds SSS 70
2 x 9 hole Par 3 courses
Recs Am–66 M McNally
V'trs U SOC
Fees £3.75 (WE/BH £4.75)
Loc M1 Junction 15, 3 miles (A508)
Mis Pitch and putt. Driving range

Kettering (1891)

Private
Headlands, Kettering
Tel **(0536) 512074**
Mem 370 100(L) 45(J) 50(5)
Sec T Cave (0536) 511104
Pro K Theobald (0536) 81014
Holes 18 L 6035 yds SSS 69
Recs Am–67 J Campbell
Pro–67 J Gallagher
V'trs WD–U WE/BH–M SOC
Fees £9
Loc South boundary of Kettering

Kingsthorpe (1908)

Private
Kingsley Road, Northampton NN2 7BU
Tel **(0604) 711173**
Mem 450
Sec NC Liddington (0604) 710610
Pro P Smith (0604) 719602
Holes 18 L 6006 yds SSS 69
Recs Am–63 S McDonald
Pro–64 B Larratt
V'trs WD–U WE/BH–MH SOC–WD
Fees £12 R/D
Loc Northampton

Northampton (1893)

Private
Kettering Road, Northampton
Tel **(0604) 711054**
Mem 500 100(L) 70(J)
Sec TCA Knight (0604) 719453
Pro R Lovelady (0604) 714897
Holes 18 L 6002 yds SSS 69
Recs Am–66 C Cieslewicz (1972)
Pro–64 M Gallagher (1983)
V'trs WD–U WE–M
Fees £10
Loc 2 miles E of town on A43

Northamptonshire County (1909)

Private
Church Brampton, Northampton
Tel (0604) 842170
Mem 600
Sec GG Morley (0604) 843025
Pro SD Brown (0604) 842226
Holes 18 L 6503 yds SSS 71
Recs Am–67 C Poxon (1986)
Pro–65 M Ingham (1987)
V'trs WD–H WE–I H XL before 3.30pm Sat and 11.15am Sun
Fees £13 (£15)
Loc 5 miles NW of Northampton off A50

Oundle (1894)

Private
Oundle
Tel (0832) 73267
Mem 500
Sec R Davis
Holes 18 L 5507 yds SSS 67
Recs Am–68
Pro–67
V'trs WD–U WE–M before 10.30am U after 10.30am
Fees £8 (£10)

Priors Hall (1965)

Public
Stamford Road, Weldon, nr Corby
Tel (0536) 60756
Mem 300
Sec M Evans (0536) 67546
Pro M Summers
Holes 18 L 6677 yds SSS 72
Recs Am–75 R Beekie, M Scott, WF Kearney
Pro–70 RH Kemp
V'trs U
Fees £2.60 (£3.80)
Loc A43

Rushden (1919)

Private
Kimbolton Road, Chelveston, Wellingborough
Tel (0933) 312581
Mem 350
Sec R Tomlin (0933) 312197
Holes 9 L 6381 yds SSS 70
Recs Am–67
V'trs WD–U exc Wed pm WE–M Sat pm/Sun am–XL BH–U SOC
Fees £10
Loc On A45, 2 miles E of Higham Ferrers

Staverton Park (1977)

Private
Staverton, nr Daventry
NN11 6JJ
Mem (0327) 705911
Sec AL McLundie
Pro B Mudge (0327) 705506
Holes 18 L 6634 yds SSS 72
Recs Am–67
Pro–64
V'trs H SOC
Fees £10 (£15)
Loc 1 mile S of Daventry off A425. M1 Junctions 16/18, 15 mins

Wellingborough (1893)

Private
Harrowden Hall, Great Harrowden, Wellingborough
NN9 5AD
Tel (0933) 673022/677234
Mem 850
Sec Maj. AS Furnival (0933) 677234
Pro D Clifford (0933) 678752
Holes 18 L 6604 yds SSS 72
Recs Am–69 AI Marshall
Pro–69 D Clifford
V'trs W–U exc Tues pm I WE–M SOC Wed & Thurs
Fees £12 D–£16
Loc 2 miles N of Wellingborough on A509 to Kettering

Woodlands Vale (1974)

Private
Farthingstone, nr Towcester
Tel (032 736) 291
Mem 650
Sec DC Donaldson (Prop)
Pro M Gallagher
Holes 18 L 6330 yds SSS 71
Recs Am–69 A Deakin (1984)
Pro–66 D Thorp (1985)
M Gallagher (1986)
V'trs U SOC
Fees £9 (£12)
Loc 6 miles W of M1 Junction 16. 3 miles W of A5 at Weedon, on Farthingstone –Everdon road
Mis Buggies for hire

Northumberland

Allendale (1923)

Private
Thornley Gate, Allendale, Hexham
NE47 9LG
Mem 90 20(L) 9(J)
Sec JC Hall (091) 2675875
Holes 9 L 4410 yds SSS 63
V'trs U SOC
Fees £3 (£4) W–£16.50
Loc 10 miles SW of Hexham

Alnmouth (1869)

Private
Foxton Hall, Alnmouth
Tel (0665) 830231
Mem 600
Sec FK Marshall (0665) 830368
Holes 18 L 6414 yds SSS 71
Recs Am–65 P Deeble
V'trs U SOC–Mon–Thurs
Fees £9 (£12)
Loc 5 miles SE of Alnwick
Mis Dormy House accommodation

Alnmouth Village (1869)

Private
Marine Road, Alnmouth
Tel (0665) 830370
Mem 340
Sec W Maclean (0665) 602096
Holes 9 L 6020 yds SSS 70
Recs Am–63 D Weddell
V'trs U
Fees £4 (£6) W–£15

Alnwick (1907)

Private
Swansfield Park, Alnwick
Tel (0665) 602632
Mem 400
Sec LE Stewart (0665) 602499
Holes 9 L 5387 yds SSS 66
Recs Am–62 P Deeble
V'trs U
Fees £5 R/D (£5 R/D)
Loc Swansfield Park Road, Alnwick

Arcot Hall (1909)

Private
Dudley Cramlington NE23 7QP
Mem 540
Sec AG Bell (091) 236 2794
Pro GM Cant (091) 236 2147
Holes 18 L 6389 yds SSS 70
Recs Am–67 N McDonald (1986), J Metcalfe (1987)
Pro–67 S & P Harrison
V'trs WD–U SOC
Fees £12 (£15)
Loc 7 miles N of Newcastle

Bamburgh Castle (1904)

Private
Bamburgh NE69 7DE
Tel (066 84) 378
Mem 650
Sec TC Osborne (066 84) 321
Holes 18 L 5465 yds SSS 67
Recs Am–63 RS Rutter (1984)
V'trs U BH–NA SOC
Fees £9 (£11) W–£30
Loc Bamburgh, on coast of N Northumberland. 7 miles E of A1 via B1341 or B1342
Mis Buggy for hire (summer)

Bedlingtonshire (1972)

Public
Acorn Bank, Bedlington
Tel (0670) 822457
Mem 652
Sec R Partis
Pro J Mathews (0670) 822087
Holes 18 L 6224 metres SSS 73
Recs Am–68 D Gray
Pro–65 K Waters
V'trs U
Fees £4.50 D–£6 (£6 D–£8)
Loc 12 miles N of Newcastle

Bellingham (1893)

Private
Bellingham NE48 2DT
Tel **(0660) 20530**
Mem 120 24(L) 15(J)
Sec TH Thompson (0660) 20281
Holes 9 L 5226 yds SSS 66
Recs Am–63 I Wilson
V'trs U exc comp Sun SOC
Fees £4 (£5)
Loc 15 miles N of Hexham

Berwick-upon-Tweed (1892)

Private
Goswick Beal, Berwick-upon-Tweed TD15 2RW
Tel **(0289) 87256**
Mem 425
Sec (0289) 87348
Pro M Leighton (0289) 87380
Holes 18 L 6399 yds SSS 71
Recs Am–64 A Cotton
V'trs WD–U WE–NA 10am–2.30pm (1st tee) SOC
Fees £7 D–£10 (£10 D–£14) W–£28
Loc 5 miles S of town

Blyth (1905)

Private
New Delaval, Blyth
Tel **(0670) 367728**
Mem 580 120(L) 120(J)
Sec WJF Lightley
Pro K Phillips (0670) 356514
Holes 18 L 6498 yds SSS 71
Recs Am–67 K Nixon (1988)
V'trs WD–U WE–M BH–NA SOC–WD
Fees £7 D–£8 WE–M
Loc W end of Plessey Road, Blyth

Dunstanburgh Castle (1907)

Private
Embleton NE66 3XQ
Tel **(066 576) 562**
Mem 256
Sec PFC Gilbert
Holes 18 L 6357 yds SSS 70
Recs Am–69
V'trs U
Fees £7 (£9)
Loc 7 miles NE of Alnwick on B1339

Hexham (1906)

Private
Spital Park, Hexham NE46 3RZ
Tel **(0434) 602057**
Mem 700
Sec JC Oates (0434) 603072
Pro I Waugh (0434) 604904
Holes 18 L 6272 yds SSS 70
Recs Am–67 D Black, JP Arnott, M Nicholson, G Gilhespy
Pro–67 I Waugh
V'trs U
Fees £8 (£11) W–£32 M–£70
Loc 21 miles W of Newcastle –upon–Tyne

Magdalene Fields (1903)

Public
Berwick–upon–Tweed
Tel **(0289) 306384**
Mem 160
Sec R Patterson (0289) 305758
Holes 18 L 6551 yds SSS 71
Recs Am–70 J Patterson
V'trs U
Fees £5 (1987)
Loc Berwick centre 5 mins

Morpeth (1907)

Private
The Common, Morpeth
Tel **(0670) 519980**
Mem 500
Sec T Weddell (0670) 55828
Pro MR Jackson (0670) 512065
Holes 18 L 5671 metres SSS 70
V'trs H
Fees £6.50 (£8)
Loc 1 mile S of town on A197

Newbiggin-by-the-Sea (1884)

Private
Newbiggin-by-the-Sea
Tel **(0670) 817344**
Mem 500
Sec WR Dent (0670) 816078
Pro D Fletcher (0670) 817833
Holes 18 L 6450 yds SSS 71
Recs Am–67 B Bennett
Pro–68 K Saint
V'trs U
Fees £4.50 (£6) W–£20
Loc Newbiggin Village, near Church Point

Ponteland (1927)

Private
53 Bell Villas, Ponteland, Newcastle–upon–Tyne NE20 9BD
Tel **(0661) 72844/71872**
Mem 460 150(L) 90(J) 30(5)
Sec G Weetman (0661) 22689
Pro I Clark (0661) 22689
Holes 18 L 6512 yds SSS 71
Recs Am–66 J Hayes, WMM Jenkins, DG Potter (1987)
Pro–66 G Burrows
V'trs WD–U WE/BH–M
Fees £9 D–£12
Loc 1 mile beyond Airport. 6 miles NW of city on A696

Prudhoe (1930)

Private
Eastwood Park, Prudhoe-on-Tyne NE42 5DX
Tel **(0661) 32466**
Mem 400
Sec GB Garratt (0661) 34134
Pro J Crawford (0661) 36188
Holes 18 L 5812 yds SSS 68
Recs Am–65 DH Curry
Pro–65 A Crosby
V'trs WD–U WE–M SOC
Fees £7 (£8)
Loc 15 miles W of Newcastle–upon–Tyne

Rothbury (1890)

Private
Old Race Course, Rothbury, Morpeth
Tel **(0669) 20718**
Mem 200
Sec WT Bathgate
Holes 9 L 5108 metres SSS 67
Recs Am–67 D Weddell
V'trs WD–U WE–U before noon NA–after noon
Fees £2.50 (£4) W–£7
Loc W side of Rothbury. 15 miles N of Morpeth on A1

Seahouses (1913)

Private
Beadnell Road, Seahouses NE68 7XT
Tel **(0665) 720794**
Mem 260
Sec G Hogg (0665) 720091
Holes 18 L 5374 yds SSS 66
Recs Am–64 RS Rutter (1984)
V'trs U SOC
Fees £6 (£8)
Loc 14 miles N of Alnwick. 9 miles off A1

Stocksfield (1913)

Private
New Ridley NE43 7RE
Tel **(0661) 843041**
Mem 341 79(L) 70(J)
Sec DB Moon (0661) 842264
Pro K Driver (0661) 842264
Holes 18 L 5594 yds SSS 68
Recs Am–61 GED Bradley
Pro–66 P Harrison
V'trs U SOC
Fees £7 (£10)
Loc 3 miles E of A68. 1 mile S of A686

Tynedale (1908)

Public
Tyne Green, Hexham
Mem 250
Sec K Peacock (0434) 605701
Holes 9 L 5706 yds SSS 68
Recs Am–64 A Varty
V'trs U exc Sun (bookings only)
Fees £2 (£3) W–£6
Loc S side of Hexham

Warkworth (1891)

Private
The Links, Warkworth, Morpeth
Tel **(0665) 711596**
Mem 400
Sec HE Slaughter (0670) 760270
Holes 9 L 5817 yds SSS 68
Recs Am–67 AB Barrett
V'trs U
Fees £5 (£7)
Loc 15 miles NE of Morpeth

Wooler (1975)

Private
Doddington, Wooler
Mem 200
Sec RJ Macdonald (0668) 81408
Holes 9 L 6327 yds SSS 71
Recs Am–75 K Fairbairn (1986)
V'trs U SOC
Fees D–£4 W–£15
Loc 2 miles NE of Wooler on Berwick Road

Nottinghamshire

Beeston Fields (1923)

Private
Beeston, Nottingham
Tel **(0602) 257062**
Mem 400 150(L) 65(J)
Sec DW Newbold
Pro M Pashley (0602) 257503
Holes 18 L 6404 yds SSS 71
Recs Am–66 P Benson
V'trs U SOC
Fees £12 (£14)
Loc 4 miles W of Nottingham. M1 Junction 25

Bulwell Forest (1902)

Public
Nottingham
Tel **(0602) 278008**
Mem 500
Sec D Stubbs
Pro CD Hall (0602) 763172
Holes 18 L 5746 yds SSS 68
Recs Am–62 DN Smedley, J Dawes, G Shepherd
Pro–64 D Snell
V'trs U
Fees £3.20
Loc 4 miles N of city centre. M1 Junction 26

Chilwell Manor (1906)

Private
Meadow Lane, Chilwell, Nottingham NG9 5AE
Tel **(0602) 257050**
Mem 620
Sec GA Spindley (0602) 258958
Pro E McCausland (0602) 258993
Holes 18 L 6379 yds SSS 69
18 L 5438 yds SSS 67
Recs Am–67 C Gray
Pro–66 B Waites
V'trs WD–U WE–NA SOC
Fees £9 D–£12
Loc 4 miles W of Nottingham

Coxmoor (1913)

Private
Coxmoor Road, Sutton-in-Ashfield NG17 5LF
Tel **(0623) 557359**
Mem 650
Sec R Allsop
Pro DJ Ridley (0623) 559906
Holes 18 L 6501 yds SSS 72
Recs Am–67 M Nunn
Pro–65 B Waites
V'trs H SOC (Ladies Day–Tues)
Fees £13 (£16)
Loc $1^1/_2$ miles S of Mansfield

Edwalton (1982)

Public
Edwalton, Nottingham
Tel **(0602) 234775**
Pro R Wiseman
Holes 9 L 3336 yds SSS 36
9 hole Par 3 course
V'trs U
Fees £1.80 (£2.20)
Loc 2 miles S of Nottingham

Kilton Forest (1978)

Public
Blyth Road, Worksop S81 0TL
Tel **(0909) 472488**
Mem 422
Sec EL James (0909) 477427
Pro PW Foster (0909) 486563
Holes 18 L 6569 yds SSS 72
Recs Am–69 SJ Thorpe (1988)
Pro–72 DJ Ridley (1988)
V'trs U
Fees £3 (£4)
Loc 1 mile NE of Worksop on B6045

Mapperley (1913)

Private
Central Avenue, Plains Road, Mapperley, Nottingham NG3 5RH
Tel **(0602) 265611**
Mem 600
Sec JH Seddon
Pro R Daibell (0602) 202227
Holes 18 L 6224 yds SSS 70
Recs Am–68 B Jones (1986)
Pro–68 R Daibell (1986)
V'trs U SOC
Fees £6.50 (£7.50)
Loc 3 miles NE of centre

Newark (1901)

Private
Kelwick, Coddington, Newark
Tel **(0636 84) 241**
Mem 575
Sec JN Simpson (0636 84) 282
Pro A Bennett (0636 84) 492
Holes 18 L 6486 yds SSS 71
Recs Am–70 C Bentley
Pro–69 CW Gray, DJ Britten
V'trs I H
Fees £10 (£15)
Loc 4 miles E of Newark on A17

Nottingham City (1910)

Public
Lawton Drive, Bulwell, Nottingham NG6 8BL
Tel **(0602) 278021**
Mem 350
Sec DA Griffiths
Pro CR Jepson (0602) 272767
Holes 18 L 6218 yds SSS 70
Recs Am–66 T Payne (1987)
Pro–67 R Daibell
V'trs WD–U WE–NA before noon SOC
Fees £3.75
Loc M1 Junction 28, 3 miles

Notts (1887)

Private
Hollinwell, Kirby-in-Ashfield NG17 7QR
Tel **(0623) 753225/752042**
Mem 500
Sec JR Walker (0623) 753225
Pro BJ Waites (0624) 753087
Holes 18 L 7020 yds SSS 74
Recs Am–67 IT Simpson, I MacKenzie
Pro–64 John Bland
V'trs WD–H WE/BH–M
Fees On application
Loc 4 miles S of Mansfield. M1 Junction 27

Oxton (1974)

Private
Oaks Lane, Oxton
Tel **(0602) 653545**
Mem 550
Sec GC Norton
Pro GC Norton
Holes 18 L 6600 yds SSS 72
9 L 3300 yds SSS 35
Recs Am–70 J Vaughan
Pro–68 D Dunk, B Waites, D Snell, D Ridley
V'trs WD–U WE/BH–arrange times with Mgr SOC
Fees £7.50 (£9)
Loc 9 miles N of Nottingham on A614 to Doncaster
Mis Floodlit driving range

Radcliffe on Trent (1909)

Private
Dewberry Lane, Cropwell Road, Radcliffe on Trent NG12 2JH
Tel **(060 73) 3000**
Mem 650
Sec PJ Newton
Pro P Hinton (060 73) 2396
Holes 18 L 6423 yds SSS 71
V'trs U H
Fees £11 (£15)
Loc 6 miles E of Nottingham off A52

Retford (1921)

Private
Brecks Road, Ordsall, Retford DN22 7UA
Tel **(0777) 703733**
Mem 360
Sec A Harrison (0777) 703389
Holes 9 L 6230 yds SSS 70
Recs Am–68 MD Walker (1987)
V'trs WD–U WE–M SOC–WD
Fees £4 (£6)
Loc 2 miles SW of Retford off A638 or A620. 16 miles E of M1 Junction 30

Ruddington Grange

Private
Wilford Road, Ruddington, Nottingham NG11 6NB
Tel **(0602) 846141**
Mem 500
Sec JA Small
Pro RJ Ellis (0602) 211951
Holes 18 L 6531 yds SSS 72
Recs Am–72 DJT Johnson (1988)
V'trs UH BH–U exc comp days SOC
Fees £15 D–£20 (£18 D–£24)
Loc 3 miles S of Nottingham

Rushcliffe (1910)

Private
East Leake, nr Nottingham
Tel **(050 982) 2209**
Mem 500
Sec MG Booth (050 982) 2959
Pro T Smart (050 982) 2701
Holes 18 L 6090 yds SSS 69
Recs Am–66 R Davenport, D Kirkland
Pro–63 GL Hunt
V'trs U
Fees £6 (£8)
Loc 9 miles S of Nottingham

Serlby Park (1905)

Private
Serlby, Doncaster, S Yorks DN10 6BA
Tel **(0777) 818268**
Mem 250
Sec M Hunter (0302) 851349
Holes 9 L 5370 yds SSS 66
Recs Am–63 A Pugsley (1988)
Pro–65 M Bembridge (1965)
V'trs M
Loc 12 miles S of Doncaster between A614 and A638

Sherwood Forest (1904)

Private
Eakring Road, Mansfield NG18 3EW
Tel **(0623) 23327**
Mem 600
Sec (0623) 26689
Pro K Hall (0623) 27403
Holes 18 L 6710 yds SSS 73
Recs Am–65 PM Baxter
Pro–68 C Gray, G Stafford
V'trs U H
Fees £14 D–£18 (£20)
Loc 2 miles N of Mansfield

Stanton-on-the-Wolds (1906)

Private
Stanton Lane, Keyworth
Tel **(060 77) 2044**
Mem 500 167(L) 100(J)
Sec HG Gray (0602) 787291
Pro KG Fear ((060 77) 2390
Holes 18 L 6437 yds SSS 71
Pro–65 D Ridley
V'trs U exc Sat comp days–NA XL SOC
Fees £8 (£11)
Loc 9 miles S of Nottingham

Wollaton Park (1927)

Private
Nottingham NG8 1BT
Tel **(0602) 787574**
Mem 600
Sec B Morris BSc PhD
Pro R Hastings (0602) 784834
Holes 18 L 6494 yds SSS 71
Recs Am–66 C Banks
Pro–65 H Weetman
V'trs U SOC
Fees £10 (£13)
Loc City centre 2 miles

Woodhouse (1973)

Public
Mansfield
Tel **(0623) 23521**
Mem 250
Sec TG Shead (0623) 641220
Holes 9
Recs Am–67 S Fisher
V'trs U
Fees £1.15
Loc 2 miles N of Mansfield

Worksop (1914)

Private
Windmill Lane, Worksop S80 2SQ
Tel **(0909) 472696**
Mem 500
Sec PG Jordan (0909) 477731
Pro JR King (0909) 477732
Holes 18 L 6651 yds SSS 72
Recs Am–70 D Bagshaw
Pro–69 A Carter
V'trs WD–U H (phone first) WE/BH–M SOC
Fees £13 R/D (£16)
Loc 1 mile SE of town off A6009. Approach from by-pass

Oxfordshire

Badgemore Park (1972)

Private
Henley-on-Thames
Tel **(0491) 572206**
Mem 750
Sec LA Booker
Pro M Howell (0491) 574175
Holes 18 L 6112 yds SSS 69
Recs Am–67 SJ Mann
Pro–65 M Howell
V'trs WD–U WE–M SOC
Fees £14 R/D
Loc 3/4 mile W of Henley-on-Thames on B290

Burford (1936)

Private
Burford OX8 4JG
Tel **(099 382) 2149**
Mem 680
Sec R Cane (099 382) 2583
Pro N Allen (099 382) 2344
Holes 18 L 6405 yds SSS 71
Recs Am–67 DE Giles
Pro–67 H Weetman
V'trs WD–U WE/BH–M H
Loc 19 miles W of Oxford on A40

Cherwell Edge (1980)

Public
Chacombe, Banbury OX17 2EN
Tel **(0295) 711591**
Sec R Davies
Pro R Davies
Holes 18 L 5925 yds SSS 69
Recs Am–71
V'trs U SOC–WD
Fees £3.60 D–£6.30 (£4.80)
Loc 3 miles E of Banbury on B4525 (A422)

Chesterton (1973)

Private
Chesterton, nr Bicester OX6 8TE
Tel **(0869) 241204**
Mem 550
Sec BT Carter
Pro JW Wilkshire (0869) 242023
Holes 18 L 6496 yds SSS 71
Recs Am–68
Pro–68
V'trs WD–U WE/BH–H SOC–WD
Fees £10 (£15)
Loc 2 miles SW of Bicester

Chipping Norton (1932)

Private
Southcombe, Chipping Norton OX7 5QH
Tel **(0608) 2383**
Mem 775
Sec AJB Norman
Pro R Gould (0608) 3356
Holes 18 L 6280 yds SSS 70
Recs Am–67 A Perrie

V'trs WD–U WE–M
Fees £12
Loc 1 mile E of town

Frilford Heath (1908)

Private
Frilford Heath, Abingdon
OX13 5NW
Tel **(0865) 390428**
Mem 750
Sec JW Kleynhans
Pro DC Craik (0865) 390887
Holes Red 18 L 6768 yds SSS 73
Green 18 L 6006 yds SSS 69
Recs Red Am–68 S Walker
Green Am–65 G Wolstenholme
V'trs WD–UH WE–MH BH–UH SOC
Fees £16 (£25)
Loc 3 miles W of Abingdon on A338 Oxford/Wantage road

Henley (1908)

Private
Harpsden, Henley-on-Thames
RG9 4HG
Tel **(0491) 573304**
Mem 750
Sec B Lovelock (0491) 575742
Pro J Cook (0491) 575710
Holes 18 L 6329 yds SSS 70
Recs Am–68 M Orris, N Farmar
Pro–65 M King (1988)
V'trs WD–H WE–M
Fees £15 R/D
Loc Station 1 mile

Huntercombe (1901)

Private
Nuffield, Henley-on-Thames
RG9 5SL
Tel **(0491) 641207**
(0492) 641472 (visitors)
Mem 700
Sec Lt Col TJ Hutchison
Pro JB Draycott (0491) 641241
Holes 18 L 6261 yds SSS 70
Recs Am–65 A Jackson
Pro–63 J Morris
V'trs WD–H WE–NA SOC
Fees £16
Loc 6 miles W of Henley–on–Thames on A423
Mis 4 ball play not allowed

North Oxford (1908)

Private
Banbury Road, Oxford
OX2 8EZ
Tel **(0865) 54415**
Mem 701
Sec W Forster (0865) 54924
Pro R Harris (0865) 53977
Holes 18 L 5805 yds SSS 67
Recs Am–64 S Donaghey
Pro–M Faulkner
V'trs U SOC
Fees £13 (£20)
Loc Between Oxford and Kidlington

RAF Benson (1975)

Private
Royal Air Force, Benson
Tel **(0491) 37766**
Mem 150
Sec Sqn Ldr WB Sowerby MVO RAF (Ret'd) (0235) 848472
Holes 9 L 4214 yds SSS 61
V'trs M
Loc 3½ miles NE of Wallingford

Southfield (1875)

Private
Hill Top Road, Oxford
OX4 1PF
Tel **(0865) 242158**
Mem 500
Sec AG Hopcraft (0865) 242158
Pro A Rees (0865) 244258
Holes 18 L 6230 yds SSS 70
Recs Am–66 CM Barrett, GL Morley
Pro–61 A Rees
V'trs WD–U WE/BH–MH SOC
Fees £15
Loc 2 miles E of city centre

Tadmarton Heath (1922)

Private
Wigginton, Banbury OX15 5HL
Tel **(0608) 737649**
Mem 600
Sec RE Wackrill (0608) 737278
Pro Les Bond (0608) 730047
Holes 18 L 5917 yds SSS 69
Recs Am–68 J Fisher
Pro–63 G Smith
V'trs WD–UH WE–M SOC
Fees £14
Loc 5 miles W of Banbury off B4035

Shropshire

Bridgnorth (1889)

Private
Stanley Lane, Bridgnorth WV16 4SF
Tel **(0746) 3315**
Mem 435
Sec EH Thomas (0746) 2400
Pro P Hinton (0746) 2045
Holes 18 L 6638 yds SSS 72
Recs Am–67 C Banks (1985)
Pro–68 A Malcolm (1981)
V'trs U SOC
Fees £12.50 (£18)
Loc 1 mile N of Bridgnorth

Church Stretton (1898)

Private
Trevor Hill, Church Stretton
Tel **(0694) 722281**
Mem 470
Sec R Broughton (0694) 722633
Holes 18 L 5008 yds SSS 66
Recs Am–63 J Griffiths (1987)
V'trs U SOC
Fees £6 (£10)
Loc ½ mile W of town off A49

Hawkstone Park (1921)

Private
Weston-under-Redcastle,
nr Shrewsbury SY4 5UY
Tel **(093924) 611**
Mem 400
Sec KL Brazier Mgr)
AWB Lyle (Golf Dir)
Pro K Williams (093924) 209
Holes Hawkstone 18 L 6465 yds SSS 71; Weston 18 L 5368 yds SSS 66
Recs Am–67 AWB Lyle, MA Smith
Pro–65 A Jacklin
V'trs U after 10.35am SOC
Fees Hawkestone £13 (£16)
Weston £8.50 (£9.50)
Loc 7 miles S of Whitchurch. 14 miles N of Shrewbury on A49
Mis Buggies for hire. Golf hotel

Hill Valley G & CC (1975)

Private
Terrick Road, Whitchurch
Tel **(0948) 3584**
Mem 400
Sec RB Walker
Pro AR Minshall (0948) 3032
Holes 18 L 6884 yds SSS 71
9 L 5106 yds SSS 65
9 hole Par 3 course
Recs Am–69 K Valentine
Pro–64 W Milne
V'trs U
Fees £9 (£14) 9 holes £6
Par 3 course £3
Loc 1 mile N of Whitchurch
Mis Wide wheel trolleys only. John Garner golf school

Lilleshall Hall (1937)

Private
Lilleshall, nr Newport TF10 9AS
Tel **(0952) 603840**
Mem 600
Sec AP Thwaite (0952) 604776
Pro NW Bramall (0952) 604104
Holes 18 L 5861 yds SSS 68
Recs Am–65 P Baker
Pro–70 J Anderson
V'trs WD–U WE–M
Fees £10 (BH+day after–£15)
Loc Abbey Road

Llanymynech (1933)

Private
Pant, nr Oswestry SY10 8LB
Tel **(0691) 830542**
Mem 720
Sec NE Clews (0691) 830983
Pro A Griffiths (0691) 830879
Holes 18 L 6114 yds SSS 69
Recs Am–68 M Evans
Pro–65 I Woosnam

V'trs U SOC
Fees £8 (£10)
Loc 5 miles S of Oswestry on A483
Mis No catering Mon

Ludlow (1889)

Private
Bromfield, nr Ludlow
Tel **(058 477) 285**
Mem 500
Sec RPJ Jones (058 477) 334
Pro G Farr (058 477) 366
Holes 18 L 6240 yds SSS 70
Recs Am–67 T Clare
Pro–65 PA Brookes
V'trs U
Fees £8 (£10)
Loc A49, 2 miles N of Ludlow

Market Drayton (1925)

Private
Sutton, Market Drayton
Tel **(0630) 2266**
Mem 450
Sec JJ Moseley (0630) 3661 (day)
Pro A Williams
Holes 18 L 6225 yds SSS 70
V'trs WD/Sat–U Sun–NA
Fees £10 (£12)
Loc 1 mile S of Market Drayton

Meole Brace (1976)

Public
Meole Brace, Shrewsbury
Tel **(0743) 64050**
Mem 250
Sec A Price (0743) 722733
Pro I Doran
Holes 9 L 2915 yds SSS 68
Recs Am–68 J Mansell
Pro–68 R Cockcroft
V'trs U
Fees 9 holes–£1.80 (£2.20)
18 holes–£2.55 (£3.20)
Loc Junction A5/A49 Meole Brace

Oswestry (1930)

Private
Aston Park, Oswestry
Tel **(069 188) 221**
Mem 700
Sec Mrs PM Lindner
(069 188) 535
Pro D Skelton (069 188) 448
Holes 18 L 6046 yds SSS 69
Recs Am–62 AL Strange
Pro–68 JW Walker
V'trs M or H SOC–WD
Fees £10 (£14)
Loc 3¼ miles E of Oswestry on A5

Shifnal (1929)

Private
Decker Hill, Shifnal
Tel **(0952) 460467/460330**
Mem 500
Sec J Bell (0952) 460330
Pro J Flanaghan (0952) 460457
Holes 18 L 6422 yds SSS 71
Recs Am–66 R Howells
Pro–67 IN Doran
V'trs WD–phone first WE/BH–M
Loc 2 miles M54 Junction 4.
1 mile NE Shifnal

Shrewsbury (1891)

Private
Condover, Shrewsbury
Tel **(074 372) 2976**
Mem 450 160(L) 75(J)
Sec JA Morrison (074 372) 2977
Pro T Simpson (074 372) 3751
Holes 18 L 6212 yds SSS 70
Recs Am–60 JR Burn
V'trs H SOC
Fees £8 (£10)
Loc 4 miles SW of town

Telford Hotel G & CC (1981)

Private
Great Hay, Sutton Hill, Telford TF7 4DT
Tel **(0952) 585642**
Mem 400
Sec Maj FE Snape
Pro S Marr (0952) 586052
Holes 18 L 6742 yds SSS 72
Recs Am–66 C Bufton (1986)
Pro–62 D Thorpe
V'trs H SOC
Fees £14 (£18)
Loc Sutton Hill, off A442

Wrekin (1905)

Private
Wellington, Telford
Tel **(0952) 244032**
Mem 500 85(L) 90(J) 30(5)
Sec S Leys
Pro K Housden
Holes 18 L 5657 yds SSS 67
Recs Am–65 GC Clayton, R Jones,
P Baker, F Tart
Pro–67 C Holmes
V'trs WD–U before 5pm
M after 5pm SOC
Fees £10 (£12)
Loc Wellington, off B5061

Somerset

Brean (1973)

Private
Coast Road, Brean TA28 2RF
Tel **(027 875) 570**
Mem 350
Sec WS Martin (027 875) 490
Holes 18 L 5566 yds SSS 67
Recs Am–67 C Clarke (1987)
V'trs WD/Sat–U Sun–M after 10am
–U after noon SOC
Fees £5 (£7.50)
Loc 3 miles N of Burnham-on-Sea

Burnham & Berrow (1890)

Private
St Christopher's Way, Burnham-on-Sea TA8 2PE
Tel **(0278) 783137**
Mem 800
Sec Mrs EL Sloman
(0278) 785760
Pro NP Blake (0278) 784545
Holes 18 L 6547 yds SSS 73
9 L 6550 yds SSS 72
Recs Medal Am–68 G Thomas
C'ship Am–66 P Baker
V'trs I SOC
Fees £15 (£15) W–£80 9 hole £5
Loc 1 mile N of Burnham-on-Sea

Enmore Park (1932)

Private
Enmore, Bridgwater
Tel **(027 867) 244**
Mem 700
Sec DB Spicer (027 867) 481
Pro N Wixon (027 867) 519
Holes 18 L 6443 yds SSS 71
Recs Am–67 CS Edwards
Pro–65 G Carter
V'trs U SOC–WD
Fees £12 (£15)
Loc 3 miles W of Bridgwater

Kingweston (1983)

Private
Somerton
Tel **(0458) 72081**
Mem 180
Sec P Mountain, 9 Behind Berry, Somerton
Holes 9 L 4516 yds SSS 62
V'trs M Closed Wed & Sat 2–5pm
Fees NA
Mis Previously Millfield School, Kingweston Club.

Mendip (1908)

Private
Gurney Slade, Bath BA3 4UT
Tel **(0749) 840570**
Mem 525 80(L) 110(J)
Sec MJ Lee
Pro RF Lee (0749) 840793
Holes 18 L 5982 yds SSS 69
Recs Am–65 RH Flower
Pro–64 N Blenkarne
V'trs WD–U WE–M H SOC–WD
Fees £10 (£15)
Loc 3 miles N of Shepton Mallet (A37)

Minehead & West Somerset (1882)

Private
Warren Road, Minehead
Tel **(0643) 2057**
Mem 473
Sec RA Lawrence
Pro I Read (0643) 4378

Holes 18 L 6130 yds SSS 70
Recs Am–68 GE Vaulter
Pro–66 BJ Hunt
V'trs U after 9.15am
Fees £12 (£15) W–£45
Loc E end of sea front

Taunton & Pickeridge (1892)

Private
Corfe, Taunton TA3 7BY
Tel (082 342) 240
Mem 550
Sec GW Sayers (082 342) 537
Pro G Glew (082 342) 790
Holes 18 L 5927 yds SSS 68
Recs Am–66 P Wathen
Pro–65 G Emerson
V'trs H SOC
Fees On application
Loc 5 miles S of Taunton on B3170

Vivary Park

Public
Taunton
Tel (0823) 3875
Mem 400
Pro R Macrow
Holes 18 L 4620 yds SSS 63
V'trs Starting time required–book through Pro; U exc Wed evenings (summer)–M
Fees £4.50
Loc Town centre
Mis Vivary Club plays here

Wells (1900)

Private
East Horrington Road, Wells
Tel (0749) 72868
Mem 670
Sec MW Davis (0749) 75005
Pro A England
Holes 18 L 5354 yds SSS 67
Recs Am–64 RW Davis (1985)
Pro–65 R Clifton (1986)
V'trs WD–U WE–H SOC–WD
Fees £8 (£10) Mon–Fri £27.50
Loc Town centre $1^1/_2$ miles, off Radstock Road

Windwhistle G & CC (1932)

Private
Cricket St Thomas, Chard
Tel (046 030) 231
Mem 300
Sec I Dodd
Pro N Morris
Holes 12 L 6055 yds SSS 69
Recs Am–71 P Knight
Pro–70 D Colgan
V'trs U WE–phone first
Fees On application
Loc On A30, opposite Cricket St Thomas Wildlife Park

Yeovil (1919)

Private
Sherborne Road, Yeovil BA21 5BW
Tel (0935) 75949
Mem 695 150(L) 70(J)
Sec J Riley (0935) 22965
Pro G Kite (0935) 73763
Holes 18 L 6139 yds SSS 69
Recs Am–64 J Pounder (1986)
Pro–65 G Laing (1987)
V'trs WD–U WE–H (phone Pro for starting time) BH–H SOC
Fees £12 (£14)
Loc Yeovil 1 mile on A30 to Sherborne

Staffordshire

Alsager G & CC (1977)

Private
Audley Road, Alsager, Stoke-on-Trent
Tel (0270) 875700
Mem 640
Sec Mrs EE Wynne
Pro D Clare (0270) 877432
Holes 18 L 6192 yds SSS 70
V'trs WD–U before 5pm –M after 5pm WE/BH–M SOC
Fees £9
Loc 2 miles E M6 Junction 16. Crewe 5 miles. Stoke 7 miles

Barlaston

Private
Meaford Road, Barlaston, Stone
Tel (078 139) 2795
Mem 450
Sec M Degg
Holes 18 L 5800 yds SSS 68
Recs Am–69 S Ashcroft (1983)
V'trs U
Fees £9 (£12)
Loc $^1/_4$ mile S of Barlaston. $^3/_4$ mile N of Stone

Beau Desert (1921)

Private
Hazel Slade, Cannock WS12 5PJ
Tel (054 38) 2773
Mem 500
Sec IE Williams (054 38) 2626
Pro B Stevens (054 38) 2492
Holes 18 L 6279 yds SSS 71
Recs Am–68 WR Probert
Pro–64 T Minshall
V'trs WD–U BH–NA WE–phone in advance SOC
Fees £15
Loc 4 miles NE of Cannock

Branston (1975)

Private
Burton Road, Branston, Burton-on-Trent
Tel (0283) 43207
Mem 390 50(L) 60(J)
Sec KL George
Pro S Warner
Holes 18 L 6480 yds SSS 71
Recs Am–69 T Bailey (1987)
Pro–67 P Kent
V'trs WD–U WE–U (M before noon) SOC
Fees £8 (£10)
Loc $^1/_2$ mile towards Burton from A38/A5121 junction

Brocton Hall (1923)

Private
Brocton, Stafford ST17 0TH
Tel (0785) 662627
Mem 500
Sec WR Lanyon (0785) 661901
Pro R Johnson (0785) 661485
Holes 18 L 6095 yds SSS 69
Recs Am–67 WB Taylor
V'trs I
Fees £15 (£17)
Loc 4 miles SE of Stafford

Burslem (1907)

Private
Wood Farm, High Lane, Stoke-on-Trent ST6 7JT
Tel (0782) 837006
Mem 250
Sec RJ Sutton (0782) 837704
Holes 11 L 5527 yds SSS 67
Recs Am–63 M Keeling (1988)
Pro–66 T Williamson
V'trs M Sun–NA
Fees £6
Loc Burslem 2 miles

Burton-on-Trent (1893)

Private
43 Ashby Road, East Burton-on-Trent DE15 0PS
Tel (0283) 68708
Mem 600
Sec A Maddock (0283) 44551
Pro JM Lower (0283) 62240
Holes 18 L 6555 yds SSS 71
Recs Am–69 JE Roberts
Pro–67 DA Stewart
V'trs I or M
Fees £9 (£13)
Loc Town centre 3 miles

Craythorne Golf Centre (1972)

Public
Craythorne Road, Stretton, Burton-on-Trent DE13 0AZ
Tel (0283) 64329
Mem 250
Sec J Bissell (Gen Mgr)
Pro BD Morris (0283) 33745
Holes 18 L 5230 yds SSS 66
9 hole course
Recs Am–62 PCR Smith (1987)
V'trs U WD/WE–SOC
Fees £5 (£7)
Loc $1^1/_2$ miles N Burton-on-Trent (A38). Junction A5121, signpost Stretton
Mis Driving range

For map index see page 203.

Drayton Park (1897)

Private
Drayton Park, Tamworth
B78 3TN
Tel **(0827) 251139**
Mem 450
Sec AO Rammell JP
Pro MW Passmore (0827) 251478
Holes 18 L 6414 yds SSS 71
Recs Am–66 M Biddle (1984)
Pro–65 DJ Russell (1987)
V'trs WD–H WE/BH–NA SOC–Tues & Thurs
Fees £14 R/D
Loc 2 miles S of Tamworth (A4091)

Goldenhill (1983)

Public
Mobberley Road, Goldenhill,
Stoke-on-Trent ST6 5SS
Mem 200
Sec DP Jones (Hon)
Pro A Clingan (078 16) 4715
Holes 18 L 5957 yds SSS 68
V'trs U WE/BH–book with Pro
Fees £3 (£3.35) 1988 prices
Loc Between Tunstall and Kidsgrove off A50

Greenway Hall (1908)

Private
Stockton Brook, Stoke-on-Trent
Tel **(0782) 503158**
Mem 390
Sec EH Jones (0782) 503095
Holes 18 L 5676 yds SSS 67
Recs Am–65 A Bailey, A Dathan
Pro–65 K Johnstone
V'trs Mon/Wed/Fri–H Tues & Thurs–M WE–M Sun pm only
Fees £8
Loc 5 miles N of Stoke

Ingestre Park (1977)

Private
nr Stafford
Tel **(0889) 270061**
Mem 500
Sec R Ashton (0889) 270845
Pro D Scullion (0889) 270304
Holes 18 L 6367 yds SSS 70
Recs Am–69 S Smith, N Jackson
Pro–68 D Scullion
V'trs WD–U WE/BH–M
Fees On application
Loc 5 miles E of Stafford

Lakeside (Rugeley) (1969)

Private
Rugeley Power Station, Rugeley
WS15 1PR
Tel **(08894) 3181**
Mem 250
Sec TA Yates (0543) 491435 (home)
Holes 9 L 4768 yds SSS 63
V'trs M
Loc Grounds of Rugeley Power Station. 2 miles SE of town centre on A513

Leek (1892)

Private
Big Birchall, Leek ST13 5RE
Tel **(0538) 385889**
Mem 400 90(L) 45(J) 100(5)
Sec F Cutts (0538) 384779
Pro P Stubbs (0538) 384767
Holes 18 L 6240 yds SSS 70
Recs Am–63 D Evans
Pro–66 CH Ward
V'trs U before 3pm–M after 3pm H SOC–Wed only
Fees £12 (£16)
Loc Leek 1/2 mile on Stone Road

Newcastle Municipal (1973)

Public
Keele Road, Newcastle-under-Lyme
Tel **(0782) 627596 (Professional)**
Mem 250
Sec RG Lane
Pro C Smith
Holes 18 L 5822 metres SSS 70
Recs Am–70 P Rowe
Pro–68 P Rowe
V'trs U
Fees £2.75 (£3.15)
Loc 2 miles NW on A525 opposite Keele University

Newcastle-under-Lyme (1908)

Private
Whitmore Road,
Newcastle-under-Lyme
Tel **(0782) 616583**
Mem 575
Sec RB Irving
Pro P Symonds (0782) 618526
Holes 18 L 6450 yds SSS 71
Recs Am–67 MC Hassall
Pro–66 AR Sadler
V'trs WD–U WE/BH–M
Fees £10
Loc Newcastle

Onneley (1968)

Private
Onneley, nr Crewe, Cheshire
Tel **(0782) 750577**
Mem 324
Sec WJ Paterson (0270) 624818
Holes 9 L 5584 yds SSS 67
Recs Am–68 D Gilford
V'trs WD–U Sat/BH–M Sun–NA
Fees £7
Loc Woore 1 mile off A51 to Newcastle

Stafford Castle (1907)

Private
Newport Road, Stafford
Tel **(0785) 3821**
Mem 250
Sec S Cowburn
Holes 9 L 6462 yds SSS 71
Recs Am–74 P Duncan
V'trs U WE after 1pm
Fees £7 (£10)
Loc 1/2 mile W of town centre

Stone (1892)

Private
Filleybrooks, Stone ST15 0NB
Tel **(0785) 813103**
Mem 170 40(L) 30(J) 15(5)
Sec MG Pharaoh (088 97) 224
Pro I Rodgers (0785) 815520
Holes 9 L 6299 yds SSS 70
Recs Am–69 A Hurst (1988)
V'trs WD–U WE/BH–M SOC–WD
Fees £7
Loc 1/2 mile W on A34

Tamworth (1978)

Public
Eagle Drive, Amington, Tamworth
B77 4EG
Tel **(0827) 53850**
Mem 400
Sec BN Jones (0827)53858
Pro BN Jones
Holes 18 L 6695 yds SSS 72
Recs Am–67 CJ Christison
Pro–65 BN Jones
V'trs U SOC–WD
Fees £3.35
Loc 2 1/2 miles E of Tamworth on B5000. M42 3 miles

Trentham (1895)

Private
14 Barlaston Old Road, Trentham,
Stoke-on-Trent ST4 8HB
Tel **(0782) 642347**
Mem 680
Sec Lt Cdr JR Smith RN(Retd) (0782) 658109
Pro D MacDonald (0782) 657309
Holes 18 L 6644 yds SSS 72
Recs Am–66 DJ Boughey (1987)
V'trs WD–U WE–M (or enquire Sec) BH–enquire Sec H SOC–WD
Fees £14 (£17) 1988 prices
Loc 3 miles S of Newcastle (Staffs) off A34. M6 Junction 15

Trentham Park (1936)

Private
Trentham Park, Stoke-on-Trent
ST4 8AE
Tel **(0782) 642245**
Mem 300 70(L) 70(J) 90(5) 84(Sen)
Sec CH Lindop (0782) 658800
Pro R Clarke (0782) 642125
Holes 18 L 6403 yds SSS 71
Recs Am–67 PG Nuthall
V'trs U SOC–Wed & Fri
Fees £10 (£12)
Loc 4 miles S of Newcastle-under-Lyme on A34. M6 Junction 15, 1 mile

Uttoxeter (1975)

Private
Wood Lane, Uttoxeter
Tel **(0889) 564884**
Mem 400
Sec Mrs G Davies
Holes 18 L 5695 yds SSS 69
Recs Am–73
V'trs U except Sun am–NA
Fees £5 (£7)
Loc Uttoxeter racecourse 1/2 mile

Westwood (1923)

Private
Newcastle Road, Walbridge, Leek
Tel **(0538) 383060**
Mem 300
Sec AJ Lawton (0782) 503780
Holes 9 L 5501 yds SSS 67
Recs Am–68 SD Spooner
V'trs WD–U Sat am–M BH–H SOC
Fees £6
Loc W boundary of Leek on A53

Whittington Barracks (1886)

Private
Tamworth Road, Lichfield WS14 9PW
Tel **(0543) 4332212**
Mem 670
Sec M Scargill (0543) 432317
Pro AR Sadler (0543) 432261
Holes 18 L 6457 yds SSS 71
Recs Am–65 CG Marks, CG Poxon
Pro–67 AR Sadler
V'trs WD–H I WE/BH–M Day after BH–M SOC–Wed & Thurs
Fees £15 R/D
Loc Lichfield 2 1/2 miles on Tamworth road

Wolstanton (1904)

Private
Dimsdale Old Hall, Newcastle ST5 9DR
Tel **(0782) 616995**
Mem 550
Sec KI Colderick (0782) 622413
Pro J Darling (0782) 622718
Holes 18 L 5807 yds SSS 68
Recs Am–65 P Sweetsur, M Hassall, R Maxfield
Pro–66 CH Ward
V'trs WD–I WE–M
Fees £8
Loc 1 1/2 miles NW of Newcastle-under-Lyme

Suffolk

Aldeburgh (1884)

Private
Aldeburgh IP15 5PE
Tel **(072 885) 2408**
Mem 750
Sec RC Van de Velde (072 885) 2890
Pro K Preston (072 885) 3309
Holes 18 L 6330 yds SSS 71
9 L 2114 yds SSS 64
Recs Am–65 J Lloyd
Pro–67 JM Johnson
V'trs I
Fees On application
Loc 6 miles E of A12, between Ipswich and Lowestoft

Beccles (1899)

Private
The Common, Beccles
Tel **(0502) 712244**
Mem 200
Sec Mrs LW Allen (0402) 712479
Pro K Allen
Holes 9 L 2696 yds SSS 67
Pro–64 K Allen
V'trs WD–U Sun–M SOC
Fees £4.50 (£5.50)
Loc Lowestoft 10 miles. Norwich 18 miles

Bungay & Waveney Valley(1889)

Private
Bungay
Tel **(0986) 2337**
Mem 600
Sec WJ Mann (0986) 2329
Pro N Whyte
Holes 18 L 5944 yds SSS 68
Recs Am–67 R Kidd
Pro–64 T Spurgeon
V'trs WD–U WE–M SOC
Fees £9 R/D
Loc Town centre 1/2 mile

Bury St Edmunds (1922)

Private
Tut Hill, Bury St Edmunds
Tel **(0284) 5979**
Mem 830 130 (L) 34(J) 100(5)
Sec CD Preece
Pro M Jillings (0284) 5978
Holes 18 L 6615 yds SSS 72
Recs Am–69 S Goodman, A Currie
Pro–68 R Kemp
V'trs WD–U WE–H NA before 10am BH–U SOC
Fees £11 (£16)
Loc 2 miles W of Bury St Edmunds on B1106

Cretingham (1983)

Public
Grove Farm, Cretingham, Woodbridge IP13 7BA
Tel **(072882) 275**
Mem 170
Sec J Austin (Prop)
Holes 9 L 1955 yds Par 30
Recs Am–28 R Watts (1986)
V'trs U
Fees £5 (£6) 18 holes
Loc 2 miles SE of Earl Soham

Diss (1903)

Private
Stuston Common, Diss
Tel **(0379) 2847**
Mem 350
Sec J Bell (0379) 2679
Pro N Taylor (0379) 4399
Holes 9 L 5900 yds SSS 68
Recs Am–68 JE Doe
Pro–T Pennock
V'trs WD–before 4pm Sat–NA Sun/BH–pm only
Fees £6 (£8)
Loc Diss 1/2 mile

Felixstowe Ferry (1880)

Private
Ferry Road, Felixstowe IP4 9RY
Tel **(0394) 286834**
Mem 750
Sec GJ Stephens
Pro I Macpherson (0394) 283975
Holes 18 L 6308 yds SSS 70
Recs Am–68 I Whinney
Pro–65 I Richardson
V'trs U WE–M before 10.30am SOC
Fees £10 (£12)
Loc 2 miles NE of town centre

Flempton (1895)

Private
Bury St Edmunds
Tel **(028 484) 291**
Mem 250
Sec PH Nunn (0638) 750100
Pro M Jillings
Holes 9 L 6704 yds SSS 69
Recs Am–67 Lt J Reynolds
Pro–69 J Arbon
V'trs WD–U WE/BH–M
Fees £12 D–£15
Loc 5 miles NW of Bury St Edmunds on A1101

Fornham Park (1974)

Private
Lark Valley Drive, Fornham St Martin, Bury St Edmunds IP28 6UG
Tel **(0284) 63426**
Mem 450
Sec JHC Clarke
Pro S Wright
Holes 18 L 6212 yds SSS 70
Recs Am–68 S Blanshard (1987)
Pro–65 S Wright (1986)
V'trs U SOC
Fees £7.50 (£11)
Loc From Cambridge, first exit on A45; from Ipswich, third exit on A45. 5 mins from A45

For map index see page 203.

Haverhill (1974)

Private
Coupals Road, Haverhill
Tel (0440) 61951
Mem 350
Sec Mrs J Webster
Pro S Mayfield
Holes 9 L 5707 yds SSS 68
Recs Am–65 T Barton
Pro–66 C Cook
V'trs U
Fees £8 (£12)
Loc Haverhill, 1 mile off A604

Ipswich (Purdis Heath) (1895)

Private
Purdis Heath, Ipswich
Tel (0473) 728941
(0473) 727474 (Steward)
Mem 700
Sec AE Howell
Pro SJ Whymark (0473) 724017
Holes 18 L 6405 yds SSS 71
9 L 1950 yds SSS 31
Recs Am–67 IP Whinney
Pro–67 RA Knight
V'trs 18 hole–H or I 9 hole–U SOC
Fees 18 holes £12 (£14)
9 holes £5 (£6)
Loc 3 miles E of Ipswich

Links (Newmarket) (1902)

Private
Cambridge Road, Newmarket CB8 0TG
Tel (0638) 662708
Mem 685
Sec JJB Saul (0638) 663000
Pro DP Thomson (0638) 662395
Holes 18 L 6402 yds SSS 71
Recs Am–69 B Jackson
Pro–70 S Barlow
V'trs WD–U WE/BH–H Sun–M before 11.30am SOC
Fees £12 (£16)
Loc 1 mile S of Newmarket

Newton Green (1907)

Private
Newton Green, Sudbury
Tel (0787) 77501/77216
Mem 400
Sec G Bright (0787) 71119
Pro C Jervis
Holes 9 L 5488 yds SSS 67
Recs Am–60 R Rowland
Pro–29 A Davey (9 holes)
V'trs WD–U WE–M
Fees £8
Loc 4 miles E of Sudbury

Rookery Park (1975)

Private
Carlton Colville, Lowestoft NR33 8HJ
Tel (0502) 560380
Mem 750
Sec J Almond
Pro M Elsworthy (0502) 515103
Holes 18 L 6649 yds SSS 72
Par 3 course
Recs Am–71 G Long (1985)
Pro–69 P Kent (1985)
V'trs WD–U WE/BH–after 11am SOC
Fees £9 (£12)
Loc West Lowestoft (A146)

Royal Worlington & Newmarket (1893)

Private
Worlington, Bury St Edmunds IP28 8SD
Tel (0638) 712216
Mem 328
Sec WN White MC MA
Pro M Hawkins (0638) 715224
Holes 9 L 6218 yds SSS 70
Recs Am–67 DJ Millensted
Pro–66 EE Beverley
V'trs U WE–NA
Fees £15
Loc Mildenhall 2 miles
Mis Phone first

Rushmere (1895)

Private
Rushmere Heath, Ipswich
Tel (0473) 727109
Mem 750
Sec RW Whiting (0473) 725648
Pro NTJ McNeill (0473) 728076
Holes 18 L 6287 yds SSS 70
Recs Am–69 F Knights (1986)
Pro–67 NTJ McNeil (1984), S Beckham (1985)
V'trs WD–U WE/BH–after 2.30pm
Fees On application
Loc Ipswich, off Woodbridge Road (A12)

Southwold (1884)

Private
The Common, Southwold
Tel (0502) 723234
Mem 450
Sec IG Guy (0502) 723248
Pro B Allen (0502) 723790
Holes 9 L 6001 yds SSS 69
Recs Am–67 S Fitzgerald
Pro–65 R Mann
V'trs U (subject to fixtures)
Fees On application
Loc 35 miles N of Ipswich

Stowmarket (1962)

Private
Lower Road, Onehouse, Stowmarket IP14 3DA
Tel (044 93) 392
Mem 600
Sec PW Rumball (044 93) 473
Pro C Aldred
Holes 18 L 6119 yds SSS 69
Recs Am–67 I Oakes
Pro–66 H Flatman
V'trs WD/WE–H SOC–Wed pm–Fri
Fees £9 (£12)
Loc $2^1/_2$ miles SW of Stowmarket

Thorpeness Hotel

Private
Thorpeness
Tel (072 885) 2176
Mem 400
Sec NW Griffin
Pro T Pennock (072 885) 2524
Holes 18 L 6208 yds SSS 71
Recs Am–66 J Marks
Pro–67 K McDonald
V'trs U
Fees £12((£17)
Loc 2 miles N of Aldeburgh
Mis Hotel adjacent to course

Waldringfield Heath (1983)

Private
Newbourne Road, Waldringfield, Woodbridge IP12 4PT
Tel (0473) 36768
Mem 450
Sec LJ McWade (0473) 36791/47569 (home)
Holes 18 L 5837 yds SSS 68
V'trs WD–U WE/BH–M before noon SOC–WD
Loc 3 miles N of Ipswich off A12

Warren Heath

Private
Bucklesham Road, Ipswich IP3 8TZ
Tel (0473) 726821
Mem 150
Sec BP Johnson
Pro JW Johnson
Holes 9 L 3162 yds SSS 34
Pro–64 JW Johnson
V'trs U SOC
Fees £2.50
Loc Between Bucklesham Road and Old Felixstowe Road

Woodbridge (1893)

Private
Bromeswell Heath, nr Woodbridge
Tel (039 43) 2038
Mem 930
Sec Capt LA Harpum RN
Pro LA Jones (039 43) 3213
Holes 18 L 6314 yds SSS 70
9 L 2243 yds SSS 31
Recs Am–64 JVT Marks
Pro–65 F Sunderland
V'trs H WE/BH–M
Fees £12 D–£16 (£16 D–£20)
1988 prices
Loc 2 miles E of Woodbridge. Follow A12 towards Lowestoft, turn off Woodbridge by-pass at roundabout towards Orford B1084

Surrey

The Addington (1913)

Private
Shirley Church Road, Croydon CR50 5AB
Tel **(01) 777 1055**
Sec (01) 777 6057
Pro E Campbell (01) 777 1701
Holes 18 L 6242 yds SSS 71
Recs Am–66 P Benka
Pro–68 F Robson
V'trs I
Fees On application
Loc E Croydon $2^1/_2$ miles

Addington Court (1931)

Public
Featherbed Lane, Addington, Croydon CR0 9AA
Tel **(01) 657 0281/2/3**
Sec Geoffrey Cotton
Pro Geoffrey Cotton
Holes Old 18 L 5577 yds SSS 67
New 18 L 5513 yds SSS 66
Lower 9 L 1812 yds SSS 62
18 hole Pitch and Putt course
Recs Pro–63 C Phillips
V'trs U
Fees Winter: Old £5 New £4.10
9 hole £3. Summer: Old £6
New £5.25 9 hole £3.50
Loc 3 miles E of Croydon

Addington Palace (1923)

Private
Gravel Hill, Addington, Croydon CR0 5BB
Tel **(01) 654 3061**
Mem 600
Sec J Robinson
Pro M Pilkington (01) 654 1786
Holes 18 L 6410 yds SSS 71
Recs Am–63 R Glading
Pro–65 AD Locke
V'trs WD–M or I WE/BH–M
Fees £18
Loc 2 miles E of Croydon Station

Banstead Downs (1890)

Private
Burdon Lane, Belmont, Sutton SM2 7DD
Tel **(01) 642 2284**
Mem 650
Sec RS Barrett
Pro I Marr (01) 642 6884
Holes 18 L 6169 yds SSS 69
Recs Am–63 PJ Stone
Pro–MLA Perry
V'trs WD–I WE/BH–M
Fees £15
Loc 1 mile S of Sutton

Barrow Hills (1970)

Private
Longcross, Chertsey
Mem 190
Sec RW Routley (0932) 848117
Holes 18 L 3090 yds SSS 53
Recs Am–58 EJ Sewell
V'trs M
Loc 4 miles W of Chertsey

Betchworth Park (1913)

Private
Reigate Road, Dorking
Tel **(0306) 882052**
Mem 750
Sec DAS Bradney
Pro A King (0306) 884334
Holes 18 L 6266 yds SSS 70
Recs Am–68 CJ Copus
Pro–65 NC Coles
V'trs WD–U exc Tues & Wed am–NA WE–by arrangement
Fees £13 (£18)
Loc 1 mile E of Dorking on A25

Bramley (1913)

Private
Bramley, nr Guildford GU5 0AL
Tel **(0483) 893042**
Mem 700
Sec Mrs M Lambert (0483) 892696
Pro G Peddie (0483) 893685
Holes 18 L 5943 yds SSS 68
Recs Am–66 MI Farmer
Pro–63 PR Gill
V'trs WD–U WE–M SOC–WD
Fees £13 D–£15
Loc 3 miles S of Guildford on A281
Mis Buggies for hire

Burhill (1907)

Private
Walton-on-Thames KT12 4BL
Tel **(0932) 227345**
Mem 1100
Sec AJ Acres
Pro Lee Johnson (0932) 221729
Holes 18 L 6224 yds SSS 70
Recs Am–66 RJ Pollitt (1987)
V'trs WD–H WE/BH–M
Fees On application
Loc Between Walton-on-Thames and Cobham

Camberley Heath (1913)

Private
Golf Drive, Camberley GU15 1JG
Tel **(0276) 23258**
Mem 725
Pro Gary Smith (0276) 27905
Holes 18 L 6402 yds SSS 71
Recs Am–66 C Laurence
Pro–67 A Perry
V'trs WD–I WE–M
Fees £12 D–£18
Loc $1^1/_4$ miles S of Camberley on Old Portsmouth Road (A325)

Centurion (1954)

Public
Richmond Park, London SW15
Tel **(01) 876 3205**
Mem 36
Sec DLR Aston (01) 870 4819
Holes Play over Richmond Park Golf Course

Chessington Golf Centre (1983)

Public
Garrison Lane, Chessington KT9 2LW
Tel **(01) 391 0948**
Mem 300
Sec A Maxted (01) 974 1705
Holes 9 hole course
Recs Am–60 N Murphy
Pro–54 R Hunter
V'trs WD–U WE–NA before noon
Fees £2.30 (£2.80) per 9 holes
Loc Off A243, 500 yards from Chessington Zoo, opposite Chessington South Station. M25 Junction 9

Chipstead (1906)

Private
How Lane, Chipstead, Coulsdon CR3 3PR
Tel **(0737) 551053**
Mem 600
Sec SLD Spencer-Skeen (0737) 555781
Pro C Jenkins (0737) 554939
Holes 18 L 5450 yds SSS 67
Recs Am–63 A Davey (1986)
Pro–63 N Child (1980)
V'trs WD–U WE/BH–M
Fees £15; after 2pm–£10
Loc Chipstead Station 200 yds

Coombe Hill (1911)

Private
Kingston Hill
Tel **(01) 942 2284**
Mem 437
Sec AL Foster
Pro C De Foy (01) 949 3713
Holes 18 L 6286 yds SSS 71
Recs Am–67 L Freedman, RL Glading
Pro–64 BJ Hunt
V'trs I or H SOC
Fees £30 H By arrangement only
Loc Off Coombe Lane West. 1 mile from New Malden. $^1/_2$ mile off A3 on A238

Coombe Wood (1904)

Private
George Road, Kingston Hill, Kingston-upon-Thames KT2 7NS
Tel **(01) 942 3828 (Steward)**
Mem 620
Sec T Duncan (01) 942 0388
Pro D Butler (01) 942 6764

For map index see page 203.

Holes 18 L 5210 yds SSS 66
Recs Am–64 M Taylor
Pro–60 D Butler (1987)
V'trs WD–UH after 9am WE/BH–M SOC–WD
Fees £15
Loc 1 mile N of Kingston-upon-Thames, off A3 at Robin Hood roundabout

Coulsdon Court (1937)

Public
Coulsdon Road CR3 2LL
Tel **(01) 660 0468**
Sec J Reed
Pro C Staff (01) 660 6083
Holes 18 L 6030 yds SSS 70
Pro–66 G Ralph
V'trs U
Fees £5 (£7.25)
Loc 5 miles S of Croydon on B2030
Mis Public course, now privately operated

Croham Hurst (1911)

Private
Croham Road, South Croydon CR2 7HJ
Tel **(01) 657 2075**
Mem 284 110(L) 80(J) 175(5)
Sec R Stallard (Sec/Mgr)
Pro E Stillwell (01) 657 7705
Holes 18 L 6274 yds SSS 70
Recs Am–64 SF Robson
Pro–66 B Firkins
V'trs WD–I WE/BH–M
Fees £16
Loc 1 mile from S Croydon. M25 Junction 6–A22–B270–B269

Crondall (1984)

Public
Oak Park, Heath Lane, Crondall, nr Farnham GU10 5PB
Tel **(0252) 850880**
Mem 350
Sec Mrs R Smythe
Pro P Rees (0252) 850066
Holes 18 L 6233 yds SSS 71
V'trs U SOC
Fees £7.50 (£10) Twilight ticket £5
Loc Off A287 Farnham to Odiham Road
Mis Covered driving range

Cuddington (1929)

Private
Banstead Road, Banstead
Tel **(01) 393 0952**
Mem 850
Sec DM Scott
Pro R Gardner (01) 393 5850
Holes 18 L 6282 yds SSS 70
Recs Am–66 NJ Woods, AP Ashworth
Pro–64 J Pinsent
V'trs WD–I WE–M
Fees £20
Loc Banstead Station 200 yds

Dorking (1897)

Private
Chart Park, Dorking
Tel **(0306) 889786**
Mem 320
Sec RM Payne (0306) 886917
Pro P Napier
Holes 9 L 5106 yds SSS 65
Recs Am–65 J Houston
Pro–62 A King
V'trs WD–U WE/BH–M SOC–WD
Fees £7.50
Loc 1 mile S of Dorking on A24

Drift (1976)

Private
The Drift, East Horsley KT24 6NU
Tel **(048 65) 4641**
Mem 700
Sec C Rose
Pro J Hagen (048 65) 4772
Holes 18 L 6414 yds SSS 71 Par 72
Recs Am–72 J Scarfe
Pro–72 TM Powell
V'trs WD–U SOC
Fees £17 before 1pm
£12 after 1pm
Loc 2 miles off A3. London 20 miles. 2 miles off M25

Dulwich & Sydenham Hill (1893)

Private
Grange Lane, College Road, London SE21 7LH
Tel **(01) 693 3961**
Mem 850
Sec B Harmer (01) 693 3961
Pro D Baillie (01) 693 8491
Holes 18 L 6051 yds SSS 69
Recs Am–62 T Bridle
Pro–63 LF Rowe
V'trs WD–I WE/BH–M SOC
Fees £15
Loc Charing Cross 5 miles

Effingham (1927)

Private
Effingham Crossroads, Effingham KT24 5PZ
Tel **(0372) 52203/4**
Mem 1200
Sec Miss SD Cousins
Pro S Hoatson (Mgr) (0372) 52606
Holes 18 L 6488 yds SSS 71
Recs Am–67 I Hawson (1986)
Pro–63 AD Locke
V'trs WD–H WE/BH–M
Fees WD–£25 before 2pm
£20 after 2pm
Loc 8 miles N of Guildford

Epsom (1889)

Private
Longdown Lane, South Epsom KT17 4JR
Tel **(037 27) 23363**
Mem 600
Sec KH Watson (037 27) 21666
Pro R Wynn (037 27) 41867
Holes 18 L 5725 yds SSS 68
Recs Am–68 R Goudie
Pro–68 R Wynn
V'trs WD–U WE/BH–U after 12 noon SOC–Wed & Fri
Fees £8 (£9)
Loc S Epsom Downs Rail Station

Farnham (1896)

Private
The Sands, Farnham GU10 1PX
Tel **(025 18) 3163**
Mem 700
Sec (025 18) 2109
Pro G Cowlishaw (025 18) 2198
Holes 18 L 6313 yds SSS 70
Recs Am–67 G Walmsley
V'trs WD–H WE–M SOC–Wed & Thurs
Fees £18 D–£21
Loc Signposted off A31, about 1 mile E of Farnham

Farnham Park (1966)

Public
Farnham Park, Farnham GU9 0AU
Tel **(0252) 715216**
Sec P Chapman
Pro P Chapman
Holes Par 3 course 9 holes
L 1163 yds SSS 54
Recs Am–61 JA Pike
Pro–56 G Wheeler
V'trs U
Fees £1.80 (£2.10)
Loc By Farnham Castle

Fernfell G & CC (1985)

Private
Barhatch Lane, Cranleigh GU6 7NG
Tel **(0483) 276626**
Mem 1000
Sec Miss GL Petersen (Mgr)
Pro C Hebdon (0483) 277188
Holes 18 L 5236 yds SSS 66
V'trs WD–U WE/BH–NA am SOC–WD
Fees £9 (£15)
Loc Off A281, 1 mile from Cranleigh. A3 8 miles. M25 11 miles

Foxhills (1975)

Private
Stonehill Road, Ottershaw KT16 0EL
Tel **(093 287) 2050**
Mem 647
Sec A Dupuy
Pro B Hunt (093 287) 3961
Holes 18 L 6880 yds SSS 73
18 L 6747 yds SSS 72
Recs Pro–65 P Dawson
V'trs U SOC
Fees £22 D–£30
Loc London 20 miles. Heathrow 10 miles
Mis Buggies for hire

Gatton Manor Hotel (1969)

Private
Ockley, nr Dorking RH5 5PQ
Tel **(030 679) 555**
Mem 250
Sec DG Heath
Pro R Sargent (030 679) 557
Holes 18 L 6903 yds SSS 72
Recs Am–72 J McLaren (1985)
Pro–73 R Sargent (1985)
V'trs U exc Sun before noon–M SOC–WD
Fees £9 (£11)
Loc $1^1/_2$ miles SW of Ockley off A29. M25 Junction 9, S on A24
Mis Buggies–£20 per day

Goal Farm (1977)

Public
Pirbright GU24 OP2
Tel **(048 67) 3183/3205**
Mem 260
Sec J Church
Holes 9 hole Par 3 course
Recs Am–27
V'trs Sat–reserved for club comps SOC–WD
Fees 18 holes £3 (£3.50)
9 holes £1.60 (£1.85)

Guildford (1886)

Private
High Path Road, Merrow, Guildford GU1 2HL
Tel **(0483) 575243**
Mem 600
Sec HJ Warburton (0483) 63941
Pro PG Hollington (0483) 66765
Holes 18 L 6080 yds SSS 70
Recs Am–66 B White
Pro–67 PG Hollington (1987)
V'trs WD–U WE–M SOC–WD
Fees £15
Loc 2 miles E of Guildford

Hankley Common (1895)

Private
Tilford, Farnham GU10 2DD
Tel **(025 125) 2493**
Mem 650
Sec JKA O'Brien
Pro W Brogden (025 125) 3761
Holes 18 L 6418 yds SSS 71
Recs Am–66 J Lee (1987)
Pro–62 H Stott (1988)
V'trs WD–I WE–At discretion of Sec
Fees £15 D–£20 (£20 after 2 pm)
Loc 3 miles SE of Farnham on Tilford Road

Hindhead (1905)

Private
Churt Road, Hindhead GU26 6HX
Tel **(042 873) 4614**
Mem 300 50(L) 100(J) 100(5)
Sec ML Brown
Pro N Ogilvy (042 873) 4458
Holes 18 L 6357 yds SSS 70
Recs Am–65 W Rowland
Pro–65 DJ Rees
V'trs WD–UH WE/BH–NA before noon SOC–Wed & Thurs only
Fees £18 (£22)
Loc $1^1/_2$ miles N of Hindhead on A287

Hoebridge Golf Centre (1982)

Public
The Club House, Old Woking Road, Old Woking GU22 8JH
Tel **(048 62) 22611**
Mem 400
Sec TD Powell
Pro TD Powell
Holes 18 L 6587 yds SSS 71
Par 3 18 L 2298 yds
V'trs U
Fees £4.70 Par 3–£2.75
Loc Between Old Woking and West Byfleet. 2 miles off A3 on A247
Mis 25 bay floodlit driving range

Home Park (1895)

Private
Hampton Wick, Kingston-upon-Thames KT1 4AD
Tel **(01) 977 6645**
Mem 500
Sec CHH Gray (01) 977 2423
Pro L Roberts (01) 977 2658
Holes 18 L 6519 yds SSS 71
V'trs U
Fees £8.50 (£13)
Loc 1 mile W of Kingston

Kingswood (1928)

Private
Sandy Lane, Kingswood, Tadworth KT20 6NE
Tel **(0737) 832188**
Mem 640
Sec M Fletcher (Admin)
Pro R Blackie (0737) 832334
Holes 18 L 6821 yds SSS 73
Recs Am–70 P Stanford
Pro–67 R Blackie
V'trs H SOC
Fees £18 (£25)
Loc 5 miles S of Sutton on A217. M25 Junction 8, 2 miles

Laleham (1907)

Private
Laleham Reach, Chertsey KT16 8RP
Tel **(093 28) 564211**
Mem 600
Sec MA Ford
Pro T Whitton (093 28) 62877
Holes 18 L 6203 yds SSS 70
Recs Am–68 C Poulton
Pro–66 R Mandeville, J Hitchcock
V'trs WD–U before 4.30pm WE–M SOC–Mon–Wed
Fees £13 D–£15
Loc 2 miles S of Staines

Leatherhead (1904)

Private
Kingston Road, Leatherhead KT22 0DP
Mem 500
Sec W Betts (037 284) 3966
Holes 18 L 6060 yds SSS 69
Recs Am–68 PW Wynn
Pro–65 R Wynn
V'trs U SOC
Fees £20 (£25)
Loc 1 mile off Leatherhead interchange of M25, on A243 to Chessington

Limpsfield Chart (1889)

Private
Limpsfield RH8 0SL
Tel **(088 388) 2106/3405**
Mem 395
Sec JC Woods (0689) 55146
Pro B A Finch
Holes 9 L 5718 yds SSS 68
Recs Am–67 N Simmons
Pro–64 B Huggett
V'trs WD–Tues/Fri/Wed pm Apr–Oct Sun–NA after 1pm
Fees On application
Loc 2 miles E of Oxted

London Scottish (1865)

Private
Windmill Enclosure, Wimbledon Common, London SW19 5NQ
Tel **(01) 788 0135**
Mem 250
Sec R Allen (01) 789 7517
Pro M Barr (01) 789 1207
Holes 18 L 5486 yds SSS 67
Recs Am–64 A Glickberg
Pro–63 D Butler, A King
V'trs WD–U WE–M BH–NA SOC–WD
Fees £6 D–£8
Loc Wimbledon Station 2 miles
Mis Club has joint use with Wimbledon Common GC

Malden (1926)

Private
Traps Lane, New Malden KT3 4RS
Tel **(01) 942 0654**
Mem 680
Sec Miss KNR Pudner
Pro G Howard (01) 942 6009
Holes 18 L 6201 yds SSS 70
Recs Am–65 G Lashford
Pro–67 A Waters
V'trs WD–U WE–restricted (apply Sec) SOC–Wed–Fri
Fees £17.50 (£22)
Loc Close to A3 between Wimbledon and Kingston

For map index see page 203.

Mitcham

Private
Carshalton Road, Mitcham Junction CR4 4HN
Tel **(01) 648 1508**
Mem 450
Sec CA McGahan (01) 648 4197
Pro JA Godfrey (01) 640 4280
Holes 18 L 5931 yds SSS 68
Recs Am–D Wilde
V'trs U WE–NA 8am–2pm SOC
Fees £5 (£6)
Loc Nr Mitcham Junction Station

Mitcham Village (1907)

Public
Tel **(01) 648 1508**
Mem 240 10(J)
Sec RL Scriven (01) 764 1861
Holes Play over Mitcham Golf Course

Moore Place (1926)

Public
Portsmouth Road, Esher KT10 9LN
Tel **(0372) 63533**
Mem 107
Sec J Darby (0932) 220575
Pro D Allen
Holes 9 L 3512 yds SSS 58
Recs Am–29 W Cavanagh
Pro–25 P Loxley
V'trs U
Fees £3 (£4)

New Zealand (1895)

Private
Woodham Lane, Woodham, Weybridge KT15 3QD
Tel **(093 23) 45049**
Mem 300
Sec MJ Wood (093 23) 42891
Pro VR Elvidge (093 23) 49619
Holes 18 L 6012 yds SSS 69
Recs Am–66 P Cannings
Pro–72 Alex Herd
V'trs WD–U BH–NA
Fees On application
Loc Woking 3 miles. West Byfleet 1 mile

North Downs (1899)

Private
Northdown Road, Woldingham
Tel **(088 385) 3298**
Mem 650
Sec SW Thomson (088 385) 2057
Pro P Ellis (088 385) 3004
Holes 18 L 5787 yds SSS 68
Recs Am–68 AS Tait (1981)
Pro–65 W Humphreys (1987)
V'trs WD–U WE–M SOC–Tues & Wed
Fees £13.50 1988 prices
Loc 3 miles E of Caterham

Oaks Sports Centre (1973)

Public
Woodmansterne Road, Carshalton
Tel **(01) 643 8363**
Mem 500
Pro G Horley
Holes 18 L 5873 yds SSS 68
9 L 1590 yds SSS 29
Recs 18–hole Pro–66 J Woodroffe
9–hole Pro–27 J Woodroffe
V'trs U
Fees 18–hole £3.75 (£4.75)
9–hole £1.65 (£2)
Loc Sutton 2 miles
Mis Floodlit driving range

Purley Downs (1894)

Private
106 Purley Downs Road, Purley CR2 0RB
Tel **(01) 657 8347**
Mem 600
Sec J Page
Pro G Wilson (01) 651 0819
Holes 18 L 6237 yds SSS 70
Recs Am–66 M Hayes
Pro–69 M Gregson
V'trs WD–I WE–M
Fees On application
Loc 3 miles S of Croydon

Puttenham (1894)

Private
Puttenham, nr Guildford
Tel **(0483) 810498**
Mem 500
Sec G Simmons
Pro G Simmons (0483) 810277
Holes 18 L 5300 yds SSS 66
Recs Am–65 P Bivona
Pro–59 R Donald
V'trs WD–H WE/BH–M SOC–Wed & Thurs
Fees On application
Loc Midway between Guildford and Farnham on Hog's Back

RAC Country Club (1913)

Private
Woodcote Park, Epsom KT18 7EW
Tel **(0372) 276311**
Sec K Symons
Pro P Butler
Holes 18 L 6672 yds SSS 72
18 L 5520 yds SSS 67
V'trs M SOC
Loc Epsom Station $1^3/_4$ miles

Redhill & Reigate (1887)

Private
Clarence Lodge, Pendleton Road, Redhill RH1 6LB
Tel **(0737) 244626/244433**
Mem 300
Sec FR Cole (0737) 240777
Pro B Davies (0737) 244433
Holes 18 L 5261 yds SSS 66
Recs Am–65 M Gander, CJ Weight, Pro–63 GW Huggett, P Deighton, R Donovan
V'trs WD–U WE–NA before 11am Sun–NA June–Sept
Fees £8 (£10)
Loc Redhill 1 mile on A23

Reigate Heath (1895)

Private
Reigate Heath RH2 8QR
Tel **(0737) 242610**
Mem 250 90(L) 50(J)
Sec Mrs DM Howard (0737) 245530
Pro WH Carter
Holes 9 L 5554 yds SSS 67
Recs Am–65 D Mahaney
Pro–65 P Loxley
V'trs U Sun/BH–M SOC–Wed & Thurs
Fees On application
Loc W boundary

Richmond (1891)

Private
Sudbrook Park, Richmond TW10 7AS
Tel **(01) 940 1463**
Mem 500
Sec JF Stocker (01) 940 4351
Pro N Job (01) 940 7792
Holes 18 L 5965 yds SSS 69
Recs Am–63 J Lawson
Pro–62 AG King
V'trs WD–U WE/BH–10am–12 noon
Fees £16 (£20)
Loc Between Richmond and Kingston-upon-Thames

Richmond Park (1923)

Public
Roehampton Gate, Richmond Park, London SW15 5JR
Tel **(01) 878 3205/1795**
Sec C Lloyd
Pro I Roberts
Holes Dukes 18 L 5940 yds SSS 68
Princes 18 L 5969 yds SSS 68
V'trs U SOC
Fees £4.50 (£6.50)
Loc 3 miles SW of Putney along Priory Lane
Mis Driving range

Roehampton (1901)

Private
Roehampton Lane, London SW15 5LR
Tel **(01) 876 5505**
Mem 900
Sec RW Varley
Pro AL Scott (01) 876 3858
Holes 18 L 6057 yds SSS 69
Recs Am–67 AL Scott
Pro–62 H Stott
V'trs WD–Introduced by member WE–M
Loc Nr Barnes

Royal Mid-Surrey (1892)

Private
Old Deer Park, Richmond TW9 2SB
Tel **(01) 940 1894**
Mem 1200
Sec MSR Lunt
Pro D Talbot (01) 940 0459
Holes Outer 18 L 6331 yds SSS 70
Inner 18 L 5446 yds SSS 71
Recs Outer Am–66 GH Micklem, JC Davies, D Gilford
Pro–64 R Charles, B Gallacher
V'trs WD–I or M WE/BH–with prior approval SOC
Fees £25 (£30)

Royal Wimbledon (1865)

Private
29 Camp Road, Wimbledon, London SW19 4UW
Tel **(01) 946 2125**
Mem 800
Sec Maj. GE Jones
Pro H Boyle (01) 946 4606
Holes 18 L 6300 yds SSS 70
Recs Am–66 JFM Connolly
Pro–71 R Burton
V'trs WD–I or M WE–M
Fees £27
Loc S of Wimbledon Common

Sandown Park (1970)

Public
More Lane, Esher KT10 8AN
Tel **(0372) 63340**
Mem 300
Sec P Barriball
Pro N Bedward
Holes 9 L 5658 yds SSS 67
9 hole Par 3
Recs Am–69 P O'Halloran
V'trs U (Closed on race day until 30 mins after last race)
Fees 9 holes £2.60 (£3.50)
Loc Sandown Park Racecourse, Esher
Mis Floodlit driving range. Sandown Park Club plays here

Selsdon Park Hotel (1929)

Private
Addington Road, Sanderstead CR2 8YA
Tel **(01) 657 8811**
Pro W Mitchell (01) 657 4129
Holes 18 L 6402 yds SSS 71
Recs Am–68 B Stevenson
Pro–65 A Lacey, J Hitchcock
V'trs U H SOC (min 12 golfers)
Fees 18 holes: £10 Sat–£15 Sun/BH–£17.80. 36 holes: WD–£15 Starting times must be prebooked
Loc 3 miles S of Croydon on A2022 Purley–Addington road
Mis Course unsuitable for novice golfers

Shillinglee Park (1980)

Public
Chiddingfold, Godalming GU8 4TA
Tel **(0428) 53237**
Mem 350
Sec R Mace
Pro R Mace
Holes 9 L 2400 yds Par 32
V'trs U SOC
Fees 9 holes £5 D–£9
Loc $2^1/_2$ miles SE of Chiddingfold

Shirley Park (1914)

Private
Addiscombe Road, Croydon CR0 7LB
Tel **(01) 654 1143**
Mem 900
Sec A Baird
Pro H Stott (01) 654 8767
Holes 18 L 6210 yds SSS 70
Recs Am–68 N Durance, R Latham
Pro–65 J Bennett
V'trs WD–U WE/BH–M SOC
Fees £16
Loc 1 mile E of Croydon Station

Silvermere (1976)

Public
Redhill Road, Cobham KT11 1EF
Tel **(0932) 67275**
Mem 600
Sec Mrs P Devereux (0932) 68122
Pro D McClelland
Holes 18 L 6333 yds SSS 71
Pro–65 S Rolley (1986)
V'trs WD–U WE–after 10.30am SOC
Fees £6 (£8.50)
Loc Between Cobham and Byfleet. $^1/_2$ mile from M25 Junction 10 on B366 to Byfleet
Mis Floodlit driving range

St George's Hill (1912)

Private
Weybridge KT13 0NL
Tel **(0932) 842406**
Mem 600
Sec MR Tapsell (0932) 847758
Pro AC Rattue (0932) 843523
Holes 18 L 6492 yds SSS 71
9 L 2360 yds SSS 35
Recs Am–65 D Swanston
Pro–65 M Faulkner
V'trs WD–IH WE/BH–NA 9 hole–U
Fees D–£28.50–£20 after 1.45pm
9 hole £6–£5 after 1.45pm
£4 after 4pm
Loc $^1/_2$ mile N of M25/A3 Junction on A245 to Woking

Surbiton (1895)

Private
Woodstock Lane, Chessington
Tel **(01) 398 3101**
Mem 670
Sec MO Wright
Pro P Milton (01) 398 6619
Holes 18 L 6211 yds SSS 70
Recs Am–64 DL Hyde
Pro–63 PE Gill
V'trs WD–U WE/BH–M
Fees £11
Loc 2 miles E of Esher

Tandridge (1925)

Private
Oxted
Tel **(0883) 712273/4**
Mem 450
Sec Air Marshal DCA Lloyd
Pro A Farquhar (0883) 713701
Holes 18 L 6250 yds SSS 70
Recs Am–68 JC Robson
Pro–69 BGC Huggett
V'trs I–Mon/–Wed/Thurs only
Fees £16.50
Loc 5 miles E of Redhill off A25. M25 Junction 6

Thames Ditton & Esher (1892)

Private
Portsmouth Road, Esher KT10 9AL
Tel **(01) 398 1551**
Mem 300
Sec BAJ Chandler
Pro R Hutton
Holes 9 L 5415 yds SSS 65
Recs Am–61 T Petitt
Pro–64 R Hutton, R Barr
V'trs WD–U WE–by arrangement
Fees £5 (£6)

Tyrrells Wood (1924)

Private
Leatherhead KT22 8QP
Tel **(0372) 376025 (2 lines)**
Mem 744
Sec GD Lawson
Pro P Taylor (0372) 375200
Holes 18 L 6219 yds SSS 70
Recs Am–67 P Earl (1988)
Pro–65 P Hoad (1988)
V'trs WD/WE/BH–I NA before noon
Loc Leatherhead 2 miles off A24 nr Headley. M25 Junction 9 1 mile

Walton Heath (1904)

Private
Tadworth KT20 7TP
Tel **(0737) 812060**
Mem 900
Sec A Heron (0737) 812380
Pro K Macpherson (0737) 812152

For map index see page 203.

Holes Old 18 L 6813 yds SSS 73
New 18 L 6659 yds SSS 72
Recs Old Am–68 R Revell
Pro–65 P Townsend
New Am–67 JK Tate
Pro–64 C Clark
V'trs WD–IH WE/BH–M SOC
Fees £25
Loc 3 miles S of Epsom.
M25 Junc 8, 2 miles

Wentworth (1924)

Private
Virginia Water GU25 4LS
Tel (099 04) 2201
Mem 1934
Sec SG Lewis
Pro B Gallacher (099 04) 3353
Holes West 18 L 6945 yds SSS 74
East 18 L 6176 yds SSS 70
Recs West Am–72 P McEvoy
Pro–64 H Clarke
East Am–65 GB Wolstenholme
Pro–62 DN Sewell, G Will
V'trs WD–H by prior arrangement
WE–M SOC–Tues–Thurs
Fees West D–£69 East D–£46 WD only
Loc 21 miles SW of London off A30 at Junction with A39
Mis 3rd 18 hole course of approx 7000 yds open 1990

West Byfleet (1922)

Private
Sheerwater Road, West Byfleet
Tel (093 23) 45230
Mem 550
Sec DG Smith (093 23) 43433
Pro D Regan (093 33) 46584
Holes 18 L 6211 yds SSS 70
Recs Am–66 W Calderwood
Pro–67 P Thomson
V'trs WD–I WE/BH–NA
Fees £15
Loc West Byfleet ½ mile on A245

West Hill (1909)

Private
Brookwood, nr Woking
Tel (04867) 4365/2110
Mem 550
Sec WD Leighton MBE
Pro JA Clements (048 67) 3172
Holes 18 L 6368 yds SSS 70
Recs Am–66 WA Murray
Pro–66 V Hood
V'trs WD–H WE–M SOC
Fees £14.50
Loc 5 miles W of Woking on A322

West Surrey (1909)

Private
Enton Green, nr Godalming GU8 5AF
Tel (048 68) 21275
Mem 743
Sec RS Fanshawe
Pro J Hoskison (048 68) 7278
Holes 18 L 6247 yds SSS 70
Recs Am–66 SD Cook
Pro–67 B Lane
V'trs H SOC–WD
Fees £13 (£24)
Loc ½ mile SE of Milford Station

White Lodge (1923)

Public
Richmond Park, London SW15
Tel (01) 876 3205
Mem 120
Sec MS McDonald (01) 876 5360
Holes Play over Richmond Park municipal courses

Wimbledon Common (1908)

Private
19 Camp Road, Wimbledon Common, London SW19 4UW
Tel (01) 946 0294
Mem 250
Sec JE Miles (01) 946 7571
Pro JE Jukes
Holes 18 L 5486 yds SSS 67
Recs Am–65 T Mahon
Pro–64 JS Jukes
V'trs WD–U WE–M Sun pm BH–NA
Fees £10
Mis Pillarbox red outer garment (can be hired) must be worn. London Scottish play here

Wimbledon Park (1898)

Private
Home Park Road, London SW19
Tel (01) 946 1002
Mem 580
Sec MK Hale (01) 946 1250
Pro FC Lucas (01) 946 4053
Holes 18 L 5465 yds SSS 67
Recs Am–66 SJ Bennett
Pro–65 A Dixon
V'trs WD–H I WE/BH–after 3pm SOC
Fees £14 (£17)
Loc Central London 8 miles

Windlemere (1978)

Public
Windlesham Road, West End, Woking
Tel (099 05) 8727
Sec CD Smith
Pro D Thomas
Holes 9 L 5346 yds SSS 66
V'trs U
Fees £3.30 (£4)
Loc A319 at Lightwater
Mis Floodlit driving range

Woking (1893)

Private
Pond Road, Hook Heath, Woking GU22 0JZ
Tel (048 62) 60053
Mem 350
Sec AW Riley
Pro J Thorne (048 62) 69582
Holes 18 L 6322 yds SSS 70
Recs Am–65 PJ Benka
V'trs WD–I WE–M
Fees £14
Loc 2½ miles W of Woking off Hollybank Road

Woodcote Park (1912)

Private
Bridle Way, Meadow Hill, Coulsdon CR3 2QQ
Tel (01) 660 0176
Mem 750
Sec BP Nazer (01) 668 2788
Pro I Martin (01) 668 1843
Holes 18 L 6300 yds SSS 71
Recs Am–66 S Keppler
Pro–66 C Bonner
V'trs WD–U WE–M
Fees £16
Loc Purley 2 miles

Worplesdon (1908)

Private
Heath House Road, Woking GU22 0RA
Tel (04867) 89876 (Steward)
Mem 560
Sec Maj REE Jones (04867) 2277
Pro J Christine (04867) 3287
Holes 18 L 6422 yds SSS 71
Recs Am–64 KE Jones (1988)
Pro–62
V'trs WD–H WE–M
Fees On application
Loc E of Woking off A322.
5 miles S of M3 Junction 3

Sussex (East)

Ashdown Forest Hotel

Private
Chapel Lane, Forest Row RH18 5BB
Tel (0342 82) 4866
Mem 150
Sec AJ Riddick, RL Pratt
Pro H Padgham (0342 82) 2247
Holes 18 L 5510 yds SSS 67
V'trs U SOC
Fees £8 (£9)
Loc 4 miles S of East Grinstead off A22. 12 miles W of Tunbridge Wells
Mis Hotel specialises in catering for golf breaks and society days

Beauport Park

Private
Battle Road, St Leonards-on-Sea TN38 0TA
Tel (0424) 52977
Mem 300
Sec DC Funnell
Holes Play over Hastings Public Course

Brighton & Hove (1887)

Private
Dyke Road, Brighton BN1 8YJ
Tel (0273) 556482
Mem 270
Sec SC Cawkwell
Holes 9 L 5722 yds SSS 68
Recs Am–67
V'trs U SOC
Fees 18 holes WD–£10 Sat–£12 Sun–£12 after 12 noon. 9 holes WD–£5 Sat–£6
Loc 15 mins N of Brighton

Cooden Beach (1912)

Private
Cooden Beach, nr Bexhill-on-Sea
Tel (042 43) 2040
Mem 650
Sec Maj PA Beacon
Pro K Benson (042 43) 3938
Holes 18 L 6411 yds SSS 71
Recs Am–67 G Burton, CM Skinner, Sir H Birkmyre
Pro–65 AG Harrison
V'trs Arrange with Sec
Fees On application
Loc W boundary of Bexhill

Crowborough Beacon (1895)

Private
Beacon Road, Crowborough
Tel (0892) 654016
Mem 600
Sec M Swatton (0892) 661511
Pro D Newnham (0892) 653877
Holes 18 L 6279 yds SSS 70
Recs Am–67 GCD Carter, SF Robson
Pro–67 K Ashdown
V'trs WD–IH WE/BH–NA before 3pm
Fees £15 (£16)
Loc 7 miles S of Tunbridge Wells on A26

Dale Hill (1973)

Private
Ticehurst, nr Wadhurst TN5 7DQ
Tel (0580) 200112
Mem 550
Sec SVC Nicholson
Pro A Collins (0580) 200577
Holes 18 L 6035 yds SSS 69
9 hole Par 3 course
Recs Pro–68 K MacDonald
V'trs WD–U WE/BH–H after 10.30am SOC
Fees £11 (£12)
Loc B2087 off A21 at Flimwell

The Dyke (1908)

Private
Dyke Road, Brighton BN1 8YJ
Tel (079 156) 296
Mem 750
Sec B Gazzard
Pro P Longmore (079 156) 260
Holes 18 L 6519 yds SSS 71
Recs Am–68 N O'Byrne
Pro–65 C Jones
V'trs U exc Sun–NA
Fees £12 D–£15 (£18)
Loc 4 miles N of Brighton

East Brighton (1894)

Private
Roedean, Brighton BN2 5RA
Tel (0273) 603989
Mem 670
Sec KR Head
Pro WH Street
Holes 18 L 6337 yds SSS 70
Recs Am–68 A Turner
Pro–63 S King
V'trs WD–U WE–NA before 11am SOC
Fees £11 (£16)
Loc N from Marina, Black Rock

Eastbourne Downs (1908)

Private
East Dean Road, Eastbourne BN20 8ES
Tel (0323) 20827
Mem 600
Sec DJ Eldrett
Pro T Marshall (0323) 32264
Holes 18 L 6635 yds SSS 72
Recs Am–67 J Collison (1988)
Pro–70 B Gallacher
V'trs U Sun–after 11am
Fees £9 (£10)
Loc 1 mile W of town on A259

Hastings (1973)

Public
Beauport Park, Battle Road, St Leonards-on-Sea TN38 0TA
Tel (0424) 52977
Sec M Barton (0424) 52981
Pro M Barton (0424) 52981
Holes 18 L 6248 yds SSS 71
Recs Am–69 V Massarella (1981)
Pro–72 S Hall (1987)
V'trs U SOC
Fees £6 (£7.50)
Loc 3 miles N of Hastings off A2100 Battle to St Leonards road
Mis Beauport Park Club plays here. Tee booking necessary

Highwoods (Bexhill) (1925)

Private
Ellerslie Lane, Bexhill-on-Sea TN39 4LJ
Tel (0424) 212625
Mem 800
Sec P Robins
Pro RJ McLean (0424) 212770
Holes 18 L 6218 yds SSS 70
Recs Am–66 JAL Smith (1987)
Pro–68 C Clark (1976)
V'trs WD/Sat–H Sun am–M Sun pm–H
Fees £16 (£20)
Loc 2 miles N of Bexhill

Hollingbury Park (Brighton) (1911)

Public
Ditching Road, Brighton BN1 7HS
Tel (0273) 552010
Mem 340
Sec JG Walling
Pro P Brown (0273) 500086
Holes 18 L 6415 yds SSS 71
Recs Am–68 G Derkson (1988)
Pro–66 B Norton (1988)
V'trs U SOC
Fees £7 (£10)
Loc Town centre 1 mile

Horam Park (1985)

Public
Chiddingly Road, Horam TN21 0JJ
Tel (04353) 3477
Mem 350
Sec M Cousins (Mgr)
Pro R Foster
Holes 9 L 5688 yds SSS 66
Pro–64 J Pinsent (1988)
V'trs U SOC Sat–M before 4pm
Fees 9 holes–£5 (£5.50)
18 holes–£8.50 (£9)
D–£10 (D–£12)
Loc 1/2 mile S of Horam towards Chiddingley. 12 miles N of Eastbourne on A267
Mis Floodlit driving range. No catering Mon

Lewes (1896)

Private
Chapel Hill, Lewes
Tel (0273) 473245
Mem 545
Sec GJ Cull (0273) 473074
Pro E Golding
Holes 18 L 5951 yds SSS 69
Recs Am–70 D Cosham
Pro–67 CA Burgess
V'trs U SOC
Fees £10 (£12)
Loc 1/2 mile from town centre at E end of Cliffe High Street

Peacehaven (1896)

Private
Brighton Road, Newhaven BN9 9UH
Tel (0273) 514049
Mem 290
Sec DT Jenkins (0273) 512571
Pro G Williams (0273) 512602
Holes 9 L 5235 yds SSS 66
Recs Am–67 A Browning (1985)
V'trs WD–U WE/BH–after 11am SOC
Fees On application
Loc 8 miles E of Brighton on A259

For map index see page 203.

Piltdown (1904)

Private
Uckfield TN22 3XB
Tel **(082 572) 2033**
Mem 350
Sec REH King (Hon)
Pro J Amos (082 572) 2389
Holes 18 L 6059 yds SSS 69
Recs Am–67 A Smith (1988)
Pro–69 S Frost, P Lovesey
V'trs I or H exc Tues/Thurs am/ Sun am
Fees £16 (£18)
Loc 1 mile W of Maresfield off A272

Royal Ashdown Forest (1888)

Private
Chapel Lane, Forest Row,
E Grinstead RH18 5LR
Tel **(034 282) 2018/3014**
(034 282) 4866 (New Course)
Mem 450
Sec KPA Mathews
Pro HA Padgham
Holes Old 18 L 6477 yds SSS 71
New 18 L 5549 yds SSS 69
Recs Am–67 RA Darlington
Pro–62 HA Padgham
V'trs On application phone first
Fees £17.50 (£22.50) 1988 prices
Loc 4 miles S of E Grinstead on B2100 Hartfield road. M25 Junction 6

Royal Eastbourne (1887)

Private
Paradise Drive, Eastbourne
BN20 8BP
Tel **(0323) 30412**
Mem 900
Sec R Passingham (0323) 29738
Pro R Wooller (0323) 36986
Holes 18 L 6109 yds SSS 69
9 L 2147 yds SSS 32
Recs Am–65 J Beland (1980)
Pro–62 J Pinsent (1987)
V'trs U H SOC
Fees 18 hole £14 (£17.50)
9 hole £7.50
Loc 1/2 mile from Town Hall

Rye (1894)

Private
Camber, Rye TN31 7QS
Tel **(0797) 225241**
Mem 800 105(L) 40(J)
Sec JM Bradley
Pro P Marsh (0797) 225218
Holes 18 L 6301 yds SSS 71
9 L 6625 yds SSS 72
Recs Am–64 P Hurring (1988)
Pro–67 C Ledger (1988)
V'trs M
Loc 3 miles E of Rye

Seaford (1887)

Private
East Blatchington, Seaford BN25 2JD
Tel **(0323) 892597**
Mem 420 110(L) 37(J) 88(5)
Sec MB Hichisson (0323) 892442
Pro P Stevens (0323) 894160
Holes 18 L 6233 yds SSS 70
Recs Am–66 EA Snow, A Flygt
Pro–67 H Weetman
V'trs WD–U WE–M
Fees £16 (£11 after 1pm)
Loc 1 mile N of Seaford Town
Mis Dormy House accommodation

Seaford Head (1907)

Public
Southdown Road, Seaford
Tel **(0323) 890139**
Mem 450
Sec AT Goodman (0323) 894843
Pro AJ Lowles
Holes 18 L 5812 yds SSS 68
Recs Am–66 J Crawford
Pro–66 M Andrews
V'trs U
Fees £4.50 (£5.60)
Loc 8 miles W of Eastbourne. 3/4 mile S of A259

Waterhall (1921)

Public
Devils Dyke Road, Brighton BN1 8YN
Tel **(0273) 508658**
Mem 343
Sec P Scarfield (Hon)
BW Pettitt (Mgr)
Pro P Charman
Holes 18 L 5692 yds SSS 67
Recs Am–66 C Wilson
Pro–64 EF Goldring
V'trs U
Fees £6 (£8)
Loc 3 miles N of Brighton between A23 and A27. 1 mile N of A2308

West Hove (1910)

Private
369 Old Shoreham Rd, Hove BN3 7GD
Tel **(0273) 413411**
Sec R Charman (0273) 419738
Pro C White (0273) 413494
Holes 18 L 6038 yds SSS 69
Recs Am–66 N O'Byrne
Pro–62 C Moody
V'trs WD–U WE–M
Fees £7 (£9)
Loc 300 yds N of Postslade & West Hove Station on A27

Willingdon (1898)

Private
Southdown Road, Eastbourne
BN20 9AA
Tel **(0323) 410983**
Mem 500
Sec B Kirby (0323) 410981
Pro DJ Ashton (0323) 410984
Holes 18 L 6049 yds SSS 69
Recs Am–64 DM Sewell (1986)
Pro–63 P Mitchell (1987)
V'trs WD–U WE–MH SOC–H
Fees 18 holes £11 (£13)
36 holes £13 (£15)
Loc 1/2 mile N of Eastbourne off A22 to London

Sussex (West)

Bognor Regis (1892)

Private
Downview Road, Felpham,
Bognor Regis PO22 8JD
Tel **(0243) 865867**
Mem 570 173(L)
Sec BD Poston (0243) 821929
Pro R Day (0243) 865209
Holes 18 L 6238 yds SSS 70
Recs Am–66 N Graves
Pro–66 R Wynn
V'trs H WE (Apr–Sept)–M
Fees £14 (£18)
Loc 2 miles E of town

Copthorne (1892)

Private
Borers Arm Road, Copthorne
RH10 3LL
Tel **(0342) 712508**
Mem 565
Sec DG Pulford
Pro J Burrell (0342) 712405
Holes 18 L 6205 yds SSS 71
Recs Am–64 HMR Deane
Pro–68 C Mason, R Boxall
V'trs H–after 2pm SOC
Fees £12 (£18)
Loc E Grinstead 1 mile on A264. M23 Junction 10

Cottesmore (1974)

Private
Buchan Hill, Crawley RH11 9AT
Tel **(0293) 28256**
Mem 1600
Sec MF Rogerson
Pro P Webster (0293) 35399
Holes 18 L 6097 yds SSS 70
18 L 5321 yds SSS 68
Recs Old Am–69 I Geddes
Pro–70 D Russel
V'trs U
Fees £14 (£18)
Loc 4 miles S of Crawley

Cowdray Park (1949)

Private
Midhurst GU29 0BB
Tel **(073 081) 2088**
Mem 700
Sec Mrs JD Huggett (073 081) 3599
Pro S Hall (073 081) 2091
Holes 18 L 6212 yds SSS 70
Recs Am–69 D Fay
Pro–68 G Ralph
V'trs Introduction by member of recognised club WE/BH–NA before 11am SOC
Fees £10–£14 (£20)
Loc 1 mile E of Midhurst on A272

Effingham Park (1980)

Private
nr Copthorne
Tel **(0342) 716528**
Mem 150
Sec AJ Lecky (0342) 713011
Pro Ian Dryden (0342) 716528
Holes 9 L 1749 yds Par 30
Recs Am–29
Pro–26
V'trs WD–U WE–M before 10.30am –U after 10.30am
Fees £4 (£5.50)
Loc B2028/B2039

Gatwick Manor (1975)

Private
Crawley
Tel **(0293) 24470**
Sec C Hemsley
Pro BC Hemsley
Holes 9 L 1109 yds SSS 27
V'trs U
Loc A23 to Crawley, 1 mile past Gatwick Airport

Goodwood (1892)

Private
Goodwood, nr Chichester
PO18 0PN
Tel **(0243) 785012 (Members)**
Mem 900
Sec M Hughes-Narborough (0243) 774968
Pro K MacDonald (0243) 774994
Holes 18 L 6383 yds SSS 70
Recs Am–69 SB Ursell (1988)
Pro–66 K MacDonald (1988)
V'trs WD–U H after 9.30pm WE–H after 10am SOC
Fees £12 (£20)
Loc 3 miles NE of Chichester

Ham Manor (1936)

Private
Angmering, nr Littlehampton
BN16 4JE
Tel **(0903) 783288**
Mem 860
Sec PH Saubergue
Pro S Buckley (0903) 783732
Holes 18 L 6216 yds SSS 70
Recs Am–64 F Wieland (1987)
Pro–62 TA Horton
V'trs WD–U WE–H
Fees On application
Loc Between Worthing and Littlehampton

Haywards Heath (1922)

Private
High Beech Lane, Haywards Heath
RH16 1SL
Tel **(0444) 414310**
Mem 625
Sec SW Cobbett (0444) 414457
Pro G Dornan (0444) 414866
Holes 18 L 6202 yds SSS 70
Recs Am–63 S Robson
Pro–65 B Firkins
V'trs WD/WE–H–restricted SOC–Wed & Thurs
Fees £13 (£17)
Loc 2 miles N of Haywards Heath

Hill Barn (1935)

Public
Hill Barn Lane, Worthing
Tel **(0903) 37301**
Pro P Higgins
Holes 18 L 6224 yds Par 70
Recs Am–66 H Francis, B Roberts
Pro–63 J Kinsella
V'trs U
Fees £7 (£8)
Loc NE of A27 at Warren Road roundabout

Ifield (1927)

Private
Rusper Road, Ifield, Crawley
RH11 0LW
Tel **(0293) 20222**
Mem 800
Sec DT Howe
Pro C Strathearn (0293) 23088
Holes 18 L 6289 yds SSS 70
Recs Am–67 M Jarvis
Pro–65 P Mitchell, G Cowlishaw
V'trs WD–H WE–M
Fees WD–£15 D–£20
Loc Nr Crawley

Littlehampton (1889)

Private
170 Rope Walk, Littlehampton
BN17 5DL
Tel **(0903) 717170**
Mem 650
Sec KR Palmer (Sec/Mgr)
Pro CA Burgess (0903) 716369
Holes 18 L 6244 yds SSS 70
Recs Am–68 S Graham
Pro–66 L Giddings
V'trs WD–U after 9.30am WE/BH–NA before noon SOC
Fees £14 (£20)
Loc W bank of River Arun, Littlehampton

Mannings Heath (1908)

Private
Mannings Heath, Horsham
Tel **(0403) 210168**
Mem 800
Sec JD Coutts (0403) 210228
Pro M Denny (0403) 210332
Holes 18 L 6402 yds SSS 71
Recs Am–66 PG Way
Pro–64 C Ralph
V'trs WD–H–M after 5pm WE–NA SOC
Fees £15
Loc 3 miles SE of Horsham (A281)

Pyecombe (1894)

Private
Pyecombe, Brighton BN4 7FF
Tel **(079 18) 4176**
Mem 550
Sec WM Wise MA (079 18) 5372
Pro CR White (079 18) 5398
Holes 18 L 6234 yds SSS 70
Recs Am–68 J Enos
Pro–67 J Debenham
V'trs WD–U exc Tues after 9.45am Sat–U after 2pm Sun–U after 3pm SOC–WD exc Tues
Fees £12.50 (£25)
Loc 6 miles N of Brighton on A272

Selsey (1906)

Private
Golf Links Lane, Selsey PO20 9DR
Tel **(0243) 602203**
Mem 400
Sec EC Rackstraw (0243) 602029
Pro P Grindley
Holes 9 L 5932 yds SSS 68
Recs Am–66 A Kelly
V'trs U
Fees £9 (£12)
Loc 7 miles S of Chichester

Tilgate (1982)

Public
Titmus Drive, Tilgate, Crawley
Tel **(0293) 30103**
Mem 235
Sec M Fearnside (0293) 30657
Pro H Spencer, D McClelland (0293) 545411
Holes 18 L 6359 yds SSS 70
Recs Am–74 (1988)
V'trs U SOC–WD only
Fees £5.60 D–£10.70 (£8.40)
Loc $1^1/_2$ miles SE of Crawley

West Chiltington (1988)

Public
Broadford Bridge Road, W. Chiltington
RH20 2YA
Tel **(07983) 3574**
Mem 750
Sec Sqn Ldr GR Linder
Pro BW Barnes (07983) 2115
Holes 18 L 5969 yds SSS 69
V'trs U SOC
Fees £7.50 (£9)
Loc 2 miles E of Pulborough
Mis Driving range

West Sussex (1930)

Private
Pulborough RH20 2EN
Tel **(079 82) 2563**
Mem 800
Sec GR Martindale
Pro T Packham (079 82) 2426
Holes 18 L 6156 yds SSS 70
Recs Am–63 DJ Harrison
V'trs I H after 9.30am Tues–M SOC–Wed & Thurs
Fees On application
Loc 2 miles from Pulborough A283

For map index see page 203.

Worthing (1905)

Private
Links Road, Worthing BN14 9QZ
Tel **(0903) 60801**
Mem 1200
Sec Maj RB Carroll
Pro S Rolley (0903) 60718
Holes Lower 18 L 6477 yds SSS 72
Upper 18 L 5243 yds SSS 66
Recs Lower Am–61 MV Jones
Pro–61 T Haliburton
V'trs WD–U WE–confirm in advance with Sec
Fees £18 (£22)
Loc Central Station $1^1/_2$ miles on A27

Tyne & Wear

Backworth (1937)

Private
The Hall, Backworth, Shiremoor, Newcastle-upon-Tyne ME27 0AH
Tel **(091) 268 1048**
Mem 400
Sec Correspondence to Hon Sec
Holes 9 L 5930 yds SSS 69
Recs Am–66
V'trs Mon & Fri–U Tues–Thurs–M after 5pm WE–after 12.30pm exc comp Sats–after 6pm
Fees £5 (£6.25)
Loc Off Tyne Tunnel link road, Holystone roundabout

Birtley (Portobello) (1922)

Private
Portobello Road, Birtley DH3 2LR
Tel **(091) 410 2207**
Mem 220
Sec GK Blain (091) 410 0710
Holes 9 L 5640 yds SSS 67
Recs Am–64 G Hammond
V'trs WD–U WE/BH–M SOC
Fees £5 (£5) W–£15
Loc Birtley service area 3 miles on A1(M)

Boldon (1912)

Private
Dipe Lane, East Boldon
Tel **(091) 536 4182**
Mem 600
Sec RE Jobes (091) 536 5360
Pro Phipps Golf (091) 536 5835
Holes 18 L 6348 yds SSS 70
Recs Am–67 GR Simpson (1987)
Pro–66 P Tupling (1980)
V'trs U
Fees £7 (£9)
Loc East Boldon

City of Newcastle (1892)

Private
Three Mile Bridge, Great North Road, Gosforth, Newcastle-upon-Tyne NE3 2DR
Tel **(091) 285 1775**
Mem 400 110(L) 60(J)
Sec AJ Mathew
Pro AJ Matthew (091) 285 5481
Holes 18 L 6508 yds SSS 71
Recs Am–67 N Graham (1985)
Pro–67 W Tyrie (1988)
V'trs U
Fees £8.50 (£12.50)
Loc A1, 3 miles N of city

Close House (1968)

Private
Close House, Heddon on the wall, Newcastle-upon-Tyne NE15 0HT
Tel **(0661) 852953**
Mem 850
Sec Mrs L Steel (0661) 852303
Holes 18 L 5511 yds SSS 67
Recs Am–66 W Parker (1984), R Ingham (1986)
V'trs M SOC–WD
Loc 9 miles W of Newcastle on A69

Garesfield (1922)

Private
Chopwell NE17 7AP
Tel **(0207) 561278/561309**
Mem 440
Sec JE Ward (091) 414 3838
Pro (0207) 561309
Holes 18 L 6196 yds SSS 70
Recs Am–69 A McClure
Pro–70 D Dunk
V'trs U SOC
Fees £4.50 (£6)
Loc 7 miles SW of Newcastle between High Spen and Chopwell

George Washington Hotel

Private
Stone Cellar Road, Washington
Mem 350
Sec D Brown (091) 417 3335
Pro G Harle D Race (091) 417 8346
Holes 18 L 6604 yds SSS 72
Recs Am–71 D Armstrong (1984)
Pro–66 N Briggs (1987)
V'trs U
Fees £4 (£5.50)
Loc By A1(M)–North turning to Washington
Mis Hotel. Driving range

Gosforth (1906)

Private
Broadway East, Gosforth, Newcastle-upon-Tyne NE3 5ER
Tel **(091) 285 6710**
Mem 360 100(L) 80(J) 40(5)
Sec HV Smith (091) 285 3495
Pro D Race (091) 285 0553
Holes 18 L 6030 yds SSS 69
Recs Am–67 J Hattrick (1987)
V'trs U SOC
Fees £7.50 (£10)
Loc 3 miles N of Newcastle on A6125

Gosforth Park (1971)

Public
High Gosforth Park, Newcastle 3
Tel **(0632) 364480/364867**
Mem 450
Sec G Garland
Pro A Mair
Holes 18 L 5807 yds SSS 68 Par 70
Recs Am–68 A Ingles
Pro–65 H Thomson
V'trs U
Fees £4 (£4.50)
Loc 5 miles N of Newcastle
Mis 9 hole pitch & putt course

Heworth (1912)

Private
Gingling Gate, Heworth, Gateshead
Tel **(091) 469 2137**
Mem 600
Sec G Holbrow (091) 469 9832
Holes 18 L 6462 yds SSS 71
Recs Am–65 D Moralee
Pro–69 P Highmoor
V'trs WD–U WE–after noon
Fees £5 (£7.50)
Loc SE boundary of Gateshead

Houghton-le-Spring (1912)

Private
Copt Hill Links, Houghton-le-Spring
Tel **(091) 584 1198**
Mem 500
Sec N Wales
Pro M Daubney (0783) 584 7421
Holes 18 L 6416 yds SSS 71
Recs Am–69 J Hogg
V'trs U SOC
Fees £8 (£12)
Loc 6 miles SW of Sunderland

Newcastle United (1890)

Private
60 Ponteland Road, Newcastle-upon-Tyne NE5 3JW
Tel **(091) 286 9998(shop)**
(091) 286 4693 (clubhouse)
Mem 500
Sec J Simpson
Holes 18 L 6484 yds SSS 71
Recs Am–69 J Simmonds
V'trs WD–U WE–M SOC
Fees £5
Loc Nuns Moor, Cowgate

Northumberland (1898)

Private
High Gosforth Park, Newcastle-upon-Tyne NE3 5HT
Tel **(091) 236 2009**
Mem 500
Sec D Lamb (091) 236 2498

Holes 18 L 6629 yds SSS 72
Recs Am–68 DP Davidson, PWS Bent, DM Moffat
Pro–65 A Jacklin, T Horton
V'trs WD–I WE/BH–M
Fees £15
Loc 4 miles N of Newcastle-upon-Tyne

Ravensworth (1906)

Private
Mossheaps, Wrekenton, Gateshead NE9 7UU
Tel **(091) 487 6014/2843**
Mem 480
Sec JN Davison (091) 469 3782
Holes 18 L 5872 yds SSS 68
Recs Am–63 IR Hornsby, B Collingwood
Pro–64 T Horton
V'trs U
Fees £5.75 (£6.90)
Loc 3 miles S of Newcastle-upon-Tyne

Ryton (1891)

Private
nr Stanners, Clara Vale NE40 3TD
Tel **(091) 413 3737**
Mem 300
Sec B Swinbanks (091) 413 2459
Holes 18 L 6300 yds SSS 69
Recs Am–69 PR Brongham
V'trs WD–U WE–U exc 8–9.30am and 12–1.30pm SOC
Fees £4 (£6)
Loc 7 miles W of Newcastle-upon-Tyne, off A69

South Shields (1893)

Private
Cleadon Hills, South Shields NE34 8EG
Tel **(091) 456 0475**
Mem 700
Sec WH Loades (091) 456 8942
Pro G Parsons (091) 456 0110
Holes 18 L 6264 yds SSS 70
Recs Am–65 J Ellwood (1988)
Pro–64 M Gregson
V'trs U SOC–WD
Fees £7 (£10)
Loc Cleadon Hills, South Shields

Tynemouth (1913)

Private
Spital Dene, Tynemouth, North Shields NE30 2ER
Tel **(091) 257 4578**
Mem 854
Sec A Turnbull (091) 257 3381
Pro J McKenna (091) 258 0728
Holes 18 L 6351 yds SSS 70
Recs Am–66 CR Hinson
Pro–64 J Ord
V'trs WD–U SOC Sat/Sun am–NA
Fees £6.50 (£8.50) W–£22 F–£40
Loc E of Newcastle-upon-Tyne

Tyneside (1879)

Private
Westfield Lane, Ryton NE40 3QE
Tel **(091) 413 2177**
Mem 660
Sec JR Watkin (091) 413 2742
Pro M Gunn (091) 413 3626
Holes 18 L 6055 yds SSS 69
Recs Am–66 J Surtees, M Dunn, PS Highmoor
Pro–65 JR Harrison
V'trs WD–U (exc 11.30–1.30pm) WE–NA before 3pm SOC
Fees £9 (£14)
Loc 7 miles W of Newcastle. S of river, off A695

Wallsend (1973)

Public
Bigges Main, Wallsend
Tel **(091) 262 4231**
Mem 800
Sec J Heddon (091) 262 8478
Pro P Eaton
Holes 18 L 6459 yds SSS 72
V'trs U
Fees £4.50 (£5.50)
Loc W boundary

Washington (1979)

Public
Stone Cellar Road, Washington
Tel **(091) 417 2626**
Mem 350
Sec D Brown
Pro D Howdon (091) 417 8346
Holes 18 L 6604 yds SSS 72
Par 3 course
Recs Am–70 R Clark (1986)
Pro–66 N Briggs (1987)
V'trs U
Fees £4.50 (£5.50)
Loc Washington District 12
Mis Driving range

Wearside (1892)

Private
Coxgreen, Sunderland SR4 9JT
Tel **(091) 534 2518**
Mem 650
Sec KD Wheldon
Pro (091) 534 4269
Holes 18 L 6315 yds SSS 70
Recs Am–67 L Naisby, D Curry, D Wood
Pro–68 A Bickerdike
V'trs WD–H WE–MH SOC
Fees £7 D–£9 (£10)
Loc 2 miles W of Sunderland, off A183. $^1/_4$ mile W of A19

Westerhope

Private
Whorlton Grange, Westerhope, Newcastle-upon-Tyne NE5 1PP
Tel **(091) 286 9125**
Mem 700
Sec RW Bate (091) 286 7636
Pro A Crosby (091) 286 0594
Holes 18 L 6407 yds SSS 71
Recs Am–66 A Morrison, R Roper
Pro–67 D Russell
V'trs U
Fees £7 (£8.50)
Loc 5 miles W of Newcastle

Whickham (1911)

Private
Hollinside Park, Whickham, Newcastle-upon-Tyne NE16 5BA
Tel **(091) 488 7309**
Mem 500
Sec N Weightman (091) 488 1576
Pro P Davies (091) 488 8591
Holes 18 L 6129 yds SSS 69
Recs Am–68
V'trs U
Fees £7 (£10)
Loc 5 miles SW of Newcastle-upon-Tyne

Whitburn (1931)

Private
Lizard Lane, South Shields NE34 7AF
Tel **(091) 529 2144**
Mem 331 73(L) 61(J) 79(5)
Sec Dr R Blakey (091) 567 4636
Pro D Stephenson (091) 529 4210
Holes 18 L 6035 yds SSS 69
Recs Am–65 KW Fleming (1988)
Pro–70 M Gunn
V'trs U SOC
Fees £6.50 (£7.50)
Loc 2 miles N of Sunderland on coast road. Bus route 539

Whitley Bay (1890)

Private
Claremount Road, Whitley Bay NE26 3UF
Tel **(091) 252 0180**
Mem 700
Sec B Dockar
Pro WJ Light (091) 252 5688
Holes 18 L 6614 yds SSS 72
Recs Am–68 GJ Clark
Pro–66 J Fourie
V'trs WD–U WE–M
Fees £10
Loc 10 miles E of Newcastle-upon-Tyne

Warwickshire

Atherstone (1894)

Private
The Outwoods, Atherstone
Tel **(0827) 713110**
Mem 224 40(L) 36(J)
Sec AG Sarson (082 77) 714579
Holes 18 L 6239 SSS 70
Recs Am–66 M Reay
Pro–65

For map index see page 203.

V'trs SOC–WD only
Fees D–£10
Loc Atherstone $^1/_2$ mile
Mis

City of Coventry (Brandon Wood) (1977)

Public
Brandon Lane, Coventry
Tel **(0203) 3141**
Mem 550
Sec RD Reynolds (0203) 85032
Pro C Gledhill
Holes 18 L 6530 yds SSS 71
Pro–68 AR Sadler
V'trs U
Fees £2.50 (£5.50)
Loc 6 miles SE of city centre

Kenilworth (1889)

Private
Crew Lane, Kenilworth
Tel **(0926) 54296**
Mem 830
Sec BV Edwards (0926) 58517
Pro S Mouland (0926) 512732
Holes 18 L 6408 yds SSS 71
Recs Am–69 P Broadbent
V'trs U
Fees £11 (£15)
Loc 5 miles S of Coventry

Ladbrook Park (1908)

Private
Poolhead Lane, Tamworth-in-Arden, Solihull B94 5ED
Tel **(056) 44 2220 (Members)**
Mem 708
Sec Mrs GP Taylor (056) 44 2264
Pro GR Taylor (056) 44 2581
Holes 18 L 6407 yds SSS 71
Recs Am–67 PJ Sant
Pro–65 RDS Livingston
V'trs WD–UH WE/BH–M
Fees £11
Loc 12 miles S of Birmingham

Leamington & County (1908)

Private
Golf Lane, Whitnash, Leamington Spa CV31 2QA
Tel **(0926) 20298**
Mem 600
Sec SM Cooknell (0926) 25961
Pro I Grant (0926) 28014
Holes 18 L 6430 yds SSS 71
Recs Am–65 RG Hiatt
Pro–66 D Thomas
V'trs U SOC
Fees £10 D–£13 (£14)
Loc $1^1/_2$ miles S of Leamington Spa

Maxstoke Park (1896)

Private
Castle Lane, Coleshill, Birmingham B46 2RD
Tel **(0675) 621518**
Mem 450
Sec JC Evans (Hon)
Pro RA Young (0675) 64915
Holes 18 L 6460 yds SSS 71
Recs Am–66 AM Allen
Pro–71 PJ Butler
V'trs WD–U WE–M
Fees £12
Loc 3 miles S of Coleshill

Newbold Comyn (1973)

Public
Newbold Terrace East, Leamington Spa
Tel **(0926) 21157**
Mem 408
Sec A Pierce (0926) 22660
Pro D Knight
Holes 18 L 6221 yds SSS 70
Recs Am–70 G Knight
Pro–S Hutchinson (1987)
V'trs U
Fees £3.20 (£4.20)
Loc Off Willes Road (B4099)

Nuneaton (1906)

Private
Golf Drive, Whitestone, Nuneaton
Tel **(0203) 347810**
(0203) 344268 (Steward)
Mem 650
Sec T Rosser
Pro PF Kowalik (0203) 340201
Holes 18 L 6412 yds SSS 71
Recs Am–67 P Broadhurst
Pro–67 C Holmes
V'trs WD–U H WE–M SOC
Fees £12
Loc 2 miles S Nuneaton

Purley Chase (1980)

Private
Pipers Lane, Ridge Lane, Nuneaton CV10 0RB
Tel **(0203) 393118**
Mem 600
Sec RG Place
Pro M Chamberlain (0203) 395348
Holes 18 L 6604 yds SSS 71
Recs Am–72 P Broadhurst
Pro–64 P Elson
V'trs WD/BH–U WE–U after 2.30pm SOC
Fees £8 (£10) D–£12 (£15)
Loc 4 miles WNW of Nuneaton on B4114 (A47). $1^1/_2$ miles SW of A5 Mancetter Island
Mis 13 bay driving range

Rugby (1891)

Private
Clifton Road, Rugby CV21 3RD
Tel **(0788) 542306**
Mem 550
Sec B Poxon (0788) 810066
Pro D Sutherland (0788) 75134
Holes 18 L 5457 yds SSS 67
Recs Am–65 R Clynick
Pro–68 D Sutherland
V'trs WD–U WE/BH–M SOC
Fees £9.50 R/D
Loc 1 mile N of Rugby on B5414

Stratford-on-Avon (1894)

Private
Tiddington Road, Stratford-on-Avon
Tel **(0789) 414546**
Mem 770
Sec JH Standbridge (0789) 205749
Pro ND Powell (0789) 205677
Holes 18 L 6309 yds SSS 70
Recs Am–67 PB Rodgers, NCF Dainton
Pro–65 J Whitehead
V'trs U
Fees On application
Loc $^1/_2$ mile E on B4086

Warwick (1971)

Public
Warwick Golf Centre, Racecourse, Warwick
Tel **(0926) 494316**
Mem 90
Sec Mrs R Dunkley
Pro S Baldwin (0926) 491284
Holes 9 L 2612 yds SSS 66
Recs Am–64 S Hill
Pro–63 S Hutchinson
V'trs No play while racing in progress
Fees £1.40 (£1.70)
Loc Centre of racecourse
Mis Driving range

Welcombe Hotel

Private
Warwick Road, Stratford-on-Avon CV37 0NR
Tel **(0789) 295252**
Sec PJ Day (Golf)
BAK Miller (Hotel)
Holes 18 L 6202 yds SSS 70
Recs Am–67 R Fletcher
V'trs WD–U(H preferred)
WE/BH–UH after noon
Fees £12 (£15)
Loc Stratford $1^1/_2$ miles (A46)

West Midlands

The Belfry (1977)

Public
Wishaw, North Warks B76 9PR
Tel **(0675) 70301**
Sec SD Butler Ext 280
Pro P McGovern Ext 267
Holes Brabazon 18 L 6975 yds SSS 73
Derby 18 L 6127 yds SSS 70
Recs Brabazon Pro–63 E Darcy
Derby Pro–69 J Brown
V'trs U
Fees Brabazon £20 (£22)
Derby £9 (£11)
Loc 4 miles N of M6 Junction 4

Bloxwich (1924)

Private
Stafford Road, Bloxwich WS3 3PQ
Tel **(0922) 405724**
Mem 475
Sec JC Minister
Pro B Janes (0922) 476889
Holes 18 L 6277 yds SSS 70
Recs Am–67 JPG Windsor
Pro–65 J Rhodes
V'trs WD–U WE–M SOC
Fees D–£11
Loc On A34 N of Walsall

Boldmere

Public
Monmouth Drive, Birmingham, Sutton Coldfield
Tel **(021) 354 3379**
Sec D Dufty
Pro T Short
Holes 18 L 4463 yds SSS 62
Recs Am–57 G Marston (1987)
Pro–57 P Weaver (1987)
V'trs U
Fees £3.80 (£4.20)
Loc By Sutton Park, 1 mile from centre of Sutton Coldfield

Brand Hall (1946)

Public
Heron Road, Oldbury, Warley
Tel **(021) 552 7475**
(Pro Shop)/2195
Mem 250
Sec WH Rushton (021) 544 6184
Pro B Bates (021) 552 2195
Holes 18 L 5813 yds SSS 68
Recs Am–66 M Curry
Pro–69 G Henderson
V'trs U exc first 2 hrs Sat/Sun
Fees £2.30
Loc 6 miles NW of Birmingham. M5 Junction 2, $1^1/_2$ miles

Calderfields

Private
Aldridge Road, Walsall
WS4 2JS
Tel **(0922) 32243**
Mem 550
Sec CA Andrews (0922) 640540
Pro A Rawlings (0922) 32243
Holes 18 L 6026 yds SSS 69
Recs Am–66 S Meek (1986)
Pro–67 S Doe (1987)
V'trs U
Fees £6 (£7.50)
Loc 1 mile N of Walsall

Cocks Moor Woods (1926)

Public
Alcester Road, South King's Heath, Birmingham BK1 6ER
Tel **(021) 444 2062**
Mem 250
Sec JW Black (021) 742 6317
Pro KF Dodsworth (021) 444 3584
Holes 18 L 5742 yds SSS 67
Recs Am–65 V Pailing
Pro–71 B Jones, K Dodsworth
V'trs U
Fees £3.50 (£3.80)
Loc $6^1/_2$ miles S of city centre

Copt Heath (1910)

Private
1220 Warwick Road, Knowle, Solihull
B93 9LN
Tel **(0564) 772650**
Mem 700
Sec W Lenton
Pro BJ Barton
Holes 18 L 6504 yds SSS 71
Recs Am–66 P McEvoy
Pro–65 BJ Barton
V'trs WD–M or I WE/BH–M
Fees £15
Loc 2 miles S of Solihull on A41

Coventry (1887)

Private
Finham Park, Coventry CV3 6PJ
Tel **(0203) 411123**
Mem 750
Sec MSH Tott (0203) 414152
Pro P Weaver (0203) 411298
Holes 18 L 6613 yds SSS 72
Recs Am–66 P Downes
Pro–66 P Weaver
V'trs WD–H
Fees £15
Loc 2 miles S of Coventry on A444

Coventry Hearsall (1896)

Private
Beechwood Avenue, Coventry
CV5 6DF
Tel **(0203) 713470**
Mem 450
Sec WG Doughty
Pro T Rouse (0203) 713156
Holes 18 L 5963 yds SSS 69
Recs Am–70 J Marley (1987)
Pro–66 B Morris (1987)
V'trs WD–U WE–M
Fees £11
Loc $1^1/_2$ miles S of city centre

Dartmouth (1910)

Private
Vale Street, West Bromwich
B71 4DW
Tel **(021) 588 2131**
Mem 250
Sec RH Smith
Holes 18 L 6060 yds SSS 69
Recs Am–68 P Griffiths
Pro–70 P Lester
V'trs WD–U WE–restricted
Fees £9
Loc 1 mile from town centre behind Churchfields High School. Nr Junction M5/M6

Druids Heath (1974)

Private
Stonnall Road, Aldridge
WS9 8JZ
Tel **(0922) 55595**
Mem 500 40(L) 35(J)
Sec LN Sedgley
Pro J Pearsall (0922) 59523
Holes 18 L 6914 yds SSS 73
Recs Am–69 M Pearce
V'trs WD–U WE–M
Fees £10 (£15)
Loc 6 miles NW of Sutton Coldfield

Dudley (1894)

Private
Turners Hill, Rowley Regis, Warley
Tel **(0384) 53719**
Mem 300
Sec RP Fortune (0384) 233877
Pro D Down (0384) 54020
Holes 18 L 5715 yds SSS 67
Recs Am–66 AA Davies
Pro–63 R Livingstone
V'trs WD–U WE–M
Fees £8.50
Loc 2 miles S of Dudley

Edgbaston (1896)

Private
Church Road, Birmingham B15 3TB
Tel **(021) 454 1736**
Mem 830
Sec Maj DB Sullivan
Pro A Bownes (021) 454 3226
Holes 18 L 6118 yds SSS 69
Recs Am–67 T Allen
Pro–65 J Rhodes
V'trs U
Fees £14.50 (£18.50)
Loc S of city centre

Enville (1935)

Private
Highgate Common, Enville,
nr Stourbridge DY7 5BN
Tel **(0384) 872551**
Mem 900
Sec RJ Bannister (Sec/Mgr)
(0384) 872074
Pro RH Hinton (0384) 872585
Holes Highgate 18 L 6451 yds SSS 72
Lodge 18 L 6207 yds SSS 70
Recs Highgate Am–68 A Stubbs
Pro–66 PH Hinton
Lodge Am–70 R Clayes
V'trs WD–U WE/BH–M H SOC
Fees £15 D–£20
Loc 6 miles W of Stourbridge
Mis Buggies for hire

Forest of Arden G & CC

Private
Maxstoke Lane, Meriden, Coventry
CV7 7HR
Tel **(0676) 22118**
Mem 600
Sec KJ Shaw (Mgr)
Pro M Tarn

Holes 18 L 6900 yds Par 72
V'trs U SOC
Fees £12 (£15)
Loc Off A45 Birmingham–Coventry road. M42 Junction 6. M6 Junction 4. NEC 3 miles

Fulford Heath (1934)

Private
Tanners Green Lane, Wythall, Birmingham B47 6BH
Tel **(0564) 822806 (clubhouse)**
(0564) 824758 (office)
Mem 675
Sec RG Bowen (021) 705 5480
Pro KA Hayward (0564) 822930
Holes 18 L 6256 yds SSS 70
Recs Am–66 KJ Miller
Pro–67 M James
V'trs WD–H WE/BH–M SOC
Fees £12 D–£15
Loc 8 miles S of Birmingham

Gay Hill (1913)

Private
Hollywood Lane, Alcester Road, Birmingham B47 5PP
Tel **(021) 430 6523/7077**
Mem 700
Sec Mrs EK Devitt (021) 430 8544
Pro A Hill (021) 474 6001
Holes 18 L 6532 yds SSS 71
Recs Am–68 MJ Duggan
Pro–66 R Livingston
V'trs WD–U WE–M SOC
Fees £12.50
Loc 7 miles S of city on A435.
M42 Junction 3, 3 miles

Grange (1924)

Private
Copsewood, Coventry CV3 1HS
Tel **(0203) 451465**
Mem 350
Sec E Soutar (0203) 446324
Pro A Bowles
Holes 9 L 6002 yds SSS 69
V'trs WD–U before 2.30pm Sat–NA Sun–NA before noon
Fees £5 D–£7
Loc East Coventry

Great Barr (1961)

Private
Chapel Lane, Birmingham B43 7BA
Tel **(021) 357 1232**
Mem 600
Sec K Pembridge (021) 358 4376
Pro SM Doe (021) 357 5270
Holes 18 L 6545 yds SSS 72
Recs Am–69 AR Eden
Pro–71 J Higgins
V'trs WD–U WE–I (h'cap max 18)
Fees £12
Loc 6 miles NW of Birmingham. M6 Junction 7

Hagley (1980)

Private
Wassell Grove, Gagley, nr Stourbridge
Tel **(0562) 883701**
Mem 600
Sec VC Lewis
Holes 18 L 6353 SSS 72
V'trs WD–U exc Wed before 1.30pm WE–M after 1pm SOC–WD
Fees £10

Halesowen (1909)

Private
The Leasowes, Halesowen B62 8QF
Tel **(021) 550 1041**
Mem 600
Sec IJ Hodgetts (021) 501 3606
Pro M Smith (021) 503 0593
Holes 18 L 5754 yds SSS 68
Recs Am–65 D Henn
Pro–66
V'trs WD–U WE–M SOC–WD exc Wed
Fees £8
Loc M5 Junction 3, 2 miles

Handsworth (1895)

Private
Sunningdale Close, Handsworth Wood, Birmingham B20 1NP
Tel **(021) 554 0599**
Mem 720
Sec RL Neale (Hon)
Pro M Hicks (021) 523 3594
Holes 18 L 6297 yds SSS 70
Recs Am–65 DJ Russell
Pro–71 HF Boyce
V'trs WD–U WE/BH–M SOC
Fees £12 (£12)
Loc 3 miles NW of city centre

Harborne (1893)

Private
40 Tennal Road, Harborne, Birmingham B32 2JE
Tel **(021) 427 1728**
Mem 500
Sec RA Eddy (021) 427 3058 (am)
Pro A Quarterman (021) 427 3512
Holes 18 L 6240 yds SSS 70
Recs Am–65 JA Fisher, R Ellis
Pro–65 E Cogle
V'trs WD–U WE/BH–M SOC
Fees £12 R/D
Loc 3 miles SW of centre. M5 Junction 3

Harborne Church Farm

Public
Vicarage Road, Harborne, Birmingham B17 0SN
Tel **(021) 427 1204**
Mem 200
Sec P Johnston (021) 501 3001
Pro S Malin
Holes 9 L 4514 yds SSS 62
Recs Am–63 J Sankey
Pro–60 PR Rudge
V'trs U
Fees 18 holes £2.50
9 holes £1.25
Loc 5 miles SW of city centre

Hatchford Brook (1969)

Public
Coventry Road, Sheldon, Birmingham B26 3PY
Tel **(021) 743 9821**
Mem 350
Sec D Williams (0676) 23383
Pro P Smith
Holes 18 L 6164 yds SSS 69
Recs Am–69 A Allen (1987)
Pro–68 P Smith (1988)
V'trs U SOC–NA
Fees £4.25
Loc City boundary close to airport. A45/M42 Junction

Hilltop (1979)

Public
Park Lane, Handsworth, Birmingham B21 8LJ
Tel **(021) 554 4463 (Pro)**
(021) 551 3229 (Members)
Sec TJ James
Pro K Highfield
Holes 18 L 6114 yds Par 71 SSS 69
Recs Am–66 H Ali
Pro–65 BN Jones
V'trs U
Fees £3.40 (£4.30)
Loc M5 West Brom opposite Hawthorns Football Ground

Himley Hall (1980)

Public
Himley Hall Park, Dudley
Tel **(0902) 895207**
Mem 80
Sec DA Baker/WG Cox
Holes 9 L 3090 yds SSS 34
V'trs WD–U WE/BH–restricted
Fees 18 holes £2.90 (£3.60)
9 holes £1.90 (£2.40)
Loc Grounds of Himley Hall Park, nr Dudley

Lickey Hills

Public
Rednal, Birmingham
Tel **(021) 453 3159**
Pro MS March
Holes 18 L 6010 yds SSS 69
Recs Am–74 MSR Lunt
Pro–72 R Livingston
V'trs U
Fees £2 (£2)
Loc 10 miles SW of city centre
Mis Rose Hill Club plays here

Little Aston (1908)

Private
Streetly, Sutton Coldfield B74 3AN
Tel **(021) 353 2066**
Mem 250
Sec NH Russell (021) 353 2942

Pro J Anderson (021) 353 2942
Holes 18 L 6724 yds SSS 73
Recs Am–66
Pro–68
V'trs WD–U WE/BH–I XL Sat/Sun am SOC
Fees £18 Apr–Oct. £14 Nov–Mar
Loc 4 miles NW of Sutton Coldfield

Moor Hall (1932)

Private
Four Oaks, Sutton Coldfield
Tel (021) 308 6130
Mem 525
Sec WC Brodie (021) 351 2232
Pro A Partridge (021) 308 5106
Holes 18 L 6219 yds SSS 70
Recs Am–66 GW Tilbrook
Pro–67 NR McDonald
V'trs WD–U after 12.30pm Thurs WE/BH–M
Fees £15
Loc 1 mile E of Sutton

Moseley (1892)

Private
Springfield Road, King's Heath, Birmingham B14 7DX
Tel (021) 444 2115
Mem 600
Sec PT Muddiman (021) 444 4957 (10am–1pm)
Pro G Edge (021) 444 2063
Holes 18 L 6227 yds SSS 70
Recs Am–64 A Forrester
Pro–64 FE Miller
V'trs M or I
Fees £20
Loc S Birmingham

North Warwickshire (1894)

Private
Hampton Lane, Meriden, Coventry CV7 7LL
Tel (0676) 22259
Mem 400
Sec EG Barnes (0676) 22915 (office)
Pro D Bradley
Holes 9 L 6362 yds SSS 70
Recs Am–67 P Broadhurst, M Biddle
V'trs WD–U WE/BH–M SOC
Fees £10 (£14)
Loc Coventry 6 miles. Birmingham 13 miles

North Worcestershire (1907)

Private
Frankley Beeches Road, Northfield, Birmingham B31 5LP
Tel (021) 475 1047
Mem 550
Sec KS Reading
Pro K Jones (021) 475 5721
Holes 18 L 5907 yds SSS 69
Recs Am–64 DJ Russell
Pro–63 K Dickens (1988)
V'trs WD–U WE/BH–M
Fees £9 plus VAT
Loc 7 miles SW of Birmingham

Olton (1893)

Private
Mirfield Road, Solihull B91 1JH
Tel (021) 705 1083
Mem 600
Sec MA Perry (0564) 777953
Pro D Playdon (021) 705 7296
Holes 18 L 6229 yds SSS 71
Recs Am–65 T Allen
Pro–66 D Llewellyn
V'trs WD–U exc Wed am WE–M
Fees £12
Loc 7 miles S of Birmingham

Oxley Park (1914)

Private
Stafford Road, Bushbury, Wolverhampton WV10 6DE
Tel (0902) 20506
Mem 400
Sec FGE Hill (0902) 25892 (mornings)
Pro LA Burlison (0902) 25445
Holes 18 L 6153 yds SSS 69
Recs Am–64 CS White
Pro–65 D Thorp, P Weaver
V'trs U SOC
Fees £9 (£12)
Loc $1\frac{1}{2}$ miles N of Wolverhampton

Patshull Park (1980)

Private
Pattingham, Shropshire WV6 7HR
Tel (0902) 700100
Mem 325
Sec T Gray
Pro D McDowall
Holes 18 L 6412 yds SSS 71
Recs Am–69 D Evans
Pro–67 R Green
V'trs U SOC
Fees £9 (£12)
Loc Wolverhampton 7 miles. M54 Junction 3, 5 miles

Penn (1908)

Private
Penn Common, Wolverhampton
Tel (0902) 341142
Mem 500
Sec PW Thorrington
Pro A Briscoe (0902) 330472
Holes 18 L 6465 yds SSS 71
Recs Am–68 RJ Green
Pro–70 J Rhodes, R Cameron
V'trs WD–U WE–M SOC
Fees £10
Loc 2 miles SW of Wolverhampton

Pype Hayes (1932)

Public
Eachelhurst Road, Walmley, Sutton Coldfield B76 8EP
Tel (021) 351 1014
Mem 400
Sec LJ Rose (021) 783 4920
Pro JF Bayliss
Holes 18 L 5811 yds SSS 68
Recs Am–62 L Jacks (1985)
Pro–59 J Cawsey (1954)
V'trs U
Fees £4
Loc 5 miles NE of Birmingham

Robin Hood (1893)

Private
St Bernards Road, Solihull B92 7DJ
Tel (021) 706 0159
Mem 650
Sec KH Ellson MBE TD (021) 706 0061
Pro FE Miller (021) 706 0806
Holes 18 L 6609 yds SSS 72
Recs Am–68 J Draper (1988)
Pro–68 A Miller
V'trs WD–U WE/BH–M SOC–WD
Fees £13.50
Loc 7 miles S of Birmingham

Rose Hill (1921)

Private
Rednal, Birmingham
Tel (021) 453 3159
Mem 275
Sec A Cushing (021) 453 2846
Holes Play over Lickey Hills Public Course

Sandwell Park (1896)

Private
Birmingham Road, West Bromwich B71 4JJ
Tel (021) 553 0260
Mem 650
Sec CP Elliott (Mgr) (021) 553 4637
Pro AW Mutton (021) 553 4384
Holes 18 L 6470 yds SSS 72
Recs Am–67 B Charlton (1983)
Pro–67 J Rhodes
V'trs WD–U WE–MH SOC–WD
Fees £10 D–£14
Loc West Bromwich/Birmingham boundary. M5 Junction 1

Shirley (1956)

Private
Stratford Road, Monkspath, Shirley, Solihull B90 4EW
Tel (021) 744 6001
Mem 450
Sec AJ Phillips
Pro C Wicketts (021) 745 4979
Holes 18 L 6510 yds SSS 71
Recs Am–68 M Payne
Pro–68
V'trs WD–U WE–M

Fees £13
Loc 8 miles S of B'ham. 400 yds city side of M42 Junction 4

South Staffordshire (1892)

Private
Danescourt Road, Tettenhall, Wolverhampton WV6 9BQ
Tel **(0902) 751065**
Mem 600
Sec H Williams
Pro J Rhodes (0902) 754816
Holes 18 L 6621 yds SSS 72
Recs Am–67 D Gifford
Pro–66 A Sadler
V'trs WD–U WE/BH–M SOC
Fees £12 D–£15
Loc 3 miles W of Wolverhampton

Sphinx (1948)

Private
Siddeley Avenue, Coventry
Tel **(0203) 458890**
Mem 400
Sec GE Brownbridge (0203) 597731
Holes 9 L 4104 yds SSS 60
Recs Am–62 PR Thorpe
V'trs U
Fees £3

Stourbridge (1892)

Private
Worcester Lane, Pedmore, Stourbridge
Tel **(0384) 393062**
Mem 720
Sec FR McLachlan (0384) 395566
Pro WH Firkins (0384) 393129
Holes 18 L 6178 yds SSS 69
Recs Am–65 J Fisher
Pro–63 WH Firkins
V'trs WD–U exc Wed before 4pm–M WE/BH–M
Fees £11

Sutton Coldfield (1889)

Private
Thornhill Road, Sutton Coldfield
Tel **(021) 353 2014**
Mem 517
Sec AJ Bishop, M McClean (021) 353 9633
Pro JK Hayes (021) 353 9633
Holes 18 L 6541 yds SSS 71
Recs Am–65 L Jacks
Pro–64 PA Elson
V'trs U
Fees £14 (£18)
Loc 9 miles N of Birmingham

Swindon (1986)

Private
Bridgnorth Road, Swindon, Dudley DY3 4PU
Tel **(0902) 897031**
Mem 500
Sec E Greenway (Mgr)
Pro P Lester (0902) 896191
Holes 18 L 6042 yds SSS 69
Recs Am–68 B Cotterill
Pro–68 K Bayliss
V'trs U SOC–WD
Fees £11 (£16.50)
Loc 5 miles from Wolverhampton, Dudley and Stourbridge on B4176
Mis Driving range

Walmley (Wylde Green) (1902)

Private
Brooks Road, Wylde Green, Sutton Coldfield B72 1HR
Tel **(021) 373 0029**
Mem 700
Sec JPG Windsor
Pro MJ Skerritt (021) 373 7103
Holes 18 L 6277 yds SSS 70
Recs Am–67 Broadhurst
Pro–68 J Higgins, A Stubbs, J Rhodes
V'trs WD–U WE–M
Fees £15
Loc N boundary of Birmingham

Walsall (1907)

Private
Broadway, Walsall
Tel **(0922) 22710**
Mem 700
Sec E Murray (0922) 613512
Pro R Lambert (0922) 26766
Holes 18 L 6232 yds SSS 70
Recs Am–66 RG Hiatt, D Blakeman
Pro–66 N Brunyard
V'trs WD–U WE–M SOC
Fees £12.50 (£18)
Loc 1 mile S of Walsall

Warley (1921)

Public
Lightwoods Hill, Warley
Tel **(021) 429 2440**
Mem 160
Sec C Lowndes (021) 236 6943
Pro D Owen
Holes 9 L 2606 yds SSS 64
Recs Am–62 M Daw
Pro–58 B Fereday
V'trs U
Fees £3.75
Loc 5 miles W of city centre

Wiltshire

Bremhill Park (1967)

Private
Shrivenham, Swindon
Tel **(0793) 782946**
Sec R Bentley (0793) 783846
Pro P Borham
Holes 18 L 5889 yds SSS 70
Recs Am–68
Pro–66 M Howell (1988)
V'trs U
Fees £8 (£10)
Loc 4 miles E of Swindon

Brinkworth (1984)

Private
Longmans Farm, Brinkworth, Chippenham SN15 5DG
Tel **(066 641) 277**
Mem 250
Sec R Sheppard
Holes 9 L 6086 yds SSS 69
V'trs U SOC
Fees £3 (£3.50) 1988 prices
Loc Brinkworth 2 miles on Wootton Bassett–Malmesbury road

Broome Manor (1976)

Public
Pipers Way, Swindon SN3 1RG
Tel **(0793) 32403**
Mem 650
Sec T Watt (Mgr)(0793) 495761
Pro B Sandry (0793) 32403
Holes 18 L 6359 yds SSS 70
9 L 2745 yds SSS 67
Recs Am–69 A Norman–Thorpe
Pro–66 M Bevan
V'trs U
Fees 18 holes £4.50 (£5)
9 holes £2.70 (£3)
Loc Swindon centre 2 miles
Mis 25 bay floodlit driving range

Chippenham (1896)

Private
Malmesbury Road, Chippenham
Tel **(0249) 652040**
Mem 600
Sec V J Carlisle
Pro W Creamer (0249) 655519
Holes 18 L 5540 yds SSS 67
Recs Am–62 M Darbyshire
Pro–64 B Sandry
V'trs H WE–M SOC
Fees £12 (£15)
Loc Town centre 1 mile. M4 Junction 17

High Post (1922)

Private
Great Durnford, Salisbury SP4 6AT
Tel **(0722) 73231**
Mem 600
Sec WWR Goodwin (0722) 73356
Pro AJ Harman (0722) 73219
Holes 18 L 6267 yds SSS 70
Recs Am–64 K Weeks, RJ Searle
Pro–65 P Alliss, N Sutton
V'trs WD–U WE/BH–H SOC
Fees £11 D–£14 (£16 R/D)
Loc 4 miles N of Salisbury on A345

Kingsdown (1880)

Private
Kingsdown, Corsham SN14 9BS
Tel **(0225) 742530**
Mem 475 100(L) 45(J)
Sec SH Phipps (0225) 743472
Pro R Emery (0225) 742634

Holes 18 L 6445 yds SSS 71
Recs Am–69 J Wallett (1988)
Pro–69 S Little (1988)
V'trs WD–U Comp days–M
Fees £12.50 (£15)
Loc 5 miles E of Bath

Marlborough (1888)

Private
The Common, Marlborough SN8 1DU
Tel (0672) 52147
Mem 710
Sec L Ross (Mgr), S Lynch (Admin)
Pro W McAdams (0672) 52493
Holes 18 L 6440 yds SSS 71
Recs Am–66 S Amor
Pro–67 J Cook
V'trs WD–U WE–H SOC
Fees £12.50 D–£15 (£20)
Loc 1 mile N of Marlborough (A345)

North Wilts (1890)

Private
Bishops' Cannings, Devizes SN10 2LP
Tel (038 086) 257
Mem 570 85(L) 28(J)
Sec Lt Cdr JBW McKelvie (038 086) 627
Pro G Laing (038 086) 330
Holes 18 L 5898 metres SSS 71
Recs Am–66 EAJ Pulleyblank
Pro–67 GJ Laing
V'trs U
Fees £10 (£12)
Loc 1 mile from A4 at Calne

RAF Upavon (1918)

Private
Upavon, Pewsey SN9 6BE
Tel (0980) 630787
Mem 300
Sec Sqn Ldr D Barnes (0980) 630351 Ext 207
Holes 9 L 5597 yds SSS 67
Recs Am–66 Wg Cdr RB Duckett
V'trs WD–U Sat am/Sun am–M SOC
Fees £6 (£8)
Loc Upavon 3 miles on A342 to Andover

RMCS Shrivenham (1953)

Private
RMCS Shrivenham, Swindon SN6 8LA
Tel (0793) 782551 Ext 2355
Mem 350
Sec GM Moss
Holes 9 L 5206 yds SSS 66
V'trs M SOC
Loc In grounds of Royal Military College of Science, Shrivenham. Entry must be arranged with Sec

Salisbury & South Wilts (1888)

Private
Netherhampton, Salisbury
Tel (0722) 742131
Mem 810
Sec Wg Cdr AW Pawson (0722) 742645
Pro G Emerson (0722) 742929
Holes 18 L 6130 yds SSS 70
9 L 2424 yds SSS 64
Recs Am–61 RS Blake
Pro–62 N Blenkarne
V'trs WD–U WE–H SOC
Fees £10 (£12)
Loc Salisbury 2 miles, Wilton 2 miles on A3094

Swindon (1907)

Private
Ogbourne St George, Marlborough, nr Swindon SN8 1TB
Tel (067 284) 217
Mem 600
Sec Mrs AL Lockwood (067 284) 327
Pro I Bolt (067 284) 287
Holes 18 L 6226 yds SSS 70
Recs Am–67 BF McCallum
Pro–65 I Bolt
V'trs U SOC–WD
Fees £8.50 (£13)
Loc On A345. 5 miles S of M4 Junction 15

West Wilts (1891)

Private
Elm Hill, Warminster BA12 0AU
Tel (0985) 212702
Mem 420 70(L) 55(J) 40(5)
Sec Maj LR Weaver (0985) 213133
Pro A Harvey (0985) 212110
Holes 18 L 5701 yds SSS 68
Recs Am–65 M Smith, C Burton
Pro–64 R Emery
V'trs U H
Fees £10.50 (£15)
Loc On A350

Yorkshire (North)

Aldwark Manor (1977)

Private
Aldwark Manor, Aldwark Alne, York YO6 2NF
Tel (03473) 353 (Golf shop)
Sec BC Horner (03473) 8146
Holes 9 L 2569 yds SSS 66
V'trs SOC
Fees £5 (£10) Hotel guests free use of course
Loc 5 miles SE of Boroughbridge off A1. 11½ miles NW of York off A19

Ampleforth College (1962)

Private
56 High Street, Helmsley, York YO6 5AE
Mem 130
Sec JE Atkinson (0439) 70678
Holes 10 L 4018 yds SSS 63
V'trs U exc WD 2–4pm SOC–WD
Fees £4 (£6)
Loc Driveway to Gilling Castle in centre of Gilling East Village. 18 miles N of York on B1363
Mis Green fees payable at Fairfax Arms, Gilling East

Bedale (1896)

Private
Leyburn Road, Bedale DL8 1EZ
Tel (0677) 22568
Mem 450 100(L) 60(J)
Sec GA Shepherdson (0677) 22451
Pro AD Johnson (0677) 22443
Holes 18 L 5599 yds SSS 66
Recs Am–66 J Swain
Pro–64 J Hughes
V'trs U SOC
Fees £8.50 (£12)
Loc N boundary of Bedale

Bentham (1922)

Private
Robin Lane, Bentham, Lancaster
Tel (05242) 61018
Mem 331
Sec JM Philipson (05242) 62455
Holes 9 L 5752 yds SSS 69
V'trs U
Fees £6 (£7.50) W–£15
Loc B6480 NE of Lancaster towards Settle. 13 miles E of M6 Junction 34

Catterick Garrison (1930)

Private
Leyburn Road, Catterick Garrison DL9 3QE
Tel (0748) 833268
Mem 600
Sec Maj. L Layton
Pro S Bradley (0748) 833671
Holes 18 L 6336 yds SSS 70
Recs Am–68 RM Roper
Pro–69 D Edwards
V'trs U
Fees £8 (£11)
Loc 3 miles SW of Scarborough off A1

Crimple Valley (1976)

Private
Hookstone Wood Road, Harrogate
Tel (0423) 883485
Mem 200
Sec J Lumb
Pro RA Lumb

Holes 9 L 2500 yds SSS 33
V'trs U
Fees £1.50
Loc Yorkshire Showground

Easingwold (1930)

Private
Stillington Road, Easingwold, York YO6 3ET
Tel **(0347) 21486**
Mem 560
Sec KC Hudson
Pro J Hughes (0347) 21964
Holes 18 L 6262 yds SSS 70
Recs Am–67 GW Mutch
Pro–67 J Hughes
V'trs U
Fees D–£12 (£15)
Loc 12 miles N of York on A19. Stillington Road, S end of town

Filey (1897)

Private
South Cliff, Filey YO14 9BQ
Tel **(0723) 513293**
Mem 890
Sec J Winship BA
Pro DW Currey (0723) 513134
Holes 18 L 6030 yds SSS 69
Recs Am–66 AS Roberts
Pro–64 AS Murray
V'trs U SOC
Fees £10 (£13)

Fulford (York) (1909)

Private
Heslington Lane, York YO1 5DY
Tel **(0904) 413579**
Mem 580
Sec JCA Gledhill (Requests for visits)
Pro B Hessay (0904) 412882
Holes 18 L 6779 yds SSS 72
Recs Am–68 P Hall (1987)
Pro–62 I Woosnam, B Dassu
V'trs By arrangement
Fees £17 (£19)
Loc 2 miles S of York centre
Mis Venue for Benson and Hedges International Open

Ganton (1891)

Private
Station Road, Ganton, Scarborough YO12 4PA
Tel **(0944) 70329**
Mem 600
Sec Air Vice Marshal RG Price CB
Pro G Brown (0944) 70260
Holes 18 L 6693 yds SSS 73
Recs Am–67 G Boardman
Pro–65 N Coles
V'trs By prior arrangement
Fees On application
Loc Scarborough 11 miles on A64

Ghyll (1907)

Private
Ghyll Brow, Thornton-in-Craven
Tel **(0282) 842466**
Mem 225
Sec H Best (0756) 2587
Holes 9 L 5708 yds SSS 68
Recs Am–67 M Davies
V'trs U
Fees £5 (£6)
Loc Barnoldswick 1 mile

Harrogate (1892)

Private
Forest Lane, Head, Harrogate HG2 7TF
Tel **(0423) 863158**
Mem 620
Sec RA Mayo (0423) 862999
Pro P Johnson (0423) 862547
Holes 18 L 6183 yds SSS 69
Recs Am–65 P Hall
Pro–64 D Durnian
V'trs WD–U WE/BH–enquire first SOC–Tues/Fri
Fees £15 (£22)
Loc Harrogate 2 miles on Knaresborough Road (A59)

Heworth (1912)

Private
Muncaster House, Muncastergate, York YO3 9JX
Tel **(0904) 424618**
Mem 245 80(L) 50(J) 70(5)
Sec KT Sawyers (0904) 421093 (home)
Pro SI Robinson (0904) 422389
Holes 11 L 6078 yds SSS 69
Recs Am–67 SJ Gledhill
Pro–72 D Durnian
Fees £7 (£10) 1988 prices
Loc NE boundary of York (A64)

Kirkbymoorside (1951)

Private
Manor Vale, Kirkbymoorside, York YO6 6EG
Tel **(0904) 31525**
Mem 400
Sec WK Ashford
Holes 18 L 5783 yds SSS 68
Recs Am–K Magson
V'trs U
Fees £6 (£7) W–£20
Loc A170 between Helmsley and Pickering

Knaresborough (1919)

Private
Boroughbridge Road, Knaresborough HG5 9XX
Tel **(0423) 863219**
Mem 662
Sec C Jones (0423) 862690
Pro K Johnstone (0423) 864865
Holes 18 L 6281 yds SSS 70
Recs Am–68 D Walker
Pro–65 J King
V'trs U
Fees £9 (£14)
Loc $1^1/_2$ miles N of Knaresborough

Malton & Norton (1923)

Private
Welham Park, Norton, Malton YO17 9QE
Tel **(0653) 692959**
Mem 700
Sec Sqn Ldr CJH Fox MBE (0653) 697912
Pro ML Henderson (0653) 693882
Holes 18 L 6401 yds SSS 71
V'trs WD–U WE–restricted on match days H
Fees £11.50 (£15.50) W–£50
Loc Between York and Scarborough, off Welham Road, Norton

Masham (1900)

Private
Burnholme, Swinton Road, Masham, Ripon HG4 4DX
Tel **(0765) 89379**
Mem 280
Sec Mrs MA Willis (0765) 89491
Holes 9 L 5244 yds SSS 66
V'trs WD–U before 5pm WE–M BH–NA
Fees £6
Loc 10 miles N of Ripon

Oakdale (1914)

Private
Oakdale, Harrogate HG1 2LN
Tel **(0423) 502806**
Mem 775
Sec JA Llewellyn MBE (0423) 67162
Pro N Summer (0423) 60510
Holes 18 L 6456 yds SSS 71
Recs Am–67 G Cuthbert (1987)
Pro–66 M Johnson (1987)
V'trs WD–U 9.30 12.30 and after 2pm SOC
Fees £12 D–£14 (£14 D–£16)
Loc $^1/_2$ mile NE of Royal Hall, Harrogate

Pannal (1906)

Private
Follifoot Road, Pannal, Harrogate HG3 1ES
Tel **(0423) 871641**
Mem 815
Sec WK Davies (0423) 872628
Pro M Burgess (0423) 872620
Holes 18 L 6659 yds SSS 72
Recs Am–66 J Whitehead (1988)
Pro–66 J Beattie, M James, D Jones
V'trs WD–H 9.30am–12 and after 1.30pm WE–after 10am and after 2.30pm
Fees £15 D–£20 (£20)
Loc $2^1/_2$ miles S of Harrogate

Pike Hills (1920)

Private
Tadcaster Road, Copmanthorpe, York YO2 3UW
Tel (0904) 706566
Mem 800
Sec G Wood
Pro I Gradwell (0904) 708756
Holes 18 L 6048 yds SSS 69
V'trs WD–UH before 4.30pm M–after 4.30pm WE/BH–M SOC
Fees Summer £12 Winter £8
Loc 3 miles W of York on Leeds Road. Parkland course around Nature Reserve

Richmond (1892)

Private
Bend Hagg, Richmond
Tel (0748) 2457
Mem 454
Sec BD Aston (0748) 4775
Pro P Jackson
Holes 18 L 5704 yds SSS 68
Recs Am–64 G Catt
Pro–64 P Tupling
V'trs U
Fees £7 (£8)
Loc 3 miles S of Scotch Corner

Ripon City (1905)

Private
Palace Road, Ripon HG4 3HH
Tel (0765) 3640
Mem 280 50(L) 30(J) 70(5)
Sec E Bentley (0765) 3991
Pro T Davis (0765) 700411
Holes 9 L 5752 yds SSS 68
Recs Am–65 M Grant
Pro–66 B Hutchinson
V'trs U
Fees £5 (£7)
Loc 1 mile N on A6108

Scarborough North Cliff (1927)

Private
North Cliff Avenue, Burniston Road, Scarborough YO12 6PP
Tel (0723) 360786
Mem 800
Sec JR Freeman
Pro SN Deller (0723) 365920
Holes 18 L 6425 yds SSS 71
Recs Am–66 MJ Kelly, R Newton
V'trs U exc Sun before 10am SOC
Fees £9.50 (£13)
Loc 2 miles N of town centre on coast road

Scarborough South Cliff (1903)

Private
Deepdale Avenue, off Filey Road, Scarborough
Tel (0723) 360522
Mem 500
Sec CH Atkinson (0723) 374737
Holes 18 L 6085 yds SSS 69
Recs Am–68 SJ Thorpe (1987)
Pro–66 MJ Slater (1987)
V'trs U
Fees £9 (£12.50)
Loc 1 mile S of centre

Selby (1907)

Private
Mill Lane, Brayton, Selby YO8 9LD
Tel (075 782) 622
Mem 691
Sec G Bywater
Pro A Smith (075 782) 785
Holes 18 L 6246 yds SSS 70
Recs Am–65 L Walker
Pro–64 D Matthew
V'trs U WE–NA SOC–Wed–Fri
Fees £12.50 WD only
Loc 3 miles SW of Selby

Settle (1896)

Private
Giggleswick, Settle
Tel (072 92) 3912
Mem 250
Sec L Whitaker
Holes 9 L 2276 yds SSS 31
Recs Am–62 P Robinson
V'trs U SOC
Fees £4 (£5)
Loc 1 mile N of Settle on A65

Skipton (1905)

Private
Short Lea Lane, off NW Bypass, Skipton BD23 1LL
Tel (0756) 3922
Mem 525
Sec JC Varley (Mgr) (0756) 2128
Pro J Hammond (0756) 3257
Holes 18 L 6087 yds SSS 70
Recs Am–71 CJ Smales (1987)
V'trs U
Fees £7.50 (£10)
Loc Centre 1 mile off NW Bypass

Thirsk & Northallerton (1914)

Private
Thornton-le-Street, Thirsk YO7 4AB
Tel (0845) 22170
Mem 300
Sec PW McCarthy (0845) 23287
Pro A Marshall
(Touring Pro D Llewellyn)
Holes 9 L 6257 yds SSS 70
Recs Am–69 R Cable
Pro–69 P Blaze
V'trs WD–U Sun–M SOC
Fees £6 D–£8 Sat/BH–£12 Sun–M
Loc 2 miles N of Thirsk

Whitby (1892)

Private
Low Straggleton, Whitby YO21 3SR
Tel (0947) 602768
Mem 500
Sec A Dyson (0947) 600660
Pro A Brook (0947) 602719
Holes 18 L 5710 yds SSS 67
Recs Am–67
Pro–68
V'trs U SOC
Fees £8 (£10)

York (1890)

Private
Lords Moor Lane, Strensall, York YO3 5XF
Tel (0904) 490304
Mem 325 110(L) 100(J)
Sec RF Harding
Pro A Mason
Holes 18 L 6275 yds SSS 70
Recs Am–64 S East
Pro–66 P Fowler
V'trs U (phone club) SOC–WD & Sun
Fees £12 (£15)
Loc 6 miles NE of York

Yorkshire (South)

Abbeydale (1895)

Private
Twentywell Lane, Dore, nr Sheffield SL17 4QA
Tel (0742) 360763
Mem 700
Sec Mrs KM Johnston
Pro SJ Cooper (0742) 365633
Holes 18 L 6419 yds SSS 71
V'trs U SOC–Tues & Fri by arrangement
Fees £11.50 (£13.50)
Loc 5 miles S of Sheffield

Austerfield Park (1974)

Private
Cross Lane, Austerfield, nr Bawtry Doncaster DN10 6RF
Tel (0302) 710841
Mem 425 45(L) 40(J) 80(5)
Sec A Bradley (0709) 540928
Pro A Stothard (0302) 710850
Holes 18 L 6824 yds SSS 73
Recs Am–73 J Pickersgill (1988)
Pro–67 J Brennand (1988)
V'trs U
Fees £7 (£10)
Loc 2 miles NE of Bawtry off A614
Mis 10–bay driving range

Barnsley (1925)

Public
Wakefield Road, Staincross, Barnsley S75 6JZ
Tel (0226) 382856
Mem 700
Sec DA Wigglesworth

Pro M Melling (0226) 382954
Holes 18 L 6048 yds SSS 69
Recs Am–64 RI Shaw (1988)
Pro–62 M Melling
V'trs U
Fees £3 (£4)
Loc 4 miles N of Barnsley on A61

Beauchief Municipal (1925)

Public
Abbey Lane, Sheffield S8 0DB
Tel (0742) 367274/620040
Mem 350
Sec JG Pearson (0742) 306720
Pro B English
Holes 18 L 5428 yds SSS 66
Recs Am–65 PW Hickinson
Pro–63 P Tupling
V'trs U
Fees £4.50 (£4.50)
Loc A621 Sheffield

Birley Wood (1974)

Private
Birley Lane, Sheffield S12 3BP
Tel (0742) 390099
Mem 400
Sec K Thompson (0742) 389198
Pro S Sherratt
Holes 18 L 6275 yds SSS 70
V'trs U
Fees £3.50 (£5)
Loc 4 miles S of Sheffield on A616 to M1

Concord Park (1952)

Public
Shiregreen Lane, Sheffield S5
Mem 147
Sec JA Bennett (0742) 613605
Holes 18 L 4280 yds SSS 61
V'trs U
Fees £2 (£2.50)
Loc M1 Junction 34, 1 mile

Crookhill Park (1973)

Public
Conisborough, nr Doncaster
Tel (0709) 862979
Mem 400
Sec DM Parry (0709) 863466
Holes 18 L 5846 yds SSS 68
Recs Am–67 R Jones
Pro–70
V'trs U
Fees £2 (£3)
Loc 3 miles W of Doncaster on A630

Doncaster (1895)

Private
Bawtry Road, Bessacarr, nr Doncaster DN4 7PD
Tel (0302) 868316
Mem 375
Sec F Colley (0302) 537815
Pro S Fox (0302) 868404
Holes 18 L 6230 yds SSS 70
Recs Am–66 H Green
Pro–66 H Clark
V'trs UH WE/BH–after 11am SOC–WD
Fees £12 (£15)
Loc $4^1/_2$ miles S of Doncaster

Doncaster Town Moor (1900)

Private
c/o Doncaster Rovers Social Club, Bellevue, Doncaster DN4 5HV
Tel (0302) 535286
Mem 400
Sec JC Padley (0302) 535458
Pro G Bailey
Holes 18 L 6314 yds SSS 69
Recs Am–66 AJ Miller (1987)
Pro–69 D Snell
V'trs U exc Sun before 11.30am SOC
Fees £7 (£8)
Loc Inside Racecourse

Dore & Totley (1913)

Private
Bradway Road, Bradway, nr Sheffield S17 4QR
Tel (0742) 360492
Mem 600
Sec Mrs C Milner (0742) 369872
Pro P Cowen (0742) 366844
Holes 18 L 6301 yds SSS 70
Recs Am–S Field
Pro–P Cowen
V'trs WD–U WE/BH–M
Fees £10
Loc 5 miles SW of town centre

Grange Park (1972)

Private
Upper Wortley Road, Rotherham S61 2SJ
Tel (0709) 559497
Mem 486
Sec R Charity (0709) 683400
Pro E Clark (0709) 559497
Holes 18 L 6461 yds SSS 71
Recs Am–68 J Beckitt
Pro–68 G Tickell
V'trs U
Fees £2.30 (£2.90)
Loc 2 miles W of town on A629

Hallamshire (1897)

Private
The Club House, Sandygate, Sheffield S10 4LA
Tel (0742) 302153
Mem 600
Sec R Burns
Pro G Tickell (0742) 305222
Holes 18 L 6396 yds SSS 71
Recs Am–66 W Bremner
Pro–63 JW Wilkinson
V'trs I
Fees £15 (£20)
Loc W boundary of Sheffield

Hickleton (1909)

Private
Hickleton, nr Doncaster
Tel (0709) 892496
Mem 485
Sec R Jowett (0709) 893506
Pro P Shepherd (0709) 895170
Holes 18 L 6403 yds SSS 71
Recs Am–71 G Beresforde (1987)
V'trs WD/Sat am/Sun pm–U SOC
Fees £5.50 (£8) Mon (exc BH)–£4.50
Loc 6 miles W of Doncaster. On A635 between Doncaster and Barnsley

Hillsborough (1920)

Private
Worrall Road, Sheffield S6 4BE
Tel (0742) 343608
Mem 710
Sec AW Platts (0742) 349151
Pro G Walker (0742) 332666
Holes 18 L 5672 metres SSS 70
V'trs U
Fees £12 (£18)
Loc Wadsley, Sheffield

Lees Hall (1907)

Private
Hemsworth Road, Norton, Sheffield S8 8LL
Tel (0742) 554402
Mem 700
Sec NE Westworth (0742) 552900
Pro JR Wilkinson
Holes 18 L 6137 yds SSS 69
Recs Am–65 AR Gellsthorpe
Pro–63 B Hutchinson
V'trs U SOC
Fees £11.50 (£17.25)
Loc $3^1/_2$ miles S of centre

Lindrick (1891)

Private
Lindrick Common, nr Worksop, Notts S81 8BH
Tel (0909) 485802
Mem 500
Sec E Taylor (0909) 475282
Pro (0909) 475820
Holes 18 L 6615 yds SSS 72
Recs Am–65 DF Livingston
Pro–65 G Bond, J Morgan
V'trs U with prior arrangement Tues am–NA SOC–WD
Fees £20 (£25) Winter £15 (£20)
Loc 4 miles W of Worksop on A57. M1 Junction 31–$4^1/_2$ miles towards Worksop

Phoenix (1932)

Private
Brinsworth, Rotherham
Tel (0709) 382624
Mem 700
Sec J Burrows (0709) 370759
Pro A Limb
Holes 18 L 6170 yds SSS 69

V'trs U
Fees D–£8 (D–£10)
Loc Rotherham 2 miles

Renishaw Park (1911)

Private
Golf House, Renishaw, Sheffield S31 9UZ
Tel (0246) 432044
Mem 400
Sec DG Rossington (0246) 811646
Pro S Elliott (0246) 435484
Holes 18 L 6253 yds SSS 70
Recs Am–65 AR Gelsthorpe
Pro–66 D Dunk, R Emery, J Rhodes
V'trs U
Fees £8.50 (£10)
Loc 7 miles from Sheffield. 2 miles from M1 Junction 30

Rotherham (1903)

Private
Thrybergh Park, Rotherham S65 4NU
Tel (0709) 850466
Mem 455
Sec F Green (0709) 850812
Pro B Ellis (0709) 850480
Holes 18 L 6500 yds SSS 70
Recs Am–66 MJ Kelly
Pro–66 B Hutchison
V'trs U
Fees £12 (£15) 1988 prices
Loc 4 miles E of Rotherham on A630

Roundwood (1976)

Private
Off Green Lane, Rawmarsh, Rotherham S62 6LA
Tel (0709) 523471
Mem 400
Sec T Barnfield (0709) 541792
Holes 9 L 5646 yds SSS 67
V'trs WE–not before 2.30pm on comp days
Fees £2 (£4)
Loc 2 miles N of Rotherham on A633

Sheffield Transport Dept (1923)

Private
Meadow Head, Sheffield
Tel (0742) 373216
Mem 100
Sec P Clarricoates
Holes 18 L 3966 yds SSS 62
Recs Am–62 VR Hutton
V'trs M

Silkstone (1905)

Private
Field Head, Silkstone, nr Barnsley
Tel (0226) 790328
Mem 450
Sec G Speight (0226) 244796
Pro K Guy (0226) 790128
Holes 18 L 6045 yds SSS 70
Recs Am–66 TG Garner, JG Clapham
V'trs WD–U WE–M SOC–WD
Fees £6
Loc 1 mile from M1

Sitwell Park (1913)

Private
Shrogs Wood Road, Rotherham
Tel (0709) 541046
Mem 500
Sec MJ Hinchcliff (0709) 364780
Pro R Swaine
Holes 18 L 6250 yds SSS 70
Recs Am–67 RN Portas
V'trs U
Fees £7 (£8)
Loc $2^1/_2$ miles E of Rotherham

Stocksbridge & District (1925)

Private
30 Royd Lane, Townend, Deepcar, nr Sheffield S30 5RZ
Tel (0742) 882003
Mem 200
Sec S Lee (0742) 882408
Holes 15 L 5055 yds SSS 65
Recs Am–61 CR Dale (1977)
Pro–61 TJ Brookes (1986)
V'trs U SOC
Fees £6 (£7)
Loc 7 miles W of Sheffield

Tankersley Park (1907)

Private
High Green, Sheffield S30 4LG
Tel (0742) 468247
Mem 574
Sec S Jessop
Pro I Kirk (0742) 455583
Holes 18 L 6241 yds SSS 70
Recs Am–66 N Grice
Pro–69 W Atkinson
V'trs WD–U WE–M SOC–WD
Fees £9 D–£11
Loc 7 miles N of Sheffield

Thorne (1980)

Private
Kirton Lane, Thorne, Doncaster DN8 5RJ
Tel (0405) 812054
Sec P Kittridge (0302) 840707
Pro RD Highfield
Holes 18 L 5522 yds SSS 67
V'trs U
Fees £3 (£4)
Loc M18 Junction 5/6

Tinsley Park (1920)

Public
Darnall, Sheffield
Tel (0742) 560237
Mem 345
Sec J Booth (0742) 422168
Pro AP Highfield
Holes 18 L 6045 yds SSS 69
Recs Am–70 D Robbins
Pro–66 D Snell
V'trs U
Fees £4
Loc M1 Junction 32, 1 mile

Wath-upon-Dearne (1904)

Private
Abdy Rawmarsh, Rotherham
Tel (0709) 872149
Mem 400
Sec B Lawrence (0709) 526727
Pro SC Poole (0709) 878677
Holes 14 L 5561 yds SS 67
V'trs WD–U WE/BH–M SOC
Fees £6
Loc Abdy Farm, $1^1/_2$ miles S of Wath-upon-Dearne

Wheatley (1913)

Private
Armthorpe Road, Doncaster DN2 5QB
Tel (0302) 831655
Mem 385 100(L) 75(J) 5(5)
Sec J Ford
Pro T Parkinson (0302) 834085
Holes 18 L 6345 yds SSS 70
Recs Am–65 B Bremner
Pro–63 G Walker
V'trs U SOC
Fees £8.50 (£11.50)
Loc 3 miles E of town

Yorkshire (West)

Alwoodley (1908)

Private
Wigton Lane, Alwoodley, Leeds LS17 8SA
Tel (0532) 681680
Mem 450
Sec TG Turnbull
Pro Ian Duncan
Holes 18 L 6686 yds SSS 72
Recs Am–68 F Haughton
Pro–68 D Fitton
V'trs WD–U SOC–WD
Fees £17 (£22)
Loc 5 miles N of Leeds

Baildon (1898)

Private
Moorgate, Baildon, Shipley BD17 5PP
Tel (0274) 584266
Mem 700
Sec D Farnsworth (0274) 584684
Pro R Masters (0274) 595162
Holes 18 L 6085 yds SSS 70
Recs Am–66 D Farnsworth
Pro–64 G Brand, D Durnian
V'trs WD–U before 5pm (limited Tues) Sat–U after 3.30pm Sun–U after 9.30am
Fees £6 (£8)
Loc 5 miles NW of Bradford

Ben Rhydding (1948)

Private
High Wood, Ben Rhydding, Ilkley
Tel **(0943) 608759**
Mem 200 70(L) 35(J)
Sec JDB Watts
Holes 9 L 4711 yds SSS 64
Recs Am–65 AG Atkins
Pro–64 GJ Brand
V'trs U
Fees £5 (£5)
Loc Ilkley

Bingley (St Ives) (1931)

Public
St Ives Estate, Bingley
Tel **(0274) 562506**
Mem 650
Sec J Crolla (0535) 274231
Pro R Firth
Holes 18 L 6466 yds SSS 71
Recs Am–70 WM Hopkinson
Pro–62 N Faldo
V'trs WD–U before 4.30pm
Fees £4.50 (£7.50)
Loc 6 miles W of Bradford

Bradford (1891)

Private
Hawksworth Lane, Guiseley, Leeds LS20 8NP
Tel **(0943) 75570**
Mem 500
Sec Maj WA Price
Pro S Weldon (0943) 73719
Holes 18 L 6259 yds SSS 70
Recs Am–68 MJ Kelly
V'trs WD–U WE–after noon
SOC–WD
Loc 8 miles N of Bradford

Bradford Moor (1907)

Private
Scarr Hall, Pollard Lane, Bradford
Tel **(0274) 638313**
Mem 375
Sec D Armitage
Pro R Hughes (0274) 631163
Holes 9 L 5854 yds SSS 68
Recs Am–68 I Helliwell
Pro–69 H Waller
V'trs U
Fees £7.50 (£8)

Bradley Park (1978)

Public
Bradley Road, Huddersfield
Tel **(0484) 539988**
Mem 300 25(L) 16(J)
Sec G Sagar (0484) 538704
Pro PE Reilly
Holes 18 L 6202 yds SSS 70
9 hole Par 3
Recs Am–69 R Hall
Pro–64 P Carman
V'trs U SOC
Fees £3.50 (£4.75)
Loc M62 Junction 25, $1^1/_2$ miles
Mis Floodlit driving range

Branshaw (1912)

Private
Branshaw Moor, Oakworth, nr Keighley BD22 7ES
Tel **(0535) 43235**
Mem 380
Sec DA Town (0535) 605003
Holes 18 L 5790 yds SSS 68
Recs Am–68 P Clayton
V'trs U
Fees £5 (£7)
Loc 2 miles SW of Keighley on B6143

Calverley (1984)

Private
Woodhall Lane, Pudsey LS28 5JX
Tel **(0532) 569244**
Mem 300
Sec A Sheard
Holes 18 L 5516 yds SSS 67
9 hole course
Recs Am–71 M Hedley
V'trs WD–U WE–pm only
Fees £3
Loc 4 miles NE of Bradford
Mis Driving range

Castle Fields (1900)

Private
Rastrick Common, Brighouse
Mem 140
Sec P Bentley (0484) 712108
Holes 6 L 2406 yds SSS 50
V'trs M
Fees £1.50
Loc 1 mile S of Brighouse

City of Wakefield (1936)

Public
Lupset Park, Horbury Road, Wakefield WF2 8QS
Tel **(0924) 374316**
Mem 500
Sec OS Ward (0924) 376214
Pro R Holland (0924) 360282
Holes 18 L 6405 yds SSS 71
Recs Am–67 D Oxley,
G Andrews
Pro–68 M Ingham
V'trs WD–U WE/BH–enquire Sec
SOC–WD
Fees £3.10 (£4.80)
Loc A642, 2 miles W of Wakefield. 2 miles E of M1 Junction 39/40

Clayton (1906)

Private
Thornton View Road, Clayton, Bradford
Tel **(0274) 880047**
Mem 180 35(L) 35(J)
Sec FV Wood (0274) 574203
Holes 9 L 5515 yds SSS 67
Recs Am–65 ND Hawkins
V'trs WD–U Sat–U Sun–after 4pm
Fees £4 (£6)
Loc 2 miles W of city centre

Cleckheaton & District (1900)

Private
483 Bradford Road, Cleckheaton
Tel **(0274) 874118**
Mem 500
Sec H Thornton (0274) 877851
Pro M Ingham (0274) 870707
Holes 18 L 5994 yds SSS 69
Recs Am–62 CA Bloice
Pro–63 GA Caygill
V'trs U
Fees £9 (£14)
Loc M62 Junction 26–A638 (Bradford) 200 yds

Crosland Heath (1914)

Private
Crosland Heath, Huddersfield
Tel **(0484) 653216**
Mem 320
Sec D Walker (0484) 653262
Pro R Jessop (0484) 653877
Holes 18 L 5961 yds SSS 70
Recs Am–66 S Ellis
Pro–65 SW Dellar
V'trs U SOC
Fees On application
Loc 3 miles W of Huddersfield

Dewsbury District (1891)

Private
The Pinnacle, Mirfield
Tel **(0924) 492399**
Mem 400
Sec P Bates (0924) 498673 (home)
Pro N Hirst (0924) 496030
Holes 18 L 6256 yds SSS 71
Recs Am–68 M Colcombe
Pro–69 G Townhill
V'trs U SOC
Fees £7 (£9)
Loc W boundary of Dewsbury

East Bierley (1928)

Private
South View Road, Bradford
Tel **(0274) 681023**
Mem 145 47(L) 38(J)
Sec Mrs M Welch
Holes 9 L 4692 yds SSS 63
Recs Am–59 R Watts
Pro–62 B Hill
V'trs U
Fees £5 (£7)
Loc 4 miles SE of Bradford

Elland (1910)

Private
Hullen Edge, Elland
Tel **(0422) 72505**
Mem 350
Sec H Wood (0484) 26085
Pro J Tindall
Holes 9 L 2763 yds SSS 66
Recs Am–64 C Hartland
V'trs U
Fees £6 (£10)
Loc Town centre $^1/_2$ mile

Ferrybridge 'C' (1976)

Private
PO Box 39, Stranglands Lane, Knottingley WF11 8SQ
Tel **(0977) 84188 Ext 256**
Mem 220
Sec NE Pugh (0977) 793884
Holes 9 L 5138 yds SSS 65
V'trs M
Loc Ferrybridge 'C' Power Station. 1/2 mile off A1 on B6136

Fulneck (1892)

Private
Pudsey
Tel **(0532) 565191**
Mem 230
Sec J Allan (0532) 663349
Holes 9 L 5564 yds SSS 67
Recs Am–64 I Holdsworth
V'trs WD–U WE/BH–M SOC
Fees £4 (£3)
Loc 5 miles W of Leeds

Garforth (1913)

Private
Long Lane, Garforth, Leeds LS25 2DS
Tel **(0532) 862021**
Mem 550
Sec FA Readman (0532) 863308
Pro K Findlater (0532) 862063
Holes 18 L 6327 yds SSS 70
Recs Am–63 AR Gelsthorpe
V'trs WD–U H WE/BH–M SOC
Fees £12 D–£15 WE–M
Loc 9 miles E of Leeds between Garforth and Barwick-in-Elmet

Gotts Park (1934)

Public
Armley Ridge Road, Armley Leeds 12
Tel **(0532) 638232**
Mem 250
Sec M Gill (0532) 562994
Pro JK Simpson (0532) 636600
Holes 18 L 4960 yds SSS 64
V'trs U
Fees £3.50
Loc 2 miles W of city centre

Halifax (1895)

Private
Union Lane, Ogden, Halifax HX2 8XR
Tel **(0422) 244171**
Mem 450
Sec JP Clark (0422) 247288
Pro SA Foster (0422) 240047
Holes 18 L 6038 yds SSS 70
Recs Am–66 J Robinson, AMA Bagott, J Rushworth
Pro–65 PW Good
V'trs U WE–parties welcome SOC
Fees £7 (£11) Reduced party rates
Loc 4 miles N of town on A629

Halifax Bradley Hall (1907)

Private
Holywell Green, Halifax
Tel **(0422) 74108**
Mem 520
Sec AM Green (0422) 646905
Pro P Wood (0422) 70231
Holes 18 L 6213 yds SSS 70
Recs Am–67 CD Doyle
V'trs U
Fees £6 (£9)
Loc S of Halifax on A6112

Halifax West End (1913)

Private
Highroad Well, Halifax HX2 0NT
Tel **(0422) 53608**
Mem 266 91(L) 44(J)
Sec BR Thomas (0422) 67145
Pro D Rishworth (0422) 63293
Holes 18 L 6003 yds SSS 69
Recs Am–65 JR Crawshaw, JR Smith
Pro–64 AJ Bickerdike
V'trs U SOC
Fees £7 (£9)
Loc 2 miles NW of Halifax

Hanging Heaton (1922)

Private
Whitecross Road, Dewsbury WF12 7DT
Tel **(0924) 461606**
Mem 550
Sec SM Simpson (0924) 461729
Pro J Allott (0924) 467077
Holes 9 L 2868 yds SSS 67
Recs Am–66 P Cockburn
Pro–AJ Bickerdyke
V'trs WD–U WE–restricted
Fees £6 (£8)
Loc Town centre 3/4 mile (A653)

Headingley (1892)

Private
Back Church Lane, Adel, Leeds LS16 8DW
Tel **(0532) 673052**
Mem 600
Sec RW Hellawell (0532) 679573
Pro (0532) 675100
Holes 18 L 6238 yds SSS 70
Recs Am–67 S Pullan
Pro–67 GR Tickell
V'trs U SOC
Fees £12 D–£15 (£18)
Loc 5 miles NW of city centre, off A660 Leeds–Otley–Skipton road

Headley (1906)

Private
Headley Lane, Thornton, nr Bradford BD13 3LX
Tel **(0274) 833481**
Mem 200
Sec JP Clark (0274) 832571
Holes 9 L 2457 yds SSS 64
Recs Am–61 A Cording (1985)
Pro–66 M Ingham
V'trs U (exc Sun)
Fees £3 (£6)
Loc 5 miles W of Bradford

Horsforth (1907)

Private
Layton Rise, Layton Road, Horsforth, Leeds LS18 5EX
Tel **(0532) 586819**
Mem 402 80(L) 74(J) 80(5)
Sec CB Carrington
Pro G Howard (0532) 585200
Holes 18 L 6293 yds SSS 70
Recs Am–67 S Lax
Pro–67 HW Muscroft
V'trs U SOC
Fees D–£10 (£14) W–£33 M–£50
Loc 6 miles NW of Leeds

Howley Hall (1900)

Private
Scotchman Lane, Morley, Leeds LS27 0NX
Tel **(0924) 472432**
Mem 465
Sec Mrs A Pepper (0924) 478417
Pro SA Spinks (0924) 473852
Holes 18 L 6209 yds SSS 69
Recs Am–66 S Hamer (1984)
V'trs U
Fees £10 D–£13 (£15 R/D)
Loc 4 miles SW of Leeds on B6123

Huddersfield (1891)

Private
Fixby Hall, Lightridge Road, Fixby, Huddersfield HD2 2EP
Tel **(0484) 20110**
Mem 685
Sec Miss D Rose (0484) 26203
Pro P Carman (0484) 26463
Holes 18 L 6424 yds SSS 71
Recs Am–66 JR Crawshaw (1978)
Pro– 66 G Thornhill(1985)
V'trs U SOC
Fees £14 (£16.50)
Loc 2 miles N of town centre. 600 yds S off A6170. M62 Junction 24

Ilkley (1889)

Private
Myddleton, Ilkley LS29 0BE
Tel **(0943) 607277**
Mem 530
Sec PS Leneghan (0943) 600214
Pro JL Hammond (0943) 607463
Holes 18 L 6249 yds SSS 70
Recs Am–65 AC Flather (1984)
Pro–64 B Hutchinson (1972)
V'trs U
Fees £15 (£20)
Loc Leeds 18 miles

Keighley (1904)

Private
Howden Park, Utley, Keighley
Tel (0535) 603179
Mem 500
Sec J Scott (0535) 604778
Pro DA Walker (0535) 65370
Holes 18 L 6134 yds SSS 70
Recs Am–66 RS Mitchell, G Smith (1987)
Pro–65 J Holchaks
V'trs U
Fees £10 (£12)
Loc 1 mile W of Keighley

Leeds (1896)

Private
Elmete Road, Roundhay, Leeds LS8 2LJ
Tel (0532) 658775
Mem 480
Sec GW Backhouse (0532) 659203
Pro S Thornhill (0532) 658786
Holes 18 L 6097 yds SSS 69
Recs Am–64 J Whiteley
Pro–64 AJ Bickerdike
V'trs WD–U WE–M
Fees £10 D–£12
Loc 4 miles NE of Leeds off A58

Lightcliffe (1907)

Private
Knowle Top Road, Lightcliffe
Tel (0422) 202459
Mem 145 92(L) 87(J)
Sec TH Gooder (0422) 201051
Pro R Parry
Holes 9 L 5368 metres SSS 68
Recs Am–66 PH Wolfe, NRA Denham
V'trs U–exc comp days Sun am–M
Fees £8 (£10)
Loc 3 miles E of Halifax

Longley Park (1911)

Private
Maple Street, off Somerset Road, Huddersfield HD5 9AX
Tel (0484) 22304
Mem 400
Sec KLW Ireland (0484) 29826
Pro D Chapman
Holes 9 L 5324 yds SSS 66
Recs Am–64 JD Oxley
Pro–65 PW Booth
V'trs WD–U exc Thurs WE–Restricted
Fees £5 (£6.50)
Loc Town centre $1/2$ mile

Low Laithes (1925)

Private
Parkmill Lane, Flushdyke, Ossett
Tel (0924) 273275
Mem 450
Sec D Walker (0924) 376553
Pro P Browning (0924) 274667
Holes 18 L 6458 yds SSS 71
Recs Pro–68
V'trs U WE–no parties
Fees £9 R/D (£14 R/D)
Loc 2 miles N of Wakefield. Motorway Junction 40

Marsden (1921)

Private
Hemplow, Marsden, nr Huddersfield
Tel (0484) 844253
Mem 165 38(L) 45(J)
Sec GC Scott (0484) 537634
Pro D Chapman
Holes 9 L 2860 yds SSS 68
Recs Am–63 AJ Bickerdike
Pro–A Bickerdike
V'trs WD–U WE–NA before 4pm
Fees £4 (£6)
Loc 8 miles S of Huddersfield

Meltham (1908)

Private
Thick Hollins Hall, Meltham, Huddersfield HD7 3DQ
Tel (0484) 850227
Mem 450
Sec BF Precious (0484) 682106
Pro S Kettlewell (0484) 851521
Holes 18 L 6145 yds SSS 70
Recs Am–68 AT Garner
Pro–69 W Casper
V'trs U
Fees £10 (£12.50)
Loc 5 miles W of Huddersfield

Middleton Park (1934)

Public
Ring Road, Beeston Park, Middleton, Leeds 10
Tel (0532) 700449
Mem 250
Sec G Hepworth (0532) 892321
Pro D Bulmer (0532) 709506
Holes 18 L 5233 yds SSS 66
V'trs U
Fees £2.80
Loc 3 miles S of city centre

Moor Allerton (1923)

Private
Coal Road, Leeds LS17 9NH
Tel (0532) 661154
Mem 1200
Sec S Mack
Pro H Clark, P Blaze (0532) 665209
Holes 18 L 6542 yds SSS
9 L 3541 yds SSS
Recs Am–68
Pro–65
V'trs WD–U Sat–24 v'trs only Sun–NA SOC
Fees £16.50 (£20) 1988 prices. Reduced Nov–Mar & after 4pm summer
Loc $5^1/_2$ miles N of Leeds

Moortown (1909)

Private
Harrogate Road, Leeds LS17 7DB
Tel (0532) 686521
Mem 500
Sec RH Brown
Pro B Hutchinson (0532) 683636
Holes 18 L 6606 yds SSS 72
Recs Am–65 D Muscroft
Pro–64 W Riley
V'trs WD–U WE/BH–M I
Fees £20 D–£25 (£25 D–£30)
Loc $5^1/_2$ miles N of Leeds

Mount Skip (1955)

Private
Wadsworth, Hebden Bridge
Tel (0422) 842896
Mem 365
Sec Dr RG Pogson (0422) 843733
Holes 9 L 5114 yds SSS 66
Recs Am–63 IS Marsland
Pro–M Ingham
V'trs U
Fees £5
Loc 1 mile N of town

Normanton (1903)

Private
Snydale Road, Normanton, Wakefield WF6 1PA
Tel (0924) 892943
Mem 250
Sec J McElhinney (0977) 702273
Pro M Evans (0924) 220134
Holes 9 L 5284 yds SSS 66
Recs Am–68 S Turner (1988)
Pro–67 A Dyson (1988)
V'trs U Sun–NA
Fees £4.50 Sat/BH–£8.50
Loc 1 mile from M62 Junction 31, A655 towards Wakefield

Northcliffe (1921)

Private
Highbank Lane, Moorhead, Shipley BD18 4LJ
Tel (0274) 584085
Mem 600
Sec R Anderson (0532) 567845
Pro S Poot (0274) 587193
Holes 18 L 6065 yds SSS 69
Recs Am–67 R Bell
Pro–67 M James
V'trs U SOC
Fees £9 (£11) 1988 prices
Loc 3 miles NW of Bradford

Otley (1906)

Private
West Busk Lane, Otley LS21 3NG
Tel (0943) 461015
Mem 600
Sec AF Flowers (0943) 465329

Pro S McNally (0943) 463403
Holes 18 L 6235 yds SSS 70
Recs Am–69 H Smith (1988)
Pro–62 GJ Brand (1988)
V'trs U SOC
Fees £12 (£15)
Loc Off Bradford Road, Otley

Outlane (1906)

Private
Slack Lane, Outlane, Huddersfield HD3 3YL
Tel (0422) 74762
Mem 325
Sec P Sykes
Pro A Dyson
Holes 18 L 5735 yds SSS 68
Recs Am–62 G Crosland
Pro–62 W Garside
V'trs U SOC
Fees £7 (£10)
Loc 4 miles W of Huddersfield nr M62

Painthorpe House (1961)

Private
Painthorpe Lane, Crigglestone, nr Wakefield
Tel (0924) 255083
Mem 120
Sec H Kershaw (0924) 274527
Holes 9 L 4108 yds SSS 60
Recs Am–64 J Turner, J Whitehouse
V'trs U exc Sun–NA
Fees WD–£2 Sat–£3
Loc 1 mile from M1 Junction 39

Phoenix Park (1922)

Private
Phoenix Park, Thornbury, Bradford 3
Tel (0274) 667178
Mem 180
Sec G Dunn (0274) 662369
Pro B Ferguson
Holes 9 L 4982 yds SSS 64
Recs Am–66 C Lally
V'trs WD/BH–U WE–NA
Fees £3
Loc Thornbury Roundabout

Pontefract & District (1900)

Private
Park Lane, Pontefract WF8 4QS
Tel (0977) 792241
Mem 810
Sec WT Smith (0977) 792115
Pro J Coleman (0977) 706806
Holes 18 L 6227 yds SSS 70
Recs Am–63 DC Rooke
Pro–67 GW Townhill
V'trs I SOC–Tues/Thurs/Fri
Fees £12 (£15)
Loc Pontefract 1 mile on B6134. M62 Junction 32

Pontefract Park (1973)

Public
Park Road, Pontefract
Tel (0977) 702799
Holes 18 L 4068 yds SSS 62
V'trs U
Fees £2.10 (£3.10)
Loc Between town and M62 roundabout

Queensbury (1923)

Private
Queensbury, nr Bradford BD13 1QF
Tel (0274) 882155
Mem 200 45(L) 60(J) 25(5)
Sec MG Roberts
Pro D Sutcliffe
Holes 9 L 5102 yds SSS 65
Recs Am–64 S Rogers, H Wilkerson
Pro–63 P Cowan
V'trs U
Fees £4 (£7)
Loc Bradford 4 miles

Rawdon (1896)

Private
Buckstone Drive, Micklefield Lane, Rawdon LS19 6BD
Tel (0532) 506040
Mem 250 50(L) 75(J) 100(5)
Sec RA Adams
Pro S Betteridge (0502) 505017
Holes 9 L 5964 yds SSS 69
Recs Am–65 JM Clough
Pro–63 A Bickerdike
V'trs WD–U WE/BH–M
Fees £7.50 W–£25 M–£45
Loc 6 miles NW of Leeds

Riddlesden (1927)

Private
Howden Rough, Riddleston, Keighley
Tel (0535) 602148
Mem 200
Sec Mrs KM Brooksbank (0535) 607646
Holes 18 L 4150 yds SSS 61
Recs Am–60 M Mitchell (1987)
Pro–59 P Cowan (1983)
V'trs U exc Sun before 10am
Fees £3 (£5)
Loc Keighley 3 miles

Roundhay (1923)

Public
Park Lane, Leeds LS8 2EJ
Tel (0532) 662695
Mem 320 55(L) 25(J)
Sec RH McLauchlan (0532) 492523
Pro (0532) 661686
Holes 9 L 5166 yds SSS 65
Recs Am–62 AR White
Pro–62 M Bembridge
V'trs U
Fees £3.40 (£3.70)
Loc 4 miles N of city centre

Ryburn (1910)

Private
Norland, Sowerby Bridge, Halifax
Tel (0422) 831355
Mem 200
Sec J Hoyle (0422) 843070
Holes 9 L 5002 yds SSS 65
Recs Am–64 DS Lumb (1987)
Pro–61 M Pearson (1987)
V'trs U
Fees £3 (£5)
Loc 3 miles S of Halifax

Sand Moor (1926)

Private
Alwoodley Lane, Leeds LS17 7DJ
Tel (0532) 681685
Mem 541
Sec D Warboys (0532) 685180
Pro J Foss (0532) 683925
Holes 18 L 6423 yds SSS 71
Recs Am–67 R Muscroft, JM Buxton, G Harland
Pro –66 D Jagger, S McNally (1987)
V'trs WD–U by arrangement WE–NA SOC–WD
Fees £15 D–£18 (£21)
Loc 5 miles N of Leeds off A61 Harrogate Road

Scarcroft (1937)

Private
Syke Lane, Leeds LS14 3BQ
Tel (0532) 892263
Mem 500
Sec RD Barwell (0532) 892311
Pro M Ross (0532) 892780
Holes 18 L 6426 yds SSS 71
Recs Am–67 E Shaw
Pro–65 D Dunk
V'trs WD–U WE/BH–M or by arrangement SOC–WD exc Fri
Fees £16 (£22)
Loc 7 miles N of Leeds off A58

Shipley (1896)

Private
Beckfoot Lane, Cottingley Bridge, Bingley BD16 1LX
Tel (0274) 563212
Mem 575
Sec SL Holman (0274) 568652
Pro D Sutcliffe (0274) 563674
Holes 18 L 6218 yds SSS 70
Recs Am–66 GM Shaw
Pro–64 M Ingham (1987)
V'trs U exc Tues before 1.30pm & Sat before 4pm
Fees £12 (£15)
Loc 6 miles N of Bradford 6 miles (A650)

Silsden (1913)

Private
Brunthwaite, Silsden, nr Keighley
Tel **(0535) 52998**
Mem 300
Sec G Davey (0943) 601490
Holes 14 L 4870 yds SSS 64
Recs Am–61
V'trs WE–restricted Sun–U after 1pm
Fees £5 (£8)
Loc 5 miles N of Keighley

South Bradford (1906)

Private
Pearson Road, Odsal, Bradford BD6 1BH
Tel **(0274) 679195**
Mem 220
Sec HH Kellett (0274) 676911
Pro (0274) 673346
Holes 9 L 6004 yds SSS 69
Recs Am–65 GM Yarnold
Pro–67 S Miguel, A Caygill
V'trs WD–U WE–M
Fees On application
Loc Bradford 2 miles, near Odsal Stadium

South Leeds (1914)

Private
Gipsy Lane, Ring Road, Beeston, Leeds LS11 5TV
Tel **(0532) 700479**
Mem 560
Sec J McBride (0532) 771676
Pro M Lewis (0532) 702598
Holes 18 L 5835 yds SSS 68
Recs Am–66 M Guy
Pro–68 B Waites
V'trs WD–U WE–M SOC
Fees £9 (£12)
Loc 4 miles S of Leeds. 2 miles from M62 and M1

Temple Newsam (1923)

Public
Temple Newsam Road, Halton, Leeds 15
Tel **(0532) 645624**
Mem 450
Sec G Gower
Pro D Bulmer (0532) 647362
Holes Lord Irwin 18 L 6448 yds SSS 71; Lady Dorothy Wood 18 L 6029 yds SSS 70
V'trs U SOC
Fees £3.50 (£4)
Loc 5 miles NE of town centre, off Selby Road

Todmorden (1895)

Private
Rive Rocks, Cross Stone, Todmorden, Lancs 014 8RD
Tel **(070 681) 2986**
Mem 123 29(L) 19(J) 8(5)
Sec RA Ward
Holes 9 L 5818 yds SSS 68
Recs Am–68 RH Fielden, G Morgan
Pro–68 B Hunt
V'trs U SOC
Fees £4 (£6)
Loc 2 miles N of Todmorden

Wakefield (1891)

Private
Woodthorpe, Wakefield WF2 6JH
Tel **(0924) 255104**
Mem 500
Sec DT Hall (0924) 250287
Pro IM Wright (0924) 255380
Holes 18 L 6626 yds SSS 72
Recs Am–67 T Margison (1982)
Pro–68 HW Muscroft (1982)
V'trs U SOC
Fees £12 (£15)
Loc 3 miles S of Wakefield

West Bowling (1898)

Private
Newall Hall, Rooley Lane, West Bowling, Bradford BD5 8LB
Tel **(0274) 724449**
Mem 300
Sec KH Ripley (0274) 393207
Pro AP Swaine (0274) 728036
Holes 18 L 5756 yds SS 68
Recs Am–66 TJ Wade
Pro–66 G Brand
V'trs U H
Fees £8 (£12)
Loc Junction of M606 and Bradford Ring Road

West Bradford (1900)

Private
Chellow Grange, Haworth Road, Bradford BD9 6NP
Tel **(0274) 542767**
Mem 450
Pro AJ Stephenson (0274) 542102
Holes 18 L 5705 yds SSS 68
Recs Am–63
Pro–66
V'trs U
Fees £6 (£8)
Loc 3 miles W of Bradford (B6269)

Wetherby (1910)

Private
Linton Lane, Wetherby LS22 4JF
Tel **(0937) 63375**
Mem 550
Sec WF Gibb
Pro D Padgett
Holes 18 L 6235 yds SSS 70
Recs Am–69 RJ Patterson (1987)
Pro–66 MB Ingham (1985)
V'trs WE–U after 10am
SOC–Wed–Fri
Fees £10 (£13)
Loc Centre 3/4 mile

Whitwood (1987)

Public
Altofts Lane, Whitwood, Castleford WF10 5PZ
Tel **(0997) 512835**
Mem 330
Sec S Hicks (0997) 558596
Pro R Holland
Holes 9 L 6176 yds SSS 69
Recs Am–77 J Knight (1988)
V'trs WD–U WE–booking service
Loc M62 Junction 31/A655 1 mile

Woodhall Hills (1906)

Private
Calverley, Pudsey LS28 5QY
Tel **(0532) 564771/554594**
Mem 315
Sec D Harkness
Pro MD Lord (0532) 562857
Holes 18 L 6102 yds SSS 69
Recs Am–66 PA Crosby
Pro–66 M Ingham
V'trs WD–U Sat–after 4.30pm
Sun–after 10.30am
Fees £7 (£9)
Loc 4 miles W of Bradford off A647

Woodsome Hall (1922)

Private
Woodsome Hall, Fenay Bridge, Huddersfield
Tel **(0484) 602971**
Mem 394 194(L) 103(J) 65(5)
Sec EV Hartley (0484) 602739, Mrs P Bates
Pro KB Scarr (0484) 602034
Holes 18 L 6088 yds SSS 69
Recs Am–68 EW Hirst
Pro–65 D Jagger
V'trs U exc Tues–NA before 4 pm
Fees £12 (£15)
Loc 6 miles SE of Huddersfield on Sheffield/Penistone road A629

Wortley (1894)

Private
Hermit Hill Lane, Wortley, nr Sheffield S30 4DF
Tel **(0742) 885294**
Mem 300
Sec JL Dalby
Pro J Tilson (0742) 886490
Holes 18 L 5983 yds SSS 69
Recs Am–67
Pro–66
V'trs U SOC
Fees £12 (£15)
Loc 2 miles W of M1 Junction 36, off A629

Ireland

Co Antrim

Ballycastle (1890)

Private
Ballycastle BT64 6QP
Tel **(026 57) 62536**
Mem 650
Sec TJ Sheehan (Hon), ME Page (Hon)
Pro T Stewart (026 57) 62506
Holes 18 L 5882 yds SSS 69
Recs Am–66 F Fleming, J McAleese, RJ McCoy
Pro–64 F Daly
V'trs U H SOC
Fees £6 (£8) W–£35 M–£85
Loc N Antrim coast between Portrush and Cushendall

Ballyclare (1923)

Private
25 Springvale Road, Ballyclare
Tel **(096 03) 22696**
Mem 400
Sec H McConnell (096 03) 22051
Holes 9 L 6708 yds SSS 71
Recs Am–69 J Foster
Pro–72 E Jones
V'trs WD–U Sat–NA before 6pm Sun–NA before noon
Fees £3 (£6)
Loc $1^1/_2$ miles N of Ballyclare. 14 miles N of Belfast

Ballymena (1903)

Private
128 Raceview Road, Ballymena BT42 4HY
Tel **(0266) 861207/861487**
Mem 975
Sec WRG Pogue (Mgr)
Pro J Gallaher (0266) 861652
Holes 18 L 5168 yds SSS 67
Recs Am–62 D Cunning
V'trs WD/Sun–U SOC
Fees £7 (£9)
Loc 2 miles E on A42

Bushfoot (1890)

Private
Portballintrae, Bushmills
Tel **(026 57) 31317**
Mem 603
Sec RF Young
Holes 9 L 5572 yds SSS 67
Recs Am–57 A McIlroy (1987)
V'trs U Sat–NA after noon SOC
Fees £5 (£6) W–£20 M–£45
Loc 1 mile N of Bushmills

Cairndhu (1928)

Private
192 Coast Road, Ballygally, Larne BT40 2QC
Tel **(0574) 83248**
Mem 800
Sec Mrs J Robinson (0574) 83324
Pro R Walker (0574) 83417
Holes 18 L 6112 yds SSS 69
Recs Am–64 B McMillen, R Houston
Pro–64 D Jones, P Townsend
V'trs U
Fees £6 (£8.50)
Loc 4 miles N of Larne

Carrickfergus (1926)

Private
35 North Road, Carrickfergus BT38 8LP
Tel **(096 03) 63713**
Mem 800
Sec ID Jardine
Pro R Stevenson (093 03) 51803
Holes 18 L 5769 yds SSS 68
Recs Am–64 P Vizard
Pro–64 N Drew
V'trs U
Fees £5 (£7) W–£20
Loc Carrickfergus $^1/_2$ mile via Albert Road
Mis Buggies for hire

Cushendall (1937)

Private
21 Shore Road, Cushendall
Tel **(026 67) 71318**
Mem 659
Sec S McLaughlin (0266) 73366
Holes 9 L 4678 yds SSS 63
Recs Am–62 S McKillop
V'trs WE–restricted SOC
Fees £5 (£6) M–£40
Loc In village 25 miles N of Larne

Dunmurry (1905)

Private
91 Dunmurry Lane, Dunmurry, Belfast BT17 9JS
Tel **(0232) 621402**
Mem 380 120(L) 50(J)
Sec JD Porter
Pro G Bleakley (0232) 301179
Holes 18 L 5333 metres SSS 68
Recs Am–68 A Young
Pro–70 V Bruce
V'trs Tues & Thurs–NA after 5pm Sat–NA before 5pm SOC
Fees £6 (£7.50) SOC–£5 (£6)
Loc Dunmurray $^1/_2$ mile. Belfast 5 miles

Greenisland (1894)

Private
156 Upper Road, Greenisland, Carrickfergus BT38 8RW
Tel **(0232) 862236**
Mem 480
Sec J Wyness (0232) 864583
Holes 9 L 5434 metres SSS 68
Recs Am–66
V'trs WD–U Sat–NA before 5pm SOC–exc Sat
Fees £6 (£7)
Loc 9 miles NE of Belfast

Larne (1894)

Private
54 Ferris Bay Road, Islandmagee, Larne BT40 3RT
Tel **(0574) 82228**
Mem 320
Sec JB Stewart (09603) 72043
Holes 9 L 6114 yds SSS 69
Recs Am–66 IA Nesbitt
Pro–68 N Drew
V'trs WD–U WE–M after 5pm SOC–WD/Sun
Fees £4 (£8)
Loc Larne Harbour 1 mile (by sea) or 6 miles N of Whitehead on Browns Bay road

Lisburn (1891)

Private
68 Eglantine Road, Lisburn BT27 5RQ
Tel **(084 62) 72186**
Mem 1100
Sec TC McCullough (084 62) 77216
Pro BR Campbell (084 62) 77217
Holes 18 L 5708 metres SSS 72
Recs Am–68 J Boyd
V'trs WD–U WE–M SOC–Mon & Thurs
Fees £9
Loc 3 miles S of Lisburn

Massereene (1895)

Private
51 Lough Road, Antrim BT41 4DQ
Tel **(08494) 63293**
Mem 850
Sec Mrs M Agnew (08494) 62096
Pro J Smyth (08494) 64074
Holes 18 L 6614 yds SSS 72
V'trs U SOC
Fees £8.50 (£10)
Loc Antrim $^1/_2$ mile

Rathmore (1947)

Private
Bushmills Road, Portrush BT56 8JG
Tel **(0265) 2285**
Mem 299
Sec DR Williamson
Holes Play over Portrush

Royal Portrush (1888)

Private
Dunluce Road, Portrush BT56 8JQ
Tel **(0265) 822311**
Mem 864 255(L)
Sec Miss W Erskine
Pro DA Stevenson (0265) 823335
Holes Dunluce 18 L 6772 yds SSS 72
Valley 18 L 6273 yds SSS 70
9 holes L 1187 yds

For map index see page 203.

Recs Dunluce Am–68 JB Carr, M Edwards
Pro–66 J Hargreaves
Valley Am–65 MJC Hoey
V'trs WD–U Sat–NA before 2.30pm
Sun–NA before 10am SOC
Fees Dunluce £12 (£12)
Valley £8 (£11)
Loc Portrush Coastal Rd 1/2 mile

Whitehead (1904)

Private
McCrae's Brae, Whitehead, Carrickfergus BT38 9NZ
Tel **(096 03) 53792/53631**
Mem 649
Sec J Niblock, DA Dinsmore (096 03) 53631
Pro H Graham
Holes 18 L 6426 yds SSS 71
Recs Am–68 A Hope
V'trs U exc Sat SOC–exc Sat
Fees £6 (£8)
Loc 1/2 mile outside town off main road to Island Magee

Co Armagh

County Armagh (1893)

Private
Newry Road, Armagh
Tel **(0861) 522501**
Mem 799
Sec HD Somerville (0861) 523137 (home)
Pro L Fisher (0861) 525864
Holes 18 L 6184 yds SSS 69
Recs Am–68
Pro–65
V'trs U SOC
Fees £5 (£8)
Loc 40 miles SW of Belfast

Craigavon

Public
Golf/Ski Centre, Turmoyra Lane, Silverwood, Lurgan, Craigavon
Tel **(0762) 6606**
Sec MM Shanks (0762) 42413
Holes 18 L 6496 yds SSS 71
Fees Season and daily tickets
Loc Lurgan 1 1/2 miles
Mis 12 hole pitch & putt course. Floodlit driving range

Lurgan (1893)

Private
The Demesne, Lurgan BT67 9BN
Tel **(0762) 322087**
Mem 686
Sec Mrs G Turkington
Pro D Paul
Holes 18 L 5836 metres SSS 70
Recs Am–66 S Magee
Pro–66 R Carr
V'trs U SOC
Fees £9 (£11)
Loc Town centre 1/4 mile

Portadown (1906)

Private
Carrickblacker, Portadown
Tel **(0762) 355356**
Mem 748
Sec Mrs ME Holloway
Pro P Stevenson
Holes 18 L 6119 yds SSS 70
Recs Am–68
Pro–63
V'trs WD–U WE–M
Fees £5 (£7)
Loc Portadown 3 miles

Tandragee (1922)

Private
Markethill Road, Tandragee, Craigavon BT62 2ER
Tel **(0762) 840727**
Mem 850
Sec A Best (0762) 841272
Pro J Black (0762) 841761
Holes 18 L 6084 yds SSS 69
Recs Am–62 P Topley
V'trs U SOC
Fees £7 (£10)
Loc Armagh city 10 miles. Craigavon 8 miles

Belfast

Ballyearl Golf Centre

Public
585 Doagh Road, Newtownabbey BT36 8RZ
Tel **(02313) 48287**
Sec A Clements (02313) 861211
Holes 9 L 2362 yds Par 3 course
V'trs U
Fees £2 (£2.75)
Loc N of Mossley on B59
Mis Driving range

Balmoral (1914)

Private
Lisburn Road, Belfast
Tel **(0232) 381514**
Mem 500
Pro J Fisher (0232) 667747
Holes 18 L 5679 metres SSS 70
Recs Am–66 M Wilson
Pro–64 D Jones
V'trs U
Fees £6 (£9)
Loc Balmoral–Kings Hall

Belvoir Park (1927)

Private
Newtown Breda, Belfast BT8 4AN
Tel **(0232) 641159/692817**
Mem 1038
Sec WI Davidson (0232) 491693 /646113
Pro GM Kelly (0232) 646714
Holes 18 L 6476 yds SSS 71
Recs Am–66 TS Anderson
Pro–66 P Alliss, EC Brown
V'trs U Sat–M
Fees £12 (£15)
Loc City centre 3 miles

Cliftonville (1911)

Private
Westland Road, Belfast
Tel **(0232) 744158**
Mem 429
Sec JM Henderson
Holes 9 L 4678 yds SSS 69
Recs Am–66 WRA Tennant
Pro–67 S Hamill
V'trs U exc Sat
Fees On application
Loc Belfast

Fortwilliam (1894)

Private
Downview Avenue, Belfast
Tel **(0232) 370770**
Mem 1050
Sec RJ Campbell
Pro P Hanna (0232) 770980
Holes 18 L 5642 yds SSS 67
Recs Am–63 G Glover
Pro–67 F Daly, J Kinsella
V'trs U
Fees £9 (£12)
Loc 2 miles N of Belfast centre

Gilnahirk (1983)

Public
Upper Bramel Road, Belfast
Tel **(0232) 448477**
Mem 200
Sec K Gray (Mgr)
Pro K Gray
Holes 9 L 2699 metres
V'trs U
Fees £2 (£2.50)
Loc 3 miles SE of city centre

Knockbracken

Private
Ballymaconaghy Road, Knockbracken, Belfast BT8
Tel **(0232) 792108**
Mem 300
Sec P Laverty (Hon) (0232) 401811
Pro D Patterson (0232) 401811
Holes 18 L 5312 yds SSS 68
V'trs U SOC
Fees £4 (£5)
Loc 2 miles SW of Belfast, near Four Winds

Malone (1895)

Private
240 Upper Malone Road, Dunmurry, Belfast BT17 9LB
Tel **(0232) 612695**
Mem 759 379(L) 211(J) 29(5)
Sec JE Osborough (0232) 612758
Pro PM O'Hagan (0232) 614917

For explanation of abbreviations see page 202.

Holes 18 L 6499 yds SSS 71
9 L 2895 yds SSS 34
Recs Pro–68 E Jones
V'trs Wed–NA after 2pm Sat–NA before 5pm SOC–Mon & Thurs
Fees £10 (£13)
Loc 6 miles S of Belfast

Ormeau (1893)

Private
Ravenhill Road, Belfast
Tel (0232) 641069
Mem 250 70(L) 30(J) 28(5)
Sec R Burnett (0232) 59605
Holes 9 L 5308 yds SSS 65
V'trs U
Fees £4 (£5)
Loc South Belfast

Shandon Park (1926)

Private
73 Shandon Park, Belfast BT5 6NY
Tel (0232) 701799
Mem 1048
Sec LH Wallace (Mgr) (0232) 401856
Pro CP Posnett (0232) 797859
Holes 18 L 6252 yds SSS 70
Recs Am–64 N Anderson
Pro–68 CP Posnett
V'trs WD–U Sat–NA before 5pm SOC
Fees £9 (£12)
Loc City centre 3 miles

The Knock Golf Club (1895)

Private
Summerfield, Dundonald, Belfast BT16 0QX
Tel (023 18) 2249
Mem 870
Sec B Jenkins OBE MBIM (023 18) 3251
Pro G Fairweather (023 18) 3825
Holes 18 L 5845 metres SSS 71
Recs Am–67 KH Graham
Pro–69 PR McGuirk
V'trs U SOC–Mon & Thurs
Fees D–£10 (£14)
Loc 4 miles E of Belfast centre

Co Carlow

Borris (1908)

Private
Deerpark, Borris
Tel (0503) 73143
Mem 250
Sec EC Lennon
Holes 9 L 6026 yds SSS 69
Recs Am–67
V'trs WD–U Sun–M SOC–WD/Sat (Apr–Sept)
Fees £5 (£6)

Carlow (1899)

Private
Oak Park, Carlow
Tel (0503) 31695
Mem 820
Sec Mrs Meaney (0503) 42599
Pro A Gilbert
Holes 18 L 6347 yds SSS 70
Recs Am–65 P Mulcare, RD Carr
Pro–68 C O'Connor
V'trs U
Fees £7 (£10)
Loc Carlow

Co Cavan

Belturbet (1950)

Private
Erne Hill, Belturbet
Tel (049) 22287
Mem 150
Sec JC Enright
Holes 9 L 5180 yds SSS 64
Recs Am–64 J Costello (1982)
V'trs U
Fees £5
Loc Town centre 1/2 mile

Blacklion (1962)

Private
Toam, Blacklion, via Sligo
Tel (0017) 53024
Mem 120
Sec R Thompson
Holes 9 L 5544 metres SSS 69
Recs Am–66 P Cafferky
V'trs U SOC
Fees £3 (£4) W–£10
Loc 12 miles SW of Enniskillen on A4. 10 miles E of Manorhamilton

Cabra Castle (1978)

Private
Kingscourt
Mem 110
Sec F Leahy (042) 67189
Holes 9 L 5308 metres SSS 68
V'trs U
Fees D–£3 (D–£3)
Loc 2 miles E of Kingscourt

County Cavan (1894)

Private
Drumelis, Cavan
Tel (049) 31283
Mem 300 150(L) 51(J)
Sec M Murray (049) 32170
Holes 18 L 5519 metres SSS 69
Recs Am–66 A Cafferty
Pro–65 J Purcell (1987)
V'trs U
Fees £6
Loc 2 miles W of Cavan Town

Virginia (1946)

Private
Virginia
Tel (049) 44103 (Sec)
Mem 172
Sec F McEvoy
Holes 9 L 4520 yds SSS 62
Recs Am–PJ O'Reilly
V'trs U
Loc 50 miles NW of Dublin

Co Clare

Drumoland Castle

Public
Newmarket-on-Fergus
Tel (061) 71144
Mem 150
Sec M Wright
Holes 18 L 6098 yds SSS 71
Recs Am–74 Dr C Hackett (1986)
V'trs U SOC
Fees D–£10
Loc 18 miles NW of Limerick

Ennis (1907)

Private
Drumbiggle Road, Ennis
Tel (065) 24074
Mem 497
Sec J Cooney
Pro M Ward (065) 20690
Holes 18 L 5358 metres SSS 68
Recs Am–64 G Roche
Pro–66 P Skerritt
V'trs U exc Sun SOC
Fees £10 SOC–£8 (£9)
Loc 1/2 mile NW of town

Kilkee (1908)

Private
East End, Kilkee
Tel Kilkee 48
Mem 343 160(L)
Sec TM Lillis Kilkee 341
Holes 9 L 6185 yds SSS 69
Recs Am–68 D Nagle, N Cotter
V'trs U SOC (exc July/Aug)
Fees £5.50 W–£22 M–£45
Loc E end of Kilkee

Kilrush (1934)

Public
Parknamoney, Kilrush
Tel (065) 51138
Mem 150
Sec N O'Regan
Holes 9 L 2739 yds SSS 67
Recs Am–64 DF Nagle
V'trs U SOC
Fees £5
Loc Kerry–Clare route

Lahinch (1892)

Private
Lahinch
Tel **(065) 81003**
Mem 1200
Pro R McCavery (065) 81408
Holes Old 18 L 6699 yds SSS 73
Castle 18 L 5265 yds SSS 67
V'trs WD–U WE–NA 9–10.30am and 1–2pm SOC
Fees £15 (£18) Castle £10
Loc Ennistymon 2 miles on T69

Shannon (1966)

Private
Shannon Airport
Tel **(061) 61020**
Mem 403
Sec JJ Quigley (061) 61849
Pro A Pyke (061) 61551
Holes 18 L 6854 yds SSS 73
Recs Am–63 J Purcell
Pro–65 D Durnian
V'trs WD–U SOC
Fees £10
Loc Shannon Airport Terminal 300 yds

Spanish Point (1915)

Private
Miltown Malbay
Tel **(065) 84198**
Mem 100
Sec G O'Loughlin
Holes 9 L 3124 yds SSS 54
Recs Am–28 PJ Leyden
Pro–23 P Skerritt
V'trs U
Fees £4 W–£20
Loc Miltown Malbay 2 miles

Co Cork

Bandon (1910)

Private
Castlebernard, Bandon
Tel **(023) 41111**
Mem 520
Sec B O'Neill (023) 41998
Pro T O'Boyle (023) 42224
Holes 18 L 5663 metres SSS 69
Recs Am–68 J Carroll
V'trs U
Fees £7 (£9)
Loc Bandon 1½ miles

Bantry (1975)

Private
Donemark, Bantry
Tel **(027) 50579**
Mem 250
Sec B Harrington (027) 50665
Holes 9 L 6436 yds SSS 70
Pro–66 C O'Connor Jr
V'trs U
Fees D–£6
Loc Bantry 1 mile on Glengarriff Road

Charleville (1909)

Private
Smiths Road, Charleville
Tel **(011) 81257**
Mem 250
Sec T Murphy
Holes 18 L 6380 yds SSS 69
Recs Am–68 T Murphy
V'trs U
Fees £6
Loc On main road between Cork and Limerick

Cobh (1986)

Private
Ballywilliam, Cobh
Tel **(021) 812399**
Mem 200
Sec M Hennessy (021) 811372
Holes 9 L 4338 metres SSS 63
Recs Am–65 G Mellerick
Pro–64 C O'Connor Sr
V'trs WD–U WE/BH–NA before noon
Fees £4 (£5)
Loc 16 miles E of Cork. 1 mile N of Cobh

Cork (1888)

Private
Little Island
Tel **(021) 353263**
Mem 350 160 (L)
Sec M Sands (021) 353451
Pro D Higgins (021) 353037
Holes 18 L 6065 metres SSS 72
Recs Am–66 P Murphy
V'trs WD–U exc 1–2pm daily & Thurs WE–10.30am–12 and after 2.30pm SOC
Fees £12 (£15) SOC–£11
Loc 5 miles E of Cork, ½ mile off Cork–Cobh road

Doneraile (1927)

Private
Doneraile
Tel **(022) 24137**
Mem 200
Sec F Carey
Holes 9 L 5528 yds SSS 67
V'trs U
Fees £3
Loc Town ½ mile

Douglas (1909)

Private
Douglas
Tel **(021) 891086**
Mem 839
Sec B Barrett (021) 895297
Pro GS Nicholson (021) 362055
Holes 18 L 5651 metres SSS 69
Recs Am–66 D O'Herlihy
Pro–64 E Darcy
V'trs WD–U WE–NA before 11.30am SOC–WD
Fees IR£11 (IR£12)
Loc Cork 3 miles

Dunmore (1967)

Private
Dunmore, Clonakilty
Tel **(023) 33352**
Mem 127
Sec M Minihan (023) 33858
Holes 9 L 4464 yds SSS 61
Recs Am–65
Pro–62
V'trs U SOC
Fees £4
Loc 3½ miles S of Clonakilty

East Cork (1971)

Private
Gortacue, Midleton
Tel **(021) 631687/631273**
Mem 250
Sec M Moloney
Holes 18 L 5207 metres SSS 69
Recs Am–66 B O'Regan (1983)
V'trs WD–U WE–NA before noon BH–U
Fees £6
Loc 2 miles N of Midleton on L35

Fermoy (1887)

Private
Corin, Fermoy
Mem 200
Sec P McCarthy (025) 31642 (home)
Holes 18 L 5399 metres SSS 68 Par 70
Recs Am–65 T Cleary
V'trs U SOC
Fees £5
Loc Fermoy 2 miles

Glengarriff (1936)

Private
Glengarriff
Tel **(027) 63150**
Mem 67
Sec N Clarke
Holes 9 L 4328 yds SSS 61
Recs Am–62 J O'Sullivan
V'trs U
Fees £4
Loc Glengarriff 1 mile

Kanturk (1974)

Private
Fairy Hill, Kanturk
Tel **(029) 50534**
Mem 130
Sec WJ Heffernan (029) 76132
Holes 9 L 5527 yds SSS 69
Recs Am–72 D O'Riordan, M Archdeacon (1987)
V'trs U
Fees £4
Loc 1½ miles SW of Kanturk

Kinsale (1912)

Private
Ringenane, Belgooly, Kinsale
Tel **(021) 772197**
Mem 310
Sec E O'Leary
Holes 9 L 5332 metres SSS 68
Recs Am–66 C Coughlan
V'trs U WE–NA SOC
Fees £6
Loc Kinsale 2 miles. Cork 16 miles

Macroom (1924)

Private
Lackaduve, Macroom
Tel **(026) 41072**
Mem 273
Sec J O'Brien
Holes 9 L 5439 metres SSS 68
Recs Am–66 J Mills
V'trs U SOC
Fees D–IR£5
Loc Bus Depot 1/2 mile

Mallow (1948)

Private
Balleyellis, Mallow
Tel **(022) 21145**
Mem 1500
Sec JP Shannon (022) 22465
Pro S Conway
Holes 18 L 6559 yds SSS 71
Recs Am–66 J Murphy (1982)
V'trs WD–U before 5pm SOC
Fees D–£8 W–£20
Loc 1 1/2 miles SE of Mallow Bridge

Mitchelstown (1908)

Private
Mitchelstown
Tel **(025) 24072**
Mem 200
Sec PA Brennan (025) 84115
Holes 9 L 5057 metres SSS 67
Recs Am–64 A Pierce
V'trs U SOC
Fees £6
Loc 30 miles N of Cork

Monkstown (1908)

Private
Parkgarriffe, Monkstown
Tel **(021) 841225**
Mem 600
Sec JP Curtin (021) 841376
Pro B Murphy (021) 841686
Holes 18 L 5534 metres SSS 68
Recs Am–66
V'trs U
Fees £10 (£11)
Loc 7 miles S of Cork

Muskerry (1897)

Private
Carrigrohane
Tel **(021) 85297**
Mem 713
Sec JJ Moynihan
Pro WM Lehane (021) 85104
Holes 18 L 5786 metres SSS 70
Recs Am–66 J McHenry, D O'Flynn
Pro–66 J Hegerty
V'trs WD–U exc 4.30–6.30pm
WE–NA before 3.30pm
Fees £10
Loc 6 miles W of Cork

Skibbereen (1931)

Private
Skibbereen
Tel **(028) 21227**
Mem 300
Sec J Hamilton (028) 21673
Holes 9 L 5774 yds SSS 68
Recs Am–65 B McDaid
V'trs U
Fees £6 W–£42
Loc West 1 mile

Youghal (1940)

Private
Knockaverry, Youghal
Tel **(024) 92787**
Mem 230 140(L) 50(J)
Sec M O'Sullivan
Pro D Higgins
Holes 18 L 6223 yds SSS 69
Recs Am–65 F Wright
V'trs U
Fees IR£8
Loc 30 miles E of Cork

Co Donegal

Ballybofey & Stranorlar (1958)

Private
Ballybofey
Tel **(074) 31093**
Mem 206 75(L) 30(J)
Sec I Kee (074) 31050
Holes 18 L 5913 yds SSS 68
Recs Am–64 J McMenamin
V'trs U SOC
Fees £6
Loc Stranorlar 1/4 mile

Ballyliffin (1947)

Private
Ballyliffin, Clonmany
Tel **Clonmany 74417**
Mem 350
Sec KJ O'Doherty
Holes 18 L 6611 yds SSS 71
Recs Am–67 G Doherty
V'trs U SOC–arrange with Sec
Fees IR£5 (IR£6)
Loc 12 miles N of Buncrana

Buncrana (1951)

Public
Buncrana
Mem 69
Sec D Hegarty
Pro NS Doherty
Holes 9 L 2020 yds SSS 59
Recs Am–63 J McLaughlin
V'trs U

Bundoran (1894)

Private
Great Northern Hotel, Bundoran
Tel **(072) 41302**
Mem 400
Sec JC Roarty (072) 41360
Pro L Robinson (072) 41302
Holes 18 L 6328 yds
Recs Am–67 J Murray
Pro–66 E Darcy
V'trs U WE–busy SOC
Fees £8 (£9)
Loc East boundary Bundoran

Donegal (1960)

Private
Murvagh
Tel **(073) 34054**
Mem 369
Sec J Nixon (073) 22166
Holes 18 L 7271 yds SSS 73
Recs Am–68 Fr B McBride
V'trs U SOC
Fees £6 (£8)
Loc 7 miles S of Donegal on N18

Dunfanaghy (1903)

Public
Dunfanaghy
Tel **(074) 36335**
Mem 70
Sec D Arnold (074) 36142
Holes 18 L 5066 metres SSS 66
Recs Am–64 J Brogan
Pro–66 L Wallace
V'trs U SOC
Fees IR£5.50 (IR£6.50)
Loc 1/4 mile from Dunfanaghy on N56

Greencastle (1892)

Private
Via Lifford, Greencastle
Tel **(077) 81013**
Mem 300
Sec HM Morris (077) 82042
Holes 9 L 5386 yds SSS 65
Recs Am–62 C McCarroll
Pro–67 D Jones
V'trs WD–U WE–Restricted SOC
Fees £5 (£7)
Loc Nr Moville

Gweedore (1923)

Private
Derrybeg, Letterkenny
Tel **(075) 31140**
Mem 170
Sec C Campbell (075) 31545
Holes 18 L 6230 yds SSS 69
Recs Am–64 S Murphy
V'trs U
Fees £5 (£7) W–£28 M–£95
Loc West Donegal

For map index see page 203.

Letterkenny (1913)

Private
Barnhill, Letterkenny
Tel **(074) 21150**
Mem 298
Sec J McBride
Holes 18 L 6299 yds SSS 71
Recs Am–67 P Shiels
V'trs U SOC
Fees £5 (£5)
Loc NE 1 mile

Narin & Portnoo (1931)

Private
Narin, Portnoo
Tel **(075) 45107**
Mem 400
Sec S Murray
Holes 18 L 5950 yds SSS 68
Recs Am–64 B McBride
Pro–62 R Browne
V'trs WD–U Sat–restricted 1–2.30pm
Sun–restricted H SOC
Fees £6 Sun–£7 SOC–£3
Loc 6 miles N of Ardara

North West (1891)

Private
Lisfannon, Fahan
Tel **(077) 61027**
Mem 300
Sec D Coyle (077) 61843
Holes 18 L 6203 yds SSS 69
Recs Am–65 F Friel
Pro–64 M Doherty
V'trs U
Fees IR£5 (IR£6) W–IR£20 M–IR£45
Loc 12 miles W of Londonderry.
Buncrana 2 miles
Mis Links course

Otway (1893)

Private
Saltpans, Rathmullen,
Letterkenny
Tel **(074) 58319**
Mem 110
Sec H Gallagher (074) 58210
Holes 9 L 4134 yds SSS 60
Recs Am–29 F Friel
V'trs U
Fees D–£3
Loc By Lough Swilly

Portsalon (1891)

Private
Portsalon, Letterkenny
Tel **Portsalon 59102**
Mem 108
Sec M Kerr
Holes 18 L 5844 yds SSS 68
Recs Am–68 J Brogan
Pro–71 J Henderson
V'trs U
Fees £4
Loc 20 miles N of Letterkenny

Rosapenna (1898)

Private
Golf Hotel, Rosapenna
Tel **(074) 55301**
Mem 89
Sec JJ McBride
Holes 18 L 6254 yds SSS 70
Recs Am–M McGinley
Pro–68 F Daly
V'trs U
Fees £1.50 (£1.75)
Loc Via Letterkenny

Co Down

Ardglass (1896)

Private
Castle Place, Ardglass
Tel **(0396) 841219**
Mem 676
Sec Mrs P Rooney
Holes 18 L 5462 metres SSS 69
Recs Am–66 J Milligan
Pro–69 H Jackson
V'trs U
Fees £5 (£8)
Loc Downpatrick 7 miles

Banbridge (1913)

Private
Huntly Road, Banbridge
Tel **(082 06) 22342**
Mem 400
Sec TF Fee (082 06) 23831
Holes 12 L 5879 yds SSS 68
Recs Am–65 K Stevenson
V'trs U SOC
Fees £5 (£6)
Loc Banbridge 1 mile

Bangor (1903)

Private
Broadway, Bangor
Tel **(0247) 465133**
Mem 1100
Sec EA Bolster (0247) 270922
Pro N Drew (0247) 462164
Holes 18 L 6372 yds SSS 71
Recs Am–67 N Anderson
Pro–66 C O'Connor
V'trs U
Fees £7.50 (£10)

Bright Castle (1979)

Private
14 Coniamstown Road, Bright,
Downpatrick
Tel **(0396) 841319**
Mem 40
Sec R Reid
Pro H Duggan
Holes 18 L 6730 yds
Recs Am–70 A Ennis
V'trs U SOC
Fees £4 Sat–£4 Sun–£5
Loc Downpatrick 5 miles on
Killough road

Carnalea (1927)

Private
Station Road, Bangor BT19 1EZ
Tel **(0247) 465004**
Mem 770
Sec JH Crozier (0247) 270368
Pro M McGee (0247) 270122
Holes 18 L 5584 yds SSS 67
Recs Am–64 P Nelson
V'trs U SOC–WD
Fees £6 (£9.50)
Loc Adjoining Carnalea Station

Clandeboye (1933)

Private
Conlig, Newtownards BT23 3PN
Tel **(0247) 271767/473706**
Mem 1077
Sec TI Marks (0247) 271767
Pro P Gregory (0247) 271750
Holes 18 L 6072 metres SSS 73
18 L 5172 metres SSS 67
Recs Am–68 D Jackson
Pro–68 J Heggarty, D Jones,
D Feherty
V'trs WD–U Sat–M Sun–M before
10am and 12.30–1.30pm
Fees Long £9 (£12) Short £8 (£10)
W–£35
Loc Bangor 2 miles on
Newtownards road

Donaghadee (1899)

Private
Warren Road, Donaghadee BT21 0PQ
Tel **(0237) 888697/883624**
Mem 1250
Sec SG Managh (0237) 883624
Pro W Hackworth (0237) 882392
Holes 18 L 5576 metres Par 71
Recs Am–65 J Nelson
Pro–69 E Clarke
V'trs U Sat–M
Fees £8 (£10)
Loc Belfast 18 miles

Downpatrick (1932)

Private
Saul Road, Downpatrick
Tel **(0396) 2152**
Mem 713
Sec A Cannon
Holes 18 L 5702 metres SSS 69
V'trs U
Fees £5 (£8)

Helen's Bay (1896)

Private
Golf Road, Helen's Bay, Bangor
BT19 1TL
Tel **(0247) 852601**
Mem 708
Sec JH Ward (0247) 852815
Holes 9 L 5176 metres SSS 67

Recs Am–68 BW Lister
Pro–67 L Esdale
V'trs WD–U Sat/BH–M Sun–U
Fees On application
Loc Belfast 12 miles

Holywood (1904)

Private
Nuns Walk, Demesne Road, Holywood
Tel **(023 17) 2138**
Mem 800
Sec GR Magennis (023 17) 3135
Pro M Bannon (023 17) 5503
Holes 18 L 5885 yds SSS 68
Recs Am–61 J Watts
Pro–64 M Bannon
V'trs WD–1.30–2.15pm
WE–Sat after 5pm
Fees £7.25 (£9.50)

Kilkeel (1948)

Public
Mourne Park, Ballyardle, Kilkeel
Tel **(069 37) 62296**
Mem 400
Sec SW Rutherford (069 37) 62293
Holes 9 L 5623 metres SSS 69
Recs Am–65 F Reilly
V'trs U
Fees £5 (£6)
Loc Kilreel 3 miles on Newry road

Kirkistown Castle (1902)

Private
142 Main Road, Cloughey, Newtownards
Tel **(024 77) 71233/71353**
Mem 800
Sec RC Vine BEM MInstAM
Pro J Peden
Holes 18 L 5628 metres SSS 70
Recs Am–68 Jas Brown
Pro–71 RJ Polley, C O'Connor
V'trs WD–U WE/BH–NA 1st tee 9.30–10.30am and 12–1.30pm SOC
Fees £7.50 (£12)
Loc 25 miles SE of Belfast

Mahee Island (1930)

Private
Comber, Belfast
Tel **(0238) 541234**
Mem 400
Sec EP Trevorrow
Holes 9 L 2790 yds SSS 67
Recs Am–65 C Boyd
Pro–66 N Drew
V'trs U Sat–NA before 4.30pm
SOC–WD exc Mon
Fees £5 (£8)
Loc 14 miles S of Belfast

Mourne (1946)

Private
36 Golf Links Road, Newcastle BT33 0AX
Tel **(039 67) 23218**
Mem 330
Sec S Keenan
Holes Play over Royal Co Down

Royal Belfast (1881)

Private
Holywood, Craigavad
Tel **(0232) 428165**
Mem 1223
Sec Ian M Piggot
Pro D Carson
Holes 18 L 6205 yds SSS 70
Recs Am–65 RAD McMillan
Pro–67 C O'Connor
V'trs I Sat–NA before 4.30pm
Fees £12 (£15)
Loc E of Belfast on A2

Royal County Down (1889)

Private
Newcastle BT33 0AN
Tel **(039 67) 23314**
Mem 450
Sec RH Cotton
Pro ET Jones (039 67) 22419
Holes C'ship 18 L 6968 yds SSS 74
No 2 18 L 4100 yds SSS 60
Recs C'ship Am–66 J Bruen, JM Jamison
Pro–67 A Compston, B Gadd
V'trs Contact Sec for information
Fees D–£15 (D–£18)
Loc Belfast 30 miles

Scrabo (1907)

Private
233 Scrabo Road, Newtownards BT23 4SL
Tel **(0247) 812355**
Mem 750
Pro W Todd
Holes 18 L 5699 metres SSS 70
Recs Am–69 W Caughey (1987)
Pro–67 N Drew (1987)
V'trs WD–U WE–after 5pm SOC
Fees £6 (£9)
Loc 2 miles W of Newtownards

The Spa (1907)

Private
20 Grove Road, Ballynahinch BT24 8BR
Tel **(0238) 562365**
Mem 350
Sec J McGlass (0232) 812340
Holes 9 L 3155 yds SSS 70
Recs Am–67 R Wallace
V'trs U exc Wed–NA after 3pm Sat–NA
Fees £4 (£5)

Warrenpoint (1893)

Private
Lr Dromore Rd, Warrenpoint
Tel **(069 37) 72219**
Mem 1100
Sec J McMahon (069 37) 73695
Pro N Shaw (069 37) 72371
Holes 18 L 5628 metres SSS 70
Recs Am–66 K Stevenson
Pro–68 D Feherty
V'trs U SOC
Fees £8 (£10)
Loc 5 miles S of Newry

Co Dublin

Balbriggan (1945)

Private
Blackhall, Balbriggan
Tel **Balbriggan 412173**
Mem 500
Sec L Cashell 412229 (office)
Holes 18 L 5717 metres SSS 70
Recs Am–68 R Nugent (1987)
Pro–71 J Burns, J Kinsella (1988)
V'trs WD–U WE–M SOC
Fees £8 (£10)
Loc 1/4 mile S of Balbriggan

Ballinascorney (1971)

Private
Ballinascorney, Tallaght
Tel **(01) 512516**
Mem 315
Sec M Walsh 829030
Holes 9 L 5322 yds SSS 66
V'trs U

Beaverstown (1985)

Private
Beaverstown, Donabate
Tel **(01) 436439**
Mem 600
Sec E Smyth
Holes 18 L 5662 metres SSS 71
Recs Am–72 M Perry (1987)
V'trs WD–U WE/BH–M SOC
Fees £8 (£10)
Loc 4 miles N of Dublin Airport

Beech Park (1973)

Private
Johnstown, Rathcoole
Tel **(01) 580522/506887**
Mem 375
Sec G Cleary
Holes 18 SSS 67
Fees £4
Loc Rathcoole 1 mile on Kilteel road

Corballis (1971)

Public
Donabate
Sec PJ Boylan (01) 436583
Holes 18 L 4971 yds SSS 64
V'trs WD–U Sat–NA before 10am
Sun–NA SOC
Fees £4 (£6)
Loc 18 miles N of Dublin. Donabate 2 miles

For map index see page 203.

Deer Park (1974)

Public
Howth
Tel (01) 322624
Mem 250
Sec JJ Leonard
Holes 18 L 6647 yds SSS 73
Recs Am–72 N Hussey
V'trs U
Fees £4.80 (£5.80)
Loc 8 miles NE of Dublin
Mis Par 3 course. Pitch and putt

Donabate (1925)

Private
Balcarrick, Donabate
Tel (01) 436059
Mem 501
Sec Mrs C Campion (01) 436346
Pro H Jackson
Holes 18 L 6187 yds SSS 69
Recs Am–67 AJ Coughlan
Pro–65 M Murphy
V'trs WE/BH–NA
Loc Dublin Airport 8 miles

Dublin & County (1979)

Public
Corballis, Donabate
Tel (01) 436228
Mem 240
Sec P Boshell
Holes Play over Corballis
Public Course

Dun Laoghaire (1910)

Private
Dun Laoghaire, Eglinton Park, Dublin
Tel (01) 801055
Mem 972
Sec T Stewart (01) 803916
Pro O Mulhall (01) 801694
Holes 18 L 5463 metres SSS 60
Recs Am–67 H McKinney
Pro–65 P Skerritt
V'trs WD–U exc 1–2pm WE–M after 5 pm SOC
Fees IR£15 (£16)
Loc 7 miles S of Dublin

Forrest Little (1972)

Private
Cloghran
Tel (01) 40118$^3/_4$01763
Mem 900
Sec V Maslin
Pro T Murphy
Holes 18 L 5852 metres SSS 70
Recs Am–67 T Judd (1984)
Pro–65 C O'Connor Jr (1984)
V'trs WD–U
Fees IR£11
Loc Adjacent to Dublin Airport

Hermitage (1905)

Private
Lucan
Tel (01) 264549
Mem 1153
Sec Miss K Russell
Pro D Daly (01) 268491
Holes 18 L 6034 metres SSS 71
Recs Am–69 T Heverin
Pro–65 R Davis
V'trs U SOC
Fees £14 (£18)
Loc City centre 8 miles.
Lucan 1 mile

The Island (1890)

Private
Corballis, Donabate
Tel (01) 436104
Mem 550
Sec LA O'Connor (01) 436205
Holes 18 L 6320 yds SSS 71
Recs Am–B Moore, B Byrne
V'trs U WE–NA before noon
Fees £10 (£15)
Loc 14 miles N of Dublin

Killiney (1903)

Private
Killiney
Tel (01) 851983
Mem 528
Sec JB Jordan
Pro P O'Boyle
Holes 9 L 6201 yds SSS 69
Recs Am–72 N Duke
Pro–65 H Bradshaw
V'trs U
Fees D–£10
Loc 8 miles S of Dublin

Kilternan Hotel (1977)

Public
Kilternan
Tel (01) 955559
Mem 255
Sec T Bradley
Pro B Malone
Holes 18 L 5413 yds SSS 66
V'trs M SOC–WD
Fees £5 (£7)
Loc 5 miles S of Dublin

Lucan (1897)

Private
Celbridge Road, Lucan
Tel (01) 280246
Mem 392
Sec M O'Halloran
Holes 9 L 6287 yds 5747 metres
SSS 70
Recs Am–63 T Rogers
Pro–67 H Bradshaw
V'trs WD–U before 3pm WE/BH–M SOC–WD exc Thurs
Fees £8
Loc 14 miles W of Dublin centre near village of Lucan

Malahide (1892)

Private
Coast Road, Malahide
Tel Malahide 450248
Mem 250
Sec B Balger
Pro C Connolly
Holes 9 L 5568 yds SSS 67
Recs Am–63 P Killeen
V'trs U WE–Restricted
Fees £6
Loc 10 miles N of Dublin.
Town centre $^1/_2$ mile

Newlands (1926)

Private
Clondalkin, Dublin 22
Tel (01) 592903
Mem 959
Sec A O'Neill (01) 593157
Pro P Heeney(01) 593538
Holes 18 L 6184 yds SSS 69
Recs Am–66 R Burdon,
P Hanley Jr
Pro–68 C O'Connor
V'trs Tues/Wed pm–NA WD–NA 1.30–2.30pm WE/BH–NA SOC
Fees IR£14
Loc 6 miles SW of Dublin

Portmarnock (1894)

Private
Portmarnock
Tel (01) 323082
Mem 971
Sec W Bornemann
Pro P Townsend (01) 325157
Holes 27 'A' L 7097 yds SSS 75
'B' L 7047 yds SSS 75
'C' L 6596 yds SSS 74
Recs Am–68 JB Carr
Pro–65 G Player
V'trs I WE–XL
Fees £20 (£25) Ladies–£10 WD only
Loc 8 miles NE of Dublin

Rush (1943)

Private
Rush
Tel (01) 437548
Mem 322
Sec BJ Clear (01) 438177 (office)
Holes 9 L 5598 metres SSS 69
Recs Am–68 PJ Dolan
V'trs WD–U WE–M
Fees £7
Loc 16 miles N of Dublin

Skerries (1906)

Private
Skerries
Tel (01) 491204
Mem 748
Sec AJB Taylor (01) 491567
Pro J Kinsella (01) 490925
Holes 18 L 5852 metres SSS 70

For explanation of abbreviations see page 202.

V'trs U
Fees IR£10 (IR£12)
Loc 20 miles N of Dublin

Slade Valley (1970)

Private
Lynch Park, Brittas
Tel **(01) 582207**
Mem 500
Sec P Maguire (01) 582183
Pro G Egan
Holes 18 L 5337 metres SSS 68 Pro–64
Fees D–£7 (£8)
Loc 8 miles W of Dublin off N4

Woodbrook (1921)

Private
nr Bray
Tel **824799**
Mem 700
Sec D Smyth
Pro W Kinsella
Holes 18 L 6007 metres SSS 71
V'trs WD–U WE–phone Sec SOC
Fees £13 (£16)
Loc Dublin 11 miles

Dublin City

Carrickmines (1900)

Private
Carrickmines
Tel **(01) 955972**
Mem 371
Sec GW McConnell (01) 863020
Holes 18 L 6044 yds SSS 69
Recs Am–68
Pro–68
V'trs M
Fees £8 Sun–£10 Sat–NA
Loc 6 miles S of Dublin

Castle (1913)

Private
Woodside Drive, Rathfarnham, Dublin 14
Tel **(01) 904207**
Mem 800
Sec LF Blackburne
Pro D Kinsella (01) 933444
Holes 18 L 6168 metres SSS 69
Recs Am–69 J Bourke
Pro–65 B Browne
V'trs Mon/Thurs/Fri–U Wed–U before 12.30pm WE/BH–M SOC
Fees £13
Loc 5 miles S of city

Clontarf (1912)

Private
Donnycarney House, Malahide Road, Dublin 3
Tel **(01) 332669**
Mem 960
Sec MG O'Brien (01) 315085
Pro J Craddock (01) 310016
Holes 18 L 5447 metres SSS 68
Recs Am–65 M O'Shea
Pro–64 H Bradshaw
V'trs WD–U WE–M SOC
Fees £12
Loc City centre 2 miles

Edmondstown (1944)

Private
Rathfarnham, Dublin 16
Tel **(01) 932461**
Mem 420
Sec S Adams (01) 931082
Pro A Crofton (01) 934602
Holes 18 L 5663 metres SSS 69
V'trs WD–U WE–NA after noon
Fees £11 (£13)
Loc 7 miles S of city

Elm Park G & SC (1927)

Private
Nutley House, Donnybrook, Dublin 4
Tel **(01) 693438/693014**
Mem 1656
Sec H Montag (01) 693014
Pro S Green (01) 692650
Holes 18 L 5485 metres SSS 68
Recs Am–63 PF Hogan
Pro–63 P Townsend
V'trs U (phone first)
Fees £13 (£18) 5D–£40
Loc 3 miles S of city centre

Foxrock (1893)

Private
Foxrock, Torquay Road, Dublin 18
Tel **(01) 895668**
Mem 550
Sec J McReynolds (01) 893992
Holes 9 L 5699 metres SSS 69
Recs Am–68 D Campbell
Pro–68 H Jackson
V'trs WD/BH/Sun–M Tues/Sat–NA
Fees £10
Loc 5 miles S of Dublin city

Grange (1911)

Private
Whitechurch, Rathfarnham, Dublin 16
Tel **(01) 932832**
Mem 1050 235(L) 210(J) 12(5)
Sec JA O'Donoghue (01) 932889
Pro WD Sullivan (01) 932299
Holes 18 L 5517 metres SSS 69
Recs Am–64 WB Buckley
Pro–62 C O'Connor Jr
V'trs WD–U exc Tues/Wed pm–NA WE–M
Fees £12
Loc Rathfarnham

Howth (1916)

Private
Carrickbrack Road, Sutton, Dublin 13
Tel **(01) 323055**
Mem 1200
Sec Mrs A MacNiece
Pro JF McGuirk
Holes 18 L 5573 metres SSS 69
Recs Am–66 M Roe
Pro–71
V'trs WD–U exc Wed WE–M
Fees £10
Loc 9 miles NE of Dublin

Milltown (1907)

Private
Lower Churchtown Road, Milltown, Dublin 14
Tel **(01) 977060**
Mem 1497
Sec B Cassidy (01) 973199/976090
Pro C Greene (01) 977072
Holes 18 L 5669 metres SSS 69
Recs Am–64 JB Carr
Pro–64 C Greene
V'trs U
Fees £5 (£13)
Loc City centre 3 miles

Rathfarnham (1896)

Private
Newton, Dublin 16
Tel **(01) 931201/931561**
Mem 561
Sec VJ Coyle (01) 931201
Pro B O'Hara
Holes 9 L 5787 metres SSS 70
Recs Am–70 C O'Carrol, N Hynes, T O'Donnell
V'trs WD–U exc Tues WE–NA
Fees £9
Loc 6 miles S of Dublin

Royal Dublin (1885)

Private
Bull Island, Dollymount, Dublin 3
Tel **(01) 336346**
Mem 760
Sec JA Lambe
Pro L Owens (01) 336477 (Tournament Pro C O'Connor)
Holes 18 L 6858 yds SSS 73
Recs Am–67 G O'Donovan (1984)
Pro–63 B Langer, G Cullen (1985)
V'trs U exc Sat
Fees £20 (£25)
Loc 3¼ miles from city centre on coast road to Howth

St Anne's (1921)

Private
Bull Island, Raheny, Dublin 5
Tel **(01) 332797**
Mem 411
Sec J Carberry (01) 336471
Pro P Skerritt
Holes 9 holes L 5813 metres SSS 70
Recs Am–67 S Rodgers
Pro–64 P Skerritt
V'trs WD–am WE–NA BH–I SOC
Fees £12
Loc Dublin city centre 5 miles

For map index see page 203.

Stackstown (1975)

Private
Kellystown Road, Rathfarnham, Dublin 16
Tel (01) 942338/941993
Mem 840
Sec PA Power (01) 555204
Holes 18 L 5952 metres SSS 72
Recs Am–72 T O'Donoghue
V'trs WD–U SOC
Fees £8 (£10)
Loc 7 miles SE of Dublin

Sutton (1890)

Private
Cush Point, Burrow Road, Sutton, Dublin 13
Tel (01) 323013
Mem 198 162(L) 95(J) 53(5)
Sec H Quirke
Pro N Lynch
Holes 9 L 5522 yds SSS 67
Recs Am–64 M Hanway
Pro–64 L Owens (1987)
V'trs Tues–NA Sat–NA before 5.30pm
Fees £8 (£10)
Loc 7 miles E of Dublin

Co Fermanagh

Enniskillen (1896)

Private
Castlecoole, Enniskillen BT74 6HZ
Tel (0365) 25250
Mem 600
Sec CJ Greaves (0365) 24444
Holes 9 L 5476 metres SSS 69
Recs Am–67 K Prenter
V'trs U SOC
Fees D–£5
Loc 1 mile SE of Enniskillen in Castlecoole Estate

Co Galway

Athenry (1957)

Private
Derrydonnel, Oranmore
Tel (091) 94466
Mem 180
Sec G Doherty (091) 44730
Holes 9 L 5448 yds SSS 67
Recs Am–69 L Gardner
V'trs WD–U Sun–M
Fees £5 Sun–NA
Loc 10 miles E of Galway City on Athenry Road

Ballinasloe (1894)

Private
Ballinasloe
Tel (0905) 42126
Mem 450
Sec W O'Rourke (0905) 42435
Holes 18 L 5800 yds SSS 66 Par 68
Recs Am–66 D Madden
Pro–66 C O'Connor
V'trs U SOC
Fees £5
Loc Town centre 2 miles

Connemara (1973)

Private
Aillebrack, Ballyconnelly, nr Clifden
Tel (095) 23502
Mem 450
Sec S Birmingham (Hon)
Holes 18 L 6186 metres SSS 73
V'trs UH SOC–exc Sun & Open weeks
Fees £8–£14
Loc 8 miles SW of Clifden

Galway (1895)

Private
Blackrock, Salthill, Galway
Tel (91) 23038
Mem 950
Sec WC Caulfield (91) 22169
Pro D Wallace
Holes 18 L 5828 metres SSS 70
Recs Am–65 S Keenan (1987)
Pro–67 C Greene
V'trs Restricted Tues & Sun
Fees £15
Loc City centre 3 miles
Mis Catering (91) 21827

Gort (1924)

Private
Laughtyshaughnessy, Gort
Tel (091) 31336
Mem 120
Sec P Grealish (091) 31375
Pro E O'Connor
Holes 9 L 4976 metres SSS 66
Recs Am–64 G Cooney
Pro–66 C O'Connor
V'trs U
Fees D–£5
Loc Gort 1 mile on Tubber Road

Loughrea (1924)

Private
Graigue, Loughrea
Tel (091) 41049
Mem 185
Holes 9 L 5578 yds SSS 67
Recs Am–67 S Glynn
V'trs U SOC
Fees IR£4 (£5)
Loc 20 miles E of Galway. 1 mile N of town centre off Dublin–Galway road

Mount Bellew (1929)

Private
Mount Bellew, Ballinasloe
Tel (0905) 9259
Mem 104
Sec LJ Smyth
Holes 9 L 5564 yds SSS 67
Recs Am–67 B Hyland
V'trs U SOC
Fees £4 (£4) W–£20 M–£40

Oughterard (1973)

Private
Oughterard
Tel (091) 82131
Mem 300
Sec J Waters (091) 82381
Pro M Ryan
Holes 18 L 6150 yds SSS 69
Recs Am–73 B Fayerty (1987)
V'trs U
Fees £6–£8
Loc 15 miles W of Galway

Portumna (1907)

Private
Portumna
Tel (0509) 41059
Mem 160
Sec G Ryan (0509) 41442
Holes 9 L 5776 yds SSS 68
Recs Am–66 M Harney (1982)
Pro–63 H Bradshaw
V'trs U
Fees £5
Loc Portumna, on road to Ennis

Tuam (1907)

Private
Barnacurragh, Tuam
Tel (093) 24354
Mem 230
Sec J Hughes
Holes 18 L 6321 yds SSS 70
Recs Am–69 DJ McGrath
Pro–68 R Rafferty (1983)
V'trs Sun–NA SOC–WD
Fees £6
Loc 20 miles N of Galway

Co Kerry

Ballybunion (1896)

Private
Ballybunion
Tel (068) 27146
Mem 800
Sec S Walsh
Pro E Higgins (068) 27209
Holes Old 18 L 6542 yds
New 18 L 6477 yds
Recs Am–67 P Mulcare
V'trs U SOC
Fees D–£20 W–£70 M–£100

Ceann Sibeal (1924)

Private
Ballyferriter, Tralee
Tel (066) 56255
Mem 102
Sec G Partington (066) 51657
Holes 9 L 6222 yds SSS 68

Recs Am–69 P Slattery, A Spring
Pro–70 L Higgins
V'trs U SOC
Fees D–£6 W–£25
Loc Dingle Peninsula

Dooks (1889)

Private
Glenbeigh
Tel (066) 68205/68200(Members)
Mem 410
Sec M Shanahan (066) 67370
Holes 18 L 5346 metres SSS 68
Recs Am–67 G Sullivan
V'trs WD–UH WE/BH–Check first SOC
Fees £10
Loc 3 miles N of Glenbeigh on Ring of Kerry

Kenmare (1903)

Private
Kenmare
Tel (064) 41291
Mem 150
Sec SW Rowe
Holes 9 L 4400 metres SSS 64
Recs Am–64 B Mulcahy
V'trs U
Fees £6

Killarney (1891)

Private
O'Mahoney's Point, Killarney
Tel (064) 31034
Mem 740
Sec T Prendergast
Pro T Coveney (064) 31615
Holes Mahoney's Point 18 L 6152 metres SSS 70; Killeen 18 L 6389 metres SSS 71
Recs Mahoney's Point: Am–68 S Coyne(1968)
Killeen: Am–73 DF O'Sullivan
V'trs U H SOC
Fees £18
Loc 3 miles W of town

Parknasilla (1974)

Private
Parknasilla
Tel (064) 45122
Mem 20
Sec M Walsh (064) 45233
Pro C McCarthy (064) 45172
Holes 9 L 4650 metres SSS 65
Recs Am–28 J Bruen, NE McCann
Pro–28 J McCarthy
V'trs U
Fees £6
Loc Great Southern Hotel

Tralee (1904)

Private
West Barrow, Ardfert
Tel (066) 36379
Mem 500
Sec JW Kleynhans
Holes 18 L 6210 metres SSS 72
Recs Am–66 G O'Sullivan
V'trs WD–U WE–U after noon
SOC–WD/Sat
Fees £12 (£14)
Loc 8 miles W of Tralee centre
Mis First Arnold Palmer course in Europe

Waterville (1889)

Private
Ring of Kerry, Waterville
Tel (0667) 4102
Mem 252
Sec LA Morrissey
Pro L Higgins (0667) 4237
Holes 18 L 7184 yds SSS 74
Pro–65 L Higgins
V'trs U H SOC
Fees £18
Loc Ring of Kerry

Co Kildare

Athy (1906)

Private
Geraldine, Athy
Tel (0507) 31729
Mem 250
Sec M Hannon (0507) 31171
Holes 9 L 6158 yds SSS 69
V'trs WD–U Sat–M SOC–WD
Fees £4 (£6)

Bodenstown (1983)

Private
Bodenstown, Sallins
Tel (045) 97096
Mem 650
Sec P Place
Pro T Halpin
Holes 18 L 7031 yds SSS 72

Cill Dara (1920)

Private
Little Curragh, Kildare Town
Tel (045) 21433
Mem 200
Sec P Gill (045) 31946
Holes 9 L 5440 metres SSS 68
Recs Am–67 NP McAlinden
V'trs U
Fees £4 (£6)
Loc 1 mile E of Kildare Town

Clongowes (1966)

Private
Clongowes Wood College, Naas
Tel Clongowes Wood 68202
Mem 100
Sec A Pierce
Holes 9 L 5374 yds SSS 65
Recs Am–67
V'trs NA
Fees Clane 2 miles

Curragh (1883)

Private
Curragh
Tel (045) 41238/41714
Mem 500 160(L)
Sec PJ Coffey (Hon)
Pro P Lawlor
Holes 18 L 6003 metres SSS 71
Recs Am–67 S Conlon
Pro–69 A Whiston
V'trs U
Fees IR£6 (IR£9) 1988 prices
Loc 3 miles S of Newbridge
Mis Golf played here since 1852. Oldest club in the Republic

Knockanally (1985)

Private
Donadea, North Kildare
Tel (045) 69322
Mem 165
Sec N Lyons
Pro P Hickey
Holes 18 L 6484 yds SSS 72
Pro–66 K O'Donnell, D James (1988)
V'trs U
Fees £8 (£10)
Loc Maynooth 7 miles. Kilcock 5 miles. Enfield 3 miles on Dublin–Galway road

Naas (1896)

Private
Kerdiffstown, Naas
Tel (45) 7509
Mem 514
Sec DJ Carbery (045) 97509
Holes 9 L 6233 yds SSS 70
Recs Am–66
V'trs U SOC
Fees £5 M–£30
Loc 2 miles N of Naas

Co Kilkenny

Callan (1930)

Private
Geraldine, Callan
Tel (056) 25136
Mem 150
Sec M Duggan (052) 54362
Holes 9 L 5844 yds SSS 68
Recs Am–70 J Madden
Pro–71 M Kavanagh
V'trs U SOC
Fees £4 (£5)
Loc 1 mile SE of Callan. Kilkenny 10 miles

Castlecomer (1935)

Private
Castlecomer
Tel (056) 41139
Mem 150
Sec S Farrell (056) 41258
Holes 9 L 6985 yds SSS 71
Recs Am–70 M Curry (1986)

For map index see page 203.

V'trs U
Fees £5
Loc 11 miles N of Kilkenny

Kilkenny (1896)

Private
Glendine, Kilkenny
Tel **(056) 22125**
Mem 900
Sec S O'Neill
Pro M Kavanagh (056) 61730
Holes 18 L 6374 yds SSS 70
Recs Am–68 D White, B Cashell
V'trs U
Fees £7 (£8)
Loc 1 mile N of Kilkenny

Co Laois

Abbey Leix (1895)

Private
Abbey Leix, Portlaoise
Mem 241
Sec E Thornton
Holes 9 L 5680 yds SSS 67
V'trs U
Fees £4
Loc 60 miles SW of Dublin on Cork road

Heath (Portlaoise) (1930)

Private
Portlaoise
Tel **(0502) 46533**
Mem 375
Sec J McNamara (0502) 21327
Pro P McDaid (0502) 46622
Holes 18 L 6247 yds SSS 70
Recs Am–67 T Tyrrell (1983)
V'trs U
Fees £6 (£9)
Loc 4 miles E of town
Mis Floodlit driving range

Mountrath (1929)

Private
Knockanina, Mountrath
Mem 74
Sec T O'Grady (0502) 32214
Pro J Delahunty (0502) 32444
Holes 9 L 5600 yds SSS 65
Recs Am–64 C Carter, T Brown
V'trs U
Fees £4
Loc Mountrath 2 miles

Portarlington (1909)

Private
Garryhinch, Portarlington
Tel **Portarlington 23115**
Mem 198
Sec D Cunningham (0502) 23482
Pro P Lawlor
Holes 9 L 5294 metres SSS 66
Recs Am–67 A Tynan
Pro–67 J Nangle
V'trs U
Fees £3 (£5)
Loc Between Portarlington and Mountmellick on L116

Rathdowney (1931)

Private
Rathdowney, Portlaoise
Tel **(0505) 46170**
Mem 97
Sec S Bolger
Holes 9 L 5722 yds SSS 68
Recs Am–67 J O'Callaghan
Pro–69 P Mahon
V'trs U SOC
Fees D–£3
Loc 1 mile S of Rathdowney

Co Leitrim

Ballinamore (1941)

Private
Ballinamore
Tel **(078) 44346**
Mem 86
Sec P Reynolds (078) 31410
Holes 9 L 5680 yds SSS 67
Recs Am–69 P Duigan
V'trs U SOC
Fees £3 W–£15
Loc $1^1/_2$ miles N of town

Carrick-on-Shannon (1910)

Private
Woodbrook, Carrick-on-Shannon
Tel **(078) 67015**
Mem 179
Sec TW Craig
Holes 9 L 5922 yds SSS 68
Recs Am–68 S Flanagan
V'trs U

Co Limerick

Adare Manor (1900)

Private
Adare
Tel **(061) 86204**
Mem 350
Sec S Ryan
Holes 9 L 5145 metres SSS 67
V'trs U WE–M
Fees D–£8
Loc 10 miles S of Limerick

Castletroy (1937)

Private
Castletroy, Limerick
Tel **(061) 335261**
Mem 1066
Sec L Hayes (061) 335753
Pro N Cassidy (061) 338283
Holes 18 L 5793 metres SSS 71
V'trs WD–U Sat am–U Sat pm/Sun–M SOC–Mon/Wed/Fri
Fees £10 (£10)
Loc $2^1/_2$ miles N of Limerick on Dublin Road

Limerick (1891)

Private
Ballyclough, Limerick
Tel **(061) 44083**
Mem 1070
Sec D McDonogh (061) 45146
Pro J Cassidy (061) 42492
Holes 18 L 5767 yds SSS 70
Recs Am–65 W Rice
Pro–67 F McGloin, J Kinsella
V'trs WD–U before 5pm exc Tues WE–M SOC–WD
Fees £10
Loc 3 miles S of Limerick City

Newcastle West (1940)

Private
Newcastle West
Tel **(069) 62015**
Mem 167
Sec R Cussen
Holes 9 L 5482 yds SSS 66
Recs Am–65 D Kennedy
V'trs U
Loc $^1/_2$ mile S of town

Co Londonderry

Castlerock (1901)

Private
Circular Road, Castlerock
Tel **(0265) 848314**
Mem 820
Sec RG McBride
Pro R Kelly
Holes 18 L 6121 metres SSS 72
9 L 2457 metres SSS 34
Recs Am–68 TBC Hoey
V'trs WD–U SOC WE–SOC after 2.30pm Sat & 10–11am Sun Tues & Fri–Ladies preference
Fees £10 (£15) 9 hole £3 (£5)
Loc 5 miles W of Coleraine on coast
on A2

City of Derry (1913)

Private
49 Victoria Road, Londonderry
Tel **(0504) 42610/46369**
Mem 846
Sec D Burgess (0504) 46369 (office) (0504) 44411 (home)
Pro M Doherty (0504) 46496
Holes Prehen 18 L 6406 yds SSS 71; Dunhugh 9 L 4708 yds SSS 63
Recs Am–68 D Ballentine
V'trs WD–U before 4pm–M after 4pm WE–U H SOC
Fees Prehen £6 (£8) Dunhugh £3
Loc 3 miles from E end of Craigavon Bridge

Kilrea (1920)

Private
Drumagarner Road, Kilrea
(All correspondence to Sec:
125 Tamlaght Road, Rasharkin)
Tel (026 653) 397
Mem 170
Sec WR McIlmoyle
Holes 9 L 4326 yds SSS 62
Recs Am–61 R Rees (1982)
V'trs WD–NA Wed after 6pm (Apr–Aug) WE–NA Sat after 12.30pm
Fees £3 (£4)
Loc Kilrea ½ mile on Kilrea–Maghera road

Moyola Park (1976)

Private
Shanemullagh, Castledawson, Magherafelt BT45 8DG
Tel (0648) 68392/68468
Mem 350
Sec M A Steele
Holes 18 L 6517 yds SSS 71
Recs Am–71 T McNeill
Pro–70 D Smyth
V'trs U SOC
Fees £6 (£10)
Loc 40 miles N of Belfast by M2

Portstewart (1894)

Private
117 Strand Road, Portstewart
Tel (026 583) 2015
Mem 1350 (500 full)
Sec M Moss BA (026 583) 3839
Pro A Hunter (026 583) 2601
Holes Strand 18 L 4784 yds SSS 72
Town 18 L 4733 yds SSS 62
Recs Strand Am–69 TBC Hoey, D Ballentine
Pro–66 E Polland
V'trs SOC–by arrangement
Fees Strand £10 (£15) W–£40
Town £4 (£6) W–£20
Loc W boundary of town

Co Longford

Co Longford (1894)

Private
Dublin Road, Longford
Tel (043) 46310
Mem 190 75(L) 50(J)
Pro J Frawley
Holes 18 L 5912 yds SSS 68
Recs Am–71 P Duignan
Pro–69 D Carson
V'trs U
Fees £4
Loc Town centre ½ mile

Co Louth

Ardee (1911)

Private
Ardee Townparks
Tel (041) 53227
Mem 250
Sec K Carrie
Holes 18 L 5833 yds SSS 68
Recs Am–74 J Higgins
Pro–71 C O'Connor Sr
V'trs U
Fees £5 (£6)
Loc ½ mile N of town

County Louth (1892)

Private
Baltray, Drogheda
Tel (041) 22327
Mem 350
Sec M Delany (041) 22329
Pro P McGuirk (041) 22444
Holes 18 L 6978 yds SSS 72
Recs Am–66 F Gannon
Pro–65 J Heggarty
V'trs By prior arrangement
Fees On request
Loc 3 miles NE of Drogheda

Dundalk (1905)

Private
Blackrock, Dundalk
Tel (042) 21379
Mem 850
Sec P Moriarty (042) 21731
Pro J Cassidy (042) 22102
Holes 18 L 6115 metres SSS 72
V'trs U SOC
Fees £8 (£10)
Loc 3 miles S of Dundalk

Greenore (1896)

Private
Greenore
Tel (042) 73212
Mem 250
Sec E McCarten (042) 34711
Holes 18 L 5614 metres SSS 69
Recs Am–67 S McParland
Pro–67 C O'Connor Sr
V'trs WD–before 5pm
WE–before noon SOC
Fees £5 (£7)
Loc 15 miles N of Dundalk on main Greenore Road

Co Mayo

Achill Island (1951)

Private
Keel, Achill Island
Tel (098) 43202
Mem 40
Sec D Quinn
Holes 9 L 5550 yds SSS 67
V'trs U
Fees £2
Loc In Keel

Ballina (1910)

Private
Mosgrove, Shanaghy, Ballina
Tel (096) 21050
Mem 128 58(L)
Sec V Frawley (096) 21795
Holes 9 L 5702 yds SSS 66
Recs Am–64 J Corcoran (1984)
Pro–66 C O'Connor
V'trs U
Fees £5 (£5) W–£20
Loc 1 mile E of town

Ballinrobe (1895)

Public
Ballinrobe, Claremorris
Tel (092) 41448
Mem 200
Sec P Holian (092) 41659
Holes 9 L 5790 yds SSS 68
Recs Am–67 B Finlay
V'trs U Sun–NA SOC
Fees £4 Sat £5 W–£15 M–£40
Loc 1½ miles NW of town on Castlebar Road

Ballyhaunis (1929)

Private
Coonaha, Ballyhaunis
Tel (0907) 30014
Mem 162
Sec J Higgins (0907) 30180
Holes 9 L 5887 yds SSS 68
Recs Am–68 W Keane
Pro–70
V'trs U SOC–WD
Fees £5
Loc 2 miles N of Ballyhaunis

Belmullet (1925)

Private
Belmullet, Ballina
Tel (097) 81093
Mem 50
Sec P McIntyre
Holes 9 L 2829 yds SSS 67
V'trs U
Fees £3
Loc 3 miles W of Belmullet

Castlebar (1910)

Private
Rocklands, Castlebar
Tel (094) 21649
Mem 211
Sec J Egan
Pro J Harnett
Holes 18 L 6109 yds SSS 69
Recs Am–67 J Langan
V'trs U
Fees £5

Claremorris (1918)

Private
Claremorris
Tel (094) 71527
Mem 140
Sec TJ Farragher (094) 71082
Holes 9 L 6454 yds SSS 69

For map index see page 203.

Recs Am–68 P Killeen
Pro–63 C O'Connor
V'trs U
Fees £4 W–£15
Loc 2 miles S of Claremorris

Mulrany (1887)

Public
Mulrany, Westport
Tel **(098) 36185**
Mem 120
Sec Fr M Kenny (098) 36107
Holes 9 L 6380 yds SSS 70
V'trs U
Fees D–£3 W–£15
Loc Castlebar 20 miles. Westport 18 miles

Swinford (1922)

Private
Brabazon Park, Swinford
Tel **(094) 51378**
Mem 103
Sec P Walsh
Holes 9 L 5230 yds SSS 65
Recs Am–68
V'trs U
Fees D–£3 W–£15
Loc Off Dublin–Castlebar road

Westport (1908)

Private
Carowholly, Westport
Tel **(098) 25113**
Mem 305
Sec S O'Malley
Holes 18 L 6950 yds SSS 73
Recs Am–73 A Joyce
V'trs U
Fees £3 (£3)
Loc Westport 2 miles

Co Meath

Gormanston College (1961)

Private
Franciscan College, Gormanston
Tel **(01) 412630**
Mem 140
Sec Fr Declan Timmons
Pro B Browne
Holes 9 L 3956 yds SSS 58
Recs Am–63 M Gannon
V'trs M
Loc 22 miles N of Dublin

Headfort (1928)

Private
Kells
Tel **(046) 40148**
Mem 450
Sec H Flanagan
Pro J Purcell (046) 40639
Holes 18 L 6350 yds SSS 69
Recs Am–67 D Snow
Pro–64 D Smyth
V'trs U
Fees £6 (£7)
Loc Kells 1/2 mile

Laytown & Bettystown (1909)

Private
Bettystown, Drogheda
Tel **(041) 27534**
Mem 750
Sec JO Carr (041) 27170
Pro RJ Browne (041) 27563 (Tournament Pro D Smyth)
Holes 18 L 6254 yds SSS 69
Pro–65 I Woosnam
V'trs U SOC–WD
Fees £7 (£10)
Loc 25 miles N of Dublin

Royal Tara (1923)

Private
Bellinter, Navan
Tel **(046) 25244/25508**
Mem 900
Sec Desmond Foley (046) 21098
Pro A Whiston
Holes 18 L 5757 metres SSS 70
Recs Am–70 D Leonard
V'trs U
Fees £8 (£10)
Loc 25 miles N of Dublin off N3

Trim (1970)

Private
Newtownmoynagh, Trim
Tel **(046) 31463**
Mem 250
Sec PJ Darby (046) 31438
Holes 9 L 6266 yds SSS 70
Recs Am–69 P Rayfus
V'trs WD–U exc Ladies day WE–restricted SOC–exc Sun
Fees £5 (£6)
Loc 2 1/2 miles SW of Trim

Co Monaghan

Castleblayney (1985)

Private
Castleblayney
Mem 140
Sec D McGlynn (042) 40197
Holes 9 L 2678 yds SSS 66
Recs Am–70 J McCarthy (1987)
V'trs U SOC
Fees £3 (£4)
Loc Town centre

Clones (1913)

Private
Hilton Park, Scotshouse, Clones
Mem 260
Sec MM Taylor (049) 52354
Holes 9 L 5570 yds SSS 67
Recs Am–66 D McGuigan
V'trs U
Fees £3

Nuremore (1961)

Private
Nuremore, Carrickmacross
Tel **(042) 61438**
Mem 107
Sec FC Lane (042) 61450
Holes 9 L 6032 yds SSS 69
V'trs U
Fees £3 (£4.50)
Loc Hotel grounds

Rossmore (1906)

Private
Rossmore Park, Monaghan
Tel **Monaghan 81316**
Mem 310
Sec B Dawson
Holes 9 L 5859 yds SSS 68
Recs Am–64 R Berry
V'trs WD–U WE/BH–U exc comp days SOC
Fees £4 (£5)
Loc 3 miles on Monaghan–Cootehill road

Co Offaly

Birr (1893)

Private
The Glenns, Birr
Tel **(0509) 20082**
Mem 320
Sec P O'Gorman (0509) 20271
Holes 18 L 6216 yds SSS 70
Recs Am–66 JB Carr
Pro–68 RJ Browne
V'trs U SOC–exc Sun
Fees D–£6
Loc Birr town 2 miles

Edenderry (1910)

Private
Boherbree, Edenderry
Tel **(0405) 31072**
Mem 230
Sec EA Moran (0405) 31342
Holes 9 L 5791 yds SSS 67
Recs Am–66 AJ McNally
V'trs U
Fees £4 (£5)
Loc 1 mile E of Edenderry

Tullamore (1896)

Private
Brookfield, Tullamore
Tel **(0506) 21439**
Mem 711
Sec WM Rossiter (0506) 21310
Pro JE Kelly
Holes 18 L 6314 yds SSS 71
Recs Am–64 D White
Pro–68 H Boyle, J Martin, D Jones

V'trs WD–U exc Tues (Ladies Day) Sat–M 12.30–3pm Sun–NA SOC
Fees £6 D–£8
Loc $2^1/_2$ miles S of Tullamore
Mis Buggies for hire

Co Roscommon

Athlone (1892)

Private
Hodson Bay, Athlone
Tel (0902) 2073
Mem 540
Sec T Collins (0902) 74796 (home)
Pro M Quinn
Holes 18 L 6000 yds SSS 70
Recs Am–63 P Egan
Pro–70 M Quinn
V'trs U SOC–WD
Fees £5 (£6)
Loc Shores of Lough Ree

Ballaghaderreen (1937)

Private
Ballaghaderreen
Mem 112
Sec JB Noonan, P Hunt
Holes 9 L 5686 yds SSS 65
Fees £2
Loc Town 3 miles

Boyle (1911)

Private
Roscommon Road, Boyle
Tel (079) 62594
Mem 150
Sec RP Nangle
Holes 9 L 4957 metres SSS 66
Recs Am–65 A Wynne (1987)
V'trs U SOC
Fees £4
Loc Boyle $1^1/_2$ miles

Castlerea (1905)

Private
Clonalis, Castlerea
Tel (0907) 20068
Mem 145
Sec B Stenson (0907) 20279
Holes 9 L 5466 yds SSS 66
Recs Am–63 R de Lacy Staunton
V'trs U
Fees £3 (£5)
Loc Town suburb Knock Road

Roscommon (1904)

Private
Mote Park, Roscommon
Tel (0903) 6382
Mem 241
Sec J Halliday (0903) 6164
Holes 9 L 6215 yds SSS 68
Recs Am–D White
V'trs U
Fees £3
Loc 1 mile E of town

Co Sligo

Ballymote (1940)

Private
Ballymote
Tel Ballymote 3460
Mem 42
Sec P Mullen
Holes 9 L 5032 yds SSS 63
Recs Am–67 P Mullen
V'trs U
Fees £2
Loc Carrigans

County Sligo (1894)

Private
Rosses Point
Tel (071) 77186
Mem 762
Sec GA Eakins (071) 77134
Pro J McGonigle (071) 77171
Holes 18 L 6003 metres SSS 72
Recs Am–65 MD O'Brien
Pro–67 C O'Connor Sr
V'trs WD–U WE/BH–M 9–10.30am and 1.30–2.45pm SOC
Fees £12 (£12) W–£50
Loc 5 miles NW of Sligo

Enniscrone (1931)

Private
Enniscrone
Tel (096) 36297
Mem 271
Sec JM Fleming
Holes 18 L 6487 yds SSS 71
Recs Am–70 J Corcoran, M Canavan
Pro–71 C O'Connor Sr, J O'Leary
V'trs U
Fees D–£7
Loc Ballina road, S of Enniscrone

Strandhill (1932)

Private
Strandhill
Tel (071) 68188
Mem 250
Sec F Carr (071) 61776
Pro B Malone (071) 68213
Holes 18 L 5937 yds SSS 68
V'trs WD–U WE/BH–restricted SOC
Fees IR£7 (IR£8)
Loc 6 miles W of Sligo

Co Tipperary

Cahir Park (1968)

Private
Kilcommon, Cahir
Tel (052) 41474
Mem 187
Sec K Murphy (052) 52155 (office)
Holes 9 L 6262 yds SSS 69
Recs Am–68
V'trs U SOC–WD/Sat
Fees £6 (£6)
Loc 1 mile S of Cahir

Carrick-on-Suir (1939)

Private
Garravone, Carrick-on-Suir
Tel (051) 40047
Mem 180
Sec MG Kelly (051) 40300 (home)
Holes 9 L 5948 yds SSS 68
Recs Am–67 C Carleton (1987)
V'trs U SOC–WD/Sat
Fees £5
Loc 2 miles on Dungarvan Road

Clonmel (1911)

Private
Lyreanearle, Mountain Road, Clonmel
Tel (052) 21138
Mem 521
Sec Mrs M Lynch (052) 21508
Pro R Hayes
Holes 18 L 6330 yds SSS 70
Recs Am–63 M O'Neill
V'trs U
Fees £6 (£8)
Loc 3 miles SW of Clonmel

Nenagh (1929)

Private
Beechwood, Nenagh
Tel (067) 31476
Mem 600
Sec B O'Brien (Hon) (067) 31099
Pro J Coyle (067) 33242
Holes 18 L 5483 metres SSS 68
Recs Am–64 P Lyons (1984)
V'trs U SOC
Fees £6 Sat–£8 Sun–£10
Loc 3 miles NE of Nenagh on Limerick–Dublin road

Rockwell College (1964)

Private
Rockwell College, Cashel
Mem 85
Sec J Ryan (062) 61444
Holes 9 L 4136 yds SSS 60
V'trs NA
Loc 3 miles S of Cashel on main Cork–Dublin road

Roscrea (1893)

Private
Roscrea
Tel Roscrea 21130
Mem 337
Sec MF Donnellan
Holes 9 L 6059 yds SSS 69
Recs Am–67 R Carr
V'trs U
Fees £5
Loc 2 miles on Dublin road

Templemore (1970)

Private
Manna South, Templemore
Tel **Templemore 53**
Mem 210
Sec JK Moloughney
(0504) 31720
Holes 9 L 5442 yds SSS 66
V'trs U exc Sun SOC
Fees £4 (£5)
Loc 1/2 mile S of town

Thurles (1909)

Private
Turtulla, Thurles
Tel **(0504) 21983/22466**
Mem 555
Sec T Ryan (0504) 23787
Pro S Hunt
Holes 18 L 5904 metres SSS 71
Recs Am–66 DF O'Sullivan
Pro–70 H Bradshaw
V'trs WD–U WE–NA
Fees £7 (£8)
Loc 1 mile S of Thurles on the Horse & Jockey road

Tipperary (1879)

Private
Rathanny, Tipperary
Tel **(062) 51119**
Mem 200
Sec P O'Donogue
Holes 9 L 6074 yds SSS 69
Recs Am–65 AD Pierse
V'trs U
Fees £3
Loc Tipperary town 1 mile

Co Tyrone

Dungannon (1890)

Private
Mullaghmore, Dungannon
Tel **(086 87) 22098**
Mem 425
Sec L Campbell (086 87) 23112
Holes 18 L 5914 yds SSS 68
Recs Am–P McAleer
V'trs U
Fees £3 (£4)
Loc 1 mile W of Dungannon

Fintona (1896)

Private
Ecclesville Demesne, Fintona
Tel **(0662) 841480**
Mem 250
Sec J Conway (036 56) 21484
Holes 9 L 5716 yds SSS 70
Recs Am–68 E Donnell
Pro–69 L Higgins, J Kinsilla, L Robinson
V'trs U exc comp days SOC–WD
Fees £3 (£5)
Loc 10 miles S of Omagh

Killymoon (1889)

Private
200 Killymoon Road, Cookstown BT80 8TW
Tel **(064 87) 63762/62254**
Mem 700
Sec Dr J McBride
Pro P Leonard
Holes 18 L 5498 metres SSS 69
Recs Am–64 A O'Neill
Pro–65 D Smyth
V'trs U
Fees £3 (£4)
Loc 1 mile S of Cookstown

Newtownstewart (1914)

Private
38 Golf Course Road, Newtownstewart BT78 4HU
Tel **(066 26) 61466**
Mem 500
Sec RTA Farrow 44262
Holes 18 L 5468 metres SSS 69
Recs Am–67 G Forbes (1987)
Pro–66 J Fisher
V'trs U SOC
Fees £4 (£6) W–£15 M–£30
Loc 2 miles SW of Newtownstewart on B84

Omagh (1910)

Private
83A Dublin Road, Omagh BT78 1HQ
Tel **(0662) 3160/41442**
Mem 462
Sec HCH Lynch (0662) 44411
Holes 18 L 5208 metres SSS 67
Recs Am–63 H Johnston (1985)
V'trs U
Fees £4 (£6) M–£25
Loc Omagh 1/2 mile

Strabane (1908)

Private
Ballycolman, Strabane
Tel **(0504) 382271**
Mem 600
Sec JJ Harron (0504) 883093
Holes 18 L 5458 metres SSS 69
Recs Am–64 C Patton
Pro–69
V'trs U
Fees £5 (£8)
Loc Strabane 1/2 mile.
Fir Trees Hotel 400 yds

Co Waterford

Dungarvan (1924)

Private
Ballinacourty, Dungarvan
Tel **(058) 41605**
Mem 340
Sec J Murphy (058) 41811
Holes 9 L 5721 metres SSS 69
Recs Am–66 J McHenry (1984)
V'trs U SOC–WD (Apr–Sept)
SOC–WE (Oct–Mar)
Fees D–£5 SOC–£4
Loc 3 miles E of Dungarvan.
30 miles W of Waterford

Lismore (1965)

Private
Lismore, Ballyin
Tel **(058) 54026**
Mem 200
Sec M O'Shea (058) 54184
Pro T Maher (058) 54026
Holes 9 L 5127 metres SSS 67
Recs Am–65 T Murphy (1987)
Pro–65 L Higgins (1978)
V'trs U SOC–exc Sun
Fees £5 W–£20
Loc 1 mile N of Lismore

Tramore (1894)

Private
Tramore
Tel **(051) 86170**
Mem 550
Sec R Brennan(051) 81616 (home)
Pro C Butler
Holes 18 L 5977 yds SSS 71
Recs Am–66 E Power
Pro–66 H Boyle
V'trs U
Fees £10 (£12) 1988 prices
Loc 7 miles S of Waterford

Waterford (1912)

Private
Newrath, Waterford
Tel **(051) 74182**
Mem 500
Sec PJ Burke (051) 32842
Pro J Condon (051) 76748
Holes 18 L 6232 metres SSS 70
Recs Am–66 P O'Rourke
Pro–70 C Kane
V'trs U
Fees £7 (£10)

Co Westmeath

Moate (1940)

Private
Moate
Tel **(0902) 81271**
Mem 176
Sec J Flynn
Holes 9 L 5348 yds SSS 65
Recs Am–68 T O'Brien
V'trs U
Fees £2
Loc 1 mile N of town

Mullingar (1896)

Private
Belvedere, Mullingar
Tel **(044) 48366**
Mem 472
Sec S Donoghue
Pro J Burns
Holes 18 L 6370 yds SSS 70
Recs Am–64 R Carr
Pro–64 P Tupling
V'trs U
Fees £1.50 (£2)
Loc 3 miles S of Mullingar

Co Wexford

Courtown (1936)

Private
Courtown Harbour, Gorey
Tel **(055) 25166**
Mem 480
Sec J Sheehan (055) 21533
Pro A Judd
Holes 18 L 6398 yds SSS 70
Recs Am–67 J McGill (1987)
Pro–68 M Murphy (1976)
V'trs U SOC
Fees £6 (£9)
Loc 2½ miles SE of Gorey

Enniscorthy (1908)

Private
Knockmarshal, Enniscorthy
Tel **(054) 33191**
Mem 300
Sec J Winters (054) 35257 (home)
Holes 9 L 6368 yds SSS 70
Recs Am–67 N Delaney
V'trs U SOC–exc Sun
Fees £4 (£5)
Loc 1 mile SW of town centre

New Ross (1917)

Private
Tinneranny, New Ross
Tel **(051) 21433**
Mem 250
Sec (051) 21451
Holes 9 L 5578 metres SSS 69
Recs Am–66 M O'Brien
Pro–65 C O'Connor
V'trs U exc Sun SOC
Fees £5 (£7)
Loc West 1 mile

Rosslare (1908)

Private
Strand, Rosslare
Tel **(053) 32113**
Mem 400
Sec Miss A O'Keefe (053) 32203
Pro A Skerritt (053) 32238
Holes 18 L 6502 yds SSS 71
Recs Am–65 D Noonan (1978)
V'trs U SOC
Fees £8 (£10)
Loc 10 miles S of Wexford

Wexford (1966)

Private
Mulgannon, Wexford
Tel **(053) 42238**
Mem 300
Sec A Doyle (053) 44720
Holes 18 L 6109 yds SSS 69
V'trs U SOC
Fees £6 (£7)
Loc Wexford town ½ mile

Co Wicklow

Arklow (1927)

Private
Abbeylands, Arklow
Tel **(0402) 32492**
Mem 310
Sec B Timmons
Pro K Daly
Holes 18 L 5770 yds SSS 68
Recs Am–66 T Dowling
Pro–66 T Halpin
V'trs WD–U Sat–U after 5pm
Sun–NA SOC–Mon–Sat
Fees £4 (£6)
Loc Town centre ½ mile

Baltinglass (1928)

Private
Baltinglass
Tel **Baltinglass 52**
Mem 350
Sec D Lord (0508) 81350
Pro M Murphy
Holes 9 L 6070 yds SSS 68
Recs Am–66 D Kilcoyne,
Rev McDonnell
Pro–70 S Hunt
V'trs U SOC
Fees £4 (£6)
Loc 38 miles S of Dublin

Blainroe (1978)

Private
Blainroe
Tel **(0404) 68168**
Mem 600
Sec W O'Sullivan
Pro J McDonald
Holes 18 L 6681 yds SSS 72
V'trs U
Fees £7 (£12) W–£35
Loc 3½ miles S of Wicklow
on coast

Bray (1897)

Private
Ravenswell Road, Bray
Tel **Bray 862484**
Mem 272 (151 Associates)
Sec JM McStravick
Pro M Walby
Holes 9 L 5230 metres SSS 70
V'trs U before 6pm SOC–WD
Fees £8
Loc 12 miles S of Dublin

Coollattin (1950)

Private
Coollattin, Shillelagh
Tel **(055) 29125**
Mem 240
Sec J O'Shea (055) 26290
Holes 9 L 6070 yds SSS 69
Fees £3 (£4)

Delgany (1908)

Private
Delgany
Tel **(404) 874645/874833**
Mem 800
Sec J Deally (404) 874536
Pro J Bradshaw (404) 874536
Holes 18 L 5249 yds SSS 69
Recs Am–63
V'trs U exc comp days
SOC–Mon/Thurs/Fri
or after 3.30pm WD/WE
Fees £9 (£11.50)
Loc Greystones 2 miles

Greystones (1895)

Private
Greystones
Tel **(01) 876624**
Mem 750
Sec O Walsh (01) 874136
Pro K Daly
Holes 18 L 5387 metres SSS 68
Recs Am–67
Pro–66
V'trs Mid–week
Fees £8 (£9)
Loc Greystones

Wicklow (1904)

Private
Dunbur Road, Wicklow
Tel **(0404) 67379**
Mem 408
Sec J Kelly
Holes 9 L 5536 yds SSS 66
Recs Am–65 W Mitchell,
LJ Mooney
V'trs I
Fees £6 (£10)

Woodenbridge (1884)

Private
Arklow
Tel **(0402) 5202**
Mem 210
Sec TH Crummy
Holes 9 L 6104 yds SSS 68
Recs Am–67 M Holden, J Kavanagh
V'trs U exc Sat
Fees £8 (£10)
Loc 45 miles S from Dublin.
4 miles W of Arklow

Scotland

Angus
Tayside Region

Arbroath (1877)

Public
Elliot, by Arbroath
Tel **(0241) 72272**
Mem 200
Sec AR Small (0241) 72666
Pro L Ewart (0241) 75837
Holes 18 L 6078 yds SSS 69
Recs Am–65 R Cargill
V'trs U
Fees £3 (£4.50) W–£12 (Mon–Fri)
Loc 1 mile S of Arbroath

Brechin Golf & Squash Club (1893)

Private
Trinity, Brechin DD9 7PD
Tel **(035 62) 2383**
Mem 650
Sec AB May (035 62) 2326
Pro B Mason (035 62) 5270
Holes 18 L 5267 yds SSS 66
Recs Am–61 A Helmsley
V'trs U ex Wed SOC
Fees £7 D–£10 (£8 D–£11) Mon–Fri £25
Loc 1 mile N of town on Aberdeen road (B966)

Buddon Links (1981)

Public
Carnoustie Golf Links, Links Parade, Carnoustie DD7 7JE
Tel **(0241) 53249 (Starter's Box)**
Sec EJC Smith (0241) 53789
Holes 18 L 5732 yds SSS 68
V'trs U
Fees £5
Loc 12 miles E of Dundee by A92 or A930

Burnside

Public
Carnoustie Golf Links, Links Parade, Carnoustie DD7 7JE
Tel **(0241) 53249 (Starter's Box)**
Sec EJC Smith (0241) 53789
Holes 18 L 6020 yds SSS 69
V'trs WD–U WE–U after 10.30am
Fees £9
Loc 12 miles E of Dundee by A92 or A930

Caird Park (1926)

Public
Dundee
Tel **(0382) 453606**
Mem 413
Sec D Farquhar Jr (0382) 457217
Pro J Black (0382) 459438
Holes 18 L 6303 yds SSS 70
Recs Am–66 W Thompson (1987)
V'trs U
Loc Off Kingsway bypass at Mains Loan

Caird Park (1982)

Public
City of Dundee Parks Dept, 353, Clepington Road, Dundee
Tel **(0382) 23141 ext 414 (Advance bookings ext 295)**
Pro K Todd
Holes Yellow 9 L 1692 yds SSS 29
Red 9 L 1983 yds SSS 29
V'trs U
Loc Caird Park Dundee

Caledonia (1887)

Private
Links Parade, Carnoustie DD7 7JF
Tel **(0241) 52115**
Mem 401
Sec DC Thomson
Holes Play over Carnoustie courses

Camperdown (1960)

Public
Camperdown Park, Dundee
Tel **(0382) 623398**
Mem 600
Sec JF Hart (0382) 68340
Pro R Brown
Holes 18 L 6561 yds SSS 72
Recs Am–68 A Morgan
V'trs U
Fees £2 (£3)
Loc 2 miles NW of Dundee

Carnoustie (1842)

Private
Links Parade, Carnoustie
Tel **(0241) 52480**
Mem 900
Sec DW Curtis
Holes Play over Carnoustie courses

Carnoustie Championship

Public
Links Parade, Carnoustie DD7 7JE
Tel **(0241) 53249 (Starter's Box)**
Sec EJC Smith (0241) 53789
Holes 18 L 6936 yds SSS 74
Recs Pro–65 J Newton
V'trs WD–U Sat–U after 1.30pm Sun–U after 10.30am
Fees £19 W–£80
Loc 12 miles E of Dundee by A92 or A930

Carnoustie Ladies (1873)

Private
Links Parade, Carnoustie
Tel **(0241) 55252**
Mem 106
Sec Mrs S Macdonald (0241) 52073
Holes Play over Carnoustie Championship, Burnside and Buddon Links

Dalhousie (1868)

Private
Links Parade, Carnoustie
Tel **(0241) 53208**
Mem 262
Sec GW Ellis
Holes Play over Carnoustie courses

Downfield (1932)

Private
Turnberry Ave, Dundee DD2 3QP
Tel **(0382) 825595**
Mem 766
Sec GD Lumsden
Pro C Waddell (0382) 89246
Holes 18 L 6804 yds SSS 73
Recs Am–67
Pro–67
V'trs WD–U 9.30am–12 noon and 2.18–4pm WE–M
Fees £12 D–£17
Loc North end of Dundee off A923 (Timex Circle)

Edzell (1895)

Private
High St, Edzell, by Brechin DD9 7TF
Tel **(035 64) 235**
Mem 650
Sec JM Hutchison (035 64) 7283
Pro JB Webster (035 64) 462
Holes 18 L 6299 yds SSS 70
Recs Am–65 JKA Bruce (1985)
Pro–66 AJ Webster (1975)
V'trs WD–NA 5–6.15pm WE–NA 8–10.30am & 12–2.30pm SOC
Fees £8 D–£12 (£10 D–£14) W–£40 M–£90
Loc 6 miles NW of Brechin

Forfar (1871)

Private
Cunninghill, Forfar DD8 2RL
Tel **(0307) 62120**
Mem 525 175(L) 150(J)
Sec PH Wallace (0307) 63773
Pro P McNiven (0307) 65683
Holes 18 L 5537 metres SSS 69
Recs Am–66 DM Chapman, CC Sinclair
Pro–65 E Brown
V'trs U exc Sat
Fees £9.50 (£15)
Loc $1^1/_2$ miles E of Forfar

Kirriemuir (1908)

Private
Kirriemuir
Tel **(0575) 72144**
Mem 600
Sec Irvine, Adamson & Co (0575) 72729
Pro A Caira (0575) 73317
Holes 18 L 5541 yds SSS 67
Recs Am–63 JL Adamson, J Murray
V'trs WD–U WE–M SOC
Fees D–£8.50
Loc NE outskirts of town

Letham Grange (1987)

Private
Colliston, Arbroath DD11 4RL
Tel **(024) 189373**
Mem 400
Sec D Scott (024) 189377
Holes 18 L 6789 yds SSS 73
Recs Am–73 W Taylor (1987)
Pro–72 J Farmer (1988)
V'trs WD–U H exc Tues before 10am WE–M before 10.30am & 1–2pm BH–U SOC
Fees £12 D–£18 (£15)
Loc 4 miles N of Arbroath on A993

Mercantile (1896)

Private
Links Parade, Carnoustie
Tel **(0241) 52525**
Mem 500
Sec R Campbell (0241) 52020
Holes Play over Carnoustie courses

Mercantile (1897)

Private
East Links, Montrose DD10 82W
Tel **(0674) 72408**
Mem 450
Sec RS West (0674) 75447
Holes Play over Montrose and Broomfield courses

Monifieth Golf Links

Private
Princes Street, Monifieth, Dundee
Tel **(0382) 532767**
Mem 1200
Sec JAR Fraser (0382) 532321
Pro I McLeod (0382) 532945
Holes Medal 18 L 6650 yds SSS 72
Ashludie 18 L 5123 SSS 66
Recs Am–63 JL Adamson
Pro–64 S Sewgolum
V'trs WD–U Sat–NA Sun–restricted SOC
Fees Medal £7 D–£14 (£10 D–£15)
Ashludie £7 D–£10 (£8 D–£12)
Loc 6 miles E of Dundee
Mis Abertay, Broughty, Grange /Dundee and Monifieth clubs have playing rights over both courses

Montrose

Public
Traill Drive, Montrose DD10 8SW
Tel **(0674) 72932**
Sec Mrs M Stewart
Pro AJ Webster (0674) 72634
Holes Medal 18 L 6451 yds SSS 71
Broomfield 18 L 4815 yds SSS 63
Recs Pro–Medal 63 G Cunningham, D Huish
V'trs WD–U Sat–no 4 ball until 3pm (Apr–Sept) WE–NA before 2pm Sat & 10am Sun (Medal Course)
Fees Medal £6.50 (£8)
Broomfield £4 (£5.50)
Loc 1 mile off A92
Mis Royal Montrose, Caledonia and Mercantile clubs play here

Montrose Caledonia (1896)

Private
Dorward Road, Montrose
Tel **(0674) 72313**
Sec G Hall (0674) 5485
Holes Play over Montrose and Broomfield courses

New Taymouth

Private
Taymouth St, Carnoustie
Tel **(0241) 52425**
Mem 450
Sec G Dunton
Holes Play over Carnoustie courses

Panmure (1845)

Private
Barry, by Carnoustie
Tel **(0241) 53120**
Mem 480
Sec Capt JC Ray
Pro T Shiel
Holes 18 L 6317 ydsss SSS 70
Recs Am–68 S Macdonald, DMA Steel, RDBM Shade
Pro–65 R de Vicenzo, R Cole, D Webster
V'trs WD/Sun–U Sat–NA
Fees £9 D–£14
Loc 2 miles W of Carnoustie

Royal Montrose (1810)

Private
Tel **(0674) 72376**
Mem 650
Sec JD Sykes (0674) 73528
Holes Play over Montrose and Broomfield courses

Argyll and Bute
Strathclyde Region

Blairmore and Strone (1896)

Private
Strone-by-Dunoon
Tel **(036 984) 676**
Mem 160
Sec AB Horton (036 984) 217
Holes 9 L 2122 yds SSS 62
Recs Am–63 JA Kirby (1987)
V'trs Mon–NA after 6pm Sat–NA 12–4pm
Fees £3 (£3) W–£12
Loc High Road at Strone, N of Dunoon

Bute (1888)

Private
Kingarth, Isle of Bute
Mem 115
Sec J Burnside (070083) 648
Holes 9 L 2497 yds SSS 64
V'trs U
Fees D–£2.50 W–£9
Loc Stravanan Bay, off A845 Rothesay–Kilchattan Bay road

Carradale (1900)

Private
Carradale PA28 6QT
Tel **(05833) 387**
Mem 172
Sec Dr JA Duncan
Holes 9 L 2387 yds SSS 63
Recs Am–62 S Campbell
V'trs U
Fees D–£3
Loc Carradale

Colonsay

Public
Isle of Colonsay PA61 7YP
Tel **(09512) 316**
Mem 100
Sec K Byrne
Holes 18 L 4775 yds SSS 72
V'trs U
Fees Full membership £5 per family per annum
Loc Machrins

Cowal (1890)

Private
Ardenslate Road, Dunoon
Tel **(0369) 2216**
Mem 432
Sec J Fletcher (0369) 5673
Pro RD Weir (0369) 2395
Holes 18 L 6251 yds SSS 70
Recs Am–64 A Brodie
V'trs U
Fees On application
Loc NE boundary of Dunoon

Craignure (1981)

Private
Isle of Mull Hotel, Mull
Tel **(068 02) 370/351**
Mem 60
Sec Mrs S Campbell (068 02) 370
Holes 9 L 4436 metres SSS 64
V'trs U
Fees D–£4 W–£12
Loc Craignure 1 mile

Dunaverty (1889)

Private
Southend
Mem 220
Sec JE Sayers
Pro WM Millan

For map index see page 203.

Holes 18 L 4597 yds SSS 63
Recs Am–61 S Campbell
Pro–65 EC Brown
V'trs U
Fees £1.10 W–£6.50
Loc 10 miles S of Campbeltown

Glencruitten (1905)

Private
Oban
Tel **(0631) 62868**
Mem 350 105(L) 115(J)
Sec CM Jarvie (0631) 62308
Pro I Auld (0631) 64115
Holes 18 L 4452 yds SSS 63
Recs Am–55 JM Wilson
Pro–60 H Bannerman, G Cunningham
V'trs U
Fees £6.50 (£8)
Loc Town centre 1 mile

Innellan (1895)

Private
Innellan
Tel **(0369) 3546**
Mem 200
Sec JG Arden
Holes 9 L 4878 yds SSS 63
Recs Am–63
V'trs U SOC
Fees £3
Loc 4 miles S of Dunoon

Islay (1891)

Private
Tigh Rhaonastil, Kildalton, Isle of Islay
Tel **(0496) 2310**
Sec DF Stone
Holes 18 L 6226 yds SSS 70
Recs Am–67 SW Morrison
Pro–67 M Seymour
V'trs U
Fees £5 D–£9 W–£45
Mis Play over Machrie course

Kyles of Bute (1907)

Private
Tighnabruaich
Tel **(0700) 811355**
Mem 160
Sec DW Gieve
Holes 9 L 2389 yds SSS 32
V'trs U
Fees D–£4 W–£16
Loc 26 miles W of Dunoon

Lochgilphead (1963)

Private
Blarbuie Road, Lochgilphead
Tel **(0546) 2340**
Mem 210
Sec PW Tait (0546) 2149
Holes 9 L 4484 yds SSS 63
Recs Am–63 T Armour
V'trs U SOC
Fees £4 (£6)
Loc Town centre ½ mile

Machrihanish (1876)

Private
Campbeltown, Machrihanish
Tel **(0586) 81 213**
Mem 516 158(L) 125(J)
Sec Mrs A Anderson
Pro K Campbell (0586) 81 277
Holes 18 L 6228 yds SSS 70
plus 9 hole course
Recs Am–66 SJ Campbell
Pro–65 R Walker
V'trs U
Fees £8.50 D–£10 (£11)
Loc 5 miles W of Campbeltown

Millport (1888)

Private
Millport, Isle of Cumbrae KA28
Tel **(0475) 530311**
Mem 267 97(L) 73(J)
Sec WD Patrick (0475) 530308
Holes 18 L 5831 yds SSS 68
Recs Am–64 AD Harrington
V'trs U
Fees £5.50 D–£7.50 (£6 D–£8) W–£24 F–£33 M–£47
Loc Isle of Cumbrae–Car ferry from Largs

Port Bannatyne (1968)

Private
Port Bannatyne, Isle of Bute
Mem 170
Sec IL MacLeod (0700) 2009
Holes 13 L 4730 yds SSS 63
Recs Am–61 J Ewing
Pro–64 W Watson
V'trs U
Fees £5 (£5) W–£20
Loc 2 miles N of Rothesay, Isle of Bute

Rothesay (1892)

Public
Canada Hill, Rothesay, Isle of Bute
Tel **(0700) 2244**
Mem 300
Sec R Strong (0700) 3493
Pro G McKinlay (0700) 3554
Holes 18 L 5358 yds SSS 67
Recs Am–63 G Murray (1984)
Pro–72 RDBM Shade (1968)
V'trs U Parties welcome
Fees £6 (£8) W–£20 £105 per annum
Loc Rothesay, in town

Tarbert (1910)

Private
Kilberry Road, Tarbert
Tel **(088 02) 565**
Mem 106
Sec JB Sinclair (088 02) 676
Holes 9 L 4460 yds SSS 64
Recs Am–64 D Lamont (1988)
V'trs U
Fees £3 D–£5 W–£20
Loc 1 mile W of Tarbert

Tobermory (1896)

Private
Tobermory, Isle of Mull
Mem 150
Sec Dr WH Clegg (0688) 2020
Holes 9 L 2460 yds SSS 64
Recs Am–70 D Brown (1988)
V'trs U
Fees D–£4 W–£16
Loc Tobermory, Isle of Mull

Vaul

Private
Scarinish, Isle of Tiree, by Oban
Mem 100
Sec Mrs P Boyd (087 92) 344
Holes 9 L 3123 yds SSS 70
V'trs U Sun–NA
Fees £3

Ayrshire

including Isle of Arran, Strathclyde Region

Annanhill (1957)

Public
Irvine Road, Kilmarnock
Tel **(0563) 21644**
Mem 280
Sec JA Murdoch (0563) 27542
Holes 18 L 6270 yds SSS 70
Recs Am–65 I McKenzie
Pro–65 J Farmer
V'trs WD/Sun–U Sat–NA SOC–exc Sat
Fees D–£3.75 (D–£7.20)
Loc 1 mile W of Kilmarnock

Ardeer (1880)

Private
Greenhead, Stevenston
Tel **(0294) 64542**
Mem 500
Sec P Watson (0294) 63630
Holes 18 L 6630 yds SSS 72
Recs Am–67 NG Walker
Pro–68 A Brooks, I Stanley, R Walker
V'trs U exc Sat–NA
Fees £9 (Sun £11)
Loc ½ mile off A78 N of Stevenston

Auchenharvie (1981)

Public
Moor Park Road, West Brewery Park, Saltcoats
Mem 100
Sec WJ Thomson
Pro R Rodgers (0292) 603103
Holes 9 L 5300 yds SSS 66
Recs Am–67 R Galloway, J Murphy, P Rodgers, A Wylie

V'trs U WE–U after 9.30am
Fees £2.40 (£3.60)
Loc Low road between Saltcoats and Stevenston

Ballochmyle (1937)

Private
Ballochmyle, Mauchline KA5 6RR
Tel (0290) 50469
Mem 860
Sec A Binnie (0292) 79503
Holes 18 L 5952 yds SSS 69
Recs Am–66 NC Brown, I Guthrie
Pro–65 A Hunter (1987)
V'trs WD/WE–U BH–M
Fees D–£10 (£15)
Loc By A70 Kilmarnock–Dumfries road. 1 mile S of Mauchline
Mis Buggies available

Beith (1896)

Private
Bigholm Road, Beith
Tel (050 55) 3166
Mem 380
Sec M Rattray (050 55) 2011
Holes 9 L 5580 yds SSS 67
Recs Am–64 K Ross
V'trs U exc Sat & Sun pm
Fees D–£5
Loc 1 mile E of Beith

Belleisle Course (1927)

Public
Ayr
Tel (0292) 41258
Sec H Diamond
Pro J Easey (0292) 41314
Holes 18 L 6540 yds SSS 71
Recs Am–63 K Gimson
Pro–65 D McLelland, J Farmer
V'trs U
Fees £4.80 D–£7.60 (£5.80 D–£9.20)
Loc 1½ miles SW of town centre
Mis Belleisle Club plays here

Belleisle Club (1928)

Private
Ayr
Tel (0292) 41258
Mem 250
Sec AF Wilson (0292) 42136
Holes Play over Belleisle and Seafield courses

Brodick (1897)

Private
Brodick, Isle of Arran
Tel (0770) 2349
Mem 525
Sec GI Jameson
Pro PS McCalla (0770) 2513
Holes 18 L 4404 yds SSS 62
Recs Am–61 D Bell
V'trs U
Fees D–£5.50
Loc Pier 1 mile

Caprington

Public
Kilmarnock Municipal, Ayr Road, Kilmarnock
Tel (0563) 21915
Mem 400
Sec F McCulloch
Holes 18 L 5460 yds SSS 69
9 hole course
Recs Am–63 S Fraser
Pro–66 E Brown
V'trs U

Corrie (1892)

Private
Corrie, Isle of Arran
Tel (077 081) 223
Mem 220
Sec J Long (077 083) 678
Holes 9 L 1948 yds SSS 61
Recs Am–62 JC Reid
V'trs U
Fees D–£3 W–£12 M–£20
Loc 6 miles N of Brodick

Dalmilling Course (1960)

Public
Westwood Avenue, Whitletts, Ayr
Tel (0292) 63893
Pro D Gemmell
Holes 18 L 5401 yds SSS 66
Recs Am–61 G McKay
V'trs U
Fees £3.50 D–£4.40 (£4.30 D–£6.90) (1986 prices)
Loc NE boundary of Ayr
Mis Dalmilling Club plays here

Dalmilling Club (1960)

Public
Westwood Avenue, Whitletts, Ayr
Tel (0292) 63893
Mem 232
Sec CAH King (0292) 268180
Holes Plays over Dalmilling

Girvan (1900)

Public
Golf Course Road, Girvan
Tel (0465) 4272
Mem 180
Sec Mrs V Connor (0465) 2144
Holes 18 L 5075 SSS 65
Recs Am–61 J Cannon
Pro–61 K Stevely
V'trs U
Fees £3.80 (£4.80)
Loc N side of town

Glasgow Gailes (1787)

Private
Gailes, Irvine
Tel (0294) 311347
Mem 1100
Sec IAD Mann (041) 942 2011
Pro J Steven (041) 942 8507
Holes 18 L 6447 yds SSS 71
Recs Am–62 CW Green
Pro–67 R Brownlie
V'trs WD–I WE–M SOC
Fees £20 (£20)
Loc 1 mile S of Irvine

Irvine (1887)

Private
Bogside, Irvine
Tel (0294) 78139
Mem 450
Sec A MacPherson (0294) 75979
Pro K Erskine (0294) 75626
Holes 18 L 6454 yds SSS 71
Recs Am–65 DA Roxburgh (1981)
Pro–66 R Weir (1987)
V'trs SOC–Mon–Thurs
Fees £9 D–£12

Irvine Ravenspark (1907)

Public
Irvine
Tel (0294) 79550
Mem 400
Sec RC Palmer (0294) 76983
Pro P Bond (0294) 76467
Holes 18 L 6496 yds SSS 71
Recs Am–66 F Moore
V'trs U
Fees £1.60 (£3.70)

Kilbirnie Place (1922)

Private
Largs Road, Kilbirnie
Tel (0505) 683398
Mem 300
Sec JF Galt
Holes 18 L 5411 yds SSS 67
Recs Am–64 G McLean
V'trs U exc Sat
Fees £3.50 Sun–£5.50
Loc ½ mile W of Kilbirnie

Kilmarnock (Barassie) (1887)

Private
29 Hillhouse Road, Barassie, Troon KA10 6SY
Tel (0292) 311077
Mem 430
Sec RL Bryce (0292) 313920
Pro WR Lockie (0292) 311322
Holes 18 L 6473 yds SSS 71
Recs Am–66 JW Milligan (1988)
Pro–68 P Bond (1988)
V'trs WE/Wed–NA SOC–Tues & Thurs
Fees On application
Loc Opposite Barassie Station

Lamlash (1889)

Private
Lamlash, Isle of Arran
Tel (077 06) 296
Mem 435
Sec J Henderson (077 06) 272
Holes 18 L 4681 yds SSS 63

For map index see page 203.

Recs Am–62 B Morrison
Pro–64 R Burke
V'trs U
Fees D–£5 After 4.30pm–£3 W–£25
Loc $3^1/_2$ miles S from Brodick Pier on A841

Largs (1891)

Private
Irvine Road, Largs KA30 8EU
Tel **(0475) 673594**
Mem 700
Sec F Gilmour (0475) 672497
Pro R Stewart (0475) 686192
Holes 18 L 6257 yds SSS 70
Recs Am–AO Harrington
V'trs U
Fees £9 D–£14
Loc 1 mile S of town centre

Lochranza

Private
Lochranza, Isle of Arran
Tel **(077 083) 273**
Mem 20
Sec Mrs R McAllister
Pro DJ McAllister
Holes 9 L 1700 yds SSS
Recs Am–26 GM Anserson
V'trs U

Loudoun Gowf Club (1909)

Private
Galston
Tel **(0563) 820551**
Mem 475
Sec CA Bruce (0563) 821993
Holes 18 L 5854 metres SSS 68
Recs Pro–64 G Davidson
V'trs WD–U WE–M SOC
Fees £5 D–£8 (1985)
Loc 5 miles E of Kilmarnock

Machrie Bay

Private
Machrie Bay, Brodick, Isle of Arran KA27 8DZ
Tel **(077 084) 267**
Mem 160
Sec M Hood
Holes 9 L 2082 yds SSS 61
Recs Am–62 A Kelso
Pro–59 W Hagen
V'trs U
Fees D–£2 W–£8 M–£10
Loc W coast, 9 miles from Brodick

Maybole

Public
Memorial Park, Maybole
Mem 100
Sec H McKay (0655) 83530
Holes 9 L 2635 yds SSS 65 (for 18)
Recs Am–64 WW McCulloch
V'trs U
Fees £2.20 (£3)
Loc Off Glasgow–Stranraer road (A77), S of Maybole

New Cumnock (1901)

Private
New Cumnock
Mem 125
Sec H Smith
Holes 9 L 2365 yds SSS 63
Recs Am–66 D Blackwood
V'trs U
Loc Cumnock Road

Prestwick (1851)

Private
Links Road, Prestwick KA9 1QG
Tel **(0292) 77404**
Mem 400
Sec JA Reid
Pro FC Rennie (0292) 79483
Holes 18 L 6631 yds SSS 72
Recs Am–68 PM Mayo, P Deeble, B Andrade (1987)
Pro–67 EC Brown, C O'Connor
V'trs I WD–on application only
Fees On application
Loc Prestwick Airport 1 mile, nr Railway Station

Prestwick St Cuthbert (1899)

Private
East Road, Prestwick KA9 2SX
Tel **(0292) 77101**
Mem 698
Sec RM Tonner (0292) 79120
Holes 18 L 6470 yds SSS 71
Recs Am–66 G Hogg (1984)
V'trs WD/BH–U WE–M SOC–WD
Fees £7 D–£12
Loc $^1/_2$ mile E side of Prestwick

Prestwick St Nicholas (1851)

Private
Grangemuir Road, Prestwick KA9 1SN
Tel **(0292) 77608**
Mem 600 125(L) 62(J)
Sec JR Leishman
Pro I Parker (0292) 79755
Holes 18 L 5926 yds SSS 68
Recs Am–63 P Girvan
Pro–63 A Johnstone
V'trs WD–I WE/BH–NA
Fees On application
Loc Prestwick

Routenburn (1914)

Private
Largs
Tel **(0475) 673230**
Mem 400
Sec JE Smeaton (0475) 674171
Pro R Torrance (0475) 674289
Holes 18 L 5650 yds SSS 67
Recs Am–65 AO Harrington
Pro–65 S Torrance
V'trs U SOC–WD
Fees £2.60 D–£3.70 (£6.30) W–£19

Royal Troon (1878)

Private
Craigend Road, Troon KA10 6EP
Tel **(0292) 311555**
Mem 800
Sec JD Montgomerie
Pro RB Anderson (0292) 313281
Holes Old (Medal) 18 L 6641 yds SSS 73; Old (C'ship) 18 L 7067 yds SSS 74; Portland 18 L 6274 yds SSS 71
Recs Old Am–70 CW Green, J Harkis
Pro–66 R Clampett, S Lyle, T Purtzer
Portland Am–66 IR Harris, JH McKay
V'trs WD–I H Mon–Thurs only (Handicap limit–18)
Old course–XL WE–NA both courses. Booking req.
Fees D–£30 Old & Portland
D–£20 Portland only
Loc Prestwick Airport 3 miles

Seafield (1930)

Public
Ayr
Tel **(0292) 41258**
Sec H Diamond
Pro JS Easey (0292) 41314
Holes 18 L 5244 yds SSS 66
Recs Am–64 D Wilkie
V'trs U
Fees £3.40 D–£5.40 (£4 D–£6.40)
Loc S boundary of Ayr in Belleisle Park
Mis Belleisle Club plays here

Shiskine (1896)

Private
Blackwaterfoot, Isle of Arran
Tel **(077 086) 226**
Mem 300 76(L) 22(J)
Sec JR Liddell (Match Sec) (077 086) 313
Holes 12 L 3089 yds Par 43
Recs Am–39 J Melvin, J Brown
Pro–36 DH McGillivray
V'trs U SOC
Fees £3.50 (£3.50) W–£20 1988 prices
Loc 11 miles from Brodick
Mis Links course

Skelmorlie (1891)

Private
Skelmorlie PA17 5ES
Tel **(0475) 520152**
Mem 300
Sec J Morrison (0475) 521969
Holes 13 L 5056 yds SSS 65
Recs Am–63 J Paton
Pro–69 J Braid, G Duncan

V'trs U exc Sat (Apr–Oct)
Fees D–£5 Sun–£10
Loc Wemyss Bay Station 1½ miles

Troon Municipal

Public
Harling Drive, Troon
Tel **(0292) 312464**
Pro G Cunningham
Holes Lochgreen 18 L 6687 yds SSS 72; Darley 18 L 6327 yds SSS 70; Fullarton 18 L 4784 yds SSS 63
Recs Lochgreen Am–66 R Milligan
Pro–65 J Chillas
Darley Am–66 M Rossi
Pro–66 J White
Fullarton Am–58 A McQueen
V'trs U SOC–exc Sat
Fees Lochgreen/Darley £4.80 D–£7.60 (£5.80 D–£8.60)
Fullarton £3 D–£3.90 (£3.60 D–£6)
Loc 4 miles N of Prestwick at Station Brae

Troon Portland (1894)

Private
1 Crosbie Road, Troon
Tel **(0292) 311555**
Mem 120
Sec J Currie (0292) 311863
Holes Play over Troon Portland of Troon GC

Troon St Meddans (1907)

Private
Harling Drive, Troon KA10 6NF
Mem 200
Sec DG Baxter (0292) 313291
Holes Play over Troon Municipal courses Lochgreen SSS 72 and Darley SSS 70

Turnberry Hotel (1906)

Private
Turnberry KA26 9LT
Tel **(0655) 31000**
Sec CJ Rouse (Gen Mgr)
Pro RS Jamieson
Holes Ailsa 18 L 6950 yds SSS 70
Arran 18 L 6276 yds SSS 69
Recs Ailsa Am–70 GK MacDonald
Pro–63 M Hayes, G Norman
Arran Am–66 AP Parkin
Pro–66 J McTear
V'trs H U after 12 noon (WD/WE)
Fees On application
Loc 5 miles N of Girvan
Mis Turnberry Club plays here

West Kilbride (1893)

Private
West Kilbride KA23 9HT
Tel **(0294) 823128**
Mem 1000
Sec ED Jefferies (0294) 823911
Pro G Howie (0294) 823042
Holes 18 L 6452 yds SSS 71
Recs Am–63 BW Aitken
Pro–67 J Panton
V'trs WD–I WE–M BH–NA SOC
Fees On application
Loc West Kilbride

Western Gailes (1897)

Private
Gailes, Irvine
Tel **(0294) 311649**
Mem 475
Sec JA Clement, B Cole ACFA
Holes 18 L 6614 yds SSS 72
Recs Am–68 ME Lewis
Pro–66 DJ Russell
V'trs I
Fees £15–£18
Loc 3 miles N of Troon

Whiting Bay (1895)

Private
Whiting Bay, Isle of Arran
Tel **(077 07) 487**
Mem 290
Sec WA Jones (077 07) 305
Holes 18 L 4405 yds SSS 63
Recs Am–63 JD Simpson, D Burn
V'trs U
Fees D–£4 W–£17 F–£25 M–£40
Loc Rear of village

Borders

Berwickshire, Peebleshire, Roxburghshire & Selkirkshire

Duns (1898)

Private
Hardens Road, Duns
Mem 200
Sec A Campbell (0361) 82717
Holes 9 L 5826 yds SSS 68
Recs Am–66 WV Paton, G Clark
V'trs U SOC
Fees £5 (£5)
Loc 1 mile W of Duns off A6105

Eyemouth (1880)

Private
Gunsgreen House, Eyemouth
Tel **(089 07) 50551**
Mem 180
Sec JW Fleming
Pro C Maltman
Holes 9 L 5500 yds SSS 67
Recs Am–60 J Patterson
V'trs U
Fees D–£3 (£4)

Galashiels (1884)

Public
Ladhope Recreation Ground, Galashiels
Tel **(0896) 3724**
Mem 250 60(J)
Sec WD Millar (0750) 21669
Holes 18 L 5309 yds SSS 67
Recs Am–62 KW Simpson
Pro–70 J Braid
V'trs U SOC
Fees £4.20 (£4.70)
Loc ¼ mile NE of town

Hawick (1877)

Private
Vertish Hill, Hawick
Tel **(0450) 72293**
Mem 510
Sec JG Brown (0450) 73183
Holes 18 L 5929 yds SSS 69
Recs Am–63 AJ Ballantyne
Pro–65 R McDonald
V'trs U
Fees £5 D–£8 (£8)
Loc 1½ miles S of Hawick
Mis Golfing package D–£15

The Hirsel (1948)

Private
Coldstream
Tel **(0890) 2678**
Mem 175
Sec IF Sproule (0890) 2251
Holes 9 L 5680 yds SSS 68
Recs Am–66 J Martin (1987)
V'trs U SOC
Fees £3.50 (£4.50)
Loc ½ mile W of Coldstream

Innerleithen (1886)

Private
Leithen Water, Leithen Road, Innerleithen
Tel **(0896) 830951**
Mem 175
Sec S Wyse (0896) 830071
Holes 9 L 5820 yds SSS 68
Recs Am–66 WN Smith
V'trs U
Fees £5 (£5) W–£18
Loc Innerleithen 1½ miles on Heriot Road

Jedburgh (1892)

Private
Dunion Road, Jedburgh
Tel **(0835) 63587**
Mem 200
Sec K McDonald (0835) 63587
Holes 9 L 5492 yds SSS 67
Recs Am–64 E Redpath (1987)
V'trs U
Fees £5 (£6)
Loc Jedburgh 1 mile

Kelso (1887)

Private
Berrymoss Racecourse Road, Kelso, Roxburghshire
Tel **(0573) 23009**
Mem 350
Sec JP Payne (0573) 23259
Holes 18 L 6066 yds SSS 69

Recs Am–64
V'trs U SOC
Fees £5.50 D–£8 (£6.50 D–£10) 1988 prices
Loc Inside Kelso racecourse, 1 mile from town centre

Langholm (1892)

Private
Laaangholm, Dumfriesshire
Tel (0541) 80559
Mem 150
Sec T Hutton (0541) 80429
Holes 9 L 2872 yds SSS 68
Recs Am–65 I Borthwick
V'trs U
Fees £4 (£4)
Loc Within Burgh of Langholm

Lauder (1896)

Public
Lauder
Tel (057 82) 409
Mem 95
Sec G Bryson
Holes 9 L 6002 yds SSS 70
Recs Am–70 JFC Jeffries
V'trs U
Fees £3 (£3.50) Honesty Box
Loc 1/2 mile W of Lauder

Melrose (1880)

Private
Dingleton, Melrose
Tel (089 682) 2855
Mem 300
Sec LM Wallace (089 684) 617
Holes 9 L 5464 yds SSS 68
Recs Am–63 DF Campbell
V'trs U
Fees £4 (£5)
Loc S boundary of Melrose

Minto (1926)

Private
Denholm, Hawick, Roxburghshire
Tel (0450) 87220
Mem 300
Sec IR Welch (0450) 72267
Pro D Dunlop (08356) 2686
Holes 18 L 5460 yds SSS 68
Recs Am–64 I Oliver
V'trs U SOC
Fees £5 (£6)
Loc 6 miles E of Hawick. Denholm 1/2 mile

Peebles (1892)

Public
Kirkland Street, Peebles
Tel (0721) 20197
Mem 600
Sec G Garvie (0721) 20153 ext 214
Holes 18 L 6137 yds SSS 69
Recs Am–64 D Campbell
Pro–70 RDBM Shade
V'trs U
Fees £5 D–£7 (£7 D–£9) W–£28
Loc 23 miles S of Edinburgh

St Boswells (1899)

Private
St Boswells, Roxburghshire
Tel (0835) 22359
Mem 245
Sec GB Ovens
Holes 9 L 5206 yds SSS 65
Recs Am–61 CI Ovens
V'trs U SOC
Fees £4
Loc 1/4 mile off A68 at St Boswells Green

Selkirk (1883)

Private
Selkirk
Tel (0750) 20621
Mem 250
Sec R Davies (0750) 20427
Holes 9 L 5560 yds SSS 67
Recs Am–60 MD Cleghorn
V'trs U SOC
Fees £5 (£7)
Loc 1 mile S of Selkirk on A7

Torwoodlee (1895)

Private
Galashiels
Tel (0896) 2260
Mem 280
Sec A Wilson
Holes 9 L 5800 yds SSS 68
Recs Am–64 RV Rutherford
Pro–64 A Wilson
V'trs U exc Sat–NA SOC
Fees £6 D–£8
Loc 1 mile N of Galashiels on A7

Clackmannanshire
Central Region

Alloa (1891)

Private
Schawpark, Sauchie, Alloa
Tel (0259) 722745
Mem 535 80(L) 130(J)
Sec AM Frame
Pro W Bennett (0259) 724476
Holes 18 L 6240 yds SSS 70
Recs Am–63 AJ Liddle
Pro–66 R Weir, G Harvey
V'trs U WE–no parties
Fees £7 D–£11 (£12)
Loc Alloa

Alva

Private
Beauclerc Street, Alva FK12 5LE
Tel (0259) 60431
Mem 200
Sec D Davidson (0259) 51427
Holes 9 L 2407 yds SSS 64
Recs Am–63 R Lyon
V'trs U
Fees £2 (£3)
Loc Back Road, Alva

Braehead (1891)

Private
Cambus, Alloa
Tel (0259) 722078
Mem 500
Sec JA Henderson (0259) 215135
Holes 18 L 6013 yds SSS 69 Par 70
Recs Am–64 D Mackison
V'trs U
Fees £7.50 (£9) W–£25
Loc 2 miles W of Alloa (A907)

Dollar (1890)

Private
Brewlands House, Dollar
Tel (025 94) 2400
Mem 300
Sec MB Shea (02594) 2666 (day)
Holes 18 L 5144 yds SSS 66
V'trs U SOC
Fees £5 D–£6 (£8)
Loc In town

Tillicoultry (1899)

Private
Alva Road, Tillicoultry
FK13 6BL
Tel (0259) 50124
Mem 400
Sec R Whitehead
Holes 9 L 2528 yds SSS 66
Recs Am–62 K Mitchell
V'trs WD–U Sat–NA Sun–NA before 2pm SOC
Fees £3.50 D–£5 (£5.50 D–£7)
Loc 9 miles E of Stirling

Tulliallan (1902)

Private
Kincardine, by Alloa
Tel (0259) 30396
Mem 525 53(L) 100(J) 19(5)
Sec JS McDowall (0324) 485420
Pro S Kelly (0259) 30798
Holes 18 L 5982 yds SSS 69
Recs Am–65 A Pickles, D Johnson
Pro–70 D Huish, S Walker, G Gray
V'trs U exc comp days
Fees £4 (£5)
Loc 5 miles E of Alloa

Dunbartonshire
Strathclyde Region

Balmore (1906)

Private
Balmore, by Torrance
Tel (0360) 2120240
Mem 700
Sec GP Woolard (041) 332 0392
Holes 18 L 5735 yds SSS 67
Recs Am–63 A Brodie

V'trs M SOC
Fees £8 R/D
Loc 2 miles N of Glasgow

Bearsden (1891)

Private
Thorn Road, Bearsden G61 4BE
Tel (041) 942 2351
Mem 600
Sec JD McArthur
Holes 9 L 5977 yds SSS 68
Recs Am–64 D MacLeod
V'trs M
Loc 7 miles NW of Glasgow

Cardross (1895)

Private
Cardross, Dumbarton G82 5LB
Tel (0389) 841213
Mem 800
Sec R Evans CA (0389) 841754
Pro N Cameron (0389) 841350
Holes 18 L 6466 yds SSS 71
Recs Am–65 JLS Kinloch
Pro–67 M Miller, G Weir
V'trs WD–U WE–M SOC
Fees £10 D–£15
Loc 4 miles W of town of Dumbarton

Clober (1951)

Private
Craigton Road, Milngavie, Glasgow G62 7HP
Tel (041) 956 1685
Mem 575
Sec G Buchanan (041) 956 5839
Pro G Lyle
Holes 18 L 5068 yds SSS 65
Recs Am–61 PW Smith, J Graham Jr
V'trs WD–U before 4.30pm WE–M BH–NA SOC
Fees £5
Loc 7 miles NW of Glasgow

Clydebank Municipal

Public
Overtoun Road, Dalmuir, Clydebank
Tel (041) 952 6372
Sec Clydebank District Council (041) 941 1331
Pro R Bowman (041) 952 6372
Holes 18 L 5349 yds SSS 66
Recs Am–64 FG Jardine, J Semple
Pro–64 R Bowman
V'trs U exc Sat 11am–2.30pm
Fees Mon–Sat £2 Sun–£2.40
Loc 8 miles W of Glasgow
Mis Clydebank Overtoun Club plays here

Clydebank Overtoun (1970)

Private
Overtoun Road, Dalmuir, Clydebank
Tel (041) 952 6372
Mem 160
Sec JD Byrne (041) 952 6480
Holes Play over Clydebank Municipal

Clydebank and District (1905)

Private
Hardgate, Clydebank
Tel (0389) 73289
Mem 780
Sec W Manson (0389) 72832
Pro C Elliott
Holes 18 L 5815 yds SSS 68
Recs Am–64 D Galbraith
V'trs WD–I
Fees D–£10 W–£40 M–£60
Loc 2 miles N of Clydebank

Craigmaddie (1977)

Public
Dougalston Golf Course, Milngavie, Glasgow
Tel (041) 956 5750
Mem 500
Sec G More
Holes Play over Dougalston

Cumbernauld (1977)

Public
Palacerigg Country Park, Cumbernauld G67 3HU
Tel (0236) 734969
Mem 350
Sec JH Dunsmore
Holes 18 L 6412 yds SSS 71
Recs Am–67 G Wilson
Pro–69 D Mathews
V'trs U SOC–WD only
Fees £4 (£8)
Mis Palacerigg GC plays here

Dougalston (1977)

Private
Milngavie, Glasgow
Tel (041) 956 5750
Sec W McInnes
Holes 18 L 6269 yds SSS 71
Recs Am–71 J Carnegie, J McLaren (1987)
Pro–73 B Barnes
V'trs U SOC
Fees £4 (£5)
Loc 7 miles N of Glasgow on A81
Mis Craigmaddie Club plays here

Douglas Park (1897)

Private
Hillfoot, Bearsden
Tel (041) 942 2220
Mem 400 250(L) 100(J)
Sec J Rennie Thorburn (041) 331 1837
Pro D Scott (041) 942 1482
Holes 18 L 5957 yds SSS 69
Recs Am–65 DG Carrick, BS Yuill, AR Docherty
Pro–66 A Hunter
V'trs M
Loc Bearsden, at Hillfoot Station

Dullatur (1896)

Private
Dullatur, Glasgow G68 0AR
Tel (0236) 723230
Mem 420 60(L)
Sec W Laing (0236) 27847
Pro D Sinclair
Holes 18 L 6253 yds SSS 70
Recs Am–67 JM Moffat (1985)
Pro–68 J Farmer
V'trs WD–U WE–M
Fees £10 (£6–1.30–4pm)
Loc 3 miles N of Cumbernauld

Dumbarton (1888)

Private
Broadmeadow, Dumbarton
Tel (0389) 32830
Mem 500
Sec R Turnbull
Holes 18 L 5981 yds SSS 69
Recs Am–64 CW Green
V'trs WD–U WE/BH–M
Fees D-£8
Loc 3/4 mile N of Dumbarton

Hayston (1926)

Private
Campsie Road, Kirkintilloch, Glasgow G66 1RN
Tel (041) 776 1244/1390
Mem 445 70(L) 80(J)
Sec (041) 762 0272
Pro R Graham (041) 775 0882
Holes 18 L 6042 yds SSS 69
Recs Am–62 LS Mann
Pro–69 K Stables
V'trs WD–I before 4.30pm
M after 4.30pm WE–M SOC
Fees £7
Loc 1 mile N of Kirkintilloch
Mis Buggies for hire

Helensburgh (1893)

Private
25 East Abercromby Street, Helensburgh G84 9JD
Tel (0436) 4173
Mem 825
Sec Mrs AC McEwan
Pro I Laird (0436) 5505
Holes 18 L 6058 yds SSS 69
Recs Am–64 A Scott
Pro–65 RT Drummond, D Chillas, B Marchbank
V'trs WD–U WE–NA
Fees £8 D–£12
Loc 25 miles W of Glasgow

Hilton Park (1927)

Private
Auldmarroch Estate, Stockiemuir Road, Milngavie G62 7HB
Tel (041) 956 5124/1215
Mem 1200
Sec Mrs JA Dawson (041) 956 4657

Pro W McCondichie (041) 956 5125
Holes Hilton 18 L 6003 yds SSS 70
Allander 18 L 5361 yds SSS 67
Recs Hilton Am–65 ND Kelly
Pro–64 AF Anderson
Allander Am–67 A James
Pro–63 F Morris, N Wood
V'trs WD–U before 5pm WE–M
Fees On application
Loc 8 miles N of Glasgow

Kirkintilloch (1894)

Private
Todhill, Campsie Road, Kirkintilloch G66 1RN
Tel **(041) 776 1256**
Mem 420 92(L) 104(J) 35(5)
Sec H Bannerman (041) 777 7971
Holes 18 L 5269 yds SSS 66
Recs Am–63 J Hay, R Moir
Pro–68 R Weir
V'trs M
Loc 7 miles N of Glasgow

Lenzie (1889)

Private
19 Crosshill Road, Lenzie G66 5DA
Tel **(041) 776 1535**
Mem 483 125(L) 125(J)
Sec AW Jones (041) 776 4377
Pro M Campbell (041) 777 7748
Holes 18 L 5982 yds SSS 69
Recs Am–64 S Lindsay
V'trs M SOC
Loc Glasgow 6 miles

Milngavie (1895)

Private
Laighpark, Milngavie G62 8EP
Tel **(041) 956 1619**
Mem 390
Sec WD Robertson (041) 956 2932
Holes 18 L 5818 yds SSS 68
Recs Am–64 RGB McCallum
V'trs M
Fees On application
Loc NW of Glasgow

Vale of Leven (1907)

Private
Northfield Road, Bonhill, Alexandria
Tel **(0389) 52351**
Mem 450
Sec W McKinlay (0389) 52508
Holes 18 L 5156 yds SSS 66
Recs Am–60 G Brown (1988)
Pro–63 EC Brown (1959)
V'trs U exc Sat (Apr–Sept) SOC (max 36 members)
Fees D–£6 (D–£10)
Loc Off A82 at Bonhill

Windyhill (1908)

Private
Windyhill, Bearsden
Tel **(041) 942 2349**
Mem 650
Sec PO Bell (041) 956 4970
Pro B Collinson (041) 942 7157
Holes 18 L 6254 yds SSS 70
Recs Am–66 DJ Shaw
V'trs WD–I Sun–M
Fees £8
Loc 8 miles NW of Glasgow

Fife

Fife Region

Aberdour (1904)

Private
Seaside Place, Aberdour KY3 0TX
Tel **(0383) 860688**
Mem 420 160(L)
Sec BP Drever (0383) 860353
Pro J Bennett (0383) 860256
Holes 18 L 5469 yds SSS 67
Recs Am–65 S Meiklejohn, D Miller
V'trs Sun/comp Sat–NA
Fees £8 (£11)
Loc Aberdour
Mis Visitors may make tee reservations 1 day in advance with Pro

Anstruther (1890)

Private
Marsfield Shore Road, Anstruther
Tel **(0333) 310956**
Mem 500
Sec T Reid (0333) 311966
Holes 9 L 4504 yds SSS 63
Recs Am–63 R Wallace, T Anderson, A Forrester
V'trs U SOC
Fees £4.50 (£6) 1988 prices
Loc Outskirts of town

Auchterderran (1904)

Private
Woodend Road, Cardenden
Tel **(0592) 721579**
Mem 100
Sec J Lynch
Holes 9 L 5400 yds SSS 66
Recs Am–66 C McRae
V'trs U
Fees £2 (£3.20) To be reviewed
Loc 1 mile N of town centre

Balbirnie Park (1983)

Private
Balbirnie Park, Markinch, Glenrothes
Tel **(0592) 752006**
Mem 500
Sec J Purves
Holes 18 L 6210 yds SSS 70
Recs Am–70 G Birnie
V'trs U
Fees £6.90 D–£9 (£9 D–£13.25)
Loc 2 miles E of Glenrothes

Balgove (1972)

Public
St Andrews
Holes 9 (Beginners course)
V'trs U
Fees £2
Loc St Andrews Links

Ballingry (1908)

Public
Lochore Meadows Country Park, Crosshill, Lochgelly
Tel **(0592) 860086**
Mem 100
Sec J Mackie (0592) 860927
Holes 9 L 6482 yds SSS 71
Recs Am–70 JJ Morris (1987)
V'trs U
Fees £2.90 (£3.90)

Burntisland (1797)

Private
Tel **(0592) 873865**
Mem 120
Sec AD McPherson
Holes Play over Dodhead Course, Burntisland

Burntisland Golf House Club (1898)

Private
Dodhead, Burntisland
Tel **(0592) 873247**
Mem 750
Sec AW Mann (0592) 874093
Pro A Owen (0592) 873247
Holes 18 L 5897 yds SSS 68
V'trs U
Fees £6 D–£10 (£8 D–£14)
Loc 1 mile E on B923

Canmore (1898)

Private
Venturefair, Dunfermline
Tel **(0383) 724969**
Mem 480 60(L) 80(J)
Sec JC Duncan (0383) 726098
Pro S Craig (0383) 728416
Holes 18 L 5437 yds SSS 66
Recs Am–61 R Wallace
V'trs WD–U
Fees £6 D–£9
Loc 1 mile N of Dunfermline on A823

Crail Golfing Society (1786)

Private
Balcomie Clubhouse, Crail KY10 3XN
Tel **(0333) 50278**
Mem 700 200(L)
Sec G Thomson (0333) 50686
Pro G Lennie (0333) 50960

Holes 18 L 5720 yds SSS 68
Recs Am–64 RW Malcolm
V'trs U
Fees On application
Loc 11 miles SE of St Andrews

Cupar (1855)

Private
Hillarvitt, Cupar
Tel **(0334) 53549**
Mem 475
Sec IR Wilson (0334) 53254
Holes 9 L 5074 yds SSS 65
Recs Am–62 J Fairfield, C Wilson
V'trs Sat–NA SOC–WD/Sun
Fees £4 (£5)
Loc 10 miles W of St Andrews

Dunfermline (1887)

Private
Pitfirrane, Crossford, Dunfermline KY12 8QV
Tel **(0383) 723534**
Mem 500
Sec JA Gillies
Pro J Montgomery
Holes 18 L 6217 yds SSS 70
Recs Am–65 AD Martin
Pro–65 A Brooks
V'trs WD–I 9.30–4pm SOC–WD
Fees £7.50 D–£12
Loc 2 miles W of Dunfermline on A994

Dunnikier Park (1963)

Public
Dunnikier Way, Kirkcaldy KY1 3LP
Tel **(0592) 261599**
Mem 600 35(L) 75(J)
Sec DR Caird (0592) 267462
Holes 18 L 6601 yds SSS 72
Recs Am–65 S Duthie (1988)
Pro–65 A Hunter (1988)
V'trs U SOC
Fees £2.80 (£3.95)
Loc N boundary of Kirkcaldy
Mis Dunnikier Park Club plays here

Earlsferry Thistle (1875)

Private
Melon Park, Elie
Tel **(0333) 310053**
Mem 60
Sec J Fyall (0333) 310053
Holes Play over Elie Golf House Club Course

Eden Course (1913)

Public
St Andrews
Tel **(0334) 74296 (Starter)**
Holes 18 L 5971 yds SSS 69
Recs Am–65 RDBM Shade, RD Park, K Hastie
Pro–64 W McHardy
V'trs U SOC
Fees £8 W–£45 3D–£22.50 available for unlimited play on Eden Course, Jubilee Course and New Course
Loc St Andrews Links

Falkland (1976)

Public
The Myre, Falkland KY7 7AA
Tel **(0337) 57404**
Mem 210
Sec Mrs CR Forsythe (0337) 57356
Holes 9 L 2384 metres SSS 66
Recs Am–67 W Garland (1987)
V'trs U SOC
Fees D–£3 (D–£5) W–£12.50
Loc On A912 Kirkcaldy–Perth road

Glenrothes (1958)

Public
Golf Course Road, Glenrothes KY6 2LA
Tel **(0592) 758686/758678**
Mem 600 35(L) 120(J)
Sec LD Dalrymple (0592) 754561
Holes 18 L 6444 yds SSS 71
Recs Am–65 C Birrell
Pro–69 R Craig, B Lawson
V'trs U
Fees £2.80 (£3.95)
Loc Glenrothes West

Golf House Club (1875)

Private
Elie, Leven KY9 1AS
Tel **(0333) 330327**
Mem 450
Sec GA Forgie (0333) 330301
Pro R Wilson (0333) 330955
Holes 18 L 6241 yds SSS 70
9 L 2277 yds SSS 32
Recs Am–63 AW Mathers
Pro–62 K Nagle
V'trs U July–Sept ballot
WE–no party bookings
Fees £10 D–£15 (£14 D–£20)
Loc St Andrews 12 miles

Jubilee Course (1899)

Public
St Andrews
Tel **(0334) 73938 (Starter)**
Holes 18 L 6986 yds SSS 73
V'trs U SOC
Fees £7 W–£45 3D–£22.50 (unlimited play over Jubilee, Eden and New Courses)
Loc St Andrews Links

Kinghorn (1887)

Public
Macduff Cres, Kinghorn KY3 9RE
Tel **(0592) 890345**
Holes 18 L 5246 SS 67
Recs Am–62 AJ McIntyre
V'trs U
Fees £2.80 (£3.95)
Loc 3 miles W of Kirkcaldy (A921)
Mis Kinghorn Club plays here

Kinghorn Ladies (1905)

Private
Kinghorn
Tel **(0592) 890345**
Mem 47
Sec Miss E Douglas (0592) 890512
Holes Play over Kinghorn Municipal

Kinghorn Thistle

Private
Kinghorn KY3 9RE
Tel **(0592) 890345**
Mem 180
Holes Play over Kinghorn Municipal

Kirkcaldy (1904)

Private
Balwearie Road, Kirkcaldy KY2 5LT
Tel **(0592) 260370**
Mem 450 80(L)
Sec C Taylor (0592) 266597
Pro B Lawson (0292) 203258
Holes 18 L 6007 yds SSS 70
Recs Am–67 B Glaney, R Wallace
V'trs U
Fees £5 D–£8 (£6 D–£10)
Loc SW end of town

Ladybank (1879)

Private
Annsmuir, Ladybank
Tel **(0337) 30320**
Mem 750
Sec D Downie (0337) 30814
Pro MJ Gray (0337) 30725
Holes 18 L 6617 yds SSS 72
Recs Am–65 S Syme (1987)
Pro–66 W Reilly (1984)
V'trs WD–U 9.15am–5pm M–after 5pm WE–NA 10.15am–5pm SOC
Fees £12 (£14) W–£40
Loc 6 miles S of Cupar

Leslie (Fife) (1898)

Private
Balsillie Laws, Leslie, Glenrothes KY6 3EZ
Mem 300
Sec M Burns (0592) 741449
Holes 9 L 4940 yds SSS 64
Recs Am–63 J Spital
Pro–64 J Chillas
V'trs U
Fees £3 (£4)
Loc Town boundary, 11 miles from M90 Junction 5/7

Leven Golfing Society (1820)

Private
Links Road, Leven KY8 4HS
Tel **(0333) 26096**
(0333) 21390 (starter)
Mem 350
Sec J Bennett (0333) 23898

For map index see page 203.

Holes 18 L 6434 yds SSS 71
V'trs WD–U before 5pm SOC–if 12+ phone M Innes (0333) 23509
Fees £9 (£12)
Loc ½ mile E of town centre

Leven Links (1846)

Private
Leven
Mem 700
Sec M Innes (0333) 23509 (Links Joint Committee)
Holes 18 L 6434 yds SSS 71
Recs Am–64 J Hawkesworth, K Goodwin (1986) Pro–63 P Hoad
V'trs WD–U Sat–no parties Sun–NA before 10.30am
Fees £9 (£12)
Loc Leven

Leven Municipal Course

Public
North Links, Leven KY8 1DH
Tel **(0333) 27057**
Pro J Simpson
Holes 18 L 5403 yds SSS 66
Recs Am–63 P Lamont
V'trs U
Fees £2.80 (£3.95)
Loc Adjoins Leven Links
Mis Scoonie Club plays here

Leven Thistle (1867)

Private
3 Balfour Street, Leven
Tel **(0333) 26397**
Mem 400
Sec J Scott (0333) 23798
Holes 18 L 6434 yds SSS 71 Pro–63 P Hoad (1984)
V'trs WD–U before 5pm WE–Sun only SOC
Fees £9 D–£14 (£12 D–£16)
Loc East end of promenade

Lochgelly (1910)

Private
Cartmore Road, Lochgelly
Tel **(0592) 780174**
Mem 400
Sec RF Stuart (0383) 512238
Holes 18 L 5491 yds SSS 67
Recs Am–64 D Walker (1988)
V'trs U
Fees £3.50 (£4.75)
Loc NW boundary

Lundin (1869)

Private
Golf Road, Lundin Links KY8 6BA
Tel **(0333) 320202**
Mem 700
Sec AC McBride
Pro DK Webster (0333) 320051
Holes 18 L 6377 yds SSS 71
Recs Am–65 W Bergin, D Dunk, P Brosted
V'trs WD/Sat/BH–U H Sun–M H and temp members (min. week)
Fees On application
Loc 3 miles E of Leven

Lundin Ladies (1891)

Private
Woodielea Road, Lundin Links KY8 6AR
Tel **(0333) 320022**
Mem 220
Sec Mrs H Melville (0333) 320553
Holes 9 L 4730 yds SSS 67
Recs Am–68 Miss P Baxter
V'trs U
Fees £2.50 D–£3.50 (£3.50 D–£4.50)
Loc 3 miles E of Leven

Methil (1892)

Private
Links House, Links Road, Leven
Tel **(0333) 25535**
Mem 50
Sec ATJ Traill
Holes Play over Leven Links

New Course (1894)

Public
St Andrews
Tel **(0334) 73938 (Starter)**
Holes 18 L 6604 yds SSS 72
Recs Am–67 GM Mitchell Pro–63 F Jowie
V'trs U
Fees £10 W–£45 3D–£22.50 (unlimited play over Jubilee, Eden and New courses)
Loc St Andrews Links

New Golf Club (1902)

Private
3–6 Gibson Place, St Andrews KY16 9JE
Tel **(0334) 73426**
Mem 1600
Sec C Jobson (Sec/Mgr)
Holes Play over St Andrews courses

Old Course (15th Century)

Public
St Andrews
Tel **(0334) 73393 (Starter)**
Holes 18 L 6566 yds SSS 72
Recs Am–67 J Carr Pro–62 C Strange (1987)
V'trs U H I No Sun play SOC
Fees £20
Loc St Andrews Links

Pitreavie (1923)

Private
Queensferry Road, Dunfermline KY11 5PR
Tel **(0383) 722591**
Mem 460
Sec WP Syme
Pro AD Hope (0383) 723151
Holes 18 L 6086 yds SSS 69
V'trs U (phone Pro first) SOC (Parties–max 36–must be booked in advance)
Fees £6 (£12) 1988 prices
Loc 2 miles off M90 Edinburgh–Perth, midway between Rosyth and Dunfermline

Royal and Ancient (1754)

Private
St Andrews
Tel **(0334) 72112**
Mem 1800
Sec MF Bonallack OBE
Pro L Auchterlonie (Honorary)
Holes Play over St Andrews courses

St Andrews (1843)

Private
Links House, The Links, St Andrews KY16 9JB
Tel **(0334) 74637**
Mem 1500
Sec WS Simpson (0334) 73017
Holes Play over St Andrews courses
V'trs Rules in accordance with Links Management Committee, Golf Place, St Andrews

St Andrews Courses

See Balgove, Eden, Jubilee, New and Old courses

Details from A Beveridge (Secretary) Links Management Committee of St Andrews, Golf Place, St Andrews KY16 9JA. Tel (0334) 75757.
A £35 weekly ticket allows unlimited play over the New, Eden and Jubilee courses for 7 days from date of purchase.

St Michael's (1903)

Private
Leuchars
Tel **(033 483) 365**
Mem 455
Sec AJR MacKenzie (0334) 870421 (home) (0334) 54044 (work)
Holes 9 L 5578 yds SSS 67
Recs Am–66 N Manzie (1988)
V'trs Sun am–NA (Mar–Oct) SOC
Fees Mon–Sat D–£6 Sun–£5 after 1pm
Loc 5 miles N of St Andrews on Dundee road

St Regulus Ladies' (1920)

Private
9 Pilmour Links, St Andrews KY16 9JG
Tel **(0334) 74699**
Mem 170
Sec Mrs K Ferguson
Holes Play over St Andrews courses

St Rule Ladies' (1898)

Private
12 The Links, St Andrews
Tel (0334) 72988
Mem 461
Sec Mrs R Hair
Holes Play over St Andrews Courses

Saline (1912)

Private
Kinneddar Hill, Saline
Tel (0383) 852591
Mem 300
Sec R Hutchison (0383) 852344
Holes 9 L 5302 yds SSS 66
Recs Am–S Mellon
V'trs U exc medal Sat
Fees £3 (£4)
Loc 5 miles NW of Dunfermline
Mis Catering by prior arrangement

Scoonie (1951)

Private
North Links, Leven
KY8 1DH
Tel (0333) 27057
Mem 200
Sec K Davidson (0592) 714232
Holes Play over Leven Municipal

Scotscraig (1817)

Private
Golf Road, Tayport DD6 9DZ
Tel (0382) 552515
Mem 600
Sec K Gourlay (0382) 730880
Holes 18 L 6486 yds SSS 71
Recs Am–65 M Milne Jr, W Lockie
Pro–66 J Berry, M Bembridge
V'trs WD–U WE–by prior arrangement SOC
Fees £10 D–£16 (£13 D–£19)
Loc 10 miles N of St Andrews

Thistle (1817)

Private
St Andrews
Mem 176
Sec Duncan L Joy (0334) 73749
Pro LB Ayton
Holes Play over St Andrews courses

Thornton (1921)

Private
Station Road, Thornton
Tel (0592) 771111
Mem 550
Sec AL Cowan
Holes 18 L 6175 yds SSS 69
Recs Am–65 R Malcolm
V'trs U
Fees £6 (£9) W–£18
Loc Thornton, 1 mile E of A92

Glasgow

Strathclyde Region

Alexandra Park (1880)

Public
Sannox Gardens, Alexandra Parade, Glasgow
Tel (041) 556 3711
Mem 250
Sec G McArthur
Holes 9 L 1968 yds SSS 30
V'trs U
Fees £1.10 (£1.40)
Loc 1/2 mile of E city centre

Bishopbriggs (1906)

Private
Brackenbrae Road, Bishopbriggs, Glasgow G64 2DU
Tel (041) 772 1810
Mem 400
Sec HG Simpson (041) 772 8938
Holes 18 L 6041 yds SSS 69
Recs Am–64 I Gillan, AF Dunsmore, S Finlayson
Pro–63 M Miller
V'trs M or I
Fees £12
Loc 6 miles N of Glasgow

Cathcart Castle (1895)

Private
Mearns Road, Clarkston
Tel (041) 638 0082
Mem 700
Sec WG Buchan (041) 638 9449
Pro D Naylor (041) 638 3436
Holes 18 L 5832 yds SSS 68
Recs Am–62 S Black
Pro–64 A White
V'trs M
Loc 7 miles SW Glasgow

Cathkin Braes (1888)

Private
Cathkin Road, Rutherglen, Glasgow G73 4SE
Tel (041) 634 6605
Mem 880
Sec GL Stevenson
Pro S Bree (041) 634 0650
Holes 18 L 6266 yds SSS 71
Recs Am–65 J Graham (1984)
Pro–66 W Milne (1988)
V'trs WD–I
Fees £10
Loc 5 miles S of Glasgow

Cawder (1933)

Private
Cadder Road, Bishopbriggs, Glasgow
Tel (041) 772 7101
Mem 1200
Sec GT Stoddart (041) 772 5167
Pro K Stevely (041) 772 7102
Holes Cawder 18 L 6244 yds SSS 71; Keir 18 L 5885 yds SSS 68
Recs Cawder Am–68 CW Green
Pro–65 R Weir
Keir Am–64 A Brodie, J Hay
V'trs WD–U WE–NA SOC–WD
Fees £13.50
Loc Bishopbriggs Station 1 1/4 miles

Cowglen (1906)

Private
301 Barrhead Road, Glasgow
Tel (041) 632 0556
Mem 450
Sec RJG Jamieson (0292) 266600
Pro J McTear (041) 649 9401
Holes 18 L 6006 yds SSS 69
Recs Am–63 D Barclay Howard
Pro–63 S Torrance
V'trs M
Loc S side of Glasgow

Deaconsbank (1922)

Public
Glasgow
Holes 18 L 4800 yds SSS 63
V'trs U
Fees 60p (80p)
Loc 5 miles S of Glasgow nr Thornliebank

Glasgow (1787)

Private
Killermont, Bearsden, Glasgow G61 2JW
Tel (041) 942 2340
Mem 900
Sec IAD Mann (041) 942 2011
Pro J Steven (041) 942 8507
Holes 18 L 5968 yds SSS 69
Recs Am–63 JS Cochran
Pro–65 H Weetman
V'trs M
Loc 4 miles NW of Glasgow

Haggs Castle (1910)

Private
70 Dumbreck Road, Dumbreck, Glasgow G41 4SN
Tel (041) 427 0480
Mem 1000
Sec ARC Alexander (041) 427 1157
Pro J McAlister (041) 427 3355
Holes 18 L 6464 yds SSS 71
Recs Am–66 J Semple (1987)
Pro–62 S Torrance (1984)
V'trs M SOC–Weds only
Fees SOC £11 D–£18
Loc SW Glasgow

King's Park (1934)

Public
150A Croftpark Avenue, Croftfoot, Glasgow G54
Holes 9 L 2010 yds SSS 30
Recs Am–27 I Simpson
V'trs U
Fees D–£1.50 (£1.20)
Loc Croftfoot Glasgow G54, 3 1/2 miles S of city centre

For map index see page 203.

Knightswood (1929)

Public
Lincoln Avenue, Glasgow G13
Tel **(041) 959 2131**
Mem 76
Sec M Kelly (041) 636 1225
Holes 9 L 2736 yds SSS 33
V'trs U
Fees D–£1.50 (£1.20)
Loc 4 miles W of city centre

Lethamhill (1933)

Public
Cumbernauld Road, Glasgow G3
Tel **(041) 770 6220**
Holes 18 L 5946 yds SSS 68
Recs Am–70 R Harker
V'trs U
Fees £2 (£2.60)
Loc Glasgow G3, 3 miles E of city centre

Linn Park (1924)

Public
Simshill Road, Glasgow G44
Tel **(041) 637 5871**
Mem 140
Sec M Peters
Holes 18 L 4848 yds SSS 65
Recs Am–64 B Hinds (1988)
V'trs U
Fees £2.10 (£2.80)
Loc 4 miles S city centre

Littlehill (1926)

Public
Auchinairn Road, Bishopbriggs, Glasgow
Tel **(041) 772 1916**
Holes 18 L 6199 yds SSS 69
Recs Am–66
V'trs U
Fees £1.80 D–£3 (£2.40)
Loc 3 miles N of city centre

Pollok (1892)

Private
90 Barrhead Road, Pollokshaws, Glasgow G43 1BG
Tel **(041) 632 1080**
Mem 500
Sec A Mathison Boyd (041) 632 4361
Holes 18 L 6257 yds SSS 70
Recs Am–62 G Shaw
Pro–62 G Cunningham
V'trs I XL WE–NA SOC–WD
Fees £12 D–£18
Loc 3 miles SW of Glasgow on B462

Ralston (1904)

Private
Ralston, Paisley
Tel **(041) 882 1349**
Mem 440 165(L) 100(J)
Sec JW Horne (041) 883 7045
Pro D Barbour (041) 810 4925
Holes 18 L 6100 yds SSS 69
Recs Am–63 J Armstrong
V'trs M
Loc 2 miles E of Paisley

Ruchill (1928)

Public
Brassey Street, Maryhill, Glasgow G20
Mem 60
Sec DF Campbell (041) 946 7676
Holes 9 L 2240 yds SSS 31
V'trs U
Fees D–£1.50 (£1.20)
Loc 2½ miles NW of city centre

Sandyhills (1905)

Private
223 Sandyhills Road, Glasgow G32 9NA
Tel **(041) 778 1179**
Mem 460
Sec G Muir CA (0698) 812203
Holes 18 L 6253 yds SSS 70
Recs Am–65 J Hay
V'trs M SOC
Loc 4 miles E city centre

Williamwood (1906)

Private
Clarkston Road, Glasgow G44
Tel **(041) 637 1783**
Mem 680
Sec IJ Gilchrist (041) 226 4311
Pro J Gardner (041) 637 2715
Holes 18 L 5878 yds SSS 68
Recs Am–63 I Carslaw, AA Nicol, S Dixon
Pro–61 BJ Gallacher
V'trs M
Loc 5 miles S of Glasgow

Lanarkshire
Strathclyde Region

Airdrie (1877)

Private
Rochsoles, Airdrie
Tel **(0236) 62195**
Mem 425
Sec WR Thomson (Hon)
Pro A McCloskey (0236) 54360
Holes 18 L 6004 yds SSS 69
Recs Am–64 G Russo, R Marshall
V'trs M I WE/BH–NA SOC
Fees £5.75
Loc Airdrie 1 mile

Bellshill (1905)

Private
Orbiston, Bellshill ML4 2RZ
Tel **(0698) 745124**
Mem 400
Sec A Currie
Holes 18 L 6607 yds SSS 72
Recs Am–68 J Simpson, A Megan, M Brown
Pro–70 J McCallum
V'trs U exc WD 5–6.30pm
Fees £7 (£9)
Loc 10 miles S of Glasgow between Bellshill and Motherwell

Biggar (1895)

Public
Public Park, Broughton Road, Biggar ML12
Tel **(0899) 20618**
Mem 400
Sec WS Turnbull (0899) 20566
Holes 18 L 5416 yds SSS 66
Recs Am–61 B Kerr (1987)
Pro–65 W Murray (1981)
V'trs U
Fees £4 (£6)
Loc Biggar town centre ½ mile

Blairbeth (1910)

Private
Burnside, Rutherglen
Tel **(041) 634 3355**
Mem 400
Sec FT Henderson (041) 632 0604
Holes 18 L 5448 yds SSS 67
Recs Am–60 DB Howard
Pro–69 WG Cunningham
V'trs M
Loc 1 mile S of Rutherglen

Bothwell Castle (1922)

Private
Blantyre Road, Bothwell G71
Tel **(0698) 853177**
Mem 1137
Sec ADC Watson (0698) 852395
Pro WA Walker (0698) 852052
Holes 18 L 6240 yds SSS 70
Recs Am–64 F Jardine (1977)
Pro–65 L Johnson (1986)
V'trs WD–U 8.30am–3.30pm
Fees £8 D–£12
Loc 3 miles N of Hamilton

Calderbraes (1893)

Private
57 Roundknowe Road, Uddingston
Tel **(0698) 813425**
Mem 300
Sec S McGuigan (02364) 65286
Holes 9 L 5046 yds SSS 67
Recs Am–65 D Gilchrist
V'trs M
Loc Start of M74

Cambuslang (1891)

Private
Westburn Drive, Cambuslang G72 7AN
Tel **(041) 641 3130**
Mem 200 100(L) 75(J)
Sec W Lilly
Holes 9 L 6072 yds SSS 69
Recs Am–65 AM Grant
V'trs I
Loc Cambuslang Station ¾ mile

Carluke (1894)

Private
Hallcraig, Carluke
Tel **(0555) 71070**
Mem 460
Sec J Kyle (0555) 70366
Pro A Brooks (0555) 51053
Holes 18 L 5805 yds SSS 68
Recs Am–64 K Harrison
Pro–64 G Cunningham, R Davis, W Milne
V'trs WD–U before 4pm WE–NA
Fees £6 D–£9
Loc Glasgow 20 miles

Carnwath (1907)

Private
Main Street, Carnwath
Tel **(0555) 840251**
Mem 380
Sec GP Pollock (0555) 4359
Holes 18 L 5955 yds SSS 69
Recs Am–65 B Holbrook
V'trs U exc Sat–NA
Fees £6.50 (£8.50)
Loc Lanark 7 miles

Coatbridge (1970)

Public
Townhead Road, Coatbridge
Tel **(0236) 28975**
Mem 300
Sec O Dolan (0236) 26811
Pro G Weir (0236) 21492
Holes 18 L 5877 yds SSS 68
V'trs U
Fees £1.75
Loc Townhead

Colville Park (1922)

Private
Jerviston Estate, Motherwell ML1 4UG
Tel **(0698) 63017**
Mem 540 64(L) 140(J)
Sec E Wood (0698) 66045
Pro Golf Shop (0698) 65779
Holes 18 L 6265 yds SSS 70
Recs Am–66 J Johnston, WS Bryson, A Dunsmore
Pro–66 SD Brown
V'trs M SOC–WD only
Fees £10
Loc 1 mile NE of Motherwell on A723

Crow Wood (1925)

Private
Muirhead, Chryston, Glasgow
Tel **(041) 799 2011**
Mem 558
Sec RD Britton (041) 248 7495
Pro (041) 779 1943
Holes 18 L 6249 yds SSS 70
Recs Am–64 D Chalmers
Pro–66 J McTear
V'trs M
Loc 5 miles NE of Glasgow

Douglas Water (1922)

Private
Douglas Water, Lanark
Tel **(055 588) 460**
Mem 150
Sec R McMillan
Holes 9 L 2916 yds SSS 69
Recs Am–66 H Gold
V'trs U
Fees £1.50 (£3)
Loc 7 miles SW of Lanark

Drumpellier (1894)

Private
Langloan, Coatbridge
Tel **(0236) 24139/28723**
Mem 450
Sec W Brownlie (0236) 23065 /28538
Pro I Collins (0236) 32971
Holes 18 L 6227 yds SSS 70
Recs Am–65 AD Ferguson, G Shanks, ISS Russell
Pro–64 W Milne
V'trs I
Fees £10 D–£15
Loc 8 miles E of Glasgow

East Kilbride (1900)

Private
Chapelside Road, Nerston, East Kilbride G74 4PF
Tel **(035 52) 20913**
Mem 700
Sec T McCracken (035 52) 47728
Pro A Taylor (035 52) 22192
Holes 18 L 6419 yds SSS 71
Recs Am–65 WF Bryce
Pro–64 D Ingram
V'trs M SOC
Fees £7 D–£10
Loc 8 miles S of Glasgow

Easter Moffat (1922)

Private
Plains, by Airdrie
Tel **(0236) 842289/842878**
Mem 400
Sec J Reilly (0236) 21864 (office)
Pro J Forsythe (0236) 843015
Holes 18 L 6221 yds SSS 70
Recs Am–68
Pro–66 R Shade
V'trs WD
Fees £4 D–£6
Loc 3 miles E of Airdrie

Hamilton (1892)

Private
Riccarton, Ferniegair, by Hamilton
Tel **(0698) 282872**
Mem 480
Sec PE Soutter (0698) 286131
Pro MJ Moir (0698) 282324
Holes 18 L 6255 yds SSS 70
Recs Am–62 G Hogg
V'trs M or by arrangement
Fees £10 D–£15
Loc 1½ miles S of Hamilton

Hollandbush (1954)

Public
Acre Tophead, Lesmahagow, by Coalburn
Tel **(0555) 893484**
Mem 500
Sec J Hamilton
Pro I Rae (0555) 893646
Holes 18 L 6110 yds SSS 70
Recs Am–63 G Brown
V'trs U
Fees £4 (£6)
Loc Between Coalburn and Lesmahagow

Kirkhill (1910)

Private
Greenlees Road, Cambuslang
Tel **(041) 641 3083 (clubhouse)**
(041) 641 8499 (office)
Mem 570
Sec CC Stanfield (041) 634 4276
Holes 18 L 5889 yds SSS 69
Recs Am–63 D Martin
Pro–68 R Weir (Cowal)
V'trs WD–by prior arrangement WE/BH–NA SOC
Fees £7 D–£10
Loc Cambuslang

Lanark (1851)

Private
The Moor, Lanark
Tel **(0555) 3219**
Mem 500 130(L) 200(J)
Sec WW Law
Pro R Wallace (0555) 61456
Holes 18 L 6426 yds SSS 71
9 L 1562 yds SSS 28
Recs Am–64 CV McInally
Pro–64 AS Oldcorn
V'trs WD–U until 4pm WE–M
9 hole course–U
Fees £12 D–£18 9 hole course £2
Loc 30 miles S of Glasgow off A74

Larkhall

Public
Burnhead Road, Larkhall
Tel **(0698) 881113**
Mem 400
Sec C Bruce, 8 Caradale Gardens
Holes 9 L 6236 yds SSS 70
Recs Am–70 B Easton
V'trs U exc Tues 5–8pm & Sat 7am–1pm
Loc SW of town on B7109

Leadhills (1935)

Private
Leadhills, Biggar
Tel **(0659) 74222**
Mem 100
Sec H Shaw
Holes 9 L 2031 yds SSS 62
V'trs U

For map index see page 203.

Fees D–£2.50 (£3.50)
Loc 6 miles off A74 at Abington
Mis Highest golf course in Great Britain; 1500 ft above sea level

Mount Ellen (1905)

Private
Gartcosh, Glasgow
Tel **(0236) 872277**
Mem 590
Sec WL Harvey (041) 776 0747
Holes 18 L 5525 yds SSS 68
Recs Am–63 J Brown
Pro–68 J Chillas
V'trs M SOC
Loc 8 miles NE of Glasgow

Shotts (1895)

Private
Blairhead, Benhar Road, Shotts
Tel **(0501) 20431**
Mem 600
Sec JF Thomson
Pro J Forrester (0501) 22658
Holes 18 L 6290 yds SSS 70
Recs Am–65 AJ Ferguson
Pro–65 B Gunson
V'trs WD–U Sat–NA before 4.30pm
Fees D–£10 (D–£12)
Loc Midway between Glasgow & Edinburgh. M8, $1^1/_2$ miles

Strathaven (1908)

Private
Strathaven ML10 6NL
Tel **(0357) 20539**
Mem 650
Sec AW Wallace (0357) 20421
Pro M McCrorie (0357) 21812
Holes 18 L 6226 yds SSS 70
Recs Am–66 RJC Milton, S Kirkland, AW Wallace, IA Ferguson
Pro–63 D Huish
V'trs WD–I before 4.30pm
WE/WD after 4.30pm–NA
Fees On request
Loc Outskirts of town off Glasgow road

Strathclyde Park

Public
Mote Hill, Hamilton
Mem 110
Sec AJ Duncan (0698) 459201
Pro K Davidson
Holes 9 L 6294 yds SSS 70
Recs Am–67 A Brown
V'trs U exc medal days (phone to book (0698) 60155)
Fees £1.20
Loc Within Hamilton

Torrance House (1969)

Public
Strathaven Road, East Kilbride
Tel **(035 52) 48638**
Mem 650
Sec Mrs J O'Brien
(035 52) 49320
Pro J Dunlop (035 52) 33451
Holes 18 L 6403 yds SSS 71
Recs Am–67 A Pitt
Pro–66 I Collins
V'trs U
Fees £4.50
Loc E Kilbride, on Strathaven Road

Wishaw (1897)

Private
55 Cleland Road, Wishaw
Tel **(0698) 372869**
Mem 475 100(L) 50(J)
Sec JW Douglas
Pro JG Campbell (0698) 358247
Holes 18 L 6134 yds SSS 69
Recs Am–64 W Denholm, A Brown
Pro–65
V'trs Sat/WD after 4pm–NA
Fees £6.50 D–£8.50 Sun–£12
Loc Centre of town

The Lothians

East, Mid- and West Lothian

Aberlady

Private
Aberlady
Mem 32
Sec AR Wood
Holes Play over Kilspindie course

Baberton (1893)

Private
Juniper Green, Edinburgh EH14 5DU
Tel **(031) 453 3361**
Mem 800
Sec DM McBain (031) 453 4911
Pro K Kelly
Holes 18 L 6098 yds SSS 69
Recs Am–65 HM Gilmour, D Beveridge Jr
Pro–62 B Barnes
V'trs M SOC–WD
Loc 5 miles W of Edinburgh

Bass Rock (1873)

Private
29 Marmion Road, N Berwick, E Lothian EH39 4NZ
Mem 104
Sec SH Butterworth (0620) 2038
Holes Play over North Berwick

Bathgate (1892)

Private
Edinburgh Road, Bathgate EH48 1BA
Tel **(0506) 52232**
Mem 492
Sec R Smith (0506) 630505
Pro S Strachan (0506) 630553
Holes 18 L 6326 yds SSS 70
Recs Am–64 J McLean
V'trs U
Fees £8 (£11)
Loc 400 yds E of town centre

Braidhills No 1 (1893)

Public
Edinburgh
Tel **(031) 447 6666**
(031) 661 5351 Ext 209 (Bookings)
Pro J Boath (031) 447 8205
Holes 18 L 5239 yds SSS 68
Recs Am–65
V'trs U
Loc 3 miles S of Edinburgh

Braidhills No 2 (1894)

Public
Edinburgh
Tel **(031) 447 6666**
(031) 661 5351 Ext 209 (Bookings)
Pro J Boath (031) 447 8205
Holes 18 L 4832 yds SSS 63
Recs Am–65
V'trs U
Loc 3 miles S of Edinburgh

Braids United (1897)

Public
Braid Hills Approach, Edinburgh 10
Tel **(031) 447 3327**
Mem 100
Sec JS Forson
Holes Play over Braids 1 and 2

Broomieknowe (1906)

Private
36 Golf Course Road, Bonnyrigg EH19 2HZ
Tel **(031) 663 9317**
Mem 500
Sec Dr J Symonds
Pro M Patchett (031) 660 2035
Holes 18 L 6046 yds SSS 69
Recs Am–64 P Gallagher
Pro–64 J Hamilton, A Horne, J Hume, WB Murray
V'trs WD–U WE/BH–NA
Fees £8 (£10)
Loc 7 miles S of Edinburgh

Bruntsfield Links Golfing Society (1761)

Private
32 Barnton Avenue, Davidson's Mains, Edinburgh EH4 6JH
Tel **(031) 336 2006**
Mem 1000
Sec MW Walton (031) 336 1479
Pro B Mackenzie (031) 336 4050
Holes 18 L 6407 yds SSS 71
Recs Am–69 AGG Miller
V'trs I WD–M before 5pm
H after 5pm SOC
Fees On application
Loc 3 miles W of town centre

Burgh Links (1894)
Public
East Links, North Berwick
Tel (0620) 2726
Mem 400
Sec DR Montgomery (0620) 2340
Holes 18 L 6079 yds SSS 69
Recs Am–65 D Drummond
V'trs U
Fees On application
Loc Edinburgh 23 miles
Mis Glen Club plays here

Carrick Knowe (1930)
Public
Glendevon Park, Edinburgh 12
Tel (031) 337 1096
(031) 661 5351 Ext 209 (Bookings)
Holes 18 L 6299 yds SSS 70
Recs Am–64 R Bradley
V'trs U
Fees £3.30 (Sat–£3.30 Sun–£3.50)
Loc 5 miles W of Edinburgh
Mis Carrickvale Club plays here

Carrickvale
Private
Carrick Knowe Municipal, Glendevon Park, Edinburgh EH12 5VZ
Tel (031) 337 1932
Mem 450
Sec D Pagan (031) 443 3581
Holes Play over Carrick Knowe Municipal

Craigentinny (1891)
Public
Edinburgh
Tel (031) 554 7501
(031) 661 5351 Ext 209 (Bookings)
Holes 18 L 5418 yds SSS 66
Recs Am–64
V'trs U
Fees £3.30 (Sat–£3.30 Sun–£3.50)
Loc 2½ miles E of Edinburgh
Mis Lochend Club plays here

Craigmillar Park (1895)
Private
1 Observatory Road, Edinburgh EH9 3HG
Tel (031) 667 2837
Mem 460 100(L) 70(J) 38(5)
Sec Mrs JH Smith (031) 667 0047
Pro B McGhee (031) 667 0047
Holes 18 L 5846 yds SSS 68
Recs Am–65 J Thomson
Pro–66 T Stangoe
V'trs WD–I or H before 3.30pm
WE/BH–NA
Fees On application
Loc Blackford, Edinburgh

Dalmahoy
Private
Dalmahoy, Kirknewton, Midlothian EH27 8EB
Tel (031) 333 2055
Sec Mrs I Auld
Pro B Anderson (031) 333 1436
Holes East 18 L 6639 yds SSS 72
West 18 L 5212 yds SSS 66
Recs East Am–69 G Russo
Pro–62 B Barnes
Fees On application
Loc 7 miles W of Edinburgh on A71

Deer Park CC (1978)
Private
Carmondean, Livingston EH54 9PG
Tel (0506) 38843
(Steward) (0506) 37800
Mem 400
Sec W Yule
Pro W Yule
Holes 18 L 6636 yds SSS 72
Recs Am–72
V'trs U
Fees £5 (£8.50)
Loc Bordering M8, N of Livingston New Town (Knightsridge District)

Dirleton Castle (1854)
Private
Gullane
Tel (0620) 843496
Mem 100
Sec RH Atkinson
Holes Play over Gullane courses

Duddingston (1897)
Private
Duddingston, Edinburgh EH15 3QD
Tel (031) 661 1005
Mem 580
Sec JC Small (031) 661 7688
Pro A McLean (031) 661 4301
Holes 18 L 6647 yds SSS 72
Recs Am–64 G Macgregor
Pro–65 S Torrance
V'trs WD–IH SOC–Tues & Thurs
Fees £12 Soc–£9
Loc Duddingston Road West

Dunbar (1794)
Private
East Links, Dunbar EH42 1LP
Tel (0368) 62317
Mem 650
Sec AJR Poole
Pro D Small (0368) 62086
Holes 18 L 6426 yds SSS 71
Recs Am–66 S Easingwood
Pro–65 R Weir (1988)
V'trs U SOC
Fees D–£12 (D–£18) 1988 rates
Loc ½ mile E of Dunbar

Dundas Park (1957)
Private
4 Loch Place, South Queensferry EH30 9NG
Tel (031) 331 3090
Mem 450
Sec AD Lawson (031) 331 2754
Pro (031) 331 2754
Holes 9 L 5510 metres SSS 69
Recs Am–66 J McLaren
V'trs M I SOC
Loc Dundas Estate (Private), S of Queensferry on B800

Gifford (1904)
Private
Gifford
Mem 419
Sec AC Harrison (062 081) 267
Holes 9 L 6138 yds SSS 69
V'trs Sun am/Tues am–NA
Wed after 4pm–NA
Fees D–£4
Loc 4½ miles S of Haddington

Glen (1906)
Public
East Links, North Berwick EH39 4LE
Tel (0620) 2221
Mem 400
Sec DR Montgomery (0620) 2340
Holes Play over East Links

Glencorse (1890)
Private
Milton Bridge, Penicuik, Midlothian EH26 0RD
Tel (0968) 77177
Mem 400
Sec DA McNiven (0968) 77189
Pro C Jones (0968) 76481
Holes 18 L 5205 yds SSS 66
Recs Am–62 JH Moore (1985), S Middleton (1988)
V'trs WD before 4pm SOC–WD
Fees £8 (£12) 1988 prices
Loc 8 miles S of Edinburgh

Greenburn (1953)
Private
Fauldhouse
Tel (0501) 70292
Mem 450
Sec A Morrison (0501) 70865
Holes 18 L 6223 yds SSS 70
Recs Am–68
V'trs U
Fees £3.30 (£4.40)
Loc Fauldhouse

For map index see page 203.

Gullane (1882)

Private
Gullane
Tel **(0620) 843115**
Mem 711 300(L) 50(J) 125(5)
Sec JS Kinnear (0620) 842255
Pro J Hume (0620) 843111
Holes No 1 18 L 6491 yds SSS 71
No 2 18 L 6127 yds SSS 69
No 3 18 L 5035 yds SSS 64
9-hole course available for children
Recs No 1 Am-65 ME Lewis
Pro-64 RDBM Shade
No 2 Am-64
RCH Robertson
Pro-66 H Bannerman
V'trs U
Fees No 1 £13 D-£20 (£16 D-£24) W-£75
No 2 £6.50 D-£9.50 (£7.50 D-£11.50) W-£35
No 3 £4.50 D-£6.50 (£5.50 D-£7.50) W-£25
Children's course free
Loc 18 miles E of Edinburgh

Haddington (1865)

Public
Amisfield Park, Haddington, E Lothian
Tel **(062 082) 3627**
Mem 320
Sec T Shaw (062 082) 2584/3627
Pro J Muir (062 082) 2727
Holes L 6280 yds SSS 70
Recs Am-65 S Stephens
V'trs WD-U WE-U 10am-12pm after 2pm
Fees £5.30 D-£7.50 (£6.75 D-£10) 1988 prices
Loc 17 miles E of Edinburgh on A1.3/4 mile E of Haddington

Harburn (1921)

Private
West Calder, West Lothian EH55 8RS
Tel **(0506) 871256**
Mem 485 50(L) 89(J)
Sec GR Clark (0506) 871131
Pro R Redpath (0506) 871582
Holes 18 L 5843 yds SSS 68
Recs Am-62 M Kirk
V'trs U
Fees £6.50 (£8)
Loc 2 miles S of West Calder

The Honourable Company of Edinburgh Golfers (1744)

Private
Muirfield, Gullane EH31 2EG
Tel **(0620) 842123**
Mem 695
Sec Maj JG Vanreenen
Holes 18 L 6601 yds SSS 73 (Championship 6963 yds)
Recs Am-71 DED Neave
Pro-63 R Davis (1987)
V'trs WD-Tues/Thurs/Fri am only
WE/BH-NA I H SOC
Fees £30 D-£40
Loc NE outskirts of Gullane, opposite sign for Greywalls Hotel on A198 Edinburgh-N Berwick road

Kilspindie (1867)

Private
Aberlady, Longniddry, E Lothian EH32 0QD
Tel **(087 57) 216/358**
Mem 430 150(L) 50(J)
Sec HF Brown (087 57) 358
Holes 18 L 4957 metres SSS 66
Recs Am-61 G Weir
Pro-60 L Vannet (1988)
V'trs U Advisable to phone Sec. Play subject to members' demands SOC-WD
Fees On application
Loc Aberlady

Kingsknowe (1908)

Private
326 Lanark Road, Edinburgh EH14 2JD
Tel **(031) 441 1144**
Mem 728
Sec HH Hoddinott (031) 441 1145
Pro W Bauld (031) 441 4030
Holes 18 L 5966 yds SSS 69
Recs Am-63 JJ Little
Pro-64 WB Murray
V'trs WD-U before 4.30pm WE-M
Fees £5.50 D-£8 W-£22 M-£60
Loc SW Edinburgh

Liberton (1920)

Private
297 Gilmerton Road, Edinburgh EH16 5UJ
Tel **(031) 664 8580**
Mem 815
Sec JM Jackson (031) 664 3009
Pro WV Wightman, PJ Fielding (031) 664 1056
Holes 18 L 5299 yds SSS 66
Recs Am-61 RMF Jack
Pro-63 JL Brash
V'trs Mon/Wed/Fri-NA after 5pm
WE/BH-No visiting clubs
Fees £7.50 (£9.50)
Loc 3 miles S of Edinburgh

Linlithgow (1913)

Private
Braehead, Linlithgow
Tel **(0506) 842585**
Mem 400
Pro D Smith (0506) 844356
Holes 18 L 5858 yds SSS 68
Recs Am-64 J Cuddihy (1975)
Pro-65 J White (1988)
V'trs U
Fees £6 D-£7.50 (£8.50 D-£10)
Loc SW of Linlithgow

Lochend

Private
Craigentinny Course, Edinburgh EH7 6RG
Tel **(031) 554 7960**
Mem 320
Sec DM Drysdale (031) 669 3134
Holes Play over Craigentinny Municipal Course

Longniddry (1921)

Private
Links Road, Longniddry, East Lothian EH32 0NL
Tel **(0875) 52141**
Mem 980
Sec GC Dempster CA
Pro WJ Gray (0875) 52228
Holes 18 L 6210 yds SSS 70
Recs Am-63 C Hardin (1987)
Pro-63 P Harrison (1987)
V'trs U SOC-Tues-Thurs after 9.18am and 2pm-Mon after 2pm
Fees £12 D-£18 (£24 R/D)
Loc 13 miles E of Edinburgh off A1

Lothianburn (1893)

Private
Biggar Road, Edinburgh
Tel **(031) 445 2206**
Mem 430 75(L) 75(J) 50(5)
Sec AR Roxton (031) 441 6448
Pro B Mason (031) 445 2288
Holes 18 L 5750 yds SSS 69
Recs Am-63 PW Lamb
V'trs WD-U before 5pm-M after 5pm WE-NA SOC
Fees £6 D-£8 (£7.50 D -£11)
Loc S boundary Edinburgh

Luffness New (1894)

Private
Aberlady EH32 0QA
Tel **(0620) 843114**
Mem 650
Sec Lt Col JG Tedford (0620) 843336
Holes 18 L 6122 yds SSS 69
Recs Am-67 I M Paterson
Pro-62 C O'Connor
V'trs M or by arrangement
Fees On application
Loc Gullane 1 mile. Longniddry 4 miles

Merchants of Edinburgh (1907)

Private
Craighill Gardens, Morningside, Edinburgh EH10 5PY
Tel **(031) 447 1219**
Mem 400
Sec JB More (031) 443 1470
Pro RM Smith (031) 447 8709
Holes 18 L 4889 yds SSS 65
Recs Am-61 WJ Jeffrey Jr

V'trs M or I SOC
Fees £4.50 D–£6
Loc SW of city centre

Mortonhall (1892)

Private
231 Braid Road, Edinburgh EH10 6PB
Tel **(031) 447 2411**
Mem 500
Sec PT Ricketts (031) 447 6974
Pro DB Horn (031) 447 5185
Holes 18 L 6557 yds SSS 71
Recs Am–67 H Macgregor
Pro–68 G Cunningham
V'trs I
Fees £13 (£16)
Loc Within the city

Murrayfield (1896)

Private
43 Murrayfield Road, Edinburgh EH12 6EU
Tel **(031) 337 1009**
Mem 775
Sec JP Bullen (031) 337 3478
Pro J Fisher (031) 337 3479
Holes 18 L 5727 yds SSS 68
Recs Am–64 DED Neave
Pro–63 WB Murray
V'trs WD–I WE–M
Fees £10 D–£15
Loc 2 miles W of Edinburgh

Musselburgh (1938)

Private
Monktonhall, Musselburgh
Tel **(031) 665 2005**
Mem 500
Sec JR Brown
Pro T Stangoe (031) 665 7055
Holes 18 L 6623 yds SSS 72
Recs Am–65 RS Hall
Pro–67 EC Brown, G Cunningham, A Jacklin, B Devlin
V'trs U
Loc 1 mile S of Musselburgh

Musselburgh Old Course

Private
Silver Ring Clubhouse, Millhill, Musselburgh
Mem 70
Sec W Finnigan
Pro None
Holes 9 L 5380 yds SSS 67
Recs Am–67 P Hosie
V'trs WD/BH–U WE–U after 10am
Fees £2.40 18 holes
Loc 7 miles E of Edinburgh on A1

Newbattle (1934)

Private
Abbey Road, Eskbank, Dalkeith EH22 3AD
Tel **(031) 663 2123**
Mem 600
Pro J Henderson (031) 660 1631
Holes 18 L 6012 yds SSS 69
Recs Am–65 G Macgregor, P Hardwick, J McLean
V'trs WD–U before 4pm WE–M
Fees £7.50 D–£12
Loc 6 miles S of Edinburgh on A7 and A68

Niddry Castle (1983)

Private
Winchburgh, W Lothian
Sec AM Lamont (0506) 890185
Holes 9 L 5476 yds SSS 67
V'trs U
Fees £3 (£5) 1988 prices
Loc Winchburgh

North Berwick (1832)

Private
West Links, Beach Road, North Berwick
Tel **(0620) 2135**
Mem 300
Sec R Russell
Pro D Huish (0620) 3233
Holes 18 L 6298 yds SSS 70
Recs Am–65 E O'Connell
Pro–63 G Laing
V'trs U
Fees £9 D–£14 (£14 D £20)
Loc 24 miles E of Edinburgh

Polkemmet (1981)

Public
By Whitburn, West Lothian EH47 0AD
Tel **(0501) 43905**
Holes 9 L 2967 metres SSS 37
V'trs U
Fees £1.50 (£1.90)
Loc Between Whitburn and Harthill on B7066
Mis 15-bay driving range

Portobello (1853)

Public
Stanley Street, Portobello, Edinburgh
Tel **(031) 669 4361**
(031) 661 5351 Ext 209 (Bookings)
Mem 60
Sec BJ Attenburgh
Holes 9 L 2419 yds SSS 32
Recs Am–27
V'trs U
Loc $3^1/_2$ miles E of Edinburgh on A1

Prestonfield (1920)

Private
6 Priestfield Road North, Edinburgh EH16 5HS
Tel **(031) 667 1273**
Mem 700
Sec MDAG Dillon (031) 667 9665
Pro B Commins (031) 667 8597
Holes 18 L 6216 yds SSS 70
Recs Am–62 AM Dun
V'trs Sat–NA 8–10.30am and 12–1.30pm Sun–NA before 11.30am SOC
Fees £9 D–£11 (£11 D–£13)
Loc 2 miles SE of city centre

Pumpherston (1895)

Private
Drumshoreland Road, Pumpherston
Tel **(0506) 32869**
Mem 260 6(L) 74(J)
Sec JS Lamond (0506) 32122
Holes 9 L 5154 yds SSS 65
Recs Am–61 I Loch Jr (1987)
V'trs M
Loc 14 miles W of Edinburgh

Ratho Park (1928)

Private
Ratho, Newbridge, Midlothian EH28 8NX
Tel **(031) 333 1252/1752**
Mem 550 98(L) 65(J)
Sec JC McLafferty (031) 333 1752
Pro A Pate (031) 333 1406
Holes 18 L 6028 yds SSS 69
Recs Am–64 CB Binnie
Pro–64 WG Stowe
V'trs U SOC–Tues–Thurs
Fees £8 D–£12 WE–£15
Loc 8 miles W of Edinburgh A71

Ravelston (1912)

Private
24 Ravelston Dykes Road, Edinburgh EH4 5NZ
Tel **(031) 315 2486**
Mem 420 120 (5)
Sec F Philip (031) 312 6850
Holes 9 L 5332 yds SSS 66
Recs Am–67 DE Doig (1987)
Pro–66 W Murray (1987)
V'trs M
Loc Off Queensferry Road (A90), Forth Road Bridge Road

Rhodes

Private
29 Westgate, N Berwick EH39
Sec R Walker
Holes Play over North Berwick

Royal Burgess Golfing Society of Edinburgh (1735)

Private
181 Whitehouse Road, Barnton, Edinburgh EH4 6BY
Tel **(031) 339 2012**
Mem 620 50(J)
Sec JP Audis (031) 339 2075
Pro G Yuille (031) 339 6474
Holes 18 L 6604 yds SSS 72
Recs Am–64
Pro–63

For map index see page 203.

V'trs I
Fees On request
Loc Queensferry Road

Royal Musselburgh (1774)

Private
Prestongrange House, Prestonpans
Tel **(0875) 810276**
Mem 700
Sec TH Hardie (Sec/Mgr)
Pro A Minto (0875) 810139
Holes 18 L 6237 yds SSS 70
Recs Am–66 A Roy
V'trs WD–U WE–M
Fees £7 (£8) D–£12
Loc 8 miles SE of Edinburgh on A198 North Berwick road
Mis Electric buggies for hire

Silverknowes (1947)

Public
Silverknowes, Parkway, Edinburgh EH4 5ET
Tel **(031) 336 3843**
(031) 661 5351 Ext 209 (Bookings)
Mem 450
Sec J Munro (031) 336 5359
Holes 18 L 6210 yds SSS 70
Recs Am–66
V'trs U
Loc 4 miles W of Edinburgh

Swanston (1927)

Private
111 Swanston Road, Fairmilehead, Edinburgh 10
Tel **(031) 445 2239**
Mem 400
Sec J Allan
Pro H Ferguson (031) 445 4002
Holes 18 L 5024 yds SSS 65
Recs Am–63 G Millar
V'trs U exc comp days–NA WE–NA after 1pm
Fees £3.45 D–£5.75
Loc W from city centre, Biggar Road A702

Tantallon (1853)

Private
32 Westgate, North Berwick EH39 4AH
Tel **(0620) 2114**
Mem 300
Sec GA Milne
Holes Play over North Berwick West Links

Thorntree (1856)

Private
Prestongrange House, Prestonpans
Mem 100
Sec J Hanratty
Holes Play over Royal Musselburgh course

Torphin Hill (1895)

Private
Torphin Road, Edinburgh EH13 0PG
Tel **(031) 441 1100**
Mem 450
Sec DO Campbell
Holes 18 L 5025 yds SSS 66
Recs Am–62 G Wilkie, AL Turner
V'trs WD–U WE–U exc comp days SOC
Fees £4 (£7)
Loc SW boundary of Edinburgh

Turnhouse (1909)

Private
154 Turnhouse Road, Corstorphine, Edinburgh
Tel **(031) 339 1014**
Mem 500
Sec AB Hay (031) 655 6119
Pro K Whitson (031) 339 7701
Holes 18 L 6171 yds SSS 69
Recs Am–65 various
Pro–64 D Huish
V'trs M or by arrangement
Loc Turnhouse Road (A9080)

Uphall

Private
Uphall
Tel **(0506) 856404**
Mem 500
Sec A Dobie
Holes 18 L 5567 yds SSS 67
V'trs U
Fees £6 (£10)
Loc Livingston 2 miles

West Linton (1890)

Private
West Linton, Peeblesshire EH46 7HN
Tel **(0968) 60463**
Mem 615
Sec JM Brogan (0968) 73864
Pro D Stewart (0968) 60256
Holes 18 L 6024 yds SSS 69
Recs Am–64 S MacKenzie (1987)
Pro–71 B Gallacher
V'trs U Sun–NA
Fees £7 D–£9 (£8 D–£11)
Loc NW Peebles

West Lothian (1892)

Private
Airngath Hill, by Linlithgow, West Lothian EH49 7RH
Tel **(0506) 826030**
Mem 480
Sec TB Fraser (0506) 825476
Holes 18 L 6578 yds SSS 71
Recs Am–66 CK Cox (1987)
AG O'Neill (1988)
Pro–68 J Farmer (1980)
V'trs U
Fees £5 (£6)
Loc 1 mile S of town between Bo'ness and Linlithgow

Winterfield

Public
Back Road, Dunbar
Tel **(0368) 62280**
Mem 300
Sec M O'Donnell (0368) 62564
Pro J Sandilands (0638) 63562
Holes 18 L 5053 yds SSS 65
Recs Am–61 R Walkinshaw, J Huggan
Pro–65 SWT Murray
V'trs U
Fees On application–phone Pro
Loc W side of Dunbar

North

Highland, Orkney & Shetland and Western Isles Regions including Caithness, Inverness, Morayshire (Grampian Region), Nairn, Orkney & Shetland, Ross & Cromarty, Sutherland and Western Isles

Abernethy (1895)

Private
Nethy Bridge, Inverness-shire
Tel **(047 982) 305**
Mem 200
Sec Mrs B Douglas (047 982) 637
Holes 9 L 2484 yds SSS 66
Recs Am–61 I Murray
V'trs U SOC
Fees D–£4 W–£20
Loc Aviemore 10 miles. Grantown 5 miles

Alness (1904)

Private
Ardross Rd, Alness, Ross-shire
Tel **(0349) 883877**
Mem 300
Sec JG Miller
Holes 9 L 2436 yds SSS 63
Recs Am–62 C MacIver (1983)
V'trs Mon–NA 5–7pm SOC
Fees £2.50 (£3.50)
Loc 1/4 mile N of Alness

Askernish (1891)

Private
Lochboisdale, South Uist, Western Isles
Mem 30
Holes 9 (18 tees) L 5114 yds SSS 67
Recs Am–66 K Robertson
V'trs U
Fees £2 (£2) W–£10
Loc 5 miles NW of Lochboisdale

Boat-of-Garten (1898)

Private
Boat-of-Garten, Inverness-shire PH24 3BQ
Tel **(047 983) 282 (shop)**
(047 983) 351 (clubhouse)
Mem 396
Sec JR Ingram (047 983) 684
Holes 18 L 5720 yds SSS 68
Recs Am–65 AP Thomson
Pro–70 GW McIntosh
V'trs U
Fees £6 (£8)
Loc 27 miles S of Inverness
Mis Starting Sheet at WE

Bonar-Bridge & Ardgay (1904)

Private
Bonar-Bridge, Ardgay, Sutherland
Mem 80
Sec Mrs J Gordon (086 32) 577
A Turner (054 982) 248
Holes 9 L 4616 yds SSS 63
Recs Am–70
V'trs U
Fees D–£3
Loc 1/2 mile N of Bonar-Bridge

Brora (1889)

Private
Golf Road, Brora, Sutherland KW9 62S
Tel **(0408) 21417**
Mem 250
Sec RD Smith (0408) 21475
Holes 18 L 6110 yds SSS 69
Recs Am–61 J Miller
Pro–67 D Huish
V'trs U exc comp days–H for open comps SOC
Fees £7 W–£28 F–£40 M–£50
Loc 68 miles N of Inverness (A9)

Carrbridge (1980)

Private
Carrbridge, Inverness-shire
Tel **(047 984) 674**
Mem 330
Sec EG Drayson
Holes 9 L 2623 yds SSS 66
Recs Am–63
V'trs U
Fees D–£4 (D–£4.50) W–£20
Loc Carrbridge Village

Elgin (1906)

Private
Hardhillock, Birnie Road, Elgin, Morayshire IV30 3SX
Tel **(0343) 2338**
Mem 490 150(L) 150(J)
Sec W McKay
Pro I Rodger (0343) 2884
Holes 18 L 6401 yds SSS 71
Recs Am–64 NS Grant
Pro–66 H Bannerman, R Jamieson
V'trs WD–U after 9.30am WE–U after 10am SOC
Fees £7 D–£12 (£9 D–£14)
Loc 1 mile S of Elgin

Forres (1889)

Private
Muiryshade, Forres, Morayshire IV36 0RD
Tel **(0309) 72949**
Mem 716 130(J)
Sec GA Reaper (0309) 72013
Pro S Aird (0309) 72250
Holes 18 L 6141 yds SSS 69
Recs Am–64 A Moir
V'trs U SOC
Fees £4 (£4)
Loc 1 mile S of town centre

Fort Augustus (1930)

Private
Markethill, Fort Augustus, Inverness-shire
Mem 110
Sec ID Aitchison (0320) 6460
Holes 9 L 5454 yds SSS 68
Recs Am–69 F Boyd (1985)
V'trs U
Fees £4 (£6) Mon–Fri £15
Loc W end of village

Fort William (1974)

Private
North Road, Fort William, Inverness-shire
Tel **(0397) 4464**
Mem 300
Sec J Allan
Holes 18 L 5686 metres SSS 71
V'trs U
Fees £4
Loc 3 miles N of town on A82

Fortrose & Rosemarkie (1888)

Private
Ness Road East, Fortrose, Ross-shire
Tel **(0381) 20529**
Mem 620
Sec Mrs M Collier
Pro GA Hampton (0381) 20733
Holes 18 L 5973 yds SSS 69
Recs Am–64 G Paterson
V'trs U SOC
Fees D–£7 (£7) 6D–£25
Loc Black Isle. Inverness 12 miles

Gairloch (1898)

Private
Gairloch, Ross-shire IV21 2BQ
Tel **(0445) 2407**
Mem 250
Sec WJ Pinnell
Holes 9 L 1942 yds SSS 63
V'trs U Sun–NA
Fees £4 D–£6 W–£20
Loc 60 miles W of Dingwall

Garmouth & Kingston (1932)

Private
Garmouth, Fochabers, Morayshire
Tel **(034 387) 388**
Mem 300
Sec A Robertson
Holes 18 L 5637 yds SSS 67
Recs Am–66
Pro–70
V'trs U SOC
Fees £4 D–£6
Loc NE of Elgin

Golspie (1889)

Private
Ferry Road, Golspie, Sutherland
Tel **(04083) 3266**
Mem 420
Sec IG Smith
Holes 18 L 5900 yds SSS 68
Recs Am–65 J Miller
Pro–65 D Huish
V'trs U
Fees D–£6 W–£30 F–£45
Loc 11 miles N of Dornoch

Grantown (1890)

Private
Grantown-on-Spey, Morayshire
Tel **(0479) 2079**
Mem 200
Sec D Shepherd (0479) 2667
Holes 18 L 5672 yds SSS 67
Recs Am–60 G Bain
Pro–62 D Webster
V'trs U
Fees £6 (£7)
Loc East town boundary

Helmsdale

Private
Helmsdale, Sutherland
Tel **(043) 12 240**
Sec J Mackay, Ivybank, Dunrobin Street
Holes 9
V'trs U
Fees £3 (£3)

Hopeman (1923)

Private
Hopeman, Morayshire
Tel **(0343) 830 578**
Mem 300
Sec J Blyth (0343) 830336
Holes 18 L 5439 yds SSS 66
V'trs U SOC
Fees £4 (£7)
Loc 7 miles N of Elgin

Invergordon (1954)

Private
King George Street, Invergordon Ross & Cromarty
Tel **(0349) 852116**
Mem 140 50(L) 60(J)
Sec B Gibson

For map index see page 203.

Holes 9 L 6028 yds SSS 69
Recs Am–65 D Ross
V'trs U SOC
Fees £2.50 (£3)
Loc Invergordon

Inverness (1883)

Private
Inverness, Inverness-shire
Tel **(0463) 233422**
Mem 1100
Sec CD Thew (0463) 239882
Pro AP Thomson (0463) 231989
Holes 18 L 6226 yds SSS 70
Pro–63 J Farmer
V'trs WE/BH–restricted SOC
Fees £9 D–£12 (£10 D–£15)
Loc 1 mile S of town centre

Kingussie (1890)

Private
Gynace Road, Kingussie
Inverness-shire PH21 1LR
Tel **(05402) 374 (clubhouse)**
Mem 480
Sec ND MacWilliam (05402) 600
Holes 18 L 5408 yds SSS 67
Recs Am–64 J Gunn, ND MacWilliam
Pro–68 AG Havers
V'trs U
Fees £5 D–£6
Loc 1/2 mile from village off A9

Lochcarron (1911)

Private
Lochcarron, Strathcarron, Ross-shire
Mem 68
Sec GB Jones (05202) 259
Holes 9 L 3470 yds SSS 62
V'trs U
Fees £3
Loc 1/2 mile E of village

Lybster (1926)

Private
Main Street, Lybster, Caithness
Mem 86
Sec M Bowman
Holes 9 L 1896 yds SSS 62
Recs Am–59 C Steele
V'trs U
Fees D–£3 W–£10
Loc 13 miles S of Wick on A9

Moray (1889)

Private
Stotfield Road, Lossiemouth, Moray
IV31 6QS
Tel **(034 381) 2018**
Mem 1136
Sec J Hamilton
Pro A Thomson (034 381) 3330
Holes Old 18 L 6643 yds SSS 72
New 18 L 6005 yds SSS 69
Recs Old Am–68 NS Grant,
MM Macleman
Pro–66 T Minshall, D Huish
New Am–68 NS Grant
Pro–67 AT MacKenzie, DW
Armor
V'trs U SOC
Fees Old D–£7 (D–£10) W–£30
New D–£5 (D–£7) W–£20 1988
prices
Loc 6 miles N of Elgin

Muir of Ord (1875)

Private
Great North Road, Muir of Ord
Ross & Cromarty IV6 7SX
Tel **(0463) 870825**
Mem 604
Sec Mrs C Moir
Pro JT Hamilton (0463) 870601
Holes 18 L 5202 yds SSS 65
Recs Am–64 C Dalgarno (1988)
V'trs U SOC
Fees D–£6 (£7) W–£30
Loc 15 miles N of Inverness on
A862 or A9/A832

Nairn (1887)

Private
Seabank Road, Nairn
IV12 4HB
Tel **(0667) 52103**
Mem 830
Sec D Patrick (0667) 53208
Pro R Fyfe (0667) 52787
Holes 18 L 6555 yds SSS 71
9 L 1918 yds
Recs Champ Tees Am–66
IC Hutcheon
Pro–65 D Small
Medal Tees Am–65 R Watson
V'trs U SOC
Fees £13 (£15) W–£50
Loc Nairn West Shore

Nairn Dunbar (1899)

Private
Lochloy Road, Nairn, Nairnshire
Tel **(0667) 52741**
Mem 500
Sec Mrs SJ McLennan
Pro R Phimister (0667) 53964
Holes 18 L 6431 yds SSS 71
Recs Am–67 AP Thomson
V'trs U
Fees £8 (£10) W–£35

Newtonmore (1890)

Private
Newtonmore, Inverness-shire
PH20 1AT
Tel **(05403) 328**
Mem 380
Sec GJ Fraser (05403) 328
Holes 18 L 5880 yds SSS 68
Recs Am–64 I Barclay
V'trs U
Fees D–£6 W–£25
Loc 46 miles S of Inverness

Orkney (1889)

Private
Grainbank, Kirkwall, Orkney
Tel **(0856) 2457**
Mem 214
Sec JR Sim (0856) 2435
Holes 18 L 5406 yds SSS 68
Recs Am–65 KD Peace
Pro–71 I Smith
V'trs U
Fees £5 W–£20 F–£25 M–£35
Loc 1 mile W of town

Reay (1893)

Private
Reay, by Thurso
Tel **(084 781) 288**
Mem 364 42(L) 37(J)
Sec NH McDonald (084 787) 222
Holes 18 L 5865 yds SSS 68
Recs Am–65 RS Taylor
V'trs U exc comp days
Fees D–£5 W–£18 F–£25
Loc Thurso 11 miles
Mis Most northerly sea-side links
on British mainland

Royal Dornoch (1877)

Private
Golf Road, Dornoch, Sutherland
IV25 3LW
Tel **(0862) 810219**
Mem 621 180(L) 25(J)
Sec AS Kinnear (Mgr)
Pro WE Skinner (0862) 810902
Holes 18 L 6577 yds SSS 72
9 L 2485 yds SSS 32
Recs Am–65 J Miller
Pro–66 B Gallacher
V'trs U
Fees On application
Loc 51 miles N of Inverness
Mis Helipad by clubhouse.
Airstrip nearby

Sconser (1964)

Private
Between Broadford and Sligachan,
Skye
Mem 120
Sec MN Beaton (0478) 2277
Holes 9 L 4796 yds SSS 63
Recs Am–65 JM Rodger
V'trs U
Fees £4 D–£6 W–£12
Loc Midway Broadford–Portree

Shetland (1894)

Private
PO Box 18, Lerwick
Tel **(059 584) 369**
Mem 311
Sec LE Groat (Mgr)
(059) 3065
Holes 18 L 5776 yds SSS 70
V'trs U
Fees £4 (£5)
Loc 3 1/2 miles N of Lerwick

For explanation of abbreviations see page 202.

Skeabost (1982)

Public
Skeabost Bridge, Isle of Skye IV5 19NP
Mem 150
Sec S MacNab Stuart (047 032) 202 (Skeabost House Hotel)
Holes 9 L 3224 yds SSS 62
V'trs U
Fees £3
Loc 6 miles from Portree on Dunvegan road

Stornaway (1947)

Private
Lady Lever Park, Stornaway, Outer Hebrides
Tel **(0851) 2240**
Mem 250
Sec SM MacDonald (0851) 2788
Holes 18 L 5119 yds SSS 66
Recs Am–64 KW Galloway
Pro–65 JC Farmer
V'trs U Sun–NA
Fees £5 D–£8 W–£25 F–£35

Strathpeffer Spa (1888)

Private
Strathpeffer, Ross & Cromarty IV14 9AS
Tel **(0997) 21219**
Mem 200 60(L) 80(J)
Sec N Roxburgh (0997) 21396
Holes 18 L 4792 yds SSS 65
Recs Am–60 D Krzyzanowski
Pro–66 A Herd
V'trs U SOC
Fees D–£5 (£5) 5D–£20
Loc 1/4 mile N of village square

Stromness (1890)

Private
Ness, Orkney
Tel **(0856) 850772**
Mem 120
Sec FJ Groundwater (0856) 850622
Holes 18 L 4665 yds SSS 64
Recs Am–62 CH Poke
Pro–66 R Macaskill
V'trs U
Fees £4 (£4)
Loc Stromness, Orkney

Tain (1890)

Private
Tain, Ross & Cromarty
Tel **(0862) 2314**
Mem 400
Sec J Fraser
Holes 18 L 6207 yds SSS 70
Recs Am–66 J Miller, S Shaw, K Berry
V'trs U
Fees £6 D–£9 (£8 D–£11)

Tarbat (1908)

Private
Portmahomack, Ross-shire
Tel **(0862 87) 236**
Mem 160
Sec D Wilson
Holes 9 L 2328 yds SSS 63
Recs Am–63 D Mackay
V'trs UH Sun–NA SOC
Fees D–£3 W–£10
Loc 6 miles SE of Tain

Thurso (1964)

Public
Newlands of Geise, Thurso, Caithness
Tel **(0847) 63807**
Mem 264
Sec G Bailey (0847) 63425
Holes 18 L 5818 yds SSS 69
Recs Am–65 E Newman (1983)
V'trs U
Fees £4 (£5)
Loc Railway station 2 miles

Torvean (1962)

Public
Glenurquhart Road, Inverness
Tel **(0463) 237543/225651**
Mem 400
Sec AS Menzies
Holes 18 L 4308 yds SSS 62
Recs Am–59 AS Philip
V'trs U
Fees £3.50 (£4)
Loc W side of town on A82

Traigh

Private
5 Back of Keppoch, Arisaig, Inverness-shire
Tel **(06875) 262**
Mem 20
Sec T McEachen
Holes 9 L 2100 yds SSS 68
V'trs U
Fees £1 (£3)

Westray

Private
Westray, Orkney
Tel **(085 77) 28**
Mem 12
Sec L Berstan
Holes 9 hole course
Recs Am–36 Dr W Balfour
V'trs U Sun–NA

Wick (1870)

Private
Reiss, Wick, Caithness KW1 5LJ
Tel **(0955) 2726**
Mem 265
Sec Mrs MSW Abernethy (0955) 2702
Holes 18 L 5945 yds SSS 69
Recs Am–63 R Taylor (1988)
Pro–68 Dai Rees
V'trs U
Fees £5 (£6) W–£20
Loc 3 miles N of Wick

North-East

Grampian Region including Aberdeen Banff and Kincardineshire

Aboyne (1883)

Private
Formaston Park, Aboyne, Aberdeenshire
Tel **(0339) 2328**
Mem 725 180(J)
Sec RD Gregson (0339) 2931
Pro I Wright (0339) 2469
Holes 18 L 5304 yds SSS 66
Recs Am–62 G Forbes
Pro–63 S Walker
V'trs U
Fees £8 (£12) W–£35
Loc E end of village

Auchenblae (1984)

Public
Auchenblae, Kincardineshire
Mem 56
Sec AI Robertson (056 12) 407
Holes 9 L 2174 yds SSS 30
Recs Am–60 C Whyte, R Cattanach
V'trs U exc comp nights Wed & Fri
Fees D–£2.50 (D–£3)
Loc 11 miles S of Stonehaven. 5 miles N of Laurencekirk

Auchmill (1975)

Public
Provost Rust Drive, Aberdeen
Tel **(0224) 714577**
Holes 9 L 2538 metres
V'trs U
Fees Summer £2.30 Winter £1.55
Loc 3 miles NW of city centre

Ballater (1892)

Private
Victoria Road, Ballater AB3 5QX
Tel **(0338) 55567**
Mem 600
Sec B Ingram
Pro F Mann (0338) 55658
Holes 18 L 5704 yds SSS 67
Recs Am–66 GJ Mitchell
Pro–66 G Collison, F Coutts
V'trs U
Fees £6 (£10) W–£24 F–£40
Loc 42 miles W of Aberdeen on A93

Balnagask

Public
St Fitticks Road, Aberdeen
Tel **(0224) 876407**
Pro I Smith
Holes 18 L 5468 metres SSS 69

V'trs U
Fees Summer £4.60 Winter £3.10
Loc $1^1/_2$ miles SE of city centre
Mis Nigg Bay Club plays here

Banchory (1905)

Private
Kinneskie, Banchory, Kincardineshire
Tel (033 02) 2365
Mem 700
Sec SAJ Adamson
Pro DW Smart (033 02) 2447
Holes 18 L 5284 yds SSS 66
Recs Am–61 JA Christie
Pro–61 A Thomson, D Matthew
V'trs U
Fees £8 (£10) W–£30
Loc 18 miles W of Aberdeen

Bon Accord (1872)

Public
19 Golf Road, Aberdeen
Tel (0224) 633464
Mem 950
Sec JJ Burnett
Holes Play over King's Links

Braemar (1902)

Private
Cluniebank Road, Braemar, Grampian AB3 5XX
Tel (033 97) 41618
Mem 287
Sec GA McIntosh (0224) 733836
Holes 18 L 4916 yds SSS 64
Recs Am–64 RA Cheyne (1987), H Haas, G Livingstone, N Abreau (1988)
Pro–64 L Vannet (1988)
V'trs U SOC
Fees £4 D–£6 (£5 D–£7)
Loc Town centre $^1/_2$ mile

Buckpool (1933)

Private
Barhill Road, Buckie, Banffshire AB5 1DU
Tel (0542) 32236
Mem 500
Sec F Macleod (0542) 35368
Holes 18 L 6257 yds SSS 70
V'trs U
Fees D–£4 (£D–£6) W–£20
Loc W end of town $^1/_2$ mile off A98, signpost Buckpool

Caledonian (1899)

Private
20 Golf Road, Aberdeen AB2 1QB
Tel (0224) 632443
Mem 960
Sec JA Bridgeford
Holes Play over King's Links

Cruden Bay (1791)

Private
Cruden Bay, Aberdeenshire AB4 7NN
Tel (0779) 812285
Mem 588
Sec IAD McPherson
Pro D Symington (0779) 812414
Holes 18 L 6370 yds SSS 71
9 L 4710 yds SSS 62
(St Olaf Course)
Recs Am–66 PJ Macleod (1987)
V'trs WD–U WE–H exc comp days SOC–WD
Fees £10 (£13.50)
Loc $22^1/_2$ miles NE of Aberdeen

Cullen (1879)

Private
The Links, Cullen, Banffshire
Tel (0542) 40685
Mem 224
Sec J Douglas, 103 Seatown, Cullen AB5 2SN
Holes 18 L 4610 yds SSS 62
Recs Am–58 B Main
V'trs U
Fees £4 (£4.50) W–£24

Deeside (1903)

Private
Bieldside, Aberdeen
Tel (0224) 869457
Mem 500
Sec NM Scott (0224) 867697
Pro E Shiel (0224) 861041
Holes 18 L 5972 yds SSS 69
9 L 6632 yds SSS 72
Recs Am–64 AK Pirie, RH Wilcox
Pro–64 S Torrance
V'trs I
Fees £12 (£15)
Loc 4 miles W of Aberdeen

Duff House Royal (1909)

Private
The Barnyards, Banff AB4 3SX
Tel (026 12) 2062
Mem 487 131(L) 100(J)
Sec M Pierog (026 12) 2461
Pro RS Strachan (026 12) 2075
Holes 18 L 6161 yds SSS 69
Recs Am–64 G Webster
V'trs WD–U WE–NA 8.30–10am and 12–2pm July/Aug–NA 5–6.30pm
Fees £6 (£8)
Loc Moray Firth coast

Dufftown (1896)

Private
Dufftown, Banffshire
Tel (0340) 20325
Mem 120
Sec Mrs JL Gray (0340) 20523
Holes 9 L 2265 yds SSS 63
Recs Am–61 GV Brand
Pro–63 P Smith
V'trs U
Fees £3 (£3)
Loc Dufftown 1 mile on Tomintoul Road
Mis Extension to 18 holes late 1989

Dunecht House (1925)

Private
Dunecht, Skene, Aberdeenshire AB3 7AX
Mem 340
Sec AJ Angus (0224) 743443
Holes 9 L 3135 yds SSS 71
Recs Am–72 A Angus (1987)
V'trs M
Loc 12 miles W of Aberdeen on B944

Durness (1988)

Public
Balnakeil, Durness, Sutherland
Mem 80
Sec Mrs L Mackay (097 181) 364
Holes 9 L 5468 yds SSS 67
Recs Am–73 J Miller, J Pritchard (1988)
V'trs U
Fees £4 W–£20 F–£30
Loc 57 miles NW of Lairg on A838

Fraserburgh (1881)

Private
Philorth, Fraserburgh, Aberdeenshire AB4 5TL
Tel (0346) 28287
Mem 420 72(L) 130(J)
Sec JW Love (0346) 27464
Holes 18 L 6217 yds SSS 70
Recs Am–66 A Ritchie, C McDonald, A Ironside
Pro–67 I Smith
V'trs U SOC
Fees £7 (£9)
Loc 1 mile E of Fraserburgh

Hazlehead (1927)

Public
Hazlehead, Aberdeen
Tel (0224) 321830
Sec J Murchie (0224) 315747
Pro I Smith
Holes 18 L 5673 metres SSS 70
18 L 5303 metres SSS 68
9 hole course
Recs Am–65 D Jamieson
Pro–67 P Oosterhuis
V'trs U
Fees Summer £4.60 Winter £3.10
Loc 3 miles W of city centre
Mis Hazlehead GC play here

Huntly (1900)

Private
Huntly, Aberdeenshire
Tel (0466) 2643
Mem 500
Sec G Angus

Holes 18 L 5399 yds SSS 66
Recs Am–61 N Mason
V'trs U
Fees £6 (£7) W–£20
Loc 38 miles NE of Aberdeen

Insch

Private
Golf Terrace, Insch, Aberdeenshire
Tel **(0464) 20363**
Mem 200
Sec G Miller (0464) 20252/20243
Holes 9 L 5488 yds SSS 67
Recs Am–67 H McKenzie (1982)
G Bruce (1988)
V'trs U
Fees £3 (£4) W–£10
Loc 28 miles NW of Aberdeen off A96 Inverness road

Inverallochy

Public
Inverallochy, nr Fraserburgh, Aberdeenshire
Mem 200
Sec GM Young(034 65) 2324
Holes 18 L 5137 yds SSS 65
Recs Am–60
V'trs U
Fees D–£3
Loc $3^1/_2$ miles off A92 nr Fraserburgh

Inverurie (1923)

Private
Blackhall Road, Inverurie, Aberdeenshire
Tel **(0467) 24080**
Mem 460 108(L)
Sec J Skinner (0467) 24080
Holes 18 L 5703 yds SSS 68
Recs Am–66 K Hird
V'trs U SOC–WD
Fees D–£5 (£7)
Loc 16 miles N of Aberdeen. 1 mile W of town centre

Keith (1963)

Private
Fife Park, Keith, Banffshire
Tel **(054 22) 2649**
Mem 250
Sec A Stronach
Holes 18 L 5811 yds SSS 68
Recs Am–65
V'trs U
Fees £4 (£5)

Kemnay (1908)

Private
Kemnay, Aberdeenshire
Mem 300
Sec A Findlater (0224) 634684
Holes 9 L 1865 yds SSS 29
V'trs WD–U exc after 5.30 Mon and Thur Sun–M
Fees £1 (£1.50)
Loc Aberdeen 15 miles

King's Links

Public
Golf Road, Aberdeen
Tel **(0224) 632269**
Pro R McDonald (0224) 641577
Holes 18 L 5838 metres SSS 71
V'trs U
Fees Summer £4.60 Winter £3.10
Loc 1 mile E of city centre
Mis Bon-Accord, Caledonian and Northern Clubs play here

Kintore (1911)

Private
Kintore, Aberdeenshire
Tel **(0467) 32631**
Mem 350 38(L) 60(J)
Sec Mrs C Lee
Holes 9 L 2688 yds SSS 66
Recs Am–64
V'trs WD–U before 4.30pm Mon Wed–NA 5–8pm
Fees £4 (£6)

McDonald (1927)

Private
Ellon, Aberdeenshire
Tel **(0358) 20576**
Mem 650
Sec G Ironside
Pro R Urquhart (0358) 22891
Holes 18 L 5986 yds SSS 69
Recs Am–66
Pro–69
V'trs U
Fees On application
Loc 15 miles N of Aberdeen

Murcar (1909)

Private
Bridge of Don, Aberdeen AB2 8BD
Tel **(0224) 704345**
Mem 525
Sec R Matthews (0224) 704354
Pro F Coutts (0224) 704370
Holes 18 L 6226 yds SSS 70
Recs Am–65 R Grant, J Savege, E Morrison
Pro–65 PA Smith
V'trs U
Fees Before noon £9 D–£14 (D–£16)
Loc 5 miles NE of Aberdeen
Mis 9 hole course at Strabathie

Newburgh-on-Ythan (1888)

Private
Newburgh, Aberdeenshire
Mem 200 35(L) 30(J)
Sec TW Young (03586) 89456
Holes 9 L 3202 yds SSS 71
V'trs U exc Tues after 3pm
Fees £5 (£6)
Loc 12 miles N of Aberdeen

Nigg Bay (1955)

Public
St Fitticks Road, Balnagask
Tel **(0224) 871286**
Mem 850
Sec H Hendry
Holes Play over Balnagask

Northern (1895)

Private
King's Links, Aberdeen
Tel **(0224) 21440**
Mem 900
Sec F Sutherland
Holes Play over King's Links

Oldmeldrum (1885)

Private
Oldmeldrum, Aberdeenshire
Mem 220
Sec GR Milton (065 12) 2212
Holes 9 L 5252 yds
Recs Am–63 GJ Webster
V'trs U
Fees £3 (£4)
Loc 17 miles NW of Aberdeen

Peterhead (1841)

Private
Craigewan, Peterhead
Tel **(0779) 72149**
Mem 450
Sec A Brandie (0779) 73350
Holes 18 L 6070 yds SSS 69
9 L 2600 yds SSS 32
Recs Am–64 K Buchan (1988)
Pro–64 J Farmer (1980)
V'trs U
Fees £5 (£10)
Loc 34 miles N of Aberdeen on coast

Royal Aberdeen (1780)

Private
Balgownie, Bridge of Don
Tel **(0224) 702571**
Mem 350 117(J)
Sec AW Baird (0224) 648797
Pro R MacAskill (0224) 702221
Holes 18 L 6372 yds SSS 71
18 L 4033 yds SSS 60
Recs Am–64 J Fought
Pro–65 S McAllister
V'trs I
Fees £15 (£18)
Loc Aberdeen Station 2 miles

Royal Tarlair (1926)

Private
Buchan Street, Macduff, Banffshire AB4 1TA
Tel **(0261) 32548/32897**
Mem 556

Sec Mrs L Edwards
Holes 18 L 5866 yds SSS 68
Recs Am–66 W Sim
V'trs U
Fees £5 D–£6 (£6 D–£8)
Loc Macduff

Spey Bay (1907)

Private
c/o Spey Bay Hotel, Spey Bay, Fochabers IV32 7PJ
Tel **(0343) 820424**
Mem 150 50(L) 50(J)
Holes 18 L 6059 yds SSS 69
Recs Am–68 L Newlands
Pro–71 J Farmer
V'trs U
Fees £3 W–£14 (phone hotel)
Loc 5 miles off A96 at Fochabers
Mis Seaside Links

Stonehaven (1888)

Private
Cowie, Stonehaven, Kincardineshire
Tel **(0569) 62124**
Mem 430
Sec RM Murdoch
Holes 18 L 5128 yds SSS 65
Recs Am–61 RG Forbes (1987)
V'trs Sat– NA before 3.45pm
Sun–NA before 10.45am
Fees £6.50 (£8) W–£30 1988 prices
Loc 1 mile N of Stonehaven

Strathlene (1877)

Private
Buckie, Banffshire AB5 2DJ
Tel **(0542) 31798**
Mem 300
Sec JF Weir (0542) 31707 (office)
Holes 18 L 5957 yds SSS 69
Recs Am–65 AG Ross
V'trs U SOC
Fees £4 (£6) W–£20
Loc 1/2 mile E of town

Tarland (1908)

Private
Tarland, Aberdeenshire AB3 4YN
Tel **(033 981) 413**
Mem 240
Sec JH Honeyman
Holes 9 L 5812 yds SSS 68
Recs Am–67 A Cruickshank
V'trs WD–U WE–Enquiry advisable
SOC–WD only
Fees £5 (£7)
Loc Aberdeen 30 miles.
Aboyne 5 miles

Torphins (1894)

Private
Torphins, Aberdeenshire
Tel **(033 982) 493**
Mem 250
Sec H Shepherd
Holes 9 L 2330 yds SSS 63
Recs Am–67 S Forbes, K Leslie
V'trs U SOC
Fees £3 (£4)
Loc Banchory 6 miles. 1/2 mile W of Torphins via Wester Beltie

Turriff (1899)

Private
Rosehall, Turriff, Aberdeenshire
Tel **(0888) 62745**
Mem 600
Sec JD Stott (0888) 62807
Pro A Hemsley (0888) 63025
Holes 18 L 6105 yds SSS 69
Recs Am–65 J McManus, G Malcolm
Pro–66 C Elliot (1987),
A Hunter (1988)
V'trs U SOC
Fees £5.50 D–£7 (£7 D–£9)
Loc Turriff
Mis Buggies for hire

Westhill (1977)

Private
Westhill, Skene, Aberdeenshire
Tel **(0224) 740159 (bookings)**
(0224) 743361 (clubhouse)
Mem 500
Sec JL Webster
Pro S Smith
Holes 18 L 5866 yds SSS 69
Recs Am–66 LR Fowler
V'trs WD–U before 4.30pm and after 7pm.M–4.30–7pm Sat–after 3.30pm Sun–after 10am
Fees £5 D–£8 (£7 D–£10)
Loc Aberdeen 6 miles on A944

Perthshire & Kinross

Tayside & Central Regions

Aberfeldy (1895)

Private
Taybridge Road, Aberfeldy PH15 2BH
Tel **(0887) 20535**
Mem 260
Sec HE Alexander (0887) 20203
Holes 9 L 2733 yds SSS 67
Recs Am–66 A McNeill (1987)
JM Munro (1988)
V'trs U
Fees £5 D–£7 W–£25 F–£35
Loc Central Perthshire, 10 miles off A9

Alyth (1894)

Private
Pitcrocknie, Alyth
Tel **(082 83) 2268**
Mem 850
Sec W Sullivan
Pro T Melville (082 83) 2411
Holes 18 L 6226 yds SSS 70
Recs Am–67 E Lindsay, JL Adamson
Pro–64 I Young
V'trs U
Fees £6 D–£9 (£9 D–£13)
Loc Dundee 16 miles

Auchterarder (1892)

Private
Ochil Road, Auchterarder PH3 1LS
Tel **(0764) 62804**
Mem 600
Sec JI Stewart (0764) 63840
Pro K Salmoni (0764) 63711
Holes 18 L 5737 yds SSS 68
Recs Am–68 K Gillon (1988)
Pro–65 W Guy (1988)
V'trs U SOC
Fees £5 D–£8 (£7 D–£11) 1988 prices
Loc 1 mile SW of town centre

Bishopshire (1903)

Private
Kinnesswood
Mem 170
Sec AB Moffat (0592) 860379
Holes 9 L 2180 yds SSS 63
Recs Am–63 J Morris
V'trs U
Fees £1 (£1.50)
Loc 3 miles E of Kinross off M90

Blair Atholl (1892)

Private
Blair Atholl, Perthshire
Tel **(079 681) 407**
Mem 390
Sec JA McGregor (079 681) 274
Holes 9 L 2855 yds SSS 69
Recs Am–66
V'trs U
Fees D–£5 W–£22
Loc 35 miles N of Perth off A9
Mis Buggies for hire

Blairgowrie (1889)

Private
Rosemount, Blairgowrie PH10 6LG
Tel **(0250) 2594**
Mem 1200
Sec DW Kirkland (0250) 2622
Pro GW Kinnoch (0250) 3116
Holes Rosemount 18 L 6588 yds SSS 72; Lansdowne 18 L 6895 yds SSS 73; Wee 9 L 4614 yds SSS 63
Recs Rosemount Am–66 ER Lindsay
Pro–66 G Norman
Lansdowne Am–68 BRN Grieve
Pro–69 J McAlister
V'trs U H–8.30am–12 & 2–3.30pm Mon/Tues/Thurs. Restricted Wed/Fri/WE
Fees £15 (£20)
Loc 15 miles NE of Perth off A93. 16 miles NW of Dundee, off A923

Comrie (1891)

Private
Comrie
Mem 150
Sec DG McGlashan (0764) 70544
Pro H Donaldson
Holes 9 L 2983 yds SSS 69
Recs Am–69 D Donaldson
V'trs U
Fees £5 (£6)
Loc 7 miles W of Crieff

Craigie Hill (1911)

Private
Cherrybank, Perth
Tel **(0738) 24377**
Mem 700
Sec WA Miller (0738) 22644
Pro F Smith (0738) 22644
Holes 18 L 5379 yds SSS 66
Recs Am–60 G Still (1988)
Pro–63 W Murray (1986)
V'trs U
Fees £7 (£9)
Loc W boundary of Perth

Crieff (1891)

Private
Perth Road, Crieff
PH7 3LR
Tel **(0764) 2397/2909 (bookings)**
Mem 650
Sec LJ Rundle (0764) 2397
Pro JM Stark (0764) 2909
Holes Ferntower 18 L 6402 yds SSS 71; Dornock 9 L 4772 yds SSS 63
Recs Ferntower Am–67
Pro–66
V'trs UH NA–12–2pm or after 5pm SOC
Fees Ferntower £10 (£12)
Dornock £7 (£8) 18 holes
Loc 17 miles W of Perth–A85. Town centre 1 mile

Dalmunzie (1948)

Public
Glenshee, Blairgowrie
Tel **(025 085) 226**
Mem 48
Sec S Winton
Holes 9 L 2035 yds SSS 60
V'trs U
Fees 9 holes £2.50 D–£4
Loc 22 miles N of Blairgowrie on A93 (Dalmunzie Hotel sign)

Dun Ochil (Gleneagles)

Private
Gleneagles, Perthshire
Sec Dr C Gribble (0786) 822592
Holes Play over Gleneagles courses

Dun Whinny (Gleneagles) (1936)

Private
12 Anderson Court, Dunblane
FK15 9BE
Tel **(0786) 823174**
Mem 70
Sec RAFG Mackelvie
Holes Play over Gleneagles courses

Dunkeld & Birnam (1910)

Private
Fungarth, Dunkeld
Tel **(035 02) 524**
Mem 300
Sec Mrs W Sinclair (035 02) 564
Holes 9 L 4945 yds SSS 66
Recs Am–64 I Sinclair
V'trs U
Fees £5 (£7)
Loc Dunkeld 1 mile off A923

Dunning (1953)

Private
Rollo Park, Dunning
Sec J Lester
Holes 9 L 4836 yds SSS 64
V'trs WD–U WE–M (Sat after 4pm)
Fees £2.50 (£3)

Glenalmond

Private
Trinity College, Glenalmond
Sec J Stewart (073 888) 270
Holes 9 L 5812 yds SSS 68
Recs Am–70 CMW Robertson
Pro–72 M Dennis
V'trs M
Loc 10 miles NW of Perth

Gleneagles Hotel

Private
Gleneagles
Tel **(076 46) 3543**
Sec TAK Younger
Pro I Marchbank (076 46) 2231
Holes King's 18 L 6471 yds SSS 71
Queen's 18 L 5965 yds SSS 69
Prince's 18 L 4664 yds SSS 64
Glendevon 18 L 5719 yds SSS 68
Recs King's Am–65 GM Rutherford
Pro–62 JM Olazabal
Queen's Pro–63 C Stadler
V'trs WD–K/Q reserved until 10.30am and between 1.30–2.30pm for hotel guests and members. WE–K/Q reserved for hotel guests and members. Visitors must book in advance
Fees On application
Loc 16 miles SW of Perth on A9. Bus meets train at Gleneagles Station

Glenearn

Private
c/o Gleneagles Hotel, Auchterarder, Perthshire
Sec W McIntyre (0786) 71478
Holes Play over Glendevon course, Gleneagles

Green Hotel (1900)

Private
Beeches Park, Kinross
Tel **(0577) 63467**
Mem 400
Sec Mrs M Stewart
Holes 18 L 6111 yds SSS 70
V'trs U
Fees £8 (£12)
Loc 17 miles S of Perth
Mis Kinross GC plays here

Killin (1913)

Private
Killin, Perthshire
Tel **(056 72) 312**
Mem 298
Sec J Blyth (056 72) 234
Holes 9 L 2410 yds SSS 65
Recs Am–61 G Smith
V'trs U SOC–Apr/May/Sep
Fees £4.50 (£4.50)
Loc Killin Village

King James VI (1858)

Private
Moncrieffe Island, Perth
Tel **(0738) 25170**
(Starter) (0738) 32460)
Mem 600
Pro A Coles (0738) 32460
Holes 18 L 6026 yds SSS 69
Recs Am–63 G Clark
V'trs U exc Sat
Fees D–£9.50 (£12.50)
Loc City centre, island in River Tay

Kinross

Private
Kinross
Tel **(0577) 62237**
Mem 505
Sec AR Malcolm
Holes Play over Green Hotel course

Milnathort (1910)

Private
South Street, Milnathort
Tel **(0577) 64069**
Mem 400
Holes 9 L 2959 yds SSS 68
Recs Am–66 D Murphy
V'trs U SOC
Fees £5 (£6)
Loc Between Dunfermline and Perth

For map index see page 203.

Muckhart (1908)

Private
Muckhart, by Dollar, Clackmannanshire FK14 7JH
Tel **(025 981) 423**
Mem 450 100(L) 100(J)
Sec RT Glaister
Pro K Salmoni (025 981) 493
Holes 18 L 6112 yds SSS 70
Recs Am–66 E Carnegie
V'trs U
Fees £6 (£9)
Loc A91 3 miles E of Dollar, turn right for Rumbling Bridge

Murrayshall (1981)

Private
Murrayshall, New Scone, Perth PH2 7PH
Tel **(0738) 52784**
Mem 350
Pro NIM Mackintosh
Holes 18 L 6416 yds SSS 71
Recs Am–67 G Redford
Pro–67 J Farmer
V'trs U SOC–WD/WE
Fees £10 (£12)
Loc $2^1/_2$ miles E of Perth off A94

Muthill (1935)

Private
Peat Road, Muthill PH5 2AD
Mem 375
Sec J Kilmartin (076 481) 369
Holes 9 L 2371 yds SSS 63
Recs Am–65 E Campbell
Pro–68 RM Jamieson, W Milne
V'trs U
Fees £4 (£4.50)
Loc 3 miles S of Crieff on A822

North Inch

Public
c/o Perth & Kinross District Council 3 High Street, Perth PH1 5JU
Sec R Smith (Mgr) (0738) 39911
Holes 18 L 4736 metres SSS 65
V'trs U SOC
Fees £2.65 (£4.50)
Loc Nr city centre and A9. Follow signs to Bell's Sports Centre

Pitlochry (1909)

Private
Pitlochry
Tel **(0796) 2792**
Mem 350
Sec DCM McKenzie
Pro J Wilson
Holes 18 L 5811 yds SSS 68
Recs Am–63 CP Christy, MM Niven
Pro–64
V'trs U
Fees £9 (£12)
Loc $^1/_2$ mile from W end of Main St

Royal Perth Golfing Society

Public
$^1/_2$ Atholl Crescent, Perth
Tel **(0738) 22265**
Mem 250
Sec AG Dorward (0738) 37311
Holes 18 L 5141 yds SSS 64
V'trs U No Sunday play
Fees On application

St Fillans (1903)

Private
South Lochearn Rd, St Fillans, Tayside PH6 2NG
Tel **(076 485) 312**
Mem 350
Sec AJN Abercrombie (0764) 3643
Holes 9 L 5268 yds SSS 66
Recs Am–70 TE Crudace (1987)
W Gemmell (1988)
V'trs U SOC (max 16)
Fees D–£4 (D–£5) 5D–£15
Loc 12 miles W of Crieff on A85

Strathtay (1909)

Private
Tighanoisinn, Grandtully, Perthshire PH15 2QT
Mem 120
Sec J Armstrong-Payne (08874) 367
Holes 9 L 4082 yds SSS 63
Recs Am–61 AM Deboys
V'trs U SOC
Fees D–£4 (£5)
Loc 4 miles W of Ballinluig (A827)

Taymouth Castle (1923)

Private
Kenmore, Tayside PH15 2NT
Tel **(08873) 228**
Mem 200
Pro A Marshall
Holes 18 L 6066 yds SSS 69
Recs Am–63 MM Niven
V'trs U WE–booking essential SOC
Fees £10 D–£15 (£11 D–£16)
Mon–Fri £40
Loc 6 miles W of Aberfeldy
Mis Buggies available for hire

Renfrewshire
Strathclyde Region

Barshaw

Private
Barshaw Park, Paisley
Tel **(041) 889 2908**
Mem 68
Sec W Collins (041) 884 2533
Holes 18 L 5703 yds SSS 67
V'trs U
Fees £2.30
Loc 1 mile E of Paisley Cross off A737

Bonnyton (1957)

Private
Eaglesham, Glasgow G76 0QA
Tel **(035 53) 2781**
Mem 950
Sec H Beach
Pro J Pearston (035 53) 2256
Holes 18 L 6252 yds SSS 71
Recs Am–67 F Black
Pro–69 N Wood
V'trs I SOC–WD
Fees £12
Loc SW Eaglesham

Caldwell (1903)

Private
Caldwell, Uplawmoor
Tel **(050 585) 329**
Mem 450
Sec DP MacLean (041) 333 9770
Pro K Baxter (050 585) 616
Holes 18 L 6046 yds SSS 69
Recs Am–64 JM Sharp
Pro–63 C Innes
V'trs WD–Contact in advance before 4pm–M after 4pm WE–M SOC
Fees £8 D–£11.50
Loc 5 miles SW of Barrhead on A736 Glasgow–Irvine road

Cochrane Castle (1895)

Private
Craigston, Johnstone PA5 0HF
Tel **(0505) 20146**
Mem 40
Sec JC Cowan
Pro TC Steele (0505) 28465
Holes 18 L 6226 yds SSS 70
Recs Am–68 D Abercrombie
Pro–71 S Kelly
V'trs WD–U WE–M
Fees £7 D–£10
Loc $^1/_2$ mile S of A737

East Renfrewshire (1922)

Private
Pilmuir, Newton Mearns G77 6RT
Tel **(035 55) 256**
Mem 450
Sec AL Gillespie CA
(041) 226 4311
Pro GD Clarke
(035 55) 258
Holes 18 L 6097 yds SSS 70
Recs Am–64 A Dow
Pro–65 WR Lockie
V'trs By arrangement
Loc 2 miles SW of Newton Mearns

Eastwood (1893)

Private
Muirshield, Loganswell, Newton Mearns, Glasgow G77 6RX
Tel **(035 55) 261**
Mem 650
Sec C Scouler
(035 55) 280
Pro K McWade (035 55) 285

Holes 18 L 5886 yds SSS 68
Recs Am–62 IA Carslaw
Pro–67 P Mills
V'trs M SOC
Loc 9 miles SW of Glasgow

Elderslie (1908)

Private
Elderslie
Tel **(0505) 23956**
Mem 400
Sec W Muirhead
Holes 18 L 6031 yds SSS 69
Recs Am–69 J Kyle, B Clarkson
Pro–R Weir, R Craig
V'trs M
Loc Paisley 2 miles

Erskine (1904)

Private
Bishopton PA7 5PH
Tel **(0505) 862302**
Mem 400 200(L)
Sec TA McKillop
Pro P Thomson (0505) 862108
Holes 18 L 6287 yds SSS 70
Recs Am–66 IG Riddell
Pro–64 MC Douglas
V'trs WD–I WE–M
Fees £11
Loc 5 miles NW of Paisley

Fereneze (1904)

Private
Barrhead G78 1HJ
Tel **(041) 881 1519**
Mem 650
Sec AD Gourley (041) 221 6394
Holes 18 L 5821 yds SSS 68
Recs Am–64 EH McMillan
Pro–67 R Drummond, D Huish, J McTear, R Weir
V'trs M
Loc 9 miles SW of Glasgow

Gleddoch (1974)

Private
Langbank PA14 6YE
Tel **(047 554) 304**
Mem 400
Pro K Campbell (047 554) 704
Holes 18 L 6200 yds SSS 71
Recs Am–69 DJ McDougall
Pro–67 J Chillas
V'trs WD–U WE–M
Fees £9
Loc 16 miles W of Glasgow by M8/A8

Gourock (1896)

Private
Cowal View, Gourock PA19 6HD
Tel **(0475) 31001**
Mem 660 106(L) 112(J)
Sec CM Campbell (0475) 38242
Pro RM Collinson (0475) 36834
Holes 18 L 6492 yds SSS 71
Recs Am–64 N Skinner
Pro–69 D Graham
V'trs WD–I WE–M SOC
Fees On application
Loc 3 miles SW of Gourock Station

Greenock (1890)

Private
Forsyth Street, Greenock PA1 8RE
Tel **(0475) 20793**
Mem 478 149(L) 144(J)
Sec EJ Black (0475) 26819
Holes 18 L 5888 yds SSS 68
9 L 2149 yds SSS 32
Recs Am–64 MC Mazzoni
Pro–66 H Thomson, J Panton, H Boyle
V'trs WD–U WE/BH–M
Fees D–£10 (D–£14)
Loc Town centre 10 mins

Kilmacolm (1891)

Private
Kilmacolm
Tel **(050 587) 2139**
Mem 623
Sec RF McDonald
Pro D Stewart (050 587) 2695
Holes 18 L 5890 yds SSS 68
Recs Am–64 M Stevenson
Pro–66 EC Brown
V'trs WD–U WE–M
Loc 10 miles W of Paisley

Lochwinnoch (1897)

Private
Burnfoot Road, Lochwinnoch
Tel **(0505) 842153**
Mem 500
Sec Mrs E McBride
Pro G Reilly (0505) 843029
Holes 18 L 6223 yds SSS 70
Recs Am–67 IJ Gilmour, A Hutchieson
Pro–63 M Miller (1987)
V'trs WD–U before 4.30pm WE–M SOC
Fees £8 (£10)
Loc 9 miles S of Paisley

Old Ranfurly (1905)

Private
Bridge of Weir
Tel **(0505) 613612**
Mem 375
Sec R MacCallum
Holes 18 L 6283 yds SSS 70
Recs Am–65 DB Howard (1984)
D Shaw (1988)
Pro–66 C Elliott (1984)
V'trs WD–I WE–M SOC
Loc Bridge of Weir

Paisley (1895)

Private
Braehead, Paisley PA2 8TZ
Tel **(041) 884 2292**
Mem 750
Sec WJ Cunningham (041) 884 3903
Holes 18 L 6424 yds SSS 71
Recs Am–64 DW Perrie
V'trs WD–I SOC
Fees £8 D–£12
Loc Braehead, Paisley

Port Glasgow (1895)

Private
Port Glasgow PA14 5XE
Tel **(0475) 704181**
Mem 375
Sec NL Mitchell (0475) 706273
Holes 18 L 5712 yds SSS 68
Recs Am–63 JW McKechnie
V'trs WD–U before 5pm–M after 5pm WE–NA SOC
Fees £6 D–£10
Loc 1 mile S of town centre

Ranfurly Castle (1889)

Private
Golf Road, Bridge of Weir
Tel **(0505) 612609**
Mem 360 185(L) 100(J)
Sec Mrs TJ Gemmell
Pro K Stables (0505) 614795
Holes 18 L 6284 yds SSS 70
Recs Am–65 WMB Brown
Pro–66 B Watson
V'trs WD–I WE–M SOC–WD
Loc 7 miles W of Paisley

Renfrew (1894)

Private
Blythswood Estate, Inchinnan Road, Renfrew PA4 9EG
Tel **(041) 886 6692**
Mem 450 110(L) 80(J)
Sec A Kerr
Pro J Mulgrew (041) 886 7477
Holes 18 L 6818 yds SSS 73
Recs Am–69 LR Pirie (1981), A Hunter (1982)
Pro–70 J Chillas, WB Milne
V'trs M SOC
Fees On application
Loc Glasgow Airport 2 miles

Whinhill (1911)

Private
Beith Road, Greenock
Tel **(0475) 24694**
Mem 350
Sec A Polonis
Holes 18 L 5454 yds SSS 67
Recs Am–66 W Brewster
V'trs U
Loc 2 miles S of Greenock

Whitecraigs (1905)

Private
72 Ayr Road, Giffnock, Glasgow G46 6SW
Tel **(041) 639 1681**
Mem 500
Sec RW Miller (041) 639 4530
Pro W Watson (041) 639 2140

For map index see page 203.

Holes 18 L 6230 yds SSS 70
Recs Am–65 GB Murray
V'trs WD–I WE–M SOC–WD
Fees £15 D–£18
Loc Whitecraigs Station 5 mins

South

Dumfriesshire & Galloway Regions, including Dumfriesshire, Kirkcudbrightshire &Wigtownshire

Castle Douglas (1905)

Private
Abercromby Road, Castle Douglas, Kirkcudbrightshire
Tel (0556) 2801
Mem 450
Sec WG Coulthard
Holes 9 L 5400 yds SSS 66
Recs Am–62 W Blayney
V'trs U
Fees £4 W–£15
Loc Near town centre

Colvend (1908)

Private
Sandyhills, nr Dalbeattie, Kirkcudbrightshire DG5 4PY
Tel (055 663) 398
Mem 400
Sec D McNeil (055 662) 685
Holes 9 L 2322 yds SSS 63
V'trs U exc Tues after 4.30pm & Thurs after 5pm (Apr–Sept) SOC
Fees £5 (£5)
Loc 6 miles S of Dalbeattie on A710 Solway Coast Road

Crichton Royal (1884)

Private
Dumfries
Mem 400+
Sec JP Cairns
Holes 9 L 3084 yds SSS 69
Recs Am–67 RB Shearman
Pro–67 D Gemmell
V'trs M
Loc Dumfries 1 mile on Bankend Road

Dalbeattie (1897)

Private
Dalbeattie, Kirkcudbrightshire
Mem 220
Sec AK Scott
Holes 9 L 4200 yds SSS 61
V'trs U
Fees £2 (£3)

Dumfries & County (1912)

Private
Nunfield, Edinburgh Road, Dumfries DG1 1JX
Tel (0387) 53585
Mem 600 150(L) 100(J)
Sec JK Wells (0387) 62045
Pro GD Gray (0387) 68918
Holes 18 L 5928 yds SSS 68
Recs Am–64 D James
Pro–63 A Thomson, J McAlister, F Mann
V'trs WD–U exc 12.30–2pm–NA Sat–NA Sun–NA before 10am
Fees £8.50 (£10) W–£30
Loc 1 mile NE of town centre on A701

Dumfries & Galloway (1880)

Private
Laurieston Avenue, Maxwelltown, Dumfries
Tel (0387) 53582
Mem 450
Sec J Donnachie (0387) 63848
Pro J Fergusson (0387) 56902
Holes 18 L 5782 yds SSS 68
Recs Am–64 R Shearman
Pro–63 K Baxter
V'trs U
Fees £7.50 (£10)
Loc In Dumfries

Gatehouse (1922)

Private
Gatehouse of Fleet, Kirkcudbrightshire
Mem 200
Sec EJ Bryan (055 74) 654
Holes 9 L 2398 yds SSS 63
Recs Am–60 S Martin
V'trs U
Fees £3.25 (£4) W–£10 F–£20
Loc 3/4 mile N of town

Kirkcudbright (1895)

Private
Stirling Crescent, Kirkcudbright
Mem 300
Sec A Gordon (0557) 30542
Holes 18 L 5681 yds SSS 67
Recs Am–62 S Calladine
V'trs U
Fees £5 W–£15
Loc Near town centre

Lochmaben (1926)

Private
Castlehill Gate, Lochmaben DG11 1NT
Tel (03887) 810552
Mem 350
Sec JK Purves
Holes 9 L 5304 yds SSS 66
Recs Am–62 D Hutchison
Pro–64 G Gray
V'trs WD–U before 5pm WE–U exc comp days
Fees D–£5
Loc 4 miles W of Lockerbie on A709. Dumfries 8 miles

Lockerbie (1889)

Private
Corrie Road, Lockerbie
Tel (057 62) 3363
Mem 360
Sec JA Carruthers (0387) 810352
Holes 18 L 5418 yds SSS 66
Recs Am–65 R Nairn (1988)
V'trs U
Fees £6 W–£25
Loc Town centre 1/2 mile on Corrie Road

Moffat (1884)

Private
Coatshill, Moffat DG10 9SB
Tel (0683) 20020
Mem 400
Sec TA Rankin
Holes 18 L 5218 yds SSS 66
Recs Am–60 GJ Rodaks (1979)
V'trs WD–restricted Wed after 12 noon
Fees D–£8 (D–£11)
Loc 1 mile from Beattock on A701

New Galloway (1902)

Private
New Galloway, Kirkcudbrightshire
Mem 160
Sec IW Adam (064 42) 226
Holes 9 L 2509 yds SSS 65
V'trs U
Fees £5 (£5)
Loc In New Galloway

Newton Stewart

Private
Kirroughtree Avenue, Minnigaff, Newton Stewart, Wigtownshire
Tel (0671) 2172
Mem 200
Sec DF Buchanan
Holes 9 L 5512 yds SSS 67
V'trs U
Fees £3.50 (£4.50) W–£16
Loc Edge of town

Portpatrick Dunskey (1903)

Private
Golf Course Road, Portpatrick, Wigtownshire DG9 8TB
Tel (0776) 81273
Mem 350
Sec JA Horberry (0776) 81231
Holes 18 L 5644 yds and 9 L 1442 yds
Recs Am–65 A Cunningham (1986)
Pro–67 W Guy (1988)
V'trs U SOC
Fees £8 D–£10 (£10 D–£12) W–£35 F–£45 9 hole course D–£4
Loc 21 miles SW of Stranraer

Powfoot (1903)

Private
Cummertrees, Annan
Tel (046 17) 227
Mem 820
Sec RG Anderson (046 17) 2866
Pro G Dick (046 17) 327
Holes 18 L 6283 yds SSS 70
Recs Am–66 DJ Warwick
Pro–67 J Stevens
V'trs WD–U WE–Limited
Fees Winter £4 (£5) 5D–£14
Summer £8 (£10) 5D–£32
Loc 4 miles W of Annan

St Medan (1905)

Private
Port William, Wigtownshire DG8 8NJ
Tel (098 87) 358
Mem 200
Sec D O'Neill (098 85) 555
Holes 9 L 2277 yds SSS 62
V'trs U SOC
Fees £5 W–£25
Loc 3 miles S of Port William on A747

Sanquhar (1894)

Private
Blackaddie Road, Sanquhar
Tel (0659) 50577
Mem 170
Sec DA Hamilton
Holes 9 L 5630 yds SSS 68
Recs Am–66 I Brotherston (1982)
J Copeland
V'trs U SOC
Fees £5 (£8)
Loc 1/2 mile W of Sanquhar by A76. Dumfries 30 miles.Prestwick Airport 30 miles

Southerness (1947)

Private
Southerness, Dumfries DG2 8AZ
Tel (038 788) 677
Mem 610
Sec WT Train (0387) 53588
Holes 18 L 6554 yds SSS 72
Recs Am–68 RD Ireland, I Milne
V'trs U SOC
Fees On application
Loc 16 miles SW of Dumfries

Stranraer (1906)

Private
Creachmore, Leswalt, Stranraer, Wigtownshire
Tel (0776) 87245
Mem 450
Sec WI Wilson CA
(0776) 3539
Holes 18 L 6300 yds SSS 71
Recs Am–66 CG Findlay
Pro–72 J Panton
V'trs WE–NA before 9.30am and 12.30–1.30pm
Fees £7 (£8.50) W–£32
Loc Town 2 miles

Thornhill (1892)

Private
Black Nest, Thornhill
Dumfriesshire DG3
Tel (0848) 30546
Mem 420
Sec RL Kerr
Holes 18 L 6011 yds SSS 69
Recs Am–66 BR Kerr
Pro–67 JG Fergusson
V'trs U
Fees £7 (£9)
Loc 14 miles N of Dumfries

Wigtown & Bladnoch (1960)

Private
Wigtown
Tel (098 84) 3354
Mem 250
Sec D Heggie (0671) 2556
Holes 9 L 2712 yds SSS 67
Recs Am–64 R McGinn, DT McRae
V'trs U
Fees £4.50 (£6)
Loc 200 yds S of town square

Wigtownshire County (1894)

Private
Mains of Park, Glenluce, Newton Stewart DG8
Tel (058 13) 420
Mem 192
Sec R McCubbin (058 13) 277
Holes 18 L 5715 yds SSS 68
Recs Am–67 K Hardie
V'trs U exc Wed–NA after 6pm
Fees £6 (£7)
Loc 8 miles E of Stranraer on A75

Stirlingshire
Strathclyde & Central Regions

Aberfoyle (1893)

Private
Aberfoyle
Tel (087 72) 493
Mem 200
Sec A Macdonald (087 72) 441
Holes 18 L 5204 yds SSS 66
Recs Am–64 EJ Barnard
V'trs U
Fees D–£7.50
Loc Braeval, Aberfoyle

Bonnybridge (1924)

Private
Larbert Road, Bonnybridge
Tel (0324) 812822
Mem 425
Sec JJ Keilt
Holes 9 L 6058 yds SSS 69
Recs Am–66 D Riddell
Pro–66 J McTear
V'trs I
Fees By arrangement
Loc 3 miles W of Falkirk

Bridge of Allan (1895)

Private
Sunnylaw, Bridge of Allan
Tel (0786) 832332
Mem 290
Sec JC Whaley (0786) 833914
Holes 9 L 4932 yds SSS 65
Recs Am–62 ID McFarlane
V'trs U exc Sat
Fees £5 (£7)
Loc Bridge of Allan

Buchanan Castle (1936)

Private
nr Drymen
Tel (0360) 60369
Mem 830
Sec JI Hay (0360) 60307
Pro C Dernie (0360) 60330
Holes 18 L 6015 yds SSS 69
Recs Am–62 RGB McCallum
Pro–66 D Huish, W Milne
V'trs M or by arrangement with Sec
Loc 18 miles NW of Glasgow

Callander (1890)

Private
Aveland Road, Callander, Perthshire FK17 8EN
Tel (0877) 30090
Mem 520
Sec HG Slater (0877) 30931
Pro J McCallum (0877) 30975
Holes 18 L 5091 yds SSS 66
Recs Am–62 GK MacDonald
Pro–59 D Matthew
V'trs U SOC
Fees On application
Loc 1/2 mile off A84, E end of town

Campsie (1895)

Private
Crow Road, Lennoxtown
Tel (0360) 313099
Mem 380
Sec JM Dolandson (0360) 312249
Pro D Stevenson
Holes 18 L 5517 yds SSS 67
Recs Am–70 J Hope
Pro–73 K Stevely
V'trs WD–U before 4.30pm
Fees £3
Loc B822 Fintry road

Dunblane New (1923)

Private
Dunblane, Perthshire
Tel (0786) 823711
Mem 600
Sec AG Duncan (Match sec)
Pro RM Jamieson

For map index see page 203.

Holes 18 L 5878 yds SSS 68
Recs Am–64 GK McDonald
Pro–64 RM Jamieson
V'trs WD–Mon/Tues/Thurs/Fri am
WE–M SOC
Fees £9 (£13)
Loc 6 miles N Stirling

Falkirk (1922)

Private
Stirling Road, Camelon, Falkirk
Tel **(0324) 611061**
Mem 500
Sec A Bennie (0324) 21388 (home)
(031) 225 2092 (office)
Holes 18 L 6277 yds SSS 70
V'trs WD–U until 4pm WE–NA
SOC–WD exc Wed
Fees On application
Loc 1$^1/_2$ miles W of Falkirk
town centre on A9

Falkirk Tryst (1885)

Private
86 Burnhead Road, Larbert
Tel **(0324) 562415**
Mem 450
Sec JA Gow (0324) 554721
Pro D Slicer (0324) 562091
Holes 18 L 6053 yds SSS 69
Recs Am–64 J Rankin
Pro–65 J Chillas
V'trs WD–U exc Wed–NA WE–M
SOC
Fees £6 D–£8.50
Loc 3 miles N of Falkirk

Glenbervie

Private
Stirling Road, Larbert
FK5 4SJ
Tel **(0324) 562605**
Mem 600
Sec Mrs M Purves
Pro G McKay (0324) 562725
Holes 18 L 6469 yds SSS 71
Recs Am–65 M Godfrey
Pro–63 C Innes
V'trs WD–I WE–M SOC–Tues &
Thurs
Fees £15 D–£20
Loc 1 mile N of Larbert on Stirling
Road

Grangemouth (1973)

Public
Polmonthill, Grangemouth,
Stirlingshire FK3 8TF
Tel **(0324) 711500**
Mem 680
Sec J Balfour
Pro SJ Campbell (0324) 714355
Holes 18 L 6527 yds SSS 71
Recs Am–71
Pro–68 R Weir
V'trs U
Fees £4 (£5)
Loc 3 miles E of Falkirk

Kilsyth Lennox (1900)

Private
Tak-Ma-Doon Road, Kilsyth
Tel **(0236) 822190**
Mem 250
Sec AG Stevenson (0236) 823213
Holes 9 L 5930 yds SSS 69
Recs Am–66 R Irvine (1986), W
Erskine (1987)
V'trs WD–U until 5pm–M after 5pm
Sat–NA before 4pm Sun–NA
before 2pm SOC–WD
Fees £5
Loc Glasgow 12 miles

Polmont (1901)

Private
Manuelrigg, Maddiston, Falkirk
Tel **(0324) 711277**
Mem 200
Sec P Lees (0324) 713811
Holes 9 L 3044 yds SSS 69
Recs Am–71 W Shanks
V'trs U Sat NA–before 1pm
Fees £3 Sat–£4 Sun–£5
Loc 4 miles S of Falkirk

Stirling (1869)

Private
Queen's Road, Stirling
FK8 2QY
Tel **(0786) 73801**
Mem 1000
Sec WC McArthur (0786) 64098
Pro J Chillas (0786) 71490
Holes 18 L 6409 yds SSS 71
Recs Am–64 R Gregan (1983)
Pro–64 W Milne (1988)
V'trs WD–U WE–NA SOC
Fees £8 (£10)
Loc King's Park, Stirling

Strathendrick (1901)

Private
Drymen
Mem 330
Sec ES Smart (038) 983 446
Holes 9 L 4962 yds SSS 65
Recs Am–62 P Heggarty
Pro–64 C Dernie
V'trs M
Loc Drymen

Wales

Clwyd

Abergele & Pensarn (1910)

Private
Tan-y-Goppa Road, Abergele
LL22 8DS
Tel **(0745) 824034**
Mem 1150
Sec DR Rose
Pro I Runcie (0745) 823813
Holes 18 L 6086 yds SSS 69
Recs Am–J Buckley (1980)
Pro–65 D Vaughan (1987)
V'trs U SOC
Fees £10 (£12)
Loc Abergele

Bryn Morfydd (1982)

Private
The Princess Course, Llanrhaeadr, nr Denbigh
Tel **(074 578) 313**
Mem 20
Sec W Lester
Holes 9 L 1190 yds SSS 27
Fees £2.50 D–£5

Denbigh (1922)

Private
Henllan Road, Denbigh
LL16
Tel **(074 571) 4159**
Mem 450
Sec TH Aldrich
Pro M Jones
Holes 18 L 5582 yds SSS 67
Recs Am–68 A Jones (1986)
Pro–69 C Defoy (1986)
V'trs U SOC
Fees £7 (£9)
Loc B5382, 2 miles NW of Denbigh

Flint (1966)

Private
Cornist Park, Flint
CH6 5HJ
Tel **(035 26) 2327**
Mem 348
Sec H Griffith (035 26) 2186
Pro M Staton
Holes 9 L 5829 yds SSS 68
Recs Am–68 O O'Neil
V'trs WD–U before 5pm WE–M after noon SOC–WD/Sat
Fees D–£4
Loc Railway Station $1^1/_2$ miles. Town centre 1 mile. M56 8 miles

Hawarden (1911)

Private
Groomsdale Lane, Hawarden, Deeside
CH5 3EH
Tel **(0244) 531447**
Mem 320 40 (5D)
Sec T Hinks-Edwards
(0352) 57955
Pro M Carty
Holes 9 L 5620 yds SSS 67
Recs Am–65 DA Reidford
V'trs M SOC
Loc 6 miles W of Chester

Holywell (1906)

Private
Brynford, Holywell
Tel **(0352) 710040**
Mem 300
Sec EH Jackson (0352) 710693
Pro M Carty
Holes 9 L 3117 yds SSS 70
Recs Am–69 T Davies
Pro–N Jones
V'trs WD–U WE–M
Fees £4 (£5)
Loc 2 miles S of Holywell

Mold (1909)

Private
Pantmywyn, nr Mold
Tel **(0352) 740318**
Mem 350 55(L) 110(J)
Sec A Newall
Pro M Carty
Holes 18 L 5521 yds SSS 67
Recs Am–65
Pro–64
V'trs U SOC
Fees £7 (£9)
Loc Mold 4 miles

Old Colwyn (1907)

Private
The Clubhouse, Woodland Avenue
LL29 9NL
Tel **(0492) 515581**
Mem 350
Sec M Davies
Holes 9 L 5268 yds SSS 66
Recs Am–63 C Oldham, JD Jones Roberts
Pro–67 DJ Rees
V'trs U
Fees £5 (£6)
Loc Colwyn Bay

Old Padeswood (1978)

Private
Station Road, Padeswood nr Mold
Tel **(0244) 547401**
Mem 460
Sec BV Hellen (0352) 770506
Pro A Davies
Holes 18 L 6728 yds SSS 72
Recs Am–69 L Lockett (1987)
Pro–72 P Dunn
V'trs U exc comp days SOC
Fees £7 (£8)
Loc 2 miles from Mold on A5118

Padeswood & Buckley (1933)

Private
The Caia, Station Lane, Padeswood, nr Mold
CH7 4JD
Tel **(0244) 542537**
Mem 592
Sec R McLauchlan
Pro D Ashton (0244) 543636
Holes 18 L 5775 yds SSS 68
Recs Am–66 RMA Morris
V'trs WD–U 9am–4pm M after 4pm Sat–U Sun–NA unless by prior permission SOC–WD from 9.30am and 1.30–4pm Ladies Day–Wed
Fees £9 (£11)
Loc 8 miles W of Chester off A5118. 2nd golf club on right

Prestatyn (1905)

Private
Marine Road East, Prestatyn
LL19 7HS
Tel **(074 56) 4320 / 88353**
Mem 550
Sec R Woodruff (Mgr)
Pro G Hutchinson
Holes 18 L 6714 yds SSS 73
Recs Am–68 J Bamford
V'trs U
Fees £7 (£9)
Loc 1 mile E of Prestatyn

Rhuddlan (1930)

Private
Rhuddlan, Rhyl
LL18 6LB
Tel **(0745) 590217**
Mem 435 135(L) 100(J)
Sec D Morris (0745) 590675 (home)
Pro G Cox (0745) 590898
Holes 18 L 6038 yds SSS 69
Recs Am–63 P Jones
V'trs H or I SOC–WD
Fees £9 (£12)
Loc 3 miles S of Rhyl

Rhyl (1890)

Private
Coast Road, Rhyl
Tel **(0745) 53171**
Mem 240
Sec J Smith (0745) 89450
Holes 9 L 6153 yds SSS 70
Recs Am–67 CH Rees
Pro–67 H Cotton, N von Nida, C Ward
V'trs U SOC
Fees £5 (£6)
Loc Coast road between Rhyl and Prestatyn

For map index see page 203.

Ruthin–Pwllglas (1920)

Private
nr Ruthin
Tel **(082 42) 2296**
Mem 360
Sec RD Roberts (082 42) 4658
Holes 9 L 5418 yds SSS 66
Recs Am–64 MG Hughes
V'trs U SOC
Fees £5 (£7)
Loc Pwllglas, $2^1/_2$ miles S of Ruthin

St Melyd (1922)

Private
The Paddock, Meliden Road, Prestatyn LL19 9NB
Tel **(074 56) 4405**
Mem 530
Sec PA White (074 56) 3147
Pro NH Lloyd (074 56) 88858
Holes 9 L 5857 yds SSS 68
Recs Am–67 C Davies
Pro–68 N Hill
V'trs U SOC
Fees £6 (£8)
Loc On A547 between Prestatyn and Meliden

Vale of Llangollen (1908)

Private
Holyhead Road, Llangollen LL20 7PR
Tel **(0978) 860040**
Mem 600
Sec TF Ellis (0978) 860040
Pro DI Vaughan (0978) 860040
Holes 18 L 6661 yds SSS 72
Recs Am–69
Pro–68
V'trs U
Fees £9 (£12)
Loc $1^1/_2$ miles E of Llangollen on A5

Wrexham (1906)

Private
Holt Road, Wrexham
Tel **(0978) 261033**
Mem 650
Sec KB Fisher (0978) 364268
Pro DA Larvin (0978) 351476
Holes 18 L 6038 yds SSS 69
Recs Am–67 P Williams, MS Chidley
V'trs H SOC–WD
Fees On application
Loc 2 miles NE of Wrexham on A534

Dyfed

Aberystwyth (1911)

Private
Bryn-y-Mor, Aberystwyth
Tel **(0970) 615104**
Mem 390 approx
Sec W Hughes (0970) 3826
Pro B Thomas
Holes 18 L 5868 yds SSS 68
Recs Am–66 W Pugh
Pro–64 A Hodson
V'trs U SOC
Fees £5 (£6) W–£16
Loc Aberystwyth $^1/_2$ mile

Ashburnham (1894)

Private
Cliffe Terrace, Burry Port SA16 0HN
Tel **(055 46) 2466**
Mem 800
Sec D Emrys Gravelle (055 46) 2269
Pro RJ Playe (055 46) 2269
Holes 18 L 7016 yds SSS 74
Recs Am–70 CI Morgan
Pro–67 M Cahill, S Torrance, P Townsend
V'trs H
Fees £8 D–£12 (£14 D–£16)
Loc 5 miles W of Llanelli

Borth & Ynyslas (1885)

Private
Borth
Tel **(0970 81) 202**
Mem 403
Sec JM Lewis, RB Mair
Pro JG Lewis (0970 81) 557
Holes 18 L 6094 yds SSS 70
Recs Am–70 W Pugh
Pro–68 JG Lewis
V'trs U SOC
Fees £6
Loc Aberystwyth 7 miles

Cardigan (1928)

Private
Gwbert-on-Sea SA43 1PR
Tel **(0239) 612035**
Mem 300
Sec J Rhapps
Pro C Parsons
Holes 18 L 6207 yds SSS 70
Recs 9-hole Am–68 WEG James
Pro–69 L Mouland
18 hole Am–69 P Daniel
V'trs U
Fees D–£8 (£10) W–£28
Loc $2^1/_2$ miles NW of town centre

Carmarthen (1907)

Private
Blaenycoed Road, Carmarthen
Tel **(0267) 87214**
Mem 600
Sec JH Jones (0267) 87588
Pro P Gillis
Holes 18 L 6212 yds SSS 71
Recs Am–68 M Thomas (1987)
Pro–69 B Barnes
V'trs U SOC
Fees £6.50 (£7.50)
Loc 4 miles NW of Carmarthen

Cilgwyn (1977)

Private
Llangybi, Lampeter SA48 8NN
Tel **(0570 45) 286**
Mem 120
Sec JL Jones (0267) 234847 (office)
(0570) 422784 (home)
Holes 9 L 5318 yds SSS 67
Recs Am–66 DG Evans
Pro–69 D Creamer
V'trs U SOC
Fees £5 (£6.50) W–£20
Loc 4 miles NE of Lampeter, off A485 at Llangybi

Glynhir (1909)

Private
Glynhir Road, Llandybie, nr Ammanford SA18 2TF
Tel **(0269) 850472**
Mem 319
Sec JT Thomas (0269) 850571
EP Rees (0269) 2345
Pro R Playle
Holes 18 L 6090 yds SSS 70
Recs Am–67 P Child
V'trs U SOC–WD
Fees Winter £5 (£6) W–£30
Summer £7 (£9) W–£35
Loc $3^1/_2$ miles N of Ammanford

Haverfordwest (1904)

Private
Arnolds Down, Haverfordwest SA61 2XQ
Tel **(0437) 3565**
Mem 600
Sec MA Harding
Pro A Pile (0437) 68409
Holes 18 L 5945 yds SSS 70
V'trs U SOC
Fees £7 (£9) Mon–Fri £25
Loc 1 mile E of Haverfordwest on A40 Carmarthen Road

Milford Haven (1913)

Private
Hubbertson, Milford Haven
Tel **(064 62) 2368**
Mem 189 47(L) 34(J)
Sec TA Elder (064 62) 2521
or 3424 (home)
Pro A Pile
Holes 18 L 6071 yds SSS 71
Recs Am–76
Pro–71 B Hugget
V'trs U SOC
Fees £6
Loc W boundary of Milford Haven

Newport (Pembs) (1925)

Private
Newport
Tel **(0239) 820244**
Mem 350
Sec R Dietrich
Holes 9 L 3089 yds SSS 69

V'trs U SOC
Fees £5.50 (£6.50) W–£22
Loc Newport Sands

St Davids City (1902)

Private
Whitesands Bay, St Davids
Tel (Phone Sec)
Mem 140
Sec GB Lewis (034 83) 607
Holes 9 L 5695 yds SSS 70
V'trs U SOC–WD
Fees £6
Loc 2 miles W of St Davids near Whitesands Bay
Mis Clubs for hire from Whitesands Bay Hotel

South Pembrokeshire (1970)

Private
Defensible Barracks, Pembroke Dock
Tel (0646) 683817
Mem 250
Sec GW Thomas (0646) 682035
Holes 9 L 5804 yds SSS 69
Recs Am–66 S Toy
V'trs U before 4.30pm SOC–WD
Fees D–£5 Mon–Fri–£15
Loc Pembroke Dock

Tenby (1888)

Private
The Burrows, Tenby
Tel (0834) 2787
Mem 500
Sec TR Arnold (0834) 2978
Pro T Mountford (0834) 4447
Holes 18 L 6450 yds SSS 71
Recs Am–65 G Clement
V'trs U SOC
Fees £10 (£11) W–£45
Loc Tenby

Gwent

Blackwood (1914)

Private
Cwymgelli, Blackwood
Tel (0495) 223152
Mem 300
Sec AM Reed-Gibbs (0495) 223047 (home)
Holes 9 L 5304 yds SSS 66
Recs Am–65 DL Stevens, NR Phillips Pro–64 F Hill
V'trs I SOC U
Fees £5 (£6)
Loc 1/4 mile N of Blackwood

Caerleon (1974)

Public
Broadway, Caerleon
Tel (0633) 420342
Sec A Campbell
Pro A Campbell
Holes 9 L 3092 yds SSS
Recs Am–71 C French (1988)
V'trs U
Fees 18 holes £2.90 (£4.20) 9 holes £1.90 (£2.50)
Loc M4 Junction 25, 3 miles
Mis Driving range

Greenmeadow (1980)

Private
Treherbert Road, Croesyceiliog, Cwmbran NP44 2BZ
Tel (063 33) 69321
Mem 430
Sec PJ Richardson
Pro C Coombs (063 33) 62626
Holes 15 L 5593 yds SSS 68
Recs Am–70 M Skinner (1985) Pro–66 C Jenkins (1987)
V'trs U SOC
Fees £7 (£9)
Loc Newport 4 miles on B4042 from M4 Junction 26

Llanwern (1928)

Private
Golf House, Tennyson Ave, Llanwern NP6 2DY
Tel (0633) 412380
Mem 625
Sec HE Ibbetson (0633) 279173
Pro S Price (0633) 415233
Holes 18 L 6139 yds SSS 69 9 L 5686 yds SSS 70
Recs Am–65 K Fitzgerald Pro–67 G Davies, R Richards (1987)
V'trs WD–U WE–restricted I H SOC
Fees WD–£10
Loc 2 miles W town

Monmouth (1921)

Private
Leasebrook Lane, Monmouth
Tel (0600) 2212
Mem 350
Sec KA Prichard (0594) 33394
Holes 9 L 5454 yds SSS 66
Recs Am–65 DJ Wills Pro–68 DR Hemming
V'trs U SOC
Fees £7 (£10) Mon–Fri £20
Loc Signposted 1 mile along A40 Monmouth–Ross Road

Monmouthshire (1892)

Private
Llanfoist, Abergavenny
Tel (0873) 3171
Mem 480 106(L) 90(J)
Sec GJ Swayne (0873) 2606
Pro P Worthing (0873) 2532
Holes 18 L 6045 yds SSS 69
Recs Am–66 PS Lewis Pro–62 D Thomas
V'trs U H SOC
Fees £12 (£16)
Loc Abergavenny Station 2 miles

Newport (1903)

Private
Great Oak, Rogerstone, Newport NP1 9FX
Tel (0633) 892683/894496
Mem 700
Sec RC Bentham
Pro R Skuse (0633) 893271
Holes 18 L 6370 yds SSS 71
Recs Am–67 G Davies Pro–67 M Hughes
V'trs U SOC–WD exc Tues Sat–M 1–4pm
Fees £12 (£15)
Loc Newport 3 miles on B4591. M4 Junction 27, 1 mile on B4591

Pontnewydd (1875)

Private
Maesgwyn Farm, West Pontnewydd, Cwmbran NP44 1AB
Tel (063 33) 2170
Mem 250
Sec HR Gabe (063 33) 67185
Holes 10 L 5340 yds SSS 67
Recs Am–63 M Hayward
V'trs WD–U WE–M SOC
Fees £8
Loc W outskirts of Cwmbran

Pontypool (1903)

Private
Trevethin, Pontypool
Tel (049 55) 3655
Mem 551 67(L) 73(J)
Sec WF Rostron (049 55) 56849
Pro J Howard (049 55) 55544
Holes 18 L 6070 yds SSS 69
Recs Am–64 M Hayward (1982) NR Davies (1985) Pro–A Sherborne
V'trs U
Fees £8 (£10)
Loc 1 mile N of Pontypool

Rolls of Monmouth (1982)

Private
The Hendre, Monmouth NP5 4HG
Tel (0600) 5353
Mem 300
Sec JD Ross
Holes 18 L 6723 yds SSS 72
Recs Am–71 D Wills Pro–68 M Thomas
V'trs U SOC
Fees £13.50 (£15)
Loc 3 1/2 miles W of Monmouth on B4233

St Mellons (1937)

Private
St Mellons, Cardiff CF3 8XS
Tel (0633) 680401
Mem 544 93(L) 68(J) 27(5)
Sec Mrs K Newling (0633) 680408

For map index see page 203.

Pro B Thomas (0633) 680101
Holes 18 L 6225 yds SSS 70
Recs Am–68 N Hayward
Pro–66 E Foster
V'trs WD–U WE–M
Fees WD–£12
Loc 4 miles E of Cardiff on A48

St Pierre (1962)

Private
Chepstow NP6 6YA
Tel (02912) 5261
Sec T Latty, TJ Cleary
Pro R Doig
Holes 18 L 6700 yds SSS 73
18 L 5762 yds SSS 68
Recs Old: Am–69 AM Williams
Pro–63 H Henning
New: Am–63 M Bearcroft
V'trs H SOC–WD
Fees On application
Loc 2 miles W of Chepstow (A48)

Tredegar & Rhymney (1921)

Private
Tredegar, Rhymney
Tel (0685) 840743
Mem 182
Sec V Davies
Holes 9 L 5564 yds SSS 67
Recs Am–64 CL Jones
Pro–33 WS Phillips
V'trs U
Fees £5
Loc 1½ miles W of Tredegar

Tredegar Park (1923)

Private
Bassaleg Road, Newport NP9 3PX
Tel (0633) 895219
Mem 800
Sec AA Skinner DFM
(0633) 894433
Pro ML Morgan (0633) 894517
Holes 18 L 6097 yds SSS 70
Recs Am–69 A Harrhy
Pro–69 J Lee
V'trs I
Fees £10 (£14)
Loc Off M4 Junction 27

West Monmouthshire (1906)

Private
Pond Road, Nantyglo NP3 4JX
Tel (0495) 310233
Mem 200
Sec CJ Lewis (0495) 312746
Holes 18 L 6118 yds SSS 69
V'trs U
Fees £5 (£6)
Loc Nr Dunlop Semtex, off
Brynmawr Bypass
Mis Highest tee in Wales, 14th,
1450 ft above sea level

Gwynedd

Aberdovey (1892)

Private
Aberdovey LL35 0RT
Tel (065 472) 210
Mem 800
Sec JM Griffiths
(065 472) 493
Pro J Davies (065 472) 602
Holes 18 L 6445 yds SSS 71
Recs Am–67 B Macfarlane
Pro–67 J Smith
V'trs NA–8.30–9.30am & 1–2pm
Fees £12 D–£16 (£14 D–£20)
Loc W end of Aberdovey

Abersoch (1907)

Private
Abersoch
Tel (075 881) 2622
Mem 600
Sec P Jones
Holes 9 L 5800 yds SSS 68
V'trs U SOC
Fees On application
Loc Abersoch, ½ mile S of
village centre

Bala (1973)

Private
Penlan, Bala LL23 7SW
Tel (0678) 520 359
Mem 250
Sec MJ Wright (0678) 520057
(evenings)
Holes 10 L 4934 yds SSS 64
Recs Am–64 DB Aykroyd
V'trs WD–U WE–NA pm SOC
Fees £5 (£7) W–£15
Loc ½ mile NW of Bala

Betws-y-Coed

Private
Clubhouse, Betws-y-Coed LL24
Tel (069 02) 556
Mem 250
Sec GB Archer
Holes 9 L 2515 yds SSS 32
Recs Am–64 H Greenslade
V'trs U SOC
Fees £6 (£7.50)
Loc ½ mile off A5 in village centre

Caernarfon (1907)

Private
Llanfaglan, Caernarfon LL54 5RP
Tel (0286) 3783
Mem 419
Sec JI Jones (0286) 2643
Holes 18 L 5870 yds SSS 69
Pro–66
V'trs U SOC
Fees £7
Loc 2½ miles W of Caernarfon

Conwy (Caernarvonshire) (1890)

Private
Conway
Tel (0492) 593400
Mem 700
Sec EC Roberts (0492) 592423
Pro JP Lees (0492) 593225
Holes 18 L 6901 yds SSS 73
V'trs WE–restricted SOC
Fees £10 (£12)
Loc ½ mile W of Conwy off A55

Criccieth (1905)

Private
Ednyfed Hill, Criccieth
Tel (0766) 522154
Mem 200
Sec MG Hamilton (0766) 522697
Holes 18 L 5755 yds SSS 68
V'trs U
Fees £5 W–£15
Loc 18 miles S of Caernarfon.
4 miles W of Portmadoc

Dolgellau (1911)

Private
Pencefn Road, Dolgellau
Tel (0341) 422603
Mem 300
Sec PM Jones (0341) 423116
Holes 9 L 4671 yds SSS 63
Recs Am–65 E Owen (1987)
Pro–61 L James (1937)
V'trs U SOC
Fees £5 (£6) W–£25
Loc Town ½ mile

Ffestiniog (1890)

Private
Ffestiniog
Tel (076 676) 2612
Mem 109
Sec A Pritchard
Holes 9 L 5032 metres SSS 66
V'trs U
Fees £3 W–£10
Loc Village 1 mile on Bala Road

Llandudno (Maesdu) (1915)

Private
Hospital Road, Llandudno LL30 1HU
Tel (0492) 76450
Mem 950
Sec J Hallam
Pro S Boulden (0492) 75195
Holes 18 L 6513 yds Par 73
Recs Am–67 G Jones, CT Brown
Pro–66 PJ Butler
V'trs U–recognised GC members
SOC
Fees £10 (£12)
Loc 1 mile S of Llandudno Station

Llandudno (North Wales) (1894)

Private
72 Bryniau Road, West Shore, Llandudno LL30 2DZ
Tel **(0492) 75325**
Mem 550
Sec GD Harwood
Pro JF Waugh (0492) 76878
Holes 18 L 6132 yds SSS 69
Recs Am–66 JHM Williams, S Goldspink
Pro–63 WS Collins
V'trs U SOC–phone Sec
Fees £10 (£12.50) Mon–Fri £40
Loc Llandudno town centre $^{3}/_{4}$ mile on West Shore

Llanfairfechan (1971)

Private
Llannerch Road, Llanfairfechan LL33 0EB
Tel **(0248) 680144**
Mem 320
Sec MJ Charlesworth (0248) 680524
Holes 9 L 3119 yds SSS 57
Recs Am–53 MJ Charlesworth (1983)
V'trs U
Fees £3 (£4)
Loc Bangor 7 miles off A55

Nefyn & District (1907)

Private
Nefyn
Tel **(0758) 720218**
Mem 700
Sec Lt Col RW Parry (0758) 720966
Pro JR Pilkington
Holes 18 L 6346 yds SSS 71
Recs Am–68 TG Gruffydd
Pro–67 I Woosnam
V'trs U SOC
Fees £10 (£12)
Loc 1$^{1}/_{2}$ miles W of Nefyn

Penmaenmawr (1910)

Private
Conway Old Road, Penmaenmawr LL34 6RD
Tel **(0492) 623330**
Mem 500
Sec Mrs JE Jones (0492) 622085
Holes 9 L 5143 yds SSS 66
Recs Am–65 M Bellis
V'trs U
Fees £5 (£7)
Loc 4 miles W of Conway

Portmadoc (1900)

Private
Morfa Bychan, Porthmadog LL49 9UC
Tel **(0766) 512037**
Mem 500
Sec Capt DG Thomas
Pro P Bright (0766) 513828
Holes 18 L 6309 yds SSS 71
Recs Am–63 J Morrow
V'trs U SOC
Fees D–£8 (D–£10)
Loc 2 miles W town on road to Black Rock Sands

Pwllheli (1900)

Private
Pwllheli
Tel **(0758) 612520**
Mem 550
Sec RE Williams
Pro GD Verity
Holes 18 L 6110 yds SSS 69
Recs Am–68 G Jones, P Morgan, RT Jones
Pro–67 D Screeton
V'trs U
Fees On application
Loc $^{1}/_{2}$ mile SW of town centre

Rhos-on-Sea Residential (1899)

Private
Pernrhyn Bay, Llandudno
Tel **(0492) 49641**
Mem 500
Sec T Frame
Pro M Greenough
Holes 18 L 6064 yds SSS 69
Recs Am–64 JR Jones
V'trs U
Fees On application
Loc On coast at Rhos-on-Sea

Royal St David's (1894)

Private
Harlech LL46 2UB
Tel **(0766) 780203**
(0766) 780857 (Tee bookings)
Mem 600
Sec RI Jones (0776) 780 361
Pro J Barnett
Holes 18 L 6427 yds SSS 71
Recs Am–66 JL Morgan (1951), TJ Melia (1976)
Pro–64 K Stables (1988)
V'trs U SOC
Fees £12 (£14)
Loc W of Harlech
Mis Buggies £10 per round

St Deiniol (1905)

Private
Penbryn, Bangor LL57 1PX
Tel **(0248) 353098**
Mem 400
Sec DL Davies
Pro P Lees
Holes 18 L 5048 metres SSS 67
Recs Am–63 GA Roberts (1979)
V'trs U
Fees £5 (£5)
Loc Off A5/A55 Junction, 1 mile E of Bangor

Isle of Anglesey

Anglesey (1914)

Private
Rhosneigr
Tel **(0407) 810219**
Mem 500
Sec RD Jones ((0407) 720533
Pro P Roberts (0407) 810703
Holes 18 L 6204 yds SSS 70
Recs Am–68 GW Jones, D McLean
Pro–68 D Parsonage
V'trs U
Fees £5 (£6.50)
Loc Holyhead 8 miles

Baron Hill (1895)

Private
Beaumaris LL58 8YW
Tel **(0248) 810231**
Mem 360
Sec ED Thomas
Pro P Maton
Holes 9 L 5062 metres SSS 67
Recs Am–65 AW Jones
V'trs U exc comp days SOC–WD & Sat (apply Sec)
Fees £5 (£6) W–£20
Loc 1 mile NW Beaumaris

Bull Bay (1913)

Private
Amlwch LL68 9RY
Tel **(0407) 830960**
Mem 650
Sec Sqd Ldr BC Martyn
Pro S Tarrant (0407) 831188
Holes 18 L 6160 yds SSS 70
Recs Am–66 D McLean, A Llyr
Pro–65 M Barton
V'trs U SOC
Fees £5 (£7)
Loc Amlwch $^{1}/_{2}$ mile on A5025

Holyhead (1912)

Private
Trearddur Bay, Holyhead LL65 2YG
Tel **(0407) 3279/2119**
Mem 484 225(L) 109(J)
Sec CF Hopper
Pro P Capper (0407) 2022
Recs Am–64 D McLean
Pro–69 H Gould
V'trs H SOC
Fees On application
Loc Holyhead Station 1 mile

Llangefni (1983)

Public
Llangefni
Tel **(0248) 722193**
Pro P Lovell
Holes 9 L 1467 yds
V'trs U
Fees £1.25 (£1.85)
Loc Town centre $^{1}/_{2}$ mile on B511

For map index see page 203.

Mid Glamorgan

Aberdare (1921)

Private
Abernant, Aberdare
Tel (0685) 871188
Mem 500
Sec JL Jenkins (0685) 873387
Pro AW Palmer (0685) 878735
Holes 18 L 5875 yds SSS 69
Recs Am–63 S Dodd
Pro–67 AW Palmer
V'trs U
Fees £7 (£9) W–£25
Loc Town centre 1/2 mile

Bargoed (1912)

Private
Heolddu, Bargoed
Tel (0443) 830143
Mem 400
Sec J Heath (0443) 834045
Holes 18 L 6233 yds SSS 69
Recs Am–67 ID Joseph
V'trs WD–U WE–M SOC–WD
Fees £9
Loc NW boundary of Bargoed

Bryn Meadows G & CC (1973)

Private
The Bryn, nr Hengoed CF8 7SM
Tel (0495) 225590/224103
Mem 500
Sec B Mayo
Pro P Worthing (0495) 221905
Holes 18 L 6200 yds SSS 69
Recs Am–66 G Davies
Pro–S Price
V'trs U
Fees £8.50 (£10.50)
Loc Newport, Gwent 12 miles

Caerphilly (1905)

Private
Mountain Road, Caerphilly CF8 1HJ
Tel (0222) 883481
Mem 695
Sec (0222) 863441
Pro E McDonald (0222) 869104
Holes 14 L 6063 yds SSS 71
Recs Am–67 AW Norman
Pro–68 B Huggett
V'trs WD–U WE–M
Fees £8 W–£22 M–£55
Loc 7 miles N of Cardiff off A469. Rail/bus stations 1 mile

Castell Heights (1987)

Private
Blaengwynlais, Caerphilly CF8 1NG
Tel (0222) 886666 (Bookings)
(0222) 886686 (Clubhouse)
Mem 1000
Sec J Talbot
Pro R Sandow
Holes 9 L 2688 yds SSS 66
V'trs U
Fees 9 holes £3
Loc 4 miles from M4 Junction 32, on Tongwynlais to Caerphilly road.
Adjacent to Mountain Lakes GC

Creigiau (1921)

Private
Creigiau, Cardiff CF4 8NN
Tel (0222) 890263
Mem 630
Sec DB Jones
Pro A Kerr Smith (0222) 891909
Holes 18 L 5800 yds SSS 68
Recs Am–67 D Samuel
V'trs WD–U WE/BH–M SOC–WD
Fees £9
Loc 5 miles NW of Cardiff

Llantrisant & Pontyclun (1927)

Private
Talbot Green, Llantrisant
Tel (0443) 222148
Mem 500
Sec L Duggan (0443) 224601
Pro A Kerr Smith (0443) 228169
Holes 12 L 5712 yds SSS 68
Recs Am–65 TJ Lewis (1974)
Pro–65 JJ Hastings (1982)
V'trs WD–U WE/BH–M
Fees £9
Loc 10 miles N of Cardiff.
2 miles N of M4 Junction 34

Maesteg (1912)

Private
Mount Pleasant, Maesteg
Tel (0656) 732037
Mem 390
Sec A Brace (0656) 733061
Pro M Benjamin
Holes 18 L 5818 yds SSS 69
Recs Am–69 J James
Pro–70 G Poor (1987)
V'trs U
Fees £6 (£7)
Loc 1 mile W of Maesteg

Merthyr Tydfil (1908)

Private
Cilsanws Mountain, Cefn Coed, nr Merthyr Tydfil CF48 2HW
Tel (0685) 3308
Mem 148 54(L) 27(J)
Sec DN Davies (0685) 3063
Holes 9 L 5794 yds SSS 68
Recs Am–70 N Evans
Pro–70 J Howard
V'trs U
Fees £3 (£5)
Loc Off A470

Morlais Castle (1900)

Private
Pant Dowlais, Merthyr Tydfil
Tel (0685) 2822
Mem 300
Sec G Morgan
Holes 9 L 6258 yds SSS 71
V'trs U exc Sat 12–4pm SOC–WD
Fees £4 M–£25
Loc 3 miles N of Merthyr Tydfil

Mountain Ash (1907)

Private
Cefnpennar
Tel (0443) 472265
Mem 555
Sec G Matthews (0443) 474022
Pro J Sim (0443) 478770
Holes 18 L 5535 yds SSS 68
Recs Am–63 SJ Lewis
Pro–66 R Evans
V'trs U
Fees £8 (£10)
Loc 9 miles NW of Pontypridd

Mountain Lakes (1988)

Private
Blaengwynlais, Caerphilly CF8 1NG
Tel (0222) 861128
Mem 400
Sec J Bull
Pro R Sandow (0222) 886666
Holes 18 L 6851 yds SSS 72
V'trs H SOC
Fees £12 (£15)
Loc 4 miles from M4 Junction 32, on Tongwynlais–Caerphilly road.
Adjacent to Castell Heights GC

Pontypridd (1905)

Private
Ty Gwyn Road, Pontypridd CF37 4DJ
Tel (0443) 402359
Mem 560
Sec JG Graham (0443) 409904
Pro K Gittins (0443) 491210
Holes 18 L 5650 yds SSS 68
Recs Am–63 J Olding (1979),
P Price (1985)
V'trs WD–UH WE/BH–MH SOC–WD H
Fees £6 (£8)
Loc E side of town off A470.
12 miles NW of Cardiff

Pyle & Kenfig (1922)

Private
Waun-y-Mer, Kenfig CF33 4PU
Tel (065 671) 3093
Mem 860
Sec RC Thomas
Pro R Evans (065 671) 772446
Holes 18 L 6655 yds SSS 73

Recs Am–70 S Cox, S Curiel, N Evans
Pro–68 D Matthew, C Gray, M Steadman
V'trs WD–U WE–M
Fees £10
Loc Porthcawl 2 miles

Rhondda (1910)

Private
Penrhys, Pontygwaith, Rhondda
Tel **(0443) 433204**
Mem 350
Sec CG Phillips
Holes 18 L 6428 yds SSS 71
Recs Am–K Thomas
V'trs U
Fees £6 (£9)

Royal Porthcawl (1891)

Private
Porthcawl
Tel **(065 671) 2251**
Mem 500 220(L) 85(J)
Sec Maj AH Hopkins
Pro G Poor (065 671) 6984
Holes 18 L 6643 yds SSS 74
Recs Am–70 JWH Mitchell, J Povall
Pro–65 B Barnes
V'trs I SOC
Fees £16 (£20)
Loc 14 miles E of Swansea. M4 Junction 37

Southerndown (1905)

Private
Ewenny, Bridgend CF35 5BT
Tel **(0656) 880326**
Mem 650
Sec R Brickell (0656) 880476
Pro DG McMonagle
Holes 18 L 6705 yds SSS 73
Recs Am–66 H Stott
Pro–64 G Hunt
V'trs WD/Sats–U Sun/BH–M
SOC–Tues & Thurs–H
Fees £10 (£13)
Loc Ewenny, Ogmore-by-Sea, nr Ogmore Castle ruins

Whitehall (1922)

Private
The Pavilion, Nelson, Treharris
Tel **(0443) 740245**
Mem 320
Sec VE Davies
Holes 9 L 5750 yds SSS 68
Recs Am–66 M Heames
Pro–62 I Woosnam
V'trs WD–U WE–M
Fees £6
Loc 15 miles NW of Cardiff

Powys

Brecon (1902)

Private
Llanfaes, Brecon
Tel **(0874) 2004**
Mem 210
Sec GN Pugh (0874) 3793
Holes 9 L 5218 yds SSS 66
Recs Am–61 R Dixon
Pro–66 WO Moses
V'trs U
Fees £5
Loc Town 1/2 mile on A40

Builth Wells (1923)

Private
Golf Club Road, Builth Wells LD2 3NN
Tel **(0982) 553296**
Mem 425
Sec MA Sanders
Pro W Evans (0982) 553293
Holes 18 L 5376 yds SSS 67
V'trs U SOC
Fees £8 (£10)
Loc Llandovery Road

Cradoc (1967)

Private
Penoyre Park, Cradoc, Brecon LD3 9LP
Tel **(0874) 3658**
Mem 426
Sec BI Jones, GSW Davies
Pro D Beattie (0874) 5524
Holes 18 L 6234 yds SSS 71
Recs Am–65 DK Wood (1982)
V'trs U SOC
Fees £8 (£11)
Loc 2 miles NW of Brecon off B4520

Knighton (1913)

Private
Little Ffrydd Wood, Knighton
Tel **(0547) 528646**
Mem 124
Sec EJP Bright (Hon) (0547) 528684
Holes 9 L 5320 yds SSS 66
Recs Am–66 M Caine
Pro–71 H Vardon
V'trs U SOC
Fees £3 (£5)
Loc 1/2 mile SW of Knighton

Llandrindod (1905)

Private
Llandrindod Wells
Tel **(0597) 2010**
Mem 180 30(L) 50(J)
Sec MG Williams (0597) 2059
Holes 18 L 5759 yds SSS 68
Recs Am–65 CJ Davies
V'trs U
Fees £7 (£9)
Loc 1 mile E of Llandrindod Wells

Machynlleth (1905)

Private
Maes-y-Golen, Machynlleth
Tel **(0654) 2000**
Mem 200
Sec WG Evans (0654) 2969
Holes 9 L 5726 yds SSS 67
Recs Am–65
Pro–65
V'trs WD–U WE–NA or M
Fees £5
Loc 1 mile E of town clock off A489

Old Rectory Hotel (1968)

Private
Llangattock, Crickhowell NP8 1PH
Tel **(0873) 810373**
Mem 200
Sec D Best
Holes 9 L 1409 yds SSS 54
V'trs U
Fees £6
Loc 8 miles W of Abergavenny

St Giles Newtown (1919)

Private
Pool Road, Newtown
Tel **(0686) 25844**
Mem 290
Sec NO Davies
Pro DP Owen
Holes 9 L 5864 yds SSS 68
Recs Am–64 AP Parkin
Pro–68 CB Jones
V'trs WD/BH–I WE–restricted
Fees £4 (WE/BH/SOC–£5)
Loc 3/4 mile E of town centre

St Idloes

Private
Penrhalt, Llanidloes
Tel **(055 12) 2559**
Mem 120
Sec A Wynn Edwards (055 12) 2205
Holes 9 L 5210 yds SSS 66
Recs Am–63 J Davies
V'trs U
Fees £3 (£4) W–£12
Loc 1/2 mile on Trefeglwys Road

Welshpool (1929)

Private
Golfa Hill, Welshpool
Tel **(093 883) 249**
Mem 250
Sec RGD Jones (0938) 3377
Holes 18 L 5708 yds SSS 69
Recs Am–65 DH Ryan
Pro–69 S Bowen
V'trs U
Fees £4 (£5)
Loc 4 1/2 miles from Welshpool on Dolgellau road

South Glamorgan

Brynhill (1921)

Private
Port Road, Colcot, Barry
Tel (0446) 735061
Mem 700
Sec DP Lloyd (0446) 720277
Pro P Fountain (0446) 733660
Holes 18 L 6000 yds SSS 69
Recs Am–68 P Cooper
V'trs WD/Sat–U Sun–M SOC–WD
Fees £8 Sat–£11 Sun–M SOC–£6
Loc A4050 8 miles W of Cardiff

Cardiff (1921)

Private
Sherborne Avenue, Cyncoed, Cardiff CF2 6SJ
Tel (0222) 753067
Mem 700
Pro PD Johnson (0222) 754772
Holes 18 L 6015 yds SSS 70
Recs Am–65 J Lee (1988)
Pro–63 L Farmer (1987)
V'trs WD–H WE–M
Fees £15
Loc 3 miles N of city centre. 2 miles from Pentwyn exit of A48M, after M4 Junction 29

Dinas Powis (1914)

Private
Dinas Powis
Tel (0222) 512727
Mem 650
Sec JD Hughes
Pro G Bennett
Holes 18 L 5377 yds SSS 66
Recs Am–67 Dr HD Maurice
Pro–67 P Fountain
V'trs U
Fees £7 (£9)
Loc 3 miles W of Cardiff

Glamorganshire (1890)

Private
Lavernock Road, Penarth CF6 2UP
Tel (0222) 707048
Sec GC Crimp (0222) 701185
Pro A Kerr-Smith (0222) 707401
Holes 18 L 6150 yds SSS 70
Recs Am–65 MG Mouland
Pro–65 A Jacklin
V'trs WD–H WE–H SOC
Fees £13 (£15)
Loc 5 miles SW of Cardiff

Llanishen (1905)

Private
Cwm Lisvane, nr Cardiff CF4 5UD
Tel (0222) 752205
Mem 875
Sec ET Davies (0222) 755078
Pro RA Jones (0222) 755076
Holes 18 L 5296 yds SSS 66
Recs Am–64 MJG Strange
Pro–63 JT Taylor
V'trs WD–U WE–M H SOC
Fees £15
Loc 5 miles N of Cardiff

RAF St Athan (1977)

Private
Barry CF6 9WA
Tel (0446) 751043
Mem 415
Sec DM Llewellyn (0446) 751105
Holes 9 L 5957 yds SSS 69
V'trs U Sun am–NA
Fees £6
Loc 2 miles E of Llantwit Major

Radyr (1902)

Private
Radyr, nr Cardiff CF4 8BS
Tel (0222) 842442
Mem 880
Sec Maj MB Richards (0222) 842408
Pro S Gough (0222) 842476
Holes 18 L 6031 yds SSS 70
Recs Am–64 P Price
Pro–63 PW Evans
V'trs WD–H WE–M SOC–Wed & Fri
Fees £10
Loc 5 miles NW of Cardiff

Wenvoe Castle (1936)

Private
Wenvoe, nr Cardiff
Tel (0222) 591094
Mem 525 100(L) 50(J)
Sec EJ Dew (0222) 594371
Pro MA Pycroft (0222) 593649
Holes 18 L 6422 yds SSS 71
Recs Am–69 P Jones, M Davey
Pro–68 G Davies
V'trs H SOC
Fees £12 (£15)
Loc 4 miles W of Cardiff

Whitchurch (Cardiff) (1915)

Private
Pantmawr Road, Whitchurch, Cardiff CF4 6XD
Tel (0222) 620125
Mem 438 111(L) 72(J)
Sec (0222) 620985
Pro E Clark (0222) 614660
Holes 18 L 6245 yds SSS 70
Recs Am–62 J Povall
Pro–62 I Woosnam
V'trs WD–U WE/BH–M H SOC–WD
Fees £15 (£17)
Loc 3 miles NW of Cardiff on A470. M4 Junction 32, 2 miles

West Glamorgan

Clyne (1920)

Private
118 Owls Lodge Lane, Mayals, Swansea
Tel (0792) 401989
Mem 450
Sec BR Player
Pro ES Turner (0792) 402094
Holes 18 L 6312 yds SSS 71
Recs Am–66 C Dickens
Pro–66 J Bland
V'trs U
Fees £9 (£11)
Loc Swansea

Fairwood Park (1970)

Private
Upper Killay, Swansea
Tel (0792) 203648
Mem 650
Sec GH Edmond
Pro M Evans
Holes 18 L 6606 yds SSS 72
Recs Am–69
Pro–68
V'trs U SOC
Fees £9 (£11)
Mis Swansea Airport 1/4 mile

Glynneath (1931)

Private
Penycraig, Pontneathvaughan, Glynneath SA11 5UG
Tel (0639) 720452
Mem 250
Sec RM Ellis (0639) 720679
Holes 16 L 5499 yds SSS 68
Recs Am–66 JL Davies
Pro–68 D Rees
V'trs U
Fees £4 (£7)
Loc 12 miles N of Neath

Inco (1965)

Private
Clydach, Swansea
Tel (0792) 844216
Mem 260
Sec DGS Murdoch (0792) 843336
Holes 13 L 5976 yds SSS 69
Recs Am–68 V Smith, N O'Sullivan
V'trs U
Fees £4 (£5)
Loc Swansea Valley

Langland Bay (1904)

Private
Langland Bay, Swansea SA3 4QR
Tel (0792) 66023
Mem 620
Sec SO Campbell (0792) 361721
Pro TJ Lynch (0792) 366186

Holes 18 L 5812 yds SSS 69
Recs Am–65 H Evans
Pro–69 D Ridley
V'trs U SOC
Fees £10 (£11)
Loc 6 miles W of Swansea

Morriston (1919)

Private
160 Clasemont Road, Morriston, Swansea
SA6 6AJ
Tel **(0792) 71079**
Mem 400
Sec LT Lewis (0792) 796528
Pro DA Rees (0792) 72335
Holes 18 L 5773 yds SSS 68
Recs Am–65 DR Richards
Pro–64 DA Rees
V'trs H SOC on WD U
Fees £8 (£10.35)
Loc 4 miles NW of Swansea on A48. M4 Junction 46, 1 mile

Neath (1934)

Private
Cadoxton, Neath
Tel **(0639) 3615**
Mem 400
Sec JR Evans (0639) 52759
Pro EM Bennett
Holes 18 L 6500 yds SSS 72
Recs Am–69 BOS Vanstone
Pro–66 F Hill
V'trs U
Fees £6 (£8)
Loc Neath 2 miles

Palleg (1930)

Private
Palleg Road, Lower Cwmtwrch, Swansea Valley
SA9 1QT
Tel **(0639) 842193**
Mem 200
Sec GH Thomas (0639) 842524
Holes 9 L 3209 yds SSS 72
Recs Am–71 C Williams
V'trs U
Fees £4 (£6)
Loc Upper Swansea Valley. Ystalyfer 1 mile. Ystradgynlais 1 mile

Pennard (1896)

Private
Southgate Road, Southgate, nr Swansea SA3 2BT
Tel **(044 128) 3131**
Mem 685
Sec JD Eccles (044 128) 3131/3170
Pro M Bennett (044 128) 3451
Holes 18 L 6273 yds SSS 71
Recs Am–69 H Guest
Pro–66 G Ryall (1987)
V'trs U SOC
Fees £9 (£10) W–£25
Loc 8 miles W of Swansea

Pontardawe (1924)

Private
Cefn Llan, Pontardawe, Swansea
Tel **(0792) 863118**
Mem 320
Sec J Burrington
Pro RA Ryder (0792) 830977
Holes 18 L 6061 yds SSS 69
Recs Am–66 B Fisher
Pro–71 D Thomas, R Brook
V'trs H SOC
Fees £7 (£10)
Loc 5 miles N of M4 Junction 45 (A4067)

Swansea Bay (1894)

Private
Jersey Marine, Neath SA10 6JP
Tel **(0792) 812198/814153**
Mem 400
Sec Mrs D Goatcher
Pro M Day
Holes 18 L 6302 yds SSS 70
Recs Am–67 A Evans
V'trs U
Fees £9 (£10)
Loc Between Briton Ferry and Swansea, nr A48

For map index see page 203.

Driving Ranges in Great Britain and Ireland

Bedfordshire

Tilsworth Golf Centre

Dunstable Road, Tilsworth, Leighton Buzzard, Beds. *Tel* (0525) 210721/2
Open 10am–9.30pm, 7 days per week. 30 bays. Floodlit 9 hole course. Bar, licensed restaurant. Professionals' shop. Professional.

Berkshire

Downshire GC

Easthampstead Park, Wokingham, Berks. *Tel* Bracknell (0344) 424066
Open 8am–dusk weekdays; 7am–dusk weekends. Full 18 hole course. 9 hole pitch and putt. Driving range. Free house and restaurant. Professional.

Hawthorn Hill

Drift Road, Hawthorn Hill, Nr Maidenhead Berks SL6 3ST. *Tel* (0628) 771030/75588.
36 bay covered floodlit driving range. Open 8.00am–10.00pm. Full 18 hole public course. £1.80 for 56 balls. Snooker. 90-seater restaurant/steakhouse. Clubhouse and licensed bar. Loc: 4 miles S of Maidenhead on A330.

Lavender Park Golf Centre

Swinley Road, Ascot. *Tel* (0344) 4074
Open 9am–10pm Mon–Fri; 9am–9pm weekends. 55 balls for £1. 115 balls for £1.50. Floodlit. 9 hole course, par 28.

Sindlesham Driving Range

Mole Road, Wokingham, Berks RG11 5DB. *Tel* Wokingham (0734) 788494.
Floodlit; 7 days a week, 14 hours a day; 20 bays; £1 machine operated. Professional.

Buckinghamshire

Colnbrook Golf Driving Range

Gallymead Road, Colnbrook, Slough SL3 OEN. *Tel* Slough (0753) 682670/685127
Open 7 days, 9.30am–10.30pm. Floodlit. Professional. Restaurant. Licensed. Loc: 5 mins from Junction 5 M4 or Junction 14 M25.

Windmill Hill Golf Complex

Tattenhoe Lane, Bletchley, Milton Keynes. *Tel* (0908) 78623
23 covered and 5 open bays. Floodlit. Open 9.00am–9.00pm Mon–Fri; 9.00am–8.00pm Sat/Sun. Full 18 hole golf course. Putting greens. Golf shop. Tuition. Practice bunker. Bars and restaurant. Loc: 4 miles from Junction 14 M1 on A421.

Cambridgeshire

Abbotsley Golf Range

Eynesbury Hardwicke, St Neots, Cambridgeshire PE19 4XN. *Tel* (0480) 217951
Open 8.30am–10.30pm daily. Professional. 14 covered bays. 6 open bays. Floodlit. Putting. Bunkers. £1.50 for 70 balls. Tuition. Shop. Licensed. Food. Loc: 2 miles S of St Neots (B1046). 12 miles W of Cambridge. M11 Junction 13 onto A45.

Channel Islands

Western Golf Range

St Ouen Bay, Jersey.
Open 10am–dusk. 24 bays. Putting, crazy golf. 9 hole par 3. Professional.

Essex

Chingford Golf Range

Waltham Way, Chingford E4 8AQ.
***Tel* 01-529 2409**
Two-tier golf range. 18 covered floodlit bays. Putting green. PGA Professional. Open 9.30am–10.00pm. 40 balls £1.20, 60 balls £1.50, 100 balls £2.20. Clubs for hire from G Goldie. Golf shop. Club repair service. Video lessons. Loc: 1 mile N of North Circular Road at Chingford turn-off. 2 miles S of M25 Junction 26.

Colchester Golf Range

Crown Inn, Old Ipswich Road, Ardleigh, Colchester. *Tel* (0206) 230974
Open 10am–9pm Mon–Fri. 10am–5pm Sat/Sun. 50 balls £1.50. 100 balls £2. Floodlit. Club hire. Bunkers. Putting. Professional.

Fairlop Waters

Forest Road, Barkingside, Ilford, Essex.
***Tel* 01-500 9911**
Open 9am–10.30pm. Floodlit. 36 covered bays. 18 + 9 hole courses. £1.10 for 40 balls. £1.75 for 90 balls. Golf shop. Full tuition. Bar, restaurant. Loc: 2 miles from S end of M11, by Fairlop Tube Station.

Towerlands

Panfield Road, Braintree, Essex CM7 5BJ.
***Tel* (0376) 26802**
Open 7 days 8.30am–dusk. 6 bays. 50 balls–£1.00. 9 hole course. Loc: 1 mile NW of Braintree.

Gloucestershire

Gloucester Hotel & Country Club

Robinswood Hill, Gloucester. *Tel* (0452) 25653
Open 9am–8.30pm, 7 days. 12 bays. Floodlit. £1 for 50 balls. Squash. Skittles. Ski-slope. Full 18 hole course. 9 hole par 3.

Hampshire

Portsmouth Golf Centre

Eastern Road, Portsmouth, Hampshire.
***Tel* (0705) 664549**
Open 8am–10pm, 7 days. Floodlit. 30 covered bays. Professional. Shop. Tuition. Public house and restaurant.

Hertfordshire

Watford Driving Range

Sheepcot Lane, Garston, Watford, Herts.
***Tel* (0923) 675560**
Open 10am–10.30pm, 7 days. 55 balls–£1. Floodlit. Covered tees. Professional. Licensed.

Whaddon Golf Range

Church Street, Whaddon, Royston, Herts.
***Tel* (0223) 207325**
Open 10am–9pm weekdays. 10am–dusk Sat/Sun. 14 covered bays. £1.00 for 50 balls. Club hire. Professional. Loc: 4 miles N of Royston off A14.

Welwyn Hatfield Sports Centre

Gosling Stadium Driving Range, Stanborough Road, Welwyn Garden City, Herts.
***Tel* (0707) 331056**
Open 10am daily. 9 bays. Floodlit. Large basket £1. Cafeteria. Licensed bars. Multi sports complex.

Humberside

Hull Golf Centre

National Avenue, Hull, N Humberside.
***Tel* (0482) 492720**
24 covered tees. Open Mon–Fri 9am–9pm, Sat/Sun 9am–7.30pm. Floodlit. £2 jumbo; £1.50 large; £1 small baskets. Pitch and putt. Professional. Licensed. Meals.

Kent

Chatham Golf Centre

Street-End Road, Chatham, Kent.
***Tel* (0634) 48925**
Open 7 days, 10am–10pm. Floodlit. Professional tuition. Licensed bar.

Edenbridge G & CC

Crouch House Road, Edenbridge, Kent, TN8 5LQ. *Tel* (0732) 865202
Open 8am–10pm. 16 floodlit bays. Pro shop. Teaching facilities. £1.50 per bucket. Putting Green. Par 3 course.

Ruxley Golf Centre

Sandy Lane, St Pauls Cray, Orpington, Kent BR5 3HY. *Tel* (0689) 71490
Floodlit driving range. 28 covered bays. Tuition. Club hire. Open 8am–10.30pm. Bar, restaurant, golfshop, tuition. 18 hole golf course. Loc: off Ruxley roundabout on A20 at Sidcup.

Lancashire

Kearsley Golf Range Ltd

Moss Lane, Kearsley, Bolton, Lancashire BL4 8SF. *Tel* (0204) 75726
Open 11am–10pm weekdays; 11am–5pm weekends. Floodlit. Covered tees. Grass tees. Professional. Shop. Licensed bar. 9 hole pitch and putt. Loc: 4 miles S of Bolton on A666.

Phoenix Sporting and Leisure Centre

Fleetwood Road, Norbreck, Blackpool. *Tel* (0253) 854846
Open 9am–dusk 7 days. £1.20 per basket. Floodlit. 18 bays. Bunkers, par 3. Professional. Licensed bar. Refreshment kiosk.

Leicestershire

Range Inn Golf Range

Melton Road, Leicester. *Tel* (0533) 664400
Open 10am–10pm, 7 days. Floodlit. 20 covered tees. £1 for 85 balls. Licensed. 9 hole pitch and putt, 18 hole crazy golf.

Middlesex

Ealing Golf Range

Rowdell Road, Northolt, Middlesex. *Tel* 01-845 4967
Open 10am–10.00pm, 7 days. 36 covered floodlit tees. Putting. £1 per bucket. 4 Professionals. Licensed. Clubhouse. Putting. Loc: A40 Target roundabout.

Finchley Golf Driving Range

444 High Road, Finchley, London N12. *Tel* 01-445 9697
Open 9am–10pm, 7 days. Bucket from £1.40. 24 Floodlit bays. Putting. Professional teaching. Bar and catering. Located just off North Circular Road.

Norfolk

Norwich Golf Centre

Long Lane, Bawburgh, Norwich, Norfolk
Open 8am till dusk, 7 days. Bucket of balls £1.50. 9 hole course. Pro shop. Clubhouse. Loc: S of A47 at rear of Royal Norfolk Showground.

Northamptonshire

Delapre Golf Complex

Eagle Drive, Nene Valley Way, Northampton.
36 open and 25 covered bays. Floodlit. Par 3, pitch and putt. Full 18 hole course. Golf shop. Full catering and bar facilities. 3 miles from M1 Junction 15 on A508.

Nottinghamshire

Carlton Forum Golf Target Range

Foxhill Road, Carlton, Nottingham.
Open 10am–10pm Mon–Fri; 10am–5pm Sat & Sun (last buckets of balls sold $^1/_2$ hour prior to closing). 28 covered tees. Floodlit. Licensed bar and restaurant. *Tel* 0602 872333. Professional.

Suffolk

Ipswich Golf Centre

Suffolk Show Ground, Bucklesham Road, Ipswich, Suffolk IP3 8TZ. *Tel* (0473) 726821
Open 8.30am–dusk 15 bays. Buckets of balls £1.00 and £1.50. Professional. Tuition. Shop.

Surrey

Chessington Golf Centre

Garrison Lane, Chessington, Surrey. *Tel* 01-391 0948
Open 8am–10pm. 45 balls–£1.00. 18 covered bays. Floodlit. Professional tuition. Video lessons. Repair service. Club hire. 9 hole course. Licensed bar/restaurant.

Croydon Golf Centre

175 Long Lane, Addiscombe, Surrey. *Tel* 01-656 1690
Open Mon–Fri 10am–10pm; Sat/Sun 10am–9pm. 40 balls £1.30; 80 balls £2.60; 110 balls £3. 20 covered tees. Floodlit. Professional. Licensed. Loc: 3 miles E of Croydon.

Fairmile Hotel

Portsmouth Road, Cobham, Surrey. *Tel* (0932) 64419
Open 10am–10pm WD; 9am–9pm WE. 24 covered tees. Floodlit. Bunkers. Professional. Licensed restaurant. Putting green.

Hoebridge Golf Centre

Old Woking, Surrey. *Tel* (048 62) 22611/2
25 bays, covered. Floodlit. 18 hole course, 18 hole par 3 course. Lessons and hire equipment from Professional. Shop, bar and restaurant. 12 table snooker facility. Loc: 5 mins from A3 on Woking/West Byfleet Road.

Richmond Driving Range

Twickenham Road, Richmond, Surrey TW9 2SS. *Tel* 01-940 5570
Open 9am–8.30pm Mon–Fri; 9 am–5.30pm Sat/Sun (Sept–Apr close at 12 noon Sat). 25 covered floodlit tees. £2 for 75 balls. PGA Professional – S Simpson. Loc: next to Royal Mid Surrey GC.

Sandown Golf Centre

Sandown Park, More Lane, Esher, Surrey. *Tel* (0372) 63340
33 floodlit bays. Open 10am–10pm daily. 45 balls –£1.30; 75 balls–£2.20; 110 balls–£2.60. 9 hole public golf course. Range closed during Sandown Park Race meetings.

Silvermere GC Driving Range

Redhill Road, Cobham, Surrey. *Tel* (0932) 67275
Open 10am–10pm daily. 32 floodlit bays. 70 balls–£2.00. Contoured landscape. Chipping targets and baskets. Free house bar /restaurant. Snacks. Located between Cobham and Byfleet.

Windlemere Golf Course

Windlesham Road, West End, Woking, Surrey. *Tel* (09905) 8727
Open 8am–10pm, 7 days. Floodlit. 12 covered bays. 9–hole full–length public course. Two professionals. Large golf shop with repair services. Clubhouse-licensed bar with snooker /pool. Located A319 at Lightwater near Bagshot.

Sussex (East)

Horam Park Driving Range

Chiddingly Road, Horam, East Sussex. *Tel* (04353) 3477
Open 9am–10pm all year round. Floodlit. 18 covered bays. Professional's shop with repair service. Tuition with video facilities. Lounge bar/restaurant. Large bucket of balls £2.00. Club hire. 9 hole course. Loc: $^1/_2$ mile S of Horam on Chiddingly Road

Sussex (West)

Fairway Golf Driving Range

Horsham Road, Pease Pottage, Sussex. *Tel* (0293) 33000
Open 9am–10.30pm, 7 days, 60 balls for 60p. Floodlit. Professional. Licensed.

Tyne & Wear

George Washington Hotel

Stone Cellar Road, Washington, Tyne and Wear. *Tel* 091-417 2626
Open 10am–10pm. 21 floodlit bays. Professional. Pitch and putt. 18 hole course. 10 table snooker club.

Gosforth Park Golfing Complex

High Gosforth Park, Newcastle-Upon-Tyne. *Tel* 091-236 4480
Open 8.00am–10pm. 7 days. Floodlit. 30 covered tees. Putting, pitching. Professional. Licensed. Restaurant. 9 hole pitch/putt and 18 hole putting green.

Warwickshire

Purley Chase

Pipers Lane, Nuneaton, Warwicks. *Tel* (0203) 393118/395348
Open 10am–9pm. 13 covered bays. Floodlit £1.00 per bucket balls. Loc: 4 miles NW of Nuneaton.

Warwick Golf Centre

Racecourse, Warwick. *Tel* (0926) 494316
Open 10am–9pm weekdays; 9am–5pm weekends. Small basket 65p; medium £1.10; large £1.30. 30 covered tees. Floodlit. Target. Putting. Professional. Shop. Licensed. 9 hole course, par 34.

West Midlands

Blackhill Wood

Bridgenorth Road, Swindon, Nr Dudley. *Tel* (0902) 892279
Open 8am–9pm daily. 24 floodlit bays. Professional tuition. Licensed bar. Loc: 5 miles S of Wolverhampton.

John Reay Golf Centre

Sandpits Lane, Keresley, Coventry.
***Tel* (020) 333 3404 or 3920**
Professional shop.

Three Hammers Golf Complex

Old Stafford Road, Coven, Nr Wolverhampton. WV10 7PP.
***Tel* (0902) 790428**
Open 9.30am–10pm weekdays; 9am–7.00pm weekends. Floodlit. 14 covered floodlit bays. 18 hole short course. Licensed. Loc: 5 miles N of Wolverhampton, 2 miles from M6 Junction 10.

Wiltshire

Broome Manor Driving Range

Broome Manor Golf Complex, Pipers Way, Swindon, Wilts SN3 1RG. *Tel* (0793) 32403
Open 9.30am–9.30pm, 7 days (Mondays 12 noon–9.30pm). 25 bays. Floodlit. £1.30 standard; £1.90 large bucket of balls. Hire of clubs 40p each. Professional. Licensed. Food.

Ireland

Ballyearl Golf Centre

585 Doagh Rod, Newtownabbey. BT36 8RZ.
***Tel* (023 13) 48287**
Professional. 9 hole Par 3 course, 2362 yds. WD–£2. W/E–£2.75. 2–tiered covered range, 27 bays. Club hire. Loc: 1 mile N of Mossley off B59.

Craigavon Golf Centre

Turmoyra Lane, Silverwood, Lurgan, Craigavon.
Open 9am–9.30pm weekdays. 9am–5pm weekends. 20 floodlit covered bays. Professional tuition. Putting green. Pitch and putt. Loc: 1½ miles from Lurgan.

Knockbracken Golf Centre

Ballymaconaghy Road, Belfast. *Tel* (0232) 643554
Open 9am–11pm. Floodlit. Also putting, 18 hole course. Snooker and pool tables.

Leopardstown Golf Centre

Foxrock. *Tel* (0001) 895341/895671
Manager William Hourihane. 9 holes golf course; 18 holes Par 3 course 2795 yds. Public course. Green fees: £4, W/E–£4.50 (18 holes); Par 3–£3. Driving range: 36 indoor bays, 50 outdoor bays. Floodlit. £1.30–£2. Open WD 10am–10pm, WE–9am–6pm.

Scotland

Clydeway Golf Centre

Blantye Farm Road, Uddingston, Lanarkshire.
***Tel* 041-641 8899**
Open 10am–9pm weekdays; 10am–6pm weekends. 20 indoor, 5 outdoor bays. 100 balls £1.80, 55 balls £1.10 (1988 prices). Floodlit. Golf shop. PGA Professional. Tuition. Loc: 1½ miles from Glasgow Zoo.

Normandy Golf Range

Inchinnan Road, Renfrew, PA4 9ES.
***Tel* 041-886 7477 (Mon–Fri)**
Open 9.30am–8.30pm weekdays; 9.30am–5.30pm weekends. 20 covered, 5 open bays. Video. Professional. Floodlit. 50 balls for £1; £1.60 for 100. Loc: 1 mile W of Glasgow Airport. M8, 1 mile.

Port Royal Golf Range

Ingliston, Edinburgh Lothians. *Tel* 031-333 4377
Open all year, 10am–11pm. 24 bays. Floodlit. £1.25 per bucket. 9 hole par 3 course. Professional tuition. Large putting green. Lounge and snack bar. Loc: By Edinburgh airport.

Strathclyde Park Golf Range

Mote Hill, Hamilton, Lanarkshire.
24 bays. Floodlit. Cafeteria. Licensed bar. Open 9.30am–9.30pm. Large bucket £2. Small bucket £1.50. 9 hole golf course. Professional teaching. Loc: A723 just off M74.

Continental Section

Austria

Bad Ischl

Salzkammergut (1932)

4820 Bad Ischl, Postfach 145
Tel (06132) 6340
Mem 450
Pro I Hay, F Laimer, Ch Schuster
Holes 9 L 5900 m SSS 71
Fees 250–350s
Loc Bad Ischl 6km. Strobl 6km. Salzburg 50km

Bad Kleinkircheim

Bad Kleinkircheim-Reichenau (1984)

A-9546 Bad Kleinkircheim
Tel (04274) 594
Mem 150
Pro G Manson
Holes 18 L 6127 m SSS 72
Fees 300s
Loc 50km NW of Klagenfurt

Badgastein

Badgastein (1962)

5640 Badgastein, PO Box 15
Tel (06434) 2775/2516
Mem 330
Pro S Wildman
Holes 9 L 5804 m SSS 71
Fees 250s (300s) W–1600s
Loc Badgastein 2km
Mis Open May–Oct

Enzesfeld

Enzesfeld (1970)

A-2551 Enzesfeld
Tel (02256) 81272
Mem 480
Pro S Jackson, A Graas
Holes 18 L 6176 m SSS 72
Fees 400s (500s)
Loc Vienna 32km
Mis WE–Jul/Aug–only with member. Handicap certificate required.

Graz

Murhof (1963)

A-8130 Frohnleiten, Adriach 53
Tel (03127) 2101
Mem 380
Pro GJ Mackintosh
Holes 18 L 6371 m SSS 73
Fees 350s
Loc 20km N of Graz. 150km S of Vienna
Mis Golf hotel guests–220s

Hainburg/Donau

Hainburg/Donau (1977)

Auf der Heide 762, A-2410 Hainburg
Tel (02165) 2628
Mem 195
Pro R Jerman
Holes 9 L 5950 m SSS 71
Fees 250s (350s)
Mis Open Mar–Nov

Innsbruck-Igls

Innsbruck-Igls (1956)

A-6074 Rinn, Oberdorf 11
Tel (05223) 8177
Mem 450
Pro I Shaw
Holes 18 L 5910 m SSS 71
9 L 4709 m SSS 66
Fees 240s (350s)
Loc Innsbruck–Rinn 10km

Kitzbühel

Kitzbühel (1955)

6370 Kitzbühel
Tel (05356) 3007
Mem 400
Pro S Brown, P Wagstaff
Holes 9 L 6085 m SSS 72
Fees 250s (350s)
Loc Kitzbühel 820 m

Klagenfurt

Kärntner (1927)

9082 Dellach, 16 Maria Wörth
Tel (04273) 2515
Mem 250
Pro M Brock, P Memp
Holes 18 L 5740 m SSS 70
Fees D–280s
Loc Velden 8km

Liezen

G & LC Ennstal (1978)

A-8940 Liezen, "Eisenhof", Postfach 28
Tel (03612) 24774
Pro P Mackenzie
Holes 9 L 5550 m SSS 70
Fees 300s
Loc Steiermark–Graz

Schloss Pichlarn (1972)

A-8952 Irdning, Ennstal Steiermark
Tel (03682) 2841
Mem 60
Pro A Mitchel
Holes 18 L 6123 m SSS 72
Fees D–250s

Linz

Linz-St Florian (1960)

A-4490 St Florian, Tillysburg 28
Tel (07223) 2873
Mem 520
Pro P Wright, B Ridley, H Thompson
Holes 18 L 6131 m SSS 72
Fees 300s
Loc Linz 15km. Vienna 170km

Wels (1981)

4512 Weisskirchen/Wels, Weyerbach 37
Tel (07243) 6038
Mem 380
Pro J Wraith
Holes 18 L 6100 m Par 72
Fees 300s (400s)
Loc 5km from Salzburg–Vienna highway. City centre 8km
Mis Driving range, pitch and putt. Handicap certificate required

Pertisau/Achensee

Achensee (1934)

A-6123 Pertisau, Postbox 3
Tel (05243) 5377
Mem 180
Pro I Schaffer
Holes 9 L 3916 m SSS 62
Fees D–140s W–900s M–3500s
Loc Pertisau 1/2km

Saalfelden

Güt Brandlhof (1983)

A-5760 Saalfelden, Sporthotel Güt Brandlhof
Tel (06582) 2176–555
Mem 110
Pro J Crisp
Holes 18 L 5902 m SSS 72
Fees 275s (330s)
Loc Between Salzburg and Kitzbühel. Salzburg 60km
Mis Hotel guests 20% discount

Salzburg

Salzburg Klesheim (1955)

5071 Wals, bei Salzburg
Tel **(0662) 850851**
Mem 420
Pro D Howard
Holes 9 L 5700 m SSS 70
Fees 300s (350s)
Loc Salzburg 5km

Schloss Fuschl (1964)

A–5322 Hof/Salzburg
Tel **(06229) 390**
Mem 200
Pro F Torrano
Holes 9 L 3054 m Par 62 SSS 61
Fees 150–200s (200s)
Loc Salzburg 12km
Mis Driving range

Seefeld

Golfakademie Seefeld (1987)

A–6100 Seefeld, WM Sportanlagen GmbH
Tel **(05212) 2313/2316**
Mem 238
Pro M Mawdsley
Holes 18 L 6046 m SSS 72
Fees 280s (400s)
Loc 4km W of Seefeld. 24km W of Innsbruck
Mis Hotel guests 15% reduction. Starting times necessary Jul–Sept

Steinakirchen Am Forst

Schloss Ernegg (1973)

A–3261 Steinakirchen am Forst NO
Tel **(07488) 214 (May–Oct)**
Mem 120
Pro K Waldon
Holes 18 L 5670 m SSS 69
9 L 2150 m SSS 63
Fees 150s (250s)
Loc 100km W of Vienna. Autobahn exit Ybbs
Mis Driving range, pitch and putt

Vienna

Wien (1901)

Freudenau 65a, 1020 Wien
Tel **(0222) 2189564/2189667**
Mem 660
Pro W Walters, R Lane
Holes 18 L 5861 m SSS 71
Fees D–450s
Loc Vienna centre 10 mins
Mis (0222) 2189674 (Caddymaster)

Vienna Neustadt

Föhrenwald (1968)

Postfach 105, A–2700 Wiener Neustadt
Tel **(02622) 52171**
Mem 400
Pro A Andrews, S Page
Holes 18 L 6080 m SSS 72
Fees 350s (450s)
Loc 5km S of Wiener Neustadt on Route 54

Semmering (1926)

2680 Semmering
Tel **(02664) 456**
Pro A Tonn
Holes 9 L 3860 m SSS 60
Fees 200s (250s)
Loc 90km S of Vienna
Mis Season May–Oct

Zell am See

Europa Sport Region (1983)

Golfstr 25, 5700 Zell am See
Tel **(06542) 6161**
Mem 530
Pro D Shaw
Holes 18 L 6400 m SSS 72
9 L 2910 m SSS 72
Fees 27 holes 350s (450s)
9 holes 320s (370s)
Loc Salzburg 95km. Munich 175km
Mis Driving range D–70s. Open May–Oct

Belgium

Antwerp

Rinkven G & CC (1980)

St Jobsteenweg 120, 2232 Schilde
Tel **(03) 384 0784**
Mem 1000
Pro M Waldron, V Duysters, B Janjic
Holes 27 L 6128 m SSS 73
Fees 1250fr (2500fr)
Loc 17km NE of Antwerp. 5km off E10
Mis Handicap certificate required

Royal Antwerp (1888)

Georges Capiaulei 2, B–2080 Kapellen
Tel **(03) 666 8456**
Mem 950
Pro C Mackay
Holes 18 L 6140 m SSS 73
9 L 2264 m SSS 33
Fees 1000fr (1400fr)
Loc Antwerp 20km–Kapellen–Kalmthout

Ternesse

Uilenbaan 15, B–2220 Wommelgen
Tel **(03) 353 0292**
Mem 600
Pro S Bouillon, V Waters
Holes 18 L 5876 m SSS 72
Fees 1250fr (2500fr)
Loc Antwerp 5 mins on E–39

Brussels

Duisberg Militaire

Hertswegenstraat 39, 1982 Duisburg
Tel **767 9752/3890 ext 388**
Holes 9 L 3630 m SSS 60
Fees D–200fr (300fr)
Loc Brussels 13km

Golf de Rigenée (1981)

Rue de Châtelet 10a, 6321 Villers-la-Ville
Tel **(071) 87 77 65**
Mem 540
Pro C Mitchell, Ch Ditlefsen, F Descampe (Touring)
Holes 18 L 6150 m SSS 72
Fees 600fr (1100fr)
Loc Between Charleroi, Namur and Brussels

Keerbergen

50 Vlieghavenlaan, 2850 Keerbergen
Tel **(015) 23 49 61**
Mem 820
Pro W Vanbegin, W Mann (015) 234963
Holes 18 L 5530 m SSS 69
Fees 1000fr (1500fr)
Loc Brussels 29km

Royal Golf Club de Belgique (1906)

Chateau de Ravenstein, 1980 Tervueren
Tel **(02) 767 5801**
Mem 1280
Pro J Williams, G Maxwell
Holes 18 L 6075 m SSS 72
9 L 1960 m Par 32
Fees 1550fr (2550fr)
Loc Brussels 15km
Mis 18 hole course limited to h'cap (men–20 ladies–24). Phone before visit. Handicap certificate required.

Royal Waterloo (1923)

Vieux Chemin de Wavre, 1328 Ohain
Tel **(02) 633 1850/1597**
Mem 1300
Pro G Will, J Blair
Holes 18 L 6260 m SSS 73
18 L 6440 m SSS 72
9 L 2143 m SSS 33

Fees D–1200fr (D–2000fr)
Loc Brussels 22km
Mis Handicap certificate required

Dinant

Château Royal d'Ardenne

5560 Houyet Dinant
Tel (082) 66 62 28
Mem 350
Pro F Masson
Holes 18 L 5363 m SSS 71
Fees 700fr (1000fr)
Loc 9km on Rochefort road

Ghent

Royal Latem (1909)

B–9830 St Martens-Latem
Tel (091) 82 54 11
Mem 730
Pro J Verplancke
Holes 18 L 5767 m SSS 70
Fees 800fr (1000fr)
Loc 10km SW of Ghent on route N43 Ghent–Deinze

Hasselt

Limburg G & CC (1966)

Golfstraat No 1, 3530 Houthalen
Tel (011) 38 35 43
Mem 650
Pro M Sullivan
Holes 18 L 6090 m SSS 72
Fees 1000fr (1300fr)
Loc Hasselt 15km

Knokke-Heist

Royal Zoute

Caddiespad 14 8300 Knokke-Heist
Tel (050) 60 12 27 (Sec)
(050) 60 72 11 (Caddiemaster)
(050) 60 37 81 (Starter)
Mem 1200
Pro A de Vulder
Holes 18 L 6172 m SSS 72
18 L 3607 m SSS 60
Fees D–1000–1300fr (1200–1700fr)
Loc Knokke 1km

Liège

Royal GC du Sart Tilman

541 Route du Condroz, 4200 Ougrée
Tel (041) 36 20 21
Mem 700
Pro R Braems, A Verlegh
Holes 18 L 6002 m SSS 71
Fees D–800fr (1000fr)
Loc Ardennes, 10km S of town centre on Route 620 Liège–Marche

Mons

Royal GC Du Hainaut (1934)

Route d'Ath, 7434 Erbisoeul
Tel (065) 22 96 10/22 94 74(Sec)
Mem 500
Pro F Lefever
Holes 18 L 6183 m SSS 72
Fees D–750fr (950fr)
Loc Mons 6km towards Ath

Ostend

Koninklijke GC Ostend (1903)

2 Koninklijke, 8420 De Haan
Tel (059) 23 32 83
Mem 450
Pro T Bowden
Holes 18 L 5320 m SSS 68
Fees 950fr (1150fr)
Loc Ostend 7km

Oudenaarde

Oudenaarde G & CC (1976)

Kasteel Petegem, Kortrykstraat 52
9790 Wortegem-Petegem
Tel (055) 31 54 81
Mem 650
Pro C Morton, T Welsh
Holes 18 L 6039 m SSS 73
Fees D–600fr (1000fr)
Loc 3km SW from Oudenaarde

Spa

Royal GC des Fagnes

Balmoral, 4880 Spa
Tel (087) 77 16 13
Mem 350
Pro WYS Robertson
Holes 18 L 5924 m SSS 72
Fees D–600fr f25(1200fr)
Loc Spa 5km. Liège 35km

Cyprus

Joint Services Dhekélia

BFPO 58
Tel Dhekélia 460
Mem 180 50(L)
Holes 18 L 5886 m SSS 69
Fees Summer £C2 Winter £C3
Loc 12km E of Larnaca

Czechoslovakia

Brno

TJ Lokomotiva-Ingstav Brno (1967)

Antoninska 5, 60200 Brno
Tel Brno 74 88 53
Mem 85
Pro P Bohumil
Holes 9 L 5064 m SSS 72
Fees 100kcs
Loc Brno 80km. Prague 100km

Karlovy Vary

TJ Start VD–Golf (1970)

360 69 Karlovy Vary, Manesova 3
Tel 27279
Mem 84
Sec E Stebel
Holes 18 L 6087 m SSS 72
Fees 100kcs
Loc Prague 120km. Pilsen 90km

Mariánské Lázně

Mariánské Lázně (1905)

Mariánské Lázně, Zadub 565
Tel 5195
Mem 160
Pro N Miroslav
Holes 18 L 6080 m SSS 72
Fees 100kcs (130kcs)
Loc 3km NE of Mariánské Lázně. 160km W of Prague

Ostrava

TJ NHKG (1968)

Cingrova 10, 70100 Ostrava 1
Tel Hlucín 449 (Clubhouse)
Mem 202
Holes 18 L 5773 m SSS 72
Fees 100kcs
Loc Silherovice 15km Ostrava

Poděbrady

TJ Sklo Bohemia Poděbrady (1964)

Tyršova ul 26/111, 29001 Poděbrady
Tel 0324–4383
Mem 55
Holes 9 L 3121 m SSS 72
Fees 40kcs
Loc E side of Poděbrady

Prague

TJ Golf Praha (1969)

Na Morani 4, 120 00 Praha 2
Tel 292828
Mem 220
Holes 9 L 2978 m SSS 36
Fees 100 kcs (200 kcs)
Loc Prague Motol direction Plzeň

Semily

Oddíl Golfu TJ Semily (1971)

513 01 Semily
Mem 62
Sec 8 L 4002 m SSS 64
Fees 20kcs
Loc Semily 2km

Denmark

Bornholm Island

Gudhjem

Nordbornholms (1987)

Spellingevej 3, RØ, DK 3760 Gudhjem
Tel (03) 98 42 00
Holes 18 L 5472 m SSS 69
Fees 100kr W–500kr
Loc Gudhjem 8km. Rønne 22km

Rønne

Bornholms (1971)

Plantagavej, 3700 Rønne
Tel (03) 95 68 54
Mem 260
Pro S Judge
Holes 18 L 4511 m SSS 65
Fees 80kr (100kr)
Loc 4km E of Rønne

Funen

Glamsbjerg

Vestfyns

Rønnemosegaard, Krengerupvej 27
5620 Glamsbjerg
Tel (09) 72 15 77
Pro S Tinning
Holes 9 L 5680 m SSS 71
Fees 60kr (75kr)
Loc 40km SW of Odense

Nyborg

SCT Knuds (1954)

Slipshavnsvej 16, DK 5800 Nyborg
Tel (09) 31 12 12
Mem 621
Pro H Hansen
Holes 18 L 5788 m SSS 70
Fees 110kr D–130kr (230kr)
Loc Nyborg 3km

Odense

Odense (1927)

Hestehaven 201, 5220 Odense SO
Tel (09) 95 90 00
Mem 1050
Pro P Dixon
Holes 18 L 6156 m SSS 71
9 L 4154 m SSS 60
Fees 80kr (100kr)
Loc SE outskirts of Odense

Svendborg

Svendborg (1970)

Tordengaardsvej, Sorup,
5700 Svendborg
Tel (09) 22 40 77
Mem 384
Pro S Jensen
Holes 9 L 5746 yds SSS 69
Fees 60kr (80kr)
Loc Svendborg 3km

Jutland

Aabenraa

Sønderjyllands (1970)

Uge Hedegård, 6360 Tinglev
Tel (04) 68 75 25
Mem 420
Pro T Mitchell (04) 688198
Holes 18 L 5666 m SSS 69
Fees D–100kr
Loc 13km SW of Aabenraa

Aalborg

Aalborg (1908)

Jargersprisvej, Restup Enge 9000,
Aalborg
Tel (08) 34 14 76
Mem 850
Pro H Barton
Holes 18 L 5800 m SSS 70
Fees D–100kr (120 kr)
Loc 7km SW of Aalborg

Brønderslev (1971)

PO Box 94, 9700 Brønderslev
Tel (08) 82 32 81
Mem 300
Pro M Thven
Holes 18 L 5710 m SSS 71
Fees 80kr
Loc 3km W of Brønderslev

Himmerlands G & CC

Centervej 1, Gatten, 9670 Løgstør
Tel (08) 66 16 00
Mem 620
Pro R Kristensen, S Rolner
Holes 18 L 5277 m SSS 68
9-hole Par 3 course
Fees 110kr (325kr) W–650kr
Loc Hobro 32km on Hobro–Løgstør road. Course is signposted W from Gatten

Aarhus

Aarhus (1931)

Ny Moesgaardvej 50, 8270 Hojbjerg
Tel (06) 27 63 22
Mem 1450
Pro P Greve
Holes 18 L 6043 m SSS 72
9 L 6093 m SSS 72
Fees 100kr (120kr); 9 hole 60kr (80kr)
Loc Aarhus 6km. 18 hole: Route 451 South. 9 hole: Route E3 North

Ebeltoft

Ebeltoft (1966)

Strandgaardshoej, DK 8400 Ebeltoft
Tel (06) 34 33 28
Mem 400
Pro A Scullion
Holes 18 L 5150 m SSS 67
Fees D–80kr W–300kr
Loc
Ebeltoft $^{1}/_{2}$ km

Esbjerg

Esbjerg (1921)

Sønderhedevej, Marbaek,
DK 6710 Esbjerg V
Tel (05) 26 92 19
Mem 1100
Pro A Tinning
Holes 18 L 6434 m SSS 74
Fees 100kr
Loc 15km N of Esbjerg

Fanø Island (1900)

DK 6720 Nordby
Tel (05) 16 32 82
Mem 239
Pro N Aafeldt
Holes 18 L 4642 m SSS 65
Fees D–80kr W–400 kr
Loc Take Fanø Island Ferry from Esbjerg

Grindsted

Gyttegård (1978)

Billundvej 43, DK 7250 Hejnsvig
Tel (05) 33 56 49
Mem 250
Pro A Thygesen
Holes 9 L 5442 m SSS 69
Fees WD/WE 80kr
Loc Grindsted 10km. Billund 6km

Haderslev

Haderslev (1971)

Egevej 22, 6100 Haderslev
Tel (04) 52 83 01
Mem 360
Pro E Grandison
Holes 18 L 5137 m SSS 67
Fees D–100kr
Loc $1^1/_2$ km NW of town centre

Herning

Herning (1964)

Silkeborgvej, 7400 Herning
Tel (07) 21 18 81
Mem 650
Pro P Dangerfield
Holes 18 L 5571 m SSS 70
Fees D–100kr
Loc Herning 2km E on Route 15

Holstebro

Holstebro (1970)

Råsted, 7570 Vemb
Tel (07) 48 51 55
Mem 527
Pro R Howett
Holes 18 L 5762 m SSS 70
Fees D–100kr (120kr)
Loc 13km W of Holstebro

Horsens

Horsens (1972)

Silkeborgvej, 8700 Horsens
Tel (05) 61 51 51
Mem 400
Pro G Oakley
Holes 18+ 6 L 5905 m SSS 72
Fees 100kr
Loc 1km W of Horsens towards Silkeborg

Juelsminde (1973)

Bobroholtvej 9, 7130 Juelsminde
Tel (05) 69 34 92
Mem 323
Pro K Maas
Holes 9 L 5990 m SSS 71
Fees WD/WE–60kr
Loc On coast 20km S of Horsens
Mis 6 hole par 3 course

Kolding

Kolding (1933)

Emerholtsvej, 6000 Kolding
Tel (05) 52 37 93
Mem 610
Pro F Atkinson
Holes 18 L 5376 m SSS 69
Fees 100kr (140kr)
Loc Kolding 3km

Randers

Randers (1958)

Himmelbovej, Fladbro, 8900 Randers
Tel (06) 42 88 69
Mem 570
Pro G Townhill
Holes 18 L 5453 m SSS 70
Fees 100kr W–500kr
Loc 5km from Randers towards Silkeborg by Fladbrovej. Follow signs "Golfbane".

Ribe

Ribe (1981)

Rønnehave, Snepsgårdevej 14, Postboks 37, 6760 Ribe
Tel (05) 44 12 30
Mem 250
Pro J Ekins
Holes 9 L 5092 m SSS 67
Fees WD/WE–80kr
Loc 8km SE of Ribe on Haderslev road

Silkeborg

Silkeborg (1966)

Sensommervej 15C, 8600 Silkeborg
Tel (06) 85 33 99
Mem 850
Pro M Kelly
Holes 18 L 5956 m SSS 72
Fees WD/WE–120kr
Loc Silkeborg 5km

Skagen-Frederikshavn

Hvide Klit

Hvideklitvej 28, 9982 Aalbaek
Tel (08) 48 90 21
Mem 500
Pro O Smidt (08) 48 80 08
Holes 18 L 5875 m SSS 72
Fees WD/WE–120kr W–400kr
Loc 3km N of Albaek. Frederickshavn 24km

Skjern

Dejbjerg (1968)

Public

Letagervej 1, Dejberg, 6900 Skjern
Tel (07) 35 09 59
Mem 300
Pro A Thygesen
Holes 9 L 5066 m SSS 67
Fees D–80kr (D–100kr)
Loc 25km from W coast on Skjern–Rinkøbing road. Skjern 6km

Thisted

Nordvestjysk (1971)

Nystrupvej 19, 1700 Thisted
Tel (07) 97 41 41
Mem 265
Pro S Tinning
Holes 9 L 5599 m SSS 70
Fees D–50kr (60kr)
Loc 13km NW of Thisted

Vejle

Vejle (1970)

Faellessletgaard, Ibaekvej, 7100 Vejle
Tel (05) 85 81 85
Mem 960
Pro J John
Holes 18 L 6042 yds SSS 71
Fees 120kr (140kr) W–600kr
Loc 5km SE of Vejle
Mis Driving range. Par 3 course.

Viborg

Skive

Resen, 7800 Skive
Tel (07) 52 44 09
Mem 200
Pro R Jackson
Holes 9
Fees D–30kr (40kr)
Loc 32km NW of Viborg

Viborg

Mollevej 26, Overlund, Viborg 8800
Tel (06) 61 11 19
Mem 425
Pro A Martin
Holes 13 L 5525 m SSS 69
Fees WD/WE–80kr
Loc 2km E of Viborg

Zealand

Copenhagen

Copenhagen (1898)

Dyrehaven 2, 2800 KGS Lyngby
Tel **(01) 63 04 83**
Mem 950
Pro H Kristensen, H Aafeldt
Holes 18 L 5701 m SSS 70
Fees 140kr (180kr)
Loc 13km N of city in deer park

Furesø (1974)

Hestkøbvoeenge 4, 3460 Birkerød
Tel **(02) 81 74 44**
Mem 950
Pro C Smith
Holes 18 L 5506 m SSS 69
Fees 100kr (140kr)
Loc 25km N of Copenhagen

Molleaens (1970)

Stenbaekgard, Bastrup, DK 3450 Lynge
Tel **(02) 18 86 31/18 86 79**
Mem 1205
Pro R Jackson
Holes 18 L 5555 m SSS 69
Fees 100kr (150kr)
Loc 32km NW of Copenhagen
Mis Driving range

Søllerød

Overodvej 239, 2840 Holte
Tel **(02) 80 17 84**
Mem 1100
Pro J Korfitsen (02) 801877
Holes 18 L 5872 m SSS 72
Fees 140kr (200kr)
Loc 19km N of Copenhagen

Falster

Storstrømmen (1969)

4863 Eskilstrup, Falster
Tel **(03) 83 80 80**
Mem 475
Pro A Mackay (03) 83 82 02
Holes 18 L 6195 m SSS 73
Fees D–100kr (D–120kr 3D–240kr)
Loc 15km N of Nykøbing F

Frederiksværk

Asserbo

Bodkergaardsvej 3300 Frederiksværk
Tel **(02) 120329**
Mem 350
Pro L Middelboe
Holes 9 L 5187 m SSS 69
Fees 60kr (80kr)
Loc Frederiksværk 3km

Gilleleje

Gilleleje (1970)

Ferlevej 52, 3250 Gilleleje
Tel **(02) 20 95 16**
Mem 767
Pro R Taylor
Holes Passebaekgård 9 L 3270 yds SSS 71; Ferlegård 9 L 2814 yds SSS 68
Fees D–140kr (140kr)
Loc 62km N of Copenhagen
Mis Free driving range

Helsingør

Helsingør

Gl Hellebaekvej, 3000 Helsingør
Tel **(02) 21 29 70**
Mem 950
Holes 18 L 5705 m SSS 71
Fees 150kr (200kr)
Loc Helsingør $1\frac{1}{2}$ km

Hillerød

Hillerød (1966)

Nysogard, Ny Hammersholt 3400 Hillerød
Tel **(02) 26 50 46**
Mem 1000
Pro M Tulloch (02) 25 40 30
Holes 18 L 5452 m SSS 70
Fees 140kr (200kr)
Loc 3km S of Hillerød

Holbaek

Holbaek

Kirsebaerholmen, 4300 Holbaek
Tel **(03) 43 45 79**
Mem 320
Pro M Irving
Holes 9 L 5158 m SSS 67
Fees 50kr (60kr)
Loc Kirsebaerholmen

Hørsholm

Kokkedal (1971)

2980 Kokkedal, Kokkedal Alle 9
Tel **(02) 86 99 59**
Mem 1130
Pro N Willett
Holes 18 L 5958 m SSS 72
Fees 170kr (180kr)
Loc Hørsholm, 30km N of Copenhagen
Mis WE–Visitors pm only

Rungsted (1937)

DK 2960 Rungsted Kyst
Tel **(02) 86 34 44 (Sec)**
Mem 1050
Pro R Beattie
Holes 18 L 5893 m SSS 72
Fees 160kr (200kr)
Loc Rungsted 30km N of Copenhagen

Kalundborg

Kalundborg (1974)

Kildekaergaard, Rosnaesvej 225 4400 Kalundborg
Tel **(03) 50 13 85**
Mem 370
Sec P Jacobsen
Pro M Irving
Holes 9 L 5064 m SSS 68
Fees 60kr (90kr)
Loc Rosnaes, 8km W of Kalundborg

Køge

Køge (1970)

Gl.Hastrupvej12, 4600 Køge
Tel **(03) 65 10 00**
Mem 750
Pro P Taylor
Holes 18 L 6042 m SSS 72
Fees 100kr (140kr)
Loc 3km S from Køge. Copenhagen 38km

Korsør

Korsør (1964)

Tarnborgparken, 4220 Korsør
Tel **(03) 57 18 36**
Mem 620
Pro M Irving (03) 57 40 18
Holes 18 L 5998 m SSS 72
Fees D–100–120kr (D–150kr)
Loc Korsør Bay

Naestved

Sydsjaellands

Borupgården Mogenstrup, 4700 Naestved
Tel **(03) 76 15 03**
Pro D Chad
Holes 18 L 5675 m SSS 70
Fees 80kr (100kr)
Loc 9km SE of Naestved

Nykøbing Sjælland

Odsherred (1967)

4573 Hojby Sjælland
Tel **(03) 42 20 76**
Mem 350
Pro P Jacobsen

Holes 12 L 5678 m SSS 70
Fees 40kr (60kr)
Loc 5km SW of Nykøbing

Roskilde

Hedeland

Staerkendevej 232
2640 Hedehusene
Tel (02) 13 61 69
Pro A Kristensen
Holes 12 L 5650 m Par 68
Fees 80kr (100kr)
Loc Roskilde 7km

Roskilde (1973)

Kongemarken 34, 4000 Roskilde
Tel (02) 370180
Mem 562
Pro T Card
Holes 12 L 4853 m SSS 69
Fees 80kr (120kr)
Loc 5km W of Roskilde

Sorø

Midtsjællands

Tuelsovej 20, 4180 Sorø
Tel (03) 63 27 75
Holes 9 L 3670 m Par 60
Loc Between Korsør and Ringsted

Finland

Hämeenlinna

Aulangon (1959)

Hämeenlinna
Tel Hämeenlinna 21271
Mem 150
Holes 9 L 2450 m SSS 67
Fees D–25 fmk
Loc Hämeenlinna 5km

Helsinki

Espoon Golfseura (1982)

Box 26, 02781 Espoo
Tel (90) 811 212
Mem 1100
Pro J Utter, V Kalliala
Holes 18 L 6183 m SSS 74
Fees 100fmk
Loc 24km W of Helsinki

Helsingin Golfklubi (1932)

Talin Kartano, SF–00350 Helsinki 35
Tel 550235 / 557899
Mem 1072
Pro S Nyström, J Hämäläinen
Holes 18 L 5900 m SSS 71
Fees 100fmk (120fmk)
Loc 7km W of Helsinki

Suur-Helsingin (1965)

Franzeninkatu 3B, 81 0050 Helsinki
Tel 855 8687
Mem 800
Pro M Louhio
Holes 9 L 5970 m SSS 72
Fees WD/WE–100fmk
Loc 20km N of Helsinki
Mis Season May–Sept

Tuusulan (1984)

PL 178 04301 Hyryla
Tel (90) 251464/251469
Mem 788
Pro M Luukkonen
Holes 9 L 5860 SSS 69
Fees 80fmk (100fmk)
Loc 30km N of Helsinki

Karhula

Kymen (1964)

Ilmattarenkatu 16, 48700 Kyminlinna
Tel (952) 14051
Mem 800
Pro L Hilokoski
Holes 18 L 6120 m Par 72
Fees 100fmk
Loc Kotka, Mussalo Island. 120km E of Helsinki

Kokkola

Kokkolan (1957)

Mantykangas 15, Tallasen 15, 67100 Finland
Tel (968) 18905
Mem 50
Holes 9 L 5890 m SSS 70
Fees 50 fmk (100 fmk)
Loc Kokkola 2km

Lahti

Lahden Golf (1959)

15230 Lahti Takkula
Tel (918) 841311
Mem 342
Pro V Kankkoner
Holes 9 L 6102 m SSS 73
Fees D–60fmk W–300fmk
Loc Lahti 6km

Lappeenranta

Viipurin Golf (1938)

54530 Luumäki
Tel (953) 73012
Mem 207
Pro P Ahokas
Holes 9 L 2450 m SSS 65
Fees D–50fmk
Loc Near city centre, behind Etelaac–Saimaa Hospital

Mariehamn

Alands

Haraldsby SF–22410 Godby
Holes 13 L 5350 m SSS 68

Mikkeli

Mikkelin Golf (1967)

Kalervonkatu 5, 50130 Mikkeli
Tel (955) 151759
Holes 9 L 2540 m SSS 68
Fees 50fmk (200fmk)
Loc 384km N of Helsinki. 2km from Mikkeli

Oulu

Oulu (1964)

Maakotkantie 20, B7 90250 Oulu
Tel (981) 571192
Mem 500
Pro J Alatalo
Holes 9 5218 m SSS 68
Fees 50fmk
Loc Kaukovainio, 3km from city

Pori

Porin Golfkerho

Kalafornia, 28100 Pori
Tel 415559
Mem 135
Pro P Makela
Holes 9 L 5650 m SSS 70
Fees D–50fmk
Loc Pori 5km

Tampere

Tammer Golf (1965)

Box 269, SF–33101 Tampere 10
Tel (931) 611316
Mem 450
Pro J Pentikainen
Holes 16 L 5801 m SSS 71
Fees 90fmk
Loc Ruotula, 5km from city

Turku

Aura Golf

Ruissalo 85, Turku 10
Tel (921) 306701/308667
Mem 450
Holes 18 L 5689 m SSS 72
Fees 80fmk (100fmk)
Loc Town centre 9km

Vaasa

Vaasan-Vaasa (1969)

Sandog 3, C34 65100 Vaasa 10 (Office)
Tel (961) 121742 (Sec)
269989 (Clubhouse)
Mem 206
Holes 9 L 2570 m SSS 70
Fees 50fmk
Loc 6km SE of town along Route 717 at Kraklund
Mis Driving range

France

Agen

Agen Bon-Encontre (1982)

Barre, 47240 Bon Encontre
Pro P Navarro
Holes 9 L 2759 m Par 35
Fees 80fr (120fr)
Loc 5km on N113 to Toulouse

Golf d'Albret (1986)

Barbaste, 47230 Lavaroac
Tel 53 65 53 69
Pro J Navas
Holes 18 L 6060 m SSS 72
Fees 90fr (120fr)
Loc Barbaste, 30km W of Agen

Aix-en-Provence

Château L'Arc (1985)

Rousset-sur-Arc, 13710 Fuveau
Tel 42 53 28 38
Mem 320
Pro R Pujol, R Guidetti
Holes 18 L 6300 m SSS 72
Fees 230fr (330fr) 1988 prices
Loc 15km SE of Aix

Aix-les-Bains

Aix-les-Bains (1936)

Avenue du Golf, 73100 Aix-les-Bains
Tel 79 61 23 35
Mem 430
Pro IS Lambie
Holes 18 L 5500 m SSS 71
Fees 150fr (220fr) 1988 prices
Loc 2½ km from Aix. 105km from Lyon

Amiens

Amiens (1951)

80115 Querrieu
Tel 22 91 02 04
Mem 347
Pro B Dachicourt
Holes 18 L 6110 m SSS 72
Fees 140fr (200fr)
Loc 7km NE of Amiens on Route D929

Angers

Angers (1963)

St Jean des Mauvrets, 49320 Brissac
Tel 41 91 96 56
Mem 230
Pro JM Cazaunau
Holes 18 L 5831 m SSS 69
Fees 140fr (180fr)
Loc 14km SE of Angers. Right bank of Loire.

Angoulême

Golf de L'Hirondelle

Chamfleuri 16-Angoulême
Tel 95 24 22
Mem 72
Pro JM Duhalde
Holes 9 L 2500 m SSS 34
Fees D–80fr
Loc Angoulême 1km

Annecy

Lac d'Annecy (1953)

Echarvines, 74290 Talloires
Tel 50 60 12 89
Mem 400
Pro J Noailly, D Bonnaz
Holes 18 L 5017 m SSS 68
Fees 175fr (200fr)
Loc Annecy 13km

Antibes

La Bastide-du-Roy

06410 Biot
Tel 93 65 08 48
Pro H Giraud, L Casella, R Pettavino
Holes 18 L 5064 m SSS 70
Fees 180fr (200fr)
Loc Antibes 5km. Nice 15km

Arcachon

Arcachon (1955)

35 Bd d'Arcachon
33260 La Teste De Buch
Tel 56 54 44 00
Mem 630
Pro J Cantagrel, J Artola, F du Reau
Holes 18 L 6150 m SSS 71
Fees D–160–250fr
Loc Bordeaux 60km

Bar-le-Duc

Golf de Combles

55000 Combles-en-Barrois
Tel 29 45 16 03
Pro M Vian
Holes 9 L 2700 m
Fees 100fr (120fr)
Loc Bar-le-Duc, 70km W of Nancy

Basel

Golf de Bâle (1926)

68220 Hagenthal-le-Bas, Ht Rhin
Tel 89 68 50 91
Mem 630
Pro D Creamer, A Perrone, C Bisel
Holes 18 L 6255 m SSS 74
Fees 150fr (220fr)
Loc Saint Louis 9km. Basel 15km
Mis Open Apr–Oct

La Baule

La Baule (1976)

Domaine de Saint-Denac
44117 Saint-André-des-Eaux
Tel 40 60 46 18
Mem 400
Pro E Mauger
Holes 18 L 6200 m Par 72
Fees 100–270fr
Loc La Baule 3km, nr Avrillac
Mis Driving range

Bayeux

Omaha Beach (1986)

14520 Port-en-Bessin
Tel 31 21 72 94
Mem 370
Pro S Lesne
Holes 18 L 6214 m SSS 72
9 L 2937m
Fees 150–200fr (360–390fr)
Loc 8km N of Bayeux

Bayonne

Golf d'Hossegor (1929)

40 150 Hossegor
Tel 58 43 56 99
Mem 470
Pro Y Hausseguy, M Hausseguy
Holes 18 L 6004 m SSS 71
Fees 230fr
Loc Bayonne 15km

Belle-Ile

Golf de Sauzon (1985)

Sauzon, 56360 Belle-Ile
Tel 97 31 64 65
Mem 280
Holes 18 L 6100 m SSS 72
Fees 200fr
Loc Island off S coast of Brittany near Quiberon
Mis Public course

Belvès

Golf de Lolivarie (1984)

Sagelat, 24170 Belvès
Tel 53 30 22 69
Mem 50
Pro W Moneret
Holes 9 L 2200 m SSS 35
Fees 100fr (120fr)
Loc 60km NW of Cahors. 60km E of Bergerac

Besançon

Besançon

La Chevillote, 25620 Mamirolle
Tel 81 55 73 54
Mem 380
Pro S Graham
Holes 18 L 6080 m SSS 72
Fees 150fr (180fr)
Loc Besançon 12km. Saône 3km

Biarritz

Biarritz (1888)

Av Edith Cavell, 64200 Biarritz
Tel 59 03 71 80
Mem 650
Pro R Simpson, O Leglise, Mlle S Fourment
Holes 18 L 5379 m SSS 69
Fees 150–250fr
Loc City centre 2 mins

Golf de Chiberta (1926)

Boulevard des Plages, 64600 Anglet
Tel 59 63 83 20
Mem 800
Pro P Dufourg, H Brousson
Holes 18 L 5901 m SSS 71
Fees 150–250fr
Loc Biarritz 3km. Bayonne 5km. Airport 5km
Mis Starting time necessary WE and High Season

Bitche

Bitche Expansion Golf (1988)

Rue des Prés, 57230 Bitche
Tel 87 96 15 30
Mem 500
Pro D Taylor, G Copp
Holes 18 L 6200 m SSS 72
9 L 2500 m SSS 34
Fees 18 holes 110fr (180fr)
9 holes 70fr (110fr)
Loc 75km NW of Strasbourg. 55km SE of Saarbrücken
Mis Public course

Bordeaux

Golf Bordelais (1900)

Domaine de Kater, Av d'Eysines
3320 Bordeaux-Caudéran
Tel 56 28 56 04
Mem 492
Pro M Saubaber, GB Morgan
Holes 18 L 4833 m SSS 67
Fees 160fr (200fr)
Loc Bordeaux 3km
Mis Course closed Mon

Golf Municipal de Bordeaux

Avenue de Pernon, 33300 Bordeaux
Tel 56 50 92 72
Mem 1300
Pro J Delgado, J Purgato, V Fructuoso, JM Duhalde
Holes 18 L 6083 m SSS 72
Fees 125fr
Mis Public course. Closed Tues

Sporting Club de Cameyrac (1972)

Cameyrac, 33450 Saint-Loubes
Tel 56 72 96 79
Mem 400
Pro V Bouneau
Holes 18 L 6057 m SSS 72
9 L 1600 m SSS 28
Fees 120fr (170fr)
Loc Bordeaux 15km

Bourg-St-Maurice

Golf des Arcs

Arc 1800, 73700 Bourg-St-Maurice
Tel 79 07 48 00
Mem 700
Pro A Leclerq, R Gollias, JC Bard
Holes 18 L 4900 m SSS 67
Fees D–105fr
Loc Les Arcs 90km E of Chambery on N90
Mis 4 holes pitch and putt

La Bretesche

La Bretesche (1968)

Domaine de la Bretesche
44780 Missillac
Tel 40 88 30 03
Mem 300
Pro T Mathon
Holes 18 L 6040 m SSS 72
Fees 120–250fr
Loc Pontchâteau 8km. Nantes 50km. Vannes 50km

Brive

Golf du Coiroux

Aubazine, 19190 Beynat
Tel 55 27 24 69
Pro JF Encuentra
Holes 9 L 2851 m SSS 35
Fees 70fr (80fr)
Loc 15km E of Brive
Mis Public course

Cabourg

Cabourg Lehome (1955)

38 Av Président Réné Coty, Le Home
Varaville, 14390 Cabourg
Tel 31 91 25 56
Mem 300
Pro L Allain
Holes 18 L 5122 m SSS 68
Fees On application
Loc Cabourg 2km

Clair Vallon

14510 Conneville
Tel 31 91 07 12
Pro JP Chardonnet
Holes 18 L 5830 m SSS 72
Fees 45fr (100fr)
Loc On road to Conneville

Cannes

Cannes (1891)

06210-Mandelieu-La Napoule
Tel 93 49 55 39
Mem 300
Pro A Monge, R Gorgerino, R Damiano, C Nunez
Holes 18 L 5871 m SSS 71
9 L 2852 m SSS 34
Fees 220fr (250fr)
Loc Mandelieu, 7km W of Cannes

Cannes-Mougins (1978)

175 Route d'Antibes, 06250 Mougins
Tel 93 75 79 13
Mem 330 170(L) 50(J)
Pro M Damiano, L Autiero, P Lemaire, R Sorrel
Holes 18 L 6300 m SSS 72
Fees 230fr (260fr)
Loc Cannes 8km. Nice 18km

Golf de Valbonne (1966)

06560 Valbonne
Tel 93 42 00 08
Mem 350
Pro J Norsworthy 93 42 05 29
Holes 18 L 5905 m Par 72
Fees 170fr (220fr)
Loc Cannes 15km. Nice Airport 20km

Carnac

St Laurent (1975)

Ploemel, 56400 Auray
Tel 97 56 85 18
Mem 450
Pro J Piron, L Miriel
Holes 18 L 6112 m SSS 72
9 L 3020 m SSS 35
Fees 110–180fr
Loc Ploemel, 16km from Carnac and Auray
Mis Public course

Chalon-sur Saône

Chalon-sur-Saône

Chatenoy-en-Bresse, 71380 Saint-Marcel
Tel 85 48 61 64
Pro J Vezin
Holes 18 L 5844 m SSS 71
Fees 45fr
Loc 2km SE of Chalon
Mis Public course. Pitch and putt

Chamonix

Chamonix (1934)

BP 31 74402 Chamonix Cedex
Tel 50 53 06 28
Mem 292
Pro R Marro, JC Bonnaz, G Ravanel
Holes 18 L 6087 m SSS 72
Fees 150–180fr 5D–850fr
Loc Chamonix Centre 2km on RN 506. Geneva 60km

Chaource

Troyes-la Cordelière

10210 Château de la Cordelière
Tel 25 40 11 05
Mem 362
Pro M Vian
Holes 18 L 6033 m SSS 72
Fees 180fr (450fr)
Loc NE of Chaource on N443. Troyes 30km

Charleville

Golf des Ardennes

Les Poursaudes, Villers-le-Tilleul, 08430 Poix-Terron
Holes 6 L 1605 m SSS 24
Fees 50fr
Loc 20km SE of Charleville

Châtellerault

Châtellerault (1987)

7 Rue Choisnin, 86100 Châtellerault
Tel 49 86 20 21
Pro J Ayala
Holes 18 L 5813 m SSS 71
Fees 130fr (150fr)
Loc La Roche-Posay, 20km E of Châtellerault. 40km NE of Poitiers

Chaussy

Villarceaux

Chaussy, 95710 Bray-et-Lu
Tel 34 67 73 83
Pro R Alsuguren
Holes 18 L 6213 m SSS
Fees 25fr (60fr)
Loc 40km NW of Paris

Cherbourg

Cherbourg (1973)

Domaine des Roches, 50470-La Glacerie
Tel 33 44 45 48
Mem 270
Pro J-F Lenoir
Holes 9 L 2842 m SSS 36
Fees 90fr (100fr)
Loc 6km S of Cherbourg

Clermont Ferrand

Golf de Charade (1985)

Charade 631, 30 Royat
Tel 73 35 73 09
Mem 250
Pro R Picabea
Holes 9 L 2300 m SSS 32
Fees D–70fr (90fr)
Loc 8km W of Clermont-Ferrand. Royat 3km

Golf des Volcans (1984)

La Bruyère des Moines 63870 Orcines
Tel 73 62 15 51
Mem 500
Pro L Roux, G Roux, O Roux
Holes 18 L 6242 m SSS 72
9 L 1815 m SSS 29
Fees 170fr (240fr)
Loc 12km W of Clermont-Ferrand on RN 141

Golf du Rigolet (1928)

63240 Le Mont-Dore
Tel 73 21 00 79
Pro L Mencagli
Holes 9 L 4230 m SSS 68
Fees D–30fr W–150fr
Loc 2½ km Mont-Dore. 35km SW of Clermont-Ferrand

Cognac

Cognac (1987)

Saint-Brice, 16100 Cognac
Tel 45 32 18 17
Mem 650
Pro M Vickery
Holes 18 L 6255 m SSS 72
Fees 145fr (180fr)
Loc 5km from Cognac

Compiègne

Compiègne (1895)

Avenue Royale, 60200 Compiègne
Tel (16) 44 40 15 73
Mem 800
Pro M Amat
Holes 18 L 5873 m SSS 71
Fees 150fr (300fr)
Loc Centre of town. 70km NE of Paris

Coutainville

Coutainville (1925)

Agon, 50230 Coutainville
Tel 33 47 03 31
Mem 284
Pro JF Lenoir
Holes 9 L 5360 m SSS 69
Fees 90–130fr
Loc 75km S of Cherbourg. 12km W of Coutances

Deauville

New GC Deauville (1929)

14 Saint Arnoult, 14800 Deauville
Tel 31 88 20 53
Mem 600
Pro C Hausseguy
Holes 18 L 5933 m SSS 71
9 L 3033 m SSS 72
Fees 130–160fr (200–250fr)
Loc 3km S of Deauville

Saint-Gatien (1987)

14130 Saint-Gatien-des-Bois
Tel 31 65 19 99
Mem 120
Pro D Hausseguy, M Ortega

Holes 18 L 6200 m SSS 72
9 L 3000 m SSS 36
Fees 160–200fr (240–300fr)
Loc 8km E of Deauville

Dieppe

Dieppe (1897)

76200 Dieppe
Tel 35 84 25 05
Mem 430
Pro S Ortiz
Holes 18 L 5854 m SSS 71
Fees 140–150fr (170–180fr 2D–260fr)
Loc Dieppe 1½ km

Dijon

Dijon-Bourgogne (1972)

Bois des Norges, 21490 Norges La Ville
Tel 80 35 71 10
Mem 350
Pro B Radcliffe
Holes 18 L 6164 m SSS 72
9 hole pitch and putt
Fees 140fr (200fr)
Loc 10km N of Dijon towards Langres

Dinard

Dinard

35 Saint-Briac-sur-Mer
Tel 34 32 07
Mem 150
Pro F Cavalo, A Curely, Miss Le Derff
Holes 18 L 5486 m SSS 71
Fees 150fr
Loc Dinard 8km

Divonne-les-Bains

Golf de Divonne (1931)

01220 Divonne-les-Bains
Tel 50 20 07 19
Mem 600
Pro M Alsurguren, M Suhas
Holes 18 L 6055 m SSS 72
Fees 200fr
Loc Divonne ½ km. Geneva 18km

Douai

Golf de Thumeries (1932)

Bois Lenglart, 59239 Thumeries
Tel 20 86 58 98
Mem 285
Pro B Tiradon
Holes 9 L 2923 m SSS 36
Fees 80fr (120fr)
Loc 15km S of Lille
Mis Max handicap 24

Dunkerque

Dunkerque

Public

Fort Vallières, Coudekerque-Village, 59380 Bergues
Tel 28 61 07 43
Holes 9 L 2785 m SSS 35
Fees 30–45fr (50–70fr)
Loc SE of Dunkerque
Mis Public course

Épinal

Images d'Épinal (1985)

Rue du Merle-Blanc, 88001 Épinal
Tel 29 31 45 45
Pro R Golias, D Mory
Holes 18 L 5700 m SSS 70
Fees D-60fr
Loc Épinal, 70km S of Nancy
Mis Public course

Étretat

Marin D'Étretat (1908)

BP No 7, 76790 Étretat
Tel 35 27 04 89 (Office)
27 04 56 (Clubhouse)
Mem 320
Pro J Morea
Holes 18 L 5840 m SSS 72
Fees 130–175fr (190–265fr 2D–330–400fr)
Loc 28km N of Le Havre. Étretat ½ km

Évian

Royal Club Évian (1905)

Rive Sud du lac de Genève, 74500 Évian
Tel 50 75 14 00
Mem 240
Pro J Moller, Ch Rey, Ch Victor
Holes 18 L 6005 m SSS 71
Fees 210–290fr (260–320fr)
Loc Évian 2km. Geneva Airport 40km
Mis All-inclusive stay at Royal Club Évian–free access to golf. Only 9 holes playable from Sept 1989

La Ferté Macé

Bagnoles-de-l'Orne (1925)

Route de Domfront, 61140 Bagnoles-de-l'Orne
Tel 33 37 81 42
Pro H Dauge
Holes 9 L 2200 m SSS 70
Fees D–40fr (60fr) W–180fr
Loc Bagnoles, 80km S of Caen
Mis Public course

Flaine

Flaine-les-Carroz (1984)

74300 Flaine
Tel 50 90 85 44
Mem 50
Pro M Malafosse
Holes 18 L 4180 m Par 63
Fees 130fr
Loc Flaine 4km. Geneva Airport 60km

Fontainebleau

Fontainebleau (1908)

Route d'Orleans, 77300 Fontainebleau
Tel 64 22 22 95
Mem 450
Pro JP Hirigoyen
Holes 18 L 6067 m SSS 72
Fees 300fr (580fr)
Loc City limits 2km

Granville

Golf Municipal de Bréhal (1964)

50290 Bréhal
Tel 33 51 58 88
Mem 320
Holes 9 L 2055 m Par 31
Fees 80–100fr
Loc 10km N of Granville along St Martin beach
Mis Public course

Granville (1912)

Pavillon du Golf, Bréville, 50290 Bréhal
Tel 33 50 23 06
Mem 290
Pro A Quibeuf
Holes 18 L 5854 m Par 72
9 L 2323 m Par 33
Fees 18 holes 100–150fr
9 holes 80–100fr
Loc 5km from Granville towards Coutances

Grenoble

Grenoble (1986)

"Les Alberges", Vaulnaveys-le-Haut, 38410 Uriage
Tel 76 89 03 47
Mem 500
Pro A Paligot
Holes 9 L 2235 m SSS 33
Fees 140fr
Loc 15km SE of Grenoble

Hardelot

Golf d'Hardelot

3, Avenue de Golf,
62152 Neufchâtel-Hardelot
Tel 21 83 73 10
Mem 650
Pro L Maisonnave
Holes 18 L 5870 m SSS 72
Fees 160fr (250fr)
Loc Hardelot, 15km S of Boulogne

Le Havre

Golf du Havre (1933)

Hameau Saint-Supplix
76930 Octeville-sur-Mer
Tel 35 46 36 50/46 36 11
Mem 450
Pro D Rudloff
Holes 18 L 5830 m SSS 71
Fees 130fr (300fr)
Loc 10km N of Le Havre

Hyères

Golf de Valcros (1964)

83 La Londe-les Maures
Tel 66 81 02
Pro M Berthet
Holes 18 L 5050 m SSS 70
Fees 180fr (250fr)
Loc Le Lavandou 16km

Lacanau

Golf de L'Ardilouse (1980)

Domaine de l'Ardilouse,
33680 Lacanau-Océan
Tel 56 03 25 60
Mem 220
Pro P Delaville, O Rougeot
Holes 18 L 6000 m SSS 72
Fees 130–150fr (150–200fr)
Loc Bordeaux 45km

Landerneau

Brest-Iroise

Parc des Loisirs de Lann-Rohou,
29220 Landerneau
Tel 98 85 16 17/85 19 39
Pro D Roumaud
Holes 18 L 6213 m SSS 72
Fees 100fr
Loc 15km E of Brest
Mis Public course. Closed Tues

Lannion

Saint-Samson (1964)

Route de Kérénoc,
22560 Pleumeur-Bodou
Tel 96 23 87 34
Mem 250
Pro D Fournet
Holes 18 L 5682 m SSS 72
Fees D–150fr (D–180fr)
Loc 7km N of Lannion on Tregastel Road

Laval

Laval (1972)

Le Jariel, 53000 Changé-Les-Laval
Tel (42) 201870
Holes 9 L 3050 m SSS 36
Fees D–90fr (100fr 2D–150fr)
Loc 7km N of Laval

Lille

Golf de Bondues (1968)

Chateau de la Vigne, 59910 Bondues
Tel 20 23 20 62
Mem 930
Pro P Iturrioz, A Vandamme, A White
Holes 18 L 6223 m SSS 73
9 L 3044 m SSS 36
Fees D–200fr (D–300fr)
Loc Roubaix 10km. Tourcoing 5km. Lille 10km
Mis Handicap certificate required

Golf de Brigode

36 Avenue de Golf, 59650 Villeneuve D'Ascq
Tel 20 91 17 86
Mem 600
Pro R Pollet
Holes 18 L 6182 m SSS 72
Fees 200fr (300fr)
Loc 8km NE of Lille
Mis Closed Tues

Golf des Flandres (1957)

137, Bd Clemenceau, 59700 Marcq (Lille)
Tel 20 72 20 74
Mem 370
Pro R Loth, P Delobelle
Holes 9 L 2317 m SSS 33
Fees 150fr
Loc 4km from Lille, on Croise Laroche racecourse

Golf du Sart (1910)

5 Rue Jean Jaures,
59650 Villeneuve D'Ascq
Tel 20 72 02 51
Mem 510
Pro R Loth, F Swaelens
Holes 18 L 5750 m SSS 71
Fees 200fr (2D–300fr)
Loc Motorway Lille-Ghent. Exit Wasquehal

Limoges

Golf Municipal de Limoges (1976)

Avenue du Golf, 87000 Limoges
Tel 55 31 21 02
Pro R Larretche
Holes 18 L 6218 m SSS 72
Fees 50fr
Loc S of Limoges on N20
Mis Public course

Loudun

Loudun Saint-Hilaire

Roiffe, 86120 Les Trois-Moutiers
Tel 49 98 78 06
Mem 320
Pro T Abbas
Holes 18 L 6325 m Par 72
Fees 110fr (160fr)
Loc Loudun 15km. Saumur 20km
Mis Public course

Luchon

Luchon (1908)

Route de Montauban, 31110 Luchon
Tel 61 79 03 27
Mem 200
Pro A Alcazar
Holes 9 L 2375 m SSS 66
Fees 90fr (100fr)
Loc Luchon, 90km SE of Tarbes

Lyon

La Dombes (1986)

Mionnay, 01390 St-André-de-Corcy
Tel 78 91 84 84
Mem 220
Pro F Dietsch
Holes 9 L 2484 m SSS 70
Fees 80fr (130fr)
Loc 20km N of Lyon towards Bourg

Lyon (1964)

38280 Villette-d'Anthon
Tel 78 31 11 33
Mem 750
Pro L Capoccia
Holes 27 L 6415 m SSS 72
Fees 130fr (250fr)
Loc Lyon 25km

Lyon-Verger (1977)

69360 Saint-Symphorien D'Ozon
Tel 78 02 84 20
Mem 590
Pro H Sauzet, B Lacroix, P Malartre

Holes 18 L 5900 m SSS 71
Fees 150fr (230fr)
Loc 14km S of Lyon on A7 exit Solaize, or RN7 2km S of Feyzin
Mis Closed Fri

Mâcon

Golf de la Commanderie (1964)

L'Aumusse Crottet, 01290 Pont-de-Veyle
Tel **85 33 44 12/85 30 40 24**
Mem 250
Pro C Soules, P Wakeford
Holes 18 L 5465 yds SSS 69
Fees 150fr (200fr)
Loc 7km from Mâcon on RN 79 to Bourg-en-Bresse

Manosque

Pierrevert (1986)

Domaine de la Grande-Gardette, 04860 Pierrevert
Tel **92 72 17 19**
Mem 450
Pro L Dubouexic 92 72 05 69
Holes 18 L 6040 m SSS 72
Fees 180fr (230fr)
Loc 45km NE of Aix-en-Provence. 5km from Manosque

Le Mans

Mans Mulsanne (1961)

72230 Arnage
Tel **43 42 00 36**
Mem 400
Pro M Dugue
Holes 18 L 5756 m SSS 71
Fees 120–180fr (190–285fr)
Loc Mulsanne. Le Mans 12km
Mis Handicap certificate required

Marseille

Marseille-Aix (1935)

Les Milles 13290
Tel **42 24 40 41/42 24 23 01**
Mem 550
Pro R Patrick, B Cotton
Holes 18L 6302 m SSS 72
Fees 170fr (320fr)
Loc Aix-en-Provence 7km. Marignane airport 15km. Marseille 20km

Mazamet

Golf de la Barouge (1956)

81660 Pont de l'Arn
Tel **63 61 08 00**
Mem 350
Pro J-M Roca
Holes 18 L 5623 m SSS 70
Fees 150fr (200fr)
Loc 2km N of Mazamet. 82km E of Toulouse

Megève

Mont-d'Arbois

74120 Megève
Tel **50 21 29 79**
Mem 400
Pro JB Alsuguren, G Parodi, P Provençal
Holes 18 L 6100 m SSS 72
Fees 180–260fr
Loc Megève 2km
Mis Competitions every WE

Méribel

Méribel-les-Allues

73550 Meribel Altiport
Tel **79 08 50 25 (Sec)**
Pro G Watine, G Martin
Holes 9 L 2433 m SSS 67
Fees 100fr
Loc 15km S of Moutiers

Metz

Metz-Cherisey (1964)

Château de Cherisey, 57240 Verny
Tel **87 52 70 18**
Mem 390
Pro J Gould
Holes 9 L 5800 m Par 70
Fees 100fr (150fr)
Loc 13km SE of Metz

Montargis

Golf de Vaugouard (1987)

Fontenay-sur-Loing, 45210 Ferrières
Tel **38 95 81 52**
Mem 350
Pro P Iturrioz
Holes 18 L 6103 m SSS 72
Fees 180fr (300fr)
Loc 10km N of Montargis. Paris 100km

Montbéliard

Golf de Prunevelle (1930)

Ferme des Petits-Bans, Dampierre-sur-le-Doubs
Tel **81 98 11 77/33 03 04**
Mem 300
Pro R Lesouder
Holes 18 L 6281 m SSS 73
Fees 140fr (180fr)
Loc 10km S of Montbéliard. Motorway A36 exit Montbéliard Sud via Besançon on D126 to Dampierre-sur-le-Doubs
Mis Open 15 Mar–10 Oct

Mont-de-Marsan

Golf du Marsan

40090 Saint-Avit
Tel **58 75 63 05 (Sec)**
Pro P Navaro
Holes 9 L 2413 m SSS 34
Fees 80fr
Loc Mont-de-Marsan 8km. 80km N of Pau
Mis Covered practice range

Montebourg

Fontenay-en-Cotentin (1975)

Fontenay-sur-Mer, 50310 Montebourg
Tel **33 21 44 27**
Mem 90
Pro A Quiboeuf (Summer)
Holes 9 L 3050 m Par 36
Fees 80fr (100fr)
Loc 15km SE of Valognes (station of turbo train Paris–Cherbourg). 32km SE of Cherbourg by RN13/D42

Monte Carlo

Monte Carlo (1910)

Mont Agel, La Turbie, 06320 Cap D'Ail
Tel **93 41 09 11**
Mem 420
Pro B Ducoulombier, C Houtart, R Halsall
Holes 18 L 5667 m SSS 71
Fees 220fr (350fr)
Loc La Turbie
Mis Handicap certificate required

Montluçon

Golf du Val-de-Cher

Nassigny, 03190 Vallon-en-Sully
Tel **70 06 71 15**
Mem 200
Pro JC Gassiat
Holes 18 L 5200 m
Fees 140fr (Sun–200fr 2D–350fr)
Loc Nassigny, N of Montluçon on N144
Mis Closed Tues

Montpellier

Coulondres (1984)

4, Rue des Erables, 34980 Saint-Gely-du-Fesc
Tel **67 84 13 75**
Mem 250
Pro V Schwechlen
Holes 9 L 3100 m SSS 36
Fees 110fr (130fr)
Loc 10km N of Montpellier towards Ganges

La Grande-Motte

Club-House de Golf, 34280 La Grande-Motte
Tel 67 56 05 00
Mem 300
Pro P Porquier
Holes 18 L 6200 m SSS 72
9 L 4000 m
6 hole course
Fees 180fr (230fr 2D-400fr)
Loc SE of Montpellier. 10km from Airport
Mis Public course

Montreuil

Nampont-St-Martin (1978)

Maison Forte, 80120 Nampont-St-Martin
Tel 22 29 92 90/25 00 20
Mem 300
Pro H Marconi, S Kershaw
Holes 18 L 5505 m SSS 71
Fees 100fr (120f 3D–250fr)
Loc 12km S of Montreuil sur Mer on route N1. 30km SE of Le Touquet
Mis Driving range

Mulhouse

Golf du Rhin (1969)

BP1152 F68053 Mulhouse Cedex
Tel 89 26 07 86
Mem 500
Pro JF Halliwell
Holes 18 L 6362 m SSS 72
Fees 150fr (220fr)
Loc Ile du Rhin-Chalampe, 20km E of Mulhouse

Nancy

Nancy-Aingeray

Aingeray, 54460 Liverdun
Tel 28 25 76 46
Mem 250
Pro P Delaville
Holes 18 L 5510 m SSS 69
Fees 35fr (75fr)
Loc Nancy 17km

Nantes

Nantes

44360 Vigneux de Bretagne
Tel 40 63 25 82
Mem 430
Pro N Gajan
Holes 18 L 5940 m SSS 72
Fees 130fr (200fr)
Loc Nantes 15km

Nevers

Golf du Nivernais

58400 Magny Cours
Tel 86 58 18 30
Mem 350
Pro P Raguet
Holes 15 L 2500 m SSS 70
Fees 60fr (120fr)
Loc 12km from Nevers on N7
Mis Public course

Nîmes

Golf de Campagne

Route de Saint Gilles 30, Nîmes
Tel 37 43 57
Pro M Ado, E Lassale
Holes 18 L 6200 m SSS 72
Fees 25fr (50fr)
Loc Nîmes 9km

Orléans

Les Bordes (1986)

La Ferté St Cyr, 41220 Saint-Laurent-Nouant
Tel 54 87 72 13
Pro C Young
Holes 18 L 6436 m Par 72
Fees 300fr (600fr)
Loc 30km SW of Orléans

Golf de Marcilly (1986)

45240 Marcilly-en-Villette
Tel 38 76 11 73
Mem 340
Pro G Raison, P Guichard
Holes 18 L 6324 m SSS 73
9 hole course
Fees 100fr (160fr)
Loc 20km SE of Orléans

Golf de Sologne (1955)

Country Club des Olleries, Route de Jouy-le-Potier, 45160 Ardon
Tel 38 76 57 33/76 68 79
Pro M Vickery
Holes 18 L 7200 yds Par 72
9 L 2700 yds Par 35
Fees 90fr (140fr)
Loc 25km S of Orléans on RN20. Paris 150km

Val de Loire

45450 Donnery
Tel 38 59 20 48/38 59 25 15
Pro JM Duboc
Holes 18 L 5840 m SSS 72
Fees D–180fr (250fr 2D–420fr)
Loc 16km E of Orléans

Orthez

Salies-de-Béarn (1988)

Route d'Orthez, 64270 Salies-de-Béarn
Tel 59 38 37 59
Mem 80
Holes 9 L 2300 m SSS 62
Fees 80–100fr (100–120fr)
Loc 16km W of Orthez. Pau 50km. Biarritz 60km

Paimpol

Golf de Boisgelin

Pléhédel, 22290 Lanvollon
Tel 96 22 31 24
Holes 9 L 2356 m Par 34
Fees 70fr (100fr)
Loc 10km S of Paimpol on D7. 35km from Saint-Brieuc

Paris

Chantilly (1908)

Vineuil Saint Firmin, 60500 Chantilly
Tel 44 57 04 43
Mem 450
Pro A Chardonnet, P Leglise, G Lamy
Holes 18 L 6250 m SSS 71
9 L 2625 m SSS 35
Fees WD–200fr
Loc Paris 45km
Mis WE–only with member

Chaumont-en-Vexin (1963)

60240 Chaumont-en-Vexin
Tel (1) 44 49 00 81/44 49 14 76
Mem 350
Holes 18 L 6190 m Par 72
Fees WD–150fr
Loc Paris 60km

Chevry (1976)

91190 Gif-sur-Yvette
Tel (1) 60 12 40 33
Pro D Maxwell, P Maréchal
Holes 9 L 2701 m SSS 36
9 hole Pitch and putt
Mis Public course

Coudray (1960)

91830 Le Coudray-Montceaux
Tel (1) 64 93 81 76
Mem 700
Pro JL Schneider, M Lebrun
Holes 18 L 5530 m SSS 70
9 L 1615 m
Fees 170fr (360fr)
Loc Paris 35km on A6

For explanation of abbreviations, see page 202.

Domont-Montmorency

Route de Montmorency, 95330 Domont
Tel (1) 39 91 07 50
Pro R Changart, Ch Gassiat, P Senez
Holes 18 L 5775 m SSS 71
Fees 220fr (420fr)
Loc Paris 18km
Mis Pitch and putt

Fourqueux (1963)

8 Rue St Nom, 78112 Fourqueux
Tel (1) 34 51 41 47
Mem 520
Pro H Gioux
Holes 18 and 9 L 6410 m SSS 73
Fees 200fr (300fr)
Loc St Germain-en-Laye 4km

Golf d'Isabella (1969)

RN12 Sainte-Appoline, 78370 Plaisir
Tel (1) 30 54 10 62
Mem 280
Holes 9 L 2454 m SSS 34
Fees 170fr (280fr) 1988 prices
Loc Paris 28km RN12 to Dreux

Golf d'Ormesson (1969)

94490 Ormesson-sur-Marne
Tel (1) 45 76 20 71
Mem 400
Pro G Minassian, F Leclercq
Holes 18 L 6180 m SSS 72
Fees 170fr (350fr)
Loc Paris 21km

Golf de Villennes (1985)

Public

CV 2 Route d'Orgeval, 78670 Villennes-sur-Seine
Tel (1) 39 75 30 00
Mem 3000
Pro P Guy, O Jaret
Holes 9 L 3000 m SSS 36
Fees 88fr (150fr)
Loc W of Paris of N13
Mis Driving range. Public course.

Golf de la Chapelle (1987)

Ferme de Monpichet, 77580 Crécy-la-Chapelle
Tel (1) 64 04 70 75
Mem 150
Pro P Merel
Holes 18 L 6211 m SSS 72
Fees 150fr (300fr)
Loc 20km E of Paris by A4

Golf de la Grenouillère

Île de la Grenouillère, 78290 Croissy-sur-Seine
Tel (1) 39 18 43 81
Mem 400
Pro P Lefebvre, A Alsuguren, JP Kevorkian, C Paillet
Holes 9 L 2120 m SSS 27
Fees 120fr (240fr)
Loc Paris 25km

Golf du Prieuré

78440 Gargenville Sailly
Tel (1) 476 70 12
Mem 1200
Pro J Alsuguren, M Lachaux, G Bourdy
Holes 18 L 6216 m SSS 72
18 L 6317 m SSS 72
Fees 50fr (140fr)
Loc Mantes La Jolie, 10km W of Paris. Meulan 9km

International Club du Lys

Rond-Point du Grand Cerf, 60260 Lamorlaye
Tel (1) 44 21 26 00
Pro F Saubaber
Holes 18 L 5986 m SSS 71
18 L 4798 m SSS 66
Fees 200fr (400fr)
Loc Chantilly 5km

Meaux-Boutigny (1985)

Le Bordet, Rue de Barrois, 77470 Trilport
Tel (1) 60 25 63 98
Mem 450
Pro A Delannoy
Holes 18 L 6100 m SSS 72
9L 1600 m SSS 30
Fees 160fr (300fr)
Loc 45km E of Paris Highway 4

Morfontaine (1926)

Mortefontaine, 60128 Plailly
Tel (1) 44 54 68 27
Mem 450
Pro S De Galard, M Philippon
Holes 18 L 6063 m SSS 72
9 L 2550 m SSS 36
Fees WD–300fr
Loc Senlis 10km
Mis WE–only with member

Ozoir-la-Ferrière (1926)

Château des Agneaux, 77330 Ozoir-la-Ferrière
Tel (1) 60 28 20 79
Mem 450
Pro M Alsuguren, G Henichard
Holes 18 L 6105 m SSS 72
9 L 2235 m SSS 33
Fees 18 holes 150fr (200fr)
9 holes 100fr (150fr)
Loc From Paris A4 (Sortie Val Maubuée)

Racing Club de France

La Boulie, 7800 Versailles
Tel (1) 950 59 41
Mem 950
Pro CH Bonardi, F Castel, M Garaialde, JP Quillo
Holes 18 L 6055 m SSS 72
18 L 6206 m SSS 72
9 L 1148 m
Fees 160fr (300fr)
Loc Paris 15km

Rochefort

78730 Rochefort-en-Yvelines
Tel (1) 484 31 81
Pro E Demiautte
Holes 18 L 6020 m SSS 73
Fees 35fr (85fr)
Loc Paris 35km

Saint-Aubin (1976)

91190 Saint-Aubin
Tel (1) 941 25 19
Pro C Chabrier, B Antoine
Holes 18 L 6100 m SSS 72
Fees 30fr (36fr)
Loc SW of Paris
Mis Public course

Saint-Cloud (1911)

60 Rue du 19 Janvier, Garches 92380
Tel (1) 47 01 01 85
Mem 2000
Pro R Giraud, F Berthet, A Leclerc
Holes 18 L 6145 m SSS 72
18 L 5135 m SSS 68
Fees 250fr (420fr)
Loc Porte Dauphine, Paris 9km
Mis Handicap certificate required

Saint-Germain-en-Laye (1922)

Route de Poissy, 78100 St-Germain-en-Laye
Tel (1) 34 51 75 90
Mem 800
Pro M Dallemagne, E Lafitte O St-Hilaire, D Hausseguy
Holes 18 L 6024 m SSS 72
9 L 2030 m SSS 33
Fees 300fr
Loc 20km from Paris
Mis WE–only with member

Saint-Nom-La-Bretêche (1959)

78860 Saint-Nom-La-Bretêche
Tel (1) 34 62 54 00
Mem 1600
Sec P Galitzine
Pro A Cadet, R Golias, A Ferran, P Rouquet, G Leven
Holes 18 L 6685 yds SSS 72
18 L 6712 yds SSS 72
Fees WD only–350fr
Loc Paris 24km on A–13
Mis Handicap certificate required

Saint-Quentin-en-Yvelines

Base de Loisirs RN12, 78190 Trappes
Tel (1) 30 50 86 40
Pro JP Chardonnet

Holes	18 L 5900 m SSS 71
	9 L 3063 m SSS 36
Loc	20km SW of Paris
Mis	Public course

Seraincourt

Gaillonnet, 95450 Vigny
Tel **(1) 34 75 47 28**
Mem 380
Pro G Alexandre
Holes 18 L 5811 m SSS 70
Fees 200fr (400fr)
Loc Paris 35km

St-Pierre-du-Perray (1974)

St-Pierre-du-Perray, 91100 Corbeil
Tel **(1) 075 17 47**
Pro B Antoine
Holes 18 L 6247 m SSS 72
Fees 40fr (56fr)
Loc SE of Paris off N6
Mis Public course

Vaucouleurs

78910 Civry-la-Forêt
Tel **(1) 34 87 62 29**
Mem 350
Pro D Chaumillon
Holes 18 L 6257 m SSS 73
Fees 225fr (400fr)
Loc 50km W of Paris between Mantes and Houdan

Parthenay

Golf de Mazières

Le Petit Chêne, 79310 Mazières-en-Gâtine
Tel **49 63 28 33**
Mem 150
Pro V Dufresne–Heniau
Holes 18 L 6060 m SSS 72
Fees 95fr (150fr)
Loc 15km SW of Parthenay. 25km NE of Niort
Mis Public course

Pau

Pau (1856)

Rue de Golf, 64140 Pau-Billère
Tel **59 32 02 33**
Mem 530
Pro A Harismendy
Holes 18 L 5389 m SSS 69
Fees 170fr (200fr)
Loc Pau 2km

Royal GC Artiguelouve

Domaine St Michel, 64230 Lescar
Tel **59 83 09 29**
Mem 400
Pro R Darrieumerlou, A Lopez
Holes 18 L 6063 m Par 71
Fees 150fr (180fr)
Loc 8km from Pau off Bayonne road

Périgueux

Périgueux (1980)

Domaine de Saltgourde, 24430 Marsac
Tel **53 53 02 35**
Mem 412
Pro C Campbell
Holes 18 L 6120 m SSS 71 (July 1989)
Fees 90fr W–400fr M–800fr
Loc Angoulême–Riberac road. Périgueux 3km
Mis Public course

Perpignan

St Cyprien (1974)

Le Mas D'Huston, 66750 St Cyprien Plage
Tel **68 21 01 71**
Mem 700
Pro P Lacroix, BI Diagne, E Bocau
Holes 18 L 6480 m SSS 73
9 L 2724 m SSS 35
Fees Resort guests–140fr
Others–160fr

Poitiers

Poitevin

Terrain des Chalons 86000
Tel **49 61 23 13**
Mem 100
Pro P Signeux
Holes 9 L 2660 m SSS 35
Fees 85fr (100fr)
Loc Poitiers 3km

Pornic

Pornic (1912)

49 bis, Boulevard de l'Océan, Sainte-Marie/Mer, 44210 Pornic
Tel **40 82 06 69**
Mem 280
Pro G Romain
Holes 9 L 5120 m SSS 68
Fees D–100–180fr
Loc Pornic 1km. Nantes 45km. La Baule 35km.

Quimper

Benodet-Quimper

Clohars-Fouesnant, 29118 Benodet
Tel **98 57 26 16**
Pro JP Sallat
Holes 18 L 6180 m SSS 72
9 hole course
Fees 150fr (190fr)
Loc 12km SE of Quimper
Mis Public course

Quimper-Cornouaille (1959)

Private
Manoir du Mesmeur, 29133 La Forêt-Fouesnant
Tel **98 56 97 09**
Mem 250
Pro L Salgado
Holes 9 L 5641 m SSS 69
Fees D–120fr W–545fr
Loc 15km SE of Quimper

Reims

Reims (1928)

Chateau des Dames de France, 51390 Gueux
Tel **(26) 03 60 14**
Mem 460
Pro P Harrison
Holes 18 L 6026 m SSS 72
Fees 100fr (130fr)
Loc Reims 10km

Rennes

Rennes

Saint-Jacques-de-la-Lande, 35000 Rennes
Tel **99 64 24 18**
Mem 131
Pro P Le Fur
Holes 9 L 2850 m SSS 72
Fees D–100fr (150fr)
Loc Route de Redon, 7km S of Rennes

Roanne

Champlong (1985)

43200 Villerest
Tel **77 69 70 60**
Mem 180
Pro L Moïse
Holes 9 L 2000 m Par 31
Fees 70fr (90fr)
Loc 5km SE of Roanne towards Clermont-Ferrand
Mis Public course

Rouen

Golf du Vaudreuil (1962)

27100 Le Vaudreuil
Tel **32 59 02 60**
Mem 350
Pro J Lecuellet
Holes 18 L 6411 m SSS 73
Fees 130–160fr (200–250fr)
Loc Louviers 6km. Rouen 25km. Paris 100km

Rouen

Rue Boucicaut, Mt St Aignan
Tel **Rouen 71 05 41**
Mem 250
Pro H Gassiat
Holes 18 L 5522 m SSS 71
Fees D–120fr
Loc Rouen 3½ km

Royan

Royan (1977)

Maine-Gaudin, 17420 Saint-Palais
Tel **46 23 16 24**
Mem 415
Pro J-P Prieur
Holes 18 L 6150 m SSS 72
Fees 140fr (170fr)
Loc Saint-Palais, 7km W of Royan
Mis Public course. Closed Tues

Sables-d'Or-les-Pins

Sables-d'Or-les-Pins (1925)

22240 Fréhel
Tel **96 41 42 57**
Mem 140
Pro G Frangeu
Holes 9 L 5253 m SSS 70
Fees D–140fr
Loc Dinard 30km

St Brieuc

Ajoncs d'Or (1976)

Kergrain Lantic, 22410 Saint-Quay Portrieux
Tel **96 71 90 74**
Mem 480
Pro A Pouette, P Rault-Maisonneuve
Holes 18 L 6230 m SSS 72
Fees 130–140fr
Loc 18km N of St Brieuc. Étables 6km. Binic 6km
Mis Public course

St Cast

Pen Guen

22380 Saint-Cast-le-Guildo
Tel **96 41 91 20**
Pro D Benet, L du Bouerie
Holes 9 L 2580 m SSS 70
Fees 80–100fr
Loc Dinard 25km

St Jean-de-Luz

Golf de Chantaco (1928)

Route d'Ascain, 64500 St Jean-de-Luz
Tel **59 26 14 22/26 19 22**
Mem 400
Pro R Garaialde, JC Harismendy
Holes 18 L 5690 m SSS 70
Fees D–130–200fr W–520–760fr
Loc St Jean-de-Luz 2km on Route d'Ascain

La Nivelle (1907)

Place William-Sharp, 64500 Ciboure
Tel **59 47 18 99/59 47 19 72**
Mem 400
Pro P Pée, P Palli
Holes 18 L 5490 m SSS 70
Fees 160–250fr
Loc 1½ km S of St Jean-de-Luz
Mis Max h'cap 18(men) 24(ladies)

St Malo

Golf du Tronchet (1986)

Le Tronchet, 35540 Miniac Morvan
Tel **99 58 96 69**
Mem 200
Pro A Dupas
Holes 18 L 5708 m SSS 71
9 hole course
Fees 120–150fr
Loc 20km S of St Malo off RN 137

St-Raphaël

Valescure (1896)

BP 451, 83704 St-Raphaël Cedex
Tel **98 82 40 46**
Mem 480
Pro E Cougourdan, M Bromet
Holes 18 L 5316 m Par 70
Fees 200fr (250fr)
Loc St-Raphaël 5km

St Tropez

Beauvallon-Grimaud

83120-Sainte Maxime
Tel **96 16 98**
Mem 320
Pro P Delaville
Holes 9 L 2525 m SSS 34
Fees 80–100fr
Loc Sainte Maxime 3km. St Tropez 10km

Saintes

Golf de Saintonge

Fontcouverte, 17100 Saintes
Tel **46 74 27 61**
Mem 350
Pro R Burguet
Holes 9 L 2435 m SSS 68
Fees 80fr (100fr)
Loc Saintes 3km
Mis Public course

Sens

Golf de Clairis (1974)

89150 Savigny-sur-Clairis
Tel **86 86 33 90**
Mem 180
Pro P Schilling
Holes 9
Fees 90fr (160fr)
Loc St Valérien, 12km W of Sens

Strasbourg

Strasbourg (1934)

Route du Rhin, 67400 Illkirch
Tel **88 66 17 22**
Mem 600
Pro IP Tairraz, N Madeuf
Holes 18 L 6047 m SSS 72
Fees WD only–170fr
Loc Strasbourg 10km

Sully-sur-Loire

Sully-sur-Loire

Viglain, 45600 Sully-sur-Loire
Tel **38 01 02 35**
Mem 220
Pro P Antoine
Holes 18 L 5863 m SSS 72
Fees 135fr (250fr)
Loc Sully-sur-Loire 3km

Tarbes

Golf de Laloubère

Public

65310 Laloubère
Tel **62 96 06 22**
Pro M Uturbide
Holes 9 L 3135 m SSS 36
Fees 100fr W–400fr
Loc Tarbes
Mis Public course

Golf de Lannemezan

La Demi-Lune, 65300 Lannemezan
Tel **62 98 01 01**
Pro R Lasserre
Holes 18 L 5945 m SSS 71
Fees 150fr (170fr)
Loc Tarbes 38km

Tende

Golf de Vievola (1978)

06430 Tende (A.M.)
Tel **93 04 61 02**
Mem 40
Pro N Giordano
Holes 9 L 1834 m SSS 60
Fees 90fr (130fr)
Loc 4km from Italian border on RN 204
Mis Open 1 Jun–2 Nov

Tignes

Tignes (1968)

Le Val Claret, 73320 Tignes
Tel **79 06 37 42**
Pro B Kvot, D Saadi
Holes 9 L 1820 m
Fees 100fr W–600fr

Toulouse

Toulouse (1951)

31 Vieille-Toulouse
Tel 61 73 45 48
Mem 380
Pro R Olalainty
Holes 18 L 5400 m SSS 69
Fees 100fr (120fr)
Loc Toulouse 8 mins

Toulouse-Palmola (1973)

31680 Buzet-Sur-Tarn
Tel 61 84 20 50
Pro D Barquez
Holes 18 L 6166 m SSS 72
Fees 180fr (300fr 2D–500fr)
Loc 20km NE of Toulouse

Le Touquet

Golf du Touquet (1904)

Ave du Golf, 62520 Le Touquet
Tel 21 05 20 22
Mem 660
Pro P Philippon
Holes 18 L 5895 m SSS 71
18 L 6140 m SSS 72
9 hole course
Fees 18 holes 200fr (260fr)
9 holes 100fr (140fr)
Loc 2km S of Le Touquet
Mis Brent Walker Group plc

Tours

Golf de Touraine

Château de la Touche, Ballan Miré
37510 Joué-lès-Tours
Tel 47 53 20 28
Mem 520
Pro M Vol, P Tabone 47 67 56 79
Holes 18 L 5745 m SSS 71
Fees 150fr (220fr)

Valenciennes

Valenciennes

59–Marly
Tel 46 30 10
Mem 215
Pro J Roux
Holes 9 L 5190 m SSS 66
Fees 80fr (120fr)
Loc Valenciennes 2km

Vichy

Sporting Club de Vichy (1907)

Allée Baugnies, 03700 Bellerive-sur-Allier
Tel 70 32 39 11
Mem 430
Pro Ch Roumand
Holes 18 L 5427 m SSS 70
Fees 180fr (250fr 2D–380fr)
Loc In city limits

Vigneulles

Golf de Madine

Nonsard, 55210 Vigneulles
Tel 29 89 56 00/29 89 32 50
Mem 30
Pro M Brasset
Holes 9 L 2930 m Par 36
Fees 50fr (80fr)
Loc 40km SE of Verdun.
45km SW of Metz
Mis Public course

Villeneuve-sur-Lot

Golf de Castelnaud (1987)

"La Menuisière", Castelnaud,
47290 Cancon
Tel 53 01 74 64
Mem 200
Pro G de Maugras
Holes 18 L 6349 m SSS 72
9 L 2184 m SSS 27
Fees 100–140fr (120–180fr)
Loc 10km N of Villeneuve.
40km N of Agen
Mis Driving range

Vittel

Vittel

BP 122, 88800 Vittel
Tel 29 08 18 80 (1 May–30 Sept)
Pro M Lachaux, D Mory
Holes 18 L 6236 m SSS 72
18 L 6250 m SSS 72
9 L 1510 m SSS 29
Fees 200fr (250fr)
Loc In city, 70km S of Nancy

Wimereux

Wimereux (1906)

Route d'Ambleteuse, 62930 Wimereux
Tel 21 32 43 20
Mem 500
Pro J-M Flory
Holes 18 L 6361 m Par 62
Fees 175fr (210fr)
Loc 6km N of Boulogne on D940.
30km S of Calais

Germany

Aachen

Aachener (1927)

Schürzelter Str 300, 5100 Aachen
Tel (0241) 12501
Mem 575
Pro W Van Mook
Holes 18 L 5903 m Par 71
Fees D–30DM (D–50DM)
Loc Aachen-Seffent, 5km
from centre

Ansbach

Ansbach

8800 Ansbach, Neustadt 25
Tel (0981) 5617
Pro M Woodhouse
Holes 9 L 4200 m Par 66
Fees 30DM
Loc Colmberg, Ansbach 15km

Lichtenau-Weickershof (1980)

8814 Lichtenau, Weickershof
Tel (09827) 6907
Pro J Speed
Holes 9 L 6160 m SSS 72
Fees 20DM (40DM)
Loc 15km E of Ansbach

Aschaffenburg

Aschaffenburger (1977)

8750 Aschaffenburg, Yorck-Str 28
Tel (06021) 92271/(06024) 7222
Mem 450
Pro T Paterson
Holes 9 L 5184 m SSS 67
Fees 30DM (40DM)
Loc Feldkahl, 7km E of
Aschaffenburg

Augsburg

Augsburg (1959)

Engelshofer Str 2,
8903 Bobingen-Burgwalden
Tel (08234) 5621
Mem 650
Pro P Ries
Holes 18 L 5805 m SSS 71
Fees 40DM (60DM)
Loc 18km SW of Augsburg
Munich 50km

Leitershofen (1980)

8902 Stadtbergen, Deuringerstr.
Tel (0821) 434919
Mem 125
Pro P Garnier-Bradley
Holes 9 L 3090 m SSS 72
Fees 25DM (30DM)
Loc 8901 Stadtbergen-Leitershofen

Bad Bramstedt

Bad Bramstedt (1975)

2357 Bad Bramsted, PO Box 1305,
Oschenweg 38
Tel (04192) 6376
Mem 150
Holes 9 SSS 70

Fees 25DM (30DM)
Loc S border of town by B4. 48km N of Hamburg on A7

Bad Driburg

Bad Driburger (1976)

Am Bad, 3490 Bad Driburg
Tel **(05253) 842500**
Mem 220
Pro R Issitt
Holes 9 L 6106 m SSS 72
Fees 25DM (30DM) W–150DM

Bad Ems

Mittelrheinischer (1930)

Denzerheide, 5427 Bad Ems
Tel **(02603) 6541**
Pro H Goerke
Holes 18 L 6050 m SSS 72
Fees 35DM (50DM)
Loc Bad Ems 6km. Koblenz 13km

Bad Harzburg

Harz (1972)

Am Breitenberg 107, 3388 Bad Harzburg 1
Tel **(05322) 6737/1096**
Mem 340
Pro CB Westerman
Holes 9 L 5562 m SSS 70
Fees 30DM (35DM)
Loc Centre of Bad Harzburg, 50km S of Braunschweig

Bad Homburg

G & L C Taunus (1979)

Merzhauser Landstr, 6395 Weilrod-Altweilnau
Tel **(06083) 865**
Pro M Bonn, J Wilson
Holes 18 holes SSS 72
Fees 20DM (30DM)
Loc 15km NW of Bad Homburg

Homburger (1899)

Saalburgchaussee 2, 6380 Bad Homburg
Tel **(06172) 38808**
Mem 525
Pro F Tauber, R Taylor
Holes 10 holes Par 70 SSS 69
Fees 30DM (50DM)
Loc On B456 to Usingen

Bad Kissingen

Bad Kissingen (1911)

Euerdorfer Str 11, 8730 Bad Kissingen
Tel **(0971) 3608**
Mem 550
Pro J Dibb, T Pearman
Holes 18 L 5464 m SSS 69
Fees 40DM (50DM)
Loc Bad Kissingen 2km

Bad Kreuznach

Nahetal (1970)

6552 Bad Münster a. St.-Ebernburg, Drei Buchen
Tel **(06708) 2145/3755**
Mem 655
Pro F Schmaderer, I Harris
Holes 18 L 6075 m SSS 72
Fees 35DM (50DM)
Loc Bad Kreuznach 6km. Bad Münster 3km

Bad Mergentheim

Bad Mergentheim (1971)

6990 Bad Mergentheim, Postfach 1304
Tel **(07931) 7579**
Pro H Rosenkranz
Holes 9 L 4230 m Par 64
Fees 25DM (35DM)
Loc Würzburg 40km

Bad Nauheim

Bad Nauheim

6350 Bad Nauheim, Postfach 1524
Tel **(06032) 2153**
Mem 370
Pro B Raschke (06032) 33797
Holes 9 L 5440 m SSS 68
Fees 35DM (50DM)
Loc Frankfurt/Main 40km

Bad Neuenahr

Bad Neuenahr G L C (1979)

Remagener Weg, D- 5483 Bad Neuenhar-Ahrweiler
Tel **(02641) 2325**
Mem 537
Pro M Nickel
Holes 18 L 6075 m SSS 72
Fees 40DM (50DM)
Loc From north: M'way A61 to exit Bad Neuenahr via Sinzig and Lohrsdorf. From South: M'way A61 exit Sinzig via Lohrsdorf.

Bad Pyrmont

Pyrmonter (1972)

Postfach 100 828, 3250 Hameln
Tel **(05281) 8196**
Mem 300
Pro S Russell
Holes 9 L 5720 m SSS 70
Fees 30DM (35DM)
Loc Bad Pyrmont 4km. Hameln 25km

Bad Sackingen

Rickenbach (1980)

7884 Rickenbach, Postfach 1041
Tel **(07765) 8880**
Mem 350
Pro CR Dew
Holes 9 L 2749 m Par 69
Fees 30DM (50DM)
Loc Bad Sackingen, 30km E of Basel

Bad Salzuflen

Ostwestfalen-Lippe

PO Box 225, 4902 Bad Salzuflen
Tel **(05222) 10773**
Mem 400
Pro M Skeide
Holes 9 L 6040 m Par 72
Fees 25DM (30DM)
Loc Bad Salzuflen 3km

Bad Soden-Salmünster

Spessart (1972)

Eselsweg, 6483 B S S-Alsberg
Tel **(06056) 3494**
Mem 650
Pro L Bolland, S Walker
Holes 18 L 6127 m SSS 72
Fees 30DM (50DM)
Loc 70km from Frankfurt
Mis Handicap certificate required

Bad Tölz

Bad Tölz (1973)

Strasse 124, 8170 Wackersberg
Tel **(08041) 9994**
Mem 260
Pro I Lyons, S Allan
Holes 9 L 2942 m SSS 71
Fees 30DM (40DM)
Loc 55km S of Munich. W of Bad Tölz

Bad Waldsee

Oberschwaben-Bad Waldsee (1968)

7967 Bad Waldsee, Hofgut Hopfenweiler
Tel **(07524) 5900**
Mem 480
Pro W Jersombeck, T Schinnenburg

Holes 18 L 6148 m SSS 72
Fees 35DM (50DM)
Loc Hofgut Hopfenweiler, nr B30

Bad Wiessee

Tegernseer GC Bad Wiessee (1958)

Robognerhof 1, 8182 Bad Wiessee
Tel **(08022) 8769**
Mem 538
Pro B Pringle, R Buschert
Holes 18 L 5501 m SSS 69
Fees 70DM (90DM)
Loc Bad Wiessee 1km. Munich 55km
Mis Driving range–10DM

Bad Wildungen

Bad Wildungen (1930)

3590 Bad Wildungen
Tel **(05621) 4877/2260**
Mem 100
Pro A Stein
Holes 9 L 5670 m Par 70
Fees 20DM (30DM)
Loc Bad Wildungen $1^1/_2$ km

Bad Wörishofen

Bad Wörishofen

8951 Rieden, Schlingener Str 27
Tel **(08346) 777**
Mem 520
Pro M Seidel, H Hoerenz, A Cawdron
Holes 18 L 6318 m SSS 71
Fees 50DM (70DM)
Loc 10km S of Bad Wörishofen

Baden-Baden

Bad Herrenalb-Bernbach

Golf-Club Bad Herrenalb-Bernbach
Tel **(07083) 8898**
Mem 400
Pro G Westen, D Randolf
Holes 9 L 5200 m SSS 68
Fees 30DM (35DM)
Loc Centre 1km

Baden-Baden (1901)

Fremersbergstrasse 127, Baden-Baden
Tel **(07221) 23579**
Mem 400
Pro E Totzke
Holes 18 L 4575 m Par 64
Fees 40DM (50DM) W–200DM
Loc Town $^1/_2$ km

Baden-Hills (1982)

Postfach 1153, 7558 Bischweier
Tel **(07222) 42274**
Pro R Walker
Holes 18 L 5672 m Par 72
Fees 20DM (30DM)
Loc 20km S of Rastatt
Mis Booking and handicap certificate required

Badenweiler

Rhein Badenweiler (1971)

7847 Badenweiler
Tel **(07632) 5031**
Mem 450
Pro JF Halliwell
Holes 18 L 6134 m SSS 72
Fees 40DM (60DM)
Loc Badenweiler 16km

Bamberg

Bamberg

Postfach 1525, 8600 Bamberg
Tel **(0951) 24631**
Pro I Donnelly (0951) 43973
Holes 18 L 6175 m SSS 72
Fees 35DM (50DM) W–190DM
Loc 16km from Bamberg at Gut Leimershof

Bayreuth

Oberfranken (1966)

8650 Kulmbach, Postfach 1404
Tel **(09221) 4336**
(09228) 319 (Clubhouse)
Mem 450
Pro D Entwhistle, A Parker
Holes 18 L 6152 m SSS 72
Fees 30DM (50DM 2D–80DM)
Loc Thurnau. 18km NW of Bayreuth. 14km SW of Kulmbach

Berchtesgaden

Berchtesgaden (1955)

Postfach 3460, Berchtesgaden
Tel **(08652) 2100/3787**
Mem 230
Holes 9 L 5135 m SSS 67
Fees 20DM (30DM)
Loc Berchtesgaden $3^1/_2$ km. Motorway 25km

Berlin

Berlin G & CC

APO 197442, US Forces Europe
Tel **8196533**
Mem 600
Pro L Beem
Holes 18 L 6350 yds Par 70
Fees $10 ($15)
Loc Wannsee

Berlin-Wannsee (1895)

Am Stoepchenweg, 1000 Berlin 39
Tel **8055075**
Mem 575
Pro U Tapperthofen, J Galbraith
Holes 9 L 5690 m SSS 70
Fees 30DM (40DM)
Loc City centre 17km

British GC Gatow (1969)

BFPO 45, RAF Gatow
Tel **3092670/3657660**
Mem 400
Holes 9 L 5687 m SSS 70
Fees 10DM (20DM)
Loc 16km from city centre
Mis British Forces & British Passport holders only

Bielefeld

Bielefelder (1977)

Dornbergerstrasse 375, 4800 Bielefeld-Hoberge 1
Tel **(0521) 105103**
Mem 438
Pro HW Kahre (0521) 104450
Holes 9 L SSS 72
Fees 25DM (35DM)
Mis WE–only with member

Blomberg

Lippischer GC Blomberg-Cappel (1981)

Postfach 444, 4290 Lemgo
Tel **(05236) 459**
Pro R Hauser
Holes 18 L 6110 m SSS 72
Fees 25DM (30DM)

Bocholt

Wasserburg Anholt (1972)

4294 Isselburg Anholt
Tel **(02874) 2283**
Pro H Johannsen
Holes 9 L 5920 m SSS 72
Fees 40DM (50DM)
Loc Anholt Schloss, Bocholt 15km

Bochum

Bochumer (1982)

Im Mailan 127, 4630 Bochum
Tel **(0234) 799832**
Pro E Newgas
Holes 9 L 5900 m SSS 71
Fees 25DM (30DM)
Loc Bochum-Stiepel

Bonn-Bad Godesberg

Bonn-Godesberg (1960)

Dechant-Heimbachstr 16,
5300 Bonn 2
Tel **(0228) 344003 (Clubhouse)**
(0228) 317494 (Sec)
Mem 600
Pro K Riechart, KP Vollrach
Holes 18 L 5900 m Par 71
Fees 35DM (45DM)
Loc Oberbachem, Bad Godesberg 4km

Braunfels

Schloss-Braunfels (1970)

Homburger Hof, 6333 Braunfels
Tel **(06442) 4530**
Mem 700
Pro D McLellan, M Lauermann, P Smith (06442) 5752
Holes 18 L 6288 m SSS 72
Fees 40DM (70DM)
Loc 70km N of Frankfurt am Main

Braunschweig

Braunschweig (1926)

Schwarzkopfstr 10, 3300 Braunschweig
Tel **(0531) 691369**
Mem 570
Pro MA Emery
Holes 15 L 5893 m SSS 71
Fees 30DM (40DM)
Loc City centre 5km

Gifhorn (1982)

Postfach 1341, 3170 Gifhorn
Tel **(05371) 16737**
Mem 233
Pro N Coombs
Holes 9 L 6160 m SSS 72
Fees 20DM (30DM)
Loc Hannover

Bremen

Club Zur Vahr (1905)

Bgm-Spitta-Allee 34, 2800 Bremen 41
Tel **Bremen (0421) 230041**
Garlstedt (04795) 417
Mem 850
Pro H Weber, KD Schneider, M Grantham
Holes Bremen 9 L 5862 m SSS 71
Garlstedt 18 L 6435 m SSS 75
Fees Bremen 30DM (40DM)
Garlstedt 40DM (50DM)
Loc Bremen-in city. Garlstedt-30 mins from Bremen

Worpswede (1974)

Grüner Weg 3, 2822 Schwanewede 1
Tel **(0421) 621425/(04673) 7313**
Mem 314
Pro R Prössel
Holes 9 L 6200 m SSS 72
Fees 30DM (40DM)
Loc Giehlermuhlen, B74 Osterholz –Scharmbeck to Bremen

Brüggen

RAF Germany (1956)

RAF Brüggen, BFPO 25
Tel **(02163) 881 Ext 463/5207**
Mem 600
Sec RW Powell
Pro T Foster
Holes 18 L 6522 yds SSS 71
Fees 25DM
Loc On B230 1km from Dutch/ German border. 25km W of Mönchengladbach

Burghausen

Falkenhof GLC (1983)

PO Box 1560, D–8263 Burghausen
Tel **(08677) 2394**
Mem 125
Pro S Tasker
Holes 9 L 3030 m SSS 72
Fees 30DM (40DM)
Loc Falkenhof–Marktl. 48km N of Salzburg
Mis Driving range

Burgsteinfurt

Münsterland (1950)

D–4430 Steinfurt Bagno
Tel **(02557) 5178**
Mem 243
Pro B Whittle
Holes 9 L 4960 m Par 66
Fees 25DM (30DM)
Loc Burgsteinfurt 2km

Chiemsee

Chiemsee

8210 Prien-Bauernberg
Tel **(08051)4820**
Pro R Krause
Holes 9 L 5960 m SSS 71
Fees 30DM (50DM)
Loc Prien 3km

GC im Chiemgau (1982)

Kötzing 1, 8224 Chieming
Tel **(08669) 7557**
Mem 470
Pro G Thomson
Holes 18 L 6200 m SSS 73
9 holes Par 3
Fees 45DM (70DM)
Loc Salzburg 20km

Höslwang im Chiemgau (1977)

Chiemseestr 18, 8200 Rosenheim
Tel **(08031) 12198**
Pro F Carli
Holes 9 L 6210 m SSS
Fees 25DM (40DM)

Coburg

Coburg Schloss Tambach

8636 Weitramsdorf
Tel **(09567) 1212**
Mem 265
Pro P Spencer
Holes 9 L 6150 m SSS 72
Fees 30DM (40DM)
Loc Tambach, 9km W of Coburg, opposite Animal Park

Cologne

Köln G & LC

Golfplatz 2, 5060 Bergisch Gladbach 1
Tel **(02204) 63114/63138**
Mem 630
Pro K Marx, A Stein
Holes 18 L 6045 m Par 72
Fees 40DM (60DM)
Loc Cologne centre 15km

Köln-Marienburger (1949)

Schillingsrotter Weg, Köln
Tel **(0221) 384793**
Pro H Becker, W Esser, J Grundy
Holes 9 L 3075 m Par 72
Fees 40DM (50DM)
Loc Within city limits

Schloss Georghausen (1962)

Georghausen 8,
5253 Lindlar-Hommerich
Tel **(02207) 4938**
Mem 703
Pro G Kessler, G Baum, J Kaynig
Holes 18 L 6045 m SSS 72
Fees 40DM (50DM)
Loc 30km E of Cologne

Cuxhaven

Küsten Golfclub Hohe Klint (1979)

Rosenhof 25, 2190 Cuxhaven
Tel **(04723) 3969**
Mem 700
Pro F O'Conner (04723) 2229
Holes 18 L 6150 m SSS 72

Fees 40DM (50DM)
Loc 12km SW of town centre on Route 6 nr Oxstedt

Darmstadt

Darmstadt-Traisa

Dippelshof, 6109 Mühltal-Traisa
Tel (06151) 146543
Mem 330
Pro M Rose
Holes 9 L 5150 m SSS 68
Fees 30DM (40DM)
Loc Traisa nr Darmstadt

Deggendorf

G & LC Rusel (1981)

Postfach 1321, D–8360 Deggendorf
Tel (09920) 911
Mem 320
Pro JA Taylor (09920) 1279
Holes 9 L 6070 m SSS 72
Fees 40DM (50DM)
Loc Deggendorf 10km on Route 11 towards Regen. Passau 45km
Mis Driving range, pitch and putt

Dingolfing

Schlossberg (1985)

Grünbach 4, 8386 Reisbach
Tel (08734) 7035
Mem 470
Pro P Haworth
Holes 18 L 6070 m SSS 72
Fees 35DM (45DM)
Loc Somershausen, 15km from Dingolfing. 100km NE of Munich off Route 11

Donaueschingen

L & GC Oeschberghof (1976)

Golfplatz 1, D–7710 Donaueschingen
Tel (771) 84525
Mem 500
Pro T Gerhardt, B Birch, S Hilton, D Enters
Holes 18 L 6570 m SSS 74
Fees 50DM (80DM)
Loc Stuttgart/Zurich airports 1 hr
Mis Handicap certificate required

Dortmund

Dortmund Garrison (1969)

Napier Barracks, BFPO 20
Mem 400
Holes 18 L 5196 m SSS 70
Fees 15DM (20DM)
Loc In Napier Barracks, Dortmund Brackel
Mis Not open to public; visitors by prior arrangement only

Dortmunder (1956)

4600 Dortmund-Reichsmark, Reichsmarkstr 12
Tel (0231) 774133/774609
Mem 650
Pro V Knörnschild, B Wargel, F Schneider
Holes 18 L 6240 m SSS 73
Fees 35DM (50DM)
Loc Dortmund 8km
Mis WE–only with member

Duisburg

Niederrheinischer (1956)

4100 Duisburg 28 (Bucholz) Grossenbaumer Allee 240
Tel (0203) 721469
Mem 402
Pro J Dennison
Holes 9 L 6090 m SSS 72
Fees 35DM (45DM)
Loc Duisburg centre 8km

Düren

Düren (1975)

Katherinenstr 59, 5160 Düren
Tel (02421) 800112
Mem 200
Pro H Gross, R Hamann
Holes 9 L 5706 m SSS 70
Fees 30DM (40DM)
Loc Trierbachweg

Düsseldorf

Düsseldorfer (1961)

Rommerljansweg 12, 4030 Ratingen 1
Tel Ratingen 81092
Mem 750
Pro J Kupitz, D Hollbach
Holes 18 L 5905 m SSS 71
Fees 40DM (50DM)
Loc City centre 11km

Düsseldorfer/Hösel

Grunerstr 13, 4000 Düsseldorf 1
Tel (0211) 631171/(02102) 68629
Mem 550
Pro F Eckl, M Pyatt
Holes 18 L 6160 m SSS 72
Fees 25DM (35DM)
Loc Hösel, 15km NE of Düsseldorf

Hubbelrath (1961)

Bergische Landstrasse 700, 4000 Dusseldorf 12
Tel (02104) 72178 / 71848
Mem 1350
Pro G Danz, HP Ranft, F Willemsen, HP Thuel, R Noélle, M Brock
Holes East 18 L 6040 m SSS 72
West 18 L 4235 m SSS 63
Fees 60DM (90DM)
Loc Hubbelrath, approx 13km E of town centre on Route B7

Eckernförde

Altenhof (1971)

2330 Altenhof, bei Eckernförde
Tel (04351) 41227
Mem 520
Pro N Robinson
Holes 18 L 6071 m SSS 72
Fees 30DM (40DM)
Loc Eckernförde 3km

Erlangen

Erlangen (1977)

Postfach 1767, 8520 Erlangen
Tel (09126) 5040
Mem 150
Pro P Zinterl
Holes 9 Par 72
Fees 15DM
Loc Am Schlienhof, 8542 Kleisendelbach. 15km E of Erlangen
Mis Members and guests only

Frankische Schweitz (1974)

D–8553 Ebermannstadt, Postfach 11 10
Tel (09194) 9228
Mem 230
Pro K Messingschlager
Holes 9 L 5256 m Par 68
Fees 20DM
Loc 5km E of Ebermannstadt

Herzogenaurach (1967)

Altenbergerstr 36, 8500 Nürnberg
Tel (0911) 616183
Mem 160+ 50 American members
Holes 9 L 6090 m SSS 72
Fees 10DM
Loc Next to Herzo base
Mis Guests with members only

Essen

Essen-Heidhausen (1970)

4300 Essen 16, Preutenborbeckstrasse 36
Tel (0201) 404111
Mem 710
Pro G Kothe, T McGarva, F Schefer
Holes 18 L 5702 m SSS 70
Fees 30DM (50DM)
Loc Essen 10km on B224

Essener Haus Oefte (1959)

Laupendahler Landstr, 4300 Essen
Tel **(02054) 83911**
Mem 650
Pro R Sommer (02054) 84722
Holes 18 L 6100 m SSS 72
Fees 40DM (50DM)
Loc Essen city centre 14km

Golfriege des Etuf (1962)

Freiherr-vom-Stein Str 92a, 4300 Essen 1
Tel **(0201) 441426**
Mem 320
Pro U Knappmann
Holes 9 L 4580 m SSS 64
Fees 25DM (30DM)
Loc 6km S of city centre

Feldafing

Feldafing (1926)

D–8133 Feldafing, Tutzingerstr 15
Tel **(08157) 7005**
Mem 700
Pro T Flossman, A Steinfurth, Chr Kilian
Holes 18 L 5865 m SSS 70
Fees 50DM (85DM)
Loc 32km S of Munich
Mis Driving range, pitch and putt

Flensburg

Forde Glücksburg

2392 Glücksburg-Bockholm
Tel **(04631) 2547**
Pro D Ohle
Holes 9 holes SSS 72
Fees 25DM (30DM)
Loc 10km NE of Flensburg

Föhr Island

Föhr (1966)

2270 Niebum auf Föhr
Tel **(04681) 3277**
Mem 301
Pro A Assmus
Holes 9 L 6100 m SSS 72
Fees 30DM (40DM)
Loc 3km SW of Wyk

Frankfurt

Frankfurter (1913)

6000 Frankfurt/M 71, Golfstr 41
Tel **(069) 6 66 23 18**
Mem 900
Pro H Strüver, T Gowdy, G Petermann
Holes 18 L 6455 yds Par 71
Fees D–65DM (85DM)
Loc City 6km. Airport 4km

Kronberg GLC (1954)

Schloss Friedrichshof, Hainstr 25, 6242 Kronberg/Taunus
Tel **(06173) 1426**
Mem 853
Pro A Schilling, J Harder, W Mych, J Thompson
Holes 18 L 5365 m SSS 68
Fees 40DM (60DM)
Loc 15km NW of Frankfurt

Freiburg

Freiburger (1970)

7815 Kirchzarten, Krüttweg 1
Tel **(07661) 5569**
Mem 510
Pro P Weggenmann
Holes 18 L 6100 m SSS 72
Fees 45DM (55DM)
Loc Freiburg–Kappel/Kirchzarten. 7km SE of town centre on Route L126b

Gutermann Gutach (1924)

7809 Gutach/Breisgau
Tel **(07681) 21243**
Mem 300
Pro IM Stewart
Holes 9 L 5260 m SSS 68
Fees 34DM (50DM)
Loc Freiburg 20km

Freudenstadt

Freudenstadt (1929)

Postfach 322, 7290 Freudenstadt
Tel **(07441) 3060**
Mem 370
Pro G Fischer, D Lösch
Holes 9 L 5857 m SSS 71
Fees 30DM (50DM)
Loc Freudenstadt 1km
Mis Open Apr–Oct

Fulda

Rhoen (1971)

Am Golfplatz, 6417 Hofbieber 1
Tel **(06657) 7077/1334**
Mem 520
Pro N Staples
Holes 18 L 5676 m SSS 70
Fees 30DM (40DM)
Loc Hofbieber, 11km E of Fulda

Furth im Wald

Furth im Wald (1982)

Voithenberg 1, 8492 Furth im Wald
Tel **(09973) 1240**
Mem 145
Pro J Edgar
Holes 9 holes SSS 71
Fees 25DM (35DM)
Loc 70km NE of Regensburg

Garmisch-Partenkirchen

Garmisch-Partkenkirchen (1928)

Postfach 1345 Garmisch-Partenkirchen
Tel **(08824) 8344/1632**
Mem 450
Pro A Hagl
Holes 18 L 6200 m SSS 72
Fees 35DM (50DM)
Loc Garmisch 6km

Werdenfels (1973)

Postfach 1345, 8100 Garmisch-Partenkirchen
Tel **(08821) 750626**
Mem 200
Pro B Davidson
Holes 9 L 5896 m SSS 71
Fees 40DM (50DM)
Loc 2km S of Garmisch on B23, direction Farchant

Gmund

Margarethenhof am Tegernsee (1982)

8184 Gmund am Tegernsee
Tel **(08022) 7366**
Pro F Bernardi
Holes 18 L 6056 m SSS 72
Fees 40DM (60DM)
Loc Munich 50km

Göppingen

Hohenstauffen (1959)

723 Göppingen
Tel **27361**
Mem 160
Pro R Miller
Holes 9 L 6540 yds SSS 72
Fees 25DM (30DM)
Loc Donzdorf 15km

Göttingen

Göttingen (1969)

Levershausen, 3410 Northeim 1
Tel **(05551) 61915/7952**
Mem 520
Pro W Kreuzer, P Dunn
Holes 18 L 6050 m SSS 72
Fees 30DM (40DM)
Loc Between Göttingen and Northeim

Günzburg

Schloss Klingenburg-Günzburg (1980)

Schloss Klingenburg, 8876 Jettingen-Scheppach
Tel **(08225) 3030**
Mem 450
Pro H Bessner
Holes 18 L 6065 m SSS 72
Fees 50DM (75DM)
Loc Günzburg 20km

Gütersloh

RAF Gütersloh

RAF Gütersloh, BFPO 47
Tel **(05241) 26021 ext 426**
Mem 425
Holes 9 L 5761 yds SSS 68
Fees 12DM
Loc 5km W of Gütersloh

Westfälischer Gütersloh

4830 Gütersloh
Tel **(05244) 2340**
Mem 600
Pro M Schwichtenberg
Holes 18 L 6175 m SSS 72
Fees 30DM (60DM)
Loc Gütersloh 6km

Hachenburg

Westerwald (1979)

Alexanderring 9, 5238 Hachenburg
Tel **(02662) 7077/1739**
Pro H-J Labonte (02620) 2230
Holes 9 holes SSS 72
Fees 25DM (35DM)

Hagen

Märkischer Hagen (1964)

5800 Hagen, Tiefendorferstr 48
Tel **(02334) 51778**
Mem 400
Pro D Giese, R Stehmans
Holes 9 L 6114 m SSS 72
Fees 25DM (40DM)
Loc Hagen-Berchum

Hamburg

An der Pinnau (1982)

Jebbenberg 32, 2084 Rellingen
Tel **(04106) 8 18 00**
Mem 590
Pro S & A Arrowsmith, B Griffiths
Holes 18 L 6129 m SSS 72
Fees 35DM (45DM)
Loc Motorway Hamburg–Flensburg exit Quickborn. Motorway Hamburg–Husum exit Pinneberg Nord
Mis Course address: Pinnebergerstr 81, 2085 Quickborn

Auf der Wendlohe

2000 Hamburg 61, Oldesloerstr 251
Tel **(550) 5014/5**
Mem 700
Pro K Vince, D Entwhistle, L Kelly
Holes 18 L 6060 m SSS 72
Fees 35DM (45DM)
Loc City centre 15km

Buxtehude (1982)

Zum Lehmfeld 1, 2150 Buxtehude
Tel **(04161) 81333**
Mem 420
Pro M Fitton, S Bates, D Reffin
Holes 18 L 6505 m SSS 74
Fees 30DM (50DM)
Loc 30km SW of Hamburg on Route 73 from Harburg

Grossensee (1975)

Hamburgerstrasse, 2077 Grossensee
Tel **(04154) 6261/6473**
Mem 200
Pro G Schurr
Holes 9 L 6118 m SSS 72
Fees 25DM (30DM)
Loc Hamburg 30km

Grossflottbeker (1901)

Otto-Ernst Str 32, 2000 Hamburg
Tel **(040) 827208**
Mem 300
Pro K Storrier
Holes 9 L 4945 m SSS 66
Fees D–30DM (D–40DM)
Loc City centre 10km

Gut Kaden (1984)

Kadenerstrasse, 2081 Alveslohe
Tel **(04193) 1420**
Mem 240
Pro C Smailes, L Kelly
Holes 18 L 6180 m SSS 72
Fees 40DM (50DM)
Loc Alveslohe, 30km N of Hamburg

Gut Waldhof (1969)

2359 Kisdorferwohld, Gut Waldhof
Tel **(04194) 383**
Mem 720
Pro HJ Jersombeck
Holes 18 L 6073 m Par 72
Fees 35DM (45DM)
Loc 34km N of Hamburg via Autobahn A7 to Kaltenkirchen or via route B432
Mis WE–only with member

Hamburg-Ahrensburg (1964)

Am Haidschlag 39-45, 2070 Ahrensburg
Tel **(04102) 513 09**
Mem 849
Pro H Heiser, C Kirchner, P Nitra
Holes 18 L 5782 m SSS 70
Fees 40DM (50DM)
Loc Hamburg 20km
Mis WE–only with member

Hamburg-Waldorfer (1960)

D–2075 Ammersbek, Schevenbarg
Tel **(040) 6 05 13 37**
Mem 850
Pro K Sallman, G Bennett
Holes 18 L 6154 m SSS 73
Fees 40DM (50DM)
Loc 20km N of city centre
Mis Driving range, pitch and putt

Hamburger (1906)

In de Bargen 59, 2000 Hamburg 55
Tel **(040) 812177**
Mem 1030
Pro A Mazza, S Blume
Holes 18 L 5925 m SSS 71
Fees 45DM (60DM)
Loc Blankenese, 14km from centre of Hamburg
Mis WE–only with member

Hamburger GC In der Lüneburger Heide (1957)

2105 Seevetal 1, Am Golfplatz 24
Tel **(04105) 2331**
Mem 600
Pro J Struver, S Wächter
Holes 18 L 5865 m SSS 71
Fees 40DM (40DM)
Loc Hamburg 25km

Hoisdorf (1977)

Duwockskamp 26, 2050 Hamburg 80
Tel **(040) 721 68 68**
Pro M Stewart, N Griffith
Holes 18 L 6010 m Par 71
Fees 35DM (45DM)
Loc 20km NE of Hamburg

Wentorf-Reinbeker (1901)

Golfstrasse 2, 2057 Wentorf
Tel **(040) 7202610/7202141**
Mem 380
Pro W Lloyd
Holes 9 L 5768 m SSS 70
Fees 30DM (45DM)
Loc City centre 25km
Mis Co-Founder of German Golf Union 1907

Hameln

Schloss Schwöbber (1985)

Schloss Schwöbber, 3258 Aerzen 16
Tel (05154) 2004
Mem 800
Pro R Lewington, E Runcie
Holes 18 L 6222 m SSS 73
9 hole short course
Fees 18 hole 40DM (45DM)
9 hole 25DM (30DM)
Loc 10km SW of Hameln. 60km SW of Hannover
Mis Driving range

Hanau

Hanau-Wilhelmsbad (1959)

Wilhelmsbader Allee 32, 6450 Hanau
Tel (06181) 82071
Mem 860
Pro A Payne
Holes 18 L 6227 m Par 73
Fees 50DM (70DM)
Loc 6km NW of centre on B8–40

Hannover

Burgdorfer (1970)

Waldstr 27, 3167 Burgdorf-Ehlershausen
Tel (05085) 7628/7144
Mem 400
Pro L Theeuwen
Holes 18 L 6460 m SSS 74
Fees 25DM (30DM)
Loc B3 Burgdorf-Ehlershausen

Hannover (1923)

3008 Garbsen 1, Am Blauen See
Tel (05137) 7 32 35
Mem 600
Pro H Koch, B Schul
Holes 18 L 5855 m SSS 71
Fees 30DM (45DM)
Loc Hannover 20km

Isernhagen (1983)

Im Kurzen Felde 24, 3004 Isernhagen
Tel (05139) 87564
Mem 450
Pro U Beuns, J Beuns
Holes 18 L 6334 m SSS 72
Fees 25DM (30DM)
Loc Gut Lohne, 12km NE of Hannover

Hechingen

Hechingen-Hohenzollern (1955)

Golfplatz Hagelwasen, Hechingen
Tel (07471) 2600
Mem 380
Pro K Schieban, P Eisenhut
Holes 9 SSS 70
Fees 30DM (50DM)
Loc Hechingen 2km
Mis WE–only with member

Heidelberg

G & LC Wiesloch-Hohenhardter Hof (1983)

Hohenhardter Hof, D–6908 Wiesloch-Baiertal
Tel (06222) 72081
Pro H Rübmann
Holes 18 L 6080 m SSS 72
Fees 30DM (40DM)
Loc 17km S of Heidelberg

Heidelberg (US Army)

Oftersheim ECN 1851
Tel (06202) 53767
Mem 700
Pro J Sporl
Holes 18 L 6650 m SSS 72
Fees $8 ($10)
Loc Heidelberg 10km

Heidelberg-Lobenfeld (1968)

Biddersbacherhof, 6921 Lobbach-Lobenfeld
Tel (06226) 40490
Mem 600
Pro JP Godefroy (06226) 41955
Holes 18 L 6240 m SSS 73
Fees 30DM (40DM)
Loc 20 mins E of town

Rheintal (1971)

Postfach 1140, 6906 Leimen
Tel (06224) 7 10 34
Pro A Winkler
Holes 18 L 5840 m SSS 70
Fees $10 ($15)

Heidenheim

Hochstatt Härtsfeld-Ries (1981)

7086 Neresheim
Tel (07326) 79 79
Pro P Smith
Holes 9 L 6170 m SSS 72
Fees 25DM (30DM)
Loc 30km E of Heidenheim. Munich 100km

Heilbronn

G & LC Schloss Liebenstein (1982)

Postfach 27, 7129 Neckarwestheim
Tel (07133) 16019
Mem 700
Pro W Kretschy, R Hartzheim
Holes 18 L 5847 m SSS 71
Fees 40DM (50DM)
Loc Stuttgart 35km. Heilbronn 20km

Heilbronn-Hohenlohe (1964)

Postfach 1341, 7107 Neckarsulm
Tel (07941) 78 86
Mem 380
Pro B Amara
Holes 9 L 5890 m SSS 71
Fees 25DM (40DM)
Loc Friedrichsruhe-Öhringen

Hennef

Rhein Sieg (1971)

5202 Hennef, Postfach 1216
Tel (02242) 6501/3047
Mem 280
Pro H Knopp, D MacLauchlan
Holes 18 L 6070 m Par 72
Fees 30DM (40DM)
Loc Hennef 3km

Herford

Herford (1984)

Heideholz 8, 4973 Vlotho-Exter
Tel (05228) 74 34
Mem 120
Pro G Pilkington
Holes 9 L 6184 m SSS 72
Fees 20DM (30DM)
Loc 30km NE of Bielefeld
80km W of Hannover
Mis Handicap certificate required

Hildesheim

Bad Salzdetfurth-Hildesheim (1972)

Postfach 1445, 3200 Hildesheim
Tel (05063) 1516
Pro W Müller
Holes 9 L 6210 m SSS 72
Fees 25DM (30DM)

Sieben-Berge (1983)

Schloss Str 1, 3211 Rheden/Gronau
Tel (05182) 2680
Mem 250
Pro P Scott
Holes 9 L 6126 m SSS 72
Fees 25DM (35DM)
Loc Hannover 40km
Mis Driving range

Hillesheim-Berndorf

Eifel (1977)

Kölner Str, 5533 Hillesheim
Tel (06593) 1241
Mem 350
Pro C Gess (06593) 8537
Holes 9 L 6180 m Par 72
Fees 25DM (40DM)
Loc 60km W of Koblenz
Mis Course closed Tues

Hof

Hof (1985)

Poststr 2, D–8670 Hof
Tel (09281) 43749
Mem 208
Pro N Fourie
Holes 9 L 3105 m SSS 72
Fees 30DM (40DM)
Loc 5km NE of Hof

Hohne

British Army (Hohne) (1962)

Hohne BFPO 30
Tel (05051) 4549
Mem 250
Holes 9 L 5682 m SSS 71
Fees 20DM (25DM)
Loc 6km S of Bergen Celle

Holzminden

Weserbergland (1982)

Sparenbergstr 9, 3450 Holzminden
Tel (15531) 10033
Pro S Fisher
Holes 18 holes SSS 72
Fees 20DM (30DM)
Loc 35km S of Hameln

Ingolstadt

Ingolstadt (1978)

Spitzelmühle, Gerolfingerstr. 8070 Ingolstadt
Tel (0841) 85778
Mem 320
Pro J Pugh
Holes 9 L 5500 m SSS 69
Fees 35DM (50DM)
Loc 3km from Ingolstad towards Gerolfing

Issum

Issum-Niederrhein (1973)

4174 Issum 1, Pauenweg 68
Tel (02835) 3626
Mem 628
Pro J Emery, S Tomkinson
Holes 18 L 6045 m SSS 72
Fees 35DM (50DM)
Loc 10km E of Geldern

Kassel

Kassel-Wilhelmshöhe

Wolfsschlucht 27, 3500 Kassel
Tel (0561) 3 35 09
Pro P Smith, U Wagener
Holes 18 L 5675 m SSS 70
Fees 40DM (50DM)

Kempten

Waldegg-Wiggensbach (1988)

Hof Waldegg, 8961 Wiggensbach/ Kempten
Tel (08370) 733
Mem 300
Pro A Koller
Holes 18 L 4035 m SSS 62
Fees 35DM (50DM) W–220DM
Loc Wiggensbach, 10km W of Kempten near Swiss/Austrian border
Mis Allgäu mountains, 873–1004m

Kiel

Kitzeberg (1902)

Sophienblatt 46, 2300 Kiel 1
Tel (0431) 63048/23404
Mem 360
Pro R Denton
Holes 9 L 5700 m Par 70
Fees 25DM (30DM)
Loc Kiel 10km

Kierspe

Varmert (1977)

5883 Kierspe-Varmert
Tel (02269) 7299
Mem 380
Pro G Thomas, S Bradbury, 'T' Pitts
Holes 9 L 6048 m SSS 72
Fees 25DM (35DM)
Loc 22km S of Ludenscheid. 50km NE of Köln

Konstanz

Konstanz (1965)

D7753 Allensbach 3, Langenrain, Kargegg 1
Tel (07533) 5124
Mem 550
Pro M Bingger, D Geary
Holes 18 L 6100 m SSS 72
Fees 40DM (60DM)
Loc 15km from Konstanz towards Bodmann on route B219
Mis Members of recognised golf clubs only

Krefeld

Krefelder (1930)

Eltweg 2, 4150 Krefeld 12
Tel (02151) 570071/72
Mem 600
Pro J Wilkinson, N Brunyard
Holes 18 L 6040 m SSS 72
Fees 45DM (60DM)
Loc 7km SE of Krefeld. Dusseldorf 16km

Laarbruch

Laarbruch GC RAF (1962)

Laarbruch BFPO 43
Tel Weeze 895441
Mem 200
Holes 9 L 4471 yds SSS 62
Fees 10DM
Loc Laarbruch 9 British Forces
Mis Access to course may be restricted

Lahr

Ortenau (1981)

7630 Lahr-Reichenbach, Postfach 1469
Tel (07821) 77217
Mem 320
Pro PP Jarvis
Holes 9 L 5450 m SSS 70
Fees 20DM (30DM)
Loc 35km SE of Strasbourg. 50km N of Freiburg

Lindau

Bodensee (1986)

8995 Weissenberg, Lampertsweiler 51
Tel (08389) 891 90
Pro A Gauld
Holes 18 L 6112 m SSS 71
Fees 55DM (75DM)
Loc Lindau 5km
Mis Handicap certificate required

Lindau-Bad Schachen (1954)

Kemptener Strasse 125, 8990 Lindau, Bodensee
Tel (08382) 78090
Mem 750
Pro R Richardson, H Kersting
Holes 18 L 5690 m SSS 70
Fees 40DM (50DM)
Loc Lindau centre $1^1/_2$ km

For explanation of abbreviations, see page 202.

Lingen

Emstal (1977)

Postfach 1431, 4450 Lingen
Tel (0591) 63216/64828
Mem 200
Pro D Bryan
Holes 9 L 5320 m SSS 68
Fees 30DM (40DM)
Loc 3km N town of centre, Route B70 to Meppen

Lübeck

Lübeck-Travemünder (1921)

Kowitzberg 41, 2400 HL-Travemünde
Tel (04502) 74018
Pro A Varley
Holes 9 L 6086 m SSS 72
Fees 30DM (50DM)
Loc Lübeck

Maritim Timmendorfer Strand (1973)

2408 Timmendorfer Strand
Tel (04503) 5152
Mem 720
Pro R Hinz
Holes 18 L 6440 m SSS 72
18 L 3720 m SSS 60
Fees 40DM (60DM)
Loc Am Overdiek

Lüneburg

An Der Goehrde (1968)

3139 Zernien-Braasche
Tel (05863) 556
Mem 180
Pro J Johannsen
Holes 9 L 6107 m SSS 72
Fees 25DM (30DM)
Loc 40km E of Lüneburg. 30km E of Uelzen

St Dionys (1972)

Widukindweg, 2123 St Dionys
Tel (04133) 6277
Mem 565
Pro KH Mahl, G Hillson
Holes 18 L 6225 m SSS 73
Fees 40DM (60DM)
Loc Nr Lüneburg

Schloss Lüdersburg (1985)

D-2127 Lüdersburg bei Lüneburg
Tel (04153) 6112
Mem 300
Pro M Rooney, S Griffin
Holes 18 L 6155 m SSS 72
6 hole Par 3 course
Fees 30DM (45DM) Par 3–15DM (25DM)
Loc 16km E of Lüneburg. 50km SE of Hamburg

Mannheim

Mannheim-Viernheim

68 Mannheim P7, 10–15
Tel 169 332
Mem 475
Pro C Jenkins, M Kagel, T Gutmann
Holes 9 L 3125 m SSS 72
Fees 25DM (50DM)
Loc Mannheim 10km

Marburg

Oberhessischer Marburg (1973)

Postfach 1828, 3550 Marburg/Lahn
Tel (06427) 8558
Mem 300
Pro T Rigby
Holes 9 L 6044 m SSS 72
Fees 30DM (40DM)
Loc 8km N of Marburg off B3 towards Reddehausen

Mölln

Gut Grambek (1981)

2411 Grambeck, Schlosstrasse 21
Tel (04542) 4627
Mem 350
Pro HJ Rumpf
Holes 18 L 6025 m SSS 71
Fees 30DM (40DM)
Loc 30km S of Lübeck. 40km E of Hamburg

Mönchengladbach

Schloss Myllendonk (1964)

Myllendonkerstr 113, 4052 Korschenbroich 1
Tel (02161) 641049
Mem 600
Pro G Kerkman, I Clegg
Holes 18 L 6120 m SSS 72
Fees 45DM (70DM)
Loc Korschenbroich, 5km E of Mönchengladbach

Schmitzhof-Wegberg (1977)

Schmitzhof, 5144 Wegberg
Tel (02436) 479
Pro E Theeuwen
Holes 18 L 6310 m SSS 73
Fees 30DM (50DM)
Loc 20km SW of Mönchengladbach

Much

Burg Overbach (1984)

Postfach 1213, 5203 Much
Tel (02245) 5550
Mem 650
Pro R Hauser, T Menne, N Büttner
Holes 18 L 6056 m SSS 72
Fees 40DM (60DM)
Loc 45km from Köln towards Olpe, off A4

Munich

Dachau (1947)

8060 Dachau, An der Flosslände 1
Tel (08131) 10879
Mem 250
Pro C De Castro
Holes 9 L 2960 m SSS 71
Fees 35DM (40DM)
Loc 2km E of Dachau. 17km NW of Munich

Erding-Grunbach (1973)

8058 Erding, Aribostr 2
Tel (08122) 6465
Mem 500
Pro G Warner
Holes 18 L 6140 m SSS 72
Fees 40DM (50DM)
Loc 45 mins from Munich towards Vilsbiburg

Eschenried (1983)

Kurfurstenweg 7, 8066 Eschenried
Tel (08131) 3238/79655
Mem 450
Pro G Stewart
Holes 9 L 6194 m SSS 72
Fees 35DM (50DM)
Loc 8km NW of Munich

Münchener (1910)

8021 Strasslach, Tölzerstrasse
Tel (08170) 450
Mem 1150
Pro A Castillo-Fernandez, H Fluss, E Junge, M Höcker
Holes Strasslach 18 L 6066 m SSS 72
Thalkirchen 9 L 2528 m SSS 69
Fees Strasslach 57DM (85DM)
Thalkirchen 57DM (85DM)
Loc Strasslach: 10km from Munich
Thalkirchen: Munich nr Camping Pl.

Olching (1981)

8037 Olching, Feurstrasse 89
Tel (08142) 15963
Mem 550
Pro C Knauss, D Cabus, A Steinfurth

Holes 18 L 6021 m SSS 72
Fees 40DM (60DM)
Loc Munich M'way A8. 25km to Stuttgart. B471 Dachau exit

Tutzing (1983)

8132 Tutzing-Deixlfurt
Tel (08158) 3600
Mem 600
Pro D Hennings
Holes 18 L 6159 m SSS 72
Fees 60DM (80DM)
Loc Starnberger See off B2

Wörthsee (1982)

Gut Schluifeld, 8031 Wörthsee
Tel (08153) 2425
Mem 720
Pro J Mills, P Pemöller, J Biddle
Holes 18 L 6270 m SSS 73
Fees 50DM (75DM)
Loc 25km from Munich towards Lindau on B12
Mis Pitch and putt

Münster

Münster-Wilkinghege (1963)

Postfach 3212, D-4400 Münster
Tel (0251) 211201
Mem 650
Pro E Reinhard, A Horsman
Holes 18 L 5880 m SSS 71
Fees 30DM (40DM)
Loc Münster 2km. Steinfurterstr 448

Neheim-Hüsten

Sauerland (1958)

Falkenhorst 15, 5760 Arnsberg 1
Tel (02932) 43 14
Mem 320
Pro V Knörnschild
Holes 9 L 5874 m SSS 71
Fees 25DM (30DM)
Loc Nr village of Herdringen
Mis Driving range

Neumünster

Mittelholsteinischer Aukrug (1969)

2356 Aukrug-Bargfeld
Tel (04873) 595
Mem 370
Pro M Kimberly
Holes 18 L 6140 m SSS 72
Fees 25DM (35DM)
Loc 10km W of Neumunster-Mitte exit on Route 430

Neunburg vorm Wald

Oberpfaelzer Wald GLC

Buchtalweg 7, D-8472 Schwarzenfeld
Tel (09439) 466
Mem 310
Pro D Holloway
Holes 18 L 6098 m SSS 72
Fees 40DM (50DM)
Loc Kemnath bei Fuhrn. 10km E of Schwarzenfeld on route to Neunburg

Neustadt

Pfalz (1971)

673 Neustadt, Weinstrasse
Tel (06327) 2973
Mem 750
Pro G Hopp, A Suchet
Holes 18 L 6180 m SSS 72
Fees 30DM (45DM)
Loc Geinsheim, 15km from Neustadt towards Speyer

Norderney Island

Norderney (1956)

2982 Norderney, Box 1233
Tel (04932) 680
Mem 225
Pro R Bremer
Holes 9 L 4890 m SSS 66
Fees 25DM (30DM)
Loc Norderney 7km

Nordkirchen

Nordkirchen

4717 Nordkirchen, Golfplatz 6
Tel (02596) 2495
Mem 340
Pro A Rössler
Holes 9 L 6200 m SSS 72
Fees 30DM (40DM)
Loc Münster 30km

Werl (1973)

Unnaerstr 23, 4760 Werl
Tel (02377) 6307
Mem 300
Pro A Stein
Holes 9 L 4640 m SSS 66
Fees 25DM (30DM)
Loc 30km E of Dortmund

Nürnberg

Club am Reichswald

Postfach 140101, 8500 Nürnberg 14
Tel (0911) 30 57 30
Pro J Gornert
Holes 18 L 6345 m SSS 73
Fees 40DM (60DM)
Loc Nürnberg 10km

Oberstdorf

Oberstdorf

Gebrgoibe 1, 8980 Oberstdorf
Tel (08322) 2895
Mem 304
Pro B Rowe
Holes 9 L 2795 m Par 70
Fees 30DM (35DM)
Loc Oberstdorf 3km. Nr Austrian border, 10km S of Sonthofen

Oldenburg

Oldenburgischer (1964)

2900 Oldenburg, Postbox 2928
Tel (04402) 7240
Mem 440
Pro J Walter
Holes 18 L 6100 m SSS 72
Fees 30DM (40DM)
Loc Rastede 3km

Osnabrück

Osnabrück (1955)

Karmannstrasse 1, 4500 Osnabrück
Tel (05402) 636
Mem 300
Pro H Theeuwen
Holes 18 L 5881 m Par 71
Fees 35DM (45DM)
Loc Osnabrück 13km

Tecklenburger Land (1971)

Tel (05455) 1035
Mem 260
Pro JP Laarman
Holes 9 L 6160 m SSS 72
Fees 30DM (40DM)
Loc 1½ km W of Autobahn, exit Lengerich/Ibbenbüren. 20km Osnabrück. 35km Münster.
Mis Closed Mon

Velper G & CC (1981)

Heinrich-Hensiekstr 1, 4535 Westerkappeln-Velpe
Tel (05456) 820
Mem 300
Pro SL Walker (05456) 287
Holes 9 L 5782 m SSS 70
Fees 20DM (30DM)
Loc 8km W of Osnabrück

Ottobeuren

Algäuer G & LC (1984)

8942 Ottobeuren, Hofgut Boschach
Tel (08332) 1310
Mem 530
Pro KH Marx, M Chesters
Holes 18 L 6215 m SSS 72

Fees 40DM (50DM)
Loc Ottobeuren 2km. Kempten 20km

Paderborn

Paderborner Land (1983)

Wilseder Weg 25, 4790 Paderborn
Tel **(05251) 4377**
Pro A van der Donck
Holes 9 L 5670 m SSS 70
Fees 20DM (30DM)
Loc Salzkotten/Thule between B-1 and B-64

Passau

G & LC Bayerwald (1970)

Frauenwaldstr 2, 8392 Waldkirchen
Tel **(08581) 1040**
Mem 400
Pro N Rayne
Holes 9 L 6080 m SSS 72
Fees 35DM (45DM)
Loc Nr Passau

Penzburg

Beuerberg (1982)

Höchlstr 2, 8000 München 80
Tel **(08179) 671/728**
Pro A Hahn
Holes 18 L 6518 m SSS 74
Fees 50DM (70DM)
Loc Beuerberg, SW of Munich

St Eurach LGC (1973)

Eurach 8, 8127 Iffeldorf
Tel **(08801) 1332**
Mem 489
Pro W John, D Praun
Holes 18 L 6250 m SSS 74
Fees WD-80DM
Loc 40km S of Munich
Mis WE-no guests allowed

Pfarrkirchen

Rottaler (1972)

Bergstr 17, D-8333 Linden
Tel **(08561) 2861**
Mem 450
Pro R Porter
Holes 18 L 6100 m SSS 72
Fees 40DM (50DM)
Loc 5km W of Pfarrkirchen on B388. 120km E of München

Ramstein

Woodlawn

6792 Ramstein Flugplatz
Tel **(06371) 476240**
Mem Military GC-Visitors limited
Pro E Sudy
Holes 18 L 6225 yds Par 70
Fees $8 ($10)
Loc Ramstein 3km

Recklinghausen

Vestischer Recklinghausen (1974)

4350 Recklinghausen
Tel **(02361) 26520**
Mem 650
Pro U Lechtermann, E Schilling, W Bollert
Holes 18 L 6111 m SSS 72
Fees 35DM (50DM)
Loc Nr Loemuehle Airport
Mis Driving range

Regensburg

G & LC Regensburg (1966)

Postfach 45, 8405 Donaustauf
Tel **(09403) 505**
Mem 500
Pro P Ries, W Lloyd
Holes 18 L 5685 m SSS 70
Fees 40DM (60DM)
Loc 14km from Regensburg near Walhalla

Rendsburg

Lohersand (1958)

2371 Lohe-Föhrden, Golfplatz
Tel **(04336) 3333**
Mem 284
Holes 9 L 6040 m Par 72
Fees 25DM (30DM)
Loc Sorgbrück/B77. Rendsburg 10km

Rotenburg/Wümme

Wümme (1984)

Hof Emmen, Westerholz, 2723 Scheessel
Tel **(04263) 3352**
Pro K Wright
Holes 9 L 3045 m SSS 36
Fees 20DM (25DM)
Loc Emmen, 10km N of Rotenberg between Bremen and Hamburg

Saarbrücken

Saar-Pfalz Katherinenhof (1982)

Heinrich-Böckingstr 1, D-6600 Saarbrücken
Tel **(0681) 68794**
Mem 394
Pro J Morris (06843) 88 78
Holes 9 L 6112 m Par 72
Fees 25DM D-30DM (50DM)
Loc 15km S of Saarbrücken towards Blieskastel
Mis WE-only with member

Saarbrücken (1961)

Golfplatz, 6634 Wallerfangen 7
Tel **(06837) 401**
Pro W Rappenecker, J Nixon, R Heymanns
Holes 18 L 6231 m SSS 73
Fees 40DM (60DM)
Loc B406 towards Wallerfangen. 8km from Saarlouis

St Peter-Ording

St Peter-Ording (1971)

Hauke Haien-Weg 1, 2252 St Peter-Ording
Tel **(04863) 1545/746**
Mem 150
Pro T Holroyd
Holes 9 L 5730 m SSS 70
Fees 30DM (35DM)
Loc St Peter-Bohl

Salzgitter

Salzgitter Liebenburg (1985)

Sportpark Mahner Berg, Postfach 511329, Salzgitter-Bad
Tel **(05341) 37376**
Mem 130
Pro G Dyck
Holes 9 L 6010 m SSS 71
Fees 20DM (30DM)
Loc Salzgitter Bad, 27km SW of Braunschweig

Schmidmühlen

Schmidmühlen G & CC (1970)

8450 Amberg, Lange Gasse 2
Tel **(09621) 1846**
Mem 105
Pro B Rowe
Holes 9 L 5328 m SSS 68
Fees 20DM (25DM)
Loc Between Regensburg and Amberg

Sennelager

Sennelager (British Army) (1963)

Bad Lippspringe, BFPO 16
Tel **(82) 2515**
Sec AG Bairstow
Holes 18 L 5964 m SSS 72

Fees (Forces) 20DM (30DM) W–70DM. (Civilians) 30DM (40DM) W–90DM
Loc Paderborn 9km off Route 1

Siegen

Siegen-Olpe (1966)

D–5900 Siegen, Bahnhofstr 4
Tel (0271) 5831/(02762) 7589
Mem 300
Pro K Hahn
Holes 9 L 5724 m SSS 70
Fees 25DM (30DM)
Loc Siegen 15km. Köln 80km

Soltau

Soltau (1982)

Golfplatz Hof Loh,
3040 Soltau-Tetendorf
Tel (05191) 14077
Mem 420
Holes 18 L 6224 m SSS 73
9 L 2340 m SSS 54
Fees 30DM (40DM)
Loc Tetendorf, 3km S of Soltau

Sonthofen

Sonnenalp (1976)

Hotel Sonnenalp, 8972 Ofterschwang
Tel (08321) 7276 (Sec)
(08321) 720 (Hotel)
Mem 180
Pro B Kennedy, A MacDonald
Holes 18 L 6040 m SSS 72
Fees 60DM (75DM) Discount for hotel guests
Loc Sonthofen 4km. Fischen 3km

Stuttgart

Haghof (1983)

Alfdorf 2, 7077 Haghof
Tel (07182) 3040
Pro B Reilly
Holes 9 L 2932 m SSS 71
Fees 25DM (30DM)
Loc Nr Welsheim, 50km NE of Stuttgart

Schloss Weitenburg (1984)

Sommerhalde 11, 7245 Starzach-Sulzau
Tel (07472) 8061
Mem 500
Pro P Ridley, G Pottage, D Kay
Holes 18 holes SSS 72
9 hole course
Fees 18 hole 40DM (60DM)
9 hole 20DM (25DM)
Loc 50km SW of Stuttgart in Neckar Valley
Mis Driving range

Stuttgarter Neckartal (1974)

Aldingerstr, Gebaudt 975,
7140 Ludwigsburg-Pattonville
Tel (07141) 871319
Mem 265
Holes 18 L 6084 m SSS 72
Fees 50DM (70DM)
Loc Between Stuttgart and Ludwigsburg, nr Kornwestheim
Mis WE–only with member

Stuttgarter Solitude (1927)

7256 Monsheim
Tel (07044) 6909
Mem 640
Pro F Lengsfeld
Holes 18 L 6040 m SSS 72
Fees 40DM (60DM)
Loc Stuttgart 25km

Sylt Island

Marine Westerland (1980)

2280 Westerland, Marinefliegerhorst
Tel (04651) 70 37
Mem 250
Pro A Pemöller
Holes 6 L 4770 m SSS 66
Fees 25DM (30DM)
Loc Sylt Island. 75km W of Flensburg by Danish border

Trier

Trier-Mosel (1977)

Postfach 1905, 5500 Trier
Tel (06507) 4374
Mem 370
Pro H Goerke
Holes 9 L 6100 m SSS 72
Fees 25DM (40DM)
Loc 20km NE of Trier
Mis Driving range, pitch and putt

Ulm

Ulm (1963)

Postfach 4068, D–7900 ULm
Tel (0731) 183214
Mem 315
Pro F Piater
Holes 9 L 6170 m Par 72
Fees 25DM (40DM)
Loc 15km S of Ulm between Illerkirchberg and Illerrieden

Waldsassen

Stiftland (1982)

8591 Ernestgrün
Tel (09638) 1271
Mem 120
Pro M Raab
Holes 9 L 6340 m SSS 70
Fees 20DM (35DM)
Loc 30km E of Marktredwitz. 50km N of Weiden

Walsrode

Tietlingen (1979)

Tietlingen 6c, 3032 Fallingbostel
Tel (05162) 38 89
Mem 330
Pro G MacMillan
Holes 9 L 6340 m SSS 73
Fees 25DM (35DM)
Loc 65km N of Hannover between Walsrode and Fallingbostel

Wiesbaden

Main-Taunus (1980)

Auf der Heide, 6200 Wiesbaden-Delkenheim
Tel (06122) 52399
Mem 680
Holes 18 L 6088 m SSS 72
Fees 40DM (60DM)
Loc Next US Air Force Base Wiesbaden–Erbenheim
Mis Driving range 10–20DM

Rhein-Main (1977)

Steubenstrasse 9, 6200 Wiesbaden
Tel (06121) 373014
Pro T Cary
Holes 18 L 5966 m SSS 71
Fees $20
Loc Wiesbaden 6km
Mis Members and guests only

Rheinblick

62 Wiesbaden-Marchenland
Tel Military 3889
Mem US Forces
Pro P Greenfield
Holes 18 L 6604 yds SSS 70
Fees $5 ($10)
Loc Wiesbaden 2km
Mis Guests limited

Wiesbadener (1893)

Chauseehaus, 6200 Wiesbaden
Tel (06121) 460238
Mem 470
Pro M Day, T Robinson (06121) 468316
Holes 9 L 5320 m Par 68
Fees 35DM (45DM)
Loc 8km from city centre towards Schlangenbad

Wiesmoor

Ostfriesland (1980)

D–2964 Wiesmoor, Postbox 1220
Tel (04944) 3040
Mem 400
Pro S Parry (04944) 2228
Holes 18 L 6256 m SSS 73

Fees 30DM (40DM)
Loc 25km SW of Wilhelmshaven

Wildenrath

Wildenrath

BFPO 42
Tel (02432) 48 5440
Mem 300 Service personnel
Holes 9 L 4335 yds SSS 61
Fees 10DM
Loc RAF Wildenrath

Wildeshausen

Wildeshausen (1978)

Grüne Str 3, 2870 Delmenhorst
Tel (04431) 1232
Mem 369
Pro A Greshake
Holes 9 L 6066 m SSS 72
Fees 20DM (30DM)
Loc 3km from Wildeshausen on road to Huntlosen

Wilhelmshaven

Wilhelmshaven (1980)

Parkstr 19, 2940 Wilhelmshaven
Tel (04425) 1721
Mem 530
Pro P Allen
Holes 9 L 6058 m SSS 72
Fees D–20DM
Loc 8km N of Wilhelmshaven

Windhagen

Waldbrunnen (1983)

Brunnenstr 7, 5461 Windhagen
Tel (02645) 15621
Mem 312
Pro M Butzkies
Holes 9 L 4816 m SSS 66
Fees 25DM (35DM)
Loc Bad Honnef 8km

Winterberg

Winterberg

Postfach 1140, 5788 Winterberg
Tel (0 29 81) 1770
Pro D Pugh
Holes 9 L 2945 m Par 71
Fees 25DM (30DM)
Loc Winterberg 2km

Wuppertal

Bergisch-Land

Siebeneickerst 386, 5600 Wuppertal
Tel (02053) 7177
Pro J Bauerdick, W Kothe
Holes 18 L 5920 m SSS 71
Fees 35DM (50DM)
Loc Wuppertal–Elberfeld 8km
Mis WE–only with member. Driving range

Juliana (1978)

Auf dem Golfgeläne, 5600 Wuppertal
Tel (0202) 64 70 70
Mem 650
Pro G Hillier, J Walter, G Problesch
Holes 18 L 6130 m SSS 71
Fees 25DM (30DM)
Loc Düsseldorf 30km

Würzburg

Würzburg-Kitzingen (1980)

Augustinerstr 3, 8700 Würzburg
Tel (0931) 55 77 9
Mem 160
Pro F Dziwlewski
Holes 9 L 6020 m SSS 72
Fees $8.75 ($15)
Loc Würzburg 20km

Greece

Athens

Glyfada (1963)

PO Box 70116 Glyfada, Athens, 16610 Greece
Tel (894) 6820/(893) 1721
Mem 1300
Pro J Sotiropoulos
Holes 18 L 6189 m SSS 72
Fees 3000dra (5000dra)
Loc Athens 12km

Corfu

Corfu (1972)

PO Box 71, Corfu, Greece
Tel (0661) 94220
Mem 150
Pro D Crawley
Holes 18 L 6300 m SSS 72
Fees D–3400dra W–18000dra
Loc Ermones Bay. Corfu town 15km

Halkidiki

Porto Carras G & CC (1979)

Porto Carras, Halkidiki
Tel (0375) 71381/71221 (Tx 412496)
Pro Mrs P Andrade
Holes 18 L 6086 m SSS 72
Fees D–2000dra W–10000dra
Loc Sithonia Peninsula. Thessaloniki 100km

Rhodes

Afantou (1973)

Afantou, Rhodes
Tel (0241) 51255/51256
Mem 96
Pro G Sotiropoulous, V Anasstassiou
Holes 18 L 6060 m SSS 72
Fees 2000dra (10000dra)
Loc Afantou 3km

Holland

Alkmaar

De Noordhollandse (1982)

Sluispolderweg 6, 1817 BM Alkmaar
Tel (072) 156807
Pro P Horn (072) 156175
Holes 9 L 6171 m SSS 72
Fees 25fl (35fl)
Loc 2km N of Alkmaar
Mis Public course. Driving range.

Almelo

De Koepel (1983)

Postbox 88, 7640 AB Wierden
Tel (05496) 76150
Mem 450
Pro A Young
Holes 9 L 2863 m SSS 70
Fees 40fl (50fl)
Loc 7km W of Almelo (E Holland)

Amersfoort

Leusdense De Hoge Kleij

Appelweg 4, 3832 Leusden
Tel (033) 616944
Mem 800
Pro TJ Giles
Holes 18 L 6053 m SSS 72
Fees 50fl (70fl)
Loc 20km NE of Utrecht via A28
Mis WE–max handicap 29

Amsterdam

Amsterdamse (1934)

Zwarte Laantje 4, 1099 CE Amsterdam
Tel (020) 943650
Mem 560 100(J)

Pro W Dorrestein (020) 947409
Fees 30fl (60fl)
Loc Amsterdam 8km

Olympus (1973)

Sportpark, Overamstel, Amsterdam
Tel **(020) 651863**
Mem 550
Pro CJ Broekhuysen, GW Hutchison
Holes 9 L 2236 m SSS 64
Fees 15fl
Loc E of Amstel River, nr junction with A1

Spaarnwoude (1977)

Het Hoge Land 8,1981 LT Velsen
Tel **(023) 382708**
Mem 1500
Pro AC Wessels
Holes 18 L 5406 m SSS 68
Fees 18fl (25fl)
Loc Spaarnwoude, Velsen. 14km W of Amsterdam. 10km NE of Haarlem

Apeldoorn

Veluwse (1957)

Nr 57, 7436 AC Hoog Soeren
Tel **(05769) 275**
Mem 400
Pro C Brown
Holes 9 L 6264 yds SSS 70
Fees 15fl (17.50fl)
Loc 5km W of Apeldoorn

Arnhem

Edese (1979)

Nationaal Sportcentrum Papendal, Amsterdamseweg, Arnhem
Tel **(08306) 1985**
Mem 440
Pro C Borst
Holes 9 L 3050 m SSS 72
Fees 25fl (35fl)
Loc Between Ede and Arnhem

Keppelse (1926)

Oude Zutphenseweg 15, Hoog-Keppel
Tel **(08348) 1416**
Mem 200
Pro C Butti
Holes 9 L 5402 m SSS 67
Fees 25fl (35fl)
Loc Laag Keppel $1^1/_2$ km

Rosendaelsche (1895)

Apeldoornsweg 450, 6816 SN Arnhem
Tel **(085) 421438**
Mem 800
Pro JGM Dorrestein, P Coleman (085) 437283
Holes 18 L 6037 m SSS 72
Fees 30fl (40fl)
Loc 5km N of town centre on Route N50

Breda

N-B Toxandria (1928)

Veenstraat 89, 5124 NC Molenschot
Tel **(01611) 1200**
Mem 800
Pro R Leach
Holes 18 L 5925 m SSS 71
Fees 50fl (70fl)
Loc Breda 8km
Mis Introduction necessary. Please phone in advance

Wouwse Plantage (1981)

Zoomvlietweg 66, 4725 TD Wouwse Plantage
Tel **(01657) 593**
Mem 450
Pro P Helsby, A McLean
Holes 9 L 2854 m SSS 70
Fees 35fl (45fl)
Loc Wouwse Plantage (N 13) near Bergen-op-Zoom

Deventer

Sallandsche "de Hoek" (1934)

PO Box 442, 7400 AK Deventer
Tel **(05709) 1214**
Mem 400
Pro J Balvert (05709) 2293
Holes 9 L 6122 yds SSS 69
Fees 50fl (60fl)
Loc 6km N of Deventer

Drachten

Lauswolt G & CC (1964)

Harinxmaweg 8A, 9244 CH Beetsterzwaag
Tel **(05126) 2594**
Mem 450
Pro J Too
Holes 9 L 5993 m SSS 71
Fees 50fl (60fl)
Loc Beetsterzwaag, 5km S of Drachten

Eindhoven

Eindhovensche (1930)

Eindhovensche Weg 300, 5553 VB Walkenswaard
Tel **(04902) 14816**
Mem 500 250(L) 80(J)
Pro G Jeurissen, J Renders
Holes 18 L 6106 m SSS 71
Fees 50fl (70fl)
Loc 14km S of Eindhoven

Haviksoord (1976)

Maarheezerweg Nrd 11, 5595 XG Leende (NB)
Tel **(04906) 1818/(040) 813186**
Mem 350
Pro D Marcks (04906) 1818
Holes 9 L 5856 m SSS 71
Fees 25fl (35fl)
Loc 10km S of Eindhoven
Mis Handicap certificate required

De Schoot (1973)

Schootsedijk 18, 5491 TD Sint Oedenrode
Tel **(04138) 73011**
Mem 400
Pro J Ottevanger
Holes 9 L 2392 m SSS 66
Fees 20fl (25fl)
Loc Eindhoven 20km

Emmen

Gelpenberg (1970)

Gebbeveensweg 1, 7854 TD Aalden
Tel **(05917) 1784**
Mem 375
Pro W Stevens (05917) 1525
Holes 9 L 5867 m SSS 71
Fees 50fl (60fl)
Loc 16km W of Emmen

Groningen

Noord Nederlandse G & CC (1950)

Pollselaan 5, 9756 CJ Glimmen
Tel **(05906) 1275**
Mem 700
Pro KC Visser, K MacDonald
Holes 18 L 5680 m SSS 70
Fees 60fl (90fl)
Loc Route A28, Junction Eelde towards Glimmen and Zuidlaren

Haarlem

Kennemer G & CC (1910)

PO Box 85, 2040 AB Zandvoort
Tel **(02507) 12836**
Mem 840
Pro J Buchanan
Holes 18 L 5860 m SSS 72
9 L 2901 m
Fees 60fl (80fl)
Loc Haarlem 6km

The Hague

Haagsche G & CC (1893)

Groot Haesebrokeseweg 22, 2242 EC Wassenaar
Tel **(01751) 79607**
Mem 1400
Pro A Loesberg, S van den Berg

Holes 18 L 5674 m SSS 71
Fees 70fl (90fl)
Loc Den Haag 6km
Mis Phone before play. Introduction required.

Wassenarse Rozenstein (1984)

Hoge Klei 1, 2242 XZ Wassenaar
Tel (01751) 17846
Pro GTG Janmaat
Holes 9 L 6044 m SSS 71
Fees 30fl (60fl)
Loc 14km NE of The Hague
Mis Driving range, pitch and putt

Den Helder

Marine Nieuwediep (1958)

PO Box 932, 1780AX Den Helder
Mem 300
Holes 9 L 4780 m SSS 66
Fees 6fl
Loc Nieuwe Haven
Mis Situated on naval base; entry by permit or introduction only

Hengelo

Twentsche (1930)

Enschedesestraat 381, 7552 CV Hengelo
Tel (074) 912773
Mem 400
Pro J Poppe
Holes 9 L 5444 m SSS 69
Fees 25fl (30fl)
Loc Hengelo 3km

's-Hertogenbosch

De Dommel

Zegenwerp 12, St Michielsgestel
Tel (04105) 2316
Mem 430
Pro M Groenendaal
Holes 12 L 5565 m SSS 69
Fees 20fl (30fl)
Loc 's-Hertogenbosch 10km

Hilversum

Hilversumsche (1910)

172 Soestdijkerstraatweg, 1213 XJ Hilversum
Tel (035) 857060
Mem 730
Pro M Morbey, R Cattell
Holes 18 L 6458 yds SSS 71
Fees 50fl (70fl)
Loc Hilversum 3km on road to Baarn

Zeewolde

Postbuis 1461, 1200 BL Hilversum
Tel (03242) 2103
Mem 800
Pro P van Wijk, I Flegg
Holes 18 L 5954 m SSS 71
Fees 35fl (45fl)
Loc 20km N of Hilversum. 60km NE of Amsterdam

Maastricht

Wittem G & CC

Dal-Bissenweg, 6281 NC Mechelen
Tel (04455) 1397
Mem 500
Pro AV Pinxten, WV Mook
Holes 9 L 5866 m SSS 71
Fees 25fl (30fl)
Loc Gulpen 5km

Middelburg

Domburgsche (1913)

Schelpweg 26, 4357 BP Domburg
Tel (01188) 1573
Mem 320
Pro L Verberne
Holes 9 L 5139 m SSS 67
Fees 50fl (60fl)
Loc 15km NW of Middelburg

Nijmegen

Berendonck (1987)

Panhuisweg 39, 6603 KH Wijchen
Tel (08894) 20039
Mem 300
Pro W Swart, C Tjerks
Holes 9 L 5788 m SSS 70
Fees 18 holes 25fl (35fl)
9 holes 15fl (25fl)
Loc Nijmegen 5km
Mis Public course. WE comps

Het Rijk van Nijmegen (1985)

Postweg 17, 6561 KJ Groesbeek
Tel (08891) 76644
Mem 550
Pro B Gee, G Morris, M Kavanagh
Holes 18 L 6114 m SSS 72
9 L 4824 m SSS 66
9 L 4166 m SSS 62
Fees 50fl (75fl)
Loc 5km E of Nijmegen

Noordwijk

Noordwijkse (1982)

Randweg 25, PO Box 70 2200 AB-Noordwijk
Tel (02523) 73761
Mem 910
Pro T O'Mahoney, P Horn (02523) 76993
Holes 18 L 5910 m SSS 72
Fees 60fl (80fl)
Loc 5km N of Noordwyk. 15km NW of Leiden

Rotterdam

Broekpolder (1981)

Watersportweg 100, 3138 HD Vlaardingen
Tel (010) 4750011/4748140/4748142
Mem 840
Pro J Stoop, J Hage, M Maddison
Holes 18 L 6048 m SSS 72
Fees 30–45fl (50–70fl)
Loc Rotterdam 15km by A20 Rotterdam–Hoek van Holland

Kleiburg (1974)

c/o Vredenburchlaan 47, 2661 HE Bergenshenhoek
Tel (01810) 14225
Pro W Koudijs
Holes 18 L 5534 m SSS 69
Fees 25fl
Loc 25km W of Rotterdam
Mis Public course

Openbare GC Kralingen (1933)

Kralingseweg 200, 3062 CG Rotterdam
Tel (010) 4527646
Mem 300
Pro R Heijkant, C Kuysters
Holes 9 L 5277 yds SSS 66
Fees 16fl (25fl)
Loc Rotterdam centre 5km

Oude Maas (1975)

Veerweg 2, 3161 EX Rhoon
Tel (01890) 18058
Pro R Goor
Holes 9 L 5876 m SSS 71
9 hole Par 3
Fees 20fl (32fl)
Loc 10km S of Rotterdam

Utrecht

De Haar (1974)

PO Box 104, Parkweg 5, 3450 AC Vleuten
Tel (03407) 2860
Mem 450
Pro B McColl
Holes 9 L 6650 yds SSS 71
Fees 50fl (70fl)
Loc 10km NW of Utrecht

Utrechtse "De Pan' (1894)

Amersfoortseweg 1, 3735 LJ Bosch en Duin
Tel (03404) 55223 (Sec)
(03404) 56225 (Clubhouse)
Mem 800
Pro C Dorrestein (03404) 56427

Holes 18 L 6088 m SSS 70
Fees 50fl (70fl)
Loc Utrecht 10km on A28 Utrecht–Amersfoort
Mis Advisable to ring first

Venlo

Geysteren G & CC (1974)

Het Spekt 2, Geysteren (L) 5862 AZ
Tel (04784) 1809/2592
Mem 700
Pro LG van Mook
Holes 18 L 5984 m SSS 71
Fees 60fl (70fl)
Loc N271 Venlo–Nymegen via Well and Wanssum

Zwolle

Hattemse G & CC (1930)

Veenwal 11, 8051 AS Hattem
Tel (05206) 41909
Mem 385
Holes 9 L 5808 yds SSS 68
Fees 40fl (50fl)
Loc Off Zwolle–Apeldoorn road

Iceland

Akranes

Leynir (1965)

PO Box 9, Akranes
Tel (93) 2711
Mem 80
Holes 9 L 2640 m SSS 69
Fees 100 Ikr
Loc Akranes

Akureyri

Akureyri (1935)

PO Box 896, 602 Akureyri
Tel (96) 22974
Mem 500
Pro DG Barnwell
Holes 18 L 5851 m SSS 72
Fees £15 (£20)
Loc 1km from Akureyri at North Innland
Mis World's most northern 18-hole course (with Luleå, Sweden). Home of the Arctic Open

Borgarnes

Borgarness (1973)

PO Box 112, 310 Borgarnes
Tel (95) 7663
Mem 60
Holes 18 L 5260 m SSS 69
9 L 2630 m SSS 69
Fees 300 Ikr
Loc Borgarnes centre 5km

Éskifjördur

Éskifjardar (1976)

735 Éskifjördur
Mem 45
Holes 9 L 2206 m SSS 66
Fees D–500 Ikr
Loc 3km W of town

Hafnarfjördur

Keilir (1967)

Hvaleyri, Hafnarfjördur
Tel 53360
Mem 300
Pro T Asgeirsson
Holes 18 L 5090 m SSS 68
Fees 500 Ikr
Loc S side of town. Reykjavik 10km

Hornafjördur

Hornafjardar

Hornafirdi
Tel (97) 8030
Mem 44
Holes 9 L 3610 m SSS 63
Fees 200 Ik
Loc Hofn

Huolsvelli

Hellu (1974)

Austurveg 1, Huolsvelli
Tel 8166
Mem 74
Holes 9 L 3886 m SSS 61
Fees 100 Ikr
Loc South Innland

Húsavík

Húsavíkur

PO Box 23, Kötlum, 640 Húsavík
Tel (96) 41000
Mem 90
Holes 9 L 2686 m SSS 70
Fees 700 Ikr
Loc Húsavík 2km

Ísafjördur

Ísafjardar (1978)

PO Box 367, Ísafjördur
Tel (94) 3035 (Captain)
Mem 75
Holes 9 L 4860 m SSS 67
Fees D–500 Ikr 1988 prices
Loc 3km W of town
Mis Course closed most WE for competitions

Keflavik

Sudurnesja (1964)

PO Box 112, 230 Keflavik
Tel (92) 14100
Mem 165
Holes 18 L 5961 m SSS 73
Loc N of Keflavik. Airport 5km
Mis Links course

Ólafsfjördur

Ólafsfjardar (1967)

Ólafsfjördur
Mem 25
Holes 9 L 4652 m SSS 65

Ólafsvík

Jökull (1973)

Ólafsvík
Mem 38
Holes 9 L 4800 m SSS 65
Loc 5km SE of town

Reykjavík

Ness (1964)

PO Box 66, 172 Seltjarnes
Tel 611930
Mem 170
Pro TH Asgeirsson
Holes 9 L 4986 m SSS 68
Fees WD/WE–800 Ikr
Loc 3km W from city

Reykjavíkur (1934)

Grafarholti, Box 4071, 124 Reykjavík
Tel 84735
Mem 816
Pro J Drummond 82815
Holes 18 L 5956 m SSS 70
Fees 1000 Ikr
Loc 8km E of Reykjavík

Saudárkrókur

Saudárkróks (1970)

Saudárkrókur
Tel (95) 5075
Mem 50
Holes 9 L 5708 m SSS 71
Fees 150 Ikr
Loc $1\frac{1}{2}$ km W of town

For explanation of abbreviations, see page 202.

Selfoss

Selfoss (1971)

Selfoss
Mem 48
Holes 9 L 5070 m SSS 69
Loc South Innland

Siglufjördur

Siglufjardar (1970)

Siglufjördur
Mem 35
Holes 9 L 4950 m SSS 66

Vestmannaeyjar

Vestmannaeyja (1938)

Tel 12363
Mem 221
Pro P Grünwell
Holes 9 L 2881 m SSS 69
Fees 300 Ikr
Loc 2km W of town centre. Large island off S coast. 20 min flight from Reykjavík.

Italy

Alassio

Garlenda (1965)

17030 Garlenda (Savona)
Tel (0182) 580012
Mem 600 130(L) 85(J)
Pro F Zanini, F Picco
Holes 18 L 5973 m SSS 71
Fees 50000L (75000L) 5D–180000L
Loc 15km N of Alassio

Alessandria

Margara (1975)

Via Tenuta Margara 5, 15043 Fubine (AL)
Tel (0131) 772377
Mem 170
Pro G Sità
Holes 18 L 6218 m SSS 72
Fees 10000L (15000L)
Loc 15km NW of Alessandria

La Serra

Via Astigliano 42, 15048 Valenza (AL)
Tel (0131) 954778
Mem 313
Pro A Caputo
Holes 9 L 2820 m SSS 70
Fees 25000L (35000L)
Loc Valenza 4km. AAleeessandria 6km
Mis Open Mar–Nov. Driving range

Bergamo

Bergamo L'Albenza (1960)

Via Longoni 12, 24030 Almenno San Bartolomeo
Tel (035) 640028/640707
Mem 480
Pro S Locatelli, M Rendina, F Ripamonti, C Rocca
Holes 18 L 6198 m SSS 72
9 L 2962 m SSS 36
Fees 40000L (60000L)
Loc Bergamo 13km. Milan 45km
Mis Closed Mon

La Rossera

Via Montebello 4, 24060 Chiuduno
Tel (035) 838600
Pro R Giglioni, G Watson
Holes 9 L 2510 m SSS 68
Fees 20000L (40000L)
Loc 18km SE of Bergamo

Biella

Biella "Le Betulle" (1958)

Valcarozza, 13050 Magnano (VC)
Tel 679151
Mem 300
Pro M Guersoli, A Reale
Holes 18 L 6100 m SSS 72
Fees 45000L (70000L)
Loc 17km SW of Biella

Bologna

Bologna (1959)

Via Sabatini 69, 40050 Chiesa Nuova di Monte S Pietro
Tel (051) 756154
Mem 280
Pro B Chezzo
Holes 18 L 5860 m SSS 71
Fees 4000L (5000L)
Loc 15km W of Bologna

Brescia

Bogliaco (1912)

Via Golf 11, 25088 Toscolano Maderno (Brescia)
Tel (0365) 643006
Mem 300
Pro L Tavernini
Holes 9 L 2572 m SSS 67
Fees 35000L (50000L)
Loc Lake Garda, 40km NE of Brescia
Mis Driving range

Gardagolf (1985)

Via Angelo Omodeo 2, 25080 Soiano Del Lago (BS)
Tel (0365) 674707 (Sec)
Mem 380
Pro F Maestroni, F Ghezzo, B Maestroni
Holes 18 L 6505 m SSS 74
9 L 2415 m Par 34
Fees 40000L (50000L)
Loc Lake Garda, 30km NE of Brescia.
Mis Driving range

Catanzaro Lido

Porto d'Orra (1977)

PB 102, 88063 Catanzaro Lido
Tel (0961) 791045
Mem 141
Pro L de Gori
Holes 9 L 2492 m SSS 70
Fees WD/WE–25000L
Loc 9km N of Catanzaro Lido

Cervinia

Cervino (1955)

11021 Cervinia-Breuil (AO)
Tel (0116) 949131
Mem 300
Holes 9 L 2397 m SSS 66
Fees 35000L–50000L
Loc 53km NE of Aosta

Como

Carimate (1962)

Via Airoldi, 22060 Carimate
Tel (031) 790226
Mem 500
Pro E Songia, M Frigerio, B Molteni
Holes 18 L 5982 m SSS 71
Fees 40000L (60000L)
Loc Como 15km. Milan 27km

Lanzo Intelvi (1962)

22024 Lanzo Intelvi (CO)
Tel (031) 840169
Mem 188
Pro G Frigerio
Holes 9 L 2438 m SSS 66
Fees 25000L (50000L)
Loc 32km N of Como. Campione d'Italia 10km
Mis Open May–Oct

Menaggio & Cadenabbia (1907)

Via Golf 12, 22010 Grandola E Uniti (CO)
Tel (0344) 32103/31564
Mem 260
Pro G Delfino

Holes 18 L 5277 m SSS 69
Fees 35000L (55000L)
Loc 5km W of Menaggio. Lugano 27km. Milan 80km

Monticello (1975)

Via Volta 4, 22070 Cassina Rizzardi
Tel (031) 928055
Mem 1200
Pro A Croce, V Damonte, E Bianchi, A Schiroli, A Ferlito
Holes 18 L 6413 m SSS 72
18 L 6056 m SSS 72
Fees 40000L (70000L)
Loc 10km SE of Como

La Pinetina (1971)

Via al Golf 4, 22070 Appiano Gentile
Tel (031) 933202
Mem 420
Pro M Sabbatino
Holes 18 L 6001 m SSS 71
Fees 35000L (50000L)
Loc Como 12km. Milan 25km

Royal Sant'Anna (1978)

22040 Annone di Brianza (CO)
Tel (0341) 577551
Holes 9 L 5370 m SSS 69
Fees 25000L (30000L)
Loc 15km SE of Como. Milano 40km

Villa D'Este (1926)

Via Cantù 13, 22030 Montorfano (CO)
Tel (031) 200200
Mem 406
Pro GC Frigerio, P Molteni, G Ciprandi
Holes 18 L 5750 m SSS 71
Fees 50000L (70000L)
Loc Montorfano, Como 7km
Mis Driving range

Courmayeur

Courmayeur & Grandes Jorasses

Courmayeur 11013 (AO)
Tel (0165) 89103
Pro F Venier
Holes 9 L 2650 m SSS 67
Fees D–4000L
Loc 5km NE of Courmayeur
Mis Driving range. Open Jul–Sept

Elba

Acquabona

57037 Portoferraio, Isola di Elba (LI)
Tel (0565) 940066
Mem 220
Pro G Ciprandi, M Barbi
Holes 9 L 5144 m SSS 67
Fees 20000–40000L
Loc 5km NW of Porto Azzurro

Fiuggi Fonte

Fiuggi (1926)

Superstrada Anlicolana 1, 03015 Fiuggi Fonte (FR)
Tel (0775) 55250
Mem 200
Pro R Terrinoni
Holes 9 L 5697 m SSS 70
Fees 20000L (25000L)
Mis Driving range

Florence

Ugolino

Strada Chiantigiana 3, 50015 Grassina
Tel (055) 205 1009
Mem 700
Pro F Rosi, R Campagnoli, C Poletti
Holes 18 L 5785 m SSS 70
Fees 40000L (60000L)
Loc Florence 12km

Genoa

Arenzano Della Pineta

Piazza del Golf, 16011 Arenzano (GE)
Tel (010) 9111817
Mem 672
Pro S Gori, A Mori, V Mori
Holes 9 L 5540 m SSS 70
Fees 25000L (40000L)
Loc 20km W of Genoa

Grosseto

Punta Ala (1964)

Via del Golf 1, 58040 Punta Ala (GR)
Tel (0564) 922121
Mem 330
Pro M Mulas, P Manca, F Rosi, GC Poletti
Holes 18 L 6190 m SSS 72
Fees 35000L–50000L
Loc 40km NW of Grosseto. Pisa 145km. Florence 150km

Madonna Di Campiglio

Campo Carlo Magno (1922)

c/o Golf Hotel, Madonna di Campiglio (TN)
Tel (0465) 41003
Mem 45
Pro A Silva
Holes 9 L 4992 m SSS 68
Fees D–8000L
Loc Madonna di Campiglio 1km. 74km NW of Trento
Mis Open Jul–Sept

Milan

Barlassina CC (1952)

Via Privata Golf 42, 20030 Birago di Camnago (MI)
Tel (0362) 560621/2/3
Mem 300
Pro N Rendina, S Betti
Holes 18 L 6073 m SSS 71
Fees 50000L (60000L)
Loc 22km N of Milan

Milano (1928)

20052 Parco di Monza (MI)
Tel (039) 303081/303082
Mem 1050
Pro G Grappasonni (039) 304561
Holes 18 L 6239 m SSS 73
9 L 2976 m SSS 36
Fees 50000L (60000L)
Loc 6km N of Monza. Milan 17km

Molinetto CC

SS Padana Superiore 11, 20063 Cernusco sul Naviglio (MI)
Tel (02) 9238500/9249373
Pro F Perini, M Taricone, B Giordano
Holes 18 L 6010 m Par 72
Fees 40000L (50000L)
Loc 10km E of Milan
Mis Driving range

Le Rovedine (1978)

Public

Via C Marx, 20090 Noverasco di Opera (MI)
Tel (02) 5242730
Mem 450
Pro R Benassi, L Marsala, L Ghirardo, G Veronelli
Holes 9 L 2890 m SSS 71
Fees 17500L (21500L)
Loc 4km S of Milan
Mis Public course

Zoate

20067 Zoate di Tribiano (MI)
Tel (02) 90632183/90631861
Pro L Grappasoni, S Zerega
Holes 18 L 6116 m Par 72
Loc 17km SE of Milan

Montecatini

Montecatini Golf (1985)

Via Dei Brogi, Loc. Pievaccia, 51005 Monsummano Terme (PT)
Tel (0572) 62218
Mem 184
Pro M Ravinetto

Holes 18 L 6140 m SSS 72
Fees 20000L (25000L)
Loc Montecatini Terme 9km. 40km NW of Florence on A11

Naples

Circolo Golf Napoli

Via Campiglione 11, 80072 Arco Felice (NA)
Tel **(081) 8674296**
Holes 9 L 4776 m SSS 68
Fees 30000L (35000L)
Loc Pozzuoli, 10km W of Naples
Mis Guests with members only.

Novara

Castelconturbia (1984)

Via Suno, 28010 Agrate Conturbia (NO)
Tel **(0322) 802093**
Mem 516
Pro A Angelini, A Ferraloni, B Murdaca
Holes Red 9 L 3330 m Par 36
Yellow 9 L 3070 m Par 36
Blue 9 L 3210 m Par 36
Loc 23km N of Novara. Milan 60km
Mis Driving range

Vigevano "Santa Martretta" (1974)

Via Chitola 49, 27029 Vigevano (PV)
Tel **(0381) 76872**
Mem 208
Pro A Zito
Holes 9 L 5880 m Par 72
Fees 25000L (40000L)
Loc 25km SE of Novara. Milan 35km. Pavia 35km

Padua

Padova (1966)

35050 Valsanzibio di Galzigano
Tel **(049) 9130078**
Mem 600
Pro A Lionello, P Bernardini
Holes 18 L 6053 m SSS 72
Fees 40000L (45000L)
Loc 20km S of Padua

Parma

La Rocca (1985)

Via Campi 8, 43038 Sala Baganza
Tel **(0521) 834037**
Mem 300
Pro R Bolognesi
Holes 9 L 2891 m SSS 70
Fees £10 (£14)
Loc 8km S of Parma

Perugia

Perugia (1970)

06074 Santa Sabina-Ellera (PG)
Tel **(075) 79704**
Mem 220
Pro R Paris
Holes 9 L 2890 m SSS 35
Fees 20000L
Loc 6km NW of Perugia

Piacenza

Croara (1977)

29010 Croara di Gazzola (PC)
Tel **(0523) 977105/977148**
Mem 290
Pro G Turrini, E Vergari
Holes 18 L 6040 m SSS 72
Fees 30000L (40000L)
Loc 16km SW of Piacenza

Pisa

Tirrenia (1968)

56018 Tirrenia (PI)
Tel **(050) 37518**
Mem 320
Pro M Ravinetto
Holes 9 L 3065 m SSS 72
Fees 20000L (25000L)
Loc On coast between Pisa and Livorno

Rapallo

Rapallo (1930)

Via Mameli 377, 16035 Rapallo (GE)
Tel **(0185) 50210/57187**
Mem 769
Pro M Canessa, M Erbisti, C Costa, A Brizzolari, M Avanzino
Holes 18 L 5694 m SSS 70
Fees 50000L (Sat–70000L)
Loc Rapallo

Ravenna

Adriatic GC Cervia (1985)

Via Ielenia Gora, 48016 Milano Marittima (RA)
Tel **(0544) 992786**
Mem 420
Pro R Paris
Holes 18 L 6275 m SSS 72
Fees 35000L (45000L)
Loc 20km SE of Ravenna

Rome

Fioranello

Casella Postale 96, 00040 Santa Maria delle Mole (Roma)
Tel **(06) 608291/608058**
Mem 250
Pro R Croce, A Pelliccioni
Holes 9 L 5276 m SSS 68
Fees 25000L (30000L)
Loc 17km SE of Rome
Mis Driving range

Olgiata (1961)

Largo Olgiata 15, 00123 Roma
Tel **(06) 3789141**
Mem 800
Pro U Grappasonni
Holes 18 L 6396 m SSS 72
9 L 2968 m SSS 71
Fees 40000L (50000L)
Loc Via Cassia Rome 19km
Mis Driving range

Roma (1903)

Via Appia Nuova 716, 00178 Roma
Tel **(06) 783407/7886159**
Mem 1300
Pro P Manca, C Croce, M Peri
Holes 18 L 5707 m SSS 70
Fees 5000L (8000L)
Loc 7½ km from city centre towards Ciampino

Rovigo

Albarella (1988)

Isola de Albarella, 45010 Rosolino (RO)
Tel **(0426) 67124**
Pro L Paolillo
Holes 18 L 6065 m SSS 72
Fees 40000L (50000L)
Loc 64km S of Venice
Mis Driving range

San Remo

Degli Ulivi (1932)

Via Campo Golf 59, 18038 San Remo
Tel **(0184) 557093/71945**
Mem 360
Pro M Bianco, G Ammirati
Holes 18 L 5230 m SSS 67
Fees 35000L (60000L)
Loc City centre 5km

Sardinia

Is Molas (1975)

Casella postale 49, 09010 Pula
Tel **(070) 9209062/9208427**
Mem 300
Pro L Cau
Holes 18 L 6992 yds SSS 72
Fees 40000–50000L
Loc Pula, 35km S of Cagliari.

Pevero (1972)

07020 Porto Cervo, Sardegna
Tel **(0789) 96072/95210**
Mem 279
Pro DB Mills (0789) 96222
Holes 18 L 6186 m SSS 72

Fees D–43000L
Loc Porto Cervo, 30km N of Olbia, on Costa Smeralda

Sestrieres

Sestrieres (1932)

Piazza Agnelli 4, 10058 Sestrieres (TO)
Tel (0122) 76276/ 76243
Mem 400
Pro M Vinzi, S Bertaina
Holes 18 L 4598 m SSS 65
Fees 35000L (45000L)
Loc Sestrieres, 96km W of Turin
Mis Highest course in Europe
Open Jun–Sept

La Spezia

Marigola

Via Vallata 5, 19032 Lerici (SP)
Tel (0187) 970193
Mem 60
Pro CA Le Chevallier
Holes 9 L 2120 m Par 54
Loc 6km SE of La Spezia

Stresa

Alpino Di Stresa (1925)

28040 Vezzo (Novara)
Tel (0323) 20101/20642
Mem 280
Pro P Giacono
Holes 9 L 5359 m SSS 67
Fees 30000L (40000L)
Loc 7km W of Stresa

Piandisole (1964)

Via Pineta 1, 28057 Premeno (NO)
Tel (0323) 47100
Mem 180
Pro V Viero
Holes 9 L 2830 m SSS 67
Fees 30000L (40000L)
Loc Promeno, 30km N of Stresa

Taranto

Riva Dei Tessali (1971)

74025 Marina di Ginosa (TA)
Tel (099) 6439251
Mem 120
Pro B Cosenza
Holes 18 L 6016 m SSS 71
Fees 5000L (7000L)
Loc 34km SW of Taranto

Tarquinia

Marina Velca

01016 Marina Velca Tarquinia (VT)
Tel (0766) 812109
Mem 150
Pro R Napoleoni
Holes 9 L 2604 m SSS 50
Fees D–5000L
Loc On coast, 80km N of Rome

Trieste

Trieste (1954)

Via Padriciano 80, 34012 Trieste
Tel (040) 226159/227062
Mem 200
Pro E Pavan
Holes 9 L 2725 m SSS 69
Fees 20000L (22000L)
Loc Padriciano, 7km from centre

Turin

Claviere (1926)

Strada Nazionale, 10050 Claviere (TO)
Tel (0122) 878917 (Clubhouse)
(011) 2398346 (Sec)
Mem 850
Pro L Merlino, F Giacotto
Holes 9 L 4428 m SSS 63
Fees 30000L (40000L)
Loc 96km W of Turin
Mis Open Jun–Oct

Le Chioccole CC

Loc Fraschetta, Cascina Roma, 12062 Cherasco (CN)
Tel (0172) 48772
Pro A Fiammengo, V Pelle
Holes 18 L 5863 m SSS 71
Loc 45km S of Turin

Le Fronde (1975)

Via Sant–Agostino 68, 10051 Avigliana (TO)
Tel (011) 938053/930540
Mem 350
Pro M Rolando, A Merletti
Holes 18 L 6081 m SSS 72
Fees 35000L (50000L)
Loc 20km W ofTurin
Mis Driving range

I Roveri (1971)

Rotta Cerbiatta 24, 10070 Fiano (TO)
Tel (011) 923571
Pro M Vinzi, G Colombatto
Holes 18 L 6218 m SSS 72
9 L 3107 m SSS 36
Fees 50000L (80000L)
Loc 16km NW of Turin

Stupinigi (1972)

Corso Unione Sovietica 506, 10135 Torino
Tel (011) 343975
Pro D Canonica, F Luzi
Holes 9 L 1975 m SSS 63
Loc Mirafiore, Turin
Mis Closed Aug

Torino (1924)

Via Grange 137, 10070 Fiano Torinese
Tel (011) 9235440/9235670
Mem 800
Pro O Bolognesi, L Merlino, S Bertaina
Holes 18 L 6216 m SSS 72
18 L 6211 m SSS 72
Fees 40000L (60000L)
Loc 23km NW of Turin

Udine

San Floriano–Gorizia (1987)

Via Oslavia 5, 34070 S Floriano del Collio (GO)
Tel (0481) 884131/884051
Mem 100
Pro E Pavan
Holes 9 L 2600 m SSS 58
Fees 20000L (25000L)
Loc 6km NW of Gorizia. 50km SE of Udine, nr Yugoslav border
Mis Open Mar–Dec. Driving range. Closed Mon

Udine (1971)

33034 Fagagna–Villaverde (UD)
Tel (0432) 800418
Mem 210
Pro L Tavarini
Holes 9 L 2944 m SSS 71
Fees 30000L
Loc 15km NW of Udine

Varese

Varese (1934)

Via Vittorio Veneto 32, 21020 Luvinate (VA)
Tel (0332) 227394/229302
Mem 622
Pro S Abbiati, M Ballarin
Holes 18 L 5936 m SSS 72
Fees 40000L (60000L)
Loc 5km NW of Varese

Venice

Ca' della Nave (1986)

Piazza Vittoria 14, 30030 Martellago (Venezia)
Tel (041) 5410555
Mem 400
Pro M Napeoleoni
Holes 27 holes SSS 72
Fees 40000L (50000L)
Loc Venice 20km

Circolo Golf Venezia (1928)

Via del Forte, 30011 Alberoni (Venezia)
Tel (041) 731015
Mem 430
Pro T Scarso, R Pavan, R Trentin
Holes 18 L 6126 m SSS 72
Fees 40000L (50000L)
Loc Venice Lido

Villa Condulmer

Via della Croce 3, 31021 Zerman di Mogliano Veneto (TV)
Tel (041) 457062
Mem 350
Pro S Ugo
Holes 18 L 5880 m SSS 71
Fees 18000L (Sun–20000L)
Loc 17km N of Venice

Verona

Verona (1967)

Ca' del Sale 15,
37066 Sommacampagna (VR)
Tel (045) 510060
Mem 430
Pro E Ridolfi, M Bolognesi
Holes 18 L 6307 m SSS 72
Fees 40000L (50000L)
Loc 7km W of Verona

Vicenza

Asiago (1967)

Via Meltar 2,36012 Asiago (VI)
Tel (0424) 62721
Mem 200
Pro M Bolognesi
Holes 9 L 2873 m SSS 70
Fees 5000L (6000L)
Loc 3km N of Asiago. 50km N of Vicenza
Mis Open Jun–Oct

Vittorio Veneto

Cansiglio (1956)

c/o A.A.S.T, 31029 Vittorio Veneto
Tel (0438) 585398
Mem 233
Pro U Scafa
Holes 9 L 5666 m SSS 69
Fees 36000L (40000L) 1988 prices
Loc 21km NE of Vittorio Veneto

Luxembourg

CC Grand-Ducal De Luxembourg (1936)

1, Route de Treves,
2633 Senningerberg
Tel Luxembourg 34090
Mem 1200
Pro E Saquet, S Clough, A Bruce
Holes 18 L 5765 m SSS 71
Fees 900fr (1250fr)
Loc Luxembourg 7km

Malta

Marsa Sports Club (1888)

Marsa, Malta
Tel (231809) 232842/233851
Mem 350
Pro R Josie
Holes 18 L 5800 yds SSS 67
Fees D–£M4

Norway

Bergen

Bergen

PO Box 470, 5001 Bergen
Tel 182077
Mem 300
Pro S Norris
Holes 9 L 4461 m SSS 33
Fees D–100kr
Loc Bergen 8km

Drammen

Kjekstad (1976)

PO Box 201, 3440 Royken
Tel (02) 855850/855353
Mem 1125
Pro D Craig
Holes 14 L 5100 yds SSS 68
Fees WD/WE–100kr
Loc 40km SW of Oslo. 12km SE of Drammen on Route 282

Hamar

Hedmark

PO Box 1131, 2301 Hamar
Tel (064) 13588
Mem 141
Holes 9 L 3200 m SSS 36
Fees 60kr
Loc Elverum, 35km E of Hamar. 150km N of Oslo

Kristiansand

Kristiansand (1973)

PO Box 31, N–4601 Kristiansand
Tel (042) 45863
Mem 350
Pro DR Clark
Holes 9 L 2485 m SSS 70
Fees WD/WE 100kr
Loc 8km E of K'sand off E18

Oslo

Oslo (1924)

Bogstad, 0757 Oslo 7
Tel (02) 504402
Mem 2917
Pro S Newey
Holes 18 L 6574 yds SSS 72
Fees 180kr (220kr)
Loc 8km NW of Oslo centre. Follow signs to "Bogstad Camping".
Mis Handicap certificate required. V'trs restricted WD–9am–1pm WE–3–7pm.

Oustoen

PO Box 1166–Sentrum, 6107 Oslo 1
Tel 535295/486563 (Sec)
Mem 360
Holes 11
Fees 100kr
Loc Small island in Oslofjord, W of Oslo
Mis Private club. V'trs must be accompanied by a member.

Sarpsborg

Borregaard (1927)

PO Box 348, 1701 Sarpsborg
Tel (09) 157401
Mem 500
Pro F Mudie
Holes 9 L 4500 m SSS 64
Fees D–80kr
Loc Opsund, 1km N of town.

Skien

Grenland (1983)

PO Box 433, 3701 Skien
Mem 127
Pro P Congreve
Holes 6 SSS 57
Fees 50kr
Loc Jarseng Sportstve

Stavanger

Stavanger (1956)

Longebakke 45, N–4042 Hafrsfjord
Tel 555431
Mem 850
Pro R Lees
Holes 18 L 5090 m SSS 68
Fees 100kr
Loc 6km SW of Stavanger

Tønsberg

Vestfold (1958)

PO Box 64, 3101 Tønsberg
Tel (033) 65655 (Sec)
Mem 1050
Pro G Beal

Holes 18 L 5860 m SSS 72
Fees D–120kr (180kr)
Loc Tønsberg 8km

Trondheim

Trondheim (1950)

PO Box 169, 7001 Trondheim
Tel **531885**
Mem 330
Pro K Dudmann
Holes 9 L 5632 m SSS 72
Fees 100kr
Loc Trondheim 3km

Portugal

Algarve

Alto (1987)

PO Box 1, Alvor, Portimão, Algarve
Tel **(082) 20119**
Holes 18 L 6659 yds SSS
Loc Portimão 5km

Palmares

Palmares, Lagos, Algarve
Tel **62961/62953**
Mem 250
Pro L Espadinha
Holes 18 L 5961 m SSS 72
Fees 4300esc
Loc Lagos 5km

Parque da Floresta (1987)

Budens, 8650 Vila do Bispo, Algarve
Tel **(082) 65333/4/5**
Holes 18 L 6476 yds SSS
Fees WD/WE–3500esc
Loc 16km W of Lagos, nr Salema

Penina (1966)

PO Box 146, Penina, Portimão, 8502 Algarve
Tel **(82) 22051/58**
Mem 220
Pro R Liddle, J Lourenco
Holes 18 L 6889 yds SSS 73
9 L 3500 yds SSS 36
9 L 2278 yds SSS 33
Fees 18 hole course D–5500esc
9 hole courses D–3700esc
Loc Portimão 5km

Quinta Do Lago (1974)

Quinta Do Lago, Almancil, 8100 Loule, Algarve
Tel **(089) 94782/94529**
Mem 300
Pro DG Silva
Holes 3=9 holes:
A+B L 6362 m Par 72
B+C L 6488 m Par 72
C+A L 6400 m Par 72
Fees WD/WE–6000esc
Loc Faro 20km
Mis Driving range

Vale Do Lobo (1968)

Vale Do Lobo, Almancil, Algarve
Tel **(089) 94444**
Mem 375
Pro S Walker
Holes Green 9 L 2813 m SSS 35
Orange 9 L 2975 m SSS 36
Yellow 9 L 3036 m SSS 36
Fees D–5600esc; Hotel Don Filipa–4200esc; Villa guests–2800esc
Loc Faro Airport 19km
Mis Par 3 course, driving range

Vilamoura (1969)

Vilamoura, 8125 Quarteira, Algarve
Tel **Vilamoura 1 (089) 33652**
Vilamoura 2 (089) 35562
Mem 300
Pro J Catarino
Holes Vilamoura 1 18 L 6331 m SSS 72; Vilamoura 2 18 L 6192 m SSS 71
Fees 4500esc (Discounts for Vilamoura guests)
Loc 25km W of Faro Airport
Mis Vilamoura 2 was originally Dom Pedro golf course

Azores

São Miguel

PO Box 55, 9501 Ponta Delgada, Azores
Tel **31925/54341**
Holes 9 L 5492 m SSS 71
Loc São Miguel Island
Mis Driving range

Terceira Island (1954)

9760 Praia da Vitória, Azores
Tel **25847**
Mem 800
Pro E Mendes Correia
Holes 18 L 6332 yds SSS 70
Fees D–US$ 6 (D–US$ 8)
Loc 13km from Angra do Heroismo, Praia da Victória and Lajes international airport

Cascais

Quinta da Marinha (1984)

Quinta da Marinha, 2750 Cascais
Tel **289881/289901**
Mem 500
Pro A Dantas
Holes 18 L 5606 m SSS 71
Fees WD/WE–4000esc
Loc 32km W of Lisbon
Mis Driving range

Estoril

Estoril (1945)

Avenida República, 2765 Estoril
Tel **2680176/2681376**
Mem 800
Pro J Rodrigues, H Paulino, C Aleixo
Holes 18 L 5210 m SSS 68
9 L 2350 m SSS 65
Fees 18 holes 3440esc
9 holes 1740esc
Loc Estoril, 30km W of Lisbon
Mis WE–guests only. Driving range

Estoril Sol (1976)

Linhó, 2710 Sintra
Tel **(923) 2461**
Mem 65
Pro D Moita
Holes 9 L 4228 m Par 66
Fees WD/WE 2500esc
Loc 7km N of Estoril. Lisbon 35km

Lisbon

Lisboa CC

Quinta da Aroeira, 2825 Monte da Caparica
Tel **2263244/2261358**
Pro A Paulino
Holes 18 L 6171 m SSS 73
Fees 3000esc
Loc 17km S of Lisbon

Lisbon Sports Club (1922)

Casal da Carragueira Belas, 2475 Queluz
Tel **4310077**
Mem 900
Pro J Baltazar
Holes 14+4 L 5866 m SSS 68
Fees D–3000esc
Loc Belas–Queluz 5km. 20km E of Lisbon

Madeira

Santo Da Serra (1967)

Sto Antonio da Serra, 9100 Santa Cruz, Madeira
Tel **55139**
Mem 130
Pro J de Sousa
Holes 9 L 2622 yds SSS 67
Fees 1500esc
Loc 22km E of Funchal. Airport 6km

Porto

Miramar (1934)

Praia de Miramar, 4405 Valadares
Tel **7622067**
Mem 500
Pro M Ribeiro
Holes 9 L 5064 m SSS 66

For explanation of abbreviations, see page 202.

Fees D–2000esc
Loc 12km S of Porto

Oporto (1890)

Sisto–Paramos, 4500 Espinho
Tel 722008
Mem 600
Pro CA Agostinho, E Maganinho
Holes 18 L 5780 m SSS 70
Fees 3000esc (3500esc)
Loc Espinho, 15km from Oporto
Mis Links course

Setúbal

Tróia Golf

Torralta, Tróia, 2900 Setúbal
Tel (065) 44151/44236
Pro F Pina
Holes 18 L 6338 m SSS 74
Fees D–3700esc
Loc 40km S of Lisbon

Torres Vedras

Vimeiro

Praia do Porto Novo, Vimeiro, 2560 Torres Vedras
Tel (061) 98157
Holes 9 L 2466 m SSS 35
Fees D–700esc 1985 prices
Loc Torres Vedras 20km. Lisbon 65km

Vidago

Vidago

Pavilhão Golf, 5425 Vidago
Tel 97106
Mem 400
Pro M Carneiro
Holes 9 L 2449 m SSS 63
Fees D–750esc 1985 prices
Loc 130km NE of Porto. Vila Real 45km

Spain

Algeciras

La Duquesa G & CC (1987)

Urb El Hacho, Manilva, Málaga
Tel (952) 890425/6
Mem 200
Pro JM Canizares, S Ruiz
Holes 18 L 6142 m SSS 72
Fees 4500P
Loc Estepona 15km. Gibraltar 25km

Sotogrande (1964)

Paseo del Parque, Sotogrande, (Cádiz)
Tel (956) 79 20 50/79 20 51
Mem 1000
Pro T Gonzalez, J Quiros
Holes 18 L 5885 m SSS 72
18 L 6263 m SSS 72
9 L 1299 m SSS 29
Fees 8000P (10000P)
Loc San Roque, Gibraltar 18km

Valderrama (1985)

Sotogrande, Cádiz
Tel (56) 79 27 75
Mem 112
Pro J Zumaquero
Holes 18 L 6326 m SSS 72
Fees D–7000P
Loc Gibraltar 30km

Alicante Region

Don Cayo (1974)

Conde de Altea 49, Altea, Alicante
Tel (96) 5840716/5848046
Pro G Sanz
Holes 9 L 6044 m SSS 72
Fees D–2800P
Loc Altea 4km

Ifach (1974)

Ctra Moraira–Calpe Km 3, Urb San Jaime, Benisa (Alicante)
Holes 9 L 3408 m SSS 59
Fees D–1500P
Loc Calpe 13km. Moraira 5km

Jávea (1981)

Ctra Benitachell Km4, Jávea, (Alicante)
Tel (96) 579 25 84
Mem 600
Pro G Sanz, JA Moyano
Holes 9 L 6070 m SSS 72
Fees D–3000P
Loc Between Valencia (100km) and Alicante (90km)

Villa Martín (1972)

Apartado 35, Torrevieja, Alicante
Tel (965) 32 03 50 54 58
Pro E Pareja
Holes 18 L 5899 m SSS 72
Fees WD/WE–3500P
Loc Torrevieja

Almería

Almerimar (1976)

Urb Almerimar, 04700 El Ejido, Almería
Tel (951) 48 02 34
Pro J Parrón
Holes 18 L 5928 m SSS 72
Fees 4000P W–20000P
Loc Almeria 36km
Mis Very flat course designed by Gary Player.

Cortijo Grande (1976)

Turre, Almería
Mem 72
Holes 18 L 5545 m SSS 70
Fees D–1500P 1988 prices
Loc 3km W of Turre. 85km N of Almería, nr Mojácar

Playa Serena (1979)

Urb Roquetas de Mar, Almería
Tel (951) 32 20 55
Mem 300
Pro F Parrón, A Parrón
Holes 18 L 5905 m SSS 72
Fees D–4500P
Loc 20km S of Almería

Barcelona Region

Llavaneras (1945)

Camino del Golf, 08392 Sant Andrés de Llavaneras
Tel (93) 792 60 50
Mem 870
Pro F González, J Bertrán, J Pérez
Holes 9 L 4298 m SSS 63
Fees 2500–3500P (6000P)
Loc Barcelona 32km on N–1

Real Golf "El Prat" (1956)

8820 El Prat de Llobregat, (Barcelona)
Tel (93) 379 02 78
Mem 2200
Pro P Marin, M Rodriguez
Holes 3 ×9 holes 5944–6256 m SSS 72–74
Fees 3640P (6048P)
Loc El Prat, Airport 3km. Barcelona 15km

Sant Cugat (1914)

Sant Cugat del Vallés
Tel (93) 674 39 08/674 39 58
Mem 1500
Pro A Demelo
Holes 18 L 5209 m SSS 68
Fees 2800P (5600P)
Loc Barcelona 20km

Vallromanes (1969)

08188 Vallromanes
Tel (93) 568 03 62
Mem 1200
Pro J Gallardo
Holes 18 L 6038 m SSS 72
Fees D–2240P (5600P)
Loc 23km from Barcelona between Alella and Granollers. A17 Junction 13/A19 Junction 5

Bilbao

La Bilbaina (1976)

Laucariz, Munguía, Vizcaya
Tel (94) 674 08 58/674 04 62
Pro F García, S Larrázabal, E Garaizar
Holes 18 L 6112 m SSS 72
Fees D–4000P
Loc 15km N of Bilbao towards Mungía

Real Golf de Neguri (1911)

Apdo Correos 9, 49990 Algorta
Tel (94) 469 02 00/04/08
Mem 2500
Pro C Celles, L Losada, JM Fuente, JR Larrazabal
Holes 18 L 6319 m SSS 72
6 hole Par 3 course
Fees WD/WE–4000P
Loc Bilbao 20km

Cádiz

Vista Hermosa (1975)

Apartado 77, Puerto de Santa María, Cádiz
Tel (956) 85 00 11
Pro M Velasco
Holes 9 L 5680 m SSS 70
Fees 2000–4500P
Loc On bay of Cádiz

Canary Islands

Costa Teguise (1978)

Lanzarote
Tel (928) 81 35 12
Pro NG Perez
Holes 18 L 6082 m SSS 71
9 L 1455 m SSS 28
Fees D–1000P
Loc 7km N of Arrecife

Golf del Sur (1987)

San Miguel de Abona, Tenerife
Tel (922) 704555
Pro J Golding, M Golding
Holes North 9 L 2510 m SSS 36
Links 9 L 2308 m SSS 35
South course SSS 36
Fees 18 holes 4000P
9 holes 2000P
Loc Tenerife Sur airport 3km

Maspalomas (1968)

Av de Africa, Maspalomas, 35100 Las Palmas de Gran Canaria
Tel (928) 76 25 81/76 73 43
Pro A Gutierrez
Holes 18 L 6216 m SSS 72
Fees D–3000P
Loc S coast of Gran Canaria

Real Golf de Las Palmas (1891)

PO Box 183, 35000 Las Palmas de Gran Canaria
Tel (928) 35 10 50/35 01 04/35 01 08
Mem 750
Pro F Santana, E Perera, S Sanchez F Santana
Holes 18 L 5690 m SSS 71
Fees WD/WE–4500P
Loc Bandama, 14km Las Palmas
Mis Driving range, pitch and putt. Bandama Hotel guests free.

Tenerife (1932)

El Peñón, Tacoronte, Tenerife
Tel (922) 25 02 40/25 10 48
Mem 626
Pro G Gonzalez
Holes 18 L 5397 m SSS 68
Fees 3500P WD only
Loc N of island, 10 mins from Santa Cruz

Cartagena

La Manga (1971)

Ctra de Portman, Los Belones, 30385 Cartagena (Murcia)
Tel (968) 56 45 11
Mem 980
Pro S Ballesteros, M Ballesteros, J Mellado, V Ballesteros
Holes North 18 L 5873 m SSS 72
South 18 L 6238 m SSS 73
Fees WD/WE D–3600P (Residents)
Loc Cartagena 20km. Murcia 70km

Castellón de la Plana

Costa De Azahar (1960)

Ctra Grao–Benicasim, Castellón de la Plana
Tel (964) 22 70 64
Mem 600
Pro A Sanchez
Holes 9 L 2724 m SSS 70
Fees D–2000P W–8000P
Loc Castellón 5km. Benicasim 5km

Castellon de la Plana

Mediterraneo CC (1978)

Urb La Coma, Borriol, (Castellón)
Tel (964) 32 12 27
Mem 1300
Pro V Garcia
Holes 18 L 6038 m SSS 72
Fees 2000–3000P
Loc La Coma, Castellón

Córdoba

Pozoblanco (1984)

San Gregorio 2, Pozoblanco, (Córdoba)
Tel (957) 10 02 39/10 00 06
Holes 9 L 3660 m SSS 62
Loc Pozoblanco 3km

Los Villares (1976)

Avda del Generalismo 1–2, PO Box 463, Córdoba
Tel (957) 35 02 08
Mem 404
Pro JM Carriles
Holes 18 L 6087 m SSS 72
Fees 2000P
Loc Between Córdoba and Obejo

La Coruña

La Coruña (1962)

Apartado 737, 15080 La Coruña
Tel (981) 28 52 00
Mem 1500
Pro J Santiago
Holes 18 L 5782 m SSS 72
Fees 2000P
Loc La Coruña 7km

Gerona

Costa Brava (1962)

Santa Cristina de Aro, Gerona
Tel (972) 83 71 50
Mem 560
Pro M Gil
Holes 18 L 5558 m Par 70
Fees 4000–5500P
Loc Playa de Aro 5km. Barcelona 100km

Pals

Pals, Gerona
Tel (972) 63 60 06
Mem 750
Pro J Anglada, M Ramos, J Riera
Holes 18 L 6222 m SSS 72
Fees D–3400–7000P (7000P)
Loc Bagur 10km

Huelva

Bellavista (1976)

Crta Huelva–Aljaraque Km 6, 21120 Corrales (Huelva)
Tel (955) 31 90 17
Mem 620
Pro M Sanchez
Holes 9 L 6252 m SSS 72
Fees 5000P
Loc 6km from Huelva

Ibiza

Roca Llisa (1971)

Apartado 200, Ibiza, Baleares
Tel (971) 31 97 18
Mem 500
Pro G Castillo
Holes 9 L 5902 m SSS 70
Fees 3500P
Loc 8km from Ibiza towards Cala Llonga

Madrid Region

Barberán (1967)

Apartado 150.239, Cuatro Vientos, Madrid
Tel (91) 218 85 05
Pro V Hernandez
Holes 9 L 6127 m SSS 72
Fees D–1250P (1600P)
Loc Madrid 10km

Las Encinas de Boadilla (1984)

Crta Boadilla–Pozuelo Km 1400, Boadilla del Monte, Madrid
Tel (91) 633 11 00
Mem 400
Pro A Gomez
Holes 9 L 1464 m SSS 50
Fees 700P (2300P)
Loc Pozuelo, Madrid 12km

Herreria (1966)

PO Box 28200, San Lorenzo del Escorial, (Madrid)
Tel (91) 890 51 11/890 52 44
Mem 3500
Pro M Aparicio
Holes 18 L 6015 m SSS 72
Fees 3500P (5500P)
Loc 200m from Escorial monastery. Madrid 50km

Lomas–Bosque (1973)

Urb El Bosque, Villaviciosa de Odón, (Madrid)
Tel (91) 616 21 70
Mem 400
Pro M Alvarez
Holes 27 L 6075 m SSS 72
Fees 2500P (6000P)
Loc Madrid 18km

La Moraleja (1976)

La Moraleja, Alcobendas (Madrid)
Tel (91) 650 07 00
Mem 600
Pro V Barrios, M Montes
Holes 18 L 5617 m SSS 69
Fees 2500P (3000P)
Loc Madrid–Burgos road Km 85

Nuevo De Madrid (1972)

Las Matas (Madrid)
Tel (91) 630 08 20
Pro J Marimon
Holes 18 L 6037 m SSS 72
Fees 1700P (2000P)
Loc Madrid 18km

Puerta de Hierro (1904)

28305 Madrid
Tel (91) 216 1745
Mem 1442
Pro J Gallardo, J Benito
Holes 18 L 6347 m SSS 73
Fees 2000P (3000P)
Loc 4km N of Madrid on Route VI
Mis V'trs must be accompanied by a member

Real Automovil Club de España (1903)

José Abascal 10, 28003 Madrid
Tel (91) 447 32 00/652 26 00
Mem 300
Pro F Alvarez, J Alvarez, F Valera, R del Castillo
Holes 18 L 6505 m SSS 74
9 hole course
Fees 2500P (3200P)
Loc San Sebastian de los Reyes, 28km from Madrid on Burgos road.

Somosaguas (1971)

Somosaguas, 28011 Madrid
Tel (91) 212 16 47
Pro M Cabrera, A Garrido
Holes 9 L 5621 m SSS 69
Fees 2000P (3000P)
Loc Somosaguas

Valdelaguila (1975)

Apdo 9, Alcalá de Henares, Madrid
Tel 885 96 59
Pro A Puebla
Holes 9 L 5714 m SSS 70
Fees D–1000P (1500P)
Loc Alcalá de Henares 8km

Villa de Madrid CC (1984)

Crta Castilla, 28040 Madrid
Tel (91) 207 03 95
Mem 3500
Pro M Morcillo
Holes 27 L 6118 m SSS 73
Fees 1800P (3600P)
Loc Madrid 4km
Mis Municipal club from 1984. Course built 1932.

Majorca

Pollensa (1984)

Predio Son Porquer, Ctra Palma–Pollensa Km 49, Apdo No 9, Mallorca
Tel (971) 53 32 16
Mem 200
Pro S Luna
Holes 9 L 5624 m SSS 72
Fees 3500P
Loc Pollensa 3km. Palma 50km

Poniente (1978)

Costa de Calvia, Mallorca
Tel (971) 68 01 48
Mem 100
Pro B Salter, P Ruiz, P Rodriguez
Holes 18 L 6430 m SSS 74
Fees 4800P
Loc 12km from Palma towards Andraitx
Mis Driving range

Real Golf Bendinat (1986)

C. Formentera, Calvia, Mallorca
Tel 40 52 00/40 51 50
Pro R Galliano
Holes 9 L 2327 m SSS 64
Fees WD/WE–3000P
Loc 10km W of Palma

Santa Ponsa (1976)

Santa Ponsa, Mallorca
Tel (71) 69 02 11/69 08 00
Mem 350
Pro S Bruna
Holes 18 L 6520 m SSS 74
Fees 4800P
Loc 18km from Palma–motorway Andraitx
Mis Hotel guests 50% discount

Son Servera (1967)

Urb Costa de Los Pinos, 07559 Son Servera (Mallorca)
Tel (971) 56 78 02
Mem 250
Pro S Sota
Holes 9 L 5872 m SSS 72
Fees D–2850P
Loc Palma 70km via Manacor

Son Vida

Son Vida, 07013 Palma de Mallorca
Tel (971) 23 76 20
Mem 500
Pro F Fuentes
Holes 18 L 5414 m SSS 68
Fees 4000P
Loc 5km NW of Palma

Vall D'Or

Apdo 23, 07660 Cala D'Or, Mallorca
Tel 57 60 99/57 60 40
Pro A Gonzalez
Holes 9 L 5462 m SSS 70
Fees 3500P
Loc Cala D'Or 6km. Palma 40 mins drive.

Málaga

El Candado (1965)

Urb El Candado, El Palo, Málaga
Tel (952) 29 46 66
Pro M Lucas
Holes 9 L 4508 m SSS 65
Fees D–1250P
Loc Málaga 5km on Route N340

CC Málaga (1925)

Apartado 324, Málaga
Tel (952) 38 11 20/21
Pro J Sanchez
Holes 18 L 6042 m SSS 71
Fees 2900P
Loc Torremolinos 3km. Málaga 9km
Mis Parador guests 50% reduction

Mijas (1976)

Public

Apartado 138, Fuengirola, Málaga
Tel (957) 47 68 43
Pro J Rosa
Holes Los Lagos 18 L 6348 m SSS 73
Los Olivos 18 L 5896 m SSS 71
Fees D–3500P
Loc Fuengirola 4km
Mis Public course. Handicap certificate required.

Nerja G & CC

PO Box 154, Nerja, Málaga
Tel (952) 52 02 08
Pro A Carsin
Holes 9 L 3000 m SSS 59
Fees 1500P
Loc 1km E of Nerja on motorway Málaga–Almería

Torrequebrada (1977)

PO Box 67, Ctra de Cádiz Km 220, 29630 Benalmadena Costa
Tel (52) 44 27 42
Mem 200
Pro J Jimenez
Holes 18 L 5860 m SSS 72
Fees 3400–4500P
Loc By Torrequebrada Casino

Marbella

Aloha (1975)

Urb Aloha, Marbella
Tel (81) 23 89
Mem 1500
Pro J Mangas, A Jimenez
Holes 18 L 6261 m SSS 72
9 hole short course
Fees 10000P
Loc Marbella 8km

Atalaya Park G & CC (1968)

Crta Benahavis, Estepona, Marbella
Tel (952) 78 18 94
Mem 350
Pro D Strachan
Holes 18 L 6272 m SSS 73
Fees WD/WE 5000P
Loc Between Marbella/Estepona. Puerto Banus 4km. Málaga 68km. Gibraltar 45 mins
Mis Hotel guests 50% discount.

Las Brisas (1968)

Apdo 147, Urb Nueva Andalucía, Marbella
Tel 81 08 75/81 55 18
Mem 1250
Pro S Miguel
Holes 18 L 6198 m SSS 73
Fees 9000P
Loc Opposite Puerto Banus. 8km S of Marbella

Guadalmina (1959)

Guadalmina Alta, San Pedro de Alcántara, Marbella
Tel (952) 78 13 17
Mem 600
Pro A Hernandez, F Hernandez
Holes 18 L 6060 m SSS 72
18 L 6200 m SSS 72
Fees 3900P
Loc Málaga airport 68km. Gibraltar airport 70km
Mis Driving range

Los Naranjos (1977)

Apdo 64, Nueva Andalucía, Marbella
Tel (952) 81 52 06/81 14 28
Pro M Escudero
Holes 18 L 6484 m SSS 75
Fees 6000P
Loc 8km S of Marbella. 60km S of Málaga airport

El Paraiso (1974)

Ctra Cádiz–Málaga Km 167, Estepona, Marbella
Tel (952) 78 47 12/78 47 16
Mem 700
Pro J Franco
Holes 18 L 6142 m SSS 73
Fees 5250P 1988 prices
Loc Marbella 14km

Rio Real (1965)

Apartado 82, Marbella
Tel (952) 77 17 00 Ext 3086
Pro A Miguel
Holes 18 L 6130 m SSS 72
Fees D–5200P (Free for Los Monteros and Inconsol guests)
Loc Marbella 5km

Minorca

Real Golf de Menorca (1976)

Apartado 97, Mahón, Menorca
Tel (971) 36 39 00
Mem 350
Pro J Tollegrosa
Holes 9 L 5724 m SSS 70
Fees D–1500P
Loc 7km N of Mahón

Son Parc (1977)

Apto Correos 634, Mahón, Menorca
Tel (971) 36 88 06/36 20 14
Holes 9 L 2775 m SSS 69
Fees 1500P
Loc Mercadel, Mahón 18km

Motril

Los Moriscos (1974)

C. Recogidas, 18005 Granada
Tel (958) 60 04 12/60 03 06
Holes 9 L 5702 m SSS 71
Loc Motril 8km. Salobreña 5km

Oviedo

Barganiza (1982)

Apartado 277, 33080 Oviedo, Asturias
Tel (985) 25 63 61
Mem 570
Pro M Bellido
Holes 18 L 5298 m SSS 69
Fees 2000P
Loc Oviedo–Gijon Old Road. 12km from Oviedo via Noreña.

Castiello (1958)

Apartado de Correos, 161 Gijón
Tel (985) 36 63 13
Mem 450
Pro A Sierra
Holes 18 L 4817 m SSS 67
Fees WD/WE–2000P
Loc Oviedo–Gijón Old Road 4km
Mis WE–comps during summer

Pamplona

Ulzama (1965)

Guerendiain (Navarra)
Tel (948) 30 51 62
Pro R Echeverría
Holes 9 L 5984 m SSS 71
Fees 1500P
Loc 21km N of Pamplona

Pontevedra

La Toja (1970)

Isla de La Toja, Pontevedra
Tel (986) 73 07 26/73 08 18
Mem 200
Pro P Medrano
Holes 9 L 6046 m SSS 72
Fees 2500P (3500P)
Loc La Toja island. Vigo 60km. Pontevedra 30km

Puigcerda

Real Golf de Cerdaña (1929)

Apartado de Correos 63, Puigcerdá (Gerona)
Tel (972) 88 13 38/88 09 50
Mem 300
Pro S Diaz
Holes 18 L 5735 m SSS 70
Fees 2000P (2500P)
Loc Cerdaña, 1km from Puigcerdá.

San Sebastián

Real San Sebastián (1910)

PO Box 6, Fuenterrabia, Guipúzcoa
Tel (943) 61 68 45/61 68 46
Mem 2500
Pro Jesús Arruti, José Arruti, J Gorostegui
Holes 18 L 6020 m SSS 71
Fees WD/WE–5000P
Loc Jaizubia Valley. Irún 6km. San Sebastián 14km.

Real Zarauz (1916)

Apartado 82, Zarauz, Guipúzcoa
Tel (943) 83 01 45
Mem 1100
Pro N Belartieta
Holes 9 L 4882 m SSS 67
Fees D–2000–4000P
Loc Zarauz 1km. San Sebastián 25km

Santander

Real Golf de Pedreña (1928)

Apartado 233, Santander
Tel (942) 50 00 01/50 02 66
Mem 1050
Pro R Sota
Holes 18 L 5721 m SSS 70
Fees D–1300–15000P
Loc Santander 20km

Santiago

Aero Club De Santiago (1976)

General Pardiñas 34, Santiago de Compostela (La Coruña)
Tel (981) 59 24 00
Pro J Ybarra
Holes 9 L 5422 m SSS 68
Fees 1000P
Loc Santiago Airport

Seville

Pineda De Sevilla (1939)

Apartado 796, Sevilla
Tel (954) 61 14 00/61 33 99
Pro P Garrido, L Gonzalez
Holes 9 L 5684 m SSS 71
Fees 1300P (2000P)
Loc Seville 3km on Cádiz road

Sitges

Terramar (1922)

Apartado 6, 08870 Sitges, Barcelona
Tel 894 05 80/894 20 43
Mem 930
Pro A Hernandez, S Perez, J Hernandez
Holes 18 L 5578 m SSS 70
Fees 2800–4500P
Loc Barcelona 40km

Tarragona

Costa Dorada (1983)

Apartado 600, Tarragona
Tel (977) 65 54 16
Pro F Jimenez
Holes 9 L 5944 m SSS 73
Fees 1500P (2000P)

Valencia Region

Escorpión (1975)

Apartado Correos 1, Betera (Valencia)
Tel 1 60 12 11
Mem 1400
Pro A Sanchez, J Rodriguez, P Contreras
Holes 18 L 6345 m SSS 73
Fees 3000P (5000P)
Loc Betera, Valencia 20km

Manises (1964)

Apartado 22.029, Manises (Valencia)
Tel (96) 379 08 50
Mem 110
Pro FE Pinto
Holes 9 L 2607 m Par 72
Fees 1000P
Loc Manises, Valencia 8km

El Saler (1968)

Parador Luis Vives, El Saler, Valencia
Tel 323 68 50
Mem 400
Pro JA Cabo, J Navarro
Holes 18 L 6485 m SSS 75
Fees D–2400P
Loc Oliva, 18km from Valencia

Vigo

Aero Club de Vigo (1951)

Reconquista 7, Vigo
Tel (986) 22 11 60/24 24 93
Pro DS Roman
Holes 9 L 5734 m SSS 70
Fees 1500P
Loc Peinador Airport, 8km from Vigo

Zaragoza

Aero Club de Zaragoza (1966)

Coso 34, Zaragoza
Tel (976) 21 43 78
Holes 9 L 4953 m SSS 66
Fees 2000P (3000P)
Loc Zaragoza 12km

La Penaza (1973)

Apartado 3039, Zaragoza
Tel (976) 34 28 00/04
Mem 700
Pro P García, V Tapia
Holes 18 L 6161 m SSS 72
Fees D–2500P (3500P)
Loc Zaragoza 15km on Madrid road

Sweden

Åmål

Billerud

661 00 Säffle
Tel (0555) 91054/91313
Mem 520
Pro F Badri
Holes 18 L 5874 m SSS 72
Fees WD/WE–40kr
Loc Säffle, Valnas 15km

Forsbacka (1969)

Box 136, 662 00 Åmål
Tel (0532) 43055
Mem 550
Pro M El Sayed
Holes 18 L 5860 m SSS 72
Fees 40kr (45kr)
Loc 6km W on Route 164

Älmhult

Älmhults (1975)

Box 152, 343 00 AUM lmhult
Tel (0476) 14135
Mem 184 117(L) 147(J)
Pro B Mårtensson

Holes 9 L 5350 m SSS 70
Fees D–50kr
Loc Askya, AUM
Imhult

Ängelholm

Ängelholms (1973)

Box 1117, 26201 Ängelholm
Tel (0431) 30260
Mem 1050
Pro Y Mahmoud
Holes 18 L 5760 m SSS 72
Fees 65–100kr (85–100kr)
Loc 10km E of town on route 114

Mölle (1943)

260 42 Mölle
Tel (042) 47012/47520
Mem 1000
Pro J Pyk
Holes 18 L 5640 m SSS 70
Fees 150kr
Loc Mölle 3km
Mis WE–restrictions in July

Arvika

Arvika

Box 33, 671 01 Arvika 1
Tel (0570) 54133
Pro A Söderqvist
Holes 9 L 5815 m SSS 71
Fees D–15kr
Loc 11km E of Arvika on Route 61

Askersund

Askersunds (1980)

S–6903 Ammeberg, Sweden
Tel (0583) 34440
Mem 380
Pro L Johansson
Holes 9 L 5650 m SSS 72
Fees 50kr
Loc 10km SE of Askersund on road to Ammeberg. Club is 1km on road to Kärra.

Avesta

Avesta (1963)

Box 168, 77400 Avesta
Tel (0226) 10363/10866/12766
Mem 750
Pro G Long
Holes 18 L 5725 m SSS 74
Fees WD/WE 80kr
Loc Avesta 4km

Fagersta (1970)

Box 2051, 77302 Fagersta
Tel (0223) 54060
Mem 810
Holes 9 L 5775 m SSS 72
Fees WD/WE–40kr
Loc 7km W of town on Route 65

Båstad

Båstad (1929)

Box 1037, 26901 Båstad
Tel (0431) 73136
Mem 1050
Pro P Hansson
Holes 18 L 5760 m SSS 71
Fees 100kr (160kr)
Loc 4km W of town on Route 115

Torekovs (1924)

Box 81, 26093 Torekov
Tel (0431) 63572
Mem 1100
Pro G Hall
Holes 18 L 5785 m SSS 72
Fees 100–170kr (120–170kr)
Loc 3km N of Torekov

Bollnäs

Bollnäs

Box 72, 82101 Bollnäs
Tel (0278) 50920/50540
Mem 725
Pro K Hagström
Holes 14 L 5870 m Par 72
Fees 60kr
Loc 15km S of Bollnäs on Route 83

Borås

Borås (1933)

Ostra VIK Krakered, 50590 Borås
Tel (033) 50142
Mem 1100
Pro L Prick
Holes 18 L 5815 m SSS 72
Fees 100kr (120kr)
Loc 6km S of town centre on new Route 41 towards Varberg
Mis Season Apr–Oct

Marks (1962)

Brättingstorpsvägen 28, S–51158 Kinna
Tel (0320) 14220
Mem 1000
Pro G Nyberg
Holes 18 L 5310 m SSS 69
Fees 100kr (120kr)
Loc Kinna, 30km S of Borås

Borlänge

Falun–Borlänge (1956)

Box 45, S–791 21 Falun
Tel (023) 31015
Mem 960
Pro A Ryberg
Holes 18 L 6085 m SSS 72
Fees 70kr
Loc Aspeboda, between Falun 13km and Borlänge 8km. Dala Airport 15km

Eksjö

Eksjö (1938)

Hasslav 6, 57500 Eksjö
Tel (0381) 13525
Mem 550
Pro D Nicholson
Holes 18 L 5930 m SSS 72
Fees D–50kr
Loc Road to Nässjö

Emmaboda

Emmaboda (1976)

Kyrkogatan, 36060 Vissefjärda
Tel (0471) 20505/20540
Mem 612
Holes 9 L 5165 m SSS 68
Fees 50kr
Loc Emmaboda 12km

Enköping

Enköping (1970)

Box 206, 19902 Enköping
Tel (0171) 20830
Mem 630
Pro A Halim
Holes 18 L 5660 m SSS 72
Fees 80kr (120kr)
Loc 3km E of town off E18

Eskilstuna

Eskilstuna (1951)

Strängnäsvägen, 633 49 Eskilstuna
Tel (016) 142629
Mem 950
Pro A Robinson
Holes 18 L 5610 m SSS 70
Fees 100kr (120kr)
Loc Strängnäsvägen.

Nyby Bruks (1960)

PO Box 587, 63108 Eskilstuna
Tel (016) 356782
Mem 350
Holes 9 L 6013 m SSS 72
Fees 60kr (100kr)
Loc Torshälla 2km

Eslöv

Eslöv (1966)

Box 150, 241 22 Eslöv
Tel (0413) 18610/13494
Mem 1150
Pro C Wilkström (0413) 16213
Holes 18 L 5670 m SSS 71
Fees 100kr (140kr)
Loc 4km S of town on Route 113

Falkenberg

Falkenberg (1949)

Golfvagen, 311 00 Falkenberg
Tel (0346) 50287
Mem 1200
Pro SA Parson
Holes 27 L 5650–5770 m SSS 72
Fees 80–110kr (140kr)
Loc 5km S of town centre

Falköping

Falköpings

Box 99, 52100 Falköping
Tel (0515) 31270
Mem 800
Pro G Johansson
Holes 18 L 5835 m SSS 72
Fees D–80kr
Loc 7km E of Falköping on Route 46 towards Skovde

Falsterbo

Falsterbo (1909)

PO Box 71, Fyrvagen 230 11 Falsterbo
Tel (040) 470078
Mem 1000
Pro P Chamberlain
Holes 18 L 6400 yds SSS 72
Fees 100kr (200kr)
Loc 35km S of Malmö

Flommens (1935)

Falsterbo 230 11
Tel (040) 470568
Mem 1000
Pro B Kristofferson
Holes 18 L 5610 m SSS 72
Fees 90kr (120kr)
Loc Malmö 35km

Ljunghusens (1932)

Kinellsvag, Ljunghusen, S–236 00 Höllviken
Tel 040 450384
Mem 1231
Pro G Sandegard
Holes 1–18 L 5895 m SSS 73
10–27 L 5670 m SSS 71
19–9 L 5455 m SSS 70
Fees 120–150kr
Loc Falster Bo Peninsula. Malmö 30km

Filipstad

Saxa (1964)

Asphyttegatan 24, 68200 Filipstad
Tel (0590) 24070
Mem 850
Pro F Speight
Holes 9 L 5860 m SSS 73
Fees 50kr
Loc 15km E of Filipstad on Route 63

Fjällbacka

Fjällbacka (1967)

450 71 Fjällbacka
Tel (0525) 31150
Mem 830
Pro M Ericsson
Holes 18 L 5850 m SSS 72
Fees D–100–140kr
Loc 2km N of Fjällbacka on Route 163.

Gällivare

Gällivare-Malmbergets (1973)

Box 52, 972 00 Gällivare
Tel (0970) 23955/15405
Mem 1900
Pro P Mattsson
Holes 9 L 5270 m SSS 70
Fees WD/WE–40kr
Loc 4km from Gällivare towards Malmberget

Gävle

Gävle (1949)

Brannarebacken 3, 803 59 Gävle
Tel (026) 113163
Mem 650
Pro G Sandegard
Holes 18 L 5705 yds SSS 71
Fees 80kr
Loc Gävle 3km

Högbo (1962)

Daniel Tilas Väg 4, 81192 Sandviken
Tel (026) 45015
Mem 1100
Pro G Sandegard
Holes 18 L 5680 m SSS 71
Fees D–70kr
Loc 6km N of Sandviken on Route 272

Gislaved

Isaberg (1968)

Box 40, 33200 Gislaved
Tel (0370) 36330
Mem 1120
Pro S Carpenter
Holes 18 L 5800 m SSS 72
Fees 100kr (120kr) W–500kr
Loc 18km N of Anderstorp and Gislaved. 10km W of Gnosjö. 60km S of Jönköping.

Göteborg

Albatross (1973)

Lillhagsvägen, S–422 50 Hisings-Backa
Tel (031) 551901/550500
Mem 1000
Pro A Anderton (031) 555054
Holes 18 L 6020 m SSS 72
Fees WD/WE–150kr
Loc 10km N of Göteborg on Hising Island

Delsjö (1962)

Kallebäck 412, 76 Göteborg
Tel (031) 406959
Mem 900
Pro J Anderson
Holes 18 L 5785 m SSS 71
Fees 90kr (100kr)
Loc 5km E of town centre on Route 40
Mis Driving range

Göteborgs (1902)

Box 2056, 436 02 Hovås
Tel (031) 283129
Mem 950
Pro M Kennedy
Holes 18 L 5935 yds SSS 69
Fees 120kr (150kr)
Loc 11km S of Göteborg RD 158

Gullbringa (1967)

442 90 Kungalv
Tel (0303) 27872/27161
Mem 500
Pro R Bayliss
Holes 18 L 5775 m Par 72
Fees 100kr (120kr)
Loc 14km W of Kungälv on road to Marstrand.

Hulta (1972)

Box 54, 517 01 Bollebygd
Tel (033) 88180
Mem 900
Pro W Byard
Holes 18 L 6000 m SSS 72
Fees 90kr (120kr)
Loc Nr Göteborg

Kungsbacka (1971)

Hamra Gård Pl 515, 43040 Särö
Tel (031) 936277
Mem 915
Pro P Nellbeck
Holes 13 L 5855 m SSS 72
Fees 120kr (150kr)
Loc 7km N of Kungsbacka on Route 158

Lysegardens (1966)

Box 82, S–442 21 Kungälv
Tel (0303) 23426
Mem 420
Pro E Öster
Holes 18 L 5681 m SSS 71
9 L 5504 m SSS 72
Fees 18 hole 100kr; 9 hole 70kr
Loc Kungälv 10km

Öijared (1958)

Pl 1082, 448 00 Floda
Tel (0302) 30604
Mem 1542
Pro E Dawson

Holes 18 L 5875 m SSS 71
18 L 5655 m SSS 71
Fees 100kr (150kr)
Loc Alihgsås 24km. Göteborg 35km
Mis WE–Members & guests only 8am–2pm

Partille (1971)

Box 234, 433 24 Partille
Tel (031) 987004/987114
Mem 850
Pro D Olsson
Holes 18 L 5330 m SSS 70
Fees 100kr
Loc 1km outside Göteborg in Öjersjö, Partille

Särö (1899)

Box 74, 43040 Särö
Tel (031) 936317
Mem 750
Pro J Rosell
Holes 9 holes Par 27
Fees 70kr (90kr)
Loc Route 158. Göteborg 18km. Kungsbacka 10km

Stora Lundby (1983)

Pl 4035, 440 06 Grabo
Tel (0302) 44200
Mem 1200
Pro L Svensson, P Houbrandt
Holes 18 L 6040 m Par 72
9 hole course Par 27
Fees 18 holes 150kr; 9 holes 60kr
Loc On W coast, 20 mins from Göteborg
Mis Championship course

Grästorp

Ekarnas (1970)

Balders Väg 12, S–46700 Grästorp
Tel (0514) 11450
Mem 3900
Holes 9 L 4480 m SSS 64
Fees 60kr
Loc 25km E of Trollhätten. Lidköping 35km

Hagfors

Uddeholms (1965)

683 03 Rada
Tel (0563) 60335/60025
Mem 800
Pro T Palm
Holes 18 L 5833 m SSS 72
Fees D–80kr
Loc 80km N of Karlstad RD62, at Lake Rada

Halmstad

Backavattnets (1977)

Box 173, 30103 Halmstad
Tel (035) 44271
Mem 900
Pro S Grant
Holes 18 L 5770 m SSS 73
Fees 110kr
Loc 13km E of Halmstad on RD25

Halmstad (1930)

302 70 Halmstad
Tel (035) 30077
Mem 2047
Pro B Grafton, M Sorling, B Gostaffson
Holes 18 L 5980 m SSS 73
18 L 5555 m SSS 72
Fees 100–150kr
Loc Halmstad 9km

Härnösand

Härnösand (1957)

Box 52, S–871 22 Härnösand
Tel (0611) 661 69
Mem 810
Pro F Guedra
Holes 18 L 5385 m SSS 70
Fees 80kr
Loc Vängnön, 12km N of Härnösand on E4

Hässleholm

Hässleholms (1978)

Skyrup, S–282 00 Tyringe
Tel (0451) 53111 9–5pm
Mem 700
Pro P Hamblett (0451) 53266
Holes 18 L 5830 m SSS 72
Fees 80kr (110kr)
Loc Hässleholm 14km. Tyringe 7km

Wittsjö (1962)

Ubbaltsgården, 280 22 Vittsjö
Tel (0451) 22635
Mem 600
Pro W Falk
Holes 18 L 5366 m SSS 70
Fees 60kr (80kr)
Loc Vittsjö 2km

Helsingborg

Helsingborg (1924)

26040 Viken
Tel (042) 236147
Mem 450
Holes 9 L 4578 m SSS 65
Fees 50kr (60kr)
Loc 15km N of Helsingborg

Rya (1934)

Rya 5500, 225 90 Helsingborg
Tel (042) 221082
Mem 900
Pro J Grant
Holes 18 L 5775 m SSS 71
Fees 100kr (120kr)
Loc 10km S of town

Söderåsens (1966)

Box 41, 260 50 Billesholm
Tel (042) 73337
Mem 850
Pro T Lidholm
Holes 18 L 5920 m SSS 73
Fees 100kr (120kr)
Loc Helsingborg 20km

Vasatorps (1973)

25590 Helsingborg
Tel (042) 235058
Mem 1800
Pro K Davies (042) 235045
Holes 18 L 5875 m SSS 72
9 L 2940 m
Fees 120–150kr
Loc 8km E of town

Hjo

Hökensås (1962)

PO Box 116, S 54400 Hjo
Tel (0503) 16059
Mem 630
Pro G Nyberg
Holes 18 L 5540 m SSS 71
Fees 75kr (100kr)
Loc 8km S of Hjo on Route 195

Hofors

Hofors (1965)

Box 117, 813 00 Hofors
Tel (0290) 85125
Mem 750
Pro G Sandegård
Holes 18 L 5400 m SSS 70
Fees 60kr (70kr)
Loc 5km SE of Hofors

Höör

Bosjökloster (1974)

243 95 Höör
Tel (0413) 25858
Mem 975
Pro S Kvillström
Holes 18 L 5890 m SSS 72
Fees 80kr (130kr)
Loc 7km S of Höör. 40km NE of Malmö

Hudiksvall

Hudiksvall (1964)

AB Iggesunds Bruk, 825 00 Iggesund
Tel (0650) 15930
Mem 250
Pro K Finno

Holes 14 L 5690 m SSS 70
Fees 60kr
Loc Hudiksvall 5km

Jönköping

Hook (1942)

560 13 Hok
Tel (0393) 21420/21080
Mem 850
Pro A Steen
Holes 18 L 5748 m SSS 72
Fees 90kr (120kr)
Loc Vaggeryd 13km

Jönköpings (1936)

Kettilstorp, S-552 67 Jönköping
Tel (036) 76567
Mem 1250
Pro A Turnbull
Holes 18 L 6370 m SSS 70
Fees 120kr
Loc 3km S of Jönköping

Kalmar

Kalmar (1947)

Box 278, 391 23 Kalmar 1
Tel (0480) 72111
Mem 1100
Pro H Weinhofer
Holes 18 L 5950 m SSS 72
Fees 80kr (100kr)
Loc 9km N of Kalmar

Nybro (1971)

Box 235, 382 00 Nybro
Tel (0480) 55044
Mem 350
Pro J Evergren
Holes 18 L 5829 m SSS 72
Fees 60kr (80kr) W-350kr
Loc Nybro 10km

Karlshamn

Karlshamns (1962)

Karlshamn 292 00
Tel (0454) 50085
Mem 720
Pro B Fredriksson
Holes 18 L 5861 m SSS 72
Fees 75kr (100kr)
Loc Morrum

Karlskoga

Karlskoga (1975)

Bricketorp 647, S-69194 Karlskoga
Tel (0586) 28597
Mem 850
Pro P Glimaker (0586) 28663
Holes 18 L 5705 m Par 72
Fees 100kr
Loc Valåsen, 6km E of town on Route E18

Örebro (1939)

Vreta Lannabruk, 710 15 Vintrosa
Tel (019) 91065
Mem 950
Pro E Ericson
Holes 18 L 5865 m SSS 72
Fees 110kr (140kr)
Loc 20km W of Örebro on Route E18
Mis Championship course. 6 hole pitch and putt

Karlskrona

Carlskrona (1949)

PO Almo, S-370 24 Nättraby
Tel (0455) 35102
Mem 900
Pro A Malmberg
Holes 18 L 5525 m Par 70
Fees D-110kr
Loc Karlskrona 15km

Ronneby (1964)

Box 26, S-37200 Ronneby
Tel (0457) 13212
Mem 400
Pro S Ohlsson
Holes 15 L 5390 m SSS 70
Fees 100kr
Loc Ronneby 2km

Karlstad

Karlstad (1957)

PO Box 294, 651 07 Karlstad
Tel (054) 36353
Mem 1200
Holes 18 L 5900 m SSS 72
9 hole course
Fees 100kr
Loc 12km E of town centre on Route 63

Katrineholm

Katrineholms (1959)

Box 74, 641 21 Katrineholm
Tel (0150) 39011/39012
Mem 950
Pro S Eriksson
Holes 18 L 5850 m SSS 72
Fees WD/WE-100kr
Loc Katrineholm 7km

Köping

Korslöts (1963)

Box 278, 731 26 Köping
Tel (46221) 81090
Mem 950
Pro B Malmquist
Holes 18 L 5636 m SSS 71
Fees 80kr (110kr)
Loc 5km N of Köping (Route 250)

Kopparberg

Stjernfors (1973)

c/o Hagabacksvej 4, 71700 Storå
Tel (0580) 41048
Mem 475
Pro D McLean
Holes 10 L 5548 m SSS 70
Fees WD/WE-50kr
Loc Kopparberg 5km

Kristianstad

Kristianstads (1924)

Box 41, 96 00 Aan hus
Tel (044) 240656
Mem 1350
Pro D Green
Holes 18 L 5848 m SSS 72
9 L 2841 m SSS 36
Fees 80kr (100krs)
Loc 18km SW of Kristanstad. Airport 20km

Ostra Goinge (1981)

Box 114, S-289 00 Knislinge
Tel (044) 60060
Mem 650
Pro A Lindbergh
Holes 9 L 5400 m Par 68
Fees 50kr
Loc Kristianstad 20km

Skepparslovs (1984)

Udarpssäteri, 29169 Kristianstad
Tel (044) 229508
Mem 1040
Pro C Claesson
Holes 18 L 5900 m SSS 72
Fees 80kr (100kr)
Loc 7km W of town

Kristinehamn

Kristinehamns (1974)

Box 3037, 681 03 Kristinehamn
Tel (0550) 82310
Mem 650
Pro E Richter
Holes 9 L 5730 m SSS 71
Fees 60kr
Loc 3km N of Kristinehamn

Laholm

Laholm (1964)

Box 101, 1200 Laholm
Tel (0430) 30601
Mem 1000
Pro C Eklund
Holes 18 L 5430 m SSS 70

Fees 90kr (130kr)
Loc 5 miles E of Laholm on Route 24

Landskrona

Barsebäck

Box 214, S-24022 Löddeköpinge
Tel (046) 775800
Mem 1135
Pro I Christersson
Holes 18 L 5900 m SSS 72
9 L 2840 m SSS 36
Fees 110kr
Loc Malmö 35km

Landskrona (1960)

Erikstorp, S-261 61 Landskrona
Tel (0418) 19528
Mem 1800
Pro A Olsson
Holes Old 18 L 5700 m SSS 71
New 18 L 4000 m SSS 62
Fees 110kr (140kr) 1988 prices
Loc 4km N of Landskrona towards Borstahusen
Mis Season Mar–Nov

St Ibb (1972)

Ulf Ohrvik Victoriagatan 7c, S-261 35 Landskrona
Tel (0418) 72363
Mem 265
Pro H Kristensen
Holes 9 L 5180 m SSS 68
Fees 120kr
Loc Island of Hven
Mis Ferry from Landskrona

Lidköping

Lidköpings (1967)

Box 2029, 531 02 Lidköping
Tel (0510) 46122
Mem 900
Pro T Lundahl
Holes 18 L 5725 m SSS 71
Fees 100kr
Loc 5km E of town

Lindesberg

Linde (1984)

Dalkarlshyttan, 711 31 Lindesberg
Tel (0581) 13960
Mem 840
Pro P Karlsson (0581) 15917
Holes 18 L 5585 m SSS 71
Fees 80kr (100fr)
Loc 42km N of Örebro on R60.

Linköping

Åtvidaberg (1954)

Box 180, 597 00 Åtvidaberg
Tel (0120) 11425/12510
Mem 950
Pro B Nygren (0120) 12510
Holes 18 L 6010 m SSS 72
Fees 120kr
Loc Linköping 30km

Linköping (1945)

Box 10054, 580 10 Linköping
Tel (0131) 20646
Mem 1100
Pro B Lemke, B Patterson
Holes 18 L 5675 m SSS 71
Fees 100kr
Loc Linköping 1km

Ljungby

Lagans (1966)

Box 63, 34014 Lagan
Tel (0372) 30450
Mem 850
Pro J Suckling
Holes 18 L 5600 m SSS 71
Fees D-100kr
Loc 10km N of Ljungby in Lagan

Ljungbyhed

F5

c/o H Pommer Myrstigen 3, 264 00 Klippan
Tel (0435) 41467
Mem 440
Holes 9 L 5675 m SSS 71
Fees D-25kr
Loc On the airfield

Ljungskile

Lyckorna (1967)

Box 66, 45900 Ljungskile
Tel (0522) 20 176
Mem 1000
Pro R Heyman
Holes 18 L 5845 m SSS 72
Fees 100kr
Loc 20km S of Uddevalla

Ljusdal

Ljusdals (1973)

Box 151, S-827 00 Ljusdal
Tel (0651) 14366
Mem 520
Holes 9 L 5920 m SSS 72
Fees 40kr
Loc 2km E of town

Ljusnedal

Härjedalsfjällens (1972)

Vintergatan 5, 8290 95 Funäsdalen
Tel (0684) 21240
Mem 520
Pro V Agardh
Holes 18 L 5300 m SSS 72
Fees 80kr

Ludvika-Smedjebacken

Hagge (1963)

Hagge, 771 00 Ludvika
Tel (0240) 28087
Mem 610
Pro U Sandberg
Holes 9 L 5680 m SSS 71
Fees WD/WE-60kr
Loc Hagge 2km. Ludvika 6km

Luleå

Bodens (1946)

Box 110, 96121 Boden
Tel (0921) 61071
Mem 355
Pro J Gidlund
Holes 9 L 5796 m Par 72 SSS 73
Fees 50kr
Loc Boden 17km

Luleå (1955)

Box 314, 95125 Luleå
Tel (0920) 56091/56174
Mem 1050
Pro L Stewart
Holes 18 L 5995 m SSS 73
Fees 80kr
Loc Rutvik, 12km E of Luleå
Mis World's most northern 18-hole course (with Akureyri, Iceland)

Piteå (1960)

Nötön, S-94190 Piteå
Tel (0911) 14990
Mem 520
Pro A Gillard
Holes 9 L 5905 m SSS 72
Fees 50kr
Loc 2km NE of town centre
Mis Midnight sun golf Jun/Jul

Lysekil

Skaftö (1963)

Röd 4476, 450 34 Fiskebäckskil
Tel (0523) 22544
Mem 480
Pro B Malmqvist
Holes 9 L 5310 m SSS 69
Fees 100kr

Malmö

Bokskogens (1963)

Box 30, 230 40 Bara I
Tel (040) 481004
Mem 1200
Pro J Larsson
Holes 18 L 6050 m SSS 73
9 L 5490 m SSS 70

Fees 120kr (160kr)
Loc Malmö 15km

Hylliekrokens (1983)

Limhamnsveg 85, 216 18 Malmö
Tel (040) 68320/160900
Mem 2192
Holes 9 holes Par 54
Fees 55kr (75kr)
Loc SW of Malmö

Lunds Akademiska (1936)

Kungsmarken, 225 90 Lund
Tel (046) 99005
Mem 1300
Pro V MacDougall
Holes 18 L 5780 m SSS 72
Fees 100kr (140kr)
Loc 5km E of Lund

Malmö

Segesvängen Box 21068, S-20021 Malmö
Tel (040) 292945
Mem 1100
Pro H Bergdahl
Holes 18 L 5720 m SSS 71
Fees 100kr (120kr)
Loc NE of Malmö, by motorway from Gothenburg
Mis Driving range

Mariestad

Mariestads (1975)

PO Box 299, 542 01 Mariestad
Tel (0501) 17383
Mem 1000
Pro R Hutton
Holes 18 L 5890 m SSS 72
Fees 100kr
Loc 5km W of town at Lake Vänern

Mjölby

Mjölby (1983)

Box 171, S-595 00 Mjölby
Tel (0142) 12570
Mem 465
Holes 9 L 2800 m SSS 72
Fees 50kr (70kr)
Loc 35km WSW of Linköping on E4 between Stockholm and Gothenburg.

Motala

Motala (1956)

PO Box 264, S-59123 Motala
Tel (0141) 50856 (Club)
(0141) 50840 (Sec)
Mem 950
Pro O Asplund (0141) 50834/50592
Holes 18 L 5855 m SSS 72
Fees WD/WE-100kr
Loc 3km S of Motala on Route 50 or 32

Vadstena (1956)

Hagalund, 592 00 Vadstena
Tel (0143) 12743
Mem 339
Holes 9 L 5486 m SSS 70
Fees 50kr (60kr)
Loc Vadstena $2^1/_2$ km

Munkedal

Torreby (1961)

Pl Torreby, 455 00 Munkedal
Tel (0524) 21109
Mem 1050
Pro J & K Grahn
Holes 18 L 5885 m SSS 72
Fees 100kr
Loc Munkedal 8km. Uddevalla 30km.

Norrköping

Finspångs (1965)

Viberga Gård, 61200 Finspång
Tel (0122) 16574
Mem 950
Pro J Kjellvall
Holes 13 L 5935 m Par 71
Fees 80kr
Loc 3km E of Finspång on route 51. Norrköping 25km.

Norrköping (1928)

Klinga, Box 2150, 600 02 Norrköping
Tel (011) 35234
Mem 830
Pro P Karström (011) 35236
Holes 18 L 5860 m SSS 72
Fees 100kr (120kr)
Loc Klinga, 2km S of Norrköping on E4

Söderköpings (1983)

Blamestigen 3, S-61400 Söderköping
Tel (011) 70579
Mem 800
Pro L Cernold (011) 70039
Holes 18 L 4700-6135 m SSS 73
Fees WD/WE-100kr
Loc Västra Husby 9km W of Söderköping

Norrtälje

Roslagens

Box 110, 761 00 Norrtälje
Tel (0176) 37137
Mem 400
Pro L Modin
Holes 18 L 5725 m SSS 71
Fees 100kr (150kr)
Loc Norrtälje 7km

Nyköping-Oxelösund

Ärila (1951)

Nicolai, 61192 Nyköping
Tel (0155) 14967
Mem 1400
Pro O Jansson
Holes 18 L 5735 m SSS 72
Fees 120kr
Loc Nyköping 5km

Nynäshamn

Nynäshamns (1977)

Box 4,148 00 Ösmo
Tel (0752) 38666
Mem 600
Pro CJ Bernce
Holes 18 L 5720 m SSS 72
Fees 120kr
Loc Nr Nynäshamn

Öland

Ölands (1983)

c/o Tullgaten 28, 387 00 Borgholm
Tel (0485) 11200
Mem 600
Holes Källatorp 9 hole course
Fees 40kr (50kr)
Loc Källatorp, 40km N of Borgholm
Mis Driving range at Ekerum, 10km S of Borgholm

Örnsköldsvik

Öviks GC Puttom (1967)

Box 216, 891 01 Örnsköldsvik 1
Tel (0660) 64070/64091
Mem 700
Pro T Mogren (0660) 64080
Holes 18 L 5795 m SSS 72
Fees D-80kr
Loc 15km N of Örnsköldsvik by E4
Mis Season Jun-Sept

Orust

Orust (1981)

Box 108, 440 90 Henan
Tel (0304) 053170/53171
Mem 360
Pro E Richter
Holes 18 L 5860 m Par 72
Fees 60kr
Loc 80km N of Gothenburg

Oskarshamn

Oskarshamns (1972)

Box 148, 572 01 Oskarshamn
Tel (0491) 94033
Mem 900
Pro I Hult
Holes 18 L 5545 m SSS 72
Fees 100kr (120kr)
Loc 10km on Route E66 towards Fliseryd

Östersund

Östersund-Frösö (1947)

Box 40, S-83201 Frösön
Tel (063) 43001
Mem 1300
Pro G Knutsson
Holes 18 L 6000 m SSS 73
Fees 100kr
Loc Island of Frösö
Mis Open May–Sept

Perstorp

Perstorp (1964)

PO Box 87, 284 00 Perstorp
Tel (0435) 35411
Mem 800
Pro J Kennedy
Holes 18 L 5668 m SSS 71
6 hole short course
Fees 80kr (125kr) 1988 prices
Loc Perstorp 1km.
Helsingborg 48km

Rättvik

Leksands (1977)

Box 25, 793 01 Leksand
Tel (0247) 14204/10922
Mem 730
Pro P Jönsson (0247) 10749
Holes 18 L 5681 m SSS 72
Fees 80kr (100kr)
Loc 2km N of Leksand

Mora (1980)

Box 264, 79201 Mora
Tel (0250) 10182
Mem 585
Pro P Mickols
Holes 18 L 5600 m Par 72
Fees 80kr (100kr)
Loc 40km NW of Rättvik
Mis Driving range

Rättvik (1954)

Box 29, 795 00 Rättvik
Tel (0248) 10773
Mem 750
Pro T Ristola
Holes 18 L 5321 m SSS 69
Fees 100kr (120kr)
Loc Rättvik 2km

Sala

Sala (1970)

Box 16, 733 00 Sala
Tel (0224) 53077/53088
Mem 800
Pro J Long
Holes 18 L 5570 m SSS 71
Fees 80kr
Loc Fallet Sala, 8km E of Sala
towards Uppsala, Route 67/72

Simrishamn

Österlens (1945)

Lilla Vik, 272 00 Simrishamn
Tel (0414) 24230
Mem 725
Pro G Mueller (0414) 24005
Holes 18 L 5855 m SSS 72
Fees 100kr
Loc Vik, 8km N of Simrishamn

Skellefteå

Skellefteå (1967)

Box 152, S-93122 Skellefteå
Tel (0910) 79333/79866
Mem 955
Pro N Fosker
Holes 18 L 6135 m SSS 73
Fees 100kr
Loc Skellefteå 5km

Skövde

Billingens (1949)

St Kulhult, 540 17 Lerdala
Tel (0511) 80291
Mem 600
Pro B Falk (0511) 80298
Holes 18 L 5605 m Par 71
Fees 80kr (100kr)
Loc Between Skara and Skövde

Söderhamn

Söderhamns (1961)

Oxtorget 1C, 826 00 Söderhamn
Tel (0270) 51000
Mem 582
Pro M Andersson
Holes 18 L 5940 m SSS 72
Fees D–70kr WD/WE
Loc Söderhamn 8km

Södertälje

Södertälje (1952)

Box 91, 15121 Södertälje
Tel (0755) 38240
Mem 1100
Pro B Tomlinson (0755) 47674
Holes 18 L 5875 m SSS 72
Fees 120kr (150kr)
Loc 4km W of Södertälje

Trosa-Vagnhärads (1972)

Box 80, 619 00 Trosa
Tel (0156) 16020/22015
Mem 525
Pro C Rose
Holes 9 L 5860 m SSS 72
Fees 70kr (80kr)
Loc Trosa 5km toward Uttervik

Sollefteå

Sollefteå-Långsele (1970)

Box 213, 881 01 Sollefteå
Tel (0620) 21477
Mem 458
Holes 18 L 5890 m SSS 72
Fees WD/WE 60kr
Loc Österforse

Stockholm

Ågesta (1958)

Ågesta, 12352 Farsta
Tel (08) 645641
Mem 1367
Pro R Tomlinson
Holes 18 L 5705 m SSS 72
9 L 3660 m SSS 59
Fees D–150kr (D–200kr)
Loc Farsta

Björkhagens (1973)

Box 430, 12104 Johanneshov 4
Tel (08) 7730431
Mem 580
Pro K Johnson
Holes 9 L 4600 m SSS 66
Fees 50kr (75kr)
Loc 11km S of Stockholm

Bro-Balstå (1978)

Box 96, S-197 00 Bro
Tel (758) 41300/41310
Mem 1000
Pro A Sjöhagen
Holes 18 hole course
Fees 120kr (180kr)
Loc Thoresta, 30 mins NW of
Stockholm

Djursholms (1931)

Hagbardsvägen 1, 18263 Djursholm
Tel (08) 7551477
Mem 1603
Pro G Deverell
Holes 18 L 5595 m SSS 71
9 L 4400 m SSS 64
Fees 140kr (165kr)
Loc 12km N of Stockholm

Drottningholms (1956)

PO Box 173, S-170 11 Drottningholm
Tel (08) 7590085
Mem 830
Pro K Finmo
Holes 18 L 5820 m SSS 72
Fees 150kr (200kr)
Loc Stockholm 10km

Haninge (1983)

Årsta Slott, S-136 91 Haninge
Tel (0750) 32240/32360
Mem 1100
Pro B Deilert

Holes 18 L 5930 m Par 73 SSS 73
Fees 140kr (170kr 2D–280fr)
Loc 30km SE of Stockholm towards Nynäsham.

Ingarö (1962)

Fogelvik, S–130 35 Ingarö
Tel (0766) 28244
Mem 740
Pro RL Morin
Holes 18 L 5603 m SSS 71
Fees 130kr (160kr)
Loc 32km E of Stockholm by Route 74

Lidingö

Box 1035, S–181 21 Lidingö
Tel (08) 7657911
Mem 1260
Pro P Hansson, D Johnston
Holes 18 L 5770 m SSS 71
Fees 140kr (175kr)
Loc Stockholm 6km

Lindö (1978)

Box 1043, 18600 Vallentuna
Tel (0762) 72260
Mem 500
Holes 27 (3 × 9 L 2850 m) SSS 72
Fees 200kr
Loc Vallentuna, 20km N of Stockholm
Mis Lindö GC is part of the Bjorn Borg Sports Club

Salstsjöbadens (1929)

Box 51, 133 21 Saltsjöbaden
Tel (08) 7173319
Mem 1200
Pro M Sheard (08) 7171035
Holes 18 L 5685 m SSS 72
9 L 3640 m SSS 60
Fees 18 holes D–160kr (200kr)
9 holes D–120kr (150kr)
Loc 15km E of Stockholm by Route 228

Sollentuna (1967)

Skillingegården, 191 77 Sollentuna
Tel (08) 7543625
Mem 1100
Pro K Ekberg
Holes 18 L 5910 m SSS 72
Fees 140kr (170kr)
Loc 19km N of Stockholm. 1km W of E4 (Rotebro).
Mis Driving range. Handicap certificate required

Stockholm (1904)

182 31 Danderyd
Tel (08) 7550031
Mem 1020
Pro M Sheard
Holes 18 L 5525 m SSS 71
Fees 150kr (200kr)
Loc 7km NE of Stockholm

Täby (1968)

Skålhamra Gård, 183 43 Täby
Tel (0762) 23261
Mem 1200
Pro T Holmström
Holes 18 L 5776 m SSS 73
Fees 130–160kr
Loc 3km N of Stockholm

Ullna (1981)

Box 16, S–18400 AAN kersberga
Tel (0762) 26075
Mem 580
Pro N Fossett
Holes 18 L 6265 m SSS 72
Fees 125kr (150kr)
Loc 20km N of Stockholm (E3)
Mis Open Apr–Oct. Driving range.

Viksjö (1969)

Fjällens Gård, 175 90 Järfälla
Tel (0758) 16600
Mem 1280
Pro S El Cherif, G Näslund
Holes 18 L 5930 m SSS 73
Fees 120kr (150kr)
Loc Stockholm 18km

Wermdö G & CC (1966)

Torpa, 139 00 Värmdö
Tel (0766) 20849
Mem 725
Pro M Jansson
Holes 18 L 5630 m SSS 72
Fees 210kr (250kr)
Loc 25km E of Stockholm on Route 222

Strängnäs

Strängnäs (1968)

Box 21, 15201 Strängnäs
Tel (0152) 14731
Mem 900
Pro K Jansson (0152) 14702
Holes 18 L 5780 m SSS 72
Fees D–80kr (120kr)
Loc 3km S of Strängnäs

Strömstad

Strömstad (1967)

Box 129, 452 00 Strömstad 1
Tel (0526) 11788
Mem 600
Pro T Hunter (0526) 14244
Holes 18 L 5490 m SSS 71
Fees 100kr W–500kr
Loc 6km N of Strömstad
Mis Driving range

Sundsvall

Sundsvalls (1952)

Roddvägen 31, 862 00 Kvissleby
Tel (060) 561020
Mem 825
Pro T Bjornsson
Holes 18 L 5885 m SSS 72
Fees WD/WE–100kr
Loc Nr Skottsund, 15km S of Sundsvall

Sunne

Sunne (1970)

Box 108, 686 00 Sunne
Tel (0565) 60300
Mem 340
Pro A Olsson (0560) 10776
Holes 9 L 2845 m SSS 71
Fees 70kr
Loc 2km from Sunne on Route 234 to Rottneros

Töreboda

Töreboda (1965)

Box 18, S–54500 Töreboda
Tel (0506) 16240
Mem 550
Holes 15 L 5450 m SSS 70
Fees WD/WE 60kr
Loc 7km E of town

Tranås

Tranås (1952)

N Storgatan 130, 573 00 Tranås
Tel (0140) 11661
Mem 900
Pro S Drewer (0170) 16920
Holes 18 L 5830 m SSS 72
Fees WD/WE–100kr
Loc 2km N of Tranås

Trelleborg

Bedinge (1931)

Box 20, 230 21 Beddingestrand
Tel (0410) 25514
Mem 700
Pro I Persson
Holes 18 L 4500 m SSS 66
Fees D–100kr W–500kr
Loc Trelleborg 20km

Trelleborgs (1963)

Pl 3307A, 231 93 Trelleborg
Tel (0410) 30460
Mem 875
Pro M Malmstrom
Holes 18 L 5320 m SSS 70
Fees 100kr (1210kr)
Loc 5km W of Trelleborg

Trollhättan

Onsjö (1974)

Box 100, 462 00 Vänersborg
Tel (0521) 64149
Mem 750
Pro N Goodison (0521) 62575
Holes 18 L 5730 m SSS 72
Fees 80kr (100kr)
Loc 4km S of Vänersborg. 8km N of Gothenburg.

Trollhättans (1963)

Box 254, 461 26 Trollhättan
Tel (0520) 41000
Mem 700
Pro G Clark (0520) 41010
Holes 18 L 6200 m SSS 73
Fees 80kr (100kr)
Loc Koberg, 20km SE of Trollhättan

Ulricehamn

Ulricehamns (1947)

Box 179, S-52301 Ulricehamn
Tel (0321) 10021
Mem 930
Pro H Ljung
Holes 18 L 5402 m SSS 70
Fees D-100kr
Loc Backasen, 2km E of Ulricehamn

Umeå

Umeå (1954)

Vintergatan 18, 902 54 Umeå
Tel (090) 41071/116355
Mem 1025
Pro J Anderson
Holes 18 L 5752 m SSS 72
Fees 80kr
Loc 16km SE of Umeå

Uppsala

Sigtunabygdens (1961)

Box 89, 193 00 Sigtuna
Tel (0760) 54012
Mem 1070
Pro H Reis
Holes 18 L 5760 m SSS 72
Fees 100kr (150kr)
Loc 50km N of Stockholm, nr Arlanda

Upsala (1937)

Box 12015, S-750 12 Uppsala
Tel (018) 461270
Mem 1790
Pro M Lord (018) 461241
Holes 18 L 6176 m SSS 74
9 L 1643 m SSS 56
Fees 80kr (120kr)
Loc Uppsala 10km
Mis Driving range

Varberg

Varbergs (1950)

Box 39, 432 21 Varberg
Tel (0340) 37470
Mem 1000
Pro F Englund
Holes 18 L 5797 m SSS 73
Fees 120kr
Loc 15km E of Varberg

Värnamo

Värnamo (1962)

Box 146, S-33101 Värnamo
Tel (46370) 23123
Mem 625
Pro A Marshall
Holes 18 L 6253 m SSS 72
Fees 100kr (120kr)
Loc 8km E of town on Route 127
Mis Driving range

Västerås

Ängsö (1979)

Skultunavägen 7, 722 17 Västerås
Tel (0171) 41012
Mem 1075
Pro P Gullberg
Holes 18 holes SSS 72
Fees 80kr (100kr) 1988 prices
Loc 15km E of Västerås

Västerås (1931)

Bjärby, 72481 Västerås
Tel (021) 357543
Mem 1393
Pro T Ljungqvist
Holes 18 L 5380 m SSS 69
Fees 80kr (125kr)
Loc 2km N of Västerås

Västervik

Västerviks (1959)

Box 62, 593 01 Västervik
Tel (0490) 19417
Mem 400
Pro P Johansson (0490) 31521
Holes 9 L 5720 m SSS 71
Fees D-50kr
Loc Västervik 2km

Växjö

Växjö (1959)

Box 227, 351 05 Växjö
Tel (0470) 21539
Mem 975
Pro L Ibsonius (0470) 14004
Holes 18 L 5860 m SSS 72
Fees 100kr (120kr)
Loc Växjö 3km

Veberöd

Romeleåsens (1969)

Kvarnbrodda, 240 14 Veberöd
Tel (046) 82012/82014
Mem 1200
Pro J Byard
Holes 18 L 5830 m SSS 72
Fees 80kr (120kr)
Loc Veberöd-Dörröd, 6km E of Malmö

Vetlanda

Vetlanda (1983)

Box 249, 574 01 Vetlanda
Tel (0383) 18310
Mem 750
Pro S Petersson
Holes 18 holes Par 72
Fees 80kr
Loc Östanå, 3km from Vetlanda.

Vimmerby

Tobo (1971)

Tobo Gård, 598 00 Vimmerby
Tel (0492) 30028/30346
Pro L Wiberg
Holes 18 L 5950 m SSS 73
Fees WD/WE-80kr
Loc S of Vimmerby off Route 34. 280km E of Gothenburg

Visby

Visby

Box 1038, 621 21 Visby
Tel (0498) 45058
Mem 965
Pro F Bergqvist (0498) 45100
Holes 18 L 5855 m SSS 72
Fees 120kr
Loc Visby 25km

Ystad

Ystad (1930)

Box 162, 27100 Ystad
Tel (0411) 50350
Mem 800
Pro B Jones
Holes 18 L 5800 m SSS 72
Fees 100-150kr
Loc 7km E of Ystad towards Simrishamn

Switzerland

Arosa

Arosa (1947)

CH–7050 Arosa
Tel **31 22 15**
Mem 200
Pro AM Platz
Holes 9 L 4435 m SSS 63
Fees D–25fr
Loc Arosa 1km

Bad Ragaz

Bad Ragaz (1956)

Hans Albrechtstrasse, 7310 Bad Ragaz
Tel **(085) 9 15 56**
Mem 700
Pro C Gaud, M Caligari, T Smith
Holes 18 L 5766 m SSS 70
Fees 50fr (60fr)
Loc Chur 20km. Zürich 100km
Mis Handicap certificate required

Bern/Fribourg

Blumisberg (1959)

3184 Wünnewil
Tel **(037) 36 13 80**
Mem 475
Pro F Schiroli, B Marx
Holes 18 L 6048 m SSS 73
Fees 40fr (60fr)
Loc Fribourg 14km. Berne 16km.

Brig

Riederalp (1986)

CH–3981 Riederalp
Tel **(028) 27 29 32/27 14 63 (Kruger Sport)**
Mem 180
Pro M Cole
Holes 9 L 3016 m SSS 57
Fees 25fr
Loc Brig 10km
Mis Season Jun–Oct

Brugg

Schinznach-Bad (1929)

5116 Schinznach-Bad
Tel **(056) 43 12 26**
Mem 235
Pro H Zimmerman, V Krajewski
Holes 9 L 6036 m Par 72
Fees 40fr (50fr)
Loc Brugg 6km

Crans-sur-Sierre

Crans-sur-Sierre (1906)

3963 Crans-sur-Sierre-Montana
Tel **(27) 41 21 68/41 27 03**
Mem 1100
Pro J Bonvin, RJ Barras, J-M Barras, B Cordonnier, B Mittaz, A Rey, M Bonvin, A Jeanquartier
Holes 18 L 6260 m SSS 72
9 L 2667 m SSS 35
Fees 18 hole course 50fr (60fr)
9 hole course 28fr (32fr)
Loc Sion 20km. Geneva 2 hrs drive

Davos

Davos (1929)

Mattastrasse 25, CH–7270 Davos Platz
Tel **(083) 5 56 34**
Mem 400
Pro HJ Hörenz
Holes 18 L 5715 yds SSS 67
Fees 30fr (40fr)
Loc 1km outside Davos
Mis Open May–Oct

Geneva

Bonmont (1983)

Château de Bonmont, 1261 Chéserex
Tel **(022) 69 23 45**
Mem 600
Pro F Boillat, G Kaye, Y Radal
Holes 18 L 6160 m Par 71
Fees D–45fr
Loc Nyon 10 mins. Geneva 25 mins. Lausanne 35 mins

Domaine Impérial (1987)

CP 84, CH–1196 Gland
Tel **(0221) 64 45 45**
Mem 1000
Pro R Guignet, A Jeanquartier, G Martin, S Rey
Holes 18 L 6254 m SSS 74
Fees WD–80fr
Loc Between Geneva and Lausanne.
Mis No visitors until 1990. Members' guests only in 1989

G & CC Bossey

Château de Crevin, F–74160 St-Julien-en-Genevois
Tel **(50) 43 75 25**
Pro JP Charpenel, E Berthet, W Reid
Holes 18 L 6145 m Par 71
Loc Geneva 6km
Mis Driving range

Golf de Geneva (1923)

70 Route de la Capite, 1223 Cologny
Tel **(022) 35 75 40**
Mem 1000
Pro JM Larretche, PM Borgeat, P Bagnoud, J Berthet
Holes 18 L 6250 m Par 72
Fees 60fr
Loc Geneva 4km
Mis WE–only with member.

Gstaad

Gstaad (1962)

CH 3780 Saanenland, Gstaad
Tel **(030) 426 36**
Mem 196
Pro B Herrmann
Holes 9 L 2870 m Par 71
Fees 25fr (30fr)
Loc Gstaad 15km

Interlaken

Interlaken-Unterseen (1964)

Postfach 110, 3800 Interlaken
Tel **(036) 22 60 22**
Mem 400
Pro B Chenaux
Holes 18 L 5980 m SSS 72
Fees 50fr (60fr)
Loc Interlaken centre 3km
Mis Reduction for Interlaken Hotel guests

Lausanne

Lausanne (1921)

Le Chalet à Gobet, 1000 Lausanne 25
Tel **784 13 16**
Mem 850
Pro A Gallardo, M Gallardo, M More, D Ingram
Holes 18 L 6165 m SSS 74
Fees 50fr (70fr)
Loc Lausanne 7km

Lenzerheide

Lenzerheide Valbella (1950)

7078 Lenzerheide
Tel **(081) 34 13 16**
Mem 400
Pro H Schumacher, R Blaesi
Holes 18 L 5269 m Par 69
Fees 50fr
Loc Lenzerheide $2^1/_2$ km
Mis Public course

Locarno

Patriziale Ascona (1928)

Via al Lido 81, 6612 Ascona
Tel **(093) 35 21 32**
Mem 350 250(L) 50(J)
Pro V Caccia, F Codiga, F Salmina
Holes 18 L 5893 m SSS 71
Fees 40fr (60fr)
Loc Ascona 1km. Locarno 5km
Mis Public course

Lucerne

Bürgenstock (1928)

6366 Bürgenstock
Tel (041) 61 24 34
Pro G Denny
Holes 9 L 1935 m Par 34
Fees 35fr
Loc 15km from Lucerne

Lucerne (1903)

Dietschiberg CH 6006
Tel (041) 36 97 87
Mem 350
Pro L Mudry, B Lagger
Holes 18 L 5700 m SSS 71
Fees 40fr (50fr)
Loc Lucerne 2km
Mis Handicap certificate required.

Lugano

Lugano (1923)

6983 Magliaso
Tel (091) 71 15 57
Mem 900
Pro D Maina, G Parisi, I Tremolada
Holes 18 L 5740 m SSS 71
Fees 50fr (70fr)
Loc Lugano 8km towards Ponte Tresa

Montreux

Montreux (1900)

Case Post 187, 1820 Montreux
Tel (025) 26 46 16 (Dir/Sec)
Mem 491
Pro P Bagnoud, J Bagnoud, J-L Chable
Holes 18 L 6205 m SSS 73
Fees 30fr (40fr)
Loc Montreux 15km

Neuchâtel

Neuchâtel (1928)

Voens/St Blaise
Tel (038) 33 55 50
Mem 400
Pro J Kressig
Holes 18 L 5840 m SSS 70
Fees 40fr (60fr)
Loc Neuchâtel 5km

St Gallen

Ostschweizischer (1948)

9246 Niederburen
Tel (071) 81 18 56
Mem 340
Pro CB Craig
Holes 18 L 5920 m SSS 71
Fees D–50fr (60fr)
Loc St Gallen 25km

St Moritz

Engadin (1892)

CH 7503 Samedan
Tel (082) 6 52 26
Mem 410
Pro A Casera, A Chiogna, I Tremolada, J Wallwork
Holes 18 L 6350 m SSS 72
Fees WD/WE–50fr
Loc Samedan/St Moritz

Verbier

Verbier (1969)

1936 Verbier
Tel (026) 7 49 95
Mem 140
Pro C Torribio
Holes 18 hole Par 3 course
Fees D–15fr (20fr)
Loc Centre of resort
Mis Open Jun–Oct

Villars

Villars (1922)

Case Postale 152, 1884 Villars
Tel (025) 354214
Mem 400
Pro JL & G Chable
Holes 18 L 4093 m SSS 61
Fees 35fr (50fr)
Loc Villars 7km

Vulpera

Vulpera (1923)

Vulpera Spa CH 7552
Tel (084) 9 96 88
Mem 220
Pro P Jones
Holes 9 L 2021 m SSS 62
Fees 40fr (50fr) W–230fr
Loc Vulpera, 60km from St Moritz in lower Engadin

Zürich

Breitenloo (1964)

Nr Bassersdorf, 61 Bassersdorf CH, 8309 Oberwil
Tel (01) 836 40 80/836 64 86
Mem 350
Pro Th Villiger
Holes 18 L 6100 m SSS 72
Fees 50fr (70fr)
Loc Zürich Airport 8km

Dolder (1907)

Kuthausstrasse 66, 8032 Zürich
Tel (01) 47 50 45
Pro D Dieter, C Brazerol
Holes 9 L 1735 m SSS 58
Fees WD–50fr
Mis Open Apr–Nov. WE–only members and guests of Hotels Waldhaus, Dolder & Grand Dolder.

Hittnau-Zürich (1964)

PO Box CH–8700 Küsnacht
Tel (01) 950 24 42
Mem 450
Pro E Bauer, D Parini
Holes 18 L 5720 m SSS 71
Fees WD–60fr
Loc Zürich 30km
Mis WE–closed for non-members.

Schönenberg

8821 Schönenberg
Tel (01) 788 16 24
Mem 400
Pro T Charpié, J Wallwork, L Freeman
Holes 18 L 6340 m SSS 73
Fees D–60fr
Loc Centre of Zürich 20km

Zürich-Zumikon (1931)

8126 Zumikon ZH
Tel (01) 918 00 50
Mem 700
Pro R Lanz, G Denny, B Griss
Holes 18 L 6360 m SSS 74
Fees WD–60fr
Loc Zürich 10km
Mis Visitors must be introduced. WE–closed for non-members

Yugoslavia

Bled

Bled (1974)

Cesta Svobode 13, 64260 Bled
Tel (064) 78 282
Mem 350
Pro D Jurman
Holes 18 L 6320 m SSS 73
Fees WD/WE–12.60Lstg W–75.80Lstg
Loc 3km W of Bled. Ljubljana airport 30km

For explanation of abbreviations, see page 202.

Part III
Who's Who in Golf

Obituaries 1988

Sir Henry Cotton MBE 1907–1987

© Peter Dazeley Photography

The towering figure of Henry Cotton, or Sir Henry as he became a few days after his death on 22nd December 1987, was the Master of British golf for five decades. Three times Open Champion, a journalist writing all his own copy, author of many books, prolific architect and course designer, original thinker and great teacher, always a supporter of youth, he was the acknowledged leader of his profession.

It had not always been so. Early in his career he was often a controversial figure, opinionated and an individualist, but he was determined and insistent that the professional golfer should be an accepted member of the golfing community. He lived to see his hope fulfilled. He led by example. When in January 1937 he came to Ashridge, Herts, as professional, one of the conditions of his appointment he laid down was election as an honorary member of the Club. He was one of the first to open the green baize door; today it is accepted practice at many Clubs.

Champion in the making

Born in 1907 at Holmes Chapel, Cheshire, he went to Alleyn's School, Dulwich, where his independent spirit resented the discipline then in force and he left at 17 to become a golf professional. He held assistant posts at Fulwell, Rye and Cannes. This latter appointment was his first experience of life on the European continent, where he was to reside nearly half his life. His determination to be a champion golfer, even in one so young, meant many hours on the practice ground, blistered hands and cultivating a particular style which, while not natural, was adopted as classic by thousands of his pupils and admirers.

He was always grateful that an assistant was taught club making and the elements of teaching, in his opinion skills which every professional should acquire if he was to have a future in the game. No department of the game failed to interest his enquiring mind. A year before his death, at a trade exhibition in London, he was able to demonstrate the special twist of the fingers needed to fashion a perfect tee of sand; it was probably 55 years since he had used one.

He was one of the first to show that practice was essential if one was to reach the top. Even when preparing for his second Open Championship win at Carnoustie in 1937, he practised under the eye of Fred Robertson, his senior assistant at Ashridge, ironing out minor faults in his swing. Robertson's reward was to finish 16th in that Open, with yet another Ashridge assistant, Bill Laidlaw in 8th place. He was always proud of that record of three professionals from the same Club finishing so high.

Peak of career in the 30s

He was appointed professional at Langley Park in Kent at 20, but after three years of comparative success and much criticism, he moved to the Waterloo Club, Brussels, where his attitude was understood and he was accepted by Club members as an equal. He had already won several

Continental Opens and was to win more before and after the War, 11 in all, but it must be admitted that the competition on the Continent in the 1930s came as much from amateurs as from the local professionals. Cyril Tolley for instance had twice won the French Open, in 1924 and 1928.

He continued to play regularly in the few British Tournaments there were and was the most successful British professional through the 1930s, winning the Open twice, in 1934 and 1937, and the News of the World match-play title, in 1932 and 1940, having been beaten in the final in 1946. Until the middle 1950s the match-play title was considered next in line after the Open.

The 1934 Open win at Sandwich was sensational; his first two rounds of 67 and 65 remain the best first 36 holes in the Open after 44 years. The 65, the record low round for any Open up to then, is the only round of golf ever to have a golf ball, the Dunlop 65, named after it.

Back in Britain again in 1937, he won at Carnoustie when the US Ryder Cup team, which had just won the Cup at Southport and Ainsdale, were all competing. His last round of 71, played in a downpour, is considered by many one of the finest ever in such conditions.

The war and after

But for the War, in which he served in the RAF until 1945, he would probably have added at least one more to his Open wins. To prove he was still a great player at 41, the triumph at Muirfield in 1948 was outstanding. His second round of 66, a course record, was played before a large gathering which included King George VI, the only time a reigning monarch has been present at the Open.

He had been appointed professional at Royal Mid-Surrey in 1946 and Temple, at Maidenhead, in 1953. After his Muirfield victory he continued to play for a few years before he withdrew from Championship and Tournament competition. In the early 1960s he was back on the Continent, first to Portugal, then for a short period to Spain while Portugal suffered political upheaval, and afterwards back to his beloved Penina where he designed and fashioned a course with which his name will always be remembered. He was still a great teacher and he designed courses in the UK and the Continent, nearly 20 in all. His literary output, in addition to the weekly and monthly press articles, was considerable. He wrote nearly a dozen books most of which were both biographical and instructional and always well illustrated as he was a keen photographer.

One of his special interests was the Golf Foundation of which he was an original member. His concern that any keen boys or girls should have professional instruction available at little or no cost was the Foundation's objective. He supported it to the end of his life, often attending the annual meeting. To encourage young professionals he also instituted the Henry Cotton Rookie of the Year Award in 1960, which continues today. For its first 15 years, he himself provided the funding for the winner. Subsequently it was underwritten commercially. Tony Jacklin and Sandy Lyle, both later Open Champions, were among the early winners and several others have since had successful tournament careers.

Such was his stature, he was seldom out of golfing news in the 1960s, 1970s and 1980s. Indeed he was the acknowledged father-figure to today's professional and the doyen of the game in the UK and Europe. Even in his late 70s his enthusiasm was undiminished. He divided his time between Penina, Paris and London, living as always in considerable style and enjoying the company of golfers and others of all ages. Until her death in 1985 his greatest supporter, mentor and critic was his wife Toots, who herself had been a golfer skilled enough to win the Ladies Championship of Austria in 1937.

He became an Honorary Member of the Royal and Ancient in 1968, one of the élite band of professionals to be so honoured. He was Captain of the Ryder Cup team in 1947 and 1953 and of the PGA in 1934 and 1954. The world of golf was thankful that his unique service to the game was at last recognised by the Knighthood awarded in the 1988 New Year's honours a few days after his death. At least he had the satisfaction of knowing that he was to be so honoured. His many friends and admirers were delighted and only regretted that he was no longer with them to celebrate the honour, as he would so much have enjoyed the occasion they would have arranged for him.

Gerald Micklem CBE 1911–1988

Gerald Micklem had been in poor health for some years when he died on 21st May at the age of 76. Indeed it was only through his courage and refusal to give in that he continued to give his all to the game he loved.

Corinthian spirit
He was one of the last of the true Corinthian style amateurs. Having no financial worries he was able to devote all the time he wanted to furthering golf in every aspect of the game. His knowledge was profound and he was always prepared to share it with others when asked and sometimes when not. His highly individual staccato delivery was known everywhere in the world of golf, enjoyed by the great majority and imitated by some, usually not very well.

Amateur success
As a player he did not mature until after the 1939–45 War, in which he served in the Grenadier Guards, being wounded when Adjutant of the 3rd Battalion in the Western Desert. He was twice English Champion, in 1947 and 1953, second in the Brabazon in 1948, four times in the Walker Cup team 1947–55 and non-playing Captain 1957–59, a Home International for 12 years from 1947, captaining the team on the last three occasions. Winner of numerous Amateur Scratch Trophies, he never forgot lesser events such as the President's Putter at Rye and the Halford-Hewitt tournament at Deal, winning the first in 1953 and playing for the Winchester side in 1948 when they took the Cup. Perhaps he enjoyed as much as any success his several wins in the Gold and Silver Medals at the Royal and Ancient's members' meetings when, after his playing career ended, he was seldom absent from the Big Room where members listened avidly to his trenchant comments on the play and players.

Administrator extraordinary
If his playing days had covered a wide canvas, his subsequent administrative commitments were vast. He was in succession Chairman of the Royal and Ancient Rules of Golf, Selection and the Championship Committees. It was in the latter that he made his greatest contribution to the future of the game. His vision and dedication to the development of the Open from a presitge event with total prize money of £8500 when he took over in 1963, to the best-run, and most important Championship in the world that it is today with a prize fund of £800,000, must in no small measure be due to his efforts. He was Captain of the Club in 1968–69.

Nor must be forgotten his work for the English Golf Union (President 1965), the European Golf

© Action Photos, courtesy of The Golf Foundation

Association (President 1967–69) and his devoted support for the Golf Foundation. He encouraged youth to take up the game and many successful amateurs and professionals today sought his advice and received much benefit from it.

He was well-known across the Atlantic as a result of many visits to the USA. His friends there had great respect for his understanding and, appreciating his contribution to golf, nominated him for the Bobby Jones Award of the USGA in 1968. He was only the third recipient who was not a United States citizen.

There was always something new in the game in which he was interested and many are the prefaces and introductions he contributed to books about golf. In one year recently as many as four Club Histories contained a Foreword by him, commending the Club and the course. The pity is that he never put pen to paper to record his own experiences. How well worth reading they would have been.

There was never any doubt of how much his efforts for the game were appreciated. The large congregation which paid tribute at his Memorial Service in the Guards Chapel in July contained representatives of every Club and organisation of which he was a member and espoused. Nor could the address by his fellow R. and A. Captain, Tom Harvey, have better summed up the man and all he did for the game.

British Isles Players

Explanations of abbreviations used

Add Present Address
Cls Club Membership
Opn Open and US Open Championships
Tls Overseas Opens
Chp British and National Union Amateur Championships
Maj European Tours and Major Amateur Tournaments
Ove Overseas Championships (other than Opens) and Tournaments
Oth Other British Tournaments
Reg Regional and County Championships
Int International Appearances
Am Amateur Record
Jun Junior Titles
Mis Miscellaneous
WPGA Women's PGA Tour
LPGA US Ladies PGA

Aitken, Miss Wilma
See Mrs W Leburn

Alliss, Peter
Born Berlin on 28th February, 1931. Turned Professional 1946

Tls Spanish Open 1956–58. Italian Open 1958. Portuguese Open 1958. Brazilian Open 1961
Maj Daks 1954–63 (tied). Dunlop 1955–59. PGA Close 1957–62–65. Sprite 1960 (tied). Swallow-Penfold 1964. Esso Golden 1964. Jeyes 1965. Martini 1966 (tied). Rediffusion 1966. Agfa-Gevaert 1967. Piccadilly 1969
Oth West of England Open Professional 1956–58–62–66. Sunningdale Foursomes 1958–61. Wentworth Pro-Am Foursomes 1959. British Assistants 1952
Int Ryder Cup 1953–57–59–61–63–65–67–69. England in World Cup 1954–55–57–58–59–61–62–64–66–67. Home International 1967 (capt). UK v Europe 1954–55–56
Am Boy International 1946
Mis PGA Captain 1962, 1987. Harry Vardon Trophy 1964–66. Author, TV commentator

Anderson, Fiona
Born Perth on 24th August, 1954

Add 15 Grange Terrace, Edinburgh
Cls Blairgowrie, Gullane Ladies, Craigie Hill
Chp Scottish Ladies 1987. Runner-up 1980–83–88
Reg North of Scotland Ladies 1977. Scottish Universities Champion 1975
Int Vagliano Trophy 1987 (Scotland) Home Int 1977–79–80–81–83–84–86–87–88; (Eur Team Ch) 1979–83–87

Anderson, Miss Jessie
See Mrs G Valentine

Anstey, Miss Veronica
See Mrs V Beharrell

Armitage, Miss Susan
See Mrs S Langridge

Attenborough, Michael F
Born Britford, nr Salisbury in October, 1939

Add 17 Parkgate, Blackheath, London SE3
Cls Chislehurst, Royal St George's, Royal and Ancient
Maj Hampshire Hog 1960. County Champion of Champions 1964. Duncan Putter 1966. Prince of Wales Challenge Cup 1969
Ove Scandinavian Amateur 1965
Oth President's Putter 1962–66
Reg Kent Amateur 1963–64–65
Int Walker Cup 1967. GB v Europe 1966–68. England (Home Int) 1964–66–67–68; (Eur Team Ch) 1967
Jun Boy International 1957

Bailey, Mrs Diane
(formerly Mrs D Frearson, *née* Robb)
Born Wolverhampton on 31st August, 1943

Add Durlin, Abinger Common, Dorking, Surrey
Cls Enville (Hon), Reigate Heath, Betchworth Park
Chp Runner-up British Ladies 1961
Maj Avia Foursomes 1972. Worplesdon Mixed Foursomes 1971
Reg Lincolnshire Ladies 1966–67. Staffordshire Ladies 1961. Midland Ladies 1966
Int Curtis Cup 1962–72. Vagliano Trophy 1961, 1983 (captain), 1985 (captain). World Team Chp 1968. England (Home Int) 1961–62–71. Captain Curtis Cup 1984–86–88
Jun British Girls 1961. Scottish Girls Open Stroke Play 1959-61. English Girls International 1957-61.
Mis Surrey Ladies County Captain 1981–82. British Ladies Commonwealth Team 1983 (captain).

Baker, Peter
Born 7th October, 1967. Turned Professional 1986

Chp English Open Amateur Stroke Play 1985 (tied)
Maj Benson and Hedges International 1988
Oth Carris Trophy 1983–85
Reg Shropshire and Herefordshire champion 1983–84–85
Int Walker Cup 1985. GB v Europe 1986. England (Home Int) 1985
Mis Rookie of the Year 1987

Banks, Charles
Born 19th November, 1953

Chp English Open Amateur Stroke Play 1983
Reg Nottinghamshire Open 1980–81–83
Int England (Home Int) 1983

Bannerman, Harry
Born Aberdeen on 5th March, 1942. Turned Professional 1965

Oth Scottish Professional 1967–72. Northern Scottish Open 1967–69–72. East of Scotland PGA Match Play 1969. Scottish Coca Cola 1976
Int Ryder Cup 1971. Scotland World Cup 1967–72. Scotland in Double Diamond 1972–74
Am Boy International 1959. North East Scotland Stroke Play 1963–64–65. North of Scotland Stroke Play 1962
Mis Frank Moran Trophy 1972

Barber, Mrs DN (*née* Sally Bonallack)
Born Chigwell, Essex on 9th April, 1938. Turned Professional 1979. Reinstated Amateur 1982

Add 111, Wyatts Drive, Thorpe Bay, Essex
Cls Thorpe Hall, Thorndon Park, Hunstanton (Hon), Killarney (Hon)
Chp English Ladies 1968, runner-up 1970–71
Maj Astor Salver 1972. Avia Foursomes 1976. London Foursomes 1984
Ove German Ladies
Reg Essex Ladies 1958–59–60–61–62–63–66–67–70–71
Int Curtis Cup 1962. Vagliano Trophy 1961–69. England (Home Int) 1960–61–62–63–68–70–72–77 (capt), (non-playing captain 1978); (Eur Team Ch) 1969–71

Barnes, Brian
Born Addington, Surrey on 3rd June, 1945. Turned Professional 1964

Tls Dutch Open 1974. French Open 1975. Spanish Open 1978. Second in New Zealand Open 1978. Italian Open 1979. Portuguese Open 1979. Zambian Open 1979–81. Kenya Open 1981. TPC 1981. Scottish Professional Champion 1981–82
Maj Agfacolor 1969. Martini International 1972. Sun Alliance PGA Match Play 1976. Greater Manchester Open 1978
Ove Australian Masters 1970. Flame Lily (Rhodesia) 1967
Oth Coca-Cola Young Professionals 1969. East of Scotland Professional 1975. Northern Scottish Open 1978
Int Ryder Cup 1969–71–73–75–77–79. Scotland in Double Diamond 1972–73–74–75–76–77. Scotland in World Cup 1974–75–76–77. GB v Europe 1974–76–78–80; v South Africa 1976
Am Britsh Youths' 1964. Somerset Amateur 1964. South Western Counties Amateur 1964
Mis Finished 4th in inaugural Alcan Golfer of the Year 1967. Third in Doral Open 1970. European American Express 1975

Bayman, Mrs Linda (*née* Denison-Pender)
Born 10th June, 1948

Chp English Ladies 1983. British Women's Stroke Play 1987
Maj Avia Foursomes 1969–71–73–79–80. Worplesdon Mixed Foursomes 1980–84. Astor Salver 1983–84. Critchley Salver 1984
Reg Kent Champion 1968–72–73–78
Int England (Home Int) 1971–72–73–83–84–85–87–88. Vagliano Trophy 1971–73–85–87. European Team Championship 1983–85–87. Curtis Cup 1988
Jun Kent Girls 1966
Mis Avia Woman Golfer of the Year 1987

Beck, Mrs JB (*née* Pim)
Born Cantibeely, Co Dublin on 1st July, 1901

Add Felder Lodge, Worth, Deal, Kent
Cls Royal Portrush, The Berkshire, Prince's
Chp Irish Ladies 1938, runner-up 1949
Oth Ladies Veteran 1952–55–56–59
Int Ireland (Home Int) 1926 to 1950–56
Mis Curtis Cup non-playing captain 1954. Captain of LGU team to tour South Africa 1951. Irish hockey internationalist 1920

Behan, Lillian
Born Co Kildare on 12th January 1965. Turned Professional 1986

Chp British Ladies 1985
Int Vagliano Trophy 1985. Curtis Cup 1986. Ireland (Home Int) 1984–85–86

Beharrell, John Charles
Born Solihull, Warwickshire on 2nd May, 1938

Add Tracery, Little Aston, Park Road, Streetly, Sutton Coldfield, Warwickshire
Cls Royal and Ancient, Edgbaston, Aldeburgh. Hon member of Little Aston, Blackwell, Handworth
Chp Amateur Champion 1956
Maj Antlers Royal Mid-Surrey 1960. Central England Mixed Foursomes 1956–57–75
Int GB v Europe 1956; v Professionals 1956. England (Home Int) 1956
Jun English Boy International 1955
Mis EGU selector 1972 to 1974. Member of R & A Championship Committee 1976–77 and Rules of Golf Committee 1979

Beharrell, Mrs Veronica (*née* Anstey)
Born Birmingham on 14th January, 1935

Add Tracery, Little Aston, Park Road, Streetly, Sutton Coldfield, Warwickshire
Cls Edgbaston (Hon), Little Aston
Maj Central England Mixed Foursomes 1957–75
Ove Australian Ladies 1955. New Zealand Ladies 1955. Victoria (Australia) Ladies Open 1955
Reg Warwickshire Ladies 1955–56–57–58–60–71–72–75
Int Curtis Cup 1956. England (Home Int) 1955–56–58 (non-playing captain 1961)
Jun Girl International 1953

Bembridge, Maurice
Born Worksop on 21st February, 1945. Turned Professional 1960

Opn Leading British Player in Open Championship 1968 (5th)
Tls Kenya Open 1968–69–79. Second New Zealand Open 1971–72. German Open 1975

Maj PGA Match Play 1969. Sumrie 1969. Dunlop Masters 1971. Martini 1973. Piccadilly Medal 1974. Viyella PGA 1974. Double Diamond Individual 1974. Benson and Hedges International 1979
Ove Caltex (New Zealand) 1970. Lusaka Open 1972
Oth British Assistants 1967
Int Ryder Cup 1969–71–73–75. GB v South Africa 1976. England in Double Diamond 1973–74–75. England in World Cup 1974–75
Mis His 63 in the qualifying round for the 1967 Open Championship equals the lowest recorded. Second in Order of Merit 1973. Scored 64 in last round 1974 US Masters equalling record; his inward half of 30 also equalled the record

Benka, Peter
Born London on 18th September, 1946

Add Manaries, Newdigate, Surrey
Cls Addington, West Sussex
Chp Second in Scottish Open Amateur Stroke Play 1969
Maj County Champion of Champions 1967. Sunningdale Foursomes 1969. St George's Challenge Cup 1969. St George's Hill Trophy 1971–75. Mullingar Trophy 1970
Ove Dutch Amateur 1972
Reg Surrey Amateur 1967–68
Int Walker Cup 1969. GB v Europe 1970. England (Home Int) 1967–68–69–70; (Eur Team Ch) 1969
Jun British Youths 1967–68. Boy International 1964. Youth International 1966–67–68
Mis Leading Amateur Open Championship 1967

Bennett, Stephen
Born Cleethorpes on 23rd April, 1959. Turned Professional 1979

Tls Tunisian Open 1985. Zimbabwe Open 1986
Reg Lincolnshire Open 1979. Lincolnshire Amateur 1977–78

Bentley, Arnold Lewis
Born Southport on 11th June, 1911

Add 24 Sandringham Court, Lord Street, Southport, Lancs
Cls Royal and Ancient, Hesketh (Hon), Royal Birkdale
Chp English Amateur 1939
Jun Boy International 1928
Int England (Home Int) 1936–37; v France 1937-39
Mis Played for British Seniors 1969

Bentley, Harry Geoffrey
Born Manchester on 13th October, 1907

Add Bentley's House, Avenue Francois Godin, Le Touquet, Pas-de-Calais. Tel (21) 051865; and Bentley's House, 133 Guadalmina, Baja, Marbella, Andalucia, Spain
Cls Royal and Ancient, Hesketh (Hon), Le Touquet
Chp English Amateur 1936, runner-up 1954. Runner-up Irish Amateur Open 1934
Maj Royal St George's Challenge Cup 1932. Prince of Wales Cup 1935
Ove French Amateur 1931–32. German Amateur 1933–37–38–39. Italian Amateur 1954
Reg Lancashire Amateur 1931–32–39
Int Walker Cup 1934–36–38. GB v Professionals 1930–31–32–34–35. England (Home Int) 1931–32–33–34–35–36–37–38–47; v France 1934–36–37–38–39 (capt) 54
Mis Chairman Walker Cup Selectors 1953. Captain British Seniors 1967. Leading Amateur French, Belgian, German, Czechoslovakian Opens 1935

Bisgood, Miss Jeanne, CBE
Born Richmond, Surrey on 11th August, 1923

Add 12 Water's Edge, Brudenell Road, Poole, Dorset BH13 7NN
Cls Parkstone (Hon)
Chp English Ladies 1951–53–57
Maj Astor Salver 1951–52–53. Roehampton Gold Cup 1951–52–53. Daily Graphic 1945–51
Ove Norwegian Ladies 1955. Swedish Ladies 1952. Italian Ladies 1953. German Ladies 1953. Portuguese Ladies 1954
Reg South Eastern Ladies 1950–52. Surrey Ladies 1951–53–69
Int Curtis Cup 1950–52–54 (non-playing captain 1970). England (Home Int) 1949–50–51–52–53–54–56–58

Blakeman, David
Born 10th June, 1960

Chp English Amateur 1981
Int England (Home Int) 1981; v France 1982

Bloice, Cecil
Born Aberfeldy on 30th July, 1954

Int Walker Cup 1985. Scotland (Home Int) 1985–86

Bolton, Mrs SM (*née* Zara Davis)
Born London on 16th March, 1914

Add Strandmore House, Portrush, Co Antrim
Cls Hon Member of Royal Portrush, Bishop's Stortford, Maccauvlei, County Down, Castlerock, Ballycastle
Chp Runner-up English Ladies 1948
Reg Herts Ladies 1935. Kent Ladies 1948. Ulster Scratch Cup 1947–48–49–50–56–60
Int Curtis Cup 1948 (non-playing captain 1956–66–68). GB v France 1948. England (Home Int) 1939–49–50–51–55 (capt)–56
Mis Non-playing captain of British Commonwealth Team 1967. Member of LGU team to tour South Africa 1951

Bonallack, Michael Francis, OBE
Born Chigwell on 31st December, 1934

Add Clatto Lodge, Blebo Craigs, Cupar, Fife
Cls Thorpe Hall, Pine Valley, Elie. Hon member of Thorndon Park, Orsett, Royal Lytham, Royal Blackheath, The Warren, Boyce Hill, Woodhall Spa, Burnham and Berrow, Royal Porthcawl, Spalding, Clitheroe, The Berkshire, Sunningdale, Rochford and others
Chp Amateur Champion 1961–65–68–69–70. English Open Amateur Stroke Play 1964–68–69 (tied)–71, second 1959–66–67. English Amateur 1962–63–65–67–68 runner-up 1959
Maj Berkshire Trophy 1957–61–65–68–70–71 (tied). Hampshire Hog 1957–79. Lytham Trophy 1965 (tied)–72. Golf Illustrated Gold Vase 1961 (tied)–67 (tied)–68–69 (tied)–71–75. Royal St George's Challenge Cup 1965–68–81. Prince of Wales Challenge Cup 1967. Scrutton Jug 1961–64–66–68–70–71. Antlers Royal Mid-Surrey 1964. Sunningdale Foursomes 1959. Worplesdon Mixed Foursomes 1958
Reg Essex Amateur 1954–57–59–60–61–63–64–68–69–70–72. Essex Open 1969. East Anglian Open 1973
Int Walker Cup 1957–59–61–63–65–67–69 (capt)–71 (capt)–73. GB Commonwealth Team 1959–63–67–71 (captain 1967–71, non-playing captain 1975). Eisenhower Trophy 1960–62–64–66–68–70–72 (captain 1968–70–72). GB v Professionals 1957–58–59–60;

v Europe 1958–60–62–64–66–68–70–72. England (Home Int) 1957–58–59–60–61–62–63–64–65–66–67–68–69–70–71–72–74 (captain 1962–63–64–65–66–67); (Eur Team Ch) 1959–61–63–65–67–69–71

Jun British Boys 1952

Mis Leading Amateur Open Championship 1968–71. Golf Writers Trophy 1968. Bobby Jones Award 1972. Best equal individual score Eisenhower Trophy 1968. EGU selector 1974. Chairman Royal and Ancient Selection Committee 1975 to 1979 and Amateur Status Committee 1976 to 1979. PGA Chairman 1976. Chairman Golf Foundation 1977. Member of Royal and Ancient Rules of Golf Committee 1979–80. President English Golf Union 1982. Secretary Royal and Ancient GC 1983

Bonallack, Mrs Angela (*née* Ward)

Born Birchington on 7th April, 1937

Add Clatto Lodge, Blebo Craigs, Cupar, Fife

Cls Prince's, Thorpe Hall, St Rule

Chp English Ladies 1958–63, runner-up 1960–62–72. Runner-up British Ladies 1962–74

Maj Astor Salver 1957–58–60–61–66. Worplesdon Mixed Foursomes 1958. Kayser-Bondor Foursomes 1958 (tied) Astor Prince's 1968. Avia Foursomes 1976. Roehampton Gold Cup 1980.

Ove Swedish Ladies 1955. German Ladies 1955. Scandinavian Ladies 1956. Portuguese Ladies 1957

Reg Essex Ladies 1968–69–73–74–76–77–78–82. South East Ladies 1957–65. Kent Ladies' 1955–56–58

Int Curtis Cup 1956–58–60–62–64–66. Vagliano Trophy 1959–61–63. England (Home Int) 1956–57–58–59–60–61–62–63–64–66–72

Jun British Girls 1955

Mis Selected for 1974 Curtis Cup but could not be available for whole tour, so did not accept. Leading amateur Colgate European Ladies' Open 1975–76

Boomer , Aubrey Basil

Born Grouville, Jersey on 1st November, 1897. Turned Professional 1919

Opn Second in Open Championship 1927

Tls French Open 1921–22–26–29–31. Belgian Open 1922–26. Dutch Open 1924–25–26. Italian Open 1932

Maj Daily Mail 1926

Ove French International PGA 1928–29

Int Ryder Cup 1926–27–29. GB v France 1929

Bousfield, Kenneth

Born Marston Moor on 2nd October, 1919. Turned Professional 1938

Tls German Open 1955–59. Swiss Open 1958. Belgian Open 1958. Portuguese Open 1960–61

Maj News Chronicle 1951. PGA Match Play 1955. PGA Close 1955. Yorkshire Evening News 1956 (tied). Dunlop 1957. Sprite 1959. Irish Hospitals 1960 (tied). Swallow-Penfold 1961

Oth Gleneagles Pro-Am 1964. Southern England Professional 1951–57–74. Pringle Seniors 1972

Int Ryder Cup 1949–51–55–57–59–61. England in World Cup 1956–57

Bradshaw, Harry

Born Delgany, Co Wicklow on 9th October, 1913. Turned Professional 1934

Opn Tied for Open Championship 1949, lost play-off

Tls Irish Open 1947–49

Maj Dunlop Masters 1953–55. PGA Close 1958. Penfold-Swallow 1958 (tied)

Oth Irish Professional 1941–42–43–44–47–50–51–53–54–57. Irish Dunlop 1950

Int Ryder Cup 1953–55–57. Ireland in World Cup 1954–55–56–57–58 (winning team)–59

Mis Second Individual section World Cup 1958

Brand, Gordon J.

Born Cambridge on 6th August, 1955. Turned Professional 1976

Tls Nigerian Open 1983–86. Ivory Coast Open 1981–86–88. Zimbabwe Open 1987.

Ove Ivory Coast Cup 1981. Nigerian Open 1983

Int Ryder Cup 1983. England in World Cup 1983. Dunhill Cup 1986–87 (winners). Nissan Cup 1986

Mis Former English Amateur Internationalist. Won Tooting Bec Cup 1981

Brand, Gordon Jr

Born Burntisland, Fife on 19th August, 1958. Turned Professional 1981

Chp English Open Amateur Stroke Play 1978. Swedish Open Amateur Stroke Play 1979. Scottish Open Amateur Stroke Play 1980

Maj Golf Illustrated Gold Vase 1980. Sunningdale Foursomes 1981. Coral Classic, Bob Hope British Classic 1982. Celtic International, European Open 1984. Scandinavian Open, Dutch Open 1987

Reg South-Western Counties Amateur 1977–78. Gloucestershire Amateur 1977

Int Walker Cup 1979. Eisenhower Trophy 1978–80. GB v Europe 1978–80. Scotland (Home Int) 1978–80; v England 1979; v Italy 1979; v France 1980–81; v Belgium 1980; (Eur Team Ch) 1979. Youth Internationals 1977–78–79. Ryder Cup 1987. Scotland in Dunhill Cup 1985–86–87–88. World Cup 1984–85. Eur in Nissan Cup 1985

Jun British Youths 1979. Scottish Youths 1980

Mis Rookie of the Year 1982. Hon. Member of Woodhall Spa, Knowle

Branigan, Declan

Born Drogheda, Ireland on 22nd July, 1948

Add Queensboro, Drogheda, Co Louth, Ireland

Cls Laytown and Bettystown

Chp Irish Amateur 1976–81

Maj West of Ireland Open Amateur 1976–81. East of Ireland Open Amateur 1981

Int Ireland (Home Int) 1975–76–77–80–86; (Eur Team Ch) 1977–81; v France, West Germany and Sweden 1976

Jun Irish Youths 1969

Briggs, Mrs Audrey (*née* Brown)

Born Kent on 31st January, 1945

Add Manor Farm, Old Village, West Kirby, Merseyside

Cls Royal Liverpool, Rye

Chp Welsh Ladies 1970–71–73–74, runner-up 1978–79–80–81

Reg Sussex Ladies 1969. Cheshire Ladies 1971–73–76–80–81. North of England Ladies 1976

Int Vagliano Trophy 1971–73. Wales (Home Int) 1969–70–71–72–73–74–75–76–77–78–79–80–81–82–83–84,(Eur Team Ch) 1969–71–73–75–77–79–81–83; in Fiat Trophy 1978–79–80

Mis Captain of Wales 1981–83

Broadhurst, Paul

Born Staffordshire on 14th August, 1965. Turned Professional 1988

Opn Leading amateur in Open 1988

Maj Lytham Trophy 1988

Int England (Home Int) 1986–87. v France 1988. (GBI) v Europe 1988

Brodie, Allan
Born Glasgow on 25th September, 1947

Add 102 Main Street, Torrance, by Glasgow
Cls Balmore (Hon), Glasgow
Chp Scottish Amateur 1977, runner-up 1973. Second in Scottish Open Amateur Stroke Play 1970
Maj Tennant Cup 1972–80. West of Scotland Open Amateur 1974. Golf Illustrated Gold Vase 1976
Reg Dunbartonshire Amateur Stroke Play 1975–76
Int Walker Cup 1977–79. GB v Europe 1974–76–78–80. Eisenhower Trophy 1978. Scotland (Home Int) 1970–72–73–74–75–76–77–78–80; (Eur Team Ch) 1973–77–79; v Belgium 1977; v Spain 1977; v France 1978; v England 1979; v Italy 1979
Jun Youth International 1966–67

Brooks, Andrew
Born 22nd December, 1946. Turned Professional 1969

Int Walker Cup 1969. Scotland (Home Int) 1968–69; (Eur Team Ch) 1969
Jun Boy International 1964. Youth International 1965–66–67–68
Mis Represented Scotland in Double Diamond Internationals 1971. Won Skol Tournament with 4–round aggregate of 259

Brooks, Colin
Born Edinburgh on 14th July, 1965

Chp Scottish Amateur 1986
Maj Tennant Cup 1985. Gran Primo 1986. West of Scotland Open Amateur Stroke Play 1986
Int GB v Europe 1986 Scotland (Home Int) 1984–85

Brown, Miss Audrey
See Mrs A Briggs

Brown, Julie
Born 26th December, 1963. Turned Professional 1985

Chp Runner-up in Ladies Amateur 1984
Reg Staffordshire Champion 1982–83
Int Vilmorin Trophy 1984. England (Home Int) 1984
WPGA LBS Ladies German Open 1985

Brown, Kenneth
Born Harpenden, Herts on 9th January, 1957. Turned Professional 1975

Tls Dutch Open 1983. Kenya Open 1983
Maj Carrolls Irish Open 1978. Glasgow Classic 1984. Four Stars National 1985
Ove Southern Open 1987
Int Ryder Cup 1977–79–83–85–87. GB v Europe 1978. Scotland in Double Diamond 1977. Scotland in World Cup 1977–78–79–83. Hennessy-Cognac Cup 1984. Kirin Cup 1987
Am Boy International 1974. Carris Trophy 1974. Herts Open 1975

Buckley, James A
Born Ontario, Canada on 14th September, 1950. Turned Professional 1969. Reinstated Amateur 1976

Add 3 Moor Park, Abergele, Clwyd, N Wales
Cls Abergele, Killarney (Hon)
Chp Welsh Amateur 1968. Welsh Amateur Stroke Play 1968–77, second 1978. Welsh Close 1969. Welsh Professional Championship 1971–72
Reg Denbighshire Amateur 1967–68–76–78. North Wales Professional (as Amateur) 1976
Int Walker Cup 1979. Wales (Home Int) 1967–68–69–76–77–78; (Eur Team Ch) 1967–69; v Denmark 1976–77
Jun Welsh Boys 1966–67–68

Burke, Miss Ita
See Mrs E Butler

Bussell, Alan Francis
Born Glasgow on 25th February, 1937

Add Bennamie, Kirkham Lane, Fritchley, Derbyshire
Cls Whitecraigs (Hon), Coxmoor (Hon), Chevin
Maj Antlers Royal Mid-Surrey 1956. Golf Illustrated Gold Vase 1959
Reg Nottinghamshire Amateur 1959–60–62–63–64–68–69. Nottinghamshire Open 1960–62. Nottinghamshire Match Play 1960–62. Renfrewshire Amateur 1955
Int Walker Cup 1957. GB v Europe 1956–62; v Professionals 1956–57–59. Scotland (Home Int) 1956–57–58–61; v Scandinavia 1956–60
Jun British Boys 1954. Boy International 1954. British Youths 1956. Youth International 1954–55–56

Butler, Mrs E (*née* Ita Burke)
Born Nenagh, Co Tipperary

Add Kilbride, Torquay Road, Foxrock, Co Dublin
Cls Hon member of Elm Park, Killarney, Woodbrook, Nenagh
Chp Runner-up Irish Ladies 1972–78
Reg Leinster Ladies three times. Munster and Midland Ladies twice
Int Curtis Cup 1966. World Team Championship 1966. Vagliano Trophy 1965. Ireland (World Cup) 1964; (Home Int) 1962–63–64–65–66–68–71–72–73–76–77–78–79; (Eur Team Ch) 1967; in Fiat Trophy 1978

Butler, Peter J
Born Birmingham on 25th March, 1932. Turned Professional 1948

Tls French Open 1968. Colombian Open 1975
Maj Swallow-Penfold 1959. Yorkshire Evening News 1962; PGA Close 1963. Bowmaker 1963–67. Cox Moore 1964. PGA Match Play runner-up 1964–75. Martini 1965. Piccadilly 1965–67. Penfold 1968. Wills 1968. RTV 1969. Classic International 1971. Sumrie 1974
Ove Evian International 1963. Grand Bahama Invitation Open 1971–72
Oth Midland Open 1956–58–60–65–69. Midland Professional 1961. Gleneagles Pro-Am 1963. Sunningdale Foursomes 1974
Int Ryder Cup 1965–69–71–73. England in World Cup. 1969–70–73. England in Double Diamond 1971–72–76. GB v Europe 1976
Mis Equal lowest round in British events of 61. Second in Order of Merit 1968. PGA Captain 1972

Cadden, Miss Suzanne
See Mrs J McMahon

Caldwell, Ian
Born Streatham on 17th May, 1930

Add 51 Campden Hill Towers, London W11
Cls Royal and Ancient, Sunningdale, Walton Heath
Chp English Amateur 1961
Maj Prince of Wales Challenge Cup 1950–51–52
Oth Boyd Quaich 1954. Carris Trophy 1947–48
Reg Surrey Amateur 1961
Int Walker Cup 1951–55. GB Commonwealth Team 1954. GB v Europe 1955. England (Home Int) 1950–51–52–53–54–55–56–57–61

Caldwell, Mrs Ian (*née* Carole Redford)
Born Kingston, Surrey on 23rd April, 1949

Add 51 Campden Hill Towers, London W11
Cls Canterbury (Hon), Sunningdale
Maj Newmark-Avia International 1973. Roehampton Gold Cup 1973–75–78. Hampshire Rose 1973, 1984. Avia Foursomes 1974. Critchley Salver 1974. London Foursomes 1984
Ove Canadian Ladies Foursomes 1978. Portuguese Ladies 1980
Reg South Eastern Ladies 1973–78. Kent Ladies 1970–75–77–86. Berkshire Ladies 1982
Int Vagliano Trophy 1973. Curtis Cup 1978–80. England (Home Int) 1973–78–79–80
Mis Playing captain of LGU under-23 team to tour Canada 1973. Lost at 27th hole in first round of American Ladies Amateur 1978

Carr, Joseph B
Born Dublin on 18th February, 1922

Add Suncroft, Sutton, Dublin
Cls Hon member of Sutton, Portmarnock, Milltown, Dublin, Killarney, Lahinch, Royal Portrush, Macroom, Malone, Howth, Newlands, Youghal, Douglas, The Island, Malahide, Moate, Lucan, Tramore, County Cork, Dun Laoghaire, Skerries, Warrenpoint, Delgany, Ballina, Mullingar, Rosslare, Ballycastle, Portumna, Royal Lytham, Augusta, Pine Valley
Chp Amateur Champion 1953–58–60, runner-up 1968. Irish Amateur 1954–57–63–64–65–67, runner-up 1951–59. Irish Open Amateur 1946–50–54–56, runner-up 1947–48–51
Maj South of Ireland Open Amateur 1948–66–69. East of Ireland Open Amateur 1941–43–45–46–48–56–57–58–60–61–64–69. West of Ireland Open Amateur 1946–47–48–51–53–54–56–58–60–61–62–66. Gleneagles Saxone 1955. Golf Illustrated Gold Vase 1951. Berkshire Trophy 1959. Formby Hare 1962. Mullingar Trophy 1963. Antlers Royal Mid-Surrey 1970
Int Walker Cup 1947–49–51–53–55–57–59–61–63 (capt)–67 (non-playing captain 1965). GB v Europe 1954–56–64 (capt)–66 (capt)–68. Eisenhower Trophy 1958–60 (non-playing captain 1964–66). Ireland (Home Int) 1947–48–49–50–51–52–53–54–55–56–57–58–59–60–61–62–63–64–65–66–67–68–69; (Eur Team Ch) 1965–67–69
Mis Semi-finalist American Amateur 1961. Leading Amateur Open Championship 1956–58. Golf Writers Trophy 1953. Bobby Jones Award 1961. Walter Hagen Award 1967

Carr, Roderick J
Born 27th October, 1950. Turned Professional 1971. Reinstated Amateur 1983

Add Suncroft, Sutton, Dublin
Maj Antlers Royal Mid-Surrey 1970. East of Ireland Open Amateur 1970. West of Ireland Open Amateur 1971. Turnberry Pro-Am 1970
Int Walker Cup 1971. Ireland (Home Int) 1970–71; (Eur Team Ch) 1971
Jun Youth International 1970–71
Mis Leading Amatuer South African Open 1971

Carrick, David
Born Glasgow on 28th January, 1957

Chp Scottish Amateur 1985. Scottish Open Amateur Stroke Play 1987
Maj Scottish Champion of Champions 1983. Glasgow Amateur 1980–81
Reg Dunbartonshire Amateur 1979–80–82–83
Int Walker Cup 1983–87. GB v Europe 1986. Scotland (Home Int) 1981–82–83–84–85–86–88; v Italy 1988

Carslaw, Iain Alexander
Born Glasgow on 4th October, 1949

Add 4 Woodvale Avenue, Giffnock, Glasgow
Cls Williamwood (Hon), Walton Heath
Chp Scottish Amateur 1978
Maj Tennant Cup 1978. Golf Illustrated Gold Vase 1982
Reg Glasgow County Match Play 1977–78–79–80. Glasgow Amateur 1978
Int Walker Cup 1979. GB v Europe 1978. Scotland (Home Int) 1976–77–78–80–81; (Eur Team Ch) 1977–79; v Spain 1977; v Belgium 1978; v France 1978–83; in Fiat Trophy 1978; v Italy 1979; v England 1979; in Moroccan International 1979
Jun Boy International 1967. Youth International 1971

Cater, John Robert
Born Edinburgh, 1919

Add Avernish, Elie, Fife
Cls Williamwood (Hon), Royal and Ancient, Elie
Maj Gleneagles Silver Tassie 1952
Reg West of Scotland Amateur 1951–55. Glasgow County 1957
Int Walker Cup 1955. Scotland (Home Int) 1952–53–54–55–56; v South Africa 1954; v Scandinavia 1956
Mis Captain of Royal and Ancient 1986

Chadwick, Miss Elizabeth
See Mrs AD Pook

Chapman, Roger
Born in Nakuru, Kenya on 1st May, 1959. Turned Professional 1981

Tls Zimbabwe Open 1988
Chp English Amateur 1979
Maj Duncan Putter 1981 (shared). Lytham Trophy 1981
Reg Kent Open 1977
Int Walker Cup 1981. GB v Europe 1980. England (Home Int) 1980–81; (Eur Team Ch) 1981
Mis Sunningdale Open Foursomes 1979–86

Christmas, Martin J
Born 1939

Add Dean Cottage, Dean, nr Bishops Waltham, Hants
Cls West Sussex, Addington
Chp Runner-up English Amateur 1960. Second in English Open Amateur Stroke Play 1960
Maj Gleneagles Pro-Am 1961. Wentworth Pro-Am Foursomes 1962
Ove Belgian Open Amateur 1976
Reg Sussex Amateur 1962
Int Walker Cup 1961–63. Eisenhower Trophy 1962. GB v Europe 1960–62–64. England (Home Int) 1960–61–62–63–64

Chugg, Mrs Pamela Mary (*née* Light)
Born Cardiff on 10th May, 1955. Turned Professional 1979. Reinstated Amateur 1986

Add 4 Heol Briwnant, Rhiwbina, Cardiff
Cls Whitchurch (Cardiff), Royal Porthcawl
Chp Welsh Ladies 1978. Welsh Ladies Open Stroke Play 1976
Reg South Western Ladies 1976–78

Int Wales (Home Int) 1972–73–74–75–76–77–78–86–87–88; (Eur Team Ch) 1973–75–77–87
Jun Welsh Girls 1970. Girl International 1969–70–71–72–73
Mis Captain of Welsh Juniors 1988

Clark, Clive Anthony

Born Winchester, Hants on 27th June, 1945. Turned Professional 1965

Opn Third in Open Championship 1967 (leading British player)
Tls Danish Open 1966
Chp Runner-up Amateur Championship 1965. Runner-up English Amateur 1965. English Open Amateur Stroke Play 1965 (tied)
Maj Lytham Trophy 1965 (tied). Golf Illustrated Gold Vase 1965. Scrutton Jug 1965. Bowmaker 1968. Agfa-Gevaert 1968. John Player Trophy 1970. Sumrie 1974
Oth Sunningdale Foursomes 1974–76
Int Walker Cup 1965. GB v Europe 1964. England (Home Int) 1964–65. Ryder Cup 1978
Mis Lost play-off for 1972 French Open. TV commentator.

Clark, Gordon James

Born Newcastle-upon-Tyne on 15th April, 1933. Turned Professional 1974. Reinstated Amateur 1983

Chp Amateur Champion 1964. Runner-up English Amateur 1961. Scottish Open Amateur Stroke Play 1973 (tied)
Ove Portuguese Amateur 1974
Reg Northumberland Amateur 1956–71. Northumberland Amateur Stroke Play 1967–71
Int Walker Cup 1965. GB v Europe 1964–66. England (Home Int) 1961–64–65–66–67–68–71; (Eur Team Ch) 1961–65
Jun English Boy International 1950

Clark, Howard K

Born Leeds on 26th August, 1954. Turned Professional October 1973

Tls Portuguese Open 1978. Spanish Open 1986.
Maj Madrid Open 1978–84–86. PGA Championship 1984. Jersey Open 1985. Glasgow Open 1985. Moroccan Open 1987. PLM Open 1987. English Open 1988
Oth Under-25 TPD 1976. Greater Manchester Open 1975
Reg Yorkshire Amateur 1973
Int Ryder Cup 1977–81–85–87. Walker Cup 1973. England (Home Int) 1973. GB v Europe 1978. England in World Cup 1978–84–85. Hennessy-Cognac Cup 1978–84. Individual World Cup Champion 1985.
Dunhill Cup 1985–86–87 (winners). Nissan Cup 1986
Jun British Boys 1971. Boys International 1969–71. Youth International 1971–72–73

Coles, Neil

Born London on 26th September, 1934. Turned Professional 1950

Opn Third in Open Championship 1961; second in 1973; leading British player 1975 (7th)
Tls German Open 1971. Spanish Open 1973
Maj Ballantine 1961. Senior Service 1962. Daks 1963 (tied)–64–70–71 (tied). Martini 1963 (tied). Bowmaker 1964–70. PGA Match Play 1964–65–73, runner-up 1966–72–78. Carrolls 1965–71. Pringle 1966. Dunlop Masters 1966. Sumrie 1970–73. Penfold 1971. Sunbeam 1972. Wills 1974. Penfold PGA 1976. Tournament Players' Championship 1977. Sanyo Open 1982
Ove Engadine Open 1963. Shell BP Italy 1970. Walworth Aloyco Italy 1970
Oth British Assistants 1956. Sunningdale Foursomes 1962–67–80. Wentworth Pro-Am Foursomes 1963–70. Southern England Professionals 1970
Int Ryder Cup 1961–63–65–67–69–71–73–77. England in World Cup 1963–68. England in Double Diamond 1971–73–75–76–77. GB v Europe 1974–76–78–80
Mis Harry Vardon Trophy 1963–70. Second in Order of Merit 1987
Sen Seniors British Open 1987

Collingham, Janet (*née* Melville)

Born Barrow-in-Furness on 16th March, 1958

Chp Ladies Amateur 1987. Ladies Amateur Stroke Play 1978
Maj Worplesdon Mixed Foursomes 1979. Northern Foursomes 1977–78. Mary McCalley Trophy 1980
Reg Highland Open 1978. Midland Ladies 1986. Lancashire Champion 1983–86
Int Vagliano Trophy 1979–87. England (Home Int) 1978–79–81–84–86–87 (Eur Team Ch) 1979. Girls International 1976–(non playing captain)81
Mis Varsity Athlete in golf at Florida International University 1980–81

Connachan, Jane

Born Haddington, East Lothian on 25th February, 1964. Turned Professional 1984

Add 33 Grange Crescent East, Prestonpans, East Lothian
Cls Royal Musselburgh (Hon)
Chp Scottish Ladies 1982. British Ladies Stroke Play 1982
Maj Helen Holm Trophy 1983
Reg East Lothian Ladies 1978-79
Int Curtis Cup 1980–82. World Team Championship 1980–82. Scotland (Home Int) 1979–80–82–83. World Invitational, Scots Girls International, Scots Ladies International 1981. Vagliano Trophy 1981–83. World Team 1982. European Ladies Team 1983. Commonwealth Team 1983
Jun Scottish Girls 1978–79–80. Scottish Girls Open Stroke Play 1978–80. British Girls 1980–81. Australian Girls 1982. Australian Junior Championship 1982. Girl International 1976–77–78–79–80. British Girls Open 1981. Second British Ladies Stroke Open 1981–83. European Junior Ladies Team 1983
Mis Avia Golfer of the Year 1982
WPGA Jersey Open 1984. British Olivetti 1985–87. 415 Match Play 1985

Cooper, Derrick

Born Bolton on 5th May, 1955. Turned Professional 1972

Tls Cepsa Madrid Open 1988

Corridan, Tom

Chp Irish Amateur 1983
Int Ireland (Home Int) 1983–84

Cosh, Gordon B

Born Glasgow on 26th March, 1939

Add 8 Bute Court, Dirleton Drive, Glasgow
Cls Troon, Royal Aberdeen, Bruntsfield Links. Hon member of Cowglen, Killarney
Chp Scottish Amateur 1968, runner-up 1965. Second in Scottish Open Amateur Stroke Play 1968
Maj Newlands Trophy 1980
Reg West of Scotland Amateur 1961–64–65–66. Glasgow County Match Play 1965–66. Glasgow Amateur 1969. Glasgow County Stroke Play 1972–74

Int Walker Cup 1965. Eisenhower Trophy 1966–68. GB Commonwealth Team 1967. GB v Europe 1966–68. Scotland (Home Int) 1964–65–66–67–68–69; (Eur Team Ch) 1965–69 (capt)
Jun Youth International 1959–60

Craddock, Tom
Born Malahide on 16th December, 1931

Add Seamount Road, The Hill, Malahide, Co Dublin
Cls Malahide, Donabate, Sutton, The Island Malahide, Malone, Woodbrook, Mullingar, Carlow, Howth, Tara, Killarney
Chp Irish Amateur 1959, runner-up 1965. Irish Open Amateur 1958
Maj East of Ireland Open Amateur 1959–65–66. Lytham Trophy 1969
Int Walker Cup 1967–69. Ireland (Home Int) 1955–56–57–58–59–60–65–66–67–69; (Eur Team Ch) 1967–71

Critchley, Bruce
Born 9th December, 1942

Add Doone, Ridgemount Road, Sunningdale, Berkshire
Cls Sunningdale, Killarney (Hon)
Maj Worplesdon Mixed Foursomes 1961. Sunningdale Foursomes 1964. Hampshire Hog 1969. Antlers Royal Mid-Surrey 1974
Reg Surrey Amateur 1969
Int Walker Cup 1969. GB v Europe 1970. England (Home Int) 1962–69–70; (Eur Team Ch) 1969
Mis TV commentator. Co-founder annual match at Deal between former Ryder Cup v Walker Cup Players

Critchley, Mrs AC (*née* Diana Lesley Fishwick)
Born London on 12th April, 1911

Add Doone, Ridgemount Road, Sunningdale, Berkshire
Cls North Foreland, Bramley, Canterbury, Sunningdale, Sunningdale Ladies
Chp British Ladies 1930. English Ladies 1932–49, runner-up 1929
Maj Sunningdale Foursomes 1934
Ove French Ladies 1932. German Ladies 1936–38. Belgian Ladies 1938. Dutch Ladies 1946. Florida (USA) West Coast 1933
Reg Kent Ladies 1934. Surrey Ladies 1936–46
Int Curtis Cup 1932-34 (non-playing captain 1950). GB v France 1931-32-33-34 (non-playing captain 1948); v Canada 1934-50. England (Home Int) 1930-31-32-33-35-36-47
Jun British Girls 1927–28
Mis Chairman of ELGA Selection Committee 1967–68–69–70. LGU International Selector 1970–71–72–73. Member LGU Team to tour South Africa 1933

Curry, David H
Born 6th July, 1963

Chp Amateur Champion 1986
Maj Selborne Salver 1984
Int England (Home Int) 1984–86–87. v France 1988. (GB) v Europe 1986–88. Walker Cup 1987

Dalgleish, Colin R
Born Glasgow on 24th September, 1960

Add 21 East Abercromby Street, Helensburgh
Cls Helensburgh (Hon), Millstone Mills (Hon)
Chp Scottish Amateur 1981
Maj Tennant Cup 1983–88
Ove East of India Amateur 1981. Indian Amateur runner-up 1981. Lake Macquarie International Stroke-Play Champion (Australia) 1983
Oth Scottish Universities Champion 1983
Int Walker Cup 1981. Scotland (Home Int) 1981–82–83; v France 1982; (Eur Team Ch) 1981–83. GB v Europe 1982. Europe v South America 1982
Jun International Junior Masters 1977. Belgian Junior Championship 1980. Runner-up British Boys 1977. Runner-up British Youths 1979–82. Boy International 1976–77–78. Youth International 1979–80–81–82

Daly, Fred
Born Portrush on 11th October, 1911

Opn Open Champion 1947, runner-up 1948, joint third 1950, third 1952
Tls Irish Open 1946
Maj PGA Match Play 1947–48–52. Dunlop Southport 1948. Penfold 1948. Lotus 1950. Daks 1952
Oth Ulster Professional 1936–40–41–42–43–46–51–55–56–57–58. Irish Professional 1940–46–52. Irish Dunlop 1946–52
Int Ryder Cup 1947–49–51–53. Ireland 1936–37–38. World Cup 1954–55

Darcy, Eamonn
Born Delgany on 7th August, 1952. Turned Professional 1969

Tls Spanish Open 1983. Belgian Open 1987
Maj Sumrie 1976–78. Greater Manchester Open 1977
Ove Air New Zealand Open 1980. Cock o' the North Open 1981. Kenya Open 1982. Mufulira Open 1984
Oth Irish Dunlop 1976. Cacharel World Under-25 1976. Irish Match Play 1981
Int Ryder Cup 1975–77–81–87. Ireland in Double Diamond 1975–76–77. Ireland in World Cup 1976–77–84–85. GB v Europe 1976; v South Africa 1976. Hennessy-Cognac Cup 1984. Dunhill Cup 1987–88 (winners)
Mis Second in Order of Merit 1976

Davies, Glyn
Born 10th July, 1958. Turned Professional 1984

Chp Welsh Amateur Stroke Play 1983
Int Wales (Home Int) 1981–82–83

Davies, John C
Born London on 14th February, 1948

Add April Cottage, Coronation Road, Ascot, Berkshire
Cls Mid-Surrey, Sunningdale, Royal Cinque Ports, Killarney
Chp Runner-up Amateur Championship 1976. Runner-up English Amateur 1971–76. Second in English Open Amateur Stroke Play 1977
Maj Berkshire Trophy 1969–71 (tied). Royal St George's Challenge Cup 1972–73–74–75–76–77. Sunningdale Foursomes 1968–72. Antlers Royal Mid-Surrey 1969–75–77. Golf Illustrated Gold Vase 1973–77. Prince of Wales Cup 1975. Berkhamsted Trophy 1976–78–79
Ove Second equal in South African Open Amateur Stroke Play 1974
Reg Surrey Amateur 1971–72–77
Int Walker Cup 1973–75–77–79. Eisenhower Trophy 1974–76 (winning team). GB v Europe 1972–74–76–78; England (Home Int) 1969–70–71–72–73–74–78; (Eur Team Ch) 1973–75–77
Mis Member of European Team to tour South Africa 1974

Davies, Karen L
Born 19th June, 1965

Oth Florida State Tournament 1985. South-Eastern USA Championship 1985
Int Curtis Cup 1986–88. Wales (Home Int) 1981–82–83 (Eur Ladies Under-22) 1981–82–83–84–85–86
Jun Welsh Girls 1980–82

Davies, Laura
Born Coventry on 5th October, 1963. Turned Professional 1985

Chp Ladies British Open 1986. US Womens Open 1987
Maj London Foursomes 1981. Welsh Open Stroke-Play 1984. English Intermediate 1983
Reg South-Eastern Champion 1983–84
Int England (Home Int) 1983–84. Vilmorin Trophy 1984. Curtis Cup 1984.
Jun Surrey Girls 1982
Mis Order of Merit leader 1985–86
WPGA Belgian Ladies Open 1985. McEwan's Lager Classic 1986. Greater Manchester Tournament 1986. Italian Open 1987–88. Ford Ladies Classic 1988. Biarritz Ladies Open 1988
LPGA Tucson Open 1988. Toledo Classic 1988

Davies, Miss Pamela
See Mrs Large

Davies, Miss Zara
See Mrs SM Bolton

Davis, Mark
Born 4th July, 1964. Turned Professional 1986

Chp English Open Amateur Stroke Play 1984
Maj Golf Illustrated Gold Vase 1985. Prince of Wales Cup 1983. Lagonda Trophy 1984
Reg Essex Amateur 1983
Int England (Home Int) 1984–85

Dawson, Peter
Born Doncaster on 9th May, 1950. Turned Professional 1970

Maj Double Diamond Individual 1975
Int Ryder Cup 1977. England in World Cup 1977. England in Double Diamond 1977
Am Runner-up English Amateur 1969. England in Home International 1969. Carris Trophy 1968. Youth International 1969–70. Boy International 1967
Mis Plays left-handed

De Bendern, Count John (John de Forest)
Born 1907

Add Villa Roveray, 1602 La Croix/Lutry, Vaud-1602, Switzerland
Cls Royal and Ancient, Sunningdale, Addington, Lausanne
Chp Amateur Champion 1932, runner-up 1931
Ove Austrian Amateur 1937. Czechoslovakian Amateur 1937
Reg Surrey Amateur 1931–49
Int Walker Cup 1932. England (Home Int) 1931

Deeble, Peter George
Born Alnwick on 27th February, 1954

Add 19 The Maltings, Alnwick, Northumberland
Cls Alnmouth, Alnwick, Ponteland (Hon), Hexham (Hon), Rothbury (Hon), Washington (Hon), Tynedale (Hon)
Chp English Amateur 1976–80
Maj Antlers Royal Mid-Surrey 1976. Lytham Trophy 1977. Berkhamsted Trophy 1975. EGUC of C Tour 1982. County Champion of Champions 1982
Reg Northumberland Amateur 1975–82–83. Northumberland Stroke Play 1973–75–77–78–79. Northumberland and Durham Open 1976
Int Walker Cup 1977–81. GB v Europe 1978. Europe v South America 1980. GB in Colombian International 1978. England (Home Int) 1975–76–77–78–80–81–83; (Eur Team Ch) 1979–81; v Scotland 1979; v France 1982. England in Fiat Trophy 1980
Jun Boy International 1970–71. Youth International 1973–75–76

Deighton, Dr FWG
Born Glasgow on 21st May, 1927

Add 4 Hatfield Drive, Glasgow W2
Cls Royal and Ancient, Western Gailes, Elie, Glasgow, Hilton Park (Hon), North Hants
Chp Scottish Amateur 1956–59
Maj Edward Trophy 1954. Gleneagles Silver Tassie 1956. Tennant Cup 1958–60–64
Oth Boyd Quaich 1947 (tied). Royal and Ancient Silver Cross 1953–60–63–70–73. Royal Medal 1956–59–61–63–66–73. Glennie Medal 1956–58–59–60–66–70–73
Reg West of Scotland Amateur 1959. Dunbartonshire Amateur 1949–50–53–54. Glasgow Amateur 1951–55
Int Walker Cup 1951–57. GB Commonwealth Team 1954–59. GB v Professionals 1956–57. Scotland (Home Int) 1950–52–53–56–58–59–60; v South Africa 1954; v New Zealand 1954; v Scandinavia 1956
Mis Member of British Touring Team to South Africa 1952

Douglas, Kitrina
Born Bristol on 6th September, 1960. Turned Professional 1984

Chp British Ladies 1982
Maj Critchley Salver 1983
Ove Portuguese Champion 1983
Reg Gloucestershire Champion 1980–81–82–83–84
Int England (Home Int) 1981–82. Curtis Cup 1982. European Team Championship 1983. Vagliano Trophy 1983
Jun Scottish Girls Stroke-Play 1981
WPGA Ford Classic 1984. Swedish Ladies Open 1984. Rookie of the Year 1984

Dowling, Deborah
Born Wimbledon on 26th July, 1962. Turned Professional 1981

Reg Surrey Champion 1980
Int England (Home Int) 1981 (Eur Team Ch) 1981
WPGA Jersey Open, Woodhall Hills 1983. Portuguese Ladies Open 1985. Eastleigh Classic 1986. Laing Ladies Classic 1986

Downes, Paul
Born Coventry on 27th September, 1959

Add 105 Mantilla Drive, Styvechale Grange, Coventry CV3 6LJ
Cls Coventry (Hon)
Chp English Amateur 1978. English Amateur Stroke Play 1982
Maj Berkshire Trophy 1980
Ove Leading Amateur Malaysian Dunlop Masters 1977. Leading Amateur Singapore Open Championship 1978
Reg Midland Open Amateur Stroke Play 1976–77–80. Warwickshire Match Play 1977–82. Warwickshire Open 1982

Int England (Home Int) 1976–77–78–80–81–82; (Eur Team Ch) 1977–79–81. GB v Europe 1980
Jun Boy International 1974–75–76–77. Youth International 1976–77–78–79–80–81

Draper, Mrs Marjorie Lilian (formerly Mrs Peel, *née* Thomas)
Born Edinburgh on 18th June, 1905

Add Broadbury, Gullane, East Lothian
Cls Gullane
Chp Scottish Ladies 1954, runner-up 1952-62
Maj Worplesdon Mixed Foursomes 1952
Reg East of Scotland Ladies 1951–52–54–55–56–57–61. East Lothian Ladies 1950
Int Curtis Cup 1954. GB v France and Belgium 1955. Scotland (Home Int) 1929–34–37–49–50–51–52–53–54–55–56–57–58–62 (non playing captain 1961–63–65)
Mis Non-playing captain Vagliano Trophy Team 1963. President Scottish Ladies Golfing Association 1973–75

Drew , Norman Vico
Born Belfast on 25th May, 1932. Turned Professional 1958

Chp Irish Open Amateur 1952–53
Maj North of Ireland Open Amateur 1950–52. East of Ireland Open Amateur 1952. Yorkshire Evening News 1959
Oth Irish Professional 1959. Irish Dunlop 1959. Ulster Professional 1966–72
Int Walker Cup 1953. Ireland (Home Int) 1952–53. Ryder Cup 1959. Ireland in World Cup 1960-61

Duncan, Colonel Anthony Arthur, OBE
Born Cardiff on 10th December, 1914

Add Steepways Corner, Churt Road, Hindhead, Surrey
Cls Royal and Ancient, Southerndown, Hindhead, Royal Porthcawl
Chp Runner-up Amateur Championship 1939. Welsh Amateur 1938–48–52–54, runner-up 1933
Maj Worplesdon Mixed Foursomes 1946–47. Hampshire Hog 1959
Oth President's Putter 1948–58
Int Wales (Home Int) 1933–34–36–38–47–48–49 (capt)–50–51–52–53–54–55–56–57–58 (capt)–59
Mis Walker Cup 1953 (capt). Chairman Walker Cup Selection Committee 1954–55. Won all six matches in 1956 Home Internationals. President Oxford and Cambridge Golfing Society 1979–83

Easingwood, Stephen
Born Edinburgh on 23rd June 1965

Add 39 Newhouse Avenue, Dunbar, East Lothian
Cls Dunbar, Winterfield
Chp Scottish Amateur Stroke Play 1988
Maj Edward Trophy 1987
Reg Lothians Champion 1985, South-East District Champion 1987–88, Craigmillar Park Open 1986
Int Scotland (Home Int) 1986–87–88; v France 1987; v Italy 1988
Jun Scottish Boys v England 1982. Scottish Youths 1983–86

Eggo, Bobby
Born 5th July, 1961

Chp English Amateur Stroke Play 1988
Maj Hampshire Hog 1986. Golf Illustrated Gold Vase 1986. Channel Islands Amateur 1984
Int Walker Cup 1987. England (Home Int) 1986–87–88; v France 1988. (GBI) v Europe 1988

Evans, Albert David
Born Newton, Brecon, South Wales on 28th August, 1911

Add Newton House, Kilcot, Newent, Gloucestershire
Cls Royal and Ancient, Royal Porthcawl. Hon member of Brecon, Ross-on-Wye, Hereford, Worcestershire, Builth Wells, Pennard, Monmouth, Killarney
Chp Welsh Amateur 1949–61
Reg Herefordshire Amateur 1938–46–49–51–53–54–55–59–60–61–62. Breconshire Amateur 1929–31–32–33–34–37
Int Wales (Home Int) 1931–32–33–34–35–38–39–47–48–49–50–51–52–53–54–55–56, capt 1960–61–62–63–64–65; v Australia 1954
Mis Walker Cup Selector 1964–75

Evans, Duncan
Born Crewe on 23rd January, 1959

Add 9 Lancaster Avenue, Leek, Staffordshire ST13 8AX
Cls Leek (Hon), Conway (Hon), Holyhead (Hon), Royal Porthcawl (Hon), Westwood (Hon)
Chp Amateur Champion 1980. Second in Welsh Amateur Stroke Play 1980. Welsh Amateur Stroke Play Championship 1981
Reg Staffordshire Amateur 1979. Aberconwy Trophy 1981
Int GB v Europe. Europe v South America 1980. Wales (Home Int) 1978–80; v Ireland 1979; in Fiat Trophy 1980. Walker Cup 1981; (Eur Team Ch) 1981
Jun Youth International 1980

Evans, Hugh
Born Swansea on 19th May, 1957

Add 25 Beaufort Drive, Kittle, Swansea
Cls Langland Bay
Chp Welsh Amateur Stroke Play 1978
Maj Duncan Putter 1979
Int Wales (Home Int) 1976–77–78–79–80–81–84–85–87–88; (Eur Team Ch) 1979–81
Reg Glamorgan County Champion 1978
Mis Glamorgan County 1974 to 88 (captain 83–85)

Everard, Mrs D Mary
Born Sheffield on 8th October, 1942

Add Holly Cottage, Rowland, Nr Bakewell, Derbyshire
Cls Hallamshire (Hon), Woodhall Spa (Hon), Kilton Forest (Hon), Lindrick
Chp Runner-up British Ladies Amateur 1967. British Ladies Amateur Stroke Play 1970, second 1971–73. Second in British Ladies Open 1977. English Ladies 1972, runner-up 1964–77
Maj Astor Salver 1967–68–78. Hovis Ladies 1967. Roehampton Gold Cup 1970. Sunningdale Foursomes 1973. Hoylake Mixed Foursomes 1965–67–71–76. Avia Foursomes 1978
Reg North of England Ladies 1972. Yorkshire Ladies 1964–67–72–73–77
Int Curtis Cup 1970–72–74–78. Vagliano Trophy 1967–69–71–73. GB Commonwealth Team 1971. World Team Championship 1968–72 (capt)–78, England (Home Int) 1964–67–70–72–73–77–78; (Eur Team Ch) 1967–71–73–77
Mis Member of British team to tour Australia 1973. Captain English team to tour Kenya 1973

Faldo, Nicholas Alexander
Born Welwyn Garden City on 18th July, 1957. Turned Professional 1976

Opn Open Champion 1987
Tls French Open 1983–88. Swiss Open 1983. Spanish Open 1987
Chp English Amateur 1975

Maj Berkshire Trophy 1975. Scrutton Jug 1975. County Champion of Champions 1975. Skol Lager 1977. Colgate PGA 1978. Sun Alliance PGA 1980-81. Tour Players Championship 1982. Martini International 1983. Lawrence Batley International 1983. CarCare International 1983-84.
Ove South African Golf Union Special Stroke Championship 1975. ICL International (SA) 1979. Heritage Classic (USA) 1984
Reg Hertfordshire Amateur 1975
Int GB Commonwealth Team 1975. England (Home Int) 1975. Ryder Cup 1977–79–81–83–85-87. GB v Europe 1978–80. England in World Cup 1977. England in Double Diamond 1977. Hennessy–Cognac Cup 1984. Dunhill Cup 1985–86-87 (winners) –88. Nissan Cup 1986. Kirin Cup 1987
Jun British Youths 1975. Boy International 1974. Youth International 1975
Mis Rookie of the Year 1977. Harry Vardon Trophy 1983

Faulkner, Max
Born Bexhill, Sussex on 29th July, 1916. Turned Professional June 1933

Opn Open Championship 1951
Tls Spanish Open 1952–53–57. Portuguese Open 1968
Maj Dunlop Southport 1946. Dunlop 1949–52. Penfold Foursomes 1949. Lotus 1949. Dunlop Masters 1951. PGA Match Play 1953. Irish Hospitals 1959
Oth West of England Open Professional 1947. Sunningdale Foursomes 1950. Southern England Professional 1964. Pringle Seniors 1968–70
Int Ryder Cup 1947–49–51–53–57

Feherty, David
Born in Bangor, NI on 13th August, 1958. Turned Professional 1976

Tls Italian Open 1986. Lexington PGA 1988
Maj Scottish Open 1986
Oth ICL International, SA
Int Ireland; Dunhill Cup 1986

Ferguson, Mrs AJR (*née* Marjory Fowler)
Born North Berwick on 15th May, 1937

Add Clova, Westgate, North Berwick
Cls North Berwick, Gullane, Killarney (Hon)
Chp Runner-up Scottish Ladies 1966–71
Ove Portuguese Ladies 1960
Reg East of Scotland Ladies 1959–60–62–75. East Lothian Ladies 1957–58–59–60–61–62–63–64–66–67–69–74–81
Int Curtis Cup 1966. Vagliano Trophy 1965. Scotland (Home Int) 1959–62–63–64–65–66–67–69–70; (Eur Team Ch) 1965–67–71

Le Feuvre, Miss Carol
See Mrs R Gibbs

Fiddian, Eric Westwood
Born Stourbridge on 28th March, 1910

Add Jasmine, Hanbury, Redditch, Worcestershire
Cls Stourbridge, Handsworth, Lindrick
Chp Runner-up Amateur Championship 1932. English Amateur 1932, runner-up 1935. Runner-up Irish Open Amateur 1933
Reg Worcestershire Amateur 1928–30–50. Midland Counties 1931
Int Walker Cup 1932–34. England (Home Int) 1929–30–31–32–33–34–35
Jun Boys Champion 1927. England Boy International 1926–27
Mis Had two holes-in-one in the Final of 1933 Irish Open Amateur

Fishwick, Miss Diana L
See Mrs AC Critchley

Foster, Rodney
Born Shipley, Yorkshire on 13th October, 1941

Add 5 Cliffestone Drive, Morton, Keighley, Yorkshire
Cls Royal and Ancient Hon member of Bradford, Halifax, Leeds, West Bowling, Ilkley, East Bierley
Chp Runner-up English Amateur 1964. English Open Amateur Stroke Play 1969 (tied)–70, second 1965
Maj Berkshire Trophy 1964. Lytham Trophy 1967–68. County Champion of Champions 1963 (tied)
Reg Yorkshire Amateur 1963–64–65–67–70
Int Walker Cup 1965–67–69–71–73 (non-playing captain 1979). GB v Europe 1964–66–68–70 (non-playing captain 1980). Eisenhower Trophy 1964–70 (non-playing captain 1980). GB Commonwealth Team 1967–71. England (Home Int) 1963–64–66–67–68–69–70–71–72 (non-playing captain 1976–77–78); (Eur Team Ch) 1963–65–67–69–71–73 (non-playing captain 1977)
Jun Boy International 1958. Youth International 1959

Fowler, Miss Marjory
See Mrs AJR Ferguson

Francis, Craig
Born London on 18th March, 1950

Add Bird Cay, PO Box N626, Nassau, Bahamas
Cls Sunningdale, Lyford Cay, Geneva, Lausanne
Maj Third in Golf Illustrated Gold Vase 1973. Runner-up Berkshire Trophy 1974
Ove Luxembourg Amateur 1972–75–82. Swiss Amateur 1973–74–77. Swiss Amateur Stroke Play 1982. Belgian Amateur 1975. Italian Amateur 1982, runner-up 1972–81. Runner-up Dutch Amateur 1976

Frearson, Mrs Diane (*née* Robb)
See Mrs Bailey

Furby, Joanne

Chp English Ladies Amateur 1987. British Ladies 1988
Int England (Home Int) 1987–88; (Eur Team Ch) 1987

Gallacher, Bernard
Born Bathgate on 9th February, 1949. Turned Professional end of 1967

Tls Spanish Open 1977. French Open 1979
Chp Scottish Open Amateur Stroke Play 1967
Maj Tennant Cup 1967. Schweppes 1969. Wills 1969. Martini International 1971–82. Carrolls International 1974. Dunlop Masters 1974–75. Tournament Players' Championship 1980. Greater Manchester Open 1981. Jersey Open 1982–84
Ove Zambia Eagle Open 1969. Zambia Cock o' the North 1969. Mufulira Open 1970
Oth Scottish Professional 1971–73–74–77. Coca-Cola Young Professionals 1973
Reg Lothians Amateur 1967
Int Scotland (Home Int) 1967. Ryder Cup 1969–71–73–75–77–79–81–83. Scotland in World Cup 1969–71–74–82–83. Scotland in Double Diamond 1971–72–73–74–75–76–77. GB v Europe 1974–78–82; v South Africa 1976. Hennessy-Cognac Cup 1984

Jun Boy International 1965–66
Mis Harry Vardon Trophy 1969 (then youngest ever winner). Scottish Sportsman of the Year 1969. Frank Moran Trophy 1973. Rookie of the Year 1968

Gannon, Mark Andrew
Born Drogheda, Ireland on 15th July, 1952

Add 39 Broadmeadows, Swords, Co Dublin
Cls Co Louth (Hon)
Chp Irish Amateur 1977, runner-up 1974–79
Maj South of Ireland Open Amateur 1973. Mullingar Trophy 1973. West of Ireland Open Amateur 1974. East of Ireland Open Amateur 1978
Int GB v Europe 1974–78. Ireland (Home Int) 1973–74–77–78–80; (Eur Team Ch) 1979; v France, West Germany and Sweden 1978–80; in Fiat Trophy 1979; (Eur Team Ch) 1981
Jun Irish Boys 1968. Irish Youths 1971–72. Youth International 1971

Garner, Mrs Maureen (*née* Madill)
Born Coleraine, Co Derry on 1st February, 1958. Turned Professional 1986

Add 8 Larkhill Road, Portstewart, Co Derry
Cls Hon member of Portstewart, Royal Portrush, Milltown, Co Down, Brancepeth Castle, Delamere Forest
Chp British Ladies 1979. British Ladies Open Amateur Stroke Play 1980. Irish Foursomes 1980
Maj Avia Foursomes 1980–85. Ulster Champion 1983
Reg North-West Scratch Cup 1978. Ulster Ladies 1980
Int Vagliano Trophy 1979–81–85. GB Commonwealth Team 1979. Curtis Cup 1980. World Team Championship 1980. Ireland (Home Int) 1978–79–80–81–82–83; (Eur Team Ch) 1979–81–83
Jun Girl International 1972–73–74–75–76

Garrett, Mrs Maureen (*née* Ruttle)
Born 22nd August, 1922

Chp French Ladies 1964
Int Curtis Cup 1960 (Captain). England (Home Int) 1960 (Captain). Vagliano Trophy 1961 (Captain)
Mis LGU President 1982–85. Bobby Jones Award 1983

Garvey, Miss Philomena K
Born Drogheda, Co Louth on 26th April, 1927. Turned Professional 1964, subsequently reinstated Amateur

Add 11 Whitehorn Road, Clonskeagh, Dublin
Cls Co Down, Co Louth, Portrush, Milltown
Chp British Ladies 1957, runner-up 1946–53–60–63. Irish Ladies 1946–47–48–50–51–53–54–55–57–58–59–60–62–63–70
Maj Worplesdon Mixed Foursomes 1955
Reg Munster Ladies 1951
Int Curtis Cup 1948–50–52–54–56–60. GB v France 1949–51–53–55; v Belgium 1951–53. Vagliano Trophy 1959–63. Ireland (Home Int) 1947–48–49–50–51–52–53–54–55–56–59–60–61–62–63–69; v Australia 1950
Mis Quarter-finalist US Ladies 1950.

Gemmill, Alison
Born 13th September, 1958

Chp Scottish Ladies 1981–85
Maj Helen Holm Trophy 1988
Reg Ayrshire Champion 1980–81–82–83–84–86
Int European Team Championship 1981. Scotland (Home Int) 1981–82–84–85–86–87–88
Jun Scottish Girl Stroke-play 1979

Gibbs, Mrs Roderick (*née* Carol Le Feuvre)
Born Jersey on 18th October, 1951

Add Les Arches, 14 Brackenborough, Brixworth, Northampton
Cls Jersey, Lee-on-the-Solent
Chp Runner-up English Ladies 1973
Maj Avia Foursomes 1974
Ove Dutch Ladies 1972
Reg Jersey Ladies 1966-67-68. Hampshire Ladies 1970-71-72-73-74-76. South-Eastern Ladies 1974
Int Curtis Cup 1974. Vagliano Trophy 1973. England (Home Int) 1971–72–73–74; (Eur Team Ch) 1973
Jun English Girls 1969–70. British Girls 1970. Girl International 1968–69–70
Mis Member of LGU Team to tour Australia 1973, and Under-25 team to tour Canada 1973

Gilford, David
Born 14th September, 1965. Turned Professional 1986

Chp English Amateur 1984
Maj Lagonda Trophy 1986
Oth Carris Trophy 1981. Silvermere Satellite Tournament 1987
Int Walker Cup 1985. GB v Europe 1986. England (Home Int) 1983–84–85
Jun British Youths 1986

Girvan, Paul
Born Ayr on 2nd October, 1965

Reg Ayrshire Champion 1985
Int Walker Cup 1987. Scotland (Home Int) 1986

Glover, John
Born Belfast on 3rd March, 1933

Add Braetrees, 96A Hepburn Gardens, St Andrews, Fife
Cls Killarney (Hon), New Club, St Andrews
Chp Carris Trophy 1950. British Universities 1954–55
Maj Formby Hare 1963
Reg Lancashire Amateur 1970
Int Ireland (Home Int) 1951–52–53–55–59-60–62–70
Jun Boy Champion 1950
Mis Secretary Royal and Ancient Rules of Golf Committee

Godwin, Geoffrey Frank
Born Wanstead on 28th July, 1950

Add 5 Wyses Cottage, Wyses Road, Highwood Quarter, Chelmsford, Essex
Cls Thorndon Park
Maj Royal St George's Challenge Cup 1979. Prince of Wales Challenge Cup 1979. Hampshire Hog 1978
Reg Essex Amateur 1978–80
Int Walker Cup 1979–81. Europe v South America 1978. England (Home Int) 1976–77–78–80–81; (Eur Team Ch) 1979–81; v Scotland 1979; v France 1982

Gorry, Miss Mary Philomena
Born Baltinglass, Co Wicklow on 11th June, 1952

Add Main Street, Baltinglass, Co Wicklow
Cls Baltinglass (Hon), Grange (Hon)
Chp Irish Ladies 1975–78
Maj Hermitage Scratch Cup 1978
Reg South of Ireland Scratch Cup 1975–78–80. Irish Midland Ladies 1974–79. Leinster Ladies 1977–79. Ulster Ladies 1979. Connaught Ladies 1979

Int Vagliano Trophy 1977. Ireland (Home Int)1971–72–73–74–75–76–77–78–79–80–88 (capt); (Eur Team Ch) 1971–73–75–77–79; in Fiat Trophy 1978
Jun Girl International 1970
Mis Irish Lady Golfer of the Year 1977–78. Non-playing captain of Irish team for European Ladies' Junior Championship 1983

Gourlay, Miss Mary Perceval (Molly), OBE

Born Kempshott Park, Basingstoke on 14th May, 1898

Add Queries, 51 Brackendale Road, Camberley, Surrey. Tel (0276) 23315
Cls Hon member of Camberley Heath, Temple, Basingstoke, Dorset, Sunningdale Ladies, Beaconsfield, Winchester, Maccauvlei, Bastad
Chp English Ladies 1926–29, runner-up 1931
Maj Worplesdon Mixed Foursomes 1929–30–34
Ove French Ladies 1923–28–29. Belgian Ladies 1925–26. Swedish Ladies 1932–36–39
Oth Veteran Ladies 1962
Reg Surrey Ladies 1923–26–27–31–33–34–38
Int Curtis Cup 1932–34. GB v Canada 1934; v France 1931–32–33–39. England (Home Int) 1923–24–27–28–29–31–32–33–34
Mis Member LGU team to tour South Africa 1933. Non-playing captain English Ladies 1957. Chairman LGU 1957–58–59. President ELGA 1963–65. Retired from playing aged 73 when handicap was 4

Green, Charles Wilson

Born Dumbarton on 2nd August, 1932

Add 51 Napier Avenue, Cardross, Dunbartonshire
Cls Dumbarton, Cardross, Helensburgh
Chp Scottish Amateur 1970–82–83, runner-up 1971–80. Scottish Open Amateur Stroke Play 1975, 1984, second 1967–83. British Seniors 1988
Maj Lytham Trophy 1970 (tied)–74. Eden Tournament 1959. Tennant Cup 1968–70–75. Edward Trophy 1968–73–74–75
Reg West of Scotland Amateur 1962–70–79. Dunbartonshire Amateur 1960–67–68–73–77. Dunbartonshire Match Play 1965–67–69–71–74. Glasgow Amateur 1979
Int Walker Cup 1963–69–71–73–75 (non-playing captain 1983–85). GB v Scandinavia 1962; v Europe 1962–66–68–70–72–74–76. Eisenhower Trophy 1970–72 (captain) 84–86. GB Commonwealth Team 1971. Scotland (Home Int) 1961–62–63–64–65–67–68–69–70–71–72–73–74–75–76–77–78 (non-playing captain 1980); v Australia 1964, (Eur Team Ch) 1965–67–69–71–73–75–77–79 (captain) 81–83; v Belgium 1973–75–77–78; v Spain 1977; v Italy 1979; v England 1979
Mis Leading Amateur Open Championship 1962, Frank Moran Trophy 1974. British Selector 1980. Scottish Sports Photographer Award 1983

Greenhalgh, Miss Julia

Born Bolton on 6th January, 1941

Add Woodliving, Under Billinge Lane, Blackburn BB2 6RL
Cls Hon member of Pleasington, Killarney, Ganton, Hermitage
Chp British Ladies Stroke Play 1974–75. Runner-up British Ladies Open Amateur 1978. English Ladies 1966–79. Welsh Ladies Open Amateur Stroke Play 1977
Maj Astor Salver 1969–79. Hermitage Cup 1977. Hampshire Rose 1977. Sunningdale Foursomes 1978
Ove New Zealand Ladies 1963
Reg Lancashire Ladies 1961–62–66–68–73–75–76–77–78. Northern Ladies 1961–62
Int Curtis Cup 1964–70–74–76–78. Vagliano Trophy 1961–65–75–77. GB Commonwealth Team 1963–75. World Team 1970 (capt)–74 (capt)–78. England (Home Int) 1960–61–63–66–69–70–71–76–77–78; (Eur Team Ch) 1971–75–77–79
Jun Scottish Girls Open Stroke Play 1960. Girl International 1957–58–59
Mis Leading Amateur (4th) in Australian Wills Ladies Open Stroke Play 1974. Daks Woman Golfer of the Year 1974. Selected for 1966 Curtis Cup and 1979 Vagliano Trophy but withdrew due to wrist injury

Gregson, Malcolm Edward

Born Leicester on 15th August, 1943. Turned Professional 1961

Maj Schweppes 1967. RTV 1967. Daks 1967–68. Martini 1967 (tied). Sumrie 1972
Ove Zambia Cock o' the North 1974. Gambian Open 1981
Oth Pannal Foursomes 1964. British Assistants 1964
Int Ryder Cup 1967. England in World Cup 1967. England 1967. GB v France 1966. England in Double Diamond 1975
Am Boy International 1959–60
Mis Harry Vardon Trophy 1967

Greig, David G

Born Broughty Ferry on 24th January, 1950

Add 12 Church Street, Carnoustie, Angus
Cls Carnoustie (Hon), Caledonia
Chp Scottish Amateur 1975
Oth Boyd Quaich 1972. British Universities Stroke Play 1969
Reg Angus Stroke Play 1978. Angus Match Play 1978. Scottish Counties Champion of Champions 1978. East of Scotland Open Amateur 1980
Int GB Commonwealth Team 1975. Scotland (Home Int) 1972–73–75
Jun Scottish Boys 1967. Boy International 1967. Youth International 1969–71

Grice-Whittaker, Penny

Born Sheffield on 11th October, 1964. Turned Professional 1985

Chp English Intermediate Champion 1984. English Stroke-Play 1984
Reg Yorkshire Champion 1981–82–83. Northern Foursomes 1984
Int England (Home Int) 1983–84. European Team Championship 1983. Curtis Cup 1984. Vilmorin Trophy 1984. Espirito Santo 1984
Jun English Girls 1983
WPGA Belgian Open 1986

Hargreaves, Jack

Born Fleetwood on 12th February, 1914. Turned Professional 1930

Opn Third in Open Championship 1948
Maj Spalding 1951. Swallow-Harrogate 1953. Goodwin Foursomes 1953
Oth Midland Professional 1952–60
Int Ryder Cup 1951
Mis Secretary Midland PGA. Captain PGA 1977

Harrington, John

Chp Irish Amateur 1979
Int Ireland (Home Int) 1960–61–74–75–76 (Eur Team Ch) 1975

Harris, Mrs Marley (formerly Mrs Spearman)
Born on 11th January, 1928

Add Broom Cottage, Exmouth Road, Budleigh Salterton, East Devon
Cls Sudbury
Chp British Ladies 1961–62. English Ladies 1964
Maj Sunningdale Foursomes 1965. Kayser-Bondor Foursomes 1958 (tied). Casa Pupo Foursomes 1965. Worplesdon Mixed Foursomes runner-up 1956–64. Roehampton Gold Cup 1965. Astor Salver 1964–65. Astor Princes' Trophy 1964–65. Hovis Ladies 1965. Spalding Ladies 1956. London Ladies Foursomes 1960
Ove New Zealand Ladies Stroke Play 1963
Reg Middlesex Ladies 1955–56–57–58–59–61–64–65. South-East Ladies 1956–58–61
Int Curtis Cup 1960–62–64. Vagliano Trophy 1959–61. GB Commonwealth Team 1959–63. England (Home Int) 1955–56–57–58–59–60–61–62–63–64–65
Mis Golf Writers' Trophy 1962. Non-playing captain English Team European Team Championship 1971

Harrold, Miss J Lynne
Born London on 9th November, 1956. Turned Professional 1977

Cls Gerrards Cross (Hon), Wentworth
Chp English Ladies 1976, runner-up 1975
Maj Roehampton Gold Cup 1974
Reg South-Eastern Ladies 1976. Bucks Ladies 1974–75–76–77
Int GB in Colombian International 1977. England (Home Int) 1974–75–76; (Eur Team Ch) 1975
Jun Girl International 1973–74–75

Hastings, Miss Joan
See Mrs J Rennie

Hastings, Mrs JL (*née* Dorothea Sommerville)
Born Glasgow on 21st June, 1934

Add 13 Calside Avenue, Paisley, Renfrewshire
Cls Haggs Castle (Hon), Troon Ladies (Hon), Erskine
Chp Scottish Ladies 1958, runner-up 1960
Reg West of Scotland Ladies 1961. Renfrewshire Ladies 1956–57–58–59–61–63–83
Int Curtis Cup 1958. Vagliano Trophy 1963. Scotland (Home Int) 1955–56–57–58–59–60–61 62–63
Jun Junior International 1953. Junior Tour of Australasia 1955

Hawksworth, John
Born 27th March, 1961. Turned Professional 1986

Maj Berkhamsted Trophy 1983. Hampshire Hog 1984. Lytham Trophy 1984
Oth (Pro) Peugeot-Talbot Assistants Championship 1987. Broadstone Satellite 1988
Int Walker Cup 1985. England (Home Int) 1984-85

Heathcoat-Amory, Lady (*née* Joyce Wethered)
Born 17th November, 1901

Add Knightshayes House, Tiverton, Devon. Tel (08842) 2438
Cls Worplesdon
Chp British Ladies 1922–24–25–29, runner-up 1921. English Ladies 1920–21–22–23–24
Maj Worplesdon Mixed Foursomes 1922–23–27–28–31–32–33–36. Sunningdale Foursomes 1935–36
Reg Surrey Ladies 1921–22–24–29–32
Int Curtis Cup 1932. GB v France 1931. England (Home Int) 1921–22–23–24–25–29
Mis Forfeited Amateur status and toured USA in 1935. Reinstated as Amateur after the war

Hedges, Peter J
Born 30th March, 1947

Add 21 The Rise, Sevenoaks, Kent
Cls Langley Park (Hon), Royal Cinque Ports, Addington, Wildernesse, Royal and Ancient
Chp English Open Amateur Stroke Play 1976
Maj Royal St George's Challenge Cup 1970. Prince of Wales Challenge Cup 1972–73–74–77. Berkshire Trophy 1973–76–78. Golf Illustrated Gold Vase 1974. Scrutton Jug 1976
Reg Kent Amateur 1968–71–79. Kent Open 1970–74
Int Walker Cup 1973–75. GB v Europe 1974-76 Eisenhower Trophy 1974. England (Home Int) 1970–73–74–75–76–77–78–82; (Eur Team Ch) 1973–75–77
Jun Youth International 1968
Mis Member of European Team to tour South Africa 1974

Hedges, Mrs Susan Claire (*née* Whitlock)
Born Beckenham, Kent on 8th May, 1947

Add 8 Stuart Close, Maidstone, Kent
Cls Wrotham Heath (Hon), Royal Cinque Ports, Langley Park
Chp Welsh Ladies Open Amateur Stroke Play 1978. Runner-up English Ladies 1979
Maj Central England Mixed Foursomes 1977–81; Hoylake Mixed Foursomes 1982
Ove Belgian Ladies 1974. Luxembourg Ladies 1976–77. Zaire Ladies 1980
Reg Kent Ladies 1976–79
Int Vagliano Trophy 1979. GB Commonwealth Team 1979. England (Home Int) 1979; (Eur Team Ch) 1979
Mis Leading Amateur (3rd) British Ladies Open 1979

Henson, Mrs Dinah (*née* Oxley)
Born Dorking on 17th October, 1948

Add No 12, The Birches, Heathside Road, Woking, Surrey
Cls West Byfleet (Hon), Killarney (Hon), Fairfield, US (Hon)
Chp British Ladies 1970. English Ladies 1970-71, runner-up 1968. Second in British Ladies Stroke Play 1969
Maj Wills Ladies 1969–70–71. Worplesdon Mixed Foursomes 1968–77. Newmark International 1975 (tied)–77
Reg Surrey Ladies 1967–70–71–76
Int Curtis Cup 1968–70–72–76. Vagliano Trophy 1967–69–71. World Team 1970. GB Commonwealth Team 1967–71. England (Home Int) 1967–68–69–70–75–76–77–78; (Eur Team Ch) 1971–77
Jun British Girls 1963. English Girls 1965. French Girls 1969. Girl International 1964–65–66
Mis Daks Woman Golfer of the Year 1970. Leading Amateur Colgate European Ladies Open 1974

Hetherington, Mrs GW (*née* McClure)
See Mrs Jean Holmes

Hill, George Alec, DSO
Born Northwood, Middlesex in 1908

Add Two Trees, Bowling Street, Sandwich, Kent
Cls Royal and Ancient, Royal St George's, Hon Company of Edinburgh Golfers, Sandy Lodge
Int Walker Cup 1936, non-playing captain 1955. England (Home Int) 1936–37

Jun Boy International 1926
Mis Chairman R and A Championship Committee 1955. Chairman Rules of Golf Committee 1958–59. Captain Royal and Ancient 1964–65

Hoey, T Brian C

Chp Irish Amateur 1984
Reg North of Ireland Amateur 1979–83
Int Ireland (Home Int) 1970–71–72–73–77–84

Holmes, Mrs Jean (formerly Mrs GW Hetherington, *née* McClure)
Born Wanstead, Essex on 17th August, 1923

Add Elder House, 25 Mill Lane, Wateringbury, Kent ME18 5SP
Cls Wanstead, Hunstanton, Thorndon Park
Chp British Ladies 1946, runner-up 1958. English Ladies 1966
Reg Nottinghamshire Ladies 1949-50-51. Essex Ladies 1956-57
Int England (Home Int) 1957–66 (non-playing captain 1967)

Homer, Trevor Walter Brian
Born Bloxwich on 8th September, 1943. Turned Professional July 1974. Reinstated as Amateur in 1978

Chp Amateur Champion 1972–74
Maj Leicestershire Fox 1972. Harlech Gold Cross 1970
Int Walker Cup 1973. Eisenhower Trophy 1972. GB v Europe 1972. England (Home Int) 1972–73; (Eur Team Ch) 1973

Hope, Miss Lesley Alexandra
Born Gullane, East Lothian on 22nd May, 1955

Add 16 Muirfield Drive, Gullane, East Lothian
Cls Gullane Ladies, Catterick
Chp Scottish Ladies Amateur 1975, runner-up 1979
Reg East of Scotland Ladies 1977–78
Int Scotland (Home Int) 1975–76–80; (Eur Team Ch) 1975–77–79; in Fiat Trophy 1979

Horton, Tommy
Born St Helens, on 16th June, 1941. Turned Professional 1957

Opn Joint leading British player in Open Championship 1976 (5th)–1977 (9th)
Tls South African Open 1970. Nigerian Open 1973. Zambian Open 1977
Maj Carrolls 1956–57. RTV 1968. PGA Match Play 1970. Gallaher Ulster 1971. Piccadilly 1972. Penfold 1974. Uniroyal International 1976. Dunlop Masters 1978
Ove Tobago Open 1975. Gambian Open 1975
Int Ryder Cup 1975–77. GB v France 1966. England in World Cup 1976. England in Double Diamond 1971–74–75–76–77. GB v Europe 1974–76
Mis Second in Order of Merit 1967. PGA Captain 1978

Hourihane, Claire
Born 18th February, 1958

Chp Irish Ladies 1983–84–85. British Ladies Stroke Play 1986
Maj Hampshire Rose 1986
Ove South Atlantic (USA) 1983
Reg South Ireland Cup 1977. Leinster Ladies 1980
Int Ireland (Home Int) 1979–80–81–82–83–84–85–86–87–88. Vagliano Trophy 1981-83-85-87. European Team Championship 1981–83–85–87; Curtis Cup 1984–86–88

Howard, Mrs Ann (*née* Phillips)
Born Prestwich on 22nd October, 1934

Add 4 Homefield Park, Ballasalla, Isle of Man
Cls Whitefield (Hon), Royal Birkdale, Castletown
Ove Danish Ladies 1955
Reg Lancashire Ladies 1957. Manx Ladies 1977–78
Int Curtis Cup 1956–68. GB v France and Belgium 1955–57. England (Home Int) 1953–54–55–56 (non-playing captain 1979–80). Non-playing captain Senior European 1981
Jun British Girls 1952

Huggett, Brian George Charles, MBE
Born Porthcawl on 18th November, 1936. Turned Professional 1951

Opn Second in Open Championship 1965. Third in 1962
Tls Dutch Open 1962. German Open 1963. Portuguese Open 1974
Maj Cox-Moore 1963. Smart-Weston 1965. Sumrie 1968–72. PGA Close 1967. Martini 1967 (tied)–68. Shell Winter Tournament 1967–68. PGA Match Play 1968, runner-up 1977. Daks 1969–71 (tied). Bowmaker 1969 (tied). Carrolls 1970. Dunlop Masters 1970. British Airways-Avis 1978
Ove Singapore International 1962. Algarve Open 1970
Oth Sunningdale Foursomes 1957. British Assistants 1958. Gleneagles Pro-Am 1961–65. East Anglian Open 1962–67. Turnberry Pro-Am 1968. Welsh Professional 1978
Int Ryder Cup 1963–67–69–71–73–75 (non-playing captain 1977). Wales in World Cup 1963–64–65–68–69–70–71–76–79. Wales in Double Diamond 1971–72–73–74–75–76–77. GB v Europe 1974–78 (capt)
Mis Vardon Trophy 1968. European American Express 1972

Hughes, Miss Ann
See Mrs JS Johnson

Huke, Beverly Joan Mary
Born Great Yarmouth on 10th May, 1951. Turned Professional 1978

Add 302 Brook Street, Broughty Ferry, Dundee
Cls Cotswold Hills (Hon), Windmill Hill (Hon), Leighton Buzzard, Panmure Barry
Chp Runner-up British Ladies 1971. English Ladies 1975
Maj Roehampton Gold Cup 1971. Renfrew Rose Bowl 1976–77–78. Helen Holm Trophy 1977
Reg Gloucestershire Ladies 1972. Angus Ladies 1976
Int Curtis Cup 1972. Vagliano Trophy 1971–75. England (Home Int) 1971–72–75–76–77; (Eur Team Ch) 1975–77
Jun Scottish Girls Open Stroke Play 1970–71. Girl International 1966–67–68
Mis Chairman WPGA Eur Tour 1988
WPGA Carlsberg (Ballater) 1979. Carlsberg (Rosemount) 1980. NABS Pro-Am 1st Pro Individual 1981. Winner Brickendon Grange and Stourbridge Pro-Am 1983; co-winner Lark Valley Classic 1983; Winner White Horse Whisky Challenge Trophy 1983. Trusthouse Forte Classic 1985. German Ladies Open 1984. Wester Volkswagen Classic 1986

Humphreys, Warren
Born Kingston, Surrey on 1st April, 1952

Chp English Amateur 1971
Maj Sunningdale Foursomes 1968. Antlers Royal Mid-Surrey 1969. Duncan Putter 1971. Lytham Trophy 1971

Int Walker Cup 1971. GB v Europe 1970. England (Home Int) 1970–71; (Eur Team Ch) 1971
Jun Boy International 1967–68–69 (capt). Youth International 1969–70–71
Mis Turned Professional Autumn 1971. Accles and Pollock Award 1972. Portuguese Open 1985

Hunt, Bernard John, MBE
Born Atherstone on 2nd February, 1930. Turned Professional 1946

Opn Third in Open Championship 1960. Leading British player (4th) 1964
Tls Egyptian Open 1956. Belgian Open 1957. German Open 1961. Brazilian Open 1962. French Open 1967
Maj Spalding 1953–57. Goodwin Foursomes 1953–54. PGA Match Play runner-up 1958. Bowmaker 1958 (tied). Martini 1961. Daks 1961. Carrolls 1963. Swallow-Penfold 1963. Smart-Weston 1963. Gevacolour 1963. Dunlop Masters 1963–65. Gallaher Ulster 1965–67. Rediffusion 1964. Piccadilly 1966. Penfold 1970. Sumrie 1970–73. Agfacolor 1970. Wills 1971
Ove Algarve Open 1969. BP Italy 1969
Oth British Assistants 1953. Gleneagles–Saxone 1953. Southern England Professional 1959–60–62–67. West of England Open Professional 1960–61
Int Ryder Cup 1953–57–59–61–63–65–67–69, non-playing captain 1973–75. England in World Cup 1958–59–60–62–63–64–68. England in Double Diamond 1971–72–73
Mis In Spalding Tournament 1953 scored 28 for first nine holes in second round. Harry Vardon Trophy 1958–60–65. Second (equal) in Order of Merit 1964

Hutcheon, Ian C
Born Monifieth, Angus on 22nd February, 1942

Add 10 Laird Street, Monifieth, Angus
Cls Monifieth (Hon), Grange and Dundee (Hon)
Chp Scottish Amateur 1973. Scottish Open Amateur Stroke Play 1971–74–79
Maj Tennant Cup 1976. Lytham Trophy 1980. Scottish Champion of Champions 1980–81–86–88
Ove North of Spain Stroke Play 1972
Reg Scottish Central District Amateur 1972. Angus Match Play 1965–70–72. Angus Stroke Play 1968–71–72–74. North of Scotland District Amateur Stroke Play 1975–76–82
Int GB v Europe 1974–76. Eisenhower Trophy 1974–76 (winning team and joint winning individual)–80. Scotland (Home Int) 1971–72–73–74–75–76–77–78–80; (Eur Team Ch) 1973–75–77–79–81; v Spain 1972–77; v Belgium 1973–75–77–78–80; v France 1978–80–81; v Italy 1979; in Fiat Trophy 1979. GB in Dominican International 1973. Walker Cup 1975–77–79–81. GB in Colombian International 1975. GB Comonwealth Team 1975
Mis Frank Moran Trophy 1976

Irvin, Miss Ann Lesley
Born 11th April, 1943

Add 177 Victoria Road, Thornton, Lancashire
Cls Lytham (Hon), Lytham Green Drive (Hon)
Chp British Ladies 1973, runner-up 1969. English Ladies 1967–74. British Ladies Stroke Play 1969. Second British Girls Championship 1961
Maj Roehampton Gold Cup 1967–68–69–72–76. Hovis Ladies 1966–68–70. Avia Foursomes 1968
Reg Northern Ladies 1963–64. Lancashire Ladies 1965–67–69–71–72–74. Northern Foursomes Championship 1973
Int Curtis Cup 1962–68–70–76. Vagliano Trophy 1961–63–65–67–69–71–73–75. GB Commonwealth Team 1967–75. England (Home Int) 1962–63–65–67–68–69–70–71–72–73–75; (Eur Team Ch) 1965–67–69–71–73–75
Jun French Girls 1963. Girl International 1960–61
Mis Daks Woman Golfer of the Year 1968–69. Captain of British Team to tour Australia 1973. Selected for 1974 Curtis Cup but withdrew through injury. Lancashire 1981. County Captain 1979. England Junior Captain. 1981–82. International Selector 1981–82. England Selector 1981–82. County Selector and Junior Organiser

Jack, Robert Reid
Born Cumbernauld on 17th January, 1924

Add The Stell, Muirton, Drem, North Berwick
Cls Hon Company of Edinburgh Golfers, Gullane. Hon member of Buchanan Castle, Dullatur, Bearsden
Chp Amateur Champion 1957. Scottish Amateur 1955
Maj Edward Trophy 1959. Tennant Cup 1961
Oth Royal and Ancient Royal Medal 1965–67. Silver Cross 1956–66. Glennie Medal 1965
Reg Glasgow Amateur 1953-54-58. Dunbartonshire Match Play 1949
Int Walker Cup 1957–59. Eisenhower Trophy 1958. GB Commonwealth Team 1959. GB v Europe 1956. Scotland (Home Int) 1950–51–54–55–56–57–58–59–61; v Scandinavia 1956-58
Mis Leading Amateur Open Championship 1959

Jacklin, Tony, OBE
Born Scunthorpe on 7th July, 1944. Turned Professional 1962

Opn Open Champion 1969. Third 1971–72. Leading British player 1970 (5th). US Open Champion 1970
Tls Italian Open 1973. German Open 1979
Maj Blaxnit 1966. Pringle 1967. Dunlop Masters 1967–73. Wills 1970. Benson & Hedges Festival 1971. Viyella PGA Close 1972. Kerrygold International Classic 1976. Jersey Open 1981. Sun Alliance PGA 1982
Ove Forest Products, New Zealand 1967. Kimberley (SA) 1966 (tied), New Zealand PGA 1967. Greater Jacksonville Open, USA 1968–72. Lancome Trophy 1970. Dunlop International Australia 1972. Los Lagartos Open 1973–74. Scandinavian Enterprises Open 1974. Venezuelan Open 1979
Oth British Assistants 1965. English Professional 1977
Int Ryder Cup 1967–69–71–73–75–77–79–83 (captain)–85 (captain)–87 (captain). GB v Europe 1976. England in World Cup 1966–70–71–72. England in Double Diamond 1972–73–74–76–77
Am Lincolnshire Open 1961
Mis Became the first British player since Harry Vardon to hold the Open and US Open titles simultaneously and the first British player to hold the US Open since Ted Ray in 1920. Hon Life President PGA. Rookie of the Year 1963

Jackson, Miss Barbara Amy Bridget
Born Birmingham on 10th July, 1936

Add 15 Kesteven Close, Edgbaston, Birmingham
Cls Royal St David's Edgbaston. Hon member of Handsworth, Hunstanton, Killarney
Chp Runner-up British Ladies 1964. English Ladies 1956, runner-up 1958
Maj Fairway and Hazard Foursomes 1954. Kayser Bondor Foursomes 1962. Avia Foursomes 1967. Worplesdon Mixed Foursomes 1960. Astor Prince's 1963
Ove German Ladies 1956. Canadian Ladies 1967

Reg Midland Ladies 1954–56–57–58–59–60–69. Staffordshire Ladies 1954–56–57–58–59–63–64–67–69–76
Int Curtis Cup 1958–64–68. Vagliano Trophy 1959–63–65–67 (non-playing captain 1973–75). GB Commonwealth Team 1959–67. GB v Belgium 1957; v France 1957. World Team Championship 1964. England (Home Int) 1955–56–57–58–59–63–64–65–66 (non-playing captain 1973–74); (Eur Team Ch) 1975 (non-playing captain); v France 1964–66
Jun British Girls 1954
Mis LGU International Selector 1983. English and GBI Selector 1983 to 1988. Chairman of English Ladies Association 1970–71

Jacobs, John Robert Maurice
Born Lindrick, Yorkshire on 14th March, 1925. Turned Professional 1947

Tls Dutch Open 1957
Ove South African Match Play 1957
Int Ryder Cup 1955 (non-playing captain 1979–81). GB v Continent 1954–55–58
Mis Former PGA Tournament Director-General. TV commentator. Coach to many International Teams

James, Mark H
Born Manchester on 28th October, 1953. Turned Professional 1975

Opn Leading British player 1976 (tied 5th)-79 (4th)
Tls Italian Open 1982. Spanish Open 1988
Chp English Amateur 1974. Runner-up Amateur Championship 1975
Maj Leicestershire Fox 1974. PGA Match Play 1978. Carrolls Irish Open 1979–80. Welsh Classic 1979. GSI Open 1985. Benson & Hedges 1986
Ove Lusaka Open 1977. Tunisian Open 1983. Danglo TPC 1988
Reg Lincs Match Play 1972. Lincs Amateur 1975
Int England (Home Int) 1974–75; (Eur Team Ch) 1975. Walker Cup 1975. Ryder Cup 1977–79–81. GB v Europe 1978–80. England in World Cup 1978–79–82–84. Hennessy-Cognac Cup 1984. Dunhill Cup 1988
Jun Boy International 1971. Youth International 1974–75
Mis Rookie of the Year 1976

Jamieson, Donald
Born Aberdeen

Chp Scottish Amateur 1980
Int Scotland (Home Int) 1980

Johnson, Mrs JS (*née* Ann Hughes)
Born Llandudno, Gwynedd on 18th October, 1946

Add 36 Churchill Road, Church Stretton, Shropshire
Cls Ludlow, Killarney (Hon)
Chp Welsh Ladies 1966–72–75, runner-up 1969–76
Reg Caernarvonshire and Anglesey Ladies 1964–68–69–72–78
Int Wales (Home Int) 1964–66-67-68-69-70-71-72-73-74-75-76-78-79; (Eur Team Ch) 1965-67-69-71-75-79
Jun Welsh Girls 1960–63–64–65. Girl International 1965

Johnson, Patricia
Born 17th January, 1966. Turned Professional 1987

Chp English Ladies 1985. English Ladies Stroke-Play 1985
Maj Roehampton Gold Cup 1986
Reg South-Western Ladies 1984
Int England (Home Int) 1984–85
Jun Devon Girls 1982

Jones, Emyr O
Born 28th January, 1965

Chp Welsh Amateur 1985
Maj Wales (Home Int) 1983–85–86

Jones, John Roger
Born Old Colwyn, Denbighshire on 14th June, 1944

Add 8 Northway Court, Bishopton, Swansea, West Glamorgan
Cls Langland Bay (Hon)
Chp Welsh Amateur Stroke Play 1972–73–82, runner-up 1983. Welsh Amateur Championship 1983
Maj Harlech Gold Cross 1976
Reg Denbighshire Amateur 1969–71. Caernarvonshire and Anglesey Amateur 1970 (tied)–72–74–75. Glamorgan Amateur 1977–79. North Wales Amateur 1976. Carmarthenshire Amateur 1979–80. Landsdowne Trophy (Channel League) Stroke-Play 1979–80–83
Int Wales (Home Int) 1970–72–73–77–78–80–81–82–83; (Eur Team Ch) 1973–79–81–83; v Denmark 1976–80; v Ireland 1979; v Switzerland 1980; v Spain 1980; in Asian Team Championship 1979

Jones, Keith Glyn
Born Brentwood on 19th July, 1969

Add 1 Brooklyn Close, Woking, Surrey
Cls Worplesdon, The Berkshire, Lansdown
Chp Welsh Amamteur 1988
Reg Bristol Open 1988. Whitchurch Silver Dragon 1988. WI Tucker Trophy 1988
Int Wales (Home Int) 1988
Jun Prince of Wales Trophy 1988

Jones, Stephen P
Born 30th January, 1961

Chp Welsh Amateur 1981
Int Wales (Home Int) 1981–82–83–84–85–86

Kelley, Michael John
Born Scarborough on 6th February, 1945

Add Red Gates, 108 Stepney Road, Scarborough
Cls Ganton, Hon member of Scarborough North Cliff, Bridlington, Bradford
Maj Lytham Trophy 1976. Antlers Royal Mid-Surrey 1972
Reg Yorkshire Amateur 1969–74–81. Yorkshire Open 1969–75. Champion of Champions 1981
Int Walker Cup 1977–79. Eisenhower Trophy 1976 (winning team). GB v Europe 1976–78–82; GB in Colombian International 1978 England (Home Int) 1974–75–76–77–78–80–81–82–88 (captain); (Eur Team Ch) 1977–79; v France 1982
Jun Boy International 1962. Youth International 1965–66

Keppler, Steven D
Born 17th February, 1961

Maj Berkshire Trophy 1982. Golf Illustrated Gold Vase 1983
Reg Surrey Amateur 1981
Int Walker Cup 1983. England (Home Int) 1982–83

King, Michael
Born 15th February, 1950. Turned Professional 1974

Maj St George's Hill Trophy 1970. County Champion of Champions 1970. Sunningdale Foursomes 1972. Lytham Trophy 1973 (tied). Tournament Players Championship 1979

Reg Berks, Bucks and Oxon Amateur 1968–69–70–73–74. Berks, Bucks and Oxon Open 1968–73
Int Walker Cup 1969–73. GB Commonwealth Team 1971. GB v Europe 1972. England (Home Int) 1971–72–73; (Eur Team Ch) 1971–73. Ryder Cup 1979. England in World Cup 1979

King, Samuel Leonard
Born Godden Green, Sevenoaks, Kent on 27th March, 1911

Opn Third in Open Championship 1939
Maj Daily Mail 1937. Yorkshire Evening News 1944–49
Oth British Assistants 1933. Dunlop–Southern 1936–37. Sunningdale Foursomes 1948. Teachers Senior 1961–62
Int Ryder Cup 1937–47–49. England 1934–36–37–38

Kyle, Alexander Thomson
Born Hawick on 16th April, 1907

Add 15 Burnbridge, Harrogate
Cls Royal and Ancient, Easingwold, Sandmoor, Moortown, Harrogate, Knaresborough, Peebles, Fulford (Hon)
Chp Amateur Champion 1939. Runner–up Irish Open Amateur 1946. Second in English Open Amateur Stroke Play 1952
Maj Newlands Trophy 1930
Reg Borders Amateur 1929–30. Yorkshire Amateur 1935–36
Int Walker Cup 1938–47–51. GB v South Africa 1952. Scotland (Home Int) 1938–47–49–50–51–52–53
Mis Played for British Seniors 1969–75

Lane, Barry
Born Hayes, Middlesex on 21st June, 1960. Turned Professional 1976

Eur Equity and Law Challenge 1987. Scottish Open 1988
Ove Jamaica Open 1983
Int (England) Dunhill Cup 1988

Langley, John DA
Born Northwood, Middlesex on 25th April, 1918

Add c/o Lloyds Bank Ltd, Law Courts Branch, 222 Strand, London WC2
Cls Sunningdale, Burnham (Hon), Swinley Forest, Fulwell (Hon), Metropolitan (Aus)
Chp English Amateur 1950, runner–up 1936
Maj Golf Illustrated Gold Vase 1952–53. St George's Hill Trophy 1952
Oth Carris Trophy 1936
Int Walker Cup 1936–51–53. England (Home Int) 1950–51–52–53; v France 1950–52
Jun British Boys 1935. Boy International 1932–33–34–35
Mis Chairman Royal and Ancient Selection Committee 1967 to 1969

Langmead, Jonathan
Born 3rd November, 1967

Chp English Amateur 1986
Int England (Home Int) 1986
Jun Youth International v Scotland 1987

Langridge, Mrs Susan (*née* Armitage)
Born Huddersfield on 5th April, 1943

Add Johannesburg, South Africa
Cls Walsall, Whittington Barracks (Hon)
Reg Midland Ladies 1961–65
Int Curtis Cup 1964–66. Vagliano Trophy 1963–65–67. England (Home Int) 1963–64–65–66–67
Jun Scottish Girls Open Stroke Play 1962

Large, Mrs Pamela (*née* Davies)
Born Coventry on 12th April, 1930

Add Springfield, Crackley Lane, Kenilworth, Warwickshire
Cls Coventry (Hon)
Chp English Ladies 1952, runner–up 1950
Reg Midland Ladies 1952. Warwickshire Ladies 1952
Int England (Home Int) 1950–51–52; v Australia 1950
Jun British Girls 1949
Mis Captain English Ladies (Home Int) Team 1981–82

Laurence, Craig
Born 3rd August, 1963. Turned Professional

Chp English Amateur 1983
Int English (Home Int) 1983–84–85

Lawrence, Miss Joan B
Born Kinghorn, Fife on 20th April, 1930

Add 36 Venturefair Avenue, Dunfermline, Fife
Cls Hon member Dunfermline, Aberdour, Killarney
Chp Scottish Ladies 1962–63–64, runner–up 1965. Scottish Veteran Ladies Champion 1982
Reg East of Scotland Ladies 1971–72. Fife Ladies 1953–57–58–59–60–61–62–63–64–65–67–68–69
Int Curtis Cup 1964. World Team Champion 1964. GB Commonwealth Team 1971 (captain). Vagliano Trophy 1963–65. Scotland (Home Int) 1959–60–61–62–63–64–65–66–67–68–69–70 (non–playing captain 1977); (Eur Team Ch) 1965–67–69 (captain)–71 (non–playing captain 1977)
Jun Girl International 1949
Mis LGU International Selector 1973–74–75–76–80–81–82–83. Treasurer Scottish Ladies Golfing Association from 1980

Lawson, Shirley
Born 1965

Chp Scottish Ladies Amateur 1988
Int Curtis Cup 1988. Scotland (Home Int) 1985–86–87–88; (Eur Team Ch) 1987
Jun Scottish Girls 1982. Scottish Girls Stroke Play 1983–84

Leburn, Mrs Wilma (*née* Aitken)
Born 24th January, 1959

Chp British Girls 1977.
Maj Helen Holm Trophy 1978 80–82. Avia Foursomes 1982
Reg West of Scotland 1978–80–81. Renfrewshire Champion 1978–79–80–81–82
Int Scotland (Home Int) 1978–79–80–81–82–83. Vilmorin Cup 1979. (Eur Team Ch 1979–81–83. Curtis Cup 1982. Vagliano Trophy 1981–83
Jun Scottish Girls 1975–77. West of Scotland Girls 1977. Scottish International 1975–77–78

Lee, Robert
Born in London on 12th October, 1961. Turned Professional 1982

Tls Brazilian Open 1985. Portuguese Open 1987
Maj Cannes Open 1985

Lee Smith, Miss Jennifer
Born Newcastle-upon-Tyne on 2nd December, 1948. Turned Professional 1977

Add 41 Kirkbride Place, Eastfield Dale, Cramlington
Cls Gosforth (Hon), Ponteland (Hon), Wideopen (Hon), Ganton (Hon), Hexham (Hon), Dunstanburgh Castle
Chp British Ladies Open Stroke Play 1976

Maj Wills Match Play 1974. Newmark 1976
Oth Hoylake Mixed Foursomes 1969
Reg Northumberland Ladies 1972-73-74
Int Curtis Cup 1974–76. England (Home Int) 1973–74–75–76; (Eur Team Ch) 1975. GB in Colombian International 1975. World Team Championship 1976. GB Commonwealth Team 1975
WPGA Carlsberg (Arcot Hall) 1979. Volvo Swedish Invitational 1980. Carlsberg (Shifnal), Robert Winsor, Manchester Evening News Classic. Sports Space 1981. McEwans Lager Welsh Classic 1981. Lambert and Butler Match Play 1982. Ford Classic 1982. Hambro Life Order of Merit winner 1981–82. British Open 1984
Mis Daks Woman Golfer of the Year 1976 (joint)

Lees, Arthur
Born Sheffield on 21st February, 1908

Tls Irish Open 1939
Maj Dunlop Masters 1947. Penfold 1951–53
Oth Midland Professional 1948–49. Southern England Professional 1956. Wentworth Pro-Am Foursomes 1957. Teachers Seniors 1959
Int Ryder Cup 1947–49–51–55. England 1938

Lewis, Malcolm
Born 8th January, 1959

Maj Dutch International Amateur 1982. India Amateur 1981.
Oth Boyd Quaich 1980–82. British Universities 1980–81
Int Walker Cup 1983. England (Home Int) 1980–81–82

Light, Miss Pamela Mary
See Mrs PM Chugg

Llewellyn, David
Born Dover on 18th November, 1951. Turned Professional 1968

Tls Ivory Coast Open 1985. Kenya Open 1972. Biarritz Open 1988. Zambian Open 1988
Oth Vernons Open 1987
Int Wales in World Cup 1974–85–87 (winners). Dunhill Cup 1985–88
Mis Rookie of the Year 1971

Long, David Charles
Born Belfast on 13th October, 1952

Add 4A Kensington Park, Belfast 5
Cls Shandon Park
Chp English Open Amateur Stroke Play 1979
Maj South of Ireland Open Amateur 1974. West of Ireland Open Amateur 1979. North of Ireland Open Amateur 1981–82
Int Europe v South America 1979. Ireland (Home Int) 1973–74–80–81–82–83; (Eur Team Ch) 1979; v Wales 1979

Longmuir, Bill
Born Essex on 10th June, 1953. Turned Professional 1968

Tls Nigerian Open 1976–80–85. Ivory Coast Open 1983
Mis Tooting Bec Cup 1979

Lucas, Percy Belgrave, CBE, DSO, DFC
Born Sandwich Bay, Kent on 2nd September, 1915

Add 11 Onslow Square, London
Cls Sandy Lodge, Walton Heath, Prince's, Royal West Norfolk
Maj Berkshire Trophy 1947–49. Royal St George's Challenge Cup 1947. Prince of Wales Challenge Cup 1947
Oth President's Putter 1949
Reg Herts Amateur 1946–47
Int Walker Cup 1936–47 (non-playing captain 1949). GB v Professionals 1935. England (Home Int) 1936–48–49 (captain); v France 1936–47
Jun British Boys 1933. Boys International 1930–31–32–33
Mis President Golf Foundation 1963 to 1966. President National Golf Clubs Advisory Association 1963 to 1969. President Association of Golf Club Secretaries 1968 to 1974. Member UK Sports Council 1971 to 1983

Lugton, Miss Constance J, MVO
Born Edinburgh on 17th November, 1936

Add Crabtree Cottage, 45 Hopetoun Terrace, Gullane, East Lothian
Cls Gullane Ladies, Musselburgh
Chp Scottish Ladies Amateur 1977, runner-up 1972
Reg East of Scotland Ladies 1974, East Lothian Ladies 1965–68–70–71–72–73–76–77–80
Int Scotland (home Int) 1965-68-72-73-77-78-80 (non-playing captain 1975–76); (Eur Team Ch) 1977
Jun Girl International 1955

Lumb, Mrs JCN (*née* Kathryn Phillips)
Born Bradford on 24th February, 1952

Cls Hon member of Bradford, West Bowling, Killarney, Filton
Maj Central England Mixed Foursomes 1966–70
Reg Yorkshire Ladies 1968–69
Int Curtis Cup 1970–72. Vagliano Trophy 1969–71. England (Home Int) 1968–69–70–71; (Eur Team Ch) 1969
Jun English Girls 1968. Scottish Girls Open Stroke Play 1968–69. French Girls 1970. Girl International 1967–68–69

Lunt, Michael Stanley Randle
Born Birmingham on 20th May, 1935

Add Smugglers Wood, Sandy Lane, Kingswood, Surrey
Cls Royal and Ancient, Walton Heath, St Enodoc, Hon member of Blackwell, Royal St David's, Moseley, Edgbaston, Stourbridge, Willesley Park, Kibworth, Handsworth, King's Norton, Dudley
Chp Amateur Champion 1963, runner-up 1964. English Amateur 1966, runner up 1962. Second in English Open Amateur Stroke Play 1961
Maj Golf Illustrated Gold Vase 1958. Harlech Gold Cross 1959–61–64–65–66–67. Leicestershire Fox 1966
Reg Midland Counties Amateur 1960–62
Int Walker Cup 1959–61–62–65. Eisenhower Trophy 1964 GB Commonwealth Team 1963. England (Home Int) 1956–57–58–59–60–62–63–64–66 (non-playing captain 1972–73–74–75). Non-playing captain in Eur Team Ch 1973–75
Jun Boy International 1949–50–51–52
Mis Golf Writers' Trophy 1963. President Midland Counties Golf Association 1978 to 1980

Lunt, Stanley
Born Moseley, Birmingham on 14th November, 1900

Add Love Lyne Farm, Hunt End, nr Redditch, Worcestershire
Cls Royal and Ancient, Hon member of Stourbridge, Moseley, Handsworth, Edgbaston, Barnehurst, Shifnal, Killarney, Aberdovey, Blackwell

Chp English Amateur 1934
Maj Harlech Gold Cross 1953
Reg Midland Counties Amateur 1934. Worcestershire Amateur 1925–36
Int British Amateurs v Professionals 1932–35. England (Home Int) 1932–33–34–35 (captain), (non-playing captain 1952–53); v France 1934–35–39
Mis President English Golf Union 1960. Senior Golfers Society v USA and Canada 1957–59–61–63–65. Captain Senior Golfers' Society 1964

Lyle, Alexander Walter Barr (Sandy)

Born Shrewsbury on 9th February, 1958. Turned Professional 1977

Opn Open Champion 1985. US Masters 1988
Chp English Open Amateur Stroke Play 1975–77
Maj County Champion of Champions, Midland Amateur 1974; Midland Open 1975; Shropshire and Herefordshire Amateur 1974–76; Hampshire Hog, Berkshire Trophy, Scrutton Jug, Berkhamsted Trophy 1977
Int Walker Cup 1977. GB Commonwealth Team 1975. GBI v Europe 1976. England (Home Int) 1975–76–77; (Eur Team Ch) 1977.
Jun British Youths 1977. Carris Trophy 1975. Boy International. 1972–73–74–75
Mis In 1975 represented England at boy, youth and full international.
Eur Jersey Open, Scandinavian Enterprise Open, European Open 1979; Coral Classic 1980; French Open, Lawrence Batley International 1981; Lawrence Batley International 1982; Madrid Open 1983; Italian Open, Lancôme Trophy 1984; Benson & Hedges International 1985; German Masters 1987; Dunhill British Masters, Suntory World Match Play 1988
USC Greater Greensboro Open 1986; Tournament Players Championship 1987; Phoenix Open, Greater Greensboro Open 1988
Jap Casio World Open 1984
Saf Nigerian Open 1978
Oth Kapalua International (Hawaii) 1984; Scottish Professional 1979
Int Ryder Cup 1979–81–83–85–87. Hennessy-Cognac Cup 1980–84. World Cup 1979–80 (Individual winner) –87 (runners-up). Dunhill Cup 1985–86–87–88. Nissan Cup 1985–86. Kirin Cup 1987
Mis Vardon Trophy 1979–80–85. Frank Moran Trophy 1985. Benson & Hedges Golfer's Handbook Golfer of the Year 1985

Macara, Michael

Born 31st October, 1965

Chp Welsh Amateur Stroke Play 1985–87
Int Wales (Home Int) 1983–84–85–87

McCann, Mrs PG (*née* Catherine Smye)

Born Clonmel, Co Tipperary in 1922

Add Colbert House, O'Moore Street, Tullamore, Offaly, Eire
Cls Tullamore
Chp British Ladies 1951. Irish Ladies 1949–61, runner-up 1947–52–57–60
Reg Munster Ladies 1958, Irish Midland Ladies 1952–57–58
Int Curtis Cup 1952. Ireland (Home Int) 1947–48–49–50–51–52–53–54–56–57–58–60–61–62; v New Zealand 1953; v Canada 1953

McClure, Miss Jean

See Mrs J Holmes

McCorkindale, Miss Isabella

See Mrs IC Robertson

Macdonald, JS

Born St Andrews on 9th July, 1944

Add 109 Duncan Drive, Elgin, Moray IV30 2NH
Cls Elgin, Baberton, Killarney (Hon), Frigate Bay (Hon)
Chp Scottish Amateur Open Stroke Play 1969. Second in English Open Amateur Stroke Play 1970–71. Kuwait Open Champion 1977
Oth Boyd Quaich 1963–65. British Universities 1965
Reg South East Scotland Amateur 1969–71. North of Scotland Open Amateur Stroke Play 1984–85
Int Walker Cup 1971. GB v Europe 1970. Scotland (Home Int) 1969–70–71–72; (Eur Team Ch) 1971; v Belgium 1973
Jun Boy International 1961. Youth International 1962–64–65

McEvoy, Peter

Born London on 22nd March, 1953

Add 12 Kensington Avenue, Cheltenham, Gloucestershire
Cls Copt Heath (Hon), Handsworth (Hon), City of Derry (Hon), St Annes (Hon), Chantilly (Hon), L'Ancresse (Hon), Cotswold Hills
Chp Amateur Champion 1977–78. English Open Amateur Stroke Play 1980 (tied), second 1978. Runner-up English Amateur 1980
Maj Duncan Putter 1978–80–87. Scrutton Jug 1978–80. Lytham Trophy 1979. Selborne Salver 1979–80. Leics Fox 1976. Lagonda Trophy 1980. Berkshire Trophy 1985. County Champion of Champions 1984 (shared). Berkhamsted Trophy 1986
Oth British Universities Stroke Play 1973
Reg Warwickshire Match Play 1973–75–81. Warwickshire Amateur 1974–76–77–80. Warwickshire Open 1973–74. West of England Open Amateur Stroke Play 1977–80–83. Midland Open Amateur Stroke Play 1978
Int Walker Cup 1977–79–81–85. Eisenhower Trophy 1978–80–88 (winners). GBI v Europe 1978–80–88. England (Home Int) v Europe 1976–77–78–80–81–83–84–85–86–87–88; (Eur Team Ch) 1977–79–81–83; v Scotland 1979; in Fiat Trophy 1980. England v France 1983–88
Jun Youth International 1974
Mis Leading amateur Open Championship 1978–79. First British amateur to complete 72 holes in US Masters (1978). Golf Writers' Trophy 1978

McGimpsey, Garth M

Born 17th July, 1955

Add 15 Portview Lane, Ballymaconnell Road, Bangor, Co Down
Cls Bangor, Royal Portrush, Royal Co Down
Chp Amateur Champion 1985
Maj Irish Close Champion 1985
Reg North of Ireland Champion 1978–84, West of Ireland Champion 1984–88, East of Ireland Champion 1988 runner-up 1979–80
Int Walker Cup 1985. GBI v Europe 1984–86–88. Eisenhower Trophy 1984–86–88 (winners). Ireland (Home Int) 1978–80–81–82–83–84–85–86–87–88. (Eur Team Ch) 1981
Mis Irish long-driving champion 1977; UK long-driving champion 1979

Macgregor, George
Born Edinburgh on 19th August, 1944

Add Esklea, Milton Bridge, Penicuik, Midlothian
Cls Glencorse, Killarney (Hon), West Linton (Hon)
Chp Scottish Open Amateur Stroke Play 1982. Runner-up 1975–79–80
Maj Lytham Trophy 1975
Reg Lothians Amateur 1968. South-East Scotland Amateur 1972–75–79–80–81. East of Scotland Open Amateur 1979–82
Int Walker Cup 1971–75–83–85–87. GB v Europe 1970–74. GB Commonwealth Team 1971–75. Scotland (Home Int) 1969–70–71–72–73–74–75–76–80–81–82–83–84–85–86–87; (Eur Team Ch) 1971–73–75–81–83; v Belgium 1973–75–80; v England 1979; v France 1981–82; Scotland v Sweden 1983
Jun Youth International 1964–65–66
Mis Leading Amateur Wills PGA Open 1970–71

Macintosh, Keith William
Born Cardross, Dunbartonshire on 21st June, 1949

Add 106A Sinclair Street, Helensburgh G84 9QE
Cls Cardross (Hon), Glasgow
Chp Scottish Amateur 1979. Second in Scottish Open Amateur Stroke Play 1978 (tied)
Ove Belgian Open Amateur 1980
Oth Scottish Universities 1969. Cameron Corbett Vase 1979. Cadzow Cup 1968
Reg Glasgow District Amateur 1973. Dunbartonshire Match Play 1980
Int GB v Europe 1980. Scotland (Home Int) 1980; v England 1979; v France 1980; v Belgium 1980; in Fiat Trophy 1980. Moroccan Amateur Team Champion 1980. Simon Bolivar Trophy 1979
Jun Youth International 1964

McHenry, John
Born Cork on 14th March, 1964. Turned Professional 1987

Chp Irish Amateur 1986
Reg South of Ireland 1976
Int Ireland (Home Int) 1985–86. Walker Cup 1987

McKellar, Paul James
Born Clarkston, Glasgow on 6th April, 1956

Cls East Renfrewshire (Hon)
Chp Runner-up Amateur Championship 1978. Scottish Open Amateur Stroke Play 1977. Runner-up Scottish Amateur 1977–79
Reg West of Scotland Close 1980
Int Walker Cup 1977. GB v Europe 1978. Europe v South America 1979. Scotland (Home Int) 1976–77–78; v Belgium 1978; v France 1978; v England 1979; in Caracas International 1979
Jun Youth International 1974–75–76–77
Mis Non-playing captain Scottish Youths Team 1978–79

McKenna, Miss Mary A
Born Dublin on 29th April, 1949

Add Moyola, Cloghran, Co Dublin
Cls Donabate, Hermitage, Woodbrook, Killarney (Hon), Milltown, Moseley, Clontarf, Fairfield (USA) (Hon)
Chp British Ladies Open Amateur Stroke Play 1979, second 1976. Irish Ladies 1969–72–74–77–79–81–82, runner-up 1968–73–76. Irish Women's Close Championship 1981
Maj Dorothy Grey Stroke Play 1970-71–73. Players No 6 Cup 1971–72–74. Avia Foursomes 1977–84–86. Hermitage Scratch Cup 1975–79
Reg South of Ireland Scratch Cup 1973–74–76–79
Int Curtis Cup 1970–72–74–76–78–80–82–84–86. Vagliano Trophy 1969–71–73–75–77–79–81–85–87. World Team Championship 1970–74–76–86 (captain). Ireland (Home Int) 1968 to 88 inclusive; (Eur Team Ch) 1969–71–73–75–77–79–81–83–85–87; in Fiat Trophy 1979
Mis Semi-finalist US Women's Western 1972, Broadmoor Tournament 1972 and US Women's Amateur 1980. Captain of LGU Touring Team to South Africa 1974. Leading Amateur Colgate European LPGA 1977 (tied)–79. Daks Woman Golfer of the Year 1979

McLean, David
Born Holyhead on 30th January, 1947

Add Cleneagles, Four Mile Bridge, Valley Anglesey
Cls Holyhead, Baron Hill, Killarney
Chp Welsh Amateur 1973–78. Welsh Amateur Stroke Play 1975–79
Maj Duncan Putter 1982
Reg North Wales Amateur 1971–75–77–81. Caernarvonshire Amateur 1966–68–69–70 (tied)–77–79–81–82. Anglesey Amateur 1965–67–68–69–70–72–73–74–76–78–79–80–81–82
Int Wales (Home Int) 1968–69–70–71–72–73–74–75–76–77–78–80–81–82–83–85–86–88; (Eur Team Ch) 1975–77–79–81–83; v France 1975–76; v Denmark 1976–80–82; v Ireland 1979; v Spain 1980; v Austria 1982; v Switzerland 1980–82; in Fiat Trophy 1978–79; in Asian Team Championship 1979

McMahon, Mrs J (*née* Suzanne Cadden)
Born Old Kilpatrick, Dunbartonshire on 8th October, 1957

Add 340 Dumbarton Road, Dalmuir, Glasgow G81
Cls Troon
Chp Runner-up British Ladies 1975. Second in British Ladies Stroke Play 1975
Maj Scottish Ladies Foursomes 1972
Ove World Junior Championship 1973
Reg Dunbartonshire Ladies 1976–77–79
Int Curtis Cup 1976. Vagliano Trophy 1975. Scotland (Home Int) 1974–75–76–77–79; (Eur Team Ch) 1975
Jun Scottish Girls 1974–76. Scottish Girls Open Stroke Play 1976–77. British Girls 1975. Girl International 1972–73–74–75–76
Mis Daks Woman Golfer of the Year 1975

Madill, Mrs Maureen
See Mrs Garner

Maher, Mrs S (*née* Sheila Vaughan)
Born Whiston, Liverpool on 9th March, 1942

Add 25 Knowsley Road, Rainhill, Merseyside L35 0PA
Cls Huyton and Prescot
Reg Lancashire Ladies 1958–63–64
Int Curtis Cup 1962–64. Vagliano Trophy 1961–65. GB Commonwealth Team 1963. England (Home Int) 1960–61–62–63–64
Jun British Girls 1959. England Girl International 1956-57-58-59
Mis In 1963 on tour of Australasia as member of GB Commonwealth Team, tied first in Australian Ladies Foursomes, won New Zealand Ladies Foursomes and won New Zealand Junior Stroke Play

Mann, Lindsay S
Born 28th February, 1962

Maj Tennant Cup 1982
Int Walker Cup 1983. Scotland (Home Int) 1982–83

Marchbank, Brian
Born Perth on 20th April, 1958. Turned Professional 1979

Add Rosemount, Tulibardine Crescent, Auchterarder, Perthshire
Cls Auchterarder (Hon)
Chp Second equal in English Open Amateur Stroke Play 1979
Maj Lytham Trophy 1978. Scottish Champion of Champions 1979
Int Walker Cup 1979. GB v Europe 1976–78. Eisenhower Trophy 1978. Scotland (Home Int) 1978; (Eur Team Ch) 1979; v Italy 1979
Jun British Boys 1975. Scottish Boys 1976. British Youths 1978. Boy International 1973–74–75. Youth International 1976–77–78–79

Marks, Geoffrey C
Born Hanley, Stoke-on-Trent, in November, 1938

Add Bar Hill House, Madeley, nr Crewe, Cheshire
Cls Hon member of Trentham, Trentham Park, Greenway Hall, Killarney, Walsall, Newcastle, Trevose, Stone. Royal and Ancient
Chp Second in English Open Amateur Stroke Play 1973–75
Maj Scrutton Jug 1967. Prince of Wales Challenge Cup 1968. Leicestershire Fox 1968. Lytham Trophy 1970 (tied). Harlech Gold Cup 1974. Homer Salver 1977
Reg Midland Amateur 1967. Staffordshire Amateur1959–60–63–66–67–68–69–73
Int Walker Cup 1969–71–87 (Captain). Eisenhower Trophy 1970. GB v Europe 1968–70. England (Home Int) 1963–67–68–69–70–71–74–75 (non-playing captain 1980–81–82–83); (Eur Team Ch) 1967–69–71–75. GB Commonwealth Team 1975. GB in Colombian International 1975
Jun Boy International 1955–56. Youth International 1957–58–59–60
Mis England Selector 1980–81–82–83 (chairman)

Marsh, Dr David Max
Born Southport on 29th April, 1934

Add 26 Blundell Drive, Southport, Lancashire
Cls Royal and Ancient, Hon member of Southport and Ainsdale, Ormskirk, West Lancashire, Worlington and Newmarket, Hillside, Clitheroe, Whalley
Chp English Amateur 1964–70
Maj Antlers Royal Mid-Surrey 1964–66. Formby Hare 1968
Oth Boyd Quaich 1957
Int Walker Cup 1959–71 (non-playing captain 1973–75); GB v Europe 1958 (non-playing captain 1972–74). GB v Professionals 1959. England (Home Int) 1956–57–58–59–60–64–65–66–68–69–70–71–72 (captain 1968–69–70–71); (Eur Team Ch) 1971
Jun Boy International 1951
Mis EGU Selector 1974. British Selector 1975. Chairman Royal and Ancient Selection Committee 1979–83. President EGU 1987

Martin, Steve W
Born Dundee on 21st December, 1955. Turned Professional 1977

Chp Scottish Open Amateur Stroke Play 1976
Maj East of Scotland Open Amateur Stroke Play 1976. Tennant Cup 1977
Reg Central District Amateur 1973. Angus Amateur 1973
Int Walker Cup 1977. Eisenhower Trophy 1976 (winning team). GB v Europe 1976. Scotland (Home Int) 1975–76–77; (Eur Team Ch) 1977; v Belgium 1977; v Spain 1977
Jun Scottish Boys Stroke Play 1972–73. Boy International 1972–73. Youth International 1973–75–76–77
Mis Represented Scotland in World Cup 1980

Marvin, Miss Vanessa Price
Born Cosford on 30th December, 1954. Turned Professional 1978

Add 24 Bradford Road, Otley, West Yorkshire, LS21 3EQ
Cls Easingwold (Hon)
Chp English Ladies Amateur 1977–78. Runner-up British Ladies Amateur 1977
Maj Hampshire Rose 1975–78 (tied). Roehampton Gold Cup 1976. Newmark-Avia 1978
Reg Yorkshire Ladies 1975–78. North of England Ladies 1975
Int Curtis Cup 1978. Vagliano Trophy 1977. England (Home Int) 1977–78; (Eur Team Ch) 1977; in Fiat Trophy 1978
Mis Leading amateur Colgate European LPGA 1977. Daks Woman Golfer of the Year 1978.

Mayo, Paul M
Born Newport, Gwent on 6th January, 1963

Opn Leading Amateur in Open 1987
Chp Amateur Champion 1987; Welsh Amateur 1987
Reg Gwent Amateur 1982
Int Walker Cup 1985–87; GB v Europe 1986; Wales (Home Int) 1982–87
Jun British Youths 1983; Welsh Boys 1979

Melia, Terry J
Born Wrexham on 7th July, 1955

Add 39 Hampton Crescent, West Cyncoed, Cardiff
Cls Cardiff
Chp Welsh Amateur 1979. Welsh Amateur Stroke Play 1980
Reg Glamorgan County 1981–82
Int Wales (Home Int) 1976–77–78–80–81–82; (Eur Team Ch) 1977–79; v Denmark 1976–80; v Ireland 1979; v Switzerland 1980; v Spain 1980; v S America 1979

Milligan, James W
Born Irvine on 15th June, 1963

Add 30 Holyoke Court, Hurlford, Ayrshire
Cls Kilmarnock (Barassie)
Chp Scottish Amateur 1988
Int Scotland (Home Int) 1986–87–88. v West Germany 1987; v Italy 1988. GBI v Europe 1988. World Cup (Eisenhower) 1988 (winners)
Jun Scottish Youths 1984

Milne, William TG
Born Perth on 13th July, 1951. Turned Professional 1973

Maj Newlands Trophy 1972
Reg North of Scotland Stroke Play 1971. Perthshire Stroke Play 1973
Int Walker Cup 1973. Scotland (Home Int) 1972–73; (Eur Team Ch) 1973; v Belgium 1973
Jun Scotland Youth International 1970–71–72
Mis Won Lusaka Eagle Open 1974 and Northern Scottish Open 1974-75

Milton, Mrs John C (*née* Moira Paterson)
Born 18th December, 1923

Add White Willows, Theale, Wedmore, Somerset, BS28 4SR
Cls Turnhouse, Hon Member of Gullane, Lenzie, Maccauvlei
Chp British Ladies 1952. Runner-up Scottish Ladies 1951

Reg Dunbartonshire Ladies 1949. Midlothian Ladies 1962
Int Curtis Cup 1952. GB v France 1949–50; v Belgium 1950. Scotland (Home Int) 1949–50–51–52; v Australia 1951; v South Africa 1951
Mis Member of LGU Team to South Africa 1951. Non-playing captain Scotland in Eur Team Championship 1973

Moir, Angus

Born Edinburgh, on 1st May, 1963

Chp Scottish Amateur 1984
Int Scotland (Home Int) 1983–84

Montgomerie, Colin S

Born Glasgow on 23rd June, 1963. Turned Professional 1987

Chp Scottish Amateur 1987; Scottish Open Amateur Stroke Play 1985
Int Walker Cup 1985–87; GB v Europe 1986; Eisenhower Trophy 1984–86; Scotland (Home Int) 1984–85–86, v Sweden 1984–86, v France 1985; (Eur Team Ch) 1985. Dunhill Cup 1988

Montgomerie, John Speir

Born Cambuslang on 7th August, 1913

Add 6 Cavendish Drive, Newton Mearns, Glasgow
Cls Royal and Ancient, Cambuslang, Kilmarnock (Barassie), Pollok
Chp Scottish Amateur 1957
Reg Lanarkshire Amateur 1951–54
Int Scotland (Home Int) 1957, (non-playing captain) 1962–63; v Scandinavia 1958
Mis Non-playing captain Scottish Team (Eur Team Ch) 1965. Walker Cup Selector 1957 to 1965. President Scottish Golf Union 1965–66

Moody, Chris

Born Uxbridge on 19th October, 1953. Turned Professional 1973

Ove Ebel European Masters
Tls Swiss Open 1988

Moore, Miss Linda

See Mrs L Simpson

Morgan, John

Born Oxford on 3rd September, 1943. Turned Professional 1968

Tls Nigerian Open 1979. Ivory Coast 1982
Maj Lusaka Open 1979. Jersey Open 1986

Morgan, John Llewellyn

Born Llandrindod Wells on 23rd June, 1918

Add 2 Kinver Crescent, Aldridge, Staffordshire
Cls Llandrindod Wells, Sutton Coldfield, Builth Wells, Little Aston, Aberystwyth, Killarney, St Deiniol, Ashburnham
Chp Welsh Amateur 1950–51, runner-up 1952
Maj Berkshire Trophy 1953. Duncan Putter 1968. Harlech Gold Cross 1951–55
Oth British Seniors 1974
Reg Midlands Amateur 1949–50–52. Midlands Open 1950. Warwickshire Amateur 1951
Int Walker Cup 1951–53–55. Wales (Home Int) 1948–49–50–51–52–53–54–56–57–58–59–60–61–62–63–64–66–67. (Eur Team Ch) 1965
Mis Professional for 4 years subsequently reinstated as Amateur

Morgan, Miss Wanda

Born Lymm, Cheshire on 22nd March, 1910

Add 67 Russell Drive, Swalecliffe, Whitstable, Kent CT5 2RG. Tel (022 779) 2319
Cls Canterbury, Westgate, St Enodoc, Herne Bay, Belmont, Chestfield, Rochester and Cobham Park, Cooden Beach, Littlestone, Prince's, Seasalter, Barnehurst, Hon Life member of *ALL* clubs listed
Chp British Ladies 1935, runner-up 1931. English Ladies 1931-36-37
Maj Sunningdale Foursomes 1948. Worplesdon Mixed Foursomes 1948. Fairway and Hazard Foursomes 1956. Daily Graphic 1941–42
Reg Kent Ladies 1930–31–33–35–36–37–53
Int Curtis Cup 1932–34–36. GB v France 1932–33–34–35–36–37; v Canada 1934. England (Home Int) 1931–32–33–34–35–36–37–53

Morris, Mick F

Chp Irish Amateur 1978
Int Ireland (Home Int) 1978–80–82–83–84 (Eur Team Ch) 1979

Mosey, Ian

Born Keighley on 29th August, 1951. Turned Professional 1972

Maj Monte Carlo Open 1984
Oth Merseyside International 1980. Kalahari Classic 1980. Holiday Inns, SA 1981

Mouland, Mark

Born Wales on 23rd April, 1961. Turned Professional 1981

Maj Car Care Plan International 1986. KLM Open 1988
Reg Midland Professional Stroke Play 1984
Int Wales: in Dunhill Cup 1986–87–88

Mulcare, Pat

Born Ballybunion, 1945

Add 35 Beech Lawn, Dundrum, Dublin 14
Cls Woodbrook (Hon), Dublin (Hon)
Maj East of Ireland Open Amateur 1971–72–73. South of Ireland Open Amateur 1971
Int Walker Cup 1975. Ireland (Home Int) 1968–69–70–71–72–73–74–78–80; (Eur Team Ch) 1975–79; v France, West Germany and Sweden 1978–80

Murray, Gordon H

Born Paisley on 19th December, 1936

Add 78 Braeside Drive, Barrhead, Renfrewshire
Cls Fereneze (Hon)
Chp Scottish Amateur 1974–76, runner-up 1975
Maj West of Scotland Open Amateur 1973–76–78. Scottish Stroke Play 1983
Reg West of Scotland Amateur 1971
Int Walker Cup 1977. GB v Europe 1978. Scotland (Home Int) 1973–74–75–76–77–78–83 (Eur Team Ch) 1975–77; v Spain 1974–77; v Belgium 1975–77

Murray, Stuart WT

Born Paisley on 10th November, 1933. Turned Professional 1963

Chp Scottish Amateur 1962, runner-up 1961
Maj Tennant Cup 1963. Edward Trophy 1960–61
Reg West of Scotland Amateur 1958. Renfrewshire Amateur 1958–59. Glasgow Amateur 1960. Hampshire Amateur 1963. Midland Professional 1964-67-68. Middlesex Open 1973

Int Walker Cup 1963. GB Commonwealth Team 1963 GB v Europe. 1958–62. Scotland (Home Int) 1959–60–61–62–63, v Scandinavia 1960

Needham, Miss Sandra Claire
See Mrs Roy

Nesbitt, Miss Claire
See Mrs C Robinson

New, Beverley Jayne
Born Bristol on 30th July, 1960. Turned Professional 1984

Add 3 Willow Close, Wick, Bristol
Cls Lansdown (Hon)
Chp English Ladies 1980. Second in Welsh Ladies Open Stroke Play 1979
Maj Hampshire Rose 1980. Runner-up Roehampton Gold Cup 1981–82. Winner Roehampton Gold Cup 1983. WPGA United Friendly Insurance Tour 1982. Worplesdon Mixed Foursomes 1982–83
Oth Martin Bowl 1983. Runner-up Keighly Trophy 1983
Reg Somerset Ladies 1979–80–82–83; Somerset Ladies Champion 1981–83. Runner-up South West Ladies Championship 1981–82–83. Bristol and District Open 1983
Int (Home Int) 1980–81–82–83; in Fiat Trophy 1980. England (Eur Team Ch) 1981–83. Vagliano Team 1983. Curtis Cup 1984.
Jun England Under 22 International 1979–80–81. South West Under 21 Champion 1980, runner-up Under 23 English Championship 1982

Nichol, Miss Margaret
See Mrs A Pickard

Nicholas, Alison
Born Gibraltar on 6th March, 1962. Turned Professional 1984

Chp Ladies Open 1987. Ladies Open Amateur Stroke Play 1983
Reg Yorkshire Champion 1984. Northern Foursomes 1983
Jun North of England Girls 1982–83
WPGA Laing Ladies Classic 1987. Variety Club Classic 1988. British Olivetti 1988. Guernsey Open 1988

O'Connor, Christy
Born Galway on 21st December, 1924

Opn Second in Open Championship 1965, third in 1961. Leading British player 1963 (6th)
Maj Swallow-Penfold 1955. Dunlop Masters 1956–59. Spalding 1956 (tied). PGA Match Play 1957. Daks 1959. Ballantine 1960. Irish Hospitals 1960–62. Carling-Caledonian 1961. Martini 1963 (tied)–64. Jeyes 1964. Carrolls 1964–66–67–72. Senior Service 1965; Gallaher Ulster 1966–68–69. Alcan International 1968 (tied). Bowmaker 1970. John Player Classic 1970. PGA Seniors 1981–82.
Oth Ulster Professional 1953–54. Irish Professional 1958–60–61–62–63–65–66–71–75–77. Irish Dunlop 1962–65–66–67. Gleneagles Pro-Am 1962. Southern Ireland Professional 1969–76. Sean Connery Pro-Am 1970. PGA Seniors 1976–77–79. World Seniors 1976–77
Int Ryder Cup 1955–57–59–61–63–65–67–69–71–73. GB v Commonwealth 1956. Ireland in World Cup 1956–57–58 (winning team)–59–60–61–62–63–64–66–67–68–69–71–75. Ireland in Double Diamond 1971–72–73–74–75–76–77
Mis Harry Vardon Trophy 1961–62. Second in order of Merit 1964 (equal)–65–66–69–70. Represented Great Britain and Ireland in the Ryder Cup ten times. Golf Writers Trophy 1977

O'Connor, Christy, Jr
Born Galway on 19th August, 1948. Turned Professional 1965

Opn Joint leading British player (5th) in Open Championship 1976. 3rd in Open 1985
Tls Zambian Open 1974
Maj Martini 1975 (tied). Carrolls Irish Open 1975. Sumrie 1976–78
Oth Irish Dunlop 1974. Carrolls Irish Match Play 1975–77
Int Ireland in Double Diamond 1974–75–76–77. Ireland in World Cup 1974–75–78–85. GB v Europe 1974: Ryder Cup 1975. GB v South Africa 1976. Dunhill Cup 1985

Oldcorn, Andrew
Born Bolton on 31st March, 1960. Turned Professional 1983

Chp English Amateur 1982
Int Walker Cup 1983. England (Home Int) 1982–83

O'Leary, John E
Born Dublin on 19th August, 1949. Turned Professional 1970

Maj Sumrie 1975. Greater Manchester Open 1976. Carrolls Irish Open 1982
Ove Holiday Inns (Swaziland) 1975
Oth Irish Dunlop 1972
Int Ryder Cup 1975. Ireland in World Cup 1972–80–82. Ireland in Double Diamond 1972–73–74–75–76–77. GB v Europe 1976–78
Am South of Ireland Amateur 1970. Youth Int 1970. Ireland (Home Int) 1969–70; (Eur Team Ch) 1969

O'Reilly, Mrs Therese (*née* Moran)
Born 29th January, 1954

Chp Irish Ladies' Amateur 1986
Reg Leinster Ladies 1975–78. Irish Midland Ladies 1974
Int Ireland (Home Int) 1977–78–86–88; (Eur Team Ch) 1988

O'Sullivan, Denis

Chp Irish Amateur 1985
Int Ireland (Home Int) 1985-86–87

O'Sullivan, Dr William M
Born Killarney on 13th March, 1911

Add Inch House, Killarney, Co Kerry
Cls Killarney (Hon), Dooks (Hon), Tralee (Hon), Muskerry (Hon), Cork (Hon), Ballybunion (Hon), Waterville
Chp Irish Open Amateur 1949, runner-up 1936–53. Runner-up Irish Amateur 1940
Int Ireland (Home Int) 1934–35–36–37–38–47–48–49–50–51–53–54. President Golfing Union of Ireland 1959–60

Oosterhuis, Peter A
Born London on 3rd May, 1948. Turned Professional November 1968

Opn Second in Open Championship 1974. Leading British player 1975(7th)–78(6th)–82(third)
Tls French Open 1973–74. Italian Open 1974. Canadian Open 1981. Third in US Masters in 1973.
Maj Berkshire Trophy 1966. Agfacolor 1971. Sunbeam Pro-Am 1971. Piccadilly 1971–73. Penfold 1972. Viyella PGA 1973

Ove General Motors, South Africa 1970. Transvaal Open 1971. Schoeman Park 1971. Rhodesian Dunlop Masters 1971. Glen Anil Classic (SA) 1972. Rothmans Match Play (SA) 1973. Maracaibo Open 1973. El Paraiso Open 1974. Canadian Open 1981
Oth Sunningdale Foursomes 1969. Under 23's PGA 1970. Coca Cola Young Professionals 1970–72. Southern England Professional 1971
Int Walker Cup 1967. Eisenhower Trophy 1968. England (Home Int) 1966–67–68. Ryder Cup 1971–73–75–77–79–81.England in World Cup 1971–73. England in Double Diamond 1973–74. GB v Europe 1974
Jun British Youths 1966. Youth Int 1966-67-68. Boy Int 1964-65
Mis Vardon Trophy 1971–72–73–74. Golf Writers Trophy 1973–74. In addition to three victories on 1974 British-European circuit, was second five times (Open included) and lost play-off in 1974 US Tournament-Monsanto Open. European American Express 1974. Qualified for USPGA tour November 1974. Finished second in the 1975 New Orleans Open 28th on US Tour Money List 1981

Oxley, Miss Dinah
See Mrs D Henson

Panton, Catherine Rita
Born Bridge of Allan, Stirlingshire on 14th June, 1955. Turned Professional 1978

Add 116C Nether Street, West Finchley, London N12
Cls Glenbervie (Hon), Pitlochry (Hon), Silloth (Hon), South Herts
Chp British Ladies 1976
Reg East of Scotland Ladies 1976
Int World Team Championship 1976. Vagliano Trophy 1977. Scotland (Home Int) 1972–73–76–77–78; (Eur Team Ch) 1973–77
Jun Scottish Girls 1969. Girl Int 1969-70-71-72-73
Mis Scottish Sportswoman of the Year 1976. Member of LGU under-25 team to tour Canada 1973
WPGA Carlsberg Tournament 1979. State Express Ladies Championship 1979 and headed WPGA Order of Merit. In 1980 won Elizabeth Ann Classic. European Ladies Champion 1981, also won two WPGA events. Moben Kitchens Classic 1982. Qualified for USLPGA Tour, January 1983. Won Smirnoff Irish Classic 1983. UBM Northern Classic 1983, Dunham Forest Pro-Am 1983. McEwans Wirral Caldy Classic 1985. Delsjö Open 1985. Portuguese Open 1986. Scottish Open 1988

Panton, John MBE
Born Pitlochry, Perthshire on 9th October, 1916. Turned Professional 1935

Opn Leading British player in 1956 Open Championship (5th)
Maj Silver King 1950. Daks 1951. North-British-Harrogate 1952. Goodwin Foursomes 1952. Yorkshire Evening News 1954. PGA Match Play 1956, runner-up 1968
Ove Woodlawn Invitation Open (Germany) 1958–59–60
Oth West of Scotland Professional 1947–48–52–54–55–61–63. Scottish Professional 1948–49–50–51–54–55–59–66 (tied). Northern Open 1948–51–52–56–59–60–62. West of Scotland PGA Match Play 1954–55–56–64. Goodwin Foursomes 1952. Gleneagles-Saxone 1956. Pringle Seniors 1967–69. World Seniors 1967
Int Ryder Cup 1951–53–61. Scotland in World Cup 1955–56–57–58–59–60–62–63–64–65–66–68
Mis Harry Vardon Trophy 1951. Golf Writers Trophy 1967. Hon Professional to Royal and Ancient from 1988

Parkin, Philip
Born Doncaster on 12th December, 1961. Turned Professional 1984

Chp Amateur Champion 1983
Int Walker Cup 1983. Wales (Home Int) 1980–81–82. Wales in World Cup 1984. Dunhill Cup 1985–86–87
Jun British Youths 1982

Paterson, Miss Moira
See Mrs JC Milton

Peel, Mrs M
See Mrs M Draper

Perkins, Miss Tegwen
See Mrs Thomas

Perowne, Arthur Herbert
Born Norwich on 21st February, 1930

Add Bawburgh Villa, Bawburgh, Norwich
Cls Royal Norwich, Hunstanton, West Norfolk
Chp English Open Amateur Stroke Play 1958
Maj Berkshire Trophy 1958 (tied)
Ove Swedish Amateur 1974
Oth Carris Trophy 1946
Reg East Anglia Open 1952. Norfolk Amateur 1948–51–52–53–54–55–56–57–58–60–61. Norfolk Open 1964
Int Walker Cup 1949–53–59. Eisenhower Trophy 1958. GB v Denmark 1955; v Professionals 1956–58. England (Home Int) 1947–48–49–50–51–53–54–55–57; v France 1950–54–56–59; v Sweden 1947; v Denmark 1947
Jun Boy International 1946

Phillips, Miss Ann
See Mrs A Howard

Phillips, Miss Kathryn
See Mrs JCN Lumb

Pickard, Mrs A (*née* Margaret Nichol)
Born on 25th April, 1938

Add East Farm , Eshott, Felton, Morpeth, Northumberland
Cls Hexham (Hon), Alnmouth (Hon), Gullane
Chp English Ladies 1960, runner-up 1957–67
Reg Northern Ladies 1957–58. Northumberland Ladies 1956–57–58–61–62–64–65–66–67–69–70–71–76–77–82
Int Curtis Cup 1968–70. Vagliano Trophy 1959–61–67. England (Home Int) 1957–58–59–60–61–67–69, non-playing captain 1983. (Eur Team Ch) 1983 (non-playing captain)

Pierse, Arthur D

Maj West of Ireland Open Amateur 1980–82. North of Ireland Amateur 1987
Int Walker Cup 1983, GB v Europe 1980. Ireland (Home Int) 1976–77–78–80–81–82–83–84–85–87–88 (Eur Team Ch) 1981

Pirie, Alex Kemp
Born Aberdeen on 21st June, 1942

Add The Golf Inn, Montrose, Angus
Cls Hazelhead (Hon), Cruden Bay
Chp Runner-up Scottish Amateur 1972–74
Maj Eden Tournament 1963. Northern Scottish Open 1970. West of Scotland Open Amateur 1972. East of Scotland Open Amateur Stroke Play 1975

Reg North East Scotland Match Play 1964–66–67–68–71–73 Aberdeenshire Stroke Play 1966–68
Int Walker Cup 1967. GB v Europe 1970. Scotland (Home Int) 1966–67–68–69–70–71–72–73–74–75; (Eur Team Ch) 1967–69; v Belgium 1973–75; v Spain 1974

Polland, Eddie
Born Newcastle, Co Down on 10th June, 1947. Turned Professional 1967

Tls Spanish Open 1976–80
Maj Penfold 1973. Sun Alliance PGA Match Play 1975
Oth Irish Dunlop 1973–75. Irish Professional 1974. Carrolls Irish Match Play 1974. Ulster Professional 1976
Int Ryder Cup 1973. Ireland in World Cup 1973–74–76–77–78–79. Ireland in Double Diamond 1972–73–74–75–76–77. GB v Europe 1974–76–78–80; v South Africa 1976

Pook, Mrs Antony D (*née* Elizabeth Chadwick)
Born Inverness on 4th April, 1943

Add 9 Manor Gardens, Buckden, Huntingdon, Cambridgeshire. Tel (0480) 810922
Cls Hon member of Bramall Park (Home Club), Alderley Edge, Stockport, Anglesey
Chp British Ladies 1966–67. Runner-up English Ladies 1963
Maj Central England Mixed Foursomes 1962–63–64
Reg North of England Ladies 1965–66–67. Cheshire Ladies 1963–64–65–66–67
Int Curtis Cup 1966. GB Commonwealth 1967. GB v Europe 1963. England (Home Int) 1963–65–66–67; (Eur Team Ch) 1967; v France 1965
Jun Girl International 1961
Mis Retired from competitive golf in 1968

Porter, Miss Ruth
See Mrs Slark

Power, Eddie
Born Waterford on 17th January, 1965

Add 1 Newtown, Tramore, Co Waterford
Cls Tramore (Hon) Enniscorthy (Hon)
Chp Irish Amateur 1987. Runner-up 1983
Int Ireland (Home Int) 1987–88
Jun Boy International 1982. Youth International 1984–86. European Boys 1982. Junior World Cup 1982

Price Fisher, Mrs Elizabeth
Born London on 17th January, 1923. Turned Professional 1968, reinstated as Amateur 1971

Add Flat 1, Keep House, Castle Street, Farnham, Surrey GU9 7JB
Cls Hankley Common, Farnham, Berkshire
Chp British Ladies 1959, runner up 1954–58. Runner-up English Ladies 1947–54–55
Maj Spalding Ladies 1955–59. Astor Salver 1955–56–59. Fairway and Hazard Foursomes 1954–60. Kayser Bondor Foursomes 1958 (tied). Roehampton Gold Cup 1960. Central England Mixed Foursomes 1971–76–82
Ove Danish Ladies 1952. Portuguese Ladies 1964
Reg South Eastern Ladies 1955–59–60–69. Surrey Ladies 1954–55–56–57–58–59–60
Int Curtis Cup 1950–52–54–56–58–60. Vagliano Trophy 1959. GB v Canada 1950–54–58; v France 1953–55–57; v Belgium 1953–55–57. GB Commonwealth Team 1955–59. England (Home Int) 1948–51–52–53–54–55–56–57–58–59–60
Mis Golf Writers Trophy 1952.

Rafferty, Ronan
Born 13th January, 1964. Turned Professional 1981

Add 5 Burren Road, Warrenpoint, Co Down
Cls Warrenpoint (Hon), Ardglass
Chp Irish Amateur 1980. English Open Amateur Stroke Play 1980 (tied)
Ove S Australian Open, New Zealand Open 1987; Australian Match Play 1988
Int Eisenhower Trophy 1980. GB v Europe 1980. Ireland (Home Int) 1980; v Wales 1979; v France, Germany, Sweden 1980; in Fiat Trophy 1980. (Eur Team Ch) 1981. Walker Cup 1981. Ireland in World Cup 1983–84. Dunhill Cup 1986. Dunhill Cup 1986–87–88 (winners). Hennessy-Cognac Cup 1984
Jun British Boys 1979. Irish Youths 1979. Ulster Youths 1979. Boy International 1978-79. Youth International 1979–80
Mis Equity and Law Challenge 1988. Youngest player ever to play in Walker Cup

Rawlings, Mandy
Born Bargoed, Glamorganshire on 15th June, 1964

Add 53 John Street, Bargoed, Mid Glamorgan
Cls Bargoed, Whitchurch, Radyr (Hon)
Chp Welsh Ladies 1980–81
Int Wales (Home Int) 1978–79–80; in Fiat Trophy 1980. Girls International 1981. Senior International 1981–83–84. Vagliano 1981
Jun Welsh Girls 1979–81. Girl International 1976–77–78–79–80. De Beers Ch 1980

Rawlings, Vicki
See Mrs V Thomas

Reddan, Mrs M (*née* Clarrie Tiernan)
Born Drogheda on 3rd July, 1916

Add Baltry, Drogheda, Co Louth
Cls Co Louth
Chp Irish Ladies 1936, runner-up 1946–48. Runner-up British Ladies 1949
Ove New Jersey State Ladies 1937. Runner-up Canadian Ladies 1938
Int Curtis Cup 1938–48. GB v Canada 1938. Ireland (Home Int) 1935–36–37–38–39–47–48–49

Redford, Miss Carole
See Mrs I Caldwell

Rees, Christopher

Chp Welsh Amateur 1966
Int Wales (Home Int) 1986–88
Jun Welsh Boys 1982

Reid, Dale
Born Ladybank, Fife on 20th March, 1959. Turned Professional 1979

Int Scotland (Home Int) 1978
Jun Fife Girls 1973–75. Scottish Girls International 1974–75–76–77
WPGA Carlsberg (Coventry) 1980. Carlsberg (Gleneagles) 1981. Moben Kitchens 1981. Guernsey Open 1982. United Friendly 1983. International Classic 1983. Caldy Classic 1983. UBM Classic 1984. JS Bloor Classic 1984. Ulster Volkswagen Classic 1985–87. Volmac Open 1987. European Open 1987. Bowring Scottish Ladies Open 1987. Brend Hotels International 1985. British Olivetti 1986. European Open 1988. Toshiba Players Ch 1988.
Mis Order of Merit leader 1984

Rennie, Mrs Joan Kerr (*née* Hastings)
Born Troon on 29th May, 1941

Add 334 Queens Road, Aberdeen
Cls Aberdeen Ladies, Hon member of Troon Bentinck, Kilmarnock (Barassie), Troon Municipal
Chp Scottish Ladies 1967, runner-up 1968
Reg Ayrshire Ladies 1960–61–63–64–66–67. Aberdeenshire Ladies 1980
Int Curtis Cup 1966. Vagliano Trophy 1961–67. Scotland (Home Int) 1961–65–66–67–71–72; (Eur Team Ch) 1973
Jun Scottish Girls 1980. Girl International 1957–58–59

Richmond, Mrs Maureen (*née* Walker)
Born Kilmacolm on 22nd April, 1955

Add 8 Greenbank Place, Morningside, Edinburgh
Cls Kilmacolm (Hon), Troon, Shiskine (Hon)
Int Curtis Cup 1974. Vagliano Trophy 1975. Scotland (Home Int) 1972–73–74–75–77–78; (Eur Team Ch) 1973–75
Jun British Girls 1972. Scottish Girls 1970–71–73. Girl International 1969–70–71–72–73
Mis Member of LGU Under-25 Team to tour Canada 1973. Selected for World Team Championship 1974 but declined due to studies

Robb, Miss Diane
See Mrs D Bailey

Roberts, Sharon
Born Penmaenmawr on 8th June, 1964

Add 1 Blaen Cwm, Llandudno, Gwynedd
Cls Llandudno (Maesdu)
Maj Keighley Open 1987. Birkdale Open 1988
Reg Midlands Match Play 1987–88
Chp Welsh Ladies Amateur 1984–88 runner-up 1987
Int Wales (Home Int) 1983–84–85–86–87–88; (Eur Team Ch) 1983–87

Robertson, Mrs IC, MBE (*née* Isabella McCorkindale)
Born Southend, Argyll, on 11th April, 1936

Add 15 Buchanan Drive, Bearsden, Glasgow G61 2EW
Cls Hon member of Dunaverty, Troon, Machrihanish, Carradale, Hermitage, Trophil Hill, Silloth-on-Solway, Fairfield CC (USA), Caernarvonshire, Trevose
Chp British Ladies Open Amateur 1981. British Ladies Stroke Play 1971–72–85. Runner-up British Ladies 1959–65–70. Scottish Ladies 1965–66–71–72–78–80, runner-up 1959–63–70. Second in British Ladies Open 1980 (also top Amateur). 2nd in British Ladies Open 1981 (also top Amateur).
Maj Sunningdale Foursomes 1960. Avia Foursomes 1972–81–84–86. Helen Holm Trophy 1973–79–86. Player's No 6 Cup 1973–76. Roehampton Gold Cup 1978 (tied)–79–81–82
Ove New Zealand Ladies Match Play 1971
Reg West of Scotland Ladies 1957–64–66–69. Dunbartonshire Ladies 1958–59–60–61–62–63–65–66–68–69–78
Int Curtis Cup 1960–66–68–70–72–82–86 (non-playing captain 1974–76). Vagliano Trophy 1959–63–65-69–71–81. World Team Championship (for Scotland) 1964, (for GB) 1966–68 (captain)–72–80–82. GB Commonwealth Team 1971, (non-playing captain 1975). Scotland (Home Int) 1958–59–60–61–62–63–64–65–66–69–72–73–78–80–81–82; (Eur Team Ch) 1965–67 (capt)–69–71–73–81–83; in Fiat Trophy 1978–80
Mis Daks Woman Golfer of the Year 1971–81. Frank Moran Trophy 1971. Leading qualifier in US Ladies Amateur 1978. Scottish Sportswoman of the Year 1968–71–78–81. Avia Golfer of the Year 1985

Robertson, Miss Janette
See Mrs I Wright

Robinson, Jeremy
Born 21st January, 1966. Turned Professional 1987

Chp English Amateur Stroke Play (Brabazon Trophy) 1987
Maj Lagonda Trophy 1985
Int Walker Cup 1987. England (Home Int) 1986

Robinson, Mrs Claire (*née* Nesbitt)
Born 7th March, 1953

Chp Irish Ladies Amateur 1976–80
Reg Ulster Ladies 1976–78
Int Curtis Cup 1980. Eur Team Ch 1975–77–79. Vagliano Trophy 1979

Roderick, R Neil
Born Swansea on 8th March, 1966

Add 1 Ael-y-Fro, Rhyd-y-Fro, Pontardawe, Swansea
Cls Pontardawe
Chp Welsh Amateur Stroke Play 1984–88
Reg Tenby Eagle 1988. Harlech Gold Cross 1986. Southerndown Silver Ram 1984–85–86
Int Wales (Home Int) 1983–84–85–86–87–88. GBI v Europe 1988
Jun Welsh Boys 1982–83

Roper, Roger
Born 15th April, 1962

Chp English Open Amateur Stroke Play 1985 (shared)
Int England (Home Int) 1984–85–86–87

Roy, Mrs Sandra Clair (*née* Needham)
Born Bishopton, Renfrewshire on 8th March, 1946

Add 4 Carron Crescent, Lenzie, Glasgow G66 5PJ
Cls Cawder (Hon), Machrihanish (Hon), Troon
Chp Scottish Ladies 1976
Maj Helen Holm Trophy 1974
Reg West of Scotland Ladies 1967–71–72–73–75. Lanarkshire Ladies 1969–72–73–77–83–84
Int Vagliano Trophy 1973–75, Scotland (Home Int) 1969–71–72–73–74–75–76–83; (Eur Team Ch) 1969–75–77
Mis Member of LGU team to tour South Africa 1974

Russell, David J
Born Birmingham on 2nd May, 1954. Turned Professional 1973

Maj Car Care Plan International 1985

Saddler, AC
Born Forfar, Angus on 11th August, 1935

Add Little Vantage, Forfar, Angus
Cls Forfar, Carnoustie
Chp Runner-up Scottish Amateur 1960
Maj Berkshire Trophy 1962

Int Walker Cup 1963–65–67 (non-playing captain 1977). Eisenhower Trophy 1962 (non-playing captain 1976) (winning team)–78. GB Commonwealth Team 1959–63–67; v Europe 1960–62–66 (non-playing captain 1976–78); v Professionals 1959–61. Scotland (Home Int) 1959–60–61–62–63–65 (non-playing captain 1974–75–76–77); (Eur Team Ch) (non-playing captain 1975–77)

Saunders, Miss Vivien Inez
Born Sutton on 24th November, 1946. Turned Professional 1969

Add Hunters Moon, Spicers Field, Oxshott, Surrey KT22 0UT. Tel (0372) 2389
Cls Tyrrells Wood, Fulwell
Chp British Ladies Open 1977. Runner-up British Ladies Amateur 1966
Maj Avia Foursomes 1967–78. Keighley Trophy 1981. In 1980 won British Car Auctions
Int Curtis Cup 1968. Vagliano Trophy 1967. GB Commonwealth Team 1967. England (Home Int) 1967–68; (Eur Team Ch) 1967; v France 1966–67
Jun Girl International 1964–65–66–67
Mis Qualified for USLPGA tour 1969, the first European to do so. Won Schweppes–Tarax Open (Australia) 1973 and Chrysler Open (Australia) 1973. Founder WPGA and Chairman 1978–79

Sewell, Douglas
Born Woking on 19th November, 1929. Turned Professional 1960

Chp English Amateur 1958–60. English Open Amateur Stroke Play 1957–59
Maj Sunningdale Foursomes 1959. Golf Illustrated Gold Vase 1960. Scrutton Jug 1959. Martini International 1970 (tied)
Oth Wentworth Pro-Am Foursomes 1968. West of England Open Professional 1968–70
Reg Surrey Amateur 1954–56–58
Int Walker Cup 1957–59. Eisenhower Trophy 1960. GB Commonwealth Team 1959. England (Home Int) 1956–57–58–59–60

Shapcott, Susan
Born 2nd November, 1969

Chp English Women's Stroke Play 1986. Welsh Open Amateur Stroke Play 1987–88
Reg Gloucestershire Ladies 1986
Int England (Home Int) 1986–88. Curtis Cup 1988

Sharp, Mrs Christine (*née* Holroyd)
Born 21st January, 1954. Turned Professional 1978

Jun Essex Girls 1971–72
WPGA Billingham South Staffs 1980. Clandeboye Classic 1983. JS Bloor Eastleigh Classic 1985

Shaw, Graeme
Born Glasgow on 6th June, 1960

Reg Glasgow Amateur 1986. Scottish Champion of Champions 1987
Int Walker Cup 1987. (Scotland) Home Int 1984–86–87–88

Sheahan, Dr David B
Born Southsea, England on 25th February, 1940

Add 57 Terenure Road East, Dublin 6. Tel (0001) 908204
Cls Grange
Chp Irish Amateur 1961–66–70
Maj Jeyes Professional 1962 (as an Amateur)
Oth Boyd Quaich 1962
Int Walker Cup 1963. GB v Europe 1962–64. Ireland (Home Int) 1961–62–63–64–65–66–67–70; (Eur Team Ch) 1965–67 (winning team on both occasions)

Shepperson, AE
Born Sutton-in-Ashfield on 8th April, 1936

Add Orchard House, High Oakham Road, Mansfield, Nottinghamshire
Cls Coxmoor (Hon), Notts
Chp Second in English Open Amateur Stroke Play 1958–62
Oth President's Putter 1957
Reg Nottinghamshire Amateur 1955–58–61–65. Nottinghamshire Open 1955–58
Int Walker Cup 1957–59. England (Home Int) 1956–57–58–59–60–62
Jun British Boys 1953

Shingler, Terence Robert
Born Kearsley, Lancashire on 9th August, 1935

Add Westways, 55 Sandhills Lane, Barnt Green, nr Birmingham B45 8NU
Cls Blackwell (Hon), Handsworth (Hon)
Chp English Amateur 1977. Worcestershire Amateur 1983
Maj Homer Salver 1972. Formby Hare 1974
Reg Leicester & Rutland Amateur 1962–63–64. Leicester & Rutland Open 1965–66. Worcestershire Amateur 1972–73. Worcestershire Open 1970–74. Worcestershire Amateur Match Play 1975–76–79
Int England (Home Int) 1977

Simpson, Linda (*née* Moore)
Born 7th October, 1961

Reg Cornwall Ladies 1979–80–81. South-West Ladies 1981
Int Curtis Cup 1980. Eur Team Ch 1981

Sinclair, Alexander
Born West Kilbride, Ayrshire on 6th July, 1920

Add 17 Blairston Avenue, Bothwell, Glasgow
Cls Royal and Ancient, West Kilbride (Hon), Drumpellier (Hon), Bothwell Castle (Hon), Royal Troon (Hon)
Maj Newlands Trophy 1950
Oth Royal and Ancient Silver Cross 1972. Royal Medal 1977. Scottish Open Amateur Seniors 1979
Reg West of Scotland Amateur 1950. Lanarkshire Amateur 1952–59–61. Glasgow Amateur 1961
Int Scotland (Home Int) 1950, (non-playing captain 1966–67). Non-playing captain Eur Team Ch 1967
Mis Chairman R & A Selection Committee from 1969 to 1975. Leading Amateur (joint second) in Northern Open 1948. President Scottish Golf Union 1976–78. Frank Moran Trophy 1978. Chairman R & A Amateur Status Committee 1979–81. President European Golf Association 1981–82–83. Captain of Royal and Ancient 1988

Slark, Mrs WA (*née* Ruth Porter)
Born Chesterfield on 6th May, 1939

Add 2 Shagbrook, Reigate Heath, Reigate, Surrey
Cls Long Ashton (Hon), Bath, Burnham and Berrow, Reigate Heath, Walton Heath
Chp English Ladies 1959–61–65, runner-up 1978
Maj Astor Prince's 1961. Fairway and Hazard Foursomes 1958. Roehampton Gold Cup 1963. Astor Salver 1962–63. Hovis Ladies 1966 (tied). Avia Foursomes 1968
Ove Australian Ladies runner-up 1963
Reg South Western Ladies 1956–57–60–61–62–64–65–66–67–69–72–77–79. Gloucestershire Ladies 1957–59–61–62–63–64–66–67–69–73–74–75–76–77

Int Curtis Cup 1960–62–64. Vagliano Trophy 1959–61–65. GB Commonwealth Team 1963. World Team Ch 1964–66. England (Home Int) 1959–60–61–62–64–65–66–68–75–78; (Eur Team Ch) 1965
Jun British Girls 1956. Scottish Girls Open Stroke Play 1958. Girls International 1955–56–57

Smith, Mrs Anne (formerly Stant, *née* Willard)
Born Calcutta, India on 23rd May, 1950

Add 19 Broadway, Walsall, West Midlands
Cls Walsall, Hon member of Gorleston, Purdis Heath (Ipswich), Ganton, Beau Desert
Chp British Ladies Stroke Play 1973
Maj Sunningdale Foursomes 1970. Central England Mixed Foursomes 1968. Hoylake Mixed Foursomes 1978
Reg Suffolk Ladies 1967–69–70–71. Midland Ladies 1973–75. Staffordshire Ladies 1975–78–79, runner-up 1977
Int England (Home Int) 1974–75–76; (Eur Team Ch) 1975. Vagliano Trophy 1975. GB Commonwealth Team 1975. Curtis Cup 1976
Jun British Girls 1965. English Girls 1967. Girl International 1965–66–67–68
Mis Member of LGU Touring Team to South Africa 1974

Smith, William Dickson
Born Glasgow on 2nd February, 1918

Add 12 Douglas Court, Beach Road, Troon
Cls Prestwick (Hon), Royal and Ancient, Royal Troon, Selkirk (Hon), Southerness, Gullane
Chp Scottish Amateur 1958. Scottish Senior Open Amateur 1983
Maj Worplesdon Mixed Foursomes 1957
Ove Indian Open Amateur 1945. Portuguese Open Amateur 1967–70
Oth Royal and Ancient Royal Medal 1971
Reg Border Amateur 1949–51–57–63. Dumfriesshire Amateur 1956
Int Walker Cup 1959. GB v Europe 1958. Scotland (Home Int) 1957–58–59–60–63 (non-playing captain 1983); v Scandinavia 1958–60
Mis Leading Amateur (5th) Open Championship 1957

Smye, Miss Catherine
See Mrs PG McCann

Smyth, Des
Born Drogheda on 12th February, 1953. Turned Professional 1973

Maj PGA Match Play 1979. Newcastle Brown 900 1980. Greater Manchester Open 1980. Coral Classic 1981. Sanyo Open 1983. Jersey Open 1988
Oth Irish Professional 1979. Carrolls Irish Match Play 1980. Irish Dunlop 1980
Int Ryder Cup 1979–81. GB v Europe 1980. Ireland in World Cup 1979–80–82–83. Hennessy-Cognac Cup 1984. Dunhill Cup 1985–86–87–88 (winners)
Am Ireland (Home Int) 1972–73; (Eur Team Ch) 1973

Sommerville, Miss Dorothea
See Mrs JL Hastings

Soulsby, Janet
Born Corbridge on 25th December, 1964. Turned Professional 1985

Chp Ladies British Stroke Play 1981
Reg Northumberland Ladies 1983
Int Curtis Cup 1982

Spearman, Mrs Marley
See Mrs M Harris

Squirrell, Hew Crawford
Born Cardiff on 15th August, 1932

Add The Nut House, 8 Hill Rise, Rickmansworth, Hertfordshire
Cls Hon member of Cardiff, Moseley, Killarney
Chp Welsh Amateur 1958–59–60–64–65, runner-up 1962–71
Maj Antlers Royal Mid-Surrey 1959–61. Hampshire Hog 1961. Berkhamsted Trophy 1960–63
Oth Boyd Quaich 1955
Reg Glamorgan Amateur 1959–65. Herts Amateur 1963–73
Int Wales (Home Int) 1955–56–57–58–59–60–61–62–63–64–65–66–67–68–69–70–71 (captain 1969–70–71)–73–74–75; (Eur Team Ch) 1965–67–69–71–75; v France 1975
Mis Deputy-Director Golf Foundation

Stant, Mrs Anne
See Mrs A Smith

Stephen, Alexander R (Sandy)
Born St Andrews on 8th January, 1954. Turned Professional 1985

Add 51 Station Park, Lower Largo, Fife
Cls Lundin (Hon), Muckhart (Hon), Broomieknowe
Chp Scottish Amateur 1971
Maj East of Scotland Open Amateur 1974–77–83–84. West of Scotland Open Amateur 1975. Scottish Champion of Champions 1984
Reg North of Scotland Open Amateur 1972–77. Fife Amateur 1973. Lothians Amateur 1978
Int GB v Europe 1972. Scotland (Home Int) 1971–72–73–74–75–76–77–84–85; (Eur Team Ch) 1975; v Spain 1974; v Belgium 1975–77–78. Walker Cup 1985
Jun Scottish Boys 1970. Boys International 1970–71. Youth International 1972–73–74–75
Mis Finished third in World Boys International Trophy (USA) 1970

Stevens, David Llewellyn
Born Church Village, Glamorgan on 14th April, 1950

Add Nant-y-Garth, Gwaelod-y-Garth, Taffs Well, Cardiff
Cls Llantrisant and Pontyclun, Southerndown, Killarney (Hon)
Chp Welsh Amateur Stroke Play 1969. Welsh Amateur 1977–80
Reg Glamorgan Amateur 1974–76–80
Int Wales (Home Int) 1968–69–70–74–75–76–78–80–82; (Eur Team Ch) 1969–77; v France 1976; v Denmark 1977; in Fiat Trophy 1980

Stewart, Gillian
Born Inverness on 21st October, 1958. Turned Professional 1985

Add 14 Annfield Road, Inverness
Cls Inverness (Hon), Nairn
Chp Scottish Ladies 1979–83–84. Britsh Ladies Match Play runner-up 1982. IBM European Open 1984 (as Amateur)
Maj Helen Holm Trophy 1981–84
Reg Northern Counties Ladies 1976–78–82. North of Scotland Ladies 1975–78–80–82-83.
Int GB Commonwealth Team 1979–83. Vagliano Trophy 1979–81–83. Curtis Cup 1980–82. Scotland (Home Int) 1979–80–81–82–83–84; (Eur Team Ch) 1979–81–83. World Cup 1982–84
Jun British Girls 1976. Girl International 1975–76–77. Scottish Under-19 Stroke Play Champion 1975

Mis Member of Scottish team which won the 1980 European Junior Team Championship. Avia Golfer of the Year 1984.
WPGA Ford Ladies Classic 1985–87

Storey, Eustace Francis
Born Lancaster on 30th August, 1901

Add Flat 4, Larchwood Lodge, Larch Avenue, Sunninghill, Berkshire
Cls Swinley Forest
Chp Runner-up Amateur Championship 1924
Maj Worplesdon Mixed Foursomes 1938–48
Oth President's Putter 1926 (tied)
Int Walker Cup 1924–26–28. England (Home Int)1924–25–26–27–28–30–36; v France 1936
Mis Leading Amateur in Open Championship 1938

Stowe, Charles
Born Sandyfields, Sedgley on 11th January, 1909

Add 46 Butts Road, Penn, Wolverhampton
Cls Penn, Brocton Hall, Beau Desert, Shifnal
Chp Runner-up Amateur Championship 1948. English Open Amateur Stroke Play 1948–53. Runner-up English Amateur 1947–49
Maj Prince of Wales Challenge Cup 1937–49
Reg Midland Counties Amateur 1935–48–59–63. Staffordshire Amateur 1934–39–46–48–53–54–57–64. Staffordshire Open 1948
Int Walker Cup 1938–47. England (Home Int) 1935–36–37–38–46–49; v France 1938–39
Mis Played for British Seniors 1967

Stuart, Hugh Bannerman
Born Forres on 27th June, 1942

Add 33 Loirston Manor, Cove, Aberdeen
Cls Forres (Hon), Murcar (Hon)
Chp Scottish Amateur 1972, runner-up 1970–76
Reg North of Scotland Amateur 1967–74. Moray Amateur 1960. Nairnshire Amateur 1966
Int Walker Cup 1971–73–75. GB Commonwealth Team 1971. Eisenhower Trophy 1972. GB v Europe 1968–72–74. Scotland (Home Int) 1967–68–70–71–72–73–74–76; (Eur Team Ch) 1969–71–73–75; v Belgium 1973–75
Jun Scottish Boys 1959. Boy International 1959
Mis Won all his matches in 1971 Walker Cup. Member of European Team to tour South Africa 1974

Swallow, Carole
Born 9th August, 1967. Turned Professional 1985

Chp Welsh Ladies Open Amateur Stroke Play 1985
Int England (Eur Team Ch) 1985; (Home Int) 1985
Jun British Girls 1984. English Girls 1984

Taylor, Alastair Ramsey
Born Lanarkshire on 21st May, 1959

Add 35 Abbotsford Brae, East Mains, East Kilbride, Lanarkshire
Cls East Kilbride
Chp Scottish Open Amateur Stroke Play 1978
Int Scotland in Fiat Trophy 1978; v England 1979
Jun Boy International 1976. Youth International 1977–78–79–80

Thirlwell, Alan
Born 8th August, 1928

Add 19 Birch Green, Formby, Merseyside L37 1NG
Cls Gosforth, Formby
Chp Runner-up Amateur Championship 1958–72. English Amateur 1954–55, runner-up 1963. Second in English Open Amateur Stroke Play 1964
Maj County Champion of Champions 1962. Wentworth Pro-Am Foursomes 1960–61–68
Reg Northumberland Amateur 1952–55–62–64. Northumberland and Durham Open 1960
Int Walker Cup 1957. GB Commonwealth Team 1954–63. GB v Europe 1956–58; v Denmark 1955; v Professionals 1963. England (Home Int) 1951–52–54–55–56–57–58–59–63–64; v France 1954–56-59
Mis Semi-finalist Canadian Amateur 1957. EGU Selector 1974 to 1977,. Secretary CONGU

Thom, Kenneth Gordon
Born 1st March, 1922

Add 305 London Road, Westcliffe-on-Sea
Cls Hendon
Chp Runner-up English Amateur 1946
Reg Middlesex Amateur 1947-48
Int Walker Cup 1949. England (Home Int) 1947–48–49–53
Jun Boy International 1939

Thomas, David C
Born Newcastle-upon-Tyne on 16th August, 1934. Turned Professional 1949

Opn Second in Open Championship 1958 (lost play-off for title). Second 1966
Tls Belgian Open 1955. Dutch Open 1958. French Open 1959
Maj Esso Golden 1961 (tied)–62–66. PGA Match Play 1963. Silentnight 1965 (tied). Penfold-Swallow 1966. Jeyes 1966. Penfold 1968 (tied). Graham Textiles 1969. Pains-Wessex 1969
Ove Caltex (NZ) 1958–59. Olgiata Trophy (Rome) 1963
Oth British Assistants 1955. Wentworth Pro-Am Foursomes 1960–61
Int Ryder Cup 1959–63–65–67. Wales in World Cup 1957–58–59–60–61–62–63–66–67–69–70. Wales in Double Diamond 1972–73
Mis Won qualifying competition for US Open 1964

Thomas, Tegwen (*née* Perkins)
Born Cardiff on 2nd October, 1955

Add 35 Headland Road, Bishopston, Swansea SA3 3DH
Cls Wenvoe Castle, Porthcawl, Pennard
Chp Welsh Ladies Amateur 1976–77. Welsh Ladies Open Amateur Stroke Play 1980. Second in British Ladies Amateur Stroke Play 1974
Maj Wills Match Play 1973. Avia Foursomes 1977. Worplesdon Mixed Foursomes 1973–78
Reg South-Western Ladies 1973–74–76. Glamorganshire Ladies 1972–74–75–77–78–80–81–83
Int Curtis Cup 1974–76–78–80. Vagliano Trophy 1973–75–77–79. World Team Championship 1974. Wales (Home Int) 1972–73–74–75–76–77–78–79–80–81–82–83–84; (Eur Team Ch) 1975–77–79–81-83; in Fiat Trophy 1978. GB Commonwealth Team 1975-79. GB in Colombian International 1977-79
Jun Welsh Girls 1970. Girl International 1970–71–72-73
Mis Member of LGU Team to tour South Africa 1974. First Welsh player in Curtis Cup Team. In 1976 became first Welsh Woman player to win all matches in Home Internationals. Daks Woman Golfer of the Year 1976 (joint)

Thomas, Vicki (*née* Rawlings)
Born Northampton on 27th October, 1954

Add 9 South Close, Bishopston, Swansea
Cls Bargoed, Pennard
Chp Welsh Ladies Amateur 1979–80–83–85–86–87. Second in British Ladies Amateur Stroke Play 1979.

Welsh Ladies Open Stroke Play 1981–82, runner-up 1980
Maj Roehampton Gold Cup 1983–85. Cotswold Gold Vase 1983. Keithley Trophy 1983
Reg Glamorganshire Ladies 1970–71–79
Int GB Commonwealth Team 1979–83–87. Vagliano Trophy 1979–83–85–87. Wales (Home Int) 1971–88 inclusive; (Eur Team Ch) 1973–75–77–79–81–83–87. Curtis Cup 1982–84–86–88
Jun Welsh Girls 1973. Girl International 1969–70–71–72–73

Thompson, Martyn S
Born 27th January, 1964

Chp Amateur Champion 1982
Int Walker Cup 1983. England (Home Int) 1982

Thomson, Muriel
Born Aberdeen on 12th December, 1954. Turned Professional 1979

Cls Murcar (Hon)
Chp Runner-up Scottish Ladies 1977
Maj Helen Holm Trophy 1975–76. Winner of Elizabeth Ann Classic 1981
Ove Canadian Ladies Foursomes 1978
Reg North of Scotland Ladies 1973–74. Aberdeenshire Ladies 1977
Int Curtis Cup 1978. Vagliano Trophy 1977. World Team Championship 1978. GB in Colombian International 1979. Scotland (Home Int) 1974–75–76–77–78; (Eur Team Ch) 1957–77
Jun Girl International 1970–71–72–73
WPGA Carlsberg (Tyrrells Wood) 1980. Viscount Double Glazing 1980. Barnham Broom 1980. Headed Carlsberg and Hambro Life Order of Merit 1980. Winner of Frank Moran Trophy 1981. Order of Merit 1983. Guernsey Open 1984. Sands International 1984. Laing Ladies Classic 1985. Irish Open 1986. Ford Ladies Classic 1986

Thornhill, Jill
Born 18th August, 1942

Add 10 Wallace Fields, Epsom, Surrey
Cls Walton Heath, Silloth-on-Solway
Chp Runner-up English Ladies 1974. British Ladies' Amateur 1983
Maj Avia Foursomes 1970–83. Astor Salver 1972–75. Newmark International 1974. Worplesdon Mixed Foursomes 1975. Hampshire Rose 1982–87
Ove Belgian Ladies 1967
Reg South Eastern Ladies 1964–64–85. Surrey Ladies 1962–64–65–73–74–77–78–81–82–83–84
Int Vagliano Trophy 1965–83–85-87. England (Home Int) 1964–65–74–82–83–84–85–86–87–88. Commonwealth Team Ch 1983; (Eur Team Ch) 1983. Curtis Cup 1984–86–88. Avia Golfer of the Year 1983

Tiernan, Miss Clarrie
See Mrs Reddan

Torrance, Sam
Born Largs, Ayrshire on 24th August, 1953. Turned Professional 1970

Tls Zambian Open 1975. Colombian Open 1979. Spanish Open 1982. Portuguese Open 1982–83. Scandinavian Open 1983. Tunisian Open 1984. Italian Open 1987
Maj Piccadilly Medal 1976. Martini 1976. Benson & Hedges International Open 1984. Sanyo Open 1984. Monte Carlo Open 1985
Ove Australian PGA 1980
Oth Lord Derby's Under-25 1972. Scottish Uniroyal 1975. Scottish Professional 1978–80
Int GB v Europe 1976–78–80. Scotland in World Cup 1976–78–82–84–85. Scotland in Double Diamond 1973–76–77. Ryder Cup 1983–85. Hennessy-Cognac Cup 1982–84. Dunhill Cup 1985–86–87
Am Boy International 1970
Mis Rookie of the Year 1982

Townsend, Peter Michael Paul
Born Cambridge on 16th September, 1946. Turned Professional 1966

Tls Dutch Open 1967. Swiss Open 1971. Zambian Open 1978
Chp English Open Amateur Stroke Play 1966
Maj Duncan Putter 1965. Mullingar Trophy 1965–66. Lytham Trophy 1966. Golf Illustrated Gold Vase 1966. Prince of Wales Challenge Cup 1966. Royal St George's Challenge Cup 1966. Berkhamsted Trophy 1966. PGA Close 1968
Ove Chesterfield (USA) 1968. Western Australia Open 1968. Walworth Aloyco 1971. Los Lagaratos Open 1972–78. Caracas Open 1969. ICL International (SA) 1975. Moroccan Grand Prix 1978. Caribbean Open 1978. Laurent Perrier 1981
Oth Carris Trophy 1964. Coca-Cola Young Professionals 1968. Carrolls Irish Match Play 1971–76. Irish Dunlop 1977
Reg Herts Amateur 1964
Int Walker Cup 1965. GB v Europe 1966. Eisenhower Trophy 1966. England (Home Int) 1965–66. Ryder Cup 1969–71. England in World Cup 1969–74. England in Double Diamond 1971–72–74. GB v Europe 1974
Jun British Boys 1962–64. British Youths 1975
Mis Equalled British PGA record of 7 consecutive birdies in 1974 Viyella PGA Championship. Captain PGA 1984

Tucker, William Iestyn
Born Nantyglo, Monmouth on 9th December, 1926

Add Nant Morlais, Caeracca Villas, Pant, Merthyr Tydfil
Cls Monmouthshire, Brecon, Killarney, Morlais Castle, Tredegar and Rhymney, Pontynewydd, Llantrisant, Radyr, Whitehall
Chp Welsh Amateur 1933–36, runner-up 1951–56–64–67–75–76. Welsh Amateur Stroke Play 1976
Maj Duncan Putter 1960–61 (tied)–63–69–76
Reg Monmouthshire Amateur 1949–52–53–54–55–56–57–58–59–60–61–62–63–67–69–74. Gwent Amateur 1976
Int Wales (Home Int) 1949–50–51–52–53–54–55–56–57–58–59–60–61–62–63–64–65–66–67–68–69–70–71–72–74–75; (Eur Team Ch) 1965-67-69-75; v Australia 1953; v France 1975. Captain Welsh Team 1966-67-68
Mis Record number of consecutive international appearances for Wales – from 1949-72. On 25th October, 1972 completed a Medal round at Cardiff GC (SSS 68) in 59 strokes. Holed in one 12 times

Uzielli, Mrs WJ (*née* Angela Carrick)
Born Swanton Morley, Norfolk on 1st February, 1940

Add Buchurst Park Cottage, Buckhurst Road, Cheapside, Ascot, Berkshire
Cls Hon member of Berkshire, Denham, Trevose, Hunstanton
Chp British Ladies Open Amateur 1977. Runner-up English Ladies Amateur 1976
Maj Astor Salver 1971–73 (tied)–77–81. Roehampton Gold Cup 1977. Avia Foursomes 1982. Hampshire Rose 1985
Reg Berkshire Ladies 1976–77–78–79–80–81–83

Int Curtis Cup 1978. Vagliano Trophy 1977. England (Home Int) 1976–77–78; (Eur Team Ch) 1977
Mis Daks Woman Golfer of the Year 1977

Valentine, Mrs George, MBE (*née* Jessie Anderson)

Born Perth on 18th March, 1915. Turned Professional 1960

Add Daintree, 11 Brompton Terrace, Perth
Cls Hon member of Craigie Hill, St Rule, Hunstanton, Blairgowrie, Murrayshall
Chp British Ladies 1937–55–58, runner-up 1950–57. Scottish Ladies 1938–39–51–53–55–56, runner-up 1934–54
Maj Spalding Ladies 1957. Kayser Bondor Foursomes 1959–61. Worplesdon Mixed Foursomes 1963–64–65
Ove New Zealand Ladies 1935. French Ladies 1936
Reg East of Scotland Ladies 1936–38–39–50
Int Curtis Cup 1936–38–50–52–54–56–58. GB v France 1935–36–38–39–47–49–51–55; v Belgium 1949–51–54–55; v Canada 1938–50. GB Commonwealth Team 1953–55 (non-playing captain 1959). Scotland (Home Int) 1934–35–36–37–38–39–47–49–50–51–52–53–54–55–56–57–58
Jun British Girls 1933
Mis Semi-finalist Canadian Ladies 1938. Member of LGU Team to Australia and New Zealand 1935. Frank Moran Trophy 1967

Vaughan, Miss Sheila

See Mrs S Maher

Wade, Julie

Chp English Ladies Stroke Play 1987. English Ladies Amateur 1988
Maj World Fourball Ch with Helen Wadsworth 1987
Int England (Home Int) 1987–88. Curtis Cup 1988

Wadsworth, Helen

Born on the Gower, Swansea on 7th April, 1964

Add Grove Lodge, Manor Avenue, Deal
Cls Royal Cinque Ports
Chp Welsh Ladies Open Amateur Stroke Play 1986
Maj Astor Salver 1985. World Fourball Ch with Julie Wade 1987
Oth South-East Girls 1981
Int Wales (Home Int) 1987–88; (Eur Team Ch) 1985

Waite, Claire

Born Marlborough on 4th November, 1964. Turned Professional 1985

Chp British Girls 1982. English Ladies 1984. British Ladies Stroke-Play 1984
Ove Australian Stroke-Play Team 1982. South Atlantic (USA) 1984. Trans National (USA) 1984
Reg Wiltshire Ladies 1980–81–83
Int England (Home Int) 1981–82–83. European Team Championship 1983. Commonwealth Tournament 1983. Vagliano Trophy 1983. Curtis Cup 1984. Espirito Santo 1984
Jun English Girl International 1981–82. English Girls 1982
Mis Avia Golfer of the Year 1984

Waites, Brian J

Born Bolton on 1st March, 1940. Turned Professional 1957

Tls Kenya Open 1980
Maj Tournament Players' Championship 1978. Car Care Plan International 1982
Ove Mufulira Open (Zambia) 1980–82. Cock of North (Zambia) Open 1985
Oth Midland Open 1971–76–81. Midland Professional Stroke Play 1972–77–78–79. Midland Professional Match Play 1972–73–74. Hennessy-Cognac Cup 1984
Int GB v Europe 1980. England in World Cup 1980–82–83

Walker, Carole Michelle

Born Alwoodley, nr Leeds on 17th December, 1952. Turned Professional 1973

Add 127 Victoria Road, New Barnet, Hertfordshire EN4 9PE
Chp British Ladies 1971–72, runner-up 1973. Second in British Ladies Stroke Play 1972. English Ladies 1973. Second in British Ladies Open 1979
Maj Hovis Ladies 1972. Sunningdale Foursomes 1982
Ove Portuguese Ladies 1972. US Trans-Mississippi 1972. Spanish Ladies 1973
Reg Kent Ladies 1971
Int Curtis Cup 1972. GB Commonwealth Team 1971. World Team Championship 1972. Vagliano Trophy 1971. England (Home Int) 1970–72; (Eur Team Ch) 1971–73
Jun Girl International 1969–70–71. French Girls Under-22 Open 1971
Mis Golf Writers Trophy 1972. Undefeated in 1972 Curtis Cup. First British woman to win a major US event for 36 years. Daks Woman Golfer of the Year 1972
WPGA Awarded USLPGA card 1974, then on having to re-qualify in 1975 school, led qualifiers. Tied first in Jerry Lewis Classic 1976 but lost play-off. In 1979 won Carlsberg (Strensall), won Carlsberg (St Pierre) 1981. In 1980 won Lambert and Butler Match Play. Sunningdale Foursomes 1982. Sands International 1983. Baume & Mercier Classic, Lorne Stewart Match Play 1984. Chairman WPGA 1981–82–83–84

Walker, Mrs JB, MBE

Born Ireland on 21st June, 1896

Cls Gosforth, Hon member of Troon, Island, Malahide, Alnmouth, Foxton Hall
Chp Irish Ladies 1930, runner-up 1934
Ove Australian Ladies 1935. Runner-up New Zealand Ladies 1935
Reg Ayrshire Ladies 1934–37–38
Int Curtis Cup 1934–36–38. GB v France 1935–38–39; v Canada 1938. Ireland (Home Int) 1928–29–30–31–32–33–34–35–36–37–38–48
Mis Two holes-in-one in the same week

Walker, James

Born Bartonholme, by Irvine, on 11th February, 1921

Add 17 Greenbank Road, Irvine, Ayrshire
Cls Irvine Bogside
Chp Scottish Amateur 1961. Runner-up Amateur Championship 1961
Reg West of Scotland Amateur 1954. Ayrshire Amateur 1956 (tied)
Int Walker Cup 1961, selected 1959. GB v Europe 1958–60; v Professionals 1958–60. Scotland (Home Int) 1954–55–57–58–60–61–62–63

Walker, Kenneth

Born Edinburgh on 1st December, 1966

Chp Scottish Open Amateur Stroke Play 1986
Maj Edward Trophy 1984
Oth Scottish Universities Individual 1985
Int Scotland (Home Int) 1986

Walker, Miss Maureen
See Mrs Richmond

Walter, Julie
Born 4th December, 1952

Chp English Ladies Amateur 1982
Reg Midland Ladies 1980
Int England (Home Int) 1974–79–80–82–86

Walton, Philip
Born Dublin on 28th March, 1962. Turned Professional 1983

Chp Irish Amateur 1982
Maj Scottish Open Amateur Stroke Play 1981
Int Walker Cup 1981–83. Ireland (Home Int) 1980–81; (Eur Team Ch) 1981

Ward, Miss Angela
See Mrs A Bonallack

Ward, Charles Harold
Born Birmingham on 16th September, 1911

Opn Third in Open Championship 1948–51, leading British player (4th) 1946
Maj Daily Mail Victory 1945. Silver King 1948 (tied). Yorkshire Evening News 1948. Spalding 1949. North British-Harrogate 1949. Dunlop Masters 1949. Daily Mail 1950. Dunlop 1951. Lotus 1951. PGA Close 1956
Oth West of England Open Professional 1937. Daily Telegraph Pro-Am 1947–48. Midland Professional 1933–34–50–53–55–63. Midland Open 1949–51–52–54–57
Int Ryder Cup 1947–49–51
Mis Vardon Trophy 1948–49

Way, Paul
Born Kingsbury, Middx on 12th March, 1963. Turned Professional 1981

Tls KLM Dutch Open 1982. Whyte & McKay PGA 1985. European Open 1987
Int Ryder Cup 1983–85. England in World Cup 1985. Dunhill Cup 1985
Am Walker Cup 1981. English Open Amateur Stroke Play Champion 1981
Mis Second Lawrence Batley International 1983. Second St Mellion Time Share Tournament 1983

Weeks, Kevin

Chp English Amateur 1987
Int England (Home Int) 1987–88; v France 1988

Wethered, Miss Joyce
See Lady Heathcoat-Amory

Whelan, David
Born Sunderland on 28th August, 1961. Turned Professional 1981

Ove Barcelona Open 1988

White, Alison
Born Nairn on 27th May, 1956

Add 8 Buchanan Gardens, St Andrews, Fife
Cls Nairn, St Rule, St Regulus
Int Scottish Girls 1973–74
Mis PGA Tournament Administrator 1979–84. LGU General Administrator since 1984

White, Ronald James
Born Wallasey on 9th April, 1921

Add Lark Rise, 11 Oldfield Drive, Heswall, Wirral, Merseyside
Cls Hon member of Royal Birkdale, Woolton, Buxton and High Peak, Killarney
Chp English Amateur 1949, runner-up 1953. English Open Amateur Stroke Play 1950–51
Maj Golf Illustrated Gold Vase 1949. Daily Telegraph Pro-Am 1947–49
Oth Carris Trophy 1937. British Seniors Open Amateur 1978–79
Reg Lancashire Amateur 1948
Int Walker Cup 1947–49–51–53–55. England (Home Int) 1947–48–49–53; France 1947–48
Jun Boy International 1936–37–38

Whitlock, Miss SC
See Mrs Susan Hedges

Willard, Miss A
See Mrs A Smith

Wilson, Miss Enid
Born Stonebroom, nr Alfreton, Derbyshire on 15th March, 1910

Add The Oast, Redbridge Farm, Redbridge Lane, Crowborough, East Sussex TN6 3SR
Cls Hon member of Notts, Sherwood Forest, Chesterfield, Bramley, Sandy Lodge, Knole Park, North Hants, Crowborough
Chp British Ladies 1931–32–33. English Ladies 1928–30, runner-up 1927
Maj Roehampton Gold Cup 1930
Reg Midland Ladies 1926–28–29–30. Derbyshire Ladies 1925–26. Cheshire Ladies 1933
Int Curtis Cup 1932. England (Home Int) 1928–29–30
Jun British Girls 1925
Mis Semi-finalist US Ladies Amateur 1931–33

Winchester, Roger
Born 28th March, 1967

Chp English Amateur 1985
Int England (Home Int) 1985. Youth (GBI) v Europe 1987

Wood, David K
Born 27th March, 1963

Chp Welsh Amateur 1982
Maj Lytham Trophy 1987
Int Wales (Home Int) 1982–83–84–85–86

Woosnam, Ian
Born 2nd March, 1958. Turned Professional 1976

Tls Swiss Open 1982. Scandinavian Open 1984. Zambian Open 1985. Kenya Open 1986. Hong Kong Open 1987. Jersey Open 1987. Cepsa Madrid Open 1987. Bells Scottish Open 1987. Lancome Trophy 1987. Suntory World Match Play 1987. Volvo PGA 1988. Irish Open 1988. European Open 1988.
Maj Silk Cut Masters 1983. Lawrence Batley TPC 1986
Int GB and Ireland Team Hennessy-Cognac Cup 1982. Ryder Cup 1983–85–87. Represented Wales in World Cup 1980–82–83–84–85. Hennessy-Cognac Cup 1984. Dunhill Cup 1985–86–87–88. Nissan Cup 1986. Kirin Cup 1987
Mis News of the World Under-23 Match Play 1982. Cacharel Under-25 1982

Wright, Mrs Innes (*née* Janette Robertson)
Born Glasgow on 7th January, 1935

Add Glenelg, Aboyne, Aberdeenshire
Cls Hon member of Lenzie, Troon, Cruden Bay, Aboyne, St Rule
Chp Scottish Ladies 1959–60–61–73, runner-up 1958
Maj Kayser Bondor Foursomes 1958 (tied)–61. Worplesdon Mixed Foursomes 1959
Reg North of Scotland Ladies 1970. Lanarkshire Ladies 1954–55–56–57–58–59. West of Scotland Ladies 1956–58–59
Int Curtis Cup 1954–56–58–60. Vagliano Trophy 1959–61. GB v France 1957; v Belgium 1957; v Canada 1954. GB Commonwealth Team 1959. Scotland (Home Int) 1952–53–54–55–56–57–58–59–60–61–63–65–66–67–73 (non-playing captain 1978–79–80); (Eur Team Ch) 1965–73 (non-playing captain 1979)
Jun British Girls 1950. Girl International 1950–51–52–53

Wright, Miss Pamela
Born 24th January, 1964

Reg Aberdenshire Ladies 1982–85
Int Vilmorin Trophy 1980. European Team Championship 1981–83. Vagliano Trophy 1981. Scotland (Home Int) 1982–83–84
Jun North of Scotland Girls 1979. Scottish Girls International 1979–80. British Under-18 1980

Overseas Players

Explanations of abbreviations used

Add	Present Address
Bri	Victories (also second place in a few top events) in British events
Nat	Victories (also second place in a few top events) in major events in native country
For	Victories (also second place in a few top events) in important foreign events excluding British and native country
Eur	European Tour } excluding 4 majors
USC	United States Tour } shown separately
Jap	Japanese Tour
ANZ	Australia and New Zealand Tour
Asa	Far East Tour
SAf	South African Tour
SAm	South American Tour
Saf	Safari Tour
LPGA	Number of victories on US circuit excluding US Open, Masters and USPGA which are shown separately
Oth	Victories in less important events in native country or overseas
Sen	Senior Tour Events
Int	International Appearances
Mis	Miscellaneous

Aaron, Tommy

Born Gainesville, Georgia, USA on 22nd February, 1937. Turned Professional 1961

Nat Runner-up US Amateur 1958. US Masters 1973. USPGA second 1972
For Canadian Open 1969
USC 1970–one
Oth Lancôme Trophy 1972
Int Walker Cup 1959. Ryder Cup 1969–73
Mis Was nine times second before winning his first event

Alcott, Amy

Born Kansas City, Missouri, USA on 22nd February, 1956. Turned Professional 1975

Nat US Women's Open 1980
LPGA 1985–three, 1986–two (1975–86: 26 wins)

Aoki, Isao

Born Abiko, Chiba, Japan on 31st August, 1942. Turned Professional 1964

Nat Japan Open 1983-87. Japan Open 1987. Japan PGA 1973–81–86
For Hawaiian Open 1983. Dunlop Jap International 1987.
Eur World Match Play Championship 1978. European Open 1983
Int Japan v US 1982–83–84. Nissan Cup 1985. Dunhill Cup 1985. Kirin Cup 1987

Azinger, Paul William

Born Holyoke Massachusetts, USA on 6th January, 1960. Turned Professional 1981

Bri 2nd in Open 1987
USC 1987 – three (Phoenix Open, Las Vegas Invitation, Greater Hartford Open); 1988 – one (Hertz Bay Hill Classic)

Baiocchi, Hugh

Born Johannesburg on 17th August, 1946. Turned Professional 1971

Bri PGA Match Play 1977
Nat South African Amateur 1970. South African Open 1978. South African PGA 1980
For Brazilian Amateur 1968. Swiss Open 1973–79. Dutch Open 1975. Scandinavian Enterprises Open 1976. Zimbabwe Open 1980
Oth Glen Anil Classic 1972. Western Province Open 1973. General Motors International Classic (SA) 1973. Transvaal Open 1973–76. ICL International (SA) 1976. Holiday Inns (Swaziland) 1976. Rhodesian Masters 1976. State Express Classic 1983
Int South Africa seven times as an amateur. South Africa in World Cup 1973–77
Mis European American Express 1973. Second in Order of Merit 1977. Captain South African PGA 1978

Baker, Kathy

Born Albany, New York, USA on 20th March, 1961. Turned Professional 1983.

Baker, Kathy

Born Albany, New York, USA on 20th March, 1961. Turned Professional 1983.

Nat US Women's Open 1985
Int Curtis Cup 1982. World Cup 1982 (winners)

Baker–Finch, Ian

Born Nambour, Queensland, Australia on 24th October, 1960. Turned Professional 1979

Nat Australian Match Play 1987. Australian Masters 1988
For Scandinavian Open 1985. New Zealand Open 1983
Jap Golf Digest 1987. Pocari Sweat Open 1988
Oth West Australian Open 1984. NSW Open 1984 Queensland PGA 1984. Victoria Open 1985
Int Nissan Cup 1986. Kirin Cup 1987

Ballesteros, Severiano

Born Pedrena, Spain on 9th April, 1957. Turned Professional 1974

Opn Open Champion 1979–84–88; second 1976.
Chp US Masters 1980–83
Eur Dutch Open, Lancôme Trophy 1976; French Open, Uniroyal International, Swiss Open 1977; Martini International, German Open, Scandinavian Enterprise Open, Swiss Open 1978; English Classic 1979; Madrid Open, Martini International, Dutch Open 1980; Scandinavian Enterprise Open, Spanish Open, Suntory World Match Play 1981; Madrid Open, French Open, Suntory World Match Play 1982; Sun Alliance PGA, Irish Open, Lancôme Trophy 1983. Suntory World Match Play 1984; Irish Open, French Open, Sanyo Open, Spanish Open, Suntory World Match Play 1985; British Masters, Irish Open, Monte Carlo Open, French Open, Dutch Open, Lancôme Trophy (tied) 1986; Suze Open 1987; Open de Baleares, Scandinavian Enterprise Open, German Open, Lancôme Trophy 1988
USC Greater Greensboro Open 1978; Westchester Classic 1983; USF&G Classic 1985; Westchester Classic 1988
Jap Japanese Open, Dunlop Phoenix 1977; Japanese Open 1978; Dunlop Phoenix 1981;
ANZ Otago Classic 1977; Australian PGA 1981
Sfi Kenyan Open 1978
Int Europe v GB 1976–78–80; Spain in World Cup 1975–76 (winners) 77 (winners); Ryder Cup 1979–83–85–87; Dunhill Cup 1985–86–88
Mis Vardon Trophy 1976–77–78–86; Golf Writers Trophy 1979

Barber, Miller

Born Shreveport, Louisiana, USA on 31st March, 1931. Turned Professional 1958

USC 1964–one. 1967–one. 1968–one. 1969–one. 1970–one. 1971–one. 1972–one. 1973–one (World Open when it was the world's richest tournament) 1974–one. 1977–one. 1978–one
Sen US Seniors PGA 1981. US Seniors Open 1982. 1987–one
Int Ryder Cup 1969–71

Bean, Andy

Born Lafayette, Georgia on 13th March, 1953. Turned Professional 1975

USC 1977–one. 1978–three. 1979–one. 1980–one. 1981–one. 1982–one. 1984–one. 1986–three
Int Ryder Cup 1979–87

Beck, Chip

Born Fayetteville, North Carolina, USA on 12th September, 1956. Turned Professional 1978

Reg Carolinas Champion twice
Jun Carolinas Junior Champion twice
USC Los Angeles Open 1988; USF&G Classic 1988
Int Dunhill Cup 1988
Mis 9th on Money List in 1987

Beman, Dean R

Born Washington, DC, USA on 22nd April, 1938. Turned Professional 1987

Bri Amateur Champion 1959
Nat US Amateur 1960–63. Second in US Open 1969
USC 1969–one. 1970–one. 1972–one. 1973–one
Oth Eastern Amateur 1960–61–63–64
Int Walker Cup 1959–61–63–65. Eisenhower Trophy 1960–62–64–66
Mis Became USPGA Tour Commissioner 1974

Berg, Patty

Born Minneapolis, USA on 13th February, 1918. Turned Professional 1940

Nat US Ladies Amateur 1938. US Women's Open 1946, second 1957
LPGA 5 tournament victories
Oth Western Amateur 1938. 29 amateur wins 1934–40
Int Curtis Cup 1936–38
Mis US leading money winner 1954–55–57. Bobby Jones Award 1963. First President of USLPGA. Ben Hogan Award 1975. LPGA Hall of Fame 1951

Bland, John

Born Johannesburg on 22nd April, 1945. Turned Professional 1968

Bri Benson & Hedges International 1983
Nat South African PGA 1977. Nine SAf circuit wins. Tournament of Champions 1988
For Suze Cannes Open 1986
Int World Cup 1975

Boros, Julius

Born Fairfield, Connecticut on 3rd March, 1920. Turned Professional 1950

Nat US Open Champion 1952–63. USPGA 1968
USC 1952–one. 1954–two. 1955–one. 1958–two. 1959–one. 1960-one. 1963-two. 1964-one. 1967-three. 1968-one. USPGA Seniors 1971–77. Legends of Golf 1979
Int Ryder Cup 1959–63–65–67. USA in World Cup 1953–68
Mis US leading money winner 1952–55. USPGA Player of the Year 1952–63

Bradley, Pat

Born Westford Massachusetts, USA on 24th March, 1951. Turned Professional 1974

Nat US Women's Open 1981
LPGA 1985–three 1986–five (1974–86 21 victories). 1987-one Standard Register Turquoise Classic

Burke, Jack, Jr

Born Fort Worth, Texas, USA in January, 1923. Turned Professional 1940

Nat US Masters 1956, second 1952. USPGA 1956
USC 1950–three. 1952–five. 1953–one. 1956–two. 1958–one. 1959–one. 1961–one. 1963–one
Int Ryder Cup 1951–53–55–57 (capt)–59, non–playing captain 1973
Mis USPGA Player of the Year 1956

Calcavecchia, Mark
Born Laurel, Nebraska, USA on 12th June 1960. Turned Professional 1981

USC 1986-one (SW Golf Classic); 1987-one (Honda Classic); 1988–one (Bank of Boston Classic)
Int Ryder Cup 1987; Kirin Cup 1987

Campbell, William Cammack
Born West Virginia, USA on 5th May, 1923

Bri Amateur Championship runner-up 1954
Nat US Amateur Champion 1964
For Mexican Amateur 1956. Canadian Amateur runner-up 1952–54–65
Oth North and South Amateur 1950–53–57–67. Tam O'Shanter World Amateur 1948–49. Ontario Amateur 1967. USGA Seniors 1979–80
Int Walker Cup 1951–53–55 (capt)–57–65–67–71–75. Eisenhower Trophy 1964, non-playing captain 1968
Mis Bobby Jones Award 1956. Member of the USGA Committee 1962 to 1965. Uniform Ball Committee 1970. President USGA 1983. Captain Royal & Ancient 1987

Canizares, José–Maria
Born Madrid on 18th February, 1947. Turned Professional 1967

Bri Avis-Jersey Open 1980. Bob Hope British Classic 1980–83
Oth Lancia D'Oro 1972. Italian Open 1981. Kenya Open 1984
Int Europe v GB 1974–76–78–80. Spain in World Cup 1974–80–82–83–84. Ryder Cup 1983. Hennessy-Cognac Cup 1984. Dunhill Cup 1985–87
Mis Lowest 9-hole aggregate of 27 on Europe PGA circuit in 1978 Swiss Open

Caponi, Donna
Born Detroit, Michigan, USA on 29th January, 1945. Turned Professional 1965

Nat US Women's Open 1969–70. USLPGA 1979–81
LPGA 24 tournament wins
Oth Colgate European Open 1975
Mis LA Times Women Golfer of the Year 1970

Carner, JoAnne (*née* Gunderson)
Born Kirkland, Washington, USA on 4th April, 1939. Turned Professional 1970

Nat US Ladies Amateur 1957–60–62–66–68; runner-up 1956–64. US Women's Open 1971–76; second 75 (tied)–78 (tied)
For Australian Ladies Open 1975
LPGA 42 Victories on USLPGA circuit up to end of 1986
Oth Western Ladies Open 1959. US Girls 1956
Int Represented US in Curtis Cup four times
Mis Rookie of the Year 1970. Leading US money winner 1974. US Ladies Player of the Year 1974. Bob Jones Award 1981

Casper, Bill
Born in San Diego, California, USA on 24th June, 1931. Turned Professional 1954

Nat US Open Champion 1959–66. US Masters 1970; second 1969. USPGA second 1958–65–71
For Canadian Open 1967. Italian Open 1975
USC 1956–one. 1957–two. 1958–four. 1959–three. 1960–five. 1961–one. 1962–one. 1963–two. 1964–four. 1965–four. 1966–three. 1967–one. 1968–six. 1969–three (includes Alcan Golfer of the Year). 1970–three. 1971–one. 1973–two. 1975–one
Oth Lancôme Trophy 1974. Moroccan Grand Prix 1973–75. Lancia D'Oro 1974. Mexican Open 1977
Sen Arizona Classic 1987
Int Ryder Cup 1961–63–65–67–69–71–73–75 (non-playing captain 1979)
Mis Vardon Trophy 1960–63–65–66–68. US leading money winner 1966–68; second 1958–70. USPGA Player of the Year 1966–70. Byron Nelson Award 1966–68–70. Second player to win over one million dollars in prize money

Charles, Robert J
Born Carterton, New Zealand on 14th March, 1936. Turned Profesional 1960

Bri Open Champion 1963; second 1968–69. Bowmaker 1961. Daks 1962 (tied). Piccadilly World Match Play 1969. John Player Classic 1972. Dunlop Masters 1972
Nat New Zealand Open 1954 (as amateur)–66–70–73; second 1974. New Zealand Professional 1961–79–80
USC 1963–one. 1965–one. 1967–one. 1974–one
Oth Caltex (NZ) 1961–62–67 (tied)–68–71. Engadine Open 1962. Watties Open (NZ) 1963–66–67–68. Forest Products (NZ) 1966. Metalcraft (NZ) 1966. Wills Masters (NZ) 1967. Spalding Masters (NZ) 1968–72. Otago Classic (NZ) 1972. Auckland Classic (NZ) 1973. New Zealand Classic 1978
Sen 1987-three
For Swiss Open 1962–74. Canadian Open 1968. Second USPGA 1968. South African Open 1973. Scandinavian Open 1973
Int Eisenhower Trophy 1960. New Zealand in World Cup 1962–63–64–65–66–67–68–71–72. Dunhill Cup 1985–86
Mis First New Zealander and first left-handed golfer to win the Open

Coe, Charles R
Born Oklahoma City, USA on 26th October, 1923

Bri Amateur Champion runner-up 1951
Nat US Amateur Champion 1949–58; runner-up 1959. Second in US Masters 1961
Oth Western Amateur 1950
Int Walker Cup 1949–51–53–59–61–63. Eisenhower Trophy 1960
Mis Bobby Jones Award 1964

Cole, Robert
Born Springs, South Africa on 11th May, 1948. Turned Professional 1966

Bri Amateur Champion 1966. Second in English Amateur Stroke Play 1966
Nat South African Open 1974–80. Dunlop Masters (SA) 1969
For Rhodesian Masters 1972
USC 1977–one
Oth Natal Open 1969–70–72. Cape Classic 1970. Transvaal Open 1972. Vavasseur (SA) 1974
Int Eisenhower Trophy 1966. Winning team World Cup 1974, individual winner 1974. South Africa in World Cup 1969–74–76
Mis Won Amateur Championship at age of 18

Crenshaw, Ben
Born Austin, Texas, USA on 11th January, 1952. Turned Professional 1973

Bri Second in Open Championship 1978(tied)–79(tied). Carrolls Irish Open 1976
Nat US Masters 1984. Second US Masters 1976–83. Second USPGA 1979
For Second in Australia Open 1978. Mexican Open 1982
USC 1973–one. 1976–three. 1977–one. 1979–one. 1980–one. 1983–one. 1986–two. 1987–one.

Int Eisenhower Trophy winning team 1972. Ryder Cup 1983–87
Mis Won the first tournament he played in after turning professional, the 1973 San Antonio Open. Rookie of the Year 1974. US second money winner 1976. Byron Nelson Award 1976

Crosby, Nathaniel
Born Los Angeles, California, USA on 29th October, 1961. Turned Professional 1984

Nat US Amateur 1981
Int Walker Cup 1983. Eisenhower Trophy (winners) 1982

Daniel, Miss Beth
Born Charleston, South Carolina, USA on 14th October, 1956. Turned Professional October, 1978

Nat US Women's Amateur 1975–77
For World Ladies Championship (Japan) 1979
LPGA 1979–one. 1980–four. 1981–two. 1982–five. 1983–one. 1985–one
Int Curtis Cup 1976–78
Mis USLPGA Rookie of the Year 1979. USLPGA leading money winner 1980. USLPGA Player of the Year 1980

Davies, Richard
Born USA on 29th October, 1930

Bri Amateur Champion 1962
Int Walker Cup 1963
Mis Leading Amateur US Open 1963

Davis, Rodger
Born Sydney, New South Wales, Australia on 18th May, 1951. Turned Professional 1974

Bri 2nd in Open 1987. State Express Classic 1981. Whyte & Mackay PGA 1986. Wang Four Stars 1988
Nat Australian Open 1986
For Lost play-off for German Open 1986
Oth South Australia Open 1978. Victoria Open 1979–85.
Int World Cup 1985. Dunhill Cup 1986 (winning team)-87. Nissan Cup 1986. Kirin Cup 1987

Dibnah, Corinne
Born Brisbane, Australia on 29th July, 1962. Turned Professional 1984

Nat Australian Champion 1981. New Zealand Champion 1983
Int Commonwealth Tournament 1983 (winners)
WPGA Trusthouse Forte Ladies Classic, Kristianstad Open 1986; Guernsey Open, Spanish Open 1987; Eastleigh Classic, British Ladies Open 1988

Dickson, Robert B
Born McAlester, Oklahoma, USA on 25th January, 1944. Turned Professional 1968

Bri Amateur Champion 1967
Nat US Amateur 1967
USC 1968–one. 1973–one
Int Walker Cup 1967
Mis Joined select few to win British and US Amateur titles in the same year. Bobby Jones Award 1968

Fernandez, Vicente
Born Corrientes, Argentina on 5th April, 1946. Turned Professional 1964

Bri Benson & Hedges 1975. Colgate PGA 1979
Nat Argentine Open 1968–69–81
For Dutch Open 1970. Brazil Open 1983–84
Int World Cup 1970–72–78–84–85. Dunhill Cup 1986

Finsterwald, Dow
Born Athens, Ohio, USA on 6th September, 1929. Turned Professional 1951

Nat USPGA Champion 1958; runner-up 1957
For Canadian Open 1956
USC 1955–two. 1956–one. 1957–one. 1958–one. 1959–three. 1960–two. 1963–one
Int Ryder Cup 1957–59–61–63 (non-playing captain 1977)
Mis USPGA Player of the Year 1958

Floyd, Ray
Born Fort Bragg, North Carolina, USA on 4th September, 1942. Turned Professional 1961

Bri Second in Open Championship 1978(tied)
Nat USPGA Champion 1969–82; second 1976. US Masters 1976. US Open 1986
For Brazilian Open 1978
USC 1963–one. 1965–one. 1969–two. 1975–one. 1976–one. 1977–two. 1979–one. 1980–one. 1981–four. 1982–three. 1985–one. 1986–one.
Int Ryder Cup 1969–75–77–83 Dunhill Cup 1985–86 Nissan Cup 1985
Mis Rookie of the Year 1963

Ford, Doug
Born West Haven, Connecticut, USA on 6th August, 1922. Turned Professional 1949

Nat US Masters 1957; second 1958. USPGA Champion 1955
USC 1952–one. 1953–three. 1954–two. 1955–two. 1957–two. 1958–one. 1960–one. 1961–one. 1962–two
For Canadian Open 1959–63
Sen 1987-one
Int Ryder Cup 1955–57–59–61
Mis USPGA Player of the Year 1955

Frost, David
Born South Africa

Nat South African Open 1986
Eur Cannes Open 1984
Oth Eight 2nd places and six 3rd places in Eur, USC, SAf since 1984
USC 1988–one (Southern Open)

Garrido, Antonio
Born Madrid on 2nd February, 1944. Turned Professional 1961

Bri Benson and Hedges International 1977. Standard Four Stars National 1986
Nat Madrid Open 1973–77. Spanish Open 1972
For Tunisian Open 1982
Int Europe v GB 1976–78–80. Spain in World Cup 1977 (winning team)–78–79. Ryder Cup 1979. Hennessy-Cognac Cup 1976–78–80–82–84

Geddes, Jane
Born Huntingdon, New York, USA on 5th February, 1960. Turned Professional 1983

Chp US Women's Open 1986. LPGA Championship 1987
LPGA 1986–one (Boston Five Classic); 1987–five (Women's Kemper Open, GNA Glendale Federal Classic, LPGA Championship, Toledo Classic, Boston Five Classic)

Giles, Marvin

Bri Amateur Champion 1975
Nat US Amateur Champion 1972, second 1967–68–69
Int Walker Cup 1969–71–73–75. Eisenhower Trophy winning team 1968–70–72
Mis Leading Amateur US Open 1973

Goldschmid, Mrs Isa (*née* Bevione)
Born Italy

Bri Kayser Bondor 1963
Nat Italian Ladies' Close 1947–51–53–54–55–56–57–58–59–60–61–62–63–64–65–66–67–69–71–73–74. Italian Ladies' Open 1952–57–58–60–61–63–64–67–68–69
For Spanish Ladies 1952. French Ladies 1975
Int Vagliano Trophy 1959–61–63–65–67–69–71–73 (non-playing captain 1977). Eur v United States 1968. Italy in World Team Championship 1964–66–68–70–72

Graham, David
Born Windsor, Tasmania on 23rd May, 1946. Turned Professional 1962

Bri Piccadilly World Match Play 1976
Nat Australian Open 1977; second 1972. Australian Wills Masters 1975
For Foreign Open 1970. Thailand Open 1970. USPGA 1979. US Open 1981. Lancôme Trophy 1982
USC 1972–one. 1976–two. 1980–one. 1983–one
Oth Victoria Open 1970. Tasmanian Open 1970. Yomiuri Open 1970. Caracas Open 1971. Japanese Airlines 1971. Chunichi Crowns (Japan) 1976. West Lakes Classic (Aust) 1979. Air New Zealand Open 1979. Queensland Open 1987
Int Australia in World Cup 1970 (winning team)–71. Dunhill Cup 1985 (winning team) –1986 (winning team) –88. Nissan Cup 1985–86
Mis Australian *Sportsman of the Year* 1979

Graham, Lou
Born Nashville, Tennessee, USA on 7th January, 1938. Turned Professional 1962

Nat US Open 1975; second 1977
USC 1967–one. 1972–one. 1979–three.
Int Ryder Cup 1973–75–77. Winning team World Cup 1975

Green, Hubert
Born Birmingham, Alabama, USA on 18th December, 1946. Turned Professional 1970

Bri Carrolls Irish Open 1977
Nat US Open 1977. Second in US Masters 1978 (tied). USPGA 1985
USC 1971–one. 1973–two. 1974–four. 1975–one. 1976–three. 1978–two. 1979–two. 1984–one
Oth Dunlop Phoenix (Japan) 1975
Int Ryder Cup 1977–79–85. USA in World Cup 1977
Mis Rookie of the Year 1971

Gunderson, Miss JoAnne
See Mrs Carner

Härdin Christian
Born Sweden

Chp Amateur Champion 1988
Int (Eur) v GBI 1988

Harper, Chandler
Born Portsmouth, Virginia, USA on 10th March, 1914. Turned Professional 1934

Nat USPGA 1950
USC Won over 20 tournaments. Ten times Virginia Open Champion. USPGA Seniors 1968. National Seniors 1965
Oth World Senior Professional 1968
Int Ryder Cup 1955
Mis Elected to USPGA Hall of Fame 1969. Holder of USPGA 54- and 36-hole records (see *Record Scoring*). In 1941 scored round of 58 (29–29) on 6100 yards, Portsmouth, Virginia

Hayes, Dale
Born Pretoria, South Africa on 1st July, 1952. Turned Professional 1970

Bri English Open Amateur Stroke Play second 1969. Scottish Open Amateur Stroke Play 1970. Coca-Cola Young Professionals 1974. PGA Under-25's 1975
Nat South African Amateur Stroke Play 1969–70. Leading Amateur South African Open 1969. South African PGA 1974–75–76. South African Open 1976
For German Amateur 1969. Brazilian Open 1970. Spanish Open 1971–79. World Junior Champion 1969. Dunlop Masters (Rhod.) 1973. Swiss Open 1975. Italian Open 1978. French Open 1978
Oth Transvaal Amateur 1969. Western Province Amateur 1970. Transvaal Open 1970. Bert Hagerman (SA) 1971. Schoeman Park (SA) 1973. Rolux Open (SA) 1973. Holiday Inns (SA) 1973–75–76. Corlett Drive Classic 1973. Royal Swaziland International 1974. ICL International (SA) 1978. Cape Open 1978. Bogota Open 1979
Int South Africa Eisenhower Trophy 1970 (runner-up Individual Section). South Africa in World Cup 1974 (winning team)–76
Mis Accles and Pollock Award 1973. Second in Order of Merit 1974–78. Vardon Trophy 1975

Henning, Harold
Born Johannesburg, South Africa on 3rd October, 1934. Turned Professional 1953

Bri Third in Open Championship 1960–70. Daks 1958 (tied). Yorkshire Evening News 1958 (tied). Spalding 1959 (tied). Sprite 1960. Pringle 1964
Nat South African Open 1957–62. South African PGA 1965–66–67–72
For Italian Open 1957. Swiss Open 1960–64. Danish Open 1960–64–65. German Open 1965. Malaysian Open 1966
USC 196–one. 1970–one
Oth Transvaal Open 1957. Natal Open 1957. Western Province Open 1957–59. Cock o' the North 1959. Engadine Open 1966. South African International Classic 1972. ICL International (SA) 1980
Int South Africa in World Cup 1957–58–59–61–65 (winning team)–66–67–69–70–71

Hogan, Ben W
Born Dublin, Texas, USA on 13th August, 1912. Turned Professional 1929

Bri Open Champion 1953
Nat US Open Champion 1948–50–51–53; second 1955–56. USPGA Champion 1946–48. US Masters 1951–53; runner-up 1942–46–54–55
USC 1938–one. 1940–four. 1941–five. 1942–six. 1945–five. 1946–twelve. 1947–seven. 1948–eight. 1949–two. 1950–one. 1951–one. 1952–one. 1953–three. 1959–one
Int Ryder Cup 1947 (capt)–49 (capt)–51, non-playing captain 1967. World Cup 1956 (winning team and individual winner)–58
Mis USPGA Player of the Year 1948–50–51–53. US leading money winner 1940–41–42–46–48. Sportsman of the Decade Award 1946–56. Had a serious car crash in 1949 which seemed likely to prevent him playing golf again but returned to win more major victories. In 1965 was named the greatest professional of all time by US golf writers. Bobby Jones Award 1976

Hyndman, William III
Born 25th December, 1915

Bri Amateur Championship runner-up 1959–69–70
Nat US Amateur runner-up 1955
Oth US Seniors 1973
Int Walker Cup 1957–59–61–71. Eisenhower Trophy 1958–60 (capt)

Inkster, Juli
Born Santa Cruz, California, USA on 24th June, 1960. Turned Professional 1983

Nat US Ladies Amateur 1980–81–82
LPGA 1983–one; 1984–two; 1985–one; 1986–four; 1988–three
Int Curtis Cup 1982. World Cup 1980–82

Irwin, Hale
Born Joplin, Montana, USA on 3rd June, 1945. Turned Professional 1968

Bri Piccadilly World Match Play 1974–75. Second Open 1983
Nat US Open 1974–79
For Australian PGA 1978. South African PGA 1978. Bridestone 1981
USC 1971–one. 1973–one. 1975–two. 1976–two. 1977–three. 1981–two. 1982–one. 1983–one. 1984–one. 1985–one. 1986–one
Int Ryder Cup 1975–77–79–81. USA in World Cup 1974–79 (winning teams and individual winner)

January, Don
Born Plainview, Texas, USA on 20th November, 1929. Turned Professional 1955

Nat USPGA Champion 1967; second 1961–76
USC 1956–two. 1959–one. 1960–one. 1961–one. 1963–one. 1966–one. 1968–one. 1970–one. 1975–one. 1976–one
Sen 1987-one
Int Ryder Cup 1965–67
Mis In 1961 won 50,000 dollars for a hole-in-one

Kennedy, Edwina
Born 10th June, 1959

Nat Ladies Amateur 1978. Canadian Ladies Amateur 1980
Int World Cup 1978 (winner)–80–84–86. Commonwealth Tournament 1979–83

King, Betsy
Born Reading, Pennsylvania, USA on 13th August, 1955. Turned Professional 1977

Bri Ladies Open 1986
LPGA 1984–three. 1985–two. 1986–two. 1987–three

Kite, Tom
Born Austin, Texas, USA on 9th December, 1949. Turned Professional 1972

Bri Second in Open Championship 1978 (tied). European Open 1980
Nat Second in US Amateur 1970
USC 1976–one. 1978–one. 1981–one. 1982–one. 1983–one. 1984–one. 1985–one. 1986–one. 1987–one
Oth Auckland Classic (NZ) 1974
Int Eisenhower Trophy winning team 1970. Walker Cup 1971. Ryder Cup 1979–81–83–85–87. Kirin Cup 1987
Mis US Rookie of the Year 1973. Bobby Jones Award 1979. Vardon Trophy 1981. Leading US money winner 1981. Golf Writers Player of the Year 1981

Knight, Mrs Nancy
See Miss Nancy Lopez

Kuramoto, Masahiro
Born Hiroshima City, Hiroshima, Japan on 9th September, 1955. Turned Professional 1981

Nat Japan Amateur 1975–77–80. Japan PGA 1982
Jap 1983–two. 1984–two. 1985–two. 1986–two. 1987–two. 1988–four
Int Dunhill Cup 1985

Langer, Bernhard
Born Anhausen, West Germany on 27th August, 1957. Turned Professional 1972

Opn 2nd in 1981–84; 3rd in 1985–86
Chp US Masters 1985
Nat German Open 1981–82–85–86. German Professional Close 1979
USC Sea Pines Heritage Classic 1985
Eur Dunlop Masters 1980; Bob Hope Classic 1981; Italian Open, Glasgow Golf Classic, St Mellion TPC 1983; French Open, Dutch Open, Irish Open, Spanish Open 1984; European Open 1985; Lancôme Trophy (tied) 1986; Whyte & Mackay PGA, Irish Open 1987
Jap Casio World Open 1983; Epson Match Play 1988
ANZ Australian Masters 1985
SAf Sun City Challenge 1985
SAm Colombian Open 1980
Oth Cacherel Under 25s Championship 1979. Belgian Classic 1987
Int Ryder Cup 1981–83–85–87. Hennessy-Cognac Cup 1976–78–80–82 (captain). Germany in World Cup 1976–77–78–79–80. Nissan Cup 1985 (captain)–86 (captain). Kirin Cup 1987
Mis Harry Vardon Trophy 1981–84

Lewis, Bob

Nat Runner-up in US Amateur 1980
Int Walker Cup 1981–83–85–87. Eisenhower Trophy (winners) 1982

Littler, Gene
Born San Diego, California, USA on 21st July, 1930. Turned Professional 1954

Nat US Amateur 1953. US Open 1961; second 1954. Second US Masters 1970. Second USPGA 1977
For Canadian Open 1965. Taiheiyo Pacific Masters 1974–75. Australian Masters 1980
USC 1954–one (as amateur). 1955–four. 1956–three. 1957–one. 1959–five. 1960–two. 1962–two. 1969–two. 1971–two. 1973–one. 1975–three. 1977–one. World Series 1966
Oth Yellow Pages (SA) 1977
Sen 1987-two
Int Ryder Cup 1961–63–65–67–69–71–75
Mis USPGA second money winner 1959–62. Bobby Jones Award 1973. Ben Hogan Award 1973. Byron Nelson Award 1959

Lopez, Nancy
Born Torrance, California, USA on 6th January, 1957. Turned Professional July, 1977

Bri Colgate European 1978–79
Nat Second in US Women's Open 1975 (as amateur)–77. LPGA Championship 1978
For Colgate Far East 1978
LPGA 1978–six. 1979–seven. 1980–three. 1981–three. 1982–two. 1983–two. 1984–one. 1985–five. 1987-two. 1988–three

Int Curtis Cup 1976. World Amateur Team 1976
Mis US Girls 1972–74 USLPGA leading money winner 1978–79. USLPGA Rookie of the Year 1977. USLPGA Player of the Year 1978–79. US Sportswoman of the Year 1978. In 1978, in first full year as a professional, won nine tournaments and a then record total of 189,813 dollars

McCumber, Mark

Born Jacksonville, Florida, USA on 7th September, 1951. Turned Professional 1974

USC Doral-Eastern Open 1979; Western Open 1983; Pensacola Open 1983; Doral-Eastern Open 1985; Anheuser-Busch Classic 1987; Tournament Players Championship 1988
Int Dunhill Cup 1988

McGuire, Marnie

Born New Zealand

Nat Ladies Amateur 1986

McIntire, Miss Barbara

Bri British Ladies 1960
Nat US Ladies Amateur 1959–64. Second in US Women's Open 1956
Int Curtis Cup 1958–60–62–64–66–72

McNulty, Mark

Born Zimbabwe on 25th October, 1953. Turned Professional 1977

Nat SAf Amateur Stroke Play 1977. SAf Masters 1981–82–86. SAf Open 1987
SAf 1980-one, 1981-one, 1982-four, 1984-one, 1985-two, 1986-seven, 1987-three
Eur Greater Manchester Open 1979; German Open 1980; Portuguese Open 1986; German Open, 4 Stars Pro-Celebrity, Dunhill Masters 1987; Cannes Open 1988
Asa Malay Open 1980
Mis In nine starts won nine consecutive tournaments 1986–87

Mahaffey, John Drayton

Born Kerrville, Texas, USA on 9th May, 1948. Turned Professional 1971

Nat USPGA 1978
USC 1973–one. 1978–two. 1979–one. 1980–one. 1984–one. 1985–one. 1986–one
Int Ryder Cup 1979. US in World Cup 1978–79. Nissan Cup 1986
Mis NCAA Champion 1970

Marsh, Graham, MBE

Born Kalgoorlie, Australia on 14th January, 1944

Bri Sunbeam Electric 1973. Benson & Hedges International 1976–80. Colgate World Match Play 1977. Dunlop Masters 1979. European Open 1981. Lawrence Batley 1985
Nat Runner-up Australian Amateur 1967. Australian PGA 1982
For Swiss Open 1970–72. Indian Open 1971–73. German Open 1972. Thailand Open 1973. Malaysian Open 1974–75. Dutch Open 1979–85
USC 1977–one
Oth Watties Open (NZ) 1970. Spalding Masters (NZ) 1971. Lancôme 1977. Western Australian Open 1976. On Japanese circuit 1972–one victory. 1973–one victory. 1974–four victories (three in successive weeks). 1975–two victories. 1976–four victories. 1977–two victories. 1979–one victory. 1981–two victories
Int Dunhill Cup 1985 (winning team). Nissan Cup 1986. Kirin Cup 1987
Mis US Rookie of the Year 1977. Australian *Sportsman of the Year* 1977. Awarded MBE in 1982

Melynk, Steven Nicholas

Born Brunswick, Georgia, USA on 26th February, 1947. Turned Professional 1971

Bri Amateur Champion 1971. Leading Amateur Open Championship 1970
Nat US Amateur Champion 1969. Leading Amateur US Masters 1970
Oth Western Amateur 1969. Eastern Amateur 1971
Int Walker Cup 1969–71
Mis US Amateur Golfer of the Year 1969

Middlecoff, Cary

Born Halls, Tennessee, USA on 6th January, 1921. Turned Professional 1947

Nat US Open Champion 1949–56; second 1957. US Masters 1955, runner-up 1948. USPGA runner-up 1955
USC 1947–one. 1948–two. 1949–four. 1950–three. 1951–six. 1952–four. 1953–three. 1954–one. 1955–five. 1956–two. 1958–one. 1959–one. 1961–one
Int Ryder Cup 1953–55–59. USA in World Cup 1959
Mis Byron Nelson Award 1955

Miller, Alice

Born Marysville, California, USA on 15th May, 1956. Turned Professional 1978

LPGA 1983–one. 1984–two. 1985–four

Miller, Johnny Lawrence

Born San Francisco, USA on 29th April, 1947. Turned Professional 1969

Bri Open Championship 1976; second 1973
Nat US Open 1973. Second in US Masters 1971–75 (tied)–81 (tied)
For Dunlop Phoenix International (Japan) 1974
USC 1971–one. 1972–one. 1974–eight. 1975–four. 1976–two. 1980–one. 1982–one. 1983–one. 1984–one. 1987–one
Oth Otago Classic (NZ) 1972. Lancome Trophy 1973–79
Int USA in World Cup 1973 (winning team)–75 (winning team)–80; individual winner 1973–75. Ryder Cup 1975
Mis Lowest round (63) in US Open in 1973. USPGA Player of the Year 1974. US leading money winner 1974; second 1975. Byron Nelson Award 1974

Mize, Larry Hogan

Born Augusta, Georgia, USA on 23rd September, 1958. Turned Professional 1980

Nat US Masters 1987
USC 1983–one (Memphis Classic)
Int Ryder Cup 1987

Nagle, Kelvin DG

Born North Sydney, Australia on 21st December, 1920. Turned Professional 1946

Bri Open Championship 1960; second 1962. Irish Hospitals 1961. Dunlop 1961. Bowmaker 1962–65. Esso Golden 1963–67. British Seniors 1971–73–75
Nat Australian Open 1959. Australian Professional 1949–54–58–59–65–68
For Second in US Open 1965. Canadian Open 1964. French Open 1961. New Zealand Professional 1957–58–60–70–73–74–75. New Zealand Open 1957–58–62–64–67–68–69. World Senior 1971–75

Oth In New Zealand BP 1968; Caltex 1969, Garden City, 1969, Otago Charity Classic 1970–76. Stars Travel 1970. In Australia: West End 1968–72–74, New South Wales Open 1968. Victoria Open 1969, NBN Newcastle 1970, New South Wales Professional 1971, South Coast Open 1975, Western Australia PGA 1977
Int Australia in World Cup 1954 (winning team) 55–58–59–(winning team)–60–61–62–65–66
Mis His score of 260 in Irish Hospitals event in 1961 established a new low scoring record with rounds of 64–65–66–65. Honorary Member Royal and Ancient.

Nakajima, Tsuneyuki

Born Kiryu City, Gumma, Japan on 20th October, 1954. Turned Professional 1975

Nat Japan Amateur 1973. Japan Open 1985–86. Japan PGA 1983–84–86
Jap 1984–one. 1985–five. 1986–five. 1987–one
Oth Nissan Cup (individual) 1986
Int Dunhill Cup 1986. Nissan Cup 1986. Kirin Cup 1987

Nelson, Byron

Born Fort Worth, Texas, USA on 4th February, 1912. Turned Professional 1932

Nat US Open Champion 1939; second 1946. USPGA Champion 1940–45; second 1939–41–44. US Masters 1937–42; second 1941–47
For Canadian Open 1945. Canadian PGA 1945. French Open 1955
USC 1935–one. 1936–one. 1937–two. 1938–two. 1939–three. 1940–two. 1941–three. 1942–three. 1944–six. 1945–fifteen. 1946–five
Int Ryder Cup 1937–47
Mis Won eleven consecutive tournaments in period March to August 1945 and his total was eighteen for the year. US leading money winner 1944–45. Bobby Jones Award 1974

Nelson, Larry Gene

Born Fort Payne, Alabama, USA on 10th September, 1947. Turned Professional 1971

Nat US Open 1983. USPGA 1981–87. 1988–one
USC 1979–one. 1980–one. 1987–one. 1988–one
Int Ryder Cup 1979–81–87

Neumann, Liselotte

Born Finspang, Sweden on 20th May, 1966. Turned Professional 1985

Nat Swedish Champion 1982–83; Swedish Matchplay Champion 1983
Int Sweden (Eur Team Ch) 1984. Espirito Santo 1982–84
WPGA 1985–two (European Open, Swedish Open). 1986–one (German Open). 1987–one (French Open) also 1987 Singapore Open. 1988–one (German Open)
LPGA US Women's Open 1988

Newton, Jack

Born Sydney, Australia on 30th January, 1950. Turned Professional 1969

Bri Benson & Hedges Festival 1972. Benson & Hedges PGA Match Play 1974. Second in Open Championship 1975. Sumrie 1975
Nat Australian Open 1979
For Dutch Open 1972. Nigerian Open 1974. Second equal in New Zealand Open 1974. Second equal in US Masters 1980
USC 1978–one
Oth City of Auckland Classic (NZ) 1972. Amoco Forbes (Aust) 1972. Cock o' the North (Zambia) 1976. Mufulira Open 1976. New South Wales Open 1976–79
Mis Seriously injured on tarmac by aeroplane propeller accident 1983

Nicklaus, Jack William

Born Columbus, Ohio, USA on 21st January, 1940. Turned Professional 1961

Bri Open Champion 1966–70–78; second 1964–67–68–72–76–77–79. Piccadilly Match Play 1970. Royal St George's Challenge Cup 1959
Nat US Amateur 1959–61. US Open 1962–67–72–80; second 1960–68–82. US Masters 1963-65-66-72-75-86; second 1964-71-77-81. USPGA 1963–71–73–75–80;second 1964–65–74–83
For Australian Open 1964–68–71–75–76–78. Second in Canadian Open 1965–68–75–76
USC 1962–two. 1963–three. 1964–four. 1965–four. 1966–two. 1967–four. 1968–two. 1969–three. 1970–two. 1971–four. 1972–five. 1973–six. 1974–two. 1975–three. 1976–two. 1977–three. 1978–three. 1982–one. 1984–one. World Series 1962–63–67–70–76
Oth Dunlop International (Aust) 1971
Int Ryder Cup 1969–71–73–75–77–81–Captain 1983 Captain 1987. Walker Cup 1959–61. USA in World Cup 1963–64–65 (winning team–63–64–66–67–71–73; individual winner 1963–64–71). Eisenhower Trophy winning team 1960; individual winner 1960
Mis Rookie of the Year 1962. US leading money winner 1964–65–67–71–72–73–75–76; second 1963–66–68–74–77. USPGA Player of the Year 1967–72–73–75–76 Byron Nelson Award 1964–65–67–72–73. Bobby Jones Award 1975. By 1973 had won over two million dollars in prize money and by 1977 over three million dollars. First person to win over 300,000 dollars in one year (1972). World record of 19 major titles US Sportsman of the Year 1978. Athlete of Decade 1970s. Walter Hagen Award 1980

Norman, Greg

Born Mt Asa, Queensland, Australia on 10th February, 1955. Turned Professional 1976

Bri Open Champion 1986. Martini 1977–79–81. World Match Play 1980–83–86. Dunlop Masters 1981–82. Benson & Hedges International Open 1982. State Express Classic 1982
Nat Australian Open 1980–85. Australian Masters 1984–87. Australian PGA 1984–85. Australian TPC 1988
For Hong Kong Open 1979. Scandinavian Enterprises Open 1980. French Open 1980. Canadian Open 1984. European Open 1986. Italian Open 1988
USC 1984–two. 1986–two. 1988–one
Oth West Lakes Classic (Aust) 1976. South Seas Classic (Fiji) 1978, NSW Open 1978–83–86. Japanese circuit: 1977–one. Victorian Open 1984. Queensland Open 1986. South Australian Open 1986. Western Australian Open 1986. ESP Open 1988. Palm Meadows Cup 1988
Int Australia in World Cup 1976–78. Dunhill Cup 1985 (winning team)–86 (winning team)–87. Nissan Cup 1985–86. Kirin Cup 1987
Mis Second in Order of Merit 1980

North, Andy

Born Thorp, Wisconsin, USA on 9th March, 1950. Turned Professional 1972

Nat US Open 1978, 1985
USC 1977–one. 1978–one
Int US in World Cup 1978

Okamoto, Ayako
Born Hiroshima, Japan on 2nd April, 1951. Turned Professional 1976

Nat Ladies Open 1984
LPGA 1982–one. 1983–one. 1984–two. 1986–two. 1987–three. 1988–three

Olazabal, José–Maria
Born Spain on 5th February, 1966. Turned Professional 1984

Chp Amateur Champion 1984
Nat Spanish Open Amateur 1983
For Sanyo Open 1986. Swiss Open 1986. German Masters 1988. Belgian Open 1988
Oth Italian Open Amateur 1983. British Youths 1985
Int Dunhill Cup 1986–87–88. Ryder Cup 1987. Kirin Cup 1987

O'Meara, Mark
Born Goldsboro, North Carolina, USA on 13th January, 1957. Turned Professional 1980

Chp US Amateur 1979
Bri Lawrence Batley International 1987
USC 1984-one. 1985-three
Oth Australian Masters 1986
Int Ryder Cup 1985. Nissan Cup 1985. Dunhill Cup 1985-86-87

Ozaki, Masashi
Born Kaiman Town, Tokushima, Japan on 24th January, 1947. Turned Professional 1972

Jap 1984-one. 1986-four. 1987-three (Chunichi Crowns, Fuji Sankei Classic, Jun Classic). 1988–five
Āsa Dunlop Japan International 1988
Int Kirin Cup 1987

Palmer, Arnold
Born Latrobe, Pennsylvania, USA on 10th September, 1929. Turned Professional 1954

Bri Open Champion 1961–62; second 1960. Piccadilly World Match Play 1964–67. Penfold PGA 1975
Nat US Amateur Champion 1954. US Open 1960; second 1962–63–66–67. US Masters 1958–60–62–64; second 1961–65. USPGA second 1964–68–70
For Canadian Open 1955. Australian Open 1966. Spanish Open 1975. Canadian PGA 1980
USC 1956–four. 1957–four. 1958–two. 1959–three. 1960–six. 1961–five. 1962–six. 1963–seven. 1964–one. 1965–one. 1966–four. 1967–four. 1968–two. 1969–two. 1970–one. 1971–four. 1973–one
Oth Lancôme Trophy 1971
Int Ryder Cup 1961–63–65–67–71–73, non-playing capt. 1975. USA in World Cup 1960–62–63–64–66–67 (winning team each time; individual winner 1967)
Mis USPGA Player of the Year 1960–62. US leading money winner 1958–60–62–63; second 1961–64–67. First player ever to earn 100,000 dollars in one year (1963). US Athlete of the Year 1960. Bobby Jones Award 1971. Byron Nelson Award 1957–60–61–62–63. Made an honorary member of the Royal and Ancient GC in 1979. Athlete of the Decade 1960's. Walter Hagen Award 1981

Pate, Jerry
Born Macon, Georgia, USA on 16th September, 1953. Turned Professional 1975

Nat US Amateur 1974. US Open 1976; second 79 (tied). Second in USPGA 1978
For Canadian Open 1976. Taiheiyo Pacific Masters 1976. Brazilian Open 1980
USC 1977–two. 1978–one. 1982–one
Int Eisenhower Trophy winning team 1974, joint individual winner 1974. Walker Cup 1975. USA in World Cup 1976
Mis Rookie of the Year 1976 with then record first year prize money of 153,000 dollars on US circuit. Youngest player to make 1 million dollars on US tour

Pavin, Corey
Born Oxnard, California, USA on 16th November, 1959. Turned Professional 1981

For German Open 1983. SA PGA 1983
USC 1984–one. 1985–one. 1986–two. 1987–two. 1988 one
Int Walker Cup 1981. Nissan Cup 1985

Peete, Calvin
Born Detroit, USA on 18th July, 1943. Turned Professional 1971

USC 1979–one. 1982–four. 1983–two. 1984–one. 1985–two. 1986–two
Oth Vardon Trophy 1984
Int Ryder Cup 1983–85. Nissan Cup 1985–86

Pinero, Manuel
Born Puebla de la Calzada, Spain on 1st September, 1952. Turned Professional 1968

Bri Penfold PGA 1977. English Classic 1980. European Open 1982
Nat Madrid Open 1974–81–85
For Swiss Open 1976. Italian Open 1985
Oth Spanish Profesional 1972–73
Int Spain in World Cup 1974–76 (winning team)–78–79–80–82 (individual and team winner)–83–85. Europe v GB 1974–76–78–80. Ryder Cup 1985

Player, Gary
Born Johannesburg, South Africa on 1st November, 1935. Turned Professional 1953

Bri Open Champion 1959–68–74. Dunlop 1956. Piccadilly World Match Play 1965–66–68–71–73
Nat South Africa Open 1956–60–65–66–67–68–69–72–75–76–77–79–81. South African Masters 1959–60–64–67–71–72–73–74–76–76–(held twice)–79. South African PGA 1968–79–81
For US Open Champion 1965, second 1958–79 (tied). US Masters 1961–74–78, second 1962–65. USPGA 1962–72, second 1969. Australian Open 1958–62–63–65–69–70–74. Australian PGA 1957. Brazilian Open 1972–74. Ibergolf European Champions 1974. Chile Open 1980
USC 1958–one. 1961–two. 1962–one. 1963–one. 1964–one. 1969–one. 1970–one. 1971–two. 1972–one. 1973–one. 1974–one. 1978–two. US World Series 1965–68–72
Oth Transvaal Open 1959–60–62–66. Natal Open 1958–60–66–68. Western Province Open (SA) 1968–71–72. Wills Masters (Aust) 1968. Dunlop International (Aust) 1970. Rothmans Match Play (SA) 1973. Japan Airlines Open 1972. International Classic (SA) 1974. Lancôme 1975. General Motors (SA) 1971–75–76. ICL International (SA) 1977. Johannesburg International 1979. Sun City Classic (SA) 1979, Ivory Coast Open 1980
Sen US Seniors Open 1987. Seniors British Open 1988. Senior TPC 1987. 1987-two
Int South Africa in World Cup 1956–57–58–59–60–62–63–64–65 (winning team and individual winner)–66–67–68–71–72–73–77 (individual winner)
Mis First overseas player to win the US Open for 45 years. Third man in history to win all four Major World Professional titles. US leading money

winner 1961. In 1974 recorded his 100th win as a professional. In 1974 Brazilian Open scored 59 in second round. This was the first time 60 had been broken in a national championship. Bobby Jones Award 1966. In 1976 became the first player to be made an honorary member of the USPGA. Captain South African PGA 1977. President South African PGA 1978. Became the oldest player to win the US Masters aged 42 in 1978, in which his last round 64 and inward half of 30 equalled the record.

Ploujoux, Philippe
Born La Bouille, Seine Maritime, France on 20th February, 1955

Chp Amateur Champion 1981
Nat French Amateur Close Match Play 1977
Oth International Moroccan Stroke Play 1977
Int Continental Team (St Andrews Trophy) five times (including winning team, 1982) Continental Youth Team four times. Represented France more than fifty times
Jun French Youths Match Play 1972–73–74–75–76. French Boys 1969–70

Pohl, Dan
Born Mt Pleasant, Michigan, USA on 1st April, 1955. Turned Professional 1977

USC 1986–two
Int Ryder Cup 1987
Am Michigan State Champion 1975–77

Prado, Señora (*née* Catherine Lacoste)
Born Paris on 27th June, 1945

Bri British Ladies 1969. Astor Prince's 1966. Worplesdon Foursomes 1967. Hovis 1969
Nat French Ladies' Open 1967–69–70–72. French Ladies' Close 1968–69
For US Ladies' Open 1967. US Ladies' Amateur 1969. Western Ladies' Amateur (US) 1968. Spanish Ladies 1969–72–76
Int World Team Championship winning team 1964; winner individual section 1964–68
Mis Was first amateur, first non-American and youngest player at the time she won the US Ladies' Open in 1967

Price, Nick
Born Durban, South Africa on 28th January, 1957. Turned Professional 1977

Opn 2nd in Open 1982, 1988
Nat SA Masters 1980
For Swiss Open 1980
Oth Lancôme Trophy 1985. World Series of Golf 1983

Randolph, Sam
Turned Professional 1987

Chp US Amateur 1985
USC 1987–one (Bank of Boston Classic)
Int Walker Cup 1985

Rivero, José
Born Spain on 20th September, 1955. Turned Professional 1973

Bri Lawrence Batley International 1984
For French Open 1987. Monte Carlo Open 1988
Int Ryder Cup 1985–87. World Cup 1984 (winner). Dunhill Cup 1986–87–88

Rogers, William Charles
Born Waco, Texas, USA on 10th September, 1951. Turned Professional 1974

Bri Open 1981. Suntory World Match Play 1980
For Suntory Open 1980. Australian Open 1981
USC 1978–one. 1981–three. 1983–one
Oth Pacific Masters 1977
Int Ryder Cup 1981

Rosenthal, Jody
Born Minneapolis, Minnesota, USA on 18th October, 1962. Turned Professional 1985

Chp Ladies Amateur 1984
Int Curtis Cup 1984

Sander, Anne (formerly Mrs Wetts, Mrs Decker, *néeQuast)*

Chp Ladies Open 1980. US Ladies 1958–61–63
Int Curtis Cup 1958–60–62–66–68–74–84 World Cup (winners) 1966–68

Sarazen, Gene
Born Harrison, New York, USA on 27th February, 1902. Turned Professional 1920

Bri Open Champion 1932; second 1928. North of England Professional 1923
Nat US Open Champion 1922–32; second 1934–40. USPGA 1922–23–33; second 1930. US Masters 1935
For Australian Open 1936
USC 1922–one. 1925–one. 1927–two. 1928–two. 1930–two. 1935–one. 1936–one. 1937–two. 1938–one. 1939–one. 1941–one. USPGA Seniors 1954–58
Int Ryder Cup 1927–29–31–33–35–37
Mis One of the few to win the Open and the US Open in the same year. Honorary member of the Royal and Ancient

Segard, Mme Patrick (formerly Vcmtsse De St Sauveur *née* Lally Vagliano)

Bri British Ladies 1950. Worplesdon Foursomes 1962. British Girls 1937. Avia Foursomes 1966. Kayser-Bondor Foursomes 1960
Nat French Ladies' Open 1948–50–51–52. French Ladies' Close 1939–46–49–50–51–54
For Swiss Ladies 1949–65. Luxembourg Ladies 1949. Italian Ladies 1949–51. Spanish Ladies 1951
Int France 1937–38–39–47–48–49–50–51–52–53–54–55–56–57–58–59–60–61–62–63–64–65–70. Vagliano Trophy 1959 (capt)–61 (capt)–63–65, non-playing captain 1975
Mis Chairman of The Women's Committee of World Amateur Golf Council 1964 to 1972

Semple, Carol (Mrs Thompson)

Bri British Ladies 1974. Newmark International 1975 (tied)
Nat US Ladies' Amateur 1973
Int Curtis Cup 1974–77–80–82. World Team Championship 1974 (winning team)–80 (winning team)

Senior, Peter
Born Singapore on 31st July, 1959. Turned Professional 1978

Eur PLM Open 1986. Monte Carlo Open 1987
Oth Queensland Open, New South Wales PGA 1984; New South Wales PGA, Rich River Classic, (South Australian Open 1979). Queensland PGA 1987
Int Australia in Dunhill Cup 1987. Kirin Cup 1987

Sheehan, Patty

Born Middlebury, Vermont, USA on 27th October, 1956. Turned Professional 1980

Nat LPGA 1983
LPGA 1985–two. 1986–three. (1981–86: 17 tournament victories)
Int Curtis Cup 1980

Siderowf, R

Bri Amateur Champion 1973–76
For Canadian Amateur 1971
Int Walker Cup 1969–73–75–77 (non-playing captain 1979). Eisenhower Trophy 1968–76

Sigel, Jay

Chp Amateur Champion 1979
Nat US Amateur 1982–83
Int Walker Cup 1977–79–81–83 (captain)–85–87
Mis Most wins (14) in Walker Cup matches

Simpson, Scott William

Born San Diego, California, USA on 17th September 1955. Turned Professional 1977

Nat US Open 1987
USC 1980–one. 1984–one. 1987–one (Greater Greensboro Open). 1988–one
Jap 1984-two (Chunichi Crowns, Dunlop Phoenix)
Int Ryder Cup 1987. Kirin Cup 1987

Sluman, Jeff

Born Rochester, New York, USA on 11th September, 1957. Turned Professional 1980

Maj US PGA 1988

Snead, Samuel Jackson

Born Hot Springs, Virginia, USA on 27th May, 1912. Turned Professional 1934

Bri Open Champion 1946
Nat US Masters 1949–52–54; second 1939–57. USPGA Champion 1942–49–51; second 1938–40. Second in US Open 1937–47–49–53
For Canadian Open 1938–40–41
USC 1936–one. 1937–four. 1938–six. 1939–four. 1940–two. 1941–four. 1942–two. 1944–two. 1945–six. 1946–five. 1948–one. 1949–four. 1950–ten. 1951–one. 1952–five. 1953–three. 1954–one. 1955–four. 1956–one. 1957–one. 1958–one. 1959–one. 1960–two. 1961–two. 1964–one. 1965–one. USPGA Seniors 1964–65–67–70–72–73
Oth World Senior Professional 1964–65–70–72–73
Int Ryder Cup 1937–47–49–51 (capt)–53–55–59 (capt); non-playing captain 1969. USA in World Cup 1954–56–57–58–59–60–61–62; (winning team 56–60–61–62; individual winner 1961)
Mis US leading money winner 1938–49–50. USPGA Player of the Year 1949. Oldest professional to win a major tournament 1965. Unofficially credited with 164 victories (including 84 official USPGA tournaments) in his long career of which full details are not available. Finished 2nd equal in a 1974 USPGA tournament aged 61 and 3rd equal in 1974 USPGA Championship aged 62. 24 holes-in-one

Somerville, Charles Ross

Born London, Ontario, Canada on 4th May, 1903

Nat Canadian Amateur 1926–28–30–31–35–37; runner-up 1924–25–34-38
For US Amateur Champion 1932
Oth Ontario Amateur 1927–28–29–37. Manitoba Amateur 1926. Canadian Seniors 1960–61 (tied)–65–66 (tied)
Mis President Royal Canadian Golf Association 1957

Stacy, Hollis

Born Savannah, Georgia, USA on 16th March, 1954. Turned Professional 1974

Nat US Women's Open 1977–78–84
LPGA 1977–two. 1978–one. 1979–one. 1980–one. 1982–three. 1983–three. 1984–two. 1985–one
Int Curtis Cup 1972
Mis US Girls 1969–70–71

Stadler, Craig

Born San Diego, California, USA on 2nd June, 1953. Turned Professional 1975

Chp US Masters 1982
Nat US Amateur 1973
USC 1980–two. 1981–one. 1982–three. 1984–one
Int Walker Cup 1975. Ryder Cup 1983–85

Stephenson, Jan

Born Sydney, NSW, Australia on 22nd December 1951. Turned Professional 1973

Chp US Women's Open 1983. LPGA 1982
Nat Australian Ladies Open 1973–77
LPGA 1976–86; (13 tournament victories) 1987–two

Stewart, Payne

Born Springfield, Missouri, USA on 30th January, 1957. Turned Professional 1979

Bri 2nd in Open 1985
For Indian Open 1981. Indonesian Open 1981. Jun Classic (Japan) 1985
USC 1982–two. 1983–one. 1987–one
Int Nissan Cup 1986. Kirin Cup 1988

Stockton, Davie

Born San Bernardino, California, USA on 2nd November, 1941. Turned Professional 1964

Nat USPGA Champion 1970–76. Second equal in US Masters 1974. Second in US Open 1978 (tied)
USC 1967–two. 1968–two. 1971–one. 1973–one. 1974–three
Int Ryder Cup 1971–77. USA in World Cup 1970–76

Stranahan, Frank R

Born Toledo, Ohio, USA on 5th August, 1922. Turned Professional 1954

Bri Amateur Champion 1948–50; runner-up 1952. Second in Open Championship 1947–53; leading Amateur 1947–49–50–51–53
Nat Second in US Amateur 1950
For Canadian Amateur 1947–48
USC 1955–one. 1958–one
Oth North and South Amateur 1946–49–52. Western Amateur 1946–49–51–53. Mexican Amateur 1946-48-51. Tam O'Shanter. All American Amateur 1948–49–50–51–52–53. Tam O'Shanter World Amateur 1950–51–52–53–54
Int Walker Cup 1947–49–51

Strange, Curtis

Born Norfolk, Virginia, USA on 20th January, 1955. Turned Professional 1976

Chp US Open 1988
For Canadian Open 1985–87
USC 1979–one. 1980–two. 1983–two. 1984–one. 1985–three. 1986–one. 1987–two. 1988–two
Int Eisenhower Trophy 1974. Walker Cup 1975. Ryder Cup 1983–85–87. Dunhill Cup 1985–87–88. Nissan Cup 1985. Kirin Cup 1987–88

Streit, Mrs Marlene Stewart
Born Cereal, Alberta, Canada on 9th March, 1934

Bri British Ladies 1953
Nat Canadian Ladies' Open 1951–54–55–56–58–59–63–68–72–73. Canadian Ladies' Close 1951–52–53–54–55–56–57–63–68
For US Ladies 1956; runner-up 1966. Australian Ladies 1963
Oth Ontario Provincial 1951–56–57–58. US North and South Ladies 1956
Int Canadian Commonwealth Team 1959–63–79 (capt)
Mis Canadian Athlete of the Year 1951–53–56. Canadian Woman Athlete of the Year 1951–53–56–60–63

Suggs, Miss Louise
Born Atlanta, Georgia, USA on 7th September, 1923. Turned Professional 1948

Bri British Ladies 1948
Nat US Ladies' Amateur 1947. US Women's Open 1949–52; second 1951–55 (tied)–58–59–63 (tied). USLPGA–1957
LPGA 50 tournament victories
Int Curtis Cup 1948
Mis Leading US money winner 1953–60. LPGA Hall of Fame 1951

Sutton, Hal
Born Shreveport, Louisiana, USA on 28th April, 1958. Turned Professional 1981

Chp US PGA 1983
Nat US Amateur 1980
USC 1982-one. 1983-one. 1985-two. 1986-two
Int Walker Cup 1979–81. Ryder Cup 1985–87. Nissan Cup 1986

Sweetser, Jess W
Born St Louis, Missouri, USA on 18th April, 1902

Bri Amateur Champion 1926
Nat US Amateur Champion 1922; runner-up 1923
Int Walker Cup 1922–23–24–26–28–32; non-playing captain 1967–73. World Amateur Cup non-playing captain 1966
Mis Honorary Member Royal and Ancient

De Taya, Marie-Laure de Lorenzi
Born Biarritz on 21st January 1961. Turned Professional 1986

Nat French Close Champion 1983. Spanish Champion 1978–80–83
Int France (Eur Team Ch) 1977–83. Vagliano 1983
Jun French Girls 1976. British Girls 1978
WPGA German Open, Belgian Open 1987. French Open, Dutch Open, Hennessy Ladies Cup, Swedish Open, Laing Charity Classic 1988

Thomson, Peter W CBE
Born Melbourne, Australia on 23rd August, 1929. Turned Professional 1949

Bri Open Champion 1954–55–56–58–65; second 1952–53–57. PGA Match Play 1954–61–66–67. Yorkshire Evening News 1957–60–61. Dunlop 1958. Daks 1958 (tied)–60–65. Dunlop Masters 1961–68. Bowmaker 1960. Esso Golden 1961 (tied). Martini International 1962–70 (tied). Piccadilly 1962. Alcan International 1967. Wills 1972
Nat Australian Open 1951–67–72; second 1950. Australian Professional 1967. Leading Amateur Australian Open 1948
For New Zealand Open 1950–51–53–55–59–60–61–65–71. New Zealand Professional 1953. Italian Open 1959. Spanish Open 1959. Hong Kong Open 1960-65-67. German Open 1960. India Open 1963–76. Philippines Open 1964. On Japanese circuit; 1972–two. 1976–one
USC 1956–one. 1957–one
Oth New Zealand Caltex 1967. Victorian Open 1973
Int Australia in World Cup 1953–54 (winning team)–55–56–57–59 (winning team)–60–61–62–65–69
Mis His five victories in the Open Championship including three in succession, were unequalled until Tom Watson's 1983 victory. Honorary member of the Royal and Ancient

Trevino, Lee
Born Dallas, Texas, USA on 1st December, 1939. Turned Professional 1961

Bri Open Champion 1971–72; second 1980. Benson & Hedges International 1978. Dunhill British Masters 1985
Nat US Open Champion 1968–71. USPGA Champion 1974–84
For Canadian Open 1971–77–79. Canadian PGA 1979–83
USC 1968–one. 1969–one. 1970–two. 1971–three. 1972–three. 1973–two. 1974–one. 1975–one. 1976–one. 1978–one. 1980–three. 1981–one. World Series 1974
Oth Chrysler Classic (Aust) 1973. Mexican Open 1975. Moroccan Grand Prix 1977. Lancome 1978–80
Int Ryder Cup 1969–71–73–75–79–81–85 (captain). USA in World Cup 1968–69 (winning team and individual winner)–70–71 (winning team)–74
Mis Rookie of the Year 1967. Won three major Open titles – US Open, Canadian Open, Open – in four weeks. US leading money winner 1970; second 1971–72–80. USPGA Player of the Year 1971. Byron Nelson Award 1971. Ben Hogan Award 1979. Vardon Trophy Winner five times. Inducted into American Golf Hall of Fame 1979. World Golf Hall of Fame 1981. Benson & Hedges Golfer's Handbook Golfer of the Year 1984

Tway, Bob
Born Oklahoma City, USA on 4th May, 1959. Turned Professional 1981

Chp US PGA 1986
USC 1986–three
Int Nissan Cup 1986

Van Donck, Flory
Born Tervueren, Brussels, Belgium on 23rd June, 1912

Bri Second in Open Championship 1956–59. PGA Match Play runner-up 1947–52. Silver King 1951–53. North British-Harrogate 1951. South of England Professional 1952. Yorkshire Evening News 1953
Nat Belgian Open 1939–46–47–53–56; second 1935–51. Belgian Professional 1935–38–39–52–53–54–55–56–57–59–60–63–64–65–66–68
For Dutch Open 1936 37–46–51–53. Italian Open 1938–47–53–55. Swiss Open 1953–55. French Open 1954–57–58. German Open 1953–56. Uruguay Open 1954. Portuguese Open 1955. Danish Open 1959. Venezuelan Open 1957
Int Belgium in World Cup 1954 to 1970–72–79, individual winner 1960. Europe v GB 1954–55–56–58
Mis Harry Vardon Trophy 1983

Varangot, Mlle Brigitte
Born Biarritz, France on 1st May, 1940

Bri British Ladies 1963–65–68. Kayser Bondor Foursomes 1960–63. British Girls 1957. Casa Pupo Foursomes 1965. Avia Foursomes 1966–73

Nat French Ladies' Open 1961–62–64–65–66–73; runner-up 1960–63–67–70. French Ladies' Close 1959–61–63–70. French Girls 1959–60–61
For Italian Ladies 1970
Int France, 1956 to 1973. Vagliano Trophy 1959–61–63–65–69–71. World Team Championship 1964 (winning team)–66–68–70–72–74

Vare, Mrs Edwin H (*née* Glenna Collett)
Born New Haven, Connecticut, USA on 20th June 1903

Bri British Ladies runner-up 1929–30
Nat US Ladies' Amateur 1922–25–28–29–30–35; runner-up 1931–32
For Canadian Ladies 1923–24
Oth North and South Ladies 1922–23–24–27–29–30. Eastern Ladies 7 times
Int Curtis Cup 1932–36–38–48 (capt); non-playing captain 1950
Mis Bobby Jones Award 1965

Verplank, Scott
Born Dallas, Texas, USA on 9th July, 1964

Nat US Amateur 1984
USC 1985–one (as amateur). 1988–one (Buick Open)
Int Walker Cup 1985

Vicenzo, Roberto De
Born Buenos Aires on 14th April, 1923. Turned Professional 1938

Bri Open Champion 1967; second 1950; third 1948–49–56–60–64–69. North British-Harrogate 1948
Nat Argentine Open 1944–49–51–52–58–65–67–70–74. Argentine Professional 1944–45–47–48–49–51–52
For Chile Open 1946. Colombia Open 1947. Uruguay Open 1949. Belgian Open 1950. Dutch Open 1950. French Open 1950–60–64. Mexican Open 1951–53. Panama Open 1952–73–74. Jamaican Open 1956–57. Brazilian Open 1957–60–63–64–73. Caracas Open 1973. German Open 1964. Spanish Open 1966. US Masters second 1968. Bogota Open 1969
USC 1951–two. 1953–one. 1957–two. 1966–one
Oth USPGA Seniors 1974. World Senior Professional 1974. Legends of Golf 1979. US Senior Open 1980
Int Argentina in World Cup 1953 (winning team)–54–55–62 (individual winner)–63–64–65–66–68–69–70 (individual winner)–71–72–73–74; Mexico in World Cup 1956–59–60–61
Mis Credited with 240 victories world wide including 40 National Championships. In the last round of the 1968 US Masters signed his card for a four at a hole at which he took three and so forfeited the right to playoff for the title. Became the oldest winner of the Open Championship (Cup) in 1967 at the age of 44 years and 93 days. Bobby Jones Award 1970. Made an honorary member of the Royal and Ancient GC 1976. Walter Hagen Award 1979

Wadkins, Lanny
Born Richmond, Virginia, USA on 5th December, 1949. Turned Professional 1971

Nat US Amateur 1970. USPGA 1977
For Canadian PGA 1978
USC 1972–one. 1973–two. 1979–two. 1982–two. 1983–two. 1985–three. 1987–one. World Series 1977. 1988–two
Oth Victorian PGA (Aust) 1978
Int Eisenhower Trophy winning team 1970. Walker Cup 1969–71. Ryder Cup 1977–79–83–85–87. USA in World Cup 1977. Dunhill Cup 1986. Kirin Cup 1987
Mis Rookie of the Year 1972 winning 116,616 dollars. Runner-up 1971 Heritage Classic as amateur

Ward, Harvie
Born Tarboro, North Carolina , USA, 1926. Turned Professional 1973

Bri Amateur Champion 1952; runner-up 1953
Nat US Amateur Champion 1955–56
For Canadian Amateur 1964
Oth North and South Amateur 1948
Int Walker Cup 1953–55–59

Watson, Tom
Born Kansas City, Montana, USA on 4th September, 1949. Turned Professional 1971

Bri Open Champion 1975–77–80–82–83
Nat US Masters 1977–81, second 1978 (tied)–79 (tied). Second USPGA 1978 (tied). US Open 1982, second 1983
USC 1974–one. 1975–one. 1977–three. 1978–five. 1979–five. 1980-five. 1981–four. 1982–two. 1984–three. World Series 1975–80
Oth Phoenix Open (Japan) 1980
Int Ryder Cup 1977–81–83
Mis Byron Nelson Award 1977–78–79. US leading money winner 1977–78–79–80. His 1980 winnings of 530,808 dollars is the largest in one year. USPGA Player of the Year 1977–78–79–80. Bobby Jones Award 1986

Weiskopf, Tom
Born Ohio, USA on 9th November, 1942. Turned Professional 1964

Bri Open Champion 1973. Piccadilly World Match Play 1972
Nat Second US Master 1969–72–74 (equal)–75–(equal). Second in US Open 1976 (equal)
For Canadian Open 1973–75. South African PGA 1973. Argentine Open 1979
USC 1968-two. 1971-two. 1972-one. 1973-three. 1975-one. 1977-one. 1978-one. 1982-one. World Series 1973
Int Ryder Cup 1973–75. USA in World Cup 1972

Whitworth, Kathy
Born Monahans, Texas, USA on 27th September, 1939. Turned Professional 1959

Nat Second in US Women's Open 1971. LPGA 1967–71 Titleholders Championship 1965–66
LPGA 88 tournament victories. 10 victories in 1968
Mis US Ladies' Player of the Year 1966–67–68–69–71–72–73. Leading US money winner 1965–66–67–68–70–71–72–73; second in 1969. All-time leading money winner. Woman Athlete of the Year 1965–66

Wright, Mary Kathryn (Mickey)
Born San Diego, California, USA in 1935. Turned Professional 1954

Nat US Ladies' Amateur runner-up 1954. US Women's Open 1958–59–61–64, second 1968. USLPGA 1958–60–61–63
LPGA In 1973 recorded her 82nd win in all tournaments with her Colgate-Dinah Shore victory
Mis Woman Athlete of the Year 1963–64. Leading US money winner 1961–62–63–64. Won 13 tournaments in 1963. US Girls 1952. LPGA Hall of Fame 1964

Yates, Charles Richardson
Born Atlanta, Georgia, USA on 9th September, 1913

Bri Amateur Champion 1938
Oth Western Amateur 1935. Leading Amateur Masters 1934–39–40

Int Walker Cup 1936–38; non-playing captain 1953
Mis Bobby Jones Award 1980

Zoeller, Frank Urban

Born New Albany, Indiana, USA on 11th November, 1951. Turned Professional 1973

Nat US Open 1984. US Masters 1979; second 1981
USC 1979–two. 1983–two. 1985–one. 1986–three.
Int Ryder Cup 1983–85
Mis Won US Masters at first attempt

British Isles International Players, Professional Men

Adams, J
(Scotland): v England 1932-33-34-35-36-37-38; v Wales 1937-38; v Ireland 1937-38. (GB): v America 1947-49-51-53

Ainslie, T
(Scotland): v Ireland 1936

Alliss, Percy
(England): v Scotland 1932-33-34-35-36-37; v Ireland 1932-38; v Wales 1938. (GB): v France 1929; v America 1929-31-33-35-37

Alliss, Peter
(England): in Canada Cup 1954-55-57-58-59-61-62-64-66; in World Cup 1967. (GB): v America 1953-57-59-61-63-65-67-69

Anderson, Joe
(Scotland): v Ireland 1932

Anderson, W
(Scotland): v Ireland 1936; v England 1937; v Wales 1937

Ayton, LB
(Scotland): v England 1910-12-13-33-34

Ayton, JB, jr
(Scotland): v England 1937. (GB): v America 1949

Ballantine, J
(Scotland): v England 1932-36

Ballingall, J
(Scotland): v England 1938; Ireland 1938; v Wales 1938

Bamford, BJ
(England): in Canada Cup 1961

Bannerman, H
(Scotland): in World Cup 1967-72. (GB): v America 1971

Barber, T
(England): v Ireland 1932-33

Barnes, BW
(Scotland): in World Cup 1974-75-76-77. (GB): v America 1969-71-73-75-77-79; v Europe 1974-76-78-80; v South Africa 1976

Batley, JB
(England): v Scotland 1912

Beck, AG
(England): v Wales 1938; v Ireland 1938

Bembridge, M
(England): in World Cup 1974-75. (GB): v America 1969-71-73-75; v South Africa 1976

Boomer, A
(England): (GB): v America 1926-27-29

Bousfield, K
(England): in Canada Cup 1956-57. (GB): v America 1949-51-55-57-59-61

Boyle, HF
(Ireland): in World Cup 1967. (GB): v America 1967

Bradshaw, H
(Ireland): in Canada Cup 1954-55-56-57-58-59; v Scotland 1937-38; v Wales 1937; v England 1938. (GB): v America 1953-55-57

Braid, J
(Scotland): v England 1903-04-05-06-07-09-10-12. (GB): v America 1921

Branch, WJ
(England): v Scotland 1936

Brand, G, jr
(Scotland): in World Cup 1984-85; in Dunhill Cup 1985-86-87-88; (Eur): in Nissan Cup 1985; (GB): v America 1987

Brand,GJ
(England): in World Cup 1983; in Dunhill Cup 1986-87 (winners). (GB): v America 1983; (Eur) Nissan Cup 1986

Brown, EC
(Scotland): in Canada Cup 1954-55-56-57-58-59-60-61-62-65-66; in World Cup 1987-68. (GB): v America 1953-55-57-59

Brown, K
(Scotland): in World Cup 1977-78-79-83. (GB): v America 1977-79-83-85-87; v Europe 1978; (Eur) Kirin Cup 1987

Burns, S
(Scotland): v England 1932. (GB): v America 1929

Burton, J
(England): v Ireland 1933

Burton, R
(England): v Scotland 1935-36-37-38; v Ireland 1938; v Wales 1938. (GB): v America 1935-37-49

Busson, JH
(England): v Scotland 1938

Busson, JJ
(England): v Scotland 1934-35-36-37. (GB): v America 1935

Butler, PJ
(England): in World Cup 1969-70-73. (GB): v America 1965-69-71-73; v Europe 1976

Callum, WS
(Scotland): v Ireland 1935

Campbell, J
(Scotland): v Ireland 1936

Carrol, LJ
(Ireland): v Scotland 1937-38; v Wales 1937; v England 1938

Cassidy, J
(Ireland): v England 1933; v Scotland 1934-35

Cassidy, D
(Ireland): v Scotland 1936-37; v Wales 1937

Cawsey, GH
(England): v Scotland 1906-07

Caygill, GA
(England): (GB): v America 1969

Clark, C
(England): (GB): v America 1973

Clark, HK
(England): in World Cup 1978-84-85-87; in Dunhill Cup 1985-86-87 (winners). (GB): v America 1977-81-85-87; v Europe 1978-84. (Eur): in Nissan Cup 1985

Coles, NC
(England): in Canada Cup 1963; in World Cup 1968. (GB): v America 1961-63-65-67-69-71-73-77; v Europe 1974-76-78-80

Collinge, T
(England): v Scotland 1937

Collins, JF
(England): v Scotland 1903-04

Coltart, F
(Scotland): v England 1909

Compston, A
(England): v Scotland 1932-35; v Ireland 1932. (GB): v America 1926-27-29-31; v France 1929

Cotton, TH
(England): (GB): v America 1929-37-47; v France 1929

Cox, S
(Wales): in World Cup 1975

Cox, WJ
(England): v Scotland 1935-36-37. (GB): v America 1935-37

Curtis, D
(England): v Scotland 1934-38; v Ireland 1938; v Wales 1938

Dabson, K
(Wales): in World Cup 1972

Dailey, A
(Scotland): v England 1932-33-34-35-36-38; v Ireland 1938; v Wales 1938. (GB): v America 1933

Daly, F
(Ireland): v Scotland 1936-37-38; v England 1938; v Wales 1937; in Canada Cup 1954-55. (GB): v America 1947-49-51-53

Darcy, E
(Ireland): in World Cup 1976-77-83-84-85-87; Dunhill Cup 1987-88 (winners). (GB): v America 1975-77-81-87; v Europe 1976-84; v South Africa 1976

Davies, R
(Wales): in World Cup 1968

Davies, WH
(England): v Scotland 1932-33; v Ireland 1932-33. (GB): v America 1931-33

Davis, W
(Scotland): v Ireland 1933-34-35-36-37-38; v England 1937-38; v Wales 1937-38

Dawson, P
(England): in World Cup 1977. (GB): v America 1977

De Foy, CB
(Wales): in World Cup 1971-73-74-75-76-77-78

Denny, CS
(England): v Scotland 1936

Dobson, T
(Scotland): v England 1932-33-34-35-36-37; v Ireland 1932-33-34-35-36-37-38; v Wales 1937-38

Don, W
(Scotland): v Ireland 1935-36

Donaldson, J
(Scotland): v England 1932-35-38; v Ireland 1937; v Wales 1937

Dornan, R
(Scotland): v Ireland 1932

Drew, NV
(Ireland): in Canada Cup 1960-61. (GB): v America 1959

Duncan, G
(Scotland): v England 1906-07-09-10-12-13-32-34-35-36-37. (GB): v America 1921-26-27-29-31

Durward, JG
(Scotland): v Ireland 1934; v England 1937

Easterbrook, S
(England): v Scotland 1932-33-34-35-38; v Ireland 1933. (GB): v America 1931-33

Edgar, J
(Ireland): v Scotland 1938

Fairweather, S
(Ireland): v England 1932; v Scotland 1933. (Scotland): v England 1933-35-36; v Ireland 1938; v Wales 1938

Faldo, NA
(England): in World Cup 1977; in Dunhill Cup 1985-86-87 (winners) -88. (GB): v America 1977-79-81-83-85-87; v Europe 1978-80-82-84; v Rest of World 1982. (Eur) Nissan Cup 1986. Kirin Cup 1987

Fallon, J
(Scotland): v England 1936-37-38; v Ireland 1937-38; v Wales 1937-38. (GB): v America 1955

Faulkner, M
(England): (GB): v America 1947-49-51-53-57

Feherty, D
(Ireland): in Dunhill Cup 1985-86

Fenton, WB
(Scotland): v England 1932; v Ireland 1932-33

Fernie, TR
(Scotland): v England 1910-12-13-33

Foster, M
(England): in World Cup 1976. (GB): v Europe 1976

Gadd, B
(England): v Scotland 1933-35-38; v Ireland 1933-38; v Wales 1938

Gadd, G
(England): (GB): v America 1926-27

Gallacher, BJ
(Scotland): in World Cup 1969-71-74-82-83. (GB): v America 1969-71-73-75-77-79-81-83; v Europe 1974-78-82-84; v South Africa 1976; v Rest of World 1982

Garner, JR
(England): (GB): v America 1971-73

Gaudin, PJ
(England): v Scotland 1905-06-07-09-12-13

Good, G
(Scotland): v England 1934-36

Gould, H
(Wales): in Canada Cup 1954-55

Gow, A
(Scotland): v England 1912

Grabham, C
(Wales): v England 1938; v Scotland 1938

Grant, T
(Scotland): v England 1913

Gray, E
(England): v Scotland 1904-05-07

Green, E
(England): (GB): v America 1947

Green, T
(England): v Scotland 1935. (Wales): v Scotland 1937-38; v Ireland 1937; v England 1938

Greene, C
(Ireland): in Canada Cup 1965

Gregson, M
(England): in World Cup 1967. (GB): v America 1967

Haliburton, TB
(Scotland): v Ireland 1935-36-38; v England 1938; v Wales 1938; in Canada Cup 1954. (GB): v America 1961-63

Hamill, J
(Ireland): v Scotland 1933-34-35; v England 1932-33

Hargreaves, J
(England): (GB): v America 1951

Hastings, W
(Scotland): England 1937-38; v Wales 1937-38; v Ireland 1937-38

Havers: AG
(England): v Scotland 1932-33-34; v Ireland 1932-33. (GB): v America 1921-26-27-31-33; v France 1929

Healing, SF
(Wales): v Scotland 1938

Hepburn, J
(Scotland): v England 1903-05-06-07-09-10-12-13

Herd, A
(Scotland): v England 1903-04-05-06-09-10-12-13-32

Hill, EF
(Wales): v Scotland 1937-38; v Ireland 1937; v England 1938

Hitchcock, J
(England): (GB): v America 1965

Hodson, B
(England): v Ireland 1933. (Wales): v Scotland 1937-38; v Ireland 1937; v England 1938. (GB): v America 1931

Holley, W
(Ireland): v Scotland 1933-34-35-36-38; v England 1932-33-38

Horne, R
(England): (GB): v America 1947

Horton, T
(England): in World Cup 1976. (GB): v Europe 1974-76; v America 1975-77

Houston, D
(Scotland): v Ireland 1934

Huggett, BGC
(Wales): in Canada Cup 1963-64-65; in World Cup 1968-69-70-71-76-79. (GB): v America 1963-67-69-71-73-75; v Europe 1974-78

Huish, D
(Scotland): in World Cup 1973

Hunt, BJ
(England): in Canada Cup 1958-59-60-62-63-64; in World Cup 1968. (GB): v America 1953-57-59-61-63-65-67-69

Hunt, GL
(England): in World Cup 1972-75. (GB): v Europe 1974; v America 1975

Hunt, Geoffrey M
(England): (GB): v America 1963

Hunter, W
(Scotland): v England 1906-07-09-10

Hutton, GC
(Scotland): v Ireland 1936-37; v England 1937-38; v Wales 1937

Ingram, D
(Scotland): in World Cup 1973

Jacklin, A
(England): in Canada Cup 1966; in World Cup 1970-71-72. (GB): v America 1967-69-71-73-75-77-79-83 (captain) -85 (captain) -87 (captain); v Europe 1976-82; v Rest of World 1982

Jackson, H
(Ireland): in World Cup 1970-71

Jacobs, JRM
(England): (GB): v America 1955

Jagger, D
(England): (GB): v Europe 1976

James, G
(Wales): v Scotland 1937; v Ireland 1937

James, MH
(England): in World Cup 1978-79-82-84-87; in Dunhill Cup 1988. GB): v America 1977-79-81; v Europe 1978-80-82; v Rest of World 1982

Jarman, EW
(England): v Scotland 1935. (GB): v America 1935

Job, N
(England): (GB): v Europe 1980

Jolly, HC
(England): (GB): v America 1926-27; v France 1929

Jones, DC
(Wales): v Scotland 1937-38; v Ireland 1937; v England 1938

Jones, E
(Ireland): in Canada Cup 1965

Jones, R
(England): v Scotland 1903-04-05-06-07-09-10-12-13

Jones, T
(Wales): v Scotland 1936; v Ireland 1937; v England 1938

Kenyon, EWH
(England): v Scotland 1932; v Ireland 392

King, M
(England): in World Cup 1979. (GB): v America 1979

King, SL
(England): v Scotland 1934-36-37-38; v Wales 1938; v Ireland 1938. (GB): v America 1937-47-49

Kinsella, J
(Ireland): in World Cup 1968-69-72-73

Kinsella, W
(Ireland): v Scotland 1937-38; v England 1938

Knight, G
(Scotland): v England 1937

Lacey, AJ
(England): v Scotland 1932-33-34-36-37-38; v Ireland 1932-33-38; v Wales 1938. (GB): v America 1933-37

Laidlaw, W
(Scotland): v England 1935-36-38; v Ireland 1937; v Wales 1937

Lane, B
(England): in Dunhill Cup 1988

Lees, A
(England): v Scotland 1938; v Wales 1938; v Ireland 1938. (GB): v America 1947-49-51-55

Llewellyn, D
(Wales): in World Cup 1974-85-87 (winners); in Dunhill Cup 1985-88. (GB): v Europe 1984

Lloyd, F
(Wales): v Scotland 1937-38; v Ireland 1937; v England 1938

Lockhart, G
(Scotland): v Ireland 1934-35

Lyle, AWB
(Scotland): in World Cup 1979-80-87; in Dunhill Cup 1985-86-87-88. (GB): v America 1979-81-83-85-87; v Europe 1980-82-84; v Rest of World 1982. (Eur): in Nissan Cup 1985-86; Kirin Cup 1987

McCartney, J
(Ireland): v Scotland 1932-33-34-35-36-37-38; v England 1932-33-38; v Wales 1937

McCulloch, D
(Scotland): v England 1932-33-34-35-36-37; v Ireland 1932-33-34-35

McDermott, M
(Ireland): v England 1932; v Scotland 1932

McDowall, J
(Scotland): v England 1932-33-34-35-36; v Ireland 1933-34-35-36

McEwan, P
(Scotland): v England 1907

McIntosh, G
(Scotland): v England 1938; v Ireland 1938; v Wales 1938

McKenna, J
(Ireland): v Scotland 1936-37-38; v Wales 1937-38; v England 1938

McKenna, R
(Ireland): v Scotland 1933-35; v England 1933

McMillan, J
(Scotland): v England 1933-34-35; v Ireland 1933-34

McMinn, W
(Scotland): v England 1932-33-34

McNeill, H
(Ireland): v England 1932

Mahon, PJ
(Ireland): v Scotland 1932-33-34-35-36-37-38; v Wales 1937-38; v England 1932-33-38

Martin, J
(Ireland): in Canada Cup 1962-63-64-66; in World Cup 1970. (GB): v America 1965

Martin, S
(Scotland): in World Cup 1980

Mason, SC
(England): in World Cup 1980. (GB): v Europe 1980

Mayo, CH
(England): v Scotland 1907-09-10-12-13

Mills, RP
(England): (GB): v America 1957

Mitchell, A
(England): v Scotland 1932-33-34. (GB): v America 1921-26-29-31-33

Moffitt, R
(England): (GB): v America 1961

Montgomerie, C
(Scotland): in Dunhill Cup 1988

Mouland, M
(Wales): in Dunhill Cup 1986-87–88

Mouland, S
(Wales): in Canada Cup 1965-66; in World Cup 1967

O'Brien, W
(Ireland): v Scotland 1934-36-37; v Wales 1937

Ockenden, J
(England): (GB): v America 1921

O'Connor, C
(Ireland): in Canada Cup 1956-57-58-59-60-61-62-63-64-66; in World Cup 1967-68-69-71-73. (GB): v America 1955-57-59-61-63-65-67-69-71-73

O'Connor, C, jr
(Ireland): in World Cup 1974-75-78-85; in Dunhill Cup 1985. (GB): v Europe 1974-84; v America 1975; v South Africa 1976

O'Connor, P
(Ireland): v Scotland 1932-33-34-35-36; v England 1932-33

Oke, WG
(England): v Scotland 1932

O'Leary, JE
(Ireland): in World Cup 1972-80-82. (GB): v America 1975; v Europe 1976-78-82; v Rest of World 1982

O'Neill, J
(Ireland): v England 1933

O'Neill, M
(Ireland): v Scotland 1933-34; v England 1933

Oosterhuis, PA
(England): in World Cup 1971. (GB): v America 1971-73-75-77-79-81; v Europe 1974

Padgham, AH
(England): v Scotland 1932-33-34-35-36-37-38; v Ireland 1932-33-38; v Wales 1938. (GB): v America 1933-35-37

Panton, J
(Scotland): in Canada Cup 1955-56-57-58-59-60-61-62-63-64-65-66; in World Cup 1968. (GB): v America 1951-53-61

Park, J
(Scotland): v England 1909

Parkin, P
(Wales): in World Cup 1984; in Dunhill Cup 1985-86-87 (GB): v Europe 1984

Patterson, E
(Ireland): v Scotland 1933-34-35-36; v England 1933; v Wales 1937

Perry, A
(England); v Ireland 1932; v Scotland 1933-36-38. (GB): v America 1933-35-37

Pickett, C
(Wales): v Scotland 1937-38; v Ireland 1937; v England 1938

Platts, L
(Wales): (GB): v America 1965

Polland, E
(Ireland): in World Cup 1973-74-76-77-78-79. (GB): v America 1973; v Europe 1974-76-78-80; v South America 1976

Pope, CW
(Ireland): v England 1932; v Scotland 1932

Rafferty, R
(Ireland): in World Cup 1983-84-87; in Dunhill Cup 1986-87-88 (winners). (GB): v Europe 1984

Rainford, P
(England): v Scotland 1903-07

Ray, E
(England): v Scotland 1903-04-05-06-07-09-10-12-13. (GB): v America 1921-26-27

Rees, DJ
(Wales): v Scotland 1937-38; v Ireland 1937; England 1938; in Canada Cup 1954-56-57-58-59-60-61-62-64. (GB): v America 1937-47-49-51-53-55-57-59-61

Reid, W
(England): v Scotland 1906-07

Renouf, TG
(England): v Scotland 1903-04-05-10-13

Ritchie, WL
(Scotland): v England 1913

Robertson, F
(Scotland): v Ireland 1933; v England 1938

Robertson, P
(Scotland): v England 1932; v Ireland 1932-34

Robson, F
(England): v Scotland 1909-10. (GB): v America 1926-27-29-31

Rowe, AJ
(England): v Scotland 1903-06-07

Sayers, B, jr
(Scotland): v England 1906-07-09

Scott, SS
(England): (GB): v America 1955

Seymour, M
(England): v Scotland 1932-33; v Ireland 1932-33. (Scotland): v Ireland 1932

Shade, RDBM
(Scotland): in World Cup 1970-71-72

Sherlock, JG
(England): v Scotland 1903-04-05-06-07-09-10-12-13. (GB): v America 1921

Simpson, A
(Scotland): v England 1904

Smalldon, D
(Wales): in Canada Cup 1955-56

Smith, CR
(Scotland): v England 1903-04-07-09-13

Smith, GE
(Scotland): v Ireland 1932

Smyth, D
(Ireland): in World Cup 1979-80-82-83; in Dunhill Cup 1985-86-87-88 (winners). (GB): v America 1979-81; v Europe 1980-82-84; v Rest of World 1982

Snell, D
(England): in Canada Cup 1965

Spark, W
(Scotland): v Ireland 1933-35-37; v England 1935; v Wales 1937

Stevenson, P
(Ireland): v Scotland 1933-34-35-36-38; v England 1933-38

Sutton, M
(England): in Canada Cup 1955

Taylor, JH
(England): v Scotland 1903-04-05-06-07-09-10-12-13 (GB): v America 1921

Taylor, JJ
(England): v Scotland 1937

Taylor, Josh
(England): v Scotland 1913. (GB): v America 1921

Thomas, DC
(Wales): in Canada Cup 1957-58-59-60-61-62-63-66; in World Cup 1967-69-70. (GB): v America 1959-63-65-67

Thompson, R
(Scotland): v England 1903-04-05-06-07-09-10-12

Tingey, A
(England): v Scotland 1903-05

Torrance, S
(Scotland): in World Cup 1976-78-82-84-85-87; in Dunhill Cup 1985-86-87. (GB): v Europe 1976-78-80-82-84; v America 1981-83-85-87; v Rest of World 1982. (Eur): in Nissan Cup 1985

Townsend, P
(England): in World Cup 1969-74. (GB): v America 1969-71; v Europe 1974

Twine, WT
(England): v Ireland 1932

Vardon, H
(England): (GB): v America 1921

Vaughan, DI
(Wales): in World Cup 1972-73-77-78-79-80

Waites, BJ
(England): in World Cup 1980-82-83. (GB): v Europe 1980-82-84; v Rest of World 1982; v America 1983

Walker, RT
(Scotland): in Canada Cup 1964

Wallace, L
(Ireland): v England 1932; v Scotland 1932

Ward, CH
(England): v Ireland 1932. (GB): v America 1947-49-51

Watt, T
(Scotland): v England 1907

Watt, W
(Scotland): v England 1912-13

Way, P
(England): in Dunhill Cup 1985; in World Cup 1985. (GB): v America 1983-85

Weetman, H
(England): in Canada Cup 1954-56-60. (GB): v America 1951-53-55-57-59-61-63

Whitcombe, CA
(England): v Scotland 1932-33-34-35-36-37-38; v Ireland 1933. (GB): v America 1927-29-31-33-35-37; v France 1929

Whitcombe, EE
(England): v Scotland 1938; v Wales 1938; v Ireland 1938

Whitcombe, ER
(England): v Scotland 1932; v Ireland 1933. (GB): v America 1926-29-31-35; v France 1929

Whitcombe, RA
(England): v Scotland 1933-34-35-36-37-38. (GB): v America 1935

White, J
(Scotland): v England 1903-04-05-06-07-09-12-13

Wilcock, P
(England): in World Cup 1973

Will, G
(Scotland): in Canada Cup 1963; in World Cup 1969-70. (GB): v America 1963-65-67

Williams, K
(Wales): v Scotland 1937-38; v Ireland 1937; v England 1938

Williamson, T
(England): v Scotland 1904-05-06-07-09-10-12-13

Wilson, RG
(England): v Scotland 1913

Wilson, T
(Scotland): v England 1933-34; v Ireland 1932-33-34

Wolstenholme, GB
(England): in Canada Cup 1965

Wood, N
(Scotland): in World Cup 1975. (GB): v America 1975

Woosnam, I
(Wales): in World Cup 1980-82-83-84-85-87 (winners); Dunhill Cup 1985-86-87-88. (GB): v Europe 1982-84; v Rest of World 1982; v America 1983-85-87. (Eur): in Nissan Cup 1985-86. Kirin Cup 1987

British Isles International Players, Amateur Men

Abbreviations:

(GB) played for Great Britain or Great Britain and Ireland;
Com Tnmt Commonwealth Tournament;
Eur T Ch played in European Team Championship for home country;
Home Int played in Home International mat in a few top events) in important

Adams, MPD
(Wales): Home Int 1969-70-71-72-75-76-77; Eur T Ch 1971

Aitken, AR
(Scotland): v England 1906-07-08

Alexander, DW
(Scotland): Home Int 1958; v Scandinavia 1958

Allison, A
(Ireland): v England 1928; v Scotland 1929

Anderson, N
(Ireland): Home Int 1985-86-87-88. (GB): v Europe 1988

Anderson, RB
(Scotland): v Scandinavia 1960-62; Home Int 1962-63

Andrew, R
(Scotland): v England 1905-06-07-08-09-10

Armour, A
(Scotland): v England 1922

Armour, TD
(GB): v America 1921

Ashby, H
(England): Home Int 1972-73-74. (GB): in Dominican Int 1973. (GB): v Europe 1974

Atkinson, HN
(Wales): v Ireland 1913

Attenborough, M
(England): Home Int 1964-66-67-68; Eur T Ch 1967. (GB): v Europe 1966-68; v American 1967

Aylmer, CC
(England): v Scotland 1911-22-23-24. (GB): v America 1921-22

Babington, A
(Ireland): v Wales 1913

Baker, P
(England): Home Int 1985. (GB): v America 1985; v Europe 1986

Baker, RN
(Ireland): Home Int 1975

Ball, J
(England): v Scotland 1902-03-04-05-06-07-08-09-10-11-12

Bamford, JL
(Ireland): Home Int 1954-56

Banks, C
(England): Home Int 1983

Banks, SE
(England): Home Int 1934-38

Bannerman, S
(Scotland): Home Int 1988

Bardsley, R
(England): Home Int 1987; v France 1988

Barker, HH
(England): v Scotland 1907

Barrie, GC
(Scotland): Home Int 1981-83

Barry, AG
(England): v Scotland 1906-07

Bayliss, RP
(England): v Ireland 1929; Home Int 1933-34

Bayne, PWGA
(Wales): Home Int 1949

Beamish, CH
(Ireland): Home Int 1950-51-53-56

Beck, JB
(England): v Scotland 1926-30; Home Int 1933. (GB): v America 1928-38 (Captain) -47 (Captain)

Beddard, JB
(England): v Wales/Ireland 1925; v Ireland 1929; v Scotland 1927-28-29

Beharrell, JC
(England): Home Int 1956

Bell, HE
(Ireland): v Wales 1930; Home Int 1932

Bell, RK
(England): Home Int 1947

Benka, PJ
(England): Home Int 1967-68-69-70: Eur T Ch 1969. (GB): v America 1969; v Europe 1970

Bennett, H
(England): Home Int 1948-49-51

Bennett, S
(England): v Scotland 1979

Bentley, AL
(England): Home Int 1936-37; v France 1937-39

Bentley, HG
(England): v Ireland 1931; v Scotland 1931. Home Int 1932-33-34-35-36-37-38-47; v France 1934-35-36-37-39-54. (GB): v America 1934-36-38

Berry, P
(England): Home Int 1972. (GB): v Europe 1972

Bevan, RJ
(Wales): Home Int 1964-65-66-67-73-74

Beveridge, HW
(Scotland): v England 1908
Birtwell, SG
(England): Home Int 1968-70-73
Black, D
(Scotland): Home Int 1966-67
Black, FC
(Scotland): Home Int 1962-64-65-66-68; v Scandinavia 1962; Eur T Ch 1965-67. (GB): v Europe 1966
Black, GT
(Scotland): Home Int 1952-53; v South Africa 1954
Black, JL
(Wales): Home Int 1932-33-34-35-36
Black, WC
(Scotland): Home Int 1964-65
Blackwell, EBH
(Scotland): v England 1902-04-05-06-07-09-10-12-23-24-25
Blair, DA
(Scotland): Home Int 1948-49-51-52-53-55-56-57; v Scandinavia 1956-58-62. (GB): v America 1955-61; in Com Tnmt 1954
Blakeman, D
(England): Home Int 1981; v France 1982
Bloice, C
(Scotland): Home Int 1985-86. (GB): v America 1985
Bloxham, JA
(England): Home Int 1966
Blyth, AD
(Scotland): v England 1904
Bonallack,MF
(England): Home Int 1957-58-59-60-61-62-63-64-65-66-67-68-69-70-71-72-73-74; Eur T Ch 1969-71. (GB): v America 1957-59-61-63-65-67-69 (Captain) -71 (Captain) -73; v Europe 1958-62-64-66-68-70-72; in Com Tnmt 1959-63-67-71; in World Team Ch 1960-62-64-66-68-70-72
Bonnell, DJ
(Wales): Home Int 1949-50-51
Bookless, JT
(Scotland): v England 1930-31; v Ireland 1930; v Wales 1931
Bottomley, S
(England): Home Int 1986
Bourn, TA
(England): v Ireland 1928; v Scotland 1930; Home Int 1933-34; v France 1934. (GB): v Australia 1934
Bowen, J
(Ireland): Home Int 1961
Bowman, TH
(England): Home Int 1932
Boxall, R
(England): Home Int 1980-81-82; v France 1982
Boyd, HA
(Ireland): v Wales 1913-23
Bradshaw, AS
(England): Home Int 1932
Bradshaw, EI
(England): v Scotland 1979; Eur T Ch 1979
Braid, H
(Scotland): v England 1922-23
Bramston, JAT
(England): v Scotland 1902
Brand, GJ
(England): Home Int 1976. (GB) v Europe 1976
Brand, G
(Scotland): Home Int 1978-80; v England 1979; Eur T Ch 1979; v Italy 1979; v Belgium 1980; v France 1980. (GB); v Europe 1978-80; in World Team Ch 1978-80; v America 1979; v France 1981
Branigan, D
(Ireland): Home Int 1975-76-77-80-81-82-86; Eur T Ch 1977-81; v West Germany, France, Sweden 1976
Bretherton, CF
(England): v Scotland 1922-23-24-25; v Wales/Ireland 1925
Briscoe, A
(Ireland): v England 1928-29-30-31; v Scotland 1929-30-31; v Wales 1929-30-31; Home Int 1932-33-38
Bristowe, OC
(GB): v America 1923-24
Broad, RD
(Wales): v Ireland 1979; Home Int 1980-81-82-84; Eur T Ch 1981
Broadhurst, P
(England): Home Int 1986-87; v France 1988. (GB) v Europe 1988
Brock, J
(Scotland) v Ireland 1929; Home Int 1932
Brodie, Allan
(Scotland): Home Int 1970-72-73-74-75-76-77-78-80; Eur T Ch 1973-77-79; v England 1979; v Italy 1979; v Belgium 1977; v Spain 1977; v France 1978. (GB): v America 1977-79; v Europe 1974-76-78-80;in World Team Ch 1978
Brodie, Andrew
(Scotland): Home Int 1968-69; v Spain 1974
Bromley-Davenport, E
(England): Home Int 1938-51
Brooks, A
(Scotland): Home Int 1968-69; Eur T Ch 1969. (GB): v America 1969
Brooks, CJ
(Scotland): Home Int 1984-85. (GB): v Europe 1986
Brotherton, IR
(Scotland): Home Int 1984-85
Brough, S
(England): Home Int 1952-55-59-60; v France 1952-60. (GB): v Europe 1960
Brown, CT
(Wales): Home Int 1970-71-72-73-74-75-77-78-80-88 (captain); Eur T Ch 1973; v Denmark 1977-80; v Ireland 1979; v Switzerland, Spain 1980
Brown, D
(Wales): v Ireland 1923-30-31; v England 1925; v Scotland 1931
Brown, JC
(Ireland): Home Int 1933-34-35-36-37-38-48-52-53
Brownlow, Hon WGE
(GB): v America 1926
Bruen, J
(Ireland): Home Int 1937-38-49-50. (GB): v America 1938-49-51
Bucher, AM
(Scotland): Home Int 1954-55-56; v Scandinavia 1956
Buckley, JA
(Wales): Home Int 1967-68-69-76-77-78; Eur T Ch 1967-69; v Denmark 1976-77. (GB): v America 1979
Burch, N
(England): Home Int 1974
Burgess, MJ
(England): Home Int 1963-64-67; Eur T Ch 1967
Burke, J
(Ireland): v England 1929-30-31; v Wales 1929-30-31; v Scotland 1930-31; Home Int 1932-33-34-35-36-37-38-47-48-49. (GB): v America 1932

Burns, M
(Ireland): Home Int 1973-75-83
Burnside, J
(Scotland): Home Int 1956-57
Burrell, TM
(Scotland): v England 1924
Bussell, AF
(Scotland): Home Int 1956-57-58-61; v Scandinavia 1956-60. (GB): v America 1957; v Europe 1956-62
Butterworth, JR
(England): v France 1954

Cairnes, HM
(Ireland): v Wales 1913-25; v England 1904; v Scotland 1904-27
Caldwell, I
(England): Home Int 1950-51-52-53-54-55-56-57-58-59-61; v France 1950. (GB): v America 1951-55
Calvert, M
(Wales): Home Int 1983-84-86-87
Cameron, D
(Scotland): Home Int 1938-51
Campbell, Bart, Sir Guy C
(Scotland): v England 1909-10-11
Campbell, HM
(Scotland): Home Int 1962-64-68; v Scandinavia 1962; v Australia 1964; Eur T Ch 1965.(GB): v Europe 1964
Campbell, JGS
(Scotland): Home Int 1947-48
Campbell, W
(Scotland): v Ireland 1927-28-29-30-31; v England 1928 -29-30-31; v Wales 1931; Home Int 1933-34-35-36. (GB): v America 1930
Cannon, JHS
(England): v Ireland/Wales 1925
Cannon, JM
(Scotland): Home Int 1969; v Spain 1974
Carman, A
(England): v Scotland 1979; Home Int 1980
Carr, FC
(England): v Scotland 1911
Carr, JB
(Ireland): Home Int 1947-48-49-50-51-52-53-54-55-56-57-58-59-60-61-62-63-64-65-66-67-68-69; Eur T Ch 1965-67-69. (GB): v America 1947-49-51-53-55-57-59-61-63-65 (Captain) -67 (Captain); v Europe 1954-56-64-66-68; in World Team Ch 1958-60
Carr, JJ
(Ireland): Home Int 1981-82-83
Carr, JP
(Wales): v Ireland 1913
Carr JR
(Ireland): v Wales 1930-31; v England 1931; Home Int 1933
Carr, R
(Ireland): Home Int 1970-71; Eur T Ch 1971. (GB): v America 1971
Carrgill, PM
(England): Home Int 1978
Carrick, DG
(Scotland): Home Int 1981-82-83-84-85-86-87-88; v West Germany 1987; v Italy 1988. (GB): v America 1983-87; v Europe 1986
Carroll, CA
(Ireland): v Wales 1924
Carroll, JP
(Ireland): Home Int 1948-49-50-51-62
Carroll, W
(Ireland): v Wales 1913-23-24-25; v England 1925; v Scotland 1929; Home Int 1932
Carslaw, LA
(Scotland): Home Int 1976-77-78-80-81; Eur T Ch 1977-79; v England 1979; v Italy 1979; v Spain 1977; v Belgium 1978; v France 1978. (GB): v Europe 1978; v America 1979
Cashell, BG
(Ireland): Home Int 1978; v France, West Germany, Sweden 1978
Castle, H
(England): v Scotland 1903-04
Cater, JR
(Scotland): Home Int 1952-53-54-55-56. (GB): v America 1955
Caul, P
(Ireland): Home Int 1968-69-71-72-73-74-75
Caven, J
(Scotland): v England 1926. (GB): v America 1922
Chapman, BHG
(England): Home Int 1961-62. (GB): v America 1961; v Europe 1962
Chapman, JA
(Wales): v Ireland 1923-29-30-31; v Scotland 1931; v England 1925
Chapman, R
(Wales): v Ireland 1929; Home Int 1932-34-35-36
Chapman, R
(England): v Scotland 1979; Home Int 1980-81; Eur T Ch 1981. (GB): v Europe 1980; v America 1981
Charles, WB
(Wales): v Ireland 1924
Chillas, D
(Scotland): Home Int 1971
Christmas, MJ
(England): Home Int 1960-61-62-63-64. (GB): v America 1961-63; v Europe 1962-64; in World Team Ch 1962
Clark, CA
(England): Home Int 1964. (GB): v Europe 1964; v America 1965
Clark, D
(Ireland): Home Int 1987
Clark, GJ
(England): Home Int 1961-64-66-67-68-71. (GB): v Europe 1964-66; v America 1965.
Clark, HK
(England): Home Int 1973. (GB): v America 1973
Clark, MD
(Wales): v Ireland 1947
Clay, G
(Wales): Home Int 1962
Claydon, R
(England): Home Int 1988
Cleary, T
(Ireland): Home Int 1976-77-78-82-83-84-85-86; v Wales 1979; v France, West Germany, Sweden 1976
Clement, G
(Wales): v Ireland 1979
Cochran, JS
(Scotland): Home Int 1966
Colt, HS
(England): v Scotland 1908
Coltart, A
(Scotland): Home Int 1988
Cook, JH
(England): Home Int 1969

Corridan, T
(Ireland): Home Int 1983-84

Corcoran, DK
(Ireland): Home Int 1972-73; Eur T Ch 1973

Cosh, GB
(Scotland): Home Int 1964-65-66-67-68-69; Eur T Ch 1965-69. (GB): v America 1965; v Europe 1966-68; in Com Tnmt 1967; in World Team Ch 1966-68

Coulter, JG
(Wales): Home Int 1951-52

Coutts, FJ
(Scotland): Home Int 1980-81-82; Eur T Ch 1981; v France 1981-82

Cox, S
(Wales): Home Int 1970-71-72-73-74; Eur T Ch 1971-73

Crabbe, JL
(Ireland): v Wales 1925; v Scotland 1927-28

Craddock, T
(Ireland): Home Int 1955-56-57-58-59-60-67-68-69-70; Eur T Ch 1971. (GB): v America 1967-69

Craigan, RM
(Ireland): Home Int 1963-64

Crawley, LG
(England): v Ireland 1931; v Scotland 1931; Home Int 1932-33-34-36-37-38-47-48-49-54-55; v France 1936-37-38-49. (GB): v America 1932-34-38-47

Critchley, B
(England): Home Int 1962-69-70; Eur T Ch 1969. (GB): v America 1969; v Europe 1970

Crosbie, GF
(Ireland): Home Int 1953-55-56-57-88 (captain)

Crowley, M
(Ireland): v England 1928-29-30-31; v Wales 1929-31; v Scotland 1929-30-31; Home Int 1932

Cuddihy, J
(Scotland): Home Int 1977

Curry, DH
(England): Home Int 1984-86-87; v France 1988. (GB): v Europe 1986–88 v America 1987

Dalgleish, CR
(Scotland): Home Int 1981-82-83; v France 1982; Eur T Ch 1981. (GB): v America 1981

Darwin, B
(England): v Scotland 1902-04-05-08-09-10-23-24. (GB): v America 1922

Davies, EN
(Wales): Home Int 1959-60-61-62-63-64-65-66-67-68-69-70-71-72-73-74; Eur T Ch 1969-71-73

Davies, JC
(England) Home Int 1969-71-72-73-74-78; Eur T Ch 1973-75-77. (GB): v Europe 1972-74-76-78; v America 1973-75-77-79; in World Team Ch 1974-76

Davies, FE
(Ireland): v Wales 1923

Davies, G
(Wales): v Denmark 1977; Home Int 1981-82-83

Davies, HE
(Wales): Home Int 1933-34-36

Davies, M
(England): Home Int 1984-85

Davies, TJ
(Wales): Home Int 1954-55-56-57-58-58-60

Dawson, JE
(Scotland): v Ireland 1927-29-30-31; v England 1930-31; v Wales 1931; Home Int 1932-33-34-37

Dawson, M
(Scotland): Home Int 1963-65-66

Dawson, P
(England): Home Int 1969

Deboys, A
(Scotland): Home Int 1956-59-60; v Scandinavia 1960

Deeble, P
(England): Home Int 1975-76-77-78-80-81-83-84; v Scotland 1979; Eur T Ch 1979-81. (GB): v America 1977-81; v Europe 1978; v France 1982; in Colombian Int 1978

Deighton, FWG
(Scotland): Home Int 1950-52-53-56-57-58-59-60. (GB): v America 1951-57; v South Africa 1952; in Com Tnmt 1954-59

Denholm, RB
(Scotland): v Ireland 1929-31; v Wales 1931; v England 1931; Home Int 1932-33-34-35

Dewar, FG
(Scotland): Home Int 1952-53-55

Dick, CE
(Scotland): v England 1902-03-04-05-09-12

Dickson, HM
(Scotland): v Ireland 1929-31

Dickson, JR
(Ireland): Eur T Ch 1977; Home Int 1980

Disley, A
(Wales): Home Int 1976-77-78; v Denmark 1977; v Ireland 1979

Dodd, SC
(Wales):Home Int 1985-87-88

Donellan, B
(Ireland): Home Int 1952

Dowie, A
(Scotland): Home Int 1949

Downes, P
(England): Home Int 1976-77-78-80-81-82; Eur T Ch 1977-79-81. (GB): v Europe 1980

Downie, JJ
(England): Home Int 1974

Draper, JW
(Scotland): Home Int 1954

Drew, NV
(Ireland): Home Int 1952-53. (GB): v America 1953

Duffy, I
(Wales): Home Int 1975

Duncan, AA
(Wales): Home Int 1933-34-36-38-47-48-49-50-51-52-53-54-55-56-57-58-59. (GB): v America (Captain) 1953

Duncan, GT
(Wales): Home Int 1952-53-54-55-56-57-58

Duncan, J, jr
(Wales): v Ireland 1913

Duncan, J
(Ireland): Home Int 1959-60-61

Dunn, NW
(England): v Ireland 1928

Dunn, P
(Wales): Home Int 1957-58-59-60-61-62-63-65-66

Dunne, E
(Ireland): Home Int 1973-74-76-77; v Wales 1979; Eur T Ch 1975

Durrant, RA
(England): Home Int 1967; Eur T Ch 1967

Dykes, JM
(Scotland): Home Int 1934-35-36-48-49-51. (GB): v America 1936

Easingwood, SR
(Scotland): Home Int 1986-87-88; v Italy 1988

Eaves, CH
(Wales): Home Int 1935-36-38-47-48-49

Edwards, B
(Ireland): Home Int 1961-62-64-65-66-67-68-69-73

Edwards, M
(Ireland): Home Int 1956-57-58-60-61-62

Edwards, TH
(Wales): Home Int 1947

Egan, TW
(Ireland): Home Int 1952-53-59-60-62-67-68; Eur T Ch 1967-69

Eggo, R
(England): Home Int 1986-87-88; v France 1988. (GB): v America 1987; v Europe 1988

Elliot, C
(Scotland): Home Int 1982

Elliot, IA
(Ireland): Home Int 1975-77-78; Eur T Ch 1975, v France, West Germany, Sweden 1978

Ellis, HC
(England): v Scotland 1902-12

Ellison, TF
(England): v Scotland 1922-25-26-27

Emerson, T
(Wales): Home Int 1932

Emery, G
(Wales): v Ireland 1925; Home Int 1933-36-38

Evans, AD
(Wales): v Scotland 1931-35; v Ireland 1931; Home Int 1932-33-34-35-38-47-49-50-51-52-53-54-55-56-61

Evans, Duncan
(Wales): Home Int 1978-80-81; v Ireland 1979; Eur T Ch 1981. (GB) v Europe 1980; v America 1981

Evans, G
(England): Home Int 1961

Evans, HJ
(Wales): Home Int 1976-77-78-80-81-84-85-87-88; v France 1976; v Denmark 1977-80; v Ireland 1979; Eur T Ch 1979-81; v Switzerland, Spain 1980

Evans, M Gear
(Wales): v Ireland 1930-31; v Scotland 1931

Everett, C
(Scotland): Home Int 1988; v Italy 1988

Ewing, RC
(Ireland): Home Int 1934-35-36-37-38-47-48-49-50-51-53-54-55-56-57-58. (GB): v America 1936-38-47-49-51-55

Eyles, GR
(England): Home Int 1974-75; Eur T Ch 1975. (GB): v America 1975; v Europe 1974; in World Team Ch 1974

Fairbairn, KA
(England): Home Int 1988

Fairchild, CEL
(Wales): v Ireland 1923; v England 1925

Fairchild, LJ
(Wales): v Ireland 1924

Fairlie, WE
(Scotland): v England 1912

Faldo, N
(England): Home Int 1975. (GB): in Com Tnmt 1975

Farmer, JC
(Scotland): Home Int 1970

Ferguson, M
(Ireland): Home Int 1952

Ferguson, WJ
(Ireland): Home Int 1952-54-55-58-59-61

Fergusson, S Mure
(Scotland): v England 1902-03-04

Ffrench, WF
(Ireland): v Scotland 1929; Home Int 1932

Fiddian, EW
(England): v Scotland 1929-30-31; v Ireland 1929-30-31; Home Int 1932-33-34-35; v France 1934. (GB): v America 1932-34

Fitzgibbon, JF
(Ireland): Home Int 1955-56-57

Fitzsimmons, J
(Ireland): Home Int 1938-47-48

Flaherty, JA
(Ireland): Home Int 1934-35-36-37

Flaherty, PD
(Ireland): Home Int 1967; Eur T Ch 1967-69

Fleming, J
(Scotland): Home Int 1987

Fleury, RA
(Ireland): Home Int 1974

Flockhart, AS
(Scotland): Home Int 1948-49

Fogarty, GN
(Ireland): Home Int 1956-58-63-64-67

Fogg, HN
(England): Home Int 1933

Forest, J de (now Count J de Bendern)
(England): v Ireland 1931; v Scotland 1931. (GB): v America 1932

Foster, MF
(England): Home Int 1973

Foster, R
(England): Home Int 1963-64-66-67-68-69-70-71-72; Eur T Ch 1967-69-71-73. (GB): v Europe 1964-66-68-70; v America 1965-67-69-71-73-79 (Captain) -81 (Captain); in Com Tnmt 1967-71; in World Team Ch 1964-70

Fowler, WH
(England): v Scotland 1903-04-05

Fox, SJ
(England): Home Int 1956-57-58

Frame, DW
(England): Home Int 1958-59-60-61-62-63. (GB): v America 1961

Francis, F
(England): Home Int 1936; v France 1935-36

Frazier, K
(England): Home Int 1938

Froggatt, P
(Ireland): Home Int 1957

Fry, SH
(England): v Scotland 1902-03-04-05-06-07-09

Gairdner, JR
(Scotland): v England 1902

Gallacher, BJ
(Scotland): Home Int 1967

Galloway, RF
(Scotland): Home Int 1957-58-59; v Scandinavia 1958

Gannon, MA
(Ireland): Home Int 1973-74-77-78-80-81-83-84-87-88; v France, West Germany, Sweden 1978-80; Eur T Ch 1979-81. (GB): v Europe 1974-78

Garner, PF
(England): Home Int 1977-78-80; v Scotland 1979

Garnet, LG
(England): v France 1934. (GB): v Australia 1934

Garson, R
(Scotland): v Ireland 1928-29

Gent, J
(England): v Ireland 1930; Home Int 1938

Gibb, C
(Scotland): v England 1927; v Ireland 1928

Gibson, WC
(Scotland): Home Int 1950-51

Gilford, CF
(Wales): Home Int 1963-64-65-66-67

Gilford, D
(England): Home Int 1983-84-85. (GB): v America 1985; v Europe 1986

Gill, WJ
(Ireland): v Wales 1931; Home Int 1932-33-34-35-36-37

Gillies, HD
(England): v Scotland 1908-25-26-27

Girvan, P
(Scotland): Home Int 1986; West Germany 1987. (GB): v America 1987

Glossop, R
(Wales): Home Int 1935-37-38-47

Glover, J
(Ireland): Home Int 1951-52-53-55-59-60-70

Godwin, G
(England): Home Int 1976-77-78-80-81; v Scotland 1979; v France 1982; Eur T Ch 1979-81. (GB): v America 1979-81

Goulding, N
(Ireland): Home Int 1988

Graham, AJ
(Scotland): v England 1925

Graham, J
(Scotland): v England 1902-03-04-05-06-07-08-09-10-11

Graham, JSS
(Ireland): Home Int 1938-50-51

Gray, CD
(England): Home Int 1932

Green, CW
(Scotland): Home Int 1961-62-63-64-65-67-68-69-70-71-72-73-74-75-76-77-78; Eur T Ch 1965-67-69-71-73-75-77-79; v Scandinavia 1962; v Belgium 1973-75-77-78; v Spain 1977; v Italy 1979; v England 1979. (GB): v Europe 1962-66-68-70-72-74-76; v America 1963-69-71-73-75-83 (Captain) -85 (Captain) in Com Tnmt 1971; in World Team Ch 1970-72

Green, HB
(England): v Scotland 1979

Green, PO
(England): Home Int 1961-62-63. (GB): in Com Tnmt 1963

Greene, R
(Ireland): Home Int 1933

Greig, DG
(Scotland): Home Int 1972-73-75. (GB): in Com Tnmt 1975

Greig, K
(Scotland): Home Int 1933

Griffiths, HGB
(Wales): v Ireland 1923-24-25

Griffiths, HS
(Wales): v England 1958

Griffiths, JA
(Wales): Home Int 1933

Guild, WJ
(Scotland): v England 1925-27-28; v Ireland 1927-28

Hales, JP
(Wales): v Scotland 1963

Hall, AH
(Scotland): Home Int 1962-66-69

Hall, D
(Wales): Home Int 1932-37

Hall, K
(Wales): Home Int 1955-59

Hambro, AV
(England): v Scotland 1905-08-09-10-22

Hamilton, CJ
(Wales): v Ireland 1913

Hamilton, ED
(Scotland): Home Int 1936-37-38

Hamer, S
(England): Home Int 1983-84

Hanway, M
(Ireland): Home Int 1971-74

Hardman, RH
(England): v Scotland 1927-28. (GB): v America 1928

Hare, A
(England): Home Int 1988

Hare, WCD
(Scotland): Home Int 1953

Harrhy, A
(Wales): Home Int 1988

Harrington, J
(Ireland): Home Int 1960-61-74-75-76; Eur T Ch 1975; v Wales 1979

Harris, IR
(Scotland): Home Int 1955-56-58-59

Harris, R
(Scotland): v England 1905-08-10-11-12-22-23-24-25-26-27-28 (GB): v America 1922 (Captain) -23 (Captain) -26 (Captain)

Harrison, JW
(Wales): Home Int 1937-50

Hartley, RW
(England): v Scotland 1926-27-28-29-30-31; v Ireland 1928-29-30-31; Home Int 1933-34-35. (GB): v America 1930-32

Hartley, WL
(England): v Ireland/Wales 1925; v Scotland 1927-31; v Ireland 1928-31; Home Int 1932-33; v France 1935. (GB): v America 1932

Hassall, JE
(England): v Scotland 1923; v Ireland/Wales 1925

Hastings, JL
(Scotland): Home Int 1957-58; v Scandinavia 1958

Hawksworth, J
(England): Home Int 1984-85. (GB): v America 1985

Hay, G
(Scotland): v England 1979; Home Int 1980–88; v Belgium 1980; v France 1980; v Italy 1988. (GB): v Europe

Hay, J
(Scotland): Home Int 1972

Hayes, JA
(Ireland): Home Int 1977

Hayward, CH
(England): v Scotland 1925; v Ireland 1928

Healy, TM
(Ireland): v Scotland 1931; v England 1931

Heather, D
(Ireland): Home Int 1976; v France, West Germany, Sweden 1976

Hedges, PJ
(England): Home Int 1970-73-74-75-76-77-78-82-83; Eur T Ch 1973-75-77. (GB): v America 1973-75; v Europe 1974-76; in World Team Ch 1974

Hegarty, J
(Ireland): Home Int 1975

Hegarty, TD
(Ireland): Home Int 1957

Helm, AGB
(England): Home Int 1948

Henderson, J
(Ireland): v Wales 1923

Henderson, N
(Scotland): Home Int 1963-64

Henriques, GLQ
(England): v Ireland 1930

Henry, W
(England): Home Int 1987; v France 1988

Herlihy, B
(Ireland): Home Int 1950

Herne, KTC
(Wales): v Ireland 1913

Heverin, AJ
(Ireland): Home Int 1978; v France, West Germany, Sweden 1978

Hezlet, CO
(Ireland): v Wales 1923-25-27-29-31; v Scotland 1927-28-29-30-31; v England 1929-30-31. (GB): v America 1924-26-28; v South Africa 1927

Higgins, L
(Ireland): Home Int 1968-70-71

Hill, GA
(England): Home Int 1936-37. (GB): v America 1936-55 (Captain)

Hilton, HH
(England): v Scotland 1902-03-04-05-06-07-09-10-11-12

Hird, K
(Scotland): Home Int 1987-88

Hoad, PGJ
(England): Home Int 1978; v Scotland 1979

Hodgson, C
(England): v Scotland 1924

Hoey, TBC
(Ireland): Home Int 1970-71-72-73-77-84; Eur T Ch 1971-77

Hogan, P
(Ireland): Home Int 1985-86-87-88

Holderess, Sir EWE
(England): v Scotland 1922-23-24-25-26-28. (GB): v America 1921-23-26-30

Holmes, AW
(England): Home Int 1962

Homer, TWB
(England): Home Int 1972-73; Eur T Ch 1973. (GB): v America 1973; v Europe 1972; in World Team Ch 1972

Homewood, G
(England): Home Int 1985

Hooman, CVL
(England): v Scotland 1910-22. (GB): v America 1922-23

Hope, WL
(Scotland): v England 1923-25-26-27-28-29. (GB): v America 1923-24-28

Horne, A
(Scotland): Home Int 1971

Hosie, JR
(Scotland): Home Int 1936

Howard, DB
(Scotland): v England 1979; Home Int 1980-81-82-83; v Belgium 1980; v France 1980-81; Eur T Ch 1981. (GB): v Europe 1980.

Howell, HR
(Wales): v Ireland 1923-24-25-29-30-31; v England 1925; v Scotland 1931; Home Int 1932-34-35-36-37-38-47

Howell, H Logan
(Wales: v Ireland 1925

Huddy, G
(England): Home Int 1960-61-62. (GB): v America 1961

Huggan, J
(Scotland): Home Int 1981-82-83-84; v France 1982; Eur T Ch 1981

Hughes, I
(Wales): Home Int 1954-55-56

Hulme, WJ
(Ireland): Home Int 1955-56-57

Humphrey, JG
(Wales): v Ireland 1925

Humphreys, AR
(Ireland): v England 1957

Humphreys, DI
(Wales): Home Int 1972

Humphreys, W
(England): Home Int 1970-71; Eur T Ch 1971. (GB): v Europe 1970; v America 1971

Hunter, NM
(Scotland): v England 1903-12

Hunter, WI
(Scotland): v England 1922

Hutcheon, I
(Scotland): Home Int 1971-72-73-74-75-76-77-78-80; v Belgium 1973-75-77-78-80; v Spain 1977; v France 1978 -80-81; v Italy 1979; Eur T Ch 1973-75-77-79-81. (GB): v Europe 1974-76; v America 1975-77-79-81; in World Team Ch 1974-76-80; in Com Tnmt 1975; in Dominican Int 1973; in Colombian Int 1975

Hutchings, C
(England): v Scotland 1902

Hutchinson, HG
(England): v Scotland 1902-03-04-06-07-09

Hutchison, CK
(Scotland): v England 1904-05-06-07-08-09-10-11-12

Hyde, GE
(England): Home Int 1967-68

Illingworth, G
(England): v Scotland 1929; v France 1937

Inglis, MJ
(England): Home Int 1977

Isitt, GH
(Wales): v Ireland 1923

Jack, RR
(Scotland): Home Int 1950-51-54-55-56-57-58-59-61; v Scandinavia 1958. (GB): v America 1957-59; v Europe 1956; in World Team Ch 1958; in Com Tnmt 1959

Jack, WS
(Scotland): Home Int 1955

Jacob, NE
(Wales): Home Int 1932-33-34-35-36

James, D
(Scotland): Home Int 1985

James, M
(England): Home Int 1974-75; Eur T Ch 1975
(GB): v America 1975

James, RD
(England): Home Int 1974-75

Jameson, JF
(Ireland): v Wales 1913-24

Jamieson, A, jr
(Scotland): v England 1927-28-31; v Ireland 1928-31; v Wales 1931; Home Int 1932-33-36-37.
(GB): v America 1926

Jamieson, D
(Scotland): Home Int 1980

Jenkins, JLC
(Scotland): v England 1908-12-22-24-26-28; v Ireland 1928. (GB): v America 1921

Jermine, JG
(Wales): Home Int 1972-73-74-75-76-82; Eur T Ch 1975-77; v France 1975

Jobson, RH
(England): v Ireland 1928

Johnson, TWG
(Ireland): v England 1929

Johnston, JW
(Scotland): Home Int 1970-71

Jones, DK
(Wales): Home Int 1973

Jones, EO
(Wales): Home Int 1983-85-86

Jones, JG Parry
(Wales): Home Int 1959-60

Jones, JL
(Wales): Home Int 1933-34-36

Jones, JR
(Wales): Home Int 1970-72-73-77-78-80-81-82-83-84-85; Eur T Ch 1973-79-81; v Denmark 1976-80; v Ireland 1979; v Switzerland, Spain 1980; v Ireland 1979

Jones, JW
(England): Home Int 1948-49-50-51-52-54-55

Jones, KG
(Wales): Home Int 1988

Jones, MA
(Wales): Home Int 1947-48-49-50-51-53-54-57

Jones, Malcolm F
(Wales): Home Int 1933

Jones, SP
(Wales): Home Int 1981-82-83-84-85-86-88

Kane, RM
(Ireland): Home Int 1967-68-71-72-74-78; Eur T Ch 1971-79; v Wales 1979. (GB): v Europe 1974

Kearney, K
(Ireland): Home Int 1988

Kelleher, WA
(Ireland): Home Int 1962

Kelley, MJ
(England): Home Int 1974-75-76-77-78-80-81-82-88 (Captain); v France 1982; Eur T Ch 1977-79. (GB): v America 1977-79; v Europe 1976-78; in World Team Ch 1976; in Colombian Int 1978

Kelley, PD
(England): Home Int 1965-66-68

Kelly, NS
(Ireland): Home Int 1966

Keppler, SD
(England): Home Int 1982-83; v France 1982.
(GB): v America 1983

Kilduff, AJ
(Ireland): v Scotland 1928

Killey, GC
(Scotland): v Ireland 1928

King, M
(England): Home Int 1969-70-71-72-73; Eur T Ch 1971-73 (GB): v America 1969-73; v Europe 1970-72; in Com Tnmt 1971

Kissock, B
(Ireland): Home Int 1961-62-74-76; v France, West Germany, Sweden 1978

Kitchin, JE
(England): v France 1949

Knight, B
(Wales): Home Int 1986

Knipe, RG
(Wales): Home Int 1953-54-55-56

Knowles, WR
(Wales): v England 1948

Kyle, AT
(Scotland): Home Int 1938-47-49-50-51-52-53.
(GB): v America 1938-47-51; v South Africa 1952

Kyle, D
(Scotland): v England 1924-30. (GB): v America 1924

Kyle, EP
(Scotland): v England 1925

Laidlay, JE
(Scotland): v England 1902-03-04-05-06-07-08-09-10-11

Lake, AD
(Wales): Home Int 1958

Lang, JA
(Scotland): v England 1929-31; v Ireland 1929-30-31; v Wales 1931. (GB): v America 1930

Langley, JDA
(England): Home Int 1950-51-52-53; v France 1950.
(GB): v America 1936-51-53

Langmead, J
(England): Home Int 1986

Lassen, EA
(England): v Scotland 1909-10-11-12

Last, CN
(Wales): Home Int 1975

Laurence, C
(England): Home Int 1983-84-85

Lawrie, CD
(Scotland): Home Int 1949-50-55-56-57-58; v Scandinavia 1958. (GB): v South Africa 1952; v America 1961 (Captain) -63 (Captain)

Layton, EN
(England): v Scotland 1922-23-26; v Ireland/Wales 1925

Lee, IGF
(Scotland): Home Int 1958-59-60-61-62; v Scandinavia 1960

Lee, JN
(Wales): Home Int 1988

Lee, M
(England): Home Int 1950

Lee, MG
(England): Home Int 1965

Lehane, N
(Ireland): Home Int 1976; v France, West Germany, Sweden 1976

Lewis, DH
(Wales): Home Int 1935-36-37-38

Lewis, DR
(Wales): v Ireland 1925-29-30-31; v Scotland 1931; Home Int 1932-34

Lewis, ME
(England): Home Int 1980-81-82; v France 1982. (GB): v America 1983

Lewis, R Cofe
(Wales): v Ireland 1925

Leyden, PJ
(Ireland): Home Int 1953-55-56-57-59

Lincoln, AC
(England): v Scotland 1907

Lindsay, J
(Scotland): Home Int 1933-34-35-36

Lloyd, HM
(Wales): v Ireland 1913

Lloyd, RM de
(Wales): v Scotland 1931; v Ireland 1931; Home Int 1932-33-34-35-36-37-38-47-48

Llyr, A
(Wales): Home Int 1984-85

Lockhart, G
(Scotland): v England 1911-12

Lockley, AE
(Wales): Home Int 1956-57-58-62

Logan, GW
(England): Home Int 1973

Long, D
(Ireland): Home Int 1973-74-80-81-82-83-84; v Wales 1979; Eur T Ch 1979

Low, AJ
(Scotland): Home Int 1964-65; Eur T Ch 1965

Low, JL
(Scotland): v England 1904

Lowe, A
(Ireland): v Wales 1924; v England 1925-28; v Scotland 1927-28

Lucas, PB
(England): Home Int 1936-48-49; v France 1936. (GB): v America 1936-47-49 (Captain)

Lunt, MSR
(England): Home Int 1956-57-58-59-60-62-63-64-66. (GB): v America 1959-61-63-65; v Europe 1964; in Com Tnmt 1963; in World Team Ch 1964

Lunt, S
(England): Home Int 1932-33-34-35; v France 1934-35-39

Lygate, M
(Scotland): Home Int 1970-75-88 (Captain); Eur T Ch 1971

Lyle, AWB
(England): Home Int 1975-76-77; Eur T Ch 1977. (GB): v America 1977; in Com Tnmt 1975; v Europe 1976

Lyon, JS
(England): Home Int 1937-38

Lyons, P
(Ireland): Home Int 1986

McAllister, SD
(Scotland): Home Int 1983

Macara, MA
(Wales): Home Int 1983-84-85-87

McArthur, W
(Scotland): Home Int 1952-54

McBeath, J
(Scotland): Home Int 1964

McBride, D
(Scotland): Home Int 1932

McCallum, AR
(Scotland): v England 1929. (GB): v America 1928

McCarrol, F
(Ireland): Home Int 1968-69

McCart, DM
(Scotland): Home Int 1977; v Belgium 1978

McCarthy, L
(Ireland): Home Int 1953-54-55-56

McConnell, FP
(Ireland): v Wales 1929-30-31; v England 1929-30-31; v Scotland 1930-31; Home Int 1934

McConnell, RM
(Ireland): v Wales 1924-25-29-30-31; v England 1925-28-29-30-31; v Scotland 1927-28-29-31; Home Int 1934-35-36-37

McConnell, WG
(Ireland): v England 1925

McCormack, JD
(Ireland): v Wales 1913-24; v England 1928, Home Int 1932-33-34-35-36-37

McCrea, WE
(Ireland): Home Int 1965-66-67; Eur T Ch 1965

McCready, SM
(Ireland): Home Int 1947-49-50-52-54. (GB): v America 1949-51

McDaid, B
(Ireland): v Wales 1979

MacDonald, GK
(Scotland): Home Int 1978-81-82; v England 1979; v France 1981-82

McDonald, H
(Scotland): Home Int 1970

Macdonald, JS
(Scotland): Home Int 1969-70-71-72; v Belgium 1973; Eur T Ch 1971. (GB): v Europe 1970; v America 1971

McEvoy, P
(England): Home Int 1976-77-78-80-81-83-84-85-86-87-88; v Scotland 1979; v France 1982–88; Eur T Ch 1977-79-81. (GB): v America 1977-79-81-85; v Europe 1978-80-86-88; in World Cup 1978-80-88 (winners)

Macfarlane, CB
(Scotland): v England 1912

McGimpsey, G
(Ireland): Home Int 1978-80-81-82-83-84-85-86-87-88; v Wales 1979; Eur T Ch 1981. (GB): v America 1985; v Europe 1986-88; World Cup 1988 (winners)

Macgregor, A
(Scotland): v Scandinavia 1956

Macgregor, G
(Scotland): Home Int 1969-70-71-72-73-74-75-76-80-81-82-83-84-85-86-87; v Belgium 1973-75-80; v England 1979; Eur T Ch 1971-73-75-81. (GB): v Europe 1970-74; v America 1971-75-83-85-87; in Com Tnmt 1971-75; v France 1981-82

MacGregor, RC
(Scotland): Home Int 1951-52-53-54. (GB): v America 1953

McHenry, J
(Ireland): Home Int 1985-86. (GB): v America 1987

McInally, H
(Scotland): Home Int 1937-47-48

McInally, RH
(Ireland): Home Int 1949-51

Macintosh, KW
(Scotland): v England 1979; Home Int 1980; v France 1980; v Belgium 1980. (GB): v Europe 1980

McKay, G
(Scotland): Home Int 1969

McKay, JR
(Scotland): Home Int 1950-51-52-54

McKellar, PJ
(Scotland): Home Int 1976-77-78; v Belgium 1978; v France 1978; v England 1979. (GB): v America 1977; v Europe 1978

Mackenzie, F
(Scotland): v England 1902-03

Mackenzie, WW
(Scotland): v England 1923-26-27-29; v Ireland 1930. (GB): v America 1922-23

Mackeown, HN
(Ireland): Home Int 1973; Eur T Ch 1973

Mackie, GW
(Scotland): Home Int 1948-50

McKinna, RA
(Scotland): Home Int 1938

McKinlay, SL
(Scotland): v England 1929-30-31; v Ireland 1930; v Wales 1931; Home Int 1932-33-35-37-47. (GB): v America 1934

McKinnon, A
(Scotland): Home Int 1947-52

McLean, D
(Wales): Home Int 1968-69-70-71-72-73-74-75-76-77-78-80-81-82-83-85-86-88; Eur T Ch 1975-77-79-81; v France 1975-76; v Denmark 1976-80; v Ireland 1979; v Switzerland, Spain 1980

McLean, J
(Scotland): Home Int 1932-33-34-35-36. (GB): v America 1934-36; v Australia 1934

McLeod, AE
(Scotland): Home Int 1937-38

McLeod, WS
(Scotland): Home Int 1935-37-38-47-48-49-50-51

McMenamin, E
(Ireland): Home Int 1981

McMullan, C
(Ireland): Home Int 1933-34-35

McNair, AA
(Scotland): v Ireland 1929

MacNamara, L
(Ireland): Home Int 1977-83-84-85-86-87-88; Eur T Ch 1977

McRuvie, EA
(Scotland): v England 1929-30-31; v Ireland 1930-31; v Wales 1931; Home Int 1932-33-34-35-36. (GB): v America 1932-34

McTear, J
(Scotland): Home Int 1971

Madeley, JFD
(Ireland): Home Int 1959-60-61-62-63-64. (GB): v Europe 1962; v America 1963

Mahon, RJ
(Ireland): Home Int 1938-52-54-55

Maliphant, FR
(Wales): Home Int 1932

Malone, B
(Ireland): Home Int 1959-64-69-71-75; Eur T Ch 1971-75

Manford, GC
(Scotland): v England 1922-23

Manley, N
(Ireland): v Wales 1924; v England 1928; v Scotland 1927-28

Mann, LS
(Scotland): Home Int 1982-83. (GB): v America 1983

Marchbank, B
(Scotland): Home Int 1978; v Italy 1979; Eur T Ch 1979. (GB): v Europe 1976-78; in World Team Ch 1978; v America 1979

Marks, GC
(England): Home Int 1963-67-68-69-70-71-74-75-82; Eur T Ch 1967-69-71-75. (GB): v Europe 1968-70; v America 1969-71-87 (Captain); in World Team Ch 1970; in Com Tnmt 1975; in Colombian Int 1975. Non playing captain v France 1982

Marren, JM
(Ireland): v Wales 1925

Marsh, DM
(England): Home Int 1956-57-58-59-60-64-66-68-69-70-71-72; Eur T Ch 1971. (GB): v Europe 1958; v America 1959-71-73 (Captain) -75 (Captain)

Marshman, A
(Wales): Home Int 1952

Marston, CC
(Wales): v Ireland 1929-30-31; v Scotland 1931

Martin, DHR
(England): Home Int 1938; v France 1934-49

Martin, GNC
(Ireland): v Wales 1923-29; v Scotland 1928-29-30; v England 1929-30. (GB): v America 1928

Martin, S
(Scotland): Home Int 1975-76-77; Eur T Ch 1977; v Belgium 1977; v Spain 1977. (GB): v America 1977; v Europe 1976; in World Team Ch 1976

Mason, SC
(England): Home Int 1973

Mathias-Thomas, FEL
(Wales): v Ireland 1924-25

Matthews, RL
(Wales): Home Int 1935-37

Maxwell, R
(Scotland): v England 1902-03-04-05-06-07-09-10

Mayo, PM
(Wales): Home Int 1982-87. (GB): v America 1985-87

Meharg, W
(Ireland): Home Int 1957

Melia, TJ
(Wales): Home Int 1976-77-78-80-81-82; v Ireland 1979; Eur T Ch 1977-79; v Denmark 1976-80; v Switzerland, Spain 1980

Mellin, GL
(England): v Scotland 1922

Melville, LM Balfour
(Scotland): v England 1902-03

Melville, TE
(Scotland): Home Int 1974

Menzies, A
(Scotland): v England 1925

Mill, JW
(Scotland): Home Int 1953-54

Millensted, DJ
(England): Home Int 1966; Eur T Ch 1967. (GB): v America 1967; in Com Tnmt 1967

Miller, AC
(Scotland): Home Int 1954-55

Miller, MJ
(Scotland): Home Int 1974-75-77-78; v Belgium 1978; v France 1978

Milligan, IW
(Scotland): Home Int 1986-87-88; v West Germany 1987; v Italy 1988. (GB): v Europe 1988; World Cup 1988 (winners)

Mills, ES
(Wales): Home Int 1957

Millward, EB
(England): Home Int 1950-52-53-54-55. (GB): v America 1949-55

Milne, WTG
(Scotland): Home Int 1972-73; Eur T Ch 1973; v Belgium 1973. (GB): v America 1973

Mitchell, A
(England): v Scotland 1910-11-12

Mitchell, CS
(England): Home Int 1975-76-78

Mitchell, FH
(England): v Scotland 1906-07-08

Mitchell, JWH
(Wales): Home Int 1964-65-66

Moffat, DM
(England): Home Int 1961-63-67; v France 1959-60

Moir, A
(Scotland): Home Int 1983-84

Montgomerie, CS
(Scotland): Home Int 1984-85-86; v West Germany 1987. (GB): v America 1985-87; v Europe 1986

Montgomerie, JS
(Scotland): Home Int 1957; v Scandinavia 1958

Montgomerie, RH de
(England): v Scotland 1908; v Wales/Ireland 1925; v South Africa 1927. (GB): v America 1921

Moody, JV
(West): Home Int 1947-48-49-51-56-58-59-60-61

Moody, PH
(England): Home Int 1971-72. (GB): v Europe 1972

Moore, GJ
(Ireland): v England 1928; v Wales 1929

Morgan, JL
(Wales): 1948-49-50-51-52-53-54-55-56-57-58-59-60-61-62-64-68. (GB): v America 1951-53-55

Morris, FS
(Scotland): Home Int 1963

Morris, MF
(Ireland): Home Int 1978-80-82-83-84; v Wales 1979; Eur T Ch 1979; v France, West Germany, Sweden 1980

Morris, R
(Wales): Home Int 1983-86-87

Morris, TS
(Wales): v Ireland 1924-29-30

Morrison, JH
(Scotland): v Scandinavia 1960

Morrison, JSF
(England): v Ireland 1930

Morrow, AJC
(Ireland): Home Int 1975-83

Morrow, JM
(Wales): v Ireland 1979; Home Int 1980-81; Eur T Ch 1979-81; v Denmark, Switzerland, Spain 1980

Mosey, IJ
(England): Home Int 1971

Moss, AV
(Wales): Home Int 1965-66-68

Mouland, MG
(Wales): Home Int 1978-81; v Ireland 1979; Eur T Ch 1979

Moxon, GA
(Wales): v Ireland 1929-30

Mulcare, P
(Ireland): Home Int 1968-69-70-71-72-74-78-80; v France, West Germany, Sweden 1978-80; Eur T Ch 1975-79. (GB): v Europe 1972; v America 1975

Mulholland, D
(Ireland): Home Int 1988

Munn, E
(Ireland): v Wales 1913-23-24; v Scotland 1927

Munn, L
(Ireland): v Wales 1913-23-24; Home Int 1936-37

Munro, RAG
(Scotland): Home Int 1960

Murdoch, D
(Scotland): Home Int 1964

Murphy, AR
(Scotland): Home Int 1961-65-67

Murphy, P
(Ireland): Home Int 1985-86

Murray, GH
(Scotland): Home Int 1973-74-75-76-77-78-83; v Spain 1974-77; v Belgium 1975-77; Eur T Ch 1975-77. (GB): v America 1977; v Europe 1978

Murray, SWT
(Scotland): Home Int 1959-60-61-62-63; v Scandinavia 1960. (GB): v Europe 1958-62; v America 1963

Murray, WA
(Scotland): v England 1923-24-25-26-27. (GB): v America 1923-24

Murray, WB
(Scotland): Home Int 1967-68-69; Eur T Ch 1969

Muscroft, R
(England): Home Int 1986

Nash A
(England): Home Int 1988

Neech, DG
(England): Home Int 1961

Neill, JH
(Ireland): Home Int 1938-47-48-49

Neill, R
(Scotland): Home Int 1936

Nestor, JM
(Ireland): Home Int 1962-63-64

Nevin, V
(Ireland): Home Int 1960-63-65-67-69-72; Eur T Ch 1967-69-73

Newey, AS
(England): Home Int 1932

Newman, JE
(Wales): Home Int 1932

Newton, H
(Wales): v Ireland 1929

Nicholson, J
(Ireland): Home Int 1932

Noon, GS
(Wales): Home Int 1935-36-37

Noon, J
(Scotland): Home Int 1987

O'Boyle, P
(Ireland): Eur T Ch 1977

O'Brien, MD
(Ireland): Home Int 1968-69-70-71-72-75-76-77; Eur T Ch 1971; v France, West Germany, Sweden 1976

O'Connell, A
(Ireland): Home Int 1967-70-71 71

O'Connell, E
(Ireland): Home Int 1985. (GB): v Europe 1988; World Cup 1988 (winners)

O'Leary, JE
(Ireland): Home Int 1969-70; Eur T Ch 1969

O'Neill, JJ
(Ireland): Home Int 1968

Oldcorn, A
(England): Home Int 1982-83. (GB): v America 1983

Oosterhuis, PA
(England): Home Int 1966-67-68. (GB): v America 1967; v Europe 1968; in World Team Ch 1968

Oppenheimer, RH
(England): v Ireland 1928-29-30; v Scotland 1930. (GB): v America 1957 (Captain)

O'Rourke, P
(Ireland): Home Int 1980-81-82-84-85

O'Sullivan, D
(Ireland): Home Int 1985-86-87

O'Sullivan, DF
(Ireland): Home Int 1976; Eur T Ch 1977

O'Sullivan, WM
(Ireland): Home Int 1934-35-36-37-38-47-48-49-50-51-53-54

Osgood, TH
(Scotland): v England 1925

Owen, JB
(Wales): Home Int 1971

Owens, GF
(Wales): Home Int 1960-61

Ownes, GH
(Ireland): Home Int 1935-37-38-47

Palferman, H
(Wales): Home Int 1950-53

Palmer, DJ
(England): Home Int 1962-63

Parfitt, RWM
(Wales): v Ireland 1924

Parkin, AP
(Wales): Home Int 1980-81-82. (GB): v America 1983

Parry, JR
(Wales): Home Int 1966-75-76-77; v France 1976

Patey, IR
(England): Home Int 1952; v France 1948-49-50

Patrick, KG
(Scotland): Home Int 1937

Patterson, AH
(Ireland): v Wales 1913

Pattinson, R
(England): Home Int 1949

Payne, J
(England): Home Int 1950-51

Pearson, AG
(GB): v South Africa 1927

Pearson, MJ
(England): Home Int 1951-52

Pease, JWB (*later* Lord Wardington)
(England): v Scotland 1903-04-05-06

Pennink, JJF
(England): Home Int 1937-38-47; v France 1937-38-39. (GB): v America 1938

Perkins, TP
(England): v Scotland 1927-28-29. (GB): v America 1928

Perowne, AH
(England): Home Int 1947-48-49-50-51-53-54-55-57. (GB): v America 1949-53-59; in World Team Ch 1958

Peters, GB
(Scotland): Home Int 1934-35-36-37-38. (GB): v America 1936-38

Peters, JL
(Wales): Home Int 1987-88

Phillips, LA
(Wales): v Ireland 1913

Pierse, AD
(Ireland): Home Int 1976-77-78-80-81-82-83-84-85-87-88; v Wales 1979; v France, West Germany, Sweden 1980; Eur T Ch 1981. (GB): v Europe 1980; v America 1983

Pinch, AG
(Wales): Home Int 1969

Pirie, AK
(Scotland): Home Int 1966-67-68-69-70-71-72-73-74-75; Eur T Ch 1967-69; v Belgium 1973-75; v Spain 1974. (GB): v America 1967; v Europe 1970

Plaxton, J
(England): Home Int 1983-84

Pollin, RKM
(Ireland): Home Int 1971; Eur T Ch 1973

Pollock, VA
(England): v Scotland 1908

Povall, J
(Wales): Home Int 1960-61-62-63-65-66-67-68-69-70-71-72-73-74-75-76-77; Eur T Ch 1967-69-71-73-75-77; v France 1975-76; v Denmark 1976, (GB): v Europe 1962

Powell, WA
(England): v Scotland 1923-24; v Wales/Ireland 1925

Power, E
(Ireland): Home Int 1987-88

Power, M
(Ireland): Home Int 1947-48-49-50-51-52-54

Poxon, MA
(England): Home Int 1975-76; Eur T Ch 1975. (GB): v America 1975

Pressdee, RNG
(Wales): Home Int 1958-59-60-61-62

Pressley, J
(Scotland): Home Int 1947-48-49

Price, JP
(Wales): Home Int 1986-87-88

Pugh, RS
(Wales): v Ireland 1923-24-29

Purcell, J
(Ireland): Home Int 1973

Raeside, A
(Scotland): v Ireland 1929

Rafferty, R
(Ireland): v Wales 1979; Home Int 1980-81; v France, West Germany, Sweden 1980; Eur T Ch 1981. (GB): v Europe 1980; in World Team Ch 1980; v America 1981

Rainey, WHE
(Ireland): Home Int 1962

Rawlinson, D
(England): Home Int 1949-50-52-53

Ray, D
(England): Home Int 1982; v France 1982

Rayfus, P
(Ireland): Home Int 1986-87–88

Reade, HE
(Ireland): v Wales 1913

Reddan, B
(Ireland): Home Int 1987

Rees, CN
(Wales): Home Int 1986-88

Rees, DA
(Wales): Home Int 1961-62-63-64

Renfrew, RL
(Scotland): Home Int 1964

Renwick, G, jr
(Wales): v Ireland 1923

Revell, RP
(England): Home Int 1972-73; Eur T Ch 1973

Ricardo, W
(Wales); v Ireland 1930-31; v Scotland 1931

Rice, JH
(Ireland): Home Int 1947-52

Rice-Jones, L
(Wales): v Ireland 1924

Richards, PM
(Wales): Home Int 1960-61-62-63-71

Richardson, S
(England): Home Int 1986-87-88

Risdon, PWL
(England): Home Int 1935-36

Robb, J, jr
(Scotland): v England 1902-03-05-06-07

Robb, WM
(Scotland): Home Int 1935

Roberts, AT
(Scotland): v Ireland 1931

Roberts, G
(Scotland): Home Int 1937-38

Roberts, GP
(England): Home Int 1951-53; v France 1949

Roberts, HJ
(England): Home Int 1947-48-53

Roberts, J
(Wales): Home Int 1937

Roberts, SB
(Wales): Home Int 1932-33-34-35-37-38-47-48-49-50-51-52-53-54

Roberts, WJ
(Wales): Home Int 1948-49-50-51-52-53-54

Robertson, A
(England): Home Int 1986-87; v France 1988

Robertson, CW
(Ireland): v Wales 1930; v Scotland 1930

Robertson, DM
(Scotland): Home Int 1973-74; v Spain 1974

Robertson-Durham, JA
(Scotland): v England 1911

Robinson, J
(England): v Ireland 1928

Robinson, J
(England): Home Int 1986. (GB): v America 1987

Robinson, S
(England): v Scotland 1925; v Ireland 1928-29-30

Roderick, RN
(Wales): Home Int 1983-84-85-86-87-88. (GB) v Europe 1988

Rolfe, B
(Wales): Home Int 1963-65

Roobottom, EL
(Wales): Home Int 1967

Roper, HS
(England): v Ireland 1931; v Scotland 1931

Roper, MS
(Wales): v Ireland 1979

Roper, R
(England): Home Int 1984-85-86-87

Rothwell, J
(England): Home Int 1947-48

Rutherford, DS
(Scotland): v Ireland 1929

Rutherford, R
(Scotland): Home Int 1938-47

Saddler, AC
(Scotland): Home Int 1959-60-61-62-63-64-66; Eur T Ch 1965-67. (GB): v Europe 1960-62-64--66; v America 1963-65-67-77 (Captain); in Com Tnmt 1959-63-67; in World Team Ch 1962

Scannel, BJ
(Ireland): Home Int 1947-48-49-50-51-53-54

Scott, KB
(England): Home Int 1937-38; v France 1938

Scott, Hon M
(England): v Scotland 1911-12-23-24-25-26. (GB): v America 1924-34 (Captain); v Australia 1934

Scott, Hon O
(England): v Scotland 1902-05-06

Scott, R, jr
(Scotland): v England 1924-28. (GB): v America 1924

Scratton, EWHB
(England): v Scotland 1912

Scroggie, FH
(Scotland): v England 1910

Scrutton, PF
(England): Home Int 1950-55. (GB): v America 1955-57

Sewell, D
(England): Home Int 1956-57-58-59-60. (GB): v America 1957-59; in Com Tnmt 1959; in World Team Ch 1960

Shade, RDBM
(Scotland): Home Int 1957-60-61-62-63-64-65-66-67-68; v Scandinavia 1960-62; Eur T Ch 1965-67. (GB): v America 1961-63-65-67; v Europe 1962-64-66-68; in World Team Ch 1962-64-66-68; in Com Tnmt 1963-67

Shaw, G
(Scotland): Home Int 1984-86-87-88; v West Germany 1987. (GB): v America 1987

Sheals, HS
(Ireland): v Wales 1929; v England 1929-30-31; v Scotland 1930; Home Int 1932-33

Sheahan, D
(Ireland): Home Int 1961-62-63-64-65-66-67-70. (GB): v Europe 1962-64-67; v America 1963

Sheilds, B
(Scotland):Home Int 1986

Shepperson, AE
(England): Home Int 1956-57-58-59-60-62. (GB): v America 1957-59

Sherborne, A
(England): Home Int 1982-83-84

Shingler, TR
(England): Home Int 1977

Shorrock, TJ
(England): v France 1952

Simcox, R
(Ireland): v Wales 1930-31; v Scotland 1930-31; v England 1931; Home Int 1932-33-34-35-36-38

Simpson, AF
(Scotland): v Ireland 1928, v England 1927

Simpson, JG
(Scotland): v England 1906-07-08-09-11-12-22-24-26. (GB): v America 1921

Sinclair, A
(Scotland): Home Int 1950

Slark, WA
(England): Home Int 1957

Slater, A
(England): Home Int 1955-62

Slattery, B
(Ireland): Home Int 1947-48

Sludds, MF
(Ireland): Home Int 1982

Smith, Eric M
(England): v Ireland 1931; v Scotland 1931

Smith, Everard
(England): v Scotland 1908-09-10-12

Smith, GF
(England): v Scotland 1902-03

Smith, JN
(Scotland): v Ireland 1928-30-31; v England 1929-30-31; v Wales 1931; Home Int 1932-33-34. (GB): v America 1930

Smith, JR
(England): Home Int 1932

Smith, LOM
(England): Home Int 1963

Smith, VH
(Wales): v Ireland 1924-25

Smith, W
(England): Home Int 1972. (GB): v Europe 1972

Smith, WD
(Scotland): Home Int 1957-58-59-60-63; v Scandinavia 1958-60. (GB): v Europe 1958; v America 1959

Smyth, D
(Ireland): Home Int 1972-73; Eur T Ch 1973

Smyth, DW
(Ireland): v Wales 1923-30; v England 1930; v Scotland 1931; Home Int 1933

Smyth, HB
(Ireland): Home Int 1974-75-76-78; Eur T Ch 1975-79; v France, West Germany, Sweden 1976. (GB): v Europe 1976

Smyth, V
(Ireland): Home Int 1981-82

Snowdon, J
(England): Home Int 1934

Soulby, DEB
(Ireland): v Wales 1929-30; v England 1929-30; v Scotland 1929-30

Spiller, EF
(Ireland): v Wales 1924; v England 1928; v Scotland 1928-29

Squirrell, HC
(Wales): Home Int 1955-56-57-58-59-60-61-62-63-64-65-66-67-68-69-70-71-73-74-75; Eur T Ch 1967-69-71-75; v France 1975

Staunton, R
(Ireland): Home Int 1964-65-72; Eur T Ch 1973

Steel, DMA
(England): Home Int 1970

Stephen, AR
(Scotland): Home Int 1971-72-73-74-75-76-77-84-85; Eur T Ch 1975; v Spain 1974; v Belgium 1975-77-78. (GB): v Europe 1972; v America 1985

Stevens, DI
(Wales): Home Int 1968-69-70-74-75-76-77-78-80-82; Eur T Ch 1969-77; v France 1976; v Denmark 1977

Stevens, LB
(England): v Scotland 1912

Stevenson, A
(Scotland): Home Int 1949

Stevenson, JB
(Scotland): v Ireland 1931; Home Int 1932-38-47-49-50-51

Stevenson, JF
(Ireland): v Wales 1923-24; v England 1925

Stevenson, K
(Ireland): Home Int 1972

Stockdale, B
(England): Home Int 1964-65

Stoker, K
(Wales): v Ireland 1923-24

Stokoe, GC
(Wales): v England 1925; v Ireland 1929-30

Storey, EF
(England): v Scotland 1924-25-26-27-28-30; Home Int 1936; v France 1936. (GB): v America 1924-26-28

Stott, HAN
(England): Home Int 1976-77

Stout, JA
(England): v Scotland 1928-29-30-31; v Ireland 1929-31. (GB): v America 1930-32

Stowe, C
(England): Home Int 1935-36-37-38-47-49-54; v France 1938-39-49. (GB): v America 1938-47

Strachan, CJL
(Scotland): Home Int 1965-66-67; Eur T Ch 1967

Straker, R
(England): Home Int 1932

Stuart, HB
(Scotland): Home Int 1967-68-70-71-72-73-74-76; Eur T Ch 1969-71-73-75; v Belgium 1973-75. (GB): v Europe 1968-72-74; v America 1971-73-75; in Com Tnmt 1971; in World Team Ch 1972

Stuart, JE
(Scotland): Home Int 1959

Stubbs, AK
(England): Home Int 1982

Suneson, C
(England): Home Int 1988

Sutherland, DMG
(England): Home Int 1947

Sutton, W
(England): v Scotland 1929-31; v Ireland 1929-30-31

Symonds, A
(Wales): v Ireland 1925

Taggart, J
(Ireland): Home Int 1953

Tait, AG
(Scotland): Home Int 1987-88

Tate, JK
(England): Home Int 1954-55-56

Taylor, GN
(Scotland): Home Int 1948

Taylor, HE
(England): v Scotland 1911

Taylor, JS
(Scotland): v England 1979; Home Int 1980; v Belgium 1980; v France 1980

Taylor, LG
(Scotland): Home Int 1955-56

Taylor, TPD
(Wales): Home Int 1963

Thirlwell, A
(England): Home Int 1951-52-54-55-56-57-58-63-64. (GB): v Europe 1956-58-64; v America 1957; in Com Tnmt 1953-64

Thirsk, TJ
(England): v Ireland 1929; Home Int 1933-34-35-36-37-38; v France 1935-36-37-38-39

Thom, KG
(England): Home Int 1947-48-49-53. (GB): v America 1949

Thomas, I
(England): Home Int 1933

Thomas, KR
(Wales): Home Int 1951-52

Thompson, ASG
(England): Home Int 1935-37

Thompson, MS
(England): Home Int 1982. (GB): v America 1983

Thomson, AP
(Scotland): Home Int 1970; Eur T Ch 1971

Thomson, H
(Scotland): Home Int 1934-35-36-37-38. (GB): v America 1936-38

Thomson, JA
(Scotland): Home Int 1981-82-83-84-85-86-87-88; v West Germany 1987; v Italy 1988

Thorburn, K
(Scotland): v England 1928; v Ireland 1927

Timbey, JC
(Ireland): v Scotland 1928-31; v Wales 1931

Timmis, CW
(England): v Ireland 1930; Home Int. 1936-37

Tipping, EB
(England): v Ireland 1930

Tipple, ER
(England): v Ireland 1928-29; Home Int 1932

Tolley, CJH
(England): v Scotland 1922-23-24-25-26-27-28-29-30; Home Int 1936-37-38; v Ireland/Wales 1925; v France 1938. (GB): v America 1921-22-23-24 (Captain) -26-30-34; v South Africa 1927

Tooth, EA
(Wales): v Ireland 1913

Torrance, TA
(Scotland): v England 1922-23-25-26-28-29--30; Home Int 1933. (GB): v America 1924-28-30-32 (Captain) -34

Torrance, WB
(Scotland): v England 1922-23-24-26-27-28-30; v Ireland 1928-29-30. (GB): v America 1922

Townsend, PM
(England): Home Int 1965-66. (GB): v America 1965; v Europe 1966; in World Team Ch 1966

Toye, JL
(Wales): Home Int 1963-64-65-66-67-69-70-71-72-73-74-76-78; Eur T Ch 1971-73-75-77; v France 1975

Tredinnick, SV
(England): Home Int 1950

Tucker, WI
(Wales): Home Int 1949-50-51-52-53-54-55-56-57-58-59-60-61-62-63-64-65-66-67-68-69-70-71-72-74-75; Eur T Ch 1967-69-75; v France 1975

Tulloch, W
(Scotland): v England 1929-30-31; v Ireland 1930-31; v Wales 1931; Home Int 1932

Tupling, LP
(England): Home Int 1969; Eur T Ch 1969. (GB): v America 1969

Turnbull, CH
(Wales): v Ireland 1913-25

Turner, A
(England): Home Int 1952

Turner, GB
(Wales): Home Int 1947-48-49-50-51-52-55-56

Tweddell, W
(England): v Scotland 1928-29-30; Home Int 1935. (GB): v America 1928 (Captain) -36 (Captain)

Vannet, L
(Scotland): Home Int 1984

Waddell, G
(Ireland): v Wales 1925

Walker, J
(Scotland): Home Int 1954-55-57-58-60-61-62-63; v Scandinavia 1958-62. (GB): v Europe 1958-60; v America 1961

Walker, KH
(Scotland): Home Int 1985-86

Walker, MS
(England): v Ireland/Wales 1925

Walker, RS
(Scotland): Home Int 1935-36

Wallis, G
(Wales): Home Int 1934-36-37-38

Walls, MPD
(England): Home Int 1980-81-85

Walters, EM
(Wales): Home Int 1967-68-69; Eur T Ch 1969

Walton, AR
(England): Home Int 1934-35

Walton, P
(Ireland): v Wales 1979: Home Int 1980-81; v France, Germany, Sweden 1980; Eur T Ch 1981. (GB): v America 1981-83

Warren, KT
(England): Home Int 1962

Watt, A
(Scotland): Home Int 1987

Way, P
(England): Home Int 1981; Eur T Ch 1981, (GB): v America 1981.

Webster, A
(Scotland): Home Int 1978

Webster, F
(Ireland): Home Int 1949

Weeks, K
(England): Home Int 1987-88; v France 1988

Welch, L
(Ireland): Home Int 1936

Wemyss, DS
(Scotland): Home Int 1937

Werner, LE
(Ireland): v Wales 1925

West, CH
(Ireland): v England 1928; Home Int 1932

Wethered, RH
(England): v Scotland 1922-23-24-25-26-27-28-29-30. (GB): v America 1921-22-23-26-30 (Captain) -34

White, RJ
(England): Home Int 1947-48-49-53-54. (GB): v America 1947-49-51-53-55

Whyte, AW
(Scotland): Home Int 1934

Wilkie, D
(Scotland): Home Int 1962-63-65-67-68

Wilkie, G
(Scotland): v England 1911

Wilkie, GT
(Wales): Home Int 1938
Willcox, FS
(Wales): v Scotland 1931; v Ireland 1931
Williams, DF
(England): v Scotland 1979
Williams KH
(Wales): Home Int 1983-84-85-86-87
Williams, PG
(Wales): v Ireland 1925
Williamson, SB
(Scotland): Home Int 1947-48-49-51-52
Willison, R
(England): Home Int 1988
Wilson, F
(Scotland): Home Int 1985
Wilson, J
(Scotland): v England 1922-23-24-26. (GB): v America 1923
Wilson, JC
(Scotland): Home Int 1947-48-49-51-52-53. (GB): v America 1947-53; v South Africa 1952; in Com Tnmt 1954
Wilson, P
(Scotland): Home Int 1976; Belgium 1977
Winchester, R
(England): Home Int 1985-87
Winfield, HB
(Wales): v Ireland 1913
Wise, WS
(England): Home Int 1947
Wolstenholme, G
(England): Home Int 1953-55-56-57-58-59-60 (GB): v America 1957-59; in World Team Ch 1958-60; in Com Tnmt 1959
Wolstenholme, G
(England): Home Int 1988; v France 1988
Wood, DK
(Wales): Home Int 1982-83-84-85-86-87
Woollam, J
(England): Home Int 1933-34-35; v France 1935
Woolley, FA
(England): v Scotland 1910-11-12
Woosnam, I
(Wales): v France 1976
Worthington, JS
(England): v Scotland 1905
Wright, I
(Scotland): Home Int 1958-59-60-61; v Scandinavia 1960

Yeo, J
(England): Home 1971
Young, D
(Ireland): Home Int 1969-70-77
Young, ID
(Scotland): Home Int 1981-82; v France 1982
Young, JR
(Scotland): Home Int 1960-61-65; v Scandinavia 1960. (GB): v Europe 1960

Zacharias, JP
(England): Home Int 1935
Zoete, HW de
(England): v Scotland 1903-04-06-07

British Isles International Players, Amateur Ladies

Abbreviations:

(GB) played for Great Britain or Great Britain and Ireland; Eur L T Ch played in European Ladies Amateur Team Championship; Home Int played in Home International matches; CW played in Commonwealth International. Previous surnames are shown in brackets.

Aitken, E (Young)
(Scotland): Home Int 1954

Alexander, M
(Ireland): Home Int 1920-21-22-30

Allen, F
(England): Home Int 1952

Allington Hughes, Miss
(Wales): Home Int 1908-09-10-12-14-22-25

Anderson, E
(Scotland): Home Int 1910-11-12-21-25

Anderson, F
(Scotland): Home Int 1977-79-80-81-83-84-86-87-88; Eur L T Ch 1987. (GB): in Vagliano Trophy 1987

Anderson, H
(Scotland): Home Int 1964-65-68-69-70-71; Eur L T Ch 1969. (GB): in Vagliano Trophy 1969

Anderson, J (Donald)
(Scotland): Home Int 1947-48-49-50-51-52-53. (GB): in Curtis Cup in 1948-50-52

Anderson, L.
(Scotland): Home Int 1986-87-88; Eur L T Ch 1987

Anderson, VH
(Scotland): Home Int 1907

Arbuthnot, M
(Ireland): Home Int 1921

Archer, A (Rampton)
(England): Home Int 1968 (Captain)

Armstrong, M
(Ireland): Home Int 1906

Ashcombe, Lady [Bromley-Davenport] (Isabella Rieben)
(Wales): Home Int 1932-33-34-35-36-48-50-51-52-53-54-55

Aubertin, Mrs
(Wales): Home Int 1908-09-10

Bailey, D [Frearson] (Robb)
(England): Home Int 1961-62-71; Eur L T Ch 1968. (GB): in Curtis Cup 1962–72-84 (Captain)–86(Captain)-88(Captain); in Vagliano Trophy 1961-83(Captain)-85(Captain); CW 1983

Bald, J
(Scotland): Home Int 1968-69-71; Eur L T Ch 1969

Barber, S (Bonallack)
(England): Home Int 1960-61-62-68-70-72-77-78 (Captain); Eur L T Ch 1969-71. (GB): in Curtis Cup 1962; in Vagliano Trophy 1961-63-69

Barclay, C (Brisbane)
(Scotland): Home Int 1953-61-68

Bargh Etherington, B (Whitehead)
(England): Home Int 1974

Barlow, Mrs
(Ireland): Home Int 1921

Barron, M
(Wales): Home Int 1929-30-31-34-35-36-37-38-39-47-48-49-50-51-52-53-54-55-56-57-58-60-61-62-63

Barry, L
(England): Home Int 1911-12-13-14

Barry, P
(England): Home Int 1982

Barton, P
(England): Home Int 1935-36-37-38-39. (GB): in Curtis Cup 1934-36

Bastin, G
(England): Home Int 1920-21-22-23-24-25

Bayliss, Mrs
(Wales): Home Int 1921

Bayman, L (Denison Pender)
(England): Home Int 1971-72-73-83-84-85-87-88; Eur L T Ch 1985-87. (GB) in Curtis Cup 1988; in Vagliano Trophy 1971-85-87

Baynes, Mrs CE
(Scotland): Home Int 1921-22

Beck, B (Pim)
(Ireland): Home Int 1930-31-32-33-34-36-37-47-48-49-50-51-52-53-54-55-56-58-59-61

Beckett, J
(Ireland): Home Int 1962-66-67-68: Eur L T Ch 1967

Beddows, C [Watson] (Stevenson)
(Scotland): Home Int 1913-14-21-22-23-27-29-30-31-32-33-34-35-36-37-39-47-48-49-50-51. (GB): in Curtis Cup 1932

Behan, L
(Ireland): Home Int 1984-85-86. (GB): in Curtis Cup 1986; in Vagliano Trophy 1985

Beharrell, V (Anstey)
(England): Home Int 1955-56-57-61(Captain). (GB): in Curtis Cup 1956

Benka, P (Tredinnick)
(England): Home Int 1967. (GB): in Curtis Cup 1966-68; in Vagliano Trophy 1967

Bennett, L
(Scotland): Home Int 1977-80-81

Benton, MH
(Scotland): Home Int 1914

Birmingham, M
(Ireland): Home Int 1967(Captain)

Bisgood, J
(England) Home Int 1949-50-51-52-53-54-56-58. (GB): in Curtis Cup 1950-52-54-70(Captain)

Blair, N (Menzies)
(Scotland): Home Int 1955

Blake, Miss
(Ireland): Home Int 1931-32-34-35-36

Blaymire, J
(England): Home Int 1971-88

Bloodworth, D (Lewis)
(Wales): Home Int 1954-55-56-57-60

Bolton, L
(Ireland): Home Int 1981-82-88

Bolton, Z (Bonner Davis)
(England): Home Int 1939-48-49-50-51-55-(Captain)-56. (GB): in Curtis Cup 1948-56(Captain)-66(Captain)-68(Captain); CW 1967

Bonallack, A (Ward)
(England): Home Int 1956-57-58-59-60-61-62-63-64-65 (Captain)-66-72. (GB): in Curtis Cup 1956-58-60-62-64-66; in Vagliano Trophy 1959-61-63

Bostock, M
(England): Home Int 1954(Captain)

Bourn, Mrs
(England): Home Int 1909-12

Bowhill, M (Robertson-Durham)
(Scotland): Home Int 1936-37-38

Boyd, J
(Ireland): Home Int 1912-13-14

Bradley, K (Rawlings)
(Wales): Home Int 1975-76-77-78-79-82-83

Bradshaw, E
(Ireland): Home Int 1964-66-67-68-69-70-71-74-75-80 Captain)-81(Captain); Eur L T Ch 1969-71-75. (GB): in Vagliano Trophy 1969-71

Brandom, G
(Ireland): Home Int 1965-66-67-68; Eur L T Ch 1967. (GB) in Vagliano Trophy 1967

Brearley, M
(Wales): Home Int 1937-38

Brennan, R (Hegarty)
(Ireland): Home Int 1974-75-76-77-78-79-81

Bridges, Mrs
(Wales): Home Int 1933-38-39

Briggs, A (Brown)
(Wales): Home Int 1969-70-71-72-73-74-75-76-77-78-79-80-81(Captain)-82(Captain)-83(Captain)-84; Eur L T Ch 1971-75. (GB): in Vagliano Trophy 1971-75

Brinton, Mrs
(Ireland): Home Int 1922

Brook, D
(Wales): Home Int 1913

Brooks, E
(Ireland): Home Int 1953-54-56

Broun, JG
(Scotland): Home Int 1905-06-07-21

Brown, B
(Ireland): Home Int 1960

Brown, E (Jones)
(Wales): Home Int 1947-48-49-50-52-53-57-58-59-60-61-62-63-64-65-66-68-69-70

Brown, Mrs FW (Gilroy)
(Scotland): Home Int 1905-06-07-08-09-10-11-13-21

Brown, J
(Wales): Home Int 1960-61-62-64-65; Eur L T Ch 1965-69

Brown, J
(England): Home Int 1984

Brown, TWL
(Scotland): Home Int 1924-25

Brown, Mrs
(Wales): Home Int 1924-25-27

Brownlow, Miss
(Ireland): Home Int 1923

Bryan-Smith, S
(Wales): Home Int 1947-48-49-50-51-52-56

Burke, Mrs
(Ireland): Home Int 1948

Burrell, Mrs
(Wales): Home Int 1939

Burton, H (Mitchell)
(Scotland): Home Int 1931-55-56-59(Captain). (GB): in Vagliano Trophy 1961

Burton, M
(England): Home Int 1975-7

Butler, I (Burke)
(Ireland): Home Int 1962-63-64-65-66-68-70-71-72-73-76-77-78-79-86(Captain)-87(Captain): Eur L T Ch 1967. (GB): in Curtis Cup 1966; in Vagliano Trophy 1965; in Espirito Santo 1964-66

Byrne, A (Sweeney)
(Ireland): Home Int 1959-60-61-62-63

Cadden, G
(Scotland): Home Int 1974-75

Cairns, Lady Katherine
(England): Home Int 1947-48-50-51-52-53-54. (GB): in Curtis Cup 1952(Captain)

Caldwell, C (Redford)
(England): Home Int 1973-78-79-80. (GB): in Curtis Cup 1978-80; in Vagliano Trophy 1973

Campbell, J (Burnett)
(Scotland): Home Int 1960

Cann, M (Nuttall)
(England): Home Int 1966

Carrick, P (Bullard)
(England): Home Int 1939-47

Caryl, M
(Wales): Home Int 1929

Casement, M (Harrison)
(Ireland): Home Int 1909-10-11-12-13-14

Cautley, B (Hawtrey)
(England): Home Int 1912-13-14-22-23-24-25-27

Chambers, D
(England): Home Int 1906-07-09-10-11-12-20-24-25. (GB): in Curtis Cup 1934(Captain)-36(Captain)-38(Captain)

Christison, D
(England): Home Int 1981

Chugg, P (Light)
(Wales): Home Int 1973-74-75-76-77-78-86-87-78; Eur L T Ch 1975-87

Clark, G (Atkinson)
(England): Home Int 1955

Clarke, Mrs ML
(England): Home Int 1933-35

Clarke, P
(England): Home Int 1981

Clarke, Mrs
(Ireland): Home Int 1922

Clarkson, H (Reynolds)
(Wales): Home Int 1935-38-39

Clay, E
(Wales): Home Int 1912

Clement, V
(England): Home Int 1932-34-35

Close, M (Wenyon)
(England): Home Int 1968-69; Eur L T Ch 1969. (GB) in Vagliano Trophy 1969

Coats, Mrs G
(Scotland): Home Int 1931-32-33-34

Cochrane, K
(Scotland): Home Int 1924-25-28-29-30

Collett, P
(England): Home Int 1910

Collingham, J (Melville)
(England): Home Int 1978-79-81-84-86-87. (GB): in Vagliano Trophy 1979-87; CW 1987

Colquhoun, H
(Ireland): Home Int 1959-60-61-63

Comboy, C (Grott)
(England): Home Int 1975(Captain)-76(Captain). (GB): in Curtis Cup 1978(Captain)-80(Captain); in Vagliano Trophy 1977(Captain)-1979(Captain); in Espirito Santo 1978(Captain); CW 1979

Connachan, J
(Scotland): Home Int 1979-80-81-82-83. (GB): in Curtis Cup 1980-82; in Vagliano Trophy 1981-83; in Espirito Santo 1980-82; CW 1983

Coote, Miss
(Ireland): Home Int 1925-28-29

Copley, K (Lackie)
(Scotland): Home Int 1974-75

Corlett, E
(England): Home Int 1927-29-30-31-32-33-35-36-37-38-39. (GB): in Curtis Cup 1932-38-64(Captain)

Costello, G
(Ireland): Home Int 1973-84(Captain)-85(Captain)

Cotton, S (German)
(England): Home Int 1967-68; Eur L T Ch 1967. (GB): in Vagliano Trophy 1967

Couper, M
(Scotland): Home Int 1929-34-35-36-37-39-56

Cowley, Lady
(Wales): Home Int 1907-09

Cox, Margaret
(Wales): Home Int 1924-25

Cox, Nell
(Wales): Home Int 1954

Craik, T
(Scotland): Home Int 1988

Cramsie, F (Hezlet)
(Ireland): Home Int 1905-06-07-08-09-10-13-20-24

Crawford, I (Wylie)
(Scotland): Home Int 1970-71-72

Cresswell, K (Stuart)
(Scotland): Home Int 1909-10-11-12 14

Critchley, D (Fishwick)
(England): Home Int 1930-31-32-33-35-36-47. (GB): in Curtis Cup 1932-34-50(Captain)

Croft, A
(England): Home Int 1927

Cross, M
(Wales): Home Int 1922

Cruickshank, DM (Jenkins)
(Scotland): Home Int 1910-11-12

Crummack, Miss
(England): Home Int 1909

Cuming, Mrs
(Ireland): Home Int 1910

Cunninghame, S
(Wales): Home Int 1922-25-29-31

Cuthell, R (Adair)
(Ireland): Home Int 1908

Dampney, S
(Wales): Home Int 1924-25-27-28-29-30

David, Mrs
(Wales): Home Int 1908

Davidson, B (Inglis)
(Scotland): Home Int 1928

Davies, K
(Wales): Home Int 1981-82-83; Eur L T Ch 1987. (GB): in Curtis Cup 1986-88; in Vagliano Trophy 1987

Davies, L
(England): Home Int 1983-84. (GB): in Curtis Cup 1984; CW 1987

Davies, P (Griffiths)
(Wales): Home Int 1965-66-67-68-70-71-73; Eur L T Ch 1971

Deacon, Mrs
(Wales): Home Int 1912-14

Denny, A (Barrett)
(England): Home Int 1951

Dering, Mrs
(Ireland): Home Int 1923

Dermott, Lisa
(Wales): Home Int 1987-88

Dickson, M
(Ireland): Home Int 1909

Dobson, H
(England): Home Int 1987-88

Dod, L
(England): Home Int 1905

Douglas, K
(England): Home Int 1981-82-83. (GB): in Curtis Cup 1982; in Vagliano Trophy 1983

Dowling, D
(England): Home Int 1979

Draper, M [Peel] (Thomas)
(Scotland): Home Int 1929-34-38-49-50-51-52-53-54(Captain)-55(Captain)-56-57-58-61(Captain)-62. (GB): in Curtis Cup 1954; in Vagliano Trophy 1963(Captain)

Duncan, B
(Wales). Home Int 1907-08-09-10-12

Duncan, M
(Wales): Home Int 1922-23-28-34

Duncan, MJ (Wood)
(Scotland): Home Int 1925-27-28-39

Durlacher, Mrs
(Ireland): Home Int 1905-06-07-08-09-10-14

Durrant, B [Green] (Lowe)
(England): Home Int 1954

Dwyer, Mrs
(Ireland): 1928

Eakin, P (James)
(Ireland): 1967

Earner, M
(Ireland): Home Int 1960-61-62-63-70

Edwards, E
(Wales): Home Int 1949-50

Edwards, J
(Wales): Home Int 1932-33-34-36-37

Edwards, J (Morris)
(Wales): Home Int 1962-63-66-67-68-69-70-77(Captain)-78 (Captain)-79(Captain); Eur L T Ch 1967-69

Ellis, E
(Ireland): Home Int 1932-35-37-38

Ellis Griffiths (Mrs)
(Wales): Home Int 1907-08-09-12-13

Emery, MJ
(Wales): Home Int 1928-29-30-31-32-33-34-35-36-37-38-47

Evans, H
(England): Home Int 1908

Evans, N
(Wales): Home Int 1908-09-10-13

Everard, M
(England): Home Int 1964-67-69-70-72-73-77-78; Eur L T Ch 1967-71-77. (GB): in Curtis Cup 1970-72-74-78; in Vagliano Trophy 1967-69-71-73; in Espirito Santo 1967-71-77; CW 1971

Fairclough, L
(England): Home Int 1988

Falconer, V (Lamb)
(Scotland): Home Int 1932-36-37-47-48-49-50-51-52-53-54-55-56

Farie-Anderson, J
(Scotland): Home Int 1924

Farquharson, E
(Scotland): Home Int 1987-88

Ferguson, D
(Ireland): Home Int 1927-28-29-30-31-32-34-35-36-37-38-61 (Captain). (GB): in Curtis Cup 1958(Captain)

Ferguson, M (Fowler)
(Scotland): Home Int 1959-62-63-64-65-66-67-69-70-85; Eur L T Ch 1965-67-71. (GB): in Curtis Cup 1966; in Vagliano Trophy 1965

Ferguson R (Ogden)
(England): Home Int 1957

Fitzgibbon, M
(Ireland): Home Int 1920-21-29-30-31-32-33

FitzPatrick, O (Heskin)
(Ireland): Home Int 1967

Fletcher, P (Sherlock)
(Ireland): Home Int 1932-34-35-36-38-39-54-55-66(Captain)

Forbes, J
(Scotland): Home Int 1985-86-87-88; Eur L T Ch 1987

Foster, C
(England): Home Int 1905-06-09

Foster, J
(Wales): Home Int 1984-85-86-87; Eur L T Ch 1987

Fowler, J
(England): Home Int 1928

Franklin Thomas, E
(Wales): Home Int 1909

Freeguard, C
(Wales): Home Int 1927

Furby, J
(England): Home Int 1987-88; Eur L T Ch 1987

Fyshe, M
(England): Home Int 1938

Gallagher, S
(Scotland): Home Int 1983-84

Gardiner, A
(Ireland): Home Int 1927-29

Garfield Evans, PR (Whittaker)
(Wales): Home Int 1948-49-50-51-52-53-54-55(Captain)-56 (Captain)-57 (Captain)-58(Captain)

Garner, M (Madill)
(Ireland): Home Int 1978-79-80-81-82-83-84-85. (GB): in Curtis Cup 1980; in Vagliano Trophy 1979-81-85; in Espirito Santo 1980; CW 1979

Garon, MR
(England): Home Int 1927-28-32-33-34-36-37-38. (GB); in Curtis Cup 1936

Garrett, M (Ruttle)
(England): Home Int 1947-48-50-53-59(Captain)-60(Captain)-63(Captain). (GB): in Curtis Cup 1948-60(Captain); in Vagliano Trophy 1959

Garvey, P
(Ireland): Home Int 1947-48-49-50-51-52-53-54(Captain)-56-57(Captain) -58(Captain)-59(Captain)-60(Captain)-61-62-63-68-69. (GB): in Curtis Cup 1948-50-52-54-56-60; in Vagliano Trophy 1959-63

Gaynor Fallon, Z
(Ireland): Home Int 1952-53-54-55-56-57-58-59-60-61-62-63-64-65-68-69-70-72 (Captain). (GB): in Espirito Santo 1964

Gear Evans, A
(Wales): Home Int 1932-33-34

Gee, Hon. J (Hives)
(England): Home Int 1950-51-52

Gemmill, A
(Scotland): Home Int 1981-82-84-85-86-87-88

Gethin Griffith, S
(Wales): Home Int 1914-22-23-24-28-29-30-31-35

Gibb, M (Titterton)
(England): Home Int 1906-07-08-10-12

Gibbs, C (Le Feuvre)
(England): Home Int 1971-72-73-74. (GB): in Curtis Cup 1974; in Vagliano Trophy 1973

Gibbs, S
(Wales): Home Int 1933-34-39

Gildea, Miss
(Ireland): Home Int 1936-37-38-39

Glendinning, D
(Ireland): Home Int 1937-54

Glennie, H
(Scotland): Home Int 1959

Glover, A
(Scotland): Home Int 1905-06-08-09-12

Gold, N
(England): Home Int 1929-31-32

Gordon, J
(England): Home Int 1947-48-49-52-53. (GB): in Curtis Cup 1948

Gorman, S
(Ireland): Home Int 1976-79-80-81-82

Gorry, Mary
(Ireland): Home Int 1971-72-73-74-75-76-77-78-79-80-88; Eur L T Ch 1971-75. (GB): in Vagliano Trophy 1977

Gotto, Mrs C
(Ireland): Home Int 1923

Gotto, Mrs L
(Ireland): Home Int 1920

Gourlay, M
(England): Home Int 1923-24-27-28-29-30-32-33-34-38-57 (Captain). (GB): in Curtis Cup 1932-34

Gow, J
(Scotland): Home Int 1923-24-27-28

Graham, MA
(Scotland): Home Int 1905-06

Graham, N
(Ireland): Home Int 1908-09-10-12

Granger Harrison, Mrs
(Scotland): Home Int 1922

Grant-Suttie, E
(Scotland): Home Int 1908-10-11-14-22-23

Grant-Suttie, R
(Scotland): Home Int 1914

Green, B (Pockett)
(England): Home Int 1939

Grice-hittaker, P (Grice)
(England): Home Int 1983-84. (GB): in Curtis Cup 1984; in Espirito Santo 1984

Griffith, W
(Wales): Home Int 1981

Griffiths, M
(England): Home Int 1920-21

Greenlees, E
(Scotland): Home Int 1924

Greenlees, Y
(Scotland): Home Int 1928-30-31-33-34-35-38

Guadella, E (Leitch)
(England): Home Int 1908-10-20-21-22-27-28-29-30-33

Gubbins, Miss
(Ireland): Home Int 1905

Haig, J (Mathias Thomas)
(Wales): Home Int 1938-39

Hall, CM
(England): Home Int 1985

Hall, Mrs
(Ireland): Home Int 1927-30

Hamilton, S (McKinven)
(Scotland): Home Int 1965

Hambro, W (Martin Smith)
(England): Home Int 1914

Hamilton, J
(England): Home Int 1937-38-39

Hammond, T
(England): Home Int 1985

Hampson, M
(England): Home Int 1954

Hanna, D
(Ireland): Home Int 1987-88

Harrington, D
(Ireland): Home Int 1923

Harris, M [Spearman] (Baker)
(England): Home Int 1955-56-57-58-59-60-61-62-63-64-65; Eur L T Ch 1965-71. (GB): in Curtis Cup 1960-62-64; in Vagliano Trophy 1959-61-65; in Espirito Santo 1964

Harrold, L
(England): Home Int 1974-75-76

Hartill, D
(England): Home Int 1923

Hartley, E
(England): Home Int 1964(Captain)

Hartley, R
(Wales): Home Int 1958-59-62

Hastings, D (Sommerville)
(Scotland): Home Int 1955-56-57-58-59-60-61-62-63. (GB): in Curtis Cup 1958; in Vagliano Trophy 1963

Hay, J (Pelham Burn)
(Scotland): Home Int 1959

Hayter, J (Yuille)
(England): Home Int 1956

Hazlett, VP
(Ireland): Home Int 1956(Captain)

Head, EA [Boatman] (Collis)
(England): Home Int 1974-80-84(Captain)-85(Captain); Eur L T Ch 1985(Captain)-87(Captain)

Healy, B (Gleeson)
(Ireland): Home Int 1980-82

Heathcoat-Amory, Lady (Joyce Wethered)
(England): Home Int 1921-22-23-24-25-29. (GB): in Curtis Cup 1932(Captain)

Hedges, S (Whitlock)
(England): Home Int 1979. (GB): in Vagliano Trophy 1979; CW 1979

Hedley Hill, Miss
(Wales): Home Int 1922

Hegarty, G
(Ireland): Home Int 1955-56-64(Captain)

Helme, E
(England): Home Int 1911-12-13-20

Heming Johnson, G
(England): Home Int 1909-11-13

Henson, D (Oxley)
(England): Home Int 1967-68-69-70-75-76-77-78; Eur L T Ch 1971-77. (GB): in Curtis Cup 1968-70-72-76; in Vagliano Trophy 1967-69-71; in Espirito Santo 1970; CW 1967-71

Heskin, A
(Ireland): Home Int 1968-69-70-72-75-77-82(Captain)-83 (Captain)

Hetherington, Mrs (Gittens)
(England): Home Int 1909

Hewett, G
(Ireland): Home Int 1923-24

Hezlet, Mrs
(Ireland): Home Int 1910

Hickey, C
(Ireland): Home Int 1969-75(Captain)-76(Captain)

Higgins, E
(Ireland): Home Int 1981-82-83-84-85-86-87-88; Eur L T Ch 1987

Hill, J
(England): Home Int 1986

Hill, Mrs
(Wales): Home Int 1924

Hodgson, M
(England): Home Int 1939

Holland, I (Hurst)
(Ireland): Home Int 1958

Holm, H (Gray)
(Scotland): Home Int 1932-33-34-35-36-37-38-47-48-50-51-55-57. (GB): in Curtis Cup 1936-38-48

Holmes, A
(England): Home Int 1931

Holmes, J [Hetherington] (McClure)
(England): Home Int 1957-66-67(Captain)

Hooman, EM [Gavin]
(England): Home Int 1910-11

Hope, LA
(Scotland): Home Int 1975-76-80-84-85-86-87

Hort, K
(Wales): Home Int 1929

Hourihane, C
(Ireland): Home Int 1979-80-81-82-83-84-85-86-87-88; Eur L T Ch 1987. (GB): in Curtis Cup 1984-86-88; in Vagliano Trophy 1981-83-85-87; in Espirito Santo 1986

Howard, A (Phillips)
(England): Home Int 1953-54-55-56-57-58-79(Captain)-80 (Captain). (GB): in Curtis Cup 1956-58

Hughes, J

(Wales): Home Int 1967-71-88; Eur L T Ch 1971

Hughes, Miss
(Wales): Home Int 1907

Huke, B
(England): Home Int 1971-72-75-76-77. (GB): in Curtis Cup 1972; in Vagliano Trophy 1975

Hulton, V (Hezlet)
(Ireland): Home Int 1905-07-09-10-11-12-20-21

Humphreys, A (Coulman)
(Wales): Home Int 1969-70-71

Humphreys, D (Forster)
(Ireland): Home Int 1951-52-53-55-57

Hunter, D (Tucker)
(England): Home Int 1905

Hurd, D [Howe] (Campbell)
(Scotland): Home Int 1905-06-08-09-11-28-30

Hurst, Mrs
(Wales): Home Int 1921-22-23-25-27-28

Hyland, B
(Ireland): Home Int 1964-65-66

Imrie, K
(Scotland): Home Int 1984-85; Eur L T Ch 1987

Inghram, E (Lever)
(Wales): Home Int 1947-48-49-50-51-52-53-54-55-56-57-58-64-65

Irvin, A
(England): Home Int 1962-63-65-67-68-69-70-71-72-73-75; Eur L T Ch 1965-67-69-71. (GB): in Curtis Cup 1962-68-70-76; in Vagliano Trophy 1961-63-65-67-69-71-73-75; in Espirito Santo 1982(Captain); CW 1967-75

Irvine, Miss
(Wales): Home Int 1930

Isaac, Mrs
(Wales): Home Int 1924

Isherwood, L
(Wales): Home Int 1972-76-77-78-80-86-88

Jack, E (Philip)
(Scotland): Home Int 1962-63-64-81(Captain)-82(Captain)

Jackson, B
(Ireland): Home Int 1937-38-39-50

Jackson, B
(England): Home Int 1955-56-57-58-59-63-64-65-66-73 (Captain)-74(Captain). (GB): in Curtis Cup 1958-64-68; in Vagliano Trophy 1959-63-65-67-73(Captain)-75(Captain); Espirito Santo 1964; CW in 1959-67

Jackson, Mrs H
(Ireland): Home Int 1921

Jackson, J
(Ireland): Home Int 1912-13-14-20-21-22-23-24-25-27-28-29-30

Jackson, Mrs L
(Ireland): Home Int 1910-12-14-20-22-25

Jameson, S (Tobin)
(Ireland): Home Int 1913-14-20-24-25-27

Jenkin, B
(Wales): Home Int 1959

Jenkins, J (Owen)
(Wales): Home Int 1953-56

John, J
(Wales): Home Int 1974

Johns, A
(England): Home Int 1987-88

Johnson, A (Hughes)
(Wales): Home Int 1964-66-67-68-69-70-71-72-73-74-75-76-78-79-85; Eur L T Ch 1965-67-69-71

Johnson, J (Roberts)
(Wales): Home Int 1955

Johnson, M
(England): Home Int 1934-35

Johnson, R
(Wales): Home Int 1955

Johnson, T
(England): Home Int 1984-85-86; Eur L T Ch 1985. (GB): in Curtis Cup 1986; in Vagliano Trophy 1985; in Espirito Santo 1986

Jones, A (Gwyther)
(Wales): Home Int 1959

Jones, K
(Wales): Home Int 1959(Captain)-1960(Captain)-61(Captain)

Jones, M (De Lloyd)
(Wales): Home Int 1951

Jones, Mrs
(Wales): Home Int 1932-35

Justice, M
(Wales): Home Int 1931-32

Kaye, H (Williamson)
(England): Home Int 1986(Captain)-87(Captain)

Keiller, G [Style]
(England): Home Int 1948-49-52

Kelway Bamber, Mrs
(Scotland): Home Int 1923-27-33

Kennedy, D (Fowler)
(England): Home Int 1923-24-25-27-28-29

Kennion, Mrs (Kenyon Stow)
(England) Home Int 1910

Kerr, J
(Scotland): Home Int 1947-48-49-54

Kidd, Mrs
(Ireland): Home Int 1934-37

King Mrs
(Ireland): Home Int 1923-25-27-29

Kinloch, Miss
(Scotland): Home Int 1913-14

Kirkwood, Mrs
(Ireland): Home Int 1955

Knight, Mrs
(Scotland): Home Int 1922

Kyle, B [Rhodes] (Norris)
(England): Home Int 1937-38-39-48-49

Kyle, E
(Scotland): Home Int 1909-10

Laing, A
(Scotland): Home Int 1966-67-70-71-73(Captain)-74(Captain); Eur L T Ch 1967. (GB): in Vagliano Trophy 1967

Lambert, S (Cohen)
(England): Home Int 1979-80. (GB): in Vagliano Trophy 1979

Lambie, S
(Scotland): Home Int 1976

Laming Evans, Mrs
(Wales): Home Int 1922-23

Langford, Mrs
(Wales): Home Int 1937

Langridge, S (Armitage)
(England): Home Int 1963-64-65-66; Eur L T Ch 1965. (GB): in Curtis Cup 1964-66; in Vagliano Trophy 1963-65

Large, P (Davies)
(England): Home Int 1951-52-81(Captain)-82(Captain)

Larkin, C (McAuley)
(Ireland): Home Int 1966-67-68-69-70-71-72; Eur L T Ch 1971

Latchford, B
(Ireland): Home Int 1931-33

Latham Hall, E (Chubb)
(England): Home Int 1928

Lauder, G
(Ireland): Home Int 1911

Lauder, R
(Ireland): Home Int 1911

Lawrence, JB
(Scotland): Home Int 1959-60-61-62-63-64-65-66-67-68-69-70-77(Captain); Eur L T Ch 1965-67-69-71. (GB): in Curtis Cup 1964; in Vagliano Trophy 1963-65; in Espirito Santo 1964; CW 1971

Lawson, S
(Scotland): Home Int 1985-86-87-88; Eur L T Ch 1987. (GB): in Curtis Cup 1988

Lebrun, W (Aitken)
(Scotland): Home Int 1978-79-80-81-82-83-85. (GB): in Curtis Cup 1982; in Vagliano Trophy 1981-83

Leaver, B
(Wales): Home Int 1912-14-21

Lee Smith, J
(England): Home Int 1973-74-75-76. (GB): in Curtis Cup 1974-76; in Espirito Santo 1976; CW 1975

Leete, Mrs IG
(Scotland): Home Int 1933

Leitch, C
(England): Home Int 1910-11-12-13-14-20-21-22-24-25-27-28

Leitch, M
(England): Home Int 1912-14

Llewellyn, Miss
(Wales): Home Int 1912-13-14-21-22-23

Lloyd, J
(Wales): Home Int 1988

Lloyd, P
(Wales): Home Int 1935-36

Lloyd Davies, VH
(Wales): Home Int 1913

Lloyd Roberts, V
(Wales): Home Int 1907-08-10

Lloyd Williams, Miss
(Wales): Home Int 1909-10-12-14

Lobbett, P
(England): Home Int 1922-24-27-29-30

Lowry, Mrs
(Ireland): Home Int 1947

Luckin, B (Cooper)
(England): Home Int 1980

Lugton, C
(Scotland): Home Int 1968-72-73-75(Captain)-76(Captain)-77-78-80

Lumb, K (Phillips)
(England): Home Int 1968-69-70-71; Eur L T Ch 1969. (GB): Curtis Cup 1972; in Vagliano Trophy 1969-71

Lyons, T (Ross Steen)
(England): Home Int 1959. (GB): in Vagliano Trophy 1959

MacAndrew, F
(Scotland): Home Int 1913-14

Macbeth, M (Dodd)
(England): Home Int 1913-14-20-21-22-23-24-25

MacCann, K
(Ireland): Home Int 1984-85-86

MacCann, K (Smye)
(Ireland): Home Int 1947-48-49-50-51-52-53-54-56-57-58-60-61-62-64-65(Captain)

McCarthy, A
(Ireland): Home Int 1951-52

McCarthy, D
(Ireland): Home Int 1988

McCulloch, J
(Scotland): Home Int 1921-22-23-24-27-29-30-31-32-33-35-60(Captain)

McDaid, E (O'Grady)
(Ireland): Home Int 1959

McDaid, ER
(Ireland): Home Int 1987-88; Eur L T Ch 1987

Macdonald, K
(Scotland): Home Int 1928-29

MacGeach, C
(Ireland): Home Int 1938-39-48-49-50

McGreevy, V
(Ireland): Home Int 1987

McIntosh, B (Dixon)
(England): Home Int 1969-70; Eur L T Ch 1969. (GB): in Vagliano Trophy 1969

McIntyre, J
(England): Home Int 1949-54

MacKean, Mrs
(Wales): Home Int 1938-39-47

McKenna, M
(Ireland): Home Int 1968-69-70-71-72-73-74-75-76-77-78-79-80-81-82-83-84 -85-86-87-88; Eur L T Ch 1969-71-75-87. (GB): in Curtis Cup 1970-72-74-76-78-80-82-84-86; in Vagliano Trophy 1969-71-73-75-77-79-81-85-87; in Espirito Santo 1970-74-76-86(Captain)

Mackenzie, A
(Scotland): Home Int 1921

McLarty, E
(Scotland): Home Int 1966(Captain)-67(Captain)-68(Captain)

McMahon, S (Cadden)
(Scotland): Home Int 1974-75-76-77-79. (GB): in Curtis Cup 1976; in Vagliano Trophy 1975

McNair, W
(England): Home Int 1921

McNeil, K
(Scotland): Home Int 1969(Captain)-70(Captain)

McNeile, CL
(Ireland): Home Int 1906

McQuillan, Y
(Ireland): Home Int 1985-86

MacTier, Mrs
(Wales): Home Int 1927

Madeley, M (Coburn)
(Ireland): Home Int 1964-69; Eur L T Ch 1969

Madill, Mrs
(Ireland): Home Int 1920-24-25-27-28-29-33

Magill, J
(Ireland): Home Int 1907-11-13

Maher, S (Vaughan)
(England): Home Int 1960-61-62-63-64. (GB): in Curtis Cup 1962-64; in Vagliano Trophy 1961; CW 1963

Main, M (Farquhar)
(Scotland): Home Int 1950-51

Maitland, M
(Scotland): Home Int 1905-06-08-12-13

Mallam, Mrs S
(Ireland): Home Int 1922-23

Marks, Mrs T
(Ireland): Home Int 1950
Marks, Mrs
(Ireland): Home Int 1930-31-33-35
Marley, MV
(Wales): Home Int 1921-22-23-30-37
Marr, H (Cameron)
(Scotland): Home Int 1927-28-29-30-31
Martin, P [Whitworth Jones] (Low)
(Wales): Home Int 1948-50-56-59-60-61
Marvin, V
(England): Home Int 1977-78; Eur L T Ch 1977. (GB): in Curtis Cup 1978; in Vagliano Trophy 1977
Mason, Mrs
(Wales): Home Int 1923
Mather, H
(Scotland): Home Int 1905-09-12-13-14
Mellis, Mrs
(Scotland): Home Int 1924-27
Menton, D
(Ireland): Home Int 1949
Menzies, M
(Scotland): Home Int 1962(Captain)
Merrill, J (Greenhalgh)
(England): Home Int 1960-61-63-66-69-70-71-75-76-77-78; Eur L T Ch 1971-77. (GB): in Curtis Cup 1964-70-74-76-78; in Vagliano Trophy 1961-65-75-77; in Espirito Santo 1970-74(Captain)-78; CW 1963
Millar, D
(Ireland): Home Int 1928
Milligan, J (Mark)
(Ireland): Home Int 1971-72-73
Mills, I
(Wales): Home Int 1935-36-37-39-47-48
Milton, M (Paterson)
(Scotland): Home Int 1948-49-50-51-52. (GB): in Curtis Cup 1952
Mitchell, J
(Ireland): Home Int 1930
Mooney, M
(Ireland): Home Int 1972-73; Eur L T Ch 1971. (GB): in Vagliano Trophy 1973
Moorcroft, S
(England): Home Int 1985-86; Eur L T Ch 1985-87
Moore, S
(Ireland): Home Int 1937-38-39-47-48-49-68(Captain)
Moran, V (Singleton)
(Ireland): Home Int 1970-71-73-74-75; Eur L T Ch 1971-75
Morant, E
(England): Home Int 1906-10
Morgan, W
(England): Home Int 1931-32-33-34-35-36-37. (GB): in Curtis Cup 32-34-36
Morgan, Miss
(Wales): Home Int 1912-13-14
Moriarty, M (Irvine)
(Ireland): Home Int 1979
Morris, L (Moore)
(England): Home Int 1912-13
Morris, Mrs de B
(Ireland): Home Int 1933
Morrison, G (Cheetham)
(England): Home Int 1965-69(Captain). (GB): in Vagliano Trophy 1965
Morrison, G (Cradock-Hartopp)
(England): Home Int 1936
Murray, Rachel
(Ireland): Home Int 1952
Murray, S (Jolly)
(England): Home Int 1976
Musgrove, Mrs
(Wales): Home Int 1923-24
Myles, M
(Scotland): Home Int 1955-57-59-60-67

Neill-Fraser, M
(Scotland): Home Int 1905-06-07-08-09-10-11-12-13-14
Nes, K (Garnham)
(England): Home Int 1931-32-33-36-37-38-39
Nevile, E
(England): Home Int 1905-06-08-10
New, B
(England): Home Int 1980-81-82-83. (GB): in Curtis Cup 1984; in Vagliano Trophy 1983
Newell, B
(England): Home Int 1936
Newman, L
(Wales): Home Int 1927-31
Newton, B (Brown)
(England): Home Int 1930-33-34-35-36-37
Nicholls, M
(Wales): Home Int 1962(Captain)
Nicholson, J (Hutton)
(Scotland): Home Int 1969-70; Eur L T Ch 1971; CW 1971
Nicholson, Mrs WH
(Scotland): Home Int 1910-13
Nimmo, H
(Scotland): Home Int 1936-38-39
Norris, J (Smith)
(Scotland): Home Int 1966-67-68-69-70-71-72-75-76-77-78-79-83(Captain)-84(Captain)-84(Captain); Eur L T Ch 1971. (GB): in Vagliano Trophy 1977
Norwell, I (Watt)
(Scotland): Home Int 1954
Nutting, P (Jameson)
(Ireland): Home Int 1927-28

O'Brien, A
(Ireland): Home Int 1969
O'Brien Kenney, S
(Ireland): Home Int 1977-78-83-84-85-86
O'Donnell, M
(Ireland): Home Int 1974-77(Captain)-78(Captain)-79 (Captain); Eur L T Ch 1980(Captain). (GB): in Curtis Cup 1982; in Vagliano Trophy 1981(Captain)
O'Donohoe, A
(Ireland): Home Int 1948-49-50-51-53-73(Captain)-74 (Captain)
O'Hare, S
(Ireland): Home Int 1921-22
O'Reilly, T (Moran)
(Ireland): Home Int 1977-78-86 88; Eur L T Ch 1987
O'Sullivan, A
(Ireland): Home Int 1982-83-84
O'Sullivan, P
(Ireland): Home Int 1950-51-52-53-54-55-56-57-58-59-60-63-64-65-66-67-69 (Captain)-70(Captain)-71(Captain); Eur L T Ch 1971(Captain)
Oliver, M (Jones)
(Wales): Home Int 1955-60-61-62-63-64-65-66.
(GB): in Espirito Santo 1964

Ormsby, Miss
(Ireland): Home Int 1909-10-11

Orr, P (Boyd)
(Ireland): Home Int 1971

Orr, Mrs
(Wales): Home Int 1924

Owen, E
(Wales): Home Int 1947

Panton, C
(Scotland): Home Int 1972-73-76-77-78. (GB): in Vagliano Trophy 1977; in Espirito Santo 1976

Park, Mrs
(Scotland): Home Int 1952

Parker, S
(England): Home Int 1973

Patey, Mrs
(Scotland): Home Int 1922-23

Pearson, D
(England): Home Int 1928-29-30-31-32-34

Percy, G (Mitchell)
(Scotland): Home Int 1927-28-30-31

Perriam, A
(Wales): Home Int 1988

Phelips, M
(Wales): Home Int 1913-14-21

Phillips, ME
(England): Home Int 1905

Phillips, Mrs
(Wales): Home Int 1921

Pickard, M (Nichol)
(England): Home Int 1958-59-60-61-67-69-83(Captain). (GB): in Curtis Cup 1968-70; in Vagliano Trophy 1959-61-67

Pim, Mrs
(Ireland): Home Int 1908

Pook, E (Chadwick)
(England): Home Int 1963-65-66-67; Eur L T Ch 1967. (GB): in Curtis Cup 1966; in Vagliano Trophy 1963-67; CW 1967

Porter, D (Park)
(Scotland): Home Int 1922-25-27-29-30-31-32-33-34-35-37-38-47-48. (GB): in Curtis Cup 1932

Porter, M (Lazenby)
(England): Home Int 1931-32

Powell, M
(Wales): Home Int 1908-09-10-12

Price, M (Greaves)
(England): Home Int 1956(Captain)

Price Fisher, E (Price)
(England): Home Int 1948-51-52-53-54-55-56-57-58-59-60. (GB): in Curtis Cup 1950-52-54-56-58-60; in Vagliano Trophy 1959; CW 1959

Proctor, Mrs
(Wales): Home Int 1907

Provis, I (Kyle)
(Scotland): Home Int 1910-11

Purcell, E
(Ireland): Home Int 1965-66-67-72-73

Purvis-Russell-Montgomery, C
(Scotland): Home Int 1921-22-23-25-28-29-20-31-32-33-34-35-36-37-38-39-47-48-49-50-52

Pyman, B
(Wales): Home Int 1925-28-29-30-32-33-34-35-36-37-38

Rabbidge, R
(England): Home Int 1931

Rawlings, M
(Wales): Home Int 1979-80-81-83-84-85-86-87. (GB): in Vagliano Trophy 1981

Rawlinson, T (Walker)
(Scotland): Home Int 1970-71-73-76. (GB): in Vagliano Trophy 1973

Read, P
(England): Home Int 1922

Reddan, C (Tiernan)
(Ireland): Home Int 1935-36-38-39-47-48-49. (GB): in Curtis Cup 1938-48

Reddan, MV
(Ireland): Home Int 1955

Reece, P (Millington)
(England): Home Int 1966(Captain)

Rees, G
(Wales): Home Int 1981

Rees, MB
(Wales): Home Int 1927-31

Reid, A (Lurie)
(Scotland) Home Int 1960-61-62-63-64-66. (GB): in Vagliano Trophy 1961

Reid, A (Kyle)
(Scotland): Home Int 1923-24-25

Reid, D
(Scotland): Home Int 1978-79

Remer, H
(England): Home Int 1909

Rennie, J (Hastings)
(Scotland): Home Int 1961-65-66-67-71-72; Eur L T Ch 1967. (GB): in Curtis Cup 1966; in Vagliano Trophy 1961-67

Rhys, J
(Wales): Home Int 1979

Rice, J
(Ireland): Home Int 1924-27-29

Richards, J
(Wales): Home Int 1980-82-83-85

Richards, S
(Wales): Home Int 1967

Richardson, Mrs
(England): Home Int 1907-09

Richmond, M (Walker)
(Scotland): Home Int 1972-73-74-75-77-78. (GB): in Curtis Cup 1974; in Vagliano Trophy 1975

Rieben, Mrs
(Wales): Home Int 1927-28-29-30-31-32-33

Rigby, F (Macbeth)
(Scotland): Home Int 1912-13

Ritchie, C (Park)
(Scotland): Home Int 1939-47-48-51-52-53-64(Captain)

Roberts, B
(Wales): Home Int 1984(Captain)-85(Captain)-86(Captain)

Roberts, E (Pentony)
(Ireland): Home Int 1932-33-34-35-36-39

Roberts, E (Barnett)
(Ireland): Home Int 1961-62-63-64-65; Eur L T Ch 1964

Roberts, G
(Wales): Home Int 1949-52-53-54

Roberts, M (Brown)
(Scotland): Home Int 1965(Captain). (GB): in Espirito Santo 1964

Roberts, P
(Wales): Home Int 1950-51-53-55-56-57-58-59-60-61-62-63-64(Captain)-65 (Captain)-66(Captain)-67(Captain)-68-69-70; Eur L T Ch 1965-67-69. (GB) in Espirito Santo 1964

Roberts, S
(Wales): Home Int 1983-84-85-86-87-88; Eur L T Ch 1987

Robertson, B (McCorkindale)
(Scotland): Home Int 1958-59-60-61-62-63-64-65-66-69-72-73-78-80-81-82-84 -85-86; Eur L T Ch 1965-67(Captain)-69-71(Captain). (GB): in Curtis Cup 1960-66-68-70-72-74 (Captain)-76(Captain)-82-86; in Vagliano Trophy 1959-63-69-71-81-85; in Espirito Santo 1959-63-69-71-81-85; CW 1971-75(Captain)

Robertson, D
(Scotland): Home Int 1907

Robertson, E
(Scotland): Home Int 1924

Robertson, G
(Scotland): Home Int 1907-08-09

Robinson, C (Nesbitt)
(Ireland): Home Int 1974-75-76-77-78-79-80-81. (GB): in Curtis Cup 1980; in Vagliano Trophy 1979

Robinson, R (Bayly)
(Ireland): Home Int 1947-56-57

Roche, Mrs
(Ireland): Home Int 1922

Rogers, J
(Wales): Home Int 1972

Roskrow, M
(England): Home Int 1948-50

Ross, M (Hezlet)
(Ireland): Home Int 1905-06-07-08-11-12

Roy, S (Needham)
(Scotland): Home Int 1969-71-72-73-74-75-76-83. (GB): in Vagliano Trophy 1973-75

Rudgard, G
(England): Home Int 1931-32-50-51-52

Rusack, J
(Scotland): Home Int 1908

Sabine, D (Plumpton)
(England): Home Int 1934-35. (GB): in Curtis Cup 1934

Saunders, V
(England): Home Int 1967-68; Eur L T Ch 1967. (GB): in Curtis Cup 1968; in Vagliano Trophy 1967; CW 1967

Scott Chard, Mrs
(Wales) Home Int 1928-30

Seddon, N
(Wales): Home Int 1962-63-74(Captain)-75(Captain)-76 (Captain)

Selkirk, H
(Wales): Home Int 1925-28

Shapcott, S
(England): Home Int 1986-88; Eur L T Ch 1987. (GB): in Curtis Cup 1988; in Vagliano Trophy 1987; CW 1987

Shaw, P
(Wales): Home Int 1913

Sheldon, A
(Wales): Home Int 1981

Sheppard, E (Pears)
(England): Home Int 1947

Simpson, L (Moore)
(England): Home Int 1979-80

Singleton, B (Henderson)
(Scotland): Home Int 1939-52-53-54-55-56-57-58-60-61-62-63-64-65

Slade, Lady
(Ireland): Home Int 1906

Slark, R (Porter)
(England): Home Int 1959-60-61-62-64-65-66-68-78; Eur L T Ch 1965. (GB): in Curtis Cup 1960-62-64; in Vagliano Trophy 1959-61-65; in Espirito Santo 1964-66(Captain); CW 1963

Slocombe, E (Davies)
(Wales): Home Int 1974-75

Smalley, Mrs A
(Wales): Home Int 1924-25-31-32-33-34

Smillie, P
(England): Home Int 1985-86

Smith, A [Stant] (Willard)
(England): Home Int 1974-75-76. (GB): in Curtis Cup 1976; in Vagliano Trophy 1975; CW 1959-63

Smith, F (Stephens)
(England): Home Int 1947-48-49-50-51-52-53-54-55-59-62 (Captain)-71(Captain) -72(Captain). (GB): in Curtis Cup 1950-52-54-56-58-60-62(non-playing Captain)-72 (non-playing Captain); in Vagliano Trophy 1959-71; CW 1959-63

Smith, Mrs L
(Ireland): Home Int 1913-14-21-22-23-25

Smythe, M
(Ireland): Home Int 1947-48-49-50-51-52-53-54-55-56-58-59-62(Captain)

Sowter, Mrs
(Wales): Home Int 1923

Speir, M
(Scotland): Home Int 1957-64-68-71(Captain)-72(Captain)

Starrett, L (Malone)
(Ireland): Home Int 1975-76-77-78-80

Stavert, M
(Scotland): Home Int 1979

Steel, Mrs DC
(Scotland): Home Int 1925

Steel, E
(England): Home Int 1905-06-07-08-11

Stewart, G
(Scotland): Home Int 1979-80-81-82-83-84; Eur L T Ch 1982-84. (GB): in Curtis Cup 1980-82; in Vagliano Trophy 1979-81-83; CW 1979-83

Stewart, L (Scraggie)
(Scotland): Home Int 1921-22-23

Stocker, J
(England): Home Int 1922-23

Stockton, Mrs
(Wales): Home Int 1949

Storry, Mrs
(Wales): Home Int 1910-14

Stuart, M
(Ireland): Home Int 1905-07-08

Stuart-French, Miss
(Ireland): Home Int 1922

Sugden, J (Machin)
(England): Home Int 1953-54-55

Summers, M (Mackie)
(Scotland): Home Int 1986

Sumpter, Mrs
(England): Home Int 1907-08-12-14-24

Sutherland Pilch, R (Barton)
(England): Home Int 1947-49-50-58(Captain)

Swallow, C
(England): Home Int 1985; Eur L T Ch 1985

Tamworth, Mrs
(England): Home Int 1908

Taylor, I
(Ireland): Home Int 1930

Teacher, F
(Scotland): Home Int 1908-09-11-12-13

Temple, S
(England): Home Int 1913-14

Temple Dobell, G (Ravenscroft)
(England): Home Int 1911-12-13-14-20-21-25-30

Thomas, C (Phipps)
(Wales): Home Int 1959-63-64-65-66-67-68-69-70-71-72-73-76-77-80

Thomas, I
(Wales): Home Int 1910

Thomas, O
(Wales): Home Int 1921

Thomas, S (Rowlands)
(Wales): Home Int 1977-82-84-85

Thomas, T (Perkins)
(Wales): Home Int 1972-73-74-75-76-77-78-79-80-81-82-83-84; Eur L T Ch 1975. (GB): in Curtis Cup 1974-76-78-80; in Vagliano Trophy 1973-75-77-79; in Espirito Santo 1979; CW 1975-79

Thomas, V (Rawlings)
(Wales): Home Int 1971-72-73-74-75-76-77-78-79-80-81-82-83-84-85-86-87-88; Eur L T Ch 1975-87. (GB): in Curtis Cup 1982-84-86-88; in Vagliano Trophy 1979-83 -85-87; CW 1979-83-87.

Thompson, M
(Wales): Home Int 1937-38-39

Thompson, M (Wallis)
(England): Home Int 1948-49

Thompson, M
(Scotland): Home Int 1949

Thomson, D
(Scotland): Home Int 1982-83-85-87

Thomson, M
(Scotland): Home Int 1907

Thomson, M
(Scotland): Home Int 1974-75-76-77-78; Eur L T Ch 1978. (GB): in Curtis Cup 1978; in Vagliano Trophy 1977

Thornhill, J (Woodside)
(England): Home Int 1965-74-82-83-84-85-86-87-88; Eur L T Ch 1965-85-87. (GB): in Curtis Cup 1984-86-88; in Vagliano Trophy 1965-83-85-87; CW 1983-87

Thornhill, Miss
(Ireland): Home Int 1924-25

Thornton, Mrs
(Ireland): Home Int 1924

Todd, Mrs
(Ireland): Home Int 1931-32-34-35-36

Thomlinson, J [Evans] (Roberts)
(England): Home Int 1962-64. (GB): in Curtis Cup 1962; in Vagliano Trophy 1963

Treharne, A [Mills]
(Wales): Home Int 1952-61

Turner, B
(England): Home Int 1908

Turner, S (Jump)
(Wales): Home Int 1982-84-85-86

Tynte, V
(Ireland): Home Int 1905-06-08-09-11-12-13-14

Uzielli, A (Carrick)
(England): Home Int 1976-77-78; Eur L T Ch 1977. (GB): in Curtis Cup 1978; in Vagliano Trophy 1977

Valentine, J (Anderson)
(Scotland): Home Int 1934-35-36-37-38-39-47-49-50-51-52-53-54-55-56 (Captain)-57-58. (GB): in Curtis Cup 1938-48-50-52-54-56-58; CW 1959

Valentine, P (Whitley)
(Wales): Home Int 1973-74-75-77-78-79-80

Veitch, F
(Scotland): Home Int 1912

Wade, J
(England): Home Int 1987-88; Eur L T Ch 1987. (GB): in Curtis Cup 1988

Wadsworth, H
(Wales): Home Int 1987-88; Eur L T Ch 1987

Waite, C
(England): Home Int 1981-82-83-84, Eur L T Ch 1985. (GB): in Curtis Cup 1984; in Vagliano Trophy 1983; in Espirito Santo 1984; CW 1983

Wakelin, H
(Wales): Home Int 1955

Walker, B (Thompson)
(England): Home Int 1905-06-07-08-09-11

Walker, M
(England): Home Int 1970-72; Eur L T Ch 1971. (GB): in Curtis Cup 1972; in Vagliano Trophy 1971; CW 1971

Walker, P
(Ireland): Home Int 1928-29-30-31-32-33-34-35-36-37-38-39-48. (GB): in Curtis Cup 1934-36-38

Walker-Leigh, F
(Ireland): Home Int 1907-08-09-11-12-13-14

Wallace-Williamson, V
(Scotland): Home Int 1932. (GB): in Curtis Cup 1938 (Captain)

Walsh, R
(Ireland): Home Int 1987

Walter, J
(England): Home Int 1974-79-80-82-86

Wardlaw, N (Baird)
(Scotland): Home Int 1932-35-36-37-38-39-47-48. (GB): in Curtis Cup 1938

Watson, C (Nelson)
(England): Home Int 1982

Webster, S (Hales)
(Wales): Home Int 1968-69-72

Wesley, N
(Wales): Home Int 1986

Westall, S (Maudsley)
(England): Home Int 1973

Weston, R
(Wales): Home Int 1927

Whieldon, Miss
(Wales): Home Int 1908

Wickham, C
(Ireland): Home Int 1983

Wickham, P
(Ireland): Home Int 1976-83-87; Eur L T Ch 1987

Williams, M
(Wales): Home Int 1936

Wlliamson, C (Barker)
(England): Home Int 1979-80-81

Willock-Pollen, G
(England): Home Int 1907

Wilson, A
(Scotland): Home Int 1973-74-85 (Captain)

Wilson, E
(England): Home Int 1928-29-30. (GB): in Curtis Cup 1932

Wilson, Mrs
(Ireland): Home Int 1931

Wilson Jones, D
(Wales): Home Int 1952

Winn, J
(England): Home Int 1920-21-23-25

Wooldridge, W (Shaw)
(Scotland): Home Int 1982

Wragg, M
(England): Home Int 1929

Wright, J (Robertson)
(Scotland): Home Int 1952-53-54-55-56-57-58-59-60-61-63-65-67-73-78 (Captain-79(Captain)-80(Captain)-86(Captain); Eur L T Ch 1965. (GB): in Curtis Cup 1954-56-58-60; in Vagliano Trophy 1959-61-63; CW 1959

Wright, N (Cook)
(Wales): Home Int 1938-47-48-49-51-52-53-54-57-58-59-60-62-63-64-66-67-68-71 (Captain)-72(Captain)-73(Captain); Eur L T Ch 1965-71 (Captain). (GB): in Espirito Santo 1964

Wright, P
(Scotland): Home Int 1981-82-83-84; Eur L T Ch 1987. (GB): in Vagliano Trophy 1981

Wylie, P (Wade)
(England): Home Int 1934-35-36-37-38-47. (GB): in Curtis Cup 1938

Note: As will be seen, there is a good deal still missing in these lists. Records, particularly of the early days, are not easily found. The Editor will be pleased to receive any additions or corrections from players or their relatives.

Association of Golf Writers

Adams, Jack	*Daily Record*, Anderston Quay, Glasgow
Andrew, Harry H	Flat 2, Glenbank Court, Glenbank Drive, Giffnock G46 7EJ
(L) Baker, John E	3 Cissbury Drive, Findon Valley, Worthing, West Sussex BN14 0DT
Ballantine, John	Brick Hill Cottage, Hook Norton, Banbury, Oxon
Bisher, Firman	Atlanta-Journal Constitution, 72 Marrietta Street NW, Atlanta, Georgia 30302, USA
Blackstock, Dixon	*Sunday Mail*, Anderston Quay, Glasgow
Blighton, Bill	*Today*, News (UK) Ltd, 70 Vauxhall Bridge Road, London SW1V 2RP
Blomquist, Jan	*Golf Digest Sverige*, Luxgatan 11, S-112, 62 Stockholm, Sweden
Bolze, Gerd A	Immensweg 11D, D2 Hamburg 73, West Germany
Booth, Alan	21 Westminster Court, St Albans, Herts AL1 2DU
Bowden, Ken	56 Hermit Lane, PO Box 573, Westport, Connecticut 06881, USA
Britten, Mike	Exchange Telegraph PLC, Extel House, 298 Regents Park Road, Finchley, London N3 2LZ
(H) Butler, Frank	Robin Hill, Chislehurst Road, Orpington, Kent
Caird, Douglas	Fairway and Hazard, Gunners, Windlesham, Surrey
Callander, Colin	*Golf Monthly*, 1 Park Circus, Glasgow G3 6AP
Campbell, John G	*The Daily Telegraph*, 49 Woodend Drive, Glasgow G13
Campbell, Malcolm	*Golf Monthly*, 1 Park Circus, Glasgow
Chapman, Jeremy	*The Sporting Life*, Alexander House, 81-89 Farringdon Road, London EC1M 3LH
Clark, Bill	*Sunday Mirror*, Mark Royal House, Donegall Street, Belfast
Clough, Frank	*The Sun*, News International, 1 Virginia Street, London E1 9XP
Coffman, Ron	*Golf World*, PO Box 2000, Southern Pines, North Carolina, USA
Creighton, Brian	Reuters, 85 Fleet Street, London EC4
Davies, David	*The Guardian*, 119 Farringdon Road, London EC1R 3ER
Davies, Patricia	51 Balmoral Road, Four Oaks, Sutton Coldfield, West Midlands B74 4UF
Dobereiner, Peter	*The Observer*, St Andrews Hill, London EC4

Dodd, Richard	*The Yorkshire Post*, Wellington Street, Leeds 1
Donald, Peter	7 House o'Hill Grove, Edinburgh EH4 5DW
Ebbinge, Jan B	*Golf Benelux Tijl Tijdschriften bv*, Jaques Veltmanstraat 29, 1065 EG Amsterdam, Holland
(L) Edwards, Leslie	26 Beachcroft Road, Meols, Cheshire
Elliott, Bill	*The Star*, Fleet Street, London EC4P 4JT
Ellison, Stanley	*Turf Management*, 3 Twelve Acre Close, Great Bookham, Surrey
Elsey, Neil	Golf World Ltd, Advance House, 37 Mill Harbour, Isle of Dogs, London E14 9TX
Farquharson, Colin	Press and Journal, Lang Stracht, Mastrick, Aberdeen AB9 8AF
(H) Fenton, John	BBC Radio, 17 McAdam Drive, Enfield, Middx
Ferrier, Bob	World of Sport Ltd, Upper Rothiemay, 39a Colquhoun Street, Helensburgh G84 9JW
Figar, Jose	Adesport SA, Lopez de Hoyos 15-6D, 28006 Madrid, Spain
Fraser, Alan	*Scotland on Sunday*, North Bridge, Edinburgh
Frederick, Adrian	*The Sunday Star*, 47 Sauer Street, Johannesburg, South Africa
Garrod, Mark	Press Association, 85 Fleet Street, London EC4
Gibbon, Sidney	26 Mowlem Court, Swanage, Dorset
Gilleece, Dermot	*The Irish Times*, D'Olier Street, Dublin, Eire
Glover, Tim	*The Independent*, 40 City Road, London EC1
Goodner, Ross	*Golf Digest*, 5520 Park Avenue, Trumbull, Connecticut 06611, USA
Green, Bob	The Associated Press, 50 Rockefeller Plaza, New York, NY 10020, USA
Green, Robert	94 Priory Road, London N8
Grimsley, Will	The Associated Press, 50 Rockefeller Plaza, New York, NY 10020
Hamilton, David	*Golf Illustrated*, 47 Dartford Road, Sevenoaks, Kent TN13 3TE
Hamilton, Eddie	Netherton Court, Ayr Road, Newton Mearns, Glasgow G77 6EN
Hardy, Martin	*Daily Express*, Fleet Street, London EC4P 4JT
Haslam, Peter	*Golf World*, Advance House, 37 Mill Harbour, Isle of Dogs, London E14 9TX
(L) Hart, Maurice	11 Ivymount Road, London SE27
Hedley, Alan	*The Journal*, Groat Market, Newcastle-upon-Tyne
Hennessy, John	*The Times*, PO Box 481, Virginia Street, London E1 9XP
Herron, Allan	4 Tweedsmuir Crescent, Mosshead, Bearsden, Glasgow G61 3LE
Higgs, Peter	*Mail on Sunday*, Northcliffe House, Tudor Street, London EC4Y 0JA

Hopkins, John	*The Sunday Times*, News International, 1 Virginia Street, London E1 9XP
(L) Huggins, Percy	43 Beechlands Drive, Clarkston, nr Glasgow G76 7UZ
Ingham, John	Alfred Dunhill Ltd., 30 Duke Street, St James's, London SW1Y 6DL
Jacobs, Raymond	*Glasgow Herald*, 195 Albion Street, Glasgow G1 1QP
Jenkins, Bob	*Sunday Post*, Glasgow
Jenkins, Dan	*Golf Digest*, 495 Westport Avenue, Norwalk, Connecticut 06856, USA
Johnson, Bill	*Bolton Evening News*, Mealhouse Lane, Bolton, Lancs
Kahn, Elizabeth	The Chase, Hadley Common, Barnet, Herts
Lafaurie, Andre-Jean	*Golf European*, 19 Rue de Prony, 75017 Paris, France
Laidlaw, Renton	*Evening Standard*, Fleet Street, London EC4
Lawrenson, Derek	*Birmingham Post and Mail*, Colmore Circus, Birmingham B4 6AX
Lincoln, Stanley	260 Park Avenue, Bushey, Herts WD2 2BH
McDonnell, Michael	*Daily Mail*, Tudor Street, London EC4
(H) McKinlay, S L	92 Killermont Road, Bearsden, Glasgow
Macniven, Ian	*Edinburgh Evening News*, North Bridge, Edinburgh
MacVicar, Jock	*Scottish Daily Express*, Park House, 2-4 Park Circus Place, Glasgow G3 6AF
Mackie, Keith	Dundrennan House, 12 Woodburn Terrace, St Andrews, Fife, Scotland
Magowan, Jack	*Belfast Telegraph*, Belfast
Mair, Norman	*The Scotsman*, North Bridge, Edinburgh
Mair, Lewine	15 Dreghorn Loan, Colinton, Edinburgh 13
Maitland, Bobby	*Scottish Daily Express*, Park House, 2-4 Park Circus Place, Glasgow
Mancinelli, Piero	*Il Giorno*, Piazza Cavour 2, 20121 Milan *Golf Italiano*, 80 Lungotevere Flaminio, 00196 Rome, Italy
Mearing, Paddy	Holly Tree Cottage, Chester Road, Bucklow Hill, Mere, Cheshire IA16 6RY
Miro, Miguel	Diario Deportivo SA, Cuesta San Vicente 26, Madrid, Spain
Moody, John	Tryfan, Danybryn Avenue, Radyr, nr Cardiff
Morgan, John	Dray Lodge, Dray Corner, Headcorn, Kent TN27 9PA
Moseley, Ron	Press Association, 85 Fleet Street, London EC4
Mossop, James	*Sunday Express*, 121 Fleet Street, London EC4P 4JT
Mulqueen, Charles	*Cork Examiner*, 95 Patrick Street, Cork, Eire
(H) Neale, Bert	Action Photos, Unit 6, 21 Wren Street, London WC1X 0HB
Nicol, Alister	*Daily Record*, 90A George Street, Edinburgh
Oakley, John	10 Cairn Close, Camberley, Surrey
Ortega, Jesus Ruiz	*Golf*, Basilica 15, 80A, 28020 Madrid, Spain

Ostermann, Ted	*Golf Vertrieb*, Hamburgerstrasse 3-27/3, D 2000 Hamburg 76, West Germany
Pargeter, John	26 Princes Road, Brunton Park, Newcastle-upon-Tyne NE3 5AL
Pastor, Nuria	*La Vanguardia*, Pelayo 28, Barcelona, Spain
Pinner, John	*Golf World Wales*, Glenview, Penrhos, Raglan, Gwent NP5 2LF
(H) Place, Tom	US Tour, 100 Nina Court, Ponte Vedra Beach, Florida 32082, USA
Platts, Mitchell	*The Times*, News International, 1 Pennington Street, London E1 9XN
Plumridge, Chris	*The Illustrated London News*, 4 Bloomsbury Square, London WC1A 2RL
Price, Charles	5c Dogwood Terrace, Pinehurst, North Carolina 27374, USA
Price-Fisher, Elizabeth	*Daily Telegraph*, Fleet Street, London EC4
Ramsey, Tom	News Limited, Australia PO Box 1349, North Sydney 2059, New South Wales, Australia
Redmond, John	*Irish Press*, Burgh Quay, Dublin 2, Eire
Reece, John K	Hailstones, Broadfield Down, Redhill, nr Bristol BS18 7TL
Riach, Ian	*Scottish Sunday Express*, Park House, Park Circus Place, Glasgow G3 6AF
Richardson, Gordon	Trees, Post Office Lane, Hyde, near Fordingbridge, Hants
Roberts, Steve	7 Marsham Lodge, East Common, Gerrards Cross, Bucks SL9 7AB
Robertson, Bill	*Today's Golfer*, EMAP Pursuit Publishing Ltd, Bretton Court, Bretton, Peterborough PE3 8D2
Robertson, Jack	*Evening Times*, 195 Albion Street, Glasgow G1 1QP
Rodrigo, Robert (Bob Rodney)	4 Wragg Drive, Newmarket, Suffolk CB8 7SD
Ross, John M	Market Source Corporation, 10 Abeel Road, Cranbury, New Jersey 08512, USA
Ruddy, Pat	*Golfers Companion*, PO Box 14, Dun Laoghaire, County Dublin, Eire
Ryde, Peter	4 Phene Street, Chelsea, London SW3
Scatchard, Charles	15 Misburg Close, Shepton Mallet, Somerset BA4 5GB
Seitz, Nick	*Golf Digest*, 495 Westport Avenue, Norwalk, Connecticut 06856, USA
Severino, Dick	Golf Features Service, 10081 Mesa Madera Drive, San Diego, California 92131, USA
Simms, George	10 Melsted Road, Hemel Hempstead, Herts HP1 1SX
Simpson, Gordon	Press Association, 96 Warroch Street, Glasgow G3 8DB
Skelton, Ronald	*Dundee Courier*, Bank Street, Dundee, Scotland
Smart, Chris	Mid-Glamorgan Press Agency, Chapel Cottage, Nottage, Porthcawl, Mid Glamorgan CF36 3ST
Smith, Colm	Independent Newspapers, 91 Middle Abbey Street, Dublin 1, Eire

	Dublin 1, Eire
Sommers, Robert	United States Golf Association, Far Hills, New Jersey 07931, USA
Spander, Art	*San Francisco Examiner*, 110 5th Street, San Francisco, California 94103, USA
Steel, Donald	*Sunday Telegraph*, 135 Fleet Street, London EC4
Stobbs, John	*General Golf and Greenkeeping*. Home: 73 Vicarage Road, Marsworth, nr Tring, Herts
Taylor, Dick	*Golf World*, Box 2000, Southern Pines, N.C. 28387, USA
(H) Thornberry, Henry W	*New York Times*, News service, 229 W 43rd Street, New York, NY 10036
(H) Ullyett, Roy	*Daily Express*, 121 Fleet Street, London EC4P 4JT
Van Esbeck, Edmund	*The Irish Times*, 31 Westmoreland Street, Dublin, Eire
Ward, Barry E	*Holiday Golf International*, 16 Georgia Avenue, Worthing, West Sussex BN14 8AZ
Whitbread, John S	Surrey Herald Newspapers, 89 Eastworth Road, Chertsey, Surrey KT16 8DX
White, Gordon S	*The New York Times*, 229 West 43rd Street, New York, NY 10036, USA
Wills, Ron	*Daily Mirror*, Holborn Circus, London EC1
Williams, Michael	*Daily Telegraph*, Peterborough Court, South Quay, 181 Marsh Wall, London E14 9SR
(L) Wilson, Enid	The Oast, Redbridge Farm, Redbridge Lane, Crowborough, East Sussex TN6 3SR
Wilson, Mark	PGA European Tour, Wentworth, Virginia Water, Surrey
Wind, Herbert Warren	*The New Yorker*, 25 W 43rd Street, New York, NY 21
Wright, Ben	125 Kenmure Drive, Flat Rock, North Carolina 28731-9780 USA
Zachrisson, Goran	*Golf Store Magazine*, Danderydswagen 16F, 182 Djursholm, Stockholm, Sweden

Provincial Golfwriters Guild

Barron, Brian	*Chronicle and Echo*, Upper Mounts, Northampton
Benbow, Paul	*Reading Evening Post*, 8 Tessa Road, Reading
Blows, David	*Hull Daily Mail*, Jameson Street, Hull
Brain, Keith (President)	*Manchester Evening News*, Manchester
Davies, Bob (Captain)	*Shropshire Star*, Ketley, Telford
Godsiff, Peter (Chairman)	*Bristol Evening Post*, Temple Way, Bristol
Instone, David	*Wolverhampton Express and Star*, Queen St, Wolverhampton
McEwan, Ian	*Dumfries and Galloway Standard*, 30 Ardwall Road, Dumfries
Madsen, Duncan	*Newcastle Evening Chronicle*, Thomson House, Groat Market, Newcastle-upon-Tyne

Madsen, Duncan	*Newcastle Evening Chronicle*, Thomson House, Groat Market, Newcastle-upon-Tyne
Phillips, Robert	*South Wales Echo*, Cardiff
Poole, Barry	*Golfer Magazine*, Norden House, 37/41 Stowell Street Newcastle-upon-Tyne
Stathers, Mike (Treasurer)	*Yorkshire Post*, Regent House, Ferensway, Hull
Yeomans, Roy (Secretary)	*Evening Echo*, Richmond Hill, Bournemouth

British Association of Golf Course Architects

Members

Full

J Hamilton Stutt	Hamilton Stutt & Co, Bergen 12, Bingham Ave, Poole, Dorset BW14 8NE *Tel* (0202) 708406
Donald Harradine	CH 6987, Caslano, Switzerland *Tel* (091) 711561
Fred and Martin Hawtree	Hawtree & Son, 5 Oxford Street, Woodstock, Oxford OX7 1TQ *Tel* (0993) 811976
Donald Steel	The Forum, Stirling Road, Chichester, West Sussex, PO19 2EN *Tel* (0243) 531901
Tom McAuley	38 Moira Drive, Bangor, Co Down, N Ireland BT20 4RW *Tel* (0247) 465953
Peter Harradine	PO Box 1165, Sharjah, United Arab Emirates *Tel* (009716) 356446

Provisional

Simon Gidman, Peter Bellchambers, Steven Macfarlane,	Hawtree & Son, 5 Oxford Street, Woodstock, Oxford OX7 1TQ *Tel* (0993) 811976
Alistair Rae	26 Tannoch Road, Uplawmoor, Glasgow G78 4AD *Tel* (050 585) 371
Stephan Quenouille	c/o Tom McAuley, 38 Moira Drive, Bangor, Co Down, N Ireland BT20 4RW *Tel* (0247) 465953
Cameron Sinclair	Marsh Watson Pty Ltd, PO Box 136, Nerang, Queensland 4211, Australia *Tel* 075-58 4733
Jeremy Pern	13 Lotissement des Chênes, Aussonne 31700, Blagnac (Toulouse), France *Tel* 61 85 09 02

Overseas (Full)

Eddie Hackett	28 Ailesbury Drive, Dublin 4, Eire *Tel* (0001) 691592
Joan Dudok Van Heel	Beukenlaan 4, B-1640, St Genesius-Rode, nr Brussels, Belgium *Tel* (02) 3583387
Pier Mancinelli	21 Via Achille Papa 00195, Rome, Italy *Tel* (06) 36036-35
Jan Sederholm	K Kristoffersweg 3A, S 253 34 Helsingborg, Sweden *Tel* (042) 371 84

Overseas (Provisional)

Kurt Rossknecht	Dennenmoos 5a, 8990 Lindau-Bad, Schachen, W Germany *Tel* 08382 230 05
R Berthet	57-59 Lhomond, 75005, Paris, France, *Tel* (1) 336-77-50
Tjasa Gregoric	Kobilarna Lipica, 66 210 Sezatia, Yugoslavia
Gerard Jol	Landschapsarchitekt bnt, Middenduinerweg 75, 2082 LC Santpoort, Netherlands *Tel* (023) 376449

Honorary Members

G S Cornish	Fiddlers Green, Amherst, Mass 01002, USA

Part IV

Tournament Results

The Championships

The Open Championship

The Belt

Year	Winner	Score	Venue	Entrants
1860	W Park, Musselburgh	174	Prestwick	8
1861	Tom Morris, sen, Prestwick	163	Prestwick	12
1862	Tom Morris, sen, Prestwick	163	Prestwick	6
1863	W Park, Musselburgh	168	Prestwick	14
1864	Tom Morris, sen, Prestwick	167	Prestwick	6
1865	A Strath, St Andrews	162	Prestwick	10
1866	W Park, Musselburgh	169	Prestwick	12
1867	Tom Morris, sen, St Andrews	170	Prestwick	10
1868	Tom Morris, jun, St Andrews	157	Prestwick	10
1869	Tom Morris, jun, St Andrews	154	Prestwick	8
1870	Tom Morris, jun, St Andrews	149	Prestwick	17

The Belt having been won thrice in succession by young Tom Morris, it became his property, and the Championship remained in abeyance for one year, when the present cup was offered for yearly competition, to be held by the leading club in the district in which the winner resided.

The Cup

Year	Winner	Score	Venue	Entrants
1872	Tom Morris, jun, St Andrews	166	Prestwick	8
1873	Tom Kidd, St Andrews	179	St Andrews	26
1874	Mungo Park, Musselburgh	159	Musselburgh	32
1875	Willie Park, Musselburgh	166	Prestwick	18
1876	Bob Martin, St Andrews	176	St Andrews	34
(David Strath tied but refused to play off)				
1877	Jamie Anderson, St Andrews	160	Musselburgh	24
1878	Jamie Anderson, St Andrews	157	Prestwick	26
1879	Jamie Anderson, St Andrews	169	St Andrews	46
1880	Bob Ferguson, Musselburgh	162	Musselburgh	30
1881	Bob Ferguson, Musselburgh	170	Prestwick	22
1882	Bob Ferguson, Musselburgh	171	St Andrews	40
1883	W. Fernie, Dumfries	159	Musselburgh	41
After a tie with Bob Ferguson, Musselburgh				
1884	Jack Simpson, Carnoustie	160	Prestwick	30
1885	Bob Martin, St Andrews	171	St Andrews	51
1886	D Brown, Musselburgh	157	Musselburgh	46
1887	W. Park, jun, Musselburgh	161	Prestwick	36
1888	Jack Burns, Warwick	171	St Andrews	53
1889	W. Park, jun, Musselburgh	155	Musselburgh	42
After a tie with Andrew Kirkaldy				
1890	John Ball, Royal Liverpool (Am)	164	Prestwick	40
1891	Hugh Kirkaldy, St Andrews	166	St Andrews	82
After 1891 the competition was extended to 72 holes and for the first time entry money was imposed				
1892	HH Hilton, Royal Liverpool (Am)	305	Muirfield	66
1893	W Auchterlonie, St Andrews	322	Prestwick	72
1894	JH Taylor, Winchester	326	Sandwich	94
1895	JH Taylor, Winchester	322	St Andrews	73
1896	H Vardon, Ganton	316	Muirfield	64
After a tie with JH Taylor. Replay scores for 36 holes: H Vardon, 157; Taylor, 161				
1897	HH Hilton, Royal Liverpool (Am)	314	Hoylake	86

The Open Championship
continued

Year	Winner	Score	Venue	Entrants
1898	H Vardon, Ganton	307	Prestwick	78
1899	H Vardon, Ganton	310	Sandwich	98
1900	JH Taylor, Mid-Surrey	309	St Andrews	81
1901	James Braid, Romford	309	Muirfield	101
1902	Alex Herd, Huddersfield	307	Hoylake	112
1903	H Vardon, Totteridge	300	Prestwick	127
1904	Jack White, Sunningdale	296	Sandwich	144
1905	James Braid, Walton Heath	318	St Andrews	152
1906	James Braid, Walton Heath	300	Muirfield	183
1907	Arnaud Massy, La Boulie	312	Hoylake	193

Year	Winner	Score	Venue	Qual	Ents
1908	James Braid, Walton Heath	291	Prestwick	180	
1909	JH Taylor, Mid-Surrey	295	Deal	204	
1910	James Braid, Walton Heath	299	St Andrews	210	
1911	Harry Vardon, Totteridge	303	Sandwich	226	
After a tie with Arnaud Massy. The tie was over 36 holes, but Massy picked up at the 35th hole before holing out. He had taken 148 for 34 holes, and when Vardon holed out at the 35th hole his score was 143.					
1912	E Ray, Oxhey	295	Muirfield	215	
1913	JH Taylor, Mid-Surrey	304	Hoylake	269	
1914	Harry Vardon, Totteridge	306	Prestwick	194	
1915-19	No Championship owing to the Great War				
1920	George Duncan, Hanger Hill	303	Deal	81	190
1921	Jock Hutchison, Glenview, Chicago	296	St Andrews	85	158
After a tie with RH Wethered (Am). Royal and Ancient-Replay scores: Jock Hutchison 150; RH Wethered 159.					
1922	Walter Hagen, Detroit, USA	300	Sandwich	80	225
1923	AG Havers, Coombe Hill	295	Troon	88	222
1924	Walter Hagen, Detroit, USA	301	Hoylake	86	277
1925	Jim Barnes, USA	300	Prestwick	83	200
1926	RT Jones, USA (Am)	291	Lytham and St Annes	117	293
1927	RT Jones, USA (Am)	285	St Andrews	108	207
1928	Walter Hagen, USA	292	Sandwich	113	271
1929	Walter Hagen, USA	292	Muirfield	109	242
1930	RT Jones, USA (Am)	291	Hoylake	112	296
1931	TD Armour, USA	296	Carnoustie	109	215
1932	G Sarazen, USA	283	Prince's, Sandwich	110	224
1933	D Shute, USA	292	St Andrews	117	287
After a tie with Craig Wood, USA-Replay scores: D Shute 149; Craig Wood 154.					
1934	TH Cotton, Waterloo, Belgium	283	Sandwich	101	312
1935	A Perry, Leatherhead	283	Muirfield	109	264
1936	AH Padgham, Sundridge Park	287	Hoylake	107	286
1937	TH Cotton, Ashridge	290	Carnoustie	141	258
1938	RA Whitcombe, Parkstone	295	Sandwich	120	268
1939	R Burton, Sale	290	St Andrews	129	254
1940-45	*No Championship owing to Second World War*				
1946	S Snead, USA	290	St Andrews	100	225
1947	Fred Daly, Balmoral	293	Hoylake	100	263
1948	TH Cotton, Royal Mid-Surrey	284	Muirfield	97	272
1949	AD Locke, South Africa	283	Sandwich	96	224
After a tie with Harry Bradshaw, Kilcroney-Replay Scores: Locke 135; Bradshaw 147.					
1950	AD Locke, South Africa	279	Troon	93	262
1951	M Faulkner, GB	285	Portrush	98	180
1952	AD Locke, South Africa	287	Lytham and St Annes	96	275
1953	Ben Hogan, USA	282	Carnoustie	91	196
1954	PW Thomson, Australia	283	Birkdale	97	349
1955	PW Thomson, Australia	281	St Andrews	94	301
1956	PW Thomson, Australia	286	Hoylake	96	360
1957	AD Locke, South Africa	279	St Andrews	96	282
1958	PW Thomson, Australia	278	Lytham and St Annes	96	362
After a tie with DC Thomas, Sudbury-Replay scores: Thomson 139; Thomas 143.					
1959	GJ Player, South Africa	284	Muirfield	90	285
1960	KDG Nagle, Australia	278	St Andrews	74	410
1961	Arnold Palmer, USA	284	Birkdale	101	364
1962	Arnold Palmer, USA	276	Troon	119	379
1963	RJ Charles, New Zealand	277	Lytham and St Annes	119	261
After a tie with Phil Rodgers, USA-Replay scores: Charles 140; Rodgers 148					
1964	Tony Lema, USA	279	St Andrews	119	327
1965	PW Thomson, Australia	285	Birkdale	130	372
1966	J Nicklaus, USA	282	Muirfield	130	310
1967	R De Vicenzo, Argentina	278	Hoylake	130	326
1968	GJ Player, South Africa	289	Carnoustie	130	309

The Open Championship
continued

Year	Winner	Score	Venue	Qual	Ents
1969	A Jacklin, GB	280	Lytham and St Annes	129	424
1970	J Nicklaus USA	283	St Andrews	134	468
After a tie with Doug Sanders, USA-Replay scores: Nicklaus 72; Sanders 73.					
1971	L Trevino, USA	278	Birkdale	150	528
1972	L Trevino, USA	278	Muirfield	150	570
1973	T Weiskopf, USA	276	Troon	150	569
1974	G Player, South Africa	282	Lytham and St Annes	150	679
1975	T Watson, USA	279	Carnoustie	150	629
After a tie with J Newton. Australia-Replay scores: Watson 71; Newton 72.					
1976	J Miller, USA	279	Birkdale	150	719
1977	T Watson, USA	268	Turnberry	150	730
1978	J Nicklaus, USA	281	St Andrews	150	788
1979	S Ballesteros, Spain	283	Lytham and St Annes	150	885
1980	T Watson, USA	271	Muirfield	151	994
1981	B Rogers, USA	276	Sandwich	153	971
1982	T Watson, USA	284	Troon	176	1,121
1983	T Watson, USA	275	Birkdale	151	1,107
1984	S Ballesteros, Spain	276	St Andrews		1,413
1985	A Lyle, GB	282	Sandwich	149	1,361
1986	G Norman, Australia	280	Turnberry	152	1,347
1987	N Faldo, GB	279	Muirfield	153	1,407
1988	S Ballesteros, Spain	273	Lytham and St Annes	153	1,393

1984 at St Andrews

Entries 1,413. Regional qualifying courses: Glenbervie, Pleasington, Lindrick, Little Aston, Porters Park, Camberley Heath. Final qualifying courses: Ladybank, Leven, Lundin, Scotscraig. Qualified for final 36 holes: 94 competitors (92 Professionals, 2 Amateurs) with scores of 148 and below. Qualified for final 18 holes: 63 competitors with scores of 219 and below.

Name	Score	Prize Money £
S Ballesteros (Spain)	69, 68, 70, 69-276	55,000
B Langer (W Germany)	71, 68, 68, 71-278	31,900
T Watson (USA)	71, 68, 66, 73-278	31,900
F Couples (USA)	70, 69, 74, 68-281	19,800
L Wadkins (USA)	70, 69, 73, 69-281	19,800
N Faldo (GB)	69, 68, 76, 69-282	16,390
G Norman (Australia)	67, 74, 74, 67-282	16,390
M McCumber (USA)	74, 67, 72, 70-283	14,300
G Marsh (Australia)	70, 74, 73, 67-284	11,264
S Torrance (GB)	74, 74, 66, 70-284	11,264
R Rafferty (Ireland)	74, 72, 67, 71-284	11,264
H Baiocchi (S Africa)	72, 70, 70, 72-284	11,264
I Baker-Finch (Australia)	68, 66, 71, 79-284	11,264
A Lyle (GB)	75, 71, 72, 67-285	6,751
K Brown (GB)	74, 71, 72, 68-285	6,751
A Bean (USA)	72, 69, 75, 69-285	6,751
F Zoeller (USA)	71, 72, 71, 71-285	6,751
P Senior (Australia)	74, 70, 70, 71-285	6,751
W Bergin (USA)	75, 73, 66, 71-285	6,751
H Irwin (USA)	75, 68, 70, 72-285	6,751
L Trevino (USA)	70, 67, 75, 73-285	6,751
C Pavin (USA)	71, 74, 72, 69-286	3,850
B Crenshaw (USA)	72, 75, 70, 69-286	3,850
T Kite (USA)	69, 71, 74, 72-286	3,850
P Way (GB)	73, 72, 69, 72-286	3,850
P Jacobsen (USA)	67, 73, 73, 73-286	3,850
G Morgan (USA)	71, 71, 71, 73-286	3,850
T Gale (Australia)	71, 74, 72, 70-287	2,970
J Gonzales (Brazil)	69, 71, 76, 71-287	2,970
C Stadler (USA)	75, 70, 70, 72-287	2,970

Other Totals

P Parkin (GB), R Drummond (GB), B Gallacher (GB), J Miller (USA), J Nicklaus (USA) 288; M Pinero (Spain), J Haas (USA), G Levenson (S Africa), J Heggarty (GB), E Murray (GB), D Dunk (GB), T Nakajima (Japan), JM Canizares (Spain) 289; N Price (S Africa), M Poxon (GB), M James (GB) 290; M Calero (Spain), I Aoki (Japan), D Frost (S Africa), R Charles (New Zealand), R Chapman (GB) 291; H Clark (GB), J Chillas (GB), R Boxall (GB) 292; M Mackenzie (GB), D Russell (GB), W Longmuir (GB), E Rodriguez (Spain) 293; S Fujiki (Japan) 294; J Garner (GB), G Koch (USA), R Hartman (USA), N Ozaki (Japan) 295.

1985 at St Georges

Entries 1, 361. Regional qualifying courses: Camberley Heath, Glenbervie, Lindrick, Little Aston, Pleasington, Porters Park, Wildernesse. Final qualifying courses: Royal Cinque Ports Deal, Littlestone, North Foreland. Qualified for final 36 holes: 85 (83 Professionals, 2 Amateurs) with scores of 149 and below. Qualified for final 18 holes: 60 (59 Professionals, 1 Amateur) with scores of 221 and below.

Name	Score	Prize Money £
A Lyle (GB)	68, 71, 73, 70-282	65,000
P Stewart (USA)	70, 75, 70, 68-283	40,000
J Rivero (Spain)	74, 72, 70, 68-284	23,600
C O'Connor Jr (Ireland)	64, 76, 72, 72-284	23,600
M O'Meara (USA)	70, 72, 70, 72-284	23,600
D Graham (Australia)	68, 71, 70, 75-284	23,600
B Langer (W Germany)	72, 69, 68, 75-284	23,600
A Forsbrand (Sweden)	70, 70, 69, 70-285	15,566
DA Weibring (USA)	69, 71, 74, 71-285	15,566
T Kite (USA)	73, 73, 67, 72-285	15,566
E Darcy (Ireland)	76, 68, 74, 68-286	11,400
G Koch (USA)	75, 72, 70, 69-286	11,400
J-M Canizares (Spain)	72, 75, 70, 69-286	11,400
F Zoeller (USA)	69, 76, 70, 71-286	11,400
P Jacobsen (USA)	71, 74, 68, 73-286	11,400
S Bishop (GB)	71, 75, 72, 69-287	7,900
S Torrance (GB)	74, 74, 69, 70-287	7,900
G Norman (Australia)	71, 72, 71, 73-287	7,900
I Woosnam (GB)	70, 71, 71, 75-287	7,900
I Baker-Finch (Australia)	71, 73, 74, 70-288	5,260
J Conzales (Brazil)	72, 72, 73, 71-288	5,260
L Trevino (USA)	73, 76, 68, 71-288	5,260
G Marsh (Australia)	71, 75, 69, 73-288	5,260
M James (GB)	71, 78, 66, 73-288	5,260
P Parkin (GB)	68, 76, 77, 68-289	3,742
K Moe (USA)	70, 76, 73, 70-289	3,742
J-M Olazabal (Spain) (Am)	72, 76, 71, 70-289	3,742
M Cahill (Australia)	72, 74, 71, 72-289	3,742
D Frost (South Africa)	70, 74, 73, 72-289	3,742
G Brand Sr (GB)	73, 72, 72, 72-289	3,742
M Pinero (Spain)	71, 73, 72, 73-289	3,742
R Lee (GB)	68, 73, 74, 74-289	3,742

Other Totals

O Sellberg (Sweden), W Riley (Australia) 290; H Baiocchi (South Africa), B Crenshaw (USA), A Bean (USA), R Shearer (Australia) 291; A Johnstone (Zimbabwe), M Parsson (Sweden), J Pinsent (GB), S Ballesteros (Spain), C Pavin (USA) 292; P Senior (Australia), R Rafferty (N Ireland), D Russell (GB) 293; D Watson (South Africa), M Mouland (GB), G Brand, Jr (GB), B Gallacher (GB), H Clark (GB), T Watson (USA) 294; N Faldo (GB), E Rodriguez (Spain) 295; L Nelson (USA), P Fowler (Australia) 296; D Whelan (GB) 298; D Williams (GB) 300; V Somers (Australia) 301; R Charles (New Zealand) retired.

1986 at Turnberry

Entries 1,347. Regional qualifying courses: Glenbervie, Haggs Castle, Hankley Common, Langley Park, Lindrick, Little Aston, Ormskirk, Porters Park. Final qualifying courses: Glasgow Gailes, Kilmarnock (Barassie), Prestwick St Nicholas, Western Gailes. Qualified for final 36 holes: 77 Professionals. Non-qualifiers after 36 holes: 74 (71 Professionals, 3 Amateurs) with scores of 152 and above.

Name	Score	Prize Money £
G Norman (Australia)	74, 63, 74, 69-280	70,000
GJ Brand Jr (Eng)	71, 68, 75, 71-285	50,000
B Langer (W Germany)	72, 70, 76, 68-286	35,000
I Woosnam (GB)	70, 74, 70, 72-286	35,000
N Faldo (GB)	71, 70, 76, 70-287	25,000
S Ballesteros (Spain)	76, 75, 73, 64-288	25,000
G Koch (USA)	73, 72, 72, 71-288	25,000
F Zoeller (USA)	75, 73, 72, 69-289	17,333
B Marchbank (GB)	78, 70, 72, 69-289	17,333

The Open Championship
continued

Name	Score	Prize Money £
T Nakajima (Japan)	74, 67, 71, 77-289	17,333
C O'Connor Jr (Ireland)	75, 71, 75, 69-290	14.000
D Graham (Australia)	75, 73, 70, 72-290	14,000
J-M Canizares (Spain)	76, 68, 73, 73-290	14,000
C Strange (USA)	79, 69, 74, 69-291	11,500
A Bean (USA)	74, 73, 73, 71-291	11,500
A Forsbrand (Sweden)	71, 73, 77, 71-292	9,000
J-M Olazabal (Spain)	78, 69, 72, 73-292	9,000
R Floyd (USA)	78, 67, 73, 74-292	9,000
R Charles (New Zealand)	76, 72, 73, 72-293	7,250
M Pinero (Spain)	78, 71, 70, 74-293	7,250
R Rafferty (N Ireland)	75, 74, 75, 70-294	5,022
D Cooper (GB)	72, 79, 72, 71-294	5,022
V Somers (Australia)	73, 77, 72, 72-294	5,022
B Crenshaw (USA)	77, 69, 75, 73-294	5,022
R Lee (GB)	71, 75, 75, 73-294	5,022
P Parkin (GB)	78, 70, 72, 74-294	5,022
D Edwards (USA)	77, 73, 70, 74-294	5,022
V Fernandez (Argentina)	78, 70, 71, 75-294	5,022
S Torrance (GB)	78, 69, 71, 76-294	5,022

Other Totals

I Stanley (Australia), J Mahaffey (USA), M Karamoto (Japan), DA Weibring (USA), A Lyle (Scotland) 295; T Watson (USA), R Chapman (England), A Brooks (Scotland), R Commans (USA), M James (England), P Stewart (USA), G Player (South Africa), G Turner (New Zealand) 296; R Maltbie (USA), M O'Meara (USA), HM Chung (Taiwan) 297; J Nicklaus (USA), M O'Grady (USA), T Charnley (England), F Couples (USA), M Clayton (Australia), L Mize (USA), J Hawkes (South Africa), LS Chuen (Taiwan), R Tway (USA), T Armour III (USA) 298; S Randolph (USA), G Marsh (Australia), C Mason (England) 300; M McNulty (Zimbabwe), M Mackenzie (England), L Trevino (USA), E Darcy (Ireland), T Lamore (USA), F Nobilo (New Zealand) 301; A Chandler (England), J Heggarty (N Ireland), M Gray (Scotland), D Hammond (USA), S Simpson (USA) 302; O Moore (Australia), P Fowler (Australia) 303; D Jones (N Ireland), R Drummond (Scotland) 305; T Horton (Scotland) 306; G Weir (Scotland) 307; K Moe (USA) 314; H Green (USA) retired

1987 at Muirfield

Entries 1,407. Regional qualifying courses: Glenbervie, Haggs Castle, Hankley Common, Langley Park, Lindrick, Little Aston, Ormskirk, Porters Park. Final qualifying courses: Glasgow Gailes, Kilmarnock (Barassie), Prestwick St Nicholas, Western Gailes. Qualified for final 36 holes: 78 (76 Professionals, 2 Amateurs). Non-qualifiers after 36 holes: 75 (65 Professionals, 10 Amateurs) with scores of 147 and above.

Name	Score	Prize Money £
N Faldo (GB)	68, 69, 71, 71-279	75,000
R Davis (Australia)	64, 73, 74, 69-280	49,500
P Azinger (USA)	68, 68, 71, 73-280	49,500
B Crenshaw (USA)	73, 68, 72, 68-281	31,000
P Stewart (USA)	71, 66, 72, 72-281	31,000
D Frost (S Africa)	70, 68, 70, 74-282	26,000
T Watson (USA)	69, 69, 71, 74-283	23,000
I Woosnam (GB)	71, 69, 72, 72-284	18,666
N Price (Zimbabwe)	68, 71, 72, 73-284	18,666
C Stadler (USA)	69, 69, 71, 75-284	18,666
M McNulty (Zimbabwe)	71, 69, 75, 70-285	13,500
H Sutton (USA)	71, 70, 73, 71-285	13,500
J-M Olazabal (Spain)	70, 73, 70, 72-285	13,500
M Ozaki (Japan)	69, 72, 71, 73-285	13,500
M Calcavecchia (USA)	69, 70, 72, 74-285	13,500
G Marsh (Australia)	69, 70, 72, 74-285	13,500
W Grady (Australia)	70, 71, 76, 69-286	7,450
A Lyle (GB)	76, 69, 71, 70-286	7,450
E Darcy (Ireland)	74, 69, 72, 71-286	7,450
B Langer (W Germany)	69, 69, 76, 72-286	7,450
L Trevino (USA)	67, 74, 73, 72-286	7,450
M Roe (GB)	74, 68, 72, 72-286	7,450
K Brown (GB)	69, 73, 70, 74-286	7,450
R Floyd (USA)	72, 68, 70, 76-286	7,450
G Taylor (Australia)	69, 68, 75, 75-287	5,300
D Feherty (Ireland)	74, 70, 77, 67-288	4,933
G Brand Jr (GB)	73, 70, 75, 70-288	4,933
L Mize (USA)	68, 71, 76, 73-288	4,933

Other Totals

L Wadkins (USA), F Zoeller (USA), K Green (USA), D Edwards (USA), A Forsbrand (Sweden) 289; D Graham (Australia) 290; R Drummond (GB), M Calero (Spain), J Haas (USA), G Norman (Australia), R Tway (USA) 291; D Cooper (GB), F Couples (USA), A Bean (USA), GJ Brand (GB) 292; F Allem (S Africa), B Marshbank (GB), O Moore (Australia), C Mason (GB), L Nelson (USA), J Slaughter (USA) 294; M Lanner (Sweden), S Torrance (GB), S Ballesteros (Spain), P Walton (Ireland) 295; J O'Leary (Ireland), R Chapman (GB), W Andrade (USA) 296; O Sellberg (Sweden), P Mayo (GB) 297; B Jones (Australia), W McColl (GB), T Nakajima (Japan) 298; S Simpson (USA), N Hansen (GB), H Clark (GB), M Martin (Spain) 299; M O'Meara (USA), G Player (S Africa), T Ozaki (Japan), H Baiocchi (S Africa), B Chamblee (USA) 300; W Westner (S Africa) 301; J Nicklaus (USA), T Kite (USA) 302; J Hawkes (S Africa) 303; R Willison (GB) 305; C Moody (GB) 306; D Jones (Ireland) 307; A Stevens (GB) 312.

1988 at Lytham St. Annes

Entries 1,393. Regional qualifying courses: Glenbervie, Haggs Castle, Hankley Common, Langley Park, Lindrick, Little Aston, Ormskirk, Porters Park. Final qualifying courses: Glasgow Gailes, Kilmarnock (Barassie), Prestwick St Nicholas, Western Gailes. Qualified for final 36 holes: 78 (76 Professionals, 2 Amateurs). Non-qualifiers after 36 holes: 75 (65 Professionals, 10 Amateurs) with scores of 147 and above.

Name	Score	Prize Money £
S Ballesteros (Spa.)	67, 71, 70, 65-273	80,000
N Price (Zim.)	70, 67, 69, 69-275	60,000
N Faldo (Eng.)	71, 69, 68, 71-279	47,000
F Couples (USA)	73, 69, 71, 68-281	33,500
G Koch (USA)	71, 72, 70, 68-281	33,500
P Senior (Aus.)	70, 73, 70, 69-282	27,000
I Aoki (Jap.)	72, 71, 73, 67-283	21,000
P Stewart (USA)	73, 75, 68, 67-283	21,000
D Frost S. Africa)	71, 75, 69, 68-283	21,000
AWB Lyle (Sco.)	73, 69, 67, 74-283	21,000
D Russell (Eng.)	71, 74, 69, 70-284	16,500
B Faxon (USA)	69, 74, 70, 71-284	16,500
C Strange (USA)	79, 69, 69, 68-285	14,000
E Romero (Arg.)	72, 71, 69, 73-285	14,000
L Nelson (USA)	73, 71, 68, 73-285	14,000
J Rivero (Spa.)	75, 69, 70, 72-286	10,500
B Crenshaw (USA)	73, 73, 68, 72-286	10,500
A Bean (USA)	71, 70, 71, 74-286	10,500
D Pooley (USA)	70, 73, 69, 74-286	10,500
T Kite (USA)	75, 71, 73, 68-287	7,000
R Davis (Aus.)	76, 71, 72, 68-287	7,000
G Brand Jr (Sco.)	72, 76, 68, 71-287	7,000
B Tway (USA)	71, 71, 72, 73-287	7,000
R Charles (NZ)	71, 74, 69, 73-287	7,000
J Nicklaus (USA)	75, 70, 75, 68-288	5,500
I Woosnam (Wal.)	76, 71, 72, 69-288	5,500
M O'Meara (USA)	75, 69, 75, 70-289	5,200
H Clark (Eng.)	71, 72, 75, 72-290	4,600
M McNulty (Zim.)	73, 73, 72, 72-290	4,600
T Watson (USA)	74, 72, 72, 72-290	4,600
C Beck (USA)	72, 71, 74, 73-290	4,600
T Armour III (USA)	73, 72, 72, 73-290	4,600
J Benepe III (USA)	75, 72, 70, 73-290	4,600
W Riley (Aus.)	72, 71, 72, 76-291	4,150
L Wadkins (USA)	73, 71, 71, 76-291	4,150
G Brand (Eng.)	73, 74, 72, 73-292	3,950
J Olazabal (Spa.)	73, 71, 73, 75-292	3,950

Other Totals

J Haas (USA), N Ratcliffe (Eng.), B Marchbank (Eng.), R Rafferty (Ire), G March (Aus.), C Pavin (USA), D Russell (Eng.), W Grady (Aus.), K Brown (Eng.) 293; P Kent (Eng.), S Torrance (Sco.), P Azinger (USA), A North (USA), M McCumber (USA) 294; P Fowler (Aus.), F Zoeller (USA), P Walton
(Eng.), H Green (USA), J Miller (USA) 295; M Smith (Eng.), C Mason (Eng), P Broadhurst (Am.) (Eng.) 296; C Stadler (USA), GJ Player (S. Africa) 297; M James (Eng.), S Bishop (Eng.), A Sherborne (Eng.) 298; M Pinero (Spa.) 299; P Carman 301; G Bruckner, C-H Hsieh 302; B Langer (W. Ger.) 303; G Stafford 305; P Mitchell 308.

Ladies' British Open Championship

Instituted 1976

Year	Winner	Club/Country	Venue	Score
1976	Miss J Lee Smith	Gosforth Park	Fulford	299
1977	Miss V Saunders	Tyrrells Wood	Lindrick	306
1978	Miss J Melville	Furness	Foxhills	310
1979	Miss A Sheard	South Africa	Southport and Ainsdale	301
1980	Miss D Massey	USA	Wentworth (East)	294
1981	Miss D Massey	USA	Northumberland	295
1982	M Figueras-Dom	Spain	Birkdale	296
1983	*Not played*			
1984	A Okamoto	Japan	Woburn	289
1985	Mrs B King	USA	Moor Park	300
1986	Miss L Davies	GB	Birkdale	283
1987	Miss A Nicholas	GB	St Mellion	296
1988	Miss C Dibnah Miss S Little	Australia South Africa } tie	Lindrick	296

(Dibnah won at second play-off hole)

Amateur Championship

Year	Winner	Runner-up	Venue	By	Ent
1885	AF MacFie	HG Hutchinson	Hoylake	7 and 6	44
1886	HG Hutchinson	Henry Lamb	St Andrews	7 and 6	42
1887	HG Hutchinson	John Ball	Hoylake	1 hole	33
1888	John Ball	JE Laidlay	Prestwick	5 and 4	38
1889	JE Laidlay	LMB Melville	St Andrews	2 and 1	40
1890	John Ball	JE Laidlay	Hoylake	4 and 3	44
1891	JE Laidlay	HH Hilton	St Andrews	20th hole	50
1892	John Ball	HH Hilton	Sandwich	3 and 1	45
1893	Peter Anderson	JE Laidlay	Prestwick	1 hole	44
1894	John Ball	SM Fergusson	Hoylake	1 hole	64
1895	LMB Melville	John Ball	St Andrews	19th hole	68
1896*	FG Tait	HH Hilton	Sandwich	8 and 7	64
**36 holes played on and after this date*					
1897	AJT Allan	James Robb	Muirfield	4 and 2	74
1898	FG Tait	SM Fergusson	Hoylake	7 and 5	77
1899	John Ball	FG Tait	Prestwick	37th hole	101
1900	HH Hilton	James Robb	Sandwich	8 and 7	68
1901	HH Hilton	JL Low	St Andrews	1 hole	116
1902	C Hutchings	SH Fry	Hoylake	1 hole	114
1903	R Maxwell	HG Hutchinson	Muirfield	7 and 5	142
1904	WJ Travis (USA)	Edward Blackwell	Sandwich	4 and 3	104
1905	AG Barry	Hon O Scott	Prestwick	3 and 2	148
1906	James Robb	CC Lingen	Hoylake	4 and 3	166
1907	John Ball	CA Palmer	St Andrews	6 and 4	200
1908	EA Lassen	HE Taylor	Sandwich	7 and 6	197
1909	R Maxwell	Capt CK Hutchison	Muirfield	1 hole	170
1910	John Ball	C Aylmer	Hoylake	10 and 9	160
1911	HH Hilton	EA Lassen	Prestwick	4 and 3	146
1912	John Ball	Abe Mitchell	Westward Ho!	38th hole	134
1913	HH Hilton	R Harris	St Andrews	6 and 5	198
1914	JLC Jenkins	CO Hezlet	Sandwich	3 and 2	232
1915-19	*No Championship owing to the Great War*				
1920	CJH Tolley	RA Gardner (USA)	Muirfield	37th hole	165
1921	WI Hunter	AJ Graham	Hoylake	12 and 11	223
1922	EWW Holderness	J Caven	Prestwick	1 hole	252
1923	RH Wethered	R Harris	Deal	7 and 6	209
1924	EWE Holderness	EF Storey	St Andrews	3 and 2	201
1925	Robert Harris	KF Fradgley	Westward Ho!	13 and 12	151
1926	Jesse Sweetser (USA)	AF Simpson	Muirfield	6 and 5	216
1927	Dr W Tweddell	DE Landale	Hoylake	7 and 6	197
1928	TP Perkins	RH Wethered	Prestwick	6 and 4	220
1929	CJH Tolley	JN Smith	Sandwich	4 and 3	253
1930	RT Jones (USA)	RH Wethered	St Andrews	7 and 6	271
1931	Eric Martin Smith	J De Forest	Westward Ho!	1 hole	171
1932	J De Forest	EW Fiddian	Muirfield	3 and 1	235
1933	Hon M Scott	TA Bourn	Hoylake	4 and 3	269
1934	W Lawson Little (USA)	J Wallace	Prestwick	14 and 13	225
1935	W Lawson Little (USA)	Dr W Tweddell	Lytham St Annes	1 hole	232
1936	H Thomson	J Ferrier (Australia)	St Andrews	2 holes	283
1937	R Sweeney, Jun (USA)	LO Munn	Sandwich	3 and 2	223

Amateur Championship continued

Year	Winner	Runner-up	Venue	By	Ent
1938	CR Yates (USA)	RC Ewing	Troon	3 and 2	241
1939	AT Kyle	AA Duncan	Hoylake	2 and 1	167
1940-45	*Suspended during Second World War*				
1946	J Bruen	R Sweeny (USA)	Birkdale	4 and 3	263
1947	WP Turnesa (USA)	RD Chapman (USA)	Carnoustie	3 and 2	200
1948	FR Stranahan (USA)	C Stowe	Sandwich	5 and 4	168
1949	SM McCready	WP Turnesa (USA)	Portmarnock	2 and 1	204
1950	FR Stranahan (USA)	RD Chapman (USA)	St Andrews	8 and 6	324
1951	RD Chapman (USA)	CR Coe (USA)	Porthcawl	5 and 4	192
1952	EH Ward (USA)	FR Stranahan (USA)	Prestwick	6 and 5	286
1953	JB Carr	E Harvie Ward (USA)	Hoylake	2 holes	279
1954	DW Bachli (Australia)	WC Campbell (USA)	Muirfield	2 and 1	286
1955	JW Conrad (USA)	A Slater	Lytham St Annes	3 and 2	240
1956*	JC Beharrell	LG Taylor	Troon	5 and 4	200
1957*	R Reid Jack	HB Ridgley (USA)	Formby	2 and 1	200
**In 1956 and 1957 the Quarter Finals, Semi-Finals and Final were played over 36 holes*					
1958*	JB Carr	A Thirlwell	St Andrews	3 and 2	488
In 1958, Semi-Finals and Final only were played over 36 holes					
1959	DR Beman (USA)	W Hyndman (USA)	Sandwich	3 and 2	362
1960	JB Carr	R Cochran (USA)	Portrush	8 and 7	183
1961	MF Bonallack	J Walker	Turnberry	6 and 4	250
1962	RD Davies (USA)	J Povall	Hoylake	1 hole	256
1963	MSR Lunt	JG Blackwell	St Andrews	2 and 1	256
1964	Gordon J Clark	MSR Lunt	Ganton	39th hole	220
1965	MR Bonallack	CA Clark	Porthcawl	2 and 1	176
1966	RE Cole (S Africa)	RDBM Shade	Carnoustie (18 holes)	3 and 2	206
1967	RB Dickson (USA)	RJ Cerrudo (USA)	Formby	2 and 1	
1968	MF Bonallack	JB Carr	Troon	7 and 6	249
1969	MF Bonallack	W Hyndman (USA)	Hoylake	3 and 2	245
1970	MF Bonallack	W Hyndman (USA)	Newcastle Co Down	8 and 7	256
1971	S Melnyk (USA)	J Simons (USA)	Carnoustie	3 and 2	256
1972	T Homer	A Thirlwell	Sandwich	4 and 3	253
1973	R Siderowf (USA)	PH Moody	Porthcawl	5 and 3	222
1974	T Homer	J Gabrielsen (USA)	Muirfield	2 holes	330
1975	MM Giles (USA)	MH James	Hoylake	8 and 7	206
1976	R Siderowf (USA)	JC Davies	St Andrews	37th hole	289
1977	P McEvoy	HM Campbell	Ganton	5 and 4	235
1978	P McEvoy	PJ McKellar	Troon	4 and 3	353
1979	J Sigel (USA)	S Hoch (USA)	Hillside	3 and 2	285
1980	D Evans	D Suddards (SA)	Porthcawl	4 and 3	265
1981	P Ploujoux (France)	J Hirsch (USA)	St Andrews	4 and 2	256
1982	M Thompson	A Stubbs	Deal	4 and 3	245
1983	AP Parkin	J Holtgrieve (USA)	Turnberry	5 and 4	288
1984	JM Olazabal (Spain)	C Montgomerie	Formby	5 and 4	291
1985	G McGimpsey	G Homewood	Dornoch	8 and 7	
1986	D Curry	G Birtwell	Lytham St Annes	11 and 9	
1987	P Mayo	P McEvoy	Prestwick	3 and 1	
1988	C Hardin (Sweden)	B Fouchee (SA)	Porthcawl		

Boys' Amateur Championship

Year	Winner	Runner-up	Venue	By
1960	P Cros	PO Green	Olton	5 and 3
1961	FS Morris	C Clark	Dalmahoy	3 and 2
1962	PM Townsend	DC Penman	Mid-Surrey	1 hole
1963	AHC Soutar	DI Rigby	Prestwick	2 and 1
1964	PM Townsend	RD Gray	Formby	9 and 8
1965	GR Milne	DK Midgley	Gullane	4 and 2
1966	A Phillips	A Muller	Moortown	12 and 11
1967	LP Tupling	SC Evans	Western Gailes	4 and 2
1968	SC Evans	K Dabson	St Annes Old Links	3 and 2
1969	M Foster	M Gray	Dunbar	37th hole
1970	ID Gradwell	JE Murray	Hillside	1 hole
1971	H Clark	G Harvey	Barassie	6 and 5
1972	G Harvey	R Newsome	Moortown	7 and 5
1973	DM Robertson	S Betti	Blairgowrie	5 and 3
1974	TR Shannon	AWB Lyle	Hoylake	10 and 9
1975	B Marchbank	AWB Lyle	Bruntsfield	1 hole
1976	M Mouland	G Hargreaves	Sunningdale	6 and 5
1977	I Ford	CR Dalgleish	Downfield	1 hole
1978	S Keppler	M Stokes	Seaton Carew	3 and 2
1979	R Rafferty	D Ray	Barassie	6 and 5

Boys Amateur Championship

continued

Year	Winner	Runner-up	Venue	By
1980	D Muscroft	A Llyr	Formby	7 and 6
1981	J Lopez	R Weedon	Gullane	4 and 3
1982	M Grieve	G Hickman	Burnham and Barrow	37th hole
1983	J Olazabal	M Pendaries	Glenbervie	6 and 5
1984	L Vannett	A Mednick	Royal Porthcawl	2 and 1
1985	J Cook	W Henry	Barnton	5 and 4
1986	L Walker	G King	Seaton Carew	5 and 4
1987	C O'Carrol	P Olsson	Barassie	3 and 1
1988	S Pardoe	D Haines	Formby	3 and 2

British Youths' Open Amateur Championship

Year	Winner	Club	Venue	Score
1960	GA Caygill	Sunningdale	Pannal	279
1961	JS Martin	Kilbirnie Place	Bruntsfield	284
1962	GA Caygill	Sunningdale	Pannal	287
1963	AJ Low	St Andrews University	Pollok	283
1964	BW Barnes	Burnham and Berrow	Pannal	290
1965	PM Townsend	Porters Park	Cosforth Park	281
1966	PA Oosterhuis	Dulwich and Sydenham	Dalmahoy (54 holes)	219
1967	PJ Benka	Addington	Copt Heath	278
1968	PJ Benka	Addington	Ayr Belleisle	281
1969	JH Cook	Calcot Park	Lindrick	289
1970	B Dassu	Italy	Barnton	276
1971	P Elson	Coventry	Northamptonshire	277
1972	AH Chandler	Regent Park	Glasgow Gailes	281
1973	SC Mason	Goring and Streatley	Southport and Ainsdale	284
1974	DM Robertson	Dunbar	Downfield	284
1975	NA Faldo	Welwyn Garden City	Pannal	278
1976	ME Lewis	Henbury	Gullane	277
1977	AWB Lyle	Hawkstone Park	Moor Park	285
1978	B Marchbank	Auchterarder	East Renfrewshire	278
1979	G Brand	Knowle	Woodhall Spa	291
1980	G Hay	Hilton Park	Troon	303
1981	T Antevik	Sweden	Gullane	290
1982	AP Parkin	Newtown	St Andrews New	280
1983	P Mayo	Newport	Sunningdale	290
1984	R Morris	Padeswick and Buckley	Blairgowrie	281
1985	J-M Olazabal	Spain	Ganton	281
1986	D Gilford	GB	Carnoustie	283
1987	J Cook / O Nordberg	GB / Sweden — tie	Hollinwell	283
(Cook won play-off)				
1988	C Cassells / C Cevaer	Murcar / France — tie	Royal Aberdeen	275
(Cevaer won play-off)				

Senior Open Amateur Championship

Year	Winner	Venue	Score
1969	R Pattison	Formby	154
1970	K Bamber	Prestwick	150
1971	GH Pickard	Deal	150
1972	TC Hartley	St Andrews	147
1973	JT Jones	Hoylake	142
1974	MA Ivor-Jones	Moortown	149
1975	HJ Roberts	Turnberry	138
1976	WM Crichton	Berkshire	149
1977	Dr TE Donaldson	Panmure	228
1978	RJ White	Formby	225
1979	RJ White	Harlech	226
1980	JM Cannon	Prestwick St Nicholas	218
1981	T Branton	Hoylake	227
1982	RL Glading	Blairgowrie	218
1983	AJ Swann (USA)	Walton Heath	222
1984	JC Owens (USA)	Western Gailes	222
1985	D Morey (USA)	Hesketh	223
1986	AN Sturrock	Panmure	229
1987	B Soyars (USA)	Deal	226
1988	CW Green	Barnton, Edinburgh	221

Ladies' British Open Amateur Championship

Year	Winner	Runner-up	Venue	By
1893	Lady Margaret Scott	Miss Isette Pearson	St Annes	7 and 5
1894	Lady Margaret Scott	Miss Isette Pearson	Littlestone	3 and 2
1895	Lady Margaret Scott	Miss E Lythgoe	Portrush	5 and 4
1896	Miss Pascoe	Miss L Thomson	Hoylake	3 and 2
1897	Miss EC Orr	Miss Orr	Gullane	4 and 2
1898	Miss L Thomson	Miss EC Neville	Yarmouth	7 and 5
1899	Miss M Hezlet	Miss Magill	Newcastle Co Down	2 and 1
1900	Miss Adair	Miss Neville	Westward Ho!	6 and 5
1901	Miss Graham	Miss Adair	Aberdovey	3 and 1
1902	Miss M Hezlet	Miss E Neville	Deal	19th hole
1903	Miss Adair	Miss F Walker-Leigh	Portrush	4 and 3
1904	Miss L Dod	Miss M Hezlet	Troon	1 hole
1905	Miss B Thompson	Miss ME Stuart	Cromer	3 and 2
1906	Mrs Kennon	Miss B Thompson	Burnham	4 and 3
1907	Miss M Hezlet	Miss F Hezlet	Newcastle Co Down	2 and 1
1908	Miss M Titterton	Miss D Campbell	St Andrews	19th hole
1909	Miss D Campbell	Miss F Hezlet	Birkdale	4 and 3
1910	Miss Grant Suttie	Miss L Moore	Westward Ho!	6 and 4
1911	Miss D Campbell	Miss V Hezlet	Portrush	3 and 2
1912	Miss G Ravenscroft	Miss S Temple	Turnberry	3 and 2
(Final played over 36 holes after 1912)				
1913	Miss M Dodd	Miss Chubb	St Annes	8 and 6
1914	Miss C Leitch	Miss G Ravenscroft	Hunstanton	2 and 1
1915-18	*No Championship owing to the Great War*			
1919	*Should have been played at Burnham in October, but abandoned owing to Railway Strike*			
1920	Miss C Leitch	Miss Molly Griffiths	Newcastle Co Down	7 and 6
1921	Miss C Leitch	Miss J Wethered	Turnberry	4 and 3
1922	Miss J Wethered	Miss C Leitch	Prince's, Sandwich	9 and 7
1923	Miss D Chambers	Miss A Macbeth	Burnham, Somerset	2 holes
1924	Miss J Wethered	Mrs Cautley	Portrush	7 and 6
1925	Miss J Wethered	Miss C Leitch	Troon	37th hole
1926	Miss C Leitch	Mrs Garon	Harlech	8 and 7
1927	Miss Thion de la Chaume (France)	Miss Pearson	Newcastle Co Down	5 and 4
1928	Miss Nanette Le Blan (France)	Miss S Marshall	Hunstanton	3 and 2
1929	Miss J Wethered	Miss G Collett (USA)	St Andrews	3 and 1
1930	Miss D Fishwick	Miss G Collett (USA)	Formby	4 and 3
1931	Miss E Wilson	Miss W Morgan	Portmarnock	7 and 6
1932	Miss E Wilson	Miss CPR Montgomery	Saunton	7 and 6
1933	Miss E Wilson	Miss D Plumpton	Gleneagles	5 and 4
1934	Mrs AM Holm	Miss P Barton	Porthcawl	6 and 5
1935	Miss W Morgan	Miss P Barton	Newcastle Co Down	3 and 2
1936	Miss P Barton	Miss B Newell	Southport and Ainsdale	5 and 3
1937	Miss J Anderson	Miss D Park	Turnberry	6 and 4
1938	Mrs AM Holm	Miss E Corlett	Burnham	4 and 3
1939	Miss P Barton	Mrs T Marks	Portrush	2 and 1
1940-45	*No Championship owing to Second World War*			
1946	Mrs GW Hetherington	Miss P Garvey	Hunstanton	1 hole
1947	Mrs George Zaharias (USA)	Miss J Gordon	Gullane	5 and 4
1948	Miss Louise Suggs (USA)	Miss J Donald	Lytham St Annes	1 hole
1949	Miss Frances Stephens	Mrs Val Reddan	Harlech	5 and 4
1950	Vicomtesse de Saint Sauveur (France)	Mrs G Valentine	Newcastle Co Down	3 and 2
1951	Mrs PG MacCann	Miss Frances Stephens	Broadstone	4 and 3
1952	Miss Moira Paterson	Miss Frances Stephens	Troon	39th hole
1953	Miss Marlene Stewart (Canada)	Miss P Garvey	Porthcawl	7 and 6
1954	Miss Frances Stephens	Miss E Price	Ganton	4 and 3
1955	Mrs G Valentine	Miss B Romack (USA)	Portrush	7 and 6
1956	Miss Margaret Smith (USA)	Miss Mary P Janssen (USA)	Sunningdale	8 and 7
1957	Miss P Garvey	Mrs G Valentine	Gleneagles	4 and 3
1958	Mrs G Valentine	Miss E Price	Hunstanton	1 hole
1959	Miss E Price	Miss B McCorkindale	Ascot	37th hole
1960	Miss B McIntyre (USA)	Miss P Garvey	Harlech	4 and 2
1961	Mrs AD Spearman	Miss DJ Robb	Carnoustie	7 and 6
1962	Mrs AD Spearman	Mrs MF Bonallack	Birkdale	1 hole
1963	Miss B Varangot (France)	Miss P Garvey	Newcastle Co Down	3 and 1
1964	Miss C Sorenson (USA)	Miss BAB Jackson	Prince's, Sandwich	37th hole
1965	Miss V Varangot (France)	Mrs IC Robertson	St Andrews	4 and 3
1966	Miss E Chadwick	Miss V Saunders	Ganton	3 and 2
1967	Miss E Chadwick	Miss M Everard	Harlech	1 hole

Ladies' British Open Amateur Championship
continued

Year	Winner	Runner-up	Venue	By
1968	Miss B Varangot (France)	Mrs C Rubin (France)	Walton Heath	20th hole
1969	Miss C Lacoste (France)	Miss A Irvin	Portrush	1 hole
1970	Miss D Oxley	Mrs IC Robertson	Gullane	1 hole
1971	Miss Michelle Walker	Miss B Huke	Alwoodley	3 and 1
1972	Miss Michelle Walker	Mrs C Rubin (France)	Hunstanton	2 holes
1973	Miss A Irvin	Miss Michelle Walker	Carnoustie	3 and 2
1974	Miss C Semple (USA)	Mrs A Bonallack	Porthcawl	2 and 1
1975	Mrs N Syms (USA)	Miss S Cadden	St Andrews	3 and 2
1976	Miss C Panton	Miss A Sheard	Silloth	1 hole
1977	Mrs A Uzielli	Miss V Marvin	Hillside	6 and 5
1978	Miss E Kennedy (Australia)	Miss J Greenhalgh	Notts	1 hole
1979	Miss M Madill	Miss J Lock (Australia)	Nairn	2 and 1
1980	Mrs A Sander (USA)	Mrs L Wollin (Sweden)	Woodhall Spa	3 and 1
1981	Mrs IC Robertson	Miss W Aitken	Conway	20th hole
1982	Miss K Douglas	Miss G Stewart	Walton Heath	4 and 2
1983	Mrs J Thornhill	Miss R Lautens (Switzerland)	Silloth	4 and 2
1984	Miss J Rosenthal (USA)	J Brown	Royal Troon	4 and 3
1985	Miss L Beman (Eire)	C Waite	Ganton	1 hole
1986	Miss McGuire (NZ)	L Briars (Australia)	West Sussex	2 and 1
1987	Miss J Collingham	Miss S Shapcott	Harlech	19th hole
1988	Miss J Furby	Miss J Wade	Deal	4 and 3

Ladies' British Open Amateur Stroke Play Championship

Year	Winner	Club	Venue	Score
1969	Miss A Irvin	Lytham St Annes	Gosforth Park	295
1970	Miss M Everard	Hallamshire	Birkdale	313
1971	Mrs IC Robertson	Dunaverty	Ayr Belleisle	302
1972	Mrs IC Robertson	Dunaverty	Silloth	296
1973	Mrs A Stant	Beau Desert	Purdis Heath	298
1974	Mrs J Greenhalgh	Pleasington	Seaton Carew	302
1975	Mrs J Greenhalgh	Pleasington	Gosforth Park	298
1976*	Miss J Lee Smith	Gosforth Park	Fulford	299
1977*	Miss M Everard	Hallamshire	Lindrick	306
1978*	Miss J Melville	Furness	Foxhills	310
1979	Miss M McKenna	Donabate	Moseley	305
1980	Miss M Mahill	Portstewart	Brancepeth Castle	304
(After a tie with Miss P Wright)				
1981	Miss J Soulsby	Prudhoe	Norwich	300
1982	Miss J Connachan	Musselburgh	Downfield	294
1983	Miss A Nicholas		Moortown	292
1984	Miss C Waite	Swindon	Caernarvonshire	295
1985	Mrs IC Robertson	Dunaverty	Formby	300
1986	Miss C Hourihane		Blairgowrie	291
(After a tie with Miss P Johnson)				
1987	Mrs L Bayman	Princes	Ipswich	297
1988	Miss K Mitchell	Worthing	Porthcawl	317

**Played concurrently with Ladies' British Open Championship*

Girls' British Open Amateur Championship

Year	Winner	Runner-up	Venue	By
1960	Miss S Clarke	Miss AL Irvin	Barassie	2 and 1
1961	Miss D Robb	Miss J Roberts	Beaconsfield	3 and 2
1962	Miss S McLaren-Smith	Miss A Murphy	Foxton Hall	2 and 1
1963	Miss D Oxley	Miss B Whitehead	Gullane	2 and 1
1964	Miss P Tredinnick	Miss K Cumming	Camberley Heath	2 and 1
1965	Miss A Willard	Miss A Ward	Formby	3 and 2
1966	Miss J Hutton	Miss D Oxley	Troon Portland	20th hole
1967	Miss P Burrows	Miss J Hutton	Liphook	2 and 1
1968	Miss C Wallace	Miss C Reybroeck	Leven	4 and 3
1969	Miss J de Witt Puyt	Miss C Reybroeck	Ilkley	2 and 1

Girls' British Open Amateur Championship
continued

Year	Winner	Runner-up	Venue	By
1970	Miss C Le Feuvre	Miss Michelle Walker	North Wales	2 and 1
1971	Miss J Mark	Miss Maureen Walker	North Berwick	4 and 3
1972	Miss Maureen Walker	Miss S Cadden	Norwich	2 and 1
1973	Miss AM Palli	Miss N Jeanson	Northamptonshire	2 and 1
1974	Miss R Barry	Miss T Perkins	Dunbar	1 hole
1975	Miss S Cadden	Miss L Isherwood	Henbury	4 and 3
1976	Miss G Stewart	Miss S Rowlands	Pyle and Kenfig	5 and 4
1977	Miss W Aitken	Miss S Bamford	Formby Ladies	2 and 1
1978	Miss M De Lorenzi	Miss D Glenn	Largs	2 and 1
1979	Miss S Lapaire	Miss P Smilie	Edgbaston	19th hole
1980	Miss J Connachan	Miss L Bolton	Wrexham	2 holes
1981	Miss J Connachan	Miss P Grice	Woodbridge	20th hole
1982	Miss C Waite	Miss M Mackie	Edzell	6 and 5
1983	Miss E Orley	Miss A Walters	Leeds	7 and 6
1984	Miss C Swallow	Miss E Farquharson	Maesdu	1 hole
1985	Miss S Shapcott	Miss E Farquharson	Hesketh	3 and 1
1986	Miss S Croce	Miss S Bennett	West Kilbride	5 and 4
1987	Miss H Dobson	Miss S Croce	Barnham Broom	19th hole
1988	Miss A Macdonald	Miss J Posener	Pyle and Kenfig	3 and 2

Senior Ladies' British Open Amateur Stroke Play Championship

Instituted 1981

Year	Winner	Club	Venue	Score
1981	Mrs BM King	Pleasington	Formby	159
1982	Mrs P Riddiford	Royal Ashdown Forest	Ilkley	161
1983	Mrs M Birtwistle		Troon Portland	167
1984	Mme O Semelaigne	France	Woodbridge	152
1985	Dr G Costello	Formby Ladies	Prestatyn	158
1986	Mrs P Riddiford	Royal Ashdown Forest	Longniddry	154
1987	Mme D Semelaigne	France	Copt Heath	152
1988	Mrs C Bailey	Tandridge	Littlestone	156

English Amateur Championship

Year	Winner	Runner-up	Venue	By
1960	DN Sewell	MJ Christmas	Hunstanton	41st hole
1961	Ian Caldwell	GJ Clark	Wentworth	37th hole
1962	MF Bonallack	MSR Lunt	Moortown	2 and 1
1963	MF Bonallack	A Thirlwell	Burnham and Berrow	4 and 3
1964	Dr D Marsh	R Foster	Hollinwell	1 hole
1965	MF Bonallack	CA Clark	Berkshire	3 and 2
1966	MSR Lunt	DJ Millensted	Lytham St Annes	3 and 2
1967	MF Bonallack	GE Hyde	Woodhall Spa	4 and 2
1968	MF Bonallack	PD Kelley	Ganton	12 and 11
1969	JH Cook	P Dawson	Sandwich	6 and 4
1970	Dr D Marsh	SG Birtwell	Birkdale	6 and 4
1971	W Humphreys	JC Davies	Burnham and Berrow	9 and 8
1972	H Ashby	R Revell	Northumberland	5 and 4
1973	H Ashby	SC Mason	Formby	5 and 4
1974	M James	JA Watts	Woodhall Spa	6 and 5
1975	N Faldo	D Eccleston	Lytham St Annes	6 and 4
1976	P Deeble	JC Davies	Ganton	3 and 1
1977	TR Shingler	J Mayell	Walton Heath	4 and 3
1978	P Downes	P Hoad	Birkdale	1 hole
1979	R Chapman	A Carman	Sandwich	6 and 5
1980	P Deeble	P McEvoy	Moortown	4 and 3
1981	D Blakeman	A Stubbs	Burnham and Berrow	3 and 1
1982	A Oldcorn	I Bradshaw	Hoylake	4 and 3
1983	G Laurence	A Brewer	Wentworth	7 and 6
1984	D Gilford	M Gerrard	Woodhall Spa	4 and 3
1985	R Winchester	P Robinson	Little Aston	1 hole
1986	J Langmead	B White	Hillside	2 and 1
1987	K Weeks	R Eggo	Frilford Heath	37th hole
1988	R Claydon	D Curry	Birkdale	38th hole

American Open Championship

Year	Winner	Runner-up	Venue	By
1894	Willie Dunn	W Campbell	St Andrews, NY	2 holes

After 1894 decided by medal play

Year	Winner	Country	Venue	Score
1895	HJ Rawlins	USA	Newport	173
1896	J Foulis	USA	Southampton	152
1897	J Lloyd	USA	Wheaton, Ill	162
1898	F Herd	USA	Shinnecock Hills	328
72 holes played from 1898				
1899	W Smith	USA	Baltimore	315
1900	H Vardon	England	Wheaton, Ill	313
1901	W Anderson	USA	Myopia, Mass	315
1902	L Auchterlonie	USA	Garden City	305
1903	W Anderson	USA	Baltusrol	307
1904	W Anderson	USA	Glenview	304
1905	W Anderson	USA	Myopia	335
1906	A Smith	USA	Onwentsia	291
1907	A Ross	USA	Chestnut Hill, Pa	302
1908	F McLeod	USA	Myopia, Mass	322
1909	G Sargent	USA	Englewood, NJ	290
1910	A Smith	USA	Philadelphia	289
(After a tie with JJ McDermott and Macdonald Smith)				
1911	JJ McDermott	USA	Wheaton, Ill	307
1912	JJ McDermott	USA	Buffalo, NY	294
1913	F Ouimet (Am)	USA	Brookline, Mass	304
(After a tie with H Vardon and E Ray)				
1914	W Hagen	USA	Midlothian	297
1915	JD Travers (Am)	USA	Baltusrol	290
1916	C Evans (Am)	USA	Minneapolis	286
1917-18	No Championship.			
1919	W Hagen	USA	Braeburn	301
1920	E Ray	England	Inverness	295
1921	J Barnes	USA	Washington	289
1922	G Sarazen	USA	Glencoe	288
1923	RT Jones, jun (Am)	USA	Inwood, LI	295
(After a tie with RA Cruikshank. Play-off: 76; Cruikshank 78)				
1924	C Walker	USA	Oakland Hills	297
1925	W MacFarlane	USA	Worcester	291
1926	RT Jones, jun (Am)	USA	Scioto	293
1927	TD Armour	USA	Oakmont	301
(After a tie with H Cooper. Play-off: Armour 76; Cooper 79)				
1928	J Farrell	USA	Olympia Fields	294
(After a tie with RT Jones, jun. Play-off: Farrell 143; Jones 144)				
1929	RT Jones, jun (Am)	USA	Winged Foot, NY	294
(After a tie with A Espinosa. Play-off: Jones 141; Espinosa 164)				
1930	RT Jones, jun (Am)	USA	Interlachen	287
1931	B Burke	USA	Inverness	292
(After a tie with G von Elm. Play-off: Burke 149, 148; von Elm 149, 149)				
1932	G Sarazen	USA	Fresh Meadow	286
1933	J Goodman (Am)	USA	North Shore	287
1934	O Dutra	USA	Merion	293
1935	S Parks	USA	Oakmont	299
1936	T Manero	USA	Springfield	282
1937	R Guldahl	USA	Oakland Hills	281
1938	R Guldahl	USA	Cherry Hills	284
1939	Byron Nelson	USA	Philadelphia	284
(After a tie with Craig Wood and D Shute)				
1940	W Lawson Little	USA	Canterbury, Ohio	287
(After a tie with G Sarazen. Tie scores: Little 70; Sarazen 73)				
1941	Craig Wood	USA	Fort Worth, Texas	284
1942-45	No Championship.			
1946	Lloyd Mangrum	USA	Canterbury	284
(After a tie with Byron Nelson and Vic Ghezzie)				
1947	Lew Worsham	USA	St Louis	282
(After a tie with Sam Snead. Replay scores: Worsham 69; Snead 70)				
1948*	Ben Hogan	USA	Los Angeles	276
1949	Dr Cary Middlecoff	USA	Medinah, Ill	286
1950	Ben Hogan	USA	Merion, Pa	287
(After a tie with Lloyd Mangrum and George Fazio. Replay scores: Hogan 69; Mangrum 73; Fazio 75)				
1951	Ben Hogan	USA	Oakland Hills, Mich	287
1952	Julius Boros	USA	Dallas, Texas	281
1953	Ben Hogan	USA	Oakmont	283
1954	Ed Furgol	USA	Baltusrol	284
1955	J Fleck	USA	San Francisco	287
(After a tie with Ben Hogan. Replay scores: Fleck 69; Hogan 72)				

American Open Championship continued

Year	Winner	Runner-up	Venue	By
1956	Dr Cary Middlecoff	USA	Rochester	281
1957	Dick Mayer	USA	Inverness	282
(After a tie with Dr Cary Middlecoff. Tie scores: Mayer 72; Middlecoff 79)				
1958	Tommy Bolt	USA	Tulsa, Okla	283
1959	W Casper	USA	Winged Foot, NY	282
1960	Arnold Palmer	USA	Denver, Col	280
1961	Gene Littler	USA	Birmingham, Mich	281
1962	JW Nicklaus	USA	Oakmont	283
(After a tie with Arnold Palmer: Nicklaus 71; Palmer 74)				
1963	Julius Boros	USA	Brookline, Mass	293
(After a tie. Play-off: J Boros, 70; Jack Cupit, 73, Arnold Palmer 76)				
1964	Ken Venturi	USA	Washington	278
1965	Gary Player	South Africa	St Louis, Mo	282
(After a tie with KDG Nagle, Australia. Replay scores: Player 71; Nagle 74)				
1966	W Casper	USA	San Francisco	278
(After a tie with Arnold Palmer. Replay scores: Casper 69; Palmer 73)				
1967	JW Nicklaus	USA	Baltusrol	275
1968	Lee Trevino	USA	Rochester	275
1969	Orville Moody	USA	Houston, Texas	281
1970	A Jacklin	England	Chaska, Minn	281
1971	L Trevino	USA	Merion, Pa	280
(After a tie with J Nicklaus. Play-off: Trevino 68; Nicklaus 71)				
1972	JW Nicklaus	USA	Pebble Beach	290
1973	J Miller	USA	Oakmont, Pa	279
1974	H Irwin	USA	Winged Foot, NY	287
1975	L Graham	USA	Medinah, Ill	287
(After a tie with Mahaffey. Play-off: Graham 71; Mahaffey 73)				
1976	J Pate	USA	Atlanta, Georgia	277
1977	H Green	USA	Southern Hills, Tulsa	278
1978	A North	USA	Cherry Hills	285
1979	H Irwin	USA	Inverness, Ohio	284
1980	JW Nicklaus	USA	Baltusrol	272
1981	D Graham	Australia	Merion, Pa	273
1982	T Watson	USA	Pebble Beach	282
1983	L Nelson	USA	Oakmont, Pa	280
1984	F Zoeller	USA	Winged Foot	276
(After tie with G Norman, Australia. Play-off: Zoeller 67; Norman 75)				
1985	A North	USA	Oakland Hills, Mich	279
1986	R Floyd	USA	Shinnecock Hills, NY	279
1987	S Simpson	USA	Olympic, San Francisco, Cal	277
1988	C Strange	USA	Brookline, Mass.	278
(After a tie with N Faldo, GB. Play-off Strange 71, Faldo 75)				

American Masters' Championship

Venue – Augusta National Golf Course, Augusta, Georgia

Year	Winner	Score	Year	Winner	Score
1934	Horton Smith	284	1964	Arnold Palmer	276
1935	Gene Sarazen	282	1965	JW Nicklaus	271
1936	Horton Smith	285	1966	JW Nicklaus	288
1937	Byron Nelson	283	1967	G Brewer	280
1938	Henry Picard	285	1968	R Goalby	277
1939	Ralph Guldahl	279	1969	G Archer	281
1940	Jimmy Demaret	280	1970	W Casper	279
1941	Craig Wood	280	1971	C Coody	279
1942	Byron Nelson	280	1972	JW Nicklaus	286
1946	Herman Keiser	282	1973	T Aaron	283
1947	Jimmy Demaret	281	1974	GJ Player (SA)	278
1948	Claude Harmon	279	1975	JW Nicklaus	276
1949	Sam Snead	283	1976	R Floyd	271
1950	Jimmy Demaret	282	1977	T Watson	276
1951	Ben Hogan	280	1978	GJ Player (SA)	277
1952	Sam Snead	286	1979	F Zoeller	280
1953	Ben Hogan	274	1980	S Ballesteros (Sp)	275
1954	Sam Snead	289	1981	T Watson	280
1955	Cary Middlecoff	279	1982	C Stadler	284
1956	Jackie Burke	289	1983	S Ballesteros (Sp)	280
1957	Doug Ford	283	1984	B Crenshaw	277
1958	Arnold Palmer	284	1985	B Langer (WG)	282
1959	A Wall	284	1986	JW Nicklaus	279
1960	Arnold Palmer	282	1987	L Mize	285
1961	GJ Player (SA)	280	(After a tie)		
1962	Arnold Palmer	280	1988	AWB Lyle	281
1963	JW Nicklaus	286			

American Masters Championship
continued

Leading Scores 1988

AWB Lyle	71-67-72-71	281
M Calcavecchia	76-69-72-70	282
C Stadler	76-69-70-68	283
B Crenshaw	72-73-67-72	284
G Norman	77-73-71-64	285
D Pooley	71-72-72-70	285
F Couples	72-68-71-71	285
D Frost	73-74-71-68	286
T Watson	72-71-73-71	287
B Langer	71-72-71-73	287
L Wadkins	74-75-69-70	288
R Floyd	80-68-68-71	288
S Ballesteros	73-72-70-73	288

American PGA Championship

Year	Winner	Runner-up	Venue	By
1916	Jim Barnes	Jock Hutchison	Siwanoy	1 hole
1919	Jim Barnes	Fred McLeod	Engineers' Club	6 and 5
1920	Jock Hutchison	Douglas Edgar	Flossmoor	1 hole
1921	Walter Hagen	Jim Barnes	Inwood Club	3 and 2
1922	Gene Sarazen	Emmet French	Oakmont	4 and 3
1923	Gene Sarazen	Walter Hagen	Pelham	38th hole
1924	Walter Hagen	Jim Barnes	French Lick	2 holes
1925	Walter Hagen	WE Mehlhorn	Olympic Fields	6 and 4
1926	Walter Hagen	Leo Diegel	Salisbury	4 and 3
1927	Walter Hagen	Joe Turnesa	Dallas, Texas	1 hole
1928	Leo Diegel	Al Espinosa	Five Farms	6 and 5
1929	Leo Diegel	J Farrell	Hill Crest	6 and 4
1930	TD Armour	G Sarazen	Fresh Meadow	1 hole
1931	T Creavy	D Shute	Wannamoisett	2 and 1
1932	O Dutra	F Walsh	St Paul, Minnesota	4 and 3
1933	G Sarazen	W Goggin	Milwaukee	5 and 4
1934	P Runyan	Craig Wood	Buffalo	38th hole
1935	J Revolta	TD Armour	Oklahoma	5 and 4
1936	D Shute	J Thomson	Pinehurst	3 and 2
1937	D Shute	H McSpaden	Pittsburgh	37th hole
1938	P Runyan	S Snead	Shawnee	8 and 7
1939	H Picard	B Nelson	Pomonok	37th hole
1940	Byron Nelson	Sam Snead	Hershey, Pa	1 hole
1941	Vic Ghezzie	Byron Nelson	Denver, Colo	38th hole
1942	Sam Snead	Jim Turnesa	Atlantic City	2 and 1
1943	*No Championship*			
1944	Bob Hamilton	Byron Nelson	Spokane, Wash	1 hole
1945	Byron Nelson	Sam Byrd	Dayton, Ohio	4 and 3
1946	Ben Hogan	Ed Oliver	Portland	6 and 4
1947	Jim Ferrier	Chick Harbert	Detroit	2 and 1
1948	Ben Hogan	Mike Turnesa	Norwood Hills	7 and 6
1949	Sam Snead	Johnny Palmer	Richmond, Va	3 and 2
1950	Chandler Harper	Henry Williams	Scioto, Ohio	4 and 3
1951	Sam Snead	Walter Burkemo	Oakmont, Pa	7 and 6
1952	Jim Turnesa	Chick Harbert	Big Spring, Louisville	1 hole
1953	Walter Burkemo	Felice Lorza	Birmingham, Michigan	2 and 1
1954	Chick Harbert	Walter Burkemo	St Paul, Minnesota	4 and 3
1955	D Ford	C Middlecoff	Detroit	4 and 3
1956	J Burke	T Kroll	Boston	3 and 2
1957	L Hebert	D Finsterwald	Miami Valley, Dayton	3 and 1

Changed to Stroke Play

Year	Winner	Venue	Score
1958	D Finsterwald	Llanerch, PA	276
1959	Bob Rosburg	Minneapolis, MN	277
1960	Jay Hebert	Firestone, Akron, OH	281
1961	Jerry Barber*	Olympia Fields, IL	277
1962	GJ Player	Aronimink, PA	278
1963	JW Nicklaus	Dallas, TX	279
1964	Bobby Nichols	Columbus, OH	271
1965	D Marr	Laurel Valley, PA	280
1966	Al Geiberger	Firestone, Akron, OH	280
1967	Don January*	Columbine, CO	281
1968	Julius Boros	Pecan Valley, TX	281
1969	Ray Floyd	Dayton, OH	276
1970	Dave Stockton	Southern Hills, OK	279

American PGA Championship continued

Year	Winner	Venue	Score
1971	JW Nicklaus	PGA National, FL	281
1972	GJ Player	Oakland Hills, MI	281
1973	JW Nicklaus	Canterbury, OH	277
1974	L Trevino	Tanglewood, NC	276
1975	JW Nicklaus	Firestone, Akron, OH	276
1976	D Stockton	Congressional, MD	281
1977	L Wadkins*	Pebble Beach, CA	287
1978	J Mahaffey*	Oakmont, PA	276
1979	D Graham*	Oakland Hills, MI	272
1980	JW Nicklaus	Oak Hill, NY	274
1981	L Nelson	Atlanta, GA	273
1982	R Floyd	Southern Hills, OK	272
1983	H Sutton	Pacific Palisades, CA	274
1984	L Trevino	Shoal Creek	273
1985	H Green	Cherry Hills, Denver, CO	278
1986	R Tway	Inverness, Toledo, OH	276
1987	L Nelson*	PGA National, FL	287
*(*After a tie)*			
1988	J Sluman	Oaktree, OK	272

English Ladies' Amateur Championship

Year	Winner	Runner-up	Venue	By
1960	Miss M Nichol	Mrs MF Bonallack	Burnham	3 and 1
1961	Miss R Porter	Mrs P Reece	Littlestone	2 holes
1962	Miss J Roberts	Mrs MF Bonallack	Woodhall Spa	3 and 1
1963	Mrs MF Bonallack	Miss E Chadwick	Liphook	7 and 6
1964	Mrs AD Spearman	Miss M Everard	Lytham St Annes	6 and 5
1965	Miss R Porter	Miss C Cheetham	Whittington Barrcks	6 and 5
1966	Miss J Greenhalgh	Mrs JC Holmes	Hayling Island	3 and 1
1967	Miss A Irwin	Mrs A Pickard	Alwoodley	3 and 2
1968	Mrs S Barber	Miss D Oxley	Hunstanton	5 and 4
1969	Miss B Dixon	Miss M Wenyon	Burnham and Berrow	6 and 4
1970	Miss D Oxley	Mrs S Barber	Rye	3 and 2
1971	Miss D Oxley	Mrs S Barber	Hoylake	5 and 4
1972	Miss M Everard	Mrs MF Bonallack	Woodhall Spa	2 and 1
1973	Miss M Walker	Miss C Le Feuvre	Broadstone	6 and 5
1974	Miss A Irvin	Mrs J Thornhill	Sunningdale	1 hole
1975	Miss B Huke	Miss L Harrold	Birkdale	2 and 1
1976	Miss L Harrold	Mrs A Uzielli	Hollinwell	3 and 2
1977	Miss V Marvin	Miss M Everard	Burnham and Berrow	1 hole
1978	Miss V Marvin	Miss R Porter	West Sussex	2 and 1
1979	Miss J Greenhalgh	Mrs S Hedges	Hoylake	2 and 1
1980	Miss B New	Miss J Walker	Aldeburgh	3 and 2
1981	Miss D Christison	Miss S Cohen	Cotswold Hills	2 holes
1982	Miss J Walter	Miss C Nelson	Brancepeth Castle	4 and 3
1983	Mrs L Bayman	Miss C Mackintosh	Hayling Island	4 and 3
1984	Miss C Waite	Mrs L Bayman	Hunstanton	3 and 2
1985	Miss P Johnson	Mrs L Bayman	Ferndown	1 hole
1986	Mrs J Thornhill	Miss S Shapcott	Princes	3 and 1
1987	Miss J Furby	Miss M King	Alwoodley	4 and 3
1988	Miss J Wade	Miss S Shapcott	Little Aston	19th hole

English Ladies' Under-23 Championship

Inaugurated 1978

Year	Winner	Venue	Score
1978	Miss S Bamford	Caldy	228
1979	Miss B Cooper	Coxmoor	223
1980	Miss B Cooper	Porters Park	226
1981	Miss J Soulsby	Willesley Park	220
1982	Miss M Gallagher	Highpost	221
1983	Miss P Grice	Hallamshire	219
1984	Miss P Johnson	Moor Park	300
1985	Miss P Johnson	Northants County	301
1986	Miss S Shapcott	Broadstone	301
1987	Miss J Wade	Northumberland	296
1988	Miss J Wade	Wentworth	299

English Open Amateur Stroke Play Championship

(formerly Brabazon Trophy)

Year	Winner	Club	Venue	Score
1960	GB Wolstenholme	Sunningdale	Ganton	286
1961	RDBM Shade	Duddingston	Hoylake	284
1962	A Slater	Wakefield	Woodhall Spa	209
1963	RDBM Shade	Duddingston	Birkdale	306
1964	MF Bonallack	Thorpe Hall	Deal	290
1965	CA Clark DJ Millensted MJ Burgess	Ganton Wentworth West Sussex } tie	Formby	289
1966	PM Townsend	Porters Park	Hunstanton	282
1967	RDBM Shade	Duddingston	Saunton	299
1968	MF Bonallack	Thorpe Hall	Walton Heath	210
1969	R Foster MF Bonallack	Bradford Thorpe Hall } tie	Moortown	290
1970	R Foster	Bradford	Little Aston	287
1971	MF Bonallack	Thorpe Hall	Hillside	294
1972	PH Moody	Notts	Hoylake	296
1973	R Revell	Farnham	Hunstanton	294
1974	N Sundelson	South Africa	Moortown	291
1975	AWB Lyle	Hawkstone Park	Hollinwell	298
1976	P Hedges	Langley Park	Saunton	294
1977	AWB Lyle	Hawkstone Park	Hoylake	293
1978	G Brand	Knowle	Woodhall Spa	289
1979	D Long	Shandon Park	Little Aston	291
1980	R Rafferty P McEvoy	Warrenpoint Copt Heath } tie	Hunstanton	293
1981	P Way	Neville	Hillside	292
1982	P Downes	Coventry	Woburn	299
1983	C Banks	Stanton-on-the-Wolds	Hollinwell	294
1984	M Davis	Thorndon Park	Royal Cinque Ports	286
1985	R Roper P Baker	Catterick Garrison Lillieshall Park } tie	Seaton Carew	296
1986	R Kaplan	South Africa	Sunningdale	286
1987	JG Robinson	Woodhall Spa	Ganton	287
1988	R Eggo	L'Ancresse	Saunton	289

English Mid-Amateur Championship

Inaugurated 1988

Year	Winner	Club	Venue	Score
1988	P McEvoy	Copt Heath	Little Aston	284

English County Championship (Men)

Year	Winner	Year	Winner
1960	Northumberland	1975	Staffordshire
1961	Lancashire	1976	Warwickshire
1962	Northumberland	1977	Warwickshire
1963	Yorkshire	1978	Kent
1964	Northumberland	1979	Gloucestershire
1965	Northumberland	1980	Surrey
1966	Surrey	1981	Surrey
1967	Lancashire	1982	Yorkshire
1968	Surrey	1983	Berks, Bucks, Oxon
1969	Berks, Bucks, Oxon	1984	Yorkshire
1970	Gloucestershire	1985	Devon Hertfordshire
1971	Staffordshire	1986	Hertfordshire
1972	Berks, Bucks, Oxon	1987	Yorkshire
1973	Yorkshire	1988	Warwickshire
1974	Lincolnshire		

English Ladies' Stroke-Play Championship

Inaugurated 1984

Year	Winner	Venue	Score
1984	Miss P Grice	Moor Park	300
1985	Miss P Johnson	Northants County	301
1986	Miss S Shapcott	Broadstone	301
1987	Miss J Wade	Northumberland	296
1988	Miss S Prosser	Wentworth	297

English Seniors Championship

Inaugurated 1981

Year	Winner	Venue	Score
1983	GM Edwards	Delamere Forest	222
1984	RL Glading	Thetford	150
1985	JR Marriott	Bristol and Clifton	153
1986	R Hiatt	Northants County	153
1987	I Caldwell	North Hants, Fleet	72
(curtailed due to storm)			
1988	G Edwards	Bromborough	222

English Ladies' Seniors Championship

Inaugurated 1988

Year	Winner	Venue	Score
1988	Mrs A Thompson	Wentworth	158

English Boys Amateur Open Stroke-Play Championship

(formerly Carris Trophy)

Venue: 1934–87 Moor Park

Year	Winner	Venue	Score
1984	J Coe	Moor Park	283
1985	P Baker	Moor Park	286
1986	G Evans	Moor Park	292
1987	D Bathgate	Moor Park	289
1988	P Page	Brancepeth Castle	284

English Ladies' Intermediate Championship

Inaugurated 1982

Year	Winner	Venue	Score
1982	Miss J Rhodes	Headingley	19th hole
1983	Miss L Davies	Worksop	2 and 1
1984	Miss P Grice	Whittington Barracks	3 and 2
1985	Miss S Lowe	Caldy	2 and 1
1986	Miss S Moorcroft	Hexham	6 and 5
1987	Miss J Wade	Sherringham	2 and 1
1988	Miss S Morgan	Enville, Staffs	20th hole

English Girls' Championship

Year	Winner	Runner-up	Venue	By
1964	Miss S Ward	Miss P Tredinnick	Wollaton Park	2 and 1
1965	Miss D Oxley	Miss A Payne	Edgbaston	2 holes
1966	Miss B Whitehead	Miss D Oxley	Woodbridge	1 hole
1967	Miss A Willard	Miss G Holloway	Burhill	1 hole
1968	Miss K Phillips	Miss C le Feuvre	Harrogate	6 and 5
1969	Miss C le Feuvre	Miss K Phillips	Hawkstone Park	2 and 1
1970	Miss C le Feuvre	Miss M Walker	High Post	2 and 1
1971	Miss C Eckersley	Miss J Stevens	Liphook	4 and 3
1972	Miss C Barker	Miss R Kelly	Trentham	4 and 3
1973	Miss S Parker	Miss S Thurston	Lincoln	19th hole
1974	Miss C Langford	Miss L Harrold	Knowle	2 and 1
1975	Miss M Burton	Miss R Barry	Formby	6 and 5
1976	Miss H Latham	Miss D Park	Moseley	3 and 2
1977	Miss S Bamford	Miss S Jolly	Chelmsfsord	21st hole
1978	Miss P Smillie	Miss J Smith	Willesley Park	3 and 2
1979	Miss L Moore	Miss P Barry	Cirencester	1 hole
1980	Miss P Smillie	Miss J Soulsby	Kedleston Park	3 and 2
1981	Miss J Soulsby	Miss C Waite	Worksop	7 and 5
1982	Miss C Waite	Miss P Grice	Wilmslow	3 and 2
1983	Miss P Grice	Miss K Mitchell	West Surrey	2 and 1
1984	Miss C Swallow	Miss S Duhig	Bath	3 and 1
1985	Miss L Fairclough	Miss K Mitchell	Coventry	6 and 5
1986	Miss S Shapcott	Miss N Way	Huddersfield	7 and 6
1987	Miss S Shapcott	Miss S Morgan	Sandy Lodge	1 hole
1988	Miss H Dobson	Miss S Shapcott	Long Ashton	1 hole

England and Wales (Ladies') County Finals

Year	Winner	Year	Winner
1960	Lancashire	1974	Surrey
1961	Middlesex	1975	Glamorgan
1962	Staffordshire	1976	Staffordshire
1963	Warwickshire	1977	Essex
1964	Lancashire	1978	Glamorgan
1965	Staffordshire	1979	Essex
1966	Lancashire	1980	Lancashire
1967	Lancashire	1981	Glamorgan
1968	Surrey	1982	Surrey
1969	Lancashire	1983	Surrey
1970	Yorkshire	1984	Surrey/Yorkshire
1971	Kent	1985	Surrey
1972	Kent	1986	Glamorgan
1973	Northumberland	1987	Lancashire
		1988	Surrey

Irish Amateur Championship

Instituted 1893

Year	Winner	Runner-up	Venue	By
1960	M Edwards	N Fogarty	Portstewart	6 and 5
1961	D Sheahan	J Brown	Rosses Point	5 and 4
1962	M Edwards	J Harrington	Baltray	42nd hole
1963	JB Carr	EC O'Brien	Killarney	2 and 1
1964	JB Carr	A McDade	Co Down	6 and 5
1965	JB Carr	T Craddock	Rosses Point	3 and 2
1966	D Sheahan	J Faith	Dollymount	3 and 2
1967	JB Carr	PD Flaherty	Lahinch	1 hole
1968	M O'Brien	F McCarroll	Portrush	2 and 1
1969	V Nevin	J O'Leary	Co Sligo	1 hole
1970	DB Sheahan	M Bloom	Grange	2 holes
1971	P Kane	M O'Brien	Ballybunion	3 and 2
1972	K Stevenson	B Hoey	Co Down	2 and 1
1973	RKM Pollin	RM Staunton	Rosses Point	1 hole
1974	R Kane	M Gannon	Portmarnock	5 and 4
1975	MD O'Brien	JA Bryan	Cork	5 and 4
1976	D Brannigan	D O'Sullivan	Portrush	2 holes
1977	M Gannon	A Hayes	Westport	19th hole
1978	M Morris	T Cleary	Carlow	1 hole
1979	J Harrington	MA Gannon	Ballybunion	2 and 1
1980	R Rafferty	MJ Bannon	Co Down	8 and 7
1981	D Brannigan	E McMenamin	Co Sligo	19th hole
1982	P Walton	B Smyth	Woodbrook	7 and 6
1983	T Corridan	E Power	Killarney	2 holes
1984	CB Hoey	L McNamara	Malone	20th hole
1985	D O'Sullivan	D Branigan	Westport	1 hole
1986	J McHenry	P Rayfus	Dublin	4 and 3
1987	E Power	JP Fitzgerald	Tranmore	2 holes
1988	G McGimpsey	D Mulholland	Portrush	2 and 1

Irish National Professional Championship

Instituted 1907

Year	Winner	Club	Venue	Score
1960	C O'Connor	Royal Dublin	Warrenpoint	271
1961	C O'Connor	Royal Dublin	Lahinch	280
1962	C O'Connor	Royal Dublin	Bangor	264
1963	C O'Connor	Royal Dublin	Little Island	271
1964	E Jones	Bangor	Knock	279
1965	C O'Connor	Royal Dublin	Mullingar	283
1966	C O'Connor	Royal Dublin	Warrenpoint	269
1967	H Boyle	Jacobs Golf Centre	Tullamore (3 rounds)	214
1968	C Greene	Mill Town	Knock	282
1969	J Martin	Unattached	Dundalk	268
1970	H Jackson	Knockbracken	Massareene	283
1971	C O'Connor	Royal Dublin	Galway	278
1972	J Kinsella	Castle	Bundoran	289
1973	J Kinsella	Castle	Limerick	284
1974	E Polland	Balmoral	Portstewart	277
1975	C O'Connor	Royal Dublin	Carlow	275
1976	P McGuirk	Co Louth	Waterville	291
From 1977 sponsored by Rank Xerox				
1977	P Skerritt	St Annes	Woodbrook	281
1978	C O'Connor	Royal Dublin	Dollymount	286
1979	D Smyth	Bettystown	Dollymount (54 holes)	215
1980	D Feherty	Balmoral	Dollymount	283
1981	D Jones	Bangor	Woodbrook	283
1982	D Feherty	Balmoral	Woodbrook	287
1983	L Higgins	Waterville	Woodbrook	275
1984	M Sludds		Skerries	277
1985	DJ Smyth		Co Louth	204
(Played over 54 holes due to bad weather)				
1986	DJ Smyth		Waterville	282
1987				
1988	E Darcy		Castle, Dublin	269

Irish Girls' Championship

Year	Winner	Runner-up	Venue	By
1951	Miss Jocelyn Davies	Miss Irene Hurst	Milltown	3 and 2
1952	Miss Jane Redgate	Miss Ann B Phillips	Grange	22nd hole
1953	Miss Jane Redgate	Miss Irene Hurst	Grange	4 and 3
1954-60	*Suspended*			
1961	Miss M Coburn	Miss C McAuley	Portrush	6 and 5
1962	Miss Pearl Boyd	Miss Patricia Atkinson	Elm Park	4 and 3
1963	Miss P Atkinson	Miss C Scarlett	Donaghadee	8 and 7
1964	Miss C Scarlett	Miss A Maher	Milltown	6 and 5
1965	Miss V Sngleton	Miss P McKenzie	Ballycastle	7 and 6
1966	Miss M McConnell	Miss D Hulme	Dun Laoghaire	3 and 2
1967	Miss M McConnell	Miss C Wallace	Portrush	6 and 5
1968	Miss C Wallace	Miss A McCoy	Louth	3 and 1
1969	Miss EA McGregor	Miss M Sheenan	Knock	6 and 5
1970	Miss EA McGregor	Miss J Mark	Greystones	3 and 2
1971	Miss J Mark	Miss C Nesbitt	Belfast	3 and 2
1972	Miss P Smyth	Miss M Governey	Elm Park	1 hole
1973	Miss M Governey	Miss R Hegarty	Mullingar	3 and 1
1974	Miss R Hegarty	Miss M Irvine	Castletroy	2 holes
1975	Miss M Irvine	Miss P Wickham	Carlow	2 and 1
1976	Miss P Wickham	Miss R Hegarty	Castle	5 and 3
1977	Miss A Ferguson	Miss R Walsh	Birr	3 and 2
1978	Miss C Wickham	Miss B Gleeson	Killarney	1 hole
1979	Miss L Bolton	Miss B Gleeson	Milltown	3 and 2
1980	Miss B Gleeson	Miss L Bolton	Kilkenny	5 and 3
1981	Miss B Gleeson	Miss E Lynn	Donegal	1 hole
1982	Miss D Langan	Miss S Lynn	Headfort	5 and 4
1983	Miss E McDaid	Miss S Lynn	Ennis	20th hole
1984	Miss S Sheehan	Miss L Tormey	Thurles	6 and 4
1985	Miss S Sheehan	Miss D Hanna	Laytown/Bettystown	5 and 4
1986	Miss D Mahon	Miss T Eakin	Mallow	4 and 3
1987	Miss V Greevy	Miss B Ryan	Galway	8 and 7
1988	Miss L McCool			

Irish Ladies' Amateur Championship

Instituted 1894

Year	Winner	Runner-up	Venue	By
1946	Miss P Garvey	Mrs V Reddan	Lahinch	39th hole
1947	Miss P Garvey	Miss C Syme	Portrush	5 and 4
1948	Miss P Garvey	Mrs V Reddan	Rosslare	9 and 7
1949	Miss C Syme	Mrs J Beck	Baltray	9 and 7
1950	Miss P Garvey	Mrs T Marks	Rosses Point	6 and 4
1951	Miss P Garvey	Miss D Forster	Ballybunion	12 and 10
1952	Miss DM Forster	Mrs PG McCann	Newcastle	3 and 2
1953	Miss P Garvey	Mrs Hegarty	Rosslare	8 and 7
1954	Miss P Garvey	Mrs HV Glendinning	Portmarnock	13 and 12
1955	Miss P Garvey	Miss A O'Donohue	Rosses Point	10 and 9
1956	Miss P O'Sullivan	Mrs JF Hegarty	Killarney	14 and 12
1957	Miss P Garvey	Mrs K McGann	Portrush	3 and 2
1958	Miss P Garvey	Mrs Z Fallon	Carlow	7 and 6
1959	Miss P Garvey	Miss H Colhoun	Lahinch	12 and 10
1960	Miss P Garvey	Mrs PG McGann	Cork	5 and 3
1961	Mrs K McCann	Miss A Sweeney	Newcastle	5 and 3
1962	Miss P Garvey	Mrs M Earner	Baltray	7 and 6
1963	Miss P Garvey	Miss E Barnett	Killarney	9 and 7
1964	Mrs Z Fallon	Miss P O'Sullivan	Portrush	37th hole
1965	Miss E Purcell	Miss P O'Sullivan	Mullingar	3 and 2
1966	Miss E Bradshaw	Miss P O'Sullivan	Rosslare	3 and 2
1967	Mrs G Brandom	Miss P O'Sullivan	Castlerock	3 and 2
1968	Miss E Bradshaw	Miss M McKenna	Lahinch	3 and 2
1969	Miss M McKenna	Mrs C Hickey	Ballybunion	3 and 2
1970	Miss P Garvey	Miss M Earner	Portrush	2 and 1
1971	Miss E Bradshaw	Miss M Mooney	Baltray	3 and 1
1972	Miss M McKenna	Mrs I Butler	Killarney	5 and 4
1973	Miss M Mooney	Miss M McKenna	Bundoran	2 and 1
1974	Miss M McKenna	Miss V Singleton	Lahinch	3 and 2
1975	Miss M Gorry	Miss E Bradshaw	Tramore	1 hole
1976	Miss C Nesbitt	Miss M McKenna	Rosses Point	20th hole
1977	Miss M McKenna	Miss R Hegarty	Ballybunion	2 holes
1978	Miss M Gorry	Mrs I Butler	Grange	4 and 3

Irish Ladies' Amateur Championship
continued

Year	Winner	Runner-up	Venue	By
1979	Miss M McKenna	Miss C Nesbitt	Donegal	6 and 5
1980	Miss C Nesbitt	Miss C Hourihane	Lahinch	1 hole
1981	Miss M McKenna	Miss M Kenny	Laytown & Bettystown	1 hole
1982	Miss M McKenna	Miss M Madill	Portrush	2 and 1
1983	Miss C Hourihane	Mrs V Hassett	Cork	6 and 4
1984	Miss C Hourihane	Miss M Madill	Rosses Point	19th hole
1985	Miss C Hourihane	Miss M McKenna	Waterville	4 and 3
1986	Mrs T O'Reilly	Miss E Higgins	Castlerock	4 and 3
1987	Miss C Hourihane	Miss C Hickey	Lahinch	5 and 4
1988	Miss L Bolton	Miss E Higgins	Tramore	2 and 1

Irish Seniors' Open Amateur Championship

Year	Winner	Venue	Score
1970	C Ewing	Lahinch	153
1971	J O'Sullivan	Rosslare	159
1972	B Scannell	Co Sligo	152
1973	JW Hulme	Warrenpoint	147
1974	Rev P Walsh	Roscrea	155
1975	SA O'Connor	Athy	152
1976	BJ Scannell	Woodbrook	150
1977	DB Somers	Warrenpoint	150
1978	DP Herlihy	Limerick	150
1979	P Kelly	Tara	156
1980	GN Fogarty	Galway	144
1981	GN Fogarty	Bundoran	149
1982	J Murray	Douglas	141
1983	F Sharpe	Courtown	153
1984	J Boston	Connemara	147
1985	J Boston	Newcastle	155
1986	J Coey	Waterford	141
1987	J Murray	Castleroy	150
1988			

Irish Youths' Open Amateur Championship

Year	Winner	Venue	Score
1969	D Brannigan	Delgany	142
1970	LA Owens	Tullamore	286
1971	M Gannon	Athlone	277
1972	M Gannon	Mullingar	291
1973	J Purcell	Tullamore	289
1974	A Dunlop	Athlone	293
1975	P McNally	Edenderry	287
1976	R McCormack	Warrenpoint	294
1977	B McDaid	Athlone	290
1978	T Corridan	Thurles	279
1979	R Rafferty	Tullamore	293
1980	J McHenry	Clandeboye	296
1981	J McHenry	Westport	303
1982	K O'Donnell	Mullingar	286
1983	P Murphy	Cork	287
1984	J Morris	Bangor	292
1985	J McHenry	Co Sligo	287
1986	JC Morris	Carlow	280
1987	C Everett	Killarney	300
1988	P McGinley		

Scottish Amateur Championship

Year	Winner	Runner-up	Venue	By
1949	R Wright	H McInally	Muirfield	1 hole
1950	WC Gibson	DA Blair	Prestwick	2 and 1
1951	JM Dykes	JC Wilson	St Andrews	4 and 2
1952	FG Dewar	JC Wilson	Carnoustie	4 and 3
1953	DA Blair	JW McKay	Western Gailes	3 and 1
1954	JW Draper	WGH Gray	Nairn	4 and 3
1955	RR Jack	AC Miller	Muirfield	2 and 1
1956	Dr FWG Deighton	A MacGregor	Troon	8 and 7
1957	JS Montgomerie	J Burnside	Balgownie	2 and 1
1958	WD Smith	IR Harris	Prestwick	6 and 5
1959	Dr FWG Deighton	RMK Murray	St Andrews	6 and 5
1960	JR Young	S Saddler	Carnoustie	5 and 3
1961	J Walker	SWT Murray	Western Gailes	4 and 3
1962	SWT Murray	RDBM Shade	Muirfield	2 and 1
1963	RDBM Shade	N Henderson	Troon	4 and 3
1964	RDBM Shade	J McBeath	Nairn	8 and 7
1965	RDBM Shade	GB Cosh	St Andrews	4 and 2
1966	RDBM Shade	CJL Strachan	Western Gailes	9 and 8
1967	RDBM Shade	A Murphy	Carnoustie	5 and 4
1968	GB Cosh	RL Renfrew	Muirfield	4 and 3
1969	JM Cannon	AH Hall	Troon	6 and 4
1970	CW Green	HB Stewart	Balgownie, Aberdeen	1 hole
1971	S Stephen	CW Green	St Andrews	3 and 2
1972	HB Stuart	AK Pirie	Prestwick	3 and 1
1973	IC Hutcheon	Allan Brodie	Carnoustie	3 and 2
1974	GH Murray	AK Pirie	Western Gailes	2 and 1
1975	D Greig	GH Murray	Montrose	7 and 6
1976	GH Murray	HB Stuart	St Andrews	6 and 5
1977	Allan Brodie	PJ McKellar	Troon	1 hole
1978	IA Carslaw	J Cuddihy	Downfield	7 and 6
1979	K Macintosh	PJ McKellar	Prestwick	5 and 4
1980	D Jamieson	CW Green	Balgownie, Aberdeen (18 holes)	2 and 1
1981	C Dalgleish	A Thomson	Western Gailes	7 and 6
1982	CW Green	G McGregor	Carnoustie	1 hole
1983	CW Green	J Huggan	Gullane	1 hole
1984	A Moir	K Buchan	Renfrew	3 and 3
1985	D Carrick	D James	Southerness	4 and 2
1986	C Brooks	A Thomson	Monifieth	3 and 2
1987	C Montgomerie	AW Watt	Nairn	9 and 8
1988	J Milligan	A Colthart	Barassie	1 hole

Scottish Open Amateur Stroke Play Championship

Year	Winner	Club	Venue	Score
1967	BJ Gallacher	Bathgate	Muirfield and Gullane	291
1968	RDBM Shade	Duddingston	Prestwick and Prestwick St Nicholas	282
1969	JS Macdonald	Dalmahoy	Carnoustie and Monifieth	288
1970	D Hayes	South Africa	Glasgow Gailes and Barassie	275
1971	IC Hutcheon	Monifieth	Leven and Lundin Links	277
1972	BN Nicholas	Nairn	Dalmahoy and Ratho Park	290
1973	DM Robertson GJ Clark (tie)	Dunbar Whitley Bay	Dunbar and North Berwick	284
1974	IC Hutcheon	Monifieth	Blairgowrie and Alyth	283
1975	CW Green	Dumbarton	Nairn and Nairn Dunbar	295
1976	S Martin	Downfield	Monifieth and Carnoustie	299
1977	PJ McKellar	East Renfrewshire	Muirfield and Gullane	299

Scottish Open Amateur Stroke Play Championship continued

Year	Winner	Club	Venue	Score
1978	AR Taylor	East Kilbride	Keir and Cawder	281
1979	IC Hutcheon	Monifieth	Lansdowne and Rosemount	296
1980	G Brand	Knowle	Musselburgh and R Musselburgh (54 holes)	207
1981	P Walton	Malahide	Erskine and Renfrew	287
1982	G Macgregor	Glencourse	Downfield and Camperdown	287
1983	G Murray	Fereneze	Irvine	291
1984	CW Green	Dumbarton	Blairgowrie	287
1985	C Montgomerie	Royal Troon	Dunbar	274
1986	KH Walker	Royal Burgess	Carnoustie	289
1987	D Carrick	Douglas Park	Lundin Links	282
1988	S Easingwood	Dunbar	Cathkin Braes	277

Scottish Boys' Championship

Year	Winner	Runner-up	Venue	By
1960	L Carver	S Wilson	North Berwick	6 and 5
1961	Kelvin Thomson	G Wilson	North Berwick	10 and 8
1962	HF Urquhart	S MacDonald	North Berwick	3 and 2
1963	Finlay S Morris	Iain Clark	North Berwick	9 and 8
1964	WR Lockie	MD Cleghorn	North Berwick	1 hole
1965	RL Penman	J Wood	North Berwick	9 and 8
1966	J McTear	DG Greig	North Berwick	4 and 3
1967	DG Greig	I Cannon	North Berwick	2 and 1
1968	RD Weir	M Grubb	North Berwick	6 and 4
1969	RP Fyle	IP Doig	North Berwick	4 and 2
1970	S Stephen	M Henry	North Berwick	38th hole
1971	JE Murray	AA Mackay	North Berwick	4 and 3
1972	DM Robertson	G Cairns	North Berwick	9 and 8
1973	R Watson	H Alexander	North Berwick	8 and 7
1974	DM Robertson	J Cuddihy	North Berwick	6 and 5
1975	A Brown	J Cuddihy	North Berwick	6 and 4
1976	B Marchbank	J Cuddihy	Dunbar	2 and 1
1977	JS Taylor	GJ Webster	Dunbar	3 and 2
1978	J Huggan	KW Stables	Dunbar	2 and 1
1979	DR Weir	S Morrison	West Kilbride	5 and 3
1980	R Gregan	AJ Currie	Dunbar	2 and 1
1981	C Stewart	G Mellon	Dunbar	3 and 2
1982	A Smith	J White	Dunbar	39th hole
1983	C Gillies	C Innes	Dunbar	38th hole
1984	K Buchan	L Vannet	Dunbar	2 and 1
1985	AD McQueen	FJ McCulloch	Dunbar	1 hole
1986	AG Tait	EA McIntosh	Dunbar	6 and 5
1987	AJ Coltart	SJ Bannerman	Dunbar	37th hole
1988	CA Fraser	F Clark	Dunbar	9 and 8

Scottish Boys' Open Amateur Stroke Play Championship

Year	Winner	Club	Venue	Score
1970	D Chillas	R Aberdeen	Carnoustie	298
1971	JE Murray	Baberton	Lanark	274
1972	S Martin	Downfield	Montrose	280
1973	S Martin	Carnoustie	Barnton	284
1974	PW Gallacher	Peebles	Lundin Links	290
1975	A Webster	Edzell	Kilmarnock Barassie	286
1976	A Webster	Edzell	Forfar	292
1977	J Huggan / L Mann } tie	Winterfield	Renfrew	303

Scottish Boys' Open Amateur Stroke Play Championship continued

Year	Winner	Club	Venue	Score
1978	R Fraser	Hilton Park	Arbroath	283
1979	L Mann	Carnoustie	Stirling	289
1980	ASK Glen	Ormesson (France)	Forfar	288
1981	J Gullen	Tillicoultry	Bellshill	296
1982	D Purdie	Turriff	Monifieth	296
1983	L Vannet	Carnoustie	Barassie	286
1984	K Walker	Royal Burgess	Carnoustie	280
1985	G Matthew	Melrose	Baberton	297
1986	G Cassells	Cruden Bay	Edzell	294
1987	C Ronald	Torrance House	Lanark	287
1988	M Urquhart	Inverness	Dumfries & County	280

Scottish Girls' Amateur Championship

Year	Winner	Runner-up	Venue	By
1960	Miss J Hastings	Miss A Lurie	Kilmacolm	6 and 4
1961	Miss I Wylie	Miss W Clark	Murrayfield	3 and 1
1962	Miss I Wylie	Miss U Burnet	West Kilbride	3 and 1
1963	Miss M Norval	Miss S MacDonald	Carnoustie	6 and 4
1964	Miss JW Smith	Miss C Workman	West Kilbride	2 and 1
1965	Miss JW Smith	Miss I Walker	Leven	7 and 5
1966	Miss Jillian Hutton	Miss F Jamieson	Arbroath	2 holes
1967	Miss Jillian Hutton	Miss K Lackie	West Kilbride	4 and 2
1968	Miss M Dewar	Miss J Crawford	Dalmahoy	2 holes
1969	Miss C Panton	Miss A Coutts	Edzell	23rd hole
1970	Miss M Walker	Miss L Bennett	Largs	3 and 2
1971	Miss M Walker	Miss S Kennedy	Edzell	1 hole
1972	Miss G Cadden	Miss C Panton	Stirling	3 and 2
1973	Miss M Walker	Miss M Thomson	Cowal, Dunoon	1 hole
1974	Miss S Cadden	Miss D Reid	Arbroath	3 and 1
1975	Miss W Aitken	Miss S Cadden	Leven	1 hole
1976	MIss S Cadden	Miss D Mitchell	Dumfries and County	4 and 2
1977	Miss W Aitken	Miss G Wilson	West Kilbride	2 holes
1978	Miss J Connachan	Miss D Mitchell	Stirling	7 and 5
1979	Miss J Connachan	Miss G Wilson	Dunbar	3 and 1
1980	Miss J Connachan	Miss P Wright	Dunfries and County	21st hole
1981	Miss D Thomson	Miss P Wright	Barassie	2 and 1
1982	Miss S Lawson	Miss D Thomson	Montrose	1 hole
1983	Miss K Imrie	Miss D Martin	Leven	2 and 1
1984	Miss T Craik	Miss D Jackson	Peebles	3 and 2
1985	Miss E Farquharson	Miss E Moffat	West Kilbride	2 holes
1986	Miss C Lambert	Miss F McKay	Nairn	4 and 3
1987	Miss S Little	Miss L Moretti	Stirling	3 and 2
1988	Miss J Jenkins	Miss F McKay	Dumfries and County	4 and 3

Scottish Girls' Open Stroke Play Championship

Year	Winner	Venue
1960	Miss J Greenhalgh	Ranfurly Castle
1961	Miss D Robb	Whitecraigs
1962	Miss S Armitage	Dalmahoy
1963	Miss A Irvin	Dumfries
1964	Miss M Nuttall	Dalmahoy
1965	Miss I Wylie	Carnoustie
1966	Miss J Smith	Douglas Park
1967	Miss J Bourassa	Dunbar
1968	Miss K Phillips	Dumfries
1969	Miss K Phillips	Prestonfield
1970	Miss B Huke	Leven
1971	Miss B Huke	Dalmahoy
1972	Miss L Hope	Troon, Portland
1973	Miss G Cadden	Edzell
1974	Miss S Lambie	Stranraer
1975	Miss S Cadden	Lanark
1976	Miss S Cadden	Prestonfield
1977	Miss S Cadden	Edzell
1978	Miss J Connachan	Peebles
1979	Miss A Gemmill	Troon, Portland

Scottish Girls' Open Stroke Play Championship
continued

Year	Winner	Venue
1980	Miss J Connachan	Kirkcaldy
1981	Miss K Douglas	Downfield
1982	Miss J Rhodes	Dumfries & Galloway
1983	Miss S Lawson	Largs
1984	Miss S Lawson	Dunbar
1985	Miss K Imrie	Ballater
1986	Miss K Imrie	Dumfries & County
1987	Miss K Imrie	Douglas Park
1988		

Scottish Ladies' Amateur Championship
Instituted 1903

Year	Winner	Runner-up	Venue	By
1960	Miss JS Robertson	Miss DT Sommerville	Turnberry	2 and 1
1961	Miss I Wright (Miss Robertson)	Miss AM Lurie	St Andrews	1 hole
1962	Miss JB Lawrence	Mrs C Draper	Dornoch	5 and 4
1963	Miss JB Lawrence	Mrs IC Robertson	Troon	2 and 1
1964	Miss JB Lawrence	Mrs SM Reid	Gullane	5 and 3
1965	Mrs IC Robertson	Miss JB Lawrence	Nairn	5 and 4
1966	Mrs IC Robertson	Miss M Fowler	Machrihanish	2 and 1
1967	Miss J Hastings	Miss A Laing	North Berwick	5 and 3
1968	Miss Joan Smith	Mrs J Rennie	Carnoustie	10 and 9
1969	Mrs JH Anderson	Miss K Lackie	West Kilbride	5 and 4
1970	Miss A Laing	Mrs IC Robertson	Dunbar	1 hole
1971	Mrs IC Robertson	Mrs A Ferguson	Dornoch	3 and 2
1972	Mrs IC Robertson	Miss CJ Lugton	Machrinabish	5 and 3
1973	Mrs I Wright	Dr AJ Wilson	St Andrews	2 holes
1974	Dr AJ Wilson	Miss K Lackie	Nairn	22nd hole
1975	Miss LA Hope	Miss JW Smith	Elie	1 hole
1976	Miss S Needham	Miss T Walker	Machrihanish	3 and 2
1977	Miss CJ Lugton	Miss M Thomson	Dornoch	1 hole
1978	Mrs IC Robertson	Miss JW Smith	Prestwick	2 holes
1979	Miss G Stewart	Miss LA Hope	Gullane	2 and 1
1980	Mrs IC Robertson	Miss F Anderson	Carnoustie	1 hole
1981	Miss A Gemmill	Miss W Aitken	Stranraer	2 and 1
1982	Miss J Connachan	Miss P Wright	Troon	19th hole
1983	Miss G Stewart	Miss F Anderson	North Berwick	3 and 1
1984	Miss G Stewart	Miss A Gemmill	Dornoch	3 and 2
1985	Miss A Gemmill	Miss D Thomson	Barassie	2 and 1
1986	Mrs IC Robertson	Miss L Hope	St Andrews	3 and 2
1987	Miss F Anderson	Miss C Middleton	Nairn	4 and 3
1988	Miss S Lawson	Miss F Anderson	Southerness	3 and 1

Scottish Professional Championship
Instituted 1907

Year	Winner	Club	Venue	Score
1960	EC Brown	Buchanan Castle	West Kilbride	278
1961	RT Walker	Downfield, Dundee	Forres	271
1962	EC Brown	Unattached	Dunbar	283
1963	WM Miller	Cardross	Crieff	284
1964	RT Walker	Downfield, Dundee	Machrihanish	277
1965	EC Brown	Cruden Bay	Forfar	271
1966	EC Brown J Panton	Cruden Bay Glenbervie } tie	Cruden Bay (36 holes)	137
1967	H Bannerman	Aberdeen	Montrose	279
1968	EC Brown	Cruden Bay	Monktonhall	286
1969	G Cunningham	Troon Municipal	Machrihanish	284
1970	RDBM Shade	Duddingston	Montrose	276
1971	NJ Gallacher	Wentworth	Lundin Links	282
1972	H Bannerman	Banchory	Strathaven	268
1973	BJ Gallacher	Wentworth	Kings Links, Aberdeen	276
1974	BJ Gallacher	Wentworth	Drumpellier	276
1975	D Huish	North Berwick	Duddingston	279
1976	J Chillas	Crow Wood	Haggs Castle	286

Scottish Professional Championship
continued

Year	Winner	Club	Venue	Score
1977	BJ Gallacher	Wentworth	Barnton	282
1978	S Torrance	Caledonian Hotel	Strathaven	269
1979	AWB Lyle	Hawkstone Park	Glasgow Gailes	274
1980	S Torrance	Caledonian Hotel	East Kilbride	273
1981	B Barnes	Caledonian Hotel	Dalmahoy	275
1982	B Barnes	Caledonian Hotel	Dalmahoy	286
1983	B Gallacher	Wentworth	Dalmahoy	276
(After play-off)				
1984	I Young		Dalmahoy	276
1985	S Torrance		Dalmahoy	277
1986	R Drummond		Glenbervie	270
1987	R Drummond		Glenbervie	268
1988				

Scottish Open Amateur Seniors' Championship
Instituted 1978

Year	Winner	Club	Venue	Score
1978	JM Cannon / GR Carmichael (tie)	Irvine / Ladybank	Glasgow Killermont	149
1979	A Sinclair	Drumpellier	Glasgow Killermont	143
1980	JM Cannon	Irvine	Royal Burgess	149
1981	IR Harris / Dr J Hastings / AN Sturrock (tie)	Royal Troon / Royal Troon / Royal Troon	Glasgow Killermont	146
1982	JM Cannon / J Niven	Irvine / Newbury & Crookham	Royal Burgess	143
1983	WD Smith	Prestwick	Glasgow Killermont	145
1984	A Sinclair	Drumpellier	Royal Burgess	148
1985	AN Sturrock	Prestwick	Glasgow Killermont	143
1986	RL Glading	Mitcham	Royal Burgess	153
1987	I Hornsby	Ponteland	Glasgow Killermont	145
1988	J Hayes	Gosforth	Royal Burgess	143

Scottish Youths' Open Amateur Stroke Play Championship
Instituted 1979

Year	Winner	Club	Venue	Score
1979	A Oldcorn	Ratho Park	Dalmahoy	217
1980	G Brand	Knowle	Monifieth and Ashludie	281
1981	S Campbell	Cawder	Cawder and Keir	279
1982	LS Mann	Carnoustie	Leven and Scoonie	270
1983	A Moir	McDonald	Mortonhall	284
1984	B Shields	Bathgate	Eastwood, Renfrew	280
1985	H Kemp	Cawder	East Kilbride	282
1986	A Mednick	Sweden	Cawder	282
1987	K Walker	Royal Burgess	Bogside	291
1988	P McGinley	Grange	Ladybank & Glenrothes	281

Welsh Amateur Championship
Instituted 1895

Year	Winner	Runner-up	Venue	By
1960	HC Squirrell	P Richards	Aberdovey	2 and 1
1961	AD Evans	J Toye	Ashburnham	3 and 2
1962	J Povall	HC Squirrell	Harlech	3 and 2

Welsh Amateur Championship continued

Year	Winner	Runner-up	Venue	By
1963	WI Tucker	J Povall	Southerndown	4 and 3
1964	HC Squirrell	WI Tucker	Harlech	1 hole
1965	HC Squirrell	G Clay	Porthcawl	6 and 4
1966	WI Tucker	EN Davies	Aberdovey	6 and 5
1967	JK Povall	WI Tucker	Asburnham	3 and 2
1968	J Buckley	J Povall	Conway	8 and 7
1969	JL Toye	EN Davies	Porthcawl	1 hole
1970	EN Davies	J Povall	Harlech	1 hole
1971	CT Brown	HC Squirrell	Southerndown	6 and 5
1972	EN Davies	JL Toye	Prestatyn	40th hole
1973	D McLean	T Holder	Ashburnham	6 and 4
1974	S Cox	EN Davies	Caernarvonshire	3 and 2
1975	JL Toye	WI Tucker	Porthcawl	5 and 4
1976	MPD Adams	WI Tucker	Harlech	6 and 5
1977	D Stevens	JKD Povall	Southerndown	3 and 2
1978	D McLean	A Ingram	Caernarvonshire	11 and 10
1979	TJ Melia	MS Roper	Ashburnham	5 and 4
1980	DL Stevens	G Clement	Prestatyn	10 and 9
1981	S Jones	C Davies	Porthcawl	5 and 3
1982	D Wood	C Davies	Harlech	8 and 7
1983	JR Jones	AP Parkin	Southerndown	2 holes
1984	JR Jones	A Llyr	Prestatyn	1 hole
1985	ED Jones	MA Macara	Ashburnham	2 and 1
1986	C Rees	B Knight	Conwy	1 hole
1987	PM Mayo	DK Wood	Porthcawl	2 holes
1988	K Jones	RN Roderick	Harlech	40th hole

Welsh Amateur Stroke Play Championship

Year	Winner	Club	Venue	Score
1967	EN Davies	Llantrisant	Harlech	295
1968	JA Buckley	Rhos-on-Sea	Harlech	294
1969	DL Stevens	Llantrisant	Tenby	288
1970	JK Povall	Whitchurch	Newport	292
1971	EN Davies JL Toye	Llantrisant Radyr } tie	Harlech	296
1972	JR Jones	Wrexham	Pyle and Kenfig	299
1973	JR Jones	Caernarvonshire	Llandudno (Maesdu)	300
1974	JL Toye	Radyr	Tenby	307
1975	D McLean	Holyhead	Wrexham	288
1976	WI Tucker	Monmouthshire	Newport	282
1977	JA Buckley	Abergele and Pensarn	Prestatyn	302
1978	HJ Evans	Llangland Bay	Pyle and Kenfig	300
1979	D McLean	Holyhead	Holyhead	289
1980	TJ Melia	Cardiff	Tenby	291
1981	D Evans	Leek	Wrexham	270
1982	JR Jones	Langland Bay	Cradoc	287
1983	G Davies	Pontypool	Aberdovey	287
1984	N Roderick	Portardawe	Newport	292
1985	MA Macara	Llandudno	Harlech	291
1986	M Calvert	Aberystwyth	Pyle and Kenfig	299
1987	MA Macara	Llandudno	Llandudno (Maesdu)	290
1988	RN Roderick	Portardawe	Tenby	283

Welsh Boys' Championship

Year	Winner	Runner-up	Venue	By
1960	C Gilford	JL Toye	Llandrindod Wells	5 and 4
1961	AR Porter	JL Toye	Llandrindod Wells	3 and 2
1962	RC Waddilove	W Wadrup	Harlech	20th hole
1963	G Matthews	R Witchell	Penarth	6 and 5
1964	D Lloyd	M Walters	Conway	2 and 1
1965	G Matthews	DG Lloyd	Wenvoe Castle	7 and 6
1966	J Buckley	DP Owen	Holyhead	4 and 2
1967	J Buckley	DL Stevens	Glamorganshire	2 and 1
1968	J Buckley	C Brown	Maesdu	1 hole

Welsh Boys' Championship
continued

Year	Winner	Runner-up	Venue	By
1969	K Dabson	P Light	Glamorganshire	5 and 3
1970	P Tadman	A Morgan	Conway	2 and 1
1971	R Jenkins	T Melia	Ashburnham	3 and 2
1972	MG Chugg	RM Jones	Wrexham	3 and 2
1973	R Tate	N Duncan	Penarth	2 and 1
1974	D Williams	S Lewis	Llandudno	5 and 4
1975	G Davies	PG Garrett	Glamorganshire	20th hole
1976	JM Morrow	MG Mouland	Caernarvonshire	1 hole
1977	JM Morrow	MG Mouland	Glamorganshire	2 and 1
1978	JM Morrow	A Laking	Harlech	2 and 1
1979	P Mayo	M Hayward	Penarth	24th hole
1980	A Llyr	DK Wood	Llandudno (Maesdu)	2 and 1
1981	M Evans	P Webborn	Pontypool	5 and 4
1982	CM Rees	KH Williams	Prestatyn	2 holes
1983	MA Macara	RN Roderick	Radyr	1 hole
1984	GA Macara	D Bagg	Llandudno	1 hole
1985	B Macfarlane	R Herbert	Cardiff	1 hole
1986	C O'Carroll	GA Macara	Rhuddlan	1 hole
1987	SJ Edwards	A Herbert	Abergavenny	19th hole
1988	C Platt			

Welsh Professional Championship
Instituted 1904

Year	Winner	Club	Venue	Score
1960	RH Kemp jun	Unattached	Llandudno	288
1961	S Mouland	Glamorganshire	Southerndown	286
1962	S Mouland	Glamorganshire	Porthcawl	302
1963	H Gould	Southerndown	Wrexham	291
1964	B Bielby	Portmadoc	Tenby	297
1965	S Mouland	Glamorganshire	Penarth	281
1966	S Mouland	Glamorganshire	Conway	281
1967	S Mouland	Glamorganshire	Pyle and Kenfig (54 holes, fog)	219
1968	RJ Davies	South Herts	Southerndown	292
1969	S Mouland	Glamorganshire	Llandudno	277
1970	W Evans	Pennard	Tredegar Park	289
1971	J Buckley	North Wales	St Pierre	291
1972	J Buckley	Rhos-on-Sea	Porthcawl	298
1973	A Griffiths	Wrexham	Newport	289
1974	M Hughes	Aberystwyth	Cardiff	284
1975	C DeFoy	Bryn Meadows	Whitchurch	285
1976	S Cox	Wenvoe Castle	Radyr	284
From 1977 sponsored by Rank Xerox				
1977	C DeFoy	Calcot Park	Glamorganshire	135
1978	BCC Huggett	Cambridgeshire Hotel	Whitchurch	145
1979	*Cancelled*			
1980	A Griffiths	Llanymynech	Cardiff	139
1981	C DeFoy	Coombe Hill	Cardiff	139
1982	C DeFoy	Coombe Hill	Cardiff	137
1983	S Cox	Wenvoe Castle	Cardiff	136
1984	K Jones	Caldy	Cardiff	135
1985	D Llewellyn		Whitchurch	132
1986	P Parkin		Whitchurch	142
1987	A Dodman		Cardiff	132
1988				

Welsh Girls' Amateur Championship

Year	Winner	Runner-up	Venue	By
1957	Miss A Coulman	Miss S Wynn-Jones	Newport (Mon)	1 hole
1958	Miss S Wynn-Jones	Miss A Coulman	Conway	3 and 1
1959	Miss C Mason	Miss T Williams	Glamorgan	3 and 2
1960	Miss A Hughes	Miss D Wilson	Llandrindod Wells	6 and 4
1961	Miss Jill Morris	Miss S Kelly	North Wales	3 and 2
1962	Miss Jill Morris	Miss Peta Morgan	Southerndown	4 and 3
1963	Miss A Hughes	Miss A Brown	Conway	8 and 7
1964	Miss A Hughes	Miss M Leigh	Holyhead	5 and 3

Welsh Girls' Amateur Championship
continued

Year	Winner	Runner-up	Venue	By
1965	Miss A Hughes	Miss A Reardon-Hughes	Swansea Bay	19th hole
1966	Miss S Hales	Miss J Rogers	Prestatyn	1 hole
1967	Miss E Wilkie	Miss L Humphreys	Pyle and Kenfig	1 hole
1968	Miss L Morris	Miss J Rogers	Portmadoc	1 hole
1969	Miss L Morris	Miss L Humphreys	Wenvoe Castle	5 and 3
1970	Miss T Perkins	Miss P Light	Rhuddlan	2 and 1
1971	Miss P Light	Miss P Whitley	Glamorganshire	4 and 3
1972	Miss P Whitley	Miss P Light	Llandudno (Maesdu)	2 and 1
1973	Miss V Rawlings	Miss T Perkins	Whitchurch	19th hole
1974	Miss L Isherwood	Miss S Rowlands	Wrexham	4 and 3
1975	Miss L Isherwood	Miss S Rowlands	Swansea Bay	1 hole
1976	Miss K Rawlings	Miss C Parry	Rhuddlan	5 and 4
1977	Miss S Rowlands	Miss D Taylor	Clyne	7 and 5
1978	Miss S Rowlands	Miss G Rees	Abergele	3 and 2
1979	Miss M Rawlings	Miss J Richards	St Mellons	19th hole
1980	Miss K Davies	Miss M Rawlings	Vale of Llangollen	19th hole
1981	Miss M Rawlings	Miss F Connor	Radyr	4 and 3
1982	Miss K Davies	Miss K Beckett	Wrexham	6 and 5
1983	Miss N Wesley	Miss J Foster	Whitchurch	4 and 2
1984	Miss J Foster	Miss J Evans	Pwllheli	6 and 5
1985	Miss J Foster	Miss S Caley	Langland Bay	6 and 5
1986	Miss J Foster	Miss L Dermott	Holyhead	3 and 2
1987	Miss J Lloyd	Miss S Bibbs	Cardiff	2 and 1
1988	Miss L Dermot	Miss A Perriam	Builth Wells	2 holes

Welsh Ladies' Amateur Championship
Instituted 1905

Year	Winner	Runner-up	Venue	By
1960	Miss M Barron	Mrs E Brown	Tenby	8 and 6
1961	Mrs M Oliver	Miss N Sneddon	Aberdovey	5 and 4
1962	Mrs M Oliver	Miss P Roberts	Radyr	4 and 2
1963	Miss P Roberts	Miss N Sneddon	Harlech	7 and 5
1964	Mrs M Oliver	Mrs M Wright	Southerndown	1 hole
1965	Mrs M Wright	Mrs E Brown	Prestatyn	3 and 2
1966	Miss A Hughes	Miss P Roberts	Ashburnham	5 and 4
1967	Mrs M Wright	Miss C Phipps	Harlech	21st hole
1968	Miss S Hales	Mrs M Wright	Porthcawl	3 and 2
1969	Miss P Roberts	Miss A Hughes	Caernarvonshire	3 and 2
1970	Mrs A Briggs	Miss J Morris	Newport	19th hole
1971	Mrs A Briggs	Mrs EN Davies	Harlech	2 and 1
1972	Miss A Hughes	Miss J Rogers	Tenby	3 and 2
1973	Mrs A Briggs	Mrs J John	Holyhead	3 and 2
1974	Mrs A Briggs	Dr H Lyall	Ashburnham	3 and 2
1975	Mrs A Johnson (*née* Hughes)	Miss K Rawlings	Prestatyn	1 hole
1976	Miss T Perkins	Mrs A Johnson	Porthcawl	4 and 2
1977	Miss T Perkins	Miss P Whitley	Aberdovey	5 and 4
1978	Miss P Light	Mrs A Briggs	Newport	2 and 1
1979	Miss V Rawlings	Mrs A Briggs	Caernarvonshire	2 holes
1980	Miss M Rawlings	Mrs A Briggs	Tenby	2 and 1
1981	Miss M Rawlings	Mrs A Briggs	Harlech	5 and 3
1982	Mrs V Thomas (*née* Rawlings)	Miss M Rawlings	Ashburnham	7 and 6
1983	Mrs V Thomas	Mrs T Thomas (*née* Perkins)	Llandudno	1 hole
1984	Miss S Roberts	K Davies	Newport	5 and 4
1985	Mrs V Thomas	S Jump	Prestatyn	1 hole
1986	Mrs V Thomas	L Isherwood	Porthcawl	7 and 6
1987	Mrs V Thomas	Miss S Roberts	Aberdovey	3 and 1
1988	Miss S Roberts			

Welsh Ladies' Open Amateur Stroke Play Championship

Instituted 1976

Year	Winner	Club	Venue	Score
1976	Miss P Light	Whitchurch	Aberdovey	227
1977	Miss J Greenhalgh	Pleasington	Aberdovey	239
1978	Mrs S Hedges	Wrotham Heath	Aberdovey (49 holes, fog)	209
1979	Miss S Crowcroft	Blackwell	Aberdovey	228
1980	Mrs T Thomas (*née* Perkins)	Wenvoe Castle	Aberdovey	223
1981	Mrs V Thomas	Pennard	Aberdovey	224
1982	Mrs V Thomas	Penard	Aberdovey	225
1983	Mrs J Thornhill	Walton Heath	Aberdovey	239
1984	Miss L Davies	West Byfleet	Aberdovey	230
1985	Miss C Swallow		Aberdovey	219
1986	Miss H Wadsworth	Princes	Aberdovey	223
1987	Miss S Shapcott	Knowle	Newport	225
1988	Miss S Shapcott	Knowle	Newport	218

Welsh Seniors' Amateur Championship

Instituted 1975

Year	Winner	Club	Venue	Score
1975	A Marshaman	Brecon		77 (18 holes)
1976	AD Evans	Ross on Wye		156
1977	AE Lockley	Swansea Bay		154
1978	AE Lockley	Swansea Bay		75 (18 holes)
1979	CR Morgan	Monmouthshire		158
1980	ES Mills	Llandudno (Maesdu)		152
1981	T Branton	Newport		153
1982	WI Tucker	Monmouthshire		147
1983	WS Gronow	East Berks		153
1984	WI Tucker			
1985	NA Lycett			
1986	E Mills	Aberdovey		154
1987	WS Gronow	East Berks		146
1988	NA Lycett	Aberdovey	Aberdovey	150

Overseas National Championships

American Amateur Championship

Year	Winner	Runner-up	Venue	By
1946	SE Bishop	S Quick	Baltusrol	37th hole
1947	RH Riegel	J Dawson	Pebble Beach	2 and 1
1948	WP Turnesa	R Billows	Memphis	2 and 1
1949	CR Coe	Rufus King	Rochester	11 and 10
1950	S Urzetta	FR Stranahan	Minneapolis	39th hole
1951	WJ Maxwell	J Cagliardi	Saucon Valley, Pa	4 and 3
1952	J Westland	A Mengert	Seattle	3 and 2
1953	G Littler	D Morey	Oklahoma City	1 hole
1954	A Palmer	R Sweeney	Detroit	1 hole
1955	E Harvie Ward	W Hyndman	Richmond, Va	9 and 8
1956	E Harvie Ward	C Kocsis	Lake Forest, Ill	5 and 4
1957	H Robbins	Dr F Taylor	Brookline	5 and 4
1958	CR Coe	T Aaron	San Francisco	5 and 4
1959	JW Nicklaus	CR Coe	Broadmoor	1 hole
1960	DR Beman	R Gardner	St Louis, Mo	6 and 4
1961	JW Nicklaus	D Wysong	Pebble Beach	8 and 6
1962	LE Harris, jun	D Gray	Pinehurst	1 hole
1963	DR Beman	D Sikes	Des Moines	2 and 1
1964	W Campbell	E Tutweiler	Canterbury, Ohio	1 hole
Changed to stroke play				
1965	R Murphy		Tulsa, Okla	291
1966	G Cowan		Ardmore, Penn	285
1967	R Dickson		Colorado	285
1968	B Fleisher		Volumbus	284
1969	S Melnyk		Oakmont	286
1970	L Wadkins		Portland	280
1971	G Cowan		Wilmington	280
1972	M Giles		Charlotte, NC	285
Reverted to match play				
1973	C Stadler	D Strawn	Inverness, Toledo, Ohio	6 and 5
1974	J Pate	J Grace	Ridgewood, NJ	2 and 1
1975	F Ridley	K Fergus	Richmond, Va	2 holes
1976	B Sander	P Moore	Bel-Air	8 and 6
1977	J Fought	D Fischesser	Aronimonk, Pa	9 and 8
1978	J Cook	S Hoch	Plainfield, NJ	5 and 4
1979	M O'Meara	J Cook	Canterbury, Ohio	8 and 7
1980	H Sutton	B Lewis	North Carolina	9 and 8
1981	N Crosby	B Lyndley	San Francisco	37th hole
1982	J Sigel	D Tolley	The Country Club, Brookline	8 and 7
1983	J Sigel	C Perry	North Shore, Chicago	8 and 7
1984	S Verplank	S Randolph	Oak Tree, Okla	4 and 3
1985	S Randolph	P Persons	Montclair, NJ	1 hole
1986	S Alexander	C Kite	Shoal Creek	5 and 3
1987	W Mayfair	E Rebmann	Jupiter Hills, Fl	4 and 3
1988	E Meeks	D Yates	Hot Springs, VA	7 and 6

American Ladies' Amateur Championship

Instituted 1895

Year	Winner	Runner-up	Venue	By
1946	Mrs G Zaharias	Mrs C Sherman	Southern Hills, Tulsa	11 and 9
1947	Miss L Suggs	Miss D Kirby	Detroit	2 holes
1948	Miss Grace Lenczyk	Miss Helen Sigel	Pebble Beach	4 and 3
1949	Mrs Mark A Porter	Miss D Kielty	Merion	3 and 2
1950	Miss Beverley Hanson	Miss Mae Murray	Atlanta	6 and 4
1951	Miss Dorothy Kirby	Miss Claire Doran	St Paul, Minn	2 and 1
1952	Mrs J Pung	Miss S McFedters	Long Beach, Calif	2 and 1
1953	Miss ML Faulk	Miss P Riley	Rhode Island	3 and 2
1954	Miss B Romack	Miss M Wright	Pittsburgh	4 and 2
1955	Miss Pat Lesser	Miss J Nelson	Charlotte	7 and 6
1956	Miss Marlene Stewart	Miss J Gunderson	Indianapolis	2 and 1
1957	Miss J Gunderson	Mrs AC Johnstone	Del Paso	8 and 6
1958	Miss A Quast	Miss B Romack	Wee Burn, Darien	3 and 2
1959	Miss B McIntyre	Miss J Goodwin	Washington	4 and 3
1960	Miss J Gunderson	Miss J Ashley	Tulsa, Oklahoma	6 and 5
1961	Mrs A Decker	Miss P Preuss	Tacoma	14 and 13
1962	Miss J Gunderson	Miss A Baker	Rochester, NY	9 and 8
1963	Mrs Anne Wells (Quast)	Miss P Conley	Williamstown	2 and 1
1964	Miss B McIntyre	Miss J Gunderson	Prairie Dunes, Kansas	3 and 2
1965	Miss J Ashley	Mrs Anne Wells	Denver	5 and 4
1966	Mrs D Carner (Miss Gunderson)	Mrs JD Streit	Pittsburgh	41st hole
1967	Miss L Dill	Miss J Ashley	Annandale, Pasadena	5 and 4
1968	Mrs JA Carner	Mrs A Wells	Birmingham, Mich	5 and 4
1969	Miss C Lacoste (France)	Miss S Hamlin	Las Colinas, Texas	3 and 2
1970	Miss M Wilkinson	Miss Cynthia Hill	Darien, Conn	3 and 2
1971	Miss L Baugh	Miss B Barry	Atlanta	1 hole
1972	Miss M Budke	Miss Cynthia Hill	St Louis, Mo	5 and 4
1973	Miss C Semple	Mrs A Sander (Welts)	Montclair, NJ	1 hole
1974	Miss Cynthia Hill	Miss C Semple	Broadmoor, Seattle	5 and 4
1975	Miss Beth Daniel	Miss D Horton	Brae Burn, Mass	3 and 2
1976	Miss D Horton	Mrs M Bretton	Del Paso, California	2 and 1
1977	Miss Beth Daniel	Mrs C Sherk	Cincinnati	3 and 1
1978	Mrs C Sherk	Mrs J Oliver	Sunnybrook, Pa	4 and 3
1979	Miss Carolyn Hill	Miss P Sheehan	Memphis	7 and 6
1980	Mrs J Inkster	Miss P Rizzo	Prairie Dunes, Kansas	2 holes
1981	Mrs J Inkster	Mrs L Coggan (Aus)	Portland, Oregon	1 hole
1982	Mrs J Inkster	Miss C Hanton	Colorado Springs	4 and 3
1983	Miss J Pacillo	Miss S Quinlan	Canoe Brook, NJ	2 and 1
1984	Miss D Richard	Miss K Williams	Broadmoor, Seattle	37th hole
1985	Miss M Hattori (Japan)	Miss C Stacy	Pittsburgh, PA	5 and 4
1986	Miss K Cockerill	Miss K McCarthy	Pasatiempo, California	9 and 7
1987	Miss K Cockerill	Miss T Kerdyk	Barrington, RI	3 and 2
1988	Miss P Sinn	Miss K Noble	Minikahde, MN	6 and 5

American Women's Open Championship

(American unless stated)

Year	Winner	Venue	By
1946	Miss P Berg	Spokane	5 and 4

Changed to stroke play

Year	Winner	Venue	Score
1947	Miss B Jamieson	Greensboro	300
1948	Nrs C Zaharias	Atlantic City	300
1949	Miss Louise Suggs	Maryland	291
1950	Mrs G Zaharias	Wichita	291
1951	Miss B Rawls	Atlanta	294
1952	Miss L Suggs	Bala, Philadelphia	284
1953	Miss B Rawls	Rochester, NY	302

(After a tie with Mrs J Pung)

American Women's Open Championship
continued

Year	Winner	Venue	Score
1954	Mrs G Zaharias	Peabody, Mass	291
1955	Miss F Crocker	Wichita	299
1956	Mrs K Cornelius	Duluth	302
(After a tie with Miss B McIntire)			
1957	Miss B Rawls	Mamaroneck	299
1958	Miss M Wright	Bloomfield Hills, Mich	290
1959	Miss M Wright	Pittsburgh, Pa	287
1960	Miss B Rawls	Worchester, Mass	292
1961	Miss M Wright	Springfield, NJ	293
1962	Mrs M Lindstrom	Myrtle Beach	301
1963	Miss M Mills	Kenwood	289
1964	Miss M Wright	San Diego	290
(After a tie with Miss Ruth Jessen, Seattle)			
1965	Miss C Mann	Northfield, NJ	290
1966	Miss S Spuzich	Hazeltine National GC, Minn	297
1967	Miss C Lacoste (France)	Hot Springs, Virginia	294
1968	Mrs SM Berning	Moselem Springs, Pa	289
1969	Miss Donna Caponi	Scenic-Hills	294
1970	Miss Donna Caponi	Muskogee, Oklahoma	287
1971	Mrs J Gunderson-Cartner	Erie, Pennsylvania	288
1972	Mrs SM Berning	Mamaroneck, NY	299
1973	Mrs SM Berning	Rochester, NY	290
1974	Miss S Haynie	La Grange, Illinois	295
1975	Miss S Palmer	Northfield, NJ	295
1976	Mrs J Carner	Springfield, Pa	292
(After a tie with Miss S Palmer)			
1977	Miss H Stacy	Hazeltine, minn	292
1978	Miss H Stacy	Indianapolis	299
1979	Miss J Britz	Brooklawn, Conn	284
1980	Miss A Alcott	Richland, Tenn	280
1981	Miss P Bradley	La Grange, Illinois	279
1982	Mrs J Alex	Del Paso, Sacramento	283
1983	Miss J Stephenson (Aus)	Broken Arrow, Oklahoma	290
1984	Miss H Stacy	Salem, Mass	290
1985	Miss K Baker	Baltusrol, NJ	280
1986	Miss J Geddes	NCR	287
1987	Miss L Davies (GB)	Plainfield	285
(After a tie with Mrs J Carner and Miss A Akamoto (Japan))			
1988			

Argentine Open Championship
Instituted 1905

Year	Winner
1984	V Fernandez
1985	V Fernandez
1986	V Fernandez
1987	M Fernandez
1988	M Fernandez

Argentine Amateur Championship
Instituted 1895

Year	Winner
1984	MA Prado
1985	F Curutchet
1986	D Ventureira
1987	J Rivas
1988	J Nougues Jr

Argentine Ladies' Amateur Championship

Instituted 1904

Year	Winner
1984	Ana Maria Lagrutta
1985	Maria E Noguerol
1986	Maria M Abramoff
1987	Veronica Podrug
1988	Maria E Noguerol

Australian Open Championship

Year	Winner	Score
1984	T Watson (US)	281
1985	G Norman	212
(54 holes only—rain)		
1986	R Davies	278
1987	G Norman	
1988		

Australian Amateur Championship

Year	Winner
1984	B King
1985	S Ruangit
1986	D Ecob
1987	B Johns
1988	

Australian Professional Championship

Year	Winner
1984	G Norman
1985	G Norman
1986	G Norman
1987	R Mackay
1988	

Australian Ladies' Amateur Championshp

Instituted 1894

Year	Winner
1984	Mrs S McCaw
1985	Miss H Greenwood
1986	Mrs E Kennedy
1987	Miss E Cavill
1988	

Austrian Amateur Open Championship

Instituted 1909

Year	Winner
1984	Chin-Han Yu (Taiwan)
1985	Chin-Sheng Hsieh (Taiwan)
1986	D Carrick
1987	Yueh-Shuang Chen (Taiwan)
1988	

Austrian Ladies' Open Championship

Year	Winner
1984	Miss Mei-Chi Cheng (Taiwan)
1985	Frl P Peter
1986	Miss Wen-Lin Li (Taiwan)
1987	Miss Yun-Shin Chen (Taiwan)
1988	

Belgian Open Championship

Instituted 1987

Year	Winner
1987	E Darcy
(three rounds only—rain)	
1988	J-M Olazabal

Belgian Open Amateur Championship

Instituted 1919

Year	Winner
1984	O Buysse
1985	
1986	
1987	
1988	

Belgian Ladies' Open Championship

Year	Winner
1985	L Davies (Eng)
1986	P Grice-Whittaker (Eng)
1987	M-L de Lorenzi Taya (Fra)
1988	K Lunn (Aus)

Canadian Amateur Championship

Year	Winner
1984	W Swartz
1985	B Franklin
1986	B Franklin
1987	B Franklin
1988	

Canadian Ladies' Open Amateur Championship

Instituted 1901

Year	Winner
1984	Miss K Williams (USA)
1985	Miss K Williams (USA)
1986	Miss M O'Connor
1987	Miss T Kerdyk (USA)
1988	

Canadian Open Championship

Instituted 1904

Year	Winner
1984	G Norman
1985	C Strange
1986	B Murphy
1987	C Strange
1988	K Green

Danish Amateur Stroke Play Championship

Instituted 1981

Year	Winner
1984	J Rasmussen
1985	A Sørensen
1986	P Digebjerg
1987	M Brodersen
1988	

Danish Ladies' Open Championship

Year	Winner
1988	F Descampe (Bel)

Danish Ladies' Stroke Play Championship

Instituted 1981

Year	Winner
1984	M Meiland
1985	M Meiland
1986	M Meiland
1987	A Peitersen
1988	

Dutch Open Championship

Instituted 1912

Year	Winner
1984	B Langer
1985	G Marsh
1986	S Ballesteros
1987	G Brand Jr
1988	M Mouland

French Open Amateur Championship

Year	Winner
1984	A Godillot
1985	R Taher (Egy.)
1986	*Not played*
1987	F Lindgren (Swe.)
1988	

French Men's Close Amateur Championship

Year	Winner
1984	Y Youssin
1985	J-F Remesy
1986	J van der Velde
1987	G Brizay
1988	

French Open Championship

Year	Winner	Score
1984	B Langer	270
1985	S Ballesteros	263
1986	S Ballesteros	269
1987	J Rivero	269
1988	N Faldo	274

French Ladies' Open Amateur Championship

Instituted 1909

Year	Winner
1984	Miss LA Chen
1985	Miss M Campomanes (Sp.)
1986	*Not played*
1987	Miss S Louapre
1988	

French Ladies' Close Championship

Instituted 1908

Year	Winner
1984	Mlle C Soules
1985	Mlle V Pammard
1986	Mme L de Lorenzi Taya
1987	Mlle S Louapre
1988	

French Ladies' Open Championship

Year	Winner	Score
1987	Miss L Neumann (Swe)	293
1988	Mme M-Laure de Lorenzi Taya	285

German Open Championship

Year	Winner	Score
1984	W Grady	268
1985	B Langer	183
(54 holes only—rain)		
1986	B Langer	273
1987	M McNulty	259
1988	S Ballesteros	263

German Open Amateur Championship

Instituted 1913

Year	Winner
1984	T Hübner
1985	R Thielemann
1986	*Not played*
1987	N Sallmann
1988	

German Ladies' Open Championship

Year	Winner
1984	B Huke
1985	J Brown
1986	L Neumann
1987	M-L de Lorenzi Taya
1988	L Neumann

German Ladies' Open Amateur Championship

Instituted 1927

Year	Winner
1984	Mrs S Lampert
1985	Mrs M Koch
1986	*Not played*
1987	Miss S Lambert
1988	

German Close Amateur Championship

Instituted 1938

Year	Winner
1984	A Stamm
1985	F Schlig
1986	S Strüver
1987	H-G Reiter
1988	

German Ladies' Close Championship

Instituted 1938

Year	Winner
1984	Mrs M Koch
1985	Mrs R Ruland
1986	Miss I Bockelmann
1987	Mrs P Peter
1988	

German Close Professional Championship

Instituted 1927

Year	Winner
1984	H-J Kupitz
1985	Heinz-P Thül
1986	S Vollrath
1987	Heinz-P Thül
1988	

German Masters Championship

Year	Winner
1987	AWB Lyle (Sco)
1988	J-M Olazabal (Spa)

German Ladies' Close Professional Championship

Year	Winner
1986	S Eckrodt
1987	S Eckrodt
1988	

Hong Kong Open Championship

Instituted 1959

Year	Winner
1984	B Brask
1985	M Aebli
1986	S Kanai
1987	I Woosnam
1988	H Chin-sheng

Iceland Amateur Championship

Year	Winner
1984	S Pétursson
1985	S Pétursson
1986	U Jonsson
1987	U Jonsson
1988	

Iceland Ladies' Championship

Instituted 1967

Year	Winner
1984	A Sverrisdóttir
1985	R Sigurdardóttir
1986	S Saemundsdóttir
1987	Th. Geirsdóttir
1988	

India Open Championship

Year	Winner
1984	R Alarcon
1985	A Grimes
1986	S Saemundsdottir
1987	B Tennyson
1988	L Chien-Soon

India Men's Amateur Championship

Year	Winner
1984	Rishi Narain
1985	Andy Sharma
1986	Rajeer Mehta
1987	Lakshman Singh
1988	

India Ladies' Championship

Year	Winner
1984	Miss Shiraz Saheed
1985	Miss Nonita Lal
1986	Mrs Ranjeet Grewal
1987	Mrs E Cavill
1988	

Italian Open Amateur Championship

Instituted 1906

Year	Winner
1984	M Luzzi
1985	JM Olazabal
1986	A Binaghi
1987	
1988	

Italian Ladies' Open Championship

Year	Winner
1984	Miss R Lautens
1985	Miss R Lautens
1986	Miss S Moorcroft
1987	P Gennaro
1988	

Italian Close Amateur Championship

Instituted 1930

Year	Winner
1984	S Prati
1985	E Nistri
1986	A Binaghi
1987	M Grabau
1988	

Italian Professional Championship

Year	Winner
1984	C Rocca
1985	G Coli
1986	M Mannelli
1987	G Coli
1988	

Italian Open Championship

Year	Winner	Score
1984	AWB Lyle	277
1985	M Pinero	267
1986	D Feherty	270
(After play-off with R Rafferty)		
1987	S Torrance	271
(After play-off with J Rivero)		
1988	G Norman	270

Japan Amateur Championship

Year	Winner
1984	K Nagarta
1985	T Nakagawa
1986	Y Ito
1987	T Suzuki
1988	

Japan Open Championship

Year	Winner
1984	K Uehara
1985	T Nakajima
1986	T Nakajima
1987	I Aoki
1988	M Ozaki

Japan Professional Championship

Year	Winner
1984	T Nakajima
1985	T Ozaki
1986	I Aoki
1987	D Ishii
1988	

Kenya Open Championship

Year	Winner
1984	J Canizares
1985	G Harvey
1986	I Woosnam
1987	C Mason
1988	C Platts

Korea Open Championship

Year	Winner
1984	M Clayton
1985	Chen Tze-Chung
1986	C-T Tsao
1987	
1988	

Malaysian Open Championship

Year	Winner
1984	L Chien-Soon
1985	T Gale
1986	S Ginn
1987	T Gale
1988	T Tyner (USA)

Malaysian Women's Open Championship

Year	Winner
1988	N Neus

New Zealand Amateur Championship

Instituted 1893

Year	Winner
1984	J Wagner (Aus)
1985	G Power (Aus)
1986	P O'Malley (Aus)
1987	O Kenall
1988	B Hughes (Aus)

New Zealand Open Championship

Year	Winner
1984	B Devlin
1985	DA Weibring
1986	C Pavin
1987	R Rafferty
1988	R Rafferty

New Zealand Ladies' Open Championship

Instituted 1893

Year	Winner
1984	
1985	
1986	Miss A Kita
1987	
1988	

Nigerian Open Championship

Year	Winner
1984	E Murray
1985	W Longmuir
1986	G Brand
1987	*not played*
1988	V Singh

Nordic Ladies' Open Amateur Championship

(Previously Scandinavian Ladies' Amateur Open)

Year	Winner
1984	T Pors
1985	M Meiland (Den.)
1986	A. Öquist (Swe.)
1987	H Anderssen (Swe.)
1988	

Nordic Men's Open Amateur Championship

(Previously Scandinavian Men's Amateur Open)

Year	Winner
1984	S Tinning
1985	C Härdin (Swe.)
1986	J Ryström (Swe.)
1987	P Hedblom (Swe.)
1988	

Pakistan Open Championship

Year	Winner
1984	Ghulam Nabi
1985	Gul Muhammad
1986	Muhammad Ali
1987	Taimur Hassan (Am.)
1988	

Pakistan Men's Amateur Championship

Year	Winner
1984	Faisal Qureshi
1985	Taimur Hassan
1986	Taimur Hassan
1987	Taimur Hassan
1988	

Pakistan Ladies' Amateur Championship

Year	Winner
1984	Mrs Yasmin Mubarik
1985	Miss Nuzhat Shahban
1986	Miss Nuzhat Shahban
1987	Miss Nuzhat Shahban
1988	

Portuguese Open Amateur Championship

Year	Winner
1984	A Dantas
1985	M Grabbau (It.)
1986	R Nissen (Den.)
1987	S Struven (Ger.)
1988	

Portuguese Ladies' Open Amateur Championship

Year	Winner
1984	M Campohanes (Sp.)
1985	T Arbitbol (Sp.)
1986	MC Navarizo (Sp.)
1987	MC Navarizo (Sp.)
1988	

Portuguese Close Amateur Championship

Year	Winner
1984	J Santos
1985	C Marta
1986	JS Melo
1987	D Silva
1988	

Portuguese Open Championship

Year	Winner	Score
1984	T Johnstone	274
1985	W Humphreys	279
1986	M McNulty	270
1987	R Lee	
1988	M Harwood	280

Singapore Open Championship

Year	Winner
1984	T Sieckmann
1985	Chen Tze Ming
1986	G Turner
1987	P Fowler
1988	G Bruckner

Singapore Open Amateur Championship

Year	Winner
1984	D Ooi
1985	D Lim
1986	Sukamdi
1987	T Wiranchant
1988	

South African Amateur Championship

Year	Winner
1984	M Wiltshire
1985	N Clarke
1986	E Els
1987	B Fouchee
1988	N Clarke

South African Amateur Stroke Play Championship

Instituted 1969

Year	Winner
1984	D James
1985	D van Staden
1986	C-S Hsieh
1987	B Fouchee
1988	N Clarke

South African Open Championship

Year	Winner	Score
1984	A Johnstone	274
1985	G Levenson	280
1986	D Frost	275
1987	M McNulty	278
1988	W Westner	275

South African Masters

Year	Winner
1984	A Johnstone
1985	
1986	M McNulty
1987	M McNulty
1988	D Frost

South African PGA Championship

Year	Winner
1984	G Levenson
1985	C Williams
1986	
1987	F Allem
1988	D Feherty

South African Ladies' Championship

Year	Winner
1984	Miss S Whitfield
1985	Miss W Warrington
1986	
1987	
1988	

Spanish Open Amateur Championship

Instituted 1911

Year	Winner
1984	JM Olazabal
1985	B Quippe de Llano
1986	A Haglund
1987	M Quirke
1988	

Spanish Amateur Close Championship

Year	Winner
1984	L Garbarda
1985	L Garbarda
1986	BQ de Llano
1987	JM Arruti
1988	

Spanish Open Championship

Instituted 1912

Year	Winner
1984	B Langer
1985	S Ballesteros
1986	H Clark
1987	N Faldo
1988	M James

Spanish Ladies' Open Amateur Championship

Instituted 1911

Year	Winner
1984	Carmen Navarro
1985	Corine Espinasse
1986	R Lautens (Swi).
1987	C Hourihane (Ire.)
1988	

Spanish Ladies' Amateur Close Championship

Year	Winner
1984	Carmen Maestre
1985	Carmen Navarro
1986	Carmen Navarro
1987	Carmen Navarro
1988	

Spanish Ladies' Open

Year	Winner
1986	L Davies (GB)
1987	C Dibnah (Aus)
1988	M-L de Lorenzi Taya

Swedish Close Men's Championship

Instituted 1904 (before 1984: Close Amateur)

Year	Winner
1984	M Lanner
1985	Nillso
1986	M Grankvist
1987	C-M Strömberg
1988	

Swedish Ladies' Close Championship

Instituted 1911

Year	Winner
1984	L Neumann
1985	S Gronberg
1986	H Alfredsson
1987	H Alfredsson
1988	

Swedish Open International Stroke Play Championship

Instituted 1964 (before 1984: Amateur)

Year	Winner
1984	A Forsbrand
1985	Y Nilson
1986	M Lanner
1987	M Pendaries (Fra.)
1988	

Swedish Ladies' International Open Stroke Play Championship

Instituted 1971 (before 1984: Amateur)

Year	Winner
1984	C Montgomery
1985	
1986	P Neilsson
1987	M Hattori (Jap.)
1988	

Swedish Professional Championship

Instituted 1976

Year	Winner
1984	P Brostedt
1985	P-A Brostedt
1986	M Persson
1987	C-M Strömberg
1988	V Singh

Swiss Open Amateur Championship

Instituted 1907

Year	Winner
1984	F Illouz
1985	T Hubner
1986	A Banagni (Italy)
1987	
1988	

Swiss Ladies' Open Amateur Championship

Instituted 1907

Year	Winner
1984	E Girardi
1985	Mrs M Koch (Aus)
1986	Mrs M Koch (Aus)
1987	
1988	

Swiss Ladies' Close Amateur Championship

Year	Winner
1984	Miss R Lautens
1985	Miss E Orley
1986	Miss E Orley
1987	
1988	

Swiss Open Championship

Year	Winner
1984	J Anderson
1985	C Stadler
1986	JM Olazabal
1987	A Forsbrand
1988	C Moody

Swiss Close Amateur Championship

Year	Winner
1984	M Buchter
1985	M Gottstein
1986	M Frank
1987	
1988	

Trinidad and Tobago Open

Instituted 1972

Year	Winner
1984	
1985	J Bennett (GB)
1986	
1987	A Murray (GB)
1988	

Zambian Open Championship

Instituted 1972

Year	Winner
1984	C Mason
1985	I Woosnam
1986	G Cullen
1987	P Carrigill
1988	D Llewellyn

Professional Tournaments

Benson and Hedges International

at Fulford

Year	Winner	Score
1984	S Torrance, Britain	270
1985	S Lyle	274
1986	M James	274
1987	N Ratcliffe	275
1988	P Baker	271

Carrolls Irish Open

Formerly Carrolls International

Year	Winner	Country	Venue	Score
1984	B Langer	Germany	Dublin	267
1985	S Ballesteros	Spain	Dublin	278
1986	S Ballesteros	Spain	Portmarnock	285
1987	B Langer	Germany	Portmarnock	269
1988	I Woosnam	Wales	Portmarnock	278

Dunhill British Masters'

Formerly sponsored by Dunlop, 1946-62 (1963-83: Silk Cut)

Year	Winner	Club/Country	Venue	Score
1946	AD Locke J Adams	South Africa Beaconsfield	Stoneham	286
1947	J Lees	Dore and Totley	Little Aston	296
1948	N Von Nida	Australia	Sunningdale	272
1949	CH Ward	Little Aston	St Andrews	290
1950	DJ Rees	South Herts	Hoylake	281
1951	M Faulkner	Unattached	Wentworth	281
1952	H Weetman	Croham Hurst	Mere	281
1953	H Bradshaw	Portmarnock	Sunningdale	272
1954	AD Locke	South Africa	Prince's, Sandwich	291
1955	H Bradshaw	Portmarnock	Little Aston	277
1956	C O'Connor	Bundoran	Prestwick	276
1957	EC Brown	Buchanan Castle	Hollinwell	275
1958	H Weetman	Selsdon Park	Little Aston	276
1959	C O'Connor	Royal Dublin	Portmarnock	276
1960	J Hitchcock	Ashford Manor	Sunningdale	275
1961	PW Thomson	Australia	Porthcawl	284
1962	DJ Rees	South Herts	Wentworth	278
1963	BJ Hunt	Hartsbourne	Little Aston	282
1964	C Legrange	South Africa	Birkdale	288
1965	BJ Hunt	Hartsbourne	Portmarnock	283
1966	NC Coles	Coombe Hill	Lindrick	278

Dunhill British Masters
continued

Year	Winner	Club/Country	Venue	Score
1967	A Jacklin	Potters Bar	St George's	274
1968	PW Thomson	Australia	Sunningdale	274
1969	C Legrange	South Africa	Little Aston	281
1970	BGC Huggett	Betchworth Park	Lytham, St Annes	293
1971	M Bembridge	Little Aston	St Pierre	273
1972	R Charles	New Zealand	Northumberland	277
1973	A Jacklin	Potters Bar	St Pierre	272
1974	B Gallacher	Wentworth	St Pierre	282
1975	B Gallacher	Wentworth	Ganton	289
1976	B Dassu	Italy	St Pierre	271
1977	GL Hunt	Gloucester Hotel	Lindrick	291
1978	TA Horton	Royal Jersey	St Pierre	279
1979	G Marsh	Australia	Woburn (Dukes Course)	283
1980	B Langer	West Germany	St Pierre	270
1981	G Norman	Australia	Woburn	273
1982	G Norman	Australia	St Pierre	267
1983	I Woosnam	Wales	St Pierre	269
1984	*Not played*			
1985	L Trevino	USA	Woburn	278
1986	S Ballesteros	Spain	Woburn	275
1987	M McNulty	Zimbabwe	Woburn	274
1988	AWB Lyle	Scotland	Woburn	273

English Open
Instituted 1988

Year	Winner	Venue	Score
1988	H Clark	Birkdale	279

Equity & Law Challenge
Instituted 1987
Venue: Royal Mid-Surrey

Year	Winner	Country	Score
1987	B Lane	England	22 points
1988	R Rafferty	England	21 points

Epson Match-Play
Instituted 1986

Year	Winner	Venue
1986	O Sellberg (Sweden) beat H Clark (GB) 3 and 2	St Pierre
1987	M Lanner (Sweden) beat J Hawkes (S Africa) 1 hole	St Pierre
1988	B Langer (W. Ger) beat M McNulty (Zimbabwe) 4 and 3	St Pierre

Bells' Scottish Open
Formerly Glasgow Classic, 1983-85

Year	Winner	Venue	Score
1984	K Brown	Haggs Castle	266
1985	H Clark	Haggs Castle	274
1986	D Feherty	Haggs Castle	270
1987	I Woosnam	Gleneagles	264
1988	B Lane	Gleneagles	271

Jersey Open

at La Moye

Formerly British Airways-Avis Tournament and Billy Butlin Open

Year	Winner	Score
1984	B Gallacher	274
1985	H Clark	279
1986	J Morgan	275
1987	I Woosnam	279
1988	D Smyth	273

Lancôme Trophy

at St Nom de la Breteche

Year	Winner	Score
1984	AWB Lyle (Scot)	278
(After tie with S Ballesteros (Spain))		
1985	N Price (SA)	275
1986	S Ballesteros (Spain)	274
1987	I Woosnam (Wal)	264
1988	S Ballesteros (Spa)	269

Lawrence Batley International

Year	Winner	Country	Venue	Score
1984	J Rivero	Spain	The Belfry	280
1985	G Marsh	Australia	The Belfry	283
1986	I Woosnam	Great Britain	The Belfry	277
1987	M O'Meara	USA	Birkdale	271
1988	discontinued			

Madrid Open Championship

Year	Winner	Venue	Score
1984	H Clark (Eng)	Puerto de Hierro	274
1985	M Pinero (Spain)	Puerto de Hierro	278
1986	H Clark (Eng)	Puerto de Hierro	274
1987	I Woosnam (Wales)	Puerto de Hierro	269
1988	D Cooper (Eng)	Puerto de Hierro	275

Panasonic European Open

at Sunningdale

Year	Winner	Country	Venue	Score
1978	RL Wadkins	USA	Walton Heath	283
1979	AWB Lyle	Scotland	Turnberry	275
1980	T Kite	USA	Walton Heath	284
1981	G Marsh	Australia	Liverpool	275
1982	M Pinero	Spain	Sunningdale	266
1983	I Aoki	Japan	Sunningdale	274
1984	G Brand Jr	Scotland	Sunningdale	270
1985	B Langer	Germany	Sunningdale	269
1986	G Norman	Australia	Sunningdale	269
1987	P Way	England	Walton Heath	279
1988	I Woosnam	Wales	Sunningdale	260

PGA Championship

Formerly PGA Close Championship
1982-83 Sponsored by Sun Alliance
1984-87 by Whyte & McKay
1988 by Volvo

Year	Sponsor	Winner	Club	Venue	Score
1955		K Bousfield	Coombe Hill	Pannal	277
1956		CH Ward	Little Aston	Maesdu	282
1957		Peter Alliss	Parkstone	Maesdu	286
1958		H Bradshaw	Portmarnock	Llandudno	287
1959		DJ Rees	South Herts	Ashburnham	283
1960		AF Stickley	Ealing	Coventry)*63 holes)*	247
1961	Schweppes	BJ Bamford	Wentworth	Mid-Surrey	266
1962	Schweppes	Peter Alliss	Parkstone	Little Aston	287
1963	Schweppes	PJ Butler	Harborne	Birkdale	306
1964	Schweppes	AG Grubb (Asst)	Coombe Hill	Western Gailes	287
1965	Schweppes	Peter Alliss	Parkstone	Prince's	286
1966	Schweppes	GB Wostenholme	St George's Hill	Saunton	278
1967	PGA Vice-Presidents	BCG Huggett	Betchworth Park	Thorndon Park	271
1968	Piccadilly	PM Townsend	Porter's Park	Mid-Surrey	275
1969-71	*Not played*				
1972	Viyella	A Jacklin		Wentworth	279
1973	Viyella	P Oosterhuis		Wentworth	280
1974	Viyella	M Bembridge		Wentworth	278
1975	Penfold	A Palmer	USA	Sandwich	285
1976	Penfold	NC Coles	Great Britain	Sandwich	280
1977	Penfold	M Pinero	Spain	Sandwich	283
1978	Colgate	N Faldo	Great Britain	Birkdale	278
1979	Colgate	V Fernandez	Argentina	St Andrews	288
1980	Sun Alliance	N Faldo	Great Britain	Sandwich	283
1981	Sun Alliance	N Faldo	Great Britain	Ganton	274
1982	Sun Alliance	A Jacklin	Great Britain	Hillside	284
1983	Sun Alliance	S Ballesteros	Spain	Sandwich	278
1984	Whyte & McKay	H Clark	Great Britain	Wentworth	204
(3 rounds only due to weather)					
1985	Whyte & McKay	P Way	Great Britain	Wentworth	282
1986	Whyte & McKay	R Davis	Australia	Wentworth	281
1987	Whyte & McKay	B Langer	Germany	Wentworth	270
1988	Volvo	I Woosnam	Wales	Wentworth	274

Scandinavian Enterprises Open

at Stockholm

Year	Winner	Country	Score
1984	I Woosnam	Wales	280
1985	I Baker-Finch	Australia	274
1986	G Turner	New Zealand	270
1987	G Brand Jr	Britain	277
1988	S Ballesteros	Spain	270

Suntory World Match Play Championship

at Wentworth

Sponsored by Piccadilly until 1976 and by Colgate 1977 and 1978
Sponsored by Suntory

Year	Winner	Runner-up	By
1964	Arnold Palmer	NC Coles	2 and 1
1965	Gary Player	PW Thomson	3 and 2
1966	Gary Player	JW Nicklaus	6 and 4
1967	Arnold Palmer	PW Thomson	1 hole
1968	Gary Player	R Charles	1 hole
1969	R Charles	G Littler	37th hole

Suntory World Match Play Championship
continued

Year	Winner	Runner-up	By
1970	JW Nicklaus	L Trevino	2 and 1
1971	Gary Player	JW Nicklaus	5 and 4
1972	T Weiskopf	L Trevino	4 and 3
1973	Gary Player	G Marsh	40th hole
1974	H Irwin	Gary Player	3 and 1
1975	H Irwin	A Geiberger	4 and 2
1976	D Graham	H Irwin	38th hole
1977	G Marsh	R Floyd	5 and 3
1978	I Aoki	S Owen	3 and 2
1979	W Rogers	I Aoki	1 hole
1980	G Norman	AWB Lyle	1 hole
1981	S Ballesteros	B Crenshaw	1 hole
1982	S Ballesteros	AWB Lyle	37th hole
1983	G Norman	N Faldo	3 and 2
1984	S Ballesteros	B Langer	2 and 1
1985	S Ballesteros	B Langer	6 and 5
1986	G Norman	AWB Lyle	2 and 1
1987	I Woosnam	AWB Lyle	1 hole
1988	AWB Lyle	N Faldo	2 and 1

PGA Close Events

Assistants' Championship

Formerly PGA Under-23 Match Play

Year	Winner	Venue	By
1984	Garry Weir	Coombe Hill	286
1985	Gary Coles	Coombe Hill	284
Sponsored by Peugeot-Talbot			
1986	J Brennand	Sand Moor	280
1987	J Hawksworth	Coombe Hill	282
1988	J Oates	Coventry	284

Club Professionals' Championship

Year	Winner	Club	Venue	Score
1984	D Durnian		Bolton Old Links	278
1985	R Mann	Thorpeness	The Belfry	291
1986	D Huish	North Berwick	Birkdale	278
1987	R Weir		Sandiway	273
1988	R Weir		Harlech	269

Senior Professional Tournament

From 1957 to 1968 sponsored by Teachers; from 1969 to 1974 sponsored by Pringle; from 1975 sponsored by Ben Sayers and Allied Hotels; from 1977 by Cambridgeshire Hotel; from 1983 by Trust House Forte

Year	Winner	Club/Country	Venue	Score
1984	E Jones	Royal Co Down	Stratford-upon-Avon	280
1985	N Coles	Expotel	Pannal, Harrogate	284
1986	N Coles	Expotel	Mere, Cheshire	276
1987	N Coles	Expotel	Turnberry	279
1988	PW Thomson	Australia	North Berwick	287

Professional Internationals

Great Britain *v* USA

Year	Great Britain			USA			Venue
1921	Foursomes	4	10½	Foursomes	1	4½	Gleneagles
(June 6)	Singles	6½		Singles	3½		
1926	Foursomes	5	13½	Foursomes	0	1½	Wentworth
(June 4-5)	Singles	8½		Singles	1½		
1988							

The Ryder Cup

Instituted 1927

Year	Great Britain			USA			Venue
1927	Foursomes	1	2½	Foursomes	3	9½	Worcester, Mass
(June 3-4)	Singles	1½		Singles	6½		
1929	Foursomes	1½	7	Foursomes	2½	5	Moortown
(May 26-27)	Singles	5½		Singles	2½		
1931	Foursomes	1	3	Foursomes	3	9	
(June 26-27)	Singles	2		Singles	6		Columbus, Ohio
1933	Foursomes	2½	6½	Foursomes	1½	5½	
(June 26-27)	Singles	4		Singles	4		Southport and Ainsdale
1935	Foursomes	1	3	Foursomes	3	9	Ridgewood, NJ
(Sept 28-29)	Singles	2		Singles	6		
1937	Foursomes	1½	4	Foursomes	2½	8	
(June 29-30)	Singles	2½		Singles	5½		Southport and Ainsdale
1947	Foursomes	0	1	Foursomes	4	11	Portland, Oregon
(Nov 1-2)	Singles	1		Singles	7		
1949	Foursomes	3	5	Foursomes	1	7	Ganton
(Sept 16-17)	Singles	2		Singles	6		
1951	Foursomes	1	2½	Foursomes	3	9½	Pinehurst, N Carolina
(Nov 2 and 4)	Singles	1½		Singles	6½		
1953	Foursomes	1	5½	Foursomes	3	6½	Wentworth
(Oct 2-3)	Singles	4½		Singles	3½		
1955	Foursomes	1	4	Foursomes	3	8	
(Nov 5-6)	Singles	3		Singles	5		
1957	Foursomes	1	7½	Foursomes	3	4½	Lindrick
(Oct 4-5)	Singles	6½		Singles	1½		
1959	Foursomes	1½	3½	Foursomes	2½	8½	Eldorado, Calif
(Nov 6-7)	Singles	2		Singles	6		
1961	Foursomes	2	8	Foursomes	6	13	Lytham St Annes
(Oct 13-14)	Singles	6		Singles	7		
1963	Foursomes	1		Foursomes	5		
(Oct 11-13)	Four-ball	1	6	Four-ball	5	20	Atlanta, Ga.
	Singles	4		Singles	10		
1965	Foursomes	4		Foursomes	4		
(Oct 7-9)	Four-ball	2	11	Four-ball	4	18	Birkdale
	Singles	5		Singles	10		
1967	Foursomes	2		Foursomes	5		
(Oct 20-22)	Four-ball	0	6	Four-ball	7	21	Houston, Tex.
	Singles	4		Singles	9		
1969	Foursomes	4		Foursomes	3		
(Oct 18-20)	Four-ball	2	13	Four-ball	3	13	Birkdale
	Singles	4		Singles	7		
1971	Foursomes	4		Foursomes	3		
(Sept 16-18)	Four-ball	1	11	Four-ball	6	16	St Louis, Missouri
	Singles	6		Singles	7		

Ryder Cup
continued

Year	Great Britain			USA			Venue
1973	Foursomes	4		Foursomes	3		
(Sept 20-22)	Four-ball	3	10	Four-ball	4	16	Muirfield
	Singles	3		Singles	9		
1975	Foursomes	1		Foursomes	7		
(Sept 19-21)	Four-ball	1	8	Four-ball	4	18	Laurel Valley, Pa.
	Singles	6		Singles	7		
1977	Foursomes	1		Foursomes	3		
(Sept 15-17)	Four-ball	1	7	Four-ball	4	12	Lytham St Annes
	Singles	5		Singles	5		

At Greenbrier, West Virginia, on 14th, 15th and 16th September, 1979

From 1979 players from Europe became available for selection in addition to those from Great Britain and Ireland

First Day–Four-ball

USA	Matches	GB and Europe	Matches
L Wadkins and L Nelson (2 and 1)	1	A Garrido and S Ballesteros	0
L Trevino and F Zoeller (3 and 2)	1	K Brown and M James	0
A Bean and L Elder (2 and 1)	1	P Oosterhuis and N Faldo	0
H Irwin and J Mahaffey	0	B Gallacher and B Barnes (2 and 1)	1
	3		1

Foursomes

USA	Matches	GB and Europe	Matches
H Irwin and T Kite (7 and 6)	1	K Brown and D Smyth	0
F Zoeller and H Green	1	S Ballesteros and A Garrido (3 and 2)	1
L Trevino and G Morgan (halved)	0	A Lyle and A Jacklin (halved)	0
L Wadkins and L Nelson (4 and 3)	1	B Gallacher and B Barnes	0
	2		1

Second Day–Foursomes

USA	Matches	GB and Europe	Matches
L Elder and J Mahaffey	0	A Jacklin and A Lyle (5 and 4)	1
A Bean and T Kite	0	N Faldo and P Oosterhuis (6 and 5)	1
F Zoeller and M Hayes	0	B Gallacher and B Barnes (2 and 1)	1
L Wadkins and L Nelson (3 and 2)	1	S Ballesteros and A Garrido	0
	1		3

Four-Ball

USA	Matches	GB and Europe	Matches
L Wadkins and L Nelson (5 and 4)	1	S Ballesteros and A Garrido	0
H Irwin and T Kite (1 hole)	1	A Jacklin and A Lyle	0
L Trevino and F Zoeller	0	B Gallacher and B Barnes (3 and 2)	1
L Elder and M Hayes	0	N Faldo and P Oosterhuis (1 hole)	1
	2		2

Third Day–Singles

USA	Matches	GB and Europe	Matches
L Wadkins	0	B Gallacher (3 and 2)	1
L Nelson (3 and 2)	1	S Ballesteros	0
T Kite (1 hole)	1	A Jacklin	0
M Hayes (1 hole)	1	A Garrido	0
A Bean (4 and 3)	1	M King	0
J Mahaffey (1 hole)	1	B Barnes	0
L Elder	0	N Faldo (3 and 2)	1
H Irwin (5 and 3)	1	D Smyth	0
H Green (2 holes)	1	P Oosterhuis	0
F Zoeller	0	K Brown (1 hole)	1
L Trevino (2 and 1)	1	A Lyle	0
G Morgan (halved, match not played)	0	M James (halved, match not played, injured)	0
	8		3

Match Aggregate: USA 16; Great Britain and Europe 10; 2 halved.
Non-playing Captains: W Casper, USA; J Jacobs, Great Britain and Europe.

At Walton Heath, 18th, 19th and 20th September, 1981

Ryder Cup
continued

First Day–Foursomes

GB and Europe	Matches	USA	Matches
A Lyle and M James (2 and 1)	1	W Rogers and B Lietzke	0
B Langer and M Pinero	0	L Trevino and L Nelson (1 hole)	1
B Gallacher and D Smyth (3 and 2)	1	H Irwin and R Floyd	0
P Oosterhuis and N Faldo	0	T Watson and J Nicklaus (4 and 2)	1
	2		2

Four-ball

D Smyth and J Canizares (6 and 5)	1	W Rogers and B Leitzke	0
A Lyle and M James (3 and 2)	1	B Crenshaw and J Pate	0
S Torrance and H Clark (halved)	0	T Kite and J Miller (halved)	0
B Gallacher and E Darcy	0	H Irwin and R Floyd (2 and 1)	1
	2		1

Second Day–Foursomes

P Oosterhuis and S Torrance	0	L Trevino and J Pate (2 and 1)	1
A Lyle and M James	0	W Rogers and R Floyd (3 and 2)	1
B Langer and M Pinero	0	J Nicklaus and T Watson (3 and 2)	1
D Smyth and B Gallacher	0	T Kite and L Nelson (3 and 2)	1
	0		4

Four-Ball

N Faldo and S Torrance	0	L Trevino and J Pate (7 and 5)	1
A Lyle and M James	0	L Nelson and T Kite (1 hole)	1
B Langer and M Pinero (2 and 1)	1	R Floyd and H Irwin	0
J Canizares and D Smyth	0	J Nicklaus and T Watson (3 and 2)	1
	1		3

Third Day–Singles

S Torrance	0	L Trevino (5 and 3)	1
A Lyle	0	T Kite (3 and 2)	1
D Smyth	0	B Crenshaw (6 and 4)	1
B Gallacher (halved)	0	W Rogers (halved)	0
M James	0	L Nelson (2 holes)	1
M Pinero (4 and 2)	1	J Pate	0
B Langer (halved)	0	B Leitzke (halved)	0
N Faldo (2 and 1)	1	J Miller	0
H Clark (4 and 3)	1	T Watson	0
J Canizares	0	H Irwin (1 hole)	1
E Darcy	0	J Nicklaus (5 and 3)	1
P Oosterhuis	0	R Floyd (2 holes)	1
	3		7

Match Aggregate: Great Britain and Europe 8; USA 17; 3 halved.

At PGA National, Florida, 14th, 15th and 16th October, 1983

First Day-Foursomes

USA	Matches	GB and Europe	Matches
T Watson and B Crenshaw (4 and 2)	1	B Gallacher and A Lyle	0
L Wadkins and C Stadler	0	N Faldo and B Langer (4 and 2)	1
T Kite and C Peete (2 and 1)	1	S Ballesteros and P Way	0
R Floyd and B Gilder	0	J-M Canizares and S Torrance (4 and 3)	1
	2		2

Ryder Cup

continued

Four-Ball

	Matches		Matches
G Morgan and F Zoeller	0	B Waites and K Brown (2 and 1)	1
T Watson and J Haas (2 and 1)	1	N Faldo and B Langer	0
R Floyd and C Strange	0	S Ballesteros and P Way (1 hole)	1
B Crenshaw and C Peete	0	S Torrance and I Woosnam	0
	1		2

Second Day—Foursomes

R Floyd and T Kite	0	N Faldo and B Langer (3 and 2)	1
J Haas and C Strange (3 and 1)	1	K Brown and B Waites	0
L Wadkins and G Morgan (7 and 5)	1	S Torrance and J-M Canizares	0
B Gilder and T Watson	0	S Ballesteros and P Way (2 and 1)	1
	2		2

Four-Ball

C Stadler and L Wadkins (1 hole)	1	K Brown and B Waites	0
C Peete and B Crenshaw	0	N Faldo and B Langer (2 and 1)	1
G Morgan and J Haas	0	S Ballesteros and P Way	0
T Watson and B Gilder (5 and 4)	1	S Torrance and I Woosnam	0
	2		1

Third Day—Singles

F Zoeller	0	S Ballesteros	0
J Haas	0	N Faldo (2 and 1)	1
G Morgan	0	B Langer (2 holes)	1
B Gilder (2 holes)	1	G Brand	0
B Crenshaw (3 and 1)	1	A Lyle	0
C Peete (1 hole)	1	B Waites	0
C Strange	0	P Way (2 and 1)	1
C Stadler (3 and 2)	1	I Woosnam	0
T Kite	0	S Torrance	0
L Wadkins	0	J-M Canizares	0
R Floyd	0	K Brown (4 and 3)	1
T Watson (2 and 1)	1	B Gallacher	0
	5		4

Match Aggregate USA 12; Great Britain and Europe 11; 5 halved.
Non-playing Captains: J Nicklaus, USA; T Jacklin, Great Britain and Europe.

At The Belfry, Sutton Coldfield, 13th, 14th and 15th September, 1985

First Day-Foursomes

GB and Europe	Matches	USA	Matches
S Ballesteros and M Pinero (2 and 1)	1	C Strange and M O'Meara	0
B Langer and N Faldo	0	C Peete and T Kite (3 and 2)	1
A Lyle and K Brown	0	L Wadkins and R Floyd (4 and 3)	1
H Clark and S Torrance	0	C Stadler and H Sutton (3 and 2)	1
	1		3

Four-ball

P Way and I Woosnam (1 hole)	1	F Zoeller and H Green	0
S Ballesteros and M Pinero (2 and 1)	1	A North and P Jacobsen	0
B Langer and J-M Canizares (halved)	0	C Stadler and H Sutton (halved)	0
S Torrance and H Clark	0	R Floyd and L Wadkins (1 hole)	1
	2		1

Ryder Cup
continued

Second Day—Four-ball

S Torrance and H Clark (2 and 1)	1	T Kite and A North	0
P Way and I Woosnam (4 and 3)	1	H Green and F Zoeller	0
S Ballesteros and M Pinero	0	M O'Meara and L Wadkins (3 and 2)	1
B Langer and A Lyle (halved)	0	C Stadler and C Strange (halved)	0
	2		1

Foursomes

	Matches		Matches
J-M Canizares and J Rivero (7 and 5)	1	T Kite and C Peete	0
S Ballesteros and M Pinero (5 and 4)	1	C Stadler and H Sutton	0
P Way and I Woosnam	0	C Strange and P Jacobsen (4 and 2)	1
B Langer and K Brown (3 and 2)	1	R Floyd and L Wadkins	0
	3		1

Third Day—Singles

M Pinero (3 and 1)	1	L Wadkins	0
I Woosnam	0	C Stadler (2 and 1)	1
P Way (2 holes)	1	R Floyd	0
S Ballesteros (halved)	0	T Kite (halved)	0
A Lyle (3 and 2)	1	P Jacobsen	0
B Langer (5 and 4)	1	H Sutton	0
S Torrance (1 hole)	1	A North	0
H Clark (1 hole)	1	M O'Meara	0
N Faldo	0	H Green (3 and 1)	1
J Rivero	0	C Peete (1 hole)	1
J-M Canizares (2 holes)	1	F Zoeller	0
K Brown	0	C Strange (4 and 2)	1
	7		4

Match Aggregate: Europe 15; USA 10; 3 halved.
Non-playing Captains: T Jacklin, Europe; L Trevino, USA.

At Muirfield Village, Ohio, 25th, 26th and 27th September, 1987

First Day-Foursomes

USA	Matches	GB and Europe	Matches
C Strange and T Kite (4 and 2)	1	S Torrance and H Clark	0
H Sutton and D Pohl (2 and 1)	1	K Brown and B Langer	0
L Wadkins and L Mize	0	N Faldo and I Woosnam (2 up)	1
L Nelson and P Stewart	0	S Ballesteros and J-M Olazabal (1 up)	1
	2		2

Four-ball

B Crenshaw and S Simpson	0	G Brand Jr and J Rivero (3 and 2)	1
A Bean and M Calcavecchia	0	S Lyle and B Langer (1 up)	1
H Sutton and D Pohl	0	N Faldo and I Woosnam (2 and 1)	1
C Strange and T Kite	0	S Ballesteros and J-M Olazabal (2 and 1)	1
	0		4

Second Day—Four-ball

T Kite and C Strange	0	I Woosnam and N Faldo (5 and 4)	1
A Bean and P Stewart (3 and 2)	1	E Darcy and G Brand Jr	0
H Sutton and L Mize (2 and 1)	1	S Ballesteros and J-M Olazabal	0
L Wadkins and L Nelson	0	S Lyle and B Langer (1 up)	1
	2		2

Ryder Cup
continued

Foursomes

	Matches		Matches
C Strange and T Kite (3 and 1)	1	J Rivero and G Brand Jr	0
H Sutton and L Mize (halved)	0	N Faldo and I Woosnam	0
L Wadkins and L Nelson	0	S Lyle and B Langer (2 and 1)	1
B Crenshaw and P Stewart	0	S Ballesteros and J-M Olazabal	1
	1		2

Third Day—Singles

A Bean (1 up)	1	I Woosnam	0
D Pohl	0	H Clark (1 up)	1
L Mize (halved)	0	S Torrance	0
M Calcavecchia (1 up)	1	N Faldo	0
P Stewart (2 up)	1	J-M Olazabal	0
S Simpson (2 and 1)	1	J Rivero	0
T Kite (3 and 2)	1	S Lyle	0
B Crenshaw	0	E Darcy (1 up)	1
L Nelson (halved)	0	B Langer	0
C Strange	0	S Ballesteros (2 and 1)	1
L Wadkins (3 and 2)	1	K Brown	0
H Sutton (halved)	0	G Brand Jr	0
	6		3

Match Aggregate: USA 11; Europe 13; 4 halved.
Non-playing Captains: J Nicklaus, USA; T Jacklin, Europe.

Individual Records

(Matches were contested as Great Britain v USA from 1927-71; as Great Britain and Ireland from 1973-7; and as Europe v USA from 1979.)

Europe

Name	Year	Played	Won	Lost	Halved
Jimmy Adams	*1939-47-49-51-53	7	2	5	0
Percy Alliss	1929-31-33-35-37	6	3	2	1
Peter Alliss	1953-57-59-61-63-65-67-69	30	10	15	5
Laurie Ayton	1949	0	0	0	0
Severiano Ballesteros	1979-83-85-87	20	10	7	3
Harry Bannerman	1971	5	2	2	1
Brian Barnes	1969-71-73-75-77-79	26	11	14	1
Maurice Bembridge	1969-71-73-75	16	5	8	3
Aubrey Boomer	1927-29	4	2	2	0
Ken Bousfield	1949-51-55-57-59-61	10	5	5	0
Hugh Boyle	1967	3	0	3	0
Harry Bradshaw	1953-55-57	5	2	2	1
Gordon J Brand	1983	1	0	1	0
Gordon Brand Jr	1987	4	1	2	1
Eric Brown	1953-55-57-59	8	4	4	0
Ken Brown	1977-79-83-85-87	13	4	9	0
Stewart Burns	1929	0	0	0	0
Dick Burton	1935-37-*39-49	5	2	3	0
Jack Busson	1935	2	0	2	0
Peter Butler	1965-69-71-73	14	3	9	2
Jose-Maria Canizares	1981-83-85	9	4	3	2
Alex Caygill	1969	1	0	0	1
Clive Clark	1973	1	0	1	0
Howard Clark	1977-81-85-87	9	4	4	1
Neil Coles	1961-63-65-67-69-71-73-77	40	12	21	7
Archie Compston	1927-29-31	6	1	4	1
Henry Cotton	1929-37-*39-47	6	2	4	0
Bill Cox	1935-37	3	0	2	1
Allan Dailey	1933	0	0	0	0
Fred Daly	1947-49-51-53	8	3	4	1
Eamonn Darcy	1975-77-81-87	11	1	8	2
William Davies	1931-33	4	2	2	0
Peter Dawson	1977	3	1	2	0
Norman Drew	1959	1	0	0	1
George Duncan	1927-29-31	5	2	3	0
Syd Easterbrook	1931-33	3	2	1	0
Nick Faldo	1977-79-81-83-85-87	22	14	7	1
John Fallon	1955	1	1	0	0
Max Faulkner	1947-49-51-53-57	8	1	7	0
George Gadd	1927	0	0	0	0
Bernard Gallacher	1969-71-73-75-77-79-81-83	31	13	13	5
John Garner	1971-73	1	0	1	0

Ryder Cup
continued

Name	Year	Played	Won	Lost	Halved
Antonio Garrido	1979	5	1	4	0
Eric Green	1947	0	0	0	0
Malcolm Gregson	1967	4	0	4	0
Tom Haliburton	1961-63	6	0	6	0
Jack Hargreaves	1951	0	0	0	0
Arthur Havers	1927-31-33	6	3	3	0
Jimmy Hitchcock	1965	3	0	3	0
Bert Hodson	1931	1	0	1	0
Reg Horne	1947	0	0	0	0
Tommy Horton	1975-77	8	1	6	1
Brian Huggett	1963-67-69-71-73-75	24	8	10	6
Bernard Hunt	1953-57-59-61-63-65-67-69	28	6	16	6
Geoffrey Hunt	1963	3	0	3	0
Guy Hunt	1975	3	0	2	1
Tony Jacklin	1967-69-71-73-75-77-79	35	13	14	8
John Jacobs	1955	2	2	0	0
Mark James	1977-79-81	10	2	7	1
Edward Jarman	1935	1	0	1	0
Herbert Jolly	1927	2	0	2	0
Michael King	1979	1	0	1	0
Sam King	1937-*39-47-49	5	1	3	1
Arthur Lacey	1933-37	3	0	3	0
Bernhard Langer	1981-83-85-87	19	10	5	4
Arthur Lees	1947-49-51-55	8	4	4	0
Sandy Lyle	1979-81-83-85-87	18	7	9	2
Jimmy Martin	1965	1	0	1	0
Peter Mills	1957	1	1	0	0
Abe Mitchell	1929-31-33	6	4	2	0
Ralph Moffitt	1961	1	0	1	0
Christy O'Connor, Jr	1975	2	0	2	0
Christy O'Connor, Sr	1955-57-59-61-63-65-67-69-71-73	35	11	20	4
Jose-Maria Olazabal	1987	5	3	2	0
John O'Leary	1975	4	0	4	0
Peter Oosterhuis	1971-73-75-77-79-81	28	14	11	3
Alf Padgham	1933-35-37-*39	6	0	6	0
John Panton	1951-53-61	5	0	5	0
Alf Perry	1933-35-37	4	0	3	1
Manuel Pinero	1981-85	9	6	3	0
Lionel Platts	1965	5	1	2	2
Eddie Polland	1973	2	0	2	0
Ted Ray	1927	2	0	2	0
Dai Rees	1937-*39-47-49-51-53-55-57-59-61	18	7	10	1
Jose Rivero	1985-87	5	2	3	0
Fred Robson	1927-29-31	6	2	4	0
Syd Scott	1955	2	0	2	0
Des Smyth	1979-81	7	2	5	0
Dave Thomas	1959-63-65-67	18	3	10	5
Sam Torrance	1981-83-85-87	15	3	8	4
Peter Townsend	1969-71	11	3	8	0
Brian Waites	1983	4	1	3	0
Charlie Ward	1947-49-51	6	1	5	0
Paul Way	1983-85	9	6	2	1
Harry Weetman	1951-53-55-57-59-61-63	15	2	11	2
Charles Whitcombe	1927-29-31-33-35-37-*39	9	3	2	4
Ernest Whitcombe	1929-31-35	6	1	4	1
Reg Whitcombe	1935-*39	1	0	1	0
George Will	1963-65-67	15	2	11	2
Norman Wood	1975	3	1	2	0
Ian Woosnam	1983-85-87	12	5	5	2

(Great Britain named eight members of their 1939 side, but the match was not played because of the Second World War.)

United States of America

Name	Year	Played	Won	Lost	Halved
Tommy Aaron	1969-73	6	1	4	1
Skip Alexander	1949-51	2	1	1	0
Jerry Barber	1955-61	5	1	4	0
Miller Barber	1969-71	7	1	4	2
Herman Barron	1947	1	1	0	0
Andy Bean	1979-87	6	4	2	0
Frank Beard	1969-71	8	2	3	3
Homero Blancas	1973	4	2	1	1
Tommy Bolt	1955-57	4	3	1	0
Julius Boros	1959-63-65-67	16	9	3	4
Gay Brewer	1967-73	9	5	3	1
Billy Burke	1931-33	3	3	0	0
Jack Burke	1951-53-55-57-59	8	7	1	0
Walter Burkemo	1953	1	0	1	0
Mark Calcavecchia	1987	2	1	1	0
Billy Casper	1961-63-65-67-69-71-73-75	37	20	10	7

Ryder Cup
continued

Name	Year	Played	Won	Lost	Halved
Bill Collins	1961	3	1	2	0
Charles Coody	1971	3	0	2	1
Wilfred Cox	1931	2	2	0	0
Ben Crenshaw	1981-83-87	9	3	5	1
Jimmy Demaret	**1941-47-49-51	6	6	0	0
Gardner Dickinson	1967-71	10	9	1	0
Leo Diegel	1927-29-31-33	6	3	3	0
Dale Douglas	1969	2	0	2	0
Dave Douglas	1953	2	1	0	1
Ed Dudley	1929-33-37	4	3	1	0
Olin Dutra	1933-35	4	1	3	0
Lee Elder	1979	4	1	3	0
Al Espinosa	1927-29-31	4	2	1	1
Johnny Farrell	1927-29-31	6	3	2	1
Dow Finsterwald	1957-59-61-63	13	9	3	1
Ray Floyd	1969-75-77-81-83-85	23	7	13	3
Doug Ford	1955-57-59-61	9	4	4	1
Ed Furgol	1957	1	0	1	0
Marty Furgol	1955	1	0	1	0
Al Geiberger	1967-75	9	5	1	3
Vic Ghezzi	*1939-**41	0	0	0	0
Bob Gilder	1983	4	2	2	0
Bob Goalby	1963	5	3	1	1
Johnny Golden	1927-29	3	3	0	0
Lou Graham	1973-75-77	9	5	3	1
Hubert Green	1977-79-85	7	4	3	0
Ralph Guldahl	1937-*39	2	2	0	0
Fred Haas, Jr	1953	1	0	1	0
Jay Haas	1983	4	2	1	1
Walter Hagen	1927-29-31-33-35	9	7	1	1
Bob Hamilton	1949	2	0	2	0
Chick Harbert	1949-55	2	2	0	0
Chandler Harper	1955	1	0	1	0
Dutch (EJ) Harrison	1947-49-51	3	2	1	0
Fred Hawkins	1957	2	1	1	0
Mark Hayes	1979	3	1	2	0
Clayton Heafner	1949-51	4	3	0	1
Jay Hebert	1959-61	4	2	1	1
Lionel Hebert	1957	1	0	1	0
Dave Hill	1969-73-77	9	6	3	0
Jimmy Hines	*1939	0	0	0	0
Ben Hogan	**1941-47-51	3	3	0	0
Hale Irwin	1975-77-79-81	16	11	4	1
Tommy Jacobs	1965	4	3	1	0
Peter Jacobsen	1985	3	1	2	0
Don January	1965-77	7	2	3	2
Herman Keiser	1947	1	0	1	0
Tom Kite	1979-81-83-85-87	20	11	6	3
Ted Kroll	1953-55-57	4	3	1	0
Ky Laffoon	1935	1	0	1	0
Tony Lema	1963-65	11	8	1	2
Bruce Lietzke	1981	3	0	2	1
Gene Littler	1961-63-65-67-69-71-75	27	14	5	8
John Mahaffey	1979	3	1	2	0
Harold McSpaden	*1939-**41	0	0	0	0
Jerry McGee	1977	2	1	1	0
Tony Manero	1937	2	1	1	0
Lloyd Mangrum	**1941-47-49-51-53	8	6	2	0
Dave Marr	1965	6	4	2	0
Billy Maxwell	1963	4	4	0	0
Dick Mayer	1957	2	1	0	1
Bill Mehlhorn	1927	2	1	1	0
Dick Metz	*1939	0	0	0	0
Cary Middlecoff	1953-55-59	6	2	3	1
Johnny Miller	1975-81	6	2	2	2
Larry Mize	1987	4	1	1	2
Gil Morgan	1979-83	6	1	2	3
Bob Murphy	1975	4	2	1	1
Byron Nelson	1937-*39-**41-47	4	3	1	0
Larry Nelson	1979-81-87	13	9	3	1
Bobby Nichols	1967	5	4	0	1
Jack Nicklaus	1969-71-73-75-77-81	28	17	8	3
Andy North	1985	3	0	3	0
Ed Oliver	1947-51-53	5	3	2	0
Mark O'Meara	1985	3	1	2	0
Arnold Palmer	1961-63-65-67-71-73	32	22	8	2
Johnny Palmer	1949	2	0	2	0
Sam Parks	1935	1	0	0	1
Jerry Pate	1981	4	2	2	0
Calvin Peete	1983-85	7	4	2	1
Henry Picard	1935-37-*39	4	3	1	0
Dan Pohl	1987	3	1	2	0

Ryder Cup
continued

Name	Year	Played	Won	Lost	Halved
Johnny Pott	1963-65-67	7	5	2	0
Dave Ragan	1963	4	2	1	1
Henry Ransom	1951	1	0	1	0
Johnny Revolta	1935-37	3	2	1	0
Chi Chi Rodriguez	1973	2	0	1	1
Bill Rogers	1981	4	1	2	1
Bob Rosburg	1959	2	2	0	0
Mason Rudolph	1971	3	1	1	1
Paul Runyan	1933-35-*39	4	2	2	0
Doug Sanders	1967	5	2	3	0
Gene Sarazen	1927-29-31-33-35-37-**41	12	7	2	3
Densmore Shute	1931-33-37	6	2	2	2
Dan Sikes	1969	3	2	1	0
Scott Simpson	1987	2	1	1	0
Horton Smith	1929-31-33-35-37-*39-**41	4	3	0	1
JC Snead	1971-73-75	11	9	2	0
Sam Snead	1937-*39-**41-47-49-51-53-55-59	13	10	2	1
Ed Sneed	1977	2	1	0	1
Mike Souchak	1959-61	6	5	1	0
Craig Stadler	1983-85	8	4	2	2
Payne Stewart	1987	4	2	2	0
Ken Still	1969	3	1	2	0
Dave Stockton	1971-77	5	3	1	1
Curtis Strange	1983-85-87	12	5	6	1
Hal Sutton	1985-87	9	3	3	3
Lee Trevino	1969-71-73-75-79-81	30	17	7	6
Jim Turnesa	1953	1	1	0	0
Joe Turnesa	1927-29	4	1	2	1
Ken Venturi	1965	4	1	3	0
Lanny Wadkins	1977-79-83-85-87	21	13	7	1
Art Wall, Jnr	1957-59-61	6	4	2	0
Al Watrous	1927-29	3	2	1	0
Tom Watson	1977-81-83	12	9	3	0
Tom Weiskopf	1973-75	10	7	2	1
Craig Wood	1931-33-35-**41	4	1	3	0
Lew Worsham	1947	2	2	0	0
Fuzzy Zoeller	1979-83-85	10	1	8	1

(US teams were selected in 1939 (*) and 1941 (**), but the matches were not played because of the Second World War.)

Kirin Cup
Formerly Nissan Cup

Year	Winner	Venue	Result
1985	USPGA	Kapalua, Hawaii	10-2
1986	Japan PGA	Yomiuri, Tokyo	7-5
1987	USPGA	Yomiuri, Tokyo	10-2
1988	USPGA	Kapalua, Hawaii	8-4

World Cup of Golf
Until 1966, called Canada Cup

Year	Winner	Runners-up	Venue	Score
1984	Spain (J-M Canizares and J Rivero)	Scotland (S Torrance and G Brand Jun)	Olgiata, Rome	414
(Individual: J-M Canizares, Spain, 205. Played over 54 holes due to storm)				
1985	Canada (D Halidorson and D Barr)	England (H Clark and P Way)	La Quinta, Calif., USA	559
(Individual: H Clark, England, 272)				
1986	Not played		Kapalua, Hawaii	
1987	Wales (I Woosnam and D Llewelyn)	Scotland (S Torrance and A Lyle)	Kapalua, Hawaii	574
(Wales won play-off)				
(Individual: I Woosnam, Wales, 274)				
1988	USA (B Crenshaw and M McCumber)	Japan (T Ozaki and M Ozaki	Royal Melbourne, Australia	560

PGA Cup

Instituted 1973

Year	Winner	Venue	Result
From 1983 sponsored by Bells' Scotch Whisky			
1984	GB & I	Turnberry	12½-8½
To be played alternate years			
1986	USA	Knollwood	16-9
1988	USA	The Belfry	15½-10½

Amateur International Tournament and Matches

United States *v* Great Britain (Walker Cup Matches)

Unofficial

Year	Great Britain			USA			Venue
1921 (May 21)	Foursomes Singles	0 3	3	Foursomes Singles	4 5	9	Hoylake

The Walker Cup

Instituted 1922

Year	Great Britain			USA			Venue
1922 (August 29)	Foursomes Singles	1 3	4	Foursomes Singles	3 5	8	Long Island, NY
1923 (May 18-19)	Foursomes Singles	3 2½	5½	Foursomes Singles	1 5½	6½	St Andrews
1924 (Sept 12-13)	Foursomes Singles	1 2	3	Foursomes Singles	3 6	9	Garden City, NY
1926 (June 2-3)	Foursomes Singles	1 4½	5½	Foursomes Singles	3 3½	6½	St Andrews
1928 (Aug 30-31)	Foursomes Singles	0 1	1	Foursomes Singles	4 7	11	Chicago
1930 (May 15-16)	Foursomes Singles	1 1	2	Foursomes Singles	3 7	10	Sandwich
1932 (Sept 1-2)	Foursomes Singles	0 2½	2½	Foursomes Singles	4 5½	9½	Brookline, Mass
1934 (May 11-12)	Foursomes Singles	1 1½	2½	Foursomes Singles	3 6½	9½	St Andrews
1936 (Sept 2-3)	Foursomes Singles	1 0½	1½	Foursomes Singles	3 7½	10½	Pine Valley, NJ
1938 (June 3-4)	Foursomes Singles	2½ 5	7½	Foursomes Singles	1½ 3	4½	St Andrews
1947 (May 16-17)	Foursomes Singles	2 2	4	Foursomes Singles	2 6	8	St Andrews
1949 (Aug 19-20)	Foursomes Singles	1 1	2	Foursomes Singles	3 7	10	Winged Foot, NY
1951 (May 11-12)	Foursomes Singles	1 3½	4½	Foursomes Singles	3 4½	7½	Royal Birkdale
1953 (Sept 4-5)	Foursomes Singles	1 2	3	Foursomes Singles	3 6	9	Kittansett, Mass
1955 (May 20-21)	Foursomes Singles	0 2	2	Foursomes Singles	4 6	10	St Andrews
1957 (Sept 1-2)	Foursomes Singles	1½ 2	3½	Foursomes Singles	2½ 6	8½	Minikahda
1959 (May 15-16)	Foursomes Singles	0 3	3	Foursomes Singles	4 5	9	Muirfield
1961 (Sept 1-2)	Foursomes Singles	0 1	1	Foursomes Singles	4 7	11	Seattle, Wash.
From 1963 Foursomes and Singles matches were played on both days, each match over 18 holes.							
1963 (May 24-25)	Foursomes Singles	1 7	8	Foursomes Singles	6 6	12	Turnberry
1965 (Sept 3-4)	Foursomes Singles	4 7	11	Foursomes Singles	3 8	11	Baltimore, M'land

Walker Cup
continued

Year	Great Britain			USA			Venue
1967 (May 15-20)	Foursomes	3	7	Foursomes	4	13	Sandwich
	Singles	4		Singles	9		
1969 (Aug 22-23)	Foursomes	3	8	Foursomes	3	10	Milwaukee, Wisc.
	Singles	5		Singles	7		
1971 (May 26-27)	Foursomes	5½	13	Foursomes	2½	11	St Andrews
	Singles	7½		Singles	8½		
1973 (Aug 24-25)	Foursomes	1	10	Foursomes	7	14	Brookline, Mass.
	Singles	9		Singles	7		
1975 (May 28-29)	Foursomes	3	8½	Foursomes	5	15½	St Andrews
	Singles	5½		Singles	10½		
1977 (Aug 26-27)	Foursomes	3	8	Foursomes	5	16	Shinnecock Hills, NY
	Singles	5		Singles	11		

At Muirfield, 30th and 31st May, 1979

First Day—Foursomes

Great Britain	Matches	USA	Matches
P McEvoy and B Marchbank	0	S Hoch and J Sigel (1 hole)	1
G Godwin and IC Hutcheon (2 holes)	1	M West and H Sutton	0
G Brand and MJ Kelley	0	D Fischesser and J Holtgrieve (1 hole)	1
A Brodie and I Carslaw (2 and 1)	1	C Moody and M Gove	0
	2		2

Singles

Great Britain	Matches	USA	Matches
P McEvoy (halved)	½	J Sigel (halved	½
JC Davies	0	D Clark (8 and 7)	1
IC Hutcheon	0	J Holtgrieve (6 and 4)	1
J Buckley	0	S Hoch (9 and 7)	1
B Marchbank (1 hole)	1	M Peck	0
G Godwin (3 and 2)	1	G Moody	0
MJ Kelley (3 and 2)	1	D Fischesser	0
A Brodie	0	M Gove (3 and 2)	1
	3½		4½

First day's aggregate: Great Britain, 5½; USA, 6½.

Second Day—Foursomes

Great Britain	Matches	USA	Matches
G Godwin and G Brand	0	S Hoch and J Sigel (4 and 3)	1
P McEvoy and B Marchbank (2 and 1)	1	D Fischesser and J Holtgrieve	0
MJ Kelley and IC Hutcheon (halved)	½	M West and H Sutton (halved)	½
J Carslaw and A Brodie (halved)	½	D Clarke and M Peck (halved)	½
	2		2

Singles

Great Britain	Matches	USA	Matches
P McEvoy	0	S Hoch (3 and 1)	1
G Brand	0	D Clarke (2 and 1)	1
G Godwin	0	M Gove (3 and 2)	1
IC Hutcheon	0	M Peck (2 and 1)	1
A Brodie (3 and 2)	1	M West	0
MJ Kelley	0	G Moody (3 and 2)	1
B Marchbank	0	H Sutton (3 and 1)	1
I Carslaw	0	J Sigel (2 and 1)	1
	1		7

Second day's aggregate: Great Britain, 3; USA, 9.
Grand Match aggregate: Great Britain, 8½; USA 15½.

Walker Cup
continued

At Cypress Point, 28th and 29th August, 1981

First Day—Foursomes

USA	Matches	Great Britain and Ireland	Matches
H Sutton and J Sigel	0	P Walton and R Rafferty (4 and 2)	1
J Holtgrieve and F Fuhrer (1hole)	1	R Chapman and P McEvoy	0
B Lewis and D von Tacky (2 and 1)	1	P Deeble and T Hutcheon	0
R Commans and C Pavin (5 and 4)	1	D Evans and P Way	0
	3		1

Singles

USA	Matches	Great Britain and Ireland	Matches
H Sutton (3 and 1)	1	R Rafferty	0
J Rassett (1 hole)	1	C Dalgleish	0
R Commans	0	P Walton (1 hole)	1
B Lewis	0	R Chapman (2 and 1)	1
C Pavin (4 and 3)	1	T Hutcheon	0
J Mudd (1 hole)	1	J Godwin	0
D von Tacky	0	P Way (3 and 1)	1
J Sigel (4 and 2)	1	P McEvoy	0
	5		3

First-days' aggregate: USA, 8; Great Britain and Ireland, 4.

Second Day—Foursomes

USA	Matches	Great Britain and Ireland	Matches
H Sutton and J Sigel	0	R Chapman and P Way (1 hole)	1
J Holtgrieve and F Fuhrer	0	P Walton and R Rafferty (6 and 4)	1
B Lewis and D von Tacky	0	D Evans and C Dalgleish (3 and 2)	1
J Rassett and J Mudd (5 and 4)	1	T Hutcheon and J Godwin	0
	1		3

Singles

USA	Matches	Great Britain and Ireland	Matches
H Sutton	0	R Chapman (1 hole)	1
J Holtgrieve (2 and 1)	1	R Rafferty	0
F Fuhrer (4 and 2)	1	P Walton	0
J Sigel (6 and 5)	1	P Way	0
J Mudd (7 and 5)	1	C Dalgleish	0
R Commans (halved)	½	J Godwin (halved)	½
J Rassett (4 and 3)	1	P Deeble	0
C Pavin (halved)	½	D Evans (halved)	½
	6		2

Second-days' aggregate: USA, 7; Great Britain and Ireland, 5.
Grand Match aggregate: USA, 15; Great Britain and Ireland, 9.

At Hoylake, 25th and 26th May, 1983

First Day—Foursomes

Great Britain and Ireland	Matches	USA	Matches
M Lewis and M Thompson	0	B Lewis and J Holtgrieve (7 and 6)	1
G Macgregor and P Walton (3 and 1)	1	J Sigel and R Fehr	0
L Mann and A Oldcorn (5 and 4)	1	W Hoffer and D Tentis	0
S Keppler and A Pierse	0	W Wood and B Faxon (3 and 1)	1
	2		2

Walker Cup
continued

Singles

Great Britain and Ireland	Matches	USA	Matches
P Parkin (6 and 4)	1	N Crosby	0
L Mann	0	J Holtgrieve (6 and 5)	1
A Oldcorn (4 and 3)	1	B Tuten	0
P Walton (1 hole)	1	J Sigel	0
S Keppler	0	R Fehr (1 hole)	1
D Carrick	0	B Faxon (3 and 1)	1
G Macgregor (halved)	½	W Wood (halved)	½
A Pierse	0	B Lewis (3 and 1)	1
	3½		4½

First day's aggregate: Great Britain and Ireland, 5½; USA, 6½.

Second Day—Foursomes

Great Britain and Ireland	Matches	USA	Matches
G Macgregor and P Walton	0	N Crosby and W Hoffer (2 holes)	1
P Parkin and M Thompson (1 hole)	1	B Faxon and W Wood	0
L Mann and A Oldcorn (1 hole)	1	B Lewis and J Holtgrieve	0
S Keppler and A Pierse (halved)	½	J Sigel and R Fehr	½
	2½		1½

Singles

Great Britain and Ireland	Matches	USA	Matches
P Walton (2 and 1)	1	W Wood	0
P Parkin	0	B Faxon (3 and 2)	1
G Macgregor	0	R Fehr (2 and 1)	1
M Thompson	0	B Tuten (3 and 2)	1
L Mann (halved)	½	D Tentis (halved)	½
S Keppler	0	B Lewis (6 and 5)	1
A Oldcorn (3 and 2)	1	J Holtgrieve	0
D Carrick	0	J Sigel (3 and 1)	1
	2½		5½

Second day's aggregate: Great Britain and Ireland, 5; USA, 7.
Grand Match aggregate: Great Britain and Ireland, 10½; USA 13½.

At Pine Valley, New Jersey, 21st and 22nd August, 1985

First Day—Foursomes

Great Britain and Ireland	Matches	USA	Matches
C Montgomerie and G Macgregor	0	S Verplank and J Sigel (1 hole)	1
J Hawksworth and G McGimpsey (4 and 3)	1	D Waldorf and S Randolph	0
P Baker and P McEvoy (6 and 5)	1	R Sonnier and J Haas	0
C Bloice and S Stephen	½	M Podolak and D Love	½
	2½		1½

Walker Cup
continued

Singles

Great Britain and Ireland	Matches	USA	Matches
G McGimpsey	0	S Verplank (2 and 1)	1
P Mayo	0	S Randolph (5 and 4)	1
J Hawksworth	½	R Sonnier	½
C Montgomerie	0	J Sigel (5 and 4)	1
P McEvoy (2 and 1)	1	B Lewis	0
G Macgregor (2 holes)	1	C Burroughs	0
D Gilford	0	D Waldorf (4 and 2)	1
S Stephen (2 and 1)	1	J Haas	0
	3½		4½

First-days' aggregate: Great Britain and Ireland, 6; USA, 6.

Second Day—Foursomes

Great Britain and Ireland	Matches	USA	Matches
P Mayo and C Montgomerie	½	S Verplank and J Sigel	½
J Hawksworth and G McGimpsey	0	S Randolph and J Hass (3 and 2)	1
P Baker and P McEvoy	0	B Lewis and C Burroughs (2 and 1)	1
C Bloice and S Stephen	0	M Podolak and D Love (3 and 2)	1
	½		3½

Singles

Great Britain and Ireland	Matches	USA	Matches
G McGimpsey	½	S Randolph	½
C Montgomerie	0	S Verplank (1 hole)	1
J Hawksworth (4 and 3)	1	J Sigel	0
P McEvoy	0	D Love (5 and 3)	1
P Baker (5 and 4)	1	R Sonnier	0
G Macgregor (3 and 2)	1	C Burroughs	0
C Bloice	0	B Lewis (4 and 3)	1
S Stephen (2 and 1)	1	D Waldorf	0
	4½		3½

Second-days' aggregate: Great Britain and Ireland, 5; USA, 7.
Grand Match aggregate: Great Britain and Ireland, 11; USA, 13.

At Sunningdale, Berkshire, 27th and 28th May, 1987

First Day—Foursomes

Great Britain and Ireland	Matches	USA	Matches
C Montgomerie and G Shaw	0	B Alexander and B Mayfair (5 and 4)	1
D Curry and P Mayo	0	C Kite and L Mattice (2 and 1)	1
G Macgregor and J Robinson	0	B Lewis and B Loeffler (2 and 1)	1
J McHenry and P Girvan	0	J Sigel and B. Andrade (3 and 2)	1
	0		4

Walker Cup
continued

Singles

Great Britain and Ireland	Matches	USA	Matches
D Curry (2 holes)	1	B Alexander	0
J Robinson	0	B Andrade (7 and 5)	1
C Montgomerie (3 and 2)	1	J Sorenson	0
R Eggo	0	J Sigel (3 and 2)	1
J McHenry	0	B Montgomery (1 hole)	1
P Girvan	0	B Lewis (3 and 2)	1
D Carrick	0	B Mayfair (2 holes)	1
G Shaw (1 hole)	1	C Kite	0
	3		5

First day's aggregate: Great Britain and Ireland, 3; USA, 9.

Second Day—Foursomes

Great Britain and Ireland	Matches	USA	Matches
D Curry and D Carrick	0	B Lewis and B Loeffler (4 and 3)	1
C Montgomerie and G Shaw	0	C Kite and L Mattice (5 and 3)	1
P Mayo and G Macgregor	0	J Sorenson and B Montgomery (4 and 3)	1
J McHenry and J Robinson (4 and 2)	1	J Sigel and B Andrade	0
	1		3

Singles

Great Britain and Ireland	Matches	USA	Matches
D Currey	0	B Alexander (5 and 4)	1
C Montgomerie (4 and 2)	1	B Andrade	0
J McHenry (3 and 2)	1	B Loeffler	0
G Shaw (half)	½	J Sorenson (half)	½
J Robinson (1 hole)	1	L Mattice	0
D Carrick	0	B Lewis (3 and 2)	1
R Eggo	0	B Mayfair (1 hole)	1
P Mayo	0	J Sigel (6 and 5)	1
	3½		4½

Second day's aggregate: Great Britain and Ireland, 4½; USA, 7½.
Grand Match aggregate: Great Britain and Ireland, 7½; USA 16½.

Individual Records

Great Britain and Ireland

Name		Year	Played	Won	Lost	Halved
MF Attenborough	Eng	1967	2	0	2	0
CC Aylmer	Eng	1922	2	1	1	0
P Baker	Eng	1985	3	2	1	0
JB Beck	Eng	1928-**(38)-(47)**	1	0	1	0
PJ Benka	Eng	1969	4	2	1	1
HG Bentley	Eng	1934-36-38	4	0	2	2
DA Blair	Scot	1955-61	4	1	3	0
C Bloice	Scot	1985	3	0	2	1
MF Bonallack	Eng	(1957)-59-61-63-65-67-**69-71**-73	25	8	14	3
G Brand	Scot	1979	3	0	3	0
OC Bristowe	Eng	(1923)-24	1	0	1	0
A Brodie	Scot	1977-79	8	5	2	1
A Brooks	Scot	1969	3	2	0	1
Hon WGE Brownlow	Eng	1926	2	0	2	0
J Bruen	Ire	1938-49-51	5	0	4	1
JA Buckley	Wales	1979	1	0	1	0
J Burke	Ire	1932	2	0	1	1
AF Bussell	Scot	1957	2	1	1	0
I Caldwell	Eng	1951-55	4	1	2	1
W Campbell	Scot	1930	2	0	2	0
JB Carr	Ire	1947-49-51-53-55-57-59-61-63-**(65)-67**	20	5	14	1

Walker Cup
continued

Name		Year	Played	Won	Lost	Halved
RJ Carr	Ire	1971	4	3	0	1
DG Carrick	Scot	1983-87	5	0	5	0
IA Carslaw	Scot	1979	3	1	1	1
JR Cater	Scot	1955	1	0	1	0
J Caven	Scot	1922	2	0	2	0
BHG Chapman	Eng	1961	1	0	1	0
R Chapman	Eng	1981	4	3	1	0
MJ Christmas	Eng	1961-63	3	1	2	0
*CA Clark	Eng	1965	4	2	0	2
GJ Clark	Eng	1965	1	0	1	0
*HK Clark	Eng	1973	3	1	1	1
GB Cosh	Scot	1965	4	3	1	0
T Craddock	Ire	1967-69	6	2	3	1
LG Crawley	Eng	1932-34-38-47	6	3	3	0
B Critchley	Eng	1969	4	1	1	2
D Curry	Eng	1987	4	1	3	0
CR Dalgleish	Scot	1981	3	1	2	0
B Darwin	Eng	1922	2	1	1	0
JC Davies	Eng	1973-75-77-79	13	3	8	2
P Deeble	Eng	1977-81	5	1	4	0
FWG Deighton	Scot	(1951)-57	2	0	2	0
*NV Drew	Ire	1953	1	0	1	0
AA Duncan	Wales	**(1953)**	0	0	0	0
JM Dykes	Scot	1936	2	0	1	1
R Eggo	Eng	1987	2	0	2	0
D Evans	Wales	1981	3	1	1	1
RC Ewing	Ire	1936-38-47-49-51-55	10	1	7	2
GRD Eyles	Eng	1975	4	2	2	0
EW Fiddian	Eng	1932-34	4	0	4	0
J de Forest	Eng	1932	1	0	1	0
R Foster	Eng	1965-67-69-71-73-**(79)-(81)**	17	2	13	2
DW Frame	Eng	1961	1	0	1	0
D Gilford	Eng	1985	1	0	1	0
P Girvan	Scot	1987	3	0	3	0
G Godwin	Eng	1979-81	7	2	4	1
*CW Green	Scot	1963-69-71-73-75-**(83)-(85)**	17	4	10	3
RH Hardman	Eng	1928	1	0	1	0
R Harris	Scot	**(1922)-23-26**	4	1	3	0
RW Hartley	Eng	1930-32	4	0	4	0
WL Hartley	Eng	1932	2	0	2	0
J Hawksworth	Eng	1985	4	2	1	1
P Hedges	Eng	1973-75	5	0	2	3
CO Hezlet	Ire	1924-26-28	6	0	5	1
GA Hill	Eng	1936-**(55)**	2	0	1	1
Sir EWE Holderness	Eng	1923-26-30	6	2	4	0
TWB Homer	Eng	1973	3	0	3	0
CVL Hooman	Eng	1922-23	3	1**	2	0**
WL Hope	Scot	1923-24-28	5	1	4	0
G Huddy	Eng	1961	1	0	1	0
W Humphreys	Eng	1971	3	2	1	0
IC Hutcheon	Scot	1975-77-79-81	15	5	8	2
RR Jack	Scot	1957-59	4	2	2	0
*M James	Eng	1975	4	3	1	0
A Jamieson, jr	Scot	1926	2	1	1	0
MJ Kelley	Eng	1977-79	7	3	3	1
SD Keppler	Eng	1983	4	0	3	1
*MG King	Eng	1969-73	7	1	5	1
AT Kyle	Scot	1938-47-51	5	2	3	0
DH Kyle	Scot	1924	1	0	1	0
JA Lang	Scot	(1930)	0	0	0	0
JDA Langley	Eng	1936-51-53	6	0	5	1
CD Lawrie	Scot	**(1961)-(63)**	0	0	0	0
ME Lewis	Eng	1983	1	0	1	0
PB Lucas	Eng	(1936)-47-**(49)**	2	1	1	0
MSR Lunt	Eng	1959-61-63-65	11	2	8	1
*AWB Lyle	Scot	1977	3	0	3	0
AR McCallum	Scot	1928	1	0	1	0
SM McCready	Ire	1949-51	3	0	3	0
JS Macdonald	Scot	1971	3	1	1	1
P McEvoy	Eng	1977-79-81-85	14	3	10	1
G McGimpsey	Ire	1985	4	1	2	1
G Macgregor	Scot	1971-75-83-85-87	14	5	8	1
RC MacGregor	Scot	1953	2	0	2	0
J McHenry	Ire	1987	4	2	2	0
P McKellar	Scot	1977	1	0	1	0
WW Mackenzie	Scot	1922-23	3	1	2	0
SL McKinlay	Scot	1934	2	0	2	0
J McLean	Scot	1934-36	4	1	3	0
EA McRuvie	Scot	1932-34	4	1	2	1
JFD Madeley	Ire	1963	2	0	1	1
LS Mann	Scot	1983	4	2	1	1
B Marchbank	Scot	1979	4	2	2	0

Walker Cup

continued

Name		Year	Played	Won	Lost	Halved
GC Marks	Eng	1969-71-**(87)**	6	2	4	0
DM Marsh	Eng	(1959)-71-**(73)**-**(75)**	3	2	1	0
GNC Martin	Ire	1928	1	0	1	0
S Martin	Scot	1977	4	2	2	0
P Mayo	Wales	1985-87	4	0	3	1
GH Micklem	Eng	1947-49-53-55-**(57)**-**(59)**	6	1	5	0
DJ Millensted	Eng	1967	2	1	1	0
EB Millward	Eng	(1949)-55	2	0	2	0
WTG Milne	Scot	1973	4	2	2	0
CS Montgomerie	Scot	1985-87	8	2	5	1
JL Morgan	Wales	1951-53-55	6	2	4	0
P Mulcare	Ire	1975	3	2	1	0
GH Murray	Scot	1977	2	1	1	0
SWT Murray	Scot	1963	4	2	2	0
WA Murray	Scot	1923-24-(26)	4	1	3	0
A Oldcorn	Eng	1983	4	4	0	0
*PA Oosterhuis	Eng	1967	4	1	2	1
R Oppenheimer	Eng	**(1951)**	0	0	0	0
P Parkin	Wales	1983	3	2	1	0
JJF Pennink	Eng	1938	2	1	1	0
TP Perkins	Eng	1928	2	0	2	0
AH Perowne	Eng	1949-53-59	4	0	4	0
GB Peters	Scot	1936-38	4	2	1	1
AD Pierse	Ire	1983	3	0	2	1
AK Pirie	Scot	1967	3	0	2	1
MA Poxon	Eng	1975	2	0	2	0
R Rafferty	Ire	1981	4	2	2	0
J Robinson	Eng	1987	4	2	2	0
AC Saddler	Scot	1963-65-67-**(77)**	10	3	5	2
Hon M Scott	Eng	1924-**34**	4	2	2	0
R Scott, jr	Scot	1924	1	1	0	0
PF Scrutton	Eng	1955-57	3	0	3	0
DN Sewell	Eng	1957-59	4	1	3	0
RDBM Shade	Scot	1961-63-65-67	14	6	6	2
G Shaw	Scot	1987	4	1	2	1
DB Sheahan	Ire	1963	4	2	2	0
AE Shepperson	Eng	1957-59	3	1	1	1
AF Simpson	Scot	(1926)	0	0	0	0
JN Smith	Scot	1930	2	0	2	0
WD Smith	Scot	1959	1	0	1	0
AR Stephen	Scot	1985	4	2	1	1
EF Storey	Eng	1924-26-28	6	1	5	0
JA Stout	Eng	1930-32	4	0	3	1
C Stowe	Eng	1938-47	4	2	2	0
HB Stuart	Scot	1971-73-75	10	4	6	0
A Thirlwell	Eng	1957	1	0	1	0
KG Thom	Eng	1949	2	0	2	0
MS Thompson	Eng	1983	3	1	2	0
H Thomson	Scot	1936-38	4	2	2	0
CJH Tolley	Eng	1922-23-**24**-26-30-34	12	4	8	0
TA Torrance	Scot	1924-28-30-**32**-34	9	3	5	1
WB Torrance	Scot	1922	2	0	2	0
*PM Townsend	Eng	1965	4	3	1	0
LP Tupling	Eng	1969	2	1	1	0
W Tweddell	Eng	**1928**-**(36)**	2	0	2	0
J Walker	Scot	1961	2	0	2	0
P Walton	Ire	1981-83	8	6	2	0
*P Way	Eng	1981	4	2	2	0
RH Wethered	Eng	1922-23-26-**30**-34	9	5	3	1
RJ White	Eng	1947-49-51-53-55	10	6	3	1
J Wilson	Scot	1923	2	2	0	0
JC Wilson	Scot	1947-53	4	0	4	0
GB Wolstenholme	Eng	1957-59	4	1	2	1

Notes: Bold Type indicates captain; in brackets, did not play.
**Players who have also played in the Ryder Cup.*
***CVL Hooman and J Sweetser in 1922 were all square after 36 holes; instructions to the contrary not being readily available, they played on and Hooman won at the 37th. On all other occasions halved matches have counted as such.*

Individual Records

United States of America

Name	Year	Played	Won	Lost	Halved
*TD Aaron	1959	2	1	1	0
B Alexander	1987	3	2	1	0
DC Allen	1965-67	6	0	4	2
B Andrade	1987	4	2	2	0
ES Andrews	1961	1	1	0	0
D Ballenger	1973	1	1	0	0

Walker Cup
continued

Name	Year	Played	Won	Lost	Halved
R Baxter, jr	1957	2	2	0	0
DR Beman	1959-61-63-65	11	7	2	2
RE Billows	1938-49	4	2	2	0
SE Bishop	1947-49	3	2	1	0
AS Blum	1957	1	0	1	0
J Bohmann	1969	3	1	2	0
M Brannan	1977	3	1	2	0
GF Burns	1975	3	2	1	0
C Burroughs	1985	3	1	2	0
AE Campbell	1936	2	2	0	0
JE Campbell	1957	1	0	1	0
WC Campbell	1951-53-**(55)**-57-65-67-71-75	18	11	4	3
RJ Cerrudo	1967	4	1	1	2
RD Chapman	1947-51-53	5	3	2	0
D Cherry	1953-55-61	5	5	0	0
D Clarke	1979	3	2	0	1
RE Cochran	1961	1	1	0	0
CR Coe	1949-51-53-**(57)-59**-61-63	13	7	4	2
R Commans	1981	3	1	1	1
JW Conrad	1955	2	1	1	0
N Crosby	1983	2	1	1	0
BH Cudd	1955	2	2	0	0
RD Davies	1963	2	0	2	0
JW Dawson	1949	2	2	0	0
RB Dickson	1967	3	3	0	0
GT Dunlap, jr	1932-34-36	5	3	1	1
D Edwards	1973	4	4	0	0
HC Egan	1934	1	1	0	0
D Eichelberger	1965	3	1	2	0
J Ellis	1973	3	2	1	0
W Emery	1936	2	1	0	1
C Evans, jr	1922-24-28	5	3	2	0
J Farquhar	1971	3	1	2	0
B Faxon	1983	4	3	1	0
R Fehr	1983	4	2	1	1
JW Fischer	1934-36-38-**(65)**	4	3	0	1
D Fischesser	1979	3	1	2	0
MA Fleckman	1967	2	0	2	0
B Fleisher	1969	4	0	2	2
J Fought	1977	4	4	0	0
WC Fownes, jr	**1922**-24	3	1	2	0
F Fuhrer	1981	3	2	1	0
JR Gabrielsen	1977-**(81)**	3	1	2	0
RA Gardner	1922-**23-24-26**	8	6	2	0
RW Gardner	1961-63	5	4	0	1
M Giles	1969-71-73-75	15	8	2	5
HL Givan	1936	1	0	0	1
JG Goodman	1934-36-38	6	4	2	0
M Gove	1979	3	2	1	0
J Grace	1975	3	2	1	0
JA Grant	1967	2	2	0	0
AD Gray, jr	1963-65-67	12	5	6	1
JP Guilford	1922-24-26	6	4	2	0
W Gunn	1926-28	4	4	0	0
*F Haas, jr	1938	2	0	2	0
*J Haas	1975	3	3	0	0
J Haas	1985	3	1	2	0
G Hallberg	1977	3	1	2	0
GS Hamer, jr	(1947)	0	0	0	0
LE Harris, jr	1963	4	3	1	0
V Heafner	1977	3	3	0	0
SD Herron	1923	2	0	2	0
S Hoch	1979	4	4	0	0
W Hoffer	1983	2	1	1	0
J Holtgrieve	1979-81-83	10	6	4	0
JM Hopkins	1965	3	0	2	1
W Howell	1932	1	1	0	0
W Hyndman	1957-59-61-69-71	9	6	1	2
J Inman	1969	2	2	0	0
JG Jackson	1953-55	3	3	0	0
HR Johnston	1923-24-28-30	6	5	1	0
RT Jones, jr	1922-24-26-**28-30**	10	9	1	0
AF Kammer	1947	2	1	1	0
M Killian	1973	3	1	2	0
C Kite	1987	3	2	1	0
*TO Kite	1971	4	2	1	1
RE Knepper	(1922)	0	0	0	0
RW Knowles	1951	1	1	0	0
G Koch	1973-75	7	4	1	2
CR Kocsis	1938-49-57	5	2	2	1
B Lewis, jr	1981-83-85-87	14	10	4	0

Walker Cup
continued

Name	Year	Played	Won	Lost	Halved
JW Lewis	1967	4	3	1	0
WL Little, jr	1934	2	2	0	0
*GA Littler	1953	2	2	0	0
B Loeffler	1987	3	2	1	0
D Love	1985	3	2	0	1
MJ McCarthy, jr	(1928)-32	1	1	0	0
BN McCormick	1949	1	1	0	0
JB McHale	1949-51	3	2	0	1
RR Mackenzie	1926-28-30	6	5	1	0
MR Marston	1922-23-24-34	8	5	3	0
L Mattiace	1987	3	2	1	0
B Mayfair	1987	3	3	0	0
SN Melnyk	1969-71	7	3	3	1
AL Miller	1969-71	8	4	3	1
L Miller	1977	4	4	0	0
DK Moe	1930-32	3	3	0	0
B Montgomery	1987	2	2	0	0
G Moody	1979	3	1	2	0
GT Moreland	1932-34	4	4	0	0
D Morey	1955-65	4	1	3	0
J Mudd	1981	3	3	0	0
*RJ Murphy	1967	4	1	2	1
JF Neville	1923	1	0	1	0
*JW Nicklaus	1959-61	4	4	0	0
LW Oehmig	**(1977)**	0	0	0	0
FD Ouimet	1922-23-24-26-30-**32-34-(36)-(38)-(47)-(49)**	16	9	5	2
HD Paddock, jr	1951	1	0	0	1
*J Pate	1975	4	0	4	0
WJ Patton	1955-57-59-63-65-**(69)**	14	11	3	0
C Pavin	1981	3	2	0	1
M Peck	1979	3	1	1	1
M Pfeil	1973	4	2	1	1
M Podolak	1985	2	1	0	1
SL Quick	1947	2	1	1	0
S Randolph	1985	4	2	1	1
J Rassett	1981	3	3	0	0
*F Ridley	1977-**(87)**	3	2	1	0
RH Riegel	1947-49	4	4	0	0
H Robbins, jr	1957	2	0	1	1
W Rodgers	1973	2	1	1	0
GV Rotan	1923	2	1	1	0
*EM Rudolph	1957	2	1	0	1
B Sander	1977	3	0	3	0
CH Seaver	1932	2	2	0	0
RL Siderowf	1969-73-75-77-**(79)**	14	4	8	2
J Sigel	1977-79-81-**83**-85-87	23	14	6	3
RH Sikes	1963	3	1	2	0
JB Simons	1971	2	0	2	0
*S Simpson	1977	3	3	0	0
CB Smith	1961-63	2	0	1	1
R Smith	1936-38	4	2	2	0
R Sonnier	1985	3	0	2	1
Sorensen	1987	3	1	1	1
*C Stadler	1975	3	3	0	0
FR Stranahan	1947-49-51	6	3	2	1
*C Strange	1975	4	3	0	1
*H Sutton	1979-81	7	2	4	1
JW Sweetser	1922-23-24-26-28-32-**(67)-(73)**	12	7	4**	1**
FM Taylor	1957-59-61	4	4	0	0
D Tentis	1983	2	0	1	1
RS Tufts	**(1963)**	0	0	0	0
WP Turnesa	1947-49-**51**	6	3	3	0
B Tuten	1983	2	1	1	0
EM Tutweiler	1965-67	6	5	1	0
ER Updegraff	1963-65-69-**(75)**	7	3	3	1
S Urzetta	1951-53	4	4	0	0
K Venturi	1953	2	2	0	0
S Verplank	1985	4	3	0	1
GJ Voigt	1930-32-36	5	2	2	1
G Von Elm	1926-28-30	6	4	1	1
D von Tacky	1981	3	1	2	0
*JL Wadkins	1969-71	7	3	4	0
D Waldorf	1985	3	1	2	0
EH Ward	1953-55-59	6	6	0	0
MH Ward	1938-47	4	2	2	0
M West	1973-79	6	2	3	1
J Westland	1932-34-53-**(61)**	5	3	0	2
HW Wettlaufer	1959	2	2	0	0
E White	1936	2	2	0	0

Walker Cup
continued

Name	Year	Played	Won	Lost	Halved
OF Willing	1923-24-30	4	4	0	0
JM Winters, jr	**(1971)**	0	0	0	0
W Wood	1983	4	1	2	1
FJ Wright	1923	1	1	0	0
CR Yates	1936-38-**(53)**	4	3	0	1
RL Yost	1955	2	2	0	0

Notes: Bold type indicates captain: in brackets, did not play.
**Players who have also played in the Ryder Cup.*
***CVL Hooman and J Sweetser in 1922 were all square after 36 holes; instructions to the contrary not being readily available, they played on and Hooman won at the 37th. On all other occasions halved matches have counted as such.*

Eisenhower Trophy (World Cup)

Instituted 1958

Year	Winners	Runners-up	Venue	Score
1978	United States	Canada	Fiji	873
1980	United States	South Africa	Pinehurst, USA	848
1982	United States	Sweden	Lausanne	859
1984	Japan	United States	Hong Kong	870
1986	Canada	United States	Caracas, Venezuela	860
1988	Great Britain and Ireland	United States	Ullva, Sweden	882

St Andrews Trophy (Great Britain *v* Europe)

Match instituted 1956
Trophy presented 1962

Year	Winner	Venue	Result
1978	Great Britain	Bremen, Germany	20½-9½
1980	Great Britain	St George's	19½-10½
1982	Europe	Rosendaelsche, Netherlands	14–10
1984	Great Britain	Taunton, Devon	13-11
1986	Great Britain	Halmstead, Sweden	14½-9½
1988	Great Britain	St Andrews	15½-8½

European Amateur Team Championship

Year	Winner	Second	Venue
1979	England	Wales	Esbjerg, Denmark
1981	England	Scotland	St Andrews, Scotland
1983	Ireland	Spain	Chantilly, France
1985	Scotland	Sweden	Halmstad, Sweden
1987	Ireland	England	Murhof, Austria

Great Britain & Ireland *v* Continent of Europe, Boys

Instituted 1958

Year	Winner	Result	Venue
1984	Great Britain & Ireland	6½-5½	Porthcawl
1985	Great Britain & Ireland	7½-4½	Barnton
1986	Continent of Europe	8½-3½	Seaton Carew
1987	Great Britain & Ireland	7½-4½	Barassie
1988	Great Britain & Ireland	5½-2½	Formby

Great Britain & Ireland *v* Continent of Europe, Youths

Instituted 1967

Year	Winner	Result	Venue
1984	Halved	6-6	Blairgowrie
1985	Great Britain & Ireland	8-4	Ganton
1986	Great Britain & Ireland	13½-10½	Bilbao, Spain
1987	Continent of Europe	7-5	Hollinwell
1988	Great Britain & Ireland	13½-10½	Copenhagen, Denmark

Home International Results

Home Internationals

1984—At Troon

Ireland halved with Wales	7½ matches each
England beat Scotland	8 matches to 7
Scotland beat Ireland	10 matches to 5
England beat Wales	12½ matches to 2½
Scotland beat Wales	7 matches to 3
Ireland beat England	6 matches to 4

(Foursomes of third series of matches cancelled due to torrential rain.)

1985—At Formby

England beat Wales	11 matches to 4
England beat Scotland	8 matches to 7
England beat Ireland	8½ matches to 6½
Wales beat Scotland	8 matches to 7
Wales beat Ireland	9½ matches to 5½
Ireland beat Scotland	11½ matches to 3½

1986—At Harlech

Scotland beat England	9½ matches to 5½
Scotland beat Ireland	10½ matches to 4½
Scotland beat Wales	10 matches to 5
England beat Wales	9 matches to 6
Ireland beat England	8 matches to 7
Wales halved with Ireland	7½ matches each

1987—At Lahinch

Ireland beat England	6 matches to 4
Ireland beat Scotland	10½ matches to 4½
Ireland beat Wales	8 matches to 7
England beat Scotland	9 matches to 6
England halved with Wales	7 matches each
Scotland beat Wales	6½ matches to 3½

(On the first day the foursomes were abandoned due to bad weather, singles only being played.)

1988—At Muirfield

England beat Wales	11 matches to 4
England beat Scotland	9 matches to 6
England beat Ireland	8 matches to 7
Ireland halved with Wales	7½ matches each
Ireland beat Scotland	10 matches to 5
Wales beat Scotland	8 matches to 7

Boys' Internationals England *v* Scotland

Instituted 1928

Year	Winner	Result	Venue
1984	England	9½-5½	Porthcawl
1985	England	10-5	Barnton
1986	Scotland	8½-6½	Seaton Carew
1987	Scotland	8-7	Barassie
1988	England	11-4	Formby

Rand A Trophy

This trophy is played between the winners of the England v *Scotland and Wales* v *Ireland International Matches and was introduced in 1985.*

Year	Winner	Result	Venue
1985	England Ireland } tie	7½-7½	Barnton
1986	Ireland	8½-6½	Seaton Carew
1987	Scotland	10½-4½	Barassie
1988	England	14-1	Formby

Wales *v* Ireland

Instituted 1972

Year	Winner	Result	Venue
1984	Wales	6½-5½	Porthcawl
1985	Ireland	11½-3½	Barnton
1986	Ireland	8½-6½	Seaton Carew
1987	Wales	10½-4½	Barassie
1988	Wales	8-7	Formby

Youths' Internationals England *v* Scotland

Year	Winner	Result	Venue
1984	Scotland	9-6	Blairgowrie
1985	Halved	7½-7½	Ganton
1986	Scotland	8-7	Carnoustie
1987	England	9½-5½	Hollinwell
1988	England	10-5	R. Aberdeen

Women's Amateur International Competitions

British Isles v USA (Ladies) Curtis Cup

Instituted 1932

	British Isles			USA			Venue
1932	Foursomes Singles	0 3½	3½	Foursomes Singles	3 2½	5½	Wentworth
1934	Foursomes Singles	1½ 1	2½	Foursomes Singles	1½ 5	6½	Chevy Chase
1936	Foursomes Singles	1½ 3	4½	Foursomes Singles	1½ 3	4½	Gleneagles
1938	Foursomes Singles	2½ 1	3½	Foursomes Singles	½ 5	5½	Essex County Club
1948	Foursomes Singles	1 1½	2½	Foursomes Singles	2 4½	6½	Birkdale
1950	Foursomes Singles	1 ½	1½	Foursomes Singles	2 5½	7½	Buffalo
1952	Foursomes Singles	2 3	5	Foursomes Singles	1 3	4	Muirfield
1954	Foursomes Singles	0 3	3	Foursomes Singles	3 3	6	Merion
1956	Foursomes Singles	1 4	5	Foursomes Singles	2 2	4	Prince's, Sandwich
1958	Foursomes Singles	2 2½	4½	Foursomes Singles	1 3½	4½	Brae Burn GC
1960	Foursomes Singles	1 1½	2½	Foursomes Singles	2 4½	6½	Lindrick
1962	Foursomes Singles	0 1	1	Foursomes Singles	3 5	8	Colorado Springs
1964	Foursomes Singles	3½ 4	7½	Foursomes Singles	2½ 8	10½	Porthcawl
1966	Foursomes Singles	1½ 3½	5	Foursomes Singles	4½ 8½	13	Hot Springs

	Great Britain & Ireland			USA			Venue
1968	Foursomes Singles	2½ 5	7½	Foursomes Singles	3½ 7	10½	Newcastle, Co Down
1970	Foursomes Singles	2½ 4	6½	Foursomes Singles	3½ 8	11½	Brae Burn, USA
1972	Foursomes Singles	3½ 4½	8	Foursomes Singles	2½ 7½	10	Western Gailes
1974	Foursomes Singles	2½ 2½	5	Foursomes Singles	3½ 9½	13	San Francisco, Cal.
1976	Foursomes Singles	2 4½	6½	Foursomes Singles	4 7½	11½	Lytham St Annes
1978	Foursomes Singles	2½ 3½	6	Foursomes Singles	3½ 8½	12	Apawamis, NY

British Isles v USA (Ladies) Curtis Cup
continued

At St Pierre, 6th and 7th June, 1980

First Day–Foursomes

Great Britain & Ireland		United States	
Miss M McKenna and Miss C Nesbitt	½	Miss L Smith and Miss T Moody	½
Mrs T Thomas and Miss G Stewart	0	Miss P Sheehan and Miss L Castillo (5 and 3)	1
Miss M Madill and Mrs C Caldwell	½	Mrs J Oliver and Miss C Semple	½
	1		2

Singles

Great Britain & Ireland		United States	
Miss M McKenna	0	Miss P Sheehan (3 and 2)	1
Miss C Nesbitt	½	Miss L Smith	½
Miss J Connachan	0	Miss B Goldsmith (2 holes)	1
Miss M Madill	0	Miss C Semple (4 and 3)	1
Miss L Moore	½	Miss M Hafeman	½
Mrs C Caldwell	0	Mrs J Oliver (1 hole)	1
	1		5

Second Day–Foursomes

Great Britain & Ireland		United States	
Mrs C Caldwell and Miss M Madill	0	Miss P Sheehan and Miss L Castillo (3 and 2)	1
Miss C Nesbitt and Miss M McKenna	0	Miss L Smith and Miss T Moody (6 and 5)	1
Mrs T Thomas and Miss L Moore	0	Mrs J Oliver and Miss C Semple (1 hole)	1
	0		3

Singles

Great Britain & Ireland		United States	
Miss M Madill	0	Miss P Sheehan (5 and 4)	1
Miss M McKenna (5 and 4)	1	Miss L Castillo	0
Miss J Connachan	0	Miss M Hafeman (6 and 5)	1
Miss G Stewart (5 and 4)	1	Miss L Smith	0
Miss L Moore (1 hole)	1	Miss B Goldsmith	0
Mrs T Thomas	0	Miss C Semple (4 and 3)	1
	3		3

Aggregate: United States, 13; Great Britain and Ireland, 5

At Denver, Colorado, USA, on 5th and 6th August, 1982

First Day–Foursomes

Great Britain & Ireland		United States	
Mrs IC Robertson and Miss M McKenna	0	Mrs J Inkster and Miss C Semple (5 and 4)	1
Miss K Douglas and Miss J Soulsby	½	Miss K Baker and Mrs L Smith	½
Miss G Stewart and Miss J Connachan	0	Miss A Benz and Miss C Hanlon (2 and 1)	1
	½		2½

British Isles v USA (Ladies) Curtis Cup
continued

Singles

Great Britain & Ireland		United States	
Miss M McKenna	0	Miss A Benz (2 and 1)	1
Miss J Connachan	0	Miss C Hanlon (5 and 4)	1
Miss W Aitken	0	Mrs M McDougall (2 holes)	1
Mrs IC Robertson	0	Miss K Baker (7 and 6)	1
Miss J Soulsby (2 holes)	1	Mrs J Oliver	0
Miss K Douglas	0	Mrs J Inkster (7 and 6)	1
	1		5

Second Day–Foursomes

Great Britain & Ireland		United States	
Miss J Connachan and Miss W Aitken	0	Mrs J Inkster and Miss C Semple (3 and 2)	1
Miss K Douglas and Miss J Soulsby	0	Miss K Baker and Miss L Smith (1 hole)	1
Miss M McKenna and Mrs IC Robertson (1 hole)	1	Miss A Benz and Miss C Hanlon	0
	1		2

Singles

Great Britain & Ireland		United States	
Miss K Douglas	0	Mrs J Inkster (7 and 6)	1
Miss G Stewart	0	Miss K Baker (4 and 3)	1
Mrs V Thomas	0	Mrs J Oliver (5 and 4)	1
Miss J Soulsby	0	Mrs M McDougall (2 and 1)	1
Miss M McKenna	0	Miss C Semple (1 hole)	1
Mrs IC Robertson (5 and 3)	1	Miss L Smith	0
	1		5

Aggregate: United States, 14½; Great Britain and Ireland, 3½

At Muirfield on 8th and 9th June, 1984

First Day–Foursomes

Great Britain & Ireland		United States	
C Waite and B New (2 holes)	1	J Pacillo and A Sander	0
J Thornhill and P Grice	½	L Smith and J Rosenthal	½
M McKenna and L Davies	0	M Widman and H Farr (1 hole)	1
	1½		1½

Singles

Great Britain & Ireland		United States	
J Thornhill	½	J Pacillo	½
C Waite	0	P Hammel (4 and 2)	1
C Hourihane	0	J Rosenthal (3 and 1)	1
V Thomas (2 and 1)	1	D Howe	0
P Grice (2 holes)	1	A Sander	0
B New	0	M Widman (4 and 3)	1
	2½		3½

British Isles v USA (Ladies) Curtis Cup
continued

Second Day–Foursomes

Great Britain & Ireland		United States	
C Waite and B New	0	L Smith and J Rosenthal (3 and 1)	1
J Thornhill and P Grice (2 and 1)	1	M Widman and H Farr	0
V Thomas and C Hourihane	½	D Howe and P Hammel	½
	1½		1½

Singles

Great Britain & Ireland		United States	
J Thornhill	0	J Pacillo (3 and 2)	1
L Davies (1 hole)	1	A Sander	0
C Waite (5 and 4)	1	L Smith	0
P Grice	0	D Howe (2 holes)	1
B New	0	H Farr (6 and 5)	1
C Hourihane (2 and 1)	1	P Hammel	0
	3		3

Aggregate: Great Britain and Ireland 8½; United States 9½

At Prairie Dunes, Kansas, USA on 1st and 2nd August, 1986

First Day–Foursomes

Great Britain & Ireland		United States	
L Behan and J Thornhill (7 and 6)	1	K Kessler and C Schreyer	0
P Johnson and K Davies (2 and 1)	1	D Ammaccapane and D Mochrie	0
B Robertson and M McKenna (1 hole)	1	K Gardner and K McCarthy	0
	3		0

Singles

Great Britain & Ireland		United States	
P Johnson (1 hole)	1	L Shannon	0
J Thornhill (4 and 3)	1	K Williams	0
L Behan (4 and 3)	1	D Ammaccapane	0
V Thomas	0	K Kessler (3 and 2)	1
K Davies	½	D Mochrie	½
C Hourihane	0	C Schreyer (2 and 1)	1
	3½		2½

Second Day–Foursomes

Great Britain & Ireland		United States	
P Johnson and K Davies (1 hole)	1	D Ammaccapane and D Mochrie	0
L Behan and J Thornhill (5 and 3)	1	L Shannon and K Williams	0
B Robertson and M McKenna	½	K Gardner and K McCarthy	½
	2½		½

Singles

Great Britain & Ireland		United States	
J Thornhill	½	L Shannon	½
P Johnson (5 and 3)	1	K McCarthy	0
L Behan	0	K Gardner (1 hole)	1
V Thomas (4 and 3)	1	K Williams	0
K Davies	½	K Kessler	½
C Hourihane (5 and 3)	1	C Schreyer	0
	4		2

Aggregate: Great Britain and Ireland 13, United States 5

For details of 1988 match see page 137

British Isles v USA (Ladies) Curtis Cup
continued

Individual Records

Great Britain and Ireland

Name		Year	Played	Won	Lost	Halved
Jean Anderson (Donald)	Scot	1948	6	3	3	0
Diane Bailey [Frearson] (Robb)	Eng	1962-72-**(84)-(86)-(88)**	5	2	2	1
Sally Barber (Bonallack)	Eng	1962	1	0	1	0
Pam Barton	Eng	1934-36	4	0	3	1
Linda Bayman	Eng	1988	4	2	1	1
Baba Beck (Pym)	Ire	**(1954)**	0	0	0	0
Charlotte Beddows [Watson] (Stevenson)	Scot	1932	1	0	1	0
Lilian Behan	Ire	1986	4	3	1	0
Veronica Beharrell (Anstey)	Eng	1956	1	0	1	0
Pam Benka (Tredinnick)	Eng	1966-68	4	0	3	1
Jeanne Bisgood	Eng	1950-52-54-**(70)**	4	1	3	0
Zara Bolton (Davis)	Eng	1948-**(56)-(66)-(68)**	2	0	2	0
Angela Bonallack (Ward)	Eng	1956-58-60-62-64-66	15	6	8	1
Ita Butler (Burke)	Ire	1966	3	2	1	0
Lady Katherine Cairns	Eng	**(1952)**	0	0	0	0
Carole Caldwell (Redford)	Eng	1978-80	5	0	3	2
Doris Chambers	Eng	**(1934)-(36)-(48)**	0	0	0	0
Carol Comboy (Grott)	Eng	**(1978)-(80)**	0	0	0	0
Jane Connachan	Scot	1980-82	5	0	5	0
Elsie Corlett	Eng	1932-38-**(64)**	3	1	2	0
Diana Critchley (Fishwick)	Eng	1932-34-**(50)**	3	1	2	0
Karen Davies	Wales	1986-88	7	4	1	2
Laura Davies	Eng	1984	2	1	1	0
Kitrina Douglas	Eng	1982	4	0	3	1
Marjorie Draper [Peel] (Thomas)	Scot	1954	1	0	1	0
Daisy Ferguson	Ire	**(1958)**	0	0	0	0
Marjory Ferguson (Fowler)	Scot	1966	1	0	1	0
Elizabeth Price Fisher (Price)	Eng	1950-52-54-56-58-60	12	7	4	1
Maureen Garner (Madill)	Ire	1980	4	0	3	1
Marjorie Ross Garon	Eng	1936	2	1	0	1
Maureen Garrett (Ruttle)	Eng	1948-**(60)**	2	0	2	0
Philomena Garvey	Ire	1948-50-52-54-56-60	11	2	8	1
Carol Gibbs (Le Feuvre)	Eng	1974	3	0	3	0
Jacqueline Gordon	Eng	1948	2	1	1	0
Molly Gourlay	Eng	1932-34	4	0	2	2
Julia Greenhalgh	Eng	1964-70-74-76-78	17	6	7	4
Penny Grice-Whittaker (Grice)	Eng	1984	4	2	1	1
Marley Harris [Spearman] (Baker)	Eng	1960-62-64	6	2	2	2
Dorothea Hastings (Sommerville)	Scot	1958	0	0	0	0
Lady Heathcoat-Amory (Joyce Wethered)	Eng	**1932**	2	1	1	0
Dinah Henson (Oxley)	Eng	1968-70-72-76	11	3	6	2
Helen Holm (Gray)	Scot	1936-38-48	5	3	2	0
Claire Hourihane	Ire	1984-86-88	5	2	2	1
Ann Howard (Phillips)	Eng	1956-68	2	0	2	0
Beverley Huke	Eng	1972	2	0	2	0
Anne Irvin	Eng	1962-68-70-76	12	4	7	1
Bridget Jackson	Eng	1958-64-68	8	1	6	1
Patricia Johnson	Eng	1986	4	4	0	0
Susan Langridge (Armitage)	Eng	1964-66	6	0	5	1
Mary Laupheimer (Everard)	Eng	1970-72-74-78	15	6	7	2
Joan Lawrence	Scot	1964	2	0	2	0
Shirley Lawson	Scot	1988	2	1	1	0
Wilma Leburn (Aitken)	Scot	1982	2	0	2	0
Jenny Lee Smith	Eng	1974-76	3	0	3	0
Kathryn Lumb (Phillips)	Eng	1970-72	2	1	1	0
Mary McKenna	Ire	1970-72-74-76-78-80-82-84-86	30	10	16	4

British Isles v USA (Ladies) Curtis Cup

continued

Name		Year	Played	Won	Lost	Halved
Suzanne McMahon (Cadden)	Scot	1976	4	0	4	0
Sheila Maher (Vaughan)	Eng	1962-64	4	1	2	1
Vanessa Marvin	Eng	1978	3	1	2	0
Moira Milton (Paterson)	Scot	1952	2	1	1	0
Wanda Morgan	Eng	1932-34-36	6	0	5	1
Beverley New	Eng	1984	4	1	3	0
Maire O'Donnell	Ire	**(1982)**	0	0	0	0
Margaret Pickard (Nichol)	Eng	1968-70	5	2	3	0
Diana Plumpton	Eng	1934	2	1	1	0
Elizabeth Pook (Chadwick)	Eng	1966	4	1	3	0
Doris Porter (Park)	Scot	1932	1	0	1	0
Clarrie Reddan (Tiernan)	Ire	1938-48	3	2	1	0
Joan Rennie (Hastings)	Scot	1966	2	0	1	1
Maureen Richmond (Walker)	Scot	1974	4	2	2	0
Jean Roberts	Eng	1962	1	0	1	0
Belle Robertson (McCorkindale)	Scot	1960-66-68-70-72-**(74)**-**(76)**-82-86	24	5	12	7
Claire Robinson (Nesbitt)	Ire	1980	3	0	1	2
Vivien Saunders	Eng	1968	4	1	2	1
Susan Shapcott	Eng	1988	4	3	1	0
Linda Simpson (Moore)	Eng	1980	3	1	1	1
Ruth Slark (Porter)	Eng	1960-62-64	7	3	3	1
Anne Smith [Stant] (Willard)	Eng	1976	1	0	1	0
Frances Smith (Stephens)	Eng	1950-52-54-56-58-60-**(62)**-**(72)**	11	7	3	1
Janet Soulsby	Eng	1982	4	1	2	1
Gillian Stewart	Scot	1980-82	4	1	3	0
Tegwen Thomas (Perkins)	Wales	1974-76-78-80	14	4	8	2
Vicki Thomas (Rawlings)	Wales	1982-84-86-88	8	4	2	2
Muriel Thomson	Scot	1978	3	2	1	0
Jill Thornhill	Eng	1984-86-88	12	6	2	4
Angela Uzielli (Carrick)	Eng	1978	1	0	1	0
Jessie Valentine (Anderson)	Scot	1936-38-50-52-54-56-58	13	4	9	0
Julie Wade	Eng	1988	4	2	2	0
Claire Waite	Eng	1984	4	2	2	0
Mickey Walker	Eng	1972	4	3	0	1
Pat Walker	Ire	1934-36-38	6	2	3	1
Verona Wallace-Williamson	Scot	**(1938)**	0	0	0	0
Nan Wardlaw (Baird)	Scot	1938	1	0	1	0
Enid Wilson	Eng	1932	2	1	1	0
Janette Wright (Robertson)	Scot	1954-56-58-60	8	3	5	0
Phyllis Wylie (Wade)	Eng	1938	1	0	0	1

Bold print: captain; bold print in brackets: non-playing captain
Maiden name in parentheses, former surname in square brackets

United States of America

Player	Year	Played	Won	Lost	Halved
Roberta Albers	1968	2	1	0	1
Danielle Ammaccapane	1986	3	0	3	0
Kathy Baker	1982	4	3	0	1
Barbara Barrow	1976	2	1	0	1
Beth Barry	1972-74	5	3	1	1
Larua Baugh	1972	4	2	1	1
Judy Bell	1960-62-**(86)**-**(88)**	2	1	1	0
Peggy Kirk Bell (Kirk)	1950	2	1	1	0
Amy Benz	1982	3	2	1	0
Patty Berg	1936-38	4	1	2	1
Barbara Fay Boddie (White)	1964-66	8	7	0	1
Jane Booth (Bastanchury)	1970-72-74	12	9	3	0
Mary Budke	1974	3	2	1	0
JoAnne Carner (Gunderson)	1958-60-62-64	10	6	3	1

British Isles v USA (Ladies) Curtis Cup
continued

Player	Year	Played	Won	Lost	Halved
Lori Castillo	1980	3	2	1	0
Leona Cheney (Pressler)	1932-34-36	6	5	1	0
Sis Choate	**(1974)**	0	0	0	0
Peggy Conley	1964-68	6	3	1	2
Mary Ann Cook (Downey)	1956	2	1	1	0
Patricia Cornett	1978-88	4	1	2	1
Jean Crawford (Ashley)	1962-66-68-**(72)**	8	6	2	0
Clifford Ann Creed	1962	2	2	0	0
Grace Cronin (Lenczyk)	1948-50	3	2	1	0
Carolyn Cudone	1956-**(70)**	1	1	0	0
Beth Daniel	1976-78	8	7	1	0
Virginia Dennehy	**(1958)**	0	0	0	0
Mary Lou Dill	1968	3	1	1	1
Alice Dye	1970	2	1	0	1
Heather Farr	1984	3	2	1	0
Jane Fassinger	1970	1	0	1	0
Mary Lena Faulk	1954	2	1	1	0
Carol Sorensen Flenniken (Sorensen)	1964-66	8	6	1	1
Edith Flippin (Quier)	**(1954)-(56)**	0	0	0	0
Kim Gardner	1986	3	1	1	1
Charlotte Glutting	1934-36-38	5	3	1	1
Brenda Goldsmith	1978-80	4	2	2	0
Aniela Goldthwaite	1934-**(52)**	1	0	1	0
Joanne Goodwin	1960	2	1	1	0
Mary Hafeman	1980	2	1	0	1
Shelley Hamkin	1968-70	8	3	3	2
Penny Hammel	1984	3	1	1	1
Nancy Hammer (Hager)	1970	2	1	1	0
Cathy Hanlon	1982	3	2	1	0
Beverley Hanson	1950	2	2	0	0
Patricia Harbottle (Lesser)	1954-56	3	2	1	0
Helen Hawes	**(1964)**	0	0	0	0
Kathryn Hemphill	1938	1	0	0	1
Helen Hicks	1932	2	1	1	0
Carolyn Hill	1978	2	0	0	2
Cindy Hill	1970-74-76-78	14	5	6	3
Opel Hill	1932-34-36	6	2	3	1
Marion Hollins	**(1932)**	0	0	0	0
Dana Howe	1984	3	1	1	1
Juli Inkster	1982	4	4	0	0
Ann Casey Johnstone	1958-60-62	4	3	1	0
Mae Murray Jones (Murray)	1952	1	0	1	0
Caroline Keggi	1988	3	0	2	1
Tracy Kerdyk	1988	4	2	1	1
Kandi Kessler	1986	3	1	1	1
Dorothy Kielty	1948-50	4	4	0	0
Dorothy Kirby	1948-50-52-54	7	4	3	0
Martha Kirouac (Wilkinson)	1970-72	8	5	3	0
Nancy Knight (Lopez)	1976	2	2	0	0
Bonnie Lauer	1974	4	2	2	0
Marjorie Lindsay	1952	2	1	1	0
Patricia Lucey (O'Sullivan)	1952	1	0	1	0
Mari McDougall	1982	2	2	0	0
Barbara McIntire	1958-60-62-64-66-72-**(76)**	16	6	6	4
Lucile Mann (Robinson)	1934	1	0	1	0
Debbie Massey	1974-76	5	5	0	0
Marion Miley	1938	2	1	0	1
Dottie Mochrie (Pepper)	1986	3	0	2	1
Evelyn Monsted	**(1968)**	0	0	0	0
Terri Moody	1980	2	1	0	1
Judith Oliver	1978-80-82	8	5	1	2
Maureen Orcutt	1932-34-36-38	8	5	3	0
Joanne Pacillo	1984	3	1	1	1
Estelle Page (Lawson)	1938-48	4	3	1	0
Frances Pond (Stebbins)	**(1938)**	0	0	0	0
Dorothy Germain Porter	1950-**(66)**	2	1	0	1
Phyllis Preuss	1962-64-66-68-70-**(84)**	15	10	4	1
Betty Probasco	**(1982)**	0	0	0	0
Mildred Prunaret	**(1960)**	0	0	0	0
Polly Riley	1948-50-52-54-56-58-**(62)**	10	5	5	0
Barbara Romack	1954-56-58	5	3	2	0
Jody Rosenthal	1984	3	2	0	1
Anne Quast Sander [Welts] [Decker] (Quast)	1958-60-62-66-68-74-84	20	9	7	4
Cindy Scholefield	1988	3	0	3	0

British Isles *v* USA (Ladies) Curtis Cup
continued

Player	Year	Played	Won	Lost	Halved
Cindy Schreyer	1986	3	1	2	0
Kathleen McCarthy Scrivner (McCarthy)	1986-88	6	2	3	1
Leslie Shannon	1986-88	6	0	4	2
Patty Sheehan	1980	4	4	0	0
Pearl Sinn	1988	2	1	1	0
Grace De Moss Smith (De Moss)	1952-54	3	1	2	0
Lancy Smith	1972-78-80-82-84	16	7	5	4
Margaret Smith	1956	2	2	0	0
Hollis Stacy	1972	2	0	1	1
Claire Stancik (Doran)	1952-54	4	4	0	0
Judy Street (Eller)	1960	2	2	0	0
Louise Suggs	1948	2	0	1	1
Nancy Roth Syms (Roth)	1964-66-76-**(80)**	9	3	5	1
Carol Thompson (Semple)	1974-76-80-82	14	7	5	2
Noreen Uihlein	1978	3	1	1	1
Virginia Van Wie	1932-34	4	3	0	1
Glenna Collett Vare (Collett)	1932-**(34)-36**-38-**48-(50)**	7	4	2	1
Jane Weiss (Nelson)	1956	1	0	1	0
Donna White (Horton)	1976	2	2	0	0
Mary Anne Widman	1984	3	2	1	0
Kimberley Williams	1986	3	0	3	0
Helen Sigel Wilson (Sigel)	1950-66-**(78)**	2	0	2	0
Joyce Ziske	1954	1	0	1	0

Bold print: captain; bold print in brackets: non-playing captain.
Maiden name in parenthesis; former surname in square brackets.

Vagliano Trophy—Great Britain & Ireland *v* Europe (Ladies)

Played for biennially between teams of women amateur golfers representing the British Isles and Europe. (From 1947 to 1957 was between the British Isles and France.)

Year	Winner	Result	Venue
1979	Halved	12-12	R Porthcawl
1981	Europe	14-10	P de Hierro
1983	GB & Ireland	14-10	Woodhall Spa
1985	GB & Ireland	14-10	Hamburg
1987	GB & Ireland	15-9	The Berkshire

Commonwealth Tournament (Ladies)

Year	Winner	Venue
1959	Great Britain	St Andrews
1963	Great Britain	Royal Melbourne, Australia
1967	Great Britain	Ancaster, Ontario, Canada
1971	Great Britain	Hamilton, New Zealand
1975	Great Britain	Ganton, England
1979	Canada	Lake Karrinup, Perth Australia
1983	Australia	Glendale, Edmonton, Canada
1987	Canada	Christchurch, New Zealand

Women's World Amateur Team Championship (Espirito Santo Trophy)

Year	Winners	Runners-up	Venue	Score
1978	Australia	Canada	Fiji	596
1980	United States	Australia	Pinehurst, USA	588
1982	United States	New Zealand	Geneva, Switzerland	579
1984	United States	France	Hong Kong	585
1986	Spain	France	Caracas, Venezuela	580
1988	United States	Sweden	Drottingholm, Sweden	587

European Ladies' Amateur Team Championship

Year	Winner	Second	Venue
1979	Ireland	Germany	Hermitage, Ireland
1981	Sweden	France	Troia, Portugal
1983	Ireland	England	Waterloo, Belgium
1985	England	Italy	Stavanger, Norway
1987	Sweden	Wales	Turnberry, Scotland

Women's Home Internationals

Year	Winner	Venue
1948	England	Lytham St Annes
1949	Scotland	Harlech
1950	Scotland	Newcastle Co, Down
1951	Scotland	Broadstone
1952	Scotland	Troon
1953	England	Porthcawl
1954	England	Ganton
1955	England Scotland	Western Gailes
1956	Scotland	Sunningdale
1957	Scotland	Troon
1958	England	Hunstanton
1959	England	Hoylake
1960	England	Gullane
1961	Scotland	Portmarnock
1962	Scotland	Porthcawl
1963	England	Formby
1964	England	Troon
1965	England	Portrush
1966	England	Woodhall Spa
1967	England	Sunningdale
1968	England	Porthcawl
1969	England Scotland	Western Gailes
1970	England	Killarney
1971	England	Longniddry
1972	England	Lytham St Annes
1973	England	Harlech
1974	England Scotland Ireland	Princes
1975	England	Newport
1976	England	Troon
1977	England	Cork
1978	England	Moortown
1979	Scotland Ireland	Harlech
1980	Ireland	Cruden Bay
1981	Scotland	Portmarnock
1982	England	Burnham and Barrow
1983	*Matches abandoned due to weather*	

Women's Home Internationals
continued

At Gullane, 9th to 14th September, 1984

England beat Wales	6½ matches to 2½
Scotland beat Ireland	7½ matches to 1½
Ireland beat Wales	9 matches to 0
England beat Scotland	5½ matches to 3½
Scotland beat Wales	5½ matches to 3½
England beat Ireland	7 matches to 2

Result: England 3; Scotland 2; Ireland 1; Wales 0

At Waterville, Co Kerry, 1985

England beat Scotland	7 matches to 2
England beat Wales	6½ matches to 2½
Ireland beat England	5½ matches to 3½
Ireland beat Wales	6 matches to 3
Scotland beat Ireland	5 matches to 4
Scotland beat Wales	6 matches to 3

Result: England 2; Ireland 2; Scotland 2; Wales 0

At Whittington Barracks, Staffs, 1986

England halved with Scotland	4½ matches each
England beat Wales	7½ matches to 1½
Wales beat Ireland	5 matches to 4
Ireland beat Scotland	6½ matches to 2½
Ireland beat England	5 matches to 4
Scotland beat Wales	6 matches to 3

Result: Ireland 2; England 1½; Scotland 1½; Wales 1

At Ashburnham, Dyfed, 1987

England beat Scotland	5½ matches to 3½
England beat Ireland	5½ matches to 3½
England beat Wales	6 matches to 3
Scotland beat Ireland	6 matches to 3
Scotland beat Wales	7 matches to 2
Ireland beat Wales	8 matches to 1

Result: England 3; Scotland 2; Ireland 1; Wales 0

At Barassie, Ayshire, 1988

Scotland beat England	5½ matches to 3½
Scotland beat Ireland	5 matches to 4
Scotland beat Wales	7½ matches to 1½
England beat Ireland	6½ matches to 2½
England beat Wales	7 matches to 2
Ireland halved with Wales	4½ matches each

Result: England 2; Scotland 3; Ireland 0; Wales 0

Girls' Home Internationals: Stroyan Cup

1985 at Hesketh

England beat Scotland	5-2
England beat Ireland	5½-1½
England beat Wales	6-1
Ireland beat Scotland	4-3
Ireland beat Wales	4-3
Scotland beat Wales	6½-½

Girls Home Internationals: Stroyan Cup
continued

1986 at West Kilbride

England beat Scotland	4-3
England beat Wales	4½-2½
England beat Ireland	5-2
Scotland beat Wales	5-2
Scotland beat Ireland	5-2
Wales beat Ireland	5-2

1987 at Barnham Broom

England beat Scotland	6½-½
England beat Ireland	7-0
England beat Wales	6-1
Scotland beat Ireland	4-3
Ireland beat Wales	4½-2½
Wales beat Scotland	4-3

1988 at Pyle and Kenfig

England beat Ireland	4-3
England beat Wales	4-3
England halved with Scotland	3½-3½
Ireland beat Wales	4-3
Ireland beat Scotland	5-2
Wales beat Scotland	4-3

County and District Championships

Aberdeenshire Ladies' Championship

Year	Winner
1984	Miss J Self
1985	Miss P Wright
1986	Miss E Farquharson
1987	Miss E Farquharson
1988	Miss L Urquhart

Angus Amateur Championship

Year	Winner
1988	D Downie

Angus Ladies' Championship

Instituted pre 1935

Year	Winner
1984	Miss K Imrie
1985	M Mackie
1986	Mrs F Farquharson
1987	Mrs F Farquharson
1988	Miss C Hay

Argyll and Bute Amateur Championship

Year	Winner
1984	D MacIntyre
1985	
1986	
1987	
1988	G Bolton

Astor Salver

Instituted 1951
Venue: The Berkshire

Year	Winner	Score
1984	Mrs L Bayman	142
1985	Miss H Wadsworth	138
1986	Miss C Pierce	144
1987	Mrs V Thomas	145
1988	Mrs J Thornhill	136

Avia Ladies' International Tournament

Venue: The Berkshire

Year	Winners
1984	Miss M McKenna and Mrs IC Robertson
1985	Mrs L Bayman and Miss M Madill
1986	Mrs IC Robertson and Miss M McKenna
1987	Miss S Moorcroft and Miss T Hammond
1988	Miss K Mitchell and Miss N Way

Ayrshire Amateur Championship

Year	Winner
1984	J Milligan
1985	P Girvan
1986	G Armstrong
1987	B Gemmell
1988	G Blair

Ayrshire Ladies' Championship

Instituted 1923

Year	Winner
1984	Miss A Gemmill
1985	Miss J Leishman
1986	Miss A Gemmill
1987	Miss A Gemmill
1988	Mrs M Wilson

Bedfordshire Amateur Championship

Instituted 1923

Year	Winner
1984	MA Stokes
1985	R Harris
1986	M Wharton
1987	P Wharton
1988	P Wharton

Bedfordshire Ladies' Championship

Instituted 1926

Year	Winner
1984	Mrs S White
1985	Mrs S White
1986	Mrs C Westgate
1987	Mrs Sarat White
1988	Miss S Cormack

Berkhamsted Trophy

Year	Winner	Score
1984	R Willison	139
1985	F George	144
1986	P McEvoy	144
1987	F George	141
1988	J Cowgill	146

Berkshire Trophy

Year	Winner	Score
1984	JL Plaxton	276
1985	P McEvoy	279
1986	R Muscroft	280
1987	J Robinson	275
1988	R Claydon	276

Berkshire Ladies' Championship

Instituted 1925

Year	Winner
1984	Mrs A Uzielli
1985	Mrs A Uzielli
1986	Mrs A Uzielli
1987	Mrs A Uzielli
1988	Miss T Smith

Berks, Bucks and Oxfordshire Amateur Championship

Instituted 1924

Year	Winner
1984	NG Webber
1985	M Rapley
1986	DG Lane
1987	F George
1988	F George

Border Counties Ladies' Championship

Year	Winner
1984	Miss S Gallacher
1985	Miss S Gallacher
1986	Miss S Gallacher
1987	Mrs S Simpson
1988	Miss A Hunter

Border Golfers' Association Amateur Championship

Instituted 1893

Year	Winner
1984	A Turnbull
1985	
1986	L Wallace
1987	D Ballantyne
1988	W Renwick

Boyd Quaich Tournament

Year	Winner
1984	J Huggan
1985	S Elgie
1986	
1987	M Pask
1988	

Bucks Ladies' Championship

Instituted 1924

Year	Winner
1984	Miss J Warren
1985	Miss E Franklin
1986	Miss A Tyreman
1987	Mrs C Watson
1988	Miss C Hourihane

Caernarvonshire Amateur Championship

Instituted 1922

Year	Winner
1984	S Owen
1985	MA Macara
1986	RI Roberts
1987	D McLean
1988	

Caernarvonshire and Anglesey Ladies' Championship

Instituted 1924

Year	Winner
1984	Miss S Jump
1985	Miss A Lewis
1986	Mrs S Turner
1987	Miss S Roberts
1988	Mrs S Turner

Cambridge Area GU Amateur Championship

Year	Winner
1984	NK Hughes
1985	DWG Wood
1986	JGR Miller
1987	R Claydon
1988	R Claydon

Cambridgeshire and Hunts Ladies' Championship

Year	Winner
1984	Miss J Walter
1985	Miss J Walter
1986	Miss J Walter
1987	Mrs R Farrow
1988	Miss S Meadows

Channel Islands Ladies' Championship

Year	Winner
1984	Mrs E Roberts
1985	Miss L Cummins
1986	Miss V Bougourd
1987	Miss L Cummins
1988	Miss L Cummins

Cheshire Amateur Championship

Instituted 1921

Year	Winner
1984	I Spencer
1985	C Harrison
1986	P Bailey
1987	P Jones
1988	P Bailey

Cheshire Ladies' Championship

Instituted 1912

Year	Winner
1984	Miss J Hill
1985	Miss L Percival
1986	Miss J Hill
1987	Miss S Robinson
1988	Miss J Morley

Clackmannanshire Amateur Championship

Year	Winner
1988	R Stewart

Cornwall Amateur Championship

Instituted 1896

Year	Winner
1984	RJ Simmons
1985	CD Phillips
1986	RJ Simmons
1987	P Clayton
1988	P Clayton

Cornwall Ladies' Championship

Instituted 1896

Year	Winner
1984	Miss J Fernleigh
1985	Miss J Fern
1986	Miss J Ryder
1987	Miss J Ryder
1988	Mrs S Currie

County Champions' Tournament (England)

For President's Bowl

Year	Winner
1984	N Briggs, Hertfordshire P McEvoy, Warwickshire
1985	P Robinson, Hertfordshire
1986	A Gelsthorpe, Yorkshire
1987	F George, Berks, Bucks & Oxon D Fay, Surrey
1988	R Claydon

Cumbria Amateur Championship

Formerly Cumberland and Westmorland Amateur Championship

Year	Winner
1984	M Lowe
1985	J Longcake
1986	M Ruddick
1987	J Loncake
1988	G Waters

Cumbria Ladies' Championship

Year	Winner
1984	Miss D Thomson
1985	Miss J Currie
1986	Mrs H Porter
1987	Miss J McColl
1988	Miss D Thomson

Denbighshire and Flintshire Ladies' Championship

Year	Winner
1984	Mrs C Ellis
1985	Miss E Davies
1986	Mrs S Thomas
1987	Mrs S Thomas
1988	Mrs S Thomas

Derbyshire Amateur Championship

Instituted 1913

Year	Winner
1984	G Shaw
1985	R Davenport
1986	J Feeney
1987	RP Green
1988	NC Wylde

Derbyshire Ladies' Championship

Instituted 1921

Year	Winner
1984	Miss J Williams
1985	Miss L Holmes
1986	Miss E Robinson
1987	Miss E Clark
1988	Miss A Howe

Derbyshire Match-Play Championship

Instituted 1971

Year	Winner
1984	G Shaw
1985	CRJ Ibbotson
1986	J Feeney
1987	G Shaw
1988	MP Higgins

Derbyshire Open Championship

Year	Winner
1984	J Feeney (Am)
1985	M McLean
1986	N Furniss (Am)
1987	SA Smith
1988	G Shaw

Derbyshire Professional Championship

Instituted 1921

Year	Winner
1984	W Bird
1985	J Turnbull
1986	J Lower
1987	AR Skingle
1988	M McLean

Devon Amateur Championship

Instituted 1912

Year	Winner
1985	J Langmead
1986	P Newcombe
1987	J Langmead
1988	J Langmead

Devon Ladies' Championship

Instituted 1922

Year	Winner
1984	Miss J Hurley
1985	Miss L Lines
1986	Miss J Hurley
1987	Miss G Jenkinson
1988	Miss J Hurley

Devon Open Championship

Instituted 1923

Year	Winner
1984	
1985	
1986	
1987	
1988	G Wolstenholme

Dorset Amateur Championship

Instituted 1924

Year	Winner
1984	JD Gordon
1985	J Bloxham
1986	A Lawrence
1987	A Lawrence
1988	A Lawrence

Dorset Ladies' Championship

Instituted 1923

Year	Winner
1984	Miss S Lowe
1985	Miss S Lowe
1986	Miss H Delew
1987	Mrs J Sugden
1988	Miss H Delew

Dumfriesshire Ladies' Championship

Year	Winner
1984	Miss DM Hill
1985	Mrs R Morrison
1986	Mrs M McKerrow
1987	Mrs M McKerrow
1988	Miss D Douglas

Dunbartonshire Amateur Championship

Year	Winner
1984	T Eckford
1985	
1986	
1987	
1988	J Laird

Dunbartonshire and Argyll Ladies' Championship

Year	Winner
1984	Miss V McAlister
1985	Miss V McAlister
1986	Miss J Kinloch
1987	Miss S McDonald
1988	Miss V McAlister

Duncan Putter

Instituted 1959

Year	Winner	Score
1984	JP Price	297
1985	P McEvoy	299
1986	D Wood	300
1987	P McEvoy	278
1988	S Dodd	290

Durham Amateur Championship

Instituted 1908

Year	Winner
1984	M Ure
1985	A Robertson
1986	H Ashby
1987	P Highmoor
1988	JR Ellwood

Durham Ladies' Championship

Instituted 1923

Year	Winner
1984	Miss B Mansfield
1985	Miss M Scullan
1986	Miss L Chesterton
1987	Miss B Mansfield
1988	Miss L Chesterton

East Anglian Ladies' Championship

Year	Winner
1986	Miss J Walter
1987	Miss J Walter
1988	

East Anglian Open Championship

Year	Winner
1984	
1985	
1986	
1987	
1988	P Kent

East Lothian Ladies' Championship

Year	Winner
1984	Miss M Ferguson
1985	Miss M Ferguson
1986	Miss P Lees
1987	Miss J Ford
1988	Miss C Lugton

East of Ireland Open Amateur Championship

Year	Winner
1984	BUM Reddan
1985	F Ronan
1986	P Hogan
1987	P Rayfus
1988	G McGimpsey

Eastern Division Ladies' Championship (Scotland)

Year	Winner
1984	Miss L Hope
1985	Miss L Bennett
1986	Miss J Harrison
1987	Miss A Rose
1988	Miss J Ford

East of Scotland Open Amateur Stroke Play

Year	Winner
1984	S Stephen
1985	A McQueen
1986	S Knowles
1987	T Cochrane
1988	C Everett

Edward Trophy

Instituted 1892

Year	Winner
1984	K Walker
1985	GK MacDonald
1986	J Noon
1987	
1988	R Blair

Essex Ladies' Championship

Year	Winner
1984	Mrs S Barber
1985	Mrs S Barber
1986	Miss S Moorcroft
1987	Miss M King
1988	Miss W Dicks

Essex Amateur Championship

Year	Winner
1984	M Stokes
1985	D Wood
1986	M Davis
1987	V Cox
1988	R Scott

Fife Amateur Championship

Instituted 1925

Year	Winner
1984	C Birrell
1985	DR Weir
1986	D Spriddle
1987	SR Meiklejohn
1988	A Mathers

Fife County Ladies' Championship

Year	Winner
1984	Miss E Hunter
1985	Miss L Bennett
1986	Miss L Bennett
1987	Miss L Bennett
1988	Miss J Lawrence

Frame Trophy
Instituted 1986
Venue: Worplesdon

Year	Winner	Score
1986	DW Frame	220
1987	JRW Walinshaw	225
1988	DW Frame	229

Galloway Ladies' Championship

Year	Winner
1984	Miss S McDonald
1985	Miss M Wright
1986	Miss M Wright
1987	Miss M Wright
1988	Miss M Wright

Glamorgan Amateur Championship

Year	Winner
1984	
1985	R Brown
1986	LP Price
1987	N Roderick
1988	I Booth

Glamorgan County Ladies' Championship
Instituted 1927

Year	Winner
1984	Miss J Foster
1985	Miss P Johnson
1986	Miss P Johnson
1987	Mrs V Thomas
1988	Mrs V Thomas

Glasgow Match Play Championship
Instituted 1897

Year	Winner
1984	I Carslaw
1985	S Savage
1986	G Shaw
1987	S Dixon
1988	J Finnigan

Glasgow Stroke Play Championship

Year	Winner
1984	IA Carslaw
1985	IA Carslaw
1986	A Maclaine
1987	S Machin
1988	D Martin

Gloucestershire Amateur Championship

Instituted 1906

Year	Winner
1984	C Robinson
1985	D Carroll
1986	RD Broad
1987	M Bessell
1988	J Webber

Gloucestershire Ladies' Championship

Instituted 1923

Year	Winner
1984	Miss K Douglas
1985	Miss C Griffiths
1986	Miss S Shapcott
1987	Mrs R Page
1988	Miss S Elliott

Golf Illustrated Gold Vase

Instituted 1909

Year	Winner
1984	JV Marks
1985	M Davis
1986	R Eggo
1987	D Lane
1988	M Turner

Grafton Morrish Trophy

Public Schools Old Boys' Golf Association

Year	Winner
1984	Sedbergh
1985	Warwick
1986	Tonbridge
1987	Harrow
1988	Robert Gordon's

Gwent Amateur Championship

Formerly Monmouthshire Amateur Championship

Year	Winner
1984	P Mayo
1985	M Brimble
1986	G Hughes
1987	M Bearcroft
1988	A Williams

Halford-Hewitt Challenge Cup

Public Schools Old Boys' Tournament
Instituted 1924
Played at Deal

Year	Winner
1984	Charterhouse
1985	Harrow
1986	Repton
1987	Merchiston
1988	Stowe

Hampshire, Isle of Wight and Channel Islands Open Championship

Instituted 1967

Year	Winner
1984	M Desmond
1985	I Young
1986	M Desmond
1987	T Healey
1988	K Bowden

Hampshire, Isle of Wight and Channel Islands Amateur Championship

Instituted 1894

Year	Winner
1984	R Eggo
1985	RA Alker
1986	R Eggo
1987	A Mew
1988	S Richardson

Hampshire Ladies' Championship

Instituted 1924

Year	Winner
1984	Miss C Mackintosh
1985	Mrs C Stirling
1986	Miss C Hayllar
1987	Mrs C Stirling
1988	Mrs C Stirling

Hampshire Professional Match Play Championship

Year	Winner
1984	J Hay
1985	P Dawson
1986	K Bowden
1987	M Desmond
1988	K Bowden

Hampshire Professional Stroke Play Championship

Year	Winner
1984	G Stubbington
1985	T Healy
1986	M Desmond
1987	T Healy
1988	G Stubbington

Hampshire Hog

Played annually at North Hants GC
Instituted 1957

Year	Winner
1984	J Hawkesworth
1985	A Clapp
1986	R Eggo
1987	A Rogers
1988	S Richardson

Hampshire Rose

Instituted 1973
Played annually at North Hants GC

Year	Winner
1984	Mrs C Caldwell
1985	Mrs A Uzielli
1986	Miss C Hourihane
1987	Mrs J Thornhill
1988	Mrs J Thornhill

Helen Holm Trophy

Instituted 1973

Year	Winner
1984	Miss G Stewart
1985	Miss P Wright
1986	Mrs IC Robertson
1987	Miss E Farquharson
1988	Miss E Farquharson

Herts Amateur Championship

Year	Winner
1984	N Briggs
1985	PR Robinson
1986	PJ Cherry
1987	A Clark
1988	J Ambridge

Herts Ladies' Championship

Instituted 1924

Year	Winner
1984	Miss K Hurley
1985	Mrs H Kaye
1986	Miss T Jeary
1987	Mrs H Kaye
1988	Miss T Jeary

Isle of Wight Ladies' Championship

Instituted 1923

Year	Winner
1984	Mrs M Butler
1985	Miss G Wright
1986	Miss M Ankers
1987	Miss M Ankers
1988	Mrs M Butler

Kent Amateur Championship

Instituted 1925

Year	Winner
1984	M Lawrence
1985	J Simmance
1986	M Lawrence
1987	L Batchelor
1988	W Hodkin

Kent Ladies' Championship

Instituted 1920

Year	Winner
1984	Mrs S Kitchen
1985	Mrs L Bayman
1986	Mrs C Caldwell
1987	Mrs L Bayman
1988	Mrs C Caldwell

Kent Open Championship

Year	Winner
1984	N Terry
1985	J Bennett
1986	P Mitchell
1987	M Goodin
1988	J Bennett

Kent Professional Championship

Instituted 1912

Year	Winner
1984	R Cameron
1985	G Will
1986	J Bennett
1987	S Barr
1988	R Cameron

The Lagonda Trophy

Instituted 1975
Venue: Camberley Heath
From 1982 played over 72 holes

Year	Winner	Score
1984	M Davis	289
1985	J Robinson	283
1986	D Gilford	282
1987	DG Lane	290
1988	R Claydon	275

Lanarkshire Amateur Championship

Year	Winner
1984	WS Bryson
1985	J Reid
1986	WS Bryson
1987	S Henderson
1988	WS Bryson

Lanarkshire Ladies' County Championship

Instituted 1928

Year	Winner
1984	Mrs S Roy
1985	Miss P Hutton
1986	Mrs JC Scott
1987	Mrs A Hendry
1988	Miss F McKay

Lancashire Amateur Championship

Instituted 1910

Year	Winner
1984	SG Birtwell
1985	RA Bardsley
1986	MJ Wild
1987	T Foster
1988	M Kingsley

Lancashire Ladies' Championship

Instituted 1912

Year	Winner
1984	Mrs A Goucher
1985	Mrs A Bromilow
1986	Mrs J Collingham (*née* Melville)
1987	Mrs J Collingham
1988	Miss L Fairclough

Lancashire Open Championship

Instituted 1973

Year	Winner
1984	
1985	R Longworth
1986	R Green
1987	
1988	

Leicestershire and Rutland Amateur Championship

Instituted 1925

Year	Winner
1984	A Martinez
1985	E Hammond
1986	IR Middleton
1987	G Marshall
1988	A Martinez

Leicestershire and Rutland Open Championship

Year	Winner
1984	R Larratt
1985	R Adams
1986	
1987	
1988	D Gibson

Leicestershire and Rutland Ladies' Championship

Year	Winner
1984	Mrs P Martin
1985	Miss A Waters
1986	Mrs V Davis
1987	Miss M Page
1988	Miss A Walters

Lincolnshire Amateur Championship

Instituted 1925

Year	Winner
1984	JA Purdy
1985	ACS Robinson
1986	JA Purdy
1987	P Stenton
1988	P Stenton

Lincolnshire Ladies' Championship

Year	Winner
1984	Mrs A Burtt
1985	Miss H Dobson
1986	Miss A Johns
1987	Miss H Dobson
1988	Miss H Dobson

Lincolnshire Open Championship

Year	Winner
1984	
1985	
1986	A Carter
1987	
1988	

Lothians Amateur Championship

Year	Winner
1984	PJ Smith
1985	S Easingwood
1986	S Smith
1987	D Kirkpatrick
1988	D Neeve

The Lytham Trophy

Venue: Lytham and St Annes

Year	Winner	Score
1984	J Hawksworth	289
1985	L Macnamara	144
1986	S McKenna	297
1987	D Wood	293
1988	P Broadhurst	296

Manx Amateur Championship

Instituted 1926

Year	Winner
1984	J Sutton
1985	J Sutton
1986	AM Cain
1987	J Sutton
1988	G Kelly

Peter McEvoy Trophy

Venue: Copt Heath
Instituted 1981

Year	Winner
1984	W Henry
1985	A Morley
1986	C Mitchell
1987	W Henry
1988	P Sefton

Middlesex Amateur Championship

Instituted 1925

Year	Winner
1984	RB Willison
1985	RB Willison
1986	A Rogers
1987	RB Willison
1988	A Rogers

Middlesex Ladies' Championship

Instituted 1923

Year	Winner
1984	Miss C Nelson
1985	Miss C Nelson
1986	Mrs A Gems
1987	Mrs A Gems
1988	Miss S Keogh

Middlesex Open Championship

Year	Winner
1984	
1985	
1986	
1987	L Fickling
1988	

Midland Open Amateur Stroke Play Championship

Year	Winner
1984	K Valentine
1985	M Hassall
1986	
1987	C Suneson
1988	R Winchester

Midland Ladies' Championship

Instituted 1897

Year	Winner
1984	Miss L Waring
1985	Miss L Waring
1986	Mrs J Collingham
1987	Miss S Roberts
1988	Miss S Roberts

Midland Mid-Amateur

Year	Winner	Venue	Score
1988	P McEvoy	Little Aston	284

Midland Masters

Instituted 1988

Year	Winner
1988	B Waites

Midland Professional Stroke Play Championship

Instituted 1897

Year	Winner
1984	M Mouland
1985	K Hayward
1986	A Skingle
1987	M Mouland
1988	G Farr

Midland Professional Match Play Championship

Instituted 1899

Year	Winner
1984	P Elson
1985	D Ridley
1986	J Higgins
1987	K Hayward
1988	J Higgins

Midlothian Ladies' Championship

Instituted 1924

Year	Winner
1984	Mrs F de Vries
1985	Mrs F de Vries
1986	Mrs J Marshall
1987	Miss M Stavert
1988	Miss M Stavert

Mid-Wales Ladies' Championship

Year	Winner
1988	Miss S James

Monmouthshire Ladies' Championship

Instituted 1920

Year	Winner
1984	Miss J Lapthorne
1985	Miss P Lord
1986	Miss H Buckley
1987	Miss H Buckley
1988	MIss H Armstrong

Norfolk Amateur Championship

Instituted 1921

Year	Winner
1984	T Hurrell
1985	CJ Lamb
1986	ID Sperrin
1987	NJ Williamson
1988	NJ Williamson

Norfolk Ladies' Championship

Instituted 1912

Year	Winner
1984	Mrs L Elliott
1985	Mrs M Whybrow
1986	Mrs N Clarke
1987	Mrs AM Davies
1988	Mrs L Elliott

Norfolk Professional Championship

Instituted 1921

Year	Winner
1984	MJ Elsworthy
1985	M Spooler
1986	M Spooler
1987	MJ Elsworthy
1988	M Few

Norfolk Professional Match Play Championship

Year	Winner
1986	MT Leeder
1987	RG Foster
1988	M Few

Norfolk Open Championship

Year	Winner
1984	M Elsworthy
1985	T Hurrell
1986	M Spooner
1987	MJ Elsworthy
1988	M Few

Northamptonshire Amateur Championship

Instituted 1927

Year	Winner
1984	M Scott
1985	M McNally
1986	M Scott
1987	D Jones
1988	D Ellson

Northamptonshire Ladies' Championship

Year	Winner
1984	Mrs A Duck
1985	Mrs A Duck
1986	Mrs P Le Vai
1987	Mrs J Kendrick
1988	Mrs A Duck

Northern (England) Professional Championship

Instituted 1920

Year	Winner
1984	
1985	A Murray
1986	D Stirling
1987	S Rolley
1988	K Waters

Northern Counties (Scotland) Ladies' Championship

Year	Winner
1984	Miss J Buist
1985	Miss A Shannon
1986	Miss F McKay
1987	Mrs I McIntosh
1988	Mrs I McIntosh

North of Ireland Open Amateur Championship

Year	Winner
1984	G McGimpsey
1985	I Elliott
1986	D Ballantine
1987	A Pierse
1988	N Anderson

Northern Scottish Open Championship

Instituted 1931

Year	Winner
1984	JS Macdonald
1984	D Huish
1985	BW Barnes
1986	R Weir
1987	A Hunter
1988	D Huish

Northern Women's Championship

Year	Winner
1984	Miss C Hall
1985	Miss C Hall
1986	Miss L Fairclough
1987	Miss S Robinson
1988	Miss K Tebbet

Northumberland Amateur Championship

Instituted 1907

Year	Winner
1984	J Straker
1985	D Faulder
1986	D Martin
1987	K Fairbairn
1988	J Metcalf

Northumberland Ladies' Championship

Instituted 1921

Year	Winner
1984	Miss CM Hall
1985	Miss CM Hall
1986	Miss CM Hall
1987	Miss C Breckon
1988	Miss D Glenn

Northern Division Ladies' Championship (Scotland)

Year	Winner
1984	Miss P Wright
1985	Miss A Shannon
1986	Miss C Middleton
1987	Mrs A Murray (*née* Shannon)
1988	Miss K Imrie

North of Scotland Open Amateur Stroke Play Championship

Instituted 1970

Year	Winner
1984	JS Macdonald
1985	JS Macdonald
1986	S Cruickshank
1987	S McIntosh
1988	KS Herd

Nottinghamshire Amateur Championship

Instituted 1924

Year	Winner
1984	G Krause
1985	M Scothern
1986	G Krause
1987	R Sallis
1988	CA Banks

Nottinghamshire Ladies' Championship

Instituted 1925

Year	Winner
1984	Miss M Elswood
1985	Miss KM Horberry
1986	CG Palmer
1987	Miss M Elswood
1988	Miss A Ferguson

Nottinghamshire Open Championship

Year	Winner
1984	CD Hall
1985	C Jepson
1986	BJ Waites
1987	CD Hall
1988	C Banks (Am)

One-Armed Championship

Year	Winner
1984	ASL Robinson
1985	ASL Robinson
1986	MJ O'Grady
1987	J Cann
1988	

Oxford *v* Cambridge

Instituted 1878

Year	Winner	Venue
1984	Cambridge	Sunningdale
1985	Oxford	Rye
1986	Oxford	Ganton
1987	Cambridge	Formby
1988	Cambridge	Royal Porthcawl

Played 99; Cambridge won 55; Oxford 39; halved 5

Oxford and Cambridge Golfing Society's "President's" Putter

Instituted 1920

Year	Winner
1984	A Edmond
1985	ER Dexter
1986	J Caplan
1987	CD Meacher
1988	G Woollett

Oxfordshire Ladies' Championship

Year	Winner
1984	Miss T Craik
1985	Miss N Sparks
1986	Miss T Craik
1987	Miss T Craik
1988	Miss T Craik

Parliamentary Handicap

Instituted 1891

Year	Winner
1984	Stanley Clinton Davis
1985	Michael Morris MP
1986	Sir Anthony Grant MP
1987	Sir Anthony Grant MP
1988	Sir Peter Hordern

Perth and Kinross Ladies' Championship

Year	Winner
1984	Miss E Aitken
1985	Miss A Guthrie
1986	Mrs I Shannon
1987	Miss F Anderson
1988	Miss V Pringle

Perth and Kinross Amateur Stroke Play Championship

Instituted 1930

Year	Winner
1984	G Lowson
1985	G Lowson
1986	C Bloice
1987	BRM Grieve
1988	EJ Lindsay

HRH Prince of Wales Challenge Cup

Instituted 1927
Venue: Deal

Year	Winner	Score
1984	DH Niven and F Wood (*tied*)	146
1985	RJ Tickner	141
1986	JM Baldwin	149
1987	S Finch	148
1988	MP Palmer	144

Queen Elizabeth Coronation Schools' Trophy

Venue: Royal Burgess Golfing Society, Barnton, Edinburgh

Year	Winner
1984	Glasgow High School FP
1985	Glasgow High School FP
1986	Watsonians
1987	Stewart's-Melville FP
1988	Watsonians

Renfrewshire Amateur Championship

Year	Winner
1984	DB Howard
1985	J McDonald
1986	IG Riddell
1987	DB Howard
1988	ES Grey

Renfrewshire County Ladies' Championship

Instituted 1927

Year	Winner
1984	Dr A Wilson
1985	Miss S Lawson
1986	Miss S Lawson
1987	Miss S Lawson
1988	Miss S Lawson

Rosebery Challenge Cup

Venue: Ashridge

Year	Winner
1984	DG Lane
1985	P Wharton
1986	JE Ambridge
1987	HA Wilkerson
1988	N Leconte

St David's Gold Cross

Instituted 1930
Venue: Royal St David's, Harlech

Year	Winner
1984	RJ Green
1985	KH Williams
1986	
1987	SR Andrew
1988	M Calvert

St George's Challenge Cup

Instituted 1888
Venue: Royal St George's, Sandwich

Year	Winner
1984	SJ Wood
1985	SJ Wood
1986	R Claydon
1987	MR Goodin
1988	T Ryan

Scottish Area Team Championship

Instituted 1977

Year	Winner
1984	Glasgow
1985	Lothians
1986	Ayrshire
1987	Lothians
1988	Lothians

Scottish Champion of Champions

Instituted 1970

Year	Winner
1984	S Stephen
1985	IR Brotherston
1986	IC Hutcheon
1987	G Shaw
1988	IC Hutcheon

Scottish Foursome Tournament–*Glasgow Evening Times* Trophy

Instituted 1891

Year	Winner
1984	Royal Musselburgh
1985	East Renfrewshire
1986	Hamilton
1987	Drumpellier
1988	Irvine Ravenspark

Scottish Ladies' County Championship

Instituted 1909

Year	Winner
1984	Lanarkshire
1985	East Lothian
1986	Aberdeenshire
1987	
1988	Lanarkshire

Scottish Ladies' Foursomes

Year	Winner
1984	Gullane
1985	*No Championship*
1986	Blairgowrie
1987	Baberton
1988	Gullane

Scottish Universities' Championship

Instituted 1923

Year	Winner
1984	Edinburgh
1985	Edinburgh
1986	Stirling
1987	Stirling
1988	

Scottish Universities' Individual Championship

Instituted 1931

Year	Winner
1984	J Huggan
1985	K Walker
1986	I Menzies
1987	N Hughes
1988	

Selborne–Salver

Venue: Blackmoor GC, Hampshire

Year	Winner
1984	D Curry
1985	SM Bottomley
1986	TE Clarke
1987	
1988	N Holman

Shropshire and Herefordshire Amateur Championship

Year	Winner
1984	PA Baker
1985	PA Baker
1986	C Bufton
1987	R Dixon
1988	S Thomas

Shropshire Ladies' Championship

Instituted 1923

Year	Winner
1984	Mrs A Johnson
1985	Mrs A Johnson
1986	Mrs S Pidgeon
1987	Mrs S Pidgeon
1988	Miss A Jackson

Somerset Amateur Championship

Instituted 1911

Year	Winner
1984	CS Edwards
1985	PR Hare
1986	CS Edwards
1987	G Hickman
1988	CS Edwards

Somerset Ladies' Championship

Instituted 1913

Year	Winner
1984	Mrs M Perriam
1985	Miss K Nicholls
1986	Miss K Nicholls
1987	Miss K Nicholls
1988	Mrs C Whiting

South-Eastern Ladies' Championship

Year	Winner
1984	Miss L Davies
1985	Mrs J Thornhill
1986	Miss S Moorcroft
1987	Miss N Way
1988	Mrs C Stirling

South Region PGA Championship

Formerly Southern (England) Professional Championship

Year	Winner
1984	M McLean
1985	C Mason
1986	
1987	
1988	J Spence

South of Ireland Open Amateur Championship

Instituted 1895
Venue: Lahinch (Co Clare)

Year	Winner
1984	N Anderson
1985	P O'Rourke
1986	J McHenry
1987	B Reddan
1988	MA Gannon

South of Scotland Championship

Instituted 1932

Year	Winner
1984	D Ireland
1985	I Brotherston
1986	I Semple
1987	I Brotherston
1988	A Coltart

Southern Division Ladies' Championship (Scotland)

Year	Winner
1984	Miss FM Rennie
1985	Mrs S Simpson
1986	Miss M Wright
1987	Miss M Wright
1988	Mrs S Simpson

South of Scotland Ladies' Championship

Year	Winner
1984	Miss M Wright
1985	Miss FM Rennie
1986	Miss FM Rennie
1987	Miss S McDonald
1988	Miss M Wright

South-Western Ladies' Championship

Year	Winner
1984	Miss P Johnson
1985	Miss S Shapcott
1986	Miss K Nicholls
1987	Miss J Fernley
1988	Mrs V Thomas

South-Western Counties Amateur Championship

Instituted 1924

Year	Winner
1984	M Blaber
1985	C Phillips
1986	C Phillips
1987	
1988	J Langmead

Staffordshire Amateur Championship

Instituted 1924

Year	Winner
1984	M Hassall
1985	M Hassall
1986	M Scarrett
1987	M Hassall
1988	P Sweetsur

Staffordshire Ladies' Championship

Instituted 1926

Year	Winner
1984	Miss D Boyd
1985	Miss L Hackney
1986	Mrs A Booth
1987	Miss D Christison
1988	Miss D Boyd

Staffordshire Open Championship

Year	Winner
1984	
1985	
1986	
1987	
1988	

Staffordshire and Shropshire Professional Championship

Year	Winner
1984	
1985	
1986	J Annable
1987	J Annable
1988	

Stirlingshire Amateur Championship

Year	Winner
1984	G Barrie
1985	W Fleming
1986	RA Godfrey
1987	SA Lee
1988	H Anderson

Stirling and Clackmannan County Ladies' Championship

Year	Winner
1984	Mrs W McCallum
1985	Miss S Michie
1986	Miss S Michie
1987	Miss J Harrison
1988	Miss J Harrison

Suffolk Amateur Championship

Instituted 1924

Year	Winner
1984	S Goodman
1985	R Barrell
1986	M Clark
1987	CN Coulton
1988	J Whitby

Suffolk Ladies' Championship

Instituted 1926

Year	Winner
1984	Dr J Gibson
1985	Dr J Gibson
1986	J Wade
1987	Miss W Day
1988	Miss S Dawson

Suffolk Open Championship

Year	Winner
1984	
1985	K Preston
1986	S Beckham
1987	M Turner
1988	

Suffolk Professional Championship

Instituted 1927

Year	Winner
1984	RW Mann
1985	S Beckhoon
1986	RW Mann
1987	
1988	J Maddock

Sunningdale Open Foursomes

Year	Winners
1984	Miss M McKenna and Miss M Madill beat Miss M Walker and Miss C Langford
1985	J O'Leary and S Torrance beat B Gallacher and P Garner at 25th
1986	R Rafferty and R Chapman beat Mrs M Garner and Miss M McKenna, 1 hole
1987	I Mosey and W Humphries beat Miss G Stewart and D Huish, 3 and 2
1988	C Mason and A Chandler beat Miss M McKenna and Mrs J Garner, 5 and 3

Surrey Amateur Championship

Instituted 1924

Year	Winner
1984	PM Talbot
1985	G Walmsley
1986	B White
1987	J Paramer
1988	A Carter

Surrey Ladies' Championship

Instituted 1921

Year	Winner
1984	Mrs J Thornhill
1985	J Nicolson
1986	Miss S Prosser
1987	Mrs W Wooldridge
1988	Mrs C Bailey

Sussex Amateur Championship

Instituted 1899

Year	Winner
1984	JS Spence
1985	MS Jarvis
1986	AW Schofield
1987	D Fay
1988	DW Alderson

Sussex Ladies' Championship

Instituted 1923 (After 1936 Final over 36 holes)

Year	Winner
1984	Miss C Rolph
1985	Miss N Way
1986	Miss M Cornelius
1987	Miss K Mitchell
1988	Miss M-J Cornelius

Sussex Open Championship

Year	Winner
1984	J Dodds (Am)
1985	JS Spence (Am)
1986	C Giddins
1987	BW Barnes
1988	S Rolley

Tennant Cup

This trophy was presented by Sir Charles Tennant to the Glasgow Club in 1880. It is the oldest open amateur stroke play competition in the world

Year	Winner
1984	E Wilson
1985	CJ Brooks
1986	
1987	J Rasmussen (Den)
1988	C Dalgleish

Ulster Youths' Open Amateur Championship

Year	Winner
1984	G Clarke
1985	J Carvill
1986	DA Mulholland
1987	J Carvill
1988	

Ulster Professional Championship

Instituted 1924 (decided by stroke play 1938-39)

Year	Winner
1984	D Carson
1985	D Jones
1986	W Todd
1987	
1988	

Warwickshire Ladies' Championship

Instituted 1923

Year	Winner
1984	Miss M Stevens
1985	Mrs S Seville
1986	Miss T Hammond
1987	Mrs M Button
1988	Miss S Morgan

Warwickshire Amateur Championship

Instituted 1906

Year	Winner
1984	P McEvoy
1985	C Suneson
1986	P Downes
1987	W Bladon
1988	AM Allen

Warwickshire Professional Championship

Year	Winner
1984	A Bownes
1985	
1986	P Elson
1987	P Elson
1988	C Wicketts

Warwickshire Open Championship

Year	Winner
1984	P Broadhurst
1985	J Gould
1986	PJ Weaver
1987	P Weaver
1988	TM Allen

Welsh Team Championship

Instituted 1895

Year	Winner
1984	Whitchurch
1985	Whitchurch
1986	Pontnewydd
1987	Llandudno (Maesdu)
1988	Ashburnham

Welsh Ladies' Team Championship

Instituted 1905

Year	Winner
1984	Monmouthshire
1985	Llandudno (Maesdu)
1986	Porthcawl
1987	Whitchurch
1988	

West of England Open Amateur Championship

Instituted 1912
Venue: Burnham-on-Sea

Year	Winner
1984	GB Hickman
1985	AC Nash
1986	J Bennett
1987	D Rosier
1988	N Holman

West of England Open Amateur Stroke Play Championship

Instituted 1968

Year	Winner
1984	A Sherborne
1985	P McEvoy
1986	P Baker
1987	G Wolstenholme
1988	M Evans

West of Ireland Open Amateur Championship

Instituted 1923
Venue: Rosses Point

Year	Winner
1984	G McGimpsey
1985	J Feeney
1986	P Rayfus
1987	N McGrane
1988	G McGimpsey

West of Scotland Open Amateur Championship

Year	Winner
1984	G Shaw
1985	JA Thomson
1986	C Brooks
1987	R Jenkins
1988	S Savage

West of Scotland Close Amateur Championship

Instituted 1977

Year	Winner
1984	
1985	S Savage
1986	S Savage
1987	R Jenkins
1988	G King

Western Division Ladies' Championship (Scotland)

Year	Winner
1984	Dr A Wilson
1985	Mrs IC Robertson
1986	Miss S Lawson
1987	Mrs A Hendry
1988	Miss S Lawson

West of Scotland Girls' Championship

Year	Winner
1984	Miss D Jackson
1985	Miss K Fitzgerald
1986	Miss L Lundie
1987	Miss A Ferguson
1988	Miss A Ferguson

West of Scotland Boys' Championship

Year	Winner
1984	G Orr
1985	
1986	G King
1987	
1988	

West Region PGA Championship

Previously West of England Professional Championship

Year	Winner
1984	
1985	D Sheppard
1986	
1987	
1988	

Wigtownshire Championship

Instituted 1936

Year	Winner
1984	A Burns
1985	
1986	
1987	
1988	

Wiltshire Amateur Championship

Instituted 1924

Year	Winner
1984	NC Garfoot
1985	S Amor
1986	G Clough
1987	RE Searle
1988	G Clough

Wiltshire Ladies' Championship

Year	Winner
1984	Mrs V Morgan
1985	Miss C Waite
1986	Miss S Marks
1987	Mrs J Lawrence
1988	Mrs S Sutton

Wiltshire Professional Championship

Instituted 1925
Now known as the "Hills" Wiltshire Pro Champ

Year	Winner
1984	G Laing
1985	G Laing
1986	B Sandry
1987	G Laing
1988	R Emery

Worcestershire Amateur Championship

Instituted 1906

Year	Winner
1984	T Martin
1985	SJ Pimley
1986	DJ Eddiford
1987	D Prosser
1988	D Prosser

Worcestershire Ladies' Championship

Instituted 1924

Year	Winner
1984	Miss S Nicklin
1985	Miss L Waring
1986	Miss K Cheetham
1987	Miss L Waring
1988	Miss J Blaymire

Worcestershire Open Championship

Year	Winner
1984	K Hayward
1985	DJ Eddiford
1986	WR Painter (Am)
1987	K Hayward
1988	D Eddiford

Worcestershire Professional Championship

Year	Winner
1984	
1985	KA Hayward
1986	D Dunk
1987	
1988	C Hancock

Worplesdon Mixed Foursomes

Instituted 1921

Year	Winners
1984	Miss L Bayman and MC Hughesdon (Sunningdale) beat Miss N McCormack (Porters Park) and N Briggs (Berkhamsted) 5 and 4
1985	Mrs H Kaye (Harpenden) and D Longmuir (Verulam) beat Mrs J Collingham (Royal Birkdale) and GS Melville (Brockenhurst Manor)
1986	Miss P Johnson and RN Roderick (Ponterdawe) beat Miss C Duffy and L Hawkins (Maidenhead), 2 and 1
1987	Mrs J Nicholsen and B White beat Miss T Craik and P Hughes, 4 and 3
1988	Mme A Larrezac (St Cloud) and JJ Caplan (Worplesdon) beat Miss S Bennett (Colchester) and BK Turner (Sunningdale Artisans) 4 and 3

Yorkshire Amateur Championship

Instituted 1894

Year	Winner
1984	J Whiteley
1985	G Field
1986	AR Gelsthorpe
1987	RM Roper
1988	S Field

Yorkshire Amateur Stroke Play Championship

Instituted 1986

Year	Winner
1986	P Hall
1987	P Hall RM Roper } tied
1988	CG Rawson

Yorkshire Open Championship

Instituted 1927

Year	Winner
1984	D Jagger
1985	D Jagger
1986	*Discontinued*

Yorkshire Ladies' Championship

Instituted 1896

Year	Winner
1984	Miss A Nicholas
1985	Miss A Farmery
1986	Miss P Smillie
1987	Miss J Copley
1988	Miss J Furby

Yorkshire Professional Championship

Instituted 1921

Year	Winner
1984	D Hutchinson
1985	B Jagger
1986	M Ingham
1987	D Stirling
1988	M Higginbottom

Royal and Ancient Tournaments

Royal and Ancient Club of St Andrews

Captain 1988-89 A Sinclair

Royal Medal

presented by His Majesty King William the Fourth
(First prize at Autumn Meeting)

Instituted 1837

Year		Strokes
1984	C McLachlan	75
1985	GJ Cotla	70
1986	P Greenhough	70
1987	HM Campbell	71
1988	AM Reid	73

Silver Cross

presented by Colonel J Murray Belshes, of Buttergask
(First prize at Spring Meeting)

Instituted 1836

Year		Strokes
1984	HM Campbell	72
1985	Dr DM Lawrie	69
1986	MJ Reece	73
1987	HM Campbell	71
1988	R Foster	73

The George Glennie Medal

presented by the Royal Blackheath Golf Club
(lowest aggregate score at Spring and Autumn Meetings)

Instituted 1882

Year		Strokes
1984	HM Campbell	150
1985	Dr DM Lawrie	148
1986	DW Frame	146
1987	HM Campbell	142
1988	HM Campbell	150

Part V
The Government of the Game

Introduction

The Editor and Publishers of the Golfer's Handbook *are grateful to the General Committee of the Royal and Ancient Club for its agreement to reproduce the* Statement of Functions of the Club. *A brief history of how the Royal and Ancient came to be the Governing Body of the Game has been added, followed by a description of the important work of the Championship Committee, especially in its responsibility for The Open.*

The Royal and Ancient Golf Club

In Britain it is not unusual for the Governing Body of a Sport to have its origins in a private club, which later comes to be recognised as the authority through which the game is administered. The Royal and Ancient Golf Club of St Andrews is a prime example and enjoys a similar status to the Marylebone Cricket Club. With the world-wide spread of golf and cricket this century, both have emerged as the international body to which most other countries look for rulings and guidance.

The Royal and Ancient Club's records date back to 1754 when the Society of St Andrews Golfers adopted the rules which had been formulated in 1744 by the Gentlemen Golfers of Leith, later to become the Honourable Company of Edinburgh Golfers; the older club located across the Forth at Muirfield.

When in 1834 King William IV granted the St Andrews Gentlemen Golfers the right and privilege of using the title *Royal and Ancient*, the Honourable Company had temporarily lost cohesion and the R&A gradually acquired the status of the premier club. During the latter half of the Victorian age, in the 1880s and 1890s when, following the spread of the railway system, many new clubs were founded, they looked to the R&A for leadership and advice.

With the appointment of the first Rules of Golf Committee in 1897, the R&A became recognised as the Governing Authority in all countries except the United States and Mexico where the United States Golf Association controls the game. Golf federations of many countries are affiliated to the R&A. This is made clear in the *Statement of Functions* of the R&A, reproduced with the permission of the General Committee. The work of the Championship Committee is expanded in a note below, with particular reference to The Open Championship.

The success of The Open in recent years, both as a spectacle and financially, has meant that the R&A can now support fully the development of the game, while remaining the guardian of its traditions. Its encouragement of young players, especially through the Boys and Youths Championships and the Golf Foundation, has helped produce the higher standards of play and younger champions now so apparent to all followers of the game.

Statement of Functions of the Royal and Ancient Golf Club throughout the world

With the developing interest in golf and the increasing complexity of the administration of the game, the Royal and Ancient Golf Club feels that a statement of its activities in this field would be of interest.

The functions for which the Club is responsible fall into three clearly defined categories. First, functions of an international nature, secondly functions of a national nature, and finally, the running of a Club with wide national and international Membership.

International Functions

In 1897 the Royal and Ancient became the Governing Authority on the Rules of Golf at the suggestion of the leading Golf Clubs in the United Kingdom at the time. Since then an ever increasing number of countries have sought affiliation to it, until today they number over 60, including several other Unions or Associations (eg the Ladies' Golf Union, European Golf Association, South American Golf Federation and Asia-Pacific Golf Confederation).

The Club in its negotiations with the United States Golf Association on matters pertaining to the Rules of Golf is not merely representing Great Britain and Ireland, but these many countries as well.

In 1919, when it took over the running of the Open and Amateur Championships, the Royal and Ancient became responsible for the Rules of Amateur Status and in matters pertaining thereto likewise represents these many countries.

The Royal and Ancient also supplies one of the two Joint Chairmen and Joint Secretaries of the World Amateur Golf Council which is responsible for the organisation of all World Amateur Team Championships.

There is close liaison at all times with the Professional Golfers' Association and the PGA European Tour.

National Functions

Prior to the First World War, a group of Clubs had been responsible for the running of the Open and Amateur Championships. In 1919 a meeting of these Clubs confirmed that the Royal and Ancient should be the Governing Authority for the game and agreed it should assume responsibility for the two Championships.

The decision that the Royal and Ancient should be the Governing Authority was endorsed at a Meeting of the English, Scottish, Irish and Welsh Unions in 1924, at which Meeting what is now the Council of National Golf Unions was formed with the object amongst others of directing the system of Standard Scratch Scores and Handicaps.

In 1948 the Royal and Ancient took over the Boys and in 1963 the Youths Championship from the private interests which had previously run them; this was done at the request of the individuals concerned. In 1969 the Royal and Ancient itself inaugurated the British Seniors Amateur Championship.

In addition to the organisation of five Championships, the Royal and Ancient is also responsible for the selection of Teams to represent Great Britain & Ireland in the Walker Cup, the Eisenhower Trophy, the St Andrews Trophy, and other International Tournaments. It is responsible for the organisation of such events when they are held in Great Britain and Ireland.

Club Functions

The Membership of the Club is limited to a total of 1,800, of which 1,050 may be resident in Great Britain and Ireland and 750 elsewhere: this Overseas Membership is spread over countries throughout the world.

The Membership both at home and abroad is representative and includes many who have given and are giving great services to golf in this country and abroad to many different Unions and Associations. This permits broad and effective representation on all the Club Committees concerned with international and national functions.

Exercise of International Functions

1. Rules of Golf

(a) Committee:

The Rules of Golf Committee exists for the purpose of reviewing the Rules of Golf from time to time and of making decisions on their interpretation and publishing these decisions where necessary.

The Committee consists of twelve Members elected by the Club, of whom three retire each year and are not eligible for re-election for one year, except in the case of the Chairman and Deputy Chairman, and of up to twelve additional persons invited annually to join the Committee from Golf Authorities at home and abroad.

At present the bodies represented are:

Council of National Golf Unions
United States Golf Association
European Golf Association
Australian Golf Union
New Zealand Golf Association
Royal Canadian Golf Association
South African Golf Union
Asia-Pacific Golf Confederation
South American Golf Federation
Japan Golf Association

(b) Revision of the Rules of Golf:
As the only other Governing Authority for the Rules of Golf is the USGA, the R&A works closely with this body when amendments to the Rules are under consideration for the purpose of maintaining uniformity in the Rules and their interpretation. Every four years a Conference takes place with the USGA for the purpose of deciding on the changes to be made. The quadrennial conference held in 1987 made numerous amendments to the 1984 Rules; these were mainly to clarify points of doubt which had emerged since 1984. The changes took effect on January 1st 1988. Although the Conference takes place quadrennially, the Rules are under constant review and investigations as to possible improvements start not long after a revision has taken place, so that ample time can be given to consult with interested parties.

Two years after a revision has taken place an important meeting is held with the USGA in the United States at the time of the Walker Cup to discuss progress and to start clearing the ground for the next Conference.

(c) Decisions:
The Rules of Golf Committee has a Decisions Sub-Committee which answers queries from Clubs and from all the Unions and Associations affiliated to the R&A. Those Decisions which seem to establish important or interesting points of interpretation are available in the form of a loose-leaf Decisions Service published jointly by the R&A and the USGA and issued world-wide. The number of subscribers to this Service is about 3,500 and is increasing steadily as golf expands.

2. Implements and Ball

The Committee consists of four Members elected by the Club, one Member of the Rules of Golf Committee and one Member of the Championship Committee, together with Consultant Members invited by the Committee to advise on technical matters. One of the elected Members retires each year but the Chairman may be re-elected immediately for the sake of continuity.

The Committee works in close co-operation with the USGA I & B Committee in interpreting the Rules and Appendices relating to the control of the form and make of golf clubs and the specifications of the golf ball to ensure that the game and established golf courses are not harmed by technical developments.

3. Rules of Amateur Status

(a) Committee:
The Committee consists of five members, of which four are elected by the Club and one provided by the Council of National Golf Unions. There are also Advisory Members to the Committee, representing the same Golfing Authorities as on the Rules of Golf Committee.

(b) Revision of Rules of Amateur Status:
A procedure, similar to that for the Rules of Golf, is adopted for revision of the Rules of Amateur Status and no policy changes are made without full consultation with all the affiliated Unions, the USGA and the PGA.

(c) Decisions:
The work of the Committee consists of (a) dealing with Applications for reinstatement to Amateur Status, (b) answering inquiries about the nature of prizes, conditions for Tournaments, etc, arising out of the increased impact of commercial sponsors on Amateur golf and the issue of guidelines and Decisions, (c) answering queries from individuals regarding their own position under the Rules and (d) controlling Scholarships and other Grants-in-aid.

Exercise of National Functions

The Championship Committee

The Championship Committee is responsible for the control of the five Championships and of the International Matches and Tournaments mentioned above.

The Committee consists of twelve elected Members elected by the Club, of whom three retire annually and are not eligible for re-election for one year. Two additional Members may also be invited to join the Committee annually together with two Business Members co-opted for four years.

For the organisation of any particular event, others may be co-opted, if required.

The work of this Committee has greatly increased in recent years, as is clearly evident from the staging of the Open Championship, for which prizes in 1984 amounted to £450,000. At the same time, more substantial reserve funds have been built up to ensure the continuance of the Open Championship as a premier world event.

The Committee makes annual donations to a number of golfing bodies, especially those concerned with the training and development of junior golf and for research on greenkeeping matters.

Selection Committee

The Selection Committee consists of a Chairman, who is a Member of the Club, and other Members, who need not be Members of the Club, appointed by the General Committee. These other Members have for some years now been representative of each of the four Home Unions. Normally they hold their appointments for four years.

Exercise of Club Functions

The domestic affairs of the Club are run by Committees which it is not necessary to describe in this statement.

It is appropriate, however, to mention that the Club does not own a Golf Course. It is, nevertheless, much concerned with the maintenance and improvements of all four Golf Courses in St Andrews. These Courses are controlled by the St Andrews Links Trust and are run by the Links Management Committee. Three of the Trustees and four Members of the Management Committee are appointed by the Club and equal numbers are appointed by the North-East Fife District Council. The Chairman of the Trust is appointed by the Secretary of State for Scotland and the current MP is also a Trustee. The Club contributes an annually negotiated sum to the Trust in return for Members' playing privileges.

Finance

International Functions:

After taking into account income derived from subscriptions to the Rules of Golf Decisions Service and the sale of official Rules publications, the net expenses of the Rules of Golf, Rules of Amateur Status and Rules for Implements and Ball are borne by External Activities.

National Functions:

Income and expenditure of all Championships run by the R&A and the expenses of Teams representing Great Britain & Ireland are accounted for in separate divisions of one Account.

Surpluses of all income over expenditure in the External Activities Account are held in reserve to ensure the continuance of the running of the various events at a high standard.

The Royal and Ancient Golf Club as a private Members' Club does not in any way benefit from the External Activities Account.

General Committee

Responsibility for directing and co-ordinating the three functions of the R&A—as a private club, as a governing authority for golf and as the body responsible for organising and running the championships and international matches—rests with the Club's General Committee, which controls all matters of policy. The Committee consists of sixteen R&A Members, eight of whom are elected by the Club; the other eight *ex-officio* members are the Captain and Chairmen of the Finance, Membership, House, Green, Rules of Golf, Championship and Amateur Status Committees.

The execution of the decisions of the Club Committees and of the decisions taken by the Members at Business Meetings is in the hands of the Secretary of the R&A, who is assisted by several senior officers and the appropriate infrastructure of secretaries and clerical staff.

Contacts with Affiliated Golfing Authorities

The R&A endeavours to consult with all those Golfing Authorities concerned whenever an issue of importance arises. This covers, in particular, matters relating to Rules of Golf, Rules of Amateur Status, and the Championships.

Meetings are held when appropriate with representatives of Golfing Authorities in Great Britain & Ireland and the European Golf Association. Consultations with other Golfing Authorities abroad are regularly conducted by correspondence.

In January 1970, a Conference attended by Golfing Unions and Associations in this country and representatives of the European Golf Association was held under the auspices of the R&A to discuss all matters of mutual interest, and in particular to establish the best means of communication in the future between the Unions and Associations concerned. This was followed by a similar Conference at Chantilly, Paris in 1976.

In May 1980 the first ever International Golf Conference was held in St Andrews at which 33 countries affiliated to the R&A were represented and to which the USGA, PGA and other golfing bodies in this country sent observers. Owing to the great success of this Conference the R&A has agreed to organise a similar one every four years starting in 1985.

The R&A is represented at Meetings of the World Amateur Golf Council and the Council of National Golf Unions and on the CCPR.

January 1985 (revised)

MF Bonallack OBE
Secretary
Royal And Ancient Golf Club
of St Andrews
Fife KY16 9JD

The Championship Committee

Until 1919 the Open and Amateur Championships of Great Britain were organised by a group of leading Clubs in Scotland and England. The Club where the Championship was to be played was charged with running it for that year. In 1919, the Royal and Ancient, by then the recognised governing authority of the game, was invited to take over the responsibility for both Championships and ever since its Championship Committee has controlled both. Once the course on which a Championship is to be played has been decided, usually several years ahead, the Committee works closely with the Club concerned.

The Amateur, which is nearly as old as The Open, may have lost some of its public appeal with the growth of Professional golf and the defection of so many able young amateurs to its lucrative tour. However, the Amateur Championship is still considered the most prestigious event in the amateur game and is always played on one of the best courses.

The Championship Committee today controls several more events besides the two oldest Championships. The Boys, started privately in 1921, and the Youths, in 1954, both now come under its wing, as does the Seniors which was inaugurated by the R&A in 1969. In addition, the biennial amateur matches against the United States and the Rest of Europe for the Walker Cup and the St Andrews Trophies respectively, are run by the Committee when played in Great Britain, as also are Boys' and Youths' Internationals against the Rest of Europe. The R&A Selection Committee chooses the team for all these amateur matches, as well as the team which competes for the Eisenhower Trophy, the World Amateur Team Championship. This was first played at St Andrews in 1958 and has since been held every two years in different parts of the world.

The remarkable development of The Open to the great occasion it is today has meant heavily increased responsibilities for the Championship Committee. TV and the media have given it an audience in millions compared with the few thousand interested in the past. The R&A's determination to match the growing interest with a new attitude and astute promotion has given the event the kudos and following it now enjoys. The last 20 years has seen the winner's cheque grow from £1200 to £80,000, the total prize money from £15,000 to £708,000, with the attendance nearly five times greater at close on 200,000. The financial success of The Open has provided considerable sums of money for the development of junior golf.

The R&A works closely with the Club of the course where the Championship is to be played, whose members take on many of the essential duties necessary if it is to run smoothly. These include spectator control where local Clubs take charge of a hole each, usually providing three-hour shifts of up to 16 members at a time. This can involve as many as 800 men daily. Local volunteer stewards also cover such diverse duties as course controllers, supervision of litter collection and spectator stand control. Security, courtesy transport, car park supervision and public catering, to name a few of the mass of services necessary, are provided under contract by companies expert in these fields. Close liaison with the area police authority is vital. Facilities for the Press, Television and the vast tented village, each involving several hundred people, occupy large areas and are a major limiting factor when considering possible venues for future championships.

Important for both competitors and spectators and appreciated by both is the radio network which provides up-to-the-minute scores and positions of the leading players which appear very quickly on the leader boards erected at strategic points round the course. The system developed over many years is as quick, informative and accurate as any in existence.

The Committee consists of thirteen Royal and Ancient members, who devote much time to their tasks. It has a full-time secretary who, together with the Secretary of the Club and some of his staff, is involved in the planning of The Open and other events throughout the year. Members of the Committee work long hours during Open week. From first light at about 5am, when the Head Greenkeeper and a nominated member of the Committee tour the course deciding the pin positions on each green for the day, to dusk when the last competitor comes in, all are occupied, mostly out on the course at selected points, in two-way radio contact with the centre, ready to give a ruling when required. In the final rounds the leading players are accompanied by a member of the committee for the whole round.

The many stands erected around the course, providing seats for sometimes 18,000 spectators, often quite close to greens, make for special problems. A loose shot which ends under a stand will probably mean the ball may be dropped without penalty in an area nearby, which has been pre-designated by the committee; his shot should be of equal difficulty as it would have been if the stand had not been there. In these cases often an official decision is required.

At the end of every round each competitor's card must be immediately checked and recorded following which, in the case of a leader, he will meet the press in the interview room.

It is the Championship Committee too which decides if any round has to be halted, postponed or cancelled due to storm and tempest. Such decisions, so difficult with so many factors, consequent on a postponement, to be considered, have been eased a little with improved weather forecasting and continuous contact with the local weather bureau.

It will be seen that the work of the Committee is never ending with the myriad of tasks necessary to ensure the even flow to a Championship. The success of The Open is due to sound planning, moving with the times and the expertise of the R&A staff which is the executive arm of the Committee. The Open may be the Championship with which all are familiar; however, it must be remembered that the many other events under the R&A's control also require planning and organisation. The work for these events goes on largely unnoticed, but must not be forgotten.

Rules of Golf

As Approved by
The Royal and Ancient Golf Club
of St Andrews, Scotland
and the
United States Golf Association

25th EDITION
EFFECTIVE 1st JANUARY 1988

Rules of Golf Committee

The Rules of Golf Committee shall consist of twelve Members of the Club to be elected by the Club, and additional Members not exceeding ten in number (who need not be Members of the Club) from Golf Authorities at home and abroad invited annually to join the Committee by the twelve Members elected by the Club. Such Invited Members shall, irrespective of the date of their invitation to become Members of the Rules of Golf Committee, remain so only until the date of the first Autumn Business Meeting occurring after their being invited to become Members but may again be invited thereafter. During their term of office such Invited Members (if not Members of the Club) shall be admitted as Temporary Members of the Club.

The Rules of Golf are the subject of quadrennial review by the R&A and the USGA in order to maintain uniformity and keep abreast of changing conditions.

Queries on the Rules may only be referred to the Rules of Golf Committee through the Secretary of the Club or the Association responsible for the competition. Many queries have to be returned unanswered because they have been sent direct to the Committee by individuals.

Rules of Golf Committee 1988/89

Dr DM Marsh *(Chairman)*
JS Scrivener *(Deputy Chairman)*
WG Burleigh
Dr DM Lawrie
WJ Uzielli
WJJ Ferguson
GS Lowden
JR Boardman
MA Boddington
DJ Harrison
NC Royds
J Sim

Additional Members

DJ Miller (CONGU)
JL Dupont (EGA)
H Stahlberg (EGA)
EJH Yong (Asia Pacific Golf Confederation)
LW Clark (Australian Golf Union)
H Brownstein (Royal Canadian Golf Association)
T Kawata (Japan Golf Association)
TM Gault (New Zealand Golf Association)
JB Churcher (South African Golf Union)
JV Garasino (South American Golf Federation)
MJ Mastalir (USGA)

CONTENTS

Other Forms of Play

Administration

Foreword

to the 1988 Edition of the Rules of Golf

The Royal and Ancient Golf Club of St. Andrews and the United States Golf Association have carried out their customary quadrennial review of the Rules of Golf and have agreed upon certain amendments which they believe will improve the Rules.

The extensive changes in the Rules which were introduced in 1984 have received universal approval. Consequently, a minimal number of substantive changes were considered necessary. These are summarised on page 695.

The R.&A. and USGA would like to record their appreciation of the valuable assistance which they have received from a number of golfing bodies throughout the world. The new Rules will become effective on 1st January 1988.

The combining of the Decisions Services of the R.&A. and USGA into a single volume has proved to be an outstanding success and has done much to establish uniformity of interpretation of the Rules worldwide.

We would like to take this opportunity to express our sincere thanks to our respective Committees and all those who have in so many ways helped us in our endeavours.

W.J.F. Bryce
Chairman
Rules of Golf Committee
Royal and Ancient Golf Club of St. Andrews

C. Grant Spaeth
Chairman
Rules of Golf Committee
United States Golf Association

CHANGES

Principal Changes introduced in the 1988 Code

Rule 2. Match Play
Expanded to state that a player may concede the next stroke, a hole or the match, and that a concession may not be declined or withdrawn.

Rule 3-3. Stroke Play. Doubt as to Procedure
If a competitor fails to announce in advance his decision to invoke this Rule, the score with the original ball, rather than the higher score, will count.

Rule 4-4. Maximum of Fourteen Clubs
Amended to state that a player may borrow a club from anyone on the course, but that the person from whom it was borrowed may not thereafter use the club.

Rule 5 and Appendix III
After 1st January 1990 it will no longer be permitted to use the small (1.620") ball.

Rule 5-3. Ball Unfit for Play
A stricter definition is adopted stating that a ball is unfit for play if it is visibly cut, cracked or out of shape, but a ball is not unfit for play solely because mud or other materials adhere to it, its surface is scratched or scraped or its paint is damaged or discoloured.

Rule 18. Ball at Rest Moved
If a ball at rest moves after address (other than as a result of a stroke) the ball shall be replaced rather than played as it lies. This procedure is now consistent with that prescribed in other sub-sections of this Rule.

Rule 19-5. Ball in Motion Deflected or Stopped by Another Ball
Clarifies that when two balls in motion collide, each player shall play his ball as it lies.

Rule 25-1b (ii) and 1c (ii). Casual Water, Ground Under Repair and Certain Damage to Course. Relief. In a Hazard

Rule 26-1b. Ball in Water Hazard

Rule 28c. Ball Unplayable
Amended to state that the ball must be dropped keeping the point where the ball lay (or where it last crossed the margin of the hazard, as the case may be) between the spot on which the ball is dropped and the hole. It is no longer permitted to stand on that line and drop a ball an arm's length to the side.

The Rules of Golf

Section I Etiquette

Courtesy on the Course

Safety

Prior to playing a stroke or making a practice swing, the player should ensure that no one is standing close by or in a position to be hit by the club, the ball or any stones, pebbles, twigs or the like which may be moved by the stroke or swing.

Consideration for Other Players

The player who has the honour should be allowed to play before his opponent or fellow-competitor tees his ball.

No one should move, talk or stand close to or directly behind the ball or the hole when a player is addressing the ball or making a stroke.

In the interest of all, players should play without delay.

No player should play until the players in front are out of range.

Players searching for a ball should signal the players behind them to pass as soon as it becomes apparent that the ball will not easily be found. They should not search for five minutes before doing so. They should not continue play until the players following them have passed and are out of range.

When the play of a hole has been completed, players should immediately leave the putting green.

Priority on the Course

In the absence of special rules, two-ball matches should have precedence over and be entitled to pass any three- or four-ball match.

A single player has no standing and should give way to a match of any kind.

Any match playing a whole round is entitled to pass a match playing a shorter round.

If a match fails to keep its place on the course and loses more than one clear hole on the players in front, it should invite the match following to pass.

Care of the Course

Holes in Bunkers

Before leaving a bunker, a player should carefully fill up and smooth over all holes and footprints made by him.

Replace Divots; Repair Ball-Marks and Damage by Spikes

Through the green, a player should ensure that any turf cut or displaced by him is replaced at once and pressed down and that any damage to the putting green made by a ball is carefully repaired. Damage to the putting green caused by golf shoe spikes should be repaired *on completion of the hole.*

Damage to Greens—Flagsticks, Bags, etc.

Players should ensure that, when putting down bags or the flagstick, no damage is done to the putting green and that neither they nor their caddies damage the hole by standing close to it, in handling the flagstick or in removing the ball from the hole. The flagstick should be properly replaced in the hole before the players leave the putting green. Players should not damage the putting green by leaning on their putters, particularly when removing the ball from the hole.

Golf Carts

Local notices regulating the movement of golf carts should be strictly observed.

Damage Through Practice Swings

In taking practice swings, players should avoid causing damage to the course, particularly the tees, by removing divots.

Section II Definitions

Addressing the Ball

A player has "addressed the ball" when he has taken his stance and has also grounded his club, except/that in a hazard a player has addressed the ball when he has taken his stance.

Advice

"Advice" is any counsel or suggestion which could influence a player in determining his play, the choice of a club or the method of making a stroke.

Information on the Rules or on matter of public information, such as the position of hazards or the flagstick on the putting green, is not advice.

Ball Deemed to Move

See "Move or Moved".

Ball Holed
See "Holed".

Ball Lost
See "Lost Ball".

Ball in Play
A ball is "in play" as soon as the player has made a stroke on the teeing ground. It remains in play until holed out, except when it is lost, out of bounds or lifted, or another ball has been substituted under an applicable Rule, whether or not such Rule permits substitution; a ball so substituted becomes the ball in play.

Bunker
A "bunker" is a hazard consisting of a prepared area of ground, often a hollow, from which turf or soil has been removed and replaced with sand or the like. Grass-covered ground bordering or within a bunker is not part of the bunker. The margin of a bunker extends vertically downwards, but not upwards.

Caddie
A "caddie" is one who carries or handles a player's clubs during play and otherwise assists him in accordance with the Rules.

When one caddie is employed by more than one player, he is always deemed to be the caddie of the player whose ball is involved, and equipment carried by him is deemed to be that player's equipment, except when the caddie acts upon specific directions of another player, in which case he is considered to be that other player's caddie.

Casual Water
"Casual water" is any temporary accumulation of water on the course which is visible before or after the player takes his stance and is not in a water hazard. Snow and ice are either casual water or loose impediments, at the option of the player, except that manufactured ice is an obstruction. Dew is not casual water.

Committee
The "Committee" is the committee in charge of the competition or, if the matter does not arise in a competition, the committee in charge of the course.

Competitor
A "competitor" is a player in a stroke competition. A "fellow-competitor" is any person with whom the competitor plays. Neither is partner of the other.

In stroke play foursome and four-ball competitions, where the context so admits, the word "competitor" or "fellow-competitor" includes his partner.

Course
The "course" is the whole area within which play is permitted (see Rule 33-2).

Equipment
"Equipment" is anything used, worn or carried by or for the player except any ball he has played at the hole being played and any small object, such as a coin or a tee, when used to mark the position of a ball or the extent of an area in which a ball is to be dropped. Equipment includes a golf cart, whether or not motorised. If such a cart is shared by more than one player, its status under the Rules is the same as that of a caddie employed by more than one player. See "Caddie".

Fellow Competitor
See "Competitor".

Flagstick
The "flagstick" is a movable straight indicator, with or without bunting or other material attached, centred in the hole to show its position. It shall be circular in cross-section.

Forecaddie
A "forecaddie" is one who is employed by the Committee to indicate to players the position of balls during play. He is an outside agency.

Ground Under Repair
"Ground under repair" is any portion of the course so marked by order of the Committee or so declared by its authorised representative. It includes material piled for removal and a hole made by a greenkeeper, even if not so marked. Stakes and lines defining ground under repair are in such ground. The margin of ground under repair extends vertically downwards, but not upwards.

Note 1: Grass cuttings and other material left on the course which have been abandoned and are not intended to be removed are not ground under repair unless so marked.

Note 2: The Committee may make a Local Rule prohibiting play from ground under repair.

Hazards
A "hazard" is any bunker or water hazard.

Hole
The "hole" shall be $4^1/_4$ inches (108mm) in diameter and at least 4 inches (100mm) deep. If a lining is used, it shall be sunk at least 1 inch (25mm) below the putting green surface unless

the nature of the soil makes it impracticable to do so; its outer diameter shall not exceed $4^1/_4$ inches (108mm).

Holed

A ball is "holed" when it is at rest within the circumference of the hole and all of it is below the level of the lip of the hole.

Honour

The side entitled to play first from the teeing ground is said to have the "honour".

Lateral Water Hazard

A "lateral water hazard" is a water hazard or that part of a water hazard so situated that it is not possible or is deemed by the Committee to be impracticable to drop a ball behind the water hazard in accordance with Rule 26-1b.

That part of a water hazard to be played as a lateral water hazard should be distinctively marked.

Note: Lateral water hazards should be defined by red stakes or lines.

Loose Impediments

"Loose impediments" are natural objects such as stones, leaves, twigs, branches and the like, dung, worms and insects and casts or heaps made by them, provided they are not fixed or growing, are not solidly embedded and do not adhere to the ball.

Sand and loose soil are loose impediments on the putting green, but not elsewhere.

Snow and ice are either casual water or loose impediments, at the option of the player, except that manufactured ice is an obstruction.

Dew is not a loose impediment.

Lost Ball

A ball is "lost" if:

a. It is not found or identified as his by the player within five minutes after the player's side or his or their caddies have begun to search for it; or

b. The player has put another ball into play under the Rules, even though he may not have searched for the original ball; or

c. The player has played any stroke with a provisional ball from the place where the original ball is likely to be or from a point nearer the hole than that place, whereupon the provisional ball becomes the ball in play.

Time spent in playing a wrong ball is not counted in the five-minute period allowed for search.

Marker

A "marker" is one who is appointed by the Committee to record a competitor's score in stroke play. He may be a fellow-competitor. He is not a referee.

Matches

See "Sides and Matches".

Move or Moved

A ball is deemed to have "moved" if it leaves its position and comes to rest in any other place.

Observer

An "observer" is one who is appointed by the Committee to assist a referee to decide questions of fact and to report to him any breach of a Rule. An observer should not attend the flagstick, stand at or mark the position of the hole, or lift the ball or mark its position.

Obstructions

An "obstruction" is anything artificial, including the artificial surfaces and sides of roads and paths and manufactured ice, except:

a. Objects defining out of bounds, such as walls, fences, stakes and railings;

b. Any part of an immovable artificial object which is out of bounds; and

c. Any construction declared by the Committee to be an integral part of the course.

Out of Bounds

"Out of bounds" is ground on which play is prohibited.

When out of bounds is defined by reference to stakes or a fence or as being beyond stakes or a fence, the out of bounds line is determined by the nearest inside points of the stakes or fence posts at ground level excluding angled supports.

When out of bounds is defined by a line on the ground, the line itself is out of bounds.

The out of bounds line extends vertically upwards and downwards.

A ball is out of bounds when all of it lies out of bounds.

A player may stand out of bounds to play a ball lying within bounds.

Outside Agency

An "outside agency" is any agency not part of the match or, in stroke play, not part of a competitor's side, and includes a referee, a marker, an observer or a forecaddie. Neither wind nor water is an outside agency.

Partner

A "partner" is a player associated with another player on the same side.

In a threesome, foursome, best-ball or four-ball match, where the context so admits, the word "player" includes his partner or partners.

Penalty Stroke

A "penalty stroke" is one added to the score of a player or side under certain Rules. In a threesome or foursome, penalty strokes do not affect the order of play.

Provisional Ball

A "provisional ball" is a ball played under Rule 27-2 for a ball which may be lost outside a water hazard or may be out of bounds.

Putting Green

The "putting green" is all ground of the hole being played which is specially prepared for putting or otherwise defined as such by the Committee. A ball is on the puting green when any part of it touches the putting green.

Referee

A "referee" is one who is appointed by the Committee to accompany players to decide questions of fact and apply the Rules of Golf. He shall act on any breach of a Rule which he observes or is reported to him.

A referee should not attend the flagstick, stand at or mark the position of the hole, or lift the ball or mark its position.

Rub of the Green

A "rub of the green" occurs when a ball in motion is accidentally deflected or stopped by any outside agency (see Rule 19-1).

Rule

The term "Rule" includes Local Rules made by the Committee under Rule 33-8a.

Sides and Matches

Side: A player, or two or more players who are partners.

Single: A match in which one plays against another.

Threesome: A match in which one plays against two, and each side plays one ball.

Foursome: A match in which two play against two, and each side plays one ball.

Three-ball: A match-play competition in which three play against one another, each playing his own ball. Each player is playing two distinct matches.

Best ball: A match in which one plays against the better ball of two or the best ball of three players.

Four-ball: A match in which two play their better ball against the better ball of two other players.

Stance

Taking the "stance" consists in a player placing his feet in position for and preparatory to making a stroke.

Stipulated Round

The "stipulated round" consists of playing the holes of the course in their correct sequence unless otherwise authorised by the Committee. The number of holes in a stipulated round is 18 unless a smaller number is authorised by the Committee. As to extension of stipulated round in match play, see Rule 2-3.

Stroke

A "stroke" is the forward movement of the club made with the intention of fairly striking at and moving the ball, but if a player checks his downswing voluntarily before the clubhead reaches the ball he is not deemed to have made a stroke.

Teeing Ground

The "teeing ground" is the starting place for the hole to be played. It is a rectangular area two club-lengths in depth, the front and the sides of which are defined by the outside limits of two tee-markers. A ball is outside the teeing ground when all of it lies outside the teeing ground.

Through the Green

"Through the green" is the whole area of the course except

a. The teeing ground and putting green of the hole being played; and

b. All hazards on the course.

Water Hazard

A "water hazard" is any sea, lake, pond, river, ditch, surface drainage ditch or other open water course (whether or not containing water) and anything of a similar nature.

All ground or water within the margin of a water hazard is part of the water hazard. The margin of a water hazard extends vertically upwards and downwards. Stakes and lines defining the margins of water hazards are in the hazards.

Note: Water hazards (other than lateral water hazards should be defined by yellow stakes or lines.

Wrong Ball

A "wrong ball" is any ball other than:

a. The ball in play,

b. A provisional ball or

c. In stroke play, a second ball played under Rule 3-3 or Rule 20-7b.

Note: Ball in play includes a ball substituted for the ball in play when the player is proceeding under an applicable Rule which does not permit substitution.

Section III
The Rules of Play

THE GAME

Rule 1. The Game

1-1. General

The Game of Golf consists in playing a ball from the teeing ground into the hole by a stroke or successive strokes in accordance with the Rules.

1-2. Exerting Influence on Ball

No player or caddie shall take any action to influence the position or the movement of a ball except in accordance with the rules.

PENALTY FOR BREACH OF RULE 1-2:
Match play—Loss of hole; Stroke play—Two strokes.

Note: In the case of a serious breach of Rule 1-2, the Committee may impose a penalty of disqualification.

1-3. Agreement to Waive Rules

Players shall not agree to exclude the operation of any Rule or to waive any penalty incurred.

PENALTY FOR BREACH OF RULE 1-3:
Match play—Disqualification of both sides; Stroke play—Disqualification of competitors concerned.

(Agreeing to play out of turn in stroke play—see Rule 10-2c.)

1-4. Points Not Covered by Rules

If any point in dispute is not covered by the Rules, the decision shall be made in accordance with equity.

Rule 2. Match Play

2-1. Winner of Hole; Reckoning of Holes

In match play the game is played by holes.

Except as otherwise provided in the Rules, a hole is won by the side which holes its ball in the fewer strokes. In a handicap match the lower net score wins the hole.

The reckoning of holes is kept by the terms: so many "holes up" or "all square", and so many "to play".

A side is "dormie" when it is as many holes up as there are holes remaining to be played.

2-2. Halved Hole

A hole is halved if each side holes out in the same number of strokes.

When a player has holed out and his opponent has been left with a stroke for the half, if the player thereafter incurs a penalty, the hole is halved.

2-3. Winner of Match

A match (which consists of a stipulated round, unless otherwise decreed by the Committee) is won by the side which is leading by a number of holes greater than the number of holes remaining to be played.

The Committee may, for the purpose of settling a tie, extend the stipulated round to as many holes as are required for a match to be won.

2-4. Concession of Next Stroke, Hole or Match

When the opponent's ball is at rest or is deemed to be at rest under Rule 16-2, the player may concede the opponent to have holed out with his next stroke and the ball may be removed by either side with a club or otherwise.

A player may concede a hole or a match at any time prior to the conclusion of the hole or the match.

Concession of a stroke, hole or match may not be declined or withdrawn.

2-5. Claims

In match play, if a doubt or dispute arises between the players and no duly authorised representative of the Committee is available within a reasonable time, the players shall continue the match without delay. Any claim, if it is to be considered by the Committee, must be made before any player in the match plays from the next teeing ground or, in the case of the last hole of the match, before all players in the match leave the putting green.

No later claim shall be considered unless it is based on facts previously unknown to the player making the claim and the player making the claim had been given wrong information (Rules 6-2a and 9) by an opponent. In any case, no later claim shall be considered after the result of the match has been officially announced, unless the Committee is satisfied that the opponent knew he was giving wrong information.

2-6. General Penalty

The penalty for a breach of a Rule in match play is loss of hole except when otherwise provided.

Rule 3. Stroke Play

3-1. Winner

The competitor who plays the stipulated round or rounds in the fewest strokes is the winner.

3-2. Failure to Hole Out

If a competitor fails to hole out at any hole and does not correct his mistake before he plays a stroke from the next teeing ground or, in the case of the last hole of the round, before he leaves the putting green, *he shall be disqualified.*

3-3. Doubt as to Procedure

a. Procedure

In stroke play only, when during play of a hole a competitor is doubtful of his rights or procedure, he may, without penalty, play a second ball. After the situation which has caused the doubt has arisen, the competitor should, before taking further action, announce to his marker or a fellow-competitor his decision to invoke this Rule and the ball with which he will score if the Rules permit.

The competitor shall report the facts to the Committee before returning his score card unless he scores the same with both balls; if he fails to do so, *he shall be disqualified.*

b. Determination of Score for Hole

If the Rules allow the procedure selected in advance by the competitor, the score with the ball selected shall be his score for the hole.

If the competitor fails to announce in advance his decision to invoke this Rule or his selection, the score with the original ball or, if the original ball is not one of the balls being played, the first ball put into play shall count if the Rules allow the procedure adopted for such ball.

Note: A second ball played under Rule 3-3 is not a provisional ball under Rule 27-2.

3-4. Refusal to Comply with a Rule

If a competitor refuses to comply with a Rule affecting the rights of another competitor, *he shall be disqualified.*

3-5. General Penalty

The penalty for a breach of a Rule in stroke play is two strokes except when otherwise provided.

CLUBS AND THE BALL

The Royal and Ancient Golf Club of St. Andrews and the United States Golf Association reserve the right to change the Rules and make and change the interpretations relating to clubs, balls and other implements at any time.

Rule 4. Clubs

If there may be any reasonable basis for doubt as to whether a club which is to be manufactured conforms with Rule 4 and Appendix II, the manufacturer should submit a sample to the Royal and Ancient Golf Club of St Andrews for a ruling, such sample to become its property for reference purposes. If a manufacturer fails to do so, he assumes the risk of a ruling that the club does not conform with the Rules of Golf.

A player in doubt as to the conformity of a club should consult the Royal and Ancient Golf Club of St Andrews.

4-1. Form and Make of Clubs

A club is an implement designed to be used for striking the ball.

A putter is a club designed primarily for use on the putting green.

The player's clubs shall conform with the provisions of this Rule and with the specifications and interpretations set forth in Appendix II.

a. General

The club shall be composed of a shaft and a head. All parts of the club shall be fixed so that the club is one unit. The club shall not be designed to be adjustable except for weight. The club shall not be substantially different from the traditional and customary form and make.

b. Shaft

The shaft shall be generally straight, with the same bending and twisting properties in any direction, and shall be attached to the clubhead at the heel either directly or through a single plain neck or socket. A putter shaft may be attached to any point in the head.

c. Grip

The grip consists of that part of the shaft designed to be held by the player and any material added to it for the purpose of obtaining a firm hold. The grip shall be substantially straight and plain in form and shall not be moulded for any part of the hands.

d. Clubhead

The distance from the heel to the toe of the clubhead shall be greater than the distance from the face to the back. The clubhead shall be generally plain in shape.

The clubhead shall have only one face designed for striking the ball, except that a putter may have two such faces if their characteristics are the same, they are opposite each other and the loft of each is the same and does not exceed ten degrees.

e. Club Face

The face shall not have any degree of concavity and, in relation to the ball, shall be hard and rigid. It shall be generally smooth except for such markings as are permitted by Appendix II. If the basic structural material of the head and face of a club, other than a putter, is metal, no inset or attachment is permitted.

f. Wear

A club which conforms with Rule 4-1 when new is deemed to conform after wear through normal use. Any part of a club which has been purposely altered is regarded as new and must conform, in the altered state, with the Rules.

g. Damage

If a player's club ceases to conform with Rule 4-1 because of damage sustained in the normal course of play, the player may:

(i) use the club in its damaged state, but only for the remainder of the stipulated round during which such damage was sustained; or

(ii) without unduly delaying play, repair it.

A club which ceases to conform because of damage sustained other than in the normal course of play shall not subsequently be used during the round.

(Damage changing playing characteristics of club — see Rule 4-2.)

4-2. Playing Characteristics Changed

During a stipulated round, the playing characteristics of a club shall not be purposely changed.

If the playing characteristics of a player's club are changed during a round because of damage sustained in the normal course of play, the player may:

(i) use the club in its altered state; or

(ii) without unduly delaying play, repair it.

If the playing characteristics of a player's club are changed because of damage sustained other than in the normal course of play, the club shall not subsequently be used during the round.

Damage to a club which occurred prior to a round may be repaired during the round, provided the playing characteristics are not changed and play is not unduly delayed.

4-3. Foreign Material

No foreign material shall be applied to the club face for the purpose of influencing the movement of the ball.

PENALTY FOR BREACH OF RULE 4-1, -2 or -3:
Disqualification

4-4. Maximum of Fourteen Clubs

a. Selection and Replacement of Clubs

The player shall start a stipulated round with not more than fourteen clubs. He is limited to the clubs thus selected for that round except that, without unduly delaying play, he may:

(i) if he started with fewer than fourteen, add as many as will bring his total to that number; and

(ii) replace, with any club, a club which becomes unfit for play in the normal course of play.

b. Borrowing or Sharing Clubs

The addition or replacement of a club or clubs may be made by borrowing from anyone; only the borrower may use such club or clubs for the remainder of the round.

The sharing of a club or clubs is prohibited except that partners may share clubs, provided that the total number of clubs carried by the partners so sharing does not exceed fourteen.

PENALTY FOR BREACH OF RULE 4-4a or b, REGARDLESS OF NUMBER OF EXCESS CLUBS CARRIED:

Match play—At the conclusion of the hole at which the breach is discovered, the state of the match shall be adjusted by deducting one hole for each hole at which a breach occurred. Maximum deduction per round: two holes.

Stroke play—Two strokes for each hole at which any breach occurred; maximum penalty per round: four strokes.

Bogey and par competitions—Penalties as in match play.

Stableford competitions—see Note to Rule 32-1b.

c. Excess Club Declared Out of Play

Any club carried or used in breach of this Rule shall be declared out of play by the player immediately upon discovery that a breach has occurred and thereafter shall not be used by the player during the round.

PENALTY FOR BREACH OF RULE 4-4c:
Disqualification

Rule 5. The Ball

5-1. General

The ball the player uses shall conform to specifications set forth in Appendix III on maximum weight, minimum size, spherical symmetry, initial velocity and overall distance when tested under specified conditions.

Note: In laying down the conditions under which a competition is to be played (Rule 33-1), the Committee may stipulate that the ball to be used shall be of certain specifications, provided these specifications are within the limits prescribed by Appendix III, and that it be of a size, brand and marking as detailed on the current List of Conforming Golf Balls issued by the Royal and Ancient Golf Club of St. Andrews.

5-2. Foreign Material

No foreign material shall be applied to a ball for the purpose of changing its playing characteristics.

PENALTY FOR BREACH OF RULES 5-1 or 5-2:
Disqualification.

5-3. Ball Unfit for Play

A ball is unfit for play if it is visibly cut, cracked or out of shape. A ball is not unfit for play solely because mud or other materials adhere to it, its surface is scratched or scraped or its paint is damaged or discoloured.

If a player has reason to believe his ball has become unfit for play during play of the hole being played, he may during the play of such hole lift his ball without penalty to determine whether it is unfit, provided he announces his intention in advance to his opponent in match play or his marker or a fellow-competitor in stroke play and gives his opponent, marker or fellow-competitor an opportunity to examine the ball. If he lifts the ball without announcing his intention in advance or giving his opponent, marker or fellow-competitor an opportunity to examine the ball, *he shall incur a penalty of one stroke.*

If it is determined that the ball has become unfit for play during play of the hole being played, the player may substitute another ball, placing it on the spot where the original ball lay. Otherwise, the original ball shall be replaced.

If a ball breaks into pieces as a result of a stroke, the stroke shall be replayed without penalty (see Rule 20-5).

*PENALTY FOR BREACH OF RULE 5-3:
Match play—Loss of hole; Stroke play—Two strokes.

*If a player incurs the general penalty for breach of Rule 5-3, no additional penalty under the Rule shall be applied.

Note 1: The ball may not be cleaned to determine whether it is unfit for play — see Rule 21.

Note 2: If the opponent, marker or fellow-competitor wishes to dispute a claim of unfitness, he must do so before the player plays another ball.

PLAYER'S RESPONSIBILITIES

Rule 6. The player

Definition

A "marker" is one who is appointed by the Committee to record a competitor's score in stroke play. He may be a fellow-competitor. He is not a referee.

6-1. Conditions of Competition

The player is responsible for knowing the conditions under which the competition is to be played (Rule 33-1).

6-2. Handicap

a. Match Play

Before starting a match in a handicap competition, the players should determine from one another their respective handicaps. If a player begins the match having declared a higher handicap which would affect the number of strokes given or received, *he shall be disqualified;* otherwise, the player shall play off the declared handicap.

b. Stroke Play

In any round of a handicap competition, the competitor shall ensure that his handicap is recorded on his score card before it is returned to the Committee. If no handicap is recorded on his score card before it is returned, or if the recorded handicap is higher than that to which he is entitled and this affects the number of strokes received, *he shall be disqualified* from that round of the handicap competition; otherwise, the score shall stand.

Note: It is the player's responsibility to know the holes at which handicap strokes are to be given or received.

6-3. Time of Starting and Groups

a. Time of Starting

The player shall start at the time laid down by the Committee.

b. Groups

In stroke play, the competitor shall remain throughout the round in the group arranged by the Committee unless the Committee authorises or ratifies a change.

PENALTY FOR BREACH OF RULE 6-3:
Disqualification.
(Best-ball and four-ball play— see Rules 30-3a and 31-2.)

Note: The Committee may provide in the conditions of a competition (Rule 33-1) that, if the player arrives at his starting point, ready to play, within five minutes after his starting time, in the absence of circumstances which warrant waiving the penalty of disqualification as provided in Rule 33-7, the penalty for failure to start on time is *loss of the first hole in match play or two strokes at the first hole in stroke play* instead of disqualification.

6-4. Caddie

The player may have only one caddie at any one time, *under penalty of disqualification.*

For any breach of a Rule by his caddie, the player incurs the applicable penalty.

6-5. Ball

The responsibility for playing the proper ball rests with the player. Each player should put an identification mark on his ball.

6-6. Scoring in Stroke Play

a. Recording Scores

After each hole the marker should check the score with the competitor and record it. On completion of the round the marker shall sign the card and hand it to the competitor. If more than one marker records the scores, each shall sign for the part for which he is responsible.

b. Signing and Returning Card

After completion of the round, the competitor should check his score for each hole and settle any doubtful points with the Committee. He shall ensure that the marker has signed the card, countersign the card himself and return it to the Committee as soon as possible.

PENALTY FOR BREACH OF RULE 6-6b:
Disqualification.

c. Alteration of Card

No alteration may be made on a card after the competitor has returned it to the Committee.

d. Wrong Score for Hole

The competitor is responsible for the correctness of the score recorded for each hole. If he returns a score for any hole lower than actually taken, *he shall be disqualified.* If he returns a score for any hole higher than actually taken, the score as returned shall stand.

Note 1: The Committee is responsible for the addition of scores and application of the handicap recorded on the card—see Rule 33-5.

Note 2: In four-ball stroke play, see also Rule 31-4 and -7a.

6-7. Undue Delay

The player shall play without undue delay. Between completion of a hole and playing from the next teeing ground, the player shall not unduly delay play.

PENALTY FOR BREACH OF RULE 6-7:
Match play—Loss of hole; Stroke play—Two strokes.
For repeated offence—Disqualification.

If the player unduly delays play between holes, he is delaying the play of the next hole and the penalty applies to that hole.

6-8. Discontinuance of Play

a. When Permitted

The player shall not discontinue play unless:
(i) the Committee has suspended play;
(ii) he believes there is danger from lightning;
(iii) he is seeking a decision from the Committee on a doubtful or disputed point (see Rules 2-5 and 34-3); or
(iv) there is some other good reason such as sudden illness.

Bad weather is not of itself a good reason for discontinuing play.

If the player discontinues play without specific permission from the Committee, he shall report to the Committee as soon as practicable. If he does so and the Committee considers his reason satisfactory, the player incurs no penalty. Otherwise, *the player shall be disqualified.*

Exception in match play: Players discontinuing match play by agreement are not subject to disqualification unless by so doing the competition is delayed.

Note: Leaving the course does not of itself constitute discontinuance of play.

b. Procedure When Play Suspended by Committee

When play is suspended by the Committee, if the players in a match or group are between the play of two holes, they shall not resume play until the Committee has ordered a resumption of play. If they are in the process of playing a hole, they may continue provided they do so without delay. If they choose to continue, they shall discontinue either before or immediately after completing the hole, and shall not thereafter resume play until the Committee has ordered a resumption of play.

PENALTY FOR BREACH OF RULE 6-8b:
Disqualification

c. Lifting Ball When Play Discontinued

When during the play of a hole a player discontinues play under Rule 6-8a, he may lift his ball. A ball may be cleaned when so lifted. If a ball has been so lifted, the player shall, when play is resumed, place a ball on the spot from which the original ball was lifted.

PENALTY FOR BREACH OF RULE 6-8c:
Match Play—Loss of hole; Stroke play—Two strokes.

Rule 7. Practice

7-1. Before or Between Rounds

a. Match Play

On any day of a match play competition, a player may practise on the competition course before a round.

b. Stroke Play

On any day of a stroke competition or play-off, a competitor shall not practise on the competition course or test the surface of any putting green on the course before a round or play-off. When two or more rounds of a stroke competition are to be played over consecutive days, practice between those rounds on any competition course remaining to be played is prohibited.

Exception: Practice putting or chipping on or near the first teeing ground before starting a round or play-off is permitted.

PENALTY FOR BREACH OF RULE 7-1b:
Disqualification.

Note: The Committee may in the conditions of a competition (Rule 33-1) prohibit practice on the competition course on any day of a match play competition or permit practice on the competition course or part of the course (Rule 33-2c) on any day of or between rounds of a stroke competition.

7-2. During Round

A player shall not play a practice stroke either during the play of a hole or between the play of two holes except that, between the play of two holes, the player may practise putting or chipping on or near the putting green of the hole last played, any practice putting green or the teeing ground of the next hole to be played in the round, provided such practice stroke is not played from a hazard and does not unduly delay play (Rule 6-7).

Exception: When play has been suspended by the Committee, a player may, prior to resumption of play, practise (a) as provided in this Rule, (b) anywhere other than on the competition course and (c) as otherwise permitted by the Committee.

PENALTY FOR BREACH OF RULE 7-2:
Match play—Loss of hole; Stroke play—
Two strokes.

In the event of a breach between the play of two holes, the penalty applies to the next hole.

Note 1: A practice swing is not a practice stroke and may be taken at any place, provided the player does not breach the Rules.

Note 2: The Committee may prohibit practice on or near the putting green of the hole last played.

Rule 8. Advice; Indicating Line of Play

Definition

"Advice" is any counsel or suggestion which could influence a player in determining his play, the choice of a club or the method of making a stroke.

Information on the Rules or on matters of public information, such as the position of hazards or the flagstick on the putting green, is not advice.

8-1. Advice

A player shall not give advice to anyone in the competition except his partner. A player may ask for advice from only his partner or either of their caddies.

8-2. Indicating Line of Play

a. Other Than on Putting Green

Except on the putting green, a player may have the line of play indicated to him by anyone, but no one shall stand on or close to the line while the stroke is being played. Any mark placed during the play of a hole by the player or with his knowledge to indicate the line shall be removed before the stroke is played.

Exception: Flagstick attended or held up — see Rule 17-1.

b. On the Putting Green

When the player's ball is on the putting green, the player, his partner or either of their caddies may, before but not during the stroke, point out a line for putting, but in so doing the putting green shall not be touched. No mark shall be placed anywhere to indicate a line for putting.

PENALTY FOR BREACH OF RULE:
Match play—Loss of hole; Stroke play—
Two strokes.

Note: In a team competition without concurrent individual competition, the Committee may in the conditions of the competition (Rule 33-1) permit each team to appoint one person, e.g., team captain or coach, who may give advice (including pointing out a line for putting) to members of that team. Such person shall be identified to the Committee prior to the start of the competition.

Rule 9. Information as to Strokes Taken

9-1. General

The number of strokes a player has taken shall include any penalty strokes incurred.

9.2 Match Play

A player who has incurred a penalty shall inform his opponent as soon as practicable. If he fails to do so, he shall be deemed to have given wrong information, even if he was not aware that he had incurred a penalty.

An opponent is entitled to ascertain from the player, during the play of a hole, the number of strokes he has taken and, after play of a hole, the number of strokes taken on the hole just completed.

If during the play of a hole the player gives or is deemed to give wrong information as to the number of strokes taken, he shall incur no penalty if he corrects the mistake before his opponent has played his next stroke. If the player fails so to correct the wrong information, *he shall lose the hole.*

If after play of a hole the player gives or is deemed to give wrong information as to the number of strokes taken on the hole just completed and this affects the opponent's understanding of the result of the hole, he shall incur no penalty if he corrects his mistake before any player plays from the next teeing ground or, in the case of the last hole of the match, before all players leave the putting green. If the player fails so to correct the wrong information, *he shall lose the hole.*

9-3. Stroke Play

A competitor who has incurred a penalty should inform his marker as soon as practicable.

ORDER OF PLAY

Rule 10. Order of Play

10-1. Match Play

a. Teeing Ground

The side entitled to play first from the teeing ground is said to have the "honour".

The side which shall have the honour at the first teeing ground shall be determined by the order of the draw. In the absence of a draw, the honour should be decided by lot.

The side which wins a hole shall take the honour at the next teeing ground. If a hole has been halved, the side which had the honour at the previous teeing ground shall retain it.

b. Other Than on Teeing Ground

When the balls are in play, the ball farther from the hole shall be played first. If the balls are equidistant from the hole, the ball to be played first should be decided by lot.

Exception: Rule 30-3c (best-ball and four-ball match play).

c. Playing Out of Turn

If a player plays when his opponent should have played, the opponent may immediately require the player to cancel the stroke so played and play a ball in correct order, without penalty (see Rule 20-5).

10-2. Stroke Play

a. Teeing Ground

The competitor entitled to play first from the teeing ground is said to have the "honour".

The competitor who shall have the honour at the first teeing ground shall be determined by the order of the draw. In the absence of a draw, the honour should be decided by lot.

The competitor with the lowest score at a hole shall take the honour at the next teeing ground. The competitor with the second lowest score shall play next and so on. If two or more competitors have the same score at a hole, they shall play from the next teeing ground in the same order as at the previous teeing ground.

b. Other Than on Teeing Ground

When the balls are in play, the ball farthest from the hole shall be played first. If two or more balls are equidistant from the hole, the ball to be played first should be decided by lot.

Exceptions: Rules 22 (ball interfering with or assisting play) and 31-5 (four-ball stroke play).

c. Playing Out of Turn

If a competitor plays out of turn, no penalty is incurred and the ball shall be played as it lies. If, however, the Committee determines that competitors have agreed to play in an order other than that set forth in Clauses 2a and 2b of this Rule to give one of them an advantage, *they shall be disqualified.*

(Incorrect order of play in threesomes and foursomes stroke play—see Rule 29-3).

10-3. Provisional Ball or Second Ball from Teeing Ground

If a player plays a provisional ball or a second ball from a teeing ground, he should do so after his opponent or fellow-competitor has played his first stroke. If a player plays a provisional ball or a second ball out of turn, Clauses 1c and 2c of this Rule shall apply.

10-4. Ball Moved in Measuring

If a ball is moved in measuring to determine which ball is farther from the hole, no penalty is incurred and the ball shall be replaced.

TEEING GROUND

Rule 11. Teeing Ground

Definition

The "teeing ground" is the starting place for the hole to be played. It is a rectangular area two club-lengths in depth, the front and the sides of which are defined by the outside limits of two tee-markers. A ball is outside the teeing ground when all of it lies outside the teeing ground.

11-1. Teeing

In teeing, the ball may be placed on the ground, on an irregularity of surface created by the player on the ground or on a tee, sand or other substance in order to raise it off the ground.

A player may stand outside the teeing ground to play a ball within it.

11-2. Tee-Markers

Before a player plays his first stroke with any ball from the teeing ground of the hole being played, the tee-markers are deemed to be fixed. In such circumstances, if the player moves or allows to be moved a tee-marker for the purpose of avoiding interference with his stance, the area of his intended swing or his line of play, *he shall incur the penalty for a breach of Rule 13-2.*

11-3. Ball Falling Off Tee

If a ball, when not in play, falls off a tee or is knocked off a tee by the player in addressing it, it may be re-teed without penalty, but if a stroke is made at the ball in these circumstances, whether the ball is moving or not, the stroke counts but no penalty is incurred.

11-4. Playing Outside Teeing Ground

a. Match Play

If a player, when starting a hole, plays a ball from outside the teeing ground, the opponent may immediately require the player to cancel the stroke so played and play a ball from within the teeing ground, without penalty.

b. Stroke Play

If a competitor, when starting a hole, plays a ball from outside the teeing ground, *he shall incur a penalty of two strokes* and shall then play a ball from within the teeing ground.

If the competitor plays a stroke from the next teeing ground without first correcting his mistake or, in the case of the last hole of the round, leaves the putting green, without first declaring his intention to correct his mistake, *he shall be disqualified.*

Strokes played by a competitor from outside the teeing ground do not count in his score.

PLAYING THE BALL

Rule 12. Searching for and Identifying Ball

Definitions

A "hazard" is any bunker or water hazard.

A "bunker" is a hazard consisting of a prepared area of ground, often a hollow, from which turf or soil has been removed and replaced with sand or the like. Grass-covered ground bordering or within a bunker is not part of the bunker. The margin of a bunker extends vertically downwards, but not upwards.

A "water hazard" is any sea, lake, pond, river, ditch, surface drainage ditch or other open water course (whether or not containing water) and anything of a similar nature.

All ground or water within the margin of a water hazard is part of the water hazard. The margin of a water hazard extends vertically upwards and downwards. Stakes and lines defining the margins of water hazards are in the hazards.

12-1. Searching for Ball; Seeing Ball

In searching for his ball anywhere on the course, the player may touch or bend long grass, rushes, bushes, whins, heather or the like, but only to the extent necessary to find and identify it, provided that this does not improve the lie of the ball, the area of his intended swing or his line of play.

A player is not necessarily entitled to see his ball when playing a stroke.

In a hazard, if the ball is covered by loose impediments or sand, the player may remove by probing, raking or other means as much thereof as will enable him to see a part of the ball. If an excess is removed, no penalty is incurred and the ball shall be re-covered so that only a part of the ball is visible. If the ball is moved in such removal, no penalty is incurred; the ball shall be replaced and, if necessary, re-covered. As to removal of loose impediments outside a hazard, see Rule 23.

If a ball lying in casual water, ground under repair or a hole, cast or runway made by a burrowing animal, a reptile or a bird is accidentally moved during search, no penalty is incurred; the ball shall be replaced, unless the player elects to proceed under Rule 25-1b.

If a ball is believed to be lying in water in a water hazard, the player may probe for it with a club or otherwise. If the ball is moved in so doing, no penalty is incurred; the ball shall be replaced, unless the player elects to proceed under Rule 26-1.

PENALTY FOR BREACH OF RULE 12-1:
Match play—Loss of hole; Stroke play—Two strokes.

12-2. Identifying Ball

The responsibility for playing the proper ball rests with the player. Each player should put an identification mark on his ball.

Except in a hazard, the player may, without penalty, lift a ball he believes to be his own for the purpose of identification and clean it to the extent necessary for identification. If the ball is the player's ball, he shall replace it. Before the player lifts the ball, he shall announce his intention to his opponent in match play or his marker or a fellow-competitor in stroke play and give his opponent, marker or fellow-competitor an opportunity to observe the lifting and replacement. If he lifts his ball without announcing his intention in advance or giving his opponent, marker or fellow-competitor an opportunity to observe, or if he lifts his ball for identification in a hazard, *he shall incur a penalty of one stroke* and the ball shall be replaced.

If a player who is required to replace a ball fails to do so, *he shall incur the penalty* for a breach of Rule 20-3a, but no additional penalty under Rule 12-2 shall be applied.

Rule 13. Ball Played As It Lies; Lie, Area of Intended Swing and Line of Play; Stance

Definitions

A "hazard" is any bunker or water hazard.

A "bunker" is a hazard consisting of a prepared area of ground, often a hollow, from which turf or soil has been removed and replaced with sand or the like. Grass-covered ground bordering or within a bunker is not part of the bunker. The margin of a bunker extends vertically downwards, but not upwards.

A "water hazard" is any sea, lake, pond, river, ditch, surface drainage ditch or other open water course (whether or not containing water) and anything of a similar nature.

All ground or water within the margin of a water hazard is part of the water hazard. The margin of a water hazard extends vertically upwards and downwards. Stakes and lines defining the margins of water hazards are in the hazards.

13-1. Ball Played As It Lies

The ball shall be played as it lies, except as otherwise provided in the Rules. (Ball at rest moved – see Rule 18.)

13-2. Improving Lie, Area of Intended Swing or Line of Play

Except as provided in the Rules, a player shall not improve or allow to be improved:

the position or lie of his ball,
the area of his intended swing,
his line of play or
the area in which he is to drop or place a ball

by any of the following actions:

moving, bending or breaking anything growing or fixed (including immovable obstructions and objects defining out of bounds) or removing or pressing down sand, loose soil, replaced divots, other cut turf placed in position or other irregularities of surface

except as follows:

as may occur in fairly taking his stance,
in making a stroke or the backward movement of his club for a stroke,
on the teeing ground in creating or eliminating irregularities of surface or
on the putting green in removing sand and loose soil as provided in Rule 16-1a or in repairing damage as provided in Rule 16-1c.

The club may be grounded only lightly and shall not be pressed on the ground.

Exception: Ball lying in or touching hazard – see Rule 13-4.

13-3. Building Stance

A player is entitled to place his feet firmly in taking his stance, but he shall not build a stance.

13-4. Ball Lying in or Touching Hazard

Except as provided in the Rules, before making a stroke at a ball which lies in or touches a hazard (whether a bunker or a water hazard), the player shall not:

a. Test the condition of the hazard or any similar hazard,

b. Touch the ground in the hazard or water in the water hazard with a club or otherwise, or

c. Touch or move a loose impediment lying in or touching the hazard.

Exceptions:

1. At address or in the backward movement for the stroke, the club may touch any obstruction or any grass, bush, tree or other growing thing.

2. The player may place his clubs in a hazard, provided nothing is done which may constitute testing the soil or improving the lie of the ball.

3. The player after playing the stroke, or his caddie at any time without the authority of the player, may smooth sand or soil in the hazard, provided that, if the ball still lies in the hazard, nothing is done which improves the lie of the ball or assists the player in his subsequent play of the hole.

PENALTY FOR BREACH OF RULE:
Match play—Loss of hole; Stroke play—Two strokes.
(Searching for ball – see Rule 12-1.)

Rule 14. Striking the Ball

Definition

A "stroke" is the forward movement of the club made with the intention of fairly striking at and moving the ball, but if a player checks his downswing voluntarily before the clubhead reaches the ball he is deemed not to have made a stroke.

14-1. Ball to be Fairly Struck At

The ball shall be fairly struck at with the head of the club and must not be pushed, scraped or spooned.

14-2. Assistance

In making a stroke, a player shall not accept physical assistance or protection from the elements.

PENALTY FOR BREACH OF RULE 14-1 or -2;
Match play—Loss of hole; Stroke play—Two strokes.

14-3. Artificial Devices and Unusual Equipment

Except as provided in the Rules, during a stipulated round the player shall not use any artificial device or unusual equipment:

a. For the purpose of gauging or measuring distance or conditions which might affect his play; or

b. Which might assist him in gripping the club, in making a stroke or in his play, except that plain gloves may be worn, resin, tape or gauze may be applied to the grip (provided such application does not render the grip non-conforming under Rule 4-1c) and a towel or handkerchief may be wrapped around the grip.

PENALTY FOR BREACH OF RULE 14-3:
Disqualification.

14-4. Striking the Ball More than Once

If a player's club strikes the ball more than once in the course of a stroke, the player shall count the stroke and *add a penalty stroke*, making two strokes in all.

14-5. Playing Moving Ball

A player shall not play while his ball is moving.

Exceptions:

Ball falling off tee—Rule 11-3.
Striking the ball more than once— Rule 14-4.
Ball moving in water—Rule 14-6.

When the ball begins to move only after the player has begun the stroke or the backward movement of his club for the stroke, he shall incur no penalty under this Rule for playing a moving ball, but he is not exempt from any penalty incurred under the following Rules

Ball at rest moved by player—Rule 18-2a.
Ball at rest moving after address— Rule 18-2b.
Ball at rest moving after loose impediment touched—Rule 18-2c.

14-6. Ball Moving in Water

When a ball is moving in water in a water hazard, the player may, without penalty, make a stroke, but he must not delay making his stroke in order to allow the wind or current to improve the position of the ball. A ball moving in water in a water hazard may be lifted if the player elects to invoke Rule 26.

PENALTY FOR BREACH OF RULE 14-5 or -6:
Match play—Loss of hole; Stroke play—Two strokes.

Rule 15. Playing a Wrong Ball

Definition

A "wrong ball" is any ball other than:

a. The ball in play,

b. A provisional ball or

c. In stroke play, a second ball played under Rule 3-3 or Rule 20-7b.

Note: Ball in play includes a ball substituted for the ball in play when the player is proceeding under an applicable Rule which does not permit substitution.

15-1. General

A player must hole out with the ball played from the teeing ground unless a Rule permits him to substitute another ball. If a player substitutes another ball when proceeding under an applicable Rule which does not permit substitution, that ball is not a wrong ball; it becomes the ball in play and, if the error is not corrected as provided in Rule 20-6, *the player shall incur a penalty of loss of hole in match play or two strokes in stroke play.*

15-2. Match Play

If a player plays a stroke with a wrong ball except in a hazard, *he shall lose the hole.*

If a player plays any strokes in a hazard with a wrong ball, there is no penalty. Strokes played in a hazard with a wrong ball do not count in the player's score. If the wrong ball belongs to another player, its owner shall place a ball on the spot from which the wrong ball was first played.

If the player and opponent exchange balls during the play of a hole, the first to play the wrong ball other than from a hazard shall lose the hole; when this cannot be determined, the hole shall be played out with the balls exchanged.

15-3. Stroke Play

If a competitor plays a stroke with a wrong ball, *he shall incur a penalty of two strokes,* unless the only stroke or strokes played with such ball were played when it was lying in a hazard, in which case no penalty is incurred.

The competitor must correct his mistake by playing the correct ball. If he fails to correct his mistake before he plays a stroke from the next teeing ground or, in the case of the last hole of the round, fails to declare his intention to correct his mistake before leaving the putting green, *he shall be disqualified.*

Strokes played by a competitor with a wrong ball do not count in his score.

If the wrong ball belongs to another competitor, its owner shall place a ball on the spot from which the wrong ball was first played.

(Lie of ball to be placed or replaced altered —see Rule 20-3b.)

THE PUTTING GREEN

Rule 16. The Putting Green

Definitions

The "putting green" is all ground of the hole being played which is specially prepared for putting or otherwise defined as such by the Committee. A ball is on the putting green when any part of it touches the putting green.

A ball is "holed" when it is at rest within the circumference of the hole and all of it is below the level of the lip of the hole.

16-1. General

a. Touching Line of Putt

The line of putt must not be touched except:

(i) the player may move sand and loose soil on the putting green and other loose impediments by picking them up or by brushing them aside with his hand or a club without pressing anything down;

(ii) in addressing the ball, the player may place the club in front of the ball without pressing anything down;

(iii) in measuring—Rule 10-4;

(iv) in lifting the ball—Rule 16-1b;

(v) in pressing down a ball-marker;

(vi) in repairing old hole plugs or ball marks on the putting green—Rule 16-1c; and

(vii) in removing movable obstructions—Rule 24-1.

(Indicating line for putting on putting green —see Rule 8-2b.)

b. Lifting Ball

A ball on the putting green may be lifted and, if desired, cleaned. A ball so lifted shall be replaced on the spot from which it was lifted.

c. Repair of Hole Plugs and Ball Marks

The player may repair an old hole plug or damage to the putting green caused by the impact of a ball, whether or not the player's ball lies on the putting green. If the ball is moved in the process of such repair, it shall be replaced, without penalty.

d. Testing Surface

During the play of a hole, a player shall not test the surface of the putting green by rolling a ball or roughening or scraping the surface.

e. Standing Astride or on Line of Putt

The player shall not make a stroke on the putting green from a stance astride, or with either foot touching, the line of the putt or an extension of that line behind the ball. For the purpose of this Clause only, the line of putt does not extend beyond the hole.

f. Position of Caddie or Partner

While making the stroke, the player shall not allow his caddie, his partner or his partner's caddie to position himself on or close to an extension of the line of putt behind the ball.

g. Playing Stroke While Another Ball in Motion

A player shall not play a stroke while another ball is in motion after a stroke on the putting green.

(Lifting ball interfering with or assisting play while another ball in motion—see Rule 22.)

PENALTY FOR BREACH OF RULE 16-1:
Match play—Loss of hole; Stroke play—Two strokes.

16-2. Ball Overhanging Hole

When any part of the ball overhangs the lip of the hole, the player is allowed enough time to reach the hole without unreasonable delay and an additional ten seconds to determine whether the ball is at rest. If by then the ball has not fallen into the hole, it is deemed to be at rest. If the ball subsequently falls into the hole, the player is deemed to have holed out with his last stroke, and *he shall add a penalty stroke to his score* for the hole; otherwise there is no penalty under this Rule.

(Undue delay—see Rule 6-7.)

Rule 17. The Flagstick

17-1. Flagstick Attended, Removed or Held Up

Before and during the stroke, the player may have the flagstick attended, removed or held up to indicate the position of the hole. This may be done only on the authority of the player before he plays his stroke.

If the flagstick is attended, removed or held up by an opponent, a fellow-competitor or the caddie of either with the player's knowledge and no objection is made, the player shall be deemed to have authorised it. If a player or a caddie attends, removes or holds up the flagstick or stands near the hole while a stroke is being played, he shall be deemed to be attending the flagstick until the ball comes to rest.

If the flagstick is not attended before the stroke is played, it shall not be attended or removed while the ball is in motion.

17-2. Unauthorised Attendance

a. Match Play

In match play, an opponent or his caddie shall not attend, remove or hold up the flagstick without the player's knowledge or authority while the player is making a stroke or his ball is in motion.

b. Stroke Play

In stroke play, if a fellow-competitor or his caddie attends, removes or holds up the flagstick without the competitor's knowledge or authority while the competitor is making a stroke or his ball is in motion, *the fellow-competitor shall incur the penalty* for breach of this Rule. In such circumstances, if the competitor's ball strikes the flagstick or the person attending it, the competitor incurs no penalty and the ball shall be played as it lies, except that, if the stroke was played from the putting green, the stroke shall be replayed.

PENALTY FOR BREACH OF RULE 17-1 or -2: *Match play—Loss of hole; Stroke play—Two strokes.*

17-3. Ball Striking Flagstick or Attendant

The player's ball shall not strike:

a. The flagstick when attended, removed or held up by the player, his partner or either of their caddies, or by another person with the player's knowledge or authority; or

b. The player's caddie, his partner or his partner's caddie when attending the flagstick, or another person attending the flagstick with the player's knowledge or authority, or equipment carried by any such person; or

c. The flagstick in the hole, unattended, when the ball has been played from the putting green.

PENALTY FOR BREACH OF RULE 17-3; *Match play—Loss of hole; Stroke play—Two strokes, and the ball shall be played as it lies.*

17-4. Ball Resting Against Flagstick

If the ball rests against the flagstick when it is in the hole, the player or another person authorised by him may move or remove the flagstick and if the ball falls into the hole, the player shall be deemed to have holed out at his last stroke; otherwise the ball, if moved, shall be placed on the lip of the hole, without penalty.

BALL MOVED, DEFLECTED OR STOPPED

Rule 18. Ball At Rest Moved

Definitions

A ball is deemed to have "moved" if it leaves its position and comes to rest in any other place.

An "outside agency" is any agency not part of the match or, in stroke play, not part of a competitor's side, and includes a referee, a marker, an observer or a forecaddie. Neither wind nor water is an outside agency.

"Equipment" is anything used, worn or carried by or for the player except any ball he has played at the hole being played and any small object, such as a coin or a tee, when used to mark the position of a ball or the extent of an area in which a ball is to be dropped. Equipment includes a golf cart, whether or not motorised. If such a cart is shared by more than one player, its status under the Rules is the same as that of a caddie employed by more than one player. See "Caddie".

A player has "addressed the ball" when he has taken his stance and has also grounded his club, except that in a hazard a player has addressed the ball when he has taken his stance.

Taking the "stance" consists in a player placing his feet in position for and preparatory to making a stroke.

18-1. By Outside Agency

If a ball at rest is moved by an outside agency, the player shall incur no penalty and the ball shall be replaced before the player plays another stroke.

(Player's ball at rest moved by another ball —see Rule 18-5.)

18-2. By Player, Partner, Caddie or Equipment

a. General

When a player's ball is in play, if:

(i) the player, his partner or either of their caddies lifts or moves it, touches it purposely (except with a club in the act of addressing it) or causes it to move except as permitted by a Rule, or

(ii) equipment of the player or his partner causes the ball to move,

the player shall incur a penalty stroke. The ball shall be replaced unless the movement of the ball occurs after the player has begun his swing and he does not discontinue his swing.

Under the Rules no penalty is incurred if a player accidentally causes his ball to move in the following circumstances:

In measuring to determine which ball farther from hole—Rule 10-4

In searching for covered ball in hazard or for ball in casual water, ground under repair, etc.—Rule 12-1

In the process of repairing hole plug or ball mark—Rule 16-1c

In the process of removing loose impediment on putting green—Rule 18-2c

In the process of lifting ball under a Rule —Rule 20-1

In the process of placing or replacing ball under a Rule—Rule 20-3a

In complying with Rule 22 relating to lifting ball interfering with or assisting play

In removal of movable obstruction—Rule 24-1.

b. Ball Moving After Address

If a player's ball in play moves after he has addressed it (other than as a result of a stroke), the player shall be deemed to have moved the ball and *shall incur a penalty stroke*. The player shall replace the ball unless the movement of the ball occurs after he has begun his swing and he does not discontinue his swing.

c. Ball Moving After Loose Impediment Touched

Through the green, if the ball moves after any loose impediment lying within a club-length of it has been touched by the player, his partner or either of their caddies and before the player has addressed it, the player shall be deemed to have moved the ball and *shall incur a penalty stroke*. The player shall replace the ball unless the movement of the ball occurs after he has begun his swing and he does not discontinue his swing.

On the putting green, if the ball moves in the process of removing any loose impediment, it shall be replaced without penalty.

18-3. By Opponent, Caddie or Equipment in Match Play

a. During Search

If, during search for a player's ball, it is moved by an opponent, his caddie or his equipment, no penalty is incurred and the player shall replace the ball.

b. Other Than During Search

If, other than during search for a ball, the ball is touched or moved by an opponent, his caddie or his equipment, except as otherwise provided in the Rules, *the opponent shall incur a penalty stroke*. The player shall replace the ball.

(Ball moved in measuring to determine which ball farther from the hole—see Rule 10-4.)

(Playing a wrong ball—see Rule 15-2.)

(Ball moved in complying with Rule 22 relating to lifting ball interfering with or assisting play.)

18-4. By Fellow-Competitor, Caddie or Equipment in Stroke Play

If a competitor's ball is moved by a fellow-competitor, his caddie or his equipment, no penalty is incurred. The competitor shall replace his ball.

(Playing a wrong ball—see Rule 15-3.)

18-5. By Another Ball

If a ball in play and at rest is moved by another ball in motion after a stroke, the moved ball shall be replaced.

*PENALTY FOR BREACH OF RULE:
Match play—Loss of hole. Stroke play—Two strokes.

**If a player who is required to replace a ball fails to do so, he shall incur the general penalty for breach of Rule 18 but no additional penalty under Rule 18 shall be applied.*

Note 1: If a ball to be replaced under this Rule is not immediately recoverable, another ball may be substituted.

Note 2: If it is impossible to determine the spot on which a ball is to be placed, see Rule 20-3c.

Rule 19. Ball in Motion Deflected or Stopped

Definitions

An "outside agency" is any agency not part of the match or, in stroke play, not part of a competitor's side, and includes a referee, a marker, an observer or a forecaddie. Neither wind nor water is an outside agency.

"Equipment" is anything used, worn or carried by or for the player except any ball he has played at the hole being played and any small object, such as a coin or a tee, when used to mark the position of a ball or the extent of an area in which a ball is to be dropped. Equipment includes a golf cart, whether or not motorised. If such a cart is shared by more than one player, its status under the Rules is the same as that of a caddie employed by more than one player. See "Caddie".

19-1. By Outside Agency

If a ball in motion is accidentally deflected or stopped by any outside agency, it is a rub of the green, no penalty is incurred and the ball shall be played as it lies except:

a. If a ball in motion after a stroke other than on the putting green comes to rest in or on any moving or animate outside agency, the player shall, through the green or in a hazard, drop the ball, or on the putting green place the ball, as near as possible to the spot where the outside agency was when the ball came to rest in or on it, and

b. If a ball in motion after a stroke on the putting green is deflected or stopped by, or comes to rest in or on any moving or animate outside agency except a worm or an insect, the stroke shall be cancelled and the ball shall be replaced.

If the ball is not immediately recoverable, another ball may be substituted.

(Player's ball deflected or stopped by another ball – see Rule 19-5.)

Note: If the referee or the Committee determines that a competitor's ball has been purposely deflected or stopped by an outside agency, Rule 1-4 applies to the competitor. If the outside agency is a fellow-competitor or his caddie, Rule 1-2 applies to the fellow-competitor.

19-2. By Player, Partner, Caddie or Equipment

a. Match Play

If a player's ball is accidentally deflected or stopped by himself, his partner or either of their caddies or equipment, *he shall lose the hole.*

b. Stroke Play

If a competitor's ball is accidentally deflected or stopped by himself, his partner or either of their caddies or equipment, *the competitor shall incur a penalty of two strokes.* The ball shall be played as it lies, except when it comes to rest in or on the competitor's, his partner's or either of their caddies' clothes or equipment, in which case the competitor shall, through the green or in a hazard, drop the ball, or on the putting green place the ball, as near as possible to where the article was when the ball came to rest in or on it.

Exception: Dropped Ball – see Rule 20-2a. (Ball purposely deflected or stopped by player, partner or caddie – see Rule 1-2.)

19-3. By Opponent, Caddie or Equipment in Match Play

If a player's ball is accidentally deflected or stopped by an opponent, his caddie or his equipment, no penalty is incurred. The player may play the ball as it lies or, before another stroke is played by either side, cancel the stroke and replay it (see Rule 20-5). If the player elects to replay the stroke and the original ball is not immediately recoverable, another ball may be substituted.

If the ball has come to rest in or on the opponent's or his caddie's clothes or equipment, the player may through the green or in a hazard drop the ball, or on the putting green place the ball, as near as possible to where the article was when the ball came to rest in or on it.

Exception: Ball striking person attending flagstick—see Rule 17-3b.

(Ball purposely deflected or stopped by opponent or caddie—see Rule 1-2.)

19-4. By Fellow-Competitor, Caddie or Equipment in Stroke Play

See Rule 19-1 regarding ball deflected by outside agency.

19-5. By Another Ball

If a player's ball in motion after a stroke is deflected or stopped by a ball at rest, the player shall play his ball as it lies. In stroke play, if both balls lay on the putting green prior to the stroke, *the player incurs a penalty of two strokes.* Otherwise, no penalty is incurred.

If a player's ball in motion after a stroke is deflected or stopped by another ball in motion, the player shall play his ball as it lies. There is no penalty unless the player was in breach of Rule 16-1g, in which case *he shall incur the penalty for breach of that Rule.*

Exception: Ball in motion after a stroke on the putting green deflected or stopped by moving or animate outside agency—see Rule 19-1b.

PENALTY FOR BREACH OF RULE:
Match play—Loss of hole; Stroke play—Two strokes.

RELIEF SITUATIONS AND PROCEDURE

Rule 20. Lifting, Dropping and Placing: Playing from Wrong Place

20.1 Lifting

A ball to be lifted under the Rules may be lifted by the player, his partner or another person authorised by the player. In any such case, the player shall be responsible for any breach of the Rules.

The position of the ball shall be marked before it is lifted under a Rule which requires it to be replaced. If it is not marked, the player *shall incur a penalty of one stroke* and the ball shall be replaced. If it is not replaced, *the player shall incur the general penalty* for breach of this Rule but no additional penalty under Rule 20-1 shall be applied.

If a ball or a ball-marker is accidentally moved in the process of lifting the ball under a Rule or marking its position, no penalty is incurred and the ball or the ball-marker shall be replaced.

Note: The position of a ball to be lifted should be marked by placing a ball-marker, a small coin or other similar object immediately behind the ball. If the ball-marker interferes with the play, stance or stroke of another player, it should be placed one or more clubhead-lengths to one side.

20-2. Dropping and Re-dropping

a. By Whom and How

A ball to be dropped under the Rules shall be dropped by the player himself. He shall stand erect, hold the ball at shoulder height and arm's length and drop it. If a ball is dropped by any other person or in any other manner and the error is not corrected as provided in Rule 20-6, *the player shall incur a penalty stroke.*

If the ball touches the player, his partner, either of their caddies or their equipment before or after it strikes the ground, the ball shall be redropped, without penalty. There is no limit to the number of times a ball shall be re-dropped in such circumstances.

(Taking action to influence position or movement of ball—see Rule 1-2.)

b. Where to Drop

When a ball is to be dropped, it shall be dropped as near as possible to the spot where the ball lay, but not nearer the hole, except when a Rule permits or requires it to be dropped elsewhere. If a ball is to be dropped in a hazard, the ball shall be dropped in and come to rest in that hazard.

Note: A ball when dropped must first strike the ground where the applicable Rule requires it to be dropped. If it is not so dropped, Rules 20-6 and -7 apply.

c. When to Re-drop

A dropped ball shall be re-dropped without penalty if it:

(i) rolls into a hazard;
(ii) rolls out of a hazard;
(iii) rolls onto a putting green;
(iv) rolls out of bounds;
(v) rolls back into the condition from which relief was taken under Rule 24-2 (immovable obstruction) or Rule 25 (abnormal ground conditions and wrong putting green);
(vi) rolls and comes to rest more than two club-lengths from where it first struck the ground; or
(vii) rolls and comes to rest nearer the hole than its original position unless otherwise permitted by the Rules.

If the ball again rolls into such position, it shall be placed as near as possible to the spot where it first struck the ground when re-dropped.

If a ball to be re-dropped or placed under this Rule is not immediately recoverable, another ball may be substituted.

20-3. Placing and Replacing

a. By Whom and Where

A ball to be placed under the Rules shall be placed by the player or his partner. A ball to be replaced shall be replaced by the player, his partner or the person who lifted or moved it. In any such case, the player shall be responsible for any breach of the Rules.

If a ball or a ball-marker is accidentally moved in the process of placing or replacing the ball, no penalty is incurred and the ball or the ball-marker shall be replaced.

b. Lie of Ball to Be Placed or Replaced Altered

If the original lie of a ball to be placed or replaced has been altered:

(i) except in a hazard, the ball shall be placed in the nearest lie most similar to the original lie which is not more than one club-length from the original lie, not nearer the hole and not in a hazard;
(ii) in a water hazard, the ball shall be placed in accordance with Clause (i) above, except that the ball must be placed in the water hazard;
(iii) in a bunker, the original lie shall be recreated as nearly as possible and the ball shall be placed in that lie.

c. Spot Not Determinable

If it is impossible to determine the spot where the ball is to be placed:

(i) through the green, the ball shall be dropped as near as possible to the place where it lay but not nearer the hole or in a hazard;
(ii) in a hazard, the ball shall be dropped in the hazard as near as possible to the place where it lay but not nearer the hole;
(iii) on the putting green, the ball shall be placed as near as possible to the place where it lay but not nearer the hole or in a hazard.

d. Ball Fails to Remain on Spot

If a ball when placed fails to remain on the spot on which it was placed, it shall be replaced without penalty. If it still fails to remain on that spot:

(i) except in a hazard, it shall be placed at the nearest spot not nearer the hole or in a hazard where it can be placed at rest;
(ii) in a hazard, it shall be placed in the hazard at the nearest spot not nearer the hole where it can be placed at rest.

PENALTY FOR BREACH OF RULE 20-1,-2 or -3;
Match play—Loss of hole; Stroke play—Two strokes.

20-4. When Ball Dropped or Placed is in Play

If the player's ball in play has been lifted, it is again in play when dropped or placed.

A substituted ball becomes the ball in play if it is dropped or placed under an applicable Rule, whether or not such Rule permits substitution. A ball substituted under an inapplicable Rule is a wrong ball.

20-5. Playing Next Stroke from Where Previous Stroke Played

When, under the Rules, a player elects or is required to play his next stroke from where a previous stroke was played, he shall proceed as follows: if the stroke is to be played from the teeing ground, the ball to be played shall be played from anywhere within the teeing ground and may be teed; if the stroke is to be played from through the green or a hazard, it shall be dropped; if the stroke is to be played on the putting green, it shall be placed.

PENALTY FOR BREACH OF RULE 20-5;
Match play—Loss of hole; Stroke play—Two strokes.

20-6. Lifting Ball Wrongly Dropped or Placed

A ball dropped or placed in a wrong place or otherwise not in accordance with the Rules but not played may be lifted, without penalty, and the player shall then proceed correctly.

20-7. Playing from Wrong Place

For a ball played outside teeing ground, see Rule 11-4.

a. Match Play

If a player plays a stroke with a ball which has been dropped or placed in a wrong place, *he shall lose the hole.*

b. Stroke Play

If a competitor plays a stroke with (i) his original ball which has been dropped or placed in a wrong place, (ii) a substituted ball which has been dropped or placed under an applicable Rule but in a wrong place or (iii) his ball in play when it has been moved and not replaced in a case where the Rules require replacement, *he shall*, provided a serious breach has not occurred, *incur the penalty prescribed by the applicable Rule* and play out the hole with the ball.

If, after playing from a wrong place, a competitor becomes aware of that fact and believes that a serious breach may be involved, he may, provided he has not played a stroke from the next teeing ground or, in the case of the last hole of the round, left the putting green, declare that he will play out the hole with a second ball dropped or placed in accordance with the Rules. The competitor shall report the facts to the Committee before returning his score card; if he fails to do so, *he shall be disqualified.* The Committee shall determine whether a serious breach of the Rule occurred. If so, the score with the second ball shall count and *the competitor shall add two penalty strokes to his score with that ball.*

If a serious breach has occurred and the competitor has failed to correct it as prescribed above, *he shall be disqualified.*

Note: If a competitor plays a second ball, penalty strokes incurred by playing the ball ruled not to count and strokes subsequently taken with that ball shall be disregarded.

Rule 21. Cleaning Ball

A ball on the putting green may be cleaned when lifted under Rule 16-1b. Elsewhere, a ball may be cleaned when lifted except when it has been lifted:

a. To determine if it is unfit for play (Rule 5-3);

b. For identification (Rule 12-2), in which case it may be cleaned only to the extent necessary for identification; or

c. Because it is interfering with or assisting play (Rule 22).

If a player cleans his ball during play of a hole except as provided in this Rule, *he shall incur a penalty of one stroke* and the ball, if lifted, shall be replaced.

If a player who is required to replace a ball fails to do so, *he shall incur the penalty* for breach of Rule 20-3a, but no additional penalty under Rule 21 shall be applied.

Exception: If a player incurs a penalty for failing to act in accordance with Rule 5-3, 12-2 or 22, no additional penalty under Rule 21 shall be applied.

Rule 22. Ball Interfering with or Assisting Play

Any player may:

a. Lift his ball if he considers that it might assist any other player or

b. Have any other ball lifted if he considers that it might interfere with his play or assist the play of any other player,

but this may not be done while another ball is in motion. In stroke play, a player required to lift his ball may play first rather than lift. A ball lifted under this Rule shall be replaced.

If a ball is accidentally moved in complying with this Rule, no penalty is incurred and the ball shall be replaced.

PENALTY FOR BREACH OF RULE:
Match play—Loss of hole; Stroke play—Two strokes.

Rule 23. Loose Impediments

Definition

"Loose impediments" are natural objects such as stones, leaves, twigs, branches and the like, dung, worms and insects and casts or heaps made by them, provided they are not fixed or growing, are not solidly embedded and do not adhere to the ball.

Sand and loose soil are loose impediments on the putting green but not elsewhere.

Snow and ice are either casual water or loose impediments, at the option of the player, except that manufactured ice is an obstruction.

Dew is not a loose impediment.

23-1. Relief

Except when both the loose impediment and the ball lie in or touch a hazard, any loose impediment may be removed without penalty. If the ball moves, see Rule 18-2c.

When a player's ball is in motion, a loose impediment on his line of play shall not be removed.

PENALTY FOR BREACH OF RULE:
Match play—Loss of hole; Stroke play—Two strokes.

(Searching for ball in hazard—see Rule 12-1.)
(Touching line of putt—see Rule 16-1a.)

Rule 24. Obstructions

Definition

An "obstruction" is anything artificial, including the artificial surfaces and sides of roads and paths and manufactured ice, except:

a. Objects defining out of bounds, such as walls, fences, stakes and railings;

b. Any part of an immovable artificial object which is out of bounds; and

c. Any construction declared by the Committee to be an integral part of the course.

24-1. Movable Obstruction

A player may obtain relief from a movable obstruction as follows:

a. If the ball does not lie in or on the obstruction, the obstruction may be removed; if the ball moves, no penalty is incurred and the ball shall be replaced.

b. If the ball lies in or on the obstruction, the ball may be lifted, without penalty, and the obstruction removed. The ball shall through the green or in a hazard be dropped, or on the putting green be placed, as near as possible to the spot directly under the place where the ball lay in or on the obstruction, but not nearer the hole.

The ball may be cleaned when lifted under Rule 24-1.

When a ball is in motion, an obstruction on the player's line of play other than an attended flagstick and equipment of the players shall not be removed.

24-2. Immovable Obstruction

a. Interference

Interference by an immovable obstruction occurs when a ball lies in or on the obstruction, or so close to the obstruction that the obstruction interferes with the player's stance or the area of his intended swing. If the player's ball lies on the putting green, interference also occurs if an immovable obstruction on the putting green intervenes on his line of putt. Otherwise, intervention on the line of play is not, of itself, interference under this Rule.

b. Relief

Except when the ball lies in or touches a water hazard or a lateral water hazard, a player may obtain relief from interference by an immovable obstruction, without penalty, as follows:

(i) **Through the Green:** If the ball lies through the green, the point on the course nearest to where the ball lies shall be determined (without crossing over, through or under the obstruction) which (a) is not nearer the hole, (b) avoids interference (as defined) and (c) is not a hazard or on a putting green. The player shall lift the ball and drop it within one club-length of the point thus determined on ground which fulfils (a), (b) and (c) above.

Note: The prohibition against crossing over, through or under the obstruction does not apply to the artificial surfaces and sides of roads and paths or when the ball lies in or on the obstruction.

(ii) **In a Bunker:** If the ball lies in or touches a bunker, the player shall lift and drop the ball in accordance with Clause (i) above, except that the ball must be dropped in the bunker.

(iii) **On the Putting Green:** If the ball lies on the putting green, the player shall lift the ball and place it in the nearest position to where it lay which affords relief from interference, but not nearer the hole nor in a hazard.

The ball may be cleaned when lifted for relief under Rule 24-2b.

(Ball rolling back into condition from which relief taken—see Rule 20-2c(v).)

Exception: A player may not obtain relief under Rule 24-2b if (a) it is clearly unreasonable for him to play a stroke because of interference by anything other than an immovable obstruction or (b) interference by an immovable obstruction would occur only through use of an unnecessarily abnormal stance, swing or direction of play.

Note: If a ball lies in or touches a water hazard (including a lateral water hazard), the player is not entitled to relief without penalty from interference by an immovable obstruction. The player shall play the ball as it lies or proceed under Rule 26-1.

PENALTY FOR BREACH OF RULE:
Match play—Loss of hole; Stroke play—Two strokes.

Rule 25. Abnormal Ground Conditions and Wrong Putting Green

Definitions

"Casual water" is any temporary accumulation of water on the course which is visible before or after the player takes his stance and is not in a water hazard. Snow and ice are either casual water or loose impediments, at the option of the player, except that manufactured ice is an obstruction. Dew is not casual water.

"Ground under repair" is any portion of the course so marked by order of the Committee or so declared by its authorised representative. It includes material piled for removal and a hole made by a greenkeeper, even if not so marked. Stakes and lines defining ground under repair are in such ground. The margin of ground under repair extends vertically downwards, but not upwards.

Note 1: Grass cuttings and other material left on the course which have been abandoned and are not intended to be removed are not ground under repair unless so marked.

Note 2: The Committee may make a Local Rule prohibiting play from ground under repair.

25-1. Casual Water, Ground Under Repair and Certain Damage to Course

a. Interference

Interference by casual water, ground under repair or a hole, cast or runway made by a burrowing animal, a reptile or a bird occurs when a ball lies in or touches any of these conditions or when the condition interferes with the player's stance or the area of his intended swing.

If the player's ball lies on the putting green, interference also occurs if such condition on the putting green intervenes on his line of putt.

If interference exists, the player may either play the ball as it lies (unless prohibited by Local Rule) or take relief as provided in Clause b.

b. Relief

If the player elects to take relief, he shall proceed as follows:

(i) **Through the Green:** If the ball lies through the green, the point on the course nearest to where the ball lies shall be determined which (a) is not nearer the hole, (b) avoids interference by the condition, and (c) is not in a hazard or on a putting green. The player shall lift the ball and drop it without penalty within one club-length of the point thus determined on ground which fulfils (a), (b) and (c) above.

(ii) **In a Hazard:** If the ball lies in or touches a hazard, the player shall lift and drop the ball either:
(a) Without penalty, in the hazard, as near as possible to the spot where the ball lay, but not nearer the hole, on ground which affords maximum available relief from the condition;
or
(b) *Under penalty of one stroke*, outside the hazard, keeping the point where the ball lay directly between the hole and the spot on which the ball is dropped.

Exception: If a ball lies in or touches a water hazard (including a lateral water hazard), the player is not entitled to relief without penalty from a hole, cast or runway made by a burrowing animal, a reptile or a bird. The player shall play the ball as it lies or proceed under Rule 26-1.

(iii) **On the Putting Green:** If the ball lies on the putting green, the player shall lift the ball and place it without penalty in the nearest position to where it lay which affords maximum available relief from the condition, but not nearer the hole nor in a hazard.

The ball may be cleaned when lifted under Rule 25-1b.

(Ball rolling back into condition from which relief taken—see Rule 20-2c(v).)

Exception: A player may not obtain relief under Rule 25-1b if (a) it is clearly unreasonable for him to play a stroke because of interference by anything other than a condition covered by Rule 25-1a or (b) interference by such a condition would occur only through use of an unnecessarily abnormal stance, swing or direction of play.

c. Ball Lost Under Condition Covered by Rule 25-1

It is a question of fact whether a ball lost after having been struck toward a condition covered by Rule 25-1 is lost under such condition. In order to treat the ball as lost under such condition, there must be reasonable evidence to that effect. In the absence of such evidence, the ball must be treated as a lost ball and Rule 27 applies.

(i) **Outside a Hazard**—If a ball is lost outside a hazard under a condition covered by Rule 25-1, the player may take relief as follows: the point on the course nearest to where the ball last crossed the margin of the area shall be determined which (a) is not nearer the hole than where the ball last crossed the margin, (b) avoids interference by the condition and (c) is not in a hazard or on a putting green. He shall drop a ball without penalty within one club-length of the point thus determined on ground which fulfils (a), (b) and (c) above.

(ii) **In a Hazard**—If a ball is lost in a hazard under a condition covered by Rule 25-1, the player may drop a ball either;

(a) Without penalty, in the hazard, as near as possible to the point at which the original ball last crossed the margin of the area, but not nearer the hole, on ground, which affords maximum available relief from the condition;

or

(b) *Under penalty of one stroke*, outside the hazard, keeping the point at which the original ball last crossed the margin of the hazard directly between the hole and the spot on which the ball is dropped.

Exception: If a ball lies in a water hazard (including a lateral water hazard), the player is not entitled to relief without penalty for a ball lost in a hole, cast or runway made by a burrowing animal, a reptile or a bird. The player shall proceed under Rule 26-1.

25-2. Embedded Ball

A ball embedded in its own pitch-mark in the ground in any closely mown area through the green may be lifted, cleaned and dropped, without penalty, as near as possible to the spot where it lay but not nearer the hole. "Closely mown area" means any area of the course, including paths through the rough, cut to fairway height or less.

25-3. Wrong Putting Green

If a ball lies on a putting green other than that of the hole being played, the point on the course nearest to where the ball lies shall be determined which (a) is not nearer the hole and (b) is not in a hazard or on a putting green. The player shall lift the ball and drop it without penalty within one club-length of the point thus determined on ground which fulfils (a) and (b) above. The ball may be cleaned when so lifted.

Note: Unless otherwise prescribed by the Committee, the term "a putting green other than that of the hole being played" includes a practice putting green or pitching green on the course.

PENALTY FOR BREACH OF RULE:
Match play—Loss of hole; Stroke play—Two strokes.

Rule 26. Water Hazards (Including Lateral Water Hazards)

Definitions

A "water hazard" is any sea, lake, pond, river, ditch, surface drainage ditch or other open water course (whether or not containing water) and anything of a similar nature.

All ground or water within the margin of a water hazard is part of the water hazard. The margin of a water hazard extends vertically upwards and downwards. Stakes and lines defining the margins of water hazards are in the hazards.

Note: Water hazards (other than lateral water hazards) should be defined by yellow stakes or lines.

A "lateral water hazard" is a water hazard or that part of a water hazard so situated that it is not possible or is deemed by the Committee to be impracticable to drop a ball behind the water hazard in accordance with Rule 26-1b.

That part of a water hazard to be played as a lateral water hazard should be distinctively marked.

Note: Lateral water hazards should be defined by red stakes or lines.

26-1. Ball in Water Hazard

It is a question of fact whether a ball lost after having been struck toward a water hazard is lost inside or outside the hazard. In order to treat the ball as lost in the hazard, there must be reasonable evidence that the ball lodged in it. In the absence of such evidence, the ball must be treated as a lost ball and Rule 27 applies.

If a ball lies in, touches or is lost in a water hazard (whether the ball lies in water or not), the player may *under penalty of one stroke:*

a. Play his next stroke as nearly as possible at the spot from which the original ball was last played (see Rule 20-5);

or

b. Drop a ball behind the water hazard, keeping the point at which the original ball last crossed the margin of the water hazard directly between the hole and the spot on which the ball is dropped, with no limit to how far behind the water hazard the ball may be dropped;

or

c. *As additional options available only if the ball lies in, touches or is lost in a lateral water hazard*, drop a ball outside the water hazard within two club-lengths of (i) the point where the original ball last crossed the margin of the water hazard or (ii) a point on the opposite margin of the water hazard equidistant from the hole. The ball must be dropped and come to rest not nearer the hole than the point where the original ball last crossed the margin of the water hazard.

The ball may be cleaned when lifted under this Rule.

(Ball moving in water in a water hazard—see Rule 14-6.)

26-2. Ball Played within Water Hazard

a. Ball comes to rest in Hazard

If a ball played from within a water hazard comes to rest in the hazard after the stroke, the player may:

(i) proceed under Rule 26-1; or

(ii) *under penalty of one stroke*, play his next stroke as nearly as possible at the spot from which the last stroke from outside the hazard was played (see Rule 20-5).

b. Ball Lost or Unplayable Outside Hazard or Out of Bounds

If a ball played from within a water hazard is lost or declared unplayable outside the hazard or is out of bounds, the player, after taking a *penalty of one stroke* under Rule 27-1 or 28a, may:

(i) play a ball as nearly as possible at the spot in the hazard from which the original ball was last played (see Rule 20-5); or

(ii) *under an additional penalty of one stroke*, proceed under Rule 26-1b or, if applicable, Rule 26-1c, using as the reference point the point where the original ball last crossed the margin of the hazard before it came to rest in the hazard; or

(iii) *under an additional penalty of one stroke*, play his next stroke as nearly as possible at the spot from which the last stroke from outside the hazard was played (see Rule 20-5).

Note: If a ball played from within a water hazard is declared unplayable outside the hazard, nothing in Rule 26-2b precludes the player from proceeding under Rule 28b or c.

PENALTY FOR BREACH OF RULE:
Match play—Loss of hole; Stroke play—Two strokes.

Rule 27. Ball Lost or Out of Bounds; Provisional Ball

If the original ball is lost under a condition covered by Rule 25-1 (casual water, ground under repair and certain damage to the course), the player may proceed under that Rule. If the original ball is lost in a water hazard, the player shall proceed under Rule 26.

Such Rules may not be used unless there is reasonable evidence that the ball is lost under a condition covered by Rule 25-1 or in a water hazard.

Definitions

A ball is "lost" if:

a. It is not found or identified as his by the player within five minutes after the player's side or his or their caddies have begun to search for it; or

b. The player has put another ball into play under the Rules, even though he may not have searched for the original ball; or

c. The player has played any stroke with a provisional ball from the place where the original ball is likely to be or from a point nearer the hole than that place, whereupon the provisional ball becomes the ball in play.

Time spent in playing a wrong ball is not counted in the five-minute period allowed for search.

"Out of bounds" is ground on which play is prohibited.

When out of bounds is defined by reference to stakes or a fence, or as being beyond stakes or a fence, the out of bounds line is determined by the nearest inside points of the stakes or fence posts at ground level excluding angled supports.

When out of bounds is defined by a line on the ground, the line itself is out of bounds.

The out of bounds line extends vertically upwards and downwards.

A ball is out of bounds when all of it lies out of bounds.

A player may stand out of bounds to play a ball lying within bounds.

A "provisional ball" is a ball played under Rule 27-2 for a ball which may be lost outside a water hazard or may be out of bounds.

27-1. Ball Lost or Out of Bounds

If a ball is lost outside a water hazard or is out of bounds, the player shall play a ball, *under penalty of one stroke*, as nearly as possible at the spot from which the original ball was last played (see Rule 20-5).

PENALTY FOR BREACH OF RULE 27-1:
Match play—Loss of hole; Stroke play—Two strokes

27-2. Provisional Ball

a. Procedure

If a ball may be lost outside a water hazard or may be out of bounds, to save time the player may play another ball provisionally as nearly as possible at the spot from which the original ball was played (see Rule 20-5). The player shall inform his opponent in match play or his marker or a fellow competitor in stroke play that he intends to play a provisional ball, and he shall play it before he or his partner goes forward to search for the original ball. If he fails to do so and plays another ball, such ball is not a provisional ball and becomes the ball in play *under penalty of stroke and distance* (Rule 27-1); the original ball is deemed to be lost.

b. When Provisional Ball Becomes Ball in Play

The player may play a provisional ball until he reaches the place where the original ball is likely to be. If he plays a stroke with the provisional ball from the place where the original ball is likely to be or from a point nearer the hole than that place, the original ball is deemed to be lost and the provisional ball becomes the ball in play under *penalty of stroke and distance* (Rule 27-1).

If the original ball is lost outside a water hazard or is out of bounds, the provisional ball becomes the ball in play, *under penalty of stroke and distance* (Rule 27-1).

c. When Provisional Ball to Be Abandoned

If the original ball is neither lost outside a water hazard nor out of bounds, the player shall abandon the provisional ball and continue play with the original ball. If he fails to do so, any further strokes played with the provisional ball shall constitute playing a wrong ball and the provisions of Rule 15 shall apply.

Note: If the original ball lies in a water hazard, the player shall play the ball as it lies or proceed under Rule 26. If it is lost in a water hazard or unplayable, the player shall proceed under Rule 26 or 28, whichever is applicable.

Rule 28. Ball Unplayable

The player may declare his ball unplayable at any place on the course except when the ball lies in or touches a water hazard. The player is the sole judge as to whether his ball is unplayable.

If the player deems his ball to be unplayable, he shall, *under penalty of one stroke*:

a. Play his next stroke as nearly as possible at the spot from which the original ball was last played (see Rule 20-5);

or

b. Drop a ball within two club-lengths of the spot where the ball lay, but not nearer the hole;

or

c. Drop a ball behind the point where the ball lay, keeping that point directly between the hole and the spot on which the ball is dropped, with no limit to how far behind that point the ball may be dropped.

If the unplayable ball lies in a bunker and the player elects to proceed under Clause b or c, a ball must be dropped in the bunker.

The ball may be cleaned when lifted under this Rule.

PENALTY FOR BREACH OF RULE:
Match play—Loss of hole; Stroke play—Two strokes.

OTHER FORMS OF PLAY

Rule 29. Threesomes and Foursomes

Definitions

Threesome: A match in which one plays against two, and each side plays one ball.

Foursome: A match in which two play against two, and each side plays one ball.

29-1. General

In a threesome or a foursome, during any stipulated round the partners shall play alternately from the teeing grounds and alternately during the play of each hole. Penalty strokes do not affect the order of play.

29-2. Match Play

If a player plays when his partner should have played, *his side shall lose the hole.*

29-3. Stroke Play

If the partners play a stroke or strokes in incorrect order, such stroke or strokes shall be cancelled and *the side shall incur a penalty of two strokes.* The side shall correct the error by playing a ball in correct order at the spot from which it first played in incorrect order (see Rule 20-5). If the side plays a stroke from the next teeing ground without first correcting the error or, in the case of the last hole of the round, leaves the putting green without declaring its intention to correct the error, *the side shall be disqualified.*

Rule 30. Three-Ball, Best-Ball and Four-Ball Match Play

Definitions

Three-Ball: A match play competition in which three play against one another, each playing his own ball. Each player is playing two distinct matches.

Best-Ball: A match in which one plays against the better ball of two or the best ball of three players.

Four-Ball: A match in which two play their better ball against the better ball of two other players.

30-1. Rules of Golf Apply

The Rules of Golf, so far as they are not at variance with the following special Rules, shall apply to three-ball, best-ball and four-ball matches.

30-2. Three-Ball Match Play

a. Ball at Rest Moved by an Opponent

Except as otherwise provided in the Rules, if the player's ball is touched or moved by an opponent, his caddie or equipment other than during search, Rule 18-3b applies. *That opponent shall incur a penalty stroke in his match with the player,* but not in his match with the other opponent.

b. Ball Deflected or Stopped by an Opponent Accidentally

If a player's ball is accidentally deflected or stopped by an opponent, his caddie or equipment, no penalty shall be incurred. In his match with that opponent the player may play the ball as it lies or, before another stroke is played by either side, he may cancel the stroke and replay it (see Rule 20-5). In his match with the other opponent, the ball shall be played as it lies.

Exception: Ball striking person attending flagstick—see Rule 17-3b.

(Ball purposely deflected or stopped by opponent—see Rule 1-2.)

30-3. Best-Ball and Four-Ball Match Play

a. Representation of Side

A side may be represented by one partner for all or any part of a match; all partners need not be present. An absent partner may join a match between holes, but not during play of a hole.

b. Maximum of Fourteen Clubs

The side shall be penalised for a breach of Rule 4-4 by any partner.

c. Order of Play

Balls belonging to the same side may be played in the order the side considers best.

d. Wrong Ball

If a player plays a stroke with a wrong ball except in a hazard, *he shall be disqualified for that hole,* but his partner incurs no penalty even if the wrong ball belongs to him. The owner of the ball shall replace it on the spot from which it was played, without penalty. If the ball is not immediately recoverable, another ball may be substituted.

e. Disqualification of Side

(i) *A side shall be disqualified* for a breach of any of the following by any partner:

Rule 1-3 –	Agreement to Waive Rules.
Rule 4-1, -2 or -3 –	Clubs.
Rule 5-1 or -2 –	The Ball
Rule 6-2a –	Handicap (playing off higher handicap).
Rule 6-4 –	Caddie.
Rule 6-7 –	Undue Delay (repeated offence).
Rule 14-3 –	Artificial Devices and Unusual Equipment.

(ii) *A side shall be disqualified* for a breach of any of the following by all partners:

Rule 6-3 –	Time of Starting and Groups.
Rule 6-8 –	Discontinuance of Play.

f. Effect of Other Penalties

If a player's breach of a Rule assists his partner's play or adversely affects an opponent's play, *the partner incurs the applicable penalty in addition to any penalty incurred by the player.*

In all other cases where a player incurs a penalty for breach of a Rule, the penalty shall not apply to his partner. Where the penalty is stated to be loss of hole, the effect shall be to disqualify the player for that hole.

g. Another Form of Match Played Concurrently

In a best-ball or four-ball match when another form of match is played concurrently, the above special Rules shall apply.

Rule 31. Four-Ball Stroke Play

In four-ball stroke play two competitors play as partners, each playing his own ball. The lower score of the partners is the score for the hole. If one partner fails to complete the play of a hole, there is no penalty.

31-1. Rules of Golf Apply
The Rules of Golf, so far as they are not at variance with the following special Rules, shall apply to four-ball stroke play.

31-2. Representation of Side
A side may be represented by either partner for all or any part of a stipulated round; both partners need not be present. An absent competitor may join his partner between holes, but not during play of a hole.

31-3. Maximum of Fourteen Clubs
The side shall be penalised for, a breach of Rule 4-4 by either partner.

31-4. Scoring
The marker is required to record for each hole only the gross score of whichever partner's score is to count. The gross scores to count must be individually identifiable; otherwise *the side shall be disqualified.* Only one of the partners need be responsible for complying with Rule 6-6b.
(Wrong score—see Rule 31-7a.)

31-5. Order of Play
Balls belonging to the same side may be played in the order the side considers best.

31-6. Wrong Ball
If a competitor plays a stroke with a wrong ball except in a hazard, *he shall add two penalty strokes to his score for the hole* and shall then play the correct ball. His partner incurs no penalty even if the wrong ball belongs to him.
The owner of the ball shall replace it on the spot from which it was played, without penalty. If the ball is not immediately recoverable, another ball may be substituted.

31-7. Disqualification Penalties

a. Breach by One Partner
A side shall be disqualified from the competition for a breach of any of the following by either partner:

Rule 1-3 – Agreement to Waive Rules.
Rule 3-4 – Refusal to Comply with Rule.
Rule 4-1, -2 or -3 – Clubs.
Rule 5-1 -2 – The Ball.
Rule 6-2b – Handicap (playing off higher handicap; failure to record handicap).
Rule 6-4 – Caddie.
Rule 6-6b – Signing and Returning Card.
Rule 6-6d – Wrong Score for Hole, i.e. when the recorded lower score of the partners is lower than actually taken. If the recorded lower score of the partners is higher than actually taken, it must stand as returned.
Rule 6-7 – Undue Delay (repeated offence).
Rule 7-1 – Practice Before or Between Rounds.
Rule 14-3 – Artificial Devices and Unusual Equipment.
Rule 31-4 – Gross Scores to count Not Individually Identifiable.

b. Breach by Both Partners
A side shall be disqualified:
(i) for a breach by both partners of Rule 6-3 (Time of Starting and Groups) or Rule 6-8 (Discontinuance of Play), or
(ii) if, at the same hole, each partner is in breach of a Rule the penalty for which is disqualification from the competition or for a hole.

c. For the Hole Only
In all other cases where a breach of a Rule would entail disqualification, *the competitor shall be disqualified only for the hole at which the breach occurred.*

31-8. Effect of Other Penalties
If a competitor's breach of a Rule assists his partner's play, *the partner incurs the applicable penalty in addition to any penalty incurred by the competitor.*
In all other cases where a competitor incurs a penalty for breach of a Rule, the penalty shall not apply to his partner.

Rule 32. Bogey, Par and Stableford Competitions

32-1. Conditions
Bogey, par and Stableford competitions are forms of stroke competition in which play is against a fixed score at each hole. The Rules for stroke play, so far as they are not at variance with the following special Rules, apply.

a. Bogey and Par Competitions
The reckoning for bogey and par competitions is made as in match play. Any hole for which a competitor makes no return shall be regarded as a loss. The winner is the competitor who is most successful in the aggregate of holes.
The marker is responsible for marking only the gross number of strokes for each hole where the competitor makes a net score equal to or less than the fixed score.

Note: Maximum of 14 Clubs—Penalties as in match play—see Rule 4-4.

b. Stableford Competitions

The reckoning in Stableford competitions is made by points awarded in relation to a fixed score at each hole as follows

Hole Played in	Points
More than one over fixed score or no score returned	0
One over fixed score	1
Fixed score	2
One under fixed score	3
Two under fixed score	4
Three under fixed score	5

The winner is the competitor who scores the highest number of points.

The marker shall be responsible for marking only the gross number of strokes at each hole where the competitor's net score earns one or more points.

Note: Maximum of 14 Clubs (Rule 4-4) — Penalties applied as follows: From total points scored for the round, deduction of two points for each hole at which any breach occurred; maximum deduction per round: four points.

32-3. Disqualification Penalties

a. From the Competition

A competitor shall be disqualified from the competition for a breach of any of the following:

Rule 1-3 –	Agreement to Waive Rules.
Rule 3-4 –	Refusal to Comply with Rule.
Rule 4-1, -2 or -3 –	Clubs.
Rule 5-1 – or -2 –	The Ball.
Rule 6-2b –	Handicap (playing off higher handicap; failure to record handicap).
Rule 6-3 –	Time of Starting and Groups.
Rule 6-4 –	Caddie.
Rule 6-6b –	Signing and Returning Card.
Rule 6-6d –	Wrong Score for Hole, except that no penalty shall be incurred when a breach of this Rule does not affect the result of the hole.
Rule 6-7 –	Undue Delay (repeated offence).
Rule 6-8 –	Discontinuance of Play.
Rule 7-1 –	Practice Before or Between Rounds.
Rule 14-3 –	Artificial Devices and Unusual Equipment.

b. For a Hole

In all other cases where a breach of a Rule would entail disqualification, *the competitor shall be disqualified only for the hole at which the breach occurred.*

ADMINISTRATION

Rule 33. The Committee

33-1. Conditions; Waiving Rule

The Committee shall lay down the conditions under which a competition is to be played.

The Committee has no power to waive a Rule of Golf.

Certain special rules governing stroke play are so substantially different from those governing match play that combining the two forms of play is not practicable and is not permitted. The results of matches played and the scores returned in these circumstances shall not be accepted.

In stroke play the Committee may limit a referee's duties.

33-2. The Course

a. Defining Bounds and Margins

The Committee shall define accurately:

(i) the course and out of bounds,

(ii) the margins of water hazards and lateral water hazards,

(iii) ground under repair, and

(iv) obstructions and integral parts of the course.

b. New Holes

New holes should be made on the day on which a stroke competition begins and at such other times as the Committee considers necessary, provided all competitors in a single round play with each hole cut in the same position.

Exception: When it is impossible for a damaged hole to be repaired so that it conforms with the Definition, the Committee may make a new hole in a nearby similar position.

c. Practice Ground

Where there is no practice ground available outside the area of a competition course, the Committee should lay down the area on which players may practise on any day of a competition, if it is practicable to do so. On any day of a stroke competition, the Committee should not normally permit practice on or to a putting green or from a hazard of the competition course.

d. Course Unplayable

If the Committee or its authorised representative considers that for any reason the course is not in a playable condition or that there are circumstances which render the proper playing of the game impossible, it may, in match play or stroke play, order a temporary suspension of play or, in stroke play, declare play null and void and cancel all scores for the round in question. When play has been temporarily suspended, it shall be resumed from where it was discontinued, even though resumption occurs on a subsequent day. When a round is cancelled, all penalties incurred in that round are cancelled.

(Procedure in discontinuing play—see Rule 6-8.)

33-3. Times of Starting and Groups

The Committee shall lay down the times of starting and, in stroke play, arrange the groups in which competitors shall play.

When a match play competition is played over an extended period, the Committee shall lay down the limit of time within which each round shall be completed. When players are allowed to arrange the date of their match within these limits, the Committee should announce that the match must be played at a stated time on the last day of the period unless the players agree to a prior date.

33-4. Handicap Stroke Table

The Committee shall publish a table indicating the order of holes at which handicap strokes are to be given or received.

33-5. Score Card

In stroke play, the Committee shall issue for each competitor a score card containing the date and the competitor's name, or in foursome, or four-ball stroke play, the competitors' names.

In stroke play, the Committee is responsible for the addition of scores and application of the handicap recorded on the card.

In four-ball stroke play, the Committee is responsible for recording the better-ball score for each hole and in the process applying the handicaps recorded on the card, and adding the better-ball scores.

In bogey, par and Stableford competitions, the Committee is responsible for applying the handicap recorded on the card and determining the result of each hole and the overall result or points total.

33-6. Decision of Ties

The Committee shall announce the manner, day and time for the decision of a halved match or of a tie, whether played on level terms or under handicap.

A halved match shall not be decided by stroke play. A tie in stroke play shall not be decided by a match.

33-7. Disqualification Penalty; Committee Discretion

A penalty of disqualification may in exceptional individual cases be waived, modified or imposed if the Committee considers such action warranted.

33-8. Local Rules

a. Policy

The Committee may make and publish Local Rules for abnormal conditions if they are consistent with the policy of the Governing Authority for the country concerned as set forth in Appendix I to these Rules.

b. Waiving Penalty

A penalty imposed by a Rule of Golf shall not be waived by a Local Rule.

Rule 34. Disputes and Decisions

34-1. Claims and Penalties

a. Match Play

In match play if a claim is lodged with the Committee under Rule 2-5, a decision should be given as soon as possible so that the state of the match may, if necessary, be adjusted.

If a claim is not made within the time limit provided by Rule 2-5, it shall not be considered unless it is based on facts previously unknown to the player making the claim and the player making the claim had been given wrong information (Rules 6-2a and 9) by an opponent. In any case, no later claim shall be considered after the result of the match has been officially announced, unless the Committee is satisfied that the opponent knew he was giving wrong information.

b. Stroke Play

Except as provided below, in stroke play no penalty shall be rescinded, modified or imposed after the competition is closed. A competition is deemed to have closed when the result has been officially announced or, in stroke play qualifying followed by match play, when the player has teed off in his first match.

A penalty of disqualification shall be imposed at any time if a competitor:

(i) returns a score for any hole lower than actually taken (Rule 6-6d) for any reason other than failure to include a penalty which he did not know he had incurred; or

(ii) returns a score card on which he has recorded a handicap which he knows is higher than that to which he is entitled, and this affects the number of strokes received (Rule 6-2b).

34-2. Referee's Decision

If a referee has been appointed by the Committee, his decision shall be final.

34-3. Committee's Decision

In the absence of a referee, the players shall refer any dispute to the Committee, whose decision shall be final.

If the Committee cannot come to a decision, it shall refer the dispute to the Rules of Golf Committee of the Royal and Ancient Golf Club of St. Andrews, whose decision shall be final.

If the point in doubt or dispute has not been referred to the Rules of Golf Committee, the player or players have the right to refer an agreed statement through the Secretary of the Club to the Rules of Golf Committee for an opinion as to the correctness of the decision given. The reply will be sent to the Secretary of the Club or Clubs concerned.

If play is conducted other than in accordance with the Rules of Golf, the Rules of Golf Committee will not give a decision on any question.

APPENDIX I

LOCAL RULES (RULE 33-8) AND CONDITIONS OF THE COMPETITION (RULE 33-1)

Part A Local Rules

The Committee may make and publish Local Rules (for Specimen Local Rules see Part B) for such abnormal conditions as:

1. Obstructions

a. General

Clarifying the status of objects which may be obstructions (Rule 24).

Declaring any construction to be an integral part of the course and, accordingly, not an obstruction, e.g. built-up sides of teeing grounds, putting greens and bunkers (Rules 24 and 33-2a).

b. Stones in Bunkers

Allowing the removal of stones in bunkers by declaring them to be "movable obstructions" (Rule 24).

c. Roads and Paths

(i) Declaring artificial surfaces and sides of roads and paths to be integral parts of the course, or

(ii) Providing relief of the type afforded under Rule 24-2b from roads and paths not having artificial surfaces and sides if they could unfairly affect play.

d. Fixed Sprinkler Heads

Providing relief from intervention by fixed sprinkler heads within two club-lengths of the putting green when the ball lies within two club-lengths of the sprinkler head.

e. Temporary Immovable Obstructions

Specimen Local Rules for application in Tournament Play are available from the Royal and Ancient Golf Club of St Andrews.

2. Areas of the Course Requiring Preservation

Assisting preservation of the course by defining areas, including turf nurseries, young plantations and other parts of the course under cultivation, as "ground under repair" from which play is prohibited.

3. Unusual Damage to the Course or Accumulation of Leaves (or the like)

Declaring such areas to be "ground under repair" (Rule 25).

Note: For relief from aerification holes see Specimen Local Rule 7 in part B of this Appendix.

4. Extreme Wetness, Mud, Poor Conditions and Protection of Course

(a.) Lifting an Embedded Ball, Cleaning

Where the ground is unusually soft, the Committee may, by temporary Local Rule, allow the lifting of a ball which is embedded in its own pitch-mark in the ground in an area "through the green" which is not "closely mown" (Rule 25-2) if it is satisfied that the proper playing of the game would otherwise be prevented. The Local Rule shall be for that day only or for a short period, and if practicable shall be confined to specified areas. The Committee shall withdraw the Local Rule as soon as conditions warrant and should not print it on the score card.

In similarly adverse conditions, the Committee may, by temporary Local Rule, permit the cleaning of a ball "through the green".

(b.) "Preferred Lies" and "Winter Rules"

Adverse conditions, including the poor condition of the course or the existence of mud, are sometimes so general, particularly during winter months, that the Committee may decide to grant relief by Local Rule either to protect the course or to promote fair and pleasant play. Such Local Rule shall be withdrawn as soon as conditions warrant.

5. Other Local Conditions which Interfere with the Proper Playing of the Game

If this necessitates modification of a Rule of Golf the approval of the Governing Authority must be obtained.

Other matters which the Committee could cover by Local Rule include:

6. Water Hazards

a. Lateral Water Hazards

Clarifying the status of sections of water hazards which may be lateral water hazards (Rule 26).

b. Provisional Ball

Permitting the play of a provisional ball for a ball which may be in a water hazard of such character that it would be impracticable to determine whether the ball is in the hazard or to do so would unduly delay play. In such a case, if a provisional ball is played and the original ball is in a water hazard, the player may play the original ball as it lies or continue the provisional ball in play, but he may not proceed under Rule 26-1.

7. Defining Bounds and Margins

Specifying means used to define out of bounds, hazards, water hazards, lateral water hazards and ground under repair.

8. **Dropping Zones**
Establishing special areas in which balls may or shall be dropped when it is not feasible or practicable to proceed exactly in conformity with Rule 24-2b (Immovable Obstruction), Rule 25-1b or Rule 25-1c (Ground Under Repair), Rule 26-1 (Water Hazards and Lateral Water Hazards) or Rule 28 (Ball Unplayable).

9. **Priority on the Course**
The Committee may make regulations governing Priority on the Course (see Etiquette).

Part B Specimen Local Rules

Within the policy set out in Part A of this Appendix the Committee may adopt a Specimen Local Rule by referring, on a score card or notice board, to the examples given below. However Specimen Local Rules 4, 5 or 6 should not be printed or referred to on a score card as they are all of limited duration.

1. **Fixed Sprinkler Heads**
All fixed sprinkler heads are immovable obstructions and relief from interference by them may be obtained under Rule 24-2. In addition, if such an obstruction on or within two club-lengths of the putting green of the hole being played intervenes on the line of play between the ball and the hole, the player may obtain relief, without penalty, as follows:

If the ball lies off the putting green but not in a hazard and is within two club-lengths of the intervening obstruction, it may be lifted, cleaned and dropped at the nearest point to where the ball lay which (a) is not nearer the hole, (b) avoids such intervention and (c) is not in a hazard or on a putting green.

PENALTY FOR BREACH OF LOCAL RULE:
Match play—Loss of hole; Stroke play—Two strokes.

2. **Stones in Bunkers**
Stones in bunkers are movable obstructions. Rule 24-1 applies.

3. **Ground Under Repair: Play Prohibited**
If a player's ball lies in an area of "ground under repair" from which play is prohibited, or if such an area of "ground under repair" interferes with the player's stance or the area of his intended swing the player must take relief under Rule 25-1.

PENALTY FOR BREACH OF LOCAL RULE:
Match play—Loss of hole; Stroke play—Two strokes.

4. **Lifting an Embedded Ball**
(Specify the area if practical) . . . through the green, a ball embedded in its own pitch mark in ground other than sand may be lifted, cleaned and dropped, without penalty, as near as possible to the spot where it lay but not nearer the hole.

PENALTY FOR BREACH OF LOCAL RULE:
Match play—Loss of hole; Stroke play—Two strokes.

5. **Cleaning Ball**
(Specify the area if practicable) . . . through the green a ball may be lifted, cleaned and replaced without penalty.

Note: The position of the ball shall be marked before it is lifted under this Local Rule—see Rule 20-1.

6. **"Preferred Lies" and "Winter Rules"**
A ball lying on any "closely mown area" through the green may, without penalty, be moved or may be lifted, cleaned and placed within six inches of where it originally lay, but not nearer the hole. After the ball has been so moved or placed, it is in play.

PENALTY FOR BREACH OF LOCAL RULE:
Match play—Loss of stoke; Stroke play—Two strokes.

7. **Aerification Holes**
If a ball comes to rest in an aerification hole, the player may, without penalty, lift the ball and clean it. Through the green, the player shall drop the ball as near as possible to where it lay, but not nearer the hole. On the putting green, the player shall place the ball at the nearest spot not nearer the hole which avoids such situation.

PENALTY FOR BREACH OF LOCAL RULE:
Match play—Loss of hole; Stroke play—Two strokes

Part C Conditions of the Competition

Rule 33-1 provides, "The Committee shall lay down the conditions under which a competition is to be played". Such conditions should include many matters such as method of entry, eligibility, number of rounds to be played, settling ties, etc. which is not appropriate to deal with in the Rules of Golf or this Appendix.

However there are four matters which might be covered in the Conditions of Competition to which the Commitee's attention is specifically drawn by way of a Note to the appropriate Rule. These are:

1. **Specification of the Ball (Note to Rule 5-1)**
Arising from the regulations for ball-testing under Rule 5-1, Lists of Conforming Golf Balls will be issued from time to time.

It is recommended that the Lists should be applied to all National and County (or equivalent) Championships and to all top class events when restricted to low handicap players. In order to apply the Lists to a particular competition the Committee must lay this down in the Conditions of the Competition. This should be referred to in the Entry Form, and also a notice should be displayed on the Club notice board and at the 1st Tee along the following lines:

(Name of Event)

(Date and Club)

The ball the player uses shall be named on the current List of Conforming Golf Balls issued by the Royal and Ancient Golf Club of St. Andrews.

Note 1: A penalty statement will be required and must be either:

(a)"PENALTY FOR BREACH OF CONDITION: Disqualification"

or

(b)"PENALTY FOR BREACH OF CONDITION: *Match play—Loss of each hole at which a breach occurred:Stroke play—Two strokes for each hole at which a breach occurred."*

If option (b) is adopted this only applies to use of a ball which, whilst not on the List of Conforming Golf Balls, does conform to the specifications set forth in Rule 5 and Appendix III. The penalty for use of a ball which does not so conform is disqualification.

Note 2: In Club events it is recommended that no such condition be applied.

2. **Time of Starting (Note to Rule 6-3a)**
   If the Committee wishes to act in accordance with the Note, the following wording is recommended:

   "If, in the absence of circumstances which warrant waiving the penalty of disqualification as provided in Rule 33-7, the player arrives at his starting point, ready to play, within five minutes after his starting time, the penalty for failure to start on time is loss of the first hole in match play or two strokes at the first hole in stroke play."

3. **Practice**
   The Committee may make regulations governing practice in accordance with the Note to Rule 7-1, Exception (c) to Rule 7-2, Note 2 to Rule 7 and Rule 33-2c.

4. **Advice in Team Competitions**
   If the Committee wishes to act in accordance with the Note, the following wording is recommended:

   "In accordance with the Note to Rule 8-1 of the Rules of Golf each team may appoint one person (in addition to the persons from whom advice may be asked under that Rule) who may give advice to members of that team. Such person [*if it is desired to insert any restriction on who may be nominated insert such restriction here*] shall be identified to the Committee prior to the start of the competition."

APPENDICES II AND III

Any design in a club or ball which is not covered by Rules 4 and 5 and Appendices II and III, or which might significantly change the nature of the game, will be ruled on by the Royal and Ancient Golf Club of St Andrews and the United States Golf Association.

Note: Equipment approved for use or marketed prior to January 1st, 1984 which conformed to the Rules in effect in 1983 but does not conform to the 1984 Rules may be used until December 31st, 1989; thereafter all equipment must conform to the current Rules.

APPENDIX II

Design of Clubs

Rule 4-1 prescribes general regulations for the design of clubs. The following paragraphs, which provide some detailed specifications and clarify how Rule 4-1 is interpreted, should be read in conjunction with this rule.

4-1b. Shaft

Generally Straight. The shaft shall be at least 18 inches (457mm) in length. It shall be straight from the top of the grip to a point not more than 5 inches (127mm) above the sole, measured along the axis of the shaft and the neck or socket.

Bending and Twisting Properties. The shaft must be so designed and manufactured that at any point along its length;

(i) it bends in such a way that the deflection is the same regardless of how the shaft is rotated about its longitudinal axis; and

(ii) it twists the same amount in both directions.

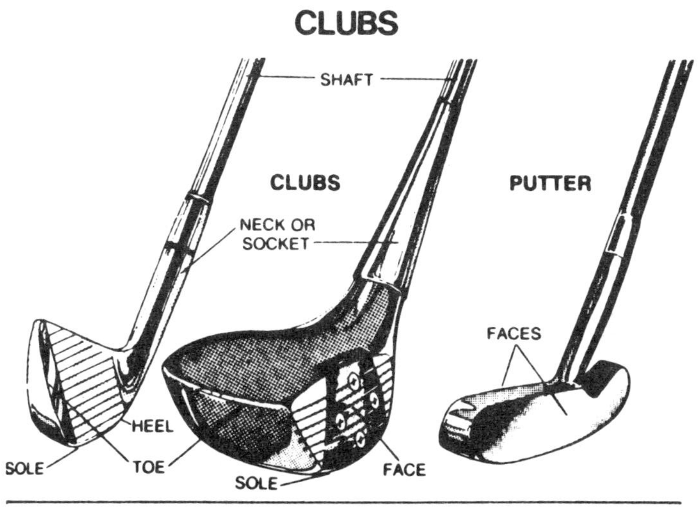

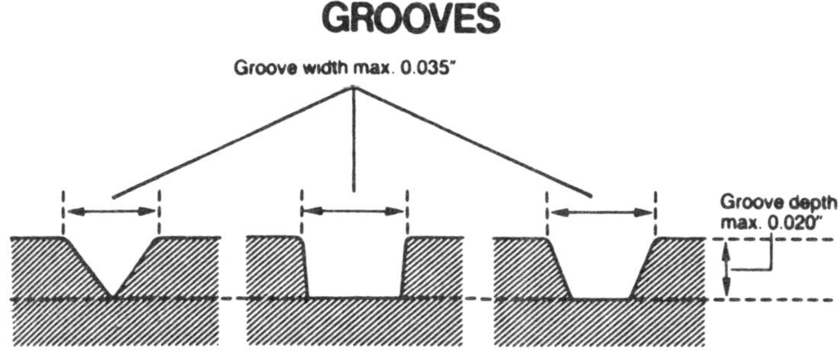

EXAMPLES OF PERMISSIBLE GROOVE CROSS SECTIONS

Attachment to Clubhead. The neck or socket must not be more than 5 inches (127mm) in length, measured from the top of the neck or socket to the sole along its axis. The shaft and the neck or socket must remain in line with the heel, or with a point to the right or left of the heel, when the club is viewed in the address position. The distance between the axis of the shaft or the neck or socket and the back of the heel must not exceed 0.625 inches (16mm).

Exception for Putters: The shaft or neck or socket of a putter may be fixed at any point in the head and need not remain in line with the heel. The axis of the shaft from the top to a point not more than 5 inches (127mm) above the sole must diverge from the vertical in the toe-heel plane by at least 10 degrees when the club is in its normal address position.

4-1c. Grip

(i) For clubs other than putters, the grip must be generally circular in cross-section, except that a continuous, straight, slightly raised rib may be incorporated along the full length of the grip.

(ii) A putter grip may have a non-circular cross-section, provided the cross-section has no concavity and remains generally similar throughout the length of the grip.

(iii) The grip may be tapered but must not have any bulge or waist.

(iv) For clubs other than putters the axis of the grip must coincide with the axis of the shaft.

4-1d. Clubhead

Dimensions. The dimensions of a clubhead (see diagram) are measured, with the clubhead in its normal address position, on horizontal lines between vertical projections of the outermost points of (i) the heel and the toe and (ii) the face and the back. If the outermost point of the heel is not clearly defined, it is deemed to be 0.625 inches (16mm) above the horizontal plane on which the club is resting in its normal address position.

Plain in Shape. The clubhead shall be generally plain in shape. All parts shall be rigid, structural in nature and functional.

Features such as holes through the head, windows or transparencies, or appendages to the main body of the head such as plates, rods or fins for the purpose of meeting dimensional specifications, for aiming or for any other purpose are not permitted. Exceptions may be made for putters.

Any furrows in or runners on the sole shall not extend into the face.

4-1e. Club Face

Hardness and Rigidity. The club face must not be designed and manufactured to have the effect at impact of a spring which would unduly influence the movement of the ball.

Markings. Except for specified markings, the surface roughness must not exceed that of decorative sandblasting. Markings must not have sharp edges or raised lips, as determined by a finger test. Markings within the area where impact is intended (the 'impact area') are governed by the following:

(i) **Grooves.** A series of straight grooves with diverging sides and a symmetrical cross-section may be used. (See diagram). The width and cross-section must be generally consistent across the face of the club and along the length of the grooves. Any rounding of groove edges shall be in the form of a radius which does not exceed 0.020 inches (0.5mm). The width of the grooves shall not exceed 0.035 inches (0.9mm), using the 30 degree method of measurement on file with the Royal and Ancient Golf Club of St Andrews. The distance between edges of adjacent grooves must not be less than three times the width of a groove, and not less than 0.075 inches (1.9mm). The depth of a groove must not exceed 0.020 inches (0.5mm).

(ii) **Punch Marks.** Punch marks may be used. The area of any such mark must not exceed 0.0044 square inches (2.8 sq mm). A mark must not be closer to an adjacent mark than 0.168 inches (4.3mm) measured from centre to centre. The depth of a punch mark must not exceed 0.040 inches (1.0mm). If punch marks are used in combination with grooves, a punch mark may not be closer to a groove than 0.168 inches (4.3mm), measured from centre to centre.

Decorative Markings. The centre of the impact area may be indicated by a design within the boundary of a square whose sides are 0.375 inches (9.5mm) in length. Such a design must not unduly influence the movement of the ball. Markings outside the impact area must not be greater than 0.040 inches (1.00mm) in depth and width.

Non-metallic Club Face Markings. The above specifications for markings do not apply to non-metallic clubs with loft angles less than 24 degrees, but markings which could unduly influence the movement of the ball are prohibited. Non-metallic clubs with a loft or face angle exceeding 24 degrees may have grooves of maximum width 0.040 inches (1.0mm) and maximum depth of $1\frac{1}{2}$ times the groove width, but must otherwise conform to the markings specifications above.

APPENDIX III

The Ball

a. Weight

The weight of the ball shall not be greater than 1.620 ounces avoirdupois (45.93gm).

b. Size

The diameter of the ball shall not be less than 1.680 inches (42.67mm). This specification will be satisfied if, under its own weight, a ball falls through a 1.680 inches diameter ring gauge in fewer than 25 out of 100 randomly selected positions, the test being carried out at a temperature of 23±1°C.

c. Spherical Symmetry

The ball shall be designed and manufactured to perform in general as if it were spherically symmetrical.

As outlined in procedures on file at the Royal and Ancient Golf Club of St. Andrews and the United States Golf Association, differences in peak angle of trajectory, carry and time of flight will be measured when 40 balls of the same types are launched, spinning 20 about one axis and 20 about another axis.

These tests will be performed using apparatus approved by the Royal and Ancient Golf Club of St. Andrews and the United States Golf Association. If in two successive tests differences in the same two or more measurements are statistically significant at the 5% level of significance and exceed the limits set forth below, the ball type will not conform to the symmetry specification.

Measurement	Maximum Absolute Difference of the Means
Peak angle of trajectory	0.9 grid units (approx. 0.4 degrees)
Carry distance	2.5 yards
Flight time	0.16 seconds

Note: Methods of determining whether a ball performs as if it were generally spherically symmetrical may be subject to change as instrumentation becomes available to measure other properties accurately, such as the aerodynamic coefficient of lift, coefficient of drag and moment of inertia.

d. Initial Velocity

The velocity of the ball shall not be greater than 250 feet (76.2m) per second when measured on apparatus approved by the Royal and Ancient Golf Club of St. Andrews. A maximum tolerance of 2% will be allowed. The temperature of the ball when tested shall be 23±1°C.

e. Overall Distance Standard

A brand of golf ball, when tested on apparatus approved by the Royal and Ancient Golf Club of St. Andrews under the conditions set forth in the Overall Distance Standard for golf balls on file with the Royal and Ancient Golf Club of St. Andrews, shall not cover an average distance in carry and roll exceeding 280 yards (256 metres) plus a tolerance of 6%.

Note: The 6% tolerance will be reduced to a minimum of 4% as test techniques are improved.

Notes to Appendix III

1: The size specification in (b) above will take effect from 1st January, 1990. Until that date the previous size specification of a diameter not less than 1.620 inches (41.15mm) will apply.

2: The Overall Distance Standard will apply only to balls which meet the new size specification of a diameter not less than 1.680 inches (42.67mm).

3: In international team competitions, until 31st December, 1989, the previous size specification of a diameter not less than 1.620 inches (41.15mm) will apply.

HANDICAPS

The Rules of Golf do not legislate for the allocation and adjustment of handicaps or their playing differentials. Such matters are within the jurisdiction and control of the National Union concerned and queries should be directed accordingly.

RULES OF AMATEUR STATUS

As approved by the Royal and Ancient Golf Club of St. Andrews

(Effective from 1st January 1987)

Definitions of an Amateur Golfer
An Amateur Golfer is one who plays the game as a non-remunerative or non-profit-making sport.

The Governing Body
The Governing Body of golf for the Rules of Amateur Status in any country is the National Union of the country concerned except in Great Britain and Ireland where the Governing Body is the Royal and Ancient Golf Club of St. Andrews.

Any person who considers any action he is proposing to take might endanger his Amateur Status should submit particulars to the Committee for consideration.

RULE 1

Forfeiture of Amateur Status at any age

The following are examples of acts which are contrary to the Definition of an Amateur Golfer and cause forfeiture of Amateur Status:

1. Professionalism.
a. Receiving payment or compensation for serving as a Professional golfer or a teaching or playing assistant to a Professional golfer.
b. Taking any action for the purpose of becoming a Professional golfer except applying unsuccessfully for the position of a teaching or playing assistant of a Professional golfer.

Note 1. Such actions including filing application to a school or competition conducted to qualify persons to play as Professionals in tournaments; receiving services from or entering into an agreement, written or oral, with a sponsor or Professional agent; agreement to accept payment or compensation for allowing one's name or likeness as a skilled golfer to be used for any commercial purpose; and holding or retaining membership in any organisation of Professional golfers.

Note 2. Receiving payment or compensation as a shop assistant is not itself a breach of the Rules, provided duties do not include playing or giving instruction.

2. Playing for Prize Money.
Playing for prize money or its equivalent in a match, tournament or exhibition.

3. Instruction.
Receiving payment or compensation for giving instruction in playing golf, either orally, in writing, by pictures or by other demonstrations, to either individuals or groups.

Exceptions:

1. Golf instruction may be given by an employee of an educational institution or system to students of the institution or system and by camp counsellors to those in their charge, provided that the total time devoted to golf instruction during a year comprises less than 50 per cent of the time spent during the year in the performance of all duties as such employee or counsellor.

2. Payment or compensation may be accepted for instruction in writing, provided one's ability or reputation as a golfer was not a major factor in his employment or in the commission or sale of his work.

4. Prizes and Testimonials
(a) Acceptance of a prize or prize voucher of retail value exceeding as follows:

	In GB & I	Elsewhere
For an event of more than 2 rounds	£170	$400 US or the equivalent
For an event of 2 rounds or less	£110	$260 US or the equivalent

or such lesser figures, if any, as may be decided by the Governing Body of golf in any country, or

(b) Acceptance of a testimonial in Great Britain and Ireland of retail value exceeding £170, elsewhere of retail value exceeding $400 US or the equivalent, or such lesser figure as may be decided by the Governing Body of golf in any country, or

(c) For a junior golfer, of such age as may be determined by the Governing Body of golf in any country, taking part in an event limited exclusively to juniors, acceptance of a prize or prize voucher in Great Britain and Ireland of retail value exceeding £50; elsewhere of retail value exceeding $120 US or the equivalent, or such lesser figure, if any, as may be decided by the Governing Body of golf in any country, or

(d) Conversion of a prize or prize voucher into money, or

(e) Accepting a gratuity in connection with a golfing event.

Exceptions:
1. Prizes of only symbolic value, provided that their symbolic nature is distinguished by distinctive permanent marking.
2. More than one testimonial award may be accepted from different donors even though their total retail value exceeds £170 or $400 U.S., provided they are not presented so as to evade such value limit for a single award.

Note 1: Events covered. The limits referred to in Clauses (a) or (c) above apply to total prize or prize vouchers received by any one person for any event or series of events in any one tournament or exhibition, including hole-in-one or other events in which golf skill is a factor.

Note 2: 'Retail value' is the price at which merchandise is available to anyone at a retail source, and the onus of proving the value of a particular prize rests with the donor.

Note 3: Purpose of prize vouchers. A prize voucher may be issued and redeemed only by the Committee in charge of a competition for the purchase of goods from a Professional's shop or other retail source, which may be specified by the Committee. It may not be used for such items as travel or hotel expenses, a bar bill, or a Club Subscription.

Note 4: Maximum Value of Prizes in any event for individuals. It is recommended that the total value of scratch or each division of handicap prizes should not exceed twice the maximum retail value of prize permitted in Rule 1-4(a) and (c) in an 18-hole competition, three times in a 36-hole competition, four times in a 54-hole competition and five times in a 72-hole competition.

Note 5: Testimonial Awards. Such awards relate to notable performances or contributions to golf as distinguished from tournament prizes.

5. Lending Name or Likeness.
Because of golf skill or golf reputation receiving or contracting to receive payment, compensation or personal benefit, directly or indirectly, for allowing one's name or likeness to be used in any way for the advertisement or sale of anything, whether or not used in or appertaining to golf except as a golf author or broadcaster as permitted by Rule 1-7.

Note: A player may accept equipment from anyone dealing in such equipment provided no advertising is involved.

6. Personal Appearance.
Because of golf skill or golf reputation, receiving payment or compensation, directly or indirectly, for a personal appearance.

Exception:
Actual expenses in connection with personal appearances may be paid or reimbursed provided no golf competition of exhibition is involved.

7. Broadcasting or Writing.
Because of golf skill or golf reputation, receiving payment or compensation, directly or indirectly, for broadcasting concerning golf, a golf event or golf events, writing golf articles or books, or allowing one's name to be advertised or published as the author of golf articles or books of which he is not actually the author.

Exceptions:
1. Broadcasting or writing as part of one's primary occupation or career, provided instruction in playing golf is not included (Rule 1-3).
2. Part-time broadcasting or writing, provided (a) the player is actually the author of the commentary, articles or books, (b) instruction in playing golf is not included and (c) the payment or compensation does not have the purpose or effect, directly or indirectly, of financing participation in a golf competition or golf competitions.

8. Expenses.
Accepting expenses, in money or otherwise, from any source to engage in a golf competition or exhibition.

Exceptions:
A player may receive expenses, not exceeding the actual expenses incurred, as follows:
1.From a member of the family or legal guardian;
or
2. As a player in a golf competition or exhibition limited exclusively to players who have not reached their 18th birthday;
or
3. As a representative of his Country, County, Club or similar body in team competitions or team training camps at home or abroad, or as a representative of his Country taking part in a National Championship abroad immediately preceding or following directly upon an international team competition, where such expenses are paid by the body he represents, or by the body controlling golf in the territory he is visiting;
or
4. As an individual nominated by a National or County Union or Club to engage in an event at home or abroad provided that:

(a) The player nominated has not reached such age as may be determined by the Governing Body of Golf in the country from which the nomination is made.
(b) The expenses shall be paid only by the National Union or County Union responsible in the area from which the nomination is made and shall be limited to twenty competitive days in any one calendar year. The expenses are deemed in include reasonable travelling time and practice days in connection with the twenty competitive days.
(c) Where the event is to take place abroad, the approval of the National Union of the country in which the event is to be staged and, if the nominating body is not the National Union of the country from which the nomination is made, the approval of the National Union shall first be obtained by the nominating body.
(d) Where the event is to take place at home, and where the nomination is made by a County Union or Club, the approval of the National Union or the County Union in the area in which the event is to be staged shall first be obtained.

(*Note:* The Term 'County Union' covers any Province, State or equivalent Union or Association;)

or

5. As a player invited for reasons unrelated to golf skill, e.g. celebrities, business associates, etc., to take part in golfing events;

or

6. As a player in an exhibition in aid of a recognised Charity provided the exhibition is not run in connection with another golfing event.

or

7. As a player in a handicap individual or handicap team sponsored golfing event where expenses are paid by the sponsor on behalf of the player to take part in the event provided the event has been approved as follows:

(a) where the event is to take place at home the approval of the Governing Body (see Definition) shall first be obtained in advance by the sponsor, and
(b) where the event is to take place both at home and abroad the approval of the two or more Governing Bodies shall first be obtained in advance by the sponsor. The application for this approval should be sent to the Governing Body of golf in the country where the competition commences.
(c) where the event is to take place abroad the approval of two or more Governing Bodies shall first be obtained by the sponsor. The application for this approval should be sent to the Governing Body of golf in the country whose players shall be taking part in the event abroad

Note 1: Business Expenses. It is permissible to play in a golf competition while on a business trip with expenses paid provided that the golf part of the expenses is borne personally and is not charged to business. Further, the business involved must be actual and substantial, and not merely a subterfuge for legitimising expenses when the primary purpose is a golf competition.

Note 2: Private Transport. Acceptance of private transport furnished or arranged for by a tournament sponsor, directly or indirectly, as an inducement for a player to engage in a golf competition or exhibition shall be considered accepting expenses under Rule 1-8.

9. Scholarships.
Because of golf skill or golf reputation, accepting the benefits of a scholarship or grant-in-aid other than ones whose terms and conditions have been approved by the Amateur Status Committee of the Royal and Ancient Golf Club of St. Andrews.

10. Membership.
Because of golf skill accepting membership in a Golf Club without full payment for the class of membership for the purpose of playing for that Club.

11. Conduct Detrimental to Golf.
Any conduct, including activities in connection with golf gambling, which is considered detrimental to the best interests of the game.

Rule 2

Procedure for Enforcement and Reinstatement

1. Decision on a Breach. Whenever information of a possible breach of the Definition of an Amateur Golfer by a player claiming to be an Amateur shall come to the attention of the appropriate Committee of the Governing Body, the Committee, after such investigation as it may deem desirable, shall decide whether a breach has occurred. Each case shall be considered on its merits. The decision of the committee shall be final.

2. Enforcement. Upon a decision that a player has acted contrary to the Definition of an Amateur Golfer, the Committee may declare the Amateur Status of the player forfeited or require the player to refrain or desist from specified actions as a condition of retaining his Amateur Status.

The Committee shall use its best endeavours to ensure that the player is notified and may notify any interested Golf Association of any action taken under this paragraph.

3. Reinstatement. The Committee shall have sole power to reinstate a player to Amateur Status or to deny reinstatement. Each application for reinstatement shall be decided on its merits. In considering an application for reinstatement, the Committee shall normally be guided by the following principles:

a. Awaiting Reinstatement.
The professional holds an advantage over the amateur by reason of having devoted himself to the game as his profession; other persons infringing the Rules of Amateur Status also obtain advantages not available to the Amateur. They do not necessarily lose such advantage merely by deciding to cease infringing the Rules. Therefore, an applicant for reinstatement to Amateur Status shall undergo a period awaiting reinstatement as prescribed by the Committee.

The period awaiting reinstatement shall start from the date of the player's last breach of the Definition of an Amateur Golfer unless the Committee decides that it shall start from the date when the player's last breach became known to the Committee.

b. Period Awaiting Reinstatement.
The period awaiting reinstatement shall normally be related to the period the player was in breach. However, no applicant shall normally be eligible for reinstatement until he has conducted himself in accordance with the Definition of an Amateur Golfer for a period of at least two consecutive years. The Committee, however, reserves the right to extend or to shorten such a period. A longer period will normally be required of applicants who have been in breach for more than five years. Players of national prominence who have been in breach for more than five years shall not normally be eligible for reinstatement.

c. One Reinstatement
A player shall not normally be reinstated more than once.

d. Status While Awaiting Reinstatement.
During the period awaiting reinstatement an applicant for reinstatement shall conform with the Definition of an Amateur Golfer.

He shall not be eligible to enter competitions as an Amateur. He may, however, enter competitions, and win a prize, solely among members of a Club of which he is a member, subject to the approval of the Club; but he may not represent such Club against other Clubs.

Forms of Application for Countries under the jurisdiction of the Royal and Ancient Golf Club

(a) Each application for reinstatement shall be submitted on the approved form to the County Union where the applicant wishes to play as an Amateur. Such Union shall, after making all necessary enquiries, forward it through the National Union (and in the case of lady applicants, the Ladies Golf Union) and the appropriate Professional Golfers' Association, with comments endorsed thereon, to the Governing Body of golf in that country. Forms of application for reinstatement may be obtained from the Royal and Ancient Golf Club or from the National or County Unions. The application shall include such information as the Royal and Ancient Golf Club may require from time to time and it shall be signed and certified by the applicant.
(b) Any application made in countries under the jurisdiction of the Royal and Ancient Golf Club of St. Andrews which the Governing Body of golf in that country considers to be doubtful or not to be covered by the above regulations may be submitted to the Royal and Ancient Golf Club of St. Andrews whose decision shall be final.

R. & A. POLICY ON GAMBLING

The Definition of an Amateur Golfer provides that an Amateur golfer is one who plays the game as a non-remunerative or non-profit-making sport. When gambling motives are introduced evils can arise to threaten the integrity of both the game and the individual players.

The R&A does not object to participation in wagering among individual golfers or teams of golfers when participation in the wagering is limited to the players, the players may only wager on themselves or their teams, the sole source of all money won by players is advanced by the players and the primary purpose is the playing of the game for enjoyment.

The distinction between playing for prize money and gambling is essential to the validity of the Rules of Amateur Status. The following constitute golf wagering and not playing for prize money:

1. Participation in wagering among individual golfers.

2. Participation in wagering among teams.
Organised Amateur events open to the general golfing public and designed and promoted to create cash prizes are not approved by the R&A. Golfers participating in such events without irrevocably waiving their right to cash prizes are deemed by the R&A to be playing for prize money.

The R&A is opposed to and urges Unions and Clubs, and all other sponsors of golf competitions to prohibit types of gambling such as: Calcuttas, auction sweepstakes and any other forms of gambling organised for general participation or permitting participants to bet on someone other than themselves or their teams.

Attention is drawn to Rule 1-11 relating to conduct detrimental to the game, under which players can forfeit their Amateur Status. It is the Club which, by permitting competitions where excessive gambling is involved, or illegal prizes are offered, bears the responsibility for which the individual is penalised and Unions have the power to invoke severe sanctions against a Club or individual for consistently ignoring this policy.

INDEX	Rule

The Standard Scratch Score and Handicapping Scheme 1983

Revised 1st January 1986

This scheme does not apply to ladies' clubs under the jurisdiction of the Ladies' Golf Union).

Published and administered by the Council of National Golf Unions and adopted by the Unions affiliated to the European Golf Association

Foreword

The Standard Scratch Score and Handicapping Scheme was prepared by the British Golf Unions' Joint Advisory Council in 1925 at the request of the Royal and Ancient Golf Club of St Andrews and has been in operation throughout Great Britain and Ireland since 1st March, 1926.

The Scheme incorporated in this book introduces a new concept in handicapping based on the system presently used by the Australian Golf Union. The Council of National Golf Unions acknowledges the assistance received from that Union and its officials in formulating the Scheme, which takes account of all scores returned by players under Medal Play conditions.

No change has been made in the present method of fixing the Standard Scratch Scores of courses but, on the principle that uniformity and equity in handicapping can be more effectively achieved if there is uniformity and equity in the fixing of Standard Scratch Scores, the Council of National Golf Unions will, as a further step, be investigating methods which would ensure closer alignment of Standard Scratch Scores throughout Great Britain and Ireland.

In view of the radically changed method of handicapping, its introduction cannot be regarded as a further revision of the existing Scheme and, for that reason, the Council of National Golf Unions has decided that the Scheme to be introduced on the 1st January 1983, will be known as the Standard Scratch Score and Handicapping Scheme 1983.

Since its introduction on 1st January 1983 amendments have been made to the Scheme. The amendments recognise that handicaps generally rose more quickly than was originally anticipated and stem from the Council's policy of keeping the effects of the Scheme's requirements constantly under review. The principal changes are (a) the introduction of a *Winter Period* (Definition Q), (b) limit of 0.1 to the increase of a player's *Exact Handicap* in all *Categories*, and (c) the establishment of a *Buffer Zone* (Definition R). These caused additions to Definitions and amendments to clauses throughout the Scheme all of which, with other minor alterations are referred to on the following page.

Principal Changes Incorporated since 1st January 1983

(a) Modification of Definition G (2).
(b) Addition of Definitions Q and R.
(c) Addition of sub clause 9.(7).
(d) Addition of sub clauses 12.(5)(i) and 12.(5)(j).
(e) Modification of sub clause 13.(8).
(f) Modification of sub clause 15.(2).
(g) Modification of sub clauses 16.(1), 16.(2), 16.(3), 16.(6), 16.(8) and 16.(11).
(h) Modification of sub clause 17.(3).
(i) A complete revision of clause 19.
(j) The deletion of clause 20.
(k) The modification of Appendices A and B.
(l) The addition of Appendix D.

Part One

Definitions

Definition
A. Union.
B. Area Authority.
C. Home Club.
D. Affiliated Club.
E. Handicapping Authority.
F. Handicap Committee.
G. Handicaps.

H. Categories of Handicap.
I. Measured Course.
J. Distance Point.
K. Medal Tee.
L. Medal Play Conditions.
M. Qualifying Competition.
N. Qualifying Score.
O. Aggregate Fourball Competition.
P. Nett Differential.
Q. Winter Period.
R. Buffer Zone.

Definitions

(Throughout the scheme whenever a word or expression is used which is defined within the following definitions the word or expression is printed in italics.)

A–Union

A *Union* is any national organisation in control of amateur golf in any country.

B–Area Authority

An *Area Authority* is any authority appointed by a *Union* to act on behalf of that *Union* for the purposes of the Scheme within a specified area.

C–Affiliated Club

An *Affiliated Club* is a club affiliated to a *Union* or *Area Authority* which pays to the *Union* and *Area Authority* a specified annual per capita fee in respect of each eligible member.

D–Home Club

A player's *Home Club* is an *Affiliated Club* of which the player is a member. If the player is a member of more than one *Affiliated Club* he shall nominate one as his *Home Club*.

E–Handicapping Authority

The *Handicapping Authority* for a player is his *Home Club* subject to the overall jurisdiction of the *Union*.

F–Handicap Committee

The *Handicap Committee* is the body appointed by an *Affiliated Club* to administer the Scheme within the club.

G–Handicaps

(1) *Exact Handicap* – a player's *Exact Handicap* is his handicap calculated in accordance with the provisions of the Scheme to one decimal place.
(2) *Playing Handicap* – a player's *Playing Handicap* is his *Exact Handicap* calculated to the nearest whole number (0.5 is rounded upwards).

H–Categories of Handicap

Handicaps are divided into the following *Categories:*
Category 1: Handicaps of 5 or less.
Category 2: Handicaps of 6 to 12 inclusive.
Category 3: Handicaps of 13 to 20 inclusive.
Category 4: Handicaps of 21 to 28 inclusive.

I–Measured Course

Any course played over by an *Affiliated Club* the measured length of which has been certified in accordance with the requirements of clause 2.

J–Distance Point

The *Distance Point* is the position of a permanent marker indicating the point from which the length of a hole is measured.

K–Medal Tee

A *Medal Tee* is a rectangular area the front of which shall not be more than 10 yards (9 metres) in front of the relevant *Distance Point* and the rear of which shall not be less than 2 yards (2 metres) behind the *Distance Point*. (NOTE: Special rules apply when the length of a *Measured Course* has been temporarily reduced by more than 100 yards (91 metres) – see clause 7(b)).

L–Medal Play Conditions

Medal Play Conditions prevail during stroke, par and Stableford competitions played with full handicap allowance over 18 holes under the Rules of Golf from *Medal Tees*. *Medal Play Conditions* shall not prevail unless the length of the course played varies by no more than 100 yards (91 metres) from the length of the *Measured Course*. (NOTE: Special rules apply when the length of a *Measured Course* has been temporarily reduced by more than 100 yards (91 metres) – see clause 7(b)).

M–Qualifying Competition

A *Qualifying Competition* is any competition in which *Medal Play Conditions* prevail subject to the restrictions and limitations contained in the Scheme or imposed by *Unions*.

N–Qualifying Score

A *Qualifying Score* is any score including a *no return* returned in a *Qualifying Competition.*

O–Aggregate Fourball Competition

An *Aggregate Fourball Competition* is a *Qualifying Competition* in which the completed scores at each hole of a team of not more than two amateur players are aggregated.

P–Nett Differential

The *Nett Differential* is the difference (+ or −) between the nett score returned by a player in a *Qualifying Competition* and the Standard Scratch Score.

Q–Winter Period

The *Winter Period* is a period of four consecutive calendar months between the months of December and April inclusive to be stipulated by *Unions* during which the *Exact Handicap* of a player who returns a score in a *Qualifying Competition* above his *Playing Handicap* shall not be increased.

R–Buffer Zone

The *Buffer Zone* is a zone which applies only to scores returned by players in *Qualifying Competitions* with *Nett Differentials* of +1 and +2 (one or two strokes above *Playing Handicaps).*

Table of Provisional Standard Scratch Scores

Standard length of course	Lengths included in standard length		Provisional Standard Scratch Score
Yards	*Yards*	*Metres*	
7100	*7001-7002*	*6402-6584*	*74*
6900	*6801-7000*	*6219-6401*	*73*
6700	*6601-6800*	*6036-6218*	*72*
6500	*6401-6600*	*5853-6035*	*71*
6300	*6201-6400*	*5670-5852*	*70*
6100	*5951-6200*	*5442-5669*	*69*
5800	*5701-5950*	*5213-5441*	*68*
5500	*5451-5700*	*4984-5212*	*67*
5300	*5201-5450*	*4756-4983*	*66*
5100	*5001-5200*	*4573-4755*	*65*
4900	*4801-5000*	*4390-4572*	*64*
4700	*4601-4800*	*4207-4389*	*63*
4500	*4401-4600*	*4024-4206*	*62*
4300	*4201-4400*	*3841-4023*	*61*
4100	*4001-4200*	*3659-3840*	*60*

1 yard = 0.91440 metre
1 metre = 1.09361 yards

Part Two
The Golf Course and the Standard Scratch Score

Clause
1. The Standard Scratch Score.
2. Course measurement.
3. Alterations to courses.
4. Tees.
5. Par.
6. Preferred lies.
7. Permitted adjustments to a *Measured Course.*

1. The Standard Scratch Score

1.(1) The Standard Scratch Score is the score which a scratch player is expected to return over a *Measured Course.* In the case of a nine-hole course it represents two rounds.
1.(2) The allocation of Standard Scratch Scores shall be the responsibility of the *Union.*
1.(3) The table above will provide a guide to officials in making their assessments.
1.(4) In assessing the Standard Scratch Score of a course, officials will take as the starting point the provisional Standard Scratch Score from the Table. They will then consider the following points:
(a) The terrain and general layout of the course.
(b) Normal ground conditions – Is run average, above average, or below average?
(c) Sizes of greens and whether watered or unwatered.
(d) Hazards – Are greens well guarded or open?
(e) Width of fairways, the effect of trees and nature of rough.
(f) Nearness of *out of bounds* to fairways and greens.
(g) Average weather conditions throughout the playing year. Is the course exposed and subject to high winds for most of the year? Is it sheltered from the full effects of adverse weather?
(h) The distance by which the length of the course varies from the standard length shown in column one of the Table.

1.(5) Having considered all these points officials will fix the Standard Scratch Score of the course by:
(a) Confirming the Provisional Standard Scratch Score as the Standard Scratch Score.

(b) Adding a stroke or strokes to the provisional Standard Scratch Score.
(c) Deducting a stroke or strokes from the Provisional Standard Scratch Score.

1.(6) The Standard Scratch Score so fixed will have taken into account the playing difficulty of the course or lack of it, and average weather conditions throughout the year and, once fixed, will remain constant.

1.(7) At the discretion of a *Union* courses of less than 4001 yards may be allocated such Standard Scratch Score as the *Union* shall determine.

2. Course Measurement

Measurement shall be by plan or projection along the horizontal plane from the *Distance Point* on the *Medal Tee* to the centre of the green of each hole.

In the case of a dog-leg hole, measurement shall be along the centre line of the fairway to the axis and then to the centre of the green. Measurement shall be carried out by a qualified surveyor, or someone competent and experienced in the handling of surveying instruments, who shall grant a certificate showing details of the length of the hole and the total playing length of the course. Subsequent alterations to the length of the course will require a certificate only for the altered hole or holes which shall be measured in the manner prescribed above.

3. Alterations to Courses

When alterations have been carried out to a course increasing or decreasing its length, the club shall submit a *Form of Application* through its *Area Authority* to the *Union*. In the case of a new course, a *Form of Application* shall be submitted by the club through its *Area Authority* to the *Union* who will fix the Standard Scratch Score. The *Union* is responsible for all Standard Scratch Scores in that country.

4. Tees

All clubs with the necessary facilities should have back and forward *Medal Tees* with a yardage measurement from each tee and a separate Standard Scratch Score as measured from back and forward *Medal Tees* permanently marked.

To facilitate the use of the correct tees, tee boxes or other objects in use to mark the teeing ground, the Royal and Ancient Golf Club of St Andrews recommends that they shall be painted as follows:

Ladies' Standard *Medal Tees*	Red
Men's Forward *Medal Tees*	Yellow
*Ladies' Back Tees	Black
Men's Back *Medal Tees*	White

**Not adopted by the Ladies' Golf Union.*

When a National Championship is being played over a course the tee markers may be coloured Blue.

5. Par

The Standard Scratch Score must not be allocated amongst the individual holes, but should be printed as a total on the card. The par figure for each hole should be printed alongside each hole on the card. Par for each hole is fixed as follows:

Par	*Yards*	*Metres*
3	Holes of 250 yards and under	Holes of 228 metres and under
4	Holes from 251 to 475 yards inclusive	Holes from 229 to 434 metres inclusive
5	Holes of 476 yards and over	Holes of 435 metres and over

The total of the Par figures for each hole of a course will not necessarily coincide with the Standard Scratch Score of that course. Par should be used for Stableford and similar competitions.

6. Preferred Lies

When preferred lies are in operation the following points shall be taken into consideration: *Medal Play Conditions* will apply notwithstanding the application of a Local Rule for preferred lies as a result of adverse conditions especially during the winter. For this purpose the winter period shall be from 1st November to 30th April. Preferred lies may be used during that period but are not mandatory upon clubs during any part thereof. The Local Rule may apply to specified holes only. Outside the winter period *Medal Play Conditions* will not apply if preferred lies are in operation unless the consent of the *Union* or *Area Authority* has been first obtained.

The Royal and Ancient Golf Club Rules of Golf Committee recommends that a Local Rule be made, worded as follows:

> *A ball lying through the green may be lifted and cleaned without penalty and placed within 6 inches of where it originally lay, but not nearer the hole and so as to preserve as nearly as possible the stance required to play from the original lie. After the ball has been so placed, it is in play.*
>
> *If however, a Club Committee considers that the term 'through the green' (Definition 35) gives too much latitude, and if it is satisfied that the area in which it wishes to apply*

the Local Rule is clearly defined by the term 'fairway', the Rules of Golf Committee would have no objection to the use of the term 'fairway' in the Local Rule, notwithstanding that it is neither defined nor used in the Rules of Golf (Decision 65/20/248) under Local Rules.

It is recommended that clubs use the term *fairway* in their Local Rule which must be posted on the Club Notice Board together with the club's definition of *fairway.*

7. Permitted Adjustments to a Measured Course

Whilst each *Affiliated Club* must endeavour to maintain the length of its *Measured Course* at all times *Medal Play Conditions* nevertheless prevail when the length of a course has been reduced in the following circumstances:

(a) When, to allow movement of the playing position on the *Medal Tee* or the use of a temporary green, the length of the course being played has been reduced by not more than 100 yards (91 metres) from the length of the *Measured Course*. The tee positions used must nevertheless be within the area defined by Definition K. (NOTE: The maximum movement forward on any *Medal Tee* must not exceed 10 yards (9 metres) – See Definition K.)

(b) When, to allow work to proceed on course alterations, or for reasons other than weather conditions, it is necessary to reduce the playing length of the *Measured Course* by between 100 and 300 yards (91 and 274 metres). In these circumstances, the club shall reduce the Standard Scratch Score of the *Measured Course* temporarily by 1 stroke and report to the *Union*, or to such other body nominated by the *Union*, the reduction in the Standard Scratch Score, and the reason for it. The club must also notify the *Union* or other body when the course has been restored to its measured length and the official Standard Scratch Score reinstated.

Part Three

Handicapping

8. Introduction.
9. Rights and obligations of the *Union*.
10. Rights and obligations of the *Area Authority*.
11. Rights and obligations of the *Affiliated Club*.
12. Rights and obligations of the *Handicap Committee*.
13. Rights and obligations of the player.
14. *Qualifying Scores*.
15. Allotment of handicaps.
16. Alteration of handicaps.
17. Suspension, lapsing and loss of handicaps.
18. Restoration of handicaps.
19. Powers of the *Handicap Committee* relating to general play.

Appendix A – Handicap record sheet.
Appendix B – Handicap adjustment table.
Appendix C – Stableford and par conversion table.
Appendix D – Decisions.

8. Introduction

8.(1) The Council of National Golf Unions Standard Scratch Score and Handicapping Scheme has been revised to achieve a uniformity and equity in handicapping throughout Great Britain and Ireland and member countries of the European Golf Association adopting the Scheme. The nature of the game of golf, with its varying playing conditions, makes handicapping a relatively inexact operation. Nevertheless if the same principles are sensibly and universally applied by *Handicap Committees*, a high degree of uniformity in handicapping can be achieved. It is therefore of paramount importance that all parties to the Scheme fulfil their obligation to it and these are set out below.

8.(2) Handicapping within the Scheme is delegated to *Affiliated Clubs* subject to the overall jurisdiction of the *Union*.

9. Rights and Obligations of the Union

The *Union:*

9.(1) Shall have overall jurisdiction for the administration of the Scheme.

9.(2) May delegate any part of that jurisdiction to an *Area Authority*.

9.(3) Shall ratify all *Playing Handicaps* reduced to scratch or below immediately after the reduction.

9.(4) Shall have the right to obtain information upon handicaps from *Affiliated Clubs* at any time.

9.(5) Shall establish within the *Union* conditions, restrictions and limitations to be imposed in respect of competitions deemed to be *Qualifying Competitions*.

9.(6) Shall settle any dispute referred to it. Its decision shall be final.

9.(7) Shall stipulate the four consecutive months which shall be the *Winter Period* in the Country over which it exercises jurisdiction. The *Winter Period* need not be the same four months throughout a Country.

10. Rights and Obligations of the Area Authority

The *Area Authority* shall:

10.(1) Administer the responsibilities delegated to it by the *Union*.

10.(2) Have the right to obtain information upon handicaps from *Affiliated Clubs* at any time.

11. Rights and Obligations of the Affiliated Club

The *Affiliated Club* shall:

11.(1) Act as the *Handicapping Authority* for all members for whom it is the *Home Club* subject to the overall jurisdiction of the *Union*.
11.(2) Ensure that the Scheme is properly applied in the club.
11.(3) Ensure that all handicaps are calculated in accordance with the Scheme.
11.(4) Appoint a *Handicap Committee* to perform the obligations set out in clause 12 below.

12. Rights and Obligations of the Handicap Committee

The *Handicap Committee* shall:
12.(1) Maintain a list in which the names of competitors must be entered prior to competing in a *Qualifying Competition* at the club.
12.(2) Ensure, so far as possible, that all cards taken out in *Qualifying Competitions* are returned to the committee including incomplete cards.
12.(3) Post on the club's notice board all changes of members' *Playing Handicaps* immediately they are made.
12.(4) Ensure that a record of members' current *Playing Handicaps* is available in a prominent position in the club house.
12.(5) When the club is a player's *Home Club:*
(a) Maintain on his behalf a handicap record sheet which shall include the information shown in Appendix A.
(b) Ensure his scores are recorded immediately after completion of each *Qualifying Competition* at the *Home Club* or the reporting of a *Qualifying Score* returned elsewhere.
(c) Keep his *Exact Handicap* up to date at all times.
(d) Notify the *Union* and *Area Authority* immediately the committee reduces a member's *Playing Handicap* to scratch or below and obtain ratification from the *Union* or, if so delegated, from the *Area Authority*. (NOTE: The reduction is effective before ratification.)
(e) Exercise the power to suspend handicaps contained in clause 17.
(f) When a member changes his *Home Club* send to the new *Home Club* a copy of the player's current handicap record sheet.
(g) Be empowered, if the committee considers that weather conditions during the play of any round of a *Qualifying Competition* were such as to render the proper playing of the game extremely difficult, to declare that that round shall not count as a *Qualifying Score*. The declaration shall be made in exceptional circumstances only and may be made at any time during the playing of the round or immediately thereafter. A player who returns a score below his *Playing Handicap* in such circumstances shall nevertheless report that score to his *Home Club* and it will be recorded in his handicap record sheet as a *Qualifying Score*. (NOTE: This power shall be exercised by *Unions, Area Authorities* and other organisations approved by a *Union* in respect of *Qualifying Competitions* organised by them.)
(h) Specify the conditions which apply when a player wishes to obtain a handicap under the provisions of clause 15.
(i) Exercise the powers to adjust players' handicaps contained in clause 19.
(j) As required by sub clause 19.(5) advise players of changes made to their handicaps under the provisions of clause 19.

13. Rights and Obligations of the Player

The player shall:

13.(1) Have one handicap only which shall be allotted and adjusted by his *Home Club*. That handicap shall apply elsewhere including other clubs of which the player is a member.
13.(2) If he is a member of more than one *Affiliated Club* select one as his *Home Club* and notify that club and the others of his choice.
13.(3) Not change his *Home Club* except by giving advance notice of the change which can take effect only at the end of a calendar year unless he has ceased to be a member of his *Home Club* or both clubs agree to the change taking place at an earlier date.
13.(4) Report to his *Home Club* the names of all other *Affiliated Clubs* of which he is, becomes, or ceases to be, a member and report to all other *Affiliated Clubs* of which he is a member:
(a) The name of his *Home Club* and any changes of his *Home Club* and
(b) Alterations to his *Playing Handicap* made by his *Home Club*.
13.(5) Ensure that before competing in a *Qualifying Competition* his entry has been inserted in the competition entry list.
13.(6) Ensure that all competition cards in *Qualifying Competitions*, whether or not complete, are returned to the organising committee.
13.(7) Report to his *Home Club* immediately all *Qualifying Scores* (including no returns) returned away from his *Home Club* advising the

Home Club of the date of the *Qualifying Competition*, the venue and the Standard Scratch Score together with the following:

(a) After a stroke play *Qualifying Competition* the gross score returned.

(b) After a Stableford *Qualifying Competition* the par of the course and the number of points scored.

(c) After a par *Qualifying Competition* the par of the course and the score versus par. (NOTE: Players are reminded that failure to report scores returned away from their *Home Clubs* (including no returns) is likely to lead to the suspension of offending players' handicaps under the provisions of clause 17.)

13.(8) Prior to playing in any competition at a club other than his *Home Club* ensure that any appropriate reductions to his *Playing Handicap* have been made or alternatively comply with the obligations set out in clause 16.(11) by either reducing his *Playing Handicap* for that competition only or informing the committee organising the competition of scores returned which may justify a reduction of his handicap.

14. Qualifying Scores

14.(1) The only scores to be recorded on a player's handicap record sheet are:

(a) *Qualifying Scores* as defined.

(b) Scores returned below his *Playing Handicap* in any abandoned round of a *Qualifying Competition* or in any round of a *Qualifying Competition* when that round has been declared by the committee under the provision of clause 12.(5)(g) not to be a *Qualifying Score*.

(c) Correct scores in a *Qualifying Competition* which are disqualified for any reason.

(d) Scores returned in a *Qualifying Competition* played over 18 holes on a course reduced in length under the provisions of clause 7.

(e) Scores returned in a *Qualifying Competition* played over a *Measured Course* when local rules are in operation for preferred lies (as permitted by clause 6) or for any other purpose provided the rules are authorised by Appendix 1 of the Rules of Golf or have been approved by the Rules of Golf Committee of the Royal and Ancient Golf Club of St Andrews.

(f) The individual scores and no returns returned by players in *Aggregate Fourball Competitions*. NOTE: The competition must be a *Qualifying Competition*.

NOTE: *Qualifying Scores* returned in Stableford and par competitions shall be converted into *Nett Differentials* by using the tables in Appendix C.

14.(2) The following returns shall not be accepted as *Qualifying Scores* in any circumstances.

(a) Scores returned in any better ball fourball competition.

(b) Scores returned in competitions over less than 18 holes.

(c) Scores returned in any competition which is not played in accordance with the Rules of Golf and authorised Local Rules.

(d) Scores returned in *running medals*. A running medal is an extended competition in which the player has the option of selecting the day or days on which he shall compete and/or how many returns he shall make. A competition extended over two or more days solely to accommodate the number of players entered is not a running medal.

(e) Subject to clause 14.(1)(b) scores returned in any round of a *Qualifying Competition* declared by the committee not to be *Qualifying Scores* under the provisions of clause 12.(5)(g).

(f) Any competition other than an *Aggregate Fourball Competition* in which competitors play in partnership with another competitor.

(g) Stableford and par competitions played with less than full handicap allowance.

15. Allotment of Handicaps

15.(1) The maximum handicap is 28. (Maximum *Exact Handicap* 28.0.)

15.(2) A handicap can be allotted only to an amateur member of an *Affiliated Club*.

15.(3) To obtain a handicap a player shall submit three cards preferably marked over a *Measured Course* which shall be adjusted by the *Handicap Committee* so that any score of more than 2 over par at any hole shall be amended to 2 over par. After these adjustments have been made, the three cards shall be averaged and the player allotted an *Exact Handicap* equivalent to the number of strokes by which the average differs from the Standard Scratch Score and rounded to the nearest whole number. The *Handicap Committee* may allot a player an initial whole number *Exact Handicap* less than the average if it has reason to consider that a lower handicap is more appropriate to the player's ability. When a player fails to return cards justifying an *Exact Handicap* of 28 he may, at the discretion of the *Handicap Committee*, be given an *Exact Handicap* of 28. The player's *Playing Handicap* shall equal the *Exact Handicap* allotted.

15.(4) A player without a handicap shall not be allotted a *Category 1 Handicap* without the written authority of the *Union*, or *Area Authority* if so delegated.

16. Alteration of Handicaps

16.(1) Definition 1 divides handicaps into the following four *Categories:*
Category 1: Handicaps of 5 or less.
Category 2: Handicaps of 6 to 12 inclusive.
Category 3: Handicaps of 13 to 20 inclusive.
Category 4: Handicaps of 21 to 28 inclusive.

16.(2) If a player plays to his *Playing Handicap* or returns a score within the *Buffer Zone* (i.e. one or two strokes above his *Playing Handicap*) his *Exact Handicap* is not changed.

16.(3) Subject to the provisions of sub clause 12.(5)(g) if a player at any time other than in the *Winter Period* returns a score with a *Nett Differential* of +3 or more (three strokes or more above his *Playing Handicap*) or records a *no return* his *Exact Handicap* is increased by 0.1 (not by an amount determined by the extent to which he was above his *Playing Handicap*). Scores returned and *no returns* recorded by a player in the *Winter Period* do not increase his *Exact Handicap*.

16.(4) If a player plays below his *Playing Handicap* his *Exact Handicap* is reduced by an amount per stroke that he was below his *Playing Handicap*, the amount per stroke being determined by his *Handicap Category*.

16.(5) The recording of scores shall be kept by *Nett Differential* i.e. the difference (+ or −) between the player's nett score and the Standard Scratch Score. The date, *Nett Differential, Exact Handicap* and *Playing Handicap* must be recorded on the player's handicap record sheet.

16.(6) *Exact Handicaps* shall be adjusted as follows, with reference to the handicap adjustment tables, Appendix B:

		If Nett Differential is:	
Category	Playing Handicap	Above Buffer Zone add *only*	Below SSS subtract for *each* stroke below
1	Up to 5	0.1	0.1
2	6 to 12	0.1	0.2
3	13 to 20	0.1	0.3
4	21 to 28	0.1	0.4

For example:

If a player on 11.2 returns a score with a *Nett Differential* of 4 his *Exact Handicap* becomes 11.3. If he then returns a score with a *Nett Differential* of −7 his *Exact Handicap* is reduced by 7 times 0.2= 1.4, i.e. to an *Exact Handicap* of 9.9 and his *Playing Handicap* is 10 which is immediately his new handicap.

16.(7) When a player's handicap is to be reduced so that it goes from a higher *Category* to a lower *Category*, it shall be reduced at the rate appropriate to the higher *Category* only so far as brings his *Playing Handicap* into the lower *Category* and the balance of the reduction shall be at the rate appropriate to the lower *Category*.

For example:

If a player on 21.2 returns a score with a *Nett Differential* of −6, i.e. 6 strokes below his *Playing Handicap* of 21, his handicap is reduced as follows:

21.2−(2 times 0.4) (i.e. −0.8)=20.4
20.4−(4 times 0.3) (i.e. −1.2)=19.2

16.(8) A player whose *Exact Handicap* contains 0.5 or over shall be given the next higher handicap, e.g. 12.5 exact would be 13 *Playing Handicap*. This applies when handicaps are to be increased or reduced.

NOTE: *Exact Handicap* −0.5 rounded upwards is *Playing Handicap* scratch and not plus one.

16.(9) Reductions shall be made on the day the score becomes known to the *Home Club*.

16.(10) Increases shall be made at the end of each calendar month or at such more frequent intervals as the *Home Club* may decide.

16.(11) If, for any reason, a player is unable to report to his *Home Club* a *Qualifying Score* or *Scores* below his *Playing Handicap* or has been unable to ascertain, after reporting such scores, whether or not his *Playing Handicap* has been reduced, he shall then, before competing in a further competition at a club other than his *Home Club*, either:

(a) For that competition only, make such reduction to his *Playing Handicap* as shall be appropriate under the Scheme, or

(b) Report to the committee organising the competition the relevant score or scores returned below his *Playing Handicap*. The committee may, for that competition only, reduce the player's *Playing Handicap*.

NOTE: Increases to *Playing Handicaps* may not be made under the provisions of this sub clause.

16.(12) The procedure for the restoration of handicaps which have been lost is contained in clause 18.

17. Suspension, Lapsing and Loss of Handicaps

17.(1) The *Handicap Committee*, or other body appointed by the *Home Club* for the purposes of this clause, shall suspend the handicap of any player who in its opinion has constantly or blatantly failed to comply with his obligations under the Scheme. The player must be notified of the period of suspension and of any other conditions imposed. No player's handicap shall be suspended without first affording him the opportunity of appearing before the committee or other body.

17.(2) If a player is suspended from membership of his *Home Club* his handicap shall lapse automatically until his membership is reinstated.

17.(3) A player's handicap is lost immediately he ceases to be a member of an *Affiliated Club* or loses his amateur status.

17.(4) Whilst a player's handicap is suspended, lapsed or has been lost he shall not enter or compete in any competition which requires a competitor to be the holder of a handicap for either entering or competing in the competition.

18. Restoration of Handicaps

18.(1) A player who has lost his handicap for any reason other than suspension or lapsing may obtain a new handicap by complying with the requirements of clause 15. When allotting him a handicap the *Handicap Committee* will give due consideration to the handicap he last held. A *Category 1 Handicap* shall not be allotted without the written approval of the *Union*, or *Area Authority* if so delegated.

18.(2) The lapsed handicap of a player suspended from membership of his *Home Club* shall be reinstated when his membership is restored and shall be the same as the handicap he held when his membership was suspended.

19. Powers of the Handicap Committee Relating to General Play

19.(1) Whenever the *Handicap Committee* of a player's *Home Club* considers that a player's *Exact Handicap* is too high and does not reflect his current playing ability the *Handicap Committee* must, subject to the provisions of sub clause (3) of this clause, reduce his *Exact Handicap* to the figure it considers appropriate.

19.(2) Whenever the *Handicap Committee* of a player's *Home Club* considers that a player's *Exact Handicap* is too low and does not reflect his current playing ability the *Handicap Committee* must, subject to the provisions of sub clause (3) of this clause, recommend to the *Union*, or *Area Authority* if so delegated, that his *Exact Handicap* should be increased to the figure it considers appropriate.

19.(3) When the *Handicap Committee* has decided that the *Exact Handicap* of a player should be reduced to less than 5.5 or that the *Exact Handicap* of a player should be increased the *Handicap Committee* must refer the matter to the *Union*, or *Area Authority* if so delegated, with its recommended adjustment. The *Union* or *Area Authority* shall then authorise the recommended variation, reject the recommendation or refer the matter back to the *Handicap Committee* for further consideration. The *Union* or *Area Authority* shall be supplied with all the information upon which the recommendation is based and with any further information required.

19.(4) When deciding whether to effect or recommend an adjustment of handicap the *Handicap Committee* of the player's *Home Club* shall consider all available information regarding the player's golfing ability.

It shall consider in particular:

(a) The frequency of *Qualifying Scores* recently returned by the player to and below his *Playing Handicap*.

(b) The player's achievements in match play, fourball better ball competitions and other non-qualifying events.

(c) *Qualifying Scores* returned by the player in stroke play competitions which are adversely affected by one or more particularly bad holes. It may prove helpful to take into account the number of points the player would have scored if these *Qualifying Scores* had been in Stableford competitions played with full handicap allowance.

19.(5) The *Handicap Committee* shall advise a player of any change of handicap under this clause and the change will become effective when the player becomes aware of the adjustment.

19.(6) The *Handicap Committee* or other body organising a competition at a Club which is not the player's *Home Club* may if it considers his handicap is too high because of scores reported pursuant to sub clause 16.(11)(b) or for any other reason reduce that handicap. Any reduction made under this sub clause shall apply only to the competition for which it is made.

19.(7) Decisions made by a *Handicap Committee, Union* or *Area Authority* under this clause shall be final.

NOTES

1. In the interests of equitable handicapping it is essential that all *Handicap Committees* keep the handicaps of the members for whom they act as the *Home Club* under review and that adjustments of handicaps are considered as soon as it comes to the committee's notice that a player's handicap may no longer correctly reflect his current general golfing ability.

2. The *Handicap Committee* should consider dealing more severely with a player whose general standard of play is known to be improving than it should with a player who it is believed has returned scores below his general ability but whose general playing ability is not considered to be improving.

Appendix A

Handicap Record Sheet

Name ______________________________

Home Club ______________________________

Other Clubs ______________________________

____

Date	Nett differential	Handicap		Date	Nett differential	Handicap		
		Exact	Playing			Exact	Playing	
May 1	B/F	21.0	21	June 30	B/F	19.4	19	
6	2	21.0	21	July				
7	4	21.1	21	8	7	19.5	19	
20	N/R	21.2	21	9	6	19.6	19	
21	−6	19.2	19	29	8	19.7	19	*Note 2*
June				30	3	19.8	20	
4	1	19.2	19	Aug				
5	4	19.3	19	6	2	19.8	20	
25	7	19.4	19	7	−6	18.0	18	
26	2	19.4	19	20	0	18.0	18	
				21	7	18.1	18	

Notes to Appendix A

1. The sheet above shows the *Playing Handicaps* when increases are made on the last day of each calendar month.
2. If increases had been made immediately the *Playing Handicap* would have been increased to 20 on the 8th July and the *Nett Differentials* of 6, 8 and 3 respectively on the 9th, 29th and 30th July would each have been reduced by 0.1. Thus, with the operation of the *Buffer Zone*, the *Exact Handicap* would have remained at 19.7 on 31st july and been 0.1 less than those shown thereafter.
3. *Nett Differential* is the difference (+ or−) between the Nett Score returned by a player in a *Qualifying Competition* and the Standard Scratch Score
4. Scores returned on places other than that of the player's *Home Club* should be distinguished by marking the *Nett Differential* thus:*.
5. Reductions of handicaps are effected immediately.
6. Increases of handicaps shall be made at the end of each calendar month or at such more frequent intervals as the *Home Club* may decide.

Appendix B

Table of Handicap Adjustments

Nett Differentials	-1	-2	-3	-4	-5	-6	-7	-8	-9	-10	-11	-12	Over Buffer Zone
Exact Handicaps Up to 5.4	-0.1	-0.2	-0.3	-0.4	-0.5	-0.6	-0.7	-0.8	-0.9	-1.0	-1.1	-1.2	0.1
5.5– 5.6	-0.2	-0.3	-0.4	-0.5	-0.6	-0.7	-0.8	-0.9	-1.0	-1.1	-1.2	-1.3	0.1
5.7– 5.8	-0.2	-0.4	-0.5	-0.6	-0.7	-0.8	-0.9	-1.0	-1.1	-1.2	-1.3	-1.4	0.1
5.9– 6.0	-0.2	-0.4	-0.6	-0.7	-0.8	-0.9	-1.0	-1.1	-1.2	-1.3	-1.4	-1.5	0.1
6.1– 6.2	-0.2	-0.4	-0.6	-0.8	-0.9	-1.0	-1.1	-1.2	-1.3	-1.4	-1.5	-1.6	0.1
6.3– 6.4	-0.2	-0.4	-0.6	-0.8	-1.0	-1.1	-1.2	-1.3	-1.4	-1.5	-1.6	-1.7	0.1
6.5– 6.6	-0.2	-0.4	-0.6	-0.8	-1.0	-1.2	-1.3	-1.4	-1.5	-1.6	-1.7	-1.8	0.1
6.7– 6.8	-0.2	-0.4	-0.6	-0.8	-1.0	-1.2	-1.4	-1.5	-1.6	-1.7	-1.8	-1.9	0.1
6.9– 7.0	-0.2	-0.4	-0.6	-0.8	-1.0	-1.2	-1.4	-1.6	-1.7	-1.8	-1.9	-2.0	0.1
7.1– 7.2	-0.2	-0.4	-0.6	-0.8	-1.0	-1.2	-1.4	-1.6	-1.8	-1.9	-2.0	-2.1	0.1
7.3– 7.4	-0.2	-0.4	-0.6	-0.8	-1.0	-1.2	-1.4	-1.6	-1.8	-2.0	-2.1	-2.2	0.1
7.5– 7.6	-0.2	-0.4	-0.6	-0.8	-1.0	-1.2	-1.4	-1.6	-1.8	-2.0	-2.2	-2.3	0.1
7.7–12.4	-0.2	-0.4	-0.6	-0.8	-1.0	-1.2	-1.4	-1.6	-1.8	-2.0	-2.2	-2.4	0.1
12.5–12.7	-0.3	-0.5	-0.7	-0.9	-1.1	-1.3	-1.5	-1.7	-1.9	-2.1	-2.3	-2.5	0.1
12.8–13.0	-0.3	-0.6	-0.8	-1.0	-1.2	-1.4	-1.6	-1.8	-2.0	-2.2	-2.4	-2.6	0.1
13.1–13.3	-0.3	-0.6	-0.9	-1.1	-1.3	-1.5	-1.7	-1.9	-2.1	-2.3	-2.5	-2.7	0.1
13.4–13.6	-0.3	-0.6	-0.9	-1.2	-1.4	-1.6	-1.8	-2.0	-2.2	-2.4	-2.6	-2.8	0.1
13.7–13.9	-0.3	-0.6	-0.9	-1.2	-1.5	-1.7	-1.9	-2.1	-2.3	-2.5	-2.7	-2.9	0.1
14.0–14.2	-0.3	-0.6	-0.9	-1.2	-1.5	-1.8	-2.0	-2.2	-2.4	-2.6	-2.8	-3.0	0.1
14.3–14.5	-0.3	-0.6	-0.9	-1.2	-1.5	-1.8	-2.1	-2.3	-2.5	-2.7	-2.9	-3.1	0.1
14.6–14.8	-0.3	-0.6	-0.9	-1.2	-1.5	-1.8	-2.1	-2.4	-2.6	-2.8	-3.0	-3.2	0.1
14.9–15.1	-0.3	-0.6	-0.9	-1.2	-1.5	-1.8	-2.1	-2.4	-2.7	-2.9	-3.1	-3.3	0.1
15.2–15.4	-0.3	-0.6	-0.9	-1.2	-1.5	-1.8	-2.1	-2.4	-2.7	-3.0	-3.2	-3.4	0.1
15.5–15.7	-0.3	-0.6	-0.9	-1.2	-1.5	-1.8	-2.1	-2.4	-2.7	-3.0	-3.3	-3.5	0.1
15.8–20.4	-0.3	-0.6	-0.9	-1.2	-1.5	-1.8	-2.1	-2.4	-2.7	-3.0	-3.3	-3.6	0.1
20.5–20.8	-0.4	-0.7	-1.0	-1.3	-1.6	-1.9	-2.2	-2.5	-2.8	-3.1	-3.4	-3.7	0.1
20.9–21.2	-0.4	-0.8	-1.1	-1.4	-1.7	-2.0	-2.3	-2.6	-2.9	-3.2	-3.5	-3.8	0.1
21.3–21.6	-0.4	-0.8	-1.2	-1.5	-1.8	-2.1	-2.4	-2.7	-3.0	-3.3	-3.6	-3.8	0.1
21.7–22.0	-0.4	-0.8	-1.2	-1.6	-1.9	-2.2	-2.5	-2.8	-3.1	-3.4	-3.7	-4.0	0.1
22.1–22.4	-0.4	-0.8	-1.2	-1.6	-2.0	-2.3	-2.6	-2.9	-3.2	-3.5	-3.8	-4.1	0.1
22.5–22.8	-0.4	-0.8	-1.2	-1.6	-2.0	-2.4	-2.7	-3.0	-3.3	-3.6	-3.9	-4.2	0.1
22.9–23.2	-0.4	-0.8	-1.2	-1.6	-2.0	-2.4	-2.8	-3.1	-3.4	-3.7	-4.0	-4.3	0.1
23.3–23.6	-0.4	-0.8	-1.2	-1.6	-2.0	-2.4	-2.8	-3.2	-3.5	-3.8	-4.1	-4.4	0.1
23.7–24.0	-0.4	-0.8	-1.2	-1.6	-2.0	-2.4	-2.8	-3.2	-3.6	-3.9	-4.2	-4.5	0.1
24.1–24.4	-0.4	-0.8	-1.2	-1.6	-2.0	-2.4	-2.8	-3.2	-3.6	-4.0	-4.3	-4.6	0.1
24.5–24.8	-0.4	-0.8	-1.2	-1.6	-2.0	-2.4	-2.8	-3.2	-3.6	-4.0	-4.4	-4.7	0.1
24.9–28.0	-0.4	-0.8	-1.2	-1.6	-2.0	-2.4	-2.8	-3.2	-3.6	-4.0	-4.4	-4.8	0.1

Appendix C

Table for converting Par and Stableford scores to nett differentials (Note: The table is based on full handicap allowance)

Scores versus PAR	**4 down**	**3 down**	**2 down**	**1 down**	**All square**	**1 up**	**2 up**	**3 up**	**4 up**	**5 up**	**6 up**	**7 up**	**8 up**	**9 up**
Stableford points scored	32	33	34	35	36	37	38	39	40	41	42	43	44	45
Par 4 less than SSS	0	-1	-2	-3	-4	-5	-6	-7	-8	-9	-10	-11	-12	-13
Par 3 less than SSS	+1	0	-1	-2	-3	-4	-5	-6	-7	-8	-9	-10	-11	-12
Par 2 less than SSS	+2	+1	0	-1	-2	-3	-4	-5	-6	-7	-8	-9	-10	-11
Par 1 less than SSS	+3	+2	+1	0	-1	-2	-3	-4	-5	-6	-7	-8	-9	-10
Par equal to SSS	+4	+3	+2	+1	0	-1	-2	-3	-4	-5	-6	-7	-8	-9
Par 1 more than SSS	+5	+4	+3	+2	+1	0	-1	-2	-3	-4	-5	-6	-7	-8
Par 2 more than SSS	+6	+5	+4	+3	+2	+1	0	-1	-2	-3	-4	-5	-6	-7
Par 3 more than SSS	+7	+6	+5	+4	+3	+2	+1	0	-1	-2	-3	-4	-5	-6
Par 4 more than SSS	+8	+7	+6	+5	+4	+3	+2	+1	0	-1	-2	-3	-4	-5
Par 5 more than SSS	+9	+8	+7	+6	+5	+4	+3	+3	+1	0	-1	-2	-3	-4
Par 6 more than SSS	+10	+9	+8	+7	+6	+5	+4	+3	+2	+1	0	-1	-2	-3
Par 7 more than SSS	+11	+10	+9	+8	+7	+6	+5	+4	+3	+2	+1	0	-1	-2
Par 8 more than SSS	+12	+11	+10	+9	+8	+7	+6	+5	+4	+3	+2	+1	0	-1
Par 9 more than SSS	+13	+12	+11	+10	+9	+8	+7	+6	+5	+4	+3	+2	+1	0

Examples:
(a) 3 up on a par 72 course with an SSS of 70. Par is 2 more than SSS so Nett Differential= −1.
(b) 37 Stableford points on a course with Par 68 and SSS 69. Par is 1 less than SSS so Nett Differential= −2.

Appendix D

Decisions

1. Non-counting Scores – Clause 12.(5)(g)

(a) A decision may be made at any time during the playing of the round in question or after completion of the round.
(b) The decision must be based on the weather conditions prevailing and the committee's view of their effect on the playing difficulty of the course.
(c) If the committee has doubts or the decision seems borderline, no decision should be made until all scores have been returned. The scores will then assist the committee to reach a decision e.g. if no competitor has played to or below his handicap *that is a clear* indication that conditions have made the playing of the game extremely difficult.
(d) If the conditions of the course are such that they alone make scoring extremely difficult the competition should be stated to be non-qualifying from the outset.
(e) A *non-counting* decision made on one day of an 18-hole *Qualifying Competition*, which is played over more than one day purely to accommodate the number of entries, will apply

to all scores returned in that *Qualifying Competition.*

NOTE: In a 36-hole *Qualifying Competition* played on one day the *non-counting* decision may apply to one round only. Similarly in a 72-hole *Qualifying Competition* played over two or more days the decision may be made in respect of one or more rounds only on any day, the decision having no effect on the remaining rounds of the competition.

2. Running Medals – Clause 14.(2)(d)

(a) Any competition which can be described as a running Medal is not a *Qualifying Competition.*
(b) The following are defined as Running Medals:
 (i) An 18-hole competition extended over two or more days for any reason other than to accommodate the number of players entered.
 (ii) An 18-hole competition played on one day or over several days in which players are allowed to return more than one score.

NOTE: If from a series of any number of scores special prizes are awarded for the best eclectic score or the best nett or gross aggregate of a prescribed number of scores, the individual scores in the series would not be regarded as constituting a *running medal* provided each score is returned under *Medal Play Conditions* in a *Qualifying Competition*, as defined in the Scheme, and not returned solely for the purpose of the eclectic, nett or gross aggregate awards.

3. Qualifying Scores

(a) If a club with a large number of *Qualifying Competitions* in the calendar year wishes to deprive certain of the competitions of their status as *Qualifying Competitions* it may do so provided competitors are so advised before play commences.
(b) It would be outside the spirit of the Handicapping Scheme to declare that all Club Medal Competitions during a specified period would not be regarded as *Qualifying Competitions*, although played under full *Medal Play Conditions.*
(c) In both (a) and (b) above it would be more appropriate to play unofficial *Medal Competitions* under conditions which would not give them the status of *Qualifying Competitions.*

NOTE: A declaration that a competition is not a *Qualifying Competition* disqualifies all scores returned in that competition for handicapping purposes. Thus a player returning a score below his handicap will not have his handicap reduced.

(d) A competition will not lose the status of *Qualifying Competition* when played under conditions when, because of work proceeding or ground conditions in the area, pegging-up has been made obligatory by the club on a restricted area of the course, provided the playing of *Qualifying Competitions* under such conditions has the prior approval of the *Union* or *Area Authority.*

4. Upwards adjustment of Handicaps

(a) Clubs may elect to adjust handicaps upwards at the end of each calendar month or at shorter intervals, including immediate adjustment after completion of each *Qualifying Competition* at the Club.
(b) There could be slight differences in *Exact Handicaps* produced by each method when comparison is made at the end of a calendar month.
(c) The procedure for recording *Nett Differentials* set out in the Scheme should be adhered to whatever method is used.
(d) There is no objection to clubs electing to adjust handicaps upwards at the end of each calendar month, or at more frequent intervals, taking steps to adjust and record *Exact* and *Playing Handicaps* so that at the end of each month they correspond with those derived by adjusting handicaps after the playing of each *Qualifying Competition.*

5. Limitation of Handicaps

Clubs have inquired whether they may impose a limit of handicap to some of their competitions e.g. insist that a 24 handicap player competes from a handicap of 18. This is permitted by Rule of Golf 33-1. However, when recording the players' scores for handicapping purposes, adjustments must be made to ensure that the *Nett Differential* is recorded from his current *Playing Handicap* i.e. in the example quoted 24 instead of 18.

This is comparatively simple for *Medal Competition*, but is impractical for Stableford and Par competitions as it is unlikely for example that a player would record a score at a hole where a stroke allowance of one from an 18 handicap gave him no points, whereas from a handicap of 24 with a stroke allowance of two at that particular hole he might have registered one point.

6. Incomplete Cards and No Returns

(a) All cards must be returned, whether complete or not.
(b) It is expected that every player who enters for an 18-hole *Qualifying Competition* intends to complete the round.

(c) Since an Incomplete Card and a No Return have the effect of increasing a player's handicap, the club would be justified in refusing to accept a card or record a *N.R.* when the player has walked in after playing only a few holes if it has reason to suppose that a genuine effort was not made to complete the 18 holes.
(d) Cards should not be issued to players when there is obviously insufficient light for them to complete the round.
(e) Sympathetic consideration should be given to players who have had to discontinue play because of injury to themselves or their markers or because of their, or their markers, being taken ill on the course.
(f) Clauses 17 and 19 of the Scheme gives clubs the discretion to deal with players who persistently submit Incomplete Cards or make No Returns if they consider they are attempting to *build a handicap*.

7. Reduction of Handicaps during a competition

Where the conditions of a competition do not provide otherwise the handicap of a player applying at the beginning of a competition shall apply throughout that competition. This provision shall apply to a competition in which supplementary prizes are awarded for the best scores returned in an individual round or in combinations of individual rounds of the competition. The provisions shall not apply in circumstances where the winner is the player returning the lowest aggregate score in two or more separate competitions. Where a player's handicap has been reduced during the course of a competition in which the original handicap continues to apply the player shall nevertheless play from his reduced handicap in all other competitions commencing after the handicap reduction.

8. Overseas Scores

Scores returned in tournaments organised by the European Golf Association are *Qualifying Scores* for handicapping purposes and must be returned to the Home Club pursuant to Clause 13.(7). Other scores returned in overseas tournaments may be returned and used, if considered appropriate, under the terms of Clause 19.

Stationery

Enquiries regarding storage binders and handicap record sheets suitable for use in connection with the Standard Scratch Score and Handicapping Scheme 1983 to be directed to Hon. Secretary of the Council of National Golf Unions: A. Thirlwell, Formby Golf Club, Formby, Liverpool L37 1LQ.
Forms of application for:

An alteration to the Basic Standard Scratch Score.

An addition for course value to the Provisional Standard Scratch Score.

The above forms may be obtained from the Secretaries of:
(a) County Golf Unions or District Committees.
(b) Area Authorities.
(c) National Golf Unions.
(d) Council of National Golf Unions.

Application of Handicaps

Stroke Index

Each club should draw up a list, called the Stroke Index, giving the order of holes at which any handicap strokes awarded should be taken. This order should be printed on the club's score card. The general principle for fixing the order of the Stroke Index is that the hole at which it is most difficult to achieve par should be Stroke Index 1, the next most difficult, Stroke Index 2 and so on until the easiest which should be Stroke Index 18.

However, certain other factors should be taken into consideration. Stroke Index 1 should not be one of the very early or very late holes on the course. The reason is that if a game were to finish all square and go on to the 19th and subsequent holes to determine the winner, the person in receipt of only one stroke would have an unfair advantage if he were to receive it at the 19th or 20th. Similarly, if Stroke Index 1 were a hole at the very end of the round, then the person in receipt of only one stroke might never be able to use it as the game might well be over by then. In general, therefore, Stroke Index 1 should not be at holes 1, 2, 17 or 18.

The other important factor to be taken into account in fixing the order of Stroke Index is that the strokes should be fairly evenly spread out over the 18 holes. If Stroke Index 1 is in the first 9 holes, Stroke Index 2 should be in the second 9 holes and so on. For example, if a person were to receive, say, four strokes, it would not be fair if he received them all in the early holes or all in the late holes.

Competition Formats and Handicap Allowances

Note 1: *In all calculations of handicap allowances, fractions under $^1/_2$ are ignored and those of $^1/_2$ or over are rounded up to the next higher figure.*

Note 2: *Handicap allowances shown are recommendations only. They are not Rules of Golf. The allowance to be used is at the discretion of the committee who should stipulate that allowance in the conditions of the competition.*

Competitions take two basic forms – match play or stroke play. In match play two players or sides compete against each other on a hole by hole basis. In stroke play a player or side competes against the whole field on his score over the whole round or rounds.

Single

Format

One player competes directly against one other player. It applies only to match play.

Handicap Allowance

The player with the higher handicap of the two receives strokes amounting to $^3/_4$ of the difference between the two players' handicaps. These strokes are taken at the holes indicated by the Stroke Index.

Foursome

Format

Two players form a side and hit alternate shots with one ball. The two players drive alternately from successive tees. Can be used for both match play and stroke play.

Handicap Allowance

Match play: The two players on each side add their handicaps together. The couple with the higher combined handicaps receive strokes amounting to $^3/_8$ of the difference between the combined handicaps of the two sides. These strokes are taken at the holes indicated by the Stroke Index.

Stroke play: The two players forming a side add their handicaps together and divide by 2. This figure is deducted from the side's gross score.

Mixed Foursome

Format

Same as Foursome except that each side must consist of a man and a woman.

Handicap Allowance

Same as Foursome.

Four-Ball Better-Ball

Format

Two players form a side, each playing his own ball throughout. The better score of the partners is the score of the side. Can be used for both match play and stroke play.

Handicap Allowance

Match play: The three players with the highest handicaps of the four each receive strokes amounting to $^3/_4$ of the difference between their own handicaps and that of the lowest handicap of the four. These strokes are taken at the holes indicated by the Stroke Index. *Example:* A–16; B–12; C–20; D–8. Player A would receive $(16–8)\times{}^3/_4=6$ strokes; B would receive $(12–8)\times{}^3/_4=3$ strokes; C would receive $(20–8)\times{}^3/_4=9$ strokes; D would receive 0 strokes.

Stroke play: $^3/_4$ of each player's full handicap is allocated at the holes according to the Stroke Index and the stroke or strokes deducted at these holes.

Four-Ball Aggregate

Format

Two players form a side, each playing his own ball throughout. The combined score of the two partners is the score for the side. Can be used for both match play and stroke play.

Handicap Allowance

Match play: Same as Four-ball Better-ball.
Stroke play: Same as Four-ball Better-ball.

Greensome

Format

Two players form a side and both drive off each tee. Either ball may be selected to continue the hole and subsequent shots are played alternately until the hole is completed. *Example:* If player A's drive is selected at any hole, B must play the second shot at that hole, A the third shot and so on alternately until the ball is holed and vice versa if player B's drive is selected. Can be used for both match play and stroke play.

Handicap Allowance

Match play: Multiply the lower handicap of the two partners by .6 and the higher handicap by .4 and add the two figures together to give the full greensome handicap of the side. The couple with the higher greensome handicap receive strokes amounting to $^3/_4$ of the difference between the greensome handicaps of the two sides. These strokes are taken at the holes indicated by the Stroke Index. *Example:* A–2; B–10; C–8; D–12. AB *v* CD: Side AB full greensome handicap$=(2\times.6)+(10\times.4)=5.2$. Side CD full greensome handicap $=(8\times.6)+(12\times.4)=9.6$. Side CD receives stroke amounting to $^3/_4$ of the difference between the two couples, i.e. $(9.6–5.2)\times{}^3/_4=3$ strokes.

Stroke play: The two players forming a side deduct their full greensome handicap (as calculated above) from their gross score.

Bogey/Par

Format

Each player or side plays against the bogey (or par) for each hole, counting a win if he holes out in less than the bogey (or par) for the hole, a half if he equals it and a loss if he holes out in more. The aggregate of wins, losses and halves is taken to give a final score of so many holes up (or down as the case may be) to bogey (or par). Suitable for stroke play only.

Handicap Allowance

Each player receives strokes amounting to $^3/_4$ of his full handicap. In the case of foursomes, each side receives strokes amounting to $^3/_8$ of the combined handicaps of the partners. In all cases these strokes are allocated at the holes according to the Stroke Index and the stroke or strokes deducted at these holes.

Stableford

Format

The Stableford system of scoring was invented in 1931 by Dr Frank Stableford of the Wallasey and Royal Liverpool Golf Clubs and the first competition was played on 16th May, 1932 at Wallasey GC. Each player or side plays against the par for each hole and receives points according to how he scores in relation to par. The scoring system is as follows: 2 or more over par–0 points; 1 over par–1 point; par–2 points; 1 under par–3 points; 2 under par–4 points; 3 under par–5 points and so on. The number of points gained at each of the 18 holes is added together to give a total points score. Suitable for stroke play only.

Handicap Allowance

$^7/_8$ of full handicap.

Eclectic

Format

Competitors play two or more rounds choosing their better or best score at each hole to make up their eclectic score. Suitable for stroke play only.

Handicap Allowance

If played over two rounds, each competitor deducts five-sixths of his full handicap from his eclectic score for the two rounds. If played over three rounds, deduct four-fifths of his handicap from his eclectic score. If played over four rounds deduct $^3/_4$, five rounds, $^2/_3$, and six or more rounds, $^1/_2$.

Round Robin

Format

This is a form of league where each competitor or side plays every other competitor or side in the league. Suitable for match play only and can be used for singles, foursomes, four-ball better-ball, four-ball aggregate or greensomes, with the appropriate handicap allowance applying according to the type of competition.

Mixed Events

In competitions where men and women compete on an equal footing, the women's handicaps should be increased by the difference between the men's and ladies' Standard Scratch Scores if the women play from the ladies' tees. If the women play from the men's tees, their handicaps should be increased by the difference between the two Standard Scratch Scores plus an equitable figure (somewhere between 2 and 6) to take account of the distance between the men's and ladies' tees, one stroke being added for every 200 yards of difference over the 18 holes.

This adjustment does not apply where each side must consist of a man and woman; it only applies where women are in direct competition with men or where a side may consist of any combination of men and women, i.e. two men, two women or one man and one woman.

Bisques

Instead of receiving strokes to be taken at holes according to the Stroke Index, in match play friendly games, a number of bisques can be agreed upon instead. A bisque is a stroke which may be used at any hole the recipient decides upon after the completion of the hole. Because bisques can be used more advantageously than strokes, which may be of no value at certain holes, a lesser number of bisques than handicap strokes allowance is usually agreed upon. A player may use any number of bisques from his quota at any hole but he must announce whether he is using any of them before any stroke is played from the next tee. The bisque form of handicapping is not used in official competitions. It is suitable only for singles or foursomes, not for four-ball games.

Callaway Handicapping

It frequently occurs in social competitions such as an office or business association outing that many of the competitors do not have official handicaps. In such cases the best solution is to use the Callaway handicapping system, so called after the name of its inventor, as it is simple to use yet has proved equitable.

Competitors complete their round marking in their gross figures at every hole and their handicaps are awarded and deducted at the end of the 18 holes using the following table:

Competitor's gross score	Handicap deduction
par or less	none
1 over par-75	1/2 worst hole
76-80	worst hole
81-85	worst hole plus 1/2 next worst
86-90	two worst holes
91-95	two worst holes plus 1/2 next
96-100	three worst holes
101-105	three worst holes plus 1/2 next
106-110	four worst holes
111-115	four worst holes plus 1/2 next
116-120	five worst holes
121-125	five worst holes plus 1/2 next
126-130	six worst holes

Note 1: ***Worst hole equals highest score at any hole regardless of the par of the hole except that the maximum score allowed for any one hole is twice the par of the hole.***

Note 2: ***The 17th and 18th holes are not allowed to be deducted.***

Example: Competitor scores 104. From the table he should deduct as his handicap the total of his three worst (i.e. highest) individual scores plus half of his fourth worst hole. If he scored one 9, one 8 and several 7s he would therefore deduct a total of 27 1/2 from his gross score of 104 to give a nett score of 76 1/2.

Draws for Match Play Competitions

Cold Draw

When the number of entries is not a whole power of 2, i.e. 4, 8, 16, 32, 64 etc, a number of first round byes are necessary. Subtract the number of entries from the nearest of these numbers above the number of entries to give the number of byes.

Example: (a) 28 entries – subtracting from 32 gives 4 first round byes; (b) 33 entries – subtracting from 64 gives 31 first round byes.

All names (or numbers representing names) are put in a hat and the requisite number of byes drawn out singly and placed in pairs in the second round of the draw, alternately at the top and bottom, i.e. the first two names go at the top of the draw, the next two at the bottom and so on until all the byes have been drawn. If there is an odd number of byes, the last drawn is bracketed to play against the winner of either the first or last first round match. Having drawn all the byes, the remaining names are then drawn and placed in pairs in the first round in the order drawn in the middle of the draw.

Automatic Draw

When a stroke play qualifying round(s) is used to determine the qualifiers for the ensuing match play, the automatic draw is used, based on the qualifying position of each qualifier, i.e. the leading qualifier is number 1 in the draw, the second qualifier is number 2 and so on.

The following table gives the automatic draw for up to 64 qualifiers. Use the first column for 64 qualifiers, the second column for 32 qualifiers, and so on.

1	1	1	1	1	1
64					
33	32				
32					
17	17	16			
48					
49	16				
16					
9	9	9	8		
56					
41	24				
24					
25	25	8			
40					
57	8				
8					
5	5	5	5	4	
60					
37	28				
28					
21	21	12			
44					
53	12				
12					
13	13	13	4		
52					
45	20				
20					
29	29	4			
36					
61	4				
4					
3	3	3	3	3	2
62					
35	30				
30					
19	19	14			
46					
51	14				
14					
11	11	11	6		
54					
43	22				
22					
27	27	6			
38					
59	6				
6					
7	7	7	7	2	
58					
39	26				
26					
23	23	10			
42					
55	10				
10					
15	15	15	2		
50					
47	18				
18					
31	31	2			
34					
63	2				
2					

The LGU System of Handicapping

Effective 1 February 1985

CONTENTS

Section 1 Summary of Principal Changes Introduced in the 1985 Edition

1. The regulations have been rearranged.
2. Definitions have been added.
3. Gaining a handicap – a marker may mark for one player only.
4. In the event of the LGU teeing ground having been moved beyond the permitted limit of ten yards from the LGU permanent mark, scores cannot count for handicap nor for LGU Competitions unless a special Scratch Score has been allotted by the National Organisation.
5. Handicap 18* has been abolished except where the * denotes a handicap limited at Revision by the Table of Permitted Increases. A player remains on 19 until the average of four scores is $18^1/_2$ or less over SS.
6. Handicap 6–4; a new category, handicap 6–4, has been introduced, requiring six scores, all returned in competition on courses with a Scratch Score of not less than 70, to average $6^1/_3$ or less over SS.
7. Handicap categories have been designated A, B, C, D, E, as follows:

A=plus to 3
B=4 to 6
C=7 to 18
D=19 to 29
E=30 to 36*

8. Handicaps 3 and under: the handicap is the average of the best *ten* differentials, all returned in competition on courses with a SS of not less than 70, only six of which may be a Home Course. Scores from at least two other courses must be included.
9. Senior Veterans' and Disabled Persons' handicaps have been abolished, but clubs may continue to award unofficial handicaps to such members. The former basis for calculation is suggested as a guide, but an SS for the nine holes used will not be allotted by the National Organisation.
10. To retain a handicap a player in Category

B must return six scores annually and in Category A ten scores annually, except when increasing from A to B or from B to C, when the number is six or four, respectively.

11. Consideration will be given by the National Organisation to all applications for increase in handicap after illness or disablement, whether or not the handicap has lapsed.

12. Clubs are no longer permitted to except Running Competitions from the regulation governing immediate reduction of handicap.

Note: Suggestions for alterations or additions to the Handicapping System must be received by the General Administrator, Ladies' Golf Union, before 1 July in order to be considered for adoption in the following year.

Section II Definitions

Throughout the text defined terms are printed as underlined capitals when used for the first time.

Committee

The term *Committee* is deemed to refer to the Committee of the Ladies' Section. The term *Club Committee* refers to the Committee in charge of the course. Where the management of the club and/or course is entirely in the hands of the Ladies' Committee the term *Club Committee* shall be deemed to refer to such.

Completed Scores

A score is deemed completed for handicap purposes when a gross score has been entered on the card for each hole and the card has been checked and signed by both marker and player. The card should also show the player's name and the date.

Differential

The differential is the difference between the gross score and the Scratch Score of the course on which it is returned.

The average differential is the sum of the differentials divided by their number.

Extra Day Scores

An Extra Day Score is one which is not returned in competition.

Handicap Advisers

Handicap Advisers and their Deputies are persons appointed by the National Organisations to assist HANDICAP SECRETARIES in dealing with problems and exceptional cases, and to keep records of all players with handicaps under 4.

Handicap Secretary

A player's Handicap Secretary is the Handicap Secretary of her HOME CLUB. The Handicap Secretary of an INDIVIDUAL MEMBER of the LGU or of a NATIONAL ORGANISATION is the Secretary, respectively, of the LGU or of the National Organisation. The Handicap Secretary of a visitor from overseas, unless she joins an affiliated club as an annual member, is the Secretary, LGU.

Home Club

The Home Club is the club which a member of more than one club has chosen to be that where her handicap records shall be maintained and of which the Handicap Secretary shall be her Handicap Secretary.

Home Course

A Home Course is any course situated at and associated with a player's Home Club.

Individual Members

a. of the LGU: Players temporarily resident overseas are entitled to apply for individual membership of the LGU.

b. of the National Organisations: Players unable to become annual playing members of an affiliated club may apply to their National Organisation for individual membership.

Lapsed Handicaps

A handicap has lapsed if four scores have not been returned in an LGU year by Category C, D and E players, six scores by Category B players (unless increasing to Category C) and ten scores by Category A players (unless increasing to Category B).

LGU Tees and Teeing Grounds

The LGU tees, indicated by a permanent mark on the right-hand side of the tee, are those from which the SCRATCH SCORE has been fixed. The actual teeing ground in play (see Rules of Golf Definition) is indicated by *red* tee markers which, for the convenience of the greenkeeper, may be moved in any direction from the permanent mark provided the hole is not altered in length by more than ten yards.

Note: In the event of the teeing ground having been accidentally or otherwise moved beyond the permitted limit the score cannot count for handicap or for LGU Competitions unless a special Scratch Score has been allotted.

Live score

A live score is one which has been returned (in accordance with Regulation IV.4) in the current LGU year (1 February to 31 January) or in the preceding LGU year.

National Organisation

The National Organisations are: the English Ladies' Golf Association, the Irish Ladies' Golf Union, the Scottish Ladies' Golfing Association and the Welsh Ladies' Golf Union. In the case of overseas affiliated clubs for *National Organisation* read *LGU*.

Scratch Score

The Scratch Score of a course is the score expected of a Scratch player in normal Spring and Autumn conditions of wind and weather.

Section III Introduction

1. Basis of the System

The chief features of the LGU System of Handicapping are: that all handicaps shall be fixed on the basis of the LGU SCRATCH SCORE; that handicaps shall be assessed on actual scores returned and not on general form; and that the player's handicap shall be the same in every club.

2. Overseas Unions and Clubs

Overseas affiliated Unions and Clubs shall be permitted to make such adjustments to these regulations as may be deemed by their Executive Committee to be necessary on account of climatic or other conditions peculiar to the territory administered by them, so long as these adjustments do not depart from the fundamental principles of the LGU System of Handicapping as stated in the paragraph above or contravene the Rules of Golf as laid down by the Royal and Ancient Golf Club of St Andrews. The LGU must be informed as and when such adjustments are made.

3. Queries

Queries on LGU Regulations or the Rules of Golf should be submitted in accordance with the following procedures:

a. Committees of Affiliated Clubs should submit queries to their NATIONAL ORGANISATION.

b. Members of Affiliated Clubs may submit queries to their National Organisation and must have their statements signed as read on behalf of the Ladies' Committee. If there is any difference of opinion the Committee or opposing party should submit their own statement in writing.

c. Secretaries of Affiliated Clubs should refer queries on handicaps to their HANDICAP SECRETARY.

d. Handicap Secretaries of Affiliated Clubs should refer queries to their HANDICAP ADVISER or National Organisation, in that order.

e. Overseas Unions and Clubs. In the case of the clubs affiliated to an affiliated Ladies' Golf Union outside Great Britain and Ireland or directly affiliated to the LGU, queries should be submitted to the LGU. Statements should be signed as read on behalf of such Union or Club Committee.

Correspondence of this nature sent to the LGU and the National Organisations is filed for reference and cannot be returned.

Section IV The Player's Responsibilities and Rights

1. General

Playing off the Correct Handicap. It is the player's responsibility to know and to apply the Handicapping Regulations and to play off the correct handicap at all times. She should be able to produce a current Handicap Certificate when required to do so. In case of doubt or disagreement between the player and her Handicap Secretary as to what is the player's correct handicap, she should play from the lower until an official decision can be obtained from the Handicap Adviser or the National Organisation.

Handicap Reduction. Any reduction in handicap is automatic and comes into force immediately, *except*

- **i.** in the event of a tie in a competition, where this is resolved by a replay or a play-off; *and*
- **ii.** in a 36-, 54- or 72-hole competition played within eight days.

Playing away from Home. A player must notify her Handicap Secretary of any score (which might affect her handicap) returned by her on any course other than at her HOME CLUB.

2. Eligibility to Hold an LGU Handicap

An LGU handicap may be obtained and held by an amateur lady golfer who is *either*

a. an annual playing member, including a country, junior or life member (whether honorary or paying) of a club affiliated to the LGU either directly or through its National Organisation; *or*

b. an individual member of either the LGU or one of the four National Organisations;

c. a temporary member of an affiliated club, provided her membership is to last for a period of not less than twelve months.

Note: Should membership cease or expire the player's LGU handicap is no longer valid, but her scores remain LIVE if returned before such cessation or expiry.

3. How to Gain an LGU Handicap

Four scores must be returned on the course or courses of an LGU affiliated club or clubs, the Scratch Score of which must be not less than 60. Play must be in twos (threes and fours are not acceptable), no more than one player per marker, and must be in accordance with Regulations IV.4(a), (b), (c), (d) and (e).

4. Scores Acceptable for LGU Handicap

To be acceptable for handicap:

a. Scores must be returned in accordance with the Rules of Golf as approved by the Royal and Ancient Golf Club of St Andrews and with the Club's Local Rules and By-Laws, which must not contravene any R. & A. Rule or LGU Regulation. The gross score must be entered for every hole.

b. Scores must be returned on the course of an LGU affiliated club with an LGU Scratch Score of not less than 60 for players with a handicap of 36*–7 and of not less than 70 for players with a handicap of less than 7. Play must be from LGU tees. Scores returned on a course of which the player is not a member must be countersigned by an official of the local ladies' committee, who should certify that the Scratch Score is correctly stated. Completed cards should either be returned in person by the player to her Handicap Secretary without delay or left in the card box of the club visited, together with the name and address of the home club and the cost of postage.

Note: Scores returned on non-affiliated courses overseas (see lists on pages 92–100 of the Lady Golfer's Handbook) *may* count for handicap at the discretion of the LGU. Such cards, duly countersigned by a local official as showing the correct Scratch Score and accompanied by relevant information about local conditions, type of soil, terrain, course difficulty, etc., should be forwarded to the Secretary, Ladies' Golf Union, The Scores, St Andrews, Fife, with a stamped, addressed envelope to the Handicap Secretary of the player's Home Club.

c. Scores must be marked by an annual playing member of a recognised golf club, who has or has had a handicap. A marker should not mark the card of more than one player.

d. A score must be that of the first round of the day on any one course, except in the case of a competition consisting of 36 holes played on one day, when both scores shall count.

e. Scores may be returned when the following conditions apply:

i. Winter Conditions. Where, for the preservation of the course, the Club Committee has made a Local Rule that the ball may be teed or placed without penalty through the green.

ii. Summer Conditions. a. Where, for the preservation of the course, the Club Committee has made a Local Rule that the ball may be placed without penalty through the green; and **b.** where, for the preservation of the course, the Club Committee has made a Local Rule that tee pegs must be used through the green and a deduction from the Scratch Score of two strokes where more than nine holes are affected, and of one stroke where nine or fewer holes are affected, has been made by the Ladies' Committee (and notified to the area Scratch Score Committee member).

iii. The Green. Where, for the preservation of the green, a temporary hole (see Rules of Golf – Definition) is off but adjacent to the green, provided this does not alter the length of the hole by more than ten yards.

Note: LGU TEES. Where, for the preservation of the course, the teeing ground has been moved beyond the permitted ten yards, scores may count for handicap only if a special Scratch Score has been allotted by the National Organisation.

f. All scores returned in Stroke Competitions, even if declared null and void, count for LGU handicap purposes, subject to Regulations IV.4(a) to (e) above and provided competitors play from LGU TEES (see Definition and Note) and the SS of the course is not less than 60 (or not less than 70 for players with handicaps less than 7). Scores may be returned in twos, threes or fours, as arranged by the Committee.

Note: The exception to this is in a competition where the best-ball or better-ball score (see Rules of Golf Definitions) is to count.

g. EXTRA DAY SCORES must be returned in accordance with Regulations IV.4(a) to (e) and should normally be marked in twos, but at the discretion of the Committee may be marked in threes, in which case a notice to this effect must be posted on the Notice Board (but see Regulation IV.3 for gaining a first handicap). Extra Day Scores marked in fours are NOT acceptable.

h. Gross scores returned in a competition from which a player has been disqualified under Rule of Golf 6–2b on her nett score shall count for handicap.

5. Calculation of an LGU Handicap

Handicaps are divided into five categories: Silver Division – A, B, C – and Bronze Division – D and E. Handicaps are calculated as follows, on the basis of live scores returned in accordance with Regulation IV.4 above:

Note 1: For handicaps 36*–7 scores must be returned on courses with a Scratch Score of not less than 60, and for handicaps 6 and under scores must be returned on courses with a Scratch Score of not less than 70.

Note 2: In all calculations above Scratch $^1/_2$, two-thirds and three-quarters count as 1 and one-third, one-quarter count as 0. In all calculations below Scratch fractions of $^1/_2$ and less count as 0, fractions greater than $^1/_2$ count as 1.

a. *Bronze Division*

(i) **Category E, 36–30.** The handicap is the difference between the player's best live score and the Scratch Score of the course on which it was played, i.e. the handicap is her best DIFFERENTIAL. If the differential is more than 36 the handicap is 36* (*Example E* [1]). If the differential is 36–30 then that is the handicap (*Example E* [2]). If the best differential is less than 30 the handicap is 30 until the average of the *two* best differentials is less than $29^1/_2$ (*Example E* [3]).

EXAMPLES:

E[1] **Best gross score**	**117**	**SS 72**	**Differential**	**45**
				Handicap 36*
E[2] **Best gross score**	**102**	**SS 69**	**Differential**	**33**
				Handicap 33
E[3] **Best gross scores**	**101**	**SS 74**	**Differential**	**27**
	106	**SS 70**	**Previous best differential**	**36**
			Average differential	**31½**
				Handicap 30

(ii) **Category D,29–19.** The handicap is the average of the two best differentials (*Examples D*[1], *D*[2]), but if the average is less than $18^1/_2$ the handicap is 19 until the average of the *four* best differentials is less than $18^1/_2$ (*Example D* [3]).

EXAMPLES:

D[1] Gross score	99	SS 73	Best differential	26
Gross score	104	SS 73	Previous best differential	31
		Average differential		28½
				Handicap 29
D[2] Gross score	95	SS 71	Best differential	24
Gross score	98	SS 70	Previous best differential	28
		Average differential		26
				Handicap 26

D[3] Gross scores	SS	Best differentials		
87	72	15		
92	72	20	Average 17½ but ...	**Handicap 19**
96	73	23		
94	71	23		
Average diff (of four)		20¼		**Handicap 19**

b. *Silver Division*

(i). **Category C,18–7.** The handicap is the average of the four best differentials (*Example C* [1]), but if this average is less than $6^1/_2$ the handicap is 7 until the conditions for Category B are fulfilled (*Example C* [2]).

EXAMPLES:

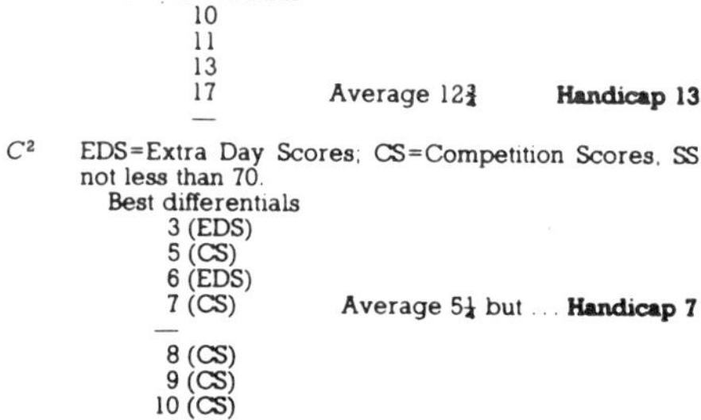

C[1] Best differentials

Best differentials		
10		
11		
13		
17	Average 12¾	**Handicap 13**

C[2] EDS=Extra Day Scores; CS=Competition Scores, SS not less than 70.

Best differentials		
3 (EDS)		
5 (CS)		
6 (EDS)		
7 (CS)	Average 5¼ but ...	**Handicap 7**
8 (CS)		
9 (CS)		
10 (CS)		
9 (CS)		

Average differential of six Comp scores = 8 **Handicap 7**

(ii) **Category B, 6–4.** The handicap is the average of the six best differentials of scores returned in competition on courses with a Scratch Score of not less than 70 (*Example B* [1]), but if this average is less than $3^1/_2$ the handicap is 4 until the conditions for Category A are fulfilled (*Example B* [2]).

EXAMPLES:

B[1] **Best differentials from competition scores on courses with a SS of not less than 70:**

7		
5		
5		
6		
4		
4	Average differential 5⅙	**Handicap 5**

B[2] **Best differentials from competition scores on courses with a SS of not less than 70: H1, H2=Home Courses, A1, A2 etc.=Away Courses.**

3 (H1)		
5 (H2)		
4 (H1)		
2 (H1)		
2 (H1)		
3 (A1)	Average differential 3⅙ but...	**Handicap 4**
6 (A1)		
7 (A2)		
6 (H2)		
8 (A1)	Average differential 4.6	**Handicap 4**

(iii) **Category A, 3 and under.** To obtain a handicap of 3 or under a player must return at least ten scores in competition, on courses with a Scratch Score of not less than 70. Only six of these scores may be from a Home Course, and the remaining four must be from at least two different Away courses. The handicap is the average of the ten best differentials so obtained (*Examples A* [1] *and A* [2]).

EXAMPLES:

A[1] **Best differentials from competition scores on courses with a SS of not less than 70:**

0 (H)
+1 (H)
+1 (H)
0 (H)
3 (H)
0 (H)
1 (A1)
0 (A1)
1 (A2)
3 (A2) Average differential 0.6

Handicap 1

A[2] Best differentials from competition scores on courses with a SS of not less than 70:

+1 (H)
+1 (H)
+2 (H)
1 (A1)
+2 (H)
+1 (A2)
0 (H)
+1 (H)
2 (A3)
0 (A1) Average differential +0.5

Handicap Scratch (+0.5=0)

6. Annual Revision of Handicaps and Lapsed Handicaps

a. General

On 31 January each year all handicaps shall be recalculated on the basis of scores returned during the preceding twelve months and in accordance with the Regulations in force during that period. Any increase in handicap resulting from such recalculation shall be limited by the Table of Permitted Increases (Table I) for Revised Handicaps set out below. At no other time during the year may a player's handicap be increased (except in accordance with Regulation IV.7(b) or (c)).

TABLE I – TABLE OF PERMITTED INCREASES FOR REVISED HANDICAPS

Handicaps plus to 6 may go up 1 stroke.
Handicaps 7 to 34 may go up 2 strokes.
Handicap 35 may go up 1 stroke.

A handicap limited by the Table of Permitted Increases for Revised Handicaps shall be marked with an asterisk until the calculation on live scores results in a handicap equal to or less than that held.

b. Minimum Number of Scores to be Returned

Handicap Categories E, D, C. To retain a handicap players with handicaps 36*–7 must have returned at least four scores.

Handicap Category B. To retain a handicap players with handicaps 6–4 must have returned at least six scores. If six scores have been returned but the other conditions for this category have not been fulfilled, the handicap shall be that held prior to Revision and shall be marked with a ∅ until the appropriate scores have been returned and the calculation results in a handicap equal to or less than that held prior to Revision.

Exception: If players with handicap 6 prior to Revision have returned at least four (not necessarily all in competition and on courses with a SS of 70 or more) and the average of the best four is 6½ or more, the handicap shall be retained and shall be calculated in accordance with Regulations governing handicaps 7–18 and the Table of Permitted Increases (Table I) for Revised Handicaps.

Handicap Category A. To retain a handicap players with handicaps 3 and under must have returned at least ten scores. If ten scores have been returned in competition on a course or courses with a SS of not less than 70, the handicap may be increased by one stroke if the scores average 0.5 or more above the handicap held prior to Revision. It shall be marked with a ∅ if the necessary scores on "away" courses are not included. If ten scores have been returned but not all in competition and on a course or courses with a SS of 70 or more, the handicap shall be that held prior to Revision and shall be marked with a ∅ until all the necessary conditions have been fulfilled and the calculation results in a handicap equal to or less than that held prior to Revision.

Exception: If players with handicap 3 prior to Revision have returned at least six scores in competition on a course or courses with a SS of not less than 70, and the average of the best six is 3½ or more, the handicap shall be retained and shall be calculated in accordance with Regulations governing handicaps 4-6 and the Table of Permitted Increases (Table I) for Revised Handicaps.

c. Lapsed Handicaps

A handicap lapses if a player has not returned the minimum number of scores necessary to retain a handicap (see **b.** above). When a player's handicap has lapsed she does not have a valid handicap until the conditions have been fulfilled to regain it (see **d.** below).

d. To Regain a Handicap which has Lapsed

Handicap Categories E, D, C. To regain a handicap which has lapsed players with handicaps 36*–7 must return the number of extra Day Scores necessary to increase the number of *live* scores to four. The handicap shall then be calculated in accordance with Regulations, but it shall be limited by the Table of Permitted Increases (Table II) for Lapsed Handicaps set out below and must be confirmed, before use, by the player's Handicap Secretary.

Handicap Category B. To regain a handicap which has lapsed players with handicaps 6–4 must return the necessary Extra Day Scores on courses with a Scratch Score of not less than 70 to increase the number of *live* scores to six. The handicap shall then be calculated in accordance with Regulations (except that the scores need not be returned in competition), but it shall be limited by the Table of Permitted Increases (Table II) for Lapsed Handicaps set out below and must be confirmed, before use, by the player's Handicap Secretary. Until scores returned fulfil all the conditions necessary for this Category of player, the handicap shall be marked with a ∅.

Handicap Category A. To regain a handicap which has lapsed players with handicaps under 4 must return the necessary Extra Day Scores on courses with a Scratch Score of not less than 70 to increase the number of *live* scores to ten.

The handicap shall then be calculated in accordance with Regulations (except that the scores need not be returned in competition), but it shall be limited by the table of Permitted Increases (Table II) for Lapsed Handicaps set out below and must be confirmed, before use, by the player's Handicap Secretary. Until scores returned fulfil all the conditions necessary for this Category of player, the handicap shall be marked with a ∅.

Transition to a Higher Category. The number of scores required to regain a handicap by players in categories A or B should be determined after taking into account the scores returned and the Table (II) of Permitted Increases for Lapsed Handicaps. For instance, a player previously in Category A, after a lapse of several years may require only six scores, and similarly a player previously in Category B may require only four, if the former handicap category is not maintained or bettered by the scores returned.

TABLE II – TABLE OF PERMITTED INCREASES FOR LAPSED HANDICAPS

(i) If lapsed for less than one year the handicap shall be limited to one stroke higher than that last held.

(ii) If lapsed for more than one year but less than two years the handicap shall be limited to two strokes higher than that last held.

(iii) For each year in excess of two the handicap may be increased by a further stroke.

EXAMPLES:

	Handicap Lapsed	*Necessary EDS Returned*	*Max Inc over Previous H'cap*
(i)	January 31 1981	1981–82 (LGU year)	1 stroke (less than one year)
(ii)		1982–83 (LGU year)	2 strokes (one-two years)
(iii)		1983–84 (LGU year)	3 strokes (two+one year)
		1984–85 (LGU year)	4 strokes (two+two years)
		1985–86 (LGU year)	5 strokes (two+three years) and so on

A handicap limited by the Table of Permitted Increases for Lapsed Handicaps shall be marked with an asterisk.

7. Special Categories of Handicap

a. Juniors. An LGU Junior handicap (limit 45) may be obtained and held by any girl who is a junior, i.e. who has not reached her twelfth birthday on 1 January, by returning two scores over nine specified holes. Any nine holes on the course may be chosen to make up the round, at the discretion of the club, and a special SS for those holes must be obtained from the National Organisation. Each score returned, and the special SS for the nine holes, shall be doubled in order to arrive at the number of strokes above SS. Handicaps will be reduced in accordance with Regulations (one card 45–30, etc.). Juniors may hold a standard LGU handicap but may not hold both.

To retain a Junior LGU handicap two scores over nine holes must be returned annually.

An LGU Junior handicap shall be acceptable for all junior competitions, and these Regulations shall apply to all players with Junior handicaps. Handicap Certificates for LGU Junior handicaps will be issued by the Handicap Secretary and *the date and year when the player will attain her twelfth birthday must be entered on the Handicap Certificate.*

b. Former Professional Golfers. On reinstatement as an amateur a player who has been a professional golfer must apply for a handicap to the Secretary, LGU. The Executive Council shall, at their discretion, allot a handicap of not more than Scratch on the basis of live scores returned during the player's period of probation in accordance with the Regulations for Extra Day Scores and those governing handicaps of 3 and under.

For the first two years after reinstatement the player's Handicap Secretary must submit all scores returned twice yearly on 1 January and 1 July to the General Administrator, LGU, The Scores, St. Andrews, Fife, KY16 9AT. Handicaps will be reviewed by the Executive Council and revised at their discretion.

c. After Serious Illness and Disablement. A person wishing to regain a handicap or have her handicap reassessed after serious illness or disablement may apply through her Club Committee to the National Organisation with all relevant details, including a minimum of four live scores returned, so that consideration may be given to the circumstances and the player may obtain a realistic handicap. Handicaps shall be adjusted in accordance with Regulations.

d. Individual Members and Visitors from Overseas. The handicaps of individual members of the LGU or of the National Organisations shall be managed by the Secretary of the LGU or of the appropriate National Organisation. All scores returned must be countersigned by the Handicap Secretary of the club at which they were returned and forwarded to the appropriate Secretary, who will act as Handicap Secretary for these players.

Handicaps of visitors from overseas who are not annual playing members of an affiliated club in Great Britain or Ireland shall be managed by the Secretary of the LGU, to whom scores should be forwarded after countersignature as above.

8. Membership of More than One Club

a. A member belonging to more than one affiliated club must inform the Ladies' Secretary and Handicap Secretary of each club of the names of other affiliated clubs to which she belongs and also of any scores (together with the Scratch Score) which may affect her handicap.

b. Handicap Secretary. If a player is a member of more than one club she must decide which club she wishes to be her Home Club for handicap purposes and notify the Ladies' Secretary of that club accordingly. A player's Handicap Secretary shall be the Handicap Secretary of her Home Club.

c. A member changing her Home Club must take her LGU4 sheet and her Handicap Certificate to the Handicap Secretary of her new Home Club.

d. A member joining an additional club must inform the Ladies' Secretary and the Handicap Secretary of such club of her existing or lapsed handicap, and of the scores, with relative dates, on which it was gained, and also the names of all clubs of which she is or has been a member.

e. A member shall play on the same handicap at all clubs.

Editor's note: Minor amendments to the above came into effect on 1 February 1989, but were not available at the time of going to press.

For details of the following, please refer to the Lady Golfer's Handbook:

Scratch Scores
LGU Tees and Teeing Grounds in Play
Starting Places
Handicap Records and Certificates
LGU Silver and Bronze Medal Competitions
LGU Gold and Silver Medal Competitions
LGU Challenge Bowl Competitions
Coronation Foursomes Competition
LGU Pendant Competition
Australian Spoons Competitions

INDEX	Section	No
Acceptable scores for handicap	IV	4.a-h
Additional club		
joining an	IV	8.d
Annual playing member		
eligible to hold LGU handicap	IV	2.a
Average differential		
Definition	II	
Away from home		
scores countersigned by local official	IV	4.b
scores returned to Handicap Secretary	IV	1 and 4.b
Basis of the System	III	1
Both scores count for handicap in 36-hole competition	IV	4.d
Bronze Division		
calculation of handicap	IV	5.a
Calculation of handicap	IV	5
Categories of handicap		
special	IV	7.a–d
Changes to the Handicapping Regulations		
summary of principal	I	
Changing Home Club	IV	8.c
Committee		
Definition	II	
Competition scores		
acceptable for handicap	IV	4.f
handicaps under 7	IV	5.b (ii) and (iii)
Competitions null and void		
scores count for handicap	IV	4.f
Completed scores		
Definition	II	
Deduction from SS in summer conditions	IV	4.e (ii)
Definitions	II	
Differential		
definition	II	
basis of handicap calculations	IV	5
Disablement		
reassessment of handicap after	IV	7.c
Eligibility to hold LGU handicap	IV	2
Extra Day Scores		
Acceptable for handicap	IV	4.g
Definition	II	
To increase lives scores to four	IV	6.d
First round of the day	IV	4.d
Former Professional golfers		
handicaps for	IV	7.b
Gaining a handicap	IV	3
Green		
temporary hole for preservation of the course	IV	4.e (iii)
Gross hole for every hole	IV	4.a
acceptable for handicap if disqualified on nett score	IV	4.h
Handicap Advisers		
Definition	II	
Queries from Handicap Secretaries	III	3.d

Governing Bodies

Home Unions

Golfing Union of Ireland

The Golfing Union of Ireland, founded in 1891, embraces 263 Clubs. Its objects are:

(1) Securing the federation of the various Clubs.

(2) Arranging Amateur Championships, Inter-Provincial and Inter-Club Competitions, and International Matches.

(3) Securing a uniform standard of handicapping.

(4) Providing for advice and assistance to affiliated Clubs in all matters appertaining to Golf, and generally to promote the game in every way, in which this can be better done by the Union than by individual Clubs.

Its functions include the holding of the *Close* Championship for Amateur Golfers and Tournaments for Team Matches.

Its organisation consists of Provincial Councils in each of the four Provinces elected by the Clubs in the Province – each province electing a limited number of delegates to the Central Council which meets annually.

Secretary Ivan ER Dickson, Glencar House, 81 Eglinton Road, Donnybrook, Dublin 4. *Tel* Dublin 694111.

Welsh Golfing Union

The Welsh Golfing Union was founded in 1895 and is the second oldest of the four National Unions. Unlike the other Unions it is an association of Golf Clubs and Golfing Organisations. The present membership is 118. For the purpose of electing the Executive Council, Wales and Gwent are divided into ten districts which between them return 22 members.

The objects of the Union are:

(a) To take any steps which may be deemed necessary to further the interests of the game in Wales and Gwent.

(b) To hold a Championship Meeting or Meetings each year.

(c) To encourage, financially and/or otherwise, Inter-Club, Inter-County, and International Matches, and such other events as may be authorised by the Council.

(d) To assist in setting up and maintaining a uniform system of Handicapping.

(e) To assist in the maintenance of the Sports Turf Research Institute.

(f) To co-operate with the Royal and Ancient Golf Club of St Andrews through the medium of the Council of National Golf Unions.

Note The union recognises the Royal and Ancient Golf Club of St Andrews as the ruling authority.

Secretary DG Lee, 5 Park Place, Cardiff, South Glamorgan. *Tel* (0222) 238467.

The Scottish Golf Union

The Scottish Golf Union was founded in 1920 and embraces 660 clubs. Subject to the stipulation and declaration that the Union recognises the Royal and Ancient Golf Club of St Andrews as the Ruling Authority in the game of golf, the objects of the Union are:

(a) To foster and maintain a high standard of Amateur Golf in Scotland and to administer and organise and generally act as the governing body of amateur golf in Scotland.

(b) To institute and thereafter carry through annually a Scottish Amateur Championship, a Scottish Open Amateur Stroke Play Championship and other such competitions and matches as they consider appropriate.

(c) To administer and apply the rules of the Standard Scratch Score and Handicapping Scheme as approved by the Council of National Golf Unions from time to time.

(d) To deal with other matters of general or local interest to amateur golfers in Scotland.

The Union's organisation consists of Area Committees covering the whole of Scotland. There are 16 Areas, each having its own Association or Committee elected by the Clubs in that particular area and each Area Association or Committee elects one delegate to serve on the Executive of the Union.

Secretary JW Hume, The Cottage, 181A Whitehouse Road, Barnton, Edinburgh EH4 6BY. *Tel* 031-339 7546.

The English Golf Union

The English Golf Union was founded in 1924 and embraces 34 County Unions with over 1,350 affiliated clubs, 22 clubs overseas, and over 130 Golfing Societies and Associations. Its objects are:

(1) To further the interests of Amateur Golf in England.
(2) To assist in maintaining a uniform system of handicapping.
(3) To arrange an English Championship; an English Stroke Play Championship; an English County Championship, International and other Matches and Competitions.
(4) To co-operate with the Royal and Ancient Golf Club of St Andrews and the Council of National Golf Unions.
(5) To co-operate with other National Golf Unions and Associations in such manner as may be decided.

Secretary K Wright, 1–3 Upper King Street, Leicester LE1 6XF. *Tel* (0533) 553042.

The Council of National Golf Unions

At a meeting of Representatives of Golf Unions and Associations in Great Britain and Ireland, called at the special request of the Scottish Golf Union, and held in York, on 14th February, 1924, resolutions were adopted from which the Council of National Golf Unions was constituted.

The Council holds an Annual Meeting in March, and such other meetings as may be necessary. Two representatives are elected from each national Home Union – England, Scotland, Ireland and Wales – and hold office until the next Annual meeting when they are eligible for re-election.

The principal function of the Council, as laid down by the York Conference, was to formulate a system of Standard Scratch Scores and Handicapping, and to co-operate with the Royal and Ancient Championship Committee in matters coming under their jurisdiction. The responsibilities undertaken by the Council at the instance of the Royal and Ancient Golf Club or the National Unions are as follows:

1. The Standard Scratch Score and Handicapping Scheme, formulated in March, 1926, approved by the Royal and Ancient, and last revised in 1983.
2. The nomination of two members on the Board of Management of The Sports Turf Research Institute, with an experimental station at St Ives, Bingley, Yorkshire.
3. The management of the Annual Amateur International Matches between the four countries – England, Scotland, Ireland and Wales.

Hon Sec Alan Thirlwell, Formby GC, Golf Road, Formby, Liverpool L37 1LQ. *Tel* (070 48) 72164.

United States Golf Association

The USGA is the national governing body of golf. Its single most important goal is preserving the integrity and values of the game.

Formed on 22nd December, 1894, a year when two clubs proclaimed different US Amateur Champions, representatives of five clubs met at a dinner at the Calumet Club in New York City. They created a central governing body to establish uniform rules, to conduct national championships and to nurture the virtues of sportsmanship in golf.

The names of the standing committees give an idea of what the USGA does:

Rules of Golf, Championship, Amateur Status and Conduct, Implements and Ball, Handicap, Women's, Sectional Affairs, Green Section, Public Links, Women's Public Links, Junior Championship, Girls' Junior, Senior Championship, Senior Women's Championship, Bob Jones Award, Museum, Green Section Award, Finance, Public Information, Membership, Regional Association, Associates, Intercollegiate Relations, Mid-Amateur Championship, International Team Selection, Development, Turfgrass Research, Nominating.

The USGA, as the governing body of the sport in the United States, makes and interprets the Rules of Golf in co-operation with the Royal & Ancient Golf Club of St Andrews, Scotland; developed and maintains the national system of handicapping; controls the standards of the ball and the implements of the game; works in turfgrass and turf management; and, generally speaking, preserves and promotes the game.

The Professional Golfers' Association

The Professional Golfers' Association was founded in 1901 to promote interest in the game of golf; to protect and advance the mutual and trade interests of its members; to arrange and hold meetings and tournaments periodically for the members; to institute and operate funds for the benefit of the members; to assist the members to obtain employment; and effect any other objects of a like nature as may be determined from time to time by the Association.

Membership Regulations

There shall be nine classes of membership:

Class A– Members engaged as the nominated professional at a PGA Training Establishment in one of the seven Regions

Class B– Members engaged by Class A and Class G members to work at PGA Establishments in one of the seven Regions
Class C– Tournament playing members
Class D– Associate Members
Class E– Special Members
Class F– Members of the Women's Professional Golf Association
Class G– Members engaged as the nominated professional at PGA Establishments with limited facilities in one of the seven Regions
Class H– Overseas members
Class HLM– Honorary Life Member

The Management of the Association is under the overall direction and control of a Board. The Association is divided into seven Regions each of which employs a full-time secretary and runs tournaments for the benefit of members within its Region.

The Association is responsible for arranging and obtaining sponsorship of the Club Professionals' Championship, PGA Cup matches, Seniors' Championship, PGA Assistants' Championship, Assistants' Match Play Championship and other National Championships.

Anyone who intends to become a club professional must serve a minimum of three years in registration and qualify at the PGA Training School before election as a full Member.

The Professional Golfers' Association: National Headquarters, Apollo House, The Belfry, Sutton Coldfield, West Midlands B76 9PT.
Tel (0675)70333. *Fax* (0675) 2881

PGA European Tour

To be eligible to become a member of the PGA European Tour a player must possess certain minimum standards which shall be determined by the Tournament Committee. In 1976 a Qualifying School for potential new members was introduced to be held annually. The leading players are awarded cards allowing them to compete in all PGA European Tour tournaments.

In 1985 the PGA European Tour became ALL EXEMPT with no more Monday pre-qualifying. Full details can be obtained from the Wentworth Headquarters: Ken Schofield, Executive Director, PGA European Tour, Wentworth Club, Wentworth Drive, Virginia Water, Surrey GU25 4LS. *Tel* (09904) 2881.

Womens Professional Golfers European Tour

The Womens Professional Golfers European Tour (WPGET) was founded in 1988 to further the development of Ladies, Professional Golf throughout Europe and its membership is open to all nationalities. An Amateur wishing to join the Tour must have a handicap of 1 or less and is on probation for 8 rounds in Tournaments, during which she must attain certain playing standards as determined by the Committee.

Full details can be obtained from Joe Flanagan, Executive Director, WPGET. The Tytherington Club, Macclesfield, Cheshire SK10 2JP. *Tel* (0625) 611444.

Government of the Amateur and Open Golf Championship

In December 1919 on the invitation of the clubs who had hitherto controlled the amateur and Open Golf Championships, the Royal and Ancient took over the government of those events. These two championships are controlled by a committee appointed by the Royal and Ancient Golf Club of St Andrews. The Committee shall be called the Royal and Ancient Golf Club Championship Committee and shall consist of twelve members (who shall be members of the Club) to be elected by the Club, and additional members not exceeding two (who shall not necessarily be members of the Club) from Golf Authorities both at home and abroad, who shall be invited annually to join the Committee by the twelve members elected by the Club. Such invited members shall, irrespective of the date of their invitation to become members of the Committee, remain members only until the date of the first Autumn Meeting occurring after the date of their invitation to become members. During their term of office, such invited members (who are not already members of the Club), shall be admitted as honorary temporary members of the Club. Two Business Members, who shall be members of the Club, shall be co-opted on the nomination of the Chairman of the Championship Committee after consultation with the Chairman of the General Committee.

Secretary: MF Bonallack OBE, Royal and Ancient Golf Club, St Andrews. Telegrams *Ancient St Andrews. Tel* 0334 72112/3. *Telex* 76348.

LGU

The Ladies' Golf Union was founded in 1893 with the following objects:

(1) To promote the interests of the game of Golf.
(2) To obtain a uniformity of the rules of the game by establishing a representative legislative authority.
(3) To establish a uniform system of handicapping.
(4) To act as a tribunal and court of reference on points of uncertainty.

(5) To arrange the Annual Championship Competition and obtain the funds necessary for that purpose.

Ninety years on only the language has changed, the present Constitution defining the objects as:

(1) To uphold the rules of the game, to advance and safeguard the interests of women's golf and to decide all doubtful and disputed points in connection therewith.
(2) To maintain, regulate and enforce the LGU system of handicapping.
(3) To employ the funds of the Union in such a manner as shall be deemed best for the interests of women's golf, with power to borrow or raise money to use for the same purpose.
(4) To maintain and regulate International events, Championships and Competitions held under the LGU regulations and to promote the interests of Great Britain and Ireland in Ladies International Golf.
(5) To make, maintain and publish such regulations as may be considered necessary for the above purposes.

The constituents of the LGU are:

Home Countries. The English Ladies' Golf Association (founded 1952), the Irish Ladies' Golf Union (founded 1893), the Scottish Ladies' Golfing Association (founded 1904), the Welsh Ladies' Golf Union (founded 1904), plus ladies' societies, girls' schools and ladies' clubs affiliated to these organisations.

Overseas. Affiliated ladies' golf unions and golf clubs in the Commonwealth and any other overseas ladies' golfing organisation affiliated to the LGU.

Individual lady members of clubs within the above categories are regarded as *members of the LGU.*

The Rules of the Game and of Amateur Status, which the LGU is bound to uphold, are those published by the Royal and Ancient Golf Club of St Andrews.

In endeavouring to fulfil its responsibilities towards advancing and safeguarding women's golf, the LGU maintains contact with other golfing organisations – the Royal and Ancient Golf Club of St Andrews, the Council of National Golf Unions, the Golf Foundation, the Central Council of Physical Recreation, the Sports Council, the Women's Professional Golf European Tour and the Women's Committee of the United States Golf Association. This contact ensures that the LGU is informed of developments and projected developments and has an opportunity to comment upon and to influence the future of the game for women.

Either directly or through its constituent national organisations the LGU advises and is the ultimate authority on doubts or disputes which may arise in connection with the handicapping system and regulations governing competitions played under LGU conditions.

The handicapping system, together with the system for assessment of Scratch Scores, is formulated and published by the LGU. The handicapping system undergoes detailed revision and is republished every four years, in the year following the revision of the Rules of Golf. Handicap Certificates are provided by the LGU and distributed through the national organisations and appointed club officials to every member of every affiliated club which has fulfilled the requisite conditions for obtaining an LGU handicap. No other form of certificate is recognised as evidence of an LGU handicap.

The funds of the LGU are administered by the Hon. Treasurer on the authority of the Executive Council, and the accounts are submitted annually for adoption in General Meeting.

All ladies' British Open Championships and the Home International matches, at both senior and junior level, are organised annually by the LGU. International events involving a British or a combined British and Irish team are organised and controlled by the LGU when held in this country and the LGU acts as the co-ordinating body for the Commonwealth Tournament in whichever of the four participating countries it is held, four-yearly, by rotation. The LGU selects and trains the teams, provides the uniforms and pays all the expenses of participation, whether held in this country or overseas. The LGU also maintains and regulates certain competitions played under handicap, such as Medal Competitions, Coronation Foursomes, Challenge Bowls, Australian Spoons and the LGU Pendant Competition.

The day-to-day administration of certain of the LGU responsibilities in the home countries is undertaken by the national organisations, such as that concerned with handicapping regulations, Scratch Scores, and the organisation of Challenge Bowls and Australian Spoons Competitions.

Membership subscriptions to the LGU are assessed on a per capita basis of the club membership. To save unnecessary expense and duplication of administrative work in the home countries LGU subscriptions are collected by the national organisations along with their own, and transmitted in bulk to the LGU.

Policy is determined and control over all the LGU's activities is exercised by an Executive Council of eight members – two each elected by the English, Irish, Scottish and Welsh national organisations. The Chairman is elected annually by the Councillors and may hold office for one year only, during which term her place on the Council is taken by her Deputy and she has no vote other than a casting vote. The President and the Hon. Treasurer of the Union also attend and take part in Council meetings but with no vote. The Council meets five times a year.

The Annual General Meeting is held in January. The formal business includes presentation of the Report of the Executive Council for the previous year and of the Accounts for the last completed financial year, the election or re-election of President, Vice-Presidents, Hon. Treasurer and Auditors, and a report of the election of Councillors and their Deputies for the ensuing year and of the European Technical Committee representative. Voting is on the following basis: Executive Council, one each (8); members in the four home countries, one per national organisation (4) and in addition one per 100 affiliated clubs or part thereof (at present 22); one per overseas Commonwealth Union with a membership of 50 or more clubs (at present 3), and one per 100 individually affiliated clubs (1).

The Lady Golfer's Handbook is published annually by the LGU and is distributed free to all affiliated clubs and organisations and to appointed Handicap Advisers. It is also available for sale to anyone interested. It contains the regulations for handicapping and Scratch Score assessment, for British Championships and international matches (with results for the past twenty years) and for LGU competitions, and sets out the Rules of the Union. It also lists every affiliated organisation, with names and addresses of officials, and every affiliated club, with Scratch Score, county of affiliation, number of members, and other useful information.

Miscellaneous Rulings

Limitation of the Golf Ball

At the Autumn Business Meeting, 1920, of the Royal and Ancient Club the following resolution was adopted:

On and after 1st May, 1921, the weight of the ball shall not be greater than 1.62 ounces avoirdupois, and the size not less than 1.62 inches in diameter. The Rules of Golf Committee and the Executive Committee of the United States Golf Association will take whatever steps they think necessary to limit the powers of the ball with regard to distance, should any ball of greater power be introduced.

The United States Golf Association intimated, May, 1929, that they had resolved to adopt *an easier and pleasanter ball for the average golfer*, and from 1st January, 1931, to 31st December, 1932, the standards of specification of the ball in competitions under their jurisdiction was not less than 1.68 inches in diameter, and not greater than 1.55 ounces in weight. In January, 1932, another alteration was made in the specification of the ball, the weight being increased to 1.62 and the size remaining the same, viz, not less than 1.68.

The Royal Canadian Golf Association adopted the USGA specification as from 1st January, 1948. The effect of this difference between the legislation of the Royal and Ancient, the Royal Canadian Golf Association, and the USGA is that golfers competing in the United States and Canada must use a ball that is larger, but no heavier, than the ball which is legal in other parts of the world.

In May, 1951, a special committee was set up by the Royal and Ancient Golf Club and the United States Golf Association to discuss the desirability of uniformity in the Rules of Golf and the form and make of clubs and balls. The committee recommended that both sizes of ball (1.62 inches and 1.68 inches in diameter both having the same weight, 1.62 ounces) be legal in all countries. At their autumn meeting the United States Golfers' Association rejected this proposal but agreed that in international team competition in the United States, the size of the ball be not less than 1.62 inches in diameter.

The matter of a uniform ball world-wide was investigated by a special committee from the R&A and the USGA but was dropped in 1974 when the two bodies could not reach agreement.

A maximum initial velocity standard of not greater than 250 feet per second on special apparatus was introduced by the R&A in 1976.

The R&A issues lists of conforming golf balls annually.

Limitation of Number of Clubs

At the Business Meeting of the Royal and Ancient Golf Club, May, 1937, the Rules of Golf Committee submitted a recommendation that on and after 1st January, 1938, the preamble to the Rules of Golf shall read: *The game of golf consists of a ball being played from a teeing ground to a hole by successive strokes with clubs (not exceeding fourteen in number) and balls made in conformity with the directions laid down in the clause on 'Form and make of golf clubs and balls'.* The recommendation was not approved by the members.

In September, 1938, at the Business Meeting of the Royal and Ancient, a similar recommendation was approved by the members, and the limitation of the number of clubs to fourteen became operative as from 1st May, 1939. The United States Golf Association decided to limit the number of clubs to fourteen as from 1st January, 1938.

Steel-Shafted Clubs

The Royal and Ancient Golf Club authorised steel shafts, November, 1929, in the following announcement: *The Rules of Golf Committee have decided that steel shafts, as approved by the Rules of Golf Committee are declared to conform with the requirements of the clause in the Rules of Golf on the form and make of golf clubs.*

Laminated Shafts

The Rules of Golf Committee on 5th December, 1932, announced that clubs with laminated shafts built entirely of wood are permissible.

Recognised Golf Clubs

The Rules of Golf Committee, in answering a query, gave the opinion that a recognised Golf Club is one which has regularly appointed office-bearers.

The English Golf Union decided that a recognised Golf Club for the purpose of competitive golf in England is a golf club affiliated to the English Golf Union through its County Union, or where there is no County Union direct to the English Golf Union as an Associate Member.

Championship Conditions

Men

The Amateur Championship

The Championship, until 1982, was decided entirely by match play over 18 holes except for the final which was over 36 holes. Since 1983 the Championship has comprised two stroke-play rounds of 18 holes each from which the top 64 scores over the 36 holes qualify for the match-play stages. Matches are over 18 holes except for the final which is over 36 holes.

Full particulars of conditions of entry and method of play can be obtained from the Secretary, Championship Committee, Royal and Ancient Golf Club, St Andrews, Fife KY16 9JD.

The Seniors' Open Amateur

The Championship consists of 18 holes on each of two days, the lowest 50 scores over the 36 holes and any tying for 50th place then playing a further 18 holes the following day.

Conditions for entry include:

Entrants must have attained the age of 55 years prior to the first day on which the Championship is played.

Entries are limited to 252 competitors, the higher handicaps being balloted out if necessary.

Full particulars of conditions of entry and method of play can be obtained from the Secretary, Championship Committee, Royal and Ancient Golf Club, St Andrews, Fife KY16 9JD.

National Championships

The English, Scottish, Irish and Welsh Amateur Championships are played by holes, each match consisting of one round of 18 holes except the final which is contested over 36 holes.

Full particulars of conditions of entry and method of play can be obtained from the secretaries of the respective national Unions.

English Open Amateur Stroke Play Championship

The Championship consists of one round of 18 holes on each of two days after which the leading 45 and those tying for 45th place play a further two rounds. The remainder are eliminated.

Conditions for entry include:

Entrants must have a handicap not exceeding three.

Where the entries exceed 130, an 18-hole qualifying round is held the day before the Championship. Certain players are exempt from qualifying.

Full particulars of conditions of entry and method of play can be obtained from the Secretary, English Golf Union, 1-3 Upper King Street, Leicester LE1 6XF.

Youths

British Youths' Open Amateur Championship

The Championship consists of 18 holes on each of two days, the lowest 40 scores over the 36 holes and any tying for 40th place then playing a further 36 holes the following day.

Conditions of entry include:

Entrants must be under 21 years of age on the last day on which the Championship is played.

Entries are limited to 150 competitors, the higher handicaps being balloted out if necessary.

Full particulars of conditions of entry and method of play can be obtained from the Secretary, Championship Committee, Royal and Ancient Golf Club, St Andrews, Fife KY16 9JD.

Boys

Boys' Amateur Championship

The Championship is played by match play, each match consisting of one round of 18 holes except for the final which is over 36 holes.

Conditions of entry include:

Entrants must be under 18 years of age on the last day on which the Championship is played.

Entries are limited to 192 competitors, the higher handicaps being balloted out if necessary.

Full particulars of conditions of entry and method of play can be obtained from the Secretary, Championship Committee, Royal and Ancient Golf Club, St Andrews, Fife KY16 9JD.

Ladies

Ladies' British Open Amateur Championship

The Championship consists of one 18 hole qualifying round on each of two days. If entries exceed 110 there will be 64 qualifiers for matchplay. If entries number 110 or less, 32 will qualify for matchplay. Handicap limit is 4.

Ladies' British Open Amateur Stroke Play Championship

The Championship consists of 72 holes stroke play; 18 holes are played on each of two days after which the first 32 and all ties for 32nd place qualify for a further 36 holes on the third day. Handicap limit is 4.

Ladies' British Open Championship

The Championship consists of 72 holes stroke play. 18 holes are played on each of four days, the field being reduced after the first 36 holes.

Entries accepted from lady amateurs with a handicap not exceeding scratch and from lady professionals.

Full particulars of conditions of entry and method of play for all three Championships can be obtained from the General Administrator, LGU, The Scores, St Andrews, Fife KY16 9AT.

National Championships

Conditions of entry and method of play for the English, Scottish, Welsh and Irish Ladies' Close Championships can be obtained from the Secretaries of the respective associations.

Other championships organised by the respective national associations, from whom full particulars can be obtained, include English Ladies', Intermediate, English Ladies' Stroke-Play, Scottish Girls' Open Amateur Stroke Play (under 21) and Welsh Ladies' Open Amateur Stroke Play.

Girls

Girls' British Open Amateur Championship

The Championship consists of two 18-hole qualifying rounds, followed by match-play in two flights each of sixteen players.

Conditions of entry include:

Entrants must be under 18 years of age on the last day of the British Girls' Championship.

Competitors are required to hold a certified LGU international handicap not exceeding 15, or to be members of their National Junior Team for the current year.

Full particulars of conditions of entry and method of play can be obtained from the General Administrator, LGU, The Scores, St Andrews, Fife KY16 9AT.

National Championships

The English, Scottish, Irish and Welsh Girls' Close Championships are open to all girls of relevant nationality and appropriate age which may vary from country to country. A handicap limit may be set by some countries.

Full particulars of conditions of entry and method of play can be obtained via the secretaries of the respective associations.

International Match Conditions

Men–Amateur

Walker Cup–Great Britain and Ireland v *United States*

Deed of Gift to United States Golf Association
International Challenge Trophy
Mr GH Walker of the United States presented a Cup for international competition to be known as *The United States Golf Association International Challenge Trophy*, popularly described as *The Walker Cup.*

The Cup shall be played for by teams of amateur golfers selected from Clubs under the jurisdiction of the United States Golf Association on the one side and from England, Scotland, Wales, Northern Ireland and Eire on the other.

The International Walker Cup Match shall be held every two years in the United States of America and Great Britain alternately.

The teams shall consist of not more than ten players and a captain.

The contest consists of 4 foursomes and 8 singles matches over 18 holes on each of two days.

Eisenhower Trophy (formerly World Cup)

Founded in 1958 in recognition of the need for an official team championship for amateurs. Each country enters a team of four players who play stroke play over 72 holes, the total of the three best individual scores to be counted each day. (One score to be discarded.) The winner to be the team with the lowest aggregate for the 72 holes. The first event was played at St Andrews in 1958 and the trophy has been played for every second year.

European Team Championship

Founded in 1959 by the European Golf Association for competition among member countries of the Association. The Championship is held biennially and played in rotation round the countries which are grouped in four geographical zones.

Each team consists of six players who play two qualifying rounds of 18 holes, the five best scores of each round constituting the team aggregate. Flights for match play are then arranged according to qualifying round rankings. For the match play, teams consist of five players, playing two foursomes in the morning and five singles in the afternoon.

A similar championship is held every year for junior teams.

Home Internationals (Raymond Trophy)

The first official International Match recorded was in 1903 at Muirfield between England and Scotland when singles only were played.

In 1932 International Week was inaugurated under the auspices of the British Golf Unions' Joint Advisory Council with the full approval of the four National Golf Unions. The Council of National Golf Unions is now responsible for running the matches.

Teams of 11 players from England, Scotland, Ireland and Wales engage in matches consisting of 5 foursomes and 10 singles over 18 holes, the foursomes being in the morning and the singles in the afternoon. Each team plays every other team.

The eligibility of players to play for their country shall be their eligibility to play in the Amateur Championship of their country.

Men–Professional

Ryder Cup

This Cup was presented by Mr Samuel Ryder, St Albans, England (who died 2nd January, 1936), for competition between a team of British professionals and a team of American professionals. The trophy was first competed for in 1927. In 1929 the original conditions were varied to confine the British team to British-born professionals resident in Great Britain, and the American team to American-born professionals resident in the United States, in the year of the match. In 1977 the British team was extended to include European players. The matches are played biennially, in alternate continents, in accordance with the conditions as agreed between the respective PGAs.

World Cup
(formerly Canada Cup)

Founded in America in 1953 as an International Team event for professional golfers with the intention of spreading international goodwill.

Each country is represented by two players, the best team score over 72 holes being the winners of the World cup and the best individual score the International Trophy. It is played annually, but not in 1986.

Ladies

Great Britain and Ireland *v United States*
(Curtis Cup)

For a trophy presented by the late Misses Margaret and Harriot Curtis of Boston, USA, for biennial competition between teams from the United States of America and Great Britain and Ireland.

The match is sponsored jointly by the United States Golf Association and the Ladies' Golf Union who may select teams of not more than 8 players.

The match consists of 3 foursomes and 6 singles of 18 holes on each of two days, the foursomes being played each morning.

Great Britain and Ireland *v Continent of Europe*
(Vagliano Trophy)

For a trophy presented to the Comité des Dames de la Fédération Française de Golf and the Ladies' Golf Union by Monsieur AA Vagliano, originally for annual competition between teams of women amateur golfers from France and Great Britain and Ireland but, since 1959, by mutual agreement, for competition between teams from the Continent of Europe and Great Britain and Ireland.

The match is played biennially, alternately in Great Britain and Ireland and on the Continent of Europe, with teams of not more than 9 players plus a non-playing captain.

The match consists of 4 foursomes and 8 singles, of 18 holes on each of two days. The foursomes are played each morning.

Women's World Amateur Team Championship
(Espirito Santo Trophy)

For the Espirito Santo Trophy presented by Mrs Ricardo Santo of Portugal for biennial competition between teams of not more than three women amateur golfers who represent a national association affiliated to the World Amateur Golf Council. First competed for in 1964.

The tournament consists of 72 holes stroke play, 18 holes on each of four days, the two best scores in each round each day constituting the team aggregate.

Commonwealth Tournament
(Lady Astor Trophy)

For a trophy presented by the late Viscountess Astor CH, and the Ladies' Golf Union for competition once in every four years between teams of women amateur golfers from Commonwealth countries.

The inaugural Commonwealth Tournament was played at St Andrews in 1959 between teams from Australia, Canada, New Zealand, South Africa and Great Britain and was won by the British team. The tournament is played in rotation in the competing countries, for the present Great Britain, Australia, Canada, and New Zealand, each country being entitled to nominate 6 players including a playing or non-playing captain.

Each team plays every other team and each team match consists of 2 foursomes and 4 singles over 18 holes. The foursomes are played in the morning and the singles in the afternoon.

European Ladies' Amateur Team Championship

The championship is held biennially between teams of amateur women golfers from the European countries. Each team consists of not more than six players who play two qualifying rounds, the five best scores in each round constituting the team aggregate. The match play draw is made in flights according to the position in the qualifying rounds. The match play consists of two foursomes and five singles on each of three days.

A similar championship is held in alternate years for junior ladies' teams, under 22 years of age.

Home Internationals

Teams from England, Scotland, Ireland and Wales compete annually for a trophy presented to the LGU by the late Mr TH Miller. The qualifications for a player being eligible to play for her country are the same as those laid down by each country for its Close Championship.

Each team plays each other team. The matches consist of 6 singles and 3 foursomes, each of 18 holes. Each country may nominate teams of not more than 8 players.

Youths

England *v Scotland*

The International Match between England and Scotland is played either one or two days before the Youths' Championship begins, depending on the location of the match between Great Britain and Ireland *v* Continent of Europe.

Great Britain and Ireland *v Continent of Europe*

The International Match between Great Britain and Ireland and the Continent of Europe is played each year. The venue of this match alternates between Great Britain and Ireland and the Continent of Europe. When held in Great Britain and Ireland it is played the day before the start of the Youths' Championship. When held on the Continent of Europe it is played over two days, one week after the Youths' Championship.

Boys

England *v Scotland; Wales v Ireland*

The International Matches between England and Scotland (10 players a side) and Wales and Ireland (10 players a side) are played on the Thursday preceding the Boys' Championship. The following day the winners of these two matches play against each other, as do the losers. To be eligible to play in these matches a boy must qualify by age to be eligible to play in the Boys' Championship.

Great Britain and Ireland *v Continent of Europe*

The International Match between Great Britain and Ireland and the Continent of Europe is played on the Saturday preceding the Boys' Championship.

Girls

Home Internationals

Teams from England, Scotland, Ireland and Wales compete annually for the Stroyan Cup. The qualifications for a player for the Girls' International Matches shall be the same as those laid down by each country for its Girls' Close Championship except that a player shall be under 18 years on the last day of the British Girls' Championship of that year.

Each team, consisting of not more than 8 players, plays each other team, a draw taking place to decide the order of play between the teams. The matches consist of 7 singles, each of 18 holes.

Golf Associations

The Golf Foundation

During the last decade, the growth of golf throughout Britain has scaled new heights with each passing year as more and more people become smitten with its addictive qualities. It was Tony Jacklin who initially sparked this explosion of interest with his victories in the Open Championship and the United States Open nearly 20 years ago and further fuel has been added by the emergence of Spain's Severiano Ballesteros as one of the most exciting players the game has ever seen. The exploits of the world's leading professionals are now regularly beamed into millions of homes via television and so people who would never have dreamed of taking an interest in the game have been fascinated and eventually drawn into finding out for themselves its magnetic qualities.

Many of these people are youngsters – girls and boys who witness the achievements of today's stars and feel that they too would like to experience the allure and charm of golf with dreams, perhaps, of emulating some of the modern day heroes and heroines. In a great many cases, these dreams are frustrated at the outset. If the parents of a child do not play golf then all the questions the child may have about starting golf can go unanswered. He or she may enquire about the game from school teachers but unless one of them is a golfer, it is unlikely that this approach will bear any fruit so the seeds of interest are soon stifled and the child turns to other games which are included in the school curriculum.

It is this gap in the education of young, potential golfers that The Golf Foundation fills. Founded in 1952, The Golf Foundation's original motives of promoting the development of junior golf throughout the country still hold good today and in the space of 35 years, thousands of junior golfers have benefited from its work. From this number have emerged some famous names such as Bernard Gallacher, Brian Barnes, Peter Oosterhuis, Michelle Walker and more recently Paul Way, Michael McLean and Ronan Rafferty all of whom received instruction and assistance under The Golf Foundation Coaching Scheme for Schools and Junior Groups.

This scheme forms the basis of the Foundation's work whereby it subsidises instruction by qualified members of the Professional Golfer's Association (PGA) to students of schools, universities and other places of higher education and to junior members of golf clubs who are in full-time education. This enables schools who do not have golf as part of their sports' programme to take advantage of giving their pupils an introduction to the game and a solid grounding in its techniques.

But the work of the Golf Foundation does not begin and end there; the Foundation realised that young people's initial interest in the game must be sustained. Thus, over the years it has expanded its field of operations to cover the development of a junior golfer right through to the adult ranks. This area includes the awarding of vouchers for individual tuition for promising girls and boys; the sponsoring of Open Coaching Centres during school holidays; the encouragement of school competitive golf and assisting the formation of National and County Schools' Golf Associations; the operation of a film and visual aids service; the organisation of the Team Championship for Schools and the Age Group Championships; the promotion of an Eclectic Competition for club juniors; the operation of a Merit Award Scheme whereby juniors can have their progress measured and rewarded. The Foundation has recently initiated the Coaching Award for Teachers in School whereby teachers who play golf themselves receive basic instruction from PGA professionals which they can then impart to pupils so that the pupils have some grounding when they receive further instruction under the Golf Foundation Coaching Scheme for Schools and Junior Groups.

The Foundation also makes an annual award to the boy or girl showing the most improvement as a result of Golf Foundation tuition and in 1983 this award was won by a 17-year-old boy who is deaf and has limited speech – proof, if any were needed, of the therapeutic powers of the game and evidence of the particular interest the Golf Foundation takes in handicapped young people.

The implementation of these activities and the running of the coaching scheme costs a great deal of money and the Golf Foundation relies heavily on club golfers for a large part of its income. Organisations within the game and companies also assist in providing funds so that its work can continue and expand.

At present, the future of British golf looks bright but in order to maintain that progress, more and more youngsters must be given the opportunity to learn about and play golf. As one old scribe once wrote, *it is a game at which you may exhaust yourself but never your subject,* and it is a game that teaches self-discipline, good manners, sportsmanship and an appreciation of other people's qualities. It is *the game of a lifetime* for it can be played by people of all ages. The Golf Foundation hopes that you too, once you have experienced the pleasures of golf, will find it a lasting source of enjoyment.

For details about the Golf Foundation's work, please apply to: The Director, The Golf Foundation, 57 London Road, Enfield, Middlesex EN2 6DU. ***Tel*** 01-367 4404.

The National Association of Public Golf Courses

(Affiliated to English Golf Union)

Hon Secretary: JHH Burdett, 948 Castle Lane East, Bournemouth BH7 6SP. ***Tel*** (0202) 483017.

1927 saw the foundation of the Association by the late FG Hawtree (Golf Course Architect) and the late JH Taylor (five times Open Champion). They were both farsighted enough to see the need for cohesion between *Private* golf, *Public* golf and the Local Councils. Up to the outbreak of World War II the Association struggled on, sustained by a small amount of very welcome financial support from the News of the World. This enabled the *unofficial* Championship to be staged.

After the War, the Association was revitalised and the Championship was recognised by the National Union – and so from a shaky start of 240 qualifiers – there are now some 3500 Public Course golfers trying to qualify, from a total estimated membership of 50,000. The success and importance of the *Public Courses Championship of England* prompted the commencement of the Championship for Ladies and then the Championship for Juniors – which share equal importance. Soon after the establishment of Individual Championships there came the introduction of various Club Team events, and these have now progressed to National Level with a vast following from the Clubs in membership. Thus the Association now organises some 14 National events each year for the total membership.

Some years ago it was realised that the Local Councils (Course Management Authorities) could not enjoy official recognition and membership of the County Unions or National Unions except through the Association, this has now been remedied and many CMA are full subscribing members of the Association, and many others permit the *Courtesy of the Course* for all our National & Zonal Tournaments. Advice is offered to CMA – when requested – on such matters as Course Construction, Club formation and integration, establishment of Standard Scratch Score and Par Values, and many other topics concerned with the management of the game of golf.

Some overseas organisations and Councils have already sought our advice and help in recent years, when forming their own Courses, Clubs and Associations.

The Constitutional aims have not changed over the years, and the Association is proud to have maintained these Aims through the activities provided by the National Executive of the Association. The aims are:

1. To unite the Clubs formed on Public Courses in England and Wales, and their Course Managements in the furtherance of the interests of Amateur Golf.
2. To promote Annual Public Courses Championships and such other matches, competitions and Tournaments as shall be authorised by the executive of the Association.
3. To afford direct representation of Public Course Interests in the National Union.

The total organisation of the Association is wholly voluntary and honorary, from the President down through Vice-Presidents, Chairmen, Secretary, Treasurer and Zone Secretaries. It is quite fantastic for an unpaid Organisation to cover such an exacting *field* of work, but most gratifying to all of us of the National Executive who have secured the steady progress of recent years.

The Association of Golf Club Secretaries

Membership is 1500, consisting of Secretaries and retired Secretaries of Clubs largely situated in Great Britain but also from 200 Clubs in other parts of the World. The Association offers from the Headquarters at Bakewell, Derbyshire advice on all aspects of Golf Club Management, together with a training course for new and intending Golf Club Secretaries. Apart from national events, including a Conference, the Association organises golfing and business meetings for its members at regional level. There are twelve regions within the British Isles.

Secretary: John Crowther, Victoria Mill, Buxton Road, Bakewell, Derbyshire DE4 1DA. ***Tel*** (062 981) 4314.

Association of Golf Writers

Secretary: Renton Laidlaw, Evening Standard, Fleet Street, London.

The Sports Turf Research Institute
(Bingley, West Yorkshire)

The Institute is officially recognised as the national centre for sports and amenity turf. Non-commercial and non-profit making, its affairs are administered by a Board of Management whose members are nominated by the sport controlling bodies in membership of the Institute. Golf is represented by nominees of the Royal and Ancient Golf Club of St Andrews, four individual National Golf Unions, and the Councils of National Golf Unions.

The institute has as its object the raising of the standard of turf used for all sports. Much valuable data is accumulated from the research activities and is incorporated in the advice given to subscribing clubs and organisations.

For further information as to subscriptions and visiting fees, etc., write to: ***The Secretary***, The Sports Turf Research Institute, Bingley, West Yorks BD16 1AU. ***Tel*** (0274) 565131.

The British Association of Golf Course Architects

Objects of the Association:

To encourage the highest standards of Golf Course Design and Construction.

To have the fullest regard to the best interests of Members' Clients.

To maintain a Register of Members fully qualified by training and experience in the design and construction of Golf Courses.

To promote the interests of its members and the game of golf.

To support research and development in golf course Design, Construction and Maintenance.

To enable members to meet together, share knowledge and experience, and discuss matters affecting their work.

To follow the best accepted principles of golf course architecture and modern design requirements with the object of providing the maximum enjoyment of the game for all standards of players.

Hon Secretary: Martin Hawtree, 5 Oxford Street, Woodstock, Oxford OX7 1TQ. ***Tel*** (0993) 811976.

The British Association of Golf Course Constructors

Objects: To promote the development of the golf course construction industry, to promote the adoption of policies which will ensure a high quality of workmanship and working practices, to collect and disseminate information of value regarding the construction of golf courses to other members of the association, to members of the allied industries and to the public at large, to promote the training and education of personnel within the industry and to maintain agreed standards of golf course construction by adherence to contractual procedures and codes of practice.

All enquiries to Howard Swan, British Association of Golf Course Constructors, Telfords Farm, Willingale, Ongar, Essex CM4 OQF. ***Tel*** (0277) 86229 ***Fax*** (0245) 461620.

British and International Golf Greenkeepers' Association

The Association was formed in 1987 and resulted from an amalgamation of the previous British, English and Scottish Associations. The Association has an official magazine, *Golf Course* which is issued free to all members.

The objects are to promote and advance all aspects of greenkeeping; to assist and encourage the proficiency of members; to arrange an International Annual Conference, educational seminars, functions and competitions; to maintain a Benevolent Fund; to act as an employment agency; to provide a magazine; to collaborate with any body or organisation which may in any way benefit the Association or its members or with which there may be a common interest; to carry out and perform any other duties or responsibilities which shall be in the general interests of the Association or its members. ***Executive Director:*** Neil Thomas, The Sports and Turf Research Institute, Bingley, West Yorkshire BD16 1AU. ***Tel*** (0274) 560556.

National Golf Clubs' Advisory Association

The National Golf Clubs' Advisory Association was founded in 1922. The objects are to protect the interests of Golf Clubs in general and to give legal advice and direction, under the opinion of Counsel, on the administrative and legal responsibilities of Golf Clubs. In cases taken to the Courts for decisions on any points which in the opinion of the Executive Committee involve principles affecting the general interests of affiliated clubs financial assistance may sometimes be given. ***Secretary:*** John Crowther, Victoria Mill, Buxton Road, Bakewell, Derbyshire DE14 1DA. ***Tel*** (062 981) 3844.

European Golf Association
Association Européenne de Golf

At a meeting held at Luxembourg, 20th November, 1937, this Association was formed.

Membership shall be restricted to European

National Amateur Golf Associations or Unions. The Association shall concern itself solely with matters of an international character. The Association shall have as its prime objects:

(a) To encourage the international development of golf and strengthen the bonds of friendship existing between the national organisations and to encourage the formation of new ones.
(b) To co-ordinate the dates of the Open and Amateur Championships of its members.
(c) To arrange when such have been decided upon, European Team Championships and Matches of international character.
(d) To decide and publish the Calendar dates of the Open and Amateur Championships and Matches.

General Secretary: John C Storjohann, En Ballègue, PO Box CH1066, Epalignes-Lausanne, Switzerland. ***Tel*** 010-41-021-32-7701. ***Fax*** 41 (21) 32 81 76

Provincial Golf Writers Guild

Secretary: Roy Yeomans, Evening Echo, Richmond Hill, Bournemouth. ***Tel*** (0202) 24601.

Golf Club Stewards' Association

The Golf Club Stewards' Association was founded as early as 1912. Its members are Stewards in Golf Clubs throughout the UK and Eire. It has a National Committee and Regional Branches in the South, North-West, Midlands, East Anglia, Yorkshire, Wales and the West, North-East Scotland and Ireland, each with its own Officers and Committee.

The objects of the Association are to promote the interests of members who are Stewards or Assistant Stewards at Golf Clubs; to administer a Benevolent Fund for members in need and to arrange golf competitions and matches. It also serves as an Agency for the employment of Stewards in Golf Clubs.

Hon Secretary: GW Shaw, 50 The Park, St Albans, Herts AL1 4RY. ***Tel*** (0727) 57334.

Addresses of British and Overseas Golfing Organisations

United Kingdom

National

Amateur Golf Championship
Sec, MF Bonallack, OBE, Royal and Ancient Golf Club, St Andrews.

Artisan Golfers' Association
Hon Sec, A Everett, 51 Rose Hill, Park West, Sutton, Surrey. *Tel* 01-644 7037.

Association of Golf Club Secretaries
Sec, J Crowther, Victoria Mill, Buxton Road, Bakewell, Derbyshire DE4 1DA. *Tel* (062 981) 4314.

Boys' Amateur Golf Championship
Sec, MF Bonallack, OBE, Royal and Ancient Golf Club, St Andrews.

British Association of Golf Course Architects
Hon Sec & Treas, MG Hawtree, 5 Oxford Street, Woodstock, Oxford OX7 1TQ. *Tel* (0993) 811976.

British Association of Golf Course Constructors
Howard Swan, Telford Farm, Willingale, Ongar, Essex CM5 OQF. *Tel* (0277) 86229

British & International Golf Greenkeepers' Association
Exec Dir, Neil Thomas, The Sports & Turf Research Institute, Bingley, W Yorks BD16 1AU. *Tel* (0274) 560556.

British Left-Handed Golfers' Society
Hon Sec, AC Kirkland, Squirrel Cottage, Mereheath Lane, Knutsford, Cheshire. *Tel* (0565) 4671.

Council of National Golf Unions
Hon Sec, Alan Thirlwell, Formby GC, Golf Road, Formby, Liverpool L37 1LQ. *Tel* (070 48) 72164.

Golf Club Stewards' Association
Sec, G Shaw, 50 The Park, St Albans, Herts. *Tel* (0727) 57334.

Chairman, A Reay, Robin Hood Golf Club, St Bernard's Road, Solihull, Birmingham. *Tel* 021-706 0159.

Special Events, DJ Lithgow, Great Barr Golf Club, Chapel Lane, Great Barr, Birmingham B43 7BA. *Tel* 021-357 1232.

Regional Secretaries

South Roger Gregory, Southwick Park Golf Club. *Tel* (0705) 370683.

Midlands Carol Reay, Robin Hood Golf Club. *Tel* 021-706 0159.

North East J Armstrong, Hexham Golf Club. *Tel* (0434) 602057.

Yorkshire K Millington, Whitby Golf Club. *Tel* (0947) 601632/602768.

Wales & West Peter Blackmore, Stinchcombe Hill Golf Club. *Tel* (0453) 2015.

Golf Foundation
Dir Miss Lesley Attwood, 57 London Road, Enfield, Middx EN2 6DU. *Tel* 01-367 4404.

Golf Society of Great Britain
Gleneagles, Maddox Park, Little Bookham, Surrey KT23 3BW. *Tel* (0372) 54260.

Hill Samuel School Foursomes
Competition Hon Sec, GR Scott, Yew Tree Cottage, 93 Wells Road, Malvern, Worcs WR14 4PB. *Tel* (068 45) 65605.

Hole in One Golf Society
Sec, EW Parker, 1 Vigilant Way, Gravesend, Kent. *Tel* (0474) 534298.

Ladies' Golf Union
General Administrator, Mrs Alison White, The Scores, St Andrews, Fife KY16 9AT. *Tel* (0334) 75811.

The Society of One-Armed Golfers
Hon Sec, Don Reid, 11 Coldwell Lane, Felling, Tyne and Wear NE10 9EX. *Tel* 091-469 4742.

The Professional Golfers' Association

Exec Dir, J Lindsey, National Headquarters, Apollo House, The Belfry, Sutton Coldfield, West Midlands, B76 9PT. ***Tel*** (0675) 70333 ***Telex*** 338481 (PGA G) ***Fax*** (0675) 70674.

Scottish Region ***Sec,*** Sandy Jones, Glenbervie Golf Club, Stirling Road, Larbert FK5 4SJ. ***Tel*** (0324) 562451.

Irish Region ***Sec,*** Michael McCumiskey, Dundalk Golf Club, Blackrock, Dundalk, Co Louth, Eire. ***Tel*** (010 353) 4221193/7.

North Region ***Sec,*** Norman Fletcher, Mere Golf and Country Club, Knutsford, Cheshire WA16 6LJ. ***Tel*** (0565) 830559.

West Region ***Sec,*** Bill Morton, Exeter Golf and Country Club, Topsham Road, Countess Wear, Exeter, Devon EX2 7AE. ***Tel*** (0392) 877657.

Midland Region ***Sec,*** Lawrence Thornton, PGA National Headquarters, Apollo House, The Belfry, Sutton Coldfield, West Midlands B76 9PT. ***Tel*** (0675) 70333.

South Region ***Sec,*** Jeremy Kilby, Tyrrells Wood Golf Club, Leatherhead, Surrey KT22 8QP. ***Tel*** (0372) 370111.

East Region ***Sec,*** David Wright, John O'Gaunt Golf Club, Sutton Park, Sandy, Biggleswade, Beds SG19 2LY. ***Tel*** (0767) 261888.

PGA European Tour

Executive Director, KD Schofield, PGA European Tour, The Wentworth Club, Wentworth Drive, Virginia Water, Surrey GU25 4LS. ***Tel*** Wentworth (099 04) 2881.

Women's Professional Golfers' European Tour

Exec Dir, Joe Flanagan, The Tytherington Club, Macclesfield, Cheshire SK10 2JP. ***Tel*** (0625) 611444.

Public Schools' Old Boys' Golf Association

Jt Secs, P de Pinna, Bruins, Wythwood, Haywards Heath, West Sussex. ***Tel*** (0444) 454883 and JBM Urry, Dormers, 232 Dickens Heath Road, Shirley, Solihull, West Midlands. ***Tel*** *(home)* (0564) 823114, *(office)* 021-772 5754.

Public Schools' Golfing Society

Hon Sec, JNS Lowe, Flushing House, Church Road, Great Bookham, Surrey KT23 3JT. ***Tel*** (0372) 58651.

Seniors' Championship

Sec, MF Bonallack, OBE, Royal and Ancient Golf Club, St Andrews.

Senior Golfers' Society

Sec, Brigadier D Ross CBE, Milland Farmhouse, Liphook, Hants GU30 7JP. ***Tel*** (042 876) 200.

Youths' Amateur Golf Championship

Sec, MF Bonallack, OBE, Royal and Ancient Golf Club, St Andrews.

England

Bedfordshire County Golf Union

Hon Sec, CEL Spurr, 8, Gainsborough Avenue, St Albans, Herts AL1 4NL. ***Tel*** (0727) 57834.

Bedfordshire Ladies' County Golf Association

Hon Sec, Mrs M Clark, 18 Homerton Rd, Luton, Beds LU3 2UL. ***Tel*** (0582) 575883.

Berks, Bucks and Oxon Union of Golf Clubs

Sec, RMF Fenning, The Lodge, Commonwood, Chipperfield, Herts. WD4 9BA. ***Tel*** (092 77) 63156 *(home)*, (092 77) 65319 *(office)*.

Berkshire Ladies' County Golf Association

Hon Sec, Mrs BE Baird, 11 Lynton Green, College Road, Maidenhead, Berks SL6 6AN. ***Tel*** (0628) 21462.

Buckinghamshire Ladies' County Golf Association

Hon Sec, Mrs N Williams, 15 Furze View, Chorleywood, Herts WD3 5HT. ***Tel*** (092 78) 3253.

Cambridgeshire Area Golf Union

Sec, RAC Blows, 2a Dukes Meadow, Stapleford, Cambs CB2 5BH. ***Tel*** (0223) 842062.

Cambs. and Hunts. Ladies' County Golf Association

Hon Sec, Mrs A Guy, 19 Greenfield Close, Stapleford, Cambs. CB2 5BF. ***Tel*** (0223) 843267.

Channel Islands Ladies' GA

Sec, Mrs JMT Willis, Oakebirch, Park Estate, St Brelade, Jersey.

Cheshire County Ladies' Golf Association

Hon Sec, Mrs R Btesh, 48 Melrose Crescent, Hale, Altrincham, Cheshire. ***Tel*** 061-980 6140.

Cheshire PGA

Tournament Director, Keith Brain, The Virgate, Abbey Way Hartford, Northwich, Cheshire CW8 1LY.

Cheshire Union of Golf Clubs

Hon Sec, BC Jones, 4 Curzon Mews, Wilmslow, Cheshire SK9 5JN. ***Tel*** (0625) 520894.

Cornwall Golf Union
Hon Sec, JG Rowe, 8 Lydcott Crescent, Widegates, Looe, Cornwall PL13 1QG. *Tel* (05034) 492.

Cornwall Ladies' County Golf Association
Hon Sec, Mrs A Eddy, Penmester, Hain Walk, St Ives, Cornwall. *Tel* (0736) 795392.

Cumbria Ladies' County Golf Association
Hon Sec, Miss T Turner, Cawdor, Gartsheads Road, Appleby, Cumbria CA16 6UD.

Cumbria Union of Golf Clubs
Hon Sec, T Edmondson, Thorn Lea, Lazonby, Penrith, Cumbria. *Tel* (0768) 83231.

Derbyshire Alliance
Hon Sec, R Reid, c/o Buxton & High Peak GC, Fairfield, Buxton, Derbyshire. *Tel* (0298) 3112.

Derbyshire Ladies' County Golf Association
Hon Sec, Mrs B Nix, Chevin Close, 58 Broadway, Duffield, Derby DE6 4BU. *Tel* (0332) 841703.

Derbyshire Union of Golf Clubs
Hon Sec, CF Ibbotson, 67 Portland Close, Mickleover, Derby DE3 5BR. *Tel* (0332) 841703.

Devon County Golf Union
Hon Sec, J Marshall, *Appledowne,* Keyberry Park, Newton Abbot, Devon TQ12 1DF. *Tel* (0626) 52999.

Devon County Ladies' Golf Association
Hon Sec, Miss M Saint, 28 Homer Rise, Elburton, Plymouth, Devon PL9 8NE. *Tel* (0752) 403348.

Devon Professional Golfers' Alliance
Hon Sec, Michael J Dunk, Sunhaven, 2 Landscore Close, Crediton, Devon. *Tel* (036 32) 3145.

Dorset County Golf Union
Hon Sec, Lt Col MD Hutchins, 38 Carlton Road, Bournemouth BH1 3TG. *Tel* (0202) 290821.

Dorset Ladies' County Golf Association
Miss JM Rhodes, 4 Egdon Glen Crossways, Dorchester, Dorset DT2 8BQ. *Tel* (0305) 852547.

Durham County Golf Union
Hon Sec, WP Murray, Highnam Lodge, Park Mews, Hartlepool, Cleveland TS26 0DX. *Tel* (0429) 273185.

Durham County Ladies' Golf Association
Sec, Mrs CF Anderson, 107 Harlsey Road, Hartburn, Stockton-on-Tees.

English Golf Union
Sec, K Wright, 1–3 Upper King Street, Leicester LE1 6XF. *Tel* (0533) 553042.

Midland Group *Sec,* RJW Baldwin, Chantry Cottage, Friar Street, Droitwich, Worcs. WR9 8EQ. *Tel* (0905) 778560.

Northern Group *Hon Sec,* EG Bunting, 7 Northbrook Court, Hartlepool, Cleveland TS26 ODJ. *Tel* (0429) 274828

South Eastern Group *Hon Sec,* MA Hobson, 22 Wye Court, Malvern Way, Ealing, London W13 8EA. *Tel* 01-997 7466.

South Western Group *Sec,*JT Lumley, Hartland, Potterne, Devizes, Wilts. *Tel* (0380) 3935.

English Ladies' Golf Association
Sec, Mrs MJ Carr, Edgbaston Golf Club, Church Road, Birmingham B15 3TB. *Tel* 021-456 2088.

Northern Division *Hon Sec,* Mrs L Young, 10 Cleehill Drive,North Shields, Tyne and Weir NE29 9EW.*Tel* 091-257 6925.

Midlands Division *Hon Sec,* Mrs W Earnshaw, 260 Widney Lane, Solihull, West Midlands B91 3JY. *Tel* 021-705 4285.

South-Eastern Division *Hon Sec,* Mrs E Block, 71 Parkanaur Avenue, Thorpe Bay, Essex SS1 3JA. *Tel* (0702) 588336.

South-Western Division *Hon Sec,* Mrs VJ Wilde, 19 Ferndown Close, Kingsweston, Bristol. *Tel* (0272) 683543.

English Schools' Golf Association
Hon Sec, R Snell, 20 Dykenook Close, Whickham, Newcastle-upon-Tyne. *Tel* 091-488 3538.

Essex County Amateur Golf Union
Hon Sec, EV Sadler, 9 Willow Walk, Hadleigh, Essex *Tel* (0702) 559871.

Essex Ladies' County Golf Association
Hon Sec, Mrs J Bourne, 1 The Paddocks, Stock, Essex. *Tel* (0277) 810466.

Essex Professional Golfers' Union
Sec, John Turner, 93 Beehive Lane, Ilford, Essex. *Tel* 01-554 4208 *(home).*

Gloucestershire and Somerset Professional Golfers' Association
Sec, Bob Newton, Henbury GC, Westbury-on-Trym, Bristol BS10 7QB. *Tel* (0272) 502121.

Gloucestershire Golf Union
Hon Sec, RF Crisp, 2 Hartley Close, Sandy Lane, Charlton Kings, Cheltenham. *Tel* (0242) 514024.

Gloucester Ladies' County Golf Association
Hon Sec, Mrs L Williams, 1 Avon Crescent, Cumberland Road, Bristol BS1 6XQ. ***Tel*** (0272) 264606.

Hampshire Ladies' County Golf Association
Hon Sec, Mrs E Buckley, 182 Bassett Green Road, Southampton, Hants SO2 3LW. ***Tel*** (0703) 789273.

Hampshire, Isle of Wight and Channel Islands Golf Union
Hon Sec/ Treas, JLS McCracken, *Glyngarth,* Tower Road, Hindhead, Surrey GU26 6SL. ***Tel*** (042 873) 4090.

Hampshire Professional Golfers' Association
Hon Sec, Chris Maltby, 3 Lily Close, Kempshott Down, Basingstoke, Hants RG22 5NT. ***Tel*** (0256) 466070.

Herts County Professional Golfers' Alliance
Hon Sec, RA Gurney, 1 Field Lane, Letchworth, Herts SG6 3LF ***Tel*** (0462) 682256.

Hertfordshire County Ladies' Golf Association
Hon Sec, Mrs EM Copley, 22 The Avenue, Radlett, Herts WD7 7DW. ***Tel*** (0923) 857184.

Hertfordshire Golf Union
Hon Sec, WA de Podesta, 2 The Heath, Radlett, Herts WD7 7DF. ***Tel*** (092 76) 7184.

Isle of Man Golf Union
Hon Sec, AJ Kewley, 51 Ballcriy Park, Colby, Isle of Man. ***Tel*** (0624) 832807

Isle of Wight Ladies' Golf Association
Hon Sec, Mrs F Harrison, 47 Palmers Road, Wootton, Isle of Wight. ***Tel*** (0983) 883864

Kent County Golf Union
Hon Sec, HF Darkins, Flat 7, Charing Court, 32 Shortlands Road, Bromley, Kent BR2 0XX. ***Tel.*** 01-464 0345.

Kent County Ladies' Golf Association
Hon Sec, Mrs D Hall-Thompson, Colleton House, North Road, Hythe, Kent CT21 4AS. ***Tel*** (0303) 66285.

Kent Professional Golfers' Union
Sec, E Impett, 20 The Grove, Barnham, Kent. Tel (0227) 831655.

Lancashire Ladies' County Golf Association
Hon Sec, Miss P Hurst, 25 Park Road, Golborne, Warrington, Cheshire WA3 3PU.

Lancashire Union of Golf Clubs
Sec, N Hardman, 4 Cedarwood Close, Lytham Hall Park, Lytham, Lancs SY8 4PD.

Leicestershire and Rutland Ladies' County Golf Association
Hon Sec, Mrs EK Eastabrook, 8 The Woodlands, Market Harborough, Leics LE4 4SB. ***Tel*** (0858) 63117.

Leicestershire and Rutland Golf Union
Hon Sec, GH Upward, 187 Leicester Road, Groby, Leicester. ***Tel*** (0533) 873675 *(home)*, (0533) 871313 *(office)*.

Leicestershire Professional Golfers' Association
Hon Sec, R Larratt, Glen Gorse GC, Glen Road, Oadby, Leics LE2 4RF. ***Tel*** (0533) 713748.

Lincolnshire Ladies' County Association
Hon Sec, Mrs G Newcombe, 7 Chapman Street, Market Rasen, Lincs LN8 3JU. ***Tel*** (0673) 842287.

Lincolnshire Professional Golfers' Association
Sec, MD Smith, 10 Highfield Drive, Kirton Lindsey, South Humberside. ***Tel*** (0652) 648658.

Lincolnshire Union of Golf Clubs
Hon Sec, TJ Hale *Dapselah,* Allenby Cres., Fotherby, Nr Louth LN11 0UJ. ***Tel*** (0507) 604298.

Manchester and District Golf Alliance
Hon Sec, JGF Brain, 18 Riverside, Leftwich, Northwich, Cheshire. ***Tel*** (0606) 41441.

Middlesex County Golf Union
Hon Sec, PSV Cooke, 36 Grants Close, Mill Hill, London NW7 1DD. ***Tel*** 01-349 0414 *(home)*.

Middlesex Ladies' County Golf Association
Hon Sec, Mrs C Hume, 62 Church Crescent, London N3 1BJ.

Midland Golf Union
Hon Sec, RJW Baldwin, Chantry Cottage, Friar Street, Droitwich, Worcs WR9 8EQ. ***Tel*** *(home)* (0905) 778560, *(office)* (0905) 774344.

Norfolk County Golf Union
Hon Sec/ Treas, RJ Trower, 246 Unthank Road, Norwich, Norfolk NR2 2AH. ***Tel*** (0603) 53332 *(home)*, (0603) 625854 *(office)*.

Norfolk Ladies' County Association
Hon Sec, Mrs VM Munro, 17 Taylor Avenue, Cringleford, Norfolk NR4 6XY. ***Tel*** (0603) 56049.

Norfolk PGA
Hon Sec, M Garrett, Sheringham GC, Sheringham, Norfolk. ***Tel*** (0263) 823488.

North East and North West PGA
Hon Sec, KW Reddall, 87 Parkside, Greenways, Spennymoor, Co Durham DL16 6SA.

Northamptonshire Golf Union
Joint Hon Secs, KDP Cooper and TCA Knight, c/o 75 Queens Park Parade, Northampton. ***Tel*** (0604) 715038 *(home)*, (0604) 21455 *(office)*.

Northamptonshire Ladies' County Golf Association
Hon Sec, Mrs MML Coker, 534 Wellingborough Road, Northampton NN3 3HZ. ***Tel*** (0604) 409298.

Northamptonshire PGA
Hon Sec, TJ Giles, Kingsthorpe GC, Northampton. ***Tel*** (0604) 719602.

Northumberland Ladies' County Golf Association
Hon Sec, Mrs FK Marshall, 15 Magdalene Fields, Warkworth, Morpeth, Northumberland NE65 0UF. ***Tel*** (0665) 711621.

Northumberland Union of Golf Clubs
Hon Sec, WE Procter, 5 Oakhurst Drive, Kenton Park, Gosforth, Newcastle-upon-Tyne NE3 4JS. ***Tel*** 091-285 4981 *(home)*, 091-274 5310 *(office)*.

Nottinghamshire County Ladies' Golf Association
Hon Sec, Mrs B Jackson, Cranmer Lodge, Main Street, Kinoulton, Notts, NA12 3EL. ***Tel*** (0949) 81201.

Nottinghamshire PGA
Sec, RW Futer, 52 Barden Road, Mapperley, Nottingham NG3 5QD. ***Tel*** (0602) 269635.

Nottinghamshire Union of Golf Clubs
Hon Sec, E Peters, 48 Weaverthorpe Road, Woodthorp, Notts NG5 4NB. ***Tel*** (0602) 266560.

Oxfordshire Ladies' County Golf Association
Hon Sec, Miss BM Nicklin, 532 Banbury Road, Oxford OX2 8EG. ***Tel*** (0865) 58300.

Sheffield Union of Golf Clubs
Sec, JHV Wheeler, 8 Newfield Court, 586 Fulwood Road, Sheffield S10 3QE.

Shropshire and Herefordshire Union of Golf Clubs
Hon Sec, JR Davies, 23 Poplar Crescent, Bayston Hill, Shrewsbury. ***Tel*** (074 372) 2655.

Shropshire Ladies' County Golf Association
Hon Sec, Mrs O Higgs, 122 Fieldhouse Drive, Muxton, Telford, Salop TF8 8BB. ***Tel*** (0952) 604522.

Somerset Golf Union
Hon Sec, CJE Betty, 11 Middleway Court, Middleway, Taunton, Somerset TA1 3QJ. ***Tel*** (0823) 72842.

Somerset Ladies' County Golf Association
Hon Sec, Mrs P Harker, 83 Milford Avenue, Wick, Nr Bristol, Avon BS15 5PP. ***Tel*** (027 582) 3087.

South-Western Counties Golf Association
Hon Sec/Treas, JT Lumley, Hartland, Potterne, Devizes, Wilts. SN10 5PA. ***Tel*** (0380) 3935.

Staffordshire Ladies' County Golf Association
Hon Sec, Mrs DB Banks, 11 Westhill, Finchfield, Wolverhampton WV3 9HL. ***Tel*** (0902) 753279.

Staffordshire and Shropshire Union of Professional Golfers
Sec, E Griffiths, 22 Wynn Road, Penn, Wolverhampton. ***Tel*** (0902) 332180 *(home)*.

Staffordshire Union of Golf Clubs
Hon Sec, A Smith, 19 Broadway, Walsall, W Midlands WS1 3EX. ***Tel*** (0922) 24988 *(home)*, (0902) 65454 *(office)*.

Suffolk County Golf Union
Hon Sec, JJ Kerrison, Heath View, Purdis Avenue, Ipswich, Suffolk IP3 8UE. ***Tel*** (0473) 74753.

Suffolk Ladies' County Golf Association
Hon Sec, Mrs R Stutely, The Cottage, Great Finborough, Stowmarket, Suffolk IP14 3AE. ***Tel*** (0449) 612888.

Suffolk PGA
Sec, Mark Jillings, Bury St Edmunds GC, Fornham All Saints, Bury St Edmunds, Suffolk IP28 2LG. ***Tel*** (0284) 5979.

Surrey County Golf Union
Sec, PG Cornish, The Pumphouse, Witley, Godalming, Surrey GU8 5LT. ***Tel*** (0428) 8793179.

Surrey Ladies' County Golf Association
Hon Sec, Mrs P Lloyd, The Pheasantry, Tandridge GC, Oxted, Surrey. ***Tel*** (08833) 2072.

Surrey PGA
Sec, P Bowles, 27 Lowerfield Road, Claygate, Surrey KT10 0EU. ***Tel*** (0372) 63882.

Sussex County Golf Union
DG Pulford, 12 Rodmell Avenue, Saltdean, Brighton, E Sussex BN2 8LT. ***Tel*** (0273) 304415

Sussex County Ladies' Golf Association
Sec, Miss M Cheal, Lahinch, 17 Grove Road, Seaford, E Sussex BN25 1BT. ***Tel*** (0323) 894871.

Sussex Professional Golfers' Union
Sec, C Pluck, 96 Cranston Avenue, Bexhill-on-Sea, Sussex. ***Tel*** (0424) 221298.

Tees-side and District Union of Golf Clubs
Hon Sec, F Simpson, 27 Marton Drive, Billingham, Cleveland. ***Tel*** (0642) 555374.

Warwickshire Ladies' County Golf Association
Hon Sec, Mrs J Plant, 57 White House Green, Solihull, W Midlands B91 1SP. ***Tel*** 021-705 8062.

Warwickshire Professional Golfers' Association
Sec, GL Taylor, Labrook Park GC, Poolhead Lane, Wood-End, Tanworth-in-Arden, Solihull B94 5ED. ***Tel*** (056 44) 2581.

Warwickshire Union of Golf Clubs
Hon Sec, JBM Urry, Dormers, 232 Dickens Heath Road, Shirley, Solihull B90 1QQ. ***Tel*** *(home)* (0564) 823114; *(office)* 021-772 5754.

Wiltshire County Golf Union
Hon Sec/Treas, RF Buthlay, 10 Priory Park, Bradford-on-Avon, Wilts. BA15 1QU. ***Tel*** (022 16) 6401.

Wiltshire Ladies' County Golf Association
Hon Sec, Mrs P Board, South Lodge, Northleigh, Bradford-on Avon, Wilts. ***Tel*** (02216) 3387.

Wiltshire PGA
L Ross, *Professional*, Marlborough GC, The Common, Marlborough, Wilts. ***Tel*** (0672) 52493.

Worcestershire Association of Professional Golfers
Sec, Chris Thompson, Droitwich GC, Ford Lane, Droitwich WR9 0BH, Worcs. ***Tel*** (0905) 770207.

Worcestershire County Ladies' Golf Association
Hon Sec, Mrs B Ward, Silverdale, Hunters Ride, Lawnswood, Stourbridge, Worcs DY7 5QN.

Worcestershire Union of Golf Clubs
Hon Sec, WR Painter, 70 Cardinal Drive, Kidderminster, Worcs DY10 4RY. ***Tel*** (0562) 823109.

Yorkshire Ladies' County Golf Association
Hon Sec, Mrs M Clarke, 3 Lane Head, Apperley Lane, Rawdon, Leeds, N Yorks LS19 7DX.

Yorkshire Professional Golfers' Association
Hon Sec, David Bulmer, Temple Newsam GC, Halton, Leeds 15, N Yorks. ***Tel*** (0532) 647362/641464.

Yorkshire Union of Golf Clubs
Hon Sec, Alan Cowman, 50 Bingley Road, Bradford, West Yorks BD9 6HH. ***Tel*** (0274) 42661.

Ireland

Irish Golf Union
Sec, Ivan ER Dickson, Glencar House, 81 Eglington Road, Donnybrook, Dublin 4. ***Tel*** (0001) 694111.

Ulster Branch *Sec,* Alf Collis MBE, 58a High Street, Holywood, Co Down BT18 9AE. ***Tel*** (02317) 3708.

Leinster Branch *Sec,* Ken Haughton, 1 Clonskeagh Square, Clonskeagh Road, Dublin 14. ***Tel*** Dublin (0001) 696977/696727.

Munster Branch *Hon Sec,* Richard Barry, Sunville, Dromsligo, Mallow, Co Cork. ***Tel*** *(office)* (22) 21117/21123; *(home)* (22) 22760.

Connacht Branch *Hon Sec,* D Howley, Rosses Point, 1 Wine Street, Co Sligo. ***Tel*** *(office)* Sligo (71) 62211; *(home)* (71) 77154.

Irish Ladies' Golf Union
Sec, Miss MP Turvey, 1 Clonskeagh Square, Clonskeagh Road, Dublin 14. ***Tel*** Dublin (0001) 696244.

Northern District *Hon Sec,* Mrs L Watson, 14D Adelaide Park, Belfast BT9 6FX. ***Tel*** (0232) 682152.

Southern District *Hon Sec,* Mrs N Flynn, 11 Barnstead Drive, Church Road, Blackrock, Cork. ***Tel*** Cork (21) 291698.

Eastern District *Hon Sec,* Mrs D O'Sullivan, 4 Castletown Court, Celbridge, Co. Kildare.

Western District *Hon Sec,* Mrs A Bradshaw, Dooney Rock, Cleveragh Drive, Sligo. ***Tel*** Sligo (71) 62351.

Midland District *Hon Sec,* Mrs B Jordan, 6 Glena Terrace, Spawell Road, Wexford. ***Tel*** Wexford (53) 22865.

Scotland

Aberdeen Ladies' County Golf Association
Hon Sec, Mrs J Middleton, Crochdane, Aulton Road, Cruden Bay. ***Tel*** (0779) 812315.

Angus Ladies' County Golf Association
Hon Sec, Mrs DJ Gordon, The Hawthorns, 7 Grange Avenue, Monifieth, Dundee *Tel* (0382) 532799.

Ayrshire Ladies' County Golf Association
Hon Sec, Mrs A McMillan, 8 Station Road, Prestwick KA9 1AQ. *Tel* (0292) 77330.

Border Counties' Golf Association
Hon Sec, Mrs E Wanless, Fullarton, Darnick, Melrose Roxburghshire. *Tel* (089 682) 2962.

Dumfriesshire and Galloway Lady Golfers' Association
Hon Sec, Miss MJ Greig, Strathdon, 10 Nelson Street, Dumfries DG2 9AY. *Tel* (0387) 54429.

Dumfriesshire Ladies' County Golf Association
Hon Sec, Miss MJ Greig, Strathdon, 10 Nelson Street, Dumfries. *Tel* (0387) 54429.

Dunbartonshire and Argyll Ladies' County Association
Hon Sec, Mrs AG Pairman, 19 Hutchison Drive, Bearsden G61 2JT. *Tel* 041-942 0451.

East Lothian Ladies' County Association
Hon Sec, Mrs IG Campbell, Glenlair, Main Street, Gullane. *Tel* (0620) 842534.

Fife County Ladies' Golf Association
Hon Sec, Mrs CH Matheson, Greyfriars, Greyfriars Garden, St Andrews. *Tel* (0334) 72639.

Galloway Ladies' County Golf Association
Hon Sec, Mrs W Lyon, Mossdene, Lewis Street, Stranraer. *Tel* (0776) 4517.

Lanarkshire Ladies' County Golf Association
Hon Sec, Mrs GE Duncanson, 75 Kenmure Gardens, Bishopbriggs, Glasgow G64 2BZ. *Tel* 041-772 1720.

Midlothian County Ladies' Golf Association
Hon Sec, Mrs EB Kemp, 84 Redford Loan, Edinburgh EH13 0AT. *Tel* 031-441 1800.

Northern Counties' Ladies Golf Association
Hon Sec, Mrs A Cranston, 15 Boarstone Avenue, Inverness. *Tel* (0463) 221317.

Perth and Kinross Ladies' County Golf Association
Hon Sec, J Jones, Broom, Caledonian Cresent, Auchterarder, Perthshire. *Tel* (0764) 62254.

Renfrewshire Ladies' County Golf Association
Hon Sec, Miss SC Goudie, 25 Florence Drive, Giffnock, Glasgow G46 6UN. *Tel* Glasgow 041–638 4971.

Stirling and Clackmannan Ladies' Golf Association
Hon Sec, Mrs HM Hudson, 14 Drummond Place, Stirling.

Scottish Golf Union
Sec, JW Hume, The Cottage, 181a Whitehouse Road, Barnton, Edinburgh EH4 6BY. *Tel* 031-339 7546.

Area Associations:

Angus G Hardie, Conachan, 4 Cliffburn Road, Arbroath, Angus DD11 5BB. *Tel* (0241) 73018 *(home)*, (0241) 722861 *(office)*.

Argyll and Bute J Forgreive, 6 Dulintart Drive, Oban. *Tel* (0631) 65298 *(home)*, (0631) 63626 *(office)*.

Ayrshire RL Crawford, 14 Maxwell Gardens, Hurlford, Kilmarnock, Ayrshire KA1 5BY. *Tel* (0563) 31932 *(home)*, (0563) 21190 *(office)*.

Borders AN Simpson, 7 Langlee Avenue, Galashiels TD1 2DZ. *Tel* (0896) 55526 *(home)*, (0896) 4866 *(office)*.

Clackmannanshire H Hunter, 27 Newton Crescent, Dunblane, Perthshire. *Tel* (0786) 822805.

Dunbartonshire RW Jenkins, Dunedin, 14 Hawthorn Avenue, Lenzie G66 4RA. *Tel* 041-776 1148.

Fife BR Wright, 2 West Fergus Place, Kirkcaldy, Fife KY1 1WR. *Tel* (0592) 263304 *(home)*, (0592) 206605 *(office)*.

Glasgow GO McInnes, 4 Dalziel Court, 56 Dalziel Drive, Glasgow G14. *Tel* 041-427 3156 *(home)*, 041-226 4471 *(office)*.

Lanarkshire JT Durrant, 30 Woodlands Crescent, Bothwell, Glasgow G71 8PP. *Tel* (0698) 852331.

Lothians IR Graham, 29 Morningside Grove, Edinburgh EH10 5PX. *Tel* 031-447 3281.

North JP Ford, Timbertop, Croy, Inverness IV1 2PH. *Tel* (066 78) 363.

North-East DJ Miller, 25 Albyn Place, Aberdeen AB1 1YL. *Tel* (0224) 589345 *(office)*, (0224) 732168 *(home)*.

Perth and Kinross DY Rae, 18 Carlownie Place, Auchterarder PH3 1BT *Tel* (0764) 62837.

Renfrewshire JI McCosh, *Muirfield*, 20 Williamson Place, Johnstone, Renfrewshire PA5 9DW. *Tel* (0505) 27974 *(home)*.

South JH Somerville, Cherry Cottage, Kirkcudbright. *Tel* (0557) 30445.

Stirlingshire RM McLaren, Yarrow, Touch Road, Cambusbarron, Stirling. ***Tel*** (0786) 72347 *(home)*, (0786) 73141 *(office)*.

Scottish Golfer's Alliance
Sec/Treas, Mrs ML Park, Chacewood, 49 Fullarton Drive, Troon KA10 6EL. ***Tel*** (0292) 313047

Scottish Ladies' Golfing Association
Sec, Mrs LH Park, 5 Brownhills House, St Andrews, Fife KY16 8PL. ***Tel*** (0334) 313047.

Scottish Ladies' Golfing Association—County Golf
Hon Sec, Miss MJ Greig, Strathdon, Nelson Street, Dumfries. ***Tel*** (0387) 54429.

Scottish Schools' Golf Association
Hon Sec, Mrs HM Hudson, 14 Drummond Place, Stirling FK8 2JE. ***Tel*** (0786) 72033.

West of Scotland Girls' Golfing Association
Hon Sec, Mrs PI McKay, 7 Gardenside Avenue, Uddingston, Glasgow G71 7BU.

Wales

Anglesey Golf Union
Hon Sec, GP Jones, 20 Gwelfor Estate, Cemaes Bay, Anglesey. ***Tel*** (0407) 710755.

Brecon and Radnor Golf Union
Hon Sec GL Williams, 10 Penpentre, Llanfaes, Brecon.

Caernarvonshire and Anglesey Ladies' County Golf Association
Hon Sec, Mrs BR Williams, Deunant, Llangefni, Anglesey LL7 7YP. ***Tel*** (0248) 722338.

Caernarvonshire and District Golfing Union
Hon Sec, R Eric Jones, 23 Bryn Rhos, Rhosbodrual, Caernarfon, Gwynedd LL55 2BT. ***Tel*** (0286) 3486.

Denbighshire Golfing Union
Hon Sec, J. Johnson, 15 Ffordd Elfed, Wrexham, Clwyd.

Denbighshire and Flintshire Ladies' County Golf Association
Hon Sec, Miss M Loveridge, Lincluden, 6 Brynlls East, Meliden, Prestatyn, Clwyd LL19 8PW.

Dyfed Golfing Union
Hon Sec, J Gottwaltz, Diamond Villa, Cosheston, Pembroke Dock. ***Tel*** (0646) 682434.

Flintshire Golfing Union
Hon Sec, H Griffith, Cornist Lodge, Cornist Park, Flint, Clwyd. ***Tel*** (03526) 2186.

Flintshire Ladies' Golf Association
Hon Sec, Mrs CM Scott, *Newlyn,* 46 Park Avenue, Hawarden, Deeside, Clwyd CH5 3HZ. ***Tel*** (0244) 534397.

Glamorgan County Golf Union
Hon Sec, John Banfill, 332 North Road, Cardiff. ***Tel*** (0222) 628493.

Glamorgan Ladies' County Golf Association
Mrs S Williams, 19 Trem-y-Don, Barry, South Glamorgan. ***Tel*** (0446) 734865.

Gwent Golf Union
Sec, J Huckin, 33 South Avenue, Griffithstown, Pontypool, Gwent. ***Tel*** (049 55) 55802.

Mid Wales Ladies County Golf Association
Hon Sec Mrs MA Carpenter, Castalia, Llandrindod Wells, LD1 5PH. ***Tel*** (0686) 86268.

Monmouthshire Ladies' County Golf Association
Hon Sec, Mrs M Menzies, 35 Park View Gardens, Bassales, Gwent NP1 9SZ. ***Tel*** (0633) 891843.

North Wales Counties Golf Association
Hon Sec, GP Jones, 20 Gwelfor Estate, Cemaes Bay, Anglesey LL67 0NL. ***Tel*** (0407) 710755.

North Wales Golfing Union
Hon Sec, RD Rogers, 52 Blackbrook Avenue, Upperdale, Hawarden, near Chester.

North Wales Junior Golf Association
Hon Sec, T Evans, 35 Parc Sychnant, Conwy, Gwynedd. ***Tel*** (049 263) 6270.

North Wales Professional Golfers' Alliance
Hon Sec, P Lees, Conway GC, Conway, Gwynedd. ***Tel*** (0492) 3225.

South Wales Professional Golfers' Association
Hon Sec, A Palmer, Aberdare GC, Aberdare, Mid-Glam. ***Tel*** (0685) 878735.

Welsh Golfing Union
Sec, DG Lee, 5 Park Place, Cardiff, South Glamorgan. ***Tel*** (0222) 238467.

Welsh Ladies' Golf Union
Hon Sec, Miss P Roberts, Ysgoldy Gynt, Llanhennock, Newport, Gwent NP6 1LT. ***Tel*** (0633) 420642.

Overseas

America: USA & Canada

American Ladies' Professional Golf Association
Commissioner, John D Laupheimer, 1250 Shoreline Drive, Suite 200, Sugarland, Texas, 77478, USA. ***Tel*** Houston (713) 980 5742.

American Professional Golfers' Association
Executive Director, Mark H Cox, Box 12458, 100 Avenue of the Champions, Palm Beach Gardens, Florida 33410.

Canadian Ladies' Golf Association
Executive Director, Les Whamond, 333 River Road, Ottawa, Ontario, K1L 8H9. ***Tel*** Ottawa (613) 746 5564.

Canadian Professional Golfers' Association
General Manager, Robert H Noble, 59 Berkeley Street, Toronto M5A 2W5. ***Tel*** Toronto (416) 368 6104.

Canadian (Royal) Golf Association
Golf House, RR no 2, Oakville, Ontario L6J 4Z3, Canada.

Provincial Golf Associations
British Columbia ***Sec/ Treas,*** RE Maze, Room 322, 1675 West 8th Ave, Vancouver, BC V6J 1V2.

Alberta ***Manager,*** ER Wood, 200-H Haddon Road, Calgary, Alberta T2V 2Y6.

Saskatchewan ***Exec Dir,*** WF Macrae, 2205 Victoria Avenue, Regina, Saskatchewan S4P 0S4.

Manitoba ***Exec Dir,*** DI Macdonald, 1700 Ellice Ave, Winnipeg, Manitoba R3H 0B1.

Ontario ***Exec Dir,*** WJ Williams, 400 Esna Park Drive, Unit 11, Markham, Ontario L3R 1H5.

Quebec ***Exec Director,*** CH Gribbin, 3300 Cavendish Blvd, Suite 250, Montreal, Quebec H4B 2M8.

New Brunswick ***Sec/ Treas,*** EA Trites, 3 Sunset Lane, St John, New Brunswick E2H 1C8.

Nova Scotia ***Sec/ Treas,*** W MacDonald, 14 Limardo Drive, Dartmouth, Nova Scotia B3A 3X4.

Newfoundland–Labrador ***Sec,*** CR Cook, PO Box 5361, St Johns, Newfoundland.

Prince Edward Island ***Sec/ Treas,*** David Kassner, PO Box 51, Charlottetown, PEI C1A 7K2.

Golf Course Association
111 East Wacker Drive, Chicago, Illinois 60601, USA. ***Tel*** Chicago (312) 644 6610.

International Golf Association
Room 746, Lincoln Building, 60 E 42nd Street, New York 10165.

TPA Tour
(USA), ***Commissioner,*** Deane R Beman, Sawgrass, Ponte Verde Beach, Florida 32082.

United States Golf Association
Senior Executive Director, Frank Hannigan, USGA Golf House, Liberty Corner Road, Far Hills, New Jersey 07931. ***Tel*** Jersey City (201) 234 2300.

United States Seniors' Golf Association
Suite 1306, 60 E 42nd Street, New York 10017.

Central America

Bahamas Golf Federation
Sec, Calvin Cooper, PO Box F.3854, Free Port, Grand Bahama, Bahamas.

Barbados Golf Association
Sec, TM Hanton, c/o Sandy Lane GC, St James, Barbados.

Bermuda Golf Association
Sec-Treas, Mrs Eric N Parker, PO Box 433, Hamilton 5, Bermuda. ***Tel*** 809 298 1367.

Jamaica Golf Association
Constant Spring Golf Club, Constant Spring, Kingston 8, Jamaica.

Mexican Golf Association
Cincinnati, No. 40-104, Mexico 18, DF.

Trinidad and Tobago Golf Association
Texaco Trinidad Inc, Point-a-Pierre, Trinidad, West Indies.

South America

Asociación Argentina de Golf
Gen Manager, JT Salorio; ***Hon Sec,*** Ignacio JR Soba Rojo, Corrientes 538, Piso 11, 1043 Buenos Aires, Argentina.

Argentine Professional Golfers' Association
Calle Libertad No. 956 (Local No. 22), Buenos Aires, Argentina.

Asunción Golf Union
Casilla de Correo 302, Asunción, Paraguay.

Bolivian Golf Federation (Federación Boliviana de Golf)
Sec, Raul Zabalaga, Casilia de Correo 6130, La Paz, Bolivia.

Brazilian Golf Confederation (Confederacão Brasileira de Golf),
Administrative Director, SS Marvin, Rua 7 de Abril, 282-S/84-01044, São Paulo, Brazil

Chilean Golf Federation
Casilla 13307, Correo 21, Santiago, Chile.

Colombian Golf Union (Federación Colombiana de Golf)
Sec, Louis Restrepo, Carrer 7A, 72-64 of Int 26 Apartado 90985, Bogotá, Colombia.

Ecuador Golf Federation (Asociación Equatoriana de Golf)
Casilia 521, Guayaquil, Ecuador.

Guyana Golf Union
c/o Demerara Bauxite Co Limited, Mackenzie, Guyana.

Paraguay Golf Association
Asunción GC, Casilla de Correo 302, Asunción, Paraguay.

Peru Golf Federation (Federación Peruana de Golf)
Sec, HB Sanchez, Casilla 5637, Lima, Peru.

South American Golf Federation
Hon Sec, E Anchordoqui, Guipuzcoa 486-P7, Montevideo, Uruguay.

Uruguay Golf Association (Asociación Uruguaya de Golf)
Sec, Jorge Brignoni, Casilla de Correo 1484, Montevideo.

Venezuela Golf Federation
Unidad Comercial, *La Florida,* Local 5, Avenida Avila, La Florida, Caracas 1050, Venezuela.

Asia and Far East

Asia-Pacific Golf Confederation
Sec Gen, EJH Yong, 52, 1st Floor, Jalan Hang, Lekiu 50100, Kuala Lumpur

Asia Professional Golf Circuit
Tournament Co-ordinator, Mrs LE Kim Hall, 1710 Star House, 3 Salisbury Road, Kowloon, Hong Kong. *Tel* Kowloon (3) 679927. *Telex* 75561 MIK HX.

Ceylon Golf Union
2 Gower Street, Colombo 5, Sri Lanka.

China (Republic of) Golf Association
Charles C Chang, *Sec Gen,* 71, Lane 369, Tanhua S Road, Taipei, Taiwan (106), Rep of China. *Tel* 711 3046, 711 7482.

Hong Kong Golf Association
Sec, Michael J Steele, Room 110, Yuto Sang Bldg 37, Queens Road, Central, Hong Kong.

Hong Kong Professional Golfers' Association
Hon Sec, AR Hamilton, PO Box 690, Hong Kong. *Tel* Hong Kong (5) 222111. *Telex* HX73751

Indian Golf Union
Hon Sec, Raj Bir Singh, Tata Centre (3rd Floor), 43 Chowringhee Road, Calcutta 700071.

Indonesian Golf Association
Hon Sec, MST Aziz, Jalan Rawamangun Muka Raya, Jakarta 13220. *Tel* 4891208 *Telex* 61396 DJACOM IA.

Japan Golf Association
Exec Dir, Toshizo Takeuchi, 606-6th Floor, Palace Building, Marunouchi, Chiyoda-ku, Tokyo, Japan. *Tel* Tokyo (3) 215 0003.

Japan Ladies' Professional Golfers' Association
Kuranae Kogyo Kaikan 7F, Shinbasi 2-19-10, Minato-ku, Tokyo. *Tel* Tokyo (3) 571 0928.

Japan Professional Golf Association
Shineido Building 5F, 1-5-14 Shinbashi, Minato-ku, Tokyo. *Tel* Tokyo (3) 504 3300.

Korean Golf Association
Sec General, Room 1B, 13th Floor, Manhattan Bldg, 36-2, Yeo-Eui-Do-Dowg, Yeong Deung Po-Ku, Seoul, Korea. *Tel* Seoul (2) 783 4748/783 4749.

Malaysian Golf Association
Hon Sec, TK Kee, 12A Persiaran Ampang, 55000 Kuala Lumpur, Malaysia.

New Guinea Papua Territory Amateur Golf Association
Sec, Jack Page, PO Box 382, Lae, TPNG.

Pakistan Golf Union
Hon Sec, Colonel MA Malik, PO Box No. 6103, Lahore 13, Pakistan. *Tel* Lahore (42) 372001.

Papua New Guinea Ladies' Golf Association
Mrs Mavis Harvey, PO Box 1256, Port Moresby, TPNG. *Tel* 675 214745.

Republic of the Philippines Golf Association
209 Administration Building, Rizal Memorial Sports Complex, Vito Cruz, Manila, Philippines.

Singapore Golf Association
Hon Sec, Gerald Loong, Singapore Golf Association, 4 Battery Rd, No 12-00 Bank of China Building, Singapore 0104. *Telegraphic address* Golfing Singapore; *Telex* RS 42354 Acapas.

Sri Lanka Ladies' Golf Union
c/o Royal Colombo Golf Club, PO Box 309, Colombo, Sri Lanka.

Sri Lanka Golf Union
2 Gower Street, Colombo 5, Sri Lanka.

Thailand Golf Association
Hon Sec, Likhit Sudarat, Railway Training, Vibhavadee Centre Rangsit Road, Bangkok 10900, Thailand. ***Tel*** 51 34988/9 ***Telex*** 20806 SCCFOOD TH.

Australasia

Australian Golf Union
Sec, CA Phillips, Golf Australia House, 155 Cecil Street, South Melbourne, Victoria 3205.

Members of the Union:

Victoria ***Sec,*** TS Duguid, Victorian Golf Association, PO Box 187, Elsternwick, Victoria 3185.

New South Wales ***Sec,*** B Scott, New South Wales Golf Association, 17-19 Brisbane Street, Darlinghurst, NSW 2010.

Tasmanian Golf Council, ***Sec,*** A Rollins, GPO Box 940K, Hobart 7001. ***Tel*** Hobart (02) 348315.

Queensland ***Sec,*** W Kennedy, Queensland Golf Union, PO Box 260, Mt Gravatt, Queensland 4122, Australia.

Western Australia ***Sec,*** G Fitzhardinge, Western Australian Golf Association Inc, PO Box 455 South Perth, W Aust. 6151

South Australia ***Sec,*** MH Hall, South Australia Golf Association, 249 Henley Beach Road, Torvensville, South Australia 5031.

Australian Ladies' Golf Union
Executive Director, Mrs KD Brown, 22 McKay Road, Rowville 3178, Victoria.
Tel Melbourne (3) 763 6919.

Members of the Union:

Victoria ***Sec,*** Miss K Mahlook, 589 Malvern Road, Toorak, 3142, Victoria.

New South Wales ***Sec,*** Miss Wendy V Weil, 17 Brisbane Street, Darlinghurst, NSW 2010. ***Tel*** 264 7327.

Queensland ***Sec,*** Mrs M Barnett, PO Box 83, Chermside, 4032, Queensland. ***Tel*** 221 6677.

Western Australia ***Sec,*** Mrs M Cutter, Suite 1-4, Stratham House, 49 Melville Parade, South Perth. ***Tel*** 368 2618.

South Australia ***Sec,*** Mrs GA Small, 13 Pitcairn Ave, Urrbrae, 5064. ***Tel*** 79 3200.
Tasmania ***Sec,*** Mrs IP Allen, 45 Balmoral Road, Kingston Beach, 7151. ***Tel*** 29 5120.

Australian Professional Golfers' Association
Sec, DN Johnson, 113 Queen Street, North Strathfield, New South Wales, 2137.

New Zealand Golf Association (Inc)
Dominion Sports House, Mercer Street, Wellington, PO Box 11842. ***Tel*** Wellington (4) 845 408. ***Telegrams*** Enzedgolf.

New Zealand Professional Golfers' Association
Sec, Sqn Ldr AR Bleakley, PO Box 21-482, Auckland 8. ***Tel*** Auckland (9) 836 4703.

New Zealand Ladies' Golf Union
Mrs A Rogers, PO Box 446, Waipukurau, Hawkes Bay, New Zealand.

Africa (south of Sahara)

Botswana Golf Union
Hon Sec, Robert Stewart, PO Box 1033, Gaborone, Botswana. ***Tel*** Gaborone (31) 53989 *(home).*

Ghana Golf Association
Sec, MM Ezan, PO Box 8, Achimola, Ghana.

Kenya Golf Union
PO Box 49609, Nairobi. ***Tel*** Nairobi (2) 720074.

Kenya Ladies' Golf Union
PO Box 45615, Nairobi, Kenya.

Malawi Golf Union
PO Box 1198, Blantyre, Malawi.

Malawi Ladies' Golf Union
PO Box 5319, Limbe, Malawi.

Nigerian Golf Association
Sec Ms N Chinakwe, c/o National Sports Commission, Surulere, PO Box 145, Lagos.

Sierra Leone Golf Federation
Pres, JS Baird, PO Box 575, Freetown, Sierra Leone.

South African Golf Union
Exec Dir, JM Kellie, PO Box 1537, Cape Town 8000. ***Cablegram address:*** Sagolfunion, Cape Town. ***Tel*** Cape Town (21) 467585 *(office)*, (21) 653617 *(home).*

Provincial Unions:

Border Golf Union ***Hon Sec,*** Mrs J Davenport, Box 1773, East London 5200, CP. ***Tel*** (0431) 403899.

Eastern Province Golf Union ***Hon Sec,*** CAL Fowles, PO Box 146, Port Elizabeth 6000, CP. ***Tel*** (041) 21919.

Karoo Golf Association ***Hon Sec,*** Mrs CL Hobson, PO Box 71, Middleburg 5900, CP.

OFS & Northern Cape Golf Union ***Hon Sec,*** RF Davidson, PO Box 517, Bloemfontein 9300, OFS. ***Tel*** (051) 470511.

Natal Golf Union ***Sec,*** RT Runge, PO Box 1939, Durban 4000, Natal. ***Tel*** (031) 223877.

South-West Africa Golf Union ***Hon Sec,*** H Hanstein, PO Box 2989, Windhoek 9000. (061) 222786.

Transkei Golf Union ***Sec,*** Philip Geldehuys, PO Box 210, Umtata, Transkei.

Transvaal Golf Union ***Sec,*** RC Witte, PO Box 391661, Bramley 2018, Transvaal. ***Tel*** (011) 6403714/5

Western Province Golf Union ***Sec*** BW Myles, Box 153, Howard Place, 7450, CP. ***Tel*** (021) 536728.

South African Ladies' Golf Union
Sec, Mrs E Cutler, PO Box 135, Vereeniging, Transvaal, South Africa.

South African Professional Golfers' Association
c/o Wanderers Golf Club, PO Box 55253, Northlands, Johannesburg 2116.

Swaziland Golf Union
A Rutt, PO Box 1739, Mbabane, Swaziland.

Tanzania Golf Union
Hon Sec, R Virjee, Tanzania Golf Union, c/o Dar es Salaam Gymkhana Club, PO Box 286, Dar es Salaam, Tanzania.

Uganda Golf Union
Sec, PO Box 2574, Kampala, Uganda.

Zaire Golf Federation
Pres, Tshilombo Mwin Tshitol, BP 1648, Lubumbashi, Zaire. ***Tel*** 2269

Zambian Golf Union
Hon Sec, Amon T Chibiya, PO Box 37445, Lusaka, Zambia. ***Telex*** ZA 40098

Zambia Ladies' Golf Union
Sec, Mrs C Howell, PO Box 32150, Lusaka, Zambia. ***Tel*** Lusaka (1) 251668, ***Telex*** ZA 40098

Zimbabwe Golf Association
Sec, B de Kock, PO Box 3327, Harare, Zimbabwe.

Zimbabwe Ladies' Golf Union
PO Box 3814, Harare, Zimbabwe.

Europe

Austrian Golf Federation
Sec, G Jungk, (Osterreichischer Golf-Verband) Haus des Sports, Prinz Eugen-Strasse 12, A-1040 Vienna, Austria. ***Tel*** Vienna (222) 653245; ***Telex*** 133132.

Belgian Royal Federation of Golf
Sec, Roger Duys, Route de la Marche 19, B-1328-Ohain. ***Tel*** Brussels (2) 633 2496. ***Fax*** 32 (2) 6334218.

Czechoslovak Golf Federation
Sec, H Goldscheider, Na Porici, 12, 11530 Prague 1. ***Tel*** Prague (2) 2350065-84 ***Telex*** 122650.

Danish Golf Union (Dansk Golf Union)
Gen Sec, JF Larsen, Toftevj 26, 2625 Vallensbaek, Denmark. ***Tel*** Copenhagen (2) 64 06 66.

European Golf Association
Gen Sec, C Storjohann, En Ballègue, Case Postale CH-1066, Epalignes, Lausanne, Switzerland. ***Tel*** (4121) 327705; ***Telex*** 450804 Golf; ***Fax*** 41-21-328176.

Amateur Technical Committee: ***Hon Sec,*** JL Dupont, 51 Av Victor Hugo, 93300 Aubervilliers. ***Tel*** Paris (1) 833 4949.

Finnish Golf Union (Finlands Golfforbund)
Hon Sec, J Huhtanen, Radiokatu 12, SF-00240 Helsinki. ***Tel*** Helsinki (90) 1581; ***Telex*** 121797.

French Golf Federation (Fédération Française de Golf)
Hon Sec, J Labatut, 69 Avenue Victor Hugo, 75783 Paris, Cedex 16. ***Tel*** Paris (1) 45021355; ***Telex*** 614 406 FF Golf, ***Fax*** 33 (1) 45003068.

French Professional Golfers' Association
69 Avenue Victor Hugo, 75116 Paris 16, France. ***Tel*** Paris (1) 500 43 72.

German Golf Association (Deutscher Golf Verband)
Sec, Heinz Biemer, Postfach 2106, Leberberg 25, 62 Wiesbaden, W Germany. ***Tel*** 010 49 (6121) 526041; ***Telex*** 4 186 459, ***Fax*** 49 (6121) 599493.

German PGA (Deutscher Golflehrer Verband)
Sec, Mrs Suzanne Mühlbauer, Eberlestrasse 13, 89 Augsberg, W Germany. ***Tel*** 010 49 (821) 528900.

Hellenic Golf Federation
Hon Sec, George Th Lusi, PO Box 70003, GR 16610, Glyfada, Athens, Greece. ***Tel*** Athens (1)894 6820 or Athens (1)894 1933, ***Telex*** 212493 MYLG GR or 224524 DIOR GR.

Hungarian Golf Association
President, Dr F Gati, c/o Hungerian Blue Danube Golf Club, 111 Milkos-ug 11, 12, H-1035 Budapest.

Iceland Golf Union (Golfsanband Islands)
Gen Sec, Frimann Gunlaugsson, Reykjavik 121, PO Box 1076, Iceland. ***Tel*** Reykjavik (1) 686686; ***Telex*** 2314 ISI IS.

International Greenkeepers' Assoc
Hon Sec, Mrs B Harradine, Via Golf, CH6987, Caslano, Switzerland.

Italian Golf Federation (Federazione Italiana Golf)
Sec, Luigi Orlandini, 388 Via Flaminia I-00196 Rome. ***Tel*** Rome (6) 394 641. ***Telex*** 613192 Golfed I.

Luxembourg Golf Club Grand Ducal
Sec, Miss J Schwartz, 1 Route de Treve 2633, Senningerberg, Luxembourg. ***Tel*** (352) 34090.

Netherlands Golf Federation
Gen Sec, JA van der Schraaf, Soestdijkerstraatweg 172, 1213XJ, Hilversum, Netherlands. ***Tel*** 010 3135-830565, ***Fax*** 31 (35) 834897.

Netherlands Professional Golfers' Assoc
Sec, A Wessels, Karel De Grotelaan 190, Deventer, Netherlands.

Norwegian Golf Union (Norges Golfforbund)
Gen Sec, Anna Donnestad, Hauger Skolevei 1, 1351 Rud, Norway. ***Tel*** Oslo (2) 51 88 00; ***Telex*** 18586 NIFN.

Portuguese Golf Federation (Federación Portuguesa de Golfe)
Sec, E Vieira, Rua Almeida Brandao 39, 1200 Lisbon, Portugal. ***Tel*** Lisbon (1) 661126; ***Telex*** 64044 FPGOLF P.

Spanish Golf Association (Real Federación Espanola de Golf)
Gen Sec L Alvarez De Bohorquez, Capitan Haya 9-5 Dcha, Madrid 28020, Spain. ***Tel*** 010 34 455 26 82 / 455 27 57; ***Fax*** 91-456-3290.

Swedish Golf Federation (Svenska Golf Forbundet)
Sec Gen, Lars Granberg, PO Box 84, S-182 11 Danderyd, Sweden. ***Tel*** Stockholm (8) 753 04 55; ***Telex*** 16608, ***Fax*** 08-7558439.

Swedish PGA
Executive Director, Christer Lindberg, ***Chairman,*** John Cockin. PO Box 35, S-181 21 Lidingö, Sweden. ***Tel*** Stockholm (8) 767 83 23.

Swiss Golf Association (Association Suisse de Golf)
Sec, JC Storjohann, En Ballègue, Case Postale CH-1066, Epalinges, Lausanne. ***Tel*** Lausanne (21) 32 7701. ***Telex*** 45450804.

Swiss Professional Golfers' Association
Hon Sec, Jakob Kressig, Perrelet 9, 2074 Marin, Switzerland. ***Tel*** (038) 33 23 79.

Yugoslavia Golf Federation
Golf association of Slovenia, Kublarjeva 34, Yu-61000 Ljubljana.

Middle East

Egyptian Golf Federation
c/o Gezira Sporting Club, Gezira, Cairo, Egypt. ***Tel*** Cairo (2) 80 6000.

Israel Golf Union
Sec, Alon Ben-David, PO Box 1010, Caesarea 30660, Israel.

Libyan Golf Union
PO Box 879, Tripoli, Libya.

United Arab Emirates Golf Union
c/o Gazira Sporting Club, Gazira, Cairo, Egypt. ***Tel*** Cairo (2) 80 6000.

Part VI
Golf History

The Origin of Golf

David Hamilton

Beginnings

The game of golf was not a sudden invention; it evolved and matured out of many other stick-and-ball games played in medieval Europe. France had its game of *chole* and England had a stick-and-ball game called 'cambuca'. Only two games, however, are serious contenders as the forerunner of the modern game of golf. The first was *colf* (or *koffe*), popular in the Low Countries, and the second was the game already known as 'golf' (or 'gouff' or 'gollfe' in the random, phonetic spelling of the day), which is persistently mentioned in Scottish records from medieval times onwards.

Dutch *colf*

The Dutch *colf* was popular and appears frequently in early Dutch records – of which many more have survived than the few scrappy Scottish documents of the same period – from 1300 onwards. A major study by Steven van Hengel, *Early Golf* (privately published in 1982), has at last described the game from original documents. A single iron-headed club, which had considerable loft, was used. It seems to have been mostly a town game, played towards a target such as a door, and may have been popular with children. The game became a nuisance in the towns, but only occasionally did regulations successfully move it out into the open fields nearby, where it may have been played into a hole in the ground. The Dutch towns where *colf* was popular were inland and, without adjacent coastal links, it could not be played very successfully outside the towns. When the canals were frozen, a form might be played using a post, or even a hole, in the ice as the target.

In Scotland, early records are less well preserved, and portrait and landscape painting did not exist. Nevertheless, sufficient is known about the early game of 'golf' to suggest that until about 1650 it may have resembled *colf*, as many records show that it was played in the churchyard or street. Scotland and the Low Countries were closely linked by trade, and hence there are good reasons why the games should have been similar.

Move to links

But by 1650 another version of the Scottish golf can be seen emerging as the dominant form, changing it to resemble the modern game. At this time it moved out of the towns on to the hard links – land beside the east-coast towns and ports, where in winter (and early golf was a winter game) a game of skill developed, combining lengthy shots with accuracy as the hole was neared. Wooden-headed clubs, which could be expensive, were now the kind most in use and even in the Low Countries were known as 'Scotch cleeks'. In Scotland an iron club was reserved for bunkers or ruts. The target in this long game was a hole in the ground.

REGULUS,

BAculus, Pila calvaria, *a goulf ball.* Fovea, *a goat.* Percute pilam baculo. Nimis curtâsti hunc mißum, *this is too short a stroke.* Pila tua devia est, procul excussisti pilam, *that is a good stroak.* Statumina pilam arena, *Teaz your ball on the sande* Statumen, *the teaz.* Frustra es, *that is a miss.* Vel irritus hic conatus est, percute pilam sensim, *give the ball but a little chap* Apposite *that is very well.* Immissa est pila in fovea, *the ball is goated.* Quomodo eam hinc elidam? Cedo baculum ferreum, *let see the bunkard club.* Iterum frustra es. *this is the second miss.* Tertia quarta, &c Bene tibi cessit hic ictus, *that is well stricken.* Malè tibi cessit hic ictus. Huc rectà pilam dirige. Dirige rectà versus foramen, *strick directly upon the hole.* Percute pilam sursum versus. *strike up the hill.* Percute deorsum versus, *strike down the hill.* An prætèrlapsa est foramen. Factum quod volui, *I would not wish a better stroak.* Immissa est in paludem, *it is in the mire.* Rectè evolavit, *it hath flowen directly on* Baculi caput, *the head of the club.* Baculi caulis, *the shaft of the club.* Baculi manubrium, *the handle where the wippen is.* Baculi filum, *the wippen.*

The earliest description of the Scottish game of golf, taken from a Latin grammar for schools, Aberdeen 1632. It mentions bunkers, iron clubs, holes and sand used for teeing up. (Courtesy of Aberdeen University Library.)

Why should the game have been different in Scotland from that played elsewhere in Europe and why should it have changed in this way? Perhaps the interest of the aristocracy and the Stuart monarchs was important, since they took up golf seriously; they could afford to buy the expensive equipment. For this reason golf appeared in London after the Union of the Crowns, when James VI of Scotland ascended the throne of Great Britain as James I. In Scotland too, the east-coast ports, notably Leith near Edinburgh, had links, whereas the Low Countries' *colf*-playing towns were inland, with wet, heavy land in winter.

There is no evidence that the Dutch game evolved along the same lines as its Scottish counterpart, and indeed *colf* disappeared about 1700, probably eliminated by the growth of the towns and the congestion of their streets. Ball-and-stick games in Holland developed in a different way to give *kolf*, an indoor game played over a short, formal court. It seems reasonable to conclude that, in the absence of other evidence, golf as we now know it evolved in Scotland, but perhaps later than was once supposed.

The first Clubs

In the late 1600s, golf was popular in Scotland along the east coast and two centres in particular were of interest. St Andrews had keen aristocratic student golfers, whose fathers were among those who played at Leith. Numerous diaries and local records show the popularity of Leith, and it was not surprising that here the world's first Golf Club was founded – the Honourable Company of Edinburgh Golfers. There were many golfing cliques in Leith and the club's foundation was probably a response to the fading fortunes of the town, in decline after the Union of the Parliaments. Already the Leith races were popular and a trophy had been given by the Town Council. The new Company of Golfers was also provided with a trophy – a silver club – and though this did not herald any sudden change in the game, it did mean that rules had to be drawn up for the new competition – the first rules of golf.

Other Clubs were founded in the seventeenth century, imitating the Leith golfers, and, as Scottish attitudes relaxed in an increasingly sociable century, these Clubs became known for their heavy drinking and hearty eating. They seem to have had little turnover of members, who were often bound together for reasons other than golf – often military or masonic. The Clubs played a valuable role in supporting the early club- and ballmakers, and were vigilant in protecting the rights of the townspeople to use the links for recreation. Many records show that golf was still popular with the tradespeople of the towns, who were not members of the Golf Clubs. Whether these poorer golfers played with the expensive equipment used by the rich or with a cheaper club and ball is not certain.

Temporary cessation

The early 1800s saw a crisis in the Scottish game. Industrialization brought rapid expansion to the towns without regard for amenities, and public links such as those

The Trophy for the Gentlemen Golfers of Edinburgh (later the Honourable Company) on display.

at Leith, Aberdeen, Glasgow and Leven were throttled. Some Clubs, like the Honourable Company of Edinburgh Golfers and the Glasgow Club, ceased to exist for a spell and others dispersed to new, quieter areas, such as Musselburgh. The game itself appeared to be less popular.

The game takes off

But in the year 1848 a revolution in the game occurred. The appearance of the new gutty ball, made out of malleable gutta-percha, produced a cheap, durable alternative to the short-lived featherie or the wooden ball of the common game. Less dramatic but of similar significance was the change from the brittle woods to tough hickory for club shafts. To the older men who earned their living by club- and ball-making, like Allan Robertson, it seemed that their trade was in danger, but others, like 'old' Tom Morris, realized that the new equipment might help spread the game. In this belief they were correct beyond any reasonable expectation. The new well-off middle class produced by the growth of industry flocked to Scotland for their holidays using the expanding rail network. St Andrews and North Berwick were favourite places and there the visitors imitated the games of the old leisured class. Their wives and families also learned the game on these Scottish holidays, and women's golf was born at St Andrews. Celebrities such as AJ Balfour, then Secretary of

State for Ireland, were keen players and helped its popularity further.

Back home, in England and elsewhere, they drew up plans for courses for which they hired Scottish help. From Scotland poured a stream of designers and professionals, like Willie Dunn and, later, Donald Ross. The Carnoustie Club (drawn from the artisans of the town) produced a remarkable number of young emigrés who could be found playing golf and tending the courses all over North America.

English and US expansion

Blackheath claimed great antiquity, dating back to the Stuart kings. The first English Club of the modern era, however, was perhaps the Old Manchester Club (1818), though the first of the continuous modern era was the Royal North Devon (1864) at Westward Ho!, a Club which had the distinction of raising JH Taylor who became the first professional to beat the Scots at their own game. In Ireland, Royal Belfast (1881) was the first golf club to be formed, and in Europe, Pau (1856) led the way. Britain's expanding Empire spread golf around the world. In Britain, a new burst of Club foundation occurred, reaching its peak in the 1890s. The number of clubs rose from less than 100 in 1875 to 1300 in 1900. Golf had been played in a small way in America before the foundation of the St Andrews Golf Club of Yonkers in 1888, but the Club's pioneers had met with ridicule. This Club's course was primitive, but by 1895 came America's first open championship links, at Newport, Rhode Island – although as late as 1899 leading British professionals like Harry Vardon met little opposition on tours in America.

'Old' and 'young' Tom Morris.

Early competitive play

Competitive golf dates from the inter-Club matches of the early nineteenth century, the first of which was recorded in 1818 when two of the Edinburgh Clubs playing over Bruntsfield Links, the Burgess Golfing Society and the Bruntsfield Links Club, competed against each other. In 1857 the Prestwick Club organized a successful inter-club tournament, and in 1860 they arranged an event for professional golfers, which later became known as the Open Championship. They may have wished to show the skills of the invited professionals, particularly their own man, Tom Morris, whom they had hired as a ball- and club-maker, and who looked after the Prestwick links – the first such salaried post for a golfer. Sadly, Allan Robertson did not live to play in the competition, though the year previously he was the first to have broken 80 in a round over the Old Course. The Open was unusual in being a stroke-play competition, as the early inter-Club tournaments were match play.

New horizons

Golf prospered and by the time of Willie Park's success the small number of professional golfers could hope for larger stakes in challenge matches and the rewards of occasional tournaments. Park was perhaps the first to capitalize on his fame in the modern way as a golf consultant and by publicizing his own branded clubs, notably an infallible putter, and by using mass production, advertising and postal sales he was highly successful. At St Andrews the first golf club manufacturing firm that had not been set up by a professional golfer appeared – the Forgan's firm, which survived for almost a century.

Scottish professional dominance ended in 1894 when an English-born professional, JH Taylor, won the Open. The rise of American golf was signalled when WJ Travis won the British Amateur Championship in 1904.

Though a home-bred player, JJ McDermott, had won the US Open in 1911, it was Francis Ouimet's win in 1913 that caught the popular imagination. Another feature of the growing dominance of America was the appearance of the Haskell ball in 1902, quickly capturing the market. Club design changed to suit the new ball: heads became deeper and the scarehead design changed to the socket joint.

Improved status

Professionals' status remained low until the end of the century and they were usually called by their second names only. Even Open Champions had to tee the ball up for their amateur

From George M Colville Five Open Champions and the Musselburgh Golf Story, *Musselburgh 1980.*

THE MAN WHO CAN PUTT IS A MATCH FOR ANYBODY.

If you want to putt well, use

Park's SPECIAL PUTTING-CLEEK (Patented) Price 7/6 each

AS USED BY

MR H. H. HILTON,

WINNER OF THE

OPEN CHAMPIONSHIP, 1897.

Mr Hilton writes in the "Sporting Chronicle" on 19th July 1898, as follows:

"If Willie Park, jun. did not succeed in winning the Open Championship, he at least had the satisfaction of knowing that the man who did succeed in beating him accomplished the feat with one of the Musselburgh man's patent putters; and the extraordinary run of success attained in the series of open tournaments was probably more due to his deadly execution with this club than to any other department of his game. It is needless to go farther than to say that the winner used one of Park's patent putters, as, in truth, the first three to finish all used what I have heard termed 'that wry-neck abortion of Park's.' Wry-necked or not, there can be no shadow of doubt as to the popularity of this very putter. It has outlived the prejudice which patent tools are more or less subject to contract at first, and it is in general use from one end of the kingdom to the other. I have frequently been asked what advantage it enjoys compared with the ordinary straight-faced putter. I am afraid I have always had to plead ignorance on this point, and have referred the inquirer to the patentee for information, while I have attributed my personal liking for the putter to a mere matter of fancy. The first time I tried it I was eminently successful with the implement, and although I am a great believer in an occasional change of clubs, I always find that eventually I fall back on the original 'Park' putter. Whether the fact that the face is set back behind the perpendicular of the shaft gives a better sight of the ball I cannot say, but I know that it imbues me with a feeling of confidence when playing an approach putt."

Beware of Imitations.

See that every Cleek is stamped "PARK'S SPECIAL."

WM. PARK & SON, GOLF CLUB MAKERS, Musselburgh.

CHAMPION GOLFERS,

1860, 1863, 1866, 1875, 1887, 1889.

BRANCHES AT—115 CANNON STREET, LONDON;
6 SOUTH ST ANDREW STREET, EDINBURGH;
and 118 WEST 23rd STREET, NEW YORK.

From George M Colville Five Open Champions and the Musselburgh Golf Story, *Musselburgh 1980.*

partners in exhibition matches, and even James Braid never entered Walton Heath clubhouse by the front door. JH Taylor organized the professionals in Britain, promoting their image until they became national figures even outside the narrow world of sport. Their new-found popularity was marked by an increasing number of tournaments, notably the sponsorship by the *News of the World* of the first tournament of the modern era. The changing status of professionals in Britain was pioneered and continued by Henry Cotton, who, on being appointed to Ashridge GC in 1937, made the bold stipulation that he be made an honorary member of the Club. The modern professional had arrived.

Today golf is played world-wide, and is perhaps the most popular participant outdoor sport in the world. The government of the game still bears out its Scottish origins – the Royal and Ancient Golf Club of St Andrews shares with the United States Golf Association the regulation of all golf. And only in Scotland is it still universally the game of the ordinary people.

Evolution of the Rules of Golf

J Stewart Lawson

Authors note: Revised Rules of Golf came into force on 1 January 1988, but 1984 was a significant date in the evolution of the Rules.

The late Henry Longhurst always maintained that perfectly adequate rules for the game of golf could be written on the back of a score card. When challenged to show how this could be done, Henry produced a set of ten Rules, the key one reading: *The game shall be played in the traditional manner*... Sadly, Henry was never pressed to say to which of the many different traditions he was referring. Should we, for example, be following the Leith system (*At Holling, you are to play your Ball honestly for the Hole, and not to play upon your Adversary's Ball, not lying in your way to the Hole* – The Gentlemen Golfers, 1744) or the Brunonian system (*It shall be deemed fair to play a ball against the adversary's ball, provided the player does not touch the adversary's ball with his club* – Edinburgh Burgess Golfing Society, 1814)?

No doubt there are many traditionalists who will shake their heads mournfully over the 1984 version of the Rules of Golf. Not only are the playing rules presented in an entirely new and, it is hoped, more logical order, but several important changes of principle and procedure have also been made. What many people forget, however, is that from the very outset the rules of the game have been organic: they have grown and proliferated; they have changed their form and shape many times; and, by discarding provisions as they became outmoded, they have supported Darwin's theory of the survival of the fittest. Nevertheless, through all phases of this evolution, the organism's backbone has remained unaffected: the game of golf still *consists in playing a ball from the* teeing ground *into the hole by a* stroke *or successive strokes in accordance with the Rules* – Rule 1-1.

Early rules

Golf in Scotland had managed to survive three centuries without any apparent need for written rules when, in 1744, the Gentlemen Golfers at Leith drew up thirteen Articles & Laws in Playing at Golf, the occasion being the first competition for the City of Edinburgh's Silver Club and the Gentlemen Golfers apprehending that entrants from other parts of the country might not be familiar with the Leith tradition. As other golfing societies were formed in the ensuing years, each drew up its own rules of play, but the leadership of the Gentlemen Golfers, later to become The Honourable Company of Edinburgh Golfers, was generally acknowledged. From the 1830s onwards, however, due to a temporary eclipse of the Honourable Company, this leadership gradually passed to the Society of St Andrews Golfers, which in 1834 had been granted the title of Royal and Ancient Golf Club of St Andrews. This shift of influence to the Royal and Ancient is illustrated by the fact that, whereas in 1810 the first 15 Rules of the Glasgow Golf Club were, with one minor difference, word for word the same as those of the Honourable Company, in 1851 the newly formed Prestwick Golf Club decided to adopt the St Andrews Rules of Play.

The last quarter of the nineteenth century saw a tremendous expansion of golf both at home and overseas, and there was a growing demand for a uniform code of rules. Widespread interest was shown when the Royal and Ancient announced the publication of a new set of Rules in 1891, and great importance was attached to the revisions these contained. It was natural, in these circumstances, that the leading clubs should invite the Royal and Ancient to assume responsibility for producing a uniform code, and the first Rules of Golf Committee was appointed in 1897. The United States Golf Association had been organized in 1894, and these two bodies, the Royal and Ancient and the USGA, now became the game's two governing authorities, responsible for the formulation of rules and for their interpretation. During the first half of the present century, the Royal and Ancient and the USGA shared the same basic code of rules, but each body issued its own interpretative Decisions, and many differences arose, particularly in the area of the game's equipment: the Royal and Ancient's banning of the centre-shafted putter after WJ Travis had won the

British Amateur with a Schenectady; the eventual disagreement (now at last resolved) over the minimum size of the golf ball; and the legalization of steel shafts by the USGA some years before the Royal and Ancient followed suit. Interpretation of the playing rules also differed, and the USGA, without the same long tradition of match play, had no qualms about abolishing the stymie.

Royal and Ancient–USGA co-operation

By 1950 there was a grave danger of the Royal and Ancient and the USGA drifting farther apart, but conferences held in 1951, which representatives from Canada and Australia also attended, resulted in the formulation of a uniform code, the only initial difference being over the size of the ball; a couple of minor divergencies in the playing rules which arose later did not last long and uniformity has been maintained ever since. Arrangements were also made in 1951 for the Royal and Ancient and the USGA to meet periodically to review the Rules, and these meetings now take place every four years; on the Royal and Ancient's part, only after detailed consultation with the 65 Golfing Unions and Associations affiliated to it. It would have been anomalous, however, to have uniform rules if they were not being interpreted in the same way. A comprehensive analysis of Royal and Ancient and USGA Decisions carried out a few years ago revealed several important differences of interpretation, and a Joint Decisions Committee was therefore appointed to establish uniformity in this area as well as in the Rules themselves. So successful has this new venture been that in 1984 the Royal and Ancient and the USGA jointly published a book of uniform Decisions on the Rules of Golf, now revised annually and the two bodies have co-operated in the production of films about the Rules.

One alteration in the 1984 Rules may have startled more than traditionalists: the change in the manner in which a ball is to be dropped. In future, the player *shall stand erect, hold the ball at shoulder height and arm's length and drop it* (Rule 20-2a) and there is no requirement that he must face the hole when doing so. The chief reason for this change was that the spot where the ball first strikes the ground when dropped is important (see Rule 20-2c), but under the old Rule how was the player – standing erect, facing the hole and dropping the ball over his shoulder – to identify that spot with any certainty? The change is certainly a major one, and the traditionalists might claim that the old Rule embodied a procedure hallowed by nearly two and a half centuries of usage. But would they be right?

Ways of dropping the ball

Article 8 of the 1744 code at Leith required a player whose ball was lost to *drop another Ball*, but it did not say in what manner this should be done. In 1754 at St Andrews the player was at liberty to take his ball out of *water, or any watery filth, and throw it behind the hazard six yards at least.* The Edinburgh Burgess Golfing Society varied not only the manner of dropping but even the identity of the dropper: in 1773 the ball was to be dropped by *the opposite party*, i.e. the opponent; in 1776 it was to be thrown over his head by the player; in 1807 the player was to drop it over his shoulder; and in 1839 the *right* shoulder was specified. Facing the hole when dropping was first introduced by the Honourable Company of Golfers at Leith in 1809, but the method of dropping varied again: *the player shall . . . fronting the hole to which he is playing, drop the ball over the back of his head.* Finally, in 1829 and 1834 the Musselburgh Golf Club required that the ball be dropped by *a cady.* Which of these several variations on the dropping theme would the traditionalists accept as Henry Longhurst's *traditional manner*?

The first written Rules of Golf were no more than 14 years old when it was thought necessary to amend them, but it was clear that the Gentlemen Golfers in 1758 believed that they had now got the wording absolutely right and that no further change would be required. Did not their Captain, Thomas Boswall, preface the amendment with these bold words, *That in all time Coming the Law shall be . . .*? Successive generations of legislators have been equally sanguine in believing that they have produced a perfect set of rules, and the Royal and Ancient and the USGA doubtless hope that the 1984 code has closed all loopholes and provided for all eventualities. Is evolution now complete? Has the definitive tradition at last been established? Only time will tell.

Editor's note: J Stewart Lawson was Chairman of The Rules of Golf Committee 1973-77, Trustee of the Royal and Ancient Golf Club, St Andrews, from 1979 and Captain of the Club 1979-80.

Golf Terminology

Bogey—origin of the term

The term was first used in 1891. Hugh Rotherham, Coventry, suggested what was termed the *ground score* of the Coventry course. The scheme propounded by Rotherham was taken up by the Great Yarmouth Club hon secretary, Dr T Browne, who inaugurated matches for Great Yarmouth on the lines indicated. About the time the popular music hall ditty, *Hush, hush, here comes the Bogey man*, was on almost everyone's lips, and it must have been uppermost in the mind of Major C Wellman one day when he exclaimed to Dr Browne: *This ground score player of yours is a regular 'Bogey man'.* So the expression *bogey* was at once adopted at Great Yarmouth. Dr Browne introduced *Bogey* to the United Services Club *as a quiet, modest and retiring gentleman, uniformly steady, but never over brilliant.* He was heartily welcomed, and the hon secretary, Captain Vidal, was so impressed with the personality of the newest member that he suggested it was but fitting he should hold service rank, so he was given the position of *Colonel*, which he still retains. The Royal and Ancient did not recognize the term until 1910, when the Rules of Golf Committee framed special rules for bogey competitions. It is now almost in disuse in its original sense since the general adoption of the standard scratch score and the assignment of par to each hole. However in the 1960s it came back into golfing parlance through its American use denoting one over par for any hole.

Golf terms

Birdie, Eagle and **Albatross** are words coined in America to represent, respectively, holes done in one below par, two below par and three below par. The word *birdie* is attributed to AH Smith, who, in 1903, when playing at Atlantic City, holed out for a 1-under par at one hole and exclaimed *that was a bird of a shot.*

Twosome is not a golf term. If one man plays against another, the match is a **Single**. In stroke play, two players competing together are a **Couple**.

Threesome designates a match in which one player plays against two playing alternate strokes with one ball, such a match being rare. The word does not mean three players each playing against the other; that is a **Three-ball Match**.

Foursome covers two players playing alternate strokes with one ball against two others playing one ball in match play or against the field in stroke play. There has been a tendency to use the word to cover a four-ball match, and so the term **Scotch Foursome** has been used in some cases to distinguish between the two.

Medal Play has crept into golf language as a synonym for **Stroke Play**. *Stroke play* is the correct term, according to the Rules and tradition.

Dormie is when a player, or his side, is as many holes up as there are holes remaining to play. A match consists of 18 holes or 36 holes. If extra holes are to be played to obtain a winning result, then the term *dormie* does not apply.

Editor's note: A fuller glossary of Golf terms will appear in the 1990 edition.

The Championships of Great Britain

History of the Open Championship

The Open Championship was initiated by Prestwick Golf Club in 1860 and was played there until 1870. The Club presented the Championship Belt which was to be held for a year by the winner and which would become the absolute property of any player who won three years in succession. The competition consisted of three rounds of the 12 holes Prestwick then had, to be played on one day. The Open did not become a four round contest until 1892. There were few entrants in the early years and nearly all were professionals, who were sometimes also greenkeepers and clubmakers, with a few amateurs.

Young Tom Morris won the Belt outright in 1870. There was no contest the following year, but in 1872 Prestwick, the Royal and Ancient and the Honourable Company, who were still playing at Musselburgh, subscribed to provide the present trophy, which was not to be won outright. Since then only three winners would have so earned it: Jamie Anderson and Bob Ferguson during the following ten years and Peter Thomson since in 1954-56. The Championship was to be held on the courses of the three subscribing Clubs in turn. Young Tom won the first for the new cup in 1872 at St Andrews, but died tragically young in 1875.

The three courses continued to be used until 1892 when it was first played at Muirfield to where the Honourable Company had moved. That year was also the first in which the Championship became a 72-hole contest over two days. In 1890, at Prestwick, John Ball had become the first amateur to win. Only two others have followed his success, Harold Hilton in 1892 and 1897, and Bobby Jones in 1926, 1927 and 1930. Roger Wethered tied with Jock Hutchison at St Andrews in 1920, but lost the play-off; if he had not incurred a penalty stroke through treading on his ball in the third round, he may well have won.

The Triumvirate

The year 1894 saw the first occasion the Open was played in England at Sandwich and the first English professional to win, JH Taylor. He won again the next year and for the fifth time in 1913. Harry Vardon and James Braid were the two others of the *great triumvirate* who together won sixteen Opens between 1894 and 1914. Taylor's five wins were spread over twenty years and Vardon's six over nineteen. Braid's wins were concentrated into ten years from 1901 to 1910, all of them in Scotland. Vardon won three times at Prestwick but never at St Andrews where Taylor and Braid both won twice. Only Taylor managed a win at Hoylake. No other player won more than once during their supremacy. The winning scores at the time were very high by today's standards, for although the courses were marginally shorter, the equipment and clothing were primitive compared with those in use now. At Sandwich Taylor's score was 326, or 38 over an average of 4s. His 304 at Hoylake in 1913 was played in appalling weather, wearing a tweed jacket, cap and boots, and using wooden shafts and leather grips. He had no protective clothing or umbrella and won by 8 strokes from Ted Ray. The last winning total over 300 was Hagen's 301 at Hoylake in 1924.

Better Standards

That improved equipment has defeated the greater length and heavier rough of today's Championship courses is suggested by comparing the average winning scores for decades of this century.

Decade	*Average winning score*	*Decade*	*Average winning score*
1905-14	302	1956-65	280
1920-29	295	1966-75	280
1930-39	289	1976-85	277
1946-55	284		

Of the 116 Opens held so far, twenty Scots have won, seventeen Americans, fifteen English, three Australians, two South Africans and one each from France, Ireland, New Zealand, Argentina and Spain. The Scots have won thirty-nine times but only twice since Braid in 1910 (Duncan in 1920 and Lyle in 1985), the USA thirty times, England twenty-seven, Australia and South Africa seven times each, Spain three times and each of the others once each. Since the triumvirate's day ended, the only Englishman to win more than once has been Sir Henry Cotton with three victories. The Americans have won thirty out of the last sixty-three Opens played.

It will be seen that certain nationalities tend to dominate for a decade or so; the Scots until 1893, then the English until 1914, the USA in the 1920s and until 1933 when the English had a short resuscitation. The Commonwealth were to the fore from 1949 to 1965 (Locke, Thomson, Nagle and Charles) with the Americans coming back again to win in 13 out of 18 years between 1966 and 1983. Equally dominating in their periods were Hagen and Jones in the twenties, Cotton in the thirties, Locke and Thomson the fifties, and thereafter Palmer, Nicklaus, Player, Trevino, Watson and Ballesteros.

Open Courses

Only fourteen courses have accommodated the Open. Prestwick, discarded after 1925 as unsuitable for large crowds, still leads with twenty-four occasions, twenty of them before 1900. St Andrews follows with twenty-three. The second group comprises Muirfield with thirteen, Sandwich eleven and Hoylake with ten. Hoylake's last Open was in 1967; that it is not used now is due not to any lack of quality of the course but to lack of space. Deal appeared in 1909 and 1920, and was due again in 1948 but the sea broke across the course, and Sandwich came in for the last time until 1981. Troon and Lytham St Annes each held an Open between the wars, Carnoustie two and Princes, Sandwich, when Sarazen won in 1932, one; this course, which was used as a tank training ground during the second war, has not been asked again. In 1951, Portrush, the only Irish course to stage an Open, also provided the only English winner between Cotton and Jacklin in Max Faulkner. Birkdale and Turnberry are firmly established in the rota which appears to have settled at four Scottish courses, St Andrews, Muirfield, Troon and Turnberry (this will be five if, hopefully, Carnoustie reappears), and three in England, Lytham St Annes, Birkdale and Sandwich.

Traditionally the Open is only played on Links courses. While there may yet be new venues by the sea capable of being stretched and groomed to be worthy of holding an Open, the many other considerations to be weighed, such as an adequate road system to carry vast crowds and nearly as many acres as the course covers to accommodate the tented village and services, it is not easy to see where the Championship Committee will turn. It is possible, even likely, in this present age that a links course of repute with the necessary acreage round it, will be developed by a consortium that will bid for an Open and succeed.

Qualifying

How does one qualify to play in an Open? Since qualifying was first introduced in 1914, there have been numerous changes. Regional qualifying was tried for a year in 1926. At one of the courses used, Sunningdale, Bobby Jones (and even he had to qualify!) played what many consider the classic round of golf: a 66, all 4s and 3s, never over par, 8 birdies, 33 putts and 33 other shots.

Until 1963 all competitors, even the holder, had to play two qualifying rounds on the Open course on the Monday and Tuesday of the Open week. The qualifiers then had one round on Wednesday, one on Thursday and the leading group of between 40 and 60 players finished with two rounds on Friday. In 1963 certain exemptions from qualifying were introduced. The two rounds on the Friday were dropped in 1966 in favour of one round each on Friday and Saturday; not until 1980 was the first round played on Thursday and the last on Sunday. As the entry continued to increase, in 1970 nearby courses were used for qualifying and in 1977 regional qualifying was reintroduced in up to four areas in the previous week with final qualifying on nearby courses later.

There have been surprisingly few ties involving a play-off, only eleven in 116 Championships. The first should have been in 1876 involving David Strath and Bob Martin. However, Strath took umbrage over a complaint against him and refused to play again, Martin being declared the winner. Until 1963 ties were decided over 36 holes; the last two, between Nicklaus and Sanders at St Andrews in 1971 and Watson and Newton at Carnoustie in 1975, were played over 18. Two years ago it was decided that in the event of a tie, the winner would be found immediately by a play-off over specified holes, followed by 'sudden death' if necessary.

Prize Money

In 1863 the total prize money was £10, its distribution among the fourteen entrants, six of whom were amateurs, is unknown. A year later it had risen by over 50% to £16, with the winner taking £6. By 1988 the total prize fund had risen to £700,000 of which Seve Ballesteros received £80,000. All 71 qualifiers for the last day received £2000 or more (except Paul Broadhurst, the only amateur to play the last two rounds). Additionally winners of the qualifying rounds won smaller amounts. Until about 1955, the winner's and leaders' rewards were very modest; even in 1939 the cheque for the first man was £100 out of a total of £500. With some justification the prestige of winning the Open then was adjudged to be of much more value than any monetary award. The growth since the 1950s has been astonishing and is evidence that, while it is still a tremendous asset for any man to have won the Open, the authorities have recognised that it will not maintain its leading place without substantial reward.

The rapid advance of the Open to the major spectacle it has become is due to a combination of factors. Not least of these is the TV presentation of the BBC, acknowledged as the world's best in golf, the interest and enthusiasm of thousands of spectators keen to watch on the spot rather than on the box, and the Royal and Ancient's promotion of this world fair of golf that it has become. Behind it all has been the foresight of successive Championship Committees and, in the late 1960s and 1970s, the masterly spreading of the gospel by Keith Mackenzie, Secretary of the R&A in 1966-82, that is so ably continued by his successor, Michael Bonallack.

The detailed list of Open Winners can be found on pages 189-190.

The Editor

The Amateur Championship

Early History

Golf has always been a competitive game and club medals have been keenly contested since the nineteenth century. Many of the leading amateurs were members of several clubs and, aided by an excellent railway system, they competed against each other at such venues as St Andrews, Prestwick, Hoylake and Musselburgh. An embryonic *open amateur competition* was held in the late 1850s (the first being won by Robert Chambers, the publisher, in 1858, but there seems to have been little enthusiasm for such an event and it died around the time of the first Open Championship (1860). The best amateurs began to enter the Open from 1861. By the 1870s, there was renewed interest in organising a tournament for amateurs only but nothing happened, probably because no one club took a strong enough lead. A proposal in 1877 to the membership of the R&A that it sponsor a sort of Amateur Championship (involving club members and others nominated by members) was defeated.

It fell to the Hoylake golfers to set in motion the championship we now know as *The Amateur*. In 1884 the Secretary of Royal Liverpool, Thomas Potter, proposed that an event – open to all amateurs – should be organised. This original intention was not carried out until 1886 and so the winner of 1885 (AF Macfie) triumphed over a strong but limited, field drawn from certain clubs. The clubs which were responsible for the running of the championship until the R&A took over in 1920 – and who made contributions for the purchase of the trophy – were:

Royal and Ancient
Royal Burgess Golfing Society of Edinburgh
Royal Liverpool
Royal St George's
Royal Albert, Montrose
Royal North Devon
Royal Aberdeen
Royal Blackheath
Royal Wimbledon
Royal Dublin
Alnmouth
North Berwick, New Club
Panmure, Dundee
Prestwick
Bruntsfield Links Golfing Society, Edinburgh
Dalhousie
Gullane
Formby
Honourable Company of Edinburgh Golfers
Innerleven
King James VI, Perth
Kilspindie
Luffness
Tantallon
Troon
West Lancashire

The first championship was not without its teething troubles. The format which was adopted allowed both golfers to proceed to the next round if their match was halved, so the first championship had three semi-finalists – and Macfie got a bye into the final. From 1886, the usual format was adopted.

More serious than the problem of an idiosyncratic draw, however, was the question of amateur status, raised for the first time in 1886.

The committee had to decide if it should accept the entries of John Ball III and Douglas Rolland. As a 15-year-old, Ball had finished fourth in the 1878 Open at Prestwick and on the advice of Jack Morris he accepted the prize money of 10s (50p). Rolland, a stonemason, had accepted second prize in the 1884 Open. Rolland's entry to the Amateur was refused while Ball's was accepted. Ball went on to win the championship a record eight times and the Open Championship of 1890.

The Format

After such a difficult start, the format of 18-hole matches with a 36-hole final remained until 1956. This arrangement made for many closely fought matches, as shown in 1930, the year of RT Jones' Grand Slam triumph. Jones' only victory in the event came in the right year and it is worth pointing out that, in making his way to the final, he won in the fourth round at the 19th (by laying a stymie) against Cyril Tolley, the holder, and his victories in the sixth round and in the semi-final were by the narrowest of margins. In addition, the fact that the draw was not seeded sometimes meant early meetings between top golfers; for example, in 1926 the visiting American Walker Cup Team members, von Elm and Ouimet, met in the second round and von Elm went on to meet Jesse Sweetser in the third. As a result of such events, there was some pressure for the introduction of seeding the draw but it was not until 1958 that the practice was officially adopted. In the fifties and sixties there were other changes in format in an attempt to satisfy large numbers of golfers who wished to play and to ensure a worthy winner.

The popularity of the championship has posed difficulties for the R&A. The mathematically ideal number of entrants to be fitted into a convenient format is 256. In 1950, 324 entered the championship causing golf to be played on the Old Course for 14 hours a day. In order to restrict the numbers turning up to the championship proper, an experiment in regional qualifying was held in 1958 (again a St Andrews year) and 488 players with handicaps of 5 and under played 36 holes of stroke play on 14 courses. This system was quickly replaced and in 1961 the handicap limit was lowered (to 3) and a balloting-out of higher handicaps was introduced so that 256 were left to play for the trophy. This method was followed until 1983 with the introduction of 36 holes of stroke play to find 64 players for match play, from which to find the eventual winner.

There was also pressure for the introduction of 36-hole matches. As early as 1922 the R&A's championship committee canvassed the opinion of the 252 men who played that year. Nineteen of these voted in favour of 36-hole matches, seven for district qualification, fifty-two voted for a stroke play qualification followed by 18-hole matches and the others who replied wanted no change to the system. In 1956 and 1957 the last 3 rounds were played over 36 holes, in 1958 and 1959 the semi-final and final were over 36 holes and then the old format returned.

There is constant pressure on the organisers to find a format to satisfy the needs of large numbers of home and foreign players, to take into account differences in national handicapping systems, to preserve the atmosphere of the championship, to maintain match play as a central feature of top-level amateur golf and even to take into account the vagaries of the weather. The task is almost impossible and it is unlikely that the championship will continue in its present form for all time.

The Winners

Any man who wins the Amateur is a considerable golfer but attention should be paid to certain outstanding champions. John Hall of Royal Liverpool won the title eight times between 1888 and 1912. It is interesting to note that he never successfully defended his title Michael Bonallack triumphed five times between 1961 and 1970, including an incredible hat-trick of final victories in which he successively beat Joe Carr and Bill Hyndman twice.

Several golfers have successfully defended their title: Horace Hutchinson, Harold Hilton, Lawson Little, Peter McEvoy and Philip Parkin, while others have won twice or more – Johnny Laidlay, Freddie Tait, Bob Maxwell, Cyril Tolley, Edward Holderness, Frank Stranahan, Joe Carr and Trevor Homer.

The oldest man to win was the Hon Michael Scott, at the age of 54 in 1933. The youngest winners – John Beharrell and Bobby Cole – were both 18 years and 1 month old. Cole's victory over Ronnie Shade was achieved over 18 holes – play being affected by poor visibility. The first overseas winner was Walter Travis who won in 1904 – one consequence of his victory was the banning of the use of centre-shafted putters. The first continental winner was the Frenchman, Philippe Ploujoux, who won in 1981. A visiting Walker Cup team always makes for an exciting championship and from fifteen visits to Great Britain the title has crossed the Atlantic twelve times. Indeed, on six occasions the final was an all-American affair.

No doubt there have been hundreds of thrilling matches played in the championship but few can have been as pulsating as the 1899 final at Prestwick where Johnny Ball beat Freddie Tait at the 37th hole. The victory must have been a sweet one for Ball, since Tait, the hero of Scotland, had won the previous year over Ball's home links of Hoylake. Tait was killed the following year in the Boer War. *The great battle* as Jones described his 4th round tie against Tolley in 1930 rivals the Ball-Tait final for tense excitement and for sheer brilliance of scoring Michael Bonallack's 1st round in the final of 1968 must take pride of place.

The Amateur Championship was 100 years old in 1985 and in essence it has changed remarkably little. How will the Championship react to changes such as the increasing popularity of the game at home and abroad, the lure of the professional ranks with its dependence on stroke play and the increasing commercialism of all sport? There is every reason to believe that it will continue to stand for all that is great in golf.

David Christie

Royal Golf Clubs

David Stirk

When one considers the number of names preceded, or followed by, the word 'Royal', it must, in general, appear as if the term can be tacked on to a name at will by anyone who fancies the idea. It is hard to believe that the Royal Oak public houses, the Theatre Royals and the Royal Insurance were all given the title by the reigning Monarch personally, any more than titles such as the Kings Arms and the Queen's Head were bestowed by the Monarch to honour those royal appendages.

Equally, there are certain titles of 'Royal' which, even to the uninitiated, appear to have real significance and to have been specially bestowed with royal approval.

In Queen Victoria's reign the term 'Royal' was granted only by the Queen, through the Home Secretary, to whom most of the requests were channelled. In 1881, the then Home Secretary suggested that the granting of the title should be given up, because so many bodies and institutions assumed it without permission. The Queen, however, wished to continue the custom, and her Private Secretary was instructed to deal with all applications, referring them to the Home Office.

Applications from the Empire would first be referred to the Governor of the Province, or the Governor General of the Dominion. If he approved, the matter would then be referred to the Colonial or Dominions Office and they, in turn, would pass the matter on to the Queen's Private Secretary. No doubt the Home Office would investigate the matter and make its recommendations to the Queen, submitting the necessary documents for her signature.

The designation 'Royal' was only valid during the reign of the Monarch who had bestowed it. Thus, on the Accession of a new Monarch, further application would have to be made.

King George V agreed on his accession that there was no need for institutions, societies etc, holding the title 'Royal' to re-apply for permission to continue the title at the beginning of each new reign. He also took the view that the title should only be bestowed on bodies and institutions that were pre-eminent. The policies concerning overseas requests remained the same. As far as Royal Golf Clubs are concerned, they are not entitled to the title 'Royal' unless that honour has been bestowed upon them by the reigning Monarch; such honours cannot be bestowed by the Prince of Wales nor by any other relative or member of the Royal Family. It appears, however, that in the 1880s and 1890s several members of the Royal Family 'granted' unofficially 'Royal' status to a few clubs and sought confirmation by the Queen and Home Office subsequently.

It is the intention of this article to stir the interest of the reader in Royal Golf Clubs; space does not allow of a complete detailed account of every Royal Club throughout the world. By the same token there is also no intention to make invidious comparisons between one Royal Golf Club and another, but to place before the reader some facts and statistics which may encourage him or her to investigate in more detail those aspects which are of particular interest.

An attempt to investigate the 'Royals' produces a very mixed reaction but, in general, the author acknowledges, with gratitude, the great interest shown by many clubs contacted and the information provided by many Secretaries and Club Captains, despite the fact that such requests often meant a tedious and time- consuming search of Club archives—yet more work for those who were already under considerable pressure of work.

It does seem that a letter from the reigning Monarch to a Golf Club, conferring on it the permission to call itself 'Royal', is of such interest and importance to that Golf Club that, except perhaps in the case of golf clubs that are 100 years old or more (in which case the records may have been lost) or in which a fire or some other disaster has resulted in the complete disappearance of records, any Club that has such a document will preserve it with great care—or at least have the date of conferral noted in the Minutes of the Club. It seems reasonable then to assume that a Club which can find no evidence, and which still has its Minute Books intact, has canonised itself and uses the title 'Royal' by its own tradition rather than by Royal consent.

The rules that apply to Royal Clubs in the

United Kingdom and in the Commonwealth do not, of course, apply in other countries. As an example, the Secretary to the Fédération Royale Belge de Golf, tells me that there are nine Royal Clubs in Belgium and that the title 'Royal' can be granted to any club that has been in existence more than 50 years. He goes on to say that the nine Royal Clubs listed were all made 'Royal' after only 25 years because the rules 20 years ago were different.

There are 38 'Royal' golf clubs in Great Britain, perhaps 20 in Belgium and Spain, the only other European countries to have them, and over 20 more in the Commonwealth.

In the Republic of Ireland there is the Royal Tara Golf Club. Until 1966, it was known as the Bellinter Golf Club, but then awarded itself the Royal purple, based on the premise that in the eleventh and twelfth centuries Tara was reputed to be the home of the ancient kings of Ireland, who, on the distaff side were Spanish. The whole sounds a charming piece of Irish history and, in the words of my kind informant, 'we do benefit, to a great extent, from the title, and we get invited to all Royal functions'. In the Republic also is the very authentic Royal Dublin Golf Club, though I must confess that I do not know how or when it acquired its title. Also there is the Royal Curragh which does not use the 'Royal' to which it is still entitled.

There are three Royal Clubs in Northern Ireland, Royal Belfast, Royal Portrush and Royal County Down. Whereas in England, Scotland and Northern Ireland Royal Clubs take their status pretty calmly and with such little outward evidence of pride that they appear almost complacent, in the Commonwealth, or at least in those parts of the Commonwealth which do not scorn the title 'Royal', it is regarded with every evidence of active pride. Virtually all the Commonwealth 'Royals' were readily able to give the date on which the honour was conferred and often the details of the special circumstances relating to it.

Yet in parts of what used to be the Empire, some of the Royals have also been allowed to lapse; but it is not only in the Commonwealth that this has happened. In 1931 there was a Royal Bodmin Golf Club in Cornwall, but this title has now been dropped. It is possible that they conferred the purple on themselves because the County is the Royal Duchy of Cornwall.

Of the Clubs in the United Kingdom that are Royal by tradition rather than by Royal consent, Royal Tarlair and Duff House Royal are examples. Neither can find evidence of Royal Patronage. Duff House Royal was played on by Princess Louise Duchess of Fyfe, eldest daughter of King Edward VII, who is said to have expressed a wish that the Club should be called 'Royal', but it would seem that the reigning Monarch declined to oblige.

Another Club that has awarded itself the affix 'Royal' is the Royal Forest of Dean Golf Club, situated in the Forest of that name. No doubt the title is good for business but it is not authentic. On the other hand the Royal Epping Forest is fully authorised to its Royal status and has always had a Royal Duke as its patron in its 100 years' existence.

One must not assume that only those Clubs with the title 'Royal' are important, the Honourable Company of Edinburgh Golfers, a pre-eminently important Golf Club, has no Royal title.

Golf Clubs attained Royal status at varying times in their history and some of the older Clubs were not made Royal until after Clubs junior to them had achieved it. An example of this occurs in England where Blackheath, by far the oldest Club in England, was given Royal status in 1901, whereas the North Devon and West of England Golf Club (founded 1864) became the Royal North Devon Golf Club in 1868.

In conclusion, there is no evidence of a Royal Ladies Golf Club, but there is evidence, kindly supplied to me by Mr Laurence Viney, of a Royal Ladies Golf Club in the past. On 29 April 1932, the Secretary of State informed the Ashdown Forest Ladies Club that they had been granted Royal status. At that time the Ladies Club had its own 9 hole golf course and its own Clubhouse. In 1956, owing to financial difficulties, the Club ceased to exist as a separate entity and was merged with the Royal Ashdown Forest Men's Club, thus depriving the golf world of an unique Royal Ladies Club.

'Royal' Facts

The first Golf Club to be made 'Royal' was the Royal Perth Golfing Society in 1833. The first 'Royal' Golf Club in England was the Royal North Devon Golf Club in 1868. The youngest 'Royal' Golf Club is Royal Troon, which became Royal in 1978. The list of Royal Clubs: Great Britain and the Channel Islands, 38; rest of the world, 40.

Acknowledgements

While thanks are due from the Author to those many Secretaries and Captains of Golf Clubs too numerous to mention individually who were kind enough to supply information from their Club archives, the Author wishes, particularly to thank the following:

Mr Laurence Viney, Editor of The Golfer's Handbook, *for his encouragement and for supplying much information. Elizabeth H Cuthbert, Deputy Registrar, The Royal Archives, Round Tower, Windsor Castle, for explanations concerning the use of the term 'Royal' and for historical background. The Secretary, Canadian Golf Association. Mr JM Kellie, Executive Director, South African Golf Union. Mr HE Touzel, Chairman of the History and Archives Committee of the Royal Melbourne Golf Club, who kindly supplied me with much information on the Royal Clubs of Australia.*

PGA History

George Simms

In the room at Walton Heath Golf Club in Surrey which bears his illustrious name, James Braid's portrait looks down on the modern golf scene of which he was so much a founding father. Relaxing therein today, one is encouraged to muse over what he would have thought of his profession as the end of the century approaches with its millions of pounds in European tournament prize money, and wealth undreamed of at the time when he, JH Taylor and Harry Vardon ruled the fairways as The Great Triumvirate, along with many historic contemporaries.

In 1987, when the Walton Heath Club played host to the Panasonic European Open Championship, Braid could gaze down from his wall on the leading ten players in the Order of Merit at that time who had jointly set a new record, each individually having won more than £100,000. The man of that particular year, Ian Woosnam, was to go on and amass a quarter of a million pounds. Twelve years earlier, when the PGA European Tour was first born as the Tournament Players' Division of The Professional Golfers' Association, the South African Dale Hayes had headed the 1975 Order of Merit with £20,500; it was not until eight years later that Severiano Ballesteros and Nick Faldo became the first to pass the six-figure mark in tournament prize money won in a season. The years since have seen an uninterrupted story of achievement, both on the course and in the administration of the professional game, which has combined to take golf in Europe to a point of world eminence.

Historians will point to 1901 as the base on which was built the European golf world of today. Fellow professionals of JH Taylor persuaded him to organise them into a body with a voice, and there came into being, following a 'mass meeting', the London and Counties Professional Golfers' Association, with Taylor in the chair. Mr AJ Balfour, later Prime Minister, was its first President. The meeting declared:

> "The objects of the Association shall be to promote interest in the game of golf; to protect and advance the mutual and trade interests of all its members; to hold meetings and tournaments periodically for the encouragement of the younger members; to institute a Benevolent Fund for the relief of deserving members; to act as an agency for assisting any professional or clubmaker to obtain employment; and to effect any other objects of a like nature as may be determined from time to time by the Association."

That declaration, nearly a century on, has barely changed in the written Constitution of today's Professional Golfers' Association, which is now a separate entity from the 'shop window' PGA European Tour. Before 1901 was out, membership had spread to the whole of the country and the name changed to The Professional Golfers' Association.

The first tournament, staged under the London and Counties auspices, was for the Tooting Bec Cup, a handsome silver trophy, still in existence today. Now it is awarded to the PGA member, resident in Great Britain and Ireland, who returns the lowest round in the Open Championship. Recipients of it in the modern age will no doubt reflect on the fact that when it was first contested the prize money was £15 and Taylor himself got £5 for winning with rounds of 76-73=149! Records show, however, that there was a Machrie tournament staged in 1901 with £100 for the winner, and that that, too, went to Taylor who beat Braid in the final. The Tooting Bec competition ran until 1922, and two years later it began its present connection with the Open Championship.

The arrival on the scene in 1903 of the *News of the World* Match-play Championship created great comment. The prize money was £200, about ten times that of the average tournament fund in those pioneering days, and was the PGA's first commercially-sponsored event. It was played at Sunningdale GC, and Braid took the winner's prize of £100, beating Ted Ray in the final. The tournament, which was later to become synonymous with the Walton Heath Club, was the cornerstone of PGA tournament golf. It ran unbroken, apart from the years of two World Wars, until 1969, enjoying other sponsors thereafter until its close ten years later. In 1986 open match-play golf, as distinct from invitational, was revived by the Epson computer company with their Grand Prix of Europe Championship.

By the middle of the 1920s, some half-a-dozen tournaments were producing over £5000 in prize money, while the *Daily Mail*'s £2000 event in 1936 was record prize money at that point. Unlike the consumer-orientated sponsorship of the present era, prize money prior to and just after the Second World War came mostly from publicity-conscious newspapers and the golf trade itself. For some years after the end of hostilities, annual prize money totalled around £25,000. Tournaments mostly were confined to three days, for the vast majority of the contesting professionals needed to be back in their club shop come Saturday morning. The day of the permanently touring pro was yet to be.

Landmarks of the time were the Penfold-Bournemouth Festival of Britain in 1951 with a record £3000, and the Swallow-Penfold in 1955 when Christy O'Connor of Ireland became the first to receive a winner's cheque for £1000.

O'Connor was to establish further history when he took a then world record first prize of £25,000 in the 1970 John Player Classic, played at the Notts Golf Club, Hollinwell. Earlier the American Gay Brewer had twice won around £20,000 for his Alcan Golfer of the Year victories of 1967 and 1968.

The 'Europeanisation' of the PGA tournament circuit can be traced to the 1970 French Open Championship with a history only five years less than that of the PGA itself. Traditionally at that time, following the British Open, it was accorded official Tour recognition that year, a move which touched off the incorporation into the circuit of other long-standing Continental Opens that had been funded and administered by the Amateur Federations of the countries concerned.

To this end the PGA took a decisive and historic step in 1971 in appointing John Jacobs, an international player and golf coach of distinction, to be its Tournament Director-General. His brief—to raise the status of the tournament circuit in the modern era. The move proved to be the foundation stone on which the European Tour of today has been built. At that time, prize money was at a low ebb; Tony Jacklin, having won the British and US Open titles, was campaigning mostly in America; and television was disinclined to transmit tournaments lacking 'top names' transported from across the Atlantic.

By the end of 1971 the circuit had lost the rich Alcan and John Player series, and the Daks, Agfa-Gevaert, Classic International and Bowmaker tournaments. Jacobs' determined policy was to establish minimum levels of prize money of £8000 for tournaments when he could not guarantee the player content of the field, and £15,000 in special weeks when Jacklin and Peter Oosterhuis were available—the latter dominating the domestic Order of Merit for four successive years from 1971 before heading for the United States. Not all was gloom, for in 1971 Italy, Spain, Switzerland and Germany joined France as PGA-recognised Open events with Order of Merit points, and Holland and Madrid joined the fold in 1972. Two years later, with prize money risen to £600,000 from the £250,000 level when Jacobs had taken over, another historic decision was taken, this time to form a self-administering Tournament Players' Division, a title changing later to the European TPD, and thence to the PGA European Tour.

Today The Professional Golfers' Association itself, based at The Belfry in the Midlands of England, and the PGA European Tour at Wentworth in suburban Surrey, are separately incorporated organisations, working none the less in harmony. The PGA through its seven regional establishments watches over the welfare of the club professional, his employment conditions, entry into the profession and regional tournaments.

Jacobs stood back after a year, and since 1975 the European Tour has operated and blossomed under its Executive Director, Ken Schofield, and a strong Tournament Committee under the chairmanship of Neil Coles. Tournament prize money has risen from the £600,000 level of 1974 to above £7 million in 1987. It reached the first million pounds in 1977, the second in 1982, the third in 1984, and has increased by a million pounds or more each year since. In 1989 total prize money is likely to be over £10 million.

A PGA Tour Qualifying School was introduced in 1976 and an All-Exempt Tour came into being in 1985, ending the irksome weekly round of pre-qualifying days. Television has also become firmly linked to the European Tour via long-term contracts. Selling, marketing and promotion of tournaments and other business ventures is undertaken by PGA European Tour Enterprises Ltd, a self-contained entity headed by George O'Grady, a former Tournament Administrator, as Managing Director.

Further proof of the eminent position in world golf of the PGA European Tour, reached through the achievements of among many others Ballesteros, Faldo, Langer, Lyle and Woosnam, and its Ryder Cup supremacy over America, came in 1987. In that year the Swedish car company Volvo concluded a five-year agreement with the Tour whereby Volvo became its first 'overall' or Corporate Sponsor. From 1988 the PGA European Tour became the Volvo Tour under an agreement considered by many to be worth well in excess of £10,000,000. No precise figure was given. Written into the contract is a £350,000 Volvo Masters tournament in southern Europe at the season's end, and a proviso that the Volvo finances can 'rescue' an ailing tournament, while the implications may also allow development of the long-visualised Satellite Tour for those players who cannot secure regular play in the main events.

The Volvo Tour contract was signed in May 1987; with Faldo's victory in the Open Championship at Muirfield in July following and Europe's triumph in retaining the Ryder Cup on American soil following in September, Volvo can commend themselves on their business foresight and their anticipation of the coming years.

Famous Players of the Past

In making the difficult choice of the names to be included, effort has been made to acknowledge the outstanding players and personalities of each successive era from the early pioneers to the stars of recent times.

Anderson, Jamie
Born 1842, died 1912. Winner of three consecutive Open Championships (1877-78-79). Born at St Andrews, he was the son of *Old Daw*, a St Andrews caddie and character. Jamie began golf when 10 years old, and rapidly developed into a fine player, noted for straight hitting and good putting. Anderson's method was to play steadily and on one occasion at St Andrews he remarked that he had played 90 consecutive holes without a bad shot or one stroke made otherwise than he had intended. He was for a period professional to Ardeer Club, but returned to St Andrews to follow his vocation of playing professional.

Anderson, Willie
Born in Scotland, 1878, died 1910. One of the Scottish emigrants to America, his flat swing won him the US Open in 1901, 1903, 1904 and 1905. He shares the record of four Open titles with Jones, Hogan and Nicklaus, and remains the only man to win three in a row.

Armour, Thomas D
Born Edinburgh, 1896. Died 1968. Open Champion, 1931. US Open Champion, 1927. USPGA 1930. He had a distinguished amateur career – including the French Open Amateur and tied first place in the Canadian Open. He had the unique distinction of playing in 1921 for Britain against the US as an amateur and in 1925 as a professional for the US against Britain in the unofficial international matches that preceded the inception of the Walker Cup and Ryder Cup events. When he came to the end of his tournament career he quickly gained an outstanding reputation as a coach, and books he wrote on the technique of the game were best-sellers.

Auchterlonie, William
Born St Andrews in 1872, died 1963. Won the Open title at Prestwick at the age of 21 with a set of seven clubs which he had made himself and shortly afterwards founded the famous club-making firm in St Andrews. He never played with more than his seven clubs and was a great believer that a golfer had to be master of the half, three-quarter and full shots with each club. As professional to the Royal and Ancient Golf Club from 1935 to his death he saw one of his ambitions fulfilled – the Centenary Open at St Andrews in 1960.

Ball, John
One of the greatest amateur golfers of all time. Born at Hoylake, 24th December, 1862, his father owned the Royal Hotel, Hoylake, prior to the formation of the golf links and when there was a small racecourse on the land later formed into the Royal Liverpool Links. The links became John Ball's playground. In 1878, when fifteen years old, he competed in the Open Championship, finished fourth, eight strokes behind the winner and ahead of many famous Scottish professionals of that time. Between 1888 and 1912 he won the Amateur Championship eight times. In 1890 he was the first amateur to win the Open Championship. He played for England against Scotland continuously from 1902 to 1911, captaining the side each year. He was Amateur Champion in 1899 when war with South Africa broke out and Ball served in that campaign with the Cheshire Yeomanry and did not compete in the Championships of 1900-01-02. In the First World War he served in the Home Forces. He played in his last Amateur Championship in 1921, the year of the first American invasion, and he reached the fifth round although in his fifty-eighth year. Modest and retiring, he rarely spoke about his golf. On the morning of his last round in the Championship he remarked to a friend in the clubhouse, *If only a storm of wind and rain would sweep across the links from the Welsh hills I feel I could beat all of them once again.* But it was a week of torrid heat and he failed. He retired to his farm in North Wales, where he died in December 1940.

Barton, Miss Pamela
Born London, 4th March, 1917. Died 13th November, 1943. At the age of twenty-two when the Second World War broke out, Miss Pamela Barton had already achieved great fame in the golfing world. She won the Ladies' Championship, 1936-39, runner-up, 1934-35, the American Ladies' Championship, 1936 and the French Ladies' Championship, 1934. In 1936, at the age of nineteen, she held both the British and American Ladies' Championships, the first person to do so since 1909. Miss Barton played for England in the home internationals in 1935-36-37-38-39; for Great Britain *v* United States in 1934-36; *v* France, 1934-36-37-38-39. She was a member of the Ladies' Golf Union teams which toured Canada and America, 1934, and Australia and New Zealand in 1935. Of a charming and cheerful disposition, Miss Barton, who became a Flight-Officer in the WAAF, was killed in a plane crash at an RAF airfield in Kent.

Braid, James
Born Elie, Fife, 6th February, 1870. Died London, 27th November, 1950. One of the greatest figures in golf of all times, James Braid, with Harry Vardon and JH Taylor, made up the Triumvirate which dominated British professional golf for twenty years before the First World War. He was the first person to win the Open Championship five times. This record was later equalled by Taylor and beaten by Vardon. Braid's achievements were remarkable for the short time in which they were accomplished. In ten years he won five times and was second on three occasions. His victories were in 1901, 1905, 1906, 1908, 1910. He won the Match Play Tournament four times, 1903-5-7-11, a record which was unequalled till 1950, and the French Open Championship in 1910. He played for Scotland *v* England in 1903-4-5-6-7-9-10-12 and for Great Britain against America, 1921. A joiner by trade, Braid played as an amateur in Fife and Edinburgh and in 1893 went to London and worked as a club-maker. Taylor and Vardon were well established in the golfing world before Braid turned professional in 1896 and he quickly came into prominence by finishing level with Taylor, who by that time had been Champion twice, in a challenge match. In a historic international foursomes, Braid partnered by Alex Herd lost to Vardon and Taylor in a match for £400 over four courses. A tall powerful player who lashed the ball with *divine* fury, he was famous for his imperturbability; no matter how the game was progressing he always appeared outwardly calm and it was this serenity of temperament which assisted him to his Championship victories on two occasions. A man of few words, it was once said that *Nobody could be as wise as James Braid looked.* One of the founder members of the Professional Golfers' Association, Braid did much to elevate the status of the professional golfer. Braid made a major contribution to golf architecture; Gleneagles, Rosemount, Carnoustie and Dalmahoy all bear his stamp. He was admired and respected by all who knew him, as much for his modest and kindly nature as for his prowess as a golfer. He was professional at Romford for eight years and at Walton Heath for forty-five, and was for twenty-five years an honorary member of the latter club, becoming one of its directors. He was made an honorary member of the Royal and Ancient Golf Club in the last years of his life and had the distinction of being the only honorary member of the Parliamentary Golfing Society.

Campbell, Miss Dorothy Iona
Born Edinburgh, 1883. Died in America, 1946. Won British Ladies' Championship, 1909-11; Scottish Ladies' Championship, 1905-6-8; American Ladies' Championship, 1909-10; Canadian Ladies' Championship 1910-11-12. One of only two women golfers to win the British, American and Canadian Championships, the other being Marlene Stewart (Mrs M Stewart Streit). Played for Scotland in international matches and for British Ladies *v* American Ladies.

Campbell, Willie
A native of Musselburgh, Willie Campbell never shirked a match anywhere or with anybody, and it was only on rare occasions that he did not win. He was a tall, strapping fellow, and was regarded as one of the finest match players of the time, fearless and courageous. In 1887 Campbell was professional at Prestwick, and in the Open Championship of that year he seemed destined to win but took eight strokes with three holes left. He joined the outflow of Scots professionals to the USA in 1891 where he died at the age of 33.

Compston, Archie Edward Wones
Born Penn, Wolverhampton, 14th January, 1893, died September, 1962. One of the outstanding personalities of British golf in the years between the two World Wars who fought hard to resist the developing dominance of the American invasion. He played in three Ryder Cup matches – in 1927, 1929 and 1931. In a 72 hole Challenge match he beat Hagen by 18 and 17 in 1928 at Moor Park and in the Open which followed he finished third to Hagen. He tied for second place in the Open of 1925.

Cotton, Sir Henry *see Obituary p 451*

Darwin, Bernard
One of the most respected and widely known personalities in the game died soon after his 85th birthday in 1961. As a graceful and

authoritative writer on golf and golfers he had no equal. He knew intimately every player and every course of note throughout the world, and his phenomenal memory, fluent pen and gentle humour established him as the top historian of the game over many years. In 1937 he was awarded the CBE for his services to literature, which included journalism, books of children's stories and other sports besides golf. He was captain of the Royal and Ancient Club in 1934-35, and played internationally for England from 1902 until 1924 and in the first Walker Cup match (1922). He had travelled to the US to report the match for *The Times* and had been called in to play and captain the side when Robert Harris fell ill. During his playing career he won many amateur titles and trophies. He was a grandson of Charles Darwin.

The Dolemans
Four brothers, natives of Musselburgh, who were associated with golf for seventy years. John, born 1826, died at Musselburgh 1918; AH, born 1836, died at Blackpool 1914; William born 1838, died at Glasgow 1918, and Frank born Musselburgh 1848, died Edinburgh, 1929. William was the best player. He was first amateur in the Open Championship in 1865-68, 1870 and 1872. He played in nearly every Amateur Championship up to 1911, and at Hoylake in 1910, when 73 years of age, he won his tie in the first round. AH was one of the pioneers of golf in England, and founder of golf at Lytham and St Annes. John, the eldest, introduced golf to Nottingham. In 1908 he took part in an octogenarian foursome, which was continued annually until 1914. Frank was a club-maker and for many years he carried on a golf club-making business at the ancient Wright's Houses, Bruntsfield Links, Edinburgh.

Duncan, George
Died on 15th January, 1964, aged 80. He was the last Scottish-born winner of the Open title domiciled in Britain. He won the title in 1920 and his victory was achieved after two opening rounds of 80 which left him 13 strokes behind the leader. Two years later, at Sandwich, he finished second to Hagen after one of the most exciting finishes up to that time. Hagen had finished and was already being hailed as the winner when Duncan, a very late starter, reached the 18th hole needing a 4 to tie. He failed but his round was notable as the only one under 70 in that Open and the first to break 70 in the Open since 1904. Prior to the first war, Duncan was a prominent challenger to the established Triumvirate and would probably have achieved greater fame but for the war years during which he would have been at his prime. One of the fastest players of all time, he wasted no time especially on the greens and his book *Golf at a Gallop* was appropriately titled.

The Dunns
The twin brothers Dunn, born at Musselburgh in 1821, were prominent in golf between 1840 and 1860. In 1849, old Willie Dunn and Jamie Dunn played their great match against Allan Robertson and old Tom Morris. Willie Dunn became custodian in the Blackheath Links until 1864, and he then returned to Leith, and later to North Berwick, where he died at the age of 59. Willie Dunn was celebrated for the peculiar grace of his style and, as the longest driver of his day, he was a doughty match fighter, and one of his famous games was with Allan Robertson in 1843, when he played the St Andrews champion 20 rounds, and lost by 2 rounds and 1 to play. Another famous match was in 1852, when, partnered by Sir Robert Hay, he played Allan Robertson and Old Tom. Jamie Dunn, his twin brother, was also a fine player. Willie's son went to America, and won the first Championship of America in 1894. He was among the first to experiment with the idea of steel shafts. About 1900 he inserted thin steel rods in split cane and lancewood shafts. He invented a coneshaped paper tee, the forerunner of the wooden tee, and was a pioneer of indoor golf schools. He died in London in 1952.

Ferguson, Bob
Born Musselburgh, 1848. Died 1915. Started to caddie on Musselburgh when aged 8. In 1866, when 18, he won the first prize in the Leith Tournament, in which all the great professionals of the day took part. The late Sir Charles Tennant put up the money for young Ferguson, who, in 1868 and 1869, beat Tom Morris six times. In 1875, at Hoylake, with young Tom Morris representing Scotland in a foursome, he beat Bob Kirk, Blackheath, and John Allan, Westward Ho! representing England. He won the Open Championship in 1880, 1881, and 1882. In 1883 he tied with Willie Fernie, losing the 36-hole play-off by one stroke. After this Championship he became ill with typhoid, and was never able to reproduce his great form. He became the custodian of the Musselburgh links, taught the young and was widely respected in the community.

Fernie, Willie
Born St Andrews 1851; died Troon, June 1924. In 1880 he went to Dumfries as greenkeeper. In 1882 he was second to Bob Ferguson in the Open Championship and after a tie with the same player he won the Open Championship in 1883 at Musselburgh after a 36-hole play-off. He became professional to Felixstowe and

Ardeer and in 1887 to Troon, and was there as professional until February, 1924. He was a very stylish player and in great demand as a teacher. He played in many important stake matches, the two biggest being against Andrew Kirkaldy over Troon, Prestwick and St Andrews which he won by 4 and 3, and against Willie Park over Musselburgh and Troon which he lost by 13 and 12. He played for Scotland against England in 1904.

Hagen, Walter C

Born Rochester, New York, 21st December, 1892. Died October, 1969. The first of the great golfers with star quality. People flocked to see him as much because he was a *character* as for his outstanding skill and many achievements. He did not want to be a millionaire, but merely to live like one, and this he did in dramatic style as when he used a hired Rolls-Royce as a changing room at the Open because professionals were not admitted to the clubhouse, and when he gave the whole of his first prize in the Open to his caddie. He also pioneered stylish dressing on the course. As a player he had great mastery of the recovery shot, nerves of steel beneath his debonair exterior and a fine putting touch. His best achievement was probably his four consecutive wins in the USPGA championship when the event was decided by matchplay over 36 holes. He won the US Open in 1914 and 1919 and the Open in 1922-24-28-29 and represented the US against Britain on seven occasions. His world tours with Kirkwood, his extrovert approach and the entertainment he provided on and off the course were the forerunners of the spectacular development of golf as a spectator sport. In spite of his being a contemporary of the immortal Bobby Jones, his personality was such that he was never overshadowed.

Herd, Alexander (Sandy)

Born at St Andrews in 1868, died London, 18th February, 1944. His life in the forefront of the game was more prolonged than his contemporaries of the Victorian era, and when he took part in his last Open at St Andrews in 1939 he was 71 and his appearances in the Championship covered a span of 54 years. A brilliant shot player, success often eluded him as he was prone to leave his putts short and to indecision. On his first appearance in the Open, at the age of 17, he possessed only four clubs and although he was frequently in contention it was not until 1902 that he won the Championship. He was the first player to win the Open using a rubber-cored ball. In 1920 at Deal and again the following year at St Andrews he was joint leader in the Open after three rounds. In 1926, aged 58, he won the PGA match-play tournament at Royal Mid-Surrey in a 36-hole final, having played five rounds in the previous three days to reach it. Those three achievements when he was in his fifties are convincing proof of the longevity of his game. His life in golf brought him into competition with all the great Victorians – Taylor, Vardon, Kirkaldy, Braid and Park – and continued through the Jones and Hagen era up to the days of Locke, Cotton, Rees and Sarazen and others who, over 100 years after Herd's birth, were still playing Open Championship golf.

Hilton, Harold Horsfall

Born at West Kirby, a few miles from Hoylake, 12th January, 1869. Died 5th March, 1942. He was one of the most scientific of golfers. He learned his game at Royal Liverpool, where he won success in Boys' Competitions. In 1892, the year the Open Championship was extended to 72 holes, he won, and again in 1897. He won the Amateur Championship and the Irish Open Championship four times each, the St George's Cup twice, the American Amateur Championship once and became the first player, and the only Britisher, to hold both the US and British Amateur titles at the same time. He was small, 5 feet 7 inches, but immensely powerful in build. Hilton made a major contribution to golf literature as the first editor of *Golf Monthly*.

Hunter, Charles

Born Prestwick, 1836; died Prestwick, 24th January, 1921. A caddie and club-maker under old Tom Morris at Prestwick, he was for three years professional at the Blackheath Club, London, and succeeded old Tom as the Prestwick Club professional in 1864. He played in the first Open Championship at Prestwick in 1860, and he was a conspicuous figure at every championship and tournament held at Prestwick, acting as starter and in charge of the house flag up till the time of his death. He did not take much part in professional competitions, preferring to attend to his club-making and his members. In fact, during one championship round, while playing a niblick shot, he received word that the Lord Ailsa wished him to come at once and pick him out a set of clubs. He put his niblick back in his bag, pocketed his ball and returned to his workshop. In 1919 he was presented with his portrait in oils by the Prestwick Club, and a replica hangs in the Club. At the Open Championship of 1914 at Prestwick, he was the recipient of a presentation from his brother professionals. As a man of fine integrity, his friendship was valued by all golfers of his time.

Hutchinson, Horatio Gordon

Born London, 16th May, 1859, died in London, 28th July, 1932; an eminent golfer from the early eighties until 1907. He was a stylish and attractive player. Won the Amateur Championship in 1886 and 1887, runner-up 1885 (the first year of the Championship), and he was in the final in 1903. He was a semi-finalist in 1896, 1901, and 1904. He represented England *v* Scotland 1902-3-4-6-7, and was chosen in 1905 but illness prevented him taking his place. His career in the front rank of the game extended over twenty years. He was a voluminous and pleasant writer on golf and out-door life. He was the first Englishman to captain the Royal and Ancient. In other years he was also Captain of Royal Liverpool, Royal St George's and President of Royal North Devon.

Jones, Robert Tyre
Born Atlanta, Georgia, USA, 17th March 1902. Died 18th December, 1971 after many years of a crippling spinal disease. By the time he retired from competitive golf in 1930 at the age of 28, Jones had established himself as one of the greatest golfers of all time, if not the greatest. He represented America in the Walker Cup from its inauguration in 1922 until 1930 and played in the match against Great Britain in 1921. His victories included the US Open in 1923-26-29-30 (tied in 1925 and 1928 but lost the play-off; second in 1922 and 1924); US Amateur 1924-25-27-28-30 (runner-up in 1919 and 1926); Open Championship 1926-27-30; Amateur Championship 1930. In 1930, Jones reached a pinnacle which will probably never be equalled when he achieved the Grand Slam – winning in one year the Open and Amateur Championships of America and Britain. He then retired from championship golf. His stylish swing was the subject of admiration wherever he went – full, flowing, smooth, graceful and rhythmical. Yet he was of such a nervous disposition that he was frequently physically sick and unable to eat during a championship. During his championship winning years, Jones was also a keen scholar and gained first-class honours degrees in law, English literature and mechanical engineering at three different universities. He finally settled on a legal career with his own practice in Atlanta. It was there that he and his friend Clifford Roberts conceived and developed the idea of the great Augusta National course and the Masters tournament, now a fitting memorial to the *Master Golfer* himself. In recognition of his great skill and courage, and the esteem in which he was held in Britain and St Andrews, he was made an honorary member of the Royal and Ancient in 1956 and two years later, when in St Andrews as captain of the US team in the inaugural competition for the Eisenhower Trophy, he was given the Freedom of the Burgh of St Andrews. As a final tribute, a memorial service was held for him in St Andrews. The 10th hole of the Old Course, St Andrews (previously nameless) is now called after him.

Kirkaldy, Andrew
Born Denhead, near St Andrews, 18th March, 1860. Died St Andrews, 16th April, 1934. A rugged type of the old school of Scottish professionals, he was the last survivor of that race. After army service in Egypt and India he was appointed professional at Winchester. He had no liking for the steady sedate life of an English professional and after six weeks returned to his native St Andrews, where he lived the rest of his days acting as a playing professional until he was appointed professional to the Royal and Ancient Golf Club. He was a man of powerful physique. He was a beautiful golfer to watch, particularly his iron shots. In the Open Championship, 1889, he tied with Willie Park at Musselburgh, but lost on the replay. He played in many money matches and the most notable was in 1895. JH Taylor had won the Open Championship in 1894, the first English professional to do so, and prior to the Open Championship, at St Andrews in 1895, the young English champion challenged the world for £50 a-side. Kirkaldy accepted and won by a hole. Candid, outspoken, sometimes uncouth, Kirkaldy in his old age was respected by princes and peers.

Laidlay, John Ernest
Born in East Lothian in 1860, Johnny Laidlay played high-quality golf for fifty years – a testimony to his technique and temperament. In all, he won more than 130 medals. At a time when golf was booming and the opposition tough, he won the Amateur Championship twice (1889, 1891) was runner-up three times and beaten semi-finalist three times. He was second in the 1893 Open Championship when his characteristically good putting failed. He played for Scotland every year from 1902 until 1911, when he was fifty-one. The longevity of his very individual swing was perhaps due to his early golfing experiences at Musselburgh where he saw Young Tom Morris, knew Willie Park well and played a lot with Bob Ferguson (including a famous round by moonlight). His contribution to the game was the overlapping grip – known erroneously as the Vardon grip. Laidlay played cricket for Scotland (vs Yorkshire – taking 6 wickets for 18 runs); he was a pioneer of wildlife photography and carved beautiful furniture. He died at Sunningdale in 1940.

Leitch, Miss Charlotte Cecilia Pitcairn (Cecil)
Born Silloth, Cumbria, 13th April, 1891. Died London, 16th September, 1977. Although Cecil Leitch had reached the semi-final of the British Ladies' Championship in 1908 at the age of 17

and had won the French Ladies' Championship in 1912, it was in 1914 that she really established herself as Britain's dominant woman golfer when she won the English Ladies', the French Ladies' and the British Ladies'. She retained each of these titles when they were next held after World War I (the English in 1919 and the British and French in 1920) and who can say how many times she might have won them in the intervening years. In all she won the French Ladies' in 1912-14-20-21-24, the English Ladies' in 1914-19, the British Ladies' in 1914-20-21-26 and the Canadian Ladies' in 1921. Her total of four victories in the British Ladies' has never been bettered and has been equalled only by her great rival Joyce Wethered, against whom in the 1920s she had many memorable matches. Miss Leitch was an outspoken person who occasionally battled with the golfing authorities. Her strong attacking play mirrored her personality. Aged 19, in 1910 she accepted the challenge from Harold Hilton, at his peak, to take on any woman golfer over 72 holes giving half a stroke (a stroke at every second hole). Miss Leitch won this famous challenge match by 2 and 1 and later also beat John Ball, eight times Amateur Champion. Right to the end of her life, Cecil Leitch took an active interest in golf, attending major events whenever possible.

Little, W Lawson, Jun
Born Newport, RI, 23rd June, 1910, died February, 1968. As an amateur he established two records in that he won both the Amateur and American Amateur Championships in 1934 and again in 1935. In the final of the 1934 Amateur he won by the margin of 14 and 13 and for the 23 holes played he was ten under 4's. He turned professional in 1936 and won the Canadian Open in the same year and in 1940, won the US Open after a play-off.

Locke, Arthur D'Arcy
Bobby Locke, the son of Northern Irish emigrants, was born near Johannesburg on 20th November 1917 and died on 9th March 1987. He turned professional in 1938 after a very successful amateur career, in which he won the South African Boys' Championship, the South African Amateur (twice) and Open Championship (twice) as well as finishing leading amateur in the Open Championships of 1936 and 1937. As a result of his visits to Britain, he developed a characteristic hook to increase his length and although never a long hitter, his deadly short game made him a formidable competitor. In his first year as a professional he won the Irish, Transvaal, South African and New Zealand Open Championships as well as the South African Professional title. During the war, Locke flew Liberator bombers for nearly 2000 hours. He left the South African Air Force weighing four stones heavier and immediately resumed his winning way. Second to Snead at St Andrews in the 1946 Open, he was encouraged to visit America where he was greatly successful. He beat Snead 12–2 in a series of matches and won five tournaments in 1947, two in 1948, three in 1949 and one in 1950. Locke had bad relations with the USPGA who disliked his success and they banned him from their tournaments. Locke concentrated his efforts on Europe. He won the Open Championship four times—1949-50-52-59—as well as the Open Championships of Canada (1947), France (1952-53), Germany (1954), Switzerland (1954), Egypt (1954) and South Africa (six times as a professional). He also won a number of British titles including the Dunlop Masters, Spalding, the Lotus, Daks and Bowmaker Tournaments. The 1957 Open Championship was the first to be shown on television and the first in which the leaders went out last. Locke won by 3 strokes and his score of 279 was the first time 280 had been beaten at St Andrews. Locke had to mark his ball on the 72nd hole and in front of the cameras replaced it on the wrong spot. The R and A decided to let his score stand as he had derived no advantage from his technical error and disqualification would have been inequitable and against the spirit of the game. Bobby Locke will be remembered as a beautifully dressed golfer — plus fours, white shirt and tie — with a superb temperament, especially after a disastrous hole, great self discipline, the highest standards of behaviour and a wonderful short game. He was virtually in retirement when he had a serious car crash. On recovery he continued to play golf but his competitive career was at an end. He was made an honorary member of the R and A in 1976.

Longhurst, Henry
Died 22nd July, 1978, aged 69. After leaving Cambridge University, he acquired a job as a golf writer in which he could indulge his love of the game and be paid for it. He never ceased to be amazed at his own good fortune. His regular weekly article in the *Sunday Times* became compulsory reading for the golfing cognoscenti. From writing he became involved in radio and, later, television, through which he became world famous as a commentator. Television was the perfect medium for his talents. His humour, easy manner, gifted observation and perception, mellow voice, calm delivery and economy of word were all perfectly suited to a slow-moving sport, and from his vast knowledge and understanding of the game, he was always able to fill in any gaps in the action with an apt story or two. Longhurst also wrote several amusing books about different periods

of his life, including a brief spell as an MP. He was awarded the CBE for his services to golf and was one of only a handful of people to be made an honorary member of the Royal and Ancient Golf Club. His own golf was good enough to have won the German Open Amateur in 1936 and to be runner-up in the French Open Amateur in 1937.

Massy, Arnaud
Born Biarritz in 1877, died 1958. Was the first overseas player to win the Open in 1907 from Taylor, Vardon and Braid; tied with Vardon in 1911 and lost play-off, conceding on the 35th hole.

Micklem, Gerald *see Obituary p 453*

Mitchell, Abe
Born East Grinstead, 1887, died 1947. *The finest player who never won an Open Championship* was the tribute paid by JH Taylor. He finished in the first 6 five times in the Open and was 3 times winner of the Match Play Championship. Along with Duncan and later Compston, he was one of the few British hopes against the American invasion of the twenties.

The Morrisses
Old Tom Morris and his son, young Tom Morris, played a prominent part in golf in the period from 1850 to 1875. The father was born at St Andrews on 16th June, 1821. At the age of eighteen, he was apprenticed to Allan Robertson in the ball-making trade. When Morris was thirty years of age, Colonel Fairlie of Coodham took him to Prestwick, and he remained there until 1865, when he returned to St Andrews and became greenkeeper to the Royal and Ancient Golf Club, a position he held until 1904. Young Tom was born at St Andrews in 1851, and exhibited early remarkable powers as a golfer. At the age of sixteen he won the Open Professional Tournament at Montrose against the best players in the country, and he won the Championship Belt outright by scoring three successive victories in 1868-9-70. The Championship lapsed for a year, but when it was resumed in 1872, young Tom scored his fourth successive victory. There is no doubt that young Tom was the finest golfer of his time, but the tragic death of his wife, while he was engaged playing with his father in a great golf match at North Berwick against the brothers Willie and Mungo Park, had a most depressing effect on him, and he only survived his wife by a few months. Near the finish of this match, a telegram reached North Berwick intimating that, following her confinement, young Tom's wife was dangerously ill. The telegram was held over by Provost Brodie and not handed to young Tom until the end of the match. The yacht of John Lewis, an Edinburgh golfer, was put at the service of the Morrises but before the party embarked, a second telegram brought the sad news to young Tom that his wife had died. It was a mournful party that made the voyage across the Forth to St Andrews. The brilliant young golfer never recovered from the shock, and he died on Christmas Day of the same year, 1875, at the age of twenty-four. There was a second son, JOF Morris, who played in professional tournaments, but, although a fine golfer, he never approached the brilliant execution of his elder brother. Old Tom competed in every Open Golf Championship up to and including 1896, which, curiously, was the year Harry Vardon scored his first victory in the Open Championship. Old Tom died at St Andrews in 1908. He was respected throughout the golfing world for his honest, sturdy qualities. His portrait hangs in the Royal and Ancient Clubhouse, and the home green at St Andrews is named in his memory. A monument, with a sculpted figure of Young Tom, in golfing pose, was erected by public subscription in St Andrews Cathedral Churchyard and a smaller memorial stone was placed on the grave when Old Tom died.

Ouimet, Francis D
Born Brookline, Mass, 1893, died 1967. Described as the player who started the golf boom in the US when as a young amateur he tied with Vardon and Ray for the 1913 US Open and then won the play-off. In an illustrious career he won the US Amateur twice and was a member of every Walker Cup team from 1922 to 1934 and was non-playing Captain from then until 1949. The first non-British national, to be elected Captain of the Royal and Ancient Golf Club in 1951. He was prominent in golf legislation and administration in America and a committee member of the USGA for many years.

The Parks
Brothers Willie and Mungo Park of Musselburgh are famous in the annals of golf for the numerous money matches they played. Willie had the distinction of winning the very first Open Championship in 1860 and repeated his victory in 1863, 1866 and 1875. For twenty years Willie had a standing challenge in *Bell's Life*, London, to play any man in the world for £100 a side. Willie took part in numerous matches against Tom Morris for very large stakes and in the last of these at Musselburgh in 1882, the match came to an abrupt end when Park was 2 up with 6 to play. The referee stopped play because spectators were interfering with the balls. Morris and the referee retired to Foreman's public house. Park sent a message saying if Morris did not

come out and finish the match he would play the remaining holes alone and claim the stakes. This he did. Mungo followed in his brother's footsteps by winning the Open Championship in 1874. He was for many years greenkeeper and professional at Alnmouth. Willie's son, Willie Jun, kept up the golfing tradition of the family by winning the Open in 1887 and 1889. He designed many golf courses in Europe and America, sometimes in conjunction with property development as at Sunningdale, and was the pioneer of the modern ideas of golf course construction. Like his forebears he took part in many private challenge matches, the one against Harry Vardon at North Berwick in 1899 being watched by the greatest crowd ever for that time and for many years afterwards. Willie Jun died in 1925 aged 61. The third generation of this golfing family sustained a prominent golf association through Miss Doris Park (Mrs Aylmer Porter), daughter of Willie Jun, who had a distinguished record in ladies' international and championship golf.

Philp, Hugh
The master craftsman among the half-dozen club-makers located in St Andrews in the early days of the nineteenth century. He was especially skilled in making a wooden putter with a long head of pear shaped design. He is believed to have made not many more than one hundred putters. The wooden putter was for centuries a favoured club at St Andrews for long approach putting. The creations of Hugh Philp are highly prized by golf club collectors. After his death in 1856 his business was carried on by Robert Forgan.

Ray, Edward
Born Jersey in 1877, died 1943. His early days coincided with the famous Triumvirate and it was not until 1912 that he won the Open and was runner-up the following year to Taylor. He was again runner-up in 1925 at the age of 48. In 1913 he tied for the US Open with Ouimet and Vardon, but lost the play-off. After the war he returned to America and won the US Open title in 1920 and was the last British player to hold the title until Tony Jacklin, in 1970. He and Vardon were the only British players to win both the US Open and the Open until they were joined by Jacklin. Noted for his long driving and powers of recovery, he was invariably to be seen playing with a pipe clenched between his teeth.

Rees, David James
One of Britain's outstanding golfers from the 1930s to the 1960s. He played in nine Ryder Cup matches between 1937 and 1961, and was also non-playing captain in 1967. In 1957, he captained the only British PGA team to win the Ryder Cup since 1933. He was three times a runner-up in the Open Championship and once third, and won the PGA Match-Play Championship four times, and the Dunlop Masters twice, in addition to numerous other tournament successes in Britain, on the Continent of Europe, and in Australasia. At the age of 60, in 1973, he finished third in the Martini Tournament. He was made an honorary member of the Royal and Ancient GC in 1976. Born in March, 1913, he died in November, 1983.

Robertson, Allan
Born St Andrews, 1815, died 1858. According to tradition, he was never beaten in an individual stake match on level terms. A short, thick-set man, he had a beautiful well-timed swing, and several golfers who could recall Robertson, and who saw Harry Vardon at his best, were of the opinion that there was considerable similarity in the elegance and grace of the two players. Tom Morris, senior, worked in Allan Robertson's shop, where the principal trade was making feather balls. A disagreement occurred between Robertson and Morris on the advent of the gutta ball, because Old Tom decided to play with the invention, and Allan considered the gutta might damage his trade in featheries. Allan, through agents, endeavoured to buy up all gutta balls in order to protect his industry of feather balls. Allan Robertson and Tom Morris never seem to have come together in any single match for large stakes, but it is recorded that they never lost a foursome in which they were partners.

Sayers, Bernard
Born Leith, 1857, died at North Berwick, 9th March, 1924. Of very small stature, one of the smallest professionals, and light of build, he nevertheless took a leading position in the game for over forty years with his outstanding skill and rigid physical training. He engaged in numerous stake matches and played for Scotland against England in every match form 1903 to 1913, except 1911. He played in every Open Championship from 1880 to 1923. Of a bright and sunny disposition, he contributed much to the merriment of championship and professional gatherings. He taught princes and nobles to play the game, was presented to King Edward, and received a presentation from King George, when Duke of York.

Smith, Mrs Frances (*née* Bunty Stephens)
Died July 1978, aged 53. Dominated post war women's golf by winning the British Ladies' Championship in 1949 and 1954 (runner-up 1951-52), the English Ladies' in 1948-54-55 (runner-up 1959) and the French Ladies' in 1949. She represented Great Britain in the Curtis Cup on six consecutive occasions form

1950 to 1960. A pronounced pause at the top of her swing made her style most distinctive. She was awarded the OBE for her services to golf and was president of the English Ladies' Golf Association at the time of her death.

Smith, Horton
Died October, 1963, aged 55. Came to notice first from Joplin, Missouri, when 20 years old, and brilliantly embarked on the professional circuit in the winter of 1929 when he won all but one of the open tournaments in which he played. He was promoted to that year's Ryder Cup team and also played in 1933 and 1935. He won the first US Masters Tournament in 1934 and again in 1936 as well as more than thirty other major events. On his 21st birthday he won the French Open. He was President of the American PGA, 1952-54 and received two national distinctions; the Ben Hogan Award for overcoming illness or injury, and the Bobby Jones Award for distinguished sportsmanship in golf. The day after the Ryder Cup match which he attended in Atlanta in 1963 he collapsed and died in a Detroit hospital.

Smith, Macdonald
Born at Carnoustie in 1890, died at Los Angeles in 1949. Was one of the great golfers who never won the Open Championship, in which he consistently finished in a high place, coming second in 1930 and 1932, third in 1923 and 1924, fourth in 1925 and 1934 and fifth in 1931. He went to America before he was twenty. In the Open Championship at Prestwick in 1925 he entered the last round with a lead of five strokes over the field, but a wildly enthusiastic Scottish crowd of 20,000 engulfed and overwhelmed him. The sequel to these unruly scenes was the introduction of gate money the following year and Prestwick was dropped from the rota for the Open.

Tait, Frederick Guthrie
Freddie Tait was born at 17 Drummond Place, Edinburgh (his father PG Tait was a Professor in Edinburgh University), on 11th January, 1870. He was killed in the South African War at Koodoosberg Drift, 7th February, 1900. He joined the Royal and Ancient in 1890, and on 5th August that year he beat all previous amateur records for St Andrews by holing the course in 77, and in 1894 he reduced the record to 72. He was first amateur in the Open Championship in 1894 (Sandwich), 1896 (Muirfield), 1899 (Sandwich). He was third in 1896 and 1897. He won the Amateur Championship in 1896 at Sandwich, beating in successive rounds GC Broadwood, Charles Hutchings, JE Laidlay, John Ball, Horace Hutchinson, and HH Hilton, the strongest amateurs of the day. He repeated his victory in 1898 at Hoylake, and in 1899 he fought and lost at the 37th the historic final with John Ball at Prestwick. There is a Freddie Tait Cup given annually to the best amateur in the South African Open Championship. This cup was purchased from the surplus of the fund collected during the visit of the British amateur golfers to South Africa in 1928.

Taylor, John Henry
Last survivor of the famous Triumvirate – Taylor, Braid and Vardon – died at his Devonshire home in February, 1963, within a month of his 92nd birthday. He was born at Northam, North Devon, 19th March, 1871, and had been professional at Burnham, Winchester and Royal Mid-Surrey. JH won the Open Championship five times – in 1894-95-1900-09-13 – and also tied with Harry Vardon in 1896, but lost the replay. He was runner-up also in 1904-05-06-14. His brilliant career included the French and German Open Championships and he was second in the US Open in 1900. Among the many honours he received were honorary membership of the Royal and Ancient Golf Club in 1949. He was regarded as the pioneer of British professionalism and helped to start the Professional Golfers' Association. He did much to raise the whole status of the professional and, in the words of Bernard Darwin, *turned a feckless company into a self-respecting and respected body of men*. On his retirement in 1957 the Royal North Devon Golf Club paid him their greatest compliment by electing him President.

Tolley, Cyril James Hastings
Born in 1896, Tolley was a dominant figure in amateur golf in the inter-war period. He won the first of two Amateur Championships in 1920 while still a student at Oxford and continued to win championships and represent England and Britain until 1938. Among other titles he won the Welsh Open (1921 and 1923) and remains the only amateur to have won the French Open (1924 and 1929). A powerful hitter with a delicate touch, Tolley was a crowd pleaser. He is remembered as much for a match he lost as much as for some of his victories. Having won the Amateur Championship in 1929, Tolley was a favourite to win at St Andrews in 1930. The draw was unseeded and he met Bobby Jones in the fourth round. A huge crowd turned out to watch an extremely exciting match which Jones won on the 19th with a stymie. The rest is history. Tolley was elected Captain of the R and A in 1948. He died in 1978.

Travis, Walter J
Born in Australia in 1862, died in New York 1925. Travis was the first overseas golfer to win the British Amateur, at Sandwich in 1904. He won

the title using a centre-shafted putter, which was subsequently banned for many years. He won the US Amateur Championship in 1900, having taken up the game four years previously at the age of 35. He repeated his victory in 1901 and 1903 and was a semi-finalist five times between 1898 and 1914, winning also the stroke competition six times between 1900 and 1908. The *Old Man* as he was known is reckoned to have been one of the finest judges of distance who ever played golf.

Vardon, Harry

Born Grouville, Jersey, died at South Herts on 20th March, 1937. Created a record by winning the Open Championship six times, his wins being in 1896, 1898, 1899, 1903, 1911 and 1914. He also won the American Open in 1900 and tied in 1913, subsequently losing the play-off. He had a serious illness in 1903 and it was said that he never quite regained his former dominance, particularly on the putting green. That he was the foremost golfer of his time cannot be disputed and he innovated the modern upright swing and popularised the overlapping grip invented by JE Laidlay. Had it not been for ill-health and the intervention of World War I, his outstanding records both in the UK and America would almost certainly have been added to in later years. But in any event his profound influence on the game lives on. More than 100 years after his birth his achievements are still the standard of comparison with the latter day giants of the game.

Wethered, Roger H

Born 3rd January, 1899, in Malden, Surrey and died in 1983, aged 84. He was one of the outstanding amateurs of the period between the two World Wars, winning the Amateur Championship in 1923, and being runner-up in 1928 and 1930. He won the President's Putter of the Oxford and Cambridge GS five times (once a tie) between 1926 and 1936, played against the United States six times between 1921 and 1934, and for England against Scotland every year from 1922 to 1930. He was captain of the Royal and Ancient in 1946. But he will probably be best remembered for the fact that he tied with Jock Hutchison, a Scot who had settled in the United States, for first place in the 1921 Open Championship at St Andrews, having incurred a penalty stroke in the course of the event by inadvertently stepping backwards and treading on his ball, while Hutchison, in the first round, had had a hole in one. Wethered was reluctant to stay on for the 36-hole play-off the following day because of a cricket engagement in England, but was persuaded to do so, only to be beaten by nine strokes, 150 to 159. No British amateur has come so close to winning the Open Championship since.

Wood, Craig Ralph

Born Lake Placid, New York, 18th November, 1901. Died 1968. Visited Great Britain for first time in 1933, and tied for Open Championship with Denny Shute, but lost on replay. Won American Open Championship, 1941; US Masters' Tournament, 1941; Canadian Open Championship, 1942; runner-up American PGA Championship, 1934. In 1936 second in USPGA Championship. A member of the American Ryder Cup team, 1931-33-35, and US Australian team, 1937. In 1939 tied for US Open, but lost on replay.

Zaharias, Mrs George (Mildred *Babe* Didrikson)

Born at Port Arthur, Texas, USA, in June 1915, and died of cancer at Galveston in September 1956. In the 1932 Olympic Games she established three world records for women: 80 metres hurdles, javelin, and high jump. On giving up athletics she took up golf and won the Texas Women's Open in 1940-45-46; Western Open, 1940-44-45-50; US National Women's Amateur, 1946. In 1947 won the Ladies' Championship, being the first American to do so. In August 1947 she turned professional and went on to win the US National Women's Open, 1948-50. In winning the Tampa Open, 1951, she set up a then women's world record aggregate of 288 for 72 holes. She was voted Woman Athlete of the year 1932-45-46-47-50, and in 1949 was voted Greatest Female Athlete of the Half-Century. First woman to hold the post of head professional to a golf club. The *Babe* was a courageous and fighting character who left her mark in the world of sport.

Part VII
Interesting Facts and Record Scoring

Interesting Facts and Unusual Incidents

Royal Golf Clubs

● The right to the designation *Royal* is bestowed by the favour of the Sovereign or a member of the Royal House. In most cases the title is granted along with the bestowal of royal patronage on the club. The Perth Golfing Society was the first to receive the designation *Royal*. That was accorded in June 1833. King William IV bestowed the honour on the Royal and Ancient Club in 1834. The most recent Club to be so designated is the Royal Troon in 1878.

Royal and Presidential Golfers

● In the long history of the Royal and Ancient game no reigning British monarch has played in an open competition. The Duke of Windsor, when Prince of Wales in 1922, competed in the Royal and Ancient Autumn Medal at St Andrews. He also took part in competitions at Mid-Surrey, Sunningdale, Royal St George's and in the Parliamentary Handicap. He also occasionally competed in American events, sometimes partnered by a professional, and on a private visit to London in 1952 he competed in the Autumn competition of Royal St George's at Sandwich scoring 97. As Prince of Wales he had played on courses all over the world and, after his abdication, as Duke of Windsor he continued to enjoy the game for many years.

● King George VI (when Duke of York) in 1930 and the Duke of Kent in 1937 also competed in the Autumn Meeting of the Royal and Ancient, these occasions being after they had formally played themselves into the Captaincy of the Club and each returned his card in the medal round.

● King Leopold of Belgium played in the Belgian Amateur Championship at Le Zoute, the only reigning monarch ever to have played in a national championship. The Belgian King played in many competitions subsequent to his abdication. In 1949 he reached the quarter-finals of the French Amateur Championship at St Cloud, playing as Count de Rethy.

● King Baudouin of Belgium in 1958 played in the triangular match Belgium-France-Holland and won his match against a Dutch player. He also took part in the Gleneagles Hotel tournament (playing as Mr B de Rethy), partnered by Dai Rees in 1959.

● HRH Prince Claus of the Netherlands played in the American-Express Pro-Am preceding the 1971 Dutch Open. His handicap was 18. Partnered by Peter Oosterhuis, he won the same event in 1974 with a score of 62.

● US President Gerald Ford played in the pro-am before the 1975 Jackie Gleason Classic in a group which included Jack Nicklaus. Following his defeat in the 1977 presidential election, he became a fairly frequent competitor at pro-am tournaments and succeeded in holing in one (his first ever) during the 1977 Memphis Classic.

● The King of Morocco is an enthusiastic golfer and plays frequently with top professionals, in particular Billy Casper.

● Exiled King Constantine of Greece is also a keen golfer. Since 1973 he has played in several pro-am tournaments.

● President Kaunda of Zambia is a keen supporter and player of the game. There is a 9-hole course in the grounds of the Presidential Palace at Lusaka where he plays regularly.

First Lady Golfer

● Mary Queen of Scots, who was beheaded on 8th February, 1587, was probably the first lady golfer so mentioned by name. As evidence of her indifference to the fate of Darnley, her husband who was murdered at Kirk o' Field, Edinburgh, she was charged at her trial with having played at golf in the fields beside Seton a few days after his death.

Record Championship Victories

● In the Amateur Championship at Muirfield, 1920, Captain Carter, an Irish golfer, defeated an American entrant by 10 and 8. This is the only known instance where a player has won every hole in an Amateur Championship tie.

● In the final of the Canadian Ladies Championship at Rivermead, Ottawa, 1921, Cecil Leitch defeated Mollie McBride by 17 and 15. Miss Leitch only lost 1 hole in the match, the ninth. She was 14 up at the end of the first round, and only 3 holes were necessary in the second round, Miss Leitch winning them all. She won 18 holes out of 21 played, lost 1, and halved 2.

● In the final of the French Ladies' Open Championship at Le Touquet in 1927, Mlle de la Chaume (St Cloud) defeated Mrs Alex Johnston (Moor Park) by 15 and 14, the largest victory in a European golf championship.

● At Prestwick in 1934, W Lawson Little, Presidio, San Francisco, defeated James Wallace, Troon Portland, by 14 and 13 in the final of the Amateur Championship, the record victory in the Amateur Championship. Wallace failed to win a single hole.

● The largest victory in the Walker Cup in 18-hole matches was in 1979 when American Scott Hoch beat Jim Buckley by 9 and 7. Buckley had a back injury.

Outstanding Records in Championships, International Matches and on the Professional Circuit

● The record number of victories in the Open Championship is six, held by Harry Vardon who won in 1896-98-99-1903-11-14.

● Five-time winners of the Championship are JH Taylor in 1894-95-1900-09-13; James Braid in 1901-05-06-08-10; Peter Thomson in 1954-55-56-58-65 and Tom Watson in 1975-77-80-82-83. Thomson's 1965 win was achieved when the Championship had become a truly international event. In 1957 he finished second behind Bobby Locke. By winning again in 1958 Thomson was prevented only by Bobby Locke from winning five consecutive Open Championships.

● Four successive victories in the Open by *Young* Tom Morris is a record so far never equalled. He won in 1868-69-70-72. (The Championship was not played in 1871.) Other four-time winners are Bobby Locke in 1949-50-52-57, Walter Hagen in 1922-24-28-29, Willie Park 1860-63-66-75, and *Old* Tom Morris 1861-62-64-67.

● Since the Championship began in 1860, players who have won three times in succession are Jamie Anderson, Bob Ferguson, and Peter Thomson.

● Robert Tyre Jones won the Open three times in 1926-27-30; the Amateur in 1930; the American Open in 1923-26-29-30; and the American Amateur in 1924-25-27-28-30. In winning the four major golf titles of the world in one year (1930) he achieved a feat unlikely ever to be equalled. Jones retired from competitive golf after winning the 1930 American Open, the last of these Championships, at the age of 28.

● Jack Nicklaus has had the most wins (six) in the US Masters Tournament, followed by Arnold Palmer with four.

● In modern times there are four championships generally regarded as standing above all others – the Open, US Open, US Masters, and USPGA. Four players have held all these titles, Gene Sarazen, Ben Hogan, Gary Player, and Jack Nicklaus, who in 1978 became the first player to have held each of them at least three times. His record in these events is – Open 1966-70-78; US Open 1962-67-72-80; US Masters 1963-65-66-72-75-86; USPGA 1963-71-73-75-80. His total of major championships is now 18.

The nearest approach to achieving the Grand Slam of the Open, US Open, US Masters and USPGA in one year was by Ben Hogan in 1953 when he won the first three and could not compete in the USPGA as it then overlapped with the Open Championship.

● In 1975 Jack Nicklaus came very near to winning the Grand Slam, winning the Masters and the USPGA and finishing only two shots and one shot behind the winning scores in the US Open and the Open Championship respectively.

● The record number of victories in the US Open is four, held by W Anderson, Bobby Jones, Ben Hogan and Jack Nicklaus.

● Bobby Jones (amateur), Gene Sarazen, Ben Hogan, Lee Trevino and Tom Watson are the only players to have won the Open and US Open Championships in the same year. Tony Jacklin won the Open in 1969 and the US Open in 1970 and for a few weeks was the holder of both.

● John Ball holds the record number of victories in the Amateur Championship, which he won eight times. Next comes Michael Bonallack with five wins.

● In winning the Amateur Championship in 1970 Michael Bonallack became the first player to win in three consecutive years.

● Cecil Leitch and Joyce Wethered each won the British Ladies' title four times.

● The English Amateur record number of victories is held by Michael Bonallack, who has won the title five times.

● The Scottish Amateur record is held by Ronnie Shade, who won five titles in successive years – 1963-64-65-66-67. His long reign as Champion ended when he was beaten in the fourth round of the 1968 Championship after winning 44 consecutive matches.

● Joyce Wethered established an unbeaten record by winning the English Ladies' in five successive years from 1920 to 1924 inclusive.

● In winning the Amateur Championships of Britain and America in 1934 and 1935 Lawson Little won 31 consecutive matches. Other dual winners of these championships in the same year are RT Jones (1930) and Bob Dickson (1967).

● Gary Player won the South African Open for the 13th time in 1981. He has also won the Australian Open seven times.

● Peter Thomson's victory in the 1971 New Zealand Open Championship was his ninth in that championship.

● In a four week spell in 1971, Lee Trevino won in succession the US Open, the Canadian Open and the Open Championships.

● The finalists in the 1970 Amateur Championship, MF Bonallack and W Hyndman, were the same as in 1969. This was the first time the same two players reached the final in successive years.

● Seve Ballesteros holds the record for most wins in one year on the European Tour, six in 1986; this followed his record equalling number in 1985. The best British players have been Bernard Hunt in 1963, Nick Faldo in 1983, and Ian Woosnam in 1987, each with five victories.

● On the US professional circuit the greatest number of consecutive victories is 11, achieved by Byron Nelson in 1945. Nelson also holds the record for most victories in one calendar year, again in 1945 when he won a total of 18 tournaments.

● Jack Nicklaus and the late Walter Hagen have had five wins each in the USPGA Championship. All Hagen's wins were in successive years and at match play; all Nicklaus's at stroke play.

● In 1953 Flori van Donck of Belgium had seven major victories in Europe, including the Open Championships of Switzerland, Italy, Holland, Germany and Belgium.

● In 1947 Norman von Nida (Australia) had seven major tournament victories in England.

● Mrs Anne Sander won four major amateur titles each under a different name. She won the US Ladies' in 1958 as Miss Quast, in 1961 as Mrs Decker, in 1963 as Mrs Welts and the British Ladies' in 1980 as Mrs Sander.

● The highest number of appearances in the Ryder Cup matches is held by Christy O'Connor who made his tenth appearance in 1973.

● The greatest number of appearances in the Walker Cup matches is held by Irishman Joe Carr who made his tenth appearance in 1967.

● In the Curtis Cup Mary McKenna made her ninth consecutive appearance in 1986.

● Players who have represented their country in both Walker and Ryder Cup matches are Fred Haas, Ken Venturi, Gene Littler, Jack Nicklaus, Tommy Aaron, Mason Rudolph, Bob Murphy, Lanny Wadkins, Tom Kite, Jerry Pate, Craig Stadler, Jay Haas and Bill Rodgers (US), and Norman Drew, Peter Townsend, Clive Clark, Peter Oosterhuis, Howard Clark, Mark James, Michael King, Paul Way and Sandy Lyle (British Isles).

Remarkable Recoveries in Match Play

● There have been two remarkable recoveries in the Walker Cup Matches. In 1930 at Sandwich, JA Stout, Great Britain, round in 68, was 4 up at the end of the first round against Donald Moe. Stout started in the second round, 3, 3, 3, and was 7 up. He was still 7 up with 13 to play. Moe, who went round in 67, won back the 7 holes to draw level at the 17th green. At the 18th or 36th of the match, Moe, after a long drive placed his iron shot within three feet of the hole and won the match by 1 hole.

● In 1936 at Pine Valley, George Voigt and Harry Girvan for America were 7 up with 11 to play against Alec Hill and Cecil Ewing. The British pair drew equal at the 17th hole, or the 35th of the match, and the last hole was halved.

● In the 1965 Piccadilly Match-Play Championship Gary Player beat Tony Lema after being 7 down with 17 to play.

● Bobby Cruickshank, the old Edinburgh player, had an extraordinary recovery in a 36-hole match in a USPGA Championship for he defeated Al Watrous after being 11 down with 12 to play.

● In a match at the Army GC, Aldershot, on 5th July, 1974, for the Gradoville Bowl, MC Smart was eight down with eight to play against Mike Cook. Smart succeeded in winning all the remaining holes and the 19th for victory.

Oldest Champions

Open Championship

Belt: 46 years. Tom Morrissen in 1867.

Cup: 44 years 93 days. Roberto De Vicenzo in 1967.
44 years 42 days. Harry Vardon in 1914.
42 years 97 days. JH Taylor in 1913.

Amateur Championship: Hon Michael Scott, 54 years, Hoylake 1933.

British Ladies Amateur: Mrs Jessie Valentine, 43 years, Hunstanton 1958.

Scottish Amateur: JM Cannon, 53 years, Troon 1969.

English Amateur: Terry Shingler, 41 years 11 months, Walton Heath 1977. Gerald Micklem, 41 years 8 months, Royal Birkdale 1947.

UK Professional: Dai Rees, 60 years, equal second Martini International, Barnton 1973.

US Open: Ted Ray (GB), 43 years, Inverness Ohio 1920.

US Amateur: Jack Westland, 47 years, Seattle 1952. Westland was defeated in the 1931 final, 21 years previously, by Francis Ouimet at Beverley, Chicago, Illinois.

US Masters: Jack Nicklaus, 46 years, in 1986.

USPGA: Julius Boros, 48 years, in 1968. Lee Trevino, 43 years, in 1984.

USPGA Tour: Sam Snead, 52 years, Greensborough Open in 1965. Julius Boros lost play-off in Westchester Classic 1975. Sam Snead, 61 years, equal second in Glen Campbell Open 1974.

Youngest Champions

Open Championship

Belt: 17 years 5 months. Tom Morris, jun in 1868.

Cup: 21 years 25 days. Willie Auchterlonie in 1893.
21 years 5 months. Tom Morris, jun in 1872.
22 years 103 days. Severiano Ballesteros in 1979.

Amateur Championship: JC Beharrell, 18 years 1 month, Troon 1956. R Cole (S Africa) 18 years 1 month, Carnoustie 1966.

British Ladies Amateur: May Hezlett, 17 years, Newcastle Co Down 1899. Michelle Walker, 18 years, Alwoodley 1971.

English Amateur: Nick Faldo, 18 years, Lytham St Annes 1975. Paul Downes, 18 years, Birkdale 1978.

English Amateur Stroke Play: Ronan Rafferty, 16 years, Hunstanton 1980.

British Ladies Open Stroke Play: Janet Melville, 20 years, Foxhills 1978.

Disqualifications

Disqualifications are now numerous, usually for some irregularity over signing a scorecard or for late arrival at the first tee. We therefore show here only incidents in major events involving famous players or players who were in a winning position or, alternatively, incidents which were in themselves unusual.

● JJ McDermott, the American Open Champion 1911-12, arrived for the Open Championship at Prestwick in 1914 to discover that he had made a mistake of a week in the date the championship began. The American could not play as the qualifying rounds were completed on the day he arrived.

● An amusing case was that of a competitor in the Amateur Championship at Prestwick in 1922. He boarded the train at Ayr thinking it stopped at Prestwick, but it did not halt until Troon some miles further on. The railway runs alongside the first hole at Prestwick and the player frantically yelled from the train that he would be back as soon as he could, but that was of no avail.

● The Hon Michael Scott was disqualified in the third round of the 1910 Amateur Championship for not being on the tee in time. He was also disqualified in the 1924 championship when the starting times owing to slowness on the course were nearly 40 minutes late. Scott calculated that his starting time would be at least half an hour late, but he failed to observe that there was an interval of forty-five minutes in the times for starting, and consequently starting had resumed at times given on the programme.

● In the Amateur Championship at Sandwich in 1937, Brigadier-General Critchley, arriving from New York at Southampton on the *Queen Mary*, which had been delayed by fog, flew by specially chartered aeroplane to Sandwich. He circled over the clubhouse, so that the officials knew he was nearly there, but he arrived six minutes late, and his name had been struck out. At the same championship a player, entered from Burma, who had travelled across the Pacific and the American Continent, and also was on the *Queen Mary*, travelled from Southampton by motor car and arrived four hours after his starting time to find after journeying more than halfway round the world he was *struck out*.

● Archie Compston was disqualified in the American Open Championship, 1932, for being late, and in the 1941 Championship Johnny Bulla was disqualified for starting *before* his time.

● An unprecedented disqualification was that of A Murray in the New Zealand Open Championship, 1937. Murray, who was New Zealand Champion in 1935, was playing with JP Hornabrook, New Zealand Amateur Champion, and at the 8th hole in the last round, while waiting for his partner to putt, Murray dropped a ball on the edge of the green and made a practice putt along the edge. Murray returned the lowest score in the championship, but he was disqualified for taking the practice putt.

● At the Open Championship at St Andrews in 1946, John Panton, Glenbervie, in the evening practised putting on a green on the New Course, which was one of the qualifying courses. He himself reported his inadvertence to the Royal and Ancient and he was disqualified.

● At the Open Championship, Sandwich, 1949, C Rotar, an American, qualified by four strokes to compete in the championship but he was disqualified because he had used a putter which did not conform to the accepted form and make of a golf club, the socket being bent over the centre of the club head. This is the only case where a player has been disqualified in the Open Championship for using an illegal club.

● In the 1957 American Women's Open Championship, Mrs Jackie Pung had the lowest score, 298 over four rounds, but lost the championship. The card she signed for the final round read *five* at the 4th hole instead of the correct *six*. Her total of 72 was correct but the error, under rigid rules, resulted in her disqualification. Betty Jameson, who partnered Mrs Pung and also returned a wrong score, was also disqualified.

Longest Match

● WR Chamberlain, a retired farmer, and George New, a postmaster at Chilton Foliat, on 1st August, 1922, met at Littlecote, the 9-hole course of Sir Ernest Wills, and they agreed to play every Thursday afternoon over the course. This they did until New's sudden death on 13th January, 1938. An accurate record of the matches was kept giving details of each round including wind direction and playing conditions. In the elaborate system nearly two million facts were recorded. They played 814 rounds, and aggregated 86,397 strokes, of which Chamberlain took 44,008 and New 42,371. New, therefore, was 1,637 strokes up. The last round of all was halved, a suitable end to such an unusual contest.

Longest Ties

● The longest known ties in 18-hole match play rounds in major events were in an early round of the News of the World Match Play Championship at Turnberry in 1960, when WS Collins beat WJ Branch at the 31st hole and in the third round of the same tournament at Walton Heath in 1961 when Harold Henning beat Peter Alliss also at the 31st hole.

● In the 1970 Scottish Amateur Championship at Balgownie, Aberdeen, E Hammond beat J McIvor at the 29th hole in their second round tie.

● CA Palmer beat Lionel Munn at the 28th hole at Sandwich in 1908. This is the record tie of the British Amateur Championship. Munn has also been engaged in two other extended ties in the Amateur Championship. At Muirfield, in 1932, in the semi-final, he was defeated by John de Forest, the ultimate winner, at the 26th hole, and at St Andrews, in 1936, in the second round he was defeated by JL Mitchell, again at the 26th hole.

The following examples of long ties are in a different category for they occurred in competitions, either stroke play or match play, where the conditions stipulated that in the event of a tie, a further stated number of holes had to be played – in some cases 36 holes, but mostly 18. With this method a vast number of extra holes was sometimes necessary to settle ties.

● The longest known was between two American women in a tournament at Peterson (New Jersey) when 88 extra holes were required before Mrs Edwin Labaugh emerged as winner.

● In a match on the Queensland course, Australia, in October, 1933, HB Bonney and Col HCH Robertson versus BJ Canniffe and Dr Wallis Hoare required to play a further four 18-hole matches after being level at the end of the original 18 holes. In the fourth replay Hoare and Caniffe won by 3 and 2 which meant that 70 extra holes had been necessary to decide the tie.

● After finishing all square in the final of the Dudley GC's foursomes competition in 1950, FW Mannell and AG Walker played a further three 18-hole replays against T Poole and E Jones, each time finishing all square. A further 9 holes were then arranged when Mannell and Walker won by 3 and 2 making a total of 61 extra holes to decide the tie.

● RA Whitcombe and Mark Seymour tied for first prize in the Penfold £750 Tournament at St Annes-on-Sea, in 1934. They had to play off over 36 holes and tied again. They were then required to play another 9 holes when Whitcombe won with 34 against 36. The tournament was over 72 holes. The first tie added 36 holes and the extra 9 holes made an aggregate of 117 holes to decide the winner. This is a record in first-class British golf but in no way compares with other long ties as it involved only two replays – one of 36 holes and one of 9.

● In the American Open Championship at Toledo, Ohio, in 1931, G Von Elm and Billy Burke tied for the title. Each returned aggregates of 292. On the first replay both finished in 149 for 36 holes but on the second replay Burke won with a score of 148 against 149. This is a record tie in a national open championship.

● Paul Downes was beaten by Robin Davenport at the 9th extra hole in the 4th round of the 1981 English Amateur Championship. A record marathon match for the championship.

● Severiano Ballesteros was beaten by Johnny Miller at the 9th extra hole of a sudden-death play-off at the 1982 million dollar Sun City Challenge, a record for any 72 hole professional event.

● In the semi-finals of the Wentworth Mixed Foursomes at Aldeburgh GC on 28th August, 1983, John Raison and Jackie Sheffield beat Andrew Mangeot and June Mangeot (the holders) at the 9th extra hole (the 27th).

Long Drives

It is impossible to state with any certainty what is the longest ever drive. Many long drives have never been measured and many others have most likely never been brought to our attention. Then there are several outside factors which can produce freakishly long drives, such as a strong following wind, downhill terrain or bonehard ground. Where all three of these favourable conditions prevail outstandingly long drives can be achieved. Another consideration is that a long drive made during a tournament is a different proposition from one made for length alone, either on the practice ground, a long driving competition or in a game of

no consequence. All this should be borne in mind when considering the long drives shown here.

- Tommie Campbell of Portmarnock is regarded as having hit the longest drive without any favourable conditions prevailing with a drive of 392 yards at Dun Laoghaire GC in July 1964.
- Playing in Australia, American George Bayer is reported to have driven to within chipping distance of a 589 yards hole. *It was certainly a drive of over 500 yards,* said Bayer acknowledging the strong following wind, sharp downslope where his ball landed and the bonehard ground.
- American senior professional Mike Austin, playing in the US National Seniors' Open at Las Vegas in 1974, amazingly drove his ball many yards through the 5th green at Winterwood GC, a hole measuring 450 yards. The total length of his downwind drive, which struck hard ground, was given at 515 yards.
- In September, 1934, over the East Devon course, THV Haydon, Wimbledon, drove to the edge of the 9th green which was a hole of 465 yards, giving a drive of not less than 450 yards. The hole was downhill and presumably other favourable conditions were also present. Haydon is also reported to have nearly driven the 15th hole (420 yards) at Royal Wimbledon in October, 1929. The ball finished just short of the green on a hole which was slightly uphill all the way and when the following wind was described as only a breeze.
- EC Bliss drove 445 yards at Herne Bay in August, 1913. The drive was measured by a Government Surveyor who also measured the drop in height from tee to resting place of the ball at 57 feet.
- Craig Wood of America in the play-off for the 1933 Open Championship at St Andrews drove into the bunkers in the face of the hill short of the 5th green. This was estimated at 430 yards. There was a considerable following wind and the ground was parched dry.
- At Sitwell Park, Rotherham, in 1935, W Smithson, the home professional, drove the 2nd green, a distance of 416 yards. Smithson's ball carried a dyke which ran across the hole at a distance of 380 yards from the tee. The remaining distance was a steep uphill approach to the green where his ball finished pin-high. A strong following wind was present.
- George Johnson in 1972, with the assistance of a following wind, drove a ball 413 yards at the 8th hole at Delamere Forest.
- The longest recorded drive on the US tournament circuit is 426 yards by George Bayer in the 1955 Tuscan Open. It is assumed that he was assisted by some favourable conditions but this is not established.

Long Carries

- At Sitwell Park, Rotherham, in 1935, W Smithson, the home professional, drove a ball which carried a dyke at 380 yards from the 2nd tee.
- George Bell, of Penrith GC, New South Wales, Australia, using a number 2 wood drove across the Nepean River, a certified carry of 309 yards in a driving contest in 1964.
- After the 1986 Irish Professional Championship at Waterville, Co. Kerry, four long-hitting professionals tried for the longest-carry record over water, across a lake in the Waterville Hotel grounds. Liam Higgins, the local professional, carried 310 yards and Paul Leonard 311, beating the previous record by 2 yards.
- In the 1972 Algarve Open at Penina, Henry Cotton vouched for a carry of 305 yards over a ditch at the 18th hole by long-hitting Spanish professional Francisco Abreu. There was virtually no wind assistance.
- At the Home International matches at Portmarnock in 1949 a driving competition was held in which all the players in the English, Scottish, Welsh and Irish teams competed. The actual carry was measured. The longest was 280 yards by Jimmy Bruen.
- When Walter Hagen was in Britain for the Open Championship in 1928, he drove a ball from the roof of the Savoy Hotel to the other side of the Thames.
- On 6th April, 1976, Tony Jacklin hit a number of balls into Vancouver harbour, Canada, from the 495-foot high roof of a new building complex. The longest carry was measured at 389 yards.

Long Hitting

There have been numerous long hits, not on golf courses, where an outside agency has assisted the length of the shot. Such an example was a 'drive' by Liam Higgins in 1986, on the Airport runway at Baldonal, near Dublin, of 632 yards.

Longest Albatrosses

- The longest-known albatrosses (three under par) recorded at par 5 holes are:
- 609 yards–15th hole at Mahaka Inn West Course, Hawaii, by John Eakin of California on 12th November, 1972.
- 602 yards–16th hole at Whiting Field Golf Course, Milton, Florida, by 27-year-old Bill Graham with a drive and a 3-wood, aided by a 25 mph tail wind.
- The longest-known albatrosses in Open Championships are:

580 yards–14th hole at Crans-sur-Sierre, by American Billy Casper in the 1971 Swiss Open.

558 yards–5th hole at Muirfield by American Johnny Miller in the 1972 Open Championship.

Eagles (Multiple and Consecutive)

● Wilf Jones scored three consecutive eagles at the first three holes at Moor Hall GC when playing in a competition there on August Bank Holiday Monday 1968. He scored 3, 1, 2 at holes measuring 529 yards, 176 yards and 302 yards.
● In a round of the 1980 Jubilee Cup, a mixed foursomes match play event of Colchester GC, Mrs Nora Booth and her son Brendan scored three consecutive gross eagles of 1, 3, 2 at the 8th, 9th and 10th holes.
● In the Wisconsin (USA) Oil Dealers' annual 18-hole tournament, Bernard Antisdel scored an eagle 2 at the same 285-yards hole in four consecutive years, from 1960 to 1963.
● Three players in a four-ball match at Kington GC, Herefordshire, on 22nd July, 1948, all had eagle 2s at the 18th hole (272 yards). They were RN Bird, R Morgan and V Timson.
● Four Americans from Wisconsin on holiday at Gleneagles in 1977 scored three eagles and a birdie at the 300-yard par-4 14th hole on the King's course. The birdie was by Dr Kim Lulloff and the eagles by Dr Gordon Meiklejohn, Richard Johnson and Jack Kubitz.
● In an open competition at Glen Innes GC, Australia on 13th November, 1977, three players in a four-ball scored eagle 3s at the 9th hole (442 metres). They were Terry Marshall, Roy McHarg and Jack Rohleder.

Speed of Golf Ball and Club Head and Effect of Wind and Temperature

● In *The Search for the Perfect Swing*, a scientific study of the golf swing, a first class golfer is said to have the club head travelling at 100 mph at impact. This will cause the ball to leave the club at 135 mph. An outstandingly long hitter might manage to have the club head travelling at 130 mph which would produce a ball send-off speed of 175 mph. The resultant shot would carry 280 yards.
● According to Thomas Hardman, Wilson's director of research and development, wind will reduce or increase the flight of a golf ball by approximately $1^1/_2$ yards for every mile per hour of wind. Every two degrees of temperature will make a yard difference in a ball's flight.

Highest Golf Courses

● The highest golf course in the world is thought to be the Tuctu GC in Peru which is 14,335 feet above sea-level. High courses are also found in Bolivia with the La Paz GC being about 13,500 feet. In the Himalayas, near the border with Tibet, a 9-hole course at 12,800 feet has been laid out by keen golfers in the Indian Army.
● The highest known course in Europe is at Sestriere in the Italian Alps, 6,500 feet above sea-level.
● The highest courses in Great Britain are Leadhills in Scotland at 1,500 feet, Tredegar in Wales rising to 1,300 feet and Church Stretton in England at 1,250 feet.
● Although no course exists at the place, Captain FES Adair tells of playing shots on a suitable piece of grassy ground over 16,000 feet when crossing a pass into Tibet.

Lowest Courses

● The lowest known course in the world was at Kallia, south of Jericho. No longer in existence, this 9-hole course, running along the shore of the Dead Sea, lay 1,250 feet below normal sea-level.

Coldest Courses

● Golf courses are to be found in every climate. A Scot founded the Polar Bear Club in the Arctic. Eskimos became members.
● A group of golfers at Thule air base held a competition in 1975 at the top of Mount Dundas in Greenland, some 800 miles from the North Pole. The golfers carried their own piece of carpet which served as teeing grounds and greens.
● Missionary Dave Freeman in 1975 founded the High Country Club, a 9-hole course with sand greens off the shores of the Beaufort Sea in Northern Canada, 400 miles inside the Arctic Circle. Membership is over 700. Another keen golfer in this area, Bill Josh, the base manager of the local airline at Victoria Island, each winter stakes out 9 holes on the Beaufort Sea when it freezes over. The temperature is said to fall to below minus 40 degrees.
● Although shut in for three years amid the eternal snow and ice of the Antarctic, Arbroath golfer Munro Sievwright did not neglect his practice with club and ball. His luggage included three clubs and a dozen red painted golf balls. In the light of the midnight sun he hit adventurous shots along the white wasteland on *fairways* of hard-packed snow. Munro, a physicist at the Antarctic Survey Base at Halley Bay, won the Carnoustie Craw's Nest Tassie in 1962, and was in the Edinburgh team which won the Scottish Universities' Championship in 1963.
● In September, 1956, Major Gus Watson, chief scientific officer of the British Antarctic Expedition's advance party, radioed the following account of life at the explorer's base camp: *Summer has come to the Antarctic – and with it the golfing season. Our two carpenters brought their clubs with them and now they spend much of their spare time driving, chipping and putting in the area around the hut.*

Longest Courses

● The longest course in the world is Dub's Dread GC, Piper, Kansas, USA measuring 8,101 yards (par 78).
● The longest course for the Open Championship was 7,252 yards at Carnoustie in 1968.

Longest Holes

● The longest hole in the world, as far as is known, is the 6th hole measuring 782 metres (860 yards) at Koolan Island GC, Western Australia. The par of the hole is 7. There are several holes over 700 yards throughout the world. At Teyateyaneng, South Africa, one hole measures 619 yards and another 37 yards.
● The longest hole for the Open Championship was 577 yards (6th hole) at Troon in 1973.

Longest Tournaments

● The longest tournament held was over 144 holes in the World Open at Pinehurst, N Carolina, USA, first held in 1973. Play was over two weeks with a cut imposed at the halfway mark.
● An annual tournament is played in Germany on the longest day of the year, comprising 100 holes' medal play. We are told that the players usually lose several pounds in weight during the tournament. The best return, in 1968, was 417 strokes.

Largest Entries

The Open—1413, St Andrews, 1984.
The Amateur—488, St Andrews, 1958.
British Youths'—244, Woodhall Spa, 1979.
The Boys'—247, Formby, 1980.
Ladies' British Open Amateur—157, St Andrews, 1975.
British Ladies Stroke Play—120, Formby, 1985.
British Girls'—94, Hesketh, 1985.
English Amateur—370, Moortown, 1980, also Woodhall Spa, 1984.
English Open Amateur Stroke Play—313, Royal Cinque Ports, Deal 1984.
Irish Amateur—302, Portmarnock, 1974.
Scottish Amateur—244, Gullane, 1983.
Scottish Open Amateur Stroke Play—249, Dunbar, North Berwick, 1985.
Scottish Boys'—354, North Berwick, 1973.
Welsh Amateur—108, Prestatyn, 1980.
Welsh Boys'—112, Glamorganshire, 1975.
● US Open—The US Open of 1988 received a record 5880 entries. 5775 were accepted. At 12 courses around the country 504 players, who had been successful at local qualifying venues, joined 96 players who were exempt from local qualifying. The 600 playing in sectional tournaments included 94 Amateurs. The 98 leaders joined 58 players exempt from Local Sectional qualifying to complete the 156 players in the US Open.
● The largest entry for a PGA ETPD event was 398 for the 1978 Colgate PGA Championship. Since 1985, when the all-exempt ruling was introduced, all PGA tournaments have had 144 competitors, slightly more or less.
● The 1976 Daily Mirror Amateur Tournament, which is a competition requiring a personal entry as opposed to a club entry on behalf of its members, drew an entry of 6,176 competitors.
● In 1952, Bobby Locke, the Open Champion, played a round at Wentworth, against any golfer in Britain. Cards costing 2s. 6d. each ($12\frac{1}{2}$p), were taken out by 24,000 golfers. The challenge was to beat the local par by more than Locke beat the par at Wentworth; 1,641 competitors, including women, succeeded in *beating* the Champion and each received a certificate signed by him. As a result of this challenge the British Golf Foundation benefited to the extent of £3,026, the proceeds from the sale of cards. A similar tournament was held in the United States and Canada when 87,094 golfers participated; 14,667 players bettered Ben Hogan's score under handicap. The fund benefited by $80,024.

Largest Prize Money

● The largest prize money for an event in Britain was £839,000 in the Dunhill Nations Cup at St Andrews in October 1988.
● In 1988 the total prize money at the Open at Royal Lytham and St Annes was £750,000, with a first prize of £80,000.
● The Machrie Tournament of 1901 was the first tournament with a first prize of £100. It was won by JH Taylor, then Open Champion, who beat James Braid in the final.
● The world's richest tournament is the annual Million Dollar Sun City Challenge, held at the Gary Player Country Club in Bophuthatswana, first played in 1982 with a first prize of $500,000.
● For the Glasgow Herald Tournament at Gleneagles and the Daily Mail Tournament in 1921, the prize money for each event was 1,000 guineas, the first golf meetings where the prize-money was over £1,000. The Daily Mail Tournament was restored in 1936 with total prize money of £2,000 and the first prize, £500. This was the first tournament in Europe where £2,000 was the prize fund. In 1951 the Penfold-Bournemouth Festival of Britain Golf Tournament had a prize fund of £3,000 which was the largest then offered for a professional tournament in the British Isles. The winner received £650. A first prize of £1,000 was first played for in the Swallow-Penfold Tournament in 1955.
● (For prize money in the Open Championship see under Conditions and History of Open Championship.)

Attendance and Gate Money

Open Championship

Year	Attendance
1962	37,098
1963	24,585
1964	35,954
1965	32,927
1966	40,182
1967	29,880
1968	51,819
1969	46,001
1970	81,593
1971	70,076
1972	84,746
1973	78,810
1974	92,796
1975	85,258
1976	92,021
1977	87,615
1978	125,271
1979	134,501
1980	131,610
1981	114,522
1982	133,299
1983	142,894
1984	193,126
1985	141,619
1986	134,261
1987	131,142
1988	205,285

Holing-in-One

Holing-in-One – Odds Against

● At the Wanderers Club, Johannesburg in January, 1951, forty-nine amateurs and professionals each played three balls at a hole 146 yards long. Of the 147 balls hit, the nearest was by Koos de Beer, professional at Reading Country Club, which finished $10^1/_2$ inches from the hole. Harry Bradshaw, the Irish professional who was touring with the British team in South Africa, touched the pin with his second shot, but the ball rolled on and stopped 3 feet 2 inches from the cup.

● A competition on similar lines was held in 1951 in New York when 1,409 players who had done a hole-in-one held a competition over several days at short holes on three New York golf courses. Each player was allowed a total of five shots, giving an aggregate of 7,045 shots. No player holed-in-one, and the nearest ball finished $3^1/_2$ inches from the hole.

● A further illustration of the element of luck in holing-in-one is derived from an effort by Harry Gonder, an American professional, who in 1940 stood for 16 hours 25 minutes and hit 1,817 balls trying to do a 160 yard hole-in-one. He had two official witnesses and caddies to tee and retrieve the balls and count the strokes. His 1,756th shot struck the hole but stopped an inch from the hole. This was his nearest effort.

● Cyril Wagner, another American professional, got a hole-in-one in 805 shots.

● From this and other similar information an estimate of the odds against holing-in-one at any particular hole within the range of one shot was made at somewhere between 1,500 and 2,000 to 1 by a proficient player. Subsequently, however, statistical analysis in America has come up with the following odds: a male professional or top amateur 3,708 to 1; a female professional or top amateur 4,648 to 1; an average golfer 42,952 to 1.

Hole-in-One First Recorded

● Earliest recorded hole-in-one was in 1868 at the Open Championship when Tommy Morris (Young Tom) did the 8th hole 145 yards Prestwick in one stroke. This was the first of four Open Championships won successively by Young Tom.

● The first hole-in-one recorded with the 1.66 in ball was in 1972 by John G Salvesen, a member of the R & A Championship Committee. At the time this size of ball was only experimental. Salvesen used a 7-iron for his historical feat at the 11th hole on the Old Course, St Andrews.

Holing-in-One in Important Events

Since the day of the first known hole-in-one by Tom Morris jun, at the 8th hole (145 yards) at Prestwick in the 1868 Open Championship, holes-in-one, even in championships, have become too numerous for each to be recorded. Only where other unusual or interesting circumstances prevailed are the instances shown here.

● 1878–Jamie Anderson, competing in the Open Championship at Prestwick, holed the 17th hole in one. Anderson was playing the next to last hole, and though it seemed then that he was winning easily, it turned out afterwards that if he had not taken this hole in one stroke he would very likely have lost. Anderson was just about to make his tee shot when Andy Stuart (winner of the first Irish Open Championship in 1892), who was acting as marker to Anderson, remarked he was standing outside the teeing ground, and that if he played the stroke from there he would be disqualified. Anderson picked up his ball and teed it in a proper place. Then he holed-in-one. He won the Championship by one stroke.

● 1885–AF Macfie in the fourth round of the initial competition at Hoylake for the Amateur Championship, holed the 14th or *Rushes* hole in one. Since then this particular hole at Hoylake has strangely enough been the scene of several holes-in-one in major championships – in 1898 by S Winkley Smith, West Middlesex, in the Amateur Championship; in 1902 by Daniel Brown, Musselburgh, in the Open Championship; and in 1925 by GNP Humphries, Stourbridge, in the English Amateur Championship.

● 1889–In the Open Championship at Musselburgh an amateur, who partnered Andrew Kirkaldy, holed the last hole in one. It was almost dark when the championship finished and when the player hit his cleek shot the green could scarcely be made out from the tee.

● 1906–R Johnston, North Berwick, competing in the Open Championship, did the 14th hole at Muirfield in one. Johnston played with only one club throughout – an adjustable head club.

● 1925–JH Taylor, in his second round in the Open Championship at Prestwick, did the 2nd hole in one stroke. In contrast, Murdoch (Troon Municipal), who played with Taylor, took 14 at the 1st hole.

● 1930–Maurice McCarthy, jun, in the qualifying stroke competition of the United States Amateur Championship at Merion did a hole-in-one. McCarthy tied for the last place and qualified for the Championship on the *play off.*

● 1933–In the final round of the Irish Open Championship over 36 holes at Newcastle, Co Down, on 23rd September, 1933, Eric Fiddian, Stourbridge, who was boy champion in 1927 and English champion in 1932, was opposed to Jack McLean. In the first round Fiddian did the 7th hole, 128 yards, in one stroke, and in the second round he did the 14th hole, 205 yards, also in one stroke. These remarkable strokes did not carry Fiddian to victory for he was defeated by 3 and 2.

● 1959–The first hole-in-one in the US Women's Open Championship was recorded. It was by Patty Berg on the 7th hole (170 yards) at Churchill Valley CC, Pittsburgh.

● 1962–On 6th April, playing in the second round of the Schweppes Close Championship at Little Aston, H Middleton of Shandon Park, Belfast, holed his tee shot at the 159 yards 5th hole, winning a prize of £1,000. Ten minutes later, playing two matches ahead of Middleton, RA Jowle, son of the professional, Frank Jowle, holed his tee shot at the 179 yards 9th hole. As an amateur he was rewarded by the sponsors with a £30 voucher.

● 1962–Dick Mayer, US professional, won £17,857 for scoring a hole-in-one in the Palm Springs tournament. This was the third successive year the feat had been performed in this tournament. The sponsors insured against *aces* with Lloyds of London.

● 1963–By holing out in one stroke at the 18th hole (156 yards) at Moor Park on the first day of the Esso Golden round-robin tournament, HR Henning, South Africa, won the £10,000 prize offered for this feat.

● 1907–Tony Jacklin in winning the Masters tournament at St George's, Sandwich, did the 16th hole in one. His ace has an exceptional place in the records for it was seen by millions on TV, the ball in view in its flight till it went into the hole in his final round of 64.

● 1971–John Hudson, 25-year-old professional at Hendon, achieved a near miracle when he holed two consecutive holes-in-one in the Martini Tournament at Norwich. They were at the 11th and 12th holes (195 yards and 311 yards respectively) in the second round. (See also section entitled *Holing Successive Holes-in-One.*)

● 1971–In the Open Championship at Birkdale, Lionel Platts holed-in-one at the 212-yard 4th hole in the second round. This was the first instance of an Open Championship hole-in-one being recorded by television. It was incidentally Platts' seventh ace of his career.

● 1972–Two holes-in-one were recorded at the 180-yard 5th hole at Pebble Beach in the US Open. They were achieved by Jerry McGee in the third round and Bobby Mitchell in the final round.

● 1973–Peter Butler achieved what is thought to be the first hole-in-one in the Ryder Cup when he holed out at the 16th hole at Muirfield in the 1973 match.

● 1973–In the 1973 Open Championship at Troon, two holes-in-one were recorded, both at the 8th hole, known as the Postage Stamp, in the first round. They were achieved by Gene Sarazen and amateur David Russell, who were by coincidence respectively the oldest and youngest competitors.

● Mrs Argea Tissies, whose husband Hermann took 15 at Royal Troon's Postage Stamp 8th hole in the 1950 Open, scored a hole-in-one at the 2nd hole at Punta Ala in the second round of the Italian Ladies Senior Open of 1978. Exactly 5 years later on the same date, at the same time of day, in the same round of the same tournament at the same hole, she did it again with the same club.

Holing-in-One – Longest Holes

● Bob Mitera, when a 21-year-old American student, standing 5 feet 6 inches and weighing under 12 stones, claimed the world record for the longest hole-in-one. Playing over the appropriately named Miracle Hill course at Omaha, on 7th October, 1965, Bob holed his drive at the 10th hole, 447 yards long. The ground sloped sharply downhill. He was further aided by a strong following wind and (he admits) a lot of luck.

● Two longer holes-in-one have been achieved, but because they were at dog-leg holes they are not generally accepted as being the longest holes-in-one. They were 480 yards (5th hole,

Hope CC, Arkansas) by L Bruce on 15th November, 1962 and 477 yards (14th hole, Martin County CC, Stuart, Florida) by Billy Newman on 13th August, 1972. The estimated length by cutting the corner was around 360 yards.

● In March, 1961, Lou Kretlow holed his tee shot at the 427 yards 16th hole at Lake Hefner course, Oklahoma City, USA.

● Another very long hole accomplished in one was the 9th hole at Hillcrest Golf Club, Winston-Salem, North Carolina, USA, by Mr Cardwell. The hole (425 yards) is a par four. The authenticity of this feat was vouched for by Ken C Abels, the Manager of the Hillcrest Golf Club.

● A ball driven by a driving machine holed out in one at the 435-yard 1st hole at Hermitage Country Club, Richmond, Virginia, USA.

● The longest known hole-in-one in Great Britain was the 393-yard 7th hole at West Lancashire GC, where in 1972 the assistant professional Peter Parkinson holed his tee shot.

● Other long holes-in-one recorded in Great Britain have been 380 yards (5th hole at Tankersley Park) by David Hulley in 1961; 380 yards (12th hole at White Webbs) by Danny Dunne on 30th July, 1976; 370 yards (17th hole at Chilwell Manor, distance from the forward tee) by Ray Newton in 1977; 365 yards (10th hole at Harewood Downs) by K Saunders in 1965; 365 yards (7th hole at Catterick Garrison GC) by Leslie Bruckner on 18th July, 1980.

● The longest-recorded hole-in-one by a woman was that accomplished in September, 1949 by Marie Robie – the 393-yard hole at Furnace Brook course, Wollaston, Mass, USA.

● In April 1988, Mary Anderson, a bio-chemistry student at Trinity College, Dublin, holed-in-one at the 290-yard 6th hole at the Island GC, Co Dublin, the longest known hole-in-one by a woman in Great Britain.

Holing-in-One – Greatest Number by One Person

47–Amateur Norman Manley of Long Beach, California.

42–US professional Art Wall between 1936 and April 1979.

35–Mancil Davis, professional at the Trophy Club, Forth Worth, Texas. Davis achieved his last in 1979 at the age of 25.

31–British professional CT le Chevalier who died in 1973.

20–British amateur, Jim Hay of Kirkintilloch GC.

10–Mrs Olga Penman, formerly of Harewood Downs GC.

At One Hole

10-Joe Vitullo at 16th hole of Hubbard GC, Ohio.

5–Left-hander, the late Fred Francis at 7th (now 16th) hole of Cardigan GC.

Holing-in-One – Greatest Frequency

● The greatest number of holes-in-one in a calendar year is 11, by JO Boydstone of California in 1962.

● John Putt of Frilford Heath GC had six holes-in-one in 1970, followed by three in 1971.

● Douglas Porteous, of Ruchill GC, Glasgow, achieved seven holes-in-one in the space of eight months. Four of them were scored in a five-day period from 26th to 30th September, 1974, in three consecutive rounds of golf. The first two were achieved at Ruchill GC in one round, the third there two days later, and the fourth at Clydebank and District GC after another two days. The following May, Porteous had three holes-in-one, the first at Linn Park GC incredibly followed by two more in the one round at Clober GC. (See also *Holing-in-One Twice in One Round.*)

● Mrs Kathleen Hetherington of West Essex has holed-in-one five times, four being at the 15th hole at West Essex. Four of her five aces were within seven months in 1966.

● Mrs Dorothy Hill of Dumfries and Galloway GC holed-in-one three times in 11 days in 1977.

●James C Reid of Brodick, aged 59 and 8 handicap in 1987, has achieved 14 holes-in-one, all but one on Isle of Arran courses. His success, in spite of severe physical handicaps of a stiff left knee, a damaged right ankle, two discs removed from his back and a hip replacement is remarkable. He plays regularly, walks the course, but uses a walking stick for balance.

Holing Successive Holes-in-One

● Successive holes-in-one are rare; successive par 4 holes-in-one may be classed as near miracles. NL Manley performed the most incredible feat in September, 1964, at Del Valle Country Club, Saugus, California, USA. The par 4 7th (330 yards) and 8th (290 yards) are both slightly downhill, dog-leg holes. Manley had *aces* at both, en route to a course record of 61 (par 71).

● The first recorded example in Britain of a player holing-in-one stroke at each of two successive holes was achieved on 6th February, 1964, at the Walmer and Kingsdown course, Kent. The young assistant professional at that club, Roger Game (aged 17) holed out with a No. 4 wood at the 244-yard 7th hole, and repeated the feat at the 256-yard 8th hole, using a No. 5 iron.

● The first occasion of holing-in-one at consecutive holes in a major professional event occurred when John Hudson, 25-year-old professional at Hendon, holed-in-one at the 11th and 12th holes at Norwich during the second round of the 1971 Martini tournament. Hudson used a 4-iron at the 195-yard 11th and a driver at the 311-yard downhill 12th hole.

● Assistant professional Tom Doty (23 years), playing in a friendly match on a course near Chicago in October, 1971 had a remarkable four hole score which included two consecutive holes-in-one, sandwiched either side by an albatross and an eagle: 4th hole (500 yards)–2; 5th hole (360 yards dog-leg)–1; 6th hole (175 yards)–1; 7th hole (375 yards)–2. Thus he was 10 under par for four consecutive holes.

Holing-in-One Twice (or more) in Same Round by Same Person

(See also Successive Holes-in-One)

What might be thought to be a very rare feat indeed – that of holing-in-one twice in the same round – has in fact happened on many occasions as the following instances show. It is, nevertheless, compared to the number of golfers in the world, still something of an outstanding achievement. The first occasion known to us was in 1907 when J Ireland playing in a three-ball match at Worlington holed the 5th and 18th holes in one stroke and two years later in 1909 HC Josecelyne holed the 3rd (175 yards) and the 14th (115 yards) at Acton on 24th November.

● The Rev Harold Snider, aged 75, scored his first hole-in-one on 9th June, 1976 at the 8th hole of the Ironwood course, near Pheonix. By the end of his round he had scored three holes-in-one, the other two being at the 13th (110 yards) and 14th (135 yards). Ironwood is a par-3 course, giving more opportunity of scoring holes-in-one, but, nevertheless, three holes-in-one in one round on any type of course is an outstanding achievement.

● The first mention of two holes-in-one in a round by a woman is of special note in that it was followed later by a similar feat by another lady at the same club. On 19th May, 1942, Mrs W Driver, of Balgowlah Golf Club, New South Wales, holed out in one at the 3rd and 8th holes in the same round, while on 29th July, 1948, Mrs F Burke at the same club holed out in one at the 2nd and 8th holes.

● The youngest-known person to have had two holes-in-one in one round was a 14-year-old American, Peter Townsend.

● The youngest British player was Ian Robertson in June, 1972, at Torphin Hill GC, Edinburgh, when 15 years old. The holes were the 252-yard 9th and 210-yard 14th.

● The youngest woman to have performed the feat was a 17-year-old, Marjorie Merchant, playing at the Lomas Athletic GC, Argentina, at the 4th (170 yards) and 8th (130 yards) holes.

Holes-in-One on the Same Day

●In July 1987, at the Skerries Club, Co Dublin, Rank Xerox sponsored two tournaments, a men's 18-hole four-ball with 134 pairs competing and a 9-hole mixed foursomes with 33. During the day each of the four par-3 holes on the course were holed-in-one, the 2nd by Noel Bollard, 5th by Bart Reynolds, 12th by Jackie Carr and 15th by Gerry Ellis.

Two Holes-in-One at Same Hole in Same Game

First in World

● George Stewart and Fred Spellmeyer at the 18th hole, Forest Hills, New Jersey, USA in October 1919.

First in Great Britain

● Miss G Clutterbuck and Mrs HM Robinson at the 15th hole (120 yards), St Augustine GC, Ramsgate, on 8th May, 1925.

First in Denmark

●In a Club match in August 1987 at Himmerland, Steffan Jacobsen of Aalborg and Peter Forsberg of Himmerland halved the 15th hole in one shot, the first known occasion in Denmark.

First in Australia

●Dr & Mrs B Rankine, playing in a mixed 'Canadian foursome' event at the Osmond Club near Adelaide, South Australia in April 1987, holed-in-one in consecutive shots at the 2nd hole (162 metres), he from the men's tee with a 3-iron and his wife from the Ladies' tee with a $1^1/_2$ wood.

Holing-in-One and Holing a Full Shot to Win a Championship or Match

Ending a match by holing-in-one or with a full shot is infrequent enough to be worthy of placing on record individually here.

● The most lucrative holing of a full shot to win occurred in the *Tam O'Shanter* World Championship at Chicago in 1953. Chandler Harper appeared to have victory and the first prize of $25,000 in the bag when Lew Worsham holed a full wedge shot of some 135 yards for a 2 at the 410-yard last hole of the tournament to win by one stroke.

● In the first round of the Oxford and Cambridge Society's President's Putter at Rye, January, 1937, between PHF White, the West of England Champion, 1936, and Leonard Crawley, Crawley was two up and six to play. White won the next three to take the lead and then holed the 17th – 230 yards – with his tee shot to win by 2 and 1.

● Willie Park, in 1898, at Troon in the second half of his match for £200 against Willie Fernie, holed a full brassie shot at the 7th hole – the 61st of the match – to win, the most dramatic ending to a first class professional match.

● When FE McCarroll (Queen's University), Belfast, won the Boyd Quaich at St Andrews in 1966, his 291st and last shot, played with a sand wedge, finished in the hole for an eagle 2.

● MG Milton completed a match in the Moray and Nairn league on 22nd May, 1972, at Nairn Dunbar GC by holing-in-one at the 174-yard 15th to win by 5 and 3.

●In the 1973 Welsh Amateur at Ashburnham, Ted Davies, defending champion, ended one of his matches by holing-in-one at the 13th hole.

● In the 1974 Home International matches at the Royal St David's GC, against Ireland in the top foursomes match, Sandy Pirie of Scotland holed-in-one at the last hole giving Scotland a one-hole victory.

● Two Australian golfers, John Wise and Glen Hutton, influenced by the fact that two tennis players had signed a contract for a 100 match series, agreed to play a similar golf series limited to ten matches per year. In 1967 Hutton won the 99th match to lead in the series by one match. In the 100th match Wise holed-in-one at the last hole to win the hole, the game and end the series all square.

● In the Assistants' Championship at Worsley, 1950, Harry Weetman (Hartsbourne Golf Club), who won the Championship for the second year in succession, holed his tee shot at the 172-yard 18th hole in the final round – the 72nd hole of the championship. Weetman, however, had had several strokes in hand for victory.

Holing-in-One — Miscellaneous Incidents

(See also Holing-in-One in the Championships)

● The late Harry Vardon, who scored the greatest number of victories in the Open Championship, only once did a hole-in-one. That was in 1903 at Mundesley, Norfolk, where Vardon was convalescing from a long illness.

● Walter Hagen, one of the greatest and most colourful golfers of all time, in his long career also did only one hole-in-one – at the 6th hole at Worcester, Mass, in 1925. It was the first shot played with a new ball, he used a No 1 iron and it was the first of July.

● In April 1984 Joseph McCaffrey and his son, Gordon, each holed-in-one in the Spring Medal at the 164 yard 12th hole at Vale of Leven Club, Dunbartonshire.

● Having watched Paul Hahn play a trick shot from a kneeling position, 16-year-old Jim Hadderer, of Elgin, Illinois, USA, tried the same *gag* at a 190-yard hole at the Wing Park course in 1965. He improved on Hahn's performance by popping the ball into the hole in one.

● Identical twins, John and Desmond Rosser scored holes-in-one in consecutive rounds at Auckland GC, New Zealand. Playing in a medal competition on Saturday 15th March, 1975 with his twin and two other members, John, the elder twin, holed-in-one at the 10th hole with his wedge. In their next game, the following Wednesday, the twins were again playing in a four-ball with two other members when Desmond holed-in-one at the 13th hole using his driver.

● In 1977, 14-year-old Gillian Field after a series of lessons holed-in-one at the 10th hole at Moor Place GC in her first round of golf.

● Having taken some golf lessons in Britain, Mrs Joan Birtley of Flamstead, Herts., accompanied her husband on a business trip to America in 1977. At Doral CC, Miami, Mrs Birtley hired some clubs and played her first-ever round of golf. At the 4th hole (116 yards) she holed-in-one.

● Mrs Fred Reeves (71) of Midland, Michigan, watched golf on television and thought it looked easy. So she borrowed a few clubs, went out to a little 9-hole course, and shot the 3rd hole (90 yards) in one stroke. She completed the 9 holes in 48 – or 21 over par.

● By holing-in-one at the 2nd hole in a match against D Graham in the 1979 Suntory World Match Play at Wentworth, Japanese professional Isao Aoki won himself a Bovis home at Gleneagles worth, inclusive of furnishings, £55,000.

● In the 1979 French Open, Willie Milne appeared to have won a Mercedes car when he holed-in-one. However the organisers later declared the prize had been withdrawn. Threatening to sue, Milne was subsequently presented with a Mercedes.

● When he holed-in-one at the 105-yard 14th hole at Tahoe Paradise course, USA, in the Harrah Invitational Tournament in 1965, Dick Kolbus, from Oakland, California, won an $18,500 Rolls-Royce car.

● One hour before he retired as Captain of the Guernsey Golf Club, Channel Islands, RJ Mahy (handicap 1) holed out in one at the 18th hole, while playing in a medal competition on 12th March, 1964. This was his first hole-in-one and a fitting climax to his year as captain.

● Playing a holiday round on Rotorua course, New Zealand, on 25th July, 1964, Dr AW Reid of Taumaranui, holed his tee shot at the 110-yard 6th hole. While approaching the next hole he was hit on the head by a ball driven from the eighth tee, and knocked unconscious. Recovering, he completed the round, and duly paid a double penalty – once for holing-in-one, and once for being still alive!

● JoAnn Washam twice holed in one in the 1979 Kemper Open, a USLPGA Tournament.

● R Buckell, a member of Pinner Hill GC and W Dunbar, playing together in a society outing over Pinner Hill on 30th August, 1969, each holed-in-one at the 17th hole (225 yards).

● On 30th November, 1975, her last day of office as lady captain of Alderley Edge GC, Mrs Gertrude Wright holed-in-one at the 4th hole (115 yards).

● Veteran American, Earl Hooke, of Paris, Texas, holed-in-one in the month of July in four consecutive years, 1968 to 1971.

● Golfers in three consecutive groups at Blowing Rock CC, North Carolina, one day in 1979 each holed-in-one at the 156-yard 7th hole. They were Charles Wood, Harold Beal and Wallace Brawley.

● Russell Dewald, Ray Newman and Hal Martin, players in three consecutive games, holed-in-one on 23rd January, 1980 at the 14th hole (120 yards) at Lakewood CC, Florida.

● On the morning after being elected captain for 1973 of the Norwich GC, JS Murray hit his first shot as captain straight into the hole at the 169 yards first hole.

● Bob Dellow and John Watt, of Millicent Golf Club in South Australia, playing with another two members in a competition on 24th July, 1970, each holed-in-one at the 153-yard 13th hole. The following day, one of the other members of the four, Greg Nitschke, holed-in-one at the same hole.

● Using the same club and ball, 11-handicap left-hander Christopher Smyth holed-in-one at the 2nd hole (170 yards) in two consecutive medal competitions at Headfort GC, Co Meath, in January, 1976.

● In a knock-out competition at Ely, Cambridgeshire, on 13th October, 1962, Mr Challis drove to within four feet of the 1st hole (170 yards). His opponent, Mr Delwage, pitched his second shot; his ball struck that of Mr Challis, knocking it into the hole and giving him the hole-in-one.

● Dr Tucker, New Orleans, Louisiana, 1936, put his name down for a hole-in-one golf tournament. After doing so he walked out to the contest hole – 160 yards – and hit the ball with an iron. The ball trickled into the hole. Elated, Dr Tucker rushed back to the clubhouse, only to find that the competition was not due to begin until two weeks later.

● The late Miss Gertrude Lawrence, a distinguished actress, when playing golf for the first time, holed-in-one with her first tee shot.

● In an RAF outing in 1973 at Peterborough Milton GC two holes-in-one were made with the same ball but not by the same person. The first was in the morning singles by Des Tuson at the 142-yard 11th hole. Then in the afternoon, playing in a greensome competition, his partner, Keith Schofield, holed-in-one at the 174-yard 2nd hole. The ball was then carefully put away.

● General Eisenhower, early in 1968, holed the 13th at Seven Lakes Country Club in one. It was his first ace and *13* was not an unlucky number.

● Joe Kirkwood holed-in-one on 11 occasions including one when doing a Newsreel Movie at the 5th (168 yards), Sea Island, Georgia, and another when he was performing trick shots off the face of a watch at the 1st (268 yards), Cedar Rapids, Iowa.

● A one-armed golfer, Andrew Harrison, has had three holes-in-one. The latest was achieved at the 16th hole (160 yards) at West Lothian GC in 1971.

● Another one-armed golfer, Don Reid of Ravensworth GC, has twice holed-in-one at his club's 8th hole, once in 1977 and again in 1979.

● A Wilmott, who had been the One-Armed Champion on several occasions, holed-in-one at the 3rd hole which measured 230 yards during a round of the 1979 club championship at Downfield GC.

● A woman who has only her right arm, Mrs Frank Andreucci, of Florida, holed-in-one at the 136-yard 13th hole at Crystal Lake CC in 1971.

● At Royal Hong Kong Golf Club, Susan Tonroe, aged 16, and her brother, aged 11, each did the 7th hole in one in junior competitions in the same week.

● Playing over Rickmansworth course at Easter, 1960, Mrs AE (Paddy) Martin achieved a remarkable sequence of *aces*. On Good Friday she sank her tee shot at the third hole (125 yards). The next day, using the same ball and the same No. 8 iron, at the same hole, she scored another *one*. And on the Monday (same ball, same club, same hole) she again holed out from the tee. (See also *Holing-in-One in Successive Rounds*).

● Playing in the Eastern Inter-County Foursomes in May 1974, RJ Taylor holed-in-one at the 188-yards 16th hole at Hunstanton on three consecutive days. Leading Bookmakers reckoned the odds against such a feat at 5 million to one.

● Joan Jankins, aged 12, achieved a hole-in-one at the 240-yard 3rd hole at Abersoch, Gwynedd, in October 1984.

● In January 1985 Otto Bucher of Switzerland, aged 99, holed-in-one at the 130-yard 12th hole at the La Manga Championship South course in Spain.

Bookmakers and Golf

(See also Wagers, Curious and Large)

● Wagering on a heavy scale has been associated with golf from its earliest days, but the first time a bookmaker appeared at a golf tournament and shouted the odds was in 1898 in a professional tournament at Carnoustie. In 1927, at the Open Championship at St Andrews, a Glasgow bookmaker and two assistants mixed among the crowds following the players and shouting the odds. In the Open Championship at Portrush, 1951, a bookmaker set up his stand during the qualifying rounds and shouted the odds. In 1934 various bookmakers' lists were promiscuously issued and publicly advertised, giving odds for the Amateur and Open Championships, and representatives of different commission agents attended the two championships and touted for bets, but this was carried out individually and odds were not publicly shouted. Since 1934 reputable bookmakers in London and the Provinces annually bet to any sum on the Amateur and Open Championships.

● At the John Player Classic Tournament at Turnberry in 1971 a firm of bookmakers had a stand in the tented village. A lot of bets were placed including several by competitors. There was much talk of the possibilities of malpractice this could lead to, and as a result, the authorities decided to ban on-course betting in British tournaments. Then in 1980 the PGA gave permission to the Coral Leisure Group for a mobile betting office to be situated on the course at several major tournaments but no head to head bets were allowed to be offered.

Challenge Matches

Before the days of large prize-money from sponsored tournaments professional golfers had little opportunity to augment their meagre regular income except by taking part in challenge matches. Sometimes wealthy sponsors would put up cash, but frequently the players staked their own money on a winner-take-all basis. This naturally meant a great deal of tension for the competitors and the matches created a great deal of interest in rival groups of supporters.

As will be seen from the following record of the more important of these challenge matches, the sums of money involved were very considerable for the times.

● 1843–Allan Robertson, St Andrews, beat Willie Dunn, Musselburgh, in a match of 20 rounds, 360 holes, by 2 rounds and 1 to play.

● 1849–Allan Robertson and Tom Morris, of St Andrews, beat the brothers Dunn, of Musselburgh, over Musselburgh, St Andrews and North Berwick, for a stake of £400. The Dunns won at Musselburgh by 13 and 12; but Robertson and Morris got even at St Andrews. The match, therefore, reverted to North Berwick. The Dunns were 4 up and 8 to play. Odds of 20 to 1 were laid on the Dunns at this point but Robertson and Morris won by one hole.

● 1852–Tom Morris and Allan Robertson defeated Sir Robert Hay and Willie Dunn by 6 and 5 over two rounds at St Andrews. Morris and Robertson staked £100 to £50 on the issue.

● 1853–Willie Park, sen, twice defeated Tom Morris, sen, in £100 matches. Allan Robertson was repeatedly challenged by Park, but refused to play.

● 1854–Tom Morris and Bob Anderson beat Allan Robertson and Willie Dunn for £200 by one hole, in an 18 hole match at St Andrews.

● 1854-5–Willie Park and Tom Morris played six £100 matches, and honours were about evenly divided. In the fifth match at Musselburgh the spectators interfered with Morris's ball repeatedly, and the referee stopped play. Morris and the referee, Bob Chambers, an Edinburgh publisher, retired to a nearby public house. Park waited for some time and then sent a message to Chambers and Morris that if they did not come out to play to a finish he would play the remaining holes alone and claim the stakes. Morris and Chambers remained in the public house and Park, completing the round, was subsequently awarded the stakes.

● 1857–Allan Robertson and Andrew Strath beat Tom Morris and Willie Park for £100 by six holes in two rounds.

● 1859–Willie Park, sen, beat Willie Dunn at Prestwick for £100.

● 1868–Lord Kennedy and Mr Cruikshank, of Langley Park, played a match of three holes for £500 a hole at St Andrews. Play started at 10 pm, and the only light was given by lamps stuck on the flag pins of the three holes. It is not known who won this extraordinary match.

● 1868-9–Old Tom and Bob Ferguson played six matches over Luffness and Musselburgh, and Ferguson won them all.

● 1869–Young Tom beat Bob Ferguson at Musselburgh by one hole.

● 1875–Old and Young Tom beat Willie Park and Mungo Park for £50 at North Berwick by one hole.

● This was the last big money match Young Tom played. A telegram had been received in North Berwick before the end of the match intimating that Young Tom's wife had died. The news was kept from him until he boarded John Lewis's yacht which took the St Andrews' party across the Forth. Young Tom never recovered from the shock and died on Christmas Day of the same year, aged 24.

● 1876–In October, 1875, John Ball, sen, father of John Ball, the eight times amateur champion, with David Strath, challenged any amateur and professional. AH Molesworth and John Allan, Westward Ho! accepted. The match was played at Hoylake over four rounds for a stake of £100 a side. Ball and Strath won by 7 and 5.

● 1883–Douglas Rolland (who afterwards turned

professional) beat John Ball, jun, in a home and away match over Earlsferry and Hoylake. Over the two rounds at Elie, Rolland finished nine holes up. On the first round at Hoylake, Ball reduced the lead by one hole, but Rolland finally won by 11 and 10. A fresh match of two rounds was played the following day, and this Rolland also won.

● 1894–Douglas Rolland beat Willie Park, jun, in a 36-hole match at Sandwich by 3 and 2 for £100. Park had challenged the world.

● 1895–Andrew Kirkaldy defeated JH Taylor by one hole over 36 holes at St Andrews for £50 a side. Taylor, reigning Open Champion, had never played over St Andrews when he issued his challenge. The match was played prior to the Open Championship, 1895, which Taylor retained.

● 1896–Willie Park defeated JH Taylor in a 72-hole match over Musselburgh and Sudbrook Park. The match was notable for the rowdyism of the spectators at Musselburgh, and there was so much local partisanship that three years later Harry Vardon refused to include Musselburgh as Park's home course in their great match, and Park had to take North Berwick.

● 1899–Harry Vardon, in a 72-hole match (36 holes over North Berwick and 36 holes over Ganton), defeated Willie Park, jun, by 11 and 10 for £100 a side. At the end of 36 holes at North Berwick Vardon was two holes up. The first ten holes were halved. At the 11th hole, Park had the honour and Vardon's drive pitched on Park's ball and rebounded two feet. Vardon duffed his next shot and lost the hole – the first change in the match. The spectators at North Berwick numbered over 10,000, and represented an unprecedented attendance for an individual match up to that time and for many years afterwards.

● 1899–John Ball and Harry Vardon beat FG Tait and Willie Park at Ganton by 5 and 4 in a 36-hole match.

● 1904–The brothers Harry and Tom Vardon defeated James Braid and Jack White at Sunningdale in a 36-hole match by 3 and 1. They also won the last hole.

● 1905–JH Taylor and Harry Vardon, representing England, defeated James Braid and Alex Herd, representing Scotland by 13 and 12 over four courses, for £200 a side. Results: St Andrews–Scotland 2 up; Troon–England 12 up; St Annes–England 7 up; Deal–England won by 13 and 12. At Troon the attendance equalled the great crowd at North Berwick for the Vardon-Park match.

● 1906–Harry Vardon and James Braid beat George Duncan and Charles Mayo, in a 72-hole match for £100, by 9 and 8. Results: Walton Heath – Vardon and Braid, 4 up. Timperley – Vardon and Braid, 9 and 8.

● 1926–Walter Hagen beat Abe Mitchell in a 72-hole match over Wentworth and St George's Hill by 2 and 1 for a stake of £1,000 (£500 a-side). At the end of 36 holes Mitchell was 4 up.

● 1926–Walter Hagen beat Bobby Jones in a 72-hole match at St Petersburg and Sarasota Bay by 11 and 10. Hagen was paid $5,000 for the St Petersburg half and received all the gate money at $3 per ticket at Sarasota. The gate money was $3,500. Hagen's combined fee of $8,500 was the largest ever received by a professional golfer for a challenge match. Hagen presented Jones with a set of shirt studs and cuff links.

● 1928–Archie Compston, on 27th and 28th April, at Moor Park, London, defeated Walter Hagen in a 72-hole match by 18 and 17. At the end of the 36 holes, Compston was 14 holes up. This is the greatest margin of victory ever recorded in a first class professional match. Stake £500. Hagen proceeded to Sandwich where he won for the third time the Open Championship.

● 1937–Henry Cotton, Open Champion, beat Densmore Shute, American professional champion, over 72 holes at Walton Heath. At the end of 18 holes they were all square; after 36 holes Cotton was two up; 54 holes (end third round) Cotton was five up and he won by 6 and 5. The match followed immediately after the Open Championship at Carnoustie. A sum of £500 was put up to be won outright, but the donor, when the winning cheque was handed to Cotton, also presented Shute with £100.

● 1938–Reginald Whitcombe, Open Champion of the year, and Henry Cotton accepted a challenge by AD Locke and Sid Brews, South Africa, for a 72-hole four-ball match, for £500 a side. The match was played at Walton Heath. At the end of the first round the Englishmen were one up, after two rounds two down, then two up again after three rounds, finally winning by 2 and 1.

● 1938–AD Locke, South African Champion, defeated Alf Padgham, Sunridge Park, by 2 holes in a 36-hole challenge match for £100 at Selsdon Park, Croydon. Locke did the last nine holes in 32 – 6 under bogey – and did not lead until the 35th hole.

● 1939–AD Locke (South Africa) in a 72-hole match for £500 a side at Coombe Hill, on 1st and 2nd June, beat Reginald Whitcombe, Parkstone, the Open Champion of 1938, by 6 and 5.

● 1939–Alfred Perry, Leatherhead, partnered by HJG Hare, six handicap, beat AD Locke, South Africa, and his backer, LH Oates, 10 handicap, by 4 and 2. Perry and Hare won £125; £25 on the first nine holes; £25 on the second; £50 on the match and £25 on the bye. On a rain-soaked course Perry had an individual score of 63.

● 1951–AD Locke (South Africa) beat Norman von Nida (Australia) by 11 and 9 over 144 holes, 36 holes were played at Cape Town, 36 at Durban and 72 at Johannesburg. The match was for £1,500. Locke received £1,000 and Von Nida, £500.

● 1952–Henry Cotton and Fred Daly defeated AD Locke and Eric Brown, 8 and 7, over 36 holes at Walton Heath. The winners each received £250 and the losers each £100.

Curious and Large Wagers

***(See also bets recorded under* Cross-Country Matches, *and in* Challenge Matches)**

● In the Royal and Ancient Club minutes an entry on 3rd November, 1870 was made in the following terms: *Sir David Moncreiffe, Bart, of Moncrieffe, backs his life against the life of John Whyte-Melville, Esq, of Strathkinnes, for a new silver club as a present to the St Andrews Golf Club, the price of the club to be paid by the survivor and the arms of the parties to be engraved on the club, and the present bet inscribed on it. No balls to be attached to it. In testimony of which this bet is subscribed by the parties thereto.* Thirteen years later, Mr Whyte-Melville, in a feeling and appropriate speech, expressed his deep regret at the lamented death of Sir Robert Moncrieffe, one of the most distinguished and zealous supporters of the club. Whyte-Melville, while lamenting the cause that led to it, had pleasure in fulfilling the duty imposed upon him by the bet, and accordingly delivered to the captain the silver putter. Whyte-Melville in 1883 was elected captain of the club a second time; he died in his eighty-sixth year in July, 1883, before he could take office and the captaincy remained vacant for a year. His portrait hangs in the Royal and Ancient clubhouse and is one of the finest and most distinguished pictures in the smoking room.

● In 1766, the Honourable Company of Edinburgh Golfers who then played at Leith Links passed a resolution that *no match should be played for more than 100 merks on the day's play, or a guinea the round.* A merk was worth approximately 6p and the limit of 100 merks would be approximately £5.60 in present-day money.

● Heavy wagering is frequently associated with private or golfing society matches, in which rich men are engaged and rounds on which £1,000 depended are not unknown. Amateurs playing for £100 a round are not out of the way.

● Bobby Jones won the four major championships in 1930 (the Amateur, the Open, the American Amateur and the American Open). Long odds had been laid against such a result by bookmakers, and extensive sums were paid out.

● In 1914 Francis Ouimet, who in the previous autumn had won the American Open Championship after a triangular tie with Harry Vardon and Ted Ray, came to Great Britain with Jerome D Travers, the holder of the American amateur title, to compete in the British Amateur Championship at Sandwich. An American syndicate took a bet of £30,000 to £10,000 that one or other of the two United States champions would be the winner. It only took two rounds to decide the bet against the Americans. Ouimet was beaten by a then quite unknown player, HS Tubbs, while Travers was defeated by Charles Palmer, who was fifty-six years of age at the time.

● 1907 John Ball for a wager undertook to go round Hoylake during a dense fog in under 90, in not more than two and a quarter hours and without losing a ball. Ball played with a black ball, went round in 81, and also beat the time.

● The late Ben Sayers, for a wager, played the eighteen holes of the Burgess Society course scoring a four at every hole. Sayers was about to start against an American, when his opponent asked him what he could do the course in. *Fours* replied Sayers, meaning 72, or an average of 4s for the round. A bet was made and the American then added, *Remember a three or a five is not a four.* There were eight bogey 5s and two 3s on the Burgess course at the time Old Ben achieved his feat.

● After a hole had been halved in one at Forest Hills, New Jersey, one of the players offered to bet $10,000 to $1 that the occurrence would not be repeated at the hole during his lifetime.

● Cross-country and freak matches, embraced on another page, have been fruitful of many wagers, and matches have been played between distinguished golfers using only a putting cleek against players carrying all their clubs. At Hoylake a match was fixed between a scratch golfer and a handicap 6 player. They played level, the handicap player having the right to say *Boo* three times on the round. He said *Boo* at the 13th hole and won the match easily with two *Boos* in hand, the scratch player, of course, being affected by always anticipating the *Boo*.

● A match was arranged on a south of England course for a considerable bet between a scratch player and a long-handicap man, playing level, the scratch man to drink a whisky-and-soda on each tee. On the 16th tee the scratch man, who had a hole lead, collapsed, and was not very well for some time afterwards.

● In June, 1950, Bryan Field, vice-president of the Delaware Park racecourse, USA, who had not played golf for several years, accepted a wager that, without practice, he would not go round Pine Valley, rated one of the hardest courses in the world, in less than 300 shots. With borrowed clubs, he set off at 8am planning to finish in time for lunch. He started 7, 9, 4, 11, and when he got a 10 at the 5th, one of the most testing on the course, after putting three tee shots into the lake, it was obvious that he was well on the way to winning the bet. With an 11 at the 8th, another difficult hole he reached the turn in 73. Coming home in 75, Mr Field holed the course in 148 and won his wager with 152 strokes in hand. He took two hours, fifty minutes to complete the round.

Feats of Endurance

Although golf is not a game where endurance, in the ordinary sense in which the term is employed in sport, is required, there are several instances of feats on the links which demanded great physical exertion.

● In 1971 during a 24-hour period from 6 pm on 27th November until 5.15 pm on 28th November, Ian Colston completed 401 holes over the 6,061 yards Bendigo course, Victoria, Australia. Colston was a top marathon athlete but was not a golfer. However prior to his golfing marathon he took some lessons and became adept with a 6-iron, the only club he used throughout the 401 holes. The only assistance Colston had was a team of harriers to carry his 6-iron and look for his ball, and a band of motor cyclists who provided light during the night. This is, as far as is known, the greatest number of holes played in 24 hours on foot on a full-size course.

● In 1934 Col Bill Farnham played 376 holes in 24 hours 10 minutes at the Guildford Lake Course, Guildford, Connecticut, using only a mashie and a putter.

● To raise funds for extending the Skipton GC course from 12 to 18 holes, the club professional, 24-year-old Graham Webster, played 277 holes in the hours of daylight on Monday 20th June, 1977. Playing with nothing longer than a 5-iron he averaged 81 per 18-hole round. Included in his marathon was a hole-in-one.

● Michael Moore, a 7 handicap 26-year-old member of Okehampton GC, completed on foot 15 rounds 6 holes (276 holes) there on Sunday, 25th June, 1972, in the hours of daylight. He started at 4.15 am and stopped at 9.15 pm. The distance covered was estimated at 56 miles. Nine brief stoppages for salty soup were made. His time for 6 rounds was 6 hours 2 minutes; for 12 rounds, 12 hours 58 minutes.

● On 21st June, 1976, 5-handicapper Sandy Small played 15 rounds (270 holes) over his home course Cosby GC, length 6,128 yards, to raise money for the Society of Physically Handicapped Children. Using only a 5-iron, 9-iron and putter, Small started at 4.10 am and completed his 270th hole at 10.39 pm with the aid of car headlights. His fastest round was his first (40 minutes) and slowest his last (82 minutes). His best round of 76 was achieved in the second round.

● In 1957, Bert L Scoggins, a US serviceman, played 260 holes in one day on the American golf course at Berlin. He started out at 2.30 am, and played continuously for 18 hours, walking 56 miles in the course of his marathon feat. His lowest single round score was 84.

● Bill Falkingham, jun, of Amstel GC, Victoria, Australia, played 257 holes between 12.30 am and 6.15 pm on 14th December, 1968. The first three holes were played in darkness. He was accompanied by his brother and a friend who held a torch to assist direction. Ten balls were lost but the first ball lasted eight rounds. His best round was 90 over a course measuring 6,673 yards, par 73, over which a gale force wind blew all day, in a temperature of 90 degrees. During the morning he trod on a snake but did not stop to kill it. He was sustained by only sandwiches and soft drinks and although completely exhausted when he finished he had completely recovered next morning and went out for another round.

● During the weekend of 20th-21st June, 1970, Peter Chambers of Yorkshire completed over 14 rounds of golf over the Scarborough South Cliff course. In a non-stop marathon lasting just under 24 hours, Chambers played 257 holes in 1,168 strokes, an average of 84.4 strokes per round.

● Stan Gard, a member of North Brighton Golf Club, New South Wales, in 1938 completed fourteen rounds and four holes on his home course. Gard started his marathon performance at 12.55 am, and finished with the aid of car lights at 9.30 pm. He played consistent golf, his best being 78 in the tenth round, and his worst 92 in the second round.

● Bruce Sutherland, on the Craiglockhart Links, Edinburgh, started at 8.15 pm on 21st June, 1927, and played almost continuously until 7.30 pm on 22nd June, 1927. During the night four caddies with acetylene lamps lit the way, and lost balls were reduced to a minimum. He completed fourteen rounds. Mr Sutherland, who was a physical culture teacher, never recovered from the physical strain and died a few years later.

● Sidney Gleave, motor cycle racer, and Ernest Smith, golf professional, Davyhulme Club, Manchester, on 12th June, 1939, played five rounds of golf in five different countries – Scotland, Ireland, Isle of Man, England and Wales. Smith had to play the five rounds under 80 in one day to win the £100 wager. They travelled by plane, and the following was their programme with time taken and Smith's score:

Start—Prestwick St Nicholas (Scotland), 3.40 am. Score 70. Time taken, 1 hour 35 minutes. 2nd Course—Bangor (Ireland), 7.15 am. Score 76. Time taken, 1 hour 30 minutes. 3rd Course—Castletown (Isle of Man), 10.15 am. Score 76. Time taken, 1 hour 40 minutes. 4th Course—Blackpool, Stanley Park (England), 1.30 pm. Score 72. Time taken, 1 hour 55 minutes. 5th Course—Hawarden (Wales), 6 pm. Score 68 (record). Time taken, 2 hours 15 minutes.

● On Wednesday, 3rd July, 1974, ES Wilson, Whitehead, Co Antrim and Dr GW Donaldson, Newry, Co Down, played a nine-hole match in each of seven countries in the one day. The first 9 holes was at La Moye (Channel Islands) followed by Hawarden (Wales), Chester (England), Turnberry (Scotland), Castletown (Isle of Man), Dundalk (Eire) and Warrenpoint (N Ireland). They started their first round at 4.25 am and their last round at 9.25 pm. Wilson piloted his own plane throughout.

● Rick Garcia and Don Tanner from Gallup, New Mexico, played 18 holes, selected from seven States, in one day in 1976 to raise money for muscular dystrophy. The States concerned were Texas, New Mexico, Colorado, Utah, Arizona, California and Nevada. A distance of over 2,000 miles was covered by private plane.

● In June 1986 to raise money for the upkeep of his medieval church, the Rector of Mark with Allerton, Somerset, the Rev Michael Pavey, played a sponsored 18 holes on 18 different courses in the Bath & Wells Diocese. With his partner, the well-known broadcaster on music, Antony Hopkins, they played the 1st at Minehead at 5.55 am and finished playing the 18th at Burnham and Berrow at 6.05 pm. They covered 240 miles in the 'round' including the distances to reach the correct tee for the 'next' hole on each course. Par for the 'round' was 70. Together the pair raised £10,500 for the church.

●To raise funds for the Marlborough Club's centenary year (1988), Laurence Ross, the Club professional, in June 1987, played 8 rounds in 12 hours. Against a par of 72, he completed the 576 holes in 3 under par, playing from back tees and walking all the way.

Fastest Rounds

● Dick Kimbrough, 41, completed a round on foot on 8th August, 1972, at North Platte CC, Nebraska (6,068 yards) in 30 minutes 10 seconds. He carried only a 3-iron. Earlier the same year Kimbrough played 364 holes in 24 hours.

● At Mowbray Course, Cape Town, November 1931, Len Richardson, who had represented South Africa in the Olympic Games, played a round which measured 6,248 yards in 31 minutes 22 seconds.

● The women's all-time record for a round played on a course of at least 5,250 yards is held by Dianne Taylor, 37, Jacksonville, Florida. She played the 5,692 yards University GC at Jacksonville in 55 minutes 54 seconds on 7th April, 1980.

● Faster rounds have been recorded, but they have not been done on foot. The fastest of these was achieved by 3 handicap Ken Wildey at Calcot Park GC on 20th July, 1980. Wildey, riding in a motorised cart, completed the 6,010 yards course in 24 minutes 3 seconds.

The sole purpose in each of the above instances was speed. The following are examples of fast rounds in a match or competition.

● On 14th June, 1922, Jock Hutchison and Joe Kirkwood (Australia) played round the Old Course at St Andrews in 1 hour 20 minutes. Hutchison, out in 37, led by three holes at the ninth and won by 4 and 3.

● In April, 1934, after attending a wedding in Bournemouth, Hants, Captain Gerald Moxom hurried to his club, West Hill in Surrey, to play in the captain's prize competition. With daylight fading and still dressed in his morning suit, he went round in 65 minutes and won the competition with a net 71 into the bargain.

● Fastest rounds can also take another form – the time taken for a ball to be propelled round 18 holes. The fastest known round of this type is 8 minutes 53.8 seconds on 25th August, 1979 by 42 members at Ridgemount CC Rochester, New York, a course measuring 6,161 yards. The Rules of Golf were observed but a ball was available on the following tee to be driven off the instant the ball had been holed at the preceding hole.

Slow Play

Standards have changed dramatically over the years as to what constitutes slow play as the following statement, which first appeared in the 1949 Golfer's Handbook, shows: *Slow motion golf has marred many championships, and notorious tortoises have been known to take three-and-a-half hours in a championship tie.*

Nowadays a round taking three-and-a-half hours is commonplace, but for the sake of history we record here examples of what was considered very slow play up to 1950.

● When Henry Cotton and RA Whitcombe played Bobby Locke and Sid Brews at Walton Heath, 1938, for a stake of £500 a side, the match made headlines with the slowness of play. Locke, who was engaging in his first important professional match in Great Britain, was ultra-careful, and the marshalling of the crowd — there were 5,000 spectators present during the second round – caused many delays, sometimes as much as 10 minutes being required for the players to leave one green and play off the next tee. The first round took three hours 40 minutes and the second round four hours 15 minutes. Cotton and Whitcombe won by 2 and 1. Locke, although on the defeated side, played phenomenal golf. He went round in 63. Walton Heath tees were far extended and it was a cruel test.

● In the Scottish Amateur Championship, 1922, at St Andrews, a competitor was deplorably slow and in one tie his opponent, in the hope of shaming the sloth into quickening his play brought to the links a camp bed, which was carried round by others who had been playing in the championship. The camp bed was placed at the side of each green, and while the tortoise crawled about studying the line of the putt, his opponent reclined on the bed and nonchalantly observed the antics of his rival. The attempt to secure a speed-up in the play was unsuccessful and the tortoise was even more deliberate in his play.

● The Amateur Championship, St Andrews, 1950, was remarkable for slowness of play and the inordinate time taken by some players to play their shots. The main cause of the slowness was the time taken to study putts. In some cases five minutes were spent over a stroke on the greens, although the record entry of 324 and the huge double greens of the Championship Course were also contributory to the sluggish pace. Many matches took four hours to complete and five couples waited at some tees. A record for the championship was made on the third day when play in the third and fourth rounds occupied 14 hours. The first ball was struck at 8 am and the last match finished on the 17th green in the lamplit dusk shortly before 10 pm. In the final between FR Stranahan and RD Chapman the first nine holes of the morning round took an hour and 50 minutes to play. A field telephone message was sent to the referee, Colonel CO Hezlet, Portrush, to warn the players that the second round would start at the scheduled time. This increased the pace slightly and the round was finished in three hours 40 minutes, the slowest round in the final of the championship at that time.

Curious Scoring

● Three threes, four fours, five fives and six sixes is one of only two progressive combinations that can work out for 18 holes. A player in a South African competition had this sequence and noticed the curiosity in scoring. The other combination is five fives, six sixes and seven sevens.

● RH Corbett, playing in the semi-final of the Tangye Cup at Mullim in 1916, did a score of 27. The remarkable part of Corbett's score was that it was made up of nine successive 3s, bogey being 5, 3, 4, 4, 5, 3, 4, 4, 3.

● At Little Chalfont in June 1985 Adrian Donkersley played six successive holes in 6, 5, 4, 3, 2, 1 from the 9th to the 14th holes against a par of 4, 4, 3, 4, 3, 3.

● On 2nd September, 1920, playing over Torphin, near Edinburgh, William Ingle did the first five holes in 1, 2, 3, 4, 5.

● In the summer of 1970, Keith McMillan, on holiday at Cullen, had a remarkable series of 1, 2, 3, 4, 5 at the 11th to 15th holes.

● Playing at Addington Palace, July, 1934, Ronald Jones, a member of Hendon Club, holed five consecutive holes in 5, 4, 3, 2, 1.

● Harry Dunderdale of Lincoln GC scored 5, 4, 3, 2, 1 in five consecutive holes during the first round of his club championship in 1978. The hole-in-one was the 7th, measuring 294 yards.

● At Westerhope near Newcastle in January 1986 Alan Crosby, the Club professional, played the first four holes in 4, 3, 2, 1 against the par of 4, 4, 3, 4.

● Playing in his club medal competition at Hindley Hall GC on 25h August, 1974, H Rowlance had every digit from 1 to 8 on his card. His 1 was at the 6th hole (156 yards).

● In a club competition Mr A Mitchell had every digit from 1 to 8 on his card.

● At Nairn in August 1985 Brian Crowther of Swinton Park and Andrew Watson of Kelso, each 12 handicap, completed 18 holes without halving a hole. Crowther won at the 19th.

● PC Chase and John North finished all square in their regular weekly match at Woking GC on 30th October, 1972, without having halved a single hole. An actuarial calculation put the odds against this at 1,413,398-1.

● Another instance of this occurred in a first round foursomes match in the Halford-Hewitt Cup at Deal in 1979 when a Hurstpierpoint pair beat St Bee's at the 19th hole, without any hole being halved. The first ten holes were exchanged, St Bee's winning the next four and Hurstpierpoint the following five.

● At the Open Amateur Tournament of the Royal Ashdown Forest in 1936 Bobby Locke in his morning round had a score of 72, accomplishing every hole in 4.

● Severiano Ballesteros in winning the 1978 Swiss Open scored four rounds of 68.

● In a four-ball match in 1936, Richard Chapman partnered by Joe Ezar, the *Clown* prince of golf, against the Hon Michael Scott and Bobby Locke, then 18 years old, were four down and five to play. Ezar asked Scott if he had ever seen five birdies in a row. Scott replied that he could not recall that happening and so Ezar made a bet on the same and pulled the match out 1 up by shooting five birdies to win the match.

● Henry Cotton told of one of the most extraordinary scoring feats ever. With some other professionals he was at Sestrieres in the thirties for the Italian Open Championship and Joe Ezar, a colourful character in those days on both sides of the Atlantic, accepted a wager from a club official – 1,000 lira for a 66 to break the course record; 2,000 for a 65; and 4,000 for a 64. *I'll do 64*, said Ezar, and proceeded to jot down the hole-by-hole score figures he would do next day for that total. With the exception of the ninth and tenth holes where his predicted score was 3, 4 and the actual score was 4, 3, he accomplished this amazing feat exactly as nominated.

High Scores

● In the qualifying competition at Formby for the 1976 Open Championship, Maurice Flitcroft, a 46-year-old crane driver from Barrow-in-Furness, took 121 strokes for the first round and then withdrew saying, *I have no chance of qualifying.* Flitcroft entered as a professional but had never before played 18 holes. He had taken the game up 18 months previously but, as he was not a member of a club, had been limited to practising on a local beach. His round was made up thus: 7, 5, 6, 6, 6, 6, 12, 6, 7–61; 11, 5, 6, 8, 4, 9, 5, 7, 5–60, total 121. After his round Flitcroft said, *I've made a lot of progress in the last few months and I'm sorry I did not do better. I was trying too hard at the beginning but began to put things together at the end of the round.* R and A officials who were not amused by the bogus professional's efforts, refunded the £30 entry money to Flitcroft's two fellow-competitors.

● Playing in the qualifying rounds of the 1965 Open Championship at Southport, an American self-styled professional entrant from Milwaukee, Walter Danecki, achieved the inglorious feat of scoring a total of 221 strokes for 36 holes, 81 over par. His first round over the Hillside course was 108, followed by a second round of 113. Walter, who afterwards admitted he felt *a little discouraged and sad*, declared that he entered because he was *after the money.*

● The highest individual scoring ever known in the rounds connected with the Open Championship occurred at Muirfield, 1935, when a Scottish professional started 7, 10, 5, 10, and took 65 to reach the 9th hole. Another 10 came at the 11th and the player decided to retire at the 12th hole. There he was in a bunker, and after playing four shots he had not regained the fairway.

● In 1883 in the Open Championship at Musselburgh, Willie Fernie, the winner, had a 10, the only time double figures appeared on the card of the Open Champion of the year. Fernie won after a tie with Bob Ferguson, and his score for the last hole in the tie was 2. He holed from just off the green to win by one stroke.

● In the first Open Championship at Prestwick in 1860 a competitor took 21, the highest score for one hole ever recorded in this event. The record is preserved in the archives of the Prestwick Golf Club, where the championship was founded.

● In 1938, in the final two rounds of the Open Championship, the players who had qualified for this stage had to contend with a hurricane during the greater part of the day. So fierce was the wind that the players had difficulty in keeping their stance during their swing. Scores of nine for individual holes were numerous; there were many 10's and one player had 14, the equal third highest score ever recorded for a single hole in the Open Championship.

● In the first round of the 1980 US Masters, Tom Weiskopf hit his ball into the water hazard in front of the par-3 12th hole five times and scored 13 for the hole.

● American Ben Crenshaw took 11 shots at the 16th hole at Firestone CC in the third round of the 1976 World Series. He hit three consecutive wedge shots into the lake in front of the green.

● In the French Open at St Cloud, in 1968, Brian Barnes took 15 for the short 8th hole in the second round. After missing putts at which he hurriedly snatched while the ball was moving he penalised himself further by standing astride the line of a putt. The amazing result was that he actually took 12 strokes from about three feet from the hole.

● US professional Dave Hill 6-putted the fifth green at Oakmont in the 1962 US Open Championship.

● In the 1973 Transvaal Open at Germiston GC, Canadian professional Ken Trowbridge took 16 putts on the last green in a deliberate move to protest over the condition of the greens.

● Many high scores have been made at the Road Hole at St Andrews. Davie Ayton, on one occasion, was coming in a certain winner of the Open Championship when he got on the road and took 11. In 1921, at the Open Championship, one professional took 13. In 1923, competing for the Autumn Medal of the Royal and Ancient, JB Anderson required a five and a four to win the second award, but he took 13 at the Road Hole. Anderson was close to the green in two, was twice in the bunkers in the face of the green, and once on the road. In 1935, RH Oppenheimer tied for the Royal Medal (the first award) in the Autumn Meeting of the Royal and Ancient. On the play-off he was one stroke behind Captain Aitken when they stood on the 17th tee. Oppenheimer drove three balls out of bounds and eventually took 11 to the Road Hole.

● In the English Amateur at Hunstanton in 1931, a competitor pitched five times into a ditch before giving up the hole.

● In the 1974 Tallahassee Open, Mike Reasor, a regular PGA tour competitor, qualified for the final 36 holes in which he then scored 123 and 114. After making the halfway cut, Reasor injured his left shoulder in a riding accident, but because of the automatic entry into the next tournament given to all who completed the current one, he decided to play on using only his right arm for the last two rounds.

● British professional Mark James scored 111 in the second round of the 1978 Italian Open. He played the closing holes with only his right hand due to an injury to his left hand.

● In the 1927 Shawnee Open, Tommy Armour took 23 strokes to the 17th hole. Armour had won the American Open Championship a week earlier. In an effort to play the hole in a particular way, Armour hooked ball after ball out of bounds and finished with a 21 on the card. There was some doubt about the accuracy of this figure and on reaching the clubhouse Armour stated that it should be 23. This is the highest score by a professional in a tournament.

Freak Matches

● In 1912, the late Harry Dearth, an eminent vocalist, attired in a complete suit of heavy armour, played a match at Bushey Hall. He was beaten 2 and 1.

● In 1914, at the start of the First World War, JN Farrar, a native of Hoylake, was stationed at Royston, Herts. A bet was made of 10-1 that he would not go round Royston under 100 strokes, equipped in full infantry marching order, water bottle, full field kit and haversack. Farrar went round in 94. At the camp were several golfers, including professionals, who tried the same feat but failed.

● Captain Pennington, who was killed in an air crash in 1933, took part in a match *from the air* against AJ Young, the professional at Sonning. Captain Pennington, with 80 golf balls in the locker of his machine, had to find the Sonning greens by dropping the balls as he circled over the course. The balls were covered in white cloth to ensure that they did not bounce once they struck the ground. The airman completed the course in 40 minutes, taking 29 *strokes*, while Young occupied two hours for his round of 68.

● In April 1924, at Littlehampton, Harry Rowntree, an amateur golfer, played the better ball of Edward Ray and George Duncan, receiving an allowance of 150 yards to use as he required during the round. Rowntree won by 6 and 5 and had used only 50 yards 2 feet of his handicap. At one hole Duncan had a two – Rowntree, who was 25 yards from the hole, took this distance from his handicap and won the hole in one. Ray (died 1945) afterwards declared that, conceded a handicap of one yard per round, he could win every championship in the world. And he might, when reckoning is taken of the number of times a putt just stops an inch or two or how much difference to a shot three inches will make for the lie of the ball, either in a bunker or on the fairway. Many single matches on the same system have been played. An 18 handicap player opposed to a scratch player should make a close match with an allowance of 50 yards.

● The first known instance of a golf match by telephone occurred in 1957, when the Cotswold Hills Golf Club, Cheltenham, England, won a golf tournament against the Cheltenham Golf Club, Melbourne, Australia, by six strokes. A large crowd assembled at the English club to wait for the 12,000 miles telephone call from Australia. The match had been played at the suggestion of a former member of the Cotswold Hills Club, Harry Davies, and was open to every member of the two clubs. The result of the match was decided on the aggregate of the eight best scores on each side and the English club won by 564 strokes to 570.

Golf Matches Against Other Sports

● HH Hilton and Percy Ashworth, many times racket champion, contested a driving match, the former driving a golf ball with a driver, and the latter a racket ball with a racket. Best distances: Against breeze – Golfer 182 yards; Racket player 125 yards. Down wind – Golfer 230 yards; Racket player 140 yards. Afterwards Ashworth hit a golf ball with the racket and got a greater distance than with the racket ball, but was still a long way behind the ball driven by Hilton.

● In 1913, at Wellington, Shropshire, a match between a golfer and a fisherman casting a $2^1/_2$ oz weight was played. The golfer, Rupert May, took 87; the fisherman JJD Mackinlay, required 102. The fisherman's difficulty was in his short casts. His longest cast, 105 yards, was within 12 yards of the world record at the time, held by a French angler, Decautelle. When within a rod's length of a hole he ran the weight to the rod end and dropped into the hole. Five times he broke his line, and was allowed another shot without penalty.

● In December, 1913, FMA Webster, of the London Athletic Club, and Dora Roberts, with javelins, played a match with the late Harry Vardon and Mrs Gordon Robertson, who used the regulation clubs and golf balls. The golfers conceded two-thirds in the matter of distance, and they won by 5 up and 4 to play in a contest of 18 holes. The javelin throwers had a mark of two feet square in which to *hole out* while the golfers had to get their ball into the ordinary golf hole. Mr Webster's best throw was one of 160 feet.

● Several matches have taken place between a golfer on the one side and an archer on the other. The wielder of the bow and arrow has nearly always proved the victor. In 1953 at Kirkhill Golf Course, Lanarkshire, five archers beat six golfers by two games to one. There were two special rules for the match; when an archer's arrow landed six feet from the hole or the golfer's ball three feet from the hole, they were counted as holed. When the arrows landed in bunkers or in the rough, archers lifted their arrow and added a stroke. The sixth archer in this match called off and one archer shot two arrows from each of the 18 tees.

● In 1954, at the Southbroom Club, South Africa, a match over 9 holes was played between an archer and a fisherman against two golfers. The participants were all champions of their own sphere and consisted of Vernon Adams (archer), Dennis Burd (fisherman), Jeanette Wahl (champion of Southbroom and Port Shepstone), and Ron Burd (professional at Southbroom). The conditions were that the archer had holed out when his arrows struck a small leather bag placed on the green beside the hole and in the event of his placing his approach shot within a bow's length of the pin he was deemed to have 1-putted. The fisherman, to achieve a 1-putt, had to land his sinker within a rod's length of the pin. The two golfers were ahead for brief spells, but it was the opposition who led at the deciding 9th hole where *Robin Hood* played a perfect approach for a birdie.

● An *Across England* combined match was begun on 11th October, 1965, by four golfers and two archers from Crowborough Beacon Golf Club, Sussex, accompanied by *Penny*, a white Alsatian dog, whose duty it was to find lost balls. They teed *off* from Carlisle Castle via Hadrian's Wall, the Pennine Way, finally holing out in the 18th hole at Newcastle United Golf Club in 612 teed shots. Casualties included 110 lost golf balls and 19 lost or broken arrows. The match took five-and-a-half days, and the distance travelled was about 60 miles. The golfers were Miss P Ward, K Meaney, K Ashdown and CA Macey; the archers were WH Hulme and T Scott. The first arrow was fired from the battlements of Carlisle Castle, a distance of nearly 300 yards, by Cumberland Champion R Willis, who also fired the second arrow right across the River Eden. R Clough, president of Newcastle United GC, holed the last two putts. The match was in aid of *Guide Dogs for the Blind* and *Friends of Crowborough Hospital.*

Cross-country Matches

● Taking 1 year, 114 days, Floyd Rood golfed his way from coast to coast across the United States. He took 114,737 shots including 3,511 penalty shots for the 3,397 mile *course*.

● Two Californian teenagers, Bob Aube (17) and Phil Marrone (18) went on a golfing safari in 1974 from San Francisco to Los Angeles, a trip of over 500 miles lasting 16 days. The first six days they played alongside motorways. Over 1,000 balls were used.

● In 1830, the Gold Medal winner of the Royal and Ancient backed himself for 10 sovereigns to drive from the 1st hole at St Andrews to the toll bar at Cupar, distance nine miles, in 200 teed shots. He won easily.

● In 1848, two Edinburgh golfers played a match from Bruntsfield Links to the top of Arthur's Seat – an eminence overlooking the Scottish capital, 822 feet above sea level.

● On a winter's day in 1898, Freddie Tait backed himself to play a gutta ball in 40 teed shots from Royal St George's Clubhouse, Sandwich, to the Cinque Ports Club, Deal. He was to hole out by hitting any part of the Deal Clubhouse. The distance as the crow flies was three miles. The redoubtable Tait holed out with his 32nd shot, so effectively that the ball went through a window.

● On 3rd December, 1920, P Rupert Phillips and W Raymond Thomas teed up on the first tee of the Radyr Golf Club and played to the last hole at Southerndown. The distance as the crow flies was $15^1/_2$ miles, but circumventing swamps, woods, and plough, they covered, approximately, 20 miles. The wager was that they would not do the *hole* in 1,000 strokes, but they holed out at their 608th stroke two days later. They carried large ordnance maps.

● In 1900 three members of the Hackensack (NJ) Club played a game of four-and-a-half hours over an extemporised course six miles long, which stretched from Hackensack to Paterson. Despite rain, cornfields, and wide streams, the three golfers – JW Hauleebeek, Dr ER Pfaare, and Eugene Crassons – completed the round, the first and the last named taking 305 strokes each, and Dr Pfaare 327 strokes. The players used only two clubs, the mashie and the cleek.

● On 12th March, 1921, A Stanley Turner, Macclesfield, played from his house to the Cat and Fiddle Inn, five miles distance, in 64 strokes. The route was broken and hilly with a rise of nearly 1,000 feet. Turner was allowed to tee up within two club lengths after each shot and the wagering was 6-4 against his doing the distance in 170 strokes.

● In 1919, a golfer drove a ball from Piccadilly Circus and, proceeding via the Strand, Fleet Street and Ludgate Hill, *holed out* at the Royal Exchange, London. The player drove off at 8 am on a Sunday, a time when the usually thronged thoroughfares were deserted.

● On 23rd April, 1939, Richard Sutton, a London stockbroker, played from Tower Bridge, London, to White's Club, St James's Street, in 142 strokes. The bet was he would not do *the course* in under 200 shots. Sutton used a putter, crossed the Thames at Southwark Bridge, and hit the ball short distances to keep out of trouble.

● Golfers produced the most original event in Ireland's three-week national festival of An Tostal, 1953 – a cross-country competition with an advertised £1,000,000 for the man who could hole out in one. The 150 golfers drove off from the first tee at Kildare Club to hole out eventually on the 18th green, five miles away, on the nearby Curragh course, a distance of 8,800 yards. The unusual hazards to be negotiated included the main Dublin-Cork railway line and highway, the Curragh Racecourse, hoofprints left by Irish thoroughbred racehorses out exercising on the plains from nearby stables, army tank tracks and about 150 telephone lines. The Golden Ball Trophy, which is played for annually – a standard size golf ball in gold, mounted on a black marble pillar beside the silver figure of a golfer on a green marble base, designed by Captain Maurice Cogan, Army GHQ, Dublin — was for the best gross. And it went to one of the longest hitters in international golf – Amateur Champion, Irish internationalist and British Walker Cup player Joe Carr, with the remarkable score of 52.

● Four Aberdeen University students (as a 1961 Charities Week stunt) set out to golf their way up Ben Nevis (4,406 feet). After losing 63 balls and expending 659 strokes, the quartet, about halfway up, conceded victory to Britain's highest mountain.

Long-lived Golfers

● The oldest golfer who ever lived we believe was Arthur Thompson of British Columbia, Canada. He equalled his age when 103 at Uplands GC, a course of over 6,000 yards. He died two years later aged 105 but it is not known whether he played after the age of 103. Mr Thompson also features in the section *Low Scoring Veterans.*.

● Nathaniel Vickers celebrated his 103rd birthday on Sunday, 9th October, 1949, and died the following day. He was the oldest member of the United States Senior Golf Association and until 1942 he competed regularly in their events and won many trophies in the various age divisions. When 100 years old, he apologised for being able to play only 9 holes a day. Vickers predicted he would live until 103 and he died a few hours after he had celebrated his birthday.

● American George Miller, who died in 1979 aged 102, played regularly when 100 years old.

● In his 93rd year, the Rev Harcourt Just had a daily round of six to 10 holes at St Andrews. In 1950, the Town Council gave him the *Courtesy of the Course*, which excused the venerable minister paying the yearly charge.

● George Swanwick, a member of Wallasey, celebrated his 90th birthday with a luncheon at the club on 1st April, 1971. He played golf several times a week, carrying his own clubs and had holed-in-one at the ages of 75 and 85. His ambition was to complete the sequence aged 95 . . . but he died in 1973 aged 92.

● The 10th Earl of Wemyss played a round on his 92nd birthday, in 1910, at Craigielaw. When 87 the Earl was partnered by Harry Vardon in a match at Kilspindie, the golf course on his East Lothian estate at Gosford. The venerable earl, after playing his ball, mounted a pony and rode to the next shot. He died on 30th June, 1914, in his 96th year.

● FL Callender, aged 78, in September 1932, played nine consecutive rounds in the Jubilee Vase, St Andrews. He was defeated in the ninth, the final round, by 4 and 2. Callender's handicap was 12. This is the best known achievement of a septuagenarian in golf.

Playing in the Dark

On numerous occasions it has been necessary to hold lamps, lighted candles, or torches at holes in order that players might finish a competition. Large entries, slow play, early darkness and an eclipse of the sun have all been causes of playing in darkness.

● At the Open Championship in Musselburgh in November 1889 many players finished when the light had so far gone that the adjacent street lamps were lit. The cards were checked by candlelight. Several players who had no chance of the championship were paid small sums to withdraw in order to permit others who had a chance to finish in daylight. This was the last championship at Musselburgh.

● At the Southern Section of the PGA tournament on 25th September, 1907, at Burnham Beeches, several players concluded the round by the aid of torch lights placed near the holes.

● In the Irish Open Championship at Portmarnock in September, 1907, a tie in the third round between WC Pickeman and A Jeffcott was postponed owing to darkness, at the 22nd hole. Pickeman on the following morning won at the 24th.

● The qualifying round of the American Amateur Championship in 1910 could not be finished in one day, and several competitors had to stop their round on account of darkness, and complete it early in the morning of the following day.

● On 10th January, 1926, in the final of the President's Putter, at Rye, EF Storey and RH Wethered were all square at the 24th hole. It was then 5 pm and so dark that, although a fair crowd was present, the balls could not be followed, and the tie was abandoned and the Putter held jointly for the year. The winner of the Putter each year affixes the ball he played; for 1926 there are two balls, respectively engraved with the names of the finalists.

● In the 1932 Walker Cup contest at Brooklyn, a total eclipse of the sun occurred.

● At Perth, on 14th September, 1932, a competition was in progress under good clear evening light, and a full bright moon. The moon rose at 7.10 and an hour later came under eclipse to the earth's surface. The light then became so bad that on the last three greens competitors holed out by the aid of the light from matches.

● At Carnoustie, 1932, in the competition for the *Craw's Nest* the large entry necessitated competitors being sent off in 3-ball matches. The late players had to be assisted by electric torches flashed on the greens.

● In February, 1950, Max Faulkner and his partner, R Dolman, in a Guildford Alliance event finished their round in complete darkness. A photographer's flash bulbs were used at the last hole to direct Faulkner's approach. Several others of more than 100 competitors also finished in the darkness. At the last hole they had only the light from the clubhouse to aim at and one played his approach so boldly that he put his ball through the hall doorway and almost into the dressing room.

● On the second day of the 1969 Ryder Cup contest, the last 4-ball match ended in near total darkness on the 18th green at Birkdale. With the help of the clubhouse lights the two American players, Lee Trevino and Miller Barber, and Tony Jacklin for Britain each faced putts of around five feet to win their match. All missed and their game was halved.

● The occasions mentioned above all occurred in competitions where it was not intended to play in the dark. There are, however, numerous instances where players set out to play in the dark either for bets or for novelty.

● On 29th November, 1878, RW Brown backed himself to go round the Hoylake links in 150 strokes, starting at 11 pm. The conditions of the match were that Mr Brown was only to be penalised *loss of distance* for a lost ball, and that no one was to help him to find it. He went round in 147 strokes, and won his bet by the narrow margin of three strokes.

● In 1876 David Strath backed himself to go round St Andrews under 100, in moonlight. He took 95, and did not lose a ball.

● In September 1928, at St Andrews, the first and last holes were illuminated by lanterns, and at 11 pm four members of the Royal and Ancient set out to play a foursome over the 2 holes. Electric lights, lanterns, and rockets were used to brighten the fairway, and the headlights of motor cars parked on Links Place formed a helpful battery. The 1st hole was won in four, and each side got a five at the 18th. About 1,000 spectators followed the freak match, which was played to celebrate the appointment of Angus Hambro to the captaincy of the club.

● In 1931, Rufus Stewart, professional, Kooyonga Club, South Australia, and former Australian Open Champion, played 18 holes of exhibition golf at night without losing a single ball over the Kooyonga course, and completed the round in 77.

● At Ashley Wood Golf Club, Blandford, Dorset, a night-time golf tournament is arranged annually with up to 180 golfers taking part over four nights. Over £6000 has been raised in four years for the Muscular Dystrophy Charity.

● At Pannal, 3rd July, 1937, RH Locke, playing in bright moonlight, holed his tee shot at the 15th hole, distance 220 yards, the only known case of holing-in-one under such conditions.

● In August, 1970, a group of Canadians held a stroke competition at the Summit Golf and Country Club, Ontario, in total darkness. Organised by Peter Kennedy, seven competitors took part, starting at midnight. Special rules drawn up included only a 1-stroke penalty for a lost ball, but if 12 balls were lost the competitor had to retire. The best score was 84 by Lief Pettersen.

Fatal and Other Accidents on the Links

The history of golf is, unfortunately, marred by a great number of fatal accidents on or near the course. In the vast majority of such cases they have been caused either by careless swinging of the club or by an uncontrolled shot when the ball has struck a spectator or bystander. In addition to the fatal accidents there is an even larger number on record which have resulted in serious injury or blindness. We do not propose to list these accidents, which have hitherto been recorded in the Golfer's Handbook, except where they have some unusual feature. We would remind all golfers of the tragic consequences which have so often been caused by momentary carelessness. The fatal accidents which follow have an unusual cause and other accidents given may have their humorous aspect.

● In July, 1971, 43-year-old Rudolph Roy was killed at a Montreal course when, in playing out of woods, the shaft of his club snapped, rebounded off a tree and the jagged edge plunged into his body.

● Harold Wallace, aged 75, playing at Lundin Links with two friends in 1950, was crossing the railway line which separates the fifth green and sixth tee, when a light engine knocked him down and he was killed instantly.

● Edward M Harrison, November, 1951, while playing alone on the Inglewood Country Club, Seattle, apparently broke the shaft of his driver and the split shaft pierced his groin. He tried to reach the clubhouse, but collapsed and bled to death 100 yards from the ninth tee where the accident happened.

● In the summer of 1963, Harold Kalles, of Toronto, Canada, died six days after his throat had been cut by a golf club shaft, which broke against a tree as he was trying to play out of a bunker.

● At Jacksonville, Florida, on 18th March, 1952, two women golfers were instantly killed when hit simultaneously by the whirling propellor of a navy fighter plane. They were playing together when the plane with a dead engine and coming in against the wind, out of control, hit them from behind. The pilot, who had been making a test flight from the Navy Air Station which adjoins the golf course, stepped out of the burning plane and did not know for some seconds that the plane had killed the women.

● In September, 1956, Myrl G Hanmore, aged 50, died from an accident at the Riviera Country Club, Los Angeles, apparently caused when he lost control of a golf car on a steep incline and was crushed between the vehicle he was driving and one he was towing from the first tee to a storage barn.

● On a Welsh course a player had played a shot out of a bunker and jumped up to see the result, when he was hit on the head by a ball driven from behind. He felt no ill effects at the moment, except a slight smarting of the eyes, but within a week he was totally blind.

● At Knott End Golf Club, on 20th June, 1953, Charles Langley, playing in a competition for the Captain's Prize, hit his tee shot from the 10th and struck the cone-shaped wood marker at the ladies' tee, which was approximately nine feet from where Mr Langley had teed his ball. The ball rebounded at lightning speed striking and destroying Mr Langley's left eye.

● Gary Player was accidentally pushed into a lake beside the 18th hole at Congressional CC by young spectators seeking his autograph as he came off the green after a practice round for the 1976 Championship.

● The ambulance crew responded in minutes to a call from the Point Grey Golf and CC in Vancouver, British Columbia, reporting a golfer had suffered a heart attack. But the supposed *victim* definitely was not suffering. Justice JM Coody, 95, a retired member of British Columbia's supreme court had been spotted resting in a golf car. A passing golfer asked what the problem was and he thought the judge replied, *Heart failure.* He didn't. Justice Coody's car was stalled. He'd actually said *Cart failure.*

Lightning on the Links

There have been a considerable number of fatal and serious accidents through players and caddies having been struck by lightning on the course. The Royal and Ancient and the USGA have, since 1952, provided for discontinuance of play during lightning storms under the Rules of Golf (Rule 37, 6) and the United States Golf Association have given the following guide for personal safety during thunderstorms:

(a) Do not go out of doors or remain out during thunderstorms unless it is necessary. Stay inside of a building where it is dry, preferably away from fireplaces, stoves, and other metal objects.

(b) If there is any choice of shelter, choose in the following order:

1. Large metal or metal-frame buildings.
2. Dwellings or other buildings which are protected against lightning.
3. Large unprotected buildings.
4. Small unprotected buildings.

(c) If remaining out of doors is unavoidable, keep away from:

1. Small sheds and shelters if in an exposed location.
2. Isolated trees.
3. Wire fences.
4. Hilltops and wide open spaces.

(d) Seek shelter in:

1. A cave.
2. A depression in the ground.
3. A deep valley or canyon.
4. The foot of a steep or overhanging cliff.
5. Dense woods.
6. A grove of trees.

Note – Raising golf clubs or umbrellas above the head is dangerous.

● A serious incident with lightning involving well-known golfers was at the 1975 Western Open in Chicago when Lee Trevino, Jerry Heard and Bobby Nichols were all struck and had to be taken to hospital. At the same time Tony Jacklin had a club thrown 15 feet out of his hands.

● Two well-known competitors were struck by lightning in European events in 1977. They were Mark James of Britain in the Swiss Open and Severiano Ballesteros of Spain in the Scandinavian Open. Fortunately neither appeared to be badly injured.

Spectators Interfering with Balls

● Deliberate interference by spectators with balls in play during important money matches was not unknown in the old days when there was intense rivalry between the *schools* of Musselburgh, St Andrews, and North Berwick, and disputes arose in stake matches caused by the action of spectators in kicking the ball into either a favourable or an unfavourable position.

● Tom Morris, in his last match with Willie Park at Musselburgh, refused to go on because of interference by the spectators, and in the match on the same course about 40 years later, in 1895, between Willie Park junior and JH Taylor, the barracking of the crowd and interference with play was so bad that when the Park-Vardon match came to be arranged in 1899, Vardon refused to accept Musselburgh as a venue.

● Even in modern times spectators have been known to interfere deliberately with players' balls, though it is usually by children. In the 1972 Penfold Tournament at Queen's Park, Bournemouth, Christy O'Connor jun had his ball stolen by a young boy, but not being told of this at the time had to take the penalty for a lost ball. O'Connor finished in a tie for first place, but lost the play-off.

● In 1912 in the last round of the final of the Amateur Championship at Westward Ho! between Abe Mitchell and John Ball, the drive of the former to the short 14th hit an open umbrella held by a lady protecting herself from the heavy rain, and instead of landing on the green the ball was diverted into a bunker. Mitchell, who was leading at the time by 2 holes, lost the hole and Ball won the Championship at the 38th hole.

● In the match between the professionals of Great Britain and America at Southport in 1937 a dense crowd collected round the 15th green waiting for the Sarazen-Alliss match. The American's ball landed in the lap of a woman, who picked it up and threw it so close to the hole that Sarazen got a two against Alliss' three.

● In a memorable tie between Bobby Jones and Cyril Tolley in the 1930 Amateur Championship at St Andrews, Jones' approach to the 17th green struck spectators massed at the left end of the green and led to controversy as to whether it would otherwise have gone on to the famous road. Jones himself had deliberately played for that part of the green and had requested stewards to get the crowd back. Had the ball gone on to the road, the historic Jones Quadrilateral of the year – the Open and Amateur Championships of Britain and the United States – might not have gone into the records.

● Now that golf has become such a widely enjoyed spectator sport with vast crowds lining the fairways, instances of a ball being deflected by spectators are no longer unusual, but are accepted as an almost normal occurrence in major events. In general it is thought that this is usually in favour of the player, as the ball is often destined for bad or even unplayable positions when it is stopped by impact with an onlooker. It is also to the advantage of a player that a ball is seldom lost, as its position is nearly always pin-pointed by a spectator in the area.

● In the 1983 Suntory World Match-play Championship at Wentworth Nick Faldo hit his second shot over the green at the 16th hole into a group of spectators. To everyone's astonishment and discomfiture the ball reappeared on the green about 30 ft from the hole, propelled there by a thoroughly misguided and anonymous spectator. The referee ruled that Faldo play the ball where it lay on the green. Faldo's opponent, Graham Marsh, understandably upset by the incident, took three putts against Faldo's two, thus losing a hole he might well otherwise have won. Faldo won the match 2 and 1, but lost in the final to Marsh's fellow Australian Greg Norman by 3 and 2.

Golf Balls Killing Animals and Fish, and Incidents with Animals

● An astounding fatality to an animal through being hit by a golf ball occurred at St Margaret's-at-Cliffe Golf Club, Kent on 13th June, 1934, when WJ Robinson, the professional, killed a cow with his tee shot to the 18th hole. The cow was standing in the fairway about 100 yards from the tee, and the ball struck her on the back of the head. She fell like a log, but staggered to her feet and walked about 50 yards before dropping again. When the players reached her she was dead.

● JW Perret, of Ystrad Mynach, playing with Chas R Halliday, of Ralston, in the qualifying rounds of the Society of One Armed Golfers' Championship over the Darley course, Troon, on 27th August, 1935, killed two gulls at successive holes with his second shots. The *deadly* shots were at the 1st and 2nd holes.

● On the first day of grouse shooting of the 1975 season (12th August), 11-year-old schoolboy, Willie Fraser, of Kingussie, beat all the guns when he killed a grouse with his tee shot on the local course.

● On 10th June, 1904, while playing in the Edinburgh High Constables' Competition at Kilspindie, Captain Ferguson sent a long ball into the rough at the Target hole, and on searching for it found that it had struck and killed a young hare.

● Playing in a mixed open tournament at the Waimairi Beach Golf Club in Christchurch, New Zealand, in the summer of 1961, Mrs RT Challis found her ball in fairly long spongy grass where a placing rule applied. She picked up, placed the ball and played her stroke. A young hare leaped into the air and fell dead at her feet. She had placed the ball on the leveret without seeing it and without disturbing it.

● In 1906 in the Border Championship at Hawick, a gull and a weasel were killed by balls during the afternoon's play.

● A golfer at Newark, in May, 1907, drove his ball into the river. The ball struck a trout 2lb in weight and killed it.

● On 24th April, 1975, at Scunthorpe GC, Jim Tollan's drive at the 14th hole, called *The Mallard*, struck and killed a female mallard duck in flight. The duck was stuffed and is displayed in the Scunthorpe Clubhouse.

● Playing over the Killarney Course, June, 1957, a golfer sliced his ball into one of the lakes and knocked out a trout rising to catch a fly. His friend waded into the water to get the ball – and the trout.

● A Samuel, Melbourne Club, at Sandringham, was driving with an iron club from the 17th tee, when a kitten, which had been playing in the long grass, sprang suddenly at the ball. Kitten and club arrived at the objective simultaneously, with the result that the kitten took an unexpected flight through the air, landing some 20 yards away.

● As Susan Rowlands was lining up a vital putt in the closing stages of the final of the 1978 Welsh Girls' Championship at Abergele, a tiny mouse scampered up her trouser leg. After holing the putt, the mouse ran down again. Susan, who won the final admitted that she fortunately had not known it was there.

● While on tour with British professionals 1936-37, in South Africa, Abe Mitchell, at the first hole on the Hill course at Port Elizabeth, noticed that his club struck something hard when he played his second shot from the edge of the rough. Taking another swing he *unearthed* a tortoise upon which his ball had perched from the tee shot.

Interference by Birds and Animals

● Crows, ravens, hawks and seagulls frequently carry off golf balls, sometimes dropping the ball actually on the green, and it is a common incident for a cow to swallow a golf ball. A plague of crows on the Liverpool course at Hoylake are addicted to golf balls – they stole 26 in one day – selecting only new balls. It was suggested that members should carry shotguns as a 15th club!

● A match was approaching a hole in a rather low-lying course, when one of the players made a crisp chip from about 30 yards from the hole. The ball trickled slowly across the green and eventually disappeared into the hole. After a momentary pause, the ball was suddenly ejected on to the green, and out jumped a large frog.

● In Massachusetts a goose, having been hit rather hard by a golf ball which then came to rest by the side of a water hazard, took revenge by waddling over to the ball and kicking it into the water.

● A large black crow named Jasper which frequented the Lithgow GC in New South Wales, Australia, stole 30 golf balls in the club's 1972 Easter Tournament.

● As Mrs Molly Whitaker was playing from a bunker at Beachwood course, Natal, South Africa, a large monkey leaped from a bush and clutched her round the neck. A caddie drove it off by clipping it with an iron club.

● Jimmy Stewart playing in the 1982 Singapore Open at the Bukit course approached his ball for his second shot at the 3rd hole and found a 10 foot cobra also making for his ball. He killed the snake only to see another emerge from the dead snake's mouth. This too was killed.

● In 1921, on the course at Kirkfield, Ontario, P McGregor and H Dowie were all square going to the home hole in the final, and when they reached the green McGregor needed to hole a long putt to win the match. It seemed to have stopped on the lip of the hole when a large grasshopper landed squarely on the ball and caused it to drop into the hole and decide the match in favour of McGregor.

● In the summer of 1963, SC King had a good drive to the 10th hole at the Guernsey Club. His partner, RW Clark, was in the rough, and King helped him to search. Returning to his ball, he found a cow eating it. Next day, at the same hole, the positions were reversed, and King was in the rough. Clark placed his woollen hat over his ball, remarking, *I'll make sure the cow doesn't eat mine.* On his return he found the cow thoroughly enjoying his hat; nothing was left but the pom-pom.

Armless, One-armed, Legless and Ambidextrous Players

● In September, 1933, at Burgess Golfing Society of Edinburgh, the first championship for one-armed golfers was held. There were 43 entries and 37 of the competitors had lost an arm in the 1914-18 war. Play was over two rounds and the championship was won by WE Thomson, Eastwood, Glasgow, with a score of 169 (82 and 87) for two rounds. The Burgess course was 6,300 yards long. Thomson drove the last green, 260 yards. The championship and an international match are played annually.

● In the Boys' Amateur Championship 1923, at Dunbar and 1949 at St Andrews, there were competitors each with one arm. The competitor in 1949, RP Reid, Cupar, Fife, who lost his arm working a machine in a butcher's shop, got through to the third round.

● There have been cases of persons with no arms playing golf. One, Thomas McAuliffe, who held the club between his right shoulder and cheek, once went round Buffalo CC, USA, in 108.

● Group Captain Bader, who lost both legs in a flying accident prior to the World War 1939-45, took part in golf competitions and reached a single-figure handicap in spite of his disability.

● In 1909, Scott of Silloth, and John Haskins of Hoylake, both one-armed golfers, played a home and away match for £20 a side. Scott finished five up at Silloth. He was seven up and 14 to play at Hoylake but Haskins played so well that Scott eventually only won by 3 and 1. This was the first match between one-armed golfers. Haskins in 1919 was challenged by Mr Mycock, of Buxton, another one-armed player. The match was 36 holes, home and away. The first half was played over the Buxton and High Peak Links, and the latter half over the Liverpool

Links, and resulted in a win for Haskins by 11 and 10. Later in the same year Haskins received another challenge to play against Alexander Smart of Aberdeen. The match was 18 holes over the Balgownie Course, and ended in favour of Haskins.

● In a match, November, 1926, between the Geduld and Sub Nigel Clubs – two golf clubs connected with the South African gold mines of the same names – each club had two players minus an arm. The natural consequence was that the quartet were matched. The players were – AWP Charteris and E Mitchell, Sub Nigel; and EP Coles and J Kirby, Geduld. This is the first record of four one-armed players in a foursome.

● At Joliet Country Club, USA, a one-armed golfer named DR Anderson drove a ball 300 yards.

● Left-handedness, but playing golf right-handed, is prevalent and for a man to throw with his left hand and play golf right-handed is considered an advantage, for Bobby Jones, Jesse Sweetser, Walter Hagen, Jim Barnes, Joe Kirkwood and more recently Johnny Miller were eminent golfers who were left-handed and ambidextrous.

● In a practice round for the Open Championship in July, 1927, at St Andrews, Len Nettlefold and Joe Kirkwood changed sets of clubs at the 9th hole. Nettlefold was a left-handed golfer and Kirkwood right-handed. They played the last nine, Kirkwood with the left-handed clubs and Nettlefold with the right-handed clubs.

● The late Harry Vardon, when he was at Ganton, got tired of giving impossible odds to his members and beating them, so he collected a set of left-handed clubs, and rating himself at scratch, conceded the handicap odds to them. Vardon won with the same monotonous regularity.

● Ernest Jones, who was professional at the Chislehurst Club, was badly wounded in the war in France in 1916 and his right leg had to be amputated below the knee. He persevered with the game, and before the end of the year he went round the Clacton course balanced on his one leg in 72. Jones later settled in the United States where he built fame and fortune as a golf teacher.

● Major Alexander McDonald Fraser of Edinburgh had the distinction of holding two handicaps simultaneously in the same club – one when he played left handed and the other for his right-handed play. In medal competitions he had to state before teeing up which method he would use.

● Former England test cricketer Brian Close once held a handicap of 2 playing right-handed, but after retiring from cricket in 1977 decided to apply himself as a left-handed player. His left-handed handicap at the time of his retirement was 7. Close had the distinction of once beating Ted Dexter, another distinguished test cricketer and noted golfer twice in the one day, playing right-handed in the morning and left-handed in the afternoon.

Blind and Blindfolded Golf

● Major Towse, VC, whose eyes were shot out during the South African War, 1899, was probably the first blind man to play golf. His only stipulations when playing the game were that he should be allowed to touch the ball with his hands to ascertain its position, and that his caddie could ring a small bell to indicate the position of the hole. Major Towse, who played with considerable skill, was also an expert oarsman and bridge player. He died in 1945, aged 81.

● The United States Blind Golfers' Association in 1946 promoted an Invitational Golf Tournament for the blind at Country Club, Inglewood, California. This competition is held annually and in 1953 there were 24 competitors and 11 players completed the two rounds of 36 holes. The winner was Charley Boswell who lost his eyesight leading a tank unit in Germany in 1944.

● In July, 1954, at Lambton Golf and Country Club, Toronto, the first international championship for the blind was held. It resulted in a win for Joe Lazaro, of Waltham, Mass, with a score of 220 for the two rounds. He drove the 215-yard 16th hole and just missed an ace, his ball stopping 18 inches from the hole. Charley Boswell, who won the United States Blind Golfers' Association Tournament in 1953, was second. The same Charles Boswell, of Birmingham, Alabama holed the 141-yard 14th hole at the Vestavia CC in one in October, 1970.

● Another blind person to have holed-in-one was American Ben Thomas while on holiday in South Carolina in 1978.

● Rick Sorenson undertook a bet in which, playing 18 holes blindfolded at Meadowbrook Course, Minneapolis, on 25th May, 1973, he was to pay $10 for every hole over par and receive $100 for every hole in par or better. He went round in 86 losing $70 on the deal.

● Alfred Toogood played in a match at Sunningdale in 1912 blindfolded. His opponent was Tindal Atkinson, and Toogood was beaten 8 and 7. I Millar, Newcastle-upon-Tyne, played a match, blindfolded, against AT Broughton, Birkdale, at Newcastle, County Down, in 1908. Putting matches while blindfolded have been frequently played.

● Wing-Commander *Laddie* Lucas, DSO, DFC, MP, played over Sandy Lodge golf course in

Hertfordshire on 7th August, 1954, completely blindfolded and had a score of 87.

Trick Shots

● Joe Kirkwood, Australia, specialised in public exhibitions of trick and fancy shots. He played all kinds of strokes after nominating them, and among his ordinary strokes nothing was more impressive than those hit for low flight. He played a full drive from the face of a wristlet watch, and the toe of a spectator's shoe, full strokes at a suspended ball, and played for slice and pull at will, and exhibited his ambidexterity by playing left-handed strokes with right-handed clubs. Holing six balls, stymieing, a full shot at a ball catching it as it descended, and hitting 12 full shots in rapid succession, with his face turned away from the ball, were shots among his repertoire. In playing the last named Kirkwood placed the balls in a row, about six inches apart, and moved quickly along the line. Kirkwood, who was born in Australia lived for many years in America. He died in November, 1970 aged 73.

● Joe Ezar, an American professional, who specialised in trick shots, included in his show a number of clowning acts with balls.

● On 2nd April, 1894, a 3-ball match was played over Musselburgh course between Messrs Grant, Bowden, and Waggot, the clubmaker, the latter teeing on the face of a watch at each tee. He finished the round in 41 the watch being undamaged in any way.

● At Westbrook, USA, in 1901, ET Knapp drove a ball off the top of a hen's egg. The egg was slightly dented on one end to afford a hold for the ball.

● At Esher, 23rd November, 1931, George Ashdown, the club professional, in a match played his tee shot for each of the 18 holes from a rubber tee strapped to the forehead of Miss Ena Shaw.

● EA Forrest, a South African professional in a music hall turn of trick golf shots, played blindfolded shots, one being from the ball teed on the chin of his recumbent partner.

● The late Paul Hahn, an American trick specialist could hit four balls with two clubs. Holding a club in each hand he hit two balls, hooking one and slicing the other with the same swing. Hahn had a repertoire of 30 trick shots. In 1955 he flew completely round the world, exhibiting in 14 countries and on all five continents.

Balls Colliding and Touching

● Competing in the 1980 Corfu International Championship, Sharon Peachey drove from one tee and her ball collided in mid-air with one from a competitor playing another hole. Her ball ended in a pond.

● Playing in the Cornish team championship in 1973 at West Cornwall GC Tom Scott-Brown, of West Cornwall GC, and Paddy Bradley, of Tehidy GC, saw their drives from the fourth and eighth tees collide in mid-air.

● Playing in a 4-ball match at Guernsey Club in June, 1966, all four players were near the 13th green from the tee. Two of them – DG Hare and S Machin – chipped up simultaneously; the balls collided in mid-air; Machin's ball hit the green, then the flagstick, and dropped into the hole for a birdie 2.

● Playing to the 13th hole on Carnoustie course on 6th October, 1911, the Rev AR Taylor's ball met in the air the ball of another player, who had struck off from the 14th tee. The balls met so square – if one can use such an expression – that they rebounded a long distance straight back towards the players who hit them.

● In May, 1926, during the meeting of the Army Golfing Society at St Andrews, Colonel Howard and Lieutenant-Colonel Buchanan Dunlop, while playing in the foursomes against J Rodger and J Mackie, hit full iron shots for the seconds to the 16th green. Each thought he had to play his ball first, and hidden by a bunker the players struck their balls simultaneously. The balls, going towards the hole about 20 yards from the pin and five feet in the air, met with great force and dropped either side of the hole five yards apart.

● In 1972, before a luncheon celebrating the centenary of the Ladies' Section of Royal Wimbledon GC, a 12-hole competition was held during which two competitors, Mrs L Champion and Mrs A McKendrick, driving from the eighth and ninth tees respectively, saw their balls collide in mid-air.

● In 1928, at Wentworth Falls, Australia, Dr Alcorn and EA Avery, of the Leura Club, were playing with the professional, E Barnes. The tee shots of Avery and Barnes at the 9th hole finished on opposite sides of the fairway. Unknown to each other, both players hit their seconds (chip shots) at the same time. Dr Alcorn, standing at the pin, suddenly saw two balls approaching the hole from different angles. They met in the air and then dropped into the hole.

● At Rugby, 1931, playing in a 4-ball match, H Fraser pulled his drive from the 10th tee in the direction of the ninth tee. Simultaneously a club member, driving from the ninth tee, pulled his drive. The tees were about 350 yards apart. The two balls collided in mid-air.

● Two golf balls, being played in opposite directions, collided in flight over Longniddry Golf Course on 27th June, 1953. Immediately after Stewart Elder, of Longniddry, had driven from the third tee, another ball, which had been pulled off line from the second fairway, which runs alongside the third, struck his ball about 20 feet above the ground. SJ Fleming, of Tranent, who was playing with Elder, heard a loud crack and thought Elder's ball had exploded. The balls were found undamaged about 70 yards apart.

Three and Two Balls Dislodged by One Shot

● In 1934 on the short 3rd hole (now the 13th) of Olton Course, Warwickshire, JR Horden, a scratch golfer of the club, sent his tee shot into long wet grass a few feet over the back of the green. When he played an *explosion* shot three balls dropped on to the putting green, his own and two others.

● AM Chevalier, playing at Hale, Cheshire, March, 1935, drove his ball into a grass bunker, and when he reached it there was only part of it showing. He played the shot with a niblick and to his amazement not one but three balls shot into the air. They all dropped back into the bunker and came to rest within a foot of each other. Then came another surprise. One of the *finds* was of the same manufacture and bore the same number as the ball he was playing with.

● Playing to the 9th hole, at Osborne House Club, Isle of Wight, George A Sherman lost his ball which had sunk out of sight on the sodden fairway. A few weeks later, playing from the same tee, his ball again was plugged, only the top showing. Under a local rule he lifted his ball to place it, and exactly under it lay the ball he had lost previously.

Balls in Strange Places

● Playing at the John O' Gaunt Club, Sutton, near Biggleswade (Bedfordshire), a member drove a ball which did not touch the ground until it reached London – over 40 miles away. The ball landed in a vegetable lorry which was passing the golf course and fell out of a package of cabbages when they were unloaded at Covent Garden, London.

● In the English Open Amateur Stroke Play at Moortown in 1974, Nigel Denham, a Yorkshire County player, in the first round saw his overhit second shot to the 18th green bounce up some steps into the clubhouse. His ball went through an open door, ricochetted off a wall and came to rest in the men's bar, 20 feet from the windows. As the clubhouse was not out of bounds Denham decided to play the shot back to the green and opened a window 4 feet by 2 feet through which he pitched his ball to 12 feet from the flag. (Several weeks later the R & A declared that Denham should have been penalised two shots for opening the window. The clubhouse was an immovable obstruction and no part of it should have been moved.)

● In the Open Championship at Sandwich, 1949, Harry Bradshaw, Kilcroney, Dublin, at the 5th hole in his second round, drove into the rough and found his ball inside a beer bottle with the neck and shoulder broken off and four sharp points sticking up. Bradshaw, if he had treated the ball as in an unplayable lie might have been involved in a disqualification, so he decided to play it where it lay. With his blaster he smashed the bottle and sent the ball about 30 yards. The hole, a par 4, cost him 6.

● Kevin Sharman of Woodbridge GC hit a low, very straight drive at the club's 8th hole in 1979. After some minutes' searching, his ball was found embedded in a plastic sphere on top of the direction post.

● On the Dublin Course, 16th July, 1936, in the Irish Open Championship, AD Locke, the South African, played his tee shot at the 100-yard 12th hole, but the ball could not be found on arrival on the green. The marker removed the pin and it was discovered that the ball had been entangled in the flag. It dropped near the edge of the hole and Locke holed the short putt for a *birdie* two.

● On a London course a player found his ball inside a derelict boot.

● While playing a round on the Geelong Golf Club Course, Australia, Easter, 1923, Captain Charteris topped his tee shot to the short 2nd hole, which lies over a creek with deep and steep clay banks. His ball came to rest on the near slope of the creek bank. He elected to play the ball as it lay, and took his niblick. After the shot, the ball was nowhere to be seen. It was afterwards found embedded in a mass of gluey clay stuck fast to the face of the niblick. It could not be shaken off. Charteris did what was afterwards approved by the R&A, cleaned the ball and dropped it behind without penalty.

● In October, 1929, at Blackmoor Golf Club, Bordon, Hants, a player driving from the first tee holed out his ball in the chimney of a house some 120 yards distant and some 40 yards out of bounds on the right. The owner and his wife were sitting in front of the fire when they heard a rattle in the chimney and were astonished to see a golf ball drop into the fire.

● A similar incident occurred in an inter-club match between Musselburgh and Lothianburn at Prestongrange in 1938 when a member of the former team hooked his ball at the 2nd hole and gave it up for lost. To his amazement a woman emerged from one of the houses adjacent to this part of the course and handed back the ball which she said had come down the chimney and landed on a pot which was on the fire.

● In July, 1955, J Lowrie, starter at the Eden Course, St Andrews, witnessed a freak shot. A visitor drove from the first tee just as a north-bound train was passing. He sliced the shot and the ball disappeared through an open window of a passenger compartment. Almost immediately the ball emerged again, having been thrown back on to the fairway by a man in the compartment, who waved a greeting which presumably indicated that no one was hurt.

● Many balls have been hit into the pockets of spectators, stewards, other competitors and even the players' own pockets. They have also been found in trouser turn-ups and in the folds of sweaters and waterproofs.

● At Coombe Wood Golf Club a player hit a ball towards the 16th green where it landed in the vertical exhaust of a tractor which was mowing the fairway. The greenkeeper was somewhat surprised to find a temporary loss of power in the tractor. When sufficient compression had built up in the exhaust system, the ball was forced out with tremendous velocity, hit the roof of a house nearby, bounced off and landed some three feet from the pin on the green.

● There have been many occasions when misdirected shots have finished in strange places after an unusual line of flight and bounce. At Ashford, Middlesex, John Miller, aged 69, hit his tee shot out of bounds at the 12th hole (237 yards). It struck a parked car, passed through a copse, hit more cars, jumped a canopy, flew through the clubhouse kitchen window, finishing in a cooking stock-pot, without once touching the ground. Mr Miller had previously done the hole-in-one on four occasions.

Balls Hit to and from Great Heights

● In 1798 two Edinburgh golfers undertook to drive a ball over the spire of St Giles' Cathedral, Edinburgh, for a wager. Mr Sceales, of Leith, and Mr Smellie, a printer, were each allowed six shots and succeeded in sending the balls well over the weather-cock, a height of more than 160 feet from the ground.

● Some years later Donald McLean, an Edinburgh lawyer, won a substantial bet by driving a ball over the Melville Monument in St Andrew Square, Edinburgh – height, 154 feet.

● Tom Morris in 1860, at the famous bridge of Ballochmyle, stood in the quarry beneath and, from a stick elevated horizontally, attempted to send golf balls over the bridge. He could raise them only to the pathway, 400 feet high, which was in itself a great feat with the gutta ball.

● Captain Ernest Carter, on 28th September, 1922, drove a ball from the roadway at the 1st tee on Harlech Links against the wall of Harlech Castle. The embattlements are 200 feet over the level of the roadway, and the point where the ball struck the embattlements was 180 yards from the point where the ball was teed. Captain Carter, who was laid odds of £100 to £1, used a baffy.

● In 1896 Freddie Tait, then a subaltern in the Black Watch, drove a ball from the Rookery, the highest building on Edinburgh Castle, in a match against a brother officer to hole out in the fountain in Princes Street Gardens 350 feet below and about 300 yards distant.

● Prior to the 1977 Lâncome Tournament in Paris, Arnold Palmer hit three balls from the second stage of the Eiffel Tower, over 300 feet above ground. The longest was measured at 403 yards. One ball was hooked and hit a bus but no serious damage was done as all traffic had been stopped for safety reasons.

● Long drives have been made from mountain peaks, across the gorge at Victoria Falls, from the Pyramids, high buildings in New York, and from many other similar places. As an illustration of such freakish *drives* a member of the New York Rangers' Hockey Team from the top of Mount Edith Cavell, 11,033 feet high, drove a ball which struck the Ghost Glacier 5,000 feet below and bounced off the rocky ledge another 1,000 feet – a total drop of 2,000 yards. Later, in June, 1968, from Pikes Peak, Colorado (14,110 feet), Arthur Lynskey hit a ball which travelled 200 yards horizontally but 2 miles vertically.

Remarkable Shots

● Remarkable shots are to be numbered as the grains of sand; around every 19th hole, legends are recalled of astounding shots. One shot is commemorated by a memorial tablet at the 17th hole at the Lytham and St Annes Club. It was made by Bobby Jones in the final round of the Open Championship in 1926. He was partnered by Al Watrous, another American player. They had been running neck and neck and at the end of the third round, Watrous was just leading Jones with 215 against 217. At the 16th Jones drew level then on the 17th he drove into a sandy lie in broken ground. Watrous reached the green with his second. Jones took a mashie-iron (the equivalent to a No. 4 iron today) and hit a magnificent shot to the green to get his 4. This remarkable recovery unnerved Watrous, who 3-putted, and Jones, getting another 4 at the last hole against 5, won his first Open Championship with 291 against Watrous' 293. The tablet is near the spot where Jones played his second shot.

● Arnold Palmer (USA), playing in the second round of the Australian Wills Masters tournament at Melbourne, in October, 1964, hooked his second shot at the 9th hole high into the fork of a gum tree. Climbing 20 feet up the tree, Palmer, with the head of his No. 1 iron reversed, played a *hammer* stroke and knocked the ball some 30 yards forward, followed by a brilliant chip to the green and a putt.

● In the foursome during the Ryder Cup at Moortown in 1929, Joe Turnesa hooked the American side's second shot at the last hole behind the marquee adjoining the clubhouse, Johnny Farrel then pitched the ball over the marquee on to the green only feet away from the pin and Turnesa holed out for a 4.

● In 1922, Peter Robertson, Braid Hills, Edinburgh, holed the Road Hole, St Andrews (17th, Old Course) in two shots, a drive and a brassie.

● Lew Worsham, in the *World's Championship* at Tam O'Shanter, 9th August, 1953, at the last hole from a distance of 135 yards, holed a wedge shot for a two at the 410-yard hole. This incredible shot made him the winner by one stroke and gave him the greatest jackpot in golf at that time, $25,000. The difference between the first and third prizes was equivalent to £5,000.

Miscellaneous Incidents and Strange Golfing Facts

● Gary Player of South Africa was honoured by his country by having his portrait on new postage stamps which were issued on 12th December, 1976. It was the first time a specific golfer had ever been depicted on any country's postage stamps. In 1981 the US Postal Service introduced stamps featuring Bobby Jones and Babe Zaharias. They are the first golfers to be thus honoured by the United States.

● Prior to the 1976 Curtis Cup Match, members of the British Isles and United States teams were presented to the Queen at Buckingham Palace, the first occasion this has occurred.

● In February, 1971, the first ever golf shots on the moon's surface were played by Captain Alan Shepard, commander of the Apollo 14 spacecraft. Captain Shepard hit two balls with an iron head attached to a makeshift shaft. With a one-handed swing he claimed he hit the first ball 200 yards aided by the reduced force of gravity on the moon. Subsequent findings put this distance in doubt. The second was a shank. Acknowledging the occasion the R&A sent Captain Shepard the following telegram: *Warmest congratulations to all of you on your great achievement and safe return. Please refer to Rules of Golf section on etiquette, paragraph 6, quote – before leaving a bunker a player should carefully fill up all holes made by him therein, unquote.* Shepard presented the club to the USGA Museum in 1974.

● Charles (Chick) Evans competed in every US Amateur Championship held between 1907 and 1962 by which time he was 72 years old. This amounted to 50 consecutive occasions discounting the six years of the two World Wars when the championship was not held.

● In winning the 1977 US Open at Southern Hills CC, Tulsa, Oklahoma, Hubert Green had to contend with a death threat. Coming off the 14th green in the final round, he was advised by USGA officials that a phone call had been received saying that he would be killed. Green decided that play should continue and happily he went on to win, unharmed.

● It was discovered at the 1977 USPGA Championship that the clubs with which Tom Watson had won the Open Championship and the US Masters earlier in the year were illegal, having grooves which exceeded the permitted specifications. The set he used in winning the 1975 Open Championship were then flown out to him and they too were found to be illegal. No retrospective action was taken.

● Mrs Fred Daly, wife of the former Open champion, saved the clubhouse of Balmoral GC, Belfast, from destruction when three men entered the professionals' shop on 5th August, 1976 and left a bag containing a bomb outside the shop beside the clubhouse when refused money. Mrs Daly carried the bag over to a hedge some distance away where the bomb exploded 15 minutes later. The only damage was broken windows. On the same day several hours afterwards, Dungannon GC in Co Tyrone suffered extensive damage to the clubhouse from terrorist bombs. Co Down GC, proposed venue of the 1979 home international matches suffered bomb damage in May that year and through fear for the safety of team members the 1979 matches were cancelled.

● A small plane crash-landed on the 18th fairway during the pro-am preceding the 1978 Hawaiian Open, coming to rest about 50 yards short of the 18th green where American professional Jim Simons and his amateur partners were putting.

● The Army Golfing Society and St Andrews on 21st April, 1934, played a match 200-a-side, the largest golf match ever played. Play was by foursomes. The Army won 58, St Andrews 31 and 11 were halved.

● In an issue of the PGA Official Journal in 1976, it was stated *Ladies will now be permitted full privileges of membership including sectional and national voting at Annual Meetings; be eligible for election to committees and be permitted to play in section events off the back tees with the men.*

● The government of Fiji, where the 1978 men's and women's world amateur team championships were held in 1978, refused to allow teams from South Africa to compete because of South Africa's apartheid policy.

● On the eve of the 1979 World Cup in Greece, Dale Hayes and Hugh Baiocchi, representing South Africa, were compelled to withdraw when the Greek government, on a demand from the anti-apartheid committee of the United Nations, refused permission for them to compete.

● John Cook, professional at Brickendon Grange, and former English Amateur champion, narrowly escaped death during an attempted coup against King Hassan of Morocco in July 1971. Cook had been playing in a tournament arranged by King Hassan, a keen golfer, and was at the King's birthday party in Rabat when rebels broke into the party demanding that the king give up his throne. Cook and many others present were taken hostage. Over 200 people were killed before King Hassan surrendered minutes before the group which included Cook was due for the firing squad.

● When playing from the 9th tee at Lossiemouth golf course in June, 1971, Martin Robertson struck a Royal Navy jet aircraft which was coming in to land at the nearby airfield. The plane was not damaged.

● In November, 1983, as John Gallacher (39), a 9-handicap player, was driving off at the 9th hole at Machrihanish in a winter league 4-ball tie, a Hercules transport plane from Germany coming in to land at the adjoining RAF airfield passed overhead, and was struck by Gallacher's ball. A mark that could have been caused by a golf ball was subsequently found on the aircraft's fuselage, but Gallacher's ball was never found.

● In view of the increasing number of people crossing the road (known as Granny Clark's Wynd) which runs across the first and 18th fairways of the Old Course, St Andrews, as a right of way, the St Andrews Links committee decided in 1969 to control the flow by erecting traffic lights, with appropriate green for go, yellow for caution and red for stop. The lights are controlled from the starter's box on the first tee. Golfers on the first tee must wait until the lights turn to green before driving off and a notice has been erected at the Wynd warning pedestrians not to cross at yellow or stop.

● A traffic light for golfers was also installed in 1971 on one of Japan's most congested courses. After putting on the uphill 9th hole of the Fukuoka course in Southern Japan, players have to switch on a go-ahead signal for following golfers waiting to play their shots to the green.

● A 22-year-old professional at Brett Essex GC, Brentwood, David Moore, who was playing in the Mufulira Open in Zambia in 1976, was shot dead it is alleged by the man with whom he was staying for the duration of the tournament. It appeared his host then shot himself.

● The first round of the Amateur Championship in 1887 and again in 1953, both strangely enough at Hoylake, consisted of only one tie, all the other competitors receiving byes. The first round of the English Ladies' in 1924 and the Scottish Amateur in 1932 also consisted of only one tie.

● Patricia Shepherd has won the ladies' club championship at Turriff GC Aberdeenshire 30 consecutive times from 1959 to 1988.

● Mrs Jackie Mercer won the South African Ladies' Championship in 1979, 31 years after her first victory in the event as Miss Jacqueline Smith.

● At Geelong course, near Melbourne, Australia, while FD Walter was driving off, the strap of his wrist watch broke. The watch fell on top of the ball at the exact moment of impact. The player picked up the watch unbroken 40 yards down the fairway.

● Lee Trevino, a few days after winning the 1972 Open Championship, thereby thwarting Jack Nicklaus' attempt to win all four major championships in the one year, was knocked down and kicked during an exhibition match at Scioto CC, Ohio. Ohio is the state in which Nicklaus was born.

● After playing a tee shot at Heworth, County Durham, in 1968, Mrs Helen Paterson found her ball impaled on the peg tee.

● During the Royal and Ancient medal meeting on 25th September, 1907, a member of the Royal and Ancient drove a ball which struck the sharp point of a hatpin in the hat of a lady who was crossing the course. The ball was so firmly impaled that it remained in position. The lady was not hurt.

● At the Northwest Park course, Washington, USA in 1975, fighting broke out between the members of two 4-ball games. One group claimed the other was holding them back and the other group claimed the group behind had driven into them. Clubs were used as weapons resulting in serious injuries including a fractured skull. Police had to be called.

● At a court in Inglewood, California, in 1978, Jim Brown was convicted of beating and choking an opponent during a dispute over where a ball should have been placed on the green.

● FG Tait, at St Andrews, drove a ball through a man's hat and had to pay the owner 5/- (25p) to purchase a new one. At the end of the round he was grumbling to old Tom Morris about the cost of this particular shot, when the sage of St Andrews interrupted him: *Eh, Mr Tait, you ought to be glad it was only a new hat you had to buy, and not an oak coffin.*

● During the Northern Ireland troubles a home-made hand grenade was found in a bunker at Dungannon GC, Co Tyrone, on Sunday, 12th September, 1976.

● At Rhymney and Tredegar, South Wales, on 10th September, 1934, the hard felt hat of a pedestrian who was crossing the fairway was hit by the drive of a golfer. The man fell, but his head was only slightly grazed. The ball had gone right through the hat and was found 20 yards farther on.

● To mark the centenary of the Jersey Golf Club in 1978, the Jersey Post Office issued a set of four special stamps featuring Jersey's most famous golfer, Harry Vardon. The background of the 13p stamp was a brief biography of Vardon's career reproduced from the Golfer's Handbook.

● In 1977, William Collings tried to hit his ball over a grapefruit tree at Eldorado CC, Palm Desert, California. He hit the shot thin and the ball became embedded in a grapefruit.

● Three boys who searched a pond at Buchanan Castle GC, near Glasgow, one day in 1975, found 604 old balls which were valued at £8. However, they were charged and found guilty of stealing the balls and fined £10, £20 and £30 in court.

● Driving from the 11th tee at the Belfairs Golf Course, Leigh, on 4th September, 1935, the player heard a startled exclamation. Hurrying to investigate, he discovered that his shot, at 160 yards distance, had smashed the pipe of a man taking a stroll over the course. The ball had cut the pipe clean out of the man's mouth without hurting him.

● At the international between British and American women golfers for the Curtis Cup at Chevy Chase, Washington, USA, on 27th September, 1934, a number of State policemen stood around the first tee. They were in their shirt-sleeves, with revolvers and cartridges in their ammunition belts and handcuffs dangling from their hips.

● Forty-one-year-old John Mosley went for a round of golf at Delaware Park GC, Buffalo, New York, in July, 1972. He stepped on to the first tee and was challenged over a green fee by an official guard. A scuffle developed, a shot was fired and Mosley, a bullet in his chest, died on the way to hospital. His wife was awarded $131,250 in an action against the City of Buffalo and the guard. The guard was sentenced to $7^1/_2$ years for second-degree manslaughter.

● When three competitors in a pro-am event in 1968 in Pennsylvania were about to drive from the 16th tee, two bandits (one with pistol) suddenly emerged from the bushes, struck one of the players and robbed them of wrist watches and $300.

● A 5-hole miniature course has been built on top of a seven-storey garage at Pompano Beach, Florida.

● In the 1932 Walker Cup match at Brooklyn, Leonard Crawley succeeded in denting the cup. An errant iron shot to the 18th green hit the cup, which was on display outside the clubhouse.

● A mayor in an English Midland town at the opening ceremony of a new course had to putt on the 18th green. The unfortunate man missed the ball completely.

● There has rarely been a man who played better golf than the late Harry Vardon played in 1898 and 1899. All the same, at Wheaton, Illinois, in the American Open Championship, in 1900, which he won, he made the humiliating mistake of regarding a six-inch putt with such indifference that, in trying to knock it gaily into the hole, he missed the ball entirely, and struck his club into the ground, thus counting a stroke.

● Three golf officials appeared in court in Johannesburg, South Africa, accused of violating a 75-year-old Sunday Observance Law by staging the final round of the South African PGA championship on Sunday, 28th February, 1971. The championship should have been completed on the Saturday but heavy rain prevented any play.

● At the 11th hole at Troon in the 1962 Open Championship, Max Faulkner carelessly tapped the ball against his foot, and the hole ultimately cost him 11 strokes.

● In the Open Championship of 1876, at St Andrews, Bob Martin and David Strath tied at 176. A protest was lodged against Strath alleging he played his approach to the 17th green and struck a spectator. The Royal and Ancient ordered the replay, but Strath refused to play off the tie until a decision had been given on the protest. No decision was given and Bob Martin was declared the Champion.

● At Rose Bay, New South Wales, on 11th July, 1931, DJ Bayly MacArthur, on stepping into a bunker, began to sink. MacArthur, who weighed 14 stone, shouted for help. He was rescued when up to the armpits. He had stepped on a patch of quicksand, aggravated by excess of moisture.

● The late Bobby Cruickshank was the victim of his own jubilation in the 1934 US Open at Merion. In the 4th round while in with a chance of winning he half-topped his second shot at the 11th hole. The ball was heading for a pond in front of the green but instead of ending up in the water it hit a rock and bounced on to the green. In his delight Cruickshank threw his club into the air only to receive a resounding blow on the head as it returned to earth.

● A dog with an infallible nose for finding lost golf balls was, in 1971, given honorary membership of the Waihi GC, Hamilton, New Zealand. The dog, called Chico, was trained to search for lost balls, to be sold back to the members, the money being put into the club funds.

● By 1980 Waddy, an 11-year-old beagle belonging to Bob Inglis, the secretary of Brokenhurst Manor GC, had found over 35,000 golf balls.

● On 6th July, 1938, N Bathie, playing on Downfield, Dundee, was about to hit an iron shot when the ball was suddenly whisked away. Then the player was spun completely round. He had been caught in the fringe of a whirlwind. The whirlwind lifted a wooden shelter 60 feet into the air and burst it into smithereens over the 11th green. A haystack was uprooted and a tree razed.

● In a match over Queen's Park, Bournemouth, Archie Compston, finding that his ball had finished in the branches of a tree, played a shot with his club at the full stretch of his arms, above his head. The result was a wonderful shot which almost reached the green.

● Donald Grant, a competitor in the Dornoch

Open Amateur Tournament in 1939, cycled from London and tied for second place in the first round of the competition with 74.

● Herbert M Hepworth, Headingley, Leeds, Lord Mayor of Leeds in 1906, scored one thousand holes in 2, a feat which took him 30 years to accomplish. It was celebrated by a dinner in 1931 at the Leeds club. The first 2 of all was scored on 12th June, 1901, at Cobble Hall Course, Leeds, and the 1,000th in 1931 at Alwoodley, Leeds. Hepworth died in November, 1942.

●Mrs Sara Gibbon won the Farnham (Surrey) Club's Grandmother's competition 48 hours after her first grand-child was born.

● Mrs Joy Traill of Kloof CC, South Africa, holed from off the green six times in a round there on 20th October, 1977 at the age of 70.

● Nineteen-year-old Ron Stutesman holed chips at five consecutive holes in a round at Orchard Hills CC, Washougal, USA in January, 1978.

● On Saturday, 12th July, 1975, 16-year-old, 3-handicap Colin Smith, of Cowal GC broke his handicap on three different courses. Playing in the Glasgow Youths' Championship at Cawder he scored 73 over the Cawder Course (SSS 71) and 70 over the Keir Course (SSS 68). Then in the evening in the Poseidon Trophy at his home club he scored 70 (SSS 70).

● At Carnoustie in the first qualifying round for the 1952 Scottish Amateur Championship a competitor drove three balls in succession out of bounds at the 1st hole and thereupon withdrew.

Strange Local Rules

● The Duke of Windsor, who played on an extraordinary variety of the world's courses, once took advantage of a local rule at Jinja in Uganda and lifted his ball from a hippo's footprint without penalty.

● Another local rule in Uganda read: *If a ball comes to rest in dangerous proximity to a crocodile, another ball may be dropped.*

● At the Glen Canyon course in Arizona a local rule provides that *If your ball lands within a club length of a rattlesnake you are allowed to move the ball.* It would be no surprise if players under these circumstances just gladly opted for the *unplayable ball* rule.

● Signs that have been seen in Africa intimate that *Elephants have right of way* and warn *You are in wild animal country.*

● The 6th hole at Koolan Island GC, Western Australia also serves as a local air strip and a local rule reads *Aircraft and vehicular traffic have right of way at all times.*

● A local rule at the RAF Waddington GC reads *When teeing off from the 2nd, right of way must be given to taxi-ing aircraft.*

Record Scoring

Open Championship

Lowest 72 Hole Aggregate

268 by Tom Watson at Turnberry in 1977.

Lowest 72 Holes

Birkdale	275	Tom Watson in 1983
Carnoustie	279	Tom Watson and Jack Newton in 1975
Hoylake	278	Roberto De Vicenzo in 1967
Lytham	277	Bob Charles and Phil Rodgers in 1963
Muirfield	271	Tom Watson in 1980
Prince's	283	Gene Sarazen in 1932
St Andrews	276	Severiano Ballesteros in 1984
Sandwich	276	B Rogers in 1981
Troon	276	Arnold Palmer in 1962 and Tom Weiskopf in 1973
Turnberry	268	Tom Watson in 1977

Lowest 18 Holes

63 by Mark Hayes at Turnberry in 1977, by Isao Aoki at Muirfield in 1980 and Greg Norman at Turnberry in 1986.

Scores of 64

Horacio Carbonetti, Muirfield	1980
Hubert Green, Muirfield	1980
Tom Watson, Muirfield	1980
Craig Stadler, Birkdale	1983
Graham Marsh, Birkdale	1983
Christy O'Connor Jr, Sandwich	1985
Severiano Ballesteros, Turnberry	1986
Rodger Davis, Muirfield	1987

Scores of 65

Henry Cotton, Sandwich	1934
Eric Brown, Lytham	1958
Leopoldo Ruiz, Lytham	1958
Peter Butler, Muirfield	1966
Christy O'Connor, Lytham	1969
Neil Coles, St Andrews	1970
Jack Nicklaus, Troon	1973
Jack Newton, Carnoustie	1975
Angel Gallardo, Turnberry	1977
Tom Watson, Turnberry (twice)	1977
Jack Nicklaus, Turnberry	1977
Tommy Horton, Turnberry	1977
Bill Longmuir, Lytham	1979
Severiano Ballesteros, Lytham	1979
Gordon Brand, Sandwich	1981
Severiano Ballesteros, Lytham	1988

Lowest 18 Holes

Birkdale	64	Craig Stadler and Graham Marsh in 1983
Carnoustie	65	Jack Newton in 1975
Hoylake	67	Roberto De Vicenzo and Gary Player in 1967
Lytham	65	Eric Brown and Leopoldo Ruiz in 1958; Christy O'Connor in 1969; Bill Longmuir and Severiano Ballesteros in 1979 and 1988
Muirfield	63	Isao Aoki in 1980
Prince's	68	Arthur Havers in 1932
St Andrews	65	Neil Coles in 1970
Sandwich	64	Christy O'Connor Jr in 1985
Troon	65	Jack Nicklaus in 1973
Turnberry	63	Mark Hayes in 1977 Greg Norman in 1986

Lowest 9 Holes

28 by Denis Durnian at Birkdale (outward half of second round in 1983.

29 by Tom Haliburton and Peter Thomson at Lytham (outward half) in 1963; by Tony Jacklin at St Andrews (outward half) in 1970, by Bill Longmuir at Lytham (outward half) in 1979; by David J Russell at Lytham (outward half) in 1988

Scores of 30

Eric Brown, St Andrews (outward half)	1957
Eric Brown, Lytham (inward half)	1958
Leopoldo Ruiz, Lytham (outward half)	1958
Phil Rodgers, Muirfield (inward half)	1966

Jimmy Kinsella, Birkdale (outward half)	1971
Lee Trevino, Muirfield (inward half)	1972
Harry Bannerman, Muirfield (outward half)	1972
Bert Yancey, Troon (outward half)	1973
Christy O'Connor, Jr. Birkdale (outward half)	1976
Arnold Palmer, Turnberry (inward half)	1977
Jack Nicklaus, Lytham (outward half)	1979
Denis Watson, Muirfield (inward half)	1980
Tom Watson, Muirfield (inward half)	1980
Lee Trevino, Birkdale (outward half)	1983
Sam Torrance, St Andrews (outward half)	1984
Christy O'Connor, Sandwich (outward half)	1985
Tsuneyuki Nakajima, Turnberry (inward half)	1986
Ross Drummond, Muirfield (inward half)	1987

Lowest First 36 Holes
132 by Henry Cotton at St George's in 1934.

Lowest Final 36 Holes
130 by Tom Watson at Turnberry in 1977.

Lowest 18 Holes by an Amateur
66 by Frank Stranahan at Troon in 1950.

Lowest Score in Qualifying Rounds
63 by Frank Jowle at St Andrews in 1955; by Peter Thomson at Lytham in 1958; by Maurice Bembridge at Delamere Forest in 1967; and by Malcolm Gunn at Gullane No 2 in 1972.

Lowest Qualifying Round by an Amateur
65 by Ronnie Shade at St Andrews in 1964.

Other Outstanding Scoring
In the Southern Section Qualifying competition for the Open Championship in 1926 played at Sunningdale, Bobby Jones had rounds of 68 and 66. His round of 66 (six under par) was regarded as an almost perfect round. Never over par, he missed only one green in regulation or better figures – the short 13th where he was a few yards short but achieved par with a single putt. His round consisted of 33 out, 33 in. He had 33 putts and 33 other shots, which shows the high quality of his golf through the green.

Dale Hayes of South Africa had rounds of 68 and 64 over Hesketh in the qualifying rounds for the 1971 Open Championship. Hayes at the time was aged 19 years and one week and had been a professional for only eight months.

European PGA Tour

Lowest 72 Hole Aggregate
260 by Kel Nagle (Australia) in the Irish Hospital Tournament at Woodbrook in 1961.

Lowest 18 Holes
61 by Tom Haliburton in the first round of a professional tournament at Worthing in 1952; by Tony Coop and Hugh Boyle in the Senior Service tournament at Dalmahoy East in 1965; and by Peter Butler in the Bowmaker tournament at Sunningdale in 1967.

Lowest 9 Holes
27 by Jose Canizares of Spain for the first 9 holes in the third round of the 1978 Swiss Open at Crans-sur-Sierre.

Lowest 36 Holes
126 by Tom Haliburton in the Spalding tournament at Worthing in 1952.

Lowest 54 Holes
194 by John Lister (New Zealand) in the Gallaher Ulster Open at Shandon Park in 1970 and by Vicente Fernandez (Argentina) in the Benson and Hedges Festival at Fulford in 1975.

Largest Winning Margin
17 strokes by Bernhard Langer in the 1979 Cacharel Under-25s' Championship.

Miscellaneous British

Andrew Brooks recorded a 72-hole aggregate of 259 in winning the Skol (Scotland) tournament at Williamwood in 1974.

Playing on the ladies' course (4,020 yards) at Sunningdale on 26th September, 1961, Arthur Lees, the professional there, went round in 52, 10 under par. He went out in 26 (2, 3, 3, 4, 3, 3, 3, 3, 2) and came back in 26 (2, 3, 3, 3, 2, 3, 4, 3, 3).

AE Smith, the Woolacombe Bay professional, recorded a score of 55 in a game there with a club member on 1st January, 1936. The course measured 4,248 yards. Smith went out in 29 and came back in 26 finishing with a hole-in-one at the 18th hole.

Other low scores recorded in Britain are by CC Aylmer, an English International who went round Ranelagh in 56; George Duncan, Axenfels in 56; Harry Bannerman, Banchory in 56 in 1971; Ian Connelly, Welwyn Garden City in 56 in 1972; James Braid, Hedderwick near Dunbar in 57; H Hardman, Wirral in 58; Norman Quigley, Windermere in 58 in 1937; Robert Webster, Eaglescliffe in 58, in 1970.

Harry Weetman scored 58 in a round at

Croham Hurst on 30th January, 1956. The course measured 6,171 yards.

D Sewell had a round of 60 in an Alliance Meeting at Ferndown, Bournemouth, a full-size course. He scored 30 for each half and had a total of 26 putts.

In September 1986, Jeffrey Burn, handicap 1 of Shrewsbury GC scored 60 in a club competition, made up of 8 birdies, an eagle and 9 pars. He was 30 out and 30 home and no 5 on his card.

Andrew Sherborne, a 20-year-old amateur, went round Cirencester in 60 strokes.

Dennis Gray completed a round at Broome Manor, Swindon (6,906 yards, SSS 73) in the summer of 1976 in 60 (28 out, 32 in).

Playing over Aberdour on 13th June, 1936, Hector Thomson, British Amateur champion, 1936, and Jack McLean, former Scottish Amateur champion, each did 61 in the second round of an exhibition. McLean in his first round had a 63, which gave him an aggregate 124 for 36 holes.

Steve Tredinnick in a friendly match against business tycoon Joe Hyman scored a 61 over West Sussex (6,211 yards) in 1970. It included a hole-in-one at the 12th (198 yards) and a 2 at the 17th (445 yards).

Another round of 61 on a full-size course was achieved by 18-year-old Michael Jones on his home course, Worthing GC (6,274 yards) in the first round of the President's Cup in May, 1974.

In the Second City Pro-Am tournament in 1970, at Handsworth, Simon Fogarty did the second 9 holes in 27 against the par of 36.

In the second round of a 36-hole open amateur competition at Sandyhills GC on 10th September, 1978, Barclay Howard completed the last 9 holes in 27.

RH Corbett, in 1916, in the semi-final of the Tangye Cup at Mullim did 9 holes in 27 as did Dr James Stothers of Ralston over the 2,056 yards 9-hole course at Carradale, Argyll, during the summer of 1971. In each case the total was made up of nine 3s.

US Open

Lowest 72 Hole Aggregate

272 by Jack Nicklaus at Baltusrol in 1980.

Lowest 18 Holes

63 by Johnny Miller at Oakmont in 1973 in the final round and by Jack Nicklaus and Tom Weiskopf at Baltusrol in 1980, both in the first round.

Lowest 9 Holes

30 by Jimmy McHale in 1947, Arnold Palmer in 1960, Ken Venturi in 1964, Bob Charles and Tom Shaw in 1971, and Raymond Floyd in 1980.

Lowest 36 Holes

134 by Jack Nicklaus at Baltusrol in 1980.

Lowest 54 Holes

204 by Jack Nicklaus and Isao Aoki at Baltusrol in 1980.

US Professional events

Lowest 72 Hole Aggregate

257 (60, 68, 64, 65) by Mike Souchak in the 1955 Texas Open.

Lowest 18 Holes

59 by Sam Snead in the third round of the Greenbrier Open (Sam Snead Festival) at White Sulphur Springs, West Virginia in 1959 and by Al Geiberger in the second round of the 1977 Danny Thomas Memphis Classic at Colonial CC when preferred lies were in operation.

Lowest 9 Holes

27 by Mike Souchak in the 1955 Texas Open and by Andy North in the 1975 BC Open.

Lowest First 36 Holes

126 by Tommy Bolt in 1954. (On the US mini-tour a 36-hole score of 123 was achieved by Bob Risch in the 1978 Mesa Centennial Open.)

Lowest Final 36 Holes

122 by Sam Snead in the Greenbrier Open (Sam Snead Festival) in 1959. On the USPGA Tour it is 125 by Ron Streck in the 1978 Texas Open.

Lowest 54 Holes

189 by Chandler Harper in the 1954 Texas Open (last three rounds).

192 by Bob Gilder in the 1982 Westchester Classic (first three rounds).

Largest Winning Margin

16 strokes by J Douglas Edgar in the 1919 Canadian Open Championship and by Bobby Locke in the 1948 Chicago Victory National Championship.

Miscellaneous USA

The lowest scores recorded for 18 holes in America are 55 by EF Staugaard in 1935 over the 6,419 yards Montebello Park, California, and 55 by Homero Blancas in 1962 over the 5,002 yards Premier course in Longview, Texas. Staugaard in his round had 2 eagles, 13 birdies and 3 pars.

Equally outstanding is a round of 58 (13 under par) achieved by a 13-year-old boy,

Douglas Beecher, on 6th July, 1976 at Pitman CC, New Jersey. The course measured 6,180 yards from the back tees, and the middle tees, off which Douglas played, were estimated by the club professional to reduce the yardage by under 180 yards.

In 1941 at a course in Portsmouth, Virginia, measuring 6,100 yards, Chandler Harper scored 58.

Jack Nicklaus in an exhibition match at Breakers Club, Palm Beach, California, in 1973 scored 59 over the 6,200 yards course.

Ben Hogan, practising on a 7,006-yard course at Palm Beach, Florida, went round in 61 – 11 under par.

The lowest 9-hole score in America is 25, held jointly by Bill Burke over the second half of the 6,384 yards Normandie CC, St Louis in May, 1970 at the age of 29; by Daniel Cavin who had seven 3s and two 2s on the par 36 Bill Brewer Course, Texas in September, 1959; and by Douglas Beecher over the second half of Pitman CC, New Jersey on 6th July, 1976 at the amazingly young age of 13. The back 9 holes of the Pitman course measured 3,150 yards (par 35) from the back tees, but even though Douglas played off the middle tees, the yardage was still over 3,000 yards for the 9 holes. He scored 8 birdies and 1 eagle.

Horton Smith scored 119 for two consecutive rounds in winning the Catalina Open in California in December, 1928. The course, however, measured only 4,700 yards.

National Opens – excluding Europe and USA

Lowest 72 Hole Aggregate

255 by Peter Tupling in the Nigerian Open at Lagos, 1981.

Lowest 36 Hole Aggregate

124 (18 under par) by Sandy Lyle in the 1978 Nigerian Open at Ikoyi GC, Lagos. (Lyle was in his first year as a professional.)

Lowest 18 Holes

59 by Gary Player in the second round of the 1974 Brazilian Open at Gavea GC (6,185 yards), Rio de Janeiro.

Professional Events – excluding GB and USA

Lowest 72 Hole Aggregate

260 (66, 62, 69, 63) by Bob Charles in the Spalding Masters at Tauranga, New Zealand, in 1969.

Lowest 18 Hole Aggregate

60 by Australian Billy Dunk at Merewether, NSW in November, 1970.

Lowest 9 Hole Aggregate

27 by American Bill Brask at Tauranga in the New Zealand PGA in 1976.

Miscellaneous – excluding GB and USA

Tony Jacklin won the 1973 Los Lagartos Open with an aggregate of 261, 27 under par.

Henry Cotton in 1950 had a round of 56 at Monte Carlo (29 out, 27 in).

In a Pro-Am tournament prior to the 1973 Nigerian Open, British professional David Jagger went round in 59.

Max Banbury recorded a 9-hole score of 26 at Woodstock, Ontario, playing in a competition in 1952.

Women

The lowest score recorded on a full-size course by a woman is 62 by Mary (Mickey) Wright of Dallas, Texas. This was achieved on the Hogan Park course (6,286 yards) at Midland, Texas, in November, 1964. It was equalled by 16-year-old Rae Rothfelder on 9th July, 1978 at Diamond Oak G&CC, Fort Worth, Texas, a course measuring 6,124 yards.

The lowest 72-hole score on the US Ladies' PGA circuit is 271 by Hollis Stacy in the 1977 Rail Muscular Dystrophy.

The lowest 9-hole score on the US Ladies' PGA circuit is 29, first achieved by Marlene Bauer Hagge in 1971 and equalled by Carol Mann (1975), Pat Bradley (1978 and again in 1979), Alexandra Reinhardt (1978), and Silvia Bertolaccini (1979).

The lowest score for 36 holes on the USLPGA circuit is 131 achieved by Kathy Martin in the 1976 Birmingham Classic and by Silvia Bertolaccini in the 1977 Lady Keystone Open.

The lowest 9-hole score on the WPGA circuit is 30 by Susan Moon at Valbonne in 1979.

In the Women's World Team Championship in Mexico in 1966, Mrs Belle Robertson, playing for the British team, was the only player to break 70. She scored 69 in the third round.

At Westgate-on-Sea GC (measuring 5,002 yards), Wanda Morgan scored 60 in an open tournament in 1929.

Since scores cannot properly be taken in match play no stroke records can be made in match play events. Nevertheless we record here two outstanding examples of low scoring in the finals of national championships. Mrs

Catherine Lacoste de Prado is credited with a score of 62 in the first round of the 36-hole final of the 1972 French Ladies' Open Championship at Morfontaine. She went out in 29 and came back in 33 on a course measuring 5,933 yards.

In the final of the English Ladies' Championship at Woodhall Spa in 1954, Frances Stephens (later Mrs Smith) did the first nine holes against Elizabeth Price (later Mrs Fisher) in 30. It included a hole-in-one at the 5th. The nine holes measured 3,280 yards.

Amateur National Championships

The following examples of low scoring cannot be regarded as genuine stroke play records since they took place in match play. Nevertheless they are recorded here as being worthy of note.

Michael Bonallack in beating D Kelley in the final of the English championship in 1968 at Ganton did the first 18 holes in 61 with only one putt under two feet conceded. He was out in 32 and home in 29. The par of the course was 71.

Charles McFarlane, playing in the fourth round of the Amateur Championship at Sandwich in 1914 against Charles Evans did the first nine holes in 31, winning by 6 and 5.

This score of 31 at Sandwich was equalled on several occasions in later years there. Then, in 1948, Richard Chapman of America went out in 29 in the fourth round eventually beating Hamilton McInally, Scottish Champion in 1937, 1939 and 1947, by 9 and 7.

In the fourth round of the Amateur Championship at Hoylake in 1953, Harvie Ward, the holder, did the first nine holes against Frank Stranahan in 32. The total yardage for the holes was 3,474 yards and included one hole of 527 yards and five holes over 400 yards. Ward won by one hole.

Francis Ouimet in the first round of the American Amateur Championship in 1932 against George Voigt did the first nine holes in 30. Ouimet won by 6 and 5.

Low scores by Amateurs in Open competitions

The 1970 South African Dunlop Masters Tournament was won by an amateur, John Fourie, with a score of 266, 14 under par. He led from start to finish with rounds of 65, 68, 65, 68, finally winning by six shots from Gary Player.

Jim Ferrier, Manly, won the New South Wales championship at Sydney in 1935 with 266. His rounds were: 67, 65, 70, 64, giving an aggregate 16 strokes better than that of the runner-up. At the time he did this amazing score Ferrier was 20 years old and an amateur.

Most holes below par

EF Staugaard in a round of 55 over the 6,419 yards Montbello Park, California, in 1935, had 2 eagles, 13 birdies and 3 pars.

American Jim Clouette scored 14 birdies in a round at Longhills GC, Arkansas, in 1974. The course measured 6,257 yards.

Jimmy Martin in his round of 63 in the Swallow-Penfold at Stoneham in 1961 had 1 eagle and 11 birdies.

In the Ricarton Rose Bowl at Hamilton, Scotland, in August, 1981, Wilma Aitken, a women's amateur internationalist, had 11 birdies in a round of 64, including 9 consecutive birdies from the 3rd to the 11th.

Mrs Donna Young scored 9 birdies and 1 eagle in one round in the 1975 Colgate European Women's Open.

Consecutive holes below par

Lionel Platts had 10 consecutive birdies from the 8th to 17th holes at Blairgowrie GC during a practice round for the 1973 Sumrie Better-Ball tournament.

Roberto De Vicenzo in the Argentine Centre of the Republic Championship in April, 1974 at the Cordoba GC, Villa Allende, broke par at each of the first 9 holes. (By starting his round at the 10th hole they were in fact the second 9 holes played by Vicenzo.) He had 1 eagle (at the 7th hole) and 8 birdies. The par for the 3,602 yards half was 37, completed by Vicenzo in 27.

Nine consecutive holes under par have been recorded by Claude Harmon in a friendly match over Winged Foot GC, Mamaroneck, NY, in 1931; by Les Hardie at Eastern GC, Melbourne, in April, 1934; by Jimmy Smith at McCabe GC, Nashville, Tenn, in 1969; by Jim DeForest on a 9-hole sand-green course at New Salem, North Dakota, in August, 1974; by 13-year-old Douglas Beecher, in 1976, at Pitman CC, New Jersey; and by Rick Sigda at Greenfield CC, Mass, in 1979.

TW Egan in winning the East of Ireland Championship in 1962 at Baltray had 8 consecutive birdies (2nd to 9th) in the third round.

On the USPGA circuit 8 consecutive holes below par have been achieved twice – by Bob Goalby in the 1961 St Petersburg Open, and by Fuzzy Zoeller in the 1976 Quad Cities Open.

Seven successive birdies have been recorded by Peter Thomson at Wentworth in the 1958 Dunlop; by Bernard Hunt at Wentworth in the

1958 Daks; by Angel Miguel at Wentworth (East) in the 1960 Daks; by Peter Butler at Fulford in the 1971 Benson and Hedges; by Peter Townsend at Wentworth in 1974 Viyella PGA; and by Brian Waites at the RAC in the 1980 Bob Hope Classic.

The United States Ladies' PGA record is 7 consecutive holes below par achieved by Carol Mann in the Borden Classic at Columbus, Ohio in 1975.

Miss Wilma Aitken recorded 9 successive birdies (from the 3rd to the 11th) in the 1981 Ricarton Rose Bowl.

Low scoring rarities

In the qualifying rounds of the 1956 Dunlop Tournament at Sunningdale, Arthur Lees, the resident professional, played 27 consecutive holes without taking more than a 4 at any hole. His first round was 65 and his second 69.

At Standerton GC, South Africa, in May, 1937, FF Bennett, playing for Standerton against Witwatersrand University, did the 2nd hole, 110 yards, in three 2s and a 1. Standerton is a 9-hole course, and in the match Bennett had to play four rounds.

In 1973 in the 36-hole Club Championship at Mufulira GC, Zambia, Amateur HG McQuillan, completed two rounds in 65 and 66 for a winning score of 131.

In 1957 a four-ball comprising HJ Marr, E Stevenson, C Bennett and WS May completed the 2nd hole (160 yards) in the grand total of 6 strokes. Marr and Stevenson both holed in 1 while Bennett and May both made 2.

The old Meadow Brook Club of Long Island, USA, had five par 3 holes and George Low in a round there in the 1950s scored 2 at each of them.

In a friendly match on a course near Chicago in 1971, assistant professional Tom Doty (23 years) had a remarkable low run over four consecutive holes: 4th (500 yards) 2; 5th (360 yards, dogleg) 1; 6th (175 yards) 1; 7th (375 yards) 2.

RW Bishop, playing in the Oxley Park, July medal competition in 1966, scored three consecutive 2s. They occurred at the 12th, 13th and 14th holes which measured 151, 500 and 136 yards respectively.

In the 1959 PGA Close Championship at Ashburnham, Bob Boobyer scored five 2s in one of the rounds.

American Art Wall scored three consecutive 2s in the first round of the US Masters in 1974. They were at the 4th, 5th and 6th holes, the par of which was 3, 4 and 3.

Nine consecutive 3s have been recorded by RH Corbett in 1916 in the semi-final of the Tangye Cup; by Dr James Stothers of Ralston GC over the 2,056 yards 9-hole course at Carradale, Argyll during the summer of 1971; by Irish internationalist Brian Kissock in the Homebright Open at Carnalea GC, Bangor in June, 1975; and by American club professional Ben Toski.

The most consecutive 3s in a British PGA event is seven by Eric Brown in the Dunlop at Gleneagles (Queen's Course) in 1960.

Hubert Green scored eight consecutive 3s in a round in the 1980 US Open.

The greatest number of 3s in one round in a British PGA event is 11 by Brian Barnes in the 1977 Skol Lager tournament at Gleneagles.

Fewest putts

The lowest known number of putts in one round is 14, achieved by Colin Collen-Smith in a round at Betchworth Park, Dorking in June, 1947. He single-putted 14 greens and chipped into the hole on four occasions. Professional Richard Stanwood in a round at Riverside GC, Pocatello, Idaho on 17th May, 1976 took 15 putts, chipping into the hole on five occasions. Several instances of 16 putts in one round have been recorded in friendly games.

For 9 holes, the fewest putts is 5 by Ron Stutesman for the first 9 holes at Orchard Hills G&CC, Washington, USA in 1978.

Walter Hagen in nine consecutive holes on one occasion took only seven putts. He holed long putts on seven greens and chips at the other two holes.

In competitive stroke rounds in Britain and Ireland, the lowest known number of putts in one round is 18, in a medal round at Portpatrick Dunskey GC, Wilmslow GC professional Fred Taggart is reported to have taken 20 putts in one round of the 1934 Open Championship. Padraigh Hogan (Elm Park), when competing in the Junior Scratch Cup at Carlow in 1976, took only 20 putts in a round of 67.

The fewest putts in a British PGA event is believed to be 22 by Bill Large in a qualifying round over Moor Park High Course for the 1972 Benson and Hedges Match Play.

Overseas, outside the United States of America, the fewest putts is 19 achieved by Robert Wynn (GB) in a round in the 1973 Nigerian Open and by Mary Bohen (US) in the final round of the 1977 South Australian Open at Adelaide.

The USPGA record for fewest putts in one round is 18, held by Sam Trahan in the 4th round of the 1979 Philadelphia Classic. For 9 holes the USPGA record is 8, by Jim Colbert in the 1967 Greater Jacksonville Open.

The fewest putts recorded for a 72-hole USPGA tournament is 94 by George Archer in the 1980 Heritage Classic.

The fewest putts recorded by a woman is 17, by Joan Joyce in the Lady Michelob tournament, Georgia in May, 1982.

Advertisers' Index

Index